# A Chronicle of American Music
# 1700–1995

# A Chronicle of American Music
# 1700 – 1995

Charles J. Hall

Schirmer Books
An Imprint of Simon & Schuster Macmillan
New York

Prentice Hall International
London   Mexico City   New Delhi   Singapore   Sydney   Toronto

Schirmer Books
An Imprint of Simon & Schuster Macmillan
1633 Broadway
New York, NY 10019

Library of Congress Catalog Card Number: 96-16458

Printed in the United States of America

Printing Number
 2  3  4  5  6  7  8  9  10


**Library of Congress Cataloging-in-Publication Data**

Hall, Charles, J.
    A chronicle of American music, 1700-1995 / Charles J. Hall.
      p.   cm.
    Includes index.
    ISBN 0–02–860296–X (alk. paper)
    1. Music—United States—Chronology.   I. Title.
    ML200.H15     1996                                               96-16458
    780'.973—dc20                                                    CIP
                                                                     MN

This paper meets the requirements of ANSI/NISO Z39.48–1992 (Permanence of Paper).

# Contents

# Foreword

It is with a great deal of pleasure and satisfaction that I write this foreword to Charles J. Hall's *A Chronicle of American Music*.

Those of us who are American artists, albeit in my case first generation, realize the tremendous prejudice that has been encountered especially by American classical music. When we speak of the American classical tradition, we talk about some of the most significant composers of the twentieth century. Even if we don't include nationalized composers such as Stravinsky and Schoenberg, we encounter extraordinarily gifted, imaginative, and innovative composers, rooted in a tradition that began in the eighteenth century. Yet, since the Western classical music tradition has been primarily a European art form, there is a reluctance to acknowledge the considerable significance, not so much of American performers, but of American composers.

What Dr. Hall has done in his incredibly informative, well-thought-out, and organized book is to document the extraordinary history of our distinguished musical tradition. I believe that with the proliferation of noteworthy performers from the United States, our music is finally taking hold as vitally important to the future of classical music in our country and in the world. Dr. Hall's book has given us so much information and so many tools, not only to further document but also to program these momentous works, and to better understand the historical perspective in which these composers worked—one of the book's most useful, engaging, and exciting aspects. He lists by year from 1700 to 1995 not only developments in American music but important events in all the arts, worldwide and especially in America. Thus, the reader can see which artists lived and worked in the same periods, whether in music, literature, or fine art.

He has also dealt with the important American performers, and to see this tradition in such a volume is also quite remarkable.

This book is a salute to the greatness of our American culture, and it will become indispensable for all of us who care about the future of our classical music tradition.

GERARD SCHWARZ

# Preface

The current tome is dedicated to the furtherance of American music, especially in that field that the author chooses to identify as the "Cultivated/Art Music" scene. No book on American music can ignore the presence of popular music, which falls here under the category of the "Vernacular/Commercial" scene. There can be no doubt in today's world that most facets of popular music, from folk to rock, are under the control of big business, therefore the addition of the term "commercial" to identify this field. It should be pointed out that the emphasis in this volume is on the art music of the United States, with only the highlights of the popular scene included; there is a plethora of publications of all sizes and shapes on all aspects of popular music, which are readily available at any book store.

The volume is arranged chronologically with brief highlights of history, world cultural highlights, and representative works of American art and literature; a companion volume with more detail of the art and literature scenes is being prepared. Emphasis here is especially on those literary or art works that have a direct bearing on music as well.

The **Vernacular/Commercial Music Scene** is divided into five categories:

A. **Births**—giving the person's field and date of birth

B. **Deaths**—giving the person's field and date of death

C. **Biographical**

**Performing Groups**—self-explanatory

**New Beginnings**—festivals, companies, and so on

**Honors**—Entries here are limited. Grammy winners are too numerous for this already lengthy tome; the proliferation of award ceremonies, mainly in country music, puts them also beyond the scope of this work.

**Miscellaneous**—mostly items of a more personal nature

D. **Publications**—important entries bearing on all aspects of the popular field

E. **Representative Pieces of Music**

**Musicals**—mainly by American composers, but containing the US premieres of other important works

**Songs/Number One Hits**—up to 1956, songs are given in the year they were composed along with the name of the composer/lyricist; beginning in 1956, the *Billboard* Number One Hits with performer are given, since in today's society, it is the performer who is honored.

**Other**—includes works for instrumental performance, larger "classically oriented" works and film compositions. *Note:* All prizes or awards (e.g., Oscars) are given with the work.

The **Cultivated/Art Music Scene** is divided into nine sections:

**F. Births**—giving the person's field of performance and date of birth

**G. Deaths**—giving the person's field of performance and date of death

**H. Debuts**

**United States**—with field of performance and place of debut

**Metropolitan Opera**—Since some consider a Metropolitan Opera debut to be the high point of one's career, Met debuts are listed separately, giving the nationality and field of performance. Those entries with no nationality listed are American.

**Other**—These are American performers with place of initial debut outside the United States.

**I. New Positions**

**Conductors**—self-explanatory

**Educational**—These entries must of necessity be limited, particularly in the twentieth century, to administrative positions or information on better-known artistic personalities or positions.

**Other**—critics, residencies, organists, and so on

**J. Honors and Awards**

**Honors**—given independently to honor the individual's accomplishments

**Awards**—given as a result of winning a prestigious competition

**K. Biographical**—short items of a more personal nature concerning musical personalities

**L. Musical Beginnings**

**Performing Groups**—school and civic groups as well as professional organizations

**Festivals**—basically a twentieth-century phenomenon

**Educational**—anything pertaining to educational life except performing groups

**Other**—publications, music businesses of all kinds, and miscellaneous material

**M. Publications**—Generally speaking, individual biographies are not included, but other important works of music history, music theory, and philosophy of music are given.

**N. Musical Compositions**—The date given is, as far as is possible to ascertain, the year of composition; the compositions have been listed alphabetically by composer followed by the title and any award received and arranged in the following order:

**Chamber Music**
**Choral/Vocal Music**
**Concertos**
**Electronic**
**Operas**
**Orchestra/Band**
**Piano/Organ**
**Symphonies**

The index of musical information is arranged not by page but by the year and letter of the section where the name or item may be found. The meanings of the letter codes are given at the bottom of each page of the index. This makes the index ideal for a quick reference on such things as births or deaths. For example, a look at the index tells us that Emma Abbott was born in 1850 (1850F) and died in 1891 (1891G).

Care has been taken to make the volume as truthful as possible considering the myriads of sources from which the information was taken (see Bibliography). Many of these sources contradict each other on such things as birth dates and debuts. In most instances, the compiler has taken the *New Grove Dictionary of Music* and the *Grove Dictionary of American Music* as the final say. It should also be recognized that there is a great deal of subjectivity in the choice of material in the late twentieth century—how can one tell which works will endure or which composers will be recognized in the years ahead? One can only stay with already recognized masters or go with those who manage to make the cultural news enough to be heard.

The time has come for Americans to start paying attention to our native composers and performers; for too long, we have forced our talent to head for Europe to study and then ignored them on their return for writing music that is "too Germanic" or "too European" (MacDowell, Chadwick, etc.). It is hoped that this tome can be a departure point for a closer study of our American music heritage.

picture Meal

To  my                 with
    lovely           love
    wife           Denzel
                   Andrew

# 1700

❄

## Historical Highlights

Catholic priests are banned from Massachusetts; the census shows a national population of 275,000, with Boston the largest city with approximately 7,000 inhabitants.

## World Cultural Highlights

**World Art**  Noël Coypel, *Susanna Being Denounced by the Elders;* Giuseppe-Maria Crespi, *Lucretia Threatened by Tarquin;* Andrea Pozzi, *Altar, St. Ignatius, Rome.*

**World Literature**  Susanna Centlivre, *The Perjured Husband;* John Dryden, *Fables Ancient and Modern;* George Farquhar, *The Constant Couple;* Nicholas Rowe, *The Ambitious Stepmother.*

**World Music**  Dietrich Buxtehude, *Abendmusik, BuxWV 133;* Arcangelo Corelli, *Twelve Violin Sonatas, Opus 5;* Johann Kuhnau, *Six Biblical Sonatas.*

**Miscellaneous**  Births include Lambert Sigisbert Adam, Christian Friedrich Henrici, Charles Joseph Natoire, and James Thomson; deaths include Caius Gabriel Cibber and John Dryden.

## American Art and Literature Highlights

**Births/Deaths**  Richard Lewis (poet) is born.

**Art Works**  Anonymous, *Mr. and Mrs. Provoost—William Stoughton.*

**Literature**  Cotton Mather, *Reasonable Religion;* Samuel Sewall, *The Selling of Joseph;* Solomon Stoddard, *The Doctrine of Institutional Churches.*

# 1701

❄

## Historical Highlights

Yale College is founded in New Haven, Connecticut; Fort Pontchartrain founded at site of present-day Detroit; William "Captain" Kidd is tried, convicted, and hanged for murder and piracy.

## World Cultural Highlights

**World Art**  Nicolas Coustou, *Mercury Putting Argus to Sleep;* Robert Le Lorrain, *Galatea;* Hyacinthe Rigaud, *Louis XIV.*

**World Literature**  Daniel Defoe, *The True-Born Englishman;* George Farquhar, *Sir Harry Wildair;* Charles Sedley, *The Tyrant King of Crete;* Richard Steele, *The Christian Hero.*

**World Music**  Tomaso Albinoni, *L'Inganno innocente;* Antonio Caldara, *La Partenope;* Louis Clérambault, *Te Deum in Three Parts;* Alessandro Scarlatti, *Laodicea e Berenice.*

**Miscellaneous**  Births include Johann Jakob Breitinger, Thomas Hudson and Theodor Verhaegen; deaths include Edme Boursault, Magdeleine de Scudéri (Sappho), and Charles Sedley.

### American Art and Literature Highlights

**Births/Deaths**    Deaths include authors William Fitzhugh and William Stoughton.

**Literature**    Robert Beverly, *An Essay upon the Government of the English Plantations . . . of America*; Edward Taylor, *Christographia*.

# 1702

☀

### Historical Highlights

Queen Anne's War (War of the Spanish Succession in Europe) begins; the British take St. Augustine in Florida and burn it; Cotton Mather helps form a vigilante group to quell delinquency in the colonies.

### World Cultural Highlights

**World Art**    Antoine Coysevox, *Mercury—Fame;* Godfrey Kneller, *Sir Isaac Newton;* Hyacinthe Rigaud, *Bossuet.*

**World Literature**    Colley Cibber, *She Wou'd and She Wou'd Not;* George Farquhar, *The Twin Rivals;* Alain René Lesage, *Le Point d'honneur;* Richard Steele, *The Funeral, or Grief à la Mode.*

**World Music**    Tomaso Albinoni, *Twelve Solo Cantatas, Opus 4*; Marc-Antoine Charpentier, *Judicium Salomonis;* Jeremiah Clarke, *The Harpsichord Master.*

**Miscellaneous**    The Copenhagen Opera House opens; births include Jacques Aved, Jean Étienne Liotard, Pietro Longhi, Samuel Scott, and Francesco Zuccarelli.

### American Art and Literature Highlights

**Literature**    Cotton Mather, *Magnalia Christi Americana*; William Penn, *More Fruits of Solitude.*

# 1703

☀

### Historical Highlights

Delaware declares itself a separate colony from Pennsylvania; Peter the Great lays out the foundation for St. Petersburg in Russia; almost 200,000 people are killed in a great earthquake in Tokyo.

### World Cultural Highlights

**World Art**    Francis Bird, *Henry VIII;* Nicolas de Largillière, *La belle Strasbourgeoise;* Jean-Louis Lemoyne, *Bust of Hardouin-Mansart.*

**World Literature**    Arthur Collier, *Clavis Universalis;* George Farquhar, *The Inconstant;* Nicholas Rowe, *The Fair Penitent—The Country House;* Richard Steele, *The Lying Lover.*

**World Music**    Tomaso Albinoni, *Griselda;* Francesco Bonporti, *Ten Trio Sonatas, Opus 4;* Reinhard Keiser, *Die Geburt der Minerva;* Alessandro Scarlatti, *Arminio.*

**Miscellaneous**    Lincoln's Inn Public Subscription Concerts begin in London; births include Henry Brooke, François Boucher, Robert Dodsley, Corrado Giaquinto, and Carl Heinrich Graun; deaths include John Crowne, Samuel Pepys, and Charles Perrault.

### American Art and Literature Highlights

**Births/Deaths**    Births include theologian/author Jonathan Edwards.

**Literature**    Louis-Armand Lahontan, *Nouveaux Voyages de M. le Baron de Lahontan dans l'Amérique Septentionale.*

# 1704

❄

### Historical Highlights

The French and their Indian allies take part in the Deerfield Massacre in Massachusetts while colonial forces attack the French fort at Port Royal in Nova Scotia; the British take Gibraltar from the Spanish and defeat the French and Bavarians at the Battle of Blenheim.

### World Cultural Highlights

**World Art**   André Bouys, *Marin Marais;* Guillaume Coustou, *The Death of Hercules;* Pierre Legros II, *Stanislas Kostka—St. Francis Xavier.*

**World Literature**   Joseph Addison, *The Campaign;* George Farquhar, *The Stage Coach;* Jean-François Regnard, *Les Folies amoureuses;* Jonathan Swift, *A Tale of a Tub.*

**World Music**   Nicola Haym, *Twelve Trio Sonatas, Opus 2;* Francesco Manfredini, *Twelve Concertini per camera, Opus 1;* Johann Pachelbel, *Missa Brevis in D Minor;* Domenico Scarlatti, *Irene.*

**Miscellaneous**   Births include William Hamilton, Maurice Quentin de la Tour, and Jean Baptiste Lemoyne; deaths include Marc-Antoine Charpentier, John Locke, and Joseph Parrocel.

### American Art and Literature Highlights

**Births/Deaths**   Births include artist Nathanial Emmons, and authors John Adams and Josiah Smith; deaths include historian William Hubbard.

### Music

**K. Biographical**   Christopher Witt (British organ maker/artist) comes to the colonies.

# 1705

❄

### Historical Highlights

North Carolina recognizes by law the Anglican Church; Barcelona falls to the British Navy; a Russian revolt takes place against the westernization procedures of Peter the Great.

### World Cultural Highlights

**World Art**   Donato Creti, *The Quarrel;* Claude Gillot, *Harlequin, Emperor in the Moon.*

**World Literature**   Joseph Addison, *Rosamund;* Susanna Centlivre, *The Gamester;* Colley Cibber, *The Careless Husband;* Prosper Jolyot de Crébillon, *Idoménée;* Richard Steele, *The Tender Husband.*

**World Music**   Antonio Bononcini, *La Maddalena;* George Frideric Handel, *Almira—Nero;* Johann Pachelbel, *Magnificat in G Minor;* Antonio Vivaldi, *Twelve Sonate da Camera, Opus 1.*

**Miscellaneous**   The King's (Queen's) Theatre (Her Majesty's Theatre in 1837) opens in London; births include Nicolas Sébastien Adam, Carle Van Loo, and Louis Roubiliac; deaths include Luca Giordano, Antônio José da Silva (burned at the stake by the Inquisition), and Jan van der Meer.

### American Art and Literature Highlights

**Births/Deaths**   Births include artist Robert Feke and critic Charles Chauncey; deaths include clergyman/poet Michael Wigglesworth.

**Art Works**   J. Hargreaves, *Sarah Harrison Blair—James Blair.*

**Literature**   Robert Beverley, *The History and Present State of Virginia;* Sarah Kemble Knight,

*Journals of Madam Knight and Rev. Mr. Buckingham . . .* ; Francis Makemie, *A Plain and Friendly Persuasive to the Inhabitants of Virginia and Maryland for Promoting Towns and Cohabitation.*

# 1706

❀

## Historical Highlights

French and Spanish naval forces are forced to withdraw from Charleston Harbor in South Carolina.

## World Cultural Highlights

**World Art**    Jean-Baptiste Jouvenet, *The Miraculous Draft of Fishes—Christ in the House of Simon.*

**World Literature**    David de Brueys, *L'Avocat Patelin;* Susanna Centlivre, *Love at a Venture;* George Farquhar, *The Recruiting Officer;* John Vanbrugh, *The Mistake;* Isaac Watts, *Horae Lyricae.*

**World Music**    Johann Fux, *Te Deum in F Major;* Jean-Philippe Rameau, *Premier livre de pièces de clavecin;* Alessandro Scarlatti, *Il gran Tamerlano.*

**Miscellaneous**    Births include Giovanni Bettino Cignaroli, Baldassare Galuppi, and Giovanni Battista (Padre) Martini; deaths include Giacomo Farelli, Johann Pachelbel, and Godfried Schacken.

## American Art and Literature Highlights

**Births/Deaths**    Births include Benjamin Franklin, poet Joseph Green, and author Samuel Mather.

**Literature**    George Keith, *A Journal of Travels from New Hampshire to Caratuck;* Cotton Mather, *The Negro Christianized.*

## Music

**M. Music Publications**

Kelpius, Johannes, *Hymnbook*

# 1707

❀

## Historical Highlights

A British military force tries to capture the French colony of Acadia; the Act of Union unites England and Scotland into one political entity, Great Britain.

## World Cultural Highlights

**World Art**    Louis Boulogne, *Diana Resting;* Luca Carlevaris, *Procession of the Earl of Manchester;* Claude Gillot, *The Trojan Horse;* Sebastiano Ricci, *Hercules and the Centaur.*

**World Literature**    Prosper Jolyot de Crébillon, *Atrée et Thyeste;* George Farquhar, *The Beaux' Stratagem;* Alain René Lesage, *Crispin, rival de son maître.*

**World Music**    Tomaso Albinoni, *Twelve Concerti a cinque, Opus 5;* Johann Sebastian Bach, *Aus der Tiefen rufe ich, Herr, zu dir, BWV 131;* George Frideric Handel, *Rodrigo.*

**Miscellaneous**    Births include Henry Fielding, Carlo Goldoni, and Louis-Michel Van Loo; deaths include Jan van Broekhuizen, Dietrich Buxtehude, Jeremiah Clark, Noël Coypel, and George Farquhar.

### American Art and Literature Highlights

**Births/Deaths**  Births include poet Mather Byles and author William Stith; deaths include author Samuel Willard.

**Literature**  Benjamin Colman, *The Government and Improvement of Mirth—Practical Discourses upon the Parable of the Ten Virgins;* Francis Makemie, *A Narrative of a New and Unusual American Imprisonment;* John Williams, *The Redeemed Captive, Returning unto Zion.*

# 1708

☀

## Historical Highlights

The French and their Indian allies destroy the colony of Haverhill in Massachusetts; the British take over Minorca and Sardinia and form a merger of the two East India companies to better exploit India.

## World Cultural Highlights

**World Art**  Antoine Coypel, *Ceiling, Versailles Royal Chapel;* Nicolas de Largillière, *Louis XIV and the Royal Family;* Hyacinthe Rigaud, *Cardinal de Bouillon.*

**World Literature**  Prosper Jolyot de Crébillon, *Électre;* John Gay, *Wine;* Pierre Carlet de Marivaux, *The Prudent and Equitable Father;* Jean-François Regnard, *Le Légataire universel.*

**World Music**  Johann Sebastian Bach, *Cantata: Gott ist mein König, BWV 71;* Benedetto Marcello, *Twelve Concerti a cinque, Opus 1;* Georg Philipp Telemann, *Adonis;* Antonio Vivaldi, *Gloria.*

**Miscellaneous**  Births include Pompeo Girolamo Batoni, Olof von Dalin, Friedrich von Hagedorn, and Francis Hayman; deaths include Ludolf Backhuysen and Johann Christian Wagenseil.

## American Art and Literature

**Births/Deaths**  Births include artist Joseph Badger; deaths include author Francis Makemie.

**Literature**  Ebenezer Cook, *The Sot-Weed Factor, or, A Voyage to Maryland . . . ;* John Lawson, *A New Voyage to Carolina; Containing the Exact Description and Natural History of That Country;* Cotton Mather, *Good Education of Children;* Solomon Stoddard, *Inexcusableness of Neglecting the Worship of God.*

## Music

**F. Births**  Thomas Johnston (organ builder/publisher).

**G. Deaths**  Johannes Kelpius (German-born mystic/compiler).

# 1709

☀

## Historical Highlights

Many Protestant refugees from Switzerland and Germany settle in the Carolinas; the Quakers open the first mental home in Philadelphia; peace talks begin at The Hague.

## World Cultural Highlights

**World Art**  Godfrey Kneller, *William Congreve;* Giovanni Pellegrini, *The Fall of Phaeton—Pyrrhus and Demetrius;* Andreas Schlüter, *Monument, Friedrich Wilhelm II.*

**World Literature** Susanna Centlivre, *The Busybody;* Mary de la Rivière Manley, *The New Atlantis;* Alexander Pope, *Pastorals—Poetical Miscellanies.*

**World Music** George Frideric Handel, *Agrippina;* Francesco Manfredini, *Twelve Sinfonie da Chiesa, Opus 2;* Giuseppe Torelli, *Twelve Concerti Grossi, Opus 8;* Antonio Vivaldi, *Twelve Violin Sonatas, Opus 2.*

**Miscellaneous** Richard Steele begins publication of *The Tatler;* births include John Cleland, Johann Feichtmayr, Jean-Baptiste Gresset, Samuel Johnson, and Jean-Jacques Pompignan; deaths include Meindert Hobbema, Andrea Pozzo, and Giuseppe Torelli.

### American Art and Literature Highlights

**Births/Deaths** Births include historian James Adair.

# 1710

☀

### Historical Highlights

The colonial population reaches approximately 357,000; British and colonial forces take Acadia from the French and rename it Nova Scotia—also Port Royal, which is renamed Annapolis.

### World Cultural Highlights

**World Art** Matthias Braun von Braun, *The Vision of St. Luitgard;* Antoine Coysevox, *The Duchess of Burgundy as Diana;* François de Troy, *A Reading with Molière;* Antoine Watteau, *The Bivouac.*

**World Literature** George Berkeley, *Treatise Concerning the Principles of Human Knowledge;* Colley Cibber, *The Rival Queens;* William Congreve, *Semele;* Gottfried Wilhelm Leibnitz, *Théodicée.*

**World Music** Johann Sebastian Bach, *Brandenburg Concerto No. 6*; Louis-Nicolas Clérambault, *First Book for Organ*; Johann C. Pepusch, *Six English Cantatas, Book I.*

**Miscellaneous** The Academy of Ancient Music is founded in London; births include Thomas Arne, Marie Anne du Boccage, Sarah Fielding, Johann August Nahl, Giovanni Battista Pergolesi, and Pierre Antoine Verschaffelt; deaths include Thomas Betterton and Giovanni Castiglione.

### American Art and Literature Highlights

**Births/Deaths** Births include poet Landon Carter, authors Richard Bland and Jonathan Carver; deaths include poet John Saffin.

**Art Works** Justus E. Kuhn, *Eleanor Darnall* (?).

**Literature** Cotton Mather, *Essays to Do Good (Bonifacius)—The American City of God (Theopolis Americana);* John Saffin, *John Saffin, His Book* (published 1928); John Wise, *The Churches Quarrel Espoused.*

# 1711

☀

### Historical Highlights

The Tuscarora Indians massacre 150 settlers in North Carolina; the colonial attack on Montreal and Quebec fails; over 500,000 people in Germany and Austria die from the bubonic plague.

### World Cultural Highlights

**World Art** Matthias Braun von Braun, *St. Ivo;* Godfrey Kneller, *Sir Christopher Wren.*

**World Literature**   Prosper Jolyot de Crébillon, *Rhadamiste et Zénobie;* John Gay, *The Present State of Wit;* Alexander Pope, *Essay on Criticism;* William Whiston, *Primitive Christianity Revived.*

**World Music**   Francesco Gasparini, *Merope;* Christoph Graupner, *Telemach;* George Frideric Handel, *Rinaldo;* Domenico Scarlatti, *Orlando—Tolomeo e Alessandro.*

**Miscellaneous**   Joseph Addison begins publishing *The Spectator;* births include William Boyce, Arthur Devis, David Hume, and Samuel Gotthold Lange; deaths include Jean Berain and Elisabeth Sophie Chéron.

## American Art and Literature Highlights

**Births/Deaths**   Births include poet Jupiter Hammon and educator Eleazer Wheelock; deaths include author John Lawson.

## Music

The first known organ in New England (second in the colonies) is set up in the home of Thomas Brattle in Boston.

# 1712

### ❀

## Historical Highlights

The Tuscarora Indians are massacred by colonial militia as a reprisal for their earlier raid on the settlers; slave revolts in New York cause the death of over 100 blacks; the last witchcraft trial takes place in England.

## World Cultural Highlights

**World Art**   Nicolas Coustou, *Marne—Seine;* Jean Baptiste Oudry, *Dead Birds with Cherries;* Camillo Rusconi, *The Four Apostles, St. John Lateran, Rome;* Antoine Watteau, *Ceres.*

**World Literature**   John Hughes, *Calypso and Telemachus;* Ambrose Philips, *The Distrest Mother;* Alexander Pope, *Rape of the Lock;* Jonathan Swift, *Proposal for Correcting the English Language.*

**World Music**   Evaristo Dall'Abaco, *Twelve Concerti a quattro da chiesa, Opus 2;* André Destouches, *Callirhoé;* George Frideric Handel, *Il pastor fido;* Antonio Vivaldi, *L'estro armonico I, II, Opus 3.*

**Miscellaneous**   Madrid's Biblioteca Nacional is founded; the Karlsruhe Opera opens; births include Francesco Algarotti, Francesco Guardi, Edward Moore, Christian Reutter, and Jean-Jacques Rousseau; deaths include Carlo Alessandro Guidi, Jan van der Heyden, and William King.

## American Art and Literature Highlights

**Births/Deaths**   Births include statesman/author Alexander Hamilton and poet Jona Green.

## Music

**K. Biographical**   John Tufts publishes the first known singing book in the colonies.

# 1713

### ❀

## Historical Highlights

The Tuscarora Indian War ends with the remaining Indians fleeing to Iroquois territory; the Carolina Territory is divided into North and South; England receives the Hudson Bay Territory,

Newfoundland and Nova Scotia from France; Edward Teach, following hostilities, continues on as Blackbeard, the pirate.

## World Cultural Highlights

**World Art**   Alexandre-François Desportes, *Spaniels with Dead Game;* Camillo Rusconi, *St. John the Evangelist;* Antoine Watteau, *Jupiter and Antiope—L'Indifférent.*

**World Literature**   Joseph Addison, *Cato;* George Berkeley, *Dialogues between Hylas and Philonous;* John Gay, *The Wife of Bath;* Jonathan Swift, *Journal to Stella.*

**World Music**   Johann Sebastian Bach, *Brandenburg Concerto No. 3;* Arcangelo Corelli, *Twelve Concerti Grossi, Opus 6;* George Frideric Handel, *Utrecht Te Deum and Jubilate—Silla.*

**Miscellaneous**   The Académie des Beaux-Arts opens in Paris; births include Charles Batteux, Denis Diderot, Allan Ramsay, and Laurence Sterne; deaths include Arcangelo Corelli, Johann Klostermann, and Carlo Maratti.

## American Art and Literature Highlights

**Births/Deaths**   Births include author Elizabeth Ashbridge.

**Art Works**   Anonymous, *Old Brick Meetinghouse* (Boston).

**Literature**   Samuel Sewall, *Proposals Touching the Accomplishments of Prophecies;* Richard Steere, *The Daniel Catcher, The Life of the Prophet Daniel in a Poem;* Solomon Stoddard, *The Efficacy of the Fear of Hell to Restrain Men from Sin.*

# 1714

✸

## Historical Highlights

The French build a military and trading post at Natchitoches, Louisiana; tea is introduced into the colonies; the mercury thermometer and the Fahrenheit scale are invented; Queen Anne of England dies; George I becomes the first Hanover King.

## World Cultural Highlights

**World Art**   Sebastiano Conca, *Madonna of the Rosary;* Giovanni Pellegrini, *Rebecca at the Well;* Antoine Watteau, *Love in the French Theater—Love in the Italian Theater.*

**World Literature**   Susanna Centlivre, *The Wonder! A Woman Keeps a Secret;* Mary de la Rivière Manley, *The Adventures of Rivella;* Nicholas Rowe, *The Tragedy of Jane Shore.*

**World Music**   Johann Sebastian Bach, at least eight cantatas including *Weinen, Klagen, Sorgen, Zagen;* Michele Mascitti, *Twelve Violin Sonatas, Opus 5;* Alessandro Scarlatti, *L'Amor generoso.*

**Miscellaneous**   The Lyons Academy of Fine Arts and Concerts opens; births include C. P. E. Bach, Raniero da Calzabigi, Christoph Willibald Gluck, Jean-Baptiste Pigalle, William Shenstone, and Claude-Joseph Vernet; deaths include Pierre Legros and Andreas Schlüter.

## American Art and Literature Highlights

**Births/Deaths**   Deaths include poet Benjamin Tompson.

**Literature**   Robert Hunter, *Androboros;* Solomon Stoddard, *A Guide to Christ.*

## Music

**K. Biographical**   Boston—first known advertisement for singing school and psalm singing; Mr. Thomas Brattle provides the King's Chapel in Boston with a new organ, the second church organ in the colonies.

# 1715

❀

## Historical Highlights

Indian problems arise with the Yamasee Indians in South Carolina; Louis XIV of France dies; the Jacobite Rebellion ends in Scotland; the annual rowing races on the Thames River begin.

## World Cultural Highlights

**World Art**   Antoine Coysevox, *Louis XIV;* Claude Gillot, *The Passion of Christ;* Francesco Solimena, *The Naming of John the Baptist;* Giovanni Battista Tiepolo, *The Sacrifice of Abraham.*

**World Literature**   Philippe Destouches, *Le Médisant;* Alain René Lesage, *Gil Blas de Santillane I, II;* Matthew Prior, *Solomon, or The Vanity of the World,* Nicholas Rowe, *The Tragedy of Lady Jane Grey.*

**World Music**   Johann Sebastian Bach, Eight cantatas—*Six English Suites;* Louis-Nicolas Clérambault, *Abraham;* Johann J. Fux, *Orfeo ed Euridice.*

**Miscellaneous**   Three Choirs Festivals begin in England, births include Étienne Bonnet de Condillac, Christian Fürchtegott Gellert, Richard Graves, Ewald Christian von Kleist, Amédée van Loo, and Jean-Baptiste Perronneau; deaths include François Girardon and Nahum Tate.

## American Art and Literature Highlights

**Births/Deaths**   Births include author Samuel Finley.

**Literature**   Joseph Morgan, *The History of the Kingdom of Basaruah.*

# 1716

❀

## Historical Highlights

Emperor Charles VI goes to war with Turkey, defeats their forces, and takes possession of Turkey's last hold in Europe; Japan first allows works in Western languages to be circulated in the country.

## World Cultural Highlights

**World Art**   Charles Antoine Coypel, *Scenes from Don Quixote;* Giovanni Battista Foggini, *The Flaying of Marsyas;* Jean-Baptiste Jouvenet, *The Visitation;* Antoine Watteau, *La leçon d'amour.*

**World Literature**   Joseph Addison, *The Drummer, or The Haunted House;* John Gay, *Trivia: or, The Art of Walking the Streets of London;* Lewis Theobald, *The Perfidious Brother.*

**World Music**   George Frideric Handel and Georg Philipp Telemann each write an *Oratorio: Der für die Sünde der Welt gemartete und sterbende Jesus;* Antonio Vivaldi, *Six Violin Sonatas, Opus 5.*

**Miscellaneous**   Births include Jean-Jacques Barthélemy, Étienne Maurice Falconet, Thomas Gray, and Joseph-Marie Vien; deaths include Gottfried Wilhelm von Leibnitz and William Wycherley.

## American Art and Literature Highlights

**Births/Deaths**   Births include sculptor Simeon Skillin, Sr. and author James Davenport; deaths include author George Keith.

# 1717

✦

## Historical Highlights

John Law is given a monopoly on trade rights in Louisiana by the French government and forms the Mississippi Company; smallpox inoculations are introduced into England.

## World Cultural Highlights

**World Art**    Francesco Solimena, *Massacre of the Giustiniani at Chios;* James Thornhill, *Scenes from the Life of St. Paul;* Antoine Watteau, *Embarkation for the Isle of Cythera.*

**World Literature**    Colley Cibber, *Nonjuror;* Prosper Jolyot de Crébillon, *Sémiramis;* Elijah Fenton, *Poems on Several Occasions;* Alexander Pope, *Eloise to Abelard;* Richard Savage, *The Convocation.*

**World Music**    Johann Sebastian Bach, *Brandenburg Concerto No. 1;* George Frideric Handel, *Water Music;* Antonio Vivaldi, *Twelve Concerti for Five Instruments, Books I, II, Opus 7.*

**Miscellaneous**    Births include Louis Carmontelle, Alexander Cozens, David Garrick, Adam Friedrich Öser, Horace Walpole, and Johann Joachim Winckelmann; deaths include Jean-Baptiste Jouvenet.

## American Art and Literature Highlights

**Art Works**    Anonymous (Schuyler Limner), *Mrs. David Ver Planck.*

**Literature**    Cotton Mather, *Messenger of God (Malachi);* John Wise, *A Vindication of the Government of New England Churches.*

## Music

The American publication of Isaac Watt's *Hymns and Spiritual Songs* appears.

# 1718

✦

## Historical Highlights

New Orleans is founded by the Mississippi Company with settlers from France and Canada; San Antonio, Texas, is founded as a Spanish mission; Blackbeard, the pirate (Edward Teach), is caught and executed in North Carolina; the Quadruple Alliance is formed in Europe.

## World Cultural Highlights

**World Art**    Jean-Marc Nattier, *Perseus Turning Phineas to Stone with the Head of Medusa;* Balthasar Permoser, *Three Satyrs, Dresden;* Antoine Watteau, *Les Champs Elysées.*

**World Literature**    Susanna Centlivre, *A Bold Stroke for a Wife;* Matthew Prior, *Alma, or The Progress of the Mind;* Richard Savage, *Love in a Veil;* Voltaire, *Edipe.*

**World Music**    Johann Sebastian Bach, *Brandenburg Concerto No. 2;* George Frideric Handel, *Chandos Anthems;* Francesco Manfredini, *Twelve Concerti for Two Violins, Opus 3.*

**Miscellaneous**    The Palermo Accademia dei Scienze, Lettere, ed Arti is founded; births include Maria Gaetana Agnesi, Hedvig Charlotta Nordenflycht, Alexandre Roslin, and Alexander Sumarokov; deaths include Pierre Legros (fils), Thomas Parnell, and Nicholas Rowe.

## American Art and Literature Highlights

**Births/Deaths**    Births include poet Thomas Craddock.

**Art Works**    Patroon Painter, *Johannes De Peyser III.*

**Literature**    Cotton Mather, *Psalterium Americanum.*

# 1719

❀

## Historical Highlights

Parliament passes the Declaration Act declaring Ireland to be a permanent part of England.

## World Cultural Highlights

**World Art**   James Thornhill, *The Life of the Apostle Paul* (completed); Giovanni Battista Tiepolo, *The Repudiation of Hagar;* Antoine Watteau, *Les Fêtes Vénitiennes.*

**World Literature**   Daniel Defoe, *Robinson Crusoe;* Ludvig Holberg, *Pedar Paars;* Thomas d'Urfey, *Wit and Mirth, or Pills to Purge Melancholy;* Edward Young, *Busiris.*

**World Music**   Johann Sebastian Bach, *Die Zeit, die Tag und Jahre macht, BWV 134a* (secular cantata); Georg Philipp Telemann, *Die Satyren in Arcadien.*

**Miscellaneous**   Births include John Hawkins, Scannabuc, Michel Jean Sedaine, and Jeremiah Theus; deaths include Joseph Addison, Christoph Ludwig Agricola, Carlo Cignani, and Jan Weenix.

## American Art and Literature

**Births/Deaths**   Births include author Joseph Bellamy.

# 1720

❀

## Historical Highlights

The colonial population is about 474,388 people, with Boston still the largest city with 12,000 inhabitants; the bankruptcy of the Mississippi Company causes problems for the French government.

## World Cultural Highlights

**World Art**   Nicolas Lancret, *Dance in a Pavilion;* Giacomo Serpotta, *Fortitude;* Giovanni Battista Tiepolo, *The Martyrdom of St. Bartholomew;* Antoine Watteau, *The Italian Comedians.*

**World Literature**   Daniel Defoe, *Captain Singleton;* John Gay, *Poems on Several Occasions;* Mary de la Rivière Manley, *The Power of Love;* Pierre Carlet de Marivaux, *L'Amour et la vérité.*

**World Music**   Johann Sebastian Bach, *Brandenburg Concerto No. 4;* George Frideric Handel, *Radamisto;* Johann C. Pepusch, *Six English Cantatas, Book II.*

**Miscellaneous**   The Breitkopf publishing firm is founded in Leipzig; Royal Academy of Music opens in London; births include Edme Dumont, Bernardo Canaletto, Carlo Gozzi, and Giovanni Battista Piranesi; deaths include John Hughes and Antoine Coysevox.

## American Art and Literature Highlights

**Births/Deaths**   Births include novelist Charlotte R. Lennox, authors Jonathan Mayhew and John Woolman; deaths include author Daniel Leeds and man of letters Francis Daniel Pastorius.

**Art Works**   Gansevoort Painter, *The Girl with the Red Shoes;* Gustavus Hesselius, *Bacchus and Ariadne* (?); Patroon Painter, *Anthony van Schaick.*

**Literature**   John Rogers, *The Book of the Revelation of Jesus Christ;* Thomas Walters, *A Dialogue between John Faustus, a Conjurer, and Jack Tory, His Friend.*

## Music

**K. Biographical**   Johann Beissel (Moravian composer) comes to the New World; the Ephrata

Cloister is founded in Pennsylvania by Conrad Beissel and Peter Miller; first documented singing societies are formed in New England.

**M. Music Publications**

Symmes, Rev. Thomas, *The Reasonableness of Regular Singing, or Singing by Note*

# 1721

✦

## Historical Highlights

Postal service begins between London and New England; a smallpox epidemic strikes Boston, but vaccination against the disease is resisted.

## World Cultural Highlights

**World Art**   Charles-Joseph Natoire, *Samson's Mother Offering Sacrifice;* Jean-Batiste Oudry, *The Dead Wolf;* Giambattista Pittoni, *Nero and Seneca's Corpse;* Antoine Watteau, *Gilles.*

**World Literature**   Pierre Carlet de Marivaux, *Arlequin poli par l'amour;* Charles-Louis Montesquieu, *Persian Letters;* Allan Ramsay, *Collected Poems I;* Edward Young, *The Revenge.*

**World Music**   Johann Sebastian Bach, *Brandenburg Concerto No. 5;* George Frideric Handel, *Floridante;* Pietro Locatelli, *Twelve Concerti Grossi (with fugues), Opus 1.*

**Miscellaneous**   Births include Mark Akenside, Bernardo Bellotto, Christian Friedrich Hunold (Menantes), Thomas Sandby, and Tobias Smollett; deaths include Matthew Prior and Jean-Antoine Watteau.

## American Art and Literature Highlights

**Births/Deaths**   Births include author Samuel Hopkins; deaths include poet/author Richard Steere.

**Art Works**   Anonymous, *Thomas Van Alstyne;* Anonymous ("Pollard Painter"), *Mrs. Ann Pollard;* Gustavus Hesselius, *The Last Supper.*

**Literature**   Cotton Mather, *The Christian Philosopher;* Samuel Sewall, *A Memorial Relating to the Kennebeck Indians;* John Wise, *A Word of Comfort to a Melancholy Country; or, The Bank of Credit Erected in Massachusetts Fairly Defended.*

## Music

**F. Births**   Peter Pelham III (organist/composer) December 9.

**M. Music Publications**

Mather, Cotton, *The Accomplished Singer . . .*
Tufts, John, *A Very Plain and Easy Introduction to the Art of Singing of Psalm Tunes*
Walters, Thomas, *The Grounds and Rules of Musick Explained . . .*

# 1722

✦

## Historical Highlights

The Iroquois Confederation of the Six Nations and the colony of Virginia sign a treaty making the Blue Ridge Mountains and the Potomac River their border.

## World Cultural Highlights

**World Art**   Egid Quirin Asam, *Assumption of the Virgin;* Paul Troger, *Descent from the Cross;* Giovanni Battista Tiepolo, *Madonna of the Carmelites and Saints;* Jean-François de Troy, *Lot's Daughters.*

**World Literature**   Daniel Defoe, *Moll Flanders—A Journal of the Plague Year;* Pierre Carlet de Marivaux, *La surprise de l'amour;* Richard Steele, *The Conscious Lovers.*

**World Music**   Johann Sebastian Bach, *Well-Tempered Clavier I;* François Couperin, *Piéces de clavecin, Book III;* Reinhard Keiser, *Ulysses.*

**Miscellaneous**   Johann Mattheson begins editing *Critica Musica;* births include John Home, Anna Luise Karschin, and Johann Heinrich Tischbein; deaths include Antoine Coypel, Claude Gillot, Johann Kuhnau, Ignace Parrocel, and Adriaen van der Werff.

### American Art and Literature Highlights

**Births/Deaths**   Deaths include historian Robert Beverley.

**Art Works**   William Burgis, *View of Boston* (engraving).

**Literature**   Robert Beverley, *History and Present State of Virginia* (1705 publication enlarged); James Blair, *Our Saviour's Divine Sermon on the Mount;* Cotton Mather, *The Angel of Bethesda;* Solomon Stoddard, *An Answer to Some Cases of Conscience Respecting the Country;* Thomas Walter, *The Sweet Psalmist of Israel.*

# 1723

❄

### Historical Highlights

Louis XV, coming of age, becomes sole regent in France; England and Prussia sign agreements of marriage between their two ruling houses; the Chinese ban Christianity from their country.

### World Cultural Highlights

**World Art**   François Lemoyne, *Perseus and Andromeda;* Sebastiano Ricci, *St. Peter Released from Prison;* John Rysbrack, *Monument to Matthew Prior;* Jean-François de Troy, *The Alarm.*

**World Literature**   Daniel Defoe, *The Highland Rogue (Rob Roy);* Richard Savage, *Sir Thomas Overbury;* John Thurmond, *Harlequin Dr. Faustus;* Voltaire, *La Henriade.*

**World Music**   Johann Sebastian Bach, about 30 cantatas—*Magnificat in E-Flat—Two-Part Inventions—Three-Part Sinfonias;* Jean-Marie Leclair (l'aîné), *Twelve Violin Sonatas I, Opus 1.*

**Miscellaneous**   The St. Petersburg Theater opens in Russia; births include Jean-François Marmontel and Joshua Reynolds; deaths include Susanna Centlivre, Johann Christian Günther, Godfrey Kneller, Thomas d'Urfey, and Christopher Wren.

### American Art and Literature Highlights

**Births/Deaths**   Births include author/poet Samuel Davies and author William Livingston; deaths include clergyman/educator Increase Mather.

**Art Works**   Anonymous, *Old North Church* (Boston); Pieter Vanderlyn, *Mrs. Petrus Vas.*

# 1724

❄

### Historical Highlights

The cultivation of rice by field irrigation begins in South Carolina; the first permanent white settlement in Vermont, Fort Dummer (Brattleboro), is built.

### World Cultural Highlights

**World Art**   Giacomo Ceruti, *The Beggar;* William Hogarth, *Masquerades and Operas: Burlington Gate;* François Lemoyne, *Hercules and Omphale;* Jean-Baptiste Oudry, *White Dog, Game and Fruit.*

**World Literature**   Daniel Defoe, *Roxana, or the Fortunate Mistress;* John Gay, *The Captives;* Allan Ramsay, *The Tea-Table Miscellany I;* Jonathan Swift, *The Drapier Letters.*

**World Music**   Johann Sebastian Bach, about 50 cantatas—*St. John Passion;* George Frideric Handel, *Tamerlano—Giulio Cesare in Egitto;* Johann C. Pepusch, *The Prophetess.*

**Miscellaneous**   The Toulouse Académie de Musique is founded; births include Pedro Antônio Correa Garçao, Immanuel Kant, Friedrich Gottlieb Klopstock, Franz Anton Maulpertsch, and George Stubbs; deaths include Mary de la Rivière Manley.

## American Art and Literature Highlights

**Births/Deaths**   Births include historian Isaac Backus.

**Literature**   Hugh Jones, *The Present State of Virginia;* Cotton Mather, *Parentator* (biography).

## Music

**K. Biographical**   The first known organ in New York City is installed in the Dutch Reformed Church.

# 1725
❋

## Historical Highlights

The British begin building forts in the Maine Territory to curb further French expansion southward; English Quakers publicly denounce slavery as an institution.

## World Cultural Highlights

**World Art**   Sebastiano Conca, *The Crowning of St. Cecilia;* Giovanni Battista Piazzetta, *The Glory of St. Dominic;* Francesco Solimena, *The Expulsion of Heliodorus from the Temple.*

**World Literature**   John Dyer, *Grongar Hill;* Pierre Carlet de Marivaux, *Isle of Slaves;* Allan Ramsay, *The Gentle Shepherd;* William Somerville, *The Two Springs;* Thomas Tickell, *Colin and Lucy.*

**World Music**   Johann Sebastian Bach, 30 cantatas—*Klavierbüchlein für Anna Magdalena Bach;* Antonio Vivaldi, *The Seasons* (part of his Opus 8).

**Miscellaneous**   The Spanish Steps are completed in Rome; the Concert Spirituel is founded in Paris; births include Jean-Baptiste Greuze, Ignaz Günther, Christian Bernhard Rode, and Paul Sandby; deaths include Jean Jacques Caffiéri, Giovanni Battista Foggini, and Alessandro Scarlatti.

## American Art and Literature Highlights

**Births/Deaths**   Births include author James Otis, Jr. and sculptor Patience Lowell Wright; deaths include author John Wise.

**Art Works**   Anonymous (Gansevoort Limner), *Pau De Wandlaer;* Robert Feke, *Self-Portrait;* Gustavus Hesselius, *Bacchanalian Revel* (?).

**Literature**   Roger Wolcott, *Poetical Meditations, Being the Improvement of Some Vacant Hours.*

## Music

**G. Deaths**   Thomas Walter (clergyman/compiler) Jan 10.

**K. Biographical**   Josiah Dwight writes his "Essay to silence the outcry . . . against regular singing."

# 1726

❀

## Historical Highlights

The British governor of Philadelphia uses troops to quell the food riots by the poor of that city; a printing press is set up in Annapolis by William Parks.

## World Cultural Highlights

**World Art**   James Gibbs, *St. Martin-in-the-Fields* (completed); Sebastiano/Marco Ricci, *The Adoration of the Magi;* Giovanni Battista Tiepolo, *The Judgment of Solomon.*

**World Literature**   Prosper Jolyot de Crébillon, *Pyrrhus;* Richard Savage, *Miscellaneous Poems;* Jonathan Swift, *Gulliver's Travels;* James Thomson, *Winter;* Edward Young, *The Instalment.*

**World Music**   Johann Sebastian Bach, 20+ cantatas, including *Was Gott tut, das ist wohlgetan;* François Couperin, *Les Nations* (sonatas); George Frideric Handel, *Alessandro—Scipione.*

**Miscellaneous**   The Tours Académie de Musique and the London Academy of Vocal Music are founded; births include Charles Burney, Daniel Chodowiecki, Louis Florence d'Épinay, and Sebastien Slodtz; deaths include Jeremy Collier, François Dumont, and John Vanbrugh.

## American Art and Literature Highlights

**Births/Deaths**   Deaths include historian Samuel Penhallow.

**Art Works**   William Burgis, *A View of Harvard College.*

**Literature**   Cotton Mather, *Manuductio ad Ministerium—Ratio Disciplinae;* Samuel Penhallow, *History of the Wars of New England with the Eastern Indians;* Samuel Willard, *A Compleat Body of Divinity in 250 Expository Lectures* . . . (posthumous publication).

# 1727

❀

## Historical Highlights

The first printing press in Rhode Island is set up by James Frank; George II takes the British throne on the death of George I; John Arbuthnot introduces John Bull as a symbol of Great Britain; the Spanish besiege Gibraltar.

## World Cultural Highlights

**World Art**   Luca Carlevaris, *Count Colloredo Visiting Venice;* Charles-Antoine Coypel, *Perseus Freeing Andromeda;* Noël-Nicolas Coypel, *The Rape of Europa;* John Rysbrack, *George I.*

**World Literature**   Philippe Destouches, *Le Philosophe Marié;* Christian Friedrich Hebbel, *Ernstschertzhaffte und satyrische Gedichte I;* Pierre Carlet de Marivaux, *Annibal;* James Thomson, *Summer.*

**World Music**   Johann Sebastian Bach, *St. Matthew Passion;* George Frideric Handel, *Coronation Anthems for George II;* Antonio Vivaldi, *"La Cetra" Concerti, Books I, II, Opus 9.*

**Miscellaneous**   Births include Francesco Bartolozzi, Giovanni Battista Cipriani, Thomas Gainsborough, and Giovanni Domenico Tiepolo; deaths include Cornelis Huysmans and Pier Jacopo Martelli.

### American Art and Literature Highlights

**Births/Deaths**   Births include artist John Greenwood and educator Ezra Stiles; deaths include poet Samuel Danforth, Jr. and diarist Sarah Kemble Knight.

**Art Works**   Peter Pelham, *Cotton Mather* (two portraits).

**Literature**   James Blair, *The Present State of Virginia, and the College;* Cadwallader Colden, *History of the Five Indian Nations Depending on the Province of New York;* Sarah Kemble Knight, *Journal;* Experience Mayhew, *Indian Converts.*

# 1728

❁

## Historical Highlights

Samuel Higby begins the first production of steel in the New World in Hartford; Boston forms its famous Commons to save it from carts and horses; the first Jewish synagogue in the New World is built in New York; the Spanish lift the siege of Gibraltar after 14 months.

## World Cultural Highlights

**World Art**   Jean-Baptiste Chardin, *The Skate;* Daniel Gran, *Ceiling, Schwarzenberg Palace, Vienna;* Jean-Baptiste Pater, *Soldiers Reveling;* Paul Troger, *The Agony in the Garden.*

**World Literature**   John Gay, *The Beggar's Opera;* Alexander Pope, *The Dunciad I–III;* Antoine Prévost, *Les Mémoires d'un Homme de Qualité;* Allan Ramsay, *Poems II;* John Thomson, *Spring.*

**World Music**   Jean-Marie Leclair (l'aîné), *Twelve Violin Sonatas, Book II, Opus 2;* Giuseppe Sammartini, *Six Concerti Grossi, Opus 2;* Giuseppe Tartini, *Six Concerti a 5, Opus 1.*

**Miscellaneous**   Broadwood and Sons begins making pianos in London; births include Oliver Goldsmith, Anton Raffael Mengs, and Thomas Warton; deaths include Paolo de Matteis and Camillo Rusconi.

## American Art and Literature Highlights

**Births/Deaths**   Births include artist John Hesselius and playwright Mercy Otis Warren; deaths include artist Henrietta Deering Johnston and clergyman/author Cotton Mather.

**Literature**   William Byrd, *The History of the Dividing Line* (published 1841).

## Music

**K. Biographical**   Philadelphia receives a pipe organ in the Christ Church.

**M. Music Publications** Chauncey, Nathaniel, *Regular Singing Defended and Proved to be the Only True Way of Singing the Songs of the Lord.*

# 1729

❁

## Historical Highlights

The Carolinas become Crown Colonies; Isaac Greenwood publishes the first arithmetic textbook in the colonies; Baltimore, Maryland, is founded.

## World Cultural Highlights

**World Art**   Canaletto, *Rialto Bridge from the South;* Alexander Desportes, *Still Life with Oysters;* Nicolas de Largillière, *Elizabeth Throckmorton as a Nun;* Jean-François de Troy, *Rape of the Sabines.*

**World Literature**   Robert Dodsley, *Servitude;* Henry Fielding, *The Author's Farce;* Albrecht von Haller, *Die Alpen;* Pierre Carlet de Marivaux, *The New Colony;* Richard Savage, *The Wanderer.*

**World Music**   George Frideric Handel, *Lotario;* George Philipp Telemann, *Flavius Bertaridus—Aesopus;* Antonio Vivaldi, *Six Flute Concerti, Opus 10—Six Violin Concerti, Opus 11.*

**Miscellaneous**   The Société du Caveau is founded in Paris; the St. Petersburg Court Orchestra is founded in Russia; births include Edmund Burke, Gotthold Lessing, Moses Mendelssohn, and Giuseppe Sarti; deaths include François Caffieri, William Congreve, and Richard Steele.

## American Art and Literature Highlights

**Births/Deaths**   Births include authors John Leacock and Samuel Seabury; deaths include authors Solomon Stoddard and John Williams, and poets John James and Edward Taylor.

**Art Works**   John Smibert, *Dean Berkeley, and His Entourage (The Bermuda Group)—Portrait of Samuel Sewall.*

**Literature**   Samuel Mather, *The Life of the Very Reverend and Learned Cotton Mather.*

## Music

**M. Music Publications** Watts, Isaac, *The Psalms of David Imitated in the Language of the New Testament* (American publication by Benjamin Franklin).

# 1730

❀

## Historical Highlights

The population of the colonies reaches about 655,000; the reflecting quadrant for determining position at sea is perfected in both the colonies and in England by two separate inventors; 137,000 people die in a great Tokyo earthquake.

## World Cultural Highlights

**World Art**   Edmé Bouchardon, *Barberini Faun;* William Hogarth, *Before and After;* Nicolas Lancret, *La Camargo Dancing;* Giovanni Battista Tiepolo, *Queen Zenobia Addressing Her Troops.*

**World Literature**   Henry Fielding, *Tom Thumb;* George Lillo, *Silvia;* Pierre Carlet de Marivaux, *Le Jeu de l'amour et du hasard;* James Thomson, *The Seasons* (completed)—*Sophonisba.*

**World Music**   François Couperin, *Pièces de clavecin IV;* Giuseppi Tartini, *Six Concerti a 5, Opus I, Book II;* Antonio Vivaldi, *Six Violin Concerti, Opus 12.*

**Miscellaneous**   The Strasbourg Académie de Musique is founded; births include Melchiore Cesarotti, Charles Palissot de Montenoy, Augustin Pajou, Robert Edge Pine, and Josiah Wedgwood; deaths include Elijah Fenton, Marco Ricci, Johann Michael Rottmayr, and François de Troy.

## American Art and Literature Highlights

**Births/Deaths**   Births include poet Robert Munford; deaths include poet John Danforth and diarist Samuel Sewall.

**Art Works**   Anonymous, *John van Cortlandt* (?); Anonymous ("Gansevoort Painter"), *Adam Winne;* John Smibert, *Daniel, Peter and Andrew Oliver—Nathaniel Byfield.*

**Literature**   Anthony Aston, *The Fool's Opera; or, the Taste of the Age;* Ebenezer Cook, *Sot-Weed Redivivus; or, the Planters Looking Glass;* James Ralph, *The Fashionable Lady;* Samuel Sewall, *Diary* (published 1882).

# 1731

✸

## Historical Highlights

British naturalist Mark Catesby publishes his *Natural History of Carolina and Florida;* England forbids any of its factory workers to move to America.

## World Cultural Highlights

**World Art**   Jean-Baptiste Lemoyne, *The Baptism of Christ;* John Rysbrack, *Isaac Newton Monument;* Giovanni Servandoni, *Amid the Ruins;* Jean-François de Troy, *Gathering in a Park.*

**World Literature**   George Lillo, *The London Merchant;* David Mallet, *Eurydice;* Antoine-François Prévost, *Histoire du Chevalier Des Grieux et de Manon Lescaut.*

**World Music**   C. P. E. Bach, *Five Trio Sonatas, H. 567-71;* Johann Sebastian Bach, several cantatas—*St. Mark Passion;* George Frideric Handel, *Poro, Rè dell'Indie.*

**Miscellaneous**   The Apollo Society of London is formed; births include Christian Cannabich, William Cowper, Antônio Diniz da Cruz e Silva, and Girolamo Tiraboschi; deaths include Francis Bird, Luca Carlevaris, Daniel Defoe, Antoine Houdar de La Motte, and Johann Melchior.

## American Art and Literature Highlights

**Births/Deaths**   Births include poet Jacob Bailey.

**Art Works**   Anonymous, *John Van Cortlandt*—*Pierre Van Cortlandt*—*Independence Hall* (Philadelphia).

**Literature**   Ebenezer Cook, *The Maryland Muse: The History of Colonel Nathaniel Bacon's Rebellion;* Jonathan Edwards, *God Glorified in Man's Dependence upon Him;* Samuel Johnson, *An Introduction to the Study of Philosophy;* John Seccomb, *Father Abbey's Will.*

# 1732

✸

## Historical Highlights

George Washington, first president of the United States, is born; James Oglethorpe is given a charter to found a colony in Georgia; Harvard adds departments of math and science to its curriculum.

## World Cultural Highlights

**World Art**   Jacopo Amigoni, *Juno Receiving the Head of Argus;* François Boucher, *Venus Asking Vulcan for Arms for Aeneas;* Nicola Salvi, *Trevi Fountain* (Rome).

**World Literature**   Philippe Destouches, *Le Glorieux;* Henry Fielding, *The Modern Husband;* Carlo Goldoni, *Belisario;* Johann Christoph Gottsched, *The Dying Cato.*

**World Music**   Francesco Geminiani, *Twelve Concerti Grossi, Opus 2, 3;* George Frideric Handel, *Ezio—Sosarme, Rè di Media;* Pietro Locatelli, *Twelve Flute Sonatas, Opus 2.*

**Miscellaneous**   The Dilettanti Society is formed in London and the Theatre Royal opens at Covent Gardens; births include Pierre-Augustin de Beaumarchais, Jean-Honoré Fragonard, Franz Joseph Haydn, and Julie de Lepinasse; deaths include John Gay and Baldassare Permoser.

## American Art and Literature Highlights

**Births/Deaths**   Births include author John Dickinson and artist William Johnston; deaths include artist Ebenezer Cook.

**Literature**   Richard Lewis, *Carmen Saeculare.*

## Music

**K. Biographical**    Charles Theodore Pachelbel (German organist/composer) emigrates to Boston.

**L. Musical Beginnings**

**Other**    New Theater (Rip Van Dam building, New York).

# 1733

✦

## Historical Highlights

Savannah, Georgia, is founded; the British Parliament, via the Molasses Act, seeks to curb the colonists' thriving trade with the French West Indies; the Corporation for the Propagation of the Gospel in New England is founded.

## World Cultural Highlights

**World Art**    Nicolas Bernard Lépicié, *Fanchon Rising;* Philippe Mercier, *The Prince of Wales and His Sisters in Concert;* Giovanni Battista Tiepolo, *The Life of St. John the Baptist.*

**World Literature**    Francesco Algarotti, *Newtonian Philosophy for Ladies;* Henry Fielding, *The Miser;* Pierre Carlet de Marivaux, *L'Heureux stratagème;* Alexander Pope, *Essay on Man.*

**World Music**    George Frideric Handel, *Orlando—Deborah—Athalia* (incidental music); Pietro Locatelli, *Twelve Violin Concertos (with 24 Caprices), Opus 3.*

**Miscellaneous**    Births include Sawrey Gilpin, Alessandro Longhi, Christoph Martin Wicland, and Johann Zoffany; deaths include François Couperin and Nicolas Coustou.

## American Art and Literature Highlights

**Births/Deaths**    Births include poet Benjamin Youngs Prime; deaths include poet Richard Lewis.

**Art Works**    Robert Feke, *Levinah Cock;* John Smibert, *Richard Bill.*

**Literature**    George Berkeley, *Alciphron: or, The Minute Philosopher;* Joseph Green, *The Poet's Lamentation for the Loss of His Cat, Which He Used to Call His Muse;* Samuel Johnson, *A Letter from a Minister of the Church of England to His Dissenting Parishioners.*

## Music

**K. Biographical**    Johann Gottlob Klemm (German organ builder) emigrates to the United States and settles in Philadelphia; the first known song recital is given in Charleston, South Carolina; Trinity Church in Newport, Rhode Island, receives a new pipe organ.

# 1734

✦

## Historical Highlights

Horseracing is introduced to the colonies in South Carolina; first permanent colony in Indiana is founded by the French at Vincennes; many displaced Protestants from Salzburg settle in Georgia.

## World Cultural Highlights

**World Art**    François Boucher, *Rinaldo and Armida;* André Bouys, *The Kitchen Maid;* Pietro Longhi, *The Fall of the Giants;* Sebastiano Ricci, *The Adoration of the Shepherds.*

**World Literature**    Charles Simon Favart, *Deux Jumelles;* Carlo Goldoni, *Belisario;* Alain René Lesage, *Estebanillo Gonzalez;* Emanuel Swedenborg, *Prodromus philosophiae.*

**World Music**    George Frideric Handel, *Six Concerti Grossi, Opus 3;* Jean-Marie Leclair, *Twelve Violin Sonatas, Opus 5;* Giuseppe Tartini, *Twelve Violin Sonatas, Opus 1—Six Concerti a 8, Opus 2.*

**Miscellaneous**    Births include Vicente Antonio García de la Huerta y Muñoz, François Gossec, George Romney, and Joseph Wright (of Derby); deaths include John Dennis, Sebastiano Ricci, and James Thornhill.

### American Art and Literature Highlights

**Births/Deaths**    Births include artist Matthew Pratt and poets Andrew Burnaby, Benjamin Church II, and Samuel Quincy of Massachusetts.

**Literature**    Jonathan Edwards, *Divine and Supernatural Light.*

# 1735

✸

### Historical Highlights

The publisher John Peter Zenger of the *New York Weekly Journal* is acquitted of libel in a landmark case on freedom of the press; Georgia outlaws the sale and use of spirits; William Pitt is elected to the British Parliament for the first time.

### World Cultural Highlights

**World Art**    Jean-Baptiste Chardin, *House of Cards;* Sawrey Gilpin, *The Artist's Club;* William Hogarth, *The Rake's Progress;* Jean-François de Troy, *Luncheon with Oysters.*

**World Literature**    Henry Carey, *The Honest Yorkshire-Man;* Robert Dodsley, *The Toy Shop;* John Hughes, *Poems on Several Occasions;* Alexander Pope, *Moral Essays;* John Wesley, *Journals.*

**World Music**    Johann Sebastian Bach, *Coffee Cantata—Italian Concerto, BWV 971;* George Frideric Handel, *Ariodante—Alcina;* Jean-Philippe Rameau, *Les Indes galantes.*

**Miscellaneous**    The Accademia Musicale opens in Cremona; births include Johann Christian Bach, James Beattie, Isaac Bickerstaffe, Ignacy Krasicki, Nicolas Bernard Lépicié, and Johann Musäus.

### American Art and Literature Highlights

**Births/Deaths**    Births include author Samuel Andrews Peters and historian Benjamin Trumbull; deaths include poet Jane Colman Turell.

**Art Works**    Charles Bridges, *Maria Taylor Byrd* (?); Gustavus Hesselius, *Lapowinsa, Indian Chief—Tishcohan, Indian Chief;* John Smibert, *Joseph Wanton* (?).

**Literature**    William Douglass, *Summary, Historical and Political, of the British Settlements in America;* Jane Colman Turell, *Reliquiae Turellae.*

### Music

**F. Births**    James Lyon (clergyman/compiler) July 1.

**K. Biographical**    John and Charles Wesley come to the United States for missionary work.

# 1736

✸

### Historical Highlights

Stagecoach service begins between Boston and Providence, Rhode Island; Claudius Aymand performs the first known successful appendectomy; warfare crops up again between Russia and Turkey.

## World Cultural Highlights

**World Art**   William Hogarth, *The Good Samaritan;* François Lemoyne, *The Apotheosis of Hercules;* Charles-Joseph Natoire, *The History of Clovis;* Giovanni Battista Tiepolo, *Danaë.*

**World Literature**   Prosper Jolyot de Crébillon, *The Wayward Head and Heart;* Philippe Destouches, *Le Dissipateur;* Henry Fielding, *Pasquin;* George Lillo, *Fatal Curiosity.*

**World Music**   Tomaso Albinoni, *Twelve Concerti a 5, Opus 10;* George Frideric Handel, *Alexander's Feast (Ode for St. Cecilia's Day);* Pietro Locatelli, *Six Trio Sonatas, Opus 5.*

**Miscellaneous**   The Lyons Academy of Fine Arts opens; the Théâtre du Capitole opens in Toulouse; births include Anton Graff, James Macpherson, and Lorenzo Tiepolo; deaths include Giovanni Pergolesi, Jean-Baptiste Pater, and Gaspar van Wittel (Vanvitelli).

## American Art and Literature Highlights

**Births/Deaths**   Births include poet/dramatist Thomas Godfrey.

**Literature**   James Alexander, *A Brief Narrative of the Case and Tryal of John Peter Zenger;* Thomas Prince, *A Chronological History of New England in the Form of Annals, Vol I.*

## Music

**K. Biographical**   First known fiddling contest held in Hanover County, Virginia; the first concert of which there are records is given by C. T. Pachelbel in New York (January 21—songs and instrumental works with harpsichord, flute, and violin).

# 1737

☀

## Historical Highlights

William Byrd founds the city of Richmond, Virginia; Connecticut becomes the first colony to produce copper coins; over 300,000 die in an earthquake and windstorm in Calcutta, India.

## World Cultutral Highlights

**World Art**   Lambert-Sigisbert Adam, *Neptune Calming the Waves;* Jean-Baptiste Chardin, *Young Draftsman Sharpening His Pencil;* Jean-François de Troy, *The Hunt Breakfast.*

**World Literature**   Henry Carey, *The Musical Century;* Alexander Cruden, *Concordance of the Holy Scripture;* Matthew Green, *The Spleen;* Pierre Carlet de Marivaux, *Les Fausses Confidences.*

**World Music**   Jean-Marie Leclair (l'aîné), *Six Concertos for Violin and Strings, Opus 7;* Pietro Locatelli, *Twelve Violin Sonatas (da camera), Opus 6;* Jean-Philippe Rameau, *Castor et Pollux.*

**Miscellaneous**   Parliament passes the Licensing Act imposing censorship on London theaters; births include Heinrich Wilhelm von Gerstenberg, Edward Gibbon, Matthew Green, Michael Haydn, and Nicolás Fernández de Moratín.

## American Art and Literature Highlights

**Births/Deaths**   Births include authors Jacob Duche, Francis Hopkinson, playwright Robert Munford, and poets Elizabeth Fergusson and Jonathan Odell.

**Literature**   Jonathan Edwards, *A Faithful Narrative of the Surprising Work of God;* George Whitefield, *The Nature and the Necessity of Our New Birth.*

## Music

**F. Births**   Josiah Flagg (conductor/bandmaster) May 28.

**I. New Positions**   Charles T. Pachelbel (organ, St. Philip's Church, Charleston, to 1850).

**M. Publications**   Wesley, John, *A Collection of Psalms and Hymns* (published in Charlestown).

# 1738

☀

## Historical Highlights

The colonial population reaches about 880,000; British troops are sent into Georgia to control border disputes with Spain; John Wesley and George Whitefield arrive in Georgia for the "Great Awakening" in religious affairs; excavations begin in Herculaneum, buried with Pompeii in 79 AD.

## World Cultural Highlights

**World Art**   Jean-Baptiste Chardin, *The Scullery Maid;* Nicolas Lancret, *Dance in a Park;* Jonathan Richardson, *George Vertue;* Louis-François Roubiliac, *George Frideric Handel.*

**World Literature**   Olof von Dalin, *The Envious Man;* Samuel Johnson, *London;* Alain René Lesage, *Bachelier de Salamanque;* Alexander Pope, *Imitations of Horace;* James Thomson, *Agamemnon.*

**World Music**   Thomas Arne, *Comus —The Tender Husband;* George Frideric Handel, *Faramondo—Alessandro Severo;* Rinaldo di Capua, *La commedia in commedia.*

**Miscellaneous**   The Royal Society of Musicians has its beginning in London; births include Elizabeth Bekker, Jacques Delille, and John Wolcot (Peter Pindar).

## American Art and Literature Highlights

**Births/Deaths**   Births include artists John Singleton Copley, Benjamin West, authors Ethan Allen, Jonathan Boucher, and poet Robert Bolling.

**Art Works**   Anonymous (Patroon Painter), *The De Peyster Boy.*

**Literature**   Jonathan Edwards, *Charity and Its Fruits;* James Sterling, *An Ode on the Times, address'd to the hope of Britain.*

# 1739

☀

## Historical Highlights

The colonists in the south declare war on the Spanish in Florida; the British navy begins raiding Spanish settlements through the Caribbean; Russia is forced to give up thought of a Black Sea navy.

## World Cultural Highlights

**World Art**   François Boucher, *The Luncheon;* Jean-Baptiste Chardin, *Back from the Market;* Charles-Joseph Natoire, *The Story of Psyche* (completed).

**World Literature**   Henry Brooke, *Gustavus Vasa;* David Hume, *A Treatise of Human Nature;* David Mallet, *Mustapha;* John Mottley, *Joe Miller's Jest-book;* James Thomson, *Edward and Eleanora.*

**World Music**   George Frideric Handel, *Saul—Israel in Egypt—Twelve Orchestral Concertos, Opus 6;* Jean-Marie Leclair (le cadet), *Twelve Violin Sonatas, Opus 1;* Jean-Philippe Rameau, *Dardanus.*

**Miscellaneous**   Births include Carl Ditters von Dittersdorf and Johann A. Eberhard; deaths include Johann Freylinghausen, George Lillo, and Antônio José da Silva who, with his family, is burned at the stake by the Inquisition.

## American Art and Literature Highlights

**Births/Deaths**   Births include poet James Allen, author William Bartram, and artist John Mare.

## Music

**M. Music Publications**

Watts, Isaac, *Hymns and Spiritual Songs* (American Edition)
*Zionistischer Weyrauchs Hügel* (Moravian collection)

# 1740

❈

### Historical Highlights

The British continue to harass the Spanish colonies in Florida and elsewhere; a great fire destroys half of Charleston, South Carolina; Maria Theresa becomes Empress of Austria and the War of the Austrian Succession begins.

### World Cultural Highlights

**World Art**    François Boucher, *The Triumph of Venus;* Canaletto, *The Return of the Bucintoro;* Pietro Longhi, *Shepherd Boy Standing;* Giovanni Piazzetta, *The Fortuneteller.*

**World Literature**    Olof von Dalin, *The Tale about the Horse;* Pierre Carlet de Marivaux, *L'Épreuve;* Samuel Richardson, *Pamela, or Virtue Rewarded;* Antoine-François Prévost, *Le Doyen de Killerine.*

**World Music**    William Boyce, *Te Deum and Jubilate in A;* George Frideric Handel, *L'Allegro, il Penseroso ed il Moderato (Ode after Milton);* Antonio Vivaldi, *Six Cello Sonatas, RV 473–478.*

**Miscellaneous**    The Florence Scuola di Musica opens; births include Carl Michael Bellman, James Boswell, Ferdinand Kobell, Philipp de Loutherbourg, the Marquis de Sade, and Giovanni Paisiello; deaths include Jan Kupezky and Thomas Tickell.

### Music

**F. Births**    John Antes (clergyman/composer).

# 1741

❈

### Historical Highlights

The Russian explorer Alexei Cherikov explores the territory of modern California; Vitus Bering discovers Alaska and is killed in a shipwreck on Bering Island; Russia and Sweden go to war; the Chinese population reaches 143,000,000.

### World Cultural Highlights

**World Art**    François Boucher, *Leda and the Swan;* Jean-Baptiste Chardin, *Girl with Shuttlecock;* Charles-Antoine Coypel, *The Sleep of Rinaldo;* Giovanni Piazzetta, *Idyll on the Sea Shore.*

**World Literature**    Robert Dodsley, *The Blind Beggar of Bethnal Green;* Ludvig Holberg, *Niels Klim's Subterranean Journey;* David Hume, *Essays, Moral and Political;* Voltaire, *Mahomet.*

**World Music**    Christoph Willibald Gluck, *Artaserse;* George Frideric Handel, *Messiah;* Johann Hasse, *Twelve Concertos in 6 Parts, Opus 3;* Pietro Locatelli, *Six Concerti for Strings, Opus 7.*

**Miscellaneous**    The London Madrigal Society is founded; births include William Combe, Henry Fuseli, André Grétry, Jean-Antoine Houdon, and Angelica Kauffmann; deaths include Giovanni Antonio Pellegrini and Antonio Vivaldi.

### American Art and Literature Highlights

**Births/Deaths**    Births include artist Charles Willson Peale.

**Art Works**   Robert Feke, *Isaac Royall and His Family—James Bowdoin II* (first portrait).

**Literature**   Jonathan Edwards, *Sinners in the Hands of an Angry God—The Distinguishing Marks of a Work of the Spirit of God;* Patrick Tailfer, *A True and Historical Narrative of the Colony of Georgia.*

## Music

**K. Biographical**   John Clemm installs his first American-made organ in the Trinity Church in New York; Moravians move from Georgia and settle in Bethlehem, Pennsylvania.

# 1742

❀

## Historical Highlights

The Florida Spanish attack Georgia but are defeated at the Battle of Bloody Marsh by the forces under Oglethorpe; New England's largest industry is fishing with over 1000 boats plying their trade; Anders Celsius invents the centigrade thermometer.

## World Cultural Highlights

**World Art**   François Boucher, *Diana Resting after Her Bath;* Nicolas Lancret, *Lady, Gentleman and Two Girls;* Jean-Marc Nattier, *Daughter of Louis XV as Flora;* Jean-Baptiste Oudry, *Gardens of Arcueil.*

**World Literature**   Claude Prosper de Crébillon, *The Sofa: A Moral Tale;* Henry Fielding, *Adventures of Joseph Andrews;* Friedrich von Hagedorn, *Oden und Lieder;* William Shenstone, *The Schoolmistress.*

**World Music**   C. P. E. Bach, *Six Sonatas for Frederick II of Prussia;* Johann Sebastian Bach, *Well-Tempered Clavier II—Peasant Cantata—Goldberg Variations;* Christoph Willibald Gluck, *Demetrio.*

**Miscellaneous**   Johann Haffner begins publishing music in Nuremberg; the Berlin Opera is founded; births include Clemente Bondi, Richard Cosway, and Anna Seward; deaths include Wilhelm de Groff and William Somerville.

## American Art and Literature Highlights

**Births/Deaths**   Births include poet Nathaniel Evans; deaths include author Thomas Story.

**Art Works**   Richard Munday, *Colony House* (Newport, Rhode Island); John Smibert, *Faneuil Hall* (Boston); John Wollaston, *George Whitefield Preaching.*

**Literature**   Jonathan Dickinson, *A Display of God's Special Grace;* Jonathan Edwards, *Some Thoughts Concerning the Present Revival of Religion in New England;* Thomas Story, *A Journal of the Life of Thomas Story* (published 1747).

## Music

**F. Births**   John Stickney (singer/composer).

# 1743

❀

## Historical Highlights

French explorers reach the Rocky Mountains; the first settlers reach South Dakota; future president Thomas Jefferson is born; the British defeat the French at the Battle of Dettingen.

## World Cultural Highlights

**World Art**    Canaletto, *The Horses of St. Mark's, Venice;* William Hogarth, *Marriage à la Mode;* John Rysbrack, *Hercules;* Giovanni Battista Tiepolo, *The Banquet of Cleopatra.*

**World Literature**    Henry Fielding, *Jonathan Wild the Great;* Alain René Lesage, *Mélange amusant;* Hedvig Nordenflycht, *The Sorrowing Turtledove;* Voltaire, *Mérope;* Edward Young, *Night Thoughts.*

**World Music**    George Frideric Handel, *Samson—Dettingen Te Deum;* Jean-Marie Leclair (l'aîné), *Twelve Violin Sonatas, Book IV, Opus 9;* Giuseppe Tartini, *Six Violin Sonatas, Opus 3.*

**Miscellaneous**    Births include Luigi Boccherini, Hannah Cowley, Alexandre-François Desportes, and Johannes Ewald; deaths include Vittore Ghislandi, Nicolas Lancret, Hyacinthe Rigaud, and Richard Savage.

## American Art and Literature Highlights

**Births/Deaths**    Births include artist Henry Benbridge; deaths include educator James Blair.

**Art Works**    Peter Pelham, *Reverend William Welsteed.*

**Literature**    Charles Chauncey, *Seasonable Thoughts on the State of Religion in New-England;* Benjamin Franklin, *A Proposal for Promoting Useful Knowledge.*

## Music

**I. New Positions**

**Other**    Peter Pelham III (organ, Trinity Church, Boston—first to be hired)

# 1744

❄

## Historical Highlights

The French fail in their attempt to retake Annapolis in Nova Scotia; King George's War breaks out; the Iroquois Confederation is forced to cede all the Ohio Territory north of the Ohio River to Great Britain; Ben Franklin invents the Franklin Stove (Pennsylvania Fireplace).

## World Cultural Highlights

**World Art**    Francis Hayman, *Wrestling Scene;* Joseph Highmore, *The Marriage of Pamela;* Giovanni Battista Piazzetta, *Elijah Going Up in the Chariot of Fire;* Jean-Baptiste Pigalle, *Mercury.*

**World Literature**    Mark Akenside, *Pleasures of the Imagination;* Edward Moore, *Fables for the Female Sex;* Hedvig Nordenflycht, *A Woman's Play of Thought, by a Shepherdess in the North.*

**World Music**    Christoph Willibald Gluck, *La Sofonisba—Ipermestra;* George Frideric Handel, *Joseph and His Brethren;* Pietro Locatelli, *Ten Violin Sonatas, Opus 8.*

**Miscellaneous**    Births include David Allan, Johann Gottfried von Herder, and Carlo Bartolomeo Rastrelli; deaths include Antonio Bibiena, Alexander Pope, and Lewis Theobald.

## American Art and Literature Highlights

**Births/Deaths**    Births include historian Jeremy Belknap and novelist Enos Hitchcock; deaths include author William Byrd II.

**Art Works**    John Smibert, *Holden Chapel* (Cambridge, Massachusetts); John Kearsley, *Christ Church* (Philadelphia).

**Literature**    Matthew Byles, *Poems on Several Occasions;* Pierre François de Charlevoix, *History and General Description of New France with the Historical Journal of a Voyage Made in Northern*

*America;* James Davenport, *Confession and Retractations;* Alexander Hamilton, *Itinerarium;* Experience Mayhew, *Grace Defended;* Thomas Prince, *The Christian History.*

## Music

**F. Births**    Samuel Blyth (organist/craftsman) May 13; Amos Bull (singing master/composer) February 9.

**L. Musical Beginnings**

**Performing Groups**    Collegium Musicum (Bethlehem, Pennsylvania).

# 1745

❋

## Historical Highlights

The French raid settlements in New England while the New Englanders capture Fort Louisbourg in Canada; the French capture and burn Saratoga, New York; Yale College gets a new royal charter; Charles Edward Stuart, the "Young Pretender" to the British throne, lands in Scotland.

## World Cultural Highlights

**World Art**    Edmé Bourchardon, *Fountain of the Seasons;* Jean Baptiste Oudry, *Still Life with Pheasants;* Jean-Baptiste Perroneau, *Girl with a Kitten.*

**World Literature**    Mark Akenside, *Odes on Several Subjects;* Robert Dodsley, *Trifles;* James Thomson, *Tancred and Sigismunda;* Thomas Warton, *The Pleasures of Melancholy.*

**World Music**    Christoph Willibald Gluck, *Ippolito;* George Frideric Handel, *Belshazzar;* Jean-Jacques Rousseau, *Les muses galantes;* Giuseppe Tartini, *Twelve Violin Sonatas, Opus 3.*

**Miscellaneous**    Births include Charles Dibdin, Denis Ivanovich Fonvizin, William Hayley, and Hannah More; deaths include Jean-Baptiste van Loo, Jonathan Richardson, and Jonathan Swift.

## American Art and Literature Highlights

**Births/Deaths**    Births include poet Thomas Brockway.

**Art Works**    Robert Feke, *Reverend Thomas Hiscox—Reverend John Callender;* John Smibert, *Sir William Pepperell.*

**Literature**    John Adams, *Poems on Several Occasions* (posthumous); Samuel Niles, *A Brief and Plain Essay on God's Wonder Working Providence in the Reduction of Louisburg—Tristitiae Ecclesiarum.*

# 1746

❋

## Historical Highlights

The French try once again to retake Nova Scotia from the British but fail; the College of New Jersey (Princeton University in 1896) is founded; the Jacobites are defeated at the Battle of Culloden Moor and Charles Stuart flees to France.

## World Cultural Highlights

**World Art**    Elias Haussmann, *Johann Sebastian Bach;* Jean-Baptiste Perroneau, *Mademoiselle Huquier Holding a Kitten;* Louis-François Roubiliac, *Monument to Bishop Hough.*

**World Literature**    Étienne Bonnot de Condillac, *Essay on the Origin of Human Knowledge;* Denis Diderot, *Pensées philosophiques;* Christian Gellert, *Fabeln und Erzählungen.*

**World Music**    William Boyce, *Cymbeline—The Secular Masque;* Christoph Willibald Gluck, *Artemene—La caduta dei giganti;* George Frideric Handel, *Occasional Oratorio.*

**Miscellaneous**   Births include Wilhelm Heinse, Barthélemy Imbert, and Julien de Lalande Poydras; deaths include Grizel Baillie, Robert Blair, Hector Macneil, and Thomas Southerne.

## American Art and Literature Highlights

**Births/Deaths**   Births include sculptor John Skillin, poet Elijah Fitch, and author Benjamin Rush; deaths include publisher John Peter Zenger.

**Art Works**   John Singleton Copley, *Tench Francis—Mrs. Tench Francis;* Robert Feke, *Thomas Hopkinson—Benjamin Franklin (?)—Tench Francis.*

**Literature**   David Brainerd, *Divine Grace Displayed;* Jonathan Edwards, *Treatise Concerning Religious Affections—A Vindication of the Gospel Doctrine of Justifying Faith;* Samuel Johnson, *Ethices Elementa, or the First Principles of Moral Philosophy.*

## Music

**F. Births**   William Billings (composer/singing master) October 7; Oliver Brownson (composer) May 13.

**K. Biographical**   Edward Bromfield builds a pipe organ, the first by an American builder, in New England (Boston).

# 1747

☀

## Historical Highlights

The Ohio Company is formed to encourage settlers to enter the Ohio Territory; the New York Bar Association becomes the first legal society in the New World; sugar is discovered in the beet.

## World Cultural Highlights

**World Art**   Jean-Baptiste Perroneau, *Jacques-Gabriel Huquier;* Joshua Reynolds, *Lieutenant Roberts.*

**World Literature**   Christian Gellert, *Die Kranke Frau;* Charlotte Lennox, *Poems on Several Occasions;* David Mallet, *The Hermit;* Claudine Guérin de Tencin, *Les Malheurs de l'amour;* Voltaire, *Zadig.*

**World Music**   George Frideric Handel, *Judas Maccabaeus;* Giuseppe Sammartini, *Six Concerti Grossi, Opus 5;* Giuseppe Tartini, *Twelve Violin Sonatas, Opus 4, 5.*

**Miscellaneous**   National Libraries are founded in Florence and Warsaw; births include György Bessenyei, Gottfried August Bürger, and Georges-François Mareschal; deaths include Alain René Lesage, Francesco Solimeno, and Francis Wheatley.

## American Art and Literature Highlights

**Births/Deaths**   Births include artists Winthrop Chandler, James Peale, poet Thomas Burke, humorist Timothy Dexter, and author John Filson; deaths include authors David Brainerd, Benjamin Colman, and Jonathan Dickinson.

**Art Works**   John Greenwood, *Greenwood-Lee Family*; John Smibert, *Sir William Pepperall.*

**Literature**   Jonathan Edwards, *An Humble Attempt to Promote Visible Union of God's People;* Benjamin Franklin, *Plain Truth, or Serious Consideration on the Present State of the City of Philadelphia;* William Livingston, *Philosophic Solitude, or, The Choice of a Rural Life.*

## Music

**F. Births**   Justin Morgan (singing master/composer).

**M. Music Publications**

*Das Gesang der einsamen und verlassenen Turtel Taube, das ist der christlichen Kirche* (Moravian)

# 1748

✸

## Historical Highlights

The Peace of Aix-la-Chapelle ends the War of the Austrian Succession (King George's War); France and England battle for control of India; a chair of astronomy is founded at Cambridge.

## World Cultural Highlights

**World Art**   Joseph Anton Feuchtmayr, *St. Elizabeth;* William Hogarth, *Calais Gate;* Jean-Baptiste Perroneau, *Duchess d'Ayen;* Allan Ramsay, *Norman, 22nd Chief of MacLeod.*

**World Literature**   Carlo Goldoni, *The Liar;* Carlo Gozzi, *Turandot;* Samuel Richardson, *Clarissa, or The History of a Young Lady;* Tobias Smollett, *The Adventures of Roderick Random.*

**World Music**   Christoph Willibald Gluck, *La Semiramide riconosciuta;* George Frideric Handel, *Joshua;* Giuseppe Tartini, *Twelve Violin Sonatas, Opus 6, 7.*

**Miscellaneous**   The Copenhagen Royal Theater opens; births include Thomas Day, Charles Johnson, John Logan, and Christian zu Stolberg; deaths include William Douglas and James Thomson.

## American Art and Literature Highlights

**Births/Deaths**   Births include artist George Beck, and poets Hugh H. Brackenridge and Jonathan M. Sewall.

**Art Works**   Robert Feke, *General Samuel Waldo* (?)—*Isaac Winslow—William Bowdoin;* Peter Harrison, *Redwood Library* (Newport, Rhode Island); Gustavus Hesselius, *Crucifixion.*

## Music

**F. Births**   Lewis Edson (composer) January 22.

# 1749

✸

## Historical Highlights

The first settlements are made in the Ohio Territory; the French continue harassing settlers with expeditions south and the founding of forts in New York; Giacobbo Rodriguez develops sign language for the deaf mute.

## World Cultural Highlights

**World Art**   Jean-Baptiste Perroneau, *Madame de Sorquainville;* Louis-François Roubiliac, *Monument to the Duke of Argyll;* Giovanni Domenico Tiepolo, *Life of S. Girolamo Emiliani.*

**World Literature**   John Cleland, *Fanny Hill;* Henry Fielding, *Tom Jones;* Carlo Goldoni, *The Respectable Girl;* Samuel Johnson, *Irene;* Gotthold Lessing, *Der Freigeist;* James Thomson, *Coriolanus.*

**World Music**   Johann Sebastian Bach, *Mass in B Minor;* George Frideric Handel, *Royal Fireworks Music—Susanna—Solomon;* Jean-Philippe Rameau, *Naïs—Zoroastre.*

**Miscellaneous**   Births include Vittorio Alfieri, Domenico Cimarosa, Johann Wolfgang von Goethe, and Friedrich Müller; deaths include Claudine Guérin de Tencin.

## American Art and Literature Highlights

**Births/Deaths**   Births include artists Samuel King, James Peale and historian David Ramsay (physician/historian).

**Art Works**    Robert Feke, *Self-Portrait—Mrs. Robert Feke;* Peter Harrison, *King's Chapel, Boston.*

**Literature**    Thomas Bacon, *Two Sermons, Preached to a Congregation of Black Slaves;* Jonathan Edwards, *Life and Diary of David Brainerd—An Humble Inquiry into the Rules of the Word of God;* Benjamin Franklin, *Proposals Relating to the Education of Youth in Pennsylvania;* Jonathan Mayhew, *Seven Sermons . . .*

## Music

**F. Births**    Andrew Law (singing teacher/compiler) March 21; Isaiah Thomas (publisher) January 19.

**K. Biographical**    David Tannenberg (German organ builder) settles in the Moravian community in Bethlehem, Pennsylvania.

**L. Musical Beginnings**

**Performing Groups**    Pachelbel Singing School (Charleston, South Carolina).

# 1750

✸

## Historical Highlights

The British Parliament restricts iron manufacture in the colonies; the Ohio Company begins exploring its territory; the Conestoga wagon and the river flatboat appear; the first coal mine in the colonies opens in Virginia; the University of Pennsylvania is founded.

## World Cultural Highlights

**World Art**    Edmé Bourchardon, *Cupid Making a Bow from Hercules' Club;* Thomas Gainsborough, *View of Dedham;* Giovanni Battista Tiepolo, *Anthony and Cleopatra.*

**World Literature**    Carlo Goldoni, *The Café;* Friedrich von Hagedorn, *Moralische Gedichte;* Jean-François Marmontel, *Cléopâtre;* Samuel Richardson, *Clarissa;* William Whitehead, *The Roman Father.*

**World Music**    William Boyce, *Eight Symphonies, Opus 2;* Christoph Willibald Gluck, *Ezio;* George Frideric Handel, *Theodora—The Choice of Hercules;* Franz Joseph Haydn, *Missa Brevis in F.*

**Miscellaneous**    The Venetian Academy of Fine Arts is founded; Samuel Johnson begins publishing *The Rambler;* births include Elizabeth Anspach, Tomás de Iriarte y Oropesa, and Johann Friedrich Tischbein; deaths include Johann Sebastian Bach, Cornelis Troost, and Apostolo Zeno.

## American Art and Literature Highlights

**Births/Deaths**    Births include poets Lemuel Hopkins and John Trumbull; deaths include artist Robert Feke.

**Art Works**    Shem Drowne, *Indian Weathervane* (?); John Greenwood, *Abigail Gerrish and Her Grandmother—Mrs. Henry Bromfield;* Robert Feke, *Portrait of Unknown Woman—Dr. Phineas Bond;* John Wollaston, *Mrs. Samuel Gouverneur* (?)—*Lt. Archibald Kennedy* (?).

**Literature**    Joseph Bellamy, *True Religion Delineated;* Joseph Green, *Entertainment for a Winter's Evening;* Charlotte R. Lennox, *The Life of Harriot Stuart;* Jonathan Mayhew, *Discourse Concerning Unlimited Submission and Non-Resistance to the Higher Powers;* Samuel Quincy, *Twenty Sermons Preach'd in the Parish of St. Philip, Charles-Town, South Carolina.*

## Music

**F. Births**    Elias Mann (composer/compiler) May 8.

**G. Deaths**    Charles Theodore Pachelbel (German-born organist/composer) September 15; John Tufts (clergyman/compiler) August 17.

# 1751

☀

## Historical Highlights

The British Parliament forbids the issuance of paper money by any of the colonies; English settlers in the Ohio Valley cause problems with the French; Georgia is formed as a Royal Colony; the Pennsylvania Hospital becomes the first in the colonies; the Academy and College of Philadelphia is founded; the British Parliament finally changes the English calendar to the Gregorian.

## World Cultural Highlights

**World Art**    Étienne Falconet, *Allegory of Music;* Thomas Gainsborough, *Artist, Wife and Child;* William Hogarth, *Gin Lane—Beer Street;* Pietro Longhi, *The Artist in His Studio.*

**World Literature**    Denis Diderot, *Encyclopédie I;* Henry Fielding, *Amelia;* Friedrich Gottlieb Klopstock, *Messias I;* Tobias Smollett, *The Adventures of Peregrine Pickle.*

**World Music**    Thomas Arne, *The Country Lasses;* William Boyce, *The Shepherd's Lottery;* George Frideric Handel, *Jephtha;* Johann A. Hasse, *Mass in D Minor—Te Deum in D Major.*

**Miscellaneous**    Births include Dmitri Bortniansky, Giuseppe Ceracchi, Heinrich Friedrich Füger, Johan Kellgren, Jakob Lenz, Nikolai L'vov, James Sharples, and Richard Brinsley Sheridan; deaths include Tomaso Albinoni and Nicola Salvi.

## American Art and Literature Highlights

**Births/Deaths**    Births include artist Ralph Earl, author John Ledyard, and poet Judith S. Murray; deaths include artist John Smibert.

**Art Works**    Peter Harrison (?), *St. Michael's Church (Charleston, South Carolina).*

**Literature**    John Bartram, *Observations . . . Made by Mr. John Bartram in His Travels from Pennsylvania to Lake Ontario;* Samuel Davies, *The State of Religion among the Protestant Dissenters in Virginia . . . ;* Jonathan Edwards, *Farewell Sermon;* Benjamin Franklin, *Experiments and Observations on Electricity, Made at Philadelphia.*

## Music

**F. Births**    Supply Belcher (composer) April 9; Jacob Van Vleck (Moravian violinist/organist).

**L. Musical Beginnings**

**Other**    James Logan Library (bequeathed to the city of Philadelphia).

# 1752

☀

## Historical Highlights

The "Liberty Bell" cracks on its first trial in Philadelphia and has to be recast; the Treaty of Logstown settles the Allegheny Mountain problems with the Indians and opens the territory for expansion of the colonies; Benjamin Franklin invents the lightning rod.

## World Cultural Highlights

**World Art**    Jean-Honoré Fragonard, *Jeroboam Sacrificing to Idols;* Corrado Giaquinto, *Birth of the Virgin;* Pietro Longhi, *Family Concert;* Giovanni Battista Tiepolo, *Beatrix' Arrival before the Emperor.*

**World Literature**    Friedrich von Hagedorn, *Oden und Lieder III;* Jean-François Marmontel, *Les Héraclides;* Michel-Jean Sedaine, *Poésies Fugitives;* Christopher Smart, *Poems on Several Occasions.*

**World Music**    Franz Joseph Haydn, *Der krumme Teufel;* Christoph Willibald Gluck, *La Clemenza di Tito;* Jean-Jacques Rousseau, *Le Devin du Village;* Domenico Scarlatti, *Thirty Keyboard Sonatas I, II.*

**Miscellaneous**   The Madrid Academy of Fine Arts is founded; born are Fanny Burney, Giuseppe Carpani, Thomas Chatterton, John Robert Cozens, Friedrich Maximilian von Klinger; deaths include Charles-Antoine Coypel and Jean-François de Troy.

### American Art and Literature Highlights

**Births/Deaths**   Births include literary figures Ann Eliza Bleecker, Charles Crawford, Timothy Dwight, Philip Freneau, David Humphreys, Peter Markoe, and St. George Tucker.

**Art Works**   John Wollaston, Jr., *Cadwallader Colden.*

**Literature**   Samuel Davies, *Miscellaneous Poems, Chiefly on Divine Subjects;* Samuel Johnson, *Elementa Philosophica;* Charlotte Ramsay Lennox, *The Female Quixote: or, The Adventures of Arabella;* William Smith, *Some Thoughts on Education . . . ;* James Sterling, *An Epistle to the Hon. Arthur Dobbs, Esq. in Europe, from a Clergyman in America.*

### Music

**F. Births**   Timothy Dwight (poet/hymnist) May 14; Abraham Wood (composer/compiler) July 30.

**K. Biographical**   Thomas Johnston begins his organ-building/restoring business in Boston; first record of an orchestra being used in an opera performance (Upper Marlborough, Maryland).

# 1753

❁

### Historical Highlights

George Washington is sent into the Ohio Territory to demand French withdrawal from Fort Presque Isle (present-day Erie, Pennsylvania) and other forts built in the territory; because of his work with electricity, Benjamin Franklin receives three honorary degrees and numerous international honors including the Copley Medal; first steam engine brought to the colonies in New Jersey.

### World Cultural Highlights

**World Art**   François Boucher, *Setting of the Sun;* Jean-Baptiste Chardin, *The Blind Man;* Jean-Baptiste Oudry, *Dog Guarding Dead Game;* Giovanni Domenico Tiepolo, *Frescoes, Kaisersaal, Würzburg.*

**World Literature**   Philippe Destouches, *Le Dissipateur;* Carlo Goldoni, *Mistress of the Inn;* Samuel Richardson, *History of Sir Charles Grandison;* Tobias Smollett, *Ferdinand, Count Fathom.*

**World Music**   Alessandro Scarlatti, *Alessandro nell'Indie;* Domenico Scarlatti, *Thirty Keyboard Sonatas III, IV.*

**Miscellaneous**   Hummel Music Publishing Co. is founded in Amsterdam; births include William Beechey, Elizabeth Inchbald, Joseph-Marie de Maistre, August Gottlieb Meissner, and Phillis Wheatley; deaths include George Berkeley and Georg Knobelsdorff.

### American Art and Literature Highlights

**Births/Deaths**   Births include author John Taylor.

**Art Works**   John Singleton Copley, *Reverend William Welsteed.*

**Literature**   James MacSparran, *America Dissected;* William Smith, *A General Ideal of the College of Mirania;* Charles Woodmason, *A Poetical Epistle to Benjamin Franklin . . . on His Experiments and Discoveries in Electricity.*

### Music

**K. Biographical**   William Tuckey (British singer/composer) arrives in New York and begins teaching private voice lessons.

# 1754

✺

## Historical Highlights

The Battle of Great Meadows signals the beginning of the French and Indian War in America (Seven Years' War in Europe); the colonies seek united action against the French with the Albany Plan; Fort Duquesne (present-day Pittsburgh) is built by the French; King's College (Columbia University) is founded in New York; the French pull out of India, leaving it to the British.

## World Cultural Highlights

**World Art**  François Boucher, *The Captive Cupid;* Jean-Honoré Fragonard, *Psyche with Cupid's Presents;* Jean-Baptiste Pigalle, *Louis XV;* Claude-Joseph Vernet, *Ports of France I.*

**World Literature**  Prosper Jolyot de Crébillon, *Le Triumvirat;* Salomon Gessner, *Daphnis;* Jean-Jacques Rousseau, *On the Inequality of Man;* Thomas Whitehead, *Creusa.*

**World Music**  Thomas Arne, *Eliza;* Christoph Willibald Gluck, *Le Cinesi;* Nicola Porpora, *Twelve Violin Sonatas;* Domenico Scarlatti, *Keyboard Sonatas VII, VIII, IX.*

**Miscellaneous**  Robert Bremner begins publishing music in Edinburgh; births include Asmus Jakob Carstens, George Crabbe, and Vicente Martín y Soler; deaths include Philippe Destouches, James Gibbs, Henry Fielding, Friedrich von Hagedorn, Ludvig Holberg, and Giovanni Battista Piazzetta.

## American Art and Literature Highlights

**Births/Deaths**  Births include artist Amos Doolittle, poets Joel Barlow and John Parke, and author Gilbert Imlay.

**Art Works**  John Singleton Copley, *Galatea* (?)—*Mars, Venus and Vulcan.*

**Literature**  Landon Carter, *A Letter from a Gentleman in Virginia to the Merchants of Great Britain . . . ;* Jonathan Edwards, *A Careful and Strict Enquiry into the Modern Prevailing Notions of Freedom of the Will;* George Washington, *The Journal of George Washington;* John Woolman, *Some Considerations on the Keeping of Negroes . . .*

## Music

**F. Births**  Benjamin Dearborn (singing teacher) April; Jacob French (composer) July 15 (?).

**K. Biographical**  Boston's first concert hall is built at Hanover and Court Streets; Alexander Malcolm gives his final musical performance with the Annapolis Tuesday Club.

**M. Music Publications**

Beissel, Conrad, *Paradisisches Wunderspiel* (Moravian)

**N. Musical Compositions**

**Choral/Vocal**  Francis Hopkinson, *Ode to Music* (believed to be the first piece of music written by a native-born American).

# 1755

✺

## Historical Highlights

At the Battle of the Wilderness, George Washington takes over command of the retreat following the death of General Braddock; the British deport the Arcadian French from Nova Scotia to Maryland; first municipal water system is set up in Bethlehem, Pennsylvania; first maps of the middle colonies are published; the great Lisbon Earthquake kills over 60,000 people.

## World Cultural Highlights

**World Art**   François Boucher, *Shepherd and Shepherdess;* Étienne Falconet, *The Punishment of Cupid;* Jean-Baptiste Greuze, *Father Reading the Bible to the Children.*

**World Literature**   Henry Fielding, *Journal of a Voyage to Lisbon;* Francis Hutcheson, *System of Moral Philosophy;* Gotthold Lessing, *Miss Sara Sampson;* Voltaire, *La Pucelle d'Orléans.*

**World Music**   Thomas Arne, *Britannia;* Christoph Willibald Gluck, *La danza—L'innocenza giustificata;* Domenico Scarlatti, *Keyboard Sonatas X, XI;* Georg Wagenseil, *Three Symphonies, Opus 1.*

**Miscellaneous**   The Venetian Academy of Art is founded; births include Anne Grant, Jean-François Collin d'Harleville, John Flaxman, Thomas Stothard, and Marie Anne Vigée-Lebrun; deaths include Jacques Caffiéri, Charles de Secondat Montesquieu, and Jean-Baptiste Oudry.

## American Art and Literature Highlights

**Births/Deaths**   Births include artist William Birch, Gilbert Stuart, authors Hannah Adams, Tench Coxe, Nathanel Fanning, and Anne McVickar Grant; deaths include artist Gustavus Hesselius and author Elizabeth Ashbridge.

**Art Works**   Joseph Blackburn, *Isaac Winslow and His Family;* John Singleton Copley, *Joshua Winslow.*

**Literature**   Mather Byles, *The Conflagration;* Joseph Green, *The Grand Arcanum Detected;* Alexander Hamilton, *The History of the Tuesday Club;* William Smith, *A Brief State of the Province of Pennsylvania* . . .

## Music

**1. New Positions**

**Other**   Peter Pelham III (organ, Bruton Church, Williamsburg, Virginia—to 1802).

# 1756

☀

## Historical Highlights

The French capture and destroy Fort Oswego in New York but fail to capitalize on their victory and return to Montreal; stagecoach service begins between New York City and Philadelphia; one of the country's longest running newspapers, the *New Hampshire Gazette*, begins publication; over 100 British soldiers die in the infamous Black Hole of Calcutta.

## World Cultural Highlights

**World Art**   Johann Hagenauer, *Christ Tied to the Column;* Pietro Longhi, *The Fortune Teller;* Charles-Joseph Natoire, *San Sebastian and the Angel;* Giovanni Piranesi, *Le Antichità Romane.*

**World Literature**   Thomas Amory, *The Life of John Buncle I;* Marie Anne Boccage, *La Colombiade;* Michel-Jean Sedaine, *Le Diable à Quatre;* Emanuel Swedenborg, *The Heavenly Arcana.*

**World Music**   Christoph Willibald Gluck, *Il Re Pastore—Antigono;* Franz Joseph Haydn, *Organ Concerto No. 1;* Georg Wagenseil, *Six Symphonies, Opus 2.*

**Miscellaneous**   Gottfried Härtel joins Breitkopf in music publishing in Leipzig; the Russian Royal Court Theater, first in Russia, opens; Samuel Johnson's *Literary Magazine* begins publication; births include Peter Bourgeois, William Gifford, Wolfgang Amadeus Mozart, Henry Raeburn, and Thomas Rowlandson; deaths include George Vertue, Jean-Louis Lemoyne, and Thomas Cooke.

## American Art and Literature Highlights

**Births/Deaths**    Births include artists/sculptors Samuel McIntire, William Rush, Simeon Skillin, Jr., John Trumbull, and Joseph Wright; deaths include statesman/author Alexander Hamilton.

**Art Works**    Joseph Blackburn, *Joseph Dwight—Mrs. Benjamin Pollard;* John Singleton Copley, *Ann Tyng—William Brattle;* Benjamin West, *Self-Portrait on Ivory;* John Wollaston, *Mrs. Fielding Lewis* (?).

**Literature**    William Smith, *A Brief View of the Conduct of Pennsylvania, for the Year 1755 . . .*

# 1757

❀

## Historical Highlights

General Montcalm captures Fort William Henry in upper New York—many of the English are massacred by the Indian allies of the French; Benjamin Franklin is sent to London as a special representative for the colonies; first street lights, oil lamps designed by Franklin, are introduced in Philadelphia; George Washington acquires his Mount Vernon estate.

## World Cultural Highlights

**World Art**    Étienne Falconet, *The Bather;* Pietro Longhi, *The Masked Reception;* Joshua Reynolds, *Dr. Samuel Johnson;* Giovanni Battista Tiepolo, *The Sacrifice of Iphigenia*.

**World Literature**    Johann Bodmer, *Das Nibelungenlied;* John Brown, *An Estimate of the Manners and Principles of the Times;* John Dyer, *The Fleece;* Friedrich Klopstock, *Geistliche Lieder I*.

**World Music**    Johann Christian Bach, *Requiem in F;* George Frideric Handel, *The Triumph of Time and Truth;* Ignaz Holzbauer, *Six Symphonies in 4 Parts, Opus 2;* Johann Stamitz, *Six Symphonies, Opus 2*.

**Miscellaneous**    The Bibliothek der Schönen Wissenschaften und Freien Künste begins publication in Germany; births include William Blake, Wojciech Boguslawski, Antonio Canova, and Harriet Lee; deaths include Colley Cibber, Edward Moore, Rosalba Carriera, and Domenico Scarlatti.

## American Art and Literature Highlights

**Births/Deaths**    Births include poets Robert Dinsmore, William Duke, and author Royall Tyler; deaths include author James Davenport.

**Art Works**    Joseph Blackburn, *Susan Apthorp;* John Singleton Copley, *George Scott—Reverend Arthur Browne—Mrs. Arthur Browne;* Jeremiah Theüs, *Elizabeth Rothmaler—Mrs. Peter Manigault*.

**Literature**    Benjamin Church, *The Choice, A Poem . . . ;* Benjamin Franklin, *The Way of Wealth;* William Smith, *The History of the Province of New York—A Review of the Military Operations in North America, 1753–1756*.

## Music

**F. Births**    Daniel Read (composer/compiler) November 16.

**K. Biographical**    Francis Hopkinson graduates from the College of Philadelphia, a member of the first class to receive a B.A. from that institution; Johann Gottlob Klemm moves his organ-making business to Bethlehem, Pennsylvania; David Tannenberg follows Klemm to Bethlehem in order to work with him.

**L. Musical Beginnings**

**Performing Groups**    Chamber Subscription Concert Series (Philadelphia).

# 1758

❈

## Historical Highlights

The British take Fort Duquesne from the French and rename it Fort Pitt, but fail to dislodge General Montcalm from Fort Ticonderoga; the first Indian Reservation is formed in Burlington County, New Jersey; the first Negro school opens in Philadelphia; Halley's Comet is rediscovered.

## World Cultural Highlights

**World Art**   François Boucher, *The Mill at Charenton;* Anton Mengs, *Ceiling, St. Eusebius;* Jean-Baptiste Pigalle, *Love and Friendship;* Louis-François Roubiliac, *William Shakespeare.*

**World Literature**   Salomon Gessner, *Der Tod Abels;* John Home, *Agis;* James Macpherson, *The Highlander;* Voltaire, *Candide;* Christoph Wieland, *Lady Johanna Gray.*

**World Music**   Johann Christian Bach, *Magnificat in C;* François Gossec, *Six Symphonies, Opus 4;* Franz Joseph Haydn, *Der Neue Krumme Teufel;* Georg Philipp Telemann, *St. Matthew Passion IV.*

**Miscellaneous**   Samuel Johnson begins writing the *Idler* papers; the Milan Accademia Filarmonica is founded; births include Johann Heinrich von Dannecker, John Hoppner, Alexander Nasmyth, Pierre-Paul Prud'hon, and Antoine-Carle Vernet, deaths include Françoise Grafigny and James Hervey.

## American Art and Literature Highlights

**Births/Deaths**   Births include artist Simon Fitch, authors Fisher Ames, and Noah Webster; deaths include authors Jonathan Edwards, Experience Mayhew, and historian Thomas Prince.

**Art Works**   Joseph Badger, *Jeremiah Belknap* (?); John Singleton Copley, *John Barrett—Mrs John Barrett—Mary and Elizabeth Royall* (?)—*Reverend Samuel Fayerweather;* John Greenwood, *American Sea Captains Carousing in Surinam—Jersey Nanny;* Benjamin West, *Thomas Mifflin.*

**Literature**   Jonathan Edwards, *The Great Christian Doctrine of Original Sin Defended;* Charlotte R. Lennox, *The History of Henrietta;* John Maylem, *The Conquest of Louisburg;* Benjamin Young Prime, *The Unfortunate Hero: A Pindaric Ode;* Thomas Prince, *Psalms, Hymns and Spiritual Songs of the Old and New Testaments;* John Woolman, *Considerations on Pure Wisdom and Human Policy.*

## Music

**F. Births**   Timothy Swan (composer/hymnist) July 23.

**K. Biographical**   Thomas Bacon (clergyman/musician) moves to Frederick, Maryland.

# 1759

❈

## Historical Highlights

The British take Fort Niagara and occupy Crown Point and Fort Ticonderoga; the French are defeated and lose the city of Quebec at the Battle of the Plains of Abraham but both British General Wolfe and French General Montcalm are killed; first known insurance company in the colonies opens in Philadelphia; George Washington marries the widow Martha Dandridge.

## World Cultural Highlights

**World Art**   François Boucher, *Madame de Pompadour;* William Hogarth, *The Cockpit;* Pietro Longhi, *The Tooth-Drawer;* Giovanni Battista Tiepolo, *St. Thecla Praying for the Plague-Stricken.*

**World Literature**   Oliver Goldsmith, *The Present State of Polite Learning in Europe;* Samuel Johnson, *History of Rasselas;* Gotthold Lessing, *Philotas;* Charles Macklin, *Love à la Mode.*

**World Music**   Carl Abel, *Six Symphonies in 4 Parts;* Franz Joseph Haydn, *Symphony No. 1—Six Divertimentos, Opus 1, for String Quartet;* Georg Philipp Telemann, *Passion According to St. Mark I.*

**Miscellaneous**   The Moscow Opera House opens; births include François Andrieux, Robert "Bobby" Burns, Julius Caesar Ibbetson, and Johann Friedrich von Schiller; deaths include Lambert Adam, William Collins, George Frideric Handel, Christophe Huet, and Ewald Christian von Kleist.

### American Art and Literature Highlights

**Births/Deaths**   Births include literary figures Thomas Andros, Hannah Webster Foster, Sarah Wentworth Morton, Mason Locke Weems, and Sarah S. B. Keating Wood.

**Art Works**   Benjamin West, *Thomas Mifflin* (?); Benjamin Wilson, *Benjamin Franklin—Deborah Franklin.*

**Literature**   Landon Carter, *A Letter to a Gentleman in London, from Virginia . . . ;* Benjamin Franklin, *An Historical Review of the Constitution and Government of Pennsylvania;* Thomas Godfrey, *The Prince of Parthia;* William Smith, *Discourses on Several Public Occasions during the War in America . . .*

### Music

**F. Births**   Charles Albrecht (piano maker); John Hubbard (music author/compiler) August 8; Timothy Olmstead (composer/fifer/compiler) November 13.

**K. Biographical**   James Lyon graduates from the College of New Jersey (Princeton) with a degree in theology.

**L. Musical Beginnings**

**Other**   Michael Hillegas Music Shop (Philadelphia—first known in the New World).

**N. Musical Compositions**

**Choral/Vocal**   Francis Hopkinson, "My Days Have Been So Wondrous Free" (possibly the first American song written in the New World).

# 1760

❀

### Historical Highlights

Montreal and Detroit are given up by the French, with a massacre of French troops by the Indians during their retreat from Montreal; New York passes a law requiring licenses for physicians and surgeons (first in the colonies); this is the probable date for Benjamin Franklin's invention of the bifocal glasses and of the rocking chair.

### World Cultural Highlights

**World Art**   Anton Mengs, *Augustus and Cleopatra;* George Stubbs, *Mares and Foals in Landscape;* Carle Van Loo, *Louis XV in State Robes;* Richard Wilson, *Destruction of Niobe's Children.*

**World Literature**   Adolf Klotz, *Genius Saeculi;* Charles Palissot de Montenoy, *Les Philosophes;* Johann Karl Musäus, *Grandison der Zweite;* Laurence Sterne, *Tristram Shandy I, II.*

**World Music**   Thomas Arne, *Thomas and Sally;* Jean-Philippe Rameau, *Les Paladins;* Franz X. Richter, *Twelve Symphonies, Opus 2, 3;* Georg Philipp Telemann, *Resurrection and Ascension of Jesus.*

**Miscellaneous**   The Royal Society of Arts is founded in London; births include Lemuel Abbott, Luigi Cherubini, Johann Peter Hebel, and Leandro Fernández de Moratin; deaths include Isaac Hawkins Browne, Louis de Silvestre, and Christiane von Zeigler.

## American Art and Literature Highlights

**Births/Deaths**   Births include poet George Richards; deaths include historian Hugh Jones.

**Art Works**   Joseph Badger, *Captain John Larrabee* (?)—*James Thatcher; Joseph Blackburn, Elizabeth and James Bowdoin;* John Singleton Copley, *Thaddeus Burr*—*Mrs. Thaddeus Burr*—*Col. Epes Sargent;* John Hesselius, *Mrs. Richard Brown.*

**Literature**   Benjamin Franklin, *The Interest of Great Britain Considered with Regard to Her Colonies;* Briton Hammon, *A Narrative of the Uncommon Sufferings, and Surprizing Deliverance of Briton Hammon, A Negro Man* . . .

## Music

**F. Births**   Richard Allen (compiler) February 14; Lucius Chapin (singing master) April 25; Ishmail Spicer (composer/educator) March 27.

**N. Musical Compositions**

**Choral/Vocal**   William Tuckey, *Thanksgiving Anthem.*

# 1761

☀

## Historical Highlights

A treaty between the colonists and the Cherokee Indians eases the troubles in the Carolinas; John Winthrop leads the first important scientific expedition in the New World to observe the transit of Venus; Venetian blinds and the first New World cookbook make their appearance.

## World Cultural Highlights

**World Art**   Jean Baptiste Greuze, *Village Bride;* Anton Mengs, *Parnassus;* Joshua Reynolds, *Garrick between Comedy and Tragedy;* Louis-François Roubiliac, *The Tomb of Lady Nightingale.*

**World Literature**   Charles Churchill, *Rosciad;* George Colman, *The Jealous Wife;* Carlo Gozzi, *The Love of Three Oranges;* Thomas Gray, *The Fatal Sisters;* Jean-Jacques Rousseau, *Julie.*

**World Music**   Franz Joseph Haydn becomes second Kapellmeister at Esterhazy, *Symphonies 7–10;* Wolfgang Amadeus Mozart, age 6, writes his first piece of music.

**Miscellaneous**   Johannes Zumpe begins making pianos and harpsichords in London; births include Louis-Leopold Boilly, John Hamilton, August Friedrich von Kotzebue, and John Opie; deaths include François Balthasar Adam, William Law, and Samuel Richardson.

## American Art and Literature Highlights

**Births/Deaths**   Births include artists Mather Brown, Edward Savage, poet Richard Alsop, and author Mason F. Cogswell; deaths include author/poet Samuel Davies.

**Art Works**   Joseph Blackburn, *Mary (Polly) Warner;* John Singleton Copley, *Rufus Greene*—*Mrs. Rufus Greene;* Peter Harrison, *Brick Market* (Newport, Rhode Island); John Hesselius, *Charles Calvert and His Colored Slave.*

**Literature**   Francis Hopkinson, *Exercises;* Ezra Stiles, *A Discourse on the Christian Union* . . .

## Music

**F. Births**   Jacob Kimball, Jr. (composer/compiler) February 15.

**K. Biographical**   Jeremiah Dencke (Moravian clergyman/organist/composer) comes to the United States; Francis Hopkinson is admitted to the Pennsylvania bar.

**L. Musical Beginnings**

**Performing Groups**   St. Cecilia Society of Charleston, South Carolina (believed to be the first known in the New World).

**Other**    Glassychord (Glass Harmonica, invented by Benjamin Franklin).

**M. Music Publications**

Lyons, James, *Urania, or, A Choice Collection of Psalm Tunes, Anthems and Hymns, from the Most Approved Authors*.

# 1762

❋

## Historical Highlights

The French secretly give the Louisiana Territory to Spain to prevent the British from taking it over during the war; the Ethan Allen ironworks are founded in Connecticut; the first known printing press in America is brought to Georgia; Catherine the Great becomes Empress of Russia.

## World Cultural Highlights

**World Art**    Étienne Falconet, *Christ in Gethsemane*; Pietro Longhi, *The Lion House*; Giovanni Pannini, *Trevi Fountain* (Rome); Louis-François Roubiliac, *Handel Monument, Westminster Abbey*.

**World Literature**    Oliver Goldsmith, *Letters from a Citizen of the World*; James Macpherson, *Fingal*; Jean-Jacques Rousseau, *Social Contract*; Tobias Smollett, *Adventures of Sir Lancelot Greaves*.

**World Music**    Christoph Willibald Gluck, *Orfeo ed Euridice*; Franz Joseph Haydn, *Four Divertimentos, Opus 2*; Wolfgang Amadeus Mozart, *Minuet and Trio in G Major, K. 1*.

**Miscellaneous**    Wolfgang Amadeus Mozart and his sister are taken on tour by their father; births include Joanna Baillie, George Colman, Jr., and André Marie de Chénier; deaths include Prosper Jolyot de Crébillon, Edmé Bourchardon, Louis-François Roubiliac, and Paul Troger.

## American Art and Literature Highlights

**Births/Deaths**    Births include novelists Susanna Haswell Rowson and Tabitha Gilman Tenney; deaths include author James Ralph.

**Literature**    Thomas Godfrey, *The Court of Fancy*; Francis Hopkinson, *Science*; James Otis, *A Vindication of the House of Representatives*; William Smith, *Additional Discourses and Essays. Being a Supplement to the First Edition . . .* ; John Woolman, *Considerations on Keeping Negroes II . . .*

## Music

**F. Births**    Andrew Adgate (editor/conductor) March 22; Samuel Holyoke (composer/compiler) October 15; Johann Christian Till (Moravian organist/composer) May 18.

**G. Deaths**    Johann Gottlob Klemm (German-born organ builder) May 5.

**J. Prizes and Honors**    James Lyons (MA, College of New Jersey).

**K. Biographical**    Thomas Bacon is appointed rector of All Saints Church (Frederick, Maryland); James Lyon is given a license to preach by the Presbyterian Synod of New Jersey.

# 1763

❋

## Historical Highlights

The Ottawa Indians under Chief Pontiac attack the settlers in the Ohio Territory and destroy all forts but Fort Pitt and Fort Detroit; by the Treaty of Paris, France loses all territory east of the Mississippi River; the Proclamation Line seeks to limit settlement west of the Appalachians; the first steamboat passes its trial run.

## World Cultural Highlights

**World Art**    Lambert Sigisbert Adam, *Prometheus Chained*; Francesco Guardi, *Election of the Doge*; Pietro Lorenzoni, *Wolfgang Amadeus Mozart*; Carle Van Loo, *Venus and Cupid*.

**World Literature**    Charles Churchill, *The Duellist*; Gotthold Lessing, *Minna von Barnhelm*; James Macpherson, *Temora*; Emanuel Swedenborg, *Life for the New Jerusalem*.

**World Music**    Thomas Arne, *The Birth of Hercules*; Johann Christian Bach, *Six Clavecin Concertos, Opus 1*; Johann A. Hasse, *Requiem in C Major*; Franz Joseph Haydn, *Symphonies No. 12–16*.

**Miscellaneous**    The Leipzig Liebhaber Subscription Concerts are revived; births include János Bacsányi, Jean Germain Drouais, Étienne Méhul, and Jean Paul Richter; dead are Franz A. Bustelli, Olaf von Dalin, Pierre Carlet de Marivaux, Hedvig Nordenflycht, and William Shenstone.

## American Art and Literature Highlights

**Births/Deaths**    Births include artists Jacob Maentel, Reuben Moulthrop, architect Charles Bulfinch, and author Anne Home Livingston; deaths include poets Thomas Godfrey and James Sterling.

**Art Works**    John Singleton Copley, *Colonel Jacob Fowle—Mrs. Daniel Sargent*; Peter Harrison, *Touro Synagogue* (Newport, Rhode Island).

**Literature**    Jonathan Mayhew, *Observations on the Charter and Conduct of the Society for the Propagation of the Gospel in Foreign Parts*; Eleazar Wheelock, *Plain and Faithful Narrative of the Indian Charity School at Lebanon*; John Woolman, *A Plea for the Poor*.

## Music

**G. Deaths**    Alexander Malcolm (clergyman/violinist) June 15.

**K. Biographical**    James Bremner (British organist/composer) comes to the United States and opens a music school in Philadelphia.

**M. Music Publications**

Hopkinson, Francis, *Collection of Psalm Tunes* . . .

# 1764

✸

## Historical Highlights

Colonial protests begin with the passage by the British Parliament of the Currency and Sugar Acts, passed for the purpose of raising money to pay war debts; French fur traders establish St. Louis as a trading post on the Mississippi River; Rhode Island College (Brown University) is founded.

## World Cultural Highlights

**World Art**    William Hogarth, *Finis (Bathos)*; Jean-Antoine Houdon, *St. Bruno*; Joshua Reynolds, *Mrs. Hale as Euphrosyne*; George Stubbs, *Cheetah with Two Indians*; Carle Van Loo, *Magic Lantern*.

**World Literature**    Charles Churchill, *The Candidate*; Immanuel Kant, *Observations on the Sense of the Beautiful and the Sublime*; Friedrich Klopstock, *Solomon*; Robert Lloyd, *The Capricious Lovers*.

**World Music**    Wolfgang Amadeus Mozart, *Symphony No. 1*; Franz Joseph Haydn, *Symphonies No. 21–24—Six String Quartets, Opus 3*; George Philip Telemann, *St. Luke Passion V*.

**Miscellaneous**    A Chair of Music is established at the University of Dublin; births include Jens Baggesen, André Marie de Chénier, Gabriel Marie Legouvé, Ann Radcliffe, and Johann Gottfried Schadow; deaths include Charles Churchill, William Hogarth, Jean-Marie Leclair, and Pietro Locatelli.

### American Art and Literature Highlights

**Births/Deaths**   Births include author Theodore Dwight, Sr., and poet Joseph Brown Ladd.

**Art Works**   John Singleton Copley, *Epes Sargent II—Mrs. Epes Sargent II—Mrs. John Powell—John Sparhawk*; John Trumbull, *Oath of Brutus*; Benjamin West, *Mary Hopkinson* (?).

**Literature**   John Dickinson, *Protest against the Appointment of Benjamin Franklin*; Benjamin Franklin, *Cool Thoughts on the Present Situation of Our Public Affairs*; Thomas Hutchinson, *History of the Colony of Massachusetts Bay, Volume I*; Jonathan Mayhew, *Letter of Reproof to Mr. John Cleaveland*; James Otis, *The Rights of the British Colonies*; Benjamin Y. Prime, *The Patriot Muse* . . .

### Music

**F. Births**   Jeremiah Ingalls (composer/compiler) March 1.

**K. Biographical**   Jacob Anthony (German woodwind maker) arrives in Philadelphia; James Lyon is ordained as a Presbyterian minister.

**M. Music Publications**

Bayley, Daniel, *A New and Complete Introduction to the Grounds and Rules of Music*
Flagg, Josiah, *A Collection of the Best Psalm Tunes, in Two, Three and Four Parts* . . .

# 1765

☀

### Historical Highlights

More colonial discontent is stirred up by the Stamp Act and the Quartering Act; a colonial Stamp Act Congress draws up the Declaration of Rights and Grievances and sends it to the British Parliament; the Ottawa Confederation under Chief Pontiac is defeated in the Ohio Territory; the College of Philadelphia opens the first medical school in the colonies; James Watt perfects his steam engine.

### World Cultural Highlights

**World Art**   Jean-Baptiste Chardin, *Attributes of the Arts—Attributes of Music*; Jean-Honoré Fragonard, *Corèsus and Callirrhoé*; Jean-Baptiste Greuze, *La Bonne Mère*.

**World Literature**   Dormont de Belloy, *Le Siège de Calais*; Henry Brooke, *The Fool of Quality*; Alice Cockburn, *Flowers of the Forest*; Oliver Goldsmith, *Essays*; Michel Sedaine, *The Duel*.

**World Music**   François Gossec, *Three Symphonies, Opus 8*; Franz Joseph Haydn, *Symphonies No. 25–32*; Wolfgang Amadeus Mozart, *Symphonies No. 4, 5*; Franz X. Richter, *Six Symphonies, Opus 4*.

**Miscellaneous**   The new Sadler's Wells Music House is built in London; Giovanni Artaria begins publishing music in Mainz; born are Manuel Maria du Bocage and James Grahame; deaths include George Lambert, Nicola Logroscino, Carle Van Loo, and Edward Young.

### American Art and Literature Highlights

**Births/Deaths**   Births include artist Robert Fulton, novelist William Hill Brown, and poet Samuel Low; deaths include artist Joseph Badger.

**Art Works**   John Singleton Copley, *The Boy with a Squirrel—John Hancock—Thomas Hancock—Nathaniel Hurd*; Matthew Pratt, *The American School*; Jeremiah Theüs, *Mr. and Mrs. Cuthbert*.

**Literature**   Benjamin Church, *The Times, a Poem;* John Dickinson, *The Late Regulations Respecting the British Colonies on the Continent of America*; Jonathan Edwards, *Personal Narrative*; Thomas Godfrey, *Poems on Various Subjects*; Stephen Hopkins, *The Rights of Colonies Examined*; James Otis, *A Vindication of the British Colonies*.

## Music

**F. Births**   George Crehore (instrument maker) February 18; Oliver Holden (composer/compiler) September 18; Alexander Juhan (violinist/conductor/composer).

**K. Biographical**   David Tannenberg moves his organ-building business to Lititz, Pennsylvania.

**L. Musical Beginnings**

**Other**   Ranelagh Gardens Summer Concerts, New York City (four seasons only).

**M. Music Publications**

Whitefield, George, *A Collection of Hymns for Social Worship* (American publication)

**N. Musical Compositions**

**Choral/Vocal**   Jeremiah Dencke, *Liebesmahl.*

# 1766

❋

## Historical Highlights

The Stamp Act is repealed as a result of loss of trade by English businessmen, but the Declaratory Act further fans the flames of discord; Benjamin Franklin becomes the colonists' representative to Parliament; the Mason-Dixon Line is established between Pennsylvania and Maryland; Queens College (Rutgers University) is founded, the Philadelphia Medical Society is formed.

## World Cultural Highlights

**World Art**   Jean-Honoré Fragonard, *The Swing*; Thomas Gainsborough, *The Harvest Wagon*; Michel Ollivier, *Mozart Playing Afternoon Tea*; Joseph Wright, *The Orrery*; Joshua Reynolds, *George Selwyn.*

**World Literature**   George Colman and David Garrick, *The Clandestine Marriage*; Oliver Goldsmith, *The Vicar of Wakefield*; Gotthold Lessing, *Laocoön*; Christoph Wieland, *The Story of Agathon.*

**World Music**   Carl Ditters von Dittersdorf, *Six Symphonies, Opus 1*; Franz Joseph Haydn, *Symphonies No. 16–20*; Wolfgang Amadeus Mozart, *Six Violin Sonatas, K. 26–31.*

**Miscellaneous**   The Anacreontic Society of London is founded; Franz Joseph Haydn becomes first kapellmeister at Esterhazy; births include Isaac d'Israeli, Wilhelm von Kobell and Mme. de Stael; deaths include Claudio Beaumont, Johann Christoph Gottsched, and Jean-Marc Nattier.

## American Art and Literature Highlights

**Births/Deaths**   Births include artists John Brewster, Jr., William Dunlap, and poet William Irving; deaths include authors Samuel Finley and Jonathan Mayhew.

**Art Works**   Benjamin Blyth, *John and Abigail Adams*; John Singleton Copley, *Mrs. Sylvanus Bourne—Mrs. Thomas Boylston*; Thomas McBean, *St. Paul's Chapel, New York*; Benjamin West, *Pylades and Orestes*; William Williams, *Deborah Hall—David Hall.*

**Literature**   Anthony Benezet, *A Caution to Great Britain and Her Colonies*; Richard Bland, *An Enquiry into the Rights of the British Colonies*; Jonathan Mayhew, *The Snare Broken*; John Morgan, *Dissertation on the Reciprocal Advantages of a Perpetual Union between Great Britain and Her American Colonies*; Robert Rogers, *Ponteach: or, The Savages in America.*

## Music

**K. Biographical**   John Schneider (violinist/horn performer) is in Fredericksburg, Virginia, as a concert impresario.

**L. Musical Beginnings**

**Other**   Southwark Theatre (Philadelphia).

**M. Music Publications**

Anonymous, *Hymns and Spiritual Songs* (Baptist)

Flagg, Josiah, *Sixteen Anthems . . . to Which Is Added a Few Psalm Tunes*

# 1767

☀

## Historical Highlights

British Parliament dissolves the New York Assembly for refusing to honor the Quartering Act and passes the Townshend Acts; the colonists retaliate by beginning a policy of nonimportation of British goods; Daniel Boone explores west of the Appalachian Mountains; the first planetarium in the colonies is built in Philadelphia.

## World Cultural Highlights

**World Art**    Daniel Chodowiecki, *Parting of Calas from His Dog*; Jean-Antoine Houdon, *St. Bruno*; Joshua Reynolds, *Lady Mary Bruce*; Joseph-Marie Vien, *Greek Girl at the Bath*.

**World Literature**    Jean-François Marmontel, *Bélisaire—Éléments de Littérature*; Moses Mendelssohn, *Phädon*; Louis-Sébastien Mercier, *L'Homme sauvage*; Laurence Sterne, *Letters of Yorick to Eliza*.

**World Music**    Christian Cannabich, *Six Symphonies, Opus 4*; Christoph Willibald Gluck, *Alceste*; Franz Joseph Haydn, *Symphony No. 35*; Wolfgang Amadeus Mozart, *Symphonies No. 6, 7*.

**Miscellaneous**    Longman and Broderip begin publishing music in London; births include Maria Edgeworth, Anne Louis Girodet-Trioson, Jan Helmers, and August von Schlegel; deaths include Hubert Drouais, Giovanni Battista Pittoni, and Georg Philipp Telemann.

## American Art and Literature Highlights

**Births/Deaths**    Births include artist Charles Peale Polk; deaths include poets Nathaniel Evans, Jonas Green, and Roger Wolcott.

**Art Works**    John Singleton Copley, *Nicholas Boylston —- Rebecca Boylston—Girl with Bird and Dog*; John Mare, *Portrait of the Unknown Man*; Jeremiah Platt, *John Ketaltas*; Benjamin West, *The Departure of Regulus*; William Williams, *Woman with a Book—Woman with Hour Glass and Skull*.

**Literature**    Thomas Forrest, *The Disappointment: or, the Force of Credulity*; Thomas Hutchinson, *History of the Colony of Massachusetts Bay, Vol. II*.

## Music

**G. Deaths**    Thomas Johnston (organ builder/publisher) May 8.

**I. New Positions**

**Other**    James Bremner (organ, Christ Church, Philadelphia).

**M. Music Publications**

Hopkinson, Francis, *Psalms of David for the Dutch Reformed Church*.

**N. Musical Compositions**

**Operas**    Andrew Barton, *The Disappointment, or, the Force of Credulity* (ballad opera). (See Literature above.)

**Piano/Organ**    William Selby, *Ten Organ Voluntaries* (?).

# 1768

☀

### Historical Highlights

The Massachusetts Assembly is dismissed by Parliament for refusing to collect taxes and to honor the Quartering Act; the Regulator Movement seeking tax reform is founded in North Carolina; the Cherokee Indians sign a treaty pushing the Virginia Territory westward; New York forms the first chamber of commerce; the first medical student graduates from Philadelphia Medical School.

### World Cutural Highlights

**World Art**   Hubert Robert, *Temple and Obelisk*; Alexander Roslin, *Lady with the Veil*; Joseph Wright, *Experiment with the Air Pump*; Francesco Zuccarelli, *Finding of Moses*.

**World Literature**   Oliver Goldsmith, *The Good-Natured Man*; Laurence Sterne, *Sentimental Journey*; Alexander Sumarokov, *The Usurer*; Horace Walpole, *Mysterious Mother*.

**World Music**   Domenico Cimarosa, *Mass in F Major*; Franz Joseph Haydn, *Symphony No. 49, "La Passione"*; Wolfgang Amadeus Mozart, *Bastien und Bastienne—La finta semplice*.

**Miscellaneous**   The Birmingham Music Festivals begin; births include François René de Chateaubriand, John Crome, Konrad Eberhard, and Joseph Anton Koch; deaths include (Antonio) Canaletto, Carlo Frugoni, John Runciman, Laurence Sterne, and Johann Joachim Winckelmann.

### American Art and Literature Highlights

**Births/Deaths**   Births include artist Ezra Ames, author Joseph Dennic, and poet William Littell; deaths include artist John Watson and author Thomas Bacon.

**Art Works**   John Singleton Copley, *John Amory*; Charles Willson Peale, *Mr. Pitt*; Benjamin West, *Venus Lamenting Adonis' Death—Agrippina Landing at Brindisium with the Ashes of Germanicus*.

**Literature**   John Dickinson, *Letters from a Farmer in Pennsylvania*; Arthur Lee, *The Monitor's Letters*; Samuel Quincy, *A Monody . . . to Benjamin Church, M.D., in Memory of Mr. Edmund Quincy . . .*; James Reid, *Caledoniensis Poems*; John Witherspoon, *Essays and Sermons on Important Subjects*.

### Music

**F. Births**   Amzi Chapin (singing master) March 2.

**G. Deaths**   Thomas Bacon (British-born violinist/composer) May 24; Johann C. Bissel (Moravian composer/hymnodist) July 6.

**N. Musical Compositions**

**Choral/Vocal**   John Dickinson, *The Liberty Song* (on music of William Boyce).

# 1769

☀

### Historical Highlights

The Virginia Assembly introduces the Virginia Resolves—the Colonial Governor dissolves the Assembly; the Spanish discover San Francisco bay and found their colony of Nuestra Señora la Reina de Los Angeles; Dartmouth College is founded in New Hampshire; Daniel Boone enters the Kentucky Territory for the first time; Poland is again partitioned by the European superpowers.

## World Cultural Highlights

**World Art**    Jean-Honoré Fragonard, *The Study—The Love Letter*; Jean-Baptiste Greuze, *Offering to Love*; George Stubbs, *Lion Attacking a Horse*; Joseph Wright, *The Academy by Lamplight*.

**World Literature**    Denis Fonvizin, *The Brigadier*; Johann von Herder, *Kritische Wälder*; Friedrich von Klopstock, *Hermanns Schlacht*; Tobias Smollett, *Adventures of an Atom*.

**World Music**    Carl Ditters von Dittersdorf, *Three Symphonies, Opus 5*; Franz Joseph Haydn, *Symphonies No. 36, 38*; Giovanni Paisiello, *La serva padrona*.

**Miscellaneous**    Births include François Joseph Bosio, Charles Julien de Chénedollé, Christian August Eberhard, and Thomas Lawrence; deaths include Giuseppe Bazzini, William Falconer, Christian Fürchtegott Gellert, and Johann Elias Ridinger.

## American Art and Literature Highlights

**Births/Deaths**    Births include authors Joseph Doddridge and William Emerson; deaths include author Joseph Sewall.

**Art Works**    John Singleton Copley, *Jeremiah Lee—Isaac Smith—Mrs. Isaac Smith*; Benjamin West, *Self-Portrait*.

**Literature**    Samuel Adams et al., *An Appeal to the World, or a Vindication of . . . Boston*; James Reid, *The Religion of the Bible and the Religion of King William County Compared*; John J. Zubly, *An Humble Enquiry into the Nature of the Dependency of the American Colonies upon the Parliament of Great-Britain*.

## Music

**F. Births**    Nahum Mitchell (composer).

**K. Biographical**    William Billings begins teaching choral singing in Boston; John Harris builds the first spinet piano in the colonies (Boston).

**L. Musical Beginnings**

**Other**    Composers Concerts (Philadelphia, by Giovanni Gualdo).

**M. Music Publications**

Bayley, Daniel, *American Harmony I—Universal Harmony*

# 1770

❋

## Historical Highlights

The so-called Boston Massacre takes place March 5; Parliament repeals the Townshend Acts; Carpenter's Hall is built in Philadelphia; the College of Charleston is founded in South Carolina; the first mental institution in the colonies opens in Williamsburg, Virginia; the estimated population in the colonies is approximately 2,000,000; Lord North becomes British Prime Minister.

## World Cultural Highlights

**World Art**    Saverio Dalla Rosa, *Mozart at the Keyboard*; Thomas Gainsborough, *Blue Boy*; Francisco de Goya, *The Flight into Egypt*; Giovanni Battista Tiepolo, *St. Francis Receiving the Stigmata*.

**World Literature**    James Beattie, *The Nature and Immutability of Truth*; Thomas Chatterton, *The Revenge*; Oliver Goldsmith, *The Deserted Village*; Thomas Percy, *Northern Antiquities*.

**World Music**    Johann Christian Bach, *Six Symphonies, Opus 6*; Muzio Clementi, *Six Keyboard Sonatas, Opus 1*; Franz Joseph Haydn, *Le Pescatrici*; Wolfgang Amadeus Mozart, *Symphonies No. 10, 11—Mitridate*.

**Miscellaneous**   B. Schotts Söhne begins publishing music in Mainz; births include Georg Wilhelm Hegel, Johann Friedrich Hölderlin, Bertel Thorvaldsen, and William Wordsworth; deaths include François Boucher, Thomas Chatterton, Giovanni Bettina Cignaroli, and Giovanni Battista Tiepolo.

## American Art and Literature Highlights

**Births/Deaths**   Births include artists Rufus Hathaway, Eunice Pinney, Henry Sargent, and Benjamin Troll; deaths include poet Thomas Craddock.

**Art Works**   Winthrop Chandler, *Reverend Ebenezer Devotion*; John S. Copley, *Ezekiel Goldthwait* (?)—*Paul Revere*—*Mrs. John Bacon*; Charles Willson Peale, *John Dickinson*; Paul Revere, *The Bloody Massacre* (engraving); Benjamin West, *The Death of General Wolfe*.

**Literature**   William Livingston, *America: Or, a Poem on the Settlement of the British Colonies*; Robert Mumford, *The Candidates*; Michael Smith, *Twelve Sermons, Preached upon Several Occasions*; John Trumbull, *Essay on the Uses and Advantages of the Fine Arts*; John Woolman, *Considerations on the True Harmony of Mankind, and How It Is to Be Maintained* . . .

## Music

**F. Births**   Ebenezer Child (composer/compiler); James Hewitt (composer) June 4 (in England); Samuel Worcester (compiler) November 1; John Wyeth (publisher) March 31.

**K. Biographical**   Johann Friedrich Peter (Moravian violinist/composer) and his brother Simon Peter (Moravian composer) are sent to Pennsylvania to minister to the Moravian settlements; William Tuckey presents excerpts from Handel's *Messiah*, a first in the colonies.

**M. Music Publications**

Billings, W. and Revere, P., *The New England Psalmsinger, or, American Chorister*

# 1771

☼

## Historical Highlights

The North Carolina "Regulators," mostly backwoods farmers, do battle with British troops over repressive taxes, under-representation in the councils, and what they consider unjust and suppressive laws; Captain James Cook completes the first of his round-the-world voyages.

## World Cultural Highlights

**World Art**   Daniel Chodowiecki, *The Artist's Studio*; Jacques-Louis David, *The Combat of Mars and Minerva*; Jean-Honoré Fragonard, *The Progress of Love*; Johann Zoffany, *Life School of the Royal Academy*.

**World Literature**   Richard Cumberland, *The West Indian*; Friedrich Klopstock, *Oden*; Henry Mackenzie, *The Man of Feeling*; Tobias Smollett, *The Expedition of Humphry Clinker*.

**World Music**   Luigi Boccherini, *Six Symphonies, Opus 12*; Franz Joseph Haydn, *Symphonies No. 42, 43*; Michael Haydn, *Requiem in C Minor*; Wolfgang Amadeus Mozart, *Symphonies No. 12–14*.

**Miscellaneous**   The Swedish Royal Academy of Music opens; births include Antoine-Jean Gros, Louis Jean Lemercier, Siegfried Mahlmann, Ferdinando Paër, and Walter Scott; deaths include Thomas Gray, Christian Klotz, Tobias George Smollett, and Louis Michel Van Loo.

## American Art and Literature Highlights

**Births/Deaths**   Births include literary figures Hosea Ballou, Charles Brockden Brown, Margaretta Fangeres, Thomas Green Fessenden, and Elihu Hubbard Smith; deaths include poet Michael Smith.

**Art Works**    John Singleton Copley, *Mrs. Humphrey Devereux—Thomas Gage—Mrs. Thomas Gage*; Samuel King, *Ezra Stiles*; Charles Willson Peale, *Edward Lloyd Family*; Benjamin West, *Penn's Treaty with the Indians—Sir Joseph Banks*; William Williams, *John Wiley, His Mother and Sisters*.

**Literature**    Anthony Benezet, *An Historical Account of Guinea*; Charles Chauncy, *A Compleat View of Episcopacy*; P. Freneau and H. Brackenridge, *The Rising Glory of America*; Michael Smith, *Christianity Unmasked, or, Unavoidable Ignorance Preferable to Corrupt Christianity, A Poem*; John Woolman, *Serious Considerations on Various Subjects of Importance*.

## Music

**F. Births**    Daniel Belknap (composer) February 9; Lewis Edson, Jr. (singing master/poet) January 23; Peter Erben (organist); Jonathan Huntington (composer/tenor) November 17.

**G. Deaths**    John Schneider (violinist/horn performer) October 19.

**I. New Positions**

**Other**    William Selby (organ, King's Chapel, Boston).

**K. Biographical**    William Selby (British organist/composer) emigrates to the colonies and settles in Boston; Josiah Flagg organizes Boston's first large ensemble concert with the 65th Regiment Band in a program of classical works.

**M. Music Publications**    Daniel Bayley, *American Harmony II*.

# 1772

❖

## Historical Highlights

Samuel Adams forms the Committees of Correspondence expressly to foment revolution within the colonies; Massachusetts finances are taken over by the Crown; the British revenue cutter *Gaspee* runs aground and is burned by the colonists; Captain James Cook begins his second world voyage.

## World Cultural Highlights

**World Art**    Louis Boilly, *St. Roche Healing the Plague-Stricken*; Francisco de Goya, *Allegory of the Trinity*; Johann Zoffany, *Academicians of the Royal Academy*; Joseph Wright of Derby, *The Forge*.

**World Literature**    Richard Graves, *The Spiritual Quixote*; Barthélemy Imbert, *The Judgment of Paris*; Gotthold Lessing, *Emilia Galotti*; Christoph Wieland, *Der Goldene Spiegel*.

**World Music**    Franz Joseph Haydn, *Symphonies No. 44–47—Six Divertimentos for String Quartet, Opus 20*; Wolfgang Amadeus Mozart, *Symphonies No. 15–21—Lucio Silla*.

**Miscellaneous**    The St. Petersburg Music Club is founded in Russia; Lemoine Music Publishers opens in Paris; births include Edward Bird, Sándor Kisfaludy, Friedrich von Schlegel, Friedrich von Hardenburg (Novalis), and Samuel Taylor Coleridge; deaths include Johann Feuchtmayr, Louis Touqué, and Pedro Antonio Correa Garção.

## American Art and Literature Highlights

**Births/Deaths**    Births include poets William Cliffton, John Lathrop, Jr., and author William Wirt; deaths include philosopher Samuel Johnson and author John Woolman.

**Art Works**    John Singleton Copley, *Samuel Adams*; Charles Willson Peale, *George Washington—Thomas Johnson Family—John Cadwalader Family*; Benjamin West, *The Artist's Wife and Son*; William Williams, *Imaginary Landscape*.

**Literature**   Nathaniel Evans, *Poems on Several Occasions, with Some Other Compositions*; Philip Freneau, *The American Village, a Poem*; Francis Hopkinson, *Dirtilla*; John Trumbull, *The Progress of Dulness I*; John Woolman, *The Journal of John Woolman* (published 1774); John J. Zubly, *Calm and Respectful Thoughts on the Negative of the Crown on a Speaker Chosen . . . by the People*.

## Music

**F. Births**   Bartholomew Brown (hymnist); Eliakim Doolittle (singing master); Stephen Jenks (composer/compiler) March 17.

**N. Musical Compositions**

**Choral/Vocal**   John F. Peter, *It Is a Precious Thing* (anthem).

# 1773

❀

## Historical Highlights

Parliament passes the Tea Act along with the so-called Coercive Acts—colonial reaction results in the "Boston Tea Party" when Massachusetts colonists dump British tea into Boston bay; the Virginia Congress joins the Committees of Correspondence; Boston installs first large street lighting system; the Philadelphia Museum and Charleston Museum of Natural History open.

## World Cultural Highlights

**World Art**   Antonio Canova, *Eurydice*; Jacques-Louis David, *The Death of Seneca*; Jean-Honoré Fragonard, *The Rendezvous*; Joshua Reynolds, *Graces Decorating Hymen*.

**World Literature**   Gottfried Bürger, *Lenore*; Johann Wolfgang von Goethe, *Götz von Berlichingen—Urfaust*; Oliver Goldsmith, *She Stoops to Conquer*; Albrecht von Haller, *Alfred*.

**World Music**   Carl Ditters von Dittersdorf, *Four Symphonies, Opus 7*; Wolfgang Amadeus Mozart, *Symphonies No. 22–27—Piano Concerto No. 5—Motet, "Exsultate, Jubilate."*

**Miscellaneous**   The Swedish National Opera opens in Stockholm; births include Johann Ludwig Tieck, Mihály Vitéz, and Heinrich Wilhelm Wackenroder; deaths include Philip Chesterfield, Hubert François Gravelot, George Lyttelton, and Bartolomeo Francesco Rastrelli.

## American Art and Literature Highlights

**Births/Deaths**   Births include poet Robert Treat Paine.

**Art Works**   John Singleton Copley, *Mr. and Mrs. Thomas Mifflin—John Winthrop—Mrs. John Winthrop*; John Trumbull, *Rebecca at the Well*.

**Literature**   John Allen, *An Oration upon the Beauties of Liberty*; Benjamin Church, *An Oration to Commemorate the Bloody Tragedy of the Fifth of March, 1770*; Samuel Hopkins, *An Inquiry into the Nature of True Holiness . . .* ; Samuel Mather, *Attempt to Shew That America Must Be Known to the Antients*; John Trumbull, *The Progress of Dulness II, III*; Mercy Otis Warren, *The Adulateur, a Tragedy*; Phillis Wheatley, *Poems on Various Subjects, Religious and Moral*.

## Music

**F. Births**   Joel Harmon, Jr. (educator/compiler); Abraham Maxim (hymnist).

**L. Musical Beginnings**

**Performing Groups**   Josiah Flagg Band (Boston).

**Other**   Charleston Theater (South Carolina, the largest in the New World).

**M. Music Publications**

Bayley, Daniel, *A New Royal Harmony*

# 1774

☼

### Historical Highlights

The First Continental Congress sends a Petition of Grievances to Parliament, which passes the "Intolerable Acts" to punish the colonies; the Port of Boston is closed and General Gage is made governor of Massachusetts; Shawnee Territory in Ohio is gained by force of arms; the Quebec Act pushes the Canadian border down to the Ohio River; Joseph Priestley discovers oxygen.

### World Cultural Highlights

**World Art**   Clodion, *St. Cecilia*; Henry Fuseli, *The Death of Cardinal Beaufort*; Ignaz Günther, *Pietà*; Pietro Longhi, *The Elephant*; Edward Penny, *Virtuous Comforted—Profligate Punished*.

**World Literature**   Louise Épinay, *Les Conversations d'Émilie*; Johann Wolfgang von Goethe, *The Sorrows of Young Werther*; Christoph Wieland, *Story of the Abderites*.

**World Music**   Franz Joseph Haydn, *Symphonies No. 51–60—Piano Sonatas 25–30*; Wolfgang Amadeus Mozart, *Symphonies No. 28–30—Bassoon Concerto*.

**Miscellaneous**   The *Gentlemen and Lady's Musical Companion* begins publication in London; births include Casper David Friedrich, Pierre Narcisse Guérin, Robert Southey, and Gaspare Spontini; deaths include Robert Fergusson, Oliver Goldsmith, Niccolò Jommelli, and Jean-Baptiste Lemoyne.

### American Art and Literature Highlights

**Births/Deaths**   Births include artist Raphaelle Peale and author/poets Thomas Branagan and Isaac Story (Peter Quince); deaths include artist Jeremiah Theüs.

**Art Works**   James Claypoole, *Memorial to E. R.*; John Singleton Copley, *Dr. Joseph Warren— Mr. and Mrs. Isaac Winslow—Mather Byles*; Gilbert Stuart, *John Bannister—Mrs. John Bannister and Son*.

**Literature**   Anthony Benezet, *The Mighty Destroyer Displayed*; Hugh H. Brackenridge, *A Poem on Divine Revelation*; Myles Cooper, *A Friendly Address to All Reasonable Americans*; John Dickinson, *An Essay upon the Constitutional Power of Great Britain Over the Colonies in America*; Timothy Dwight, Jr., *The Conquest of Canaan*; Thomas Jefferson, *A Summary View of the Rights of British America*; Samuel Seabury, *Free Thoughts on the Proceedings of the Continental Congress . . .* ; John Woolman, *Journal*.

### Music

**F. Births**   Thomas S. Wetmore (psalmist) August 12.

**K. Biographical**   John Behrent builds the first large American piano; William Billings marries his student, Lucy Swan; Elizabeth and Peter Albrecht von Hagen, Sr. (Dutch organists/publishers) emigrate to the colonies and settle in Charleston, South Carolina; David Tannenberg installs a new organ in the Holy Trinity Church in Lancaster, Pennsylvania.

**M. Music Publications**

*Gentlemen and Lady's Musical Companion*

# 1775

☼

### Historical Highlights

The Second Continental Congress begins in Philadelphia; Parliament imposes the New England Restraining Act on the colonies; the American Revolution begins with the Battles of Lexington,

Concord, and Bunker (Breed's) Hill and the capture of Fort Ticonderoga by Ethan Allen; George Washington is appointed Commander-in-Chief; Daniel Boone leads the first settlers into Kentucky.

## World Cultural Highlights

**World Art**    Jean-Baptiste Chardin, *Self-Portrait with Eye Shade*; Clodion, *Satyr and Bacchante*; Jean-Antoine Houdon, *Christoph Willibald Gluck*; Joshua Reynolds, *Mrs. Bowles and Her Dog*.

**World Literature**    Pierre Augustin de Beaumarchais, *The Barber of Seville*; John Burgoyne, *Maid of the Oak*; Richard Sheridan, *The Duenna—The Rivals*.

**World Music**    C. P. E. Bach, *The Israelites in the Wilderness*; Wolfgang Amadeus Mozart, *Violin Concertos No. 1–5—Il rè pastore— La finta giardiniera—Serenade, K. 204*.

**Miscellaneous**    Simon and Pierre Leduc, Music Publishers, open in Paris; births include Jane Austen, Thomas Girtin, Charles Lamb, Walter Savage Landor, Friedrich Wilhelm von Schelling, Joseph Turner, and Richard Westmacott; deaths include Pierre Dormant de Belloy and François Drouais.

## American Art and Literature Highlights

**Births/Deaths**    Births include artists Robert Salmon, Benjamin Tanner, John Vanderlyn, poet Paul Allen, and author George Tucker; deaths include poet Robert Bolling.

**Art Works**    Henry Benbridge, *Sarah Flagg* (?); John Singleton Copley, *Mr. and Mrs. Ralph Izzard—Mrs. Samuel Chase and Her Daughter*; Amos Doolittle, *The Battle of Lexington, April 19th, 1775* (engraving); Thomas Jefferson, *Monticello* (Virginia); Gilbert Stuart, *Francis Malbone and His Brother*; William Williams, *Husband and Wife in a Landscape—Conversation Piece*.

**Literature**    James Adair, *The History of the American Indians*; John Dickinson, *A Declaration by the Representatives of the United Colonies*; Philip Freneau, *General Gage's Confession*; John Leacock, *The First Book of the American Chronicles of the Times*; Samuel Seabury, *A View of the Controversy between Great Britain and Her Colonies*; Mercy Otis Warren, *The Group*.

## Music

**F. Births**    George E. Blake (publisher).

**K. Biographical**    Andrew Law graduates from Rhode Island College (Brown University).

**M. Music Publications**

Bayley, Daniel, *New Universal Harmony*

**N. Musical Compositions**

**Choral/Vocal**    Andrew Law, *The American Hero* (words by N. Niles).

# 1776

❋

## Historical Highlights

The Declaration of Independence is signed in August by the members of the Continental Congress; colonial forces leave New York; the Stars and Stripes is first flown over Philadelphia; Nathan Hale is executed by the British as a spy; New Jersey grants women suffrage; Captain James Cook begins his third world voyage; Louis XVI rejects all reforms sought by the French people.

## World Cultural Highlights

**World Art**    Antonio Canova, *Orpheus*; John Cozens, *Hannibal Crossing the Alps*; Jean-Baptiste Pigalle, *The Nude Voltaire*; Joshua Reynolds, *The Child Samuel—John the Baptist*.

**World Literature**    Vittorio Alfieri, *Antigone*; Edward Gibbon, *The Decline and Fall of the Roman Empire I*; Friedrich von Klinger, *Sturm und Drang*; Adam Smith, *The Wealth of Nations*.

**World Music**   Johann Christian Bach, *Lucio Silla*; Franz Joseph Haydn, *Symphonies No. 66, 67*; Wolfgang Amadeus Mozart, *Haffner Serenade—Serenade, "Notturna"—Concerto for Three Pianos*.

**Miscellaneous**   The Bolshoi Opera Company is founded in Russia; the Concert Spirituel begins in Leipzig; births include John Constable, E. T. A. Hoffmann, Jane Porter, and Gottlieb Schick; deaths include Alexei Egorov, Francis Hayman, David Hume, and George de Marsées.

### American Art and Literature Highlights

**Births/Deaths**   Births include artists Jacob Eichholtz and Thomas Thompson; deaths include author Richard Bland and historians Cadwallader Colden and Samuel Smith.

**Art Works**   Charles Willson Peale, *Mrs. James Smith and Grandson—John Carroll*; Benjamin West, *Helen Brought to Paris*.

**Literature**   Anonymous, *The Battle of Brooklyn*; Hugh H. Brackenridge, *The Battle of Bunkers-Hill*; Samuel Hopkins, *A Dialogue Concerning the Slavery of the Africans*; Francis Hopkinson, *The Prophecy*; Robert Munford, *The Patriots*; Thomas Paine, *Common Sense*; Mercy Otis Warren, *The Blockheads*; John Witherspoon, *The Dominion of Providence over the Passions of Men*.

### Music

**F. Births**   George Schetky (cellist/publisher) June 1.

**I. New Positions**

**Other**   William Selby (organ, Boston Trinity Church).

**K. Biographical**   Jacob Eckhard (German organist/composer) comes to the colonies and settles in Richmond, Virginia; Francis Hopkinson, dropping all his posts in order to serve as a delegate to the Continental Congress, becomes one of the signers of the Declaration of Independence; Andrew Law is licensed as a Congregational minister.

# 1777

❊

### Historical Highlights

The Stars and Stripes are officially adopted by the Continental Congress, which has to flee Philadelphia when the British take over; Washington's troops spend a hard winter at Valley Forge; victory at Saratoga encourages the French to enter the conflict on the side of the colonies; the Articles of Confederation are adopted; Vermont becomes the first state to outlaw slavery.

### World Cultural Highlights

**World Art**   Anonymous, *Mozart with the Golden Spur*; Thomas Gainsborough, *The Watering Hole*; Francisco de Goya, *The Parasol*; Jean-Antoine Houdon, *Morpheus*.

**World Literature**   György Bessenyei, *The Philosopher*; James Cook, *A Voyage toward the South Pole and Round the World*; Richard Sheridan, *A School for Scandal*; Thomas Warton, *Poems*.

**World Music**   Johann Christian Bach, *Six Keyboard Concertos, Opus 13*; Wolfgang Amadeus Mozart, *Piano Concerto No. 9—Piano Sonatas, K. 309, 311*; Christoph Willibald Gluck, *Armide*.

**Miscellaneous**   The Manchester Festivals begin in England; births include Lorenzo Bartolini, Thomas Campbell, Philipp Runge, Heinrich von Kleist, and Friedrich de La Motte-Fouqué; deaths include Claude Prosper de Crébillon, Jean-Baptiste Gresset, Charles-Joseph Natoire, and Alexander Sumarokov.

### American Art and Literature Highlights

**Births/Deaths**   Births include artists William Bennett, Edward G. Malbone, and poet John Blair Linn; deaths include artist William Johnston.

**Art Works**   John Singleton Copley, *Elizabeth, the Artist's Daughter*; Ralph Earl, *Roger Sherman* (?); John Trumbull, *The Trumbull Family*; Benjamin West, *Saul and the Witch of Endor*.

**Literature**   Isaac Backus, *History of New England, with Particular Reference to the Denomination of Christians Called Baptists*; Hugh H. Brackenridge, *The Death of General Montgomery, a Tragedy*; Francis Hopkinson, *The Political Catechism—Letter Written by a Foreigner on the Character of the English Nation*; Samuel Quincy, *Diary* (published 1882).

## Music

**F. Births**   George Catlin (instrument builder?); William Marcellus Goodrich (organ builder) July 21; Micah Hawkins (composer) January 1; John Rowe Parker (music dealer/publisher) October 24.

# 1778

❀

## Historical Highlights

France becomes the first country to recognize the new government in America; the British evacuate Philadelphia but take Savannah, Georgia; George Washington gains a victory at Monmouth and General Anthony Wayne occupies West Point; Captain Cook explores the western coast of North America and discovers the Sandwich Islands (Hawaii).

## World Cultural Highlights

**World Art**   Antonio Canova, *Daedalus und Icarus*; Henry Fuseli, *Oath on the Rütli*; Joseph Nollekens, *Venus Chiding Cupid*; Giovanni Battista Piranesi, *Vedute di Roma*.

**World Literature**   Fanny Burney, *Evelina*; George Ellis, *Poetical Tales by Sir Gregory Gander*; Johann Gottfried von Herder, *Stimmen der Völker in Liedern I*; Friedrich Müller, *Fausts Leben I*.

**World Music**   Franz Joseph Haydn, *Symphonies No. 66–69*; Wolfgang Amadeus Mozart, *"Paris" Symphony No. 31—Seven Violin Concertos, K. 296, 301–306*; John S. Smith, *To Anacreon in Heaven*.

**Miscellaneous**   The La Scala Opera House opens in Milan; births include Clemens Brentano, John James Chalon, Ugo Foscolo, and John Thomson; deaths include Nicolas-Sébastien Adam, Thomas Arne, Laurent Delvaux, George Knapton, Jean-Baptiste Lemoyne, and Voltaire.

## American Art and Literature Highlights

**Births/Deaths**   Births include art figures John Cogdell, Rembrandt Peale, and authors William Austin, James K. Paulding, and Margaret Bayard Smith; deaths include John Hesselius, Pieter Vanderlyn, and poets Landon Carter and Benjamin Church II.

**Art Works**   John Singleton Copley, *Watson and the Shark*; Joseph-Siffred Duplessis, *Benjamin Franklin*; John Trumbull, *Governor and Mrs. Jonathan Trumbull*; Benjamin West, *The Battle of The Hague*.

**Literature**   Joel Barlow, *The Prospect of Peace, a Poetical Composition Delivered in Yale-College*; Hugh Brackenridge, *Six Political Discourses Founded on the Scripture*; Landon Carter, *Diary*; Jonathan Carver, *Travels through the Interior Part of North America*; Benjamin Franklin, *The Ephemera*; Francis Hopkinson, *The Battle of the Kegs—Letter to Joseph Galloway*.

## Music

**F. Births**   Joseph Funk (composer) April 6.

**I. New Positions**

**Other**   John Hiwell (Inspector/Superintendent of Music in the Army); William Selby (organ, Stone Chapel, Boston).

**M. Music Publications**
Billings, William, *The Singing Master's Assistant*
**N. Musical Compositions**
**Choral/Vocal**   William Billings, *Chester*

# 1779

❀

## Historical Highlights

John Paul Jones, in the *Bonhomme Richard*, defeats the British frigate *Serapis* off the English coast; George Rogers Clark takes over the Old Northwest Territory; the British are defeated at Stony Point, New York; the University of Pennsylvania is founded; William and Mary College introduces student choice in selection of classes; Spain joins in the fighting against England.

## World Cultural Highlights

**World Art**   John Bacon, *Chatham Monument* (Westminster Abbey); Jacques-Louis David, *St. Jerôme*; Pietro Longhi, *The Alchemists*; Joseph Wright, *Grotto in the Kingdom of Naples*.

**World Literature**   David Hume, *Dialogues on Natural Religion*; Ignacy Krasicki, *Fables and Tales*; Gotthold Lessing, *Nathan, the Wise*; Hannah More, *Fatal Falsehood*; Richard Sheridan, *The Critic*.

**World Music**   Franz Joseph Haydn, *Symphony No. 70*; Wolfgang Amadeus Mozart, *Symphonies No. 32, 33—Posthorn Serenade—Concerto for Two Pianos—Coronation Mass*.

**Miscellaneous**   The Mannheim National Theater opens to house the newly formed National Opera Company; births include Thomas Birch, Augustus Callcott, and Adam Gottlob Oehlenschläger; deaths include William Boyce, Thomas Chippendale, Anton Raphael Mengs, and Jean-Baptiste Chardin.

## American Art and Literature Highlights

**Births/Deaths**   Births include artist Washington Allston, authors Francis Scott Key, Clement C. Moore, and William Tudor.

**Art Works**   Winthrop Chandler, *View of a River with Trees and Figures* (?); John Singleton Copley, *The Copley Family*; Ralph Earl, *William Carpenter*; Jean-Antoine Houdon, *Benjamin Franklin*; John Trumbull, *Belisarius*.

**Literature**   Ethan Allen, *Narrative of Colonel Ethan Allen's Captivity*; Jacob Duche, *Discourses on Various Subjects*; Benjamin Franklin, *The Morals of Chess*; Philip Freneau, *The House of Night*; Jonathan Odell, *Word of Congress*; Mercy Otis Warren, *The Motley Assembly, A Farce* (?).

## Music

**F. Births**   Asa Hopkins (woodwind maker); Oliver Shaw (organist/tenor/composer) March 13; Peter Von Hagen, Jr. (violinist/organist/composer?).

**K. Biographical**   Francis Hopkinson begins service as a judge, serving until his death.

**M. Music Publications**
Billings, William, *Music in Miniature*
Law, Andrew, *The Select Harmony*

# 1780

❀

## Historical Highlights

The colonies suffer a defeat at Camden but win at King's Mountain; Major André, found with the plans for surrendering West Point to the British, is hanged as a spy; Nashville, Tennessee, founded as a fort; the Dutch declare war on England; the Peruvian natives rebel against Spanish domination; Empress Maria Theresa dies, Joseph II becomes sole ruler in Austria.

## World Cultural Highlights

**World Art** Jean-Antoine Houdon, *Diana*; George Morland, *The Angler's Repast*; Élisabeth Vigée-Lebrun, *Marie Camargo*; Johann Zoffany, *Tribuna of the Uffizi Gallery*.

**World Literature** Matthias Claudius, *Lieder für das Volk*; Hannah Cowley, *The Belle's Stratagems*; George Crabbe, *The Candidate*; William Mason, *The English Garden*; Christoph Wieland, *Oberon*.

**World Music** Muzio Clementi, *Five Piano Sonatas, Opus 1*; Franz Joseph Haydn, *Symphonies No. 71, 74, 75*; Wolfgang Amadeus Mozart, *Symphony No. 34*; Luigi Cherubini, *Il Quinto Fabio*.

**Miscellaneous** The Leipzig Gewandhaus is built; births include Alfred Edward Chalon, Jean Auguste Ingres, Ferdinand Jagemann, and Anna Maria Porter; deaths include Charles Batteux, Bernardo Bellotto (Canaletto), Étienne Bonnot de Condillac, and Nicolás Fernández de Moratín.

## American Art and Literature Highlights

**Births/Deaths** Births include artists Edward Hicks, John W. Jarvis, and literary figures William E. Channing, Timothy Flint, William Ioor, and Hannah Farnham Lee; deaths include artist John V. Haidt and poet Joseph Green.

**Art Works** Winthrop Chandler, *Mrs. Samuel Chandler – Captain Samuel Chandler*; John Singleton Copley, *The Death of the Earl of Chatham in the House of Lords*; Charles Willson Peale, *George Washington* (engraving).

**Literature** Anthony Benezet, *Short Account of the People Called Quakers*; Timothy Dwight, *America: Or, a Poem on the Settlement of the British Colonies . . .*; Benjamin Franklin, *Dialogue between Franklin and the Gout*; David Humphreys, *A Poem on the Happiness of the United States*; Jonathan Odell, *The American Times*; Thomas Paine, *Public Good*.

## Music

**F. Births** Ananias Davisson (composer) February 2; Uri K. Hill (composer/educator).

**G. Deaths** James Bremner (British-born organist/composer) September.

**K. Biographical** Jacob Kimball graduates from Harvard.

**L. Musical Beginnings**

**Performing Groups** Handel Society of Dartmouth.

**N. Musical Compositions**

**Choral/Vocal** Francis Hopkinson, *Ode in Memory of James Bremner*.

# 1781

☀

## Historical Highlights

The British surrender at Yorktown following a blockade of Chesapeake Bay by the French Navy; the Articles of Confederation are ratified by Maryland, the last colony to do so; the Bank of North America is established; the Massachusetts Medical Society is founded; Joseph II of Austria abolishes slavery and grants freedom of the press and religious tolerance.

## World Cultural Highlights

**World Art** Jacques-Louis David, *Belisarius*; Johann Mansfield, *Franz Joseph Haydn*; Johann Nepomuk, *The Mozart Family*; Piat Joseph Sauvage, *The Triumph of the Infant Bacchus*.

**World Literature**   Immanuel Kant, *Critique of Pure Reason*; Charles Macklin, *The Man of the World*; Jean-Jacques Rousseau, *Confessions*; Johann Friedrich von Schiller, *The Robbers*.

**World Music**   Wolfgang Amadeus Mozart, *Idomeneo;* Franz Joseph Haydn, *Symphonies No. 72, 73, "La Chasse"—Six String Quartets, Opus 33, "Russian"*; Giovanni Paisiello, *La Serva Padrona*.

**Miscellaneous**   The Leipzig Gewandhaus Orchestra is formed; the first Broadwood Grand Piano is built; births include Achim von Arnim, Adelbert von Chamisso, Francis Chantrey, and Anton Diabelli; deaths include Gotthold Lessing and Johannes Ewald.

### American Art and Literature Highlights

**Births/Deaths**   Births include playwright George Washington Parke Custis and architect Robert Mills; deaths include author Josiah Smith.

**Art Works**   Charles Willson Peale, *George Washington at the Battle of Princeton —Walter Stewart—John Paul Jones*; John Trumbull, *St. Jerome at Parma*.

**Literature**   Joel Barlow, *A Poem, Spoken at the Public Commencement at Yale College, 1781*; Philip Freneau, *The British Prison-Ship*; Ebenezer Gay, *The Old Man's Calendar*; Samuel Andrews Peters, *General History of Connecticut, by a Gentleman of the Province*; John Witherspoon, *The Druid*.

### Music

**F. Births**   Nathaniel Duren Gould (singing master/compiler) November 26.

**G. Deaths**   William Tuckey (British-born singer/composer) September 14.

**M. Music Publications**

Billings, William, *The Psalm Singer's Amusement*

**N. Musical Compositions**

**Choral/Vocal**   Francis Hopkinson, *The Temple of Minerva* (cantata).

# 1782

☼

## Historical Highlights

A Treaty of Peace is concluded with England; the Great Seal of the United States is adopted; the bald eagle is chosen as the national bird; the Order of the Purple Heart for soldiers wounded in battle is introduced by George Washington; Harvard Medical School opens its doors; Spain fails to wrest Gibraltar from the English; James Watt builds the first rotary steam engine.

## World Cultural Highlights

**World Art**   Antonio Canova, *Theseus and the Minotaur*; Étienne Falconet, *Peter the Great*; Henry Fuseli, *The Nightmare*; Angelica Kauffmann, *Poetry Embracing Painting*.

**World Literature**   William Beckford, *Vathek*; Fanny Burney, *Cecilia*; George Colman, *The Female Dramatist*; Tomás de Iriarte y Oropesa, *Fábulas Literarias*; Hannah More, *Sacred Dramas*.

**World Music**   Giovanni Paisiello, *Barber of Seville*; Franz Joseph Haydn, *Symphonies No. 76–78— Mariazeller Messe*; Wolfgang Amadeus Mozart, *"Haffner" Symphony—Horn Concerto No. 1*.

**Miscellaneous**   The Royal Irish Academy of Music opens in Dublin; births include William Allen, John Cotman, John Field, Félicité de Lamennais, Niccolò Paganini, and Johannes de Troostwijck; deaths include Johann Christian Bach, Pietro Metastasio, and Richard Wilson.

## American Art and Literature Highlights

**Births/Deaths**   Births include artist Charles Fraser.

**Art Works**   Charles Willson Peale, *Mrs. Walter Stewart*; Gilbert Stuart, *The Gentleman Skater—James Ward*; Joseph Wright, *Benjamin Franklin*.

**Literature**   Anonymous, *The Blockheads; or, Fortunate Contractor*; Charles Chauncy, *Salvation for All Men*; St. John de Crèvecoeur, *Letters from an American Farmer*; John Trumbull, *M'Fingal, A Modern Epic Poem, in Four Cantos*.

## Music

**F. Births**   Elkanah K. Dare (clergyman/theorist/composer).

**K. Biographical**   Daniel Read settles for life in New Haven, Connecticut, and begins teaching singing schools in New England.

**M. Music Publications**

Law, Andrew, *Collection of Hymns for Social Worship*.

**N. Musical Compositions**   Johann F. Peter, *I Will Make an Everlasting Covenant*.

# 1783

❀

## Historical Highlights

The Treaty of Paris formally ends the Revolutionary War; most of the European countries recognize the new United States; the Continental Army is disbanded but the officers form the Society of the Cincinnati; Maryland and Massachusetts abolish slavery; William Pitt becomes British prime minister; Russia annexes the Crimea.

## World Cultural Highlights

**World Art**   Jacques-Louis David, *The Grief of Andromache*; Joseph Lange, *Wolfgang Amadeus Mozart*; John Opie, *The Peasant Family*; George Stubbs, *The Reapers*.

**World Literature**   William Beckford, *Dreams, Waking Thoughts and Incidents*; Hannah Cowley, *A Bold Stroke for a Husband*; George Crabbe, *The Village*; Thomas Day, *History of Sandford and Merton*.

**World Music**   Ludwig van Beethoven, *Piano Rondo in A Major*; Wolfgang Amadeus Mozart, *"Linz" Symphony No. 36—Horn Concerto No. 2—Piano Concertos No. 11, 13*.

**Miscellaneous**   The Hermitage Theater opens in St. Petersburg; Samuel Johnson forms the Essex Head Club in London; births include Peter von Cornelius, David Cox, Thomas Sully, and Stendhal; deaths include Louise Florence Épinay, Johann Hasse, Jean-Baptiste Perroneau, and Antonio Soler.

## American Art and Literature Highlights

**Births/Deaths**   Births include authors Washington Irving, George Watterston and artist Samuel Lovett Waldo; deaths include author James Adair and poets Ann Eliza Bleecker and Thomas Burke.

**Art Works**   John Singleton Copley, *The Death of Major Pierson*; Ralph Earl, *Admiral Kempenfelt*; Charles Willson Peale, *Nathaniel Greene—Artist's Mother with Her Grandchildren*; Gilbert Stuart, *Henrietta Elizabeth Frederica Vane*; Benjamin West, *The Three Sisters*.

**Literature**   Hugh H. Brackenridge, *Narratives of a Late Expedition against the Indians . . . ;* Charles Crawford, *Liberty: A Pindaric Ode*; David Humphreys, *The Glory of America: or, Peace Triumphant over War*; John Ledyard, *A Journal of Captain Cook's Last Voyage to the Pacific Ocean*; Ezra Stiles, *The United States Elevated to Glory and Honor*.

## Music

**F. Births**   Nathan Adams (brass instrument maker) August 21; Asahel Nettleton (evangelist/compiler) April 21.

**I. New Positions**

**Other**    William Billings (editor, *Boston Magazine*).

**K. Biographical**    John Jacob Astor (German music dealer) comes to the United States to bring music instruments to his brother in Baltimore; Oliver Holden receives two months' training in singing school, his only formal music training, and begins teaching his own singing schools.

**L. Musical Beginnings**

**Other**    Boston Book Store (Oliver Ditson and Co.).

**M. Music Publications**

Brownson, Oliver, *Select Harmony*
Law, Andrew, *The Rudiments of Music*

**N. Musical Compositions**

**Choral/Vocal**    John Friedrich Peter, *A Psalm of Joy*.

# 1784

❀

## Historical Highlights

The Mason-Dixon Line is extended westward into the new territories; the Potomac Company seeks to provide canal transportation for the colonies; slavery is abolished in the states of Connecticut and Rhode Island; the first law school opens in Connecticut; the British Parliament passes the British India Act, strengthening their hold on that state; Denmark abolishes serfdom within its borders.

## World Cultural Highlights

**World Art**    Jacques-Louis David, *The Oath of the Horatii*; Joshua Reynolds, *Mrs. Reynolds as the Tragic Muse*; Andreas Stöttrup, *C. P. E. Bach and the Artist*; Joseph Wright, *The Maid of Corinth*.

**World Literature**    Pierre de Beaumarchais, *The Marriage of Figaro*; Johann Wolfgang von Goethe, *Scherz, List und Rache*; Johann Friedrich von Schiller, *Kabale und Liebe*.

**World Music**    Franz Joseph Haydn, *Symphonies No. 79–81*; Wolfgang Amadeus Mozart, *Piano Concertos No. 14–19—"Hunt" String Quartet*.

**Miscellaneous**    The Italian Opera House opens in Prague; births include François Fétis, Leigh Hunt, Ernst Benjamin Raupach, François Rude, and Ludwig Spohr; deaths include Denis Diderot, Samuel Johnson, "Padre" Martini, Jean-Jacques Pompignan, Allan Ramsay, and Giuseppe Zais.

## American Art and Literature Highlights

**Births/Deaths**    Births include artist Bass Otis, Rubens Peale, and literary figures James Nelson Barker and Nathaniel Beverley Tucker; deaths include author Anthony Benezet and poets Robert Munford and Phillis Wheatley.

**Art Works**    Charles Willson Peale, *Washington at Yorktown*; Gilbert Stuart, *John Singleton Copley—Sir Joshua Reynolds*; Benjamin West, *Call of the Prophet Isaiah*.

**Literature**    Ethan Allen, *Reason the Only Oracle of Man*; Anthony Benezet, *Some Observations on the Indian Natives of This Continent*; Benjamin Franklin, *The Savages of North America*; Francis Hopkinson, *Modern Learning Exemplified*; Thomas Jefferson, *Notes on Virginia*; Samuel Low, *Winter Display'd, a Poem* . . . ; Peter Markoe, *The Patriot Chief*; Phillis Wheatley, *Liberty and Peace, a Poem*.

## Music

**F. Births**    Thomas Hastings (hymn composer) October 15; Job Plimpton (composer/organ builder) February 27.

**H. Debuts**

**United States**   William Brown (German [?] flutist—Baltimore).

**K. Biographical**   George Godfrey Müller (German Moravian violinist/composer) comes to the United States and spends most of his life in Lititz, Pennsylvania; William Smith (Scottish theologian/composer/author) comes to the United States and settles in Philadelphia.

**L. Musical Beginnings**

**Performing Groups**   Fredericksburg Harmonic Society (Virginia); Institution for the Encouragement of Church Music (Uranian Society, 1787—Philadelphia).

**M. Music Publications**

Smith, Joshua, *Divine Hymns or Spiritual Songs for the Use of Religious Assemblies and Private Christians*

**N. Musical Compositions**

**Choral/Vocal**   Abraham Wood, *A Hymn on Peace*.

# 1785

❀

## Historical Highlights

The bald eagle is added to the Great Seal of the United States; Thomas Jefferson is appointed Minister to France and John Adams Minister to Great Britain; the United States and Spain begin arguing over navigation rights on the Mississippi River; New York State outlaws slavery; Russia begins the settlement of the Aleutian Islands of Alaska.

## World Cultural Highlights

**World Art**   Jean-Honoré Fragonard, *Fountain of Love*; Thomas Gainsborough, *The Morning Walk*; Joshua Reynolds, *The Infant Hercules*; George Romney, *Lady Hamilton as a Bacchante*.

**World Literature**   Jens Baggesen, *Comical Tales*; Gottfried Bürger, *Der Wilde Jäger*; Rudolph Raspe, *Baron Münchhausen's Narrative of His Marvellous Travels and Campaigns*.

**World Music**   Franz Joseph Haydn, *Symphonies No. 83, 85, 87*; Wolfgang Amadeus Mozart, *Masonic Funeral Music—Piano Concertos No. 20–22—C Minor Piano Fantasy, K. 475*.

**Miscellaneous**   The Beefsteak Society is founded in London; births include Bettina Brentano von Arnim, Caroline Lamb, Thomas de Quincy, and David Wilkie; deaths include Gustav Creutz, Baldassare Galuppi, Pietro Longhi, Jean-Baptiste Pigalle, and William Whitehead.

## American Art And Literature Highlights

**Births/Deaths**   Births include artists Charles Bird King and Eliar Melcalf, and literary figures Mordecai M. Noah, John Pierpont, and Samuel Woodworth; deaths include authors Myles Cooper and Samuel Mather.

**Art Works**   John Singleton Copley, *Mrs. Seymour Fort (?)—The Children of George IV*; William Rush, *Benjamin Franklin* (wood carving).

**Literature**   Timothy Dwight, *The Conquest of Canaan*; Francis Hopkinson, *A Letter from a Gentleman in America*; John Marrant, *A Narrative of the Lord's Wonderful Dealings with John Marrant, a Black . . .* ; Humphrey Marshall, *Arbustum Americanum: The American Grove*; David Ramsay, *History of the Revolution of South Carolina I, II*.

## Music

**F. Births**   Thomas Appleton (organ builder) December 26; Alpheus Babcock (piano maker) September 11; John Meacham, Jr. (piano maker) May 2.

**H. Debuts**

**United States**   Henri Capron (French cellist—Philadelphia).

**K. Biographical**   John Cole (British) comes to the United States with his family and settles in Baltimore; Benjamin Dearborn develops his "Scheme for reducing the Science of Music to a more simple state . . ."; Hans Gram (Danish organist/composer) comes to the United States and settles in Boston; John Christopher Moller (German organist/composer) emigrates to the United States.

**L. Musical Beginnings**

**Educational**   Adgate Free School (Uranian Society—Academy in 1787—Philadelphia).

**Other**   Old American Co. (revival).

**M. Music Publications**

Adgate, Andrew, *Lessons for the Uranian Society*
Ballou, Silas, *New Hymns for Various Subjects*
Read, Daniel, *The American Singing Book, or A New and Easy Guide to the Art of Psalmody* . . .

# 1786

✦

## Historical Highlights

Shays' Rebellion in Massachusetts is put down by state militia; the Annapolis Convention sets the stage for the Constitutional Congress to meet; the first Indian Reservation west of the Mississippi is created; New Jersey abolishes slavery; John Fitch sails the first steamboat in the new world; Lord Cornwallis becomes Governor-General in India; Frederick the Great of Prussia dies.

## World Cultural Highlights

**World Art**   François Beaucourt, *Negro Slave Girl*; Jacques-Louis David, *Death of Ugolino*: Francisco de Goya, *The Seasons*; John Opie, *The Assassination of James I*; Salvatore Tonci, *Giuseppe Sarti*.

**World Literature**   Gottfried Bürger, *Poems*; "Bobby" Burns, *Poems, Chiefly in the Scottish Dialect*; Jean-François Collin d'Harleville, *L'Inconstant*; John Tooke, *The Diversions of Purley I*.

**World Music**   Franz Joseph Haydn, *"Paris" Symphonies*; Wolfgang Amadeus Mozart, *"Prague" Symphony No. 38—Piano Concertos No. 23–25—The Marriage of Figaro—Der Schauspieldirektor*.

**Miscellaneous**   The Salomon Concerts begin in London; births include Marceline Desbordes-Valmore, Andras Fáy, Wilhelm Grimm, Franz Riepenhausen, and Carl Maria von Weber; deaths include Michael Arne, Alexander Cozens, Gasparo Gozzi, and Moses Mendelssohn.

## American Art and Literature Highlights

**Births/Deaths**   Births include artist James Frothingham and poet Lucius Manlius Sargent; deaths include wax sculptor Patience Lowell Wright and poet Joseph Brown Ladd.

**Art Works**   Mather Brown, *Thomas Jefferson*; Ralph Earl, *The Baron von Steuben*; Gilbert Stuart, *Chief Joseph Brant—Self-Portrait* (unfinished); John Trumbull, *The Death of Montgomery in the Attack on Quebec—The Death of General Warren at the Battle of Bunker Hill*; Vallière, *Michel Guillaume Jean de Crèvecoeur*.

**Literature**   Philip Freneau, *Poems I*; Francis Hopkinson, *A Plan for the Improvement of the Art of Paper War*; Joseph B. Ladd, *The Poems of Arouet*; Thomas Paine, *Dissertations on Government*; Susanna Rowson, *Victoria, a Novel*; St. George Tucker, *The Knights and Friars: An Historical Tale*; John Witherspoon, *Essay on Money*.

## Music

**H. Debuts**   Alexander Reinagle (German pianist—Philadelphia).

**I. New Positions**

**Other**   Jacob Eckhard (organ, St. John's Lutheran, Charleston, South Carolina); John Christopher Moller (organist/composer, Zion German Lutheran Church, Philadelphia).

**K. Biographical**   John Jacob Astor opens the first music shop in New York; Johannes Herbst (Moravian composer/minister) and his wife sail for Lancaster, Pennsylvania; Andrew Law receives an honorary doctorate from Yale University; Alexander Reinagle (British-born composer/impresario) arrives in the United States and settles in Philadelphia; Charles Taws (Scottish piano and organ maker) emigrates to the United States.

**L. Musical Beginnings**

**Performing Groups**   Collegium Musicum der Germaine (Salem, North Carolina); Stoughton Musical Society (Massachusetts).

**Other**   *American Musical Magazine* (12 issues only—first in United States); Astor Music Shop (New York); Harmony Hall (Charleston, South Carolina); Philadelphia "City Concerts"; Philpot's Hill Theater (Baltimore); Richmond Theater (Virginia).

**M. Music Publications**

Billings, William, *The Suffolk Harmony*
Thomas, Isaiah, ed., *The Worcester Collection of Sacred Harmony*

**N. Musical Compositions**

**Choral/Vocal**   John F. Peter, *The Lord Is in His Holy Temple* (baritone and strings).

**Concertos**   William Brown, *Flute Concerto* (?).

# 1787

❋

## Historical Highlights

The Constitutional Convention drafts the Constitution—Delaware, Pennsylvania, and New Jersey become the first states to ratify; the Northwest Ordinance is passed; the first cotton factory is opened in Massachusetts; the Pennsylvania Society for the Encouragement of Manufactures and Useful Acts is formed; the settlement of Freetown is founded in Sierra Leone in Africa.

## World Cultural Highlights

**World Art**   Jacques-Louis David, *The Death of Socrates*; Thomas Gainsborough, *The Wood Gatherers*; George Stubbs, *Phaeton and Pair*; Johann Tischbein, *Goethe in the Roman Campagna*.

**World Literature**   Johann Wolfgang von Goethe, *Iphigenie auf Tauris*; Friedrich von Klopstock, *Hermanns Tod*; Johann Friedrich von Schiller, *Don Carlos*.

**World Music**   Franz Joseph Haydn, *"Russian" Quartets—Symphonies No. 88, 89*; Wolfgang Amadeus Mozart, *Eine Kleine Nachtmusik—A Musical Joke—Don Giovanni*.

**Miscellaneous**   The Marseilles Opera is founded; births include Konstantin Batyushkov, Mary Russell Mitford, and Johann Uhland; deaths include Pompeo Girolamo Batoni, Arthur Devis, Christoph Willibald Gluck, Leopold Mozart, and Johann Karl Musäus.

## American Art and Literature Highlights

**Births/Deaths**   Births include artist Matthew H. Jouett, author Caroline M. Warren, and poets William Crafts, Richard Henry Dana, Sr., Emma H. Willard, and author Eliza Leslie; deaths include author Charles Chauncey.

**Art Works**   Charles Willson Peale, *Benjamin Franklin* (engraving); John Trumbull, *The Declaration of Independence*.

**Literature**   Joel Barlow, *The Vision of Columbus*; Jupiter Hammon, *An Address to the Negroes of* *the State of New York*; David Humphreys, *Select Poems of Col. Humphreys, Aid-de-Camp to Gen. Washington*; Peter Markoe, *The Algerine Spy in Pennsylvania*; Royall Tyler, *May Day in Town*; Mary Wollstonecraft, *Mary: A Fiction*.

## Music

**F. Births**   F. W. Adams (violin maker); James P. Carrell (composer/compiler) February 13.

**K. Biographical**   John Aitken brings out the first compilation of Catholic music in the New World; William Brown is the composer of the first piano music to be published in the United States; Joseph Downer builds the first pipe organ west of the Alleghenies in Cookstown, Pennsylvania; Oliver Holden leaves the US Navy and settles in Charleston, South Carolina; Andrew Law is ordained as a minister in the Presbyterian and Congregational churches; Alexander Reinagle performs in Philadelphia's City Tavern with George Washington present; J. George Schetky (Scottish cellist/publisher) emigrates to the United States and begins teaching music in Philadelphia.

**L. Musical Beginnings**

**Performing Groups**   Philadelphia Uranian Society (to 1800).

**Other**   John Aitken, Music Publisher (Philadelphia).

**M. Music Publications**

Adgate, Andrew, *Select Psalms and Hymns for the Use of Mr. Adgate's Pupils*
Aitken, John, *A Compilation of the Litanies and Vesper Hymns and Anthems as They Are Sung in the Catholic Church*
Newton, J. and Cowper, W., *Olney Hymns* (American edition)
Read, Daniel, *American Singing Book Supplement*
Reinagle, Alexander, *A Selection of the Most Favorite Scots Tunes*

**N. Musical Compositions**

**Choral/Vocal**   William Tuckey, *Anthem from the 97th Psalm*.

**Piano/Organ**   William Brown, *Three Rondos for the Pianoforte or Harpsichord*; Francis Hopkinson, *Seven Songs for the Harpsichord or Forte Piano*.

# 1788

❀

## Historical Highlights

The new Constitution is ratified after pressure is brought to bear on Rhode Island and North Carolina; Virginia and Maryland donate territory for the proposed District of Columbia; Louis XVI of France, presented with a List of Grievances from the people, calls for a meeting of the Estates-General; the first boatload of British convicts are settled in Sydney, Australia.

## World Cultural Highlights

**World Art**   James Barry, *King Lear Weeping over Cordelia*; Jacques-Louis David, *Paris and Helen*; Thomas Gainsborough, *The Woodman—The Haymaker and the Sleeping Girl*.

**World Literature**   Johann Wolfgang von Goethe, *Egmont*; Immanuel Kant, *The Critique of Practical Reason*; Susanna Rowson, *The Inquisitor*; Charlotte Smith, *Emmeline*.

**World Music**   Franz Joseph Haydn, *Symphonies No. 90, 91*; Franz Kotzwara, *The Battle of Prague* (piano); Wolfgang Amadeus Mozart, *Symphonies No. 39–41—Piano Concerto No. 26, "Coronation."*

**Miscellaneous**   *The Gentleman's Musical Magazine* and *The Lady's Musical Magazine* begin publication; births include Joseph von Eichendorff, Friedrich Rückert, Arthur Schopenhauer, and George Lord Byron; deaths include C. P. E. Bach, Thomas Gainsborough, Maurice-Quentin de La Tour, and Francesco Zuccarelli.

## American Art and Literature Highlights

**Births/Deaths**   Births include artists Sarah Goodridge, Ammi Phillips, and authors Sarah Josepha Hale and Eliza Buckminster Lee; deaths include artist Robert Edge Pine, author John Filson, and poets Elijah Fitch and Mather Byles.

**Art Works**   William Dunlap, *Artist Showing a Picture from Hamlet to His Parents*; Reuben Moulthrop, *Mr. and Mrs. Samuel Hathaway* (?); Robert E. Pine, *Congress Voting Independence* (finished by E. Savage); John Trumbull, *Thomas Jefferson*; Benjamin West, *Edward the Black Prince and King John of France*.

**Literature**   Richard Alsop, *The Charms of Fancy*; John Dickinson, *The Letters of Fabius I*; Timothy Dwight, *The Triumph of Infidelity*; Philip Freneau, *The Miscellaneous Works of Philip Freneau*; Richard Henry Lee, *Letters from the Federal Farmer*; Peter Markoe, *The Times*; Susanna Rowson, *The Inquisitor—Poems on Various Subjects*; William Smith, *An Address to the General Assembly of Pennsylvania*, St. George Tucker, *Liberty, a Poem on the Independence of America*.

## Music

**G. Deaths**   John Hiwell (bandmaster/teacher) March 15.

**L. Musical Beginnings**

**Performing Groups**   New York Musical Society (till 1794).

**M. Music Publications**

Adgate, Andrew, *The Rudiments of Music*
Bayley, Daniel, *The New Harmony of Zion*
Holden, Oliver, *The Federal Harmony*
Jocelyn, Simeon, *The Chorister's Companion*
Swan, Timothy, *The Federal Harmony*

**N. Musical Compositions**

**Orchestra/Band**   Alexander Reinagle, *Federal March*.

# 1789

## Historical Highlights

The Constitution goes into effect; George Washington is the unanimous choice for president; New York City is chosen as capital; the Federalist Party is formally founded; the Federal Judiciary Act is passed; Georgetown University is founded; in France, the Bastille is stormed and the new National Assembly passes the Declaration of the Rights of Man.

## World Cultural Highlights

**World Art**   Jacques-Louis David, *Brutus Receiving His Son's Body*; François Gerard, *Joseph and His Brothers*; Jean-Baptiste Regnault, *The Descent from the Cross*; Hubert Robert, *Pulling Down of the Bastille*.

**World Literature**   William Blake, *Songs of Innocence*; Johann Wolfgang von Goethe, *Torquato Tasso*; Johann Friedrich von Schiller, *Die Künstler*.

**World Music**   Franz Joseph Haydn, *Symphony No. 92, "Oxford"—Piano Trios Nos. 8–10*; Wolfgang Amadeus Mozart, *Clarinet Quintet, K. 581—"King of Prussia" String Quartet*.

**Miscellaneous**   *Moniteur* begins publication in Paris; opening of the Théâtre de Monsieur; births include John "Mad" Martin, Johannes Riepenhausen, and Claude-Joseph and Horace Vernet; deaths include Thomas Day, Jean Étienne Liotard, Franz X. Richter, and Johann Heinrich Tischbein.

## American Art and Literature Highlights

**Births/Deaths**   Births include literary figures James Fenimore Cooper, Hannah Flagg Gould, Asa

Greene, James A. Hillhouse, Henry C. Knight, and Catharine Maria Sedgwick; deaths include literary figures Ethan Allen, John Parke, and Samuel Quincy of Massachusetts.

**Art Works**   Christian Gullager, *George Washington*; Thomas Jefferson, *Virginia Capitol, Richmond*; Charles Willson Peale, *Robert Goldsborough Family*; John Ramage, *George Washington*; William Rush, *Indian Trader* (?); John Trumbull, *The Battle of Bunker's Hill—Sortie, Garrison of Gibraltar*.

**Literature**   William H. Brown, *The Power of Sympathy*; William Dunlap, *The Father: or, American Shandy-ism*; Olaudah Equiano, *The Interesting Narrative of the Life of Olaudah Equiano*; David Humphreys, *Poems by Col. David Humphreys, Late Aid-de-Camp to His Excellency, Gen. Washington*; Thomas Johnson, Jr., *The Kentucky Miscellany*; Susanna Rowson, *The Test of Honour, a Novel*.

## Music

**F. Births**   John Firth (piano maker) October 1; Horace Meacham (piano maker) July 19; Abraham Prescott (stringed-instrument maker) July 5; William Whiteley (instrument maker).

**K. Biographical**   Samuel Holyoke graduates from Harvard and begins teaching music.

**L. Musical Beginnings**

**Other**   Charles Albrecht, Piano Maker (Philadelphia); Bacon Piano Co. (New York).

**M. Music Publications**

Adgate, Andrew, *Philadelphia Harmony*
French, Jacob, *New American Melody*
Hubbard, John, *Harmonica Selecta*
Wood, Abraham, *Divine Songs*

**N. Musical Compositions**

**Chamber Music**   Johann F. Peter, *Six String Quintets* (believed to be the oldest preserved chamber music written in the New World).

**Choral/Vocal**   Abraham Wood, *Ode to Spring*.

# 1790

✸

## Historical Highlights

The US census shows a population just short of four million in 13 states; Philadelphia becomes the next temporary capital; the US Patent Office and the US Coast Guard are formed; the Treaty of Greenville between the United States and the Indians temporarily settles the Ohio problem; the French National Assembly draws up a new constitution forming a limited monarchy.

## World Cultural Highlights

**World Art**   Henry Fuseli, *Titania and Bottom*; Francesco Guardi, *Island in the Lagoon*; Jean-Antoine Houdon, *Apollo*; George Morland, *Inside the Stable*; Johann Zoffany, *Charles Towneley Among His Marbles*.

**World Literature**   Joanna Baillie, *Fugitive Verses*; Carl Bellman, *Fredmans Epistlar*; William Bligh, *Mutiny on Board the Bounty*; "Bobby" Burns, *Tam O'Shanter*; Ann Radcliffe, *A Sicilian Romance*.

**World Music**   Ludwig van Beethoven, *Cantata on the Death of Joseph II*; Franz Joseph Haydn, *Six String Quartets, Opus 64*; Wolfgang Amadeus Mozart, *String Quartets No. 22, 23—Così fan tutte*.

**Miscellaneous**   Births include Per Daniel Atterbom, Anna Eliza Bray, John Gibson, and Alphonse de Lamartine; deaths include John Bacon, Antoine de Bertin, Adam Smith, and Thomas Warton.

## American Art and Literature Highlights

**Births/Deaths**  Births include sculptor John Frazee and literary figures Alexander Hill Everett, Francis W. Gilmer, Fitz-Greene Halleck, and Augustus B. Longstreet; deaths include artist Winthrop Chandler, authors Joseph Bellamy, and William Livingston.

**Art Works**  Anonymous, *Dr. Hezekiah Beardsley—Mrs. Hezekiah Beardsley* (?); Ralph Earl, *Colonel William Taylor*; Rufus Hathaway, *Lady with Her Pets*; Jean Antoine Houdon, *George Washington* (bust); Reuben Moulthrop, *James Reynolds—Mary Kimberly Reynolds* (?); Charles Willson Peale, *Mrs. John Nicholson and Son*; Gilbert Stuart, *George Hamilton—Mrs. George Hamilton*.

**Literature**  David Humphreys, *The Miscellaneous Works of David Humphreys*; Charlotte R. Lennox, *Euphemia*; Sarah W. Morton, *Ouabi: or, the Virtues of Nature: An Indian Tale*; Mercy Otis Warren, *Poems Dramatic and Miscellaneous*; Mary Wollstonecraft, *Vindication of the Rights of Women*; John Winthrop, *Journal I, II*.

## Music

**F. Births**  Thomas V. Wiesenthal (composer).

**H. Debuts**

**United States**  John Christopher Moller (German organist –New York).

**K. Biographical**  Congress passes the first Copyright Law with no mention made of music; Andrew Adgate has the first musical work to be printed in the United States, his earlier works being printed in England: the third edition of his *Rudiments of Music (Philadelphia Harmony)*; William Billings suffers acute financial problems; Pierre Landrin Duport (French violinist/ballet) flees France for the United States; John Christopher Moller (German organist/composer) comes to the United States and finally settles in Philadelphia; David Tannenberg installs a new organ in the Zion Lutheran church in Philadelphia.

**L. Musical Beginnings**

**Other**  Oliver Holden Music Store (Charleston, South Carolina); The New Company (by A. Reinagle and T. Wignell).

**M. Music Publications**

Read, Daniel, *An Introduction to Psalmody*

**N. Musical Compositions**

**Chamber Music**  John Antes, *String Trios, Opus 3*.

**Choral/Vocal**  Samuel Holyoke, *Washington* (song).

**Operas**  Peter Markoe, *The Reconciliation, or, The Triumph of Nature*.

**Piano/Organ**  Alexander Reinagle, *Four Piano Sonatas* (?).

# 1791

❀

## Historical Highlights

The US Bill of Rights is ratified; Vermont becomes the 14th state, the first to join the original 13; the Bank of the United States is chartered by Congressional action; the Lancaster Pike is opened; the Canada Act divides that country into Quebec, the French portion, and Ontario, the English section; Louis XVI and family are caught and put under house arrest.

## World Cultural Highlights

**World Art**  Jacques-Louis David, *Tennis Court Oath*; Carl G. Langhans, *Brandenburg Gate* (Berlin); Augustin Pajou, *Psyche Abandoned*; Elisabeth Vigée-Lebrun, *Self-Portrait*.

**World Literature**    Jens Baggesen, *Labyrinthen*; Carl Bellman, *Fredmans Sänger*; Friedrich Klinger, *Fausts Leben, Thaten und Höllenfahrt*; Ann Radcliffe, *Romance of the Forest*.

**World Music**    Franz Joseph Haydn, *London Symphonies, First Set*; Wolfgang Amadeus Mozart, *The Magic Flute—La Clemenza di Tito—Requiem* (completed by Franz Süssmayr).

**Miscellaneous**    The Berliner Singakademie is founded; births include Sergei Aksakov, Karl Czerny, Jean-Louis Géricault, Franz Grillparzer, Giacomo Meyerbeer, and Augustin T. Eugène Scribe; deaths include Étienne Maurice Falconet and Wolfgang Amadeus Mozart.

## American Art and Literature Highlights

**Births/Deaths**    Births include art figures Hezekiah Auger, Samuel F. B. Morse, Anna C. Peale, and literary figures James Athearn, John Howard Payne, Lydia Howard Sigourney, Charles Sprague, and George Ticknor; deaths include artist William Williams and poet Benjamin Young Prime.

**Art Works**    John Singleton Copley, *The Siege of Gibraltar*; Ralph Earl, *Mrs. William Moseley and Her Son Charles*; James Hoban, *Capitol Building, South Carolina*; M'Kay, *Hannah Bush*; Charles Willson Peale, *Thomas Jefferson—Alexander Hamilton—Mr. and Mrs. James Gittings and Granddaughter*; John Trumbull, *Monte Video*.

**Literature**    John Adams, *Discourses on Davila*; William Bartram, *Travels through North and South Carolina, Georgia, East and West Florida* . . . ; Jeremy Belknap, *History of New-Hampshire II*; Thomas Paine, *The Rights of Man*; Benjamin Young Prime, *Columbia's Glory or British Pride Humbled* . . . ; Susanna Rowson, *Charlotte, A Tale of Truth—Mentoria: or, The Young Lady's Friend*.

## Music

**F. Births**    Thomas Hall (organ builder).

**G. Deaths**    Francis Hopkinson (statesman/judge/musician) May 9.

**K. Biographical**    Trinity Church in New York receives a new organ from a Mr. Holland of London.

**L. Musical Beginnings**

**Performing Groups**    Boston Philo-Harmonic Society; New American Co. (Kenna Family—one season only, Philadelphia); New York St. Cecilia Society (to 1799).

**Other**    Dodds and Claus Piano Co. (New York).

**M. Music Publications**

Holyoke, Samuel, *Harmonia Americana*

**N. Musical Compositions**

**Chamber Music**    Alexander Reinagle, *Miscellaneous Quartets* (?)—*New Miscellaneous Quartett* (?).

**Choral/Vocal**    Hans Gram, *The Death Song of an Indian Chief*.

**Orchestra/Band**    Hans Gram, *America* (march).

# 1792

❀

## Historical Highlights

George Washington is re-elected as president; the Democratic-Republican Party is formed in opposition to the Federalists; the first mint is established in Philadelphia; the motto *"E Pluribus Unum"* is approved; Kentucky becomes the 15th state; the New York Stock Exchange is organized; Denmark abolishes the slave trade by its people; Francis II becomes new Austrian Emperor.

## World Cultural Highlights

**World Art**   John Flaxman, *The Fury of Athamas*; Henry Fuseli, *Falstaff in the Buck Basket*; Thomas Hardy, *Franz Joseph Haydn*; George Stubbs, *Hound and Bitch in Landscape*.

**World Literature**   Hannah More, *Village Politics*; Gabriel Legouvé, *La Mort d'Abel*; Jakob Lenz, *Pandaemonium Germanicum*; Jean-Paul Richter, *Die Unsichtbare Loge*; Charlotte Smith, *Celestina*.

**World Music**   Ludwig van Beethoven, *Two Sonatinas, Opus 163*; Domenico Cimarosa, *Il matrimonio segreto*; Franz Joseph Haydn, *Sinfonia Concertante, Opus 84*; Claude Rouget de L'Isle, *La Marseillaise*.

**Miscellaneous**   The Royal Opera Co. of Berlin is founded; Johann Gerstenberg begins publishing music; births include George Cruikshank, George Hayter, John Keble, and Gioacchino Rossini; deaths include Jean Jacques Caffieri, Denis Ivanovich Fonvizin, Jacob Lenz, and Joshua Reynolds.

## American Art and Literature Highlights

**Births/Deaths**   Births include art figures John H. I. Browere, Alvan Fisher, Anne Hall, Chester Harding, and Rufus Porter, humorist Seba Smith, and William Leete Stone; deaths include artist John Greenwood and poet Peter Markoe.

**Art Works**   Charles Bulfinch, *Hartford State House*; Ralph Earl, *Justice Oliver Ellsworth and His Wife — Mrs. Richard Alsop*; Jean-Antoine Houdon, *George Washington* (Richmond, Virginia); Samuel Jennings, *Liberty Displaying the Arts and Sciences*; Charles Willson Peale, *James Madison* (?); John Trumbull, *Alexander Hamilton by His Desk* (?).

**Literature**   Joel Barlow, *Advice to the Privileged Orders in the Several States of Europe — The Conspiracy of Kings: A Poem*; Jeremy Belknap, *The Foresters, an American Tale*; Hugh H. Brackenridge, *Modern Chivalry I, II*; Francis Hopkinson, *Miscellaneous Essays and Occasional Writing*; Susanna Rowson, *The Fille de Chambre, a Novel*

## Music

**F. Births**   Allen Dickenson Carden (teacher/compiler) October 13; Francis Johnson (bandmaster/cornetist); Lowell Mason (music educator) January 8; John Osborne (piano builder); Sylvanus Billings Pond (composer/publisher) April 5.

**G. Deaths**   Daniel Bayley (compiler/publisher) February 29.

**H. Debuts**

**United States**   Joseph Gehot (Belgian violinist—New York), John Hodgkinson (British singer—Philadelphia), and Mary Ann Pownall (British singer— New York).

**I. New Positions**

**Conductors**   James Hewitt (Park Street Theater, New York, to 1808).

**K. Biographical**   Joseph Gehot (Belgian violinist/composer) emigrates to the United States and conducts his *Overture in Twelve Movements, Expressive of a Voyage from England to America;* James Hewitt (British conductor/composer) comes to the United States and settles in New York; Samuel Holyoke receives his MA degree from Harvard; Victor Pelissier (French composer/hornist) arrives in Philadelphia; Mary Ann Pownall (British singer/actress/composer) comes to the United States with her second husband and joins the Old American Co.; Raynor Taylor (British composer/organist) leaves a successful London career and emigrates to the United States; Isaiah Thomas moves his publishing firm to Boston.

**L. Musical Beginnings**

**Other**   Boston Theater New Exhibition Room; *The Musical Magazine* (to 1801); Spectacle de la Rue St. Pierre (New Orleans theater).

**M. Music Publications**

Beeman, Anna, *Hymns on Various Subjects*

Holden, Oliver, *American Harmony*
Richards, G. and Lane, O. W., *Psalms, Hymns and Spirtual Songs: Selected and Original*
Rippon, John, *The Psalms and Hymns of Dr. Watts* . . . (American edition)

**N. Musical Compositions**

**Choral/Vocal**   Oliver Holden, *Coronation* (hymn tune "All Hail the Power of Jesus' Name").

**Operas**   Benjamin Carr, *Philander and Silvia* (pastorale).

**Piano/Organ**   James Hewitt, *Overture in 9 Movements Expressive of a Battle*.

# 1793

☼

## Historical Highlights

Congress passes the Proclamation of Neutrality in regard to the Anglo-French warfare; a Fugitive Slave Law is passed by Congress; Eli Whitney patents the cotton gin but has all his ideas stolen by big business interests; the Reign of Terror under the control of Robespierre begins in France—Louis XVI and Marie Antoinette are sent to the guillotine.

## World Cultural Highlights

**World Art**   Antonio Canova, *Cupid and Psyche*; Jacques-Louis David, *Death of Marat*; Francisco de Goya, *The Madhouse*; Giovanni Battista Tiepolo, *Pulcinellos on Holiday*.

**World Literature**   Marie Chénier, *Fénelon*; Nicolas François, *Paméla*; Richard Graves, *The Reveries of Solitude*; Charlotte Smith, *The Old Manor House*; William Wordsworth, *Descriptive Sketches*.

**World Music**   Ludwig van Beethoven, *Variations on "Se vuol ballare," Opus 46*; Franz Joseph Haydn, *Symphony No. 99—Six String Quartets, Opus 71, 74*.

**Miscellaneous**   Simrock Music House is founded in Bonn, Germany; the Haydn Monument is unveiled in Rohrau; births include Theobald Boehm, Charles Eastlake, and Ferdinand Georg Waldmüller; deaths include Carlo Goldoni, Francesco Guardi, and Pierre-Antoine Verschafelt.

## American Art and Literature Highlights

**Births/Deaths**   Births include artists Thomas Doughty, Robert Havell, and authors John Neal, and Samuel Griswold Goodrich; deaths include sculptor Joseph Wright and novelist William H. Brown.

**Art Works**   James Hoban, *U.S. White House*; James Peale, *The Ramsay-Polk Family*; William Rush, *River God* (?); William Thornton, *Plans, Capitol Rotunda, Washington* (winner of competition); John Trumbull, *Thomas Youngs Seymour—Lemuel Hopkins*; William Winstanley, *Morning, Hudson River—Evening, Hudson River*.

**Literature**   Richard Alsop, *American Poems*; Ann E. Bleecker, *The Posthumous Works of Ann Eliza Bleecker*; Margaretta Fangeres, *A Collection of Essays—Prose and Poetical*; Enos Hitchcock, *The Farmer's Friend*; George Richards, *The Declaration of Independence: A Poem*; Samuel Seabury, *Discourses on Several Subjects*; Elihu H. Smith, *American Poems, Selected and Original*.

## Music

**G. Deaths**   Andrew Adgate (editor/conductor) September 30; Philip Phile (violinist/composer) (?).

**H. Debuts**

**United States**   Miss Broadhurst (Philadelphia), George Gillingham (British violinist—New York), Georgina Oldmixon (British soprano—Philadelphia).

**K. Biographical**    George Blake (British publisher) comes to the United States; Boston's 1750 theatrical prohibition, although not repealed, is ignored; Benjamin Carr (British singer/pianist/composer) emigrates to the United States and settles in Philadelphia; George Gillingham (British violinist/conductor) comes to the United States; Alexander Reinagle assists in forming a New York stock company for comic opera; George Willig (British publisher) comes to the United States.

**L. Musical Beginnings**

**Performing Groups**    "City Concerts" (New York City—to 1797); New York Uranian Society (to 1798).

**Educational**    Groton (Lawrence) Academy (New Hampshire—by Samuel Holyoke); Moller and Capron Music School (Philadelphia).

**Other**    Boston Theatre (Federal Street Theatre); Broad Street (Charleston) Theater; Carr's Musical Repository (Philadelphia); Moller and Capron Music Store and Publishing Co. (Philadelphia); New Theater Opera House (Philadelphia).

**M. Music Publications**

French, Jacob, *The Psalmodist's Companion*
Hewitt, James and Pownall, Mary Ann, *A Book of Songs* (piano, by subscription)
Holden, Oliver, *The Union Harmony*
Kimball, Jacob, *The Rural Harmony*
Read, Daniel, *The Columbian Harmonist I*
Shumway, Nehemiah, *The American Harmony*
Wood, A. and Stone, J., *The Columbian Harmony*

**N. Musical Compositions**

**Choral/Vocal**    Benjamin Cook, *Three Songs from Shakespeare*.

**Operas**    Benjamin Carr, *The Caledonian Frolic* (pantomime); Victor Pelissier, *The Death of Captain Cook* (pantomime); Raynor Taylor, *Capocchio and Dorinna*.

**Orchestra/Band**    John Christopher Moller, *Sinfonia*.

# 1794

❁

## Historical Highlights

The Battle of Fallen Timbers finally settles the Indian problems in the Ohio Territory; the Whiskey Rebellion in Pennsylvania is put down by federal troops; the US Navy is officially formed by Congress; the Jay Treaty prevents another war with England; the University of Tennessee is founded; the Reign of Terror in France ends with the death of Robespierre.

## World Cultural Highlights

**World Art**    William Blake, *The Ancient of Days*; Francisco de Goya, *Procession of the Flagellants*; Jean-Antoine Houdon, *The Negro Girl*; Philippe de Loutherbourg, *Lord Howe's Victory at Ushant*.

**World Literature**    William Blake, *Songs of Experience;* William Gifford, *The Baviad*; Louis Lemercier, *Agamemnon*; Ann Radcliffe, *The Mysteries of Udolpho*; Jean-Paul Richter, *Hesperus*.

**World Music**    Ludwig van Beethoven, *Trio for Two Oboes and English Horn, Opus 87*; Franz Joseph Haydn, *Symphonies 100–102—Piano Trios No. 15–18*.

**Miscellaneous**    A new Drury Lane Theatre is built in London; births include Karl Begas, Julius Schnorr von Carolsfeld, Ignaz Moscheles, and Wilhelm Müller; deaths include Gottfried August Bürger, Sébastien Chamfort, André Chénier, George Colman, Sr., and Edward Gibbon.

## American Art and Literature Highlights

**Births/Deaths**   Births include poets Maria Gowen Brooks, William Cullen Bryant, Caroline Howard Hilman, and Edwin Clifford Holland; deaths include author John Witherspoon.

**Art Works**   Amos Doolittle, *A Display of the United States of America*; Richard Jennys, *Elizabeth Canfield*; Gilbert Stuart, *Chief Justice John Jay—Richard Yates—Mrs. Richard Yates—Josef de Jaudenes y Nebot—General Horatio Gates—General Matthew Clarkson*; John Trumbull, *The Declaration of Independence I*.

**Literature**   Jeremy Belknap, *American Biography I*; Caleb Bingham, *The American Preceptor*; William Dunlap, *Leicester (The Fatal Deception)*; Philip Freneau, *The Village Merchant*; Willliam Godwin, *The Adventures of Caleb Williams*; Anne K. Hatton, *Tammany*; David Humphreys, *A Poem on Industry*; Thomas Paine, *The Age of Reason*; Susanna Rowson, *Slaves in Algiers*.

## Music

**F. Births**   Samuel Graves (instrument maker) July 2; Joshua Leavitt (hymnbook compiler) September 8.

**G. Deaths**   James Lyon (clergyman/compiler) October 12.

**H. Debuts**   Benjamin Carr (singer—Philadelphia).

**I. New Positions**

**Other**   John Hodgkinson (manager, Old American Co.).

**K. Biographical**   Henri Capron (French cellist and composer) decides to settle permanently in Philadelphia.

**L. Musical Beginnings**

**Other**   Benjamin Carr's Musical Repository (New York and Baltimore branches); Joseph Carr Publishing House (Baltimore); Chestnut Street Theater (Philadelphia); George Willig, Music Publisher (buys out Moller and Capron, Philadelphia).

**M. Music Publications**

Belcher, Supply, *The Harmony of Maine*
Billings, William, *The Continental Harmony*
Law, Andrew, *The Art of Singing*
Read, Daniel, *The Columbian Harmonist II*

**N. Musical Compositions**

**Choral/Vocal**   Benjamin Carr, *Four Ballads*; John Christopher Moller, *Dank und Gebet* (cantata); Alexander Reinagle, *America, Commerce and Freedom* (song); Raynor Taylor, *An Ode to the New Year*.

**Concertos**   Alexander Reinagle, *Concerto for Piano and Orchestra* (lost).

**Operas**   James Hewitt, *Tammany, or The Indian Chief* (ballad opera)—*The Patriots* (ballad opera); Victor Pelissier, *Sophia of Brabant* (pantomime)—*Harlequin Pastry Cook* (pantomime); Alexander Reinagle, *Robin Hood* (opera)—*The Spanish Barber* (opera).

**Orchestra/Band**   Benjamin Carr, *Federal Overture*; Alexander Reinagle, *Overture, St. Patrick's Day—Slaves in Algiers* (incidental music)—*An Occasional Overture*

**Piano/Organ**   James Hewitt, *Overture, Storm at Sea*; Alexander Reinagle, *Piano Preludes in Three Classes*.

# 1795

❀

## Historical Highlights

The Treaty of San Lorenzo gives the United States navigation rights on the Mississippi River; the

Pinckney Treaty provides right of deposits at New Orleans; Congress passes a Naturalization Act; Milwaukee is founded by the Northwest Company; Napoleon Bonaparte becomes head of the French Army in Italy; the French Directory is formed to lead the nation; the Third Partition of Poland takes place.

## World Cultural Highlights

**World Art**    William Blake, *God Judging Adam*; Asmus Carstens, *Night with Her Children*; John Flaxman, *Aeschylus*; Francisco de Goya, *Duchess of Alba*; Francis Wheatley, *The Cries of London*.

**World Literature**    André Chénier, *Pensées, Maximes et Anecdotes*; William Gifford, *The Maeviad*; Johann Wolfgang von Goethe, *Wilhelm Meisters Lehrjahre*; Walter Landor, *Poems*.

**World Music**    Ludwig van Beethoven, *Piano Concerto No. 2—Three Piano Sonatas, Opus 2*; Franz Joseph Haydn, *Symphonies 103, 104, "London"*; Giovanni Viotti, *Violin Concerto No. 24.*

**Miscellaneous**    The École Royale de Chant and the Institute of Music are combined to form the Paris Conservatory; Thomas Boosey opens a book store in London; births include Thomas Carlyle, Heinrich Marschner, and John Keats; deaths include Carl Michael Bellman, James Boswell, and Friedrich Marpurg.

## American Art and Literature Highlights

**Births/Deaths**    Births include artists William Jewett, Margaretta Peale, and literary figures Joseph R. Drake, John P. Kennedy (Mark Littleton), Louisa Medina, James G. Percival, and Daniel Pierce Thompson; deaths include artist John Marc and educator Ezra Stiles.

**Art Works**    Anonymous, *Emma Van Name*; Giuseppe Ceracchi, *Bust, George Washington*; William Jennys, *Nathaniel Lamson (?)—Hannah French Bacon*; Charles W. Peale, *The Staircase Group—Angelica Peale and Her Husband*; Gilbert Stuart, *Mathilde Stoughton de Jaudenes (?)—George Washington: The Vaughn Portrait*.

**Literature**    Ebenezer Bradford, *The Art of Courting*; William Dunlap, *Fontainville Abbey*; Philip Freneau, *Poems Written between 1768 and 1794*; John B. Linn, *Miscellaneous Works, Prose and Poetical*; Judith S. Murray, *The Medium*; Robert T. Paine, *The Invention of Letters, a Poem*; Susanna Rowson, *Trials of the Human Heart*; Isaac Story, *Liberty*.

## Music

**F. Births**    George Peabody (patron of the arts) February 18.

**G. Deaths**    Samuel Blyth (organist/craftsman) January 13; Jeremias Dencke (Moravian composer); Josiah Flagg (conductor/bandmaster) January 2.

**H. Debuts**

**United States**    Johann Christian Gottlieb Graupner (Charleston, South Carolina).

**I. New Positions**

**Other**    Raynor Taylor (organ, St. Peter's Church, Philadelphia—to 1813).

**K. Biographical**    John L. Berkenhead (blind British organist) comes to the United States; Johann Christian Graupner (German composer/performer) leaves London and comes to the United States, settling in Charleston, South Carolina; David Moritz Michael (Moravian composer/educator) comes to the United States and teaches in Nazareth, Pennsylvania.

**L. Musical Beginnings**

**Performing Groups**    Columbian Anacreontic Society (New York); Norwich Anacreontic Society.

**Other**    Duncan Phyfe Shop (New York); Providence Theater (Rhode Island).

**M. Music Publications**

Bull, Amos, *The Responsory*
Holden, O., Gram, H., and Holyoke, S., *Massachusetts Compiler of Theoretical Principles*
Read, Daniel, *The Columbian Harmonist III*

### N. Musical Compositions

**Chamber Music**   John Christopher Moller, *Quartet for Glass Harmonica, Two Violas and Cello.*

**Operas**   Benjamin Carr, *Poor Jack* (pantomime); Victor Pelissier, *La forêt noire* (pantomime)— *Danaides, or Vice Punished* (pantomime); Alexander Reinagle, *Harlequin Shipwreck'd* (pantomime)—*The Purse* (melodrama)—*The Volunteers* (opera).

**Orchestra/Band**   Benjamin Carr, *Macbeth* (incidental music); Alexander Reinagle, *Overture to Auld Robin Gray—Overture, Harlequin's Invasion*; Raynor Taylor, *La Petite Piedmontese* (ballet).

# 1796

✺

## Historical Highlights

John Adams is elected President when Washington refuses a third term; Tennessee becomes the 16th state; Cleveland, Ohio, is founded on the shores of Lake Erie; the Land Act makes it possible to sell public lands by auction; Catherine the Great of Russia dies and Paul I becomes Czar; Edward Jenner introduces the smallpox vaccine.

## World Cultural Highlights

**World Art**   Antonio Canova, *The Penitent Magdalen*; Antoine-Jean Gros, *Napoleon at Arcole Bridge*; Hubert Robert, *View of the Grande Gallerie*; Joseph Turner, *Fishermen at Sea.*

**World Literature**   Fanny Burney, *Camilla*; Elizabeth Inchbald, *Nature and Art;* Matthew Lewis, *Ambrosio, or The Monk*; Jean-Paul Richter, *Siebenkás I*; William Wordsworth, *The Borderers.*

**World Music**   Franz Joseph Haydn, *Trumpet Concerto—Heiligmesse—The Seven Last Words* (choral); Ludwig van Beethoven, *Two Piano Sonatinas, Opus 43a, 44a—Ah, perfido, Opus 65.*

**Miscellaneous**   The *Musenalmanach* is founded; the Bologna Liceo Filarmonico is founded; births include Antoine-Louis Barye, Franz Berwald, Jean-Baptiste Corot, and Manuel Bretón de los Herreros; deaths include David Allan, "Bobby" Burns, James Macpherson, and Franz Anton Maulbertsch.

## American Art and Literature Highlights

**Births/Deaths**   Births include artists George Catlin, Asher Durand, Charles Ingham, John Neagle, and literary figures John G. Brainard, Thomas Bulfinch, Theodore Dwight, Jr., John Gorham Palfrey, and William H. Prescott; deaths include author Samuel Seabury.

**Art Works**   George Beck, *Potomac River Rapids* (?); John Singleton Copley, *John Quincy Adams*; Archibald Robertson, *New York from Long Island*; Edward Savage, *David Rittenhouse— Liberty Feeding the American Eagle—The Washington Family Series*; Gilbert Stuart, *George Washington: The Athenaeum Portrait—The Landsdowne Portrait—Martha Washington.*

**Literature**   Joel Barlow, *The Hasty Pudding*; Matthew Carey, *The Porcupiniad: A Hudibrastic Poem*; Joseph Dennie, *The Lay Preacher*; William Dunlap, *The Archers, or, The Mountaineers of Switzerland*; John Blair Linn, *Poetical Wanderer*; Judith S. Murray, *The Traveller Returned*: Robert T. Paine, *The Ruling Passion*; Susanna Rowson, *Americans in England*; Isaac Story, *All the World's a Stage.*

## Music

**F. Births**   William Hall (piano maker) May 13.

**G. Deaths**   Mary Ann Pownall (British-born singer/composer) August 11.

**I. New Positions**

**Conductors**   Gottlieb Graupner (orchestra, Federal St. Theater, Boston); John Christopher Moller (New York City Concerts).

**Other**  John L. Berkenhead (organ, Trinity Church, Newport—to 1804).

**K. Biographical**  Peter Albrecht and Elizabeth Von Hagen, Sr. move to Boston; Gottlieb Graupner marries singer/actress Catherine Comerford Hellyer; Dr. George J. Jackson (British organist/educator) comes to the United States; Wignell and Reinagle move to the New York area.

**L. Musical Beginnings**

**Performing Groups**  New York Harmonical Society (to 1799).

**Other**  Haymarket Theater (Boston).

**N. Musical Compositions**

**Concertos**  Raynor Taylor, *Violin Concerto.*

**Operas**  Benjamin Carr, *The Archers, or The Mountaineers of Switzerland* (see William Dunlap, American Literature preceding); Victor Pelissier, *Edwin and Angelina, or The Banditti* (libretto by E. H. Smith)—*Robinson Crusoe* (pantomime); Alexander Reinagle, *The Warrior's Welcome* (pantomime)—*The Witches of the Rock* (pantomime).

**Orchestra/Band**  Victor Pelissier, *The Mysterious Monk* (incidental music); Alexander Reinagle, *Overture to The Lucky Escape—Pierre de Province and La belle Magulone* (ballet); Raynor Taylor, *New Overture.*

**Piano/Organ**  Benjamin Carr, *Six Piano Sonatas*; James Hewitt, *Three Sonatas for the Piano Forte, Opus 5.*

# 1797

✵

## Historical Highlights

The XYZ Affair and France's interfering with U.S. shipping strain relations between the two countries; the first frigate built in the New World, the *United States*, is launched; Fort Adams (Memphis) is built on the Mississippi River; a patent is given for the iron plow; Talleyrand becomes French Foreign Minister; Fredrick William III becomes Emperor of Austria.

## World Cultural Highlights

**World Art**  William Blake, *Night Thoughts*; Francisco de Goya, *The Nude Duchess*; Thomas Lawrence, *Satan Calling His Legions*; Joseph Turner, *Millbank by Moonlight.*

**World Literature**  Samuel Taylor Coleridge, *Rhyme of the Ancient Mariner*; Johann Wolfgang von Goethe, *Hermann und Dorothea*; Harriet Lee, *Clara Lennox*; Ann Radcliffe, *The Italian.*

**World Music**  Franz Joseph Haydn, *Six String Quartets, Opus 76*; Ludwig van Beethoven, *Piano Concerto No. 1—Quintet for Piano and Woodwinds, Opus 16*; Luigi Cherubini, *Médée.*

**Miscellaneous**  The *Pianoforte Magazine* begins publication; births include Hippolyte Delaroche, Gaetano Donizetti, Heinrich Heine, Franz Schubert, Michel Jean Sedaine, and Mary Wollstonecraft Shelley; deaths include Edmund Burke, Horace Walpole and Joseph Wright.

## American Art and Literature Highlights

**Births/Deaths**  Births include authors Walter Colton, William Ware, and poet Penina Moïse.

**Art Works**  William Berczy, *Joseph Brant, Mohawk Chief*; Francis Guy, *Tontine Coffee House*; Gilbert Stuart, *Miss Dick and Her Cousin—View of Broad Street, New York.*

**Literature**  Caleb Bingham, *The Columbian Orator*; Ann E. Bleecker, *The History of Maria Kittle* (posthumous publication); Hugh H. Brackenridge, *Modern Chivalry III;* John D. Burk, *Bunker-Hill*; John Dickinson, *Letters of Fabius II*; Hannah Foster, *The Coquette*; John Blair Linn, *Bourville Castle*; Sarah W. Morton, *Beacon Hill: A Local Poem*; Royall Tyler, *The Algerine Captive.*

## Music

**F. Births**    Jonas Chickering (piano maker) April 5.

**I. New Positions**

**Conductors**    Peter Albrecht von (Van) Hagen (conductor, Haymarket Theater, New York).

**Other**    John Henry Schmidt (organ, St. Peter's Church, Philadelphia).

**K. Biographical**    Benjamin Carr sells his music store to James Hewitt; Johann Gottlieb and Catherine Graupner settle in Boston where Johann begins teaching music; Johann Geib (piano/organ builder) comes to the United States and settles in New York; George K. Jackson (British composer/teacher) emigrates to the United States and begins teaching in New Brunswick, New Jersey.

**L. Musical Beginnings**

**Performing Groups**    Essex Musical Association (Massachusetts).

**Other**    John Geib and Co., Organ Builders (New York); John and Michael Paff Publishing Co.

**M. Music Publications**

Aitken, John, ed., *Scot's Musical Museum*
Belknap, Daniel, *Harmonist's Companion*
Brownson, Oliver, *A New Collection of Sacred Harmony*
Holden, Oliver, *The Worcester Collection*
Merrill, Richard, *The Musical Practitioner: or, American Psalmody—The Pocket Hymn Book*

**N. Musical Compositions**

**Chamber Music**    Raynor Taylor, *Sonata for Piano with Violin.*

**Choral/Vocal**    Daniel Belknap, *A View of the Temple—A Masonic Ode—Spring—Summer.*

**Operas**    Victor Pelissier, *Ariadne Abandoned by Theseus in the Isle of Naxos* (melodrama); Alexander Reinagle, *Columbus* (melodrama)—*The Savoyard* (musical farce); Raynor Taylor, *The Iron Chest—The Shipwrecked, or, La Bonne Petite Fille*; Peter Van Hagen, *The Adopted Child* (musical drama).

**Orchestra/Band**    Peter Van Hagen, *Federal Overture.*

**Piano/Organ**    James Hewitt, *The Battle of Trenton.*

**Symphonies**    Raynor Taylor, *Symphony.*

# 1798

☀

## Historical Highlights

State's Rights are set forth in the Kentucky Resolutions and the Virginia Resolutions; Congress authorizes all-out naval warfare with France and passes the Alien Act and the Sedition Act; the War of the Second Coalition begins; Napoleon begins his Egyptian campaign; Lord Nelson destroys the French fleet; the pope is imprisoned by French revolutionary forces.

## World Cultural Highlights

**World Art**    Francisco de Goya, *Los Caprichos*; François Gérard, *Cupid and Psyche*; Thomas Rowlandson, *The Comforts of Bath*; George Stubbs, *A Green Monkey.*

**World Literature**    William Cowper, *The Castaways*; Friedrich Klinger, *Der Weltmann und der Dichter*; August Kotzebue, *The Stranger*; Walter Landor, *Gebir.*

**World Music**    Franz Joseph Haydn, *The Creation—Lord Nelson Mass*; Ludwig van Beethoven, *Piano Sonatas No. 5–8—Violin Sonatas No. 1–3, Opus 12*; François Boieldieu, *Zoraume et Zulnar*.

**Miscellaneous**    Broderip, Clementi and Co. begin music publishing in London and T. Mollo and Co. in Vienna; births include Ferdinand and Victor-Eugène Delacroix, August Heinrich Hoffmann, and Adam Mickiewicz; deaths include Christian Cannabich, Asmus Jacob Carstens, and Gaetano Pugnani.

## American Art and Literature Highlights

**Births/Deaths**    Births include artist Isaac Sheffield and poets McDonald Clarke and Samuel Henry Dickson; deaths include literary figures Jeremy Belknap, Jacob Duche, and Elihu H. Smith.

**Art Works**    Washington Allston, *Wieland*; Ralph Earl, *Looking East from Denny Hill*; Charles Bulfinch, *Boston State House*; Benjamin Latrobe, *Bank of Pennsylvania, Philadelphia*; Edward G. Malbone, *Self-Portrait* (?); Samuel McIntire, *Derby-Crowninshield House* (Salem, Massachusetts)—*Governor John Winthrop*.

**Literature**    Jeremy Belknap, *American Biography II*; Charles B. Brown, *Wieland—Alcuin*; John Davis, *A Tribute to the United States, a Poem*; William Dunlap, *André, a Tragedy*; William Milns, *All in a Bustle: or, the New House*; William Munford, *Prose on Several Occasions*; Susanna Rowson, *Reuben and Rachel: Tales of Old Times*; Benjamin Rush, *Essays, Literary, Moral and Philosphical*.

## Music

**G. Deaths**    Justin Morgan (composer); William Selby (British-born organist/composer) December 12.

### I. New Positions

**Other**    Peter Albrecht Von Hagen, Sr. (organ, King's Chapel, Boston—to 1803); John Hodgkinson (manager, Haymarket Theater, Boston).

**K. Biographical**    Nathaniel Gould opens the first known singing school in Stoddard, New Hampshire.

### L. Musical Beginnings

**Performing Groups**    US Marine Fife and Drum Corps.

**Other**    *The American Musical Miscellany*; Columbia Garden Summer Concerts (New York); Adam and William Geib, Organ and Piano Makers (Manhattan); Peter Albrecht von (Van) Hagen, Sr., Music Publisher (Boston); Park Theater (New York).

### M. Music Publications

Goddard, Josiah, *A New and Beautiful Collection*
Kimball, Jacob, *The Village Harmony*

### N. Musical Compositions

**Choral/Vocal**    *Hail, Columbia* (words by Joseph Hopkinson—music Philip Phile's *President's March*); Peter A. Von Hagen, Jr., *Adam and Washington* (song).

**Orchestra/Band**    Alexander Reinagle, *The Italian Monk—The Gentle Shepherd* (incidental music).

# 1799

✸

## Historical Highlights

Fries' Rebellion takes place in Pennsylvania; Congress standardizes weights and measures and passes a National Quarantine Act; negotiations begin with France over shipping problems; the first public water system is built in Philadelphia; Napoleon returns to France, overthrows the French Directory and makes himself First Consul; Alexander Humboldt begins his South American explorations.

## World Cultural Highlights

**World Art**   Jacques-Louis David, *Rape of the Sabine Women*; George Stubbs, *The Hambletonian*; Berthold Thorvaldsen, *Bacchus and Ariadne*; Joseph Turner, *Battle of the Nile*.

**World Literature**   Vittorio Alfieri, *Misogallo*; Charles Bocage, *Ormond*; Thomas Campbell, *The Pleasures of Hope*; Johann Friedrich von Schiller, *Wallenstein Trilogy*.

**World Music**   Ludwig van Beethoven, *Symphony No. 1—Septet in E-flat, Opus 20*; James Hewitt, *The Mysterious Marriage*; Franz Joseph Haydn, *Theresienmesse—"Lobkowitz" String Quartets*.

**Miscellaneous**   The Rosetta Stone is discovered in Egypt; Lübeck Opera House opens; births include Honoré de Balzac, Jacques Halévy, Karl August Nicander, and Alexander Pushkin; deaths include Pierre Augustin de Beaumarchais, Carl Ditters von Dittersdorf, Ferdinand Kobell, and Adam Friedrich Oeser.

## American Art and Literature Highlights

**Births/Deaths**   Births include literary figures Amos Bronson Alcott, Samuel B. H. Judah, Grenville Mellen, Robert Charles Sands, and Richard Penn Smith; deaths include poet William Cliffton.

**Art Works**   Amos Doolittle, *A New Display of the United States of America*; Richard Jennys, *Elisha Bostwick*; Charles Peale Polk, *Nelly Conway Madison—James Madison*; Gilbert Stuart, *Thomas Jefferson*; John Vanderlyn, *Mrs. Edward Church and Child*.

**Literature**   Charles B. Brown, *Arthur Mervyn—Ormond—Edgar Huntley*; Thomas Cooper, *Political Essays*; John Davis, *Poems, Written at Coosahatchie, in South Carolina*; Nathan Fiske, *The Moral Monitor*; Philip Freneau, *Letters on Various Interesting and Important Subjects*; Sarah W. Morton, *The Virtues of Society*; Elihu Smith, *Diary* (not published until 1973); Helena Wells, *The Stepmother*.

## Music

**F. Births**   William Darracott, Jr. (violin maker); George Washington Doane (hymnist) May 27; Sophia Henrietta Hewitt Ostinelli (pianist) June 13.

**G. Deaths**   Stephen Woolls (singer/actor).

**I. New Positions**   William Farr (director, US Marine Band—to 1804).

**K. Biographical**   Charles Frederic Hupfield (German violinist/conductor) comes to the United States and settles in Baltimore; Filippo Traetta escapes political prison in Italy and comes to the United States, settling first in Boston.

**L. Musical Beginnings**

**Performing Groups**   New York Euterpean Society; New York Philharmonic Society I (to 1816); US Marine Band.

**M. Music Publications**

*A Collection of Psalms and Hymns for Public Worship* (Unitarian)
Benjamin, Jonathan, *Harmonia coelestis*
Jenks, Stephen, *The New England Harmonist*
Merrill, David, *Psalmodist's Best Companion*
Spicer, Ishmail, *Spicer's Pocket Companion, or The Young Mason's Monitor*
Strong, N., Flint, A., and Steward, J., *Hartford Selection of Hymns*

**N. Musical Compositions**

**Choral/Vocal**   Benjamin Carr, *Three Ballads, Opus 2*; Alexander Reinagle, *I Have a Silent Sorrow Here* (song); Raynor Taylor, *Monody on the Death of George Washington*; Peter A. Von Hagen, Jr., *To Arms, Columbia* (song).

**Operas**   James Hewitt, *Columbus* (ballad opera)—*The Mysterious Marriage* (ballad opera); Victor Pelissier, *The Fourth of July* (pantomime)—*Sterne's Maria, or The Vintage*; Alexander Reinagle, *The Arabs of the Desert* (pantomime)—*The Constellation* (dramatic sketch).

# 1800

❖

## Historical Highlights

The US population stands at 5,308,000 at the latest census; Thomas Jefferson is chosen by the House of Representatives as the third president; Washington, DC, becomes the capital and the White House is finished; the Harrison Land Act opens western lands to settlers; the Louisiana Territory is secretly returned to France by Spain.

## World Cultural Highlights

**World Art**   Jean-Jacques Chalon, *Banditti at Their Repast*; Jacques-Louis David, *Napoleon Crossing the Alps*; John Flaxman, *Apollo and Marpessa*; Jean-Auguste Ingres, *Cincinnatus Receiving the Deputies*.

**World Literature**   Charles Brown, *Arthur Merwyn*; Maria Edgeworth, *Castle Rackrent*; Gabriel Legouvé, *Le Mérite des Femmes*; Johann Friedrich von Schiller, *Maria Stuart*.

**World Music**   François Boieldieu, *The Caliph of Bagdad*; Franz Joseph Haydn, *The Seasons*; Ludwig van Beethoven, *Piano Concerto No. 3—Christ on the Mount of Olives—Six String Quartets, Opus 18*.

**Miscellaneous**   Hoffmeister and Kühnel's Bureau de Musique opens in Leipzig; births include Jean-Jacques Ampère, Anna Marie Hall, Emil Cauer, Louis-Eugène Lami, and Thomas Macaulay; deaths include William Cowper, Evstigney Fomin, and Niccolò Piccinni.

## American Art and Literature Highlights

**Births/Deaths**   Births include artists Francis Alexander, Jeremiah Harder, Sarah M. Peale, and literary figures Catharine Beecher, Charles James Cannon, Caroline Lee Hentz, and John Augustus Stone; deaths include sculptor John Skillin.

**Art Works**   Anonymous, *The Sargent Family*; John J. Barralet, *Sacred to the Memory of Washington* (?); Ralph Earl, *Looking East from Leicester Hill, Worcester*; William Groombridge, *Fairmount and Schuylkill River*; Edward Savage, *Thomas Jefferson—Benjamin Rush*; Gilbert Stuart, *John Adams—Mrs. John Adams—Robert Liston—Mrs. Robert Liston*; William Thornton, *Octagon House* (DC).

**Literature**   Richard Alsop, *A Poem, Sacred to the Memory of George Washington*; William Cliffton, *Poems*; John Davis, *The Farmer of New Jersey*; John Blair Linn, *The Death of Washington: A Poem*; Samuel Low, *Poems* (2 volumes); Susanna Rowson, *The Columbian Daughter*; Jonathan Sewall, *Eulogy on the Late General Washington*; Mason Weems, *A History of the Life and Death, Virtues, and Exploits of General George Washington*.

## Music

**F. Births**   Henry Erben (organ builder) March 10; James Hemmenway (bandmaster/composer); Henry K. Oliver (organist/hymnist) November 24; Benjamin Franklin White (composer/compiler/teacher) September 20.

**G. Deaths**   William Billings (singing master/composer) September 26.

**H. Debuts**

**United States** Charles H. Gilfert (Czech pianist/composer—New York).

**I. New Positions**

**Other** Peter Albrecht Von Hagen, Jr. (organ, Trinity Church, Boston).

**K. Biographical** John Isaac Hawkins builds the first known upright piano in the United States; Samuel Holyoke moves to Salem, Massachusetts, and continues to teach music.

**L. Musical Beginnings**

**Performance Groups** Society for Cultivating Church Music (New York).

**Other** J. C. Deagan Music Bells Co. (St. Louis); Graupner Music Store and Publishing House (Boston); Mt. Vernon Garden Theatre (New York); *Musical Journal for the Piano Forte* (till 1804).

**M. Music Publications**

Belknap, Daniel, *The Evangelical Harmony*
Cole, John, *Episcopalian Harmony*
Hewitt, James, *The Musical Repository*
Holden, Oliver, *Plain Psalmody—Modern Collection of Sacred Music*
Holyoke, Samuel, *The Instrumental Assistant I*
Huntington, Jonathan, *The Albany Collection*
Kimball, Jacob, *The Essex Harmony*
Richards, George, *Hymns and Odes, Composed on the Death of George Washington*
Swan, Timothy, *Songster's Assistant*

**N. Musical Compositions**

**Choral/Vocal** Daniel Belknap, *Funeral Ode—Autumn—Winter*; Benjamin Carr, *Dead March and Monody for General Washington*; James Hewitt, *The Wounded Hussar* (song); Oliver Holden, *From Vernon's Mount Behold the Hero Rise—Dirge, or Sepulchral Service*; Alexander Reinagle, *Rosa* (song); Abraham Wood, *Funeral Elegy on the Death of General George Washington*.

**Operas** James Hewitt, *Robin Hood—The Wild Goose Chase*; Alexander Reinagle, *A Wreath for American Tars* (dramatic sketch)—*The Double Disguise* (musical farce)—*Harlequin Freemason* (pantomime); Peter Van Hagen, *Columbus* (music drama).

**Orchestra/Band** Victor Pelissier, *Virgin of the Sun* (incidental music); Alexander Reinagle, *Masonic Overture—Pizarro* (incidental music).

# 1801

☀

## Historical Highlights

Demands for tribute from the Pirates of Tripoli result in Congress sending the US fleet to the Mediterranean; Robert Fulton designs the first practical submarine; the Treaty of Luneville brings the Holy Roman Empire to an end; the governments of Ireland and Great Britain are combined in the Act of Union; the British drive the French out of Egypt.

## World Cultural Highlights

**World Art** Antonio Canova, *Perseus with the Head of Medusa*; Jean-Auguste Ingres, *The Envoys of Agamemnon*; Anne-Louis Girodet-Trioson, *Ossian Receiving the Warriors*.

**World Literature** Clemens Brentano, *Godwi*; François de Chateaubriand, *Atala*; Johann Friedrich von Schiller, *Die Jungfrau von Orleans—Don Carlos*; Robert Southey, *Thalaba*.

**World Music** John Field, *Three Piano Sonatas, Opus 1*; Franz Joseph Haydn, *Schöpfungsmesse*; Ludwig van Beethoven, *The Creatures of Prometheus—Piano Sonatas No. 12–15*.

**Miscellaneous**   The Trieste Opera House and the Bavarian Academy of Arts and Sciences open; births include Vincenzo Bellini, Richard Bonington, Thomas Cole, Cardinal Newman, and Christian Dietrich Grabbe; deaths include Daniel Chodowiecki, Domenico Cimarosa, Ignace Krasicki, and Novalis.

## American Art and Literature Highlights

**Births/Deaths**   Births include artists Henry Inman, John Quidor, and literary figures George Washington Cutter, Caroline Kirkland (Mary Clavers), and William Leggett; deaths include artist Ralph Earl and literary figures Margaretta Fangeres, Elizabeth Fergusson, and Lemuel Hopkins.

**Art Works**   William Jennys, *John Bancroft*; Rembrandt Peale, *Rubens Peale with a Geranium*; John Trumbull, *The Infant Christ and St. John*.

**Literature**   Paul Allen, *Original Poems, Serious and Entertaining*; Charles B. Brown, *Jane Talbot*; John Davis, *Poems, Written Chiefly in South Carolina*; Charles J. Ingersoll, *Edwy and Elgiva*; Jonathan Sewall, *Miscellaneous Poems*; Isaac Story, *A Parnassian Shop, Opened in the Pindaric Stile, by Peter Quince, Esq.*; William Winstanley, *The Hypocrite Unmask't*; Sarah Wood, *Dorval: or, The Speculator*.

## Music

**F. Births**   John Hill Hewitt (poet/composer) July 1?

**I. New Positions**

**Conductors**   Solomon Warriner (choir director, Old First Church, Springfield, Massachusetts).

**Other**   Benjamin Carr (organ, St. Augustine's Catholic Church, Washington, DC—to 1831).

**L. Musical Beginnings**

**Educational**   American Conservatorio (Boston); Mallet and Graupner Musical Academy and Repository of Music (Boston).

**M. Music Publications**

Allen, Richard, *A Collection of Spiritual Songs and Hymns*
Hill, Uri K., *The Vermont Harmony*
Little, W. and Smith, W., *The Easy Instructor, or A New Method of Teaching Sacred Harmony*
Rippon, D., *Psalms and Hymns of Dr. Watts Arranged by Dr. Rippon* (Baptist)
Shumway, Nehemiah, *American Harmony*
Swan, Timothy, *New England Harmony*

**N. Musical Compositions**

**Operas**   Victor Pelissier, *Obi, or Three-fingered Jack* (pantomime).

**Orchestra/Band**   Alexander Reinagle, *Edwy and Elgiva* (incidental music); George Jackson, *Overture with Double Fugue and Grand March (?)—Freedom and Our President (Jefferson's March)*.

**Piano/Organ**   James Hewitt, *The Fourth of July (A Grand Military Sonata)*.

# 1802

☀

## Historical Highlights

West Point Military Academy is formed by Congress; Cincinnati, Ohio, is incorporated; Martha Washington dies on May 22; Napoleon Bonaparte is made First Consul for life by the French; the Treaty of Amiens brings a year's peace between France and England.

## World Cultural Highlights

**World Art**    John Flaxman, *Illustrations to The Divine Comedy*; Thomas Girtin, *The Eidometropolis*; Pierre Guérin, *Phédre and Hippolyte*; Joseph Turner, *The Tenth Plague on Egypt*.

**World Literature**    François de Chateaubriand, *The Genius of Christianity*; Walter Scott, *Minstrelsy of the Scottish Border I, II*; Friedrich von Schelling, *Bruno*; Mme. de Stael, *Delphine*.

**World Music**    Ludwig van Beethoven, *Symphony No. 2*; Franz Joseph Haydn, *Harmoniemesse*; Jan Václav Stich, *Horn Concertos No. 8–10*; Carl Maria von Weber, *Jugendmesse*.

**Miscellaneous**    Beethoven, in despair over his approaching deafness, writes his "Heiligenstadt Testament"; births include Alexandre Dumas, père, Victor Hugo, Edwin Landseer, and Nicolaus Lenau; deaths include Marie Anne Boccage, Francesco Casanova, Giuseppe Ceracchi, Thomas Girtin, George Romney, and Giuseppe Sarti.

## American Art and Literature Highlights

**Births/Deaths**    Births include literary figures Horace Bushnell, William A. Caruthers, Lydia Maria Child, Dorothea Dix, George Pope Morris, and Edward C. Pinkney; deaths include playwright John Leacock.

**Art Works**    Simon Fitch, *Ephraim Starr—Hannah Beach Starr*; William Jennys, *Colonel Constant Storrs*; Raphaelle Peale, *A Deception*; Gilbert Stuart, *Mrs. Perez Morton (?)*; Benjamin West, *Death on a Pale Horse*.

**Literature**    John Davis, *Adventures of the Mammoth Cheese*; Timothy Dexter, *Pickle for the Knowing Ones—Plain Truths in a Homespun Dress*; Washington Irving, *Letters of Jonathan Oldstyle, Gent.*; John Lathrop, Jr., *The Speech of Caunonicus; or, an Indian Tradition—A Poem*; Mason Weems, *The True Patriot*; Sarah S. K. Wood, *Amelia: or, The Influence of Virtue*.

## Music

**F. Births**    Ureli Corelli Hill (violinist/conductor).

**I. New Positions**

**Other**    George K. Jackson (organ, St. George's Church, New York—to 1807).

**K. Biographical**    Congress passes a revised Copyright Act; Andrew Law devises a system of staffless music notation.

**L. Musical Beginnings**

**Performing Groups**    Massachusetts Musical Society (to 1810).

**Other**    George E. Blake, Publisher (Philadelphia); John Cole, Music Publisher (Baltimore); J. George Schetky, Music Publisher (Philadelphia).

**M. Music Publications**

Alline, Henry, *Hymns and Spiritual Songs*
Belknap, Daniel, *The Middlesex Collection*
French, Jacob, *The Harmony of Harmony*
Holyoke, Samuel, *Columbian Repository of Sacred Harmony*
Maxim, Abraham, *Oriental Harmony*

**N. Musical Compositions**

**Chamber Music**    Peter Weldon, *The New York Serenading Waltz* (piano and violin/flute).

**Choral/Vocal**    Peter A. Von Hagen, Jr., *Anna—Gentle Zephyr* (songs).

**Orchestra/Band**    Victor Pelissier, *Gil Blas* (pantomime).

**Piano/Organ**    James Hewitt, *Collection of Most Favorite Country Dances*.

**Symphonies**    James Hewitt, *Grand Sinfonie, Characteristic of the Peace of the French Republic*.

# 1803

❁

## Historical Highlights

The size of the United States is doubled with the purchase of the Louisiana Territory from Napoleon; Lewis and Clark begin their expedition to the Northwest Territory; Ohio enters the Union as the 17th state; Fort Dearborn (Chicago) is built; Buffalo, New York, is founded.

## World Cultural Highlights

**World Art**   Louis Boilly, *Arrival of the Stagecoach*; Joseph Turner, *Calais Pier*; James Ward, *Fighting Bulls by the Castle*; Benjamin Ward, *Christ Healing the Sick*.

**World Literature**   Ludwig von Arnim, *Der Wintergarten*; Jane Porter, *Thaddeus of Warsaw*; Jean-Paul Richter, *The Titan*; Johann Friedrich von Schiller, *Die Braut von Messina*.

**World Music**   Ludwig van Beethoven, *Eroica Symphony—Kreutzer Sonata*; Luigi Cherubini, *Anacréon*; Franz Joseph Haydn, *String Quartet, Opus 103*; Carl Maria von Weber, *Peter Schmoll*.

**Miscellaneous**   The French Prix de Rome in music is inaugurated; births include Adolphe Adam, Thomas Beddoes, Hector Berlioz, Edward Bulwer-Lytton, Robert Lauder, and Prosper Mérimée; deaths include Vittorio Alfieri, James Beattie, Johann von Herder, and Friedrich Klopstock.

## American Art and Literature Highlights

**Births/Deaths**   Births include artists Alexander Davis, Robert W. Weir, and literary figures Orestes A. Brownson, George Henry Calvert, Ralph Waldo Emerson, and Sarah Helen Whitman; deaths include literary figures Enos Hitchcock, Samuel Hopkins, William Smith, and Isaac Story (Peter Quince).

**Art Works**   Washington Allston, *The Deluge* (?).

**Literature**   Charles Crawford, *Poems on Several Occasions*; John Davis, *Travels of Four Years and a Half in the United States*; William Dunlap, *Ribbemont, or, The Feudal Baron*; Thomas G. Fessenden, *Terrible Tractoration*; Samuel Miller, *A Brief Retrospect of the Eighteenth Century*; William Wirt, *Letters of the British Spy*.

## Music

**F. Births**   Henry E. Moore (composer/educator); George Stevens (organ builder) April 22; Joseph C. Taws (pianist/composer?).

**G. Deaths**   Arabella Brett (Mrs. John Hodgkinson—British-born soprano); Peter Albrecht Von Hagen, Sr. (Dutch-born organist/publisher) August 20; Thomas Wignell (impresario).

**I. New Positions**

**Other**   J. J. Negrin (editor, *The Freeman's Vocal Assistant*).

**K. Biographical**   Johann Christoph Mueller (German flutist/violinist) accompanies Johann G. Rapp to the United States and helps form the Harmony Society in Pennsylvania (1805); Alexander Reinagle moves to Baltimore and marries his second wife, Anna Duport.

**L. Musical Beginnings**

**Other**   George E. Blake, Music Publisher (Philadelphia); *Songwriter's Museum*.

**M. Music Publications**

Cole, John, *Cole's Collection of Psalm Tunes and Anthems*
Hill, Uri K., *A Number of Original Airs, Duetto's and Trio's*
Holden, Oliver, *Charlestown Collection of Sacred Songs*

Swan, Timothy, *The Singster's Museum*

Zeisberger, David, *A Collection of Hymns for the Use of the Christian Indians of the Mission of the United Brethren of North America*

**N. Musical Compositions**

**Choral/Vocal**   Anonymous, *Jefferson and Liberty* (to tune, "Anacreon in Heaven"); Alexander Reinagle, *Masonic Ode*.

**Operas**   Victor Pelissier, *A Tale of Mystery* (melodrama).

**Orchestra/Band**   George K. Jackson, *President Jefferson's New March and Quick Step*; Victor Pelissier, *La fille hussar* (pantomime); Filippo Traetta, *Sinfonia Concertata*.

# 1804

☀

## Historical Highlights

Thomas Jefferson is re-elected president; the 12th Amendment, calling for a separate popular vote for vice president, is ratified; the Lewis and Clark expedition finally reaches the Pacific Ocean; war with Tripoli increases over the continuing piracy on US ships; Napoleon Bonaparte is crowned emperor of France and the Code Napoleon goes into effect for all occupied countries.

## World Cultural Highlights

**World Art**   John S. Cotman, *Viaduct*; Antoine Gros, *Napoleon at Jaffa*; Joseph Turner, *Great Falls at Reichenbach*; Antoine Vernet, *The Battle of Marengo*; David Wilkie, *Pitlessie Fair*.

**World Literature**   William Blake, *Jerusalem*; William Hayley, *The Triumphs of Music*; Jane Porter, *The Lake of Killarney*; Johann Friedrich von Schiller, *William Tell*.

**World Music**   Ludwig van Beethoven, *Triple Concerto—Piano Sonatas No. 21–23*; Henry Bishop, *Angelina*; Gioacchino Rossini, *Six Sonatas a Quattro*; Carl Maria von Weber, *Rübezahl*.

**Miscellaneous**   The Liceo Filarmonico opens in Bologna; births include Benjamin Disraeli, Michael Glinka, Eduard Mörike, Charles Sainte-Beuve, George Sand, and Johann Strauss, Sr.; deaths include Elizabeth Bekker, Immanuel Kant, George Morland, and Giovanni Domenico Tiepolo.

## American Art and Literature Highlights

**Births/Deaths**   Births include artists Thomas Cummings, Fitz Hugh Lane, and authors Nathaniel Hawthorne, John A. McClung, and William Joseph Snelling; deaths include authors Jonathan Boucher, Charlotte Ramsay Lennox, and John Blair Linn.

**Art Works**   Washington Allston, *Landscape with a Lake—Rising of a Thunderstorm at Sea*; Francis Guy, *View of Baltimore from Beech Hill—1804*; William Rollinson, *Alexander Hamilton*; Gilbert Stuart, *Dolley Madison—James Madison—General John R. Fenwick*; John Vanderlyn, *The Death of Jane McCrea*.

**Literature**   John Quincy Adams, *Letters on Silesia*; William Austin, *Letters from London*; Hugh H. Brackenridge, *Modern Chivalry II, Vol. 1*; Thomas G. Fessenden, *Original Poems*; Isaac Mitchell, *The Asylum: or, Alonzo and Melissa*; Susanna Rowson, *Miscellaneous Poems*; John Williams, *The Hamiltoniad*; Sarah S. Wood, *Ferdinand and Elmira: A Russian Story*.

## Music

**G. Deaths**   Hans Gram (Danish-born organist/composer) April 28; David Tannenberg (German organ builder) May 19; Abraham Wood (composer/compiler) August 6.

**I. New Positions**

**Conductors**  Charles S. Ashworth (US Marine Band—to 1816).

**K. Biographical**  Benjamin Carr returns to music publishing in partnership with George Schetky.

**L. Musical Beginnings**

**Performing Groups**  New Ipswich Military Band.

**Other**  William Goodrich, Organ Builder (Boston).

**M. Music Publications**

Child, Ebenezer, *The Sacred Musician*
Holyoke, Samuel, *The Christian Harmonist*

**N. Musical Compositions**

**Choral/Vocal**  George K. Jackson, *Ode for General Hamilton's Funeral—David's Psalms* (low voice and organ).

**Operas**  Victor Pelissier, *Raymond and Agnes* (pantomime); Alexander Reinagle, *The Sailor's Daughter* (musical comedy).

**Piano/Organ**  Benjamin Carr, *The Siege of Tripoli: Historical Naval Sonata, Opus 4*.

# 1805

## Historical Highlights

Trade problems in the West Indies cause a break in relations between the United States and England; officially, the war with Tripoli ends, but preying on American ships continues; the Michigan Territory is officially formed; the War of the Third Coalition begins; the British gain world naval supremacy at the Battle of Trafalgar.

## World Cultural Highlights

**World Art**  Ferdinand Jagemann, *Schiller on His Deathbed*; Joseph Koch, *Landscape with Rainbow*; Pierre-Paul Prud'hon, *Empress Josephine*; Joseph Turner, *The Shipwreck*.

**World Literature**  Jens Baggesen, *Parthenais*; Walter Scott, *Lay of the Last Minstrel* (completed); Étienne de Sénancour, *Obermann*; Robert Southey, *Madoc*; William Wordsworth, *The Prelude*.

**World Music**  Ludwig van Beethoven, *Fidelio—Leonore Overture No. 2—Piano Concerto No. 4*; Michael Haydn, *Leopoldmesse*; Ferdinando Paër, *Leonora*; Giovanni Viotti, *Violin Concerto No. 25*.

**Miscellaneous**  The G. Donizetti Musical Institute opens in Bergamo; births include Hans Christian Andersen, Esteban Echeverria, Constantin Guys, and Wilhelm von Kalmbach; deaths include Manuel du Bocage, Luigi Boccherini, Jean-Baptiste Greuze, Johann Friedrich von Schiller, and Mihály Vitéz.

## American Art and Literature Highlights

**Births/Deaths**  Births include Erastus S. Field, Horatio Greenough, Hiram Powers, novelist Charles E. Gayarre, and poet Frederic Stanhope Hill; deaths include author Nathaniel Fanning and artist Matthew Pratt.

**Art Works**  Washington Allston, *The Classical or Italian Landscape* (?)*—Self-Portrait—Diana in the Chase*; John W. Jarvis, *Thomas Paine*; Joshua Johnston, *Kennedy Long Family*; Charles Willson Peale, *Gilbert Stuart*; Rembrandt Peale, *Thomas Jefferson*; William Rush, *Eagle*; Gilbert Stuart, *General Henry Knox—John Randolph*; Benjamin West, *Angel Announcing the Resurrection to Mary*.

**Literature**  Hugh H. Brackenridge, *Modern Chivalry IV*; Thomas Branagan, *Avenia: . . . a Tragical Poem . . .* ; John Davis, *The First Settlers of Virginia; an Historical Novel*; Thomas G.

Fessenden, *Democracy Unveiled*; William Ioor, *Independence: or, Which Do You Like Best, the Peer or the Farmer?*; John Blair Linn, *Valerian, a Narrative Poem*; Caroline M. Warren, *The Gamesters: or, Ruins of Innocence*.

## Music

**F. Births**   John Sage (publisher) September 11.

**G. Deaths**   John Hodgkinson (British-born singer/impresario) September 12; Peter Pelham III (organist/harpsichordist/composer) April 28.

**I. New Positions**

**Conductors**   Nathaniel D. Gould (conductor, Middlesex Musical Society, Massachusetts); James Hewitt (municipal bands, New York).

**Other**   Uri K. Hill (organ, Brattle Street Church, Boston).

**K. Biographical**   John Bray (British composer/arranger) comes to the United States and settles in Philadelphia; Gaetano Carusi (Italian composer) arrives in the United States with his three musical sons and 18 musical companions; Anthony Philip Heinrich (Bohemian composer) visits the United States for the first time; Edward Riley (British publisher) comes to the United States; Oliver Shaw begins teaching keyboard in Dedham, Massachusetts.

**M. Music Publications**

Ingalls, Jeremiah, *The Christian Harmony*
Jenks, Stephen, *The Delights of Harmony*
Mead, Stith, *Hymns and Spiritual Songs*
Mintz, David S., *Spiritual Song Book*
Olmstead, Timothy, *The Musical Olio*

**N. Musical Compositions**

**Choral/Vocal**   George K. Jackson, *Ode to Harmony—Ode to Peace*.

**Operas**   Victor Pelissier, *Valentine and Orson* (melodrama).

**Orchestra/Band**   Alexander Reinagle, *Overture to The Wife of Two Husbands—The Voice of Nature* (incidental music).

# 1806

☀

## Historical Highlights

The Lewis and Clark expedition returns to St. Louis; Zebulon Pike discovers the peak named after him; the first federal highway, the Cumberland Road, begins construction; the Confederation of the Rhine is founded; Napoleon defeats Prussia; the British blockade the Continent.

## World Cultural Highlights

**World Art**   Johann von Dannecker, *Ariadne*; Antoine Gros, *The Battle of Aboukir*; Jean-Auguste Ingres, *Napoleon as Emperor*; Bertel Thorvaldsen, *Hebe*; Joseph Turner, *Garden of the Hesperides*.

**World Literature**   Ludwig von Arnim/Clemens Brentano, *Des Knaben Wunderhorn*; Johann Wolfgang von Goethe, *Faust I*; Heinrich von Kleist, *Der Zerbrochene Krug*; Sydney Morgan, *The Wild Irish Girl*.

**World Music**   Ludwig van Beethoven, *Symphony No. 4—Violin Concerto—Razumovsky Quartets, Opus 59—Leonore Overture No. 3*; Gioacchino Rossini, *Demetrio e Polibio*.

**Miscellaneous**   The Moscow Imperial Theater is built; the Mannheim Conservatory of Music opens; births include Elizabeth Browning, Friedrich Halm, and Heinrich Laube; deaths include James Barry, Jean-Honoré Fragonard, Carlo Gozzi, Michael Haydn, and George Stubbs.

## American Art and Literature Highlights

**Births/Deaths**   Births include art figures Francis W. Edmonds, William M. Prior, and literary figures Robert Montgomery Bird, Charles F. Hoffman, Cornelius A. Logan, William G. Simms, Frederick W. Thomas, and Nathaniel P. Willis; deaths include sculptor Simeon Skillin, Jr. and humorist Timothy Dexter.

**Art Works**   Charles Bulfinch, *Gore Place* (Waltham, Massachusetts); Edward G. Malbone, *Robert Macomb—Mary Cornell Pell*; Charles Willson Peale, *Exhumation of the Mastodon*; Gilbert Stuart, *Washington at Dorchester Heights—William King—Mrs. William King*; John Trumbull, *The Holy Family—The Vernet Family*; Benjamin West, *Robert Fulton*.

**Literature**   Thomas Branagan, *The Flowers of Literature*; Nathaniel Fanning, *Narrative of the Adventures of an American Navy Officer*; William Littell, *Epistles of William, Surnamed Littell, to the People of the Realm of Kentucky*; John Howard Payne, *Julia: or, The Wanderer*; Noah Webster, *Compendious Dictionary of the English Language*.

## Music

### I. New Positions

**Other**   Peter Erben (organ, New Dutch Reformed Church, New York—to 1807).

**K. Biographical**   Jonathan Huntington begins four years as a singing instructor in Northampton, Massachusetts; Andrew Law moves to Philadelphia; Edward Riley (British publisher) settles in New York and begins teaching instruments and singing; Samuel Priestly Taylor (British organist) emigrates to the United States (?).

### M. Music Publications

Belknap, Daniel, *The Village Compilation*  
Forbush, Abijah, *Psalmist's Assistant*  
Graupner, Gottlieb, *Rudiments of the Art of Playing the Piano Forte*  
Hill, Uri Keeler, *The Sacred Minstrel*  
Huntington, Jonathan, *The Apollo Harmony*  
Jenks, Stephen, *Laus Deo*  
Olmstead, Timothy, *Martial Music*  
Read, Daniel, *Litchfield Collection*  
Shaw, Oliver, *A Favorite Selection of Music . . .*

### N. Musical Compositions

**Operas**   Alexander Reinagle, *Mary, Queen of Scots*.

**Piano/Organ**   James Hewitt, *Theme with Thirty Variations in D Major*.

# 1807

☀

## Historical Highlights

The Chesapeake Affair strains relations with England; the Embargo Act forbids trade with any foreign nation, France and England in particular; Robert Fulton makes a sucessful first run of the steamboat *Clermont*; the US Coast Guard is formed; the slave trade is outlawed by England, France, Spain, and Portugal; the War of the Third Coalition ends with the Treaty of Tilsit.

## World Cultural Highlights

**World Art**   Philipp Runge, *Night*; Ludwig Spohr, *Self-Portrait*; Bertel Thorvaldsen, *Cupid and Psyche;* Joseph Turner, *Sun Rising in the Mist—Windsor Castle from Salt Hill*.

**World Literature**    Lord Byron, *Hours of Idleness*; George Crabbe, *Poems*; Adam Oehlenschläger, *Baldur, the Good*; Mme. de Staël, *Corinne*; William Wordsworth, *Poems*.

**World Music**    Ludwig van Beethoven, *Symphony No. 5—Mass in C Major—Coriolanus Overture—Thirty-Two Variations in C for Piano*; Carl Maria von Weber, *Symphonies No. 1, 2*.

**Miscellaneous**    The Pleyel piano factory opens in Paris; the Milan Conservatory of Music opens; births include Thomas Duncan, Gabriel Legouvé, Wincenty Pol, and Giovanni Ruffini; deaths include Angelica Kauffman, August Meissner, John Opie, and Clara Reeve.

## American Art and Literature Highlights

**Births/Deaths**    Births include artist William Sidney Mount and literary figures Theodore S. Fay, Henry W. Herbert (Frank Forester), Richard Hildreth, Henry Wadsworth Longfellow, Thomas Ward (Flaccus), and John Greenleaf Whittier; deaths include artist Edward G. Malbone and poets Thomas Brockway and Alexander Martin.

**Art Works**    Joshua Johnston, *The Westwood Children*; Charles Bird King, *Joel Barlow—Louisa Catherine Adams*; John Trumbull, *Niagara Falls, Upper Bank*; John Vanderlyn, *Marius Amid the Ruins of Carthage*.

**Literature**    Richard Alsop et al., *The Echo, and Other Poems*; Joel Barlow, *The Columbiad*; Thomas Branagan, *The Excellency of the Female Character Vindicated*; John D. Burk, *Bethlem Gabor*; William Ioor, *The Battle of Eutaw Springs*; Washington Irving, *Salmagundi: or, the Whim-Whams and Opinions of Launcelot Langstaff, Esq., and Others*.

## Music

**F. Births**    Ira Aldridge (performer/singer); George Hood (clergyman/composer/author) February 10; John W. Moore (musicologist/lexicographer) April 11.

**I. New Positions**

**Other**    Benjamin Carr (organ, St. Mary's Catholic Church, Philadelphia—to 1811); Peter Erben (organ, St. George's Chapel, New York—to 1813); Oliver Shaw (organ, First Congregational Church, Providence, Rhode Island).

**L. Musical Beginnings**

**Performing Groups**    Dartmouth Handel Society; Massachusetts Musical Society (to 1810); Pittsburgh Apollonian Society.

**Other**    Théâtre St. Philippe (New Orleans—burns down in 1817).

**M. Music Publications**

Herrick, Joseph, *The Instrumental Preceptor*
Holden, Oliver, *Vocal Companion*
Holyoke, Samuel, *Instrumental Assistant II*
Hubbard, John, *Essay on Music*
Jenks, Stephen, *The Hartford Collection of Sacred Harmony*
Mann, Elias, *Massachusetts Collection of Sacred Harmony*
Shaw, Oliver, *For the Gentleman: A Favorite Selection of Instrumental Music . . .*

**N. Musical Compositions**

**Choral/Vocal**    George K. Jackson, *Thirteen Easy Canons: Sacred to Masonry*.

**Operas**    James N. Barker and John Bray, *Tears and Smiles* (musical play); James Hewitt, *The Tars from Tripoli* (ballad opera); Alexander Reinagle, *The Travellers*.

**Orchestra/Band**    Timothy Olmstead, *Martial Music: A Collection of Marches Harmonized for Field Bands*; Oliver Shaw, *March, for the Gentlemen*.

# 1808

☀

## Historical Highlights

James Madison becomes the fourth president; the slave trade is outlawed by Congress; the American Fur Company is founded by J. J. Astor; the Union Temperate Society is founded in New York; Napoleon occupies Spain, putting his brother, Joseph, on the Spanish throne; Spain and Italy abolish the Inquisition.

## World Cultural Highlights

**World Art**   Antonio Canova, *Pauline Borghese as Venus*; Jacques-Louis David, *The Coronation of Napoleon*; Jean-Auguste Ingres, *The Bather*; Joseph Turner, *Battle of Trafalgar*.

**World Literature**   Johann Wolfgang von Goethe, *Pandora*; Heinrich von Kleist, *Penthesilea*; Charles Maturin, *The Wild Irish Boy*; Friedrich La Motte-Fouqué, *Sigurd, the Dragon Slayer*.

**World Music**   Ludwig van Beethoven, *Pastoral Symphony—Choral Fantasy*; Etienne Méhul, *Symphony No. 2*; Anton Reicha, *Symphonies No. 1, 2*; Ludwig Spohr, *Clarinet Concerto No. 1*.

**Miscellaneous**   The Naples Conservatory of Music opens; the Ricordi Music House opens in Milan; births include Michael Balfe, Honoré Daumier, Antoine Étex, Karl Lessing, and Karl Spitzweg; deaths include Melchiorre Cesarotti, Carl Langhans, Hubert Robert, and Thomas Thorild.

## American Art and Literature Highlights

**Births/Deaths**   Births include art figures William H. Brown, Seth Eastman, John F. Francis, Horatio Stone, and literary figures Willis G. Clark, William D. Gallagher, and Harriet Wilson; deaths include authors Fisher Ames, John Dickinson, and poets Jacob Bailey and Jonathan M. Sewall.

**Art Works**   J. Brown, *Mercy Barnes Hall—Calvin Hall—Laura Hall*; William Rush, *Comedy—Tragedy*.

**Literature**   Fisher Ames, *The Works of Fisher Ames*; James N. Barker, *The Indian Princess, or, La Belle Sauvage*; Thomas Branagan, *The Beauties of Philanthropy*; William Cullen Bryant, *The Embargo*; John Davis, *Walter Kennedy*; Anne McVicker Grant, *Memoirs of an American Lady*; George Watterston, *The Lawyer: or, Man as He Ought Not to Be*.

## Music

**F. Births**   Edward "Ned" Kendall (bandmaster/keyed bugler) March 21; Thomas "Daddy" Rice (minstrel).

**K. Biographical**   Johann Christian Gottlieb Graupner becomes an American citizen.

**L. Musical Beginnings**

**Performing Groups**   Pierian Sodality (Harvard Musical Association in 1837); Massachusetts Musical Society.

**Other**   Boston Athenaeum.

**M. Music Publications**

*The Missouri Songster*
Emerson, William, *A Collection of Psalms and Hymns . . . Suitable for Private Devotion and the Worship of Churches*
Hupfield, Charles, *Musical Preceptor*
Shaw, Oliver, *The Columbian Sacred Harmonist*

**N. Musical Compositions**

**Choral/Vocal**   George K. Jackson, *Ode for the Fourth of July*; David Moritz Michael, *Psalm 103*.

**Operas**   James N. Barker and John Bray, *The Indian Princess* (musical play).

# 1809

☀

## Historical Highlights

Congress, via the Non-Intercourse Act, opens trade with all countries except France and England; the *Phoenix*, first oceangoing steamship, makes its maiden voyage; the Illinois Territory is formed from the Northwest Territory; Napoleon conquers Austria; Metternich becomes Austrian prime minister; England signs the Treaty of the Dardanelles with Turkey.

## World Cultural Highlights

**World Art**   John Constable, *Malvern Hall*; John Flaxman, *Lord Nelson*; Antoine Gros, *The Surrender of Madrid*; Henry Raeburn, *Mrs. Spiers*; Joseph Turner, *Fishing on the Blythe-Sand*.

**World Literature**   Lord Byron, *English Bards and Scotch Reviewers*; Maria Edgeworth, *Tales from Fashionable Life I*; Thomas Fessenden, *Pills, Poetical, Political and Philosophical*.

**World Music**   Ludwig van Beethoven, *Emperor Concerto—Piano Sonatas No. 24–26*; Luigi Cherubini, *Mass in F*; Gioacchino Rossini, *Six Quartets for Woodwinds*; Carl Maria von Weber, *Turandot*.

**Miscellaneous**   The new Covent Garden Theater is erected; births include Roger de Beauvoir, Nikolai Gogol, Felix Mendelssohn, Frederik Paludan-Müller, Antoine Preault, and Alfred Lord Tennyson; deaths include Franz Joseph Haydn, Augustin Pajou, and Johann Anton Stamitz.

## American Art and Literature Highlights

**Births/Deaths**   Births include artists Karl Bodmer, Cephas G. Thompson, and literary figures Thomas H. Chivers, Oliver Wendell Holmes, Joseph H. Ingraham, Albert Pike, and Edgar Allen Poe; deaths include authors Samuel Cole Davis and Thomas Paine.

**Art Works**   John Singleton Copley, *George IV as Prince of Wales*; William Dunlap, *Charles Brockden Brown* (?); John W. Jarvis, *Washington Irving*; George Murray, *Buttermilk Falls*; Charles Willson Peale, *Peale Family Group—Harrison Grey Otis*; William Rush, *Water Nymph and Bittern* (?); John Trumbull, *Lamderg and Gelchossa*.

**Literature**   Thomas Branagan, *An Intellectual Telescope* . . . ; Samuel C. Davis, *Diary* (unpublished); Philip Freneau, *Poems, Written . . . during the American Revolution*; Washington Irving, *Knickerbocker's History of New York*; Henry C. Knight, *The Cypriad*; John Howard Payne, *Lovers' Vows*; Samuel S. Smith, *Lectures on the Evidences of the Christian Religion*; Royall Tyler, *The Yankey in London* . . .

## Music

**F. Births**   William Walker (composer/compiler) May 6; Edward L. White (composer/educator).

**G. Deaths**   Elizabeth Catherine von Hagen (organist/publisher); Alexander Reinagle (British-born composer/impresario) September 21.

**I. New Positions**

**Conductors**   Gottlieb Graupner (Boston Philo-Harmonic Society).

**Other**   Jacob Eckhard, Sr. (organ, St. Michael's Episcopal Church, Charleston—to 1833); Oliver Shaw (organ, First Congregational Church, Providence—to 1832).

**K. Biographical**   Frank Johnson (composer/bandmaster from Martinique) settles in Philadelphia and forms his own band; First Lady Dolly Madison purchases the first piano for the White House in Washington, DC.

**L.  Musical Beginnings**

**Performing Groups**   Boston Philo-Harmonic Society; Psallonian Society (Providence, Rhode Island); Harvard College Orchestra (first in United States); Philadelphia Haydn Society.

**Other**   Babcock Brothers Piano Co. (Boston).

**M.  Music Publications**

Belknap, Daniel, *The Middlesex Songster* (?)
Harmon, Joel, Jr., *The Columbian Sacred Minstrel*
Huntington, Jonathan, *The English Extracts*
Law, Andrew, *The Art of Playing the Organ and Pianoforte*
Moors, Hezekiah, *The Province Harmony*
Smith, William, *The Churchman's Choral Companion*
Totten, John C., *A Collection of the Most Admired Hymns and Spiritual Songs*
Watt, Solomon, *Impartial Selection of Hymns and Spiritual Songs*

**N.  Musical Compositions**

**Chamber Music**   Peter Weldon, *President Madison's March* (piano and flute/violin).

**Choral/Vocal**   Alexander Reinagle, *Paradise Lost* (unfinished oratorio); Oliver Shaw, *Thanksgiving Anthem*.

**Piano/Organ**   Daniel Belknap, *Belknap's March*; Benjamin Carr, *Applicazione adolcita, Opus 6*.

# 1810

❀

## Historical Highlights

The US population reaches 7,240,000; the United States resumes trade with France and England, but France continues to seize US ships; Florida is annexed by Congress when the occupants revolt against Spanish rule; Yale Medical School opens its doors; the Mexican Revolution begins; Napoleon marries Marie Louise of Austria and annexes the Low Countries.

## World Cultural Highlights

**World Art**   William Blake, *The Canterbury Pilgrims*; François Gérard, *The Battle of Austerlitz*; Francisco de Goya, *Disasters of War I*; Pierre Guérin, *Andromache and Pyrrhus*.

**World Literature**   George Crabbe, *The Borough*; Heinrich von Kleist, *Das Käthchen von Heilbronn*; Walter Scott, *Lady of the Lake*; Robert Southey, *The Curse of Kehama*.

**World Music**   Ludwig van Beethoven, *Egmont Music—String Quartet No. 11, "Serioso"*; Gioacchino Rossini, *La cambiale di matrimonio*; Carl Maria von Weber, *Silvana—Piano Concerto No. 1*.

**Miscellaneous**   Chapell and Co., Ltd., music publishers, opens in London; births include Frédéric Chopin, Elizabeth Gaskell, Robert Griepenkerl, Clark Mills, Otto Nicolai, and Robert Schumann; deaths include John Hoppner, Philipp Runge, Johannes de Troostwijck, and Johann Zoffany.

## American Art and Literature Highlights

**Births/Deaths**   Births include art figures Joel T. Hart, Chauncey Ives, Clark Mills, and literary figures Robert Taylor Conrad, (Sarah) Margaret Fuller, John B. Jones, Theodore Parker, and François Dominique Rouquette; deaths include authors Charles Brockden Brown and James Cheetham.

**Art Works**   Jacob Eichholtz, *Self-Portrait* (?); John Johnston, *Still Life with Fruit*; Robert Mills, *Harrisburg State House* (Pennsylvania); Rembrandt Peale, *Napoleon*.

**Literature**    William Crafts, *The Raciad and Other Occasional Poems*; William Dunlap, *The Italian Father*; Charles J. Ingersoll, *Inchiquin, the Jesuit's Letters*; Susanna Rowson, *A Present for Young Ladies; Containing Poems, Dialogues, Addresses*; Isaiah Thomas, *History of Printing in America I, II*; George Watterston, *Glencarn: or, The Disappointments of Youth*.

## Music

**F. Births**    Joel Walker Sweeney (banjo player/maker?).

**G. Deaths**    John Hubbard (music author/compiler) August 14.

**K. Biographical**    Benjamin Carr, Raynor Taylor, and George Schetky give a concert reported as "the greatest musical event that had occurred up to that time in Philadelphia"; Anthony Philip Heinrich settles in Philadelphia and attempts to begin a musical merchandising business in the United States; Uri Keeler Hill moves to New York and continues teaching music there; Charles Thibault (French pianist/composer) comes to the United States.

**L. Musical Beginnings**

**Performing Groups**    Worcester Glee Club (Massachusetts).

**Other**    Clarion (type of bass clarinet by G. Catlin); William Whiteley Instrument Shop (Utica, New York).

**M. Music Publications**

Dare, Elkanah K., *The Periodical Harmony*
Hinde, Thomas S., *The Pilgrim Songster*
Mercer, Jesse, *The Cluster* (Baptist)
Mitchell, Nahum, *Brattle Street Collection*
Wyeth, John, *Repository of Sacred Music*

**N. Musical Compositions**

**Choral/Vocal**    Benjamin Carr, *Six Ballads from "The Lady of the Lake," Opus 7*.

**Operas**    Victor Pelissier, *Mother Goose* (pantomime).

**Piano/Organ**    James Hewitt, *Yankee Doodle with Variations;* Peter K. Moran, *Variations on a Swiss Waltz*.

# 1811

☀

## Historical Highlights

The greatest earthquake in recorded history takes place in the Mississippi Valley and covers 300,000 square miles; William Henry Harrison defeats the Indian chief Tecumseh at the Battle of Tippecanoe; the first steamboat to sail the Mississippi River is the *New Orleans*; Paraguay in South America gains its independence from Spain.

## World Cultural Highlights

**World Art**    John Constable, *East Bergholt Fair*; Wilhelm von Kobell, *Horse Races at Munich*; Pierre-Paul Prud'hon, *Empress Marie-Louise*; Joseph Turner, *Apollo and Python*.

**World Literature**    Clemens Brentano, *Gockel, Hinkel und Gackeleia*; Johann Wolfgang von Goethe, *Aus Meinem Leben I*; Heinrich von Kleist, *Novellen I, II*; Friedrich La Motte Fouqué, *Undine*.

**World Music**    Ludwig van Beethoven, *The Ruins of Athens—King Stephen*; Ludwig Spohr, *Symphony No. 1*; Carl Maria von Weber, *Abu Hassan—Clarinet Concertos No. 1, 2*.

**Miscellaneous**    The Prague Conservatory of Music opens; Novello and Co., Ltd., founded in London; births include Henri Delaborde, Théophile Gautier, Franz Liszt, and William Thackeray; deaths include György Bessenyei, Heinrich von Kleist (by suicide), and John Leyden.

## American Art and Literature Highlights

**Births/Deaths**  Births include artists George C. Bingham, John Casilear, Thomas Dow Jones, William Page, and literary figures Delia Salter Bacon, Fanny Fern (Sara Payson), Henry James, Sr., Frances S. Osgood, Harriet Beecher Stowe, and Alfred B. Street; deaths include poet Robert Treat Paine and artist James Sharples.

**Art Works**  Washington Allston, *Coast Scene of the Mediterranean—Poor Author and Rich Bookseller*; John Trumbull, *Lady of the Lake*.

**Literature**  Thomas Branagan, *A Concise View of the Principal Religious Denominations in the United States of America* . . . ; William Emerson, *An Historical Sketch of the First Church in Boston* . . . ; Alexander Graydon, *Memoirs of a Life*; Robert Treat Paine, *Works in Verse and Prose* (printed 1812).

## Music

**F. Births**  Joseph Atwill (music publisher); Benjamin Franklin Baker (composer) July 16; James C. Beckel (composer) December 20; Oliver Ditson (publisher) October 20; Elbridge G. Wright (brass instrument maker) March 1.

**G. Deaths**  John Antes (composer).

**K. Biographical**  James Hewitt sells his business in New York to John Willson and moves his family to Boston where he supervises the music at the Federal Street Theater; Samuel Hale Parker buys out William Blagrove's music store in Boston; Thomas Walker (British teacher/conductor) comes to the United States.

**L. Musical Beginnings**

**Other**  Thomas Hall, Organ Builder (Philadelphia); Edward Riley, Music Publisher and Store (New York); Théâtre d'Orléans (New Orleans).

**M. Music Publications**

Dupuy, Starke, *Hymns and Spiritual Songs* (Baptist)
Pelissier, Victor, *Columbian Melodies*
Riley, Edward, *Riley's New Instructions for the German Flute*
Shaw, Oliver, *A Plain Introduction to the Art of Playing the Pianoforte*

**N. Musical Compositions**

**Choral/Vocal**  Benjamin Carr, *Lessons and Exercises in Vocal Music, Opus 8*.

# 1812

☸

## Historical Highlights

James Madison is re-elected president; Louisiana becomes the 18th state; the Missouri Territory is formed out of the remainder of the Louisiana Purchase; war breaks out between the United States and England; Napoleon invades Russia but suffers his worst defeat by the Russian winter.

## World Cultural Highlights

**World Art**  Antonio Canova, *The Italian Venus*; Jean Géricault, *Mounted Officer, Imperial Guard*; Antoine Gros, *Napoleon and the Austrian Emperor*; Joseph Turner, *Hannibal Crossing the Alps*.

**World Literature**  William Comb, *Tours of Dr. Syntax I*; Thomas DeQuincey, *Confessions of an English Opium Eater*; John Nichols, *Literary Anecdotes of the Eighteenth Century*.

**World Music**  Ludwig van Beethoven, *Symphonies No. 7, 8*; John Field, *Piano Sonata No. 4*; Gioacchino Rossini, *La scala di seta—Il Signor Bruschino*; Franz Schubert, *Der Teufel als Hydraulicus*.

**Miscellaneous**  The Gesellschaft der Musikfreunde (Vienna) and the Brussels Conservatory of

Music are founded; born are Robert Browning, Charles Dickens, Edward Lear, and Johann August Tischbein; deaths include Berthold Auerbach, Gottlieb Schick, Gabriel Legouvé, and Johann Friedrich Tischbein.

## American Art and Literature Highlights

**Births/Deaths**   Births include art figures Shobal Clevenger, James Clonney, Charles W. Jarvis, Flora B. Palmer, and literary figures Martin Robinson Delaney, Peter Hamilton Myers, and William T. Thompson; deaths include artists George Beck, Henry Benbridge, and poet Joel Barlow.

**Art Works**   Robert Mills, *Monumental Church* (Richmond, Virginia); Samuel F. B. Morse, *The Dying Hercules*; Rembrandt Peale, *Roman Daughter*; William Rush, *The Nymph of the Schuylkill*; Gilbert Stuart, *Major-General Henry Alexander Dearborn—Mrs. Henry Alexander Dearborn*; John Trumbull, *Our Saviour and Little Children*.

**Literature**   James N. Barker, *Marmion*; Thomas Branagan, *The Charms of Benevolence and Patriotic Mentor . . .*; William Dunlap, *Yankee Chronology; or, Huzza for the Constitution*; Mordecai M. Noah, *Paul and Alexis*; James K. Paulding, *The Diverting History of John Bull and Brother Jonathan*; Lucius M. Sargent, *Hubert and Ellen and Other Poems*; William Wirt, *The Old Bachelor*.

## Music

**F. Births**   William Hauser (composer/hymnist) December 23; Horace Waters (publisher).

**G. Deaths**   Johannes Herbst (Moravian clergyman/composer) Jan 15.

**I. New Positions**

**Other**   James Hewitt (organ, Trinity Church, Boston); G. K. Jackson (organ, Brattlestreet Church, Boston).

**K. Biographical**   Jonathan Huntington begins 17 years as a singing instructor in Boston; Charles F. Hupfield moves from Baltimore to Philadelphia, where he takes an active part in music activities; Lowell Mason goes to Savannah, Georgia, taking work as a bank clerk.

**L. Musical Beginnings**

**Other**   *Carr's Musical Miscellany in Occasional Numbers* (till 1825).

**M. Music Publications**

*A Selection of Psalm Tunes for Use of the Protestant Episcopal Church in New York*
Huntington, Jonathan, *Classical Church Musick*
Mitchell, Nahum, *Templi Carmina*
Pilkington, H. W., *A Musical Dictionary*

**N. Musical Compositions**

**Choral/Vocal**   Eliakim Doolittle, *The Hornet Stinging the Peacock* (song); James Sanderson, *Hail to the Chief* (?).

**Piano/Organ**   Benjamin Carr, *Six Progressive Sonatinas* (with flute or violin ad lib.).

# 1813

❂

## Historical Highlights

Captain Oliver Perry breaks the British blockade on Lake Erie; the Creek War breaks out in Alabama while the Northwest Indian Confederacy falls apart following the death of Tecumseh; "Uncle Sam" makes his first appearance in the Troy *Post*. Napoleon is defeated at the Battle of Nations and is driven out of Spain and the Netherlands; Venezuela becomes independent.

## World Cultural Highlights

**World Art**   John Constable, *Cornfield under Heavy Clouds*; Jean-Auguste Ingres, *The Betrothal of Raphael*; Johann Kraft, *Departure*; Henry Raeburn, *The Macnab*; Joseph Turner, *Frosty Morning*.

**World Literature**   Jane Austen, *Pride and Prejudice*; Lord Byron, *The Giaour*; George Crabbe, *The Parish Register*; Percy Bysshe Shelley, *Queen Mab*; Johann Wyss, *Swiss Family Robinson*.

**World Music**   Ludwig van Beethoven, *Wellington's Victory*; Gioacchino Rossini, *Tancredi—L'Italiana in Algeri*; Franz Schubert, *Symphony No. 1*; Carl Maria von Weber, *Andante and Hungarian Rondo*.

**Miscellaneous**   The London Philharmonic Society is founded; births include Georg Büchner, Friedrich Hebbel, Giuseppe Verdi, and Richard Wagner; deaths include Michel de Crèvecoeur, Anton Graff, André Grétry, Jan F. Helmers, Alessandro Longhi, and Christoph Wieland.

## American Art and Literature Highlights

**Births/Deaths**   Births include artists George P. A. Healy, William Ranney, and literary figures Charles T. Brooks, Susan Fenimore Cooper, Christopher P. Cranch, Elijah Kellogg, Epes Sargent, Henry T. Tuckerman, and Jones Very; deaths include poet Robert Proud and artist Alexander Wilson.

**Art Works**   Thomas Birch, *Naval Engagement, United States and the Macedonian*; John L. Krimmel, *Interior of an American Inn*; Raphaelle Peale, *Melons and Morning Glories*; Henry Sargent, *The Landing of the Pilgrims*; Joshua Shaw, *The Deluge* (?); Gilbert Stuart, *Paul Revere—Mrs. Paul Revere*; Thomas Sully, *Daniel La Motte*.

**Literature**   Washington Allston, *The Sylphs of the Seasons with Other Poems*; John Davis, *Life and Surprising Adventures of the Celebrated John Smith*; James Hillhouse, *Demetria*; Edwin C. Holland, *Odes, Naval Songs and Other Occasional Poems*; John H. Payne, *Juvenile Poems*; James K. Paulding, *The Lay of the Scottish Fiddle*; Susanna Rowson, *Sarah*; George Watterston, *The Scenes of Youth*.

## Music

**F. Births**   William Henry Fry (composer) August 19; John S. Dwight (music critic/author) March 13; Thomas D. Paine (instrument maker/inventor), Billy Whitlock (minstrel/banjoist/songwriter); Henry F. Williams (violinist/composer) August 13.

**G. Deaths**   Johann (John) Frederick Peter (Moravian violinist/composer) July 13.

**I. New Positions**

**Other**   Peter Erben (organ, St. John's Chapel, New York); Johann Christian Till (organ, Bethleham Moravian Congregation—to 1844).

**L. Musical Beginnings**

**Other**   Gilfert's (Charles) Music Repository (Charleston, South Carolina); *Patterson's Church Music*.

**M. Music Publications**

Warriner, Solomon, *Springfield Collection of Sacred Music*
Wyeth, John, *Repository of Sacred Music II*

**N. Musical Compositions**

**Choral/Vocal**   Benjamin Carr, *Four Ballads from Rokeby, Opus 10* (?); Jacob Eckhard, Jr., *Naval Song (The Pillar of Glory)*.

# 1814

✺

## Historical Highlights

The British set fire to Washington, DC but fail to invade New York or take Fort McHenry at Baltimore; the Treaty of Ghent ends the War of 1812; Napoleon abdicates when the British invade France and is sent to the Island of Elba; Louis XVIII becomes King of France; the Congress of Vienna begins.

## World Cultural Highlights

**World Art**　John Constable, *Cart and Horses with Dog*; Theodore Géricault, *The Wounded Cuirassier*; Jean-Auguste Ingres, *Grande Odalisque*; Thomas Lawrence, *The Congress of Vienna*.

**World Literature**　Jane Austen, *Mansfield Park*; Lord Byron, *The Corsair*; E. T. A. Hoffmann, *Phantasiestücke in Callots Manier*; Walter Scott, *Waverley*; William Wordsworth, *The Excursion*.

**World Music**　Ludwig van Beethoven, *Fidelio Overture*; John Field, *Nocturnes No. 1–3*; Gioacchino Rossini, *Il Turco in Italia*; Franz Schubert, *Mass No. 1—Gretchen am Spinnrade*.

**Miscellaneous**　C. F. Peters Co. opens in Leipzig; the Cuban Conservatory of Music opens; births include Zsigmond Kemény, Mikhail Lermontov, and Jean-François Millet; deaths include Jacques Bernadin de Saint-Pierre, Charles Burney, Clodion, and Charles Palissot de Montenoy.

## American Art and Literature Highlights

**Births/Deaths**　Births include artists Albertus de Browere, George L. Brown, John Mix Stanley, Jerome Thompson, sculptor Henry K. Brown, and literary figures Eliza Ann Dupuy, William Howe Hosmer, and Samuel Ward; deaths include artist Reuben Moulthrop, poet George Richards, and playwright Mercy Otis Warren.

**Art Works**　Washington Allston, *Dead Man Restored to Life by Touching the Bones of the Prophet Elijah*; Thomas Birch, *Perry's Victory on Lake Erie* (?); John L. Krimmel, *Country Wedding*; Samuel F. B. Morse, *The Judgment of Jupiter*; William Rush, *George Washington*; Thomas Sully, *John Myers—Mrs. Edward Hudson*; John Vanderlyn, *Ariadne Asleep on the Island of Naxos*.

**Literature**　N. Biddle and P. Allen, eds., *History of the Expedition of Captains Lewis and Clark*; Mathew Carey, *The Olive Branch; or, Faults on Both Sides, Federal and Democratic*; David Humphreys, *The Yankee in England*; Francis Scott Key, *The Star-Spangled Banner*; William Littell, *Festoons of Fancy: Consisting of Compositions Amatory, Sentimental, and Humorous in Verse and Prose*.

## Music

**F. Births**　Silas Brainard (music publisher) February 14.

**K. Biographical**　Joshua Leavitt graduates from Yale; John Stafford Smith's *To Anacreon in Heaven* becomes the music for Francis Scott Key's *Star Spangled Banner*.

**L. Musical Beginnings**

Performing Groups: Handel Society of Maine (Portland).

**M. Music Publications**

Cole, John, *The Devotional Harmony*
Harmon, Joel, Jr., *A Musical Primer*
Hill, Uri Keeler, *The Handelian Repository*
Law, Andrew, *Essays on Music*
Smith, William, *The Reasonableness of Setting Forth the Most Worthy Praise of Almighty God*

**N. Musical Compositions**

**Choral/Vocal**　Benjamin Carr, *The History of England, Opus 11* (voice and piano).

**Orchestra/Band**　Raynor Taylor, *The Aethiop* (incidental music).

# 1815

❀

## Historical Highlights

The British are defeated at the Battle of New Orleans, which takes place after the peace is signed; Stephen Decatur brings an end to the Barbary Pirates' harassing of US shipping; the *USS Fulton* becomes the world's first steam warship; Napoleon escapes from Elba, is defeated at Waterloo, and is re-exiled to St. Helena.

## World Cultural Highlights

**World Art** Antonio Canova, *The Three Graces*; John Constable, *East Bergholt Church*; Francisco de Goya, *The Third of May, 1808*; Joseph Turner, *Crossing the Brook*; James Ward, *Gordale Scar, Yorkshire*.

**World Literature** Jane Austen, *Emma*; Lord Byron, *Hebrew Melodies*; James Knowles, *Caius Gracchus*; Silvio Pellico, *Francesca da Rimini*; Walter Scott, *Guy Mannering*.

**World Music** Ludwig van Beethoven, *Calm Sea and Prosperous Voyage*; Luigi Cherubini, *Smyphony in D*; John Field, *Piano Concertos No. 1, 2*; Franz Schubert, *Symphonies No. 2, 3—Der Erlkönig*.

**Miscellaneous** Charles-Joseph Sax sets up his instrument shop in Brussels; births include Thomas Couture, Robert Franz, Ernest Meissonier, Adolf von Menzel, Giovanni Prati, and Anthony Trollope; deaths include George Ellis, Matthias Claudius, and Johann Salomon.

## American Art and Literature Highlights

**Births/Deaths** Births include artists John Banvard, James and John Bard, David G. Blythe, sculptor Emma Stebbins, and literary figures Joseph G. Baldwin, Richard Dana, Jr., Ellen Sturgis Hooper, Thomas Low Nichols, and Thomas Bangs Thorpe; deaths include artists John Singleton Copley, Robert Fulton, and poets Richard Alsop and Charles Crawford.

**Art Works** Alvan Fisher, *Activity at the River*; John Frazee, *Grief*; John W. Jarvis, *Alexander Anderson*; Charles Bird King, *Poor Artist's Cupboard* (?); Rembrandt Peale, *Candlelight Self-Portrait*; Thomas Sully, *Colonel Jonathan Williams*; Benjamin West, *Christ Healing the Sick in the Temple—Christ Rejected*.

**Literature** Richard Alsop, *A Narrative of the Adventures . . . of John R. Jewitt . . .* ; Hugh H. Brackenridge, *Modern Chivalry* (complete edition); William C. Bryant, *To a Waterfowl*; Philip Freneau, *A Collection of Poems on American Affairs and a Variety of Other Subjects*; James K. Paulding, *The United States and England*; Lydia H. Sigourney, *Moral Pieces in Prose and Verse*; G. C. Verplanck, *A Fable for Statesmen and Politicians*.

## Music

**F. Births** J. Lathrop Allen (brass instrument maker) September 24; Alfred Badger (flute maker?); E. P. Christy (minstrel/impresario); Daniel Emmett (minstrel performer/composer) October 29; Francis F. Hagen (Moravian clergyman/composer) October 30.

**G. Deaths** Daniel Belknap (composer/compiler); Oliver Brownson (composer).

**I. New Positions**

**Other** John Davis (manager, Théâtre d'Orléans, New Orleans—to 1837).

**K. Biographical** John Bray leaves Philadelphia and moves to Boston; George Catlin establishes his instrument-making business in Philadelphia; David Moritz Michael (Moravian composer) retires from teaching and returns to Germany.

**L. Musical Beginnings**

**Performing Groups** Boston Handel and Haydn Society.

**Other** Boston Musical Instrument Manufactory; John Firth Piano and Publishing Co. (New York); Adam and William Geib, Music Publishers (Manhattan); Charles H. Gilfert, Music Publisher (Charleston, South Carolina); *North American Review*; John Osborne Piano Co. (Boston).

**M. Music Publications**

Shaw, Oliver, *The Providence Selection of Psalm and Hymn Tunes*
Worcester, Samuel, *Christian Psalmody*

**N. Musical Compositions**

**Choral/Vocal** Micah Hawkins, *Backside of Albany, or, The Siege of Plattsburg* (first black-dialect song to be published in the United States); Filippo Traetta, *Peace* (oratorio).

**Piano/Organ**    Philip Laroque, *Sonata, Battle of the Memorable 8th of January*; Francesco Masi, *Piano Sonata, "Battles of Lake Champlain and Plattsburg"*; Samuel Woodsworth, *The Hunters of Kentucky* (basis for "The Battle of New Orleans" in 1959).

# 1816

❖

## Historical Highlights

James Monroe becomes the fiftth president; Indiana becomes the 19th state; Baltimore is the first city to have coal gas lights; Congress passes its first protective tariff; the American Bible Society is formed; the first known bicycle is invented in Germany by Karl von Sauerbronn; Argentina declares its independence from Spain.

## World Cultural Highlights

**World Art**    Peter von Cornelius, *Joseph and His Brothers*; John Martin, *Joshua Commanding the Sun to Stand Still*; Thomas Rowlandson, *Dance of Life—Dance of Death*.

**World Literature**    Lord Byron, *Siege of Corinth*; Charles Lamb, *Glenarron*; Giovanni Niccolini, *Nabucco*; Thomas Peacock, *Headlong Hall*; Percy Bysshe Shelley, *Alastor*.

**World Music**    Ludwig van Beethoven, *An die ferne Geliebte*; John Field, *Piano Concertos No. 3, 4*; E. T. A. Hoffmann, *Undine*; Gioacchino Rossini, *The Barber of Seville*; Franz Schubert, *Symphonies No. 4, 5*.

**Miscellaneous**    Thomas Boosey Publishing House opens in London; the Mees Music Academy opens in Brussels; births include Charlotte Brontë, Emmanuel Leutze, Bernhard Malmström, and Wolfgang Müller; deaths include Giovanni Paisiello and Richard Sheridan.

## American Art and Literature Highlights

**Births/Deaths**    Births include art figures Richard Hubbard, Daniel Huntington, John Kensett, William Rimmer, and literary figures Philip P. Cooke, Evert Augustus Duyckinck, Charles G. Eastman, and John Godfrey Saxe (humorist/poet); deaths include poets Richard Alsop and Hugh Brackenridge.

**Art Works**    Charles Bulfinch, *Old Meetinghouse Church, Lancaster, MA*; John W. Jarvis, *Oliver Hazard Perry at the Battle of Lake Erie*; Charles Willson Peale, *Mrs. Peale (Hannah Moore)—Belfield*; Raphaelle Peale, *Still Life with Celery and Wine*; Ammi Phillips, *Harriet Leavens* (?); William Rush, *Elisabeth Rush* (?); John Trumbull, *Surrender of General Burgoyne at Saratoga* (?).

**Literature**    Francis W. Gilmer, *Sketches of American Orators*; James Ogilvie, *Philosophical Essays*; John Pickering, *Vocabulary of Words and Phrases Peculiar to the United States*; D. Ramsay and S. Smith, *History of the United States*; George Tucker, *Letters from Virginia*; Alexander Wilson, *Poems: Chiefly in the Scottish Dialect*; Samuel Woodworth, *The Champion of Freedom*.

## Music

**F. Births**    William B. Bradbury (composer/organist) October 6; Charlotte Cushman (contralto) July 23; Henry W. Greatorex (organ/compiler); William Allen Johnson (organ builder) October 27.

**I. New Positions**

**Conductors**    Venerando Pulizzi (US Marine Band—two months only) followed by John Powley (US Marine Band—to 1818).

**Other**    Benjamin Carr (organ/choir director, St. Peter's Episcopal Church—to 1831); James Hewitt (organ, Trinity Church, New York).

**K. Biographical**    William Bradford begins music study with Lowell Mason; James Hewitt leaves Boston and moves back to New York; Richard Willis (Irish bandmaster/composer) moves to the United States.

**L. Musical Beginnings**

**Performing Groups**   Euterpian Society of Hartford.

**Other**   Allyn and Bacon, Music Publishers (Philadelphia).

**M. Music Publications**

Davisson, Ananias, *Kentucky Harmony*
Dow, Peggy, *A Collection of Camp-meeting Hymns*
Eckhard, Jacob, Sr., *Choral-Book*
Funk, Joseph, *Die allgemein nützliche Choral-Music*
Hastings, Thomas and Warriner, Solomon, *Musical Sacra*
Jackson, George K., *A Choice Collection of Chants*
Smith, William, *Assistant to the Evangelical Psalmodist*
Whiteley, William, *The Instrumental Preceptor*

# 1817

✸

## Historical Highlights

Mississippi becomes the 20th state; the Seminole Indian War begins in Florida; work begins on the Erie Canal; the American Society for the Return of Negroes to Africa is founded—Liberia is founded in Africa; the United States and Great Britain sign the Rush-Bagot Treaty limiting naval forces on the Great Lakes; José San Martin defeats the Spanish forces in Chile.

## World Cultural Highlights

**World Art**   Jacques-Louis David, *Cupid and Psyche*; Théodore Géricault, *The Riderless Horse Race*; Johann Kraft, *The Battle of Leipzig*; Bertel Thorvaldsen, *Ganymede with the Eagle*.

**World Literature**   Lord Byron, *Manfred—The Lament of Tasso*; Maria Edgeworth, *Ormond*; Franz Grillparzer, *Die Ahnfrau*; Thomas Moore, *Lalla Rookh*; Walter Scott, *Rob Roy*.

**World Music**   Luigi Cherubini, *Requiem in C Minor*; John Field, *Nocturnes No. 4–6*; Gioacchino Rossini, *La Cenerentola—La Gazza Ladra*; Franz Schubert, *Death and the Maiden*.

**Miscellaneous**   The Amsterdam Rijksmuseum opens; *Edinburgh Monthly (Blackwood's) Magazine* begins publication; births include Konstantin Aksakov, Neils Gade, Alexei Tolstoy, and George Watts; deaths include Andrea Appiani, Jane Austen, Étienne Méhul, and Mme. Germaine de Staël.

## American Art and Literature Highlights

**Births/Deaths**   Births include art figures Robert Duncanson, Erastus Palmer, Peter Rothermel, and literary figures Frederick Douglass, Henry B. Hirst, Cornelius Mathews, Victor Séjour, and Henry Thoreau; deaths include poet Timothy Dwight.

**Art Works**   Washington Allston, *Uriel in the Sun*; Francis Guy, *Brooklyn*; Raphaelle Peale, *Still Life with Steak*; Gilbert Stuart, *James Monroe*; John Trumbull, *Timothy Dwight*; Samuel Waldo, *Andrew Jackson—Self-Portrait*.

**Literature**   Morris Birbeck, *Notes on a Journey to the Territory of Illinois*; Thomas Branagan, *The Pleasures of Contemplation*; William C. Bryant, *Thanatopsis* (poem); Amasa Delano, *Narrative of Voyages and Travels Comprising Three Voyages Round the World*; Timothy Dwight, *Travels in New-England and New-York*; James K. Paulding, *Letters from the South I, II*.

## Music

**F. Births**   Allen Dodsworth (bandmaster); Rufus Grider (Moravian musician/historian); A. N. Johnson (theoretician/publisher/educator) June 22; Sylvester Main (editor/publisher) April 18; Alexander W. Thayer (music historian) October 22.

**G. Deaths**   Jacob French (composer) May.

**I. New Positions**

**Conductors**   Richard Willis (band, US Military Academy, West Point).

**Other**   Charles Gilfert (manager, Charleston Theater—to 1825).

**K. Biographical**   William Dubois takes over Astor's old music shop from the Paff Brothers; Anthony Philip Heinrich leads the first known American performance of a Beethoven symphony (*Symphony No. 1*) in Lexington, Kentucky; Peter K. Moran (Irish composer/pianist) comes to the United States.

**L. Musical Beginnings**

**Other**   Franklin Music Warehouse (Boston, by J. R. Parker).

**M. Music Publications**

Dyer, Samuel, *New Selections of Sacred Music*
Gillet, Wheeler, *The Virginia Sacred Minstrel*
Harrod, John J., *Social and Camp Meeting Sings for the Pious*
Hastings, Thomas, *The Musical Reader*
Jackson, George K., *The Choral Companion*
Metcalf, Samuel L., *The Kentucky Harmonist*
Mudge, Enoch, *The American Camp Meeting Hymn Book*
Rumrille, J. and Holton, H., *The Drummer's Instructor: or Martial Musician*

**N. Musical Compositions**

**Piano/Organ**   Peter K. Moran, *Variations on Stantz Waltz—Variations on "Ach du lieber Augustin"*; Filippo Traetta, *Commodore Decatur's Turkish March* (?).

# 1818

❊

## Historical Highlights

Congress approves the Stars and Stripes as the official flag and passes the Flag Act, which calls for an additional star for each new state; Illinois becomes the 21st state; Andrew Jackson helps put down the Indians in the First Seminole War; the United States and Canada settle their boundary dispute on the 49th parallel.

## World Cultural Highlights

**World Art**   John Flaxman, *The Shield of Achilles*; David Friedrich, *Traveler Overlooking a Sea of Fog*; Théodore Géricault, *The Raft of the Medusa*; Edwin Landseer, *Fighting Dogs*.

**World Literature**   John Grillparzer, *Sappho*; John Keats, *Endymion*; Thomas Peacock, *Nightmare Abbey*; Mary Wollstonecraft Shelley, *Frankenstein*; Percy Bysshe Shelley, *Prometheus Unbound*.

**World Music**   Franz Gruber, *Silent Night*; Gioacchino Rossini, *Mosè in Egitto*; Franz Schubert, *Symphony No. 6—Deutsche Trauermesse*; Carl Maria von Weber, *Jubel Overture*.

**Miscellaneous**   The Old Vic Theater Co. of London opens; the Bavarian State Opera is founded in Munich; births include Emily Brontë, Wilhelm Camphausen, Eliza Cook, Charles Gounod, Charles de Lisle, and Ivan Turgenev; deaths include Heinrich Füger and Leopold Kozeluch.

## American Art and Literature Highlights

**Births/Deaths**   Births include art figures Charles Deas, Thomas R. Gould, Thomas Le Clear, Charles Nahl, Thomas Rossiter, and literary figures William E. Channing II, Frederick S. Cozzens (Richard Haywarde), Mary H. Eastman, Elizabeth P. Prentiss, and Henry W. Shaw (Josh Billings); deaths include poets David Humphreys and Jonathan Odell.

**Art Works**   Washington Allston, *Elijah Fed by the Ravens*; Alvan Fisher, *Mishap at the Ford*; Charles Willson Peale, *Rembrandt Peale—Henry Clay—John Quincy Adams*; Henry Sargent, *Boy on a Hobby Horse*; Thomas Sully, *Lady with a Harp: Eliza Ridgely*.

**Literature**   Hannah M. Crocker, *Observations on the Rights of Women*; Timothy Dwight, *Theology, Explained and Defended*; Edwin C. Holland, *Corsair*; John P. Kennedy, *The Red Book*; James K. Paulding, *The Backwoodsman*; John Howard Payne, *Brutus: or, the Fall of Tarquin: An Historical Tragedy*; Samuel Woodworth, *Poems, Odes, Songs and Other Metrical Effusions*.

## Music

**F. Births**   Francis H. Brown (pianist/composer) April 6; Samuel P. Jackson (organist/composer) February 5; Maria Delores Nau (soprano) March 18; George A. Prince (melodeon maker) February 17.

**G. Deaths**   Johann (John) Geib (German-born piano/organ builder) October.

**H. Debuts**

**United States**   Charles Incledon (British tenor—tour), Joseph C. Taws (Philadelphia, as pianist), and Charles Thibault (French pianist—New York).

**K. Biographical**   Jonas Chickering is apprenticed to piano maker John Osborn in Boston; Oliver Holden begins 15 years as a member of the South Carolina House of Representatives; Paul Emil Johns (Polish pianist/composer) settles in New Orleans; Lowell Mason helps to found the Savannah Missionary Society; the New York Handel and Haydn Society presents the first US performance of Haydn's *The Creation*; Henry K. Oliver graduates from Dartmouth College.

**L. Musical Beginnings**

**Other**   Théâtre d'Orleans (rebuilt—New Orleans).

**M. Music Publications**

Boyd, James M., *The Virginia Sacred Musical Repository*
Jenks, Stephen, *The Harmony of Zion, or Union Compiler*
Johnson, Francis, *Collection of Cotillions*
Read, Daniel, *The New Haven Collection of Sacred Music*
Shaw, Oliver, *Sacred Melodies, Selected from Handel, Haydn . . . and Others*
Winchell, James, *Psalms, Hymns and Spiritual Songs of Watts—Sacred Harmony*

**N. Musical Compositions**

**Choral/Vocal**   Anonymous, *The Banjo Song*; "Daddy" Rice, *Jump Jim Crow*.

# 1819

❀

## Historical Highlights

The Panic of 1819 causes a four year depression; Alabama enters the Union as the 22nd state; the United States pays Spain five million dollars for the Florida Territory; Fort Snelling (Minneapolis) is built; the Universities of Cincinnati and Virginia are founded; Simón Bolívar defeats the Spanish in Venezuela; future Queen Victoria is born.

## World Cultural Highlights

**World Art**   John Constable, *The White Horse*; Francisco de Goya, *The Last Communion of St. Joseph*; Jean-Auguste Ingres, *Nicolò Paganini*; Bertel Thorvaldsen, *Christ and the Apostles*.

**World Literature**   Lord Byron, *Mazeppa—Don Juan I, II*; George Crabbe, *Tales of the Hall*; Hannah More, *Moral Sketches*; Adam Oehlenschläger, *The Gods of the North*; Walter Scott, *Bride of Lammermoor*.

**World Music**   Ludwig van Beethoven, *Hammerklavier Sonata*; Franz Schubert, *Trout Quintet—Die Zwillingsbrüder*; Carl Maria von Weber, *Invitation to the Dance—Mass in G*.

**Miscellaneous**   Norwegian violinist Ole Bull makes his debut at age nine; births include Théodore Chassériau, Gustave Courbet, George Eliot, Jacques Offenbach, Clara Schumann, and Franz von Suppé; deaths include Edward Bird, August Kotzebue, John Ruskin, and John Wolcot.

## American Art and Literature Highlights

**Births/Deaths**   Births include art figures Thomas Ball, Richard Greenough, Martin J. Heade, and literary figures Julia Ward Howe, James Russell Lowell, Herman Melville, Anna Cora Mowatt, E. D. E. N. Southworth, William Wetmore Story, Caroline S. Tappan, William R. Wallace, and Walt Whitman; deaths include artist Samuel King.

**Art Works**   Washington Allston, *Moonlit Landscape—The Flight of Florimel*; John L. Krimmel, *Fourth of July Celebration in Philadelphia*; Bass Otis, *The Mill*; Charles Willson Peale, *Yarrow Mamout*; Samuel Seymour, *War Dance in the Interior of a Konza Lodge*; Thomas Sully, *Washington at the Passage of the Delaware*; Samuel L. Waldo, *The Independent Beggar*; Benjamin West, *Self-Portrait*.

**Literature**   James N. Barker, *She Would Be a Soldier: or, The Plains of Chippewa*; Fitz-Greene Halleck, *Fanny*; James A. Hillhouse, *Percy's Masque*; Washington Irving, *The Sketch Book*; James K. Paulding, *Salmagundi II*; G. C. Verplanck, *The State Triumvirate*; Robert Waln, *The Hermit in America on a Visit to Philadelphia*; Richard H. Wilde, *The Lament of the Captive*.

## Music

**F. Births**   John W. Dadmun (hymn composer) December 20; Elizabeth Taylor Greenfield (singer/freed slave); Justin Holland (composer/guitarist); Samuel Parkman Tuckerman (organist/composer) February 11; Joseph P. Webster (popular composer/performer) February 18; Richard Storrs Willis (composer/writer) February 10; Isaac Baker Woodbury (composer/educator) October 23.

**G. Deaths**   Joseph Carr (British-born music publisher) October 27; Simon Peter (Moravian composer) May 29.

**K. Biographical**   Johann G. Klemm (German instrument maker) emigrates to Philadelphia; Newark, New Jersey gets its first church organ.

**L. Musical Beginnings**

**Performing Groups**   Beethoven Musical Society of Portland, Maine (to 1826); Haydn Society of Cincinnati.

**Other**   Dubois and Stodart, Piano Makers (New York); Klemm and Brothers, Importers and Publishers (Philadelphia); John Siegling Music Store and Publishers (Charleston, South Carolina); James Stewart, Piano Builder (Philadelphia).

**M. Music Publications**

Goodale, Ezekiel, *Instrumental Director*
Graupner, Gottlieb, *Rudiments of the Art of Playing the Pianoforte* (revised and enlarged)
Law, Andrew, *The Harmonic Companion*
Shaw, Oliver, *Melodia Sacra*
Worcester, Samuel, *The Psalms, Hymns, and Spiritual Songs of the Reverend Isaac Watts*

**N. Musical Compositions**

**Piano/Organ**   James Hemmenway, *The Philadelphia Grand Entre Waltz* (?)—*Cupid's Frolic—Miss Billing's Waltz*; Charles Thibault, *Variations on Robin Adair*.

# 1820

❀

## Historical Highlights

The US population reaches 9,683,000, with New York the largest city with a population of 124,000; James Monroe is re-elected president; Maine becomes the 23rd state; slavery in the Louisiana Territory is limited by the Missouri Compromise; Indiana University is founded; the Spanish Constitution is restored by Ferdinand VII; the continent of Antarctica is discovered.

## World Cultural Highlights

**World Art**　John Constable, *Harwich Lighthouse*; David Friedrich, *Landscape in the Silesian Mountains*; Francisco de Goya, *The Giant*; Edwin Landseer, *Alpine Mastiffs and Traveler*.

**World Literature**　Tommaso Grossi, *Ildegonda*; John Keats, *Lamia and Other Poems*; Alphonse de Lamartine, *Méditations Poétiques*; Alexander Pushkin, *Russlan and Ludmilla*; Walter Scott, *Ivanhoe*.

**World Music**　Ludwig van Beethoven, *Piano Sonata No. 30*; Gioacchino Rossini, *Messa Solenne*; Franz Schubert, *Sakuntala—Die Zauberharfe*; Carl Maria von Weber, *Preciosa* (incidental music).

**Miscellaneous**　The statue of Venus de Milo is discovered; the Toulouse Conservatory of Music opens in France; births include Anne Brontë, George Grove, Jenny Lind (the "Swedish Nightingale"), Josef Mánes, and Henri Vieuxtemps; deaths include William Drennan and Ferdinand Jagemann.

## American Art and Literature Highlights

**Births/Deaths**　Births include art figures George Durrie, Benjamin West, Thomas W. Whittredge, and literary figures Charles M. Barras, Alice Cary, Lucretia P. Hale, Margaret J. Preston, and George Vashon; deaths include artists Francis Guy, Benjamin West, and literary figures Joseph Rodman Drake, Judith S. Murray, James Ogilvie, and Benjamin Trumbull.

**Art Works**　Alvan Fisher, *Great Horseshoe Falls, Niagara*; Francis Guy, *A Winter Scene in Brooklyn* (?); Rembrandt Peale, *The Court of Death*; Thomas Sully, *The Torn Hat*; John Trumbull, *Surrender of Cornwallis at Yorktown* (begun 1787)—*The Declaration of Independence II* (DC); Benjamin West, *Franklin and the Lightning*; Micah Williams, *Woman with a Book* (?).

**Literature**　Maria Brooks, *Judith, Esther and Other Poems*; William Crafts, *Sullivan's Island and Other Poems*; Washington Irving, *The Sketch Book of Geoffrey Crayon, Gent.* (completed); Samuel Judah, *The Mountain Torrent*; Henry W. Longfellow, *The Battle of Lovewells's Pond*; John Trumbull, *The Poetical Works of John Trumbull*; William Tudor, *Letters on the Eastern States*.

## Music

**F. Births**　Fanny J. Crosby (poet/hymnist) March 24; Luther O. Emerson (composer/conductor) August 3; Isaac Fiske (brass instrument maker) December 23; Hiram Murray Higgins (music publisher) October 13; John Henry Hopkins (clergyman/hymnwriter) October 28; Elias Howe (music publisher); Robert "Father" Kemp (popular performer) June 6; Elisha J. King (composer?); George Frederick Root (composer/educator) August 30.

**G. Deaths**　Lewis Edson (composer); Joseph Gehot (violinist/composer) (?); Samuel Holyoke (composer/compiler) February 7.

**I. New Positions**

**Other**　Peter Erben (organ, Trinity Church, New York—to 1839); Lowell Mason (organ, Independent Presbyterian Church, Savannah, Georgia).

**K. Biographical**　Alexander Reinagle loses all of his theater music scores in a fire at the Philadelphia New Theatre; the Washington Theatre is destroyed by fire.

**L. Musical Beginnings**

**Performing Groups**　Musica Sacra Society of Buffalo; Philharmonic Society of Bethlehem (Pennsylvania).

**Other**　*The Euterpeiad, or Musical Intelligencer* (to 1823); William Hall Piano Co. (Firth, Hall, and Pond); Musical Fund Society of Philadelphia.

**M. Music Publications**

Carden, Allen D., *The Missouri Harmony*
Davison, Ananias, *Supplement to the Kentucky Harmony*
Harris, Cary, *Western Harmony for Singers*
Hill, Uri Keeler, *Solfeggio Americano, a System of Singing*

**N. Musical Compositions**

**Chamber Music**   Joseph C. Taws, *Air with Variations* (piano with instruments); Anthony P. Heinrich, *The Dawning of Music in Kentucky, Opus 1—The Western Minstrel, Opus 2* (piano and violin).

**Piano/Organ**   Benjamin Carr, *Musical Bagatelles, Opus 13*; Anthony P. Heinrich, *A Chromatic Ramble of the Peregrine Harmonist*; Julius Metz, *Clermont Waltz with Variations*; Charles Thibault, *Variations on a Russian Air*.

# 1821

❀

## Historical Highlights

Missouri becomes the 24th state; the United States officially begins the settlement of the Florida Territory; Texas, a state of Mexico, is opened to settlement by Moses Austin; the first public high school opens in Boston; Congress rejects the metric system; Mexico declares its independence and Santa Ana becomes president; Guatamala, Panama, and Santo Domingo declare their independence.

## World Cultural Highlights

**World Art**   Antonio Canova, *Endymion*; John Constable, *The Hay Wain*; John Flaxman, *St. Michael Overcoming Satan*; Théodore Géricault, *The Epsom Derby*; John Martin, *Belshazzar's Feast*.

**World Literature**   John Clare, *The Village Minstrel*; Franz Grillparzer, *The Golden Fleece*; Walter Scott, *Kenilworth*; Percy Bysshe Shelley, *Adonais*; Robert Southey, *Vision of Judgment*.

**World Music**   Ludwig van Beethoven, *Piano Sonata No. 31, Opus 110*; Ludwig Spohr, *Clarinet Concerto No. 3*; Carl Maria von Weber, *Der Freischütz—Konzertstücke, Opus 70*.

**Miscellaneous**   The Lower Rhine Music Festival begins at Cologne; births include Hermann Allmers, Charles Baudelaire, Champfleury, Feodor Dostoyevsky, Gustav Flaubert, Hermann von Helmholtz, and Joseph Paton; deaths include John Crome, John Keats, Joseph de Maistre, and Christian Stolberg.

## American Art and Literature Highlights

**Births/Deaths**   Births include sculptor Anne Whitney and literary figures Sylvanus Cobb, Jr., Frederick Goddard Tuckerman, and Richard Grant White; deaths include poet William Irving and artist John Lewis Krimmel.

**Art Works**   Washington Allston, *Saul and the Witch of Endor*; Charles Bulfinch, *Baltimore Cathedral* (completed); Charles B. King, *Five Pawnee Braves*; Samuel F. B. Morse, *Congress Hall: Old House of Representatives*; Henry Sargent, *The Tea Party* (?); Thomas Sully, *Thomas Jefferson*.

**Literature**   William C. Bryant, *The Ages and Other Poems*; James F. Cooper, *The Spy*; Joseph Doddridge, *Logan, The Last of the Race of Shikellemus*; Timothy Dwight, *Travels in New England and New York*; Fitz-Greene Halleck, *Marco Bozzaris*; Thomas Jefferson, *Autobiography*; Mordecai M. Noah, *Marion: or, the Hero of Lake George*; James Gates Percival, *Poems*.

## Music

**F. Births**   Charley White (minstrel/manager) June 4; John Gordon McCurry (composer/compiler); Cool White (minstrel performer) July 28.

**G. Deaths**   Catherine Comerford Graupner (actress/singer) May; Andrew Law (music educator) April 21; George Godfrey Müller (German Moravian violinist/composer) March 19; William Smith (Scottish theologian/composer) April 6.

**J. Honors**    Andrew Law (honorary doctorate, Allegheny College).

**K. Biographical**    Hall and Erben build a new organ in St. George's in New York.

**L. Musical Beginnings**

**Other**    Thomas Appleton, Organ Maker (Boston); John Cole Music Shop (Baltimore); Jackson (George K.) Music Warehouse and Variety Store (Boston).

**M. Music Publications**

Carrell, James P., *Songs of Zion*

Davisson, Ananias, *An Introduction to Sacred Music*

Humphraville, Angus, *Missouri Lays and Other Western Ditties*

Sewall, Henry, *A Collection of Psalms and Hymns for Social and Private Worship (The New York Collection)*

**N. Musical Compositions**

**Choral/Vocal**    Christopher Meineke, *Te Deum.*

**Orchestra/Band**    James Hemmenway, *Washington Grays' Bugle Quick Step* (?).

**Piano/Organ**    Joseph Taws, *Variations, The Knight Errant.*

# 1822

☀

## Historical Highlights

Boston, founded in 1630, is finally incorporated; Florida becomes an official US Territory; Congress seeks to recognize the newly independent nations in Latin America, the latest being Brazil and Peru; a slave rebellion is crushed in South Carolina; the Republic of Haiti is formed.

## World Cultural Highlights

**World Art**    Eugène Delacroix, *Dante and Virgil in Hell*; David Friedrich, *The Wreck of the Hope*; Wilhelm Hensel, *Felix Mendelssohn*; John Martin, *Destruction of Herculaneum*.

**World Literature**    Heinrich Heine, *Gedichte*; Charles Nodler, *Trilby;* Alexander Pushkin, *Eugene Onegin*; Walter Scott, *The Fortunes of Nigel*; Percy Bysshe Shelley, *The Triumph of Life*.

**World Music**    Ludwig van Beethoven, *Consecration of the House Overture—Piano Sonata No. 32*; Gioacchino Rossini, *Zelmira*; Franz Schubert, *Unfinished Symphony—Wanderer Fantasy*.

**Miscellaneous**    The Royal Academy of Music opens in London; Louis Daguerre opens his Diorama in Paris; births include Matthew Arnold, Rosa Bonheur, César Franck, and Edmond de Goncourt; deaths include Antonio Canova, Arthur Devis, E. T. A. Hoffmann, and Franz Kobell.

## American Art and Literature Highlights

**Births/Deaths**    Births include art figures Edward S. Bartholomew, William Sonntag, Lilly M. Spencer, and literary figures Edward Everett Hale, Richard M. Johnston, George Lippard, Donald Grant Mitchell, Thomas Buchanan Read, and Francis Ticknor; deaths include artists Rufus Hathaway and Charles Polk.

**Art Works**    Thomas Doughty, *View of Baltimore from "Beach Hill"*; Charles Willson Peale, *The Artist in His Museum—James Peale (The Lamplight Portrait)—Self-Portrait*; Raphaelle Peale, *Still Life with Cake*; William Rush, *Self-Portrait* (?).

**Literature**    Washington Irving, *Bracebridge Hall*; Samuel Judah, *Odofriede*; James Lawson, *Ontwa, the Son of the Forest*; Clement C. Moore, *'Twas the Night before Christmas*; Mordecai M. Noah, *The Grecian Captive*; James K. Paulding, *A Sketch of Old England*; James G. Percival, *Clio* (3 volumes); Catharine M. Sedgwick, *A New England Tale*; John Taylor, *Tyranny Unmasked*.

## Music

**F. Births**   Harvey B. Dodsworth (bandmaster/publisher); David C. Hall (brass instrument maker) May 16; James Pierpont (songwriter); George D. Russell (publisher).

**G. Deaths**   George K. Jackson (British-born composer/teacher) November 18.

**K. Biographical**   Christian F. Albrecht (German piano maker) arrives in Philadelphia; Benjamin Carr begins a series of biographical sketches on American musical figures in *The Euterpeiad*; Gaetano Carusi opens the Washington Assembly Hall on the site of the old Washington Theatre; Emilius N. Scherr (Danish organ maker) emigrates to the United States and settles in Philadelphia; Filippo Traetta finally settles down as a music teacher in Philadelphia.

**L. Musical Beginnings**

**Performing Groups**   Jubal Society of Hartford.

**Other**   Niblo's Garden (New York).

**M. Music Publications**

French, Jacob, *Harmony of Harmony*
Hastings, Thomas, *Dissertation on Musical Taste*
Mason, Lowell, *Handel and Haydn Society's Collection of Church Music*
Spencer, Peter, *African Union Hymn Book*

**N. Musical Compositions**

**Choral/Vocal**   Peter K. Moran, *The Carrier Pigeon* (song).

**Piano/Organ**   Julius Metz, *Variations on the Vesper Hymn*.

# 1823

❀

## Historical Highlights

The Monroe Doctrine, warning European nations to steer clear of the Americas, is proclaimed by the president; Fort Brook (Tampa) founded in Florida; the first teacher's training school opens in Vermont. The United Provinces of Central America and the British Anti-Slavery Society are formed.

## World Cultural Highlights

**World Art**   John Constable, *Salisbury Cathedral*; Théodore Géricault, *The Kiln*; Joseph Turner, *Bay of Baiae*; Ferdinand Waldmüller, *Ludwig van Beethoven*; James Ward, *The Deer Stealer*.

**World Literature**   Alphonse de Lamartine, *Nouvelles Méditations Poétiques*; Charles Lamb, *Essays of Elia*; Friedrich Rückert, *Liebesfrühling*; Walter Scott, *Quentin Durward*.

**World Music**   Ludwig van Beethoven, *Choral Symphony—Missa Solemnis*; Gioacchino Rossini, *Semiramide*; Franz Schubert, *Rosamunde—Die Schöne Müllerin*; Carl Maria von Weber, *Euryanthe*.

**Miscellaneous**   The Bannatyne Club under Walter Scott is founded in London; births include Théodore de Banville, Alexandre Cabanel, Edouard Lalo, and Coventry Patmore; deaths include Joseph Nollekens, Sándor Petofi, Pierre-Paul Prud'hon, and Henry Raeburn.

## American Art and Literature Highlights

**Births/Deaths**   Births include artists Jasper Cropsey, Sanford Gifford, Thomas Hicks, and literary figures George H. Boker, Mary B. Chesnut, George L. Duyckinck, E. Z. C. Judson (Ned Buntline), James M. Legaré, Elizabeth B. Stoddard, and Lydia Louise Very.

**Art Works**   Asher B. Durand, *Signing of the Declaration of Independence*; Henry Inman, *Rip Van*

*Winkle Awakening from His Sleep*; Charles Willson Peale, *Bishop Cheverus*; Raphaelle Peale, *After the Bath*; John Quidor, *Dorothea*; Robert W. Weir, *St. Paul Preaching in Athens*.

**Literature**    James F. Cooper, *The Pioneers—The Pilot*; Samuel Judah, *Gotham and the Gothamites*; James McHenry, *The Spectre of the Forest*; John Neal, *Seventy-Six* (two volumes); James K. Paulding, *Koningsmarke, the Long Finne*; John Howard Payne, *Clari—Ali Pascha*; James Thacher, *A Military Journal during the American Revolutionary War, from 1775 to 1783*.

## Music

**F. Births**    Thomas J. Bowers (tenor?); William B. Simmons (organ builder).

**K. Biographical**    Thomas Hastings settles in Utica, New York, and begins editing the religious paper, *Western Reader*.

**L. Musical Beginnings**:

**Performing Groups**    New York Choral Society.

**Educational**    American Conservatorio (Philadelphia)

**Other**    Dayton (Ohio) Pleyel Society; R. and W. Nunns (Nunns and Clark), Piano Makers (New York); Stewart and Chickering, Piano Makers (Boston).

**M. Music Publications**

Bacon, Leonard, *Hymns and Sacred Songs*
Gould, Nathaniel, *Social Harmony*
Taylor, S. P. and Hart, J., *The Uranian Harmony*

**N. Musical Compositions**

**Chamber Music**    Anthony P. Heinrich, *The Sylviad, or Minstrelsy of Nature in the Wilds of North America*.

**Choral/Vocal**    Lowell Mason, *Missionary Hymn*.

**Orchestra/Band**    James Hemmenway, *The Philadelphia Grand March (?)*.

**Piano/Organ**    Charles Thibault, *Rondo, Le Printemps, Opus 6—Variations, Le Souvenir, Opus 7* (or harp).

# 1824

❋

## Historical Highlights

From the four candidates, Congress selects John Quincy Adams to be the sixth president; the Bureau of Indian Affairs is created in the War Department; Jim Bridger becomes the first white man to visit the Great Salt Lake; the United States signs a treaty with Russia over frontier rights in the Northwest; Colombia wins its independence; civil war breaks out in Turkey.

## World Cultural Highlights

**World Art**    Jacques-Louis David, *Mars and Venus*; Eugène Delacroix, *Massacre of Chios*; Edwin Landseer, *The Cat's Paw*; Friedrich Overbeck, *Christ Entering Jerusalem*; Joseph Turner, *The Lock*.

**World Literature**    Walter Landor, *Imaginary Conversations I*; Walter Scott, *Redgauntlet*; Percy Bysshe Shelley, *The Witch of Atlas*; Alfred de Vigny, *Éloa*.

**World Music**    Ludwig van Beethoven, *String Quartet No. 12, Opus 127*; Felix Mendelssohn, *Symphony No. 1—Overture for Winds*; Franz Schubert, *String Quartet, "Death and the Maiden."*

**Miscellaneous**    The Luxembourg Philharmonic Society and the Philharmonic Society of Mexico City are founded; births include Eugène Boudin, Pierre de Chavannes, Alexander Dumas, fils, and Bedrich Smetana; deaths include Lord Byron, Théodore Géricault, and Anne-Louis Girodet-Trioson.

## American Art and Literature

**Births/Deaths**   Births include art figures William M. Hunt, Eastman Johnson and literary figures Phoebe Cary, Jessie B. Frémont, Lucy Larcom, Sarah Anna Lewis, and Mary Hayden Pike; deaths include poets Edwin Holland, William Littell, Julien de Lalande Poydras, and Susanna Rowson.

**Art Works**   John H. I. Browere, *John Adams, Age 90*; John Frazee, *John Wells*; Matthew Jouett, *Marquis de Lafayette*; Charles Bird King, *Louisa Catherine Adams at the Harp*; Charles Willson Peale, *Josiah Quincy*; William Rush, *The Marquis de Lafayette—Wisdom—Justice*; William Strickland, *Second Bank of Philadelphia*; Gilbert Stuart, *Josiah Quincy*.

**Literature**   Lydia Maria Child, *Hobomok: A Tale of Early Times*; Washington Irving, *Tales of a Traveller*; James McHenry, *O'Halloran, or, the Insurgent Chief*; Israel R. Potter, *Life and Remarkable Adventures of Israel R. Potter*; Catharine M. Sedgwick, *Redwood*; Royall Tyler, *The Chestnut Tree*.

## Music

**F. Births**   Eliza Biscaccianti (soprano); Thomas E. Chickering (piano builder) October 22; John Wesley Steere (organ builder) April 10.

**K. Biographical**   James Albrecht retires from the piano-making business.

**L. Musical Beginnings**

**Performing Groups**   New Orleans Philharmonic Society; New York Philharmonic Society II (to 1827).

**Other**   Camp Street Theater (New Orleans); Hall and Erben, Organ Builders (New York); Musical Fund Hall (Philadelphia).

**M. Music Publications**

Carden, A. D. et al., *Western Harmony*
Nettleton, Asahel, *Village Hymns for Social Worship*

**N. Musical Compositions**

**Operas**   Micah Hawkins, *The Saw-Mill, or A Yankee Trick*.

**Orchestra/Band**   James Hemmenway, *Generall LaFayette's Trumpet March and Quick Step*; James Hewitt, *LaFayette's Quick Step in D Major*.

**Piano/Organ**   Benjamin Carr, *Six Canzonets, Opus 14, for Piano*; Oliver Shaw, *Welcome the Nation's Guest*; Joseph C. Taws, *Pennsylvania LaFayette March—Triumphal March of General LaFayette*; Charles Thibault, *Variations, L'espérance, Opus 8—Variations, La Bretonne, Opus 9— The Greek March of Liberty, Opus 10—LaFayette's Return (The Hero's Welcome), Opus 12*.

# 1825

❋

## Historical Highlights

The Erie Canal is opened for shipping; Congress sets out to move all Indians to reservations west of the Mississippi River; Omaha is founded as a fur trading post; New Harmony, Indiana, is founded; a patent is granted to T. Kensett for the tin can; Bolivia gains its independence.

## World Cultural Highlights

**World Art**   John Constable, *The Leaping Horse*; Jean-Baptiste Corot, *Homer on the Isle of Patmos*; Thomas Lawrence, *The Red Boy*; Friedrich Overbeck, *Madonna and Child*.

**World Literature**   Samuel Taylor Coleridge, *Aids to Reflection*; Alphonse de Lamartine, *Le Dernier Chant du Pèlerinage d'Harold*; Alexander Pushkin, *Boris Godounov*; Walter Scott, *The Talisman*.

**World Music**  Ludwig van Beethoven, *String Quartets No. 13, 15—Grosse Fuge*; François Boieldieu, *La Dame Blanche*; Luigi Cherubini, *Coronation Mass*; Felix Mendelssohn, *Concerto for Two Pianos*.

**Miscellaneous**  The Buffet-Crampon Woodwind Co. is founded in Paris; the Elíazaga Conservatory of Music opens in Mexico City; births include Thomas Huxley, Aleksei Plescheyev, and Johann Strauss, Jr.; deaths include Giuseppe Carpani, Jacques-Louis David, Henry Fuseli, and Jean-Paul Richter.

## American Art and Literature Highlights

**Births/Deaths**  Births include art figures Benjamin Akers, George Inness, John Jackson, William Rinehart, Richard Woodville, and literary figures Caroline Chesebro', William Falkner, Frances Ellen Harper, Mary Jane Holmes, Augustus J. Requier, and Richard H. Stoddard; deaths include artist Raphaelle Peale and author Mason Locke Weems.

**Art Works**  John James Audubon, *Wild Turkey*; John H. I. Browere, *James Madison, Age 74—Lafayette, Age 82*; Thomas Cole, *Lake with Dead Trees—Kaaterskill Falls*; Sarah Goodridge, *Gilbert Stuart*; Jeremiah Hardy, *Sarah Molasses*; Samuel F. B. Morse, *The Marquis de Lafayette*; Luigi Persico, *Bust of John Quincy Adams—The Genius of America*; Henry Sargent, *The Dinner Party*.

**Literature**  John G. Brainard, *Occasional Pieces of Poetry*; Lydia Maria Child, *The Rebels: or, Boston before the Revolution*; Nicholas Heutz, *Tadeuskund, the Last King of the Lenape*; James A. Jones, *The Refugee*; William Leggett, *Leisure Hours at Sea*; Edward C. Pinckney, *Rodolph and Other Poems*; William G. Simms, *Poems I*; Samuel Woodworth, *The Forest Rose: or, American Farmers*.

## Music

**F. Births**  Eliza Biscaccianti (soprano); George Frederick Bristow (organist/composer) December 19; Henry Stephen Cutler (organist) October 13; Felipe Gutiérrez (y) Espinosa (Puerto Rican composer) May 26; Master Juba Lane (performer/singer); Henry F. Miller (piano maker); John Wheeler Tufts (organist/educator) May 12; Horace Weston (folk banjoist).

**G. Deaths**  Amos Bull (singing master/composer) August; Micah Hawkins (composer) July 29; Elias Mann (composer/compiler) May 12; Raynor Taylor (British-born organist/composer) August 17.

**H. Debuts**

**United States**  Manuel Garcia (Spanish tenor—New York), Edward Kendall (Boston), Maria Malibran (Spanish mezzo-soprano—New York).

**K. Biographical**  Thomas Dodsworth (British dancing master) brings his four sons with him to New York; Manuel Garcia brings his opera troupe to New York and presents 80 performances of mostly Rossini and Mozart operas before moving on to Mexico City; John Hill Hewitt has his first songs published.

**L. Musical Beginnings**

**Educational**  Musical Fund Society Academy of Music (Philadelphia).

**Other**  James L. Hewitt, Music Publisher (with J. A. Dickson—Boston).

**M. Music Publications**

William Moore, *Columbian Harmony*

**N. Musical Compositions**

**Choral/Vocal**  James Hewitt, *The Minstrel's Return from the War* (?); Joseph C. Taws, *My Home*.

**Orchestra/Band**  James Hemmenway, *Washington Grays' Grand March* (?).

**Piano/Organ**  Julius Metz, *West Point March*; Peter K. Moran, *Variations on "Kinlock of Kinlock"*; Charles Thibault, *Three Waltzes, Opus 13*; Samuel Woolworth, *The Meeting of the Waters of Hudson and Erie*.

# 1826

❀

## Historical Highlights

Congress remains cool to the working of the Pan-American Conference meeting in Panama; a treaty of peace is signed with the Creek Indians; Kansas City is founded as a trading post on the Missouri River; Henry Ogle builds the first working reaper.

## World Cultural Highlights

**World Art**   William Blake, *Illustrations on Job*; Eugène Delacroix, *Greece on the Ruins of Missolonghi*; Francisco de Goya, *The Butcher's Table*; John Martin, *The Deluge*.

**World Literature**   Giovanni Casanova, *Memoirs*; Benjamin Disraeli, *Vivian Grey*; Joseph von Eichendorff, *Aus dem Leben eines Taugenichts*; Karl Nicander, *The Death of Tasso*.

**World Music**   Ludwig van Beethoven, *String Quartet No. 16*; Felix Mendelssohn, *Midsummer Night's Dream Overture*; Giaocchino Rossini, *The Siege of Corinth*; Carl Maria von Weber, *Oberon*.

**Miscellaneous**   The Berlin Philharmonic Society is formed; births include Silvestro Lega, Gustave Moreau, and Josef von Scheffel; deaths include Jens Baggesen, Johannes Falk, John Flaxman, Johann Peter Hebel, Siegfried Mahlmann, and Carl Maria von Weber.

## American Art and Literature Highlights

**Births/Deaths**   Births include artists William Babcock, Frederic E. Church, and literary figures Charles M. Barras, John William De Forest, Frank B. Goodrich, and Frances Fuller Victor; deaths include poets Paul Allen, William Crafts, and authors Joseph Doddridge, Francis W. Gilmer, and Royall Tyler.

**Art Works**   Thomas Cole, *Gelyna—Falls of the Kaaterskill*; Samuel F. B. Morse, *General Lafayette*; Alexander Parris, *Quincy Market* (Boston); William Strickland, *U.S. Naval Asylum, Philadelphia*; Gilbert Stuart, *John Adams*; John Trumbull, *Asher B. Durand*.

**Literature**   James Athearn, *Tales of an Indian Camp*; James F. Cooper, *The Last of the Mohicans*; Frederic S. Hill, *The Harvest Festival and Other Poems*; Abiel Holmes, *The Annals of America*; Henry W. Longfellow, *Poems I*; George P. Morris, *Brier Cliff*; James K. Paulding, *The Merry Tales of the Three Wise Men of Gotham*; Samuel Woodworth, *Melodies, Duets, Songs and Ballads*.

## Music

**F. Births**   Armand Edward Blackmar (teacher/publisher); Stephen C. Foster (composer) July 4; Jacob Kimball, Jr. (composer/educator) February 6; Robert Lowry (hymnwriter) March 12; William F. Sherwin (composer/educator) March 14; Henry Tucker (composer/tenor?).

**G. Deaths**   Elkanah K. Dare (theorist/composer); George Gillingham (British-born violinist/conductor) September 16; Jacob Kimball, Jr. (composer/educator) February 6; John Stickney (singer/composer).

**K. Biographical**   William Henry Fry enters the Mount St. Mary's School in Maryland; Anthony Philip Heinrich begins a five-year stay in Europe; James Hewitt undergoes an unsuccessful operation for facial cancer.

**L. Musical Beginnings**

**Performing Groups**   Salem Mozart Association (Massachusetts).

**Other**   Meneely and Co., Bell Foundry (New York).

**M. Music Publications**

*Hymns of the Protestant Episcopal Church of the United States*
Carr, Benjamin, *The Analytical Instructor*

Davisson, Ananias, *A Small Collection of Sacred Music*
Mason, Lowell, *Address on Church Music*
Palmer, J. W., *Western Harmonic Companion*
Woodworth, Samuel, *Melodies, Duets, Trios, Songs and Ballads*

**N. Musical Compositions**

**Choral/Vocal**   Anonymous, *The Erie Canal;* Charles Zeuner, *Missa Solemnis in C Minor.*

**Orchestra/Band**   James Hemmenway, *The Philadelphia Serenading Grand March (?)—The Philadelphia Hop Waltz (?).*

**Piano/Organ**   Christopher Meineke, *Piano Variations on "Araby's Daughter"—Piano Variations on Weber's "Hunter's Chorus" from "Der Freischütz"*; Peter K. Moran, *Variations on "Ah beauteous Maid"*; Charles Thibault, *Scherzo, Opus 15, on Three Themes from Rossini.*

# 1827

✸

## Historical Highlights

The Baltimore and Ohio becomes the first railroad to be chartered; the Cherokee Nation forms a constitutional government within the Georgia Territory; Fort Leavenworth, Kansas, is built to protect wagon trains on the Santa Fe Trail; Russia, France, and England enter the Greek-Turkish War against Turkey—the Turkish fleet is destroyed at the Battle of Navarino.

## World Cultural Highlights

**World Art**   Jean-Baptiste Corot, *The Bridge at Narni*; Jean-Auguste Ingres, *Apotheosis of Homer*; John Martin, *Milton's Paradise Lost*; François Rude, *Neapolitan Fisher Boy.*

**World Literature**   Charles Forrester, *Absurdities in Prose and Verse*; Heinrich Heine, *Buch der Lieder*; Victor Hugo, *Cromwell*; John Keble, *The Christian Year*; Thomas More, *The Epicurean.*

**World Music**   Hector Berlioz, *La Mort d'Orphée*; Frédéric Chopin, *Nocturne and Funeral March, Opus 72*; Gioacchino Rossini, *Moïse*; Franz Schubert, *Die Winterreise—Deutsche Messe.*

**Miscellaneous**   The Christiania National Theater opens in Oslo; births include Arnold Böcklin, Jules Breton, Jean-Baptiste Carpeaux, and William Hunt; deaths include Ludwig van Beethoven, William Blake, Ugo Foscolo, Wilhelm Müller, and Thomas Rowlandson.

## American Art and Literature Highlights

**Births/Deaths**   Births include artist John W. Ehninger, sculptor Alexander Galt, and literary figures Ethel Lynn Beers, Maria S. Cummins, Francis Miles Finch, John R. Ridge, Lewis Wallace, and Anna B. Warner (Amy Lothrop); deaths include artists Matthew Jouett, Charles W. Peale, and poets St. George Tucker and Carlos Wilcox.

**Art Works**   Thomas Cole, *Scene, "The Last of the Mohicans"—View in the White Mountains of New Hampshire*; Robert Mills, *South Carolina Historical Society Building*; John Neagle, *Pat Lyon at the Forge I*; Rembrandt Peale, *George Washington* (lithograph); John Vanderlyn, *View of Niagara Falls.*

**Literature**   James F. Cooper, *The Prairie—The Red Rover*; Richard H. Dana, Sr., *The Buccaneer and Other Poems*; Sumner L. Fairfield, *The Cities of the Plain*; Samuel G. Goodrich, *The Tales of Peter Parley about America*; Fitz-Greene Halleck, *Alnwick Castle with Other Poems*; William G. Simms, *Lyrical and Other Poems*; St. George Tucker, *Poems, 1752–1827*; Sarah Wood, *Tales of the Night.*

## Music

**F. Births**   Ellsworth Phelps (organist) August 11; Caroline Richings (soprano/pianist); Lucien H. Southard (composer) February 4; Marcus Lafayette Swan (composer/hymnist); Septimus Winner (composer/publisher) May 11.

**G. Deaths**    James Hewitt (British-born composer/conductor) August 2.

**H. Debuts**

**United States**    Elizabeth Austin (British soprano—Philadelphia), Charles Edward Horn (British composer/singer—New York).

**I. New Positions**

**Conductors**    John O. Curvillier (US Marine Band—to 1829).

**Other**    Lowell Mason (president, Boston Handel and Haydn Society—to 1832).

**K. Biographical**    Charles Edward Horn (British composer/singer—born 1784) makes his first visit to New York and decides to stay; Stephen Jenks moves to Ohio; Lowell Mason moves to Boston and begins supervision of church music; Philadelphia and New York get their first authentic French opera in a visit by an opera group from New Orleans.

**L. Musical Beginnings**

**Performing Groups**    Choral Society of Hartford; Portland Band (Maine).

**Other**    Bowery Theater (New York); Firth and Hall (John Firth joined by Hall and Sylvanus Pond, maker of pianos at the Meacham Factory); Hook and Hastings, Organ Builders (Salem, Massachusetts); Tremont Theater (Boston).

**M. Music Publications**

Hastings, Thomas, *The Juvenile Psalmody*

**N. Musical Compositions**

**Choral/Vocal**    G. W. Dixon, *Long Tail Blue* (song).

**Orchestra/Band**    James Hemmenway, *The New Year and Courtsy Cotillions.*

**Piano/Organ**    Christopher Meineke, *Piano Variations on "Brignal Banks"—Piano Variations on "Au clair de la lune"—Piano Variations on "My Heart and Lute."*

# 1828

☀

## Historical Highlights

Andrew Jackson is the first president from the Democratic Party; the "spoils system" is introduced into the White House; the so-called Tariff of Abominations is passed; the B & O Railroad begins horse-drawn rail service; ground-breaking ceremonies mark the beginning of the Chesapeake and Ohio Canal; Great Britain repeals laws forbidding Catholics and Nonconformists to hold office.

## World Cultural Highlights

**World Art**    Vincenzo Camuccini, *Judith*; John Constable, *Hadleigh Castle*; Charles Eastlake, *Pilgrims in Sight of Rome*; John Martin, *The Fall of Nineveh*; Bertel Thorvaldsen, *Amor and Anacreon.*

**World Literature**    Edward Bulwer-Lytton, *Pelham*; Robert Gilfillan, *Peter M'Craw*; Charles Lamb, *The Wife's Trial*; Jean Reboul, *L'Ange et l'Enfant*; Walter Scott, *The Fair Maid of Perth.*

**World Music**    Hector Berlioz, *Overtures, Waverley—Les Francs Juges*; Heinrich Marschner, *Der Vampyr*; Franz Schubert, *Symphony No. 9—Der Hirt auf dem Felsen*; Ludwig Spohr, *Symphony No. 3.*

**Miscellaneous**    The Bösendorfer Piano Co. is founded in Vienna; Brno Music Institute opens; births include Henrik Ibsen, George Meredith, Dante Rossetti, Leo Tolstoy, and Jules Verne; deaths include Richard Bonington, Francisco de Goya, Jean-Antoine Houdon, and Franz Schubert.

## American Art and Literature Highlights

**Births/Deaths**    Births include art figures William M. Brown, Jervis McEntee, Leonard Volk,

Charles Wimar, and literary figures Oliver Bell Bunce, Martha Finley (Farquharson), Henry Timrod, and Theodore Winthrop; deaths include artist Gilbert Stuart and poets John G. Brainard and Edward Pinkney.

**Art Works**    Thomas Cole, *Landscape with Tree Trunks—Expulsion from the Garden of Eden*; William Sydney Mount, *Self-Portrait with Flute*; John Neagle, *William Strickland*; Margaretta A. Peale, *Still Life*; Rembrandt Peale, *Self-Portrait*; John Quidor, *Ichabod Crane Pursued by the Headless Horseman—The Young Artist*; William Rush, *Schuylkill River Chained—Schuylkill River Freed*.

**Literature**    Robert M. Bird, *The City Looking Glass*; James F. Cooper, *Notions of the Americans*; Timothy Flint, *The Life and Adventures of Arthur Clenning*; Nathaniel Hawthorne, *Fanshawe*; Washington Irving, *The Life and Voyages of Christopher Columbus*; Grenville Mellen, *Sad Tales and Glad Tales*; Susanna Rowson, *Charlotte's Daughter*; Margaret B. Smith, *What is Gentility?*

## Music

**F. Births**    Matthew Arbuckle (cornettist/bandmaster); Asa B. Everett (composer/compiler); J. C. D. Parker (composer/organist) June 2; George William Warren (organist/composer) August 17.

**K. Biographical**    Léopold Meignen (French composer/publisher) comes to the United States and settles in Philadelphia.

**L. Musical Beginnings**

**Performing Groups**    Portland Handel and Haydn Society (Maine—to 1831).

**Other**    New York Musical Fund Society; *Theatrical Censor and Musical Review*.

**N. Musical Compositions**

**Choral/Vocal**    Charles E. Horn, *Ode to Washington*; Filippo Traetta, *Jerusalem in Affliction* (oratorio).

**Orchestra/Band**    Alexander Reinagle, *America, Commerce and Freedom* (played at groundbreaking ceremony of the Chesapeake and Ohio Canal).

**Piano/Organ**    Christopher Meineke, *Piano Variations on "Le petit tambour"—Piano Variations on Mozart's "Non più andrai" from "Le nozze di Figaro"—The Rail Road March*; Charles Thibault, *Rondo, Les charmes de New York, Opus 19*.

# 1829

☀

## Historical Highlights

The *Tom Thumb*, first steam locomotive in the New World, begins operation; the Working Man's Party is founded; Andrew Jackson invents the "Kitchen Cabinet"; the Tremont House, first modern hotel, opens in Boston; Russia and Turkey sign the Peace of Adrianople; Greece becomes an independent republic; Louis Braille invents the Braille System for the blind.

## World Cultural Highlights

**World Art**    John Constable, *Salisbury Cathedral from the Meadows*; Eugène Delacroix, *Death of Sardanapalus*; Edwin Landseer, *High Life, Low Life*; Joseph Turner, *Ulysses Deriding Polyphemus*.

**World Literature**    Johann Wolfgang von Goethe, *Wilhelm Meisters Wanderjahre*; Victor Hugo, *Les Orientales*; Alfred de Musset, *Tales of Spain and Italy*; Alfred Lord Tennyson, *Timbuctoo*.

**World Music**    Hector Berlioz, *Cléopâtre*; Felix Mendelssohn, *"Trumpet" Overture—String Quartet No. 1*; Gioacchino Rossini, *William Tell*; Robert Schumann, *Piano Quartet in C Minor*.

**Miscellaneous**    Mendelssohn conducts the *St. Matthew Passion*, initiating a new interest in the music of Johann Sebastian Bach; births include Anselm Feuerbach, Johan Malmström, and John Everett Millais; deaths include Wojciech Boguslawski, Karl von Schlegel, and Johann H. Tischbein, Jr.

## American Art and Literature Highlights

**Births/Deaths**   Births include artists Albert Bellows, Robert Dunning, Marie Hart, Benjamin Reinhardt, and literary figures Philander Deming, Hinton Rowan Helper, Silas Weir Mitchell, Edna Dean Proctor, and Charles Dudley Warner (man of letters).

**Art Works**   William Bartlett, *The Battery and Harbor, New York*; Thomas Birch, *Shipwreck*; Thomas Cole, *Subsiding of the Waters of the Deluge*; Alvan Fisher, *Corn Husking Frolic*; Horatio Greenough, *Chanting Cherubs*; Samuel F. B. Morse, *Pat Lyon at the Forge II*; John Quidor, *The Return of Rip Van Winkle*; Robert W. Weir, *Seneca Chief Red Jacket*.

**Literature**   James F. Cooper, *The Wept of Wish-ton-Wish*; Thomas Dring, *Recollections of the Jersey Prison-Ship*; James A. Jones, *Tales of an Indian Camp*; William Leggett, *Tales and Sketches, by a Country Schoolmaster*; Edgar Allen Poe, *Al Aaraaf, Tamerlane, and Minor Poems*; John A. Stone, *Metamora, or the Last of the Wampanoags*; Nathaniel Willis, *Fugitive Poetry*.

## Music

**F. Births**   Patrick Gilmore (bandmaster/composer) December 25; Louis Moreau Gottschalk (pianist/composer) May 8; William G. Mason (composer/pianist) January 24; Harrison Millard (composer) September 10; Charles A. White (composer/publisher) March 20.

**G. Deaths**   Charles H. Gilfert (Czech-born composer/publisher) July 30; Abraham Maxim (hymnwriter); Edward Riley (British-born publisher).

**I. New Positions**

**Conductors**   Joseph Cuvillier (US Marine Band—to 1835).

**K. Biographical**   Stephen Jenks leaves music and takes up farming in Ohio; first musical convention held by the Central Musical Society of New Hampshire.

**L. Musical Beginnings**

**Other**   Asa Hopkins, Woodwind Maker (Litchfield, Connecticut); Conrad Meyer, Piano Maker (Philadelphia); Chabrier Peloubet, Woodwind Maker (New York); W. C. Peters Music Store (Louisville); George Willig, Jr., Publishing Co. (Baltimore).

**M. Music Publications**

Carden, Allen D., *United States Harmony*
Cole, J., *Union Harmony*
Mason, Lowell, *The Juvenile Psalmist*
Scott, Orange, *New and Improved Camp-Meeting Hymn Book*
Traetta, Filippo, *Introduction to the Art and Science of Music—Rudiments of Art and Singing I*

**N. Musical Compositions**

**Choral/Vocal**   Anonymous, *Coal Black Rose*; Filippo Traetta, *The Daughters of Zion* (oratorio).

**Operas**   Charles E. Horn, *The Quartette, or Interrupted Harmony*.

**Piano/Organ**   Christopher Meineke, *Piano Variations on "Malbrouk"—Grand National March for General Andrew Jackson*.

# 1830

☀

## Historical Highlights

The US population reaches 12,866,000; the Webster-Haynes debates question the subject of States's rights; a patent is given for the fountain pen; the Mexican government forbids any further colonization of Texas by US citizens; the July Revolution occurs in France and Louis Philippe replaces Charles X; Ecuador and Venezuela gain their freedom in Latin America.

## World Cultural Highlights

**World Art**  Eugène Delacroix, *Liberty Guiding the People*; François Gérard, *Pantheon Ceiling* (Paris); Samuel Palmer, *Coming from Evening Church*; Joseph Turner, *Old Chain Pier at Brighton*.

**World Literature**  Adelbert von Chamisso, *Frauenliebe und Leben*; Théophile Gautier, *Premières Poésies*; Victor Hugo, *Hernani*; Alphonse de Lamartine, *Harmonies Poétiques et Religieuses*.

**World Music**  Hector Berlioz, *Fantastic Symphony*; Frédéric Chopin, *Piano Concertos 1, 2*; Gaetano Donizetti, *Anna Bolena*; Felix Mendelssohn, *Hebrides Overture*; Robert Schumann, *Abegg Variations*.

**Miscellaneous**  The Royal Conservatory of Music opens in Madrid; Chopin leaves Poland, never to return; births include Jules Alfred de Goncourt, Paul von Heyse, Frédéric Mistral, Camille Pissarro, and Christina Rosetti; deaths include Benjamin Constant, William Hazlitt, and Johann von Müller.

## American Art and Literature Highlights

**Births/Deaths**  Births include art figures Albert Bierstadt, William Hays, Harriet Hosmer, John Q. A. Ward, and literary figures George L. Aiken, John Esten Cooke, Emily Dickinson, Paul Hamilton Hayne, Helen Hunt Jackson, and Mary V. Terhune (Marion Harland); deaths include author Mason Cogswell and playwright William Ioor.

**Art Works**  Hezekiah Augur, *Jephthah and His Daughter*; Thomas Birch, *Skating*; George Catlin, *Goes Up the River, Aged Chief*; Thomas Doughty, *The Raft*; Asher B. Durand, *American Landscape Series*; Edward Hicks, *The Peaceable Kingdom of the Branch*; Charles B. King, *Vanity of the Artist's Dream*; William S. Mount, *A Rustic Dance after a Sleigh Ride*; William Rimmer, *Despair, Seated Youth* (?).

**Literature**  John G. Brainard, *Fugitive Tales*; James F. Cooper, *The Water Witch*; William Dunlap, *A Trip to Niagara: or, Travellers in America*; Joseph P. Martin, *A Narrative . . . of a Revolutionary Soldier*; James K. Paulding, *The Lion of the West*; Catharine M. Sedgwick, *Clarence*; William J. Snelling, *Tales of the Northwest: or, Sketches of Indian Life. . . .*

## Music

**F. Births**  Clara M. Brinkerhoff (soprano?); Benjamin Franklin Quinby (brass instrument maker) July 3; John P. Thomas (songwriter).

**G. Deaths**  Richard Willis (Irish-born bandmaster/cornetist) February 1.

**I. New Positions**

**Other**  Samuel P. Jackson (organ, St. Clement's, New York—to 1842); George Webb (organ, Old South Church, Boston).

**K. Biographical**  Joel Sweeney invents the five-string banjo; George James Webb (British composer/educator) emigrates to the United States and settles in Boston; Charles Zeuner (German organist) comes to the United States (?) and also settles in Boston.

**L. Musical Beginnings**

**Performing Groups**  Buffalo Philharmonic Society I; Newark Harmonic Society.

**Other**  Samuel Graves and Co., Instrument Makers (Winchester, New Hampshire); Paul Emile Johns, Music Publisher and Store (New Orleans).

**M. Music Publications**

Greenwood, Francis, *A Collection of Psalms and Hymns for Sacred Worship*
Hastings, Thomas, *The Union Minstrel*
Mason, Lowell, *Choral Harmony*
Taylor, Samuel P., *Practical School for the Organ*

### N. Musical Compositions

**Choral/Vocal**    Anonymous, *Cape Cod Girls* (sea chantey)—*Old Rosin the Beau* (?); Benjamin Carr, *Sacred Airs, Opus 16*; Charles Zeuner, *Mass in E-flat Major*.

**Concertos**    Charles Zeuner, *Organ Concerto No. 1*.

**Piano/Organ**    Peter K. Moran, *National Guards March and Rondo*.

# 1831

❀

## Historical Highlights

Turner's Rebellion results in 50 deaths in Virginia; William Garrison's *The Liberator* begins publication; South Bend, Indiana, is founded; New York University is chartered; flanged railroad track is introduced; former president James Monroe dies; Russian troops crush the Polish Insurrection; Charles Darwin begins his five-year voyage on the *HMS Beagle*.

## World Cultural Highlights

**World Art**    Jean-Baptiste Corot, *The Quarry of La Chaise à Marie*; Alexandre Decamps, *The Turkish Patrol*; Eugéne Delacroix, *The Battle of Nancy*; Robert Lauder, *The Bride of Lammermoor*.

**World Literature**    Johann Wolfgang von Goethe, *Faust II*; Nicolai Gogol, *Evenings on a Farm I*; Franz Grillparzer, *Hero and Leander*; Victor Hugo, *Notre Dame de Paris*.

**World Music**    Vincenzo Bellini, *Norma*; Hector Berlioz, *Overtures, King Lear—Le Corsaire*; Felix Mendelssohn, *Piano Concerto No. 1*; Giacomo Meyerbeer, *Robert le Diable*; Robert Schumann, *Papillons*.

**Miscellaneous**    The Dublin Music Festivals begin; births include Jean Falguière, Joseph Joachim, Constantin Meunier, Wilhelm Raabe, and Victorien Sardou; deaths include Achim von Arnim, Willem Bilderdijk, Friedrich von Klinger, and Henry Mackenzie.

## American Art and Literature Highlights

**Births/Deaths**    Births include art figures Enoch Perry, Jr., Charles Ward, and literary figures Jane Goodwin Austin, Mary Elizabeth Dodge, Amanda Douglas, Nora Perry, and Metta Victoria Victor; deaths include artists Mather Brown, James Peale, author Hannah Adams, and poet John Trumbull.

**Art Works**    Washington Allston, *The Spanish Girl—Roman Lady Reading*; George Catlin, *Great Chief—One Sitting in the Clouds, a Boy*; Thomas Cole, *A Wild Scene*; Alvin Fisher, *Niagara Falls*; John Frazee, *John Jay*; Horatio Greenough, *Bust, Samuel F. B. Morse*; George R. Pain, *The Castle of Otranto*.

**Literature**    Delia S. Bacon, *Tales of the Puritans*; Robert M. Bird, *The Gladiator*; James F. Cooper, *The Bravo*; Washington Irving, *Voyages of the Companions of Columbus*; James McHenry, *Meredith*; James K. Paulding, *The Dutchman's Fireside*; Richard P. Smith, *Caius Marius*; John A. Stone, *The Demoniac: or, the Prophet's Bride*; John G. Whittier, *Legends of New England*.

## Music

**F. Births**    William Oscar Perkins (singer/composer) June 2.

**G. Deaths**    Richard Allen (compiler) March 26; Benjamin Carr (British-born composer/publisher) May 24; Benjamin Crehore (instrument maker) October 14; Peter K. Moran (Irish-born composer/pianist) February 10; J. George Schetky (cellist/publisher) December 11; Isaiah Thomas (publisher) April 4; Jacob Van Vleck (Moravian violinist/organist) July 3.

**K. Biographical**    Congress revises the Copyright Act making mention of music for the first time; Ureli Corelli Hill conducts the first full performance of Handel's *Messiah* in New York, complete with orchestral accompaniment; Charles Maximilian Stieff (German piano maker) emigrates to the United States and settles in Pennsylvania; Philip P. Werlein (German dealer and publisher) emigrates to the United States and settles in Vicksburg, Mississippi.

**L. Musical Beginnings**

**Performing Groups**   Newark Handel and Haydn Society.

**M. Music Publications**

Carrell, J. and Clayton, D., *The Virginia Harmony*
Hastings, T. and Mason, L., *Spiritual Songs for Social Worship*
Leavitt, Joshua, *The Christian Lyre—Supplement to The Christian Lyre*
Mason, L. and Green, D., *Manual of Christian Psalmody—The Juvenile Lyre*
Seat, J. B., *St. Louis Harmony*
Shaw, Oliver, *Oliver Shaw's Instructions for the Pianoforte*
Zeuner, Charles, *Church Music*

**N. Musical Compositions**

**Concertos**   Charles Zeuner, *Organ Concerto No. 2*.

**Orchestra/Band**   Anthony P. Heinrich, *Pushmataha—A Venerable Chief of a Western Tribe of Indians* (orchestral fantasy).

**Symphonies**   W. C. Peters, *Symphony in D Major*.

# 1832

✿

## Historical Highlights

Andrew Jackson is re-elected president and vetoes the National Bank Reform Bill; the Black Hawk War with the Indians takes place in Wisconsin; the *Ann McKim*, the first clipper ship, is launched; cities founded include Tulsa, Oklahoma, Toledo, Ohio, and Buffalo, New York; a major cholera epidemic sweeps the United States and the world.

## World Cultural Highlights

**World Art**   John Constable, *Waterloo Bridge*; Bertel Thorvaldsen, *Artist with the Statue of Hope*; Joseph Turner, *Childe Harold's Pilgrimage*; David Wilkie, *The Preaching of Knox*.

**World Literature**   Honoré de Balzac, *Louis Lambert*; Fanny Burney, *Memoirs of Doctor Burney*; Victor Hugo, *Le Roi s'Amuse*; Walter Scott, *Castle Dangerous*; Alfred Lord Tennyson, *Poems II*.

**World Music**   Hector Berlioz, *Les Nuits d'Été*; Frédéric Chopin, *Twelve Etudes, Opus 10*; Gaetano Donizetti, *L'Elisir d'amore*; Felix Mendelssohn, *Reformation Symphony*; Richard Wagner, *Symphony*.

**Miscellaneous**   The Brussels State Academy of Music is founded; births include Lewis Carroll, Gustave Doré, Édouard Manet, William Orchardson, and Theodore Watts-Dunton; deaths include Muzio Clementi, George Crabbe, Johann Wolfgang von Goethe, and Walter Scott.

## American Art and Literature Highlights

**Births/Deaths**   Births include artists Samuel Colman, Jr., Aaron Shattuck and literary figures Louisa May Alcott, Horatio Alger, Jr., Moncure D. Conway, and Fanny Herring; deaths include artist Amos Doolittle and poets Philip M. Freneau and Robert Sands.

**Art Works**   William J. Bennett, *Boston, from City Point Near Sea Street*; George Catlin, *Bird's Eye View of the Mandan Village*; Thomas Cole, *Salvator Rosa Sketching Banditti*; Horatio Greenough, *George Washington*; John Quidor, *The Money Diggers—Leatherstocking Meets the Law*; John Trumbull, *The Declaration of Independence III* (Wadsworth).

**Literature**   Robert M. Bird, *Oralloosa*; William C. Bryant, *Poems*; Lydia Maria Child, *An Appeal in Favor of That Class of Americans Called Africans*; James F. Cooper, *The Heidenmauer*; S. E. Glover, *The Cradle of Liberty: or Boston in 1775*; Caroline Lee Hentz, *Werdenberg*; Washington Irving, *The Alhambra*; John P. Kennedy, *Swallow Barn*; James K. Paulding, *Westward Ho!*

# Music

**F. Births**   Charles Converse (hymn writer) October 7; William H. Doane (hymn composer/compiler) February 3; John F. Stratton (instrument maker and dealer) September 14; Clark J. Whitney (publisher/dealer/impresario) July 12; Henry Clay Work (composer) October 1.

**G. Deaths**   Arthur Clifton (Scottish-born pianist/composer) February 19; Ishmail Spicer (composer/educator) December 22; John F. Stratton (bandmaster/publisher).

**H. Debuts**

**United States**   Luciano Fornasari (Italian bass—New York), Miss Hughes (British soprano—New York).

**K. Biographical**   John Sullivan Dwight graduates from Harvard but continues study for the ministry; Thomas Hastings moves to New York and joins Lowell Mason at the Normal Institute; Anthony Heinrich returns again to the United States and settles this time in Boston; Charles Edward Horn (British conductor/composer) returns permanently to New York as conductor at the Park Theater; Montressor's Italian Opera group lasts only one season in New York.

**L. Musical Beginnings**

**Performing Groups**   Dodsworth Brass Band (New York); New Haven Musical Society (Connecticut).

**Educational**   Boston Academy of Music.

**Other**   San Juan Municipal Theater (Puerto Rico).

**M. Music Publications**

Funk, Joseph, *A Compilation of Genuine Church Music*
Gould, Nathaniel, *National Church Harmony*
James, Uriah and Joseph, *The Aeolian Songster*
Mason, Lowell, *Lyra Sacra—The Choir: or, Union Collection of Church Music—Manual of Christian Harmony*
Read, Daniel, *Musica Ecclesia* (unpublished)
Zeuner, Charles, *The American Harp*

**N. Musical Compositions**

**Choral/Vocal**   Anonymous, *Clare de Kitchen*; Charles Zeuner, *The Feast of Tabernacles* (oratorio).

**Operas**   Charles E. Horn, *Nadir and Zuleika*.

# 1833

☀

## Historical Highlights

President Jackson takes all public funds out of the Bank of the United States; the American Anti-Slavery Society is founded in New England; Oberlin College becomes the first coed institution in the country; Chicago, Illinois, is incorporated; Great Britain bans slavery throughout its empire; the Ottoman empire, in order to avoid an Egyptian takeover, signs a treaty with Russia.

## World Cultural Highlights

**World Art**   Antoine Etex, *Cain Cursed by God*; Thomas Sully, *Fanny Kemble as Beatrice*; Joseph Turner, *Music at Petworth*; Richard Westmacott, *The Duke of York*.

**World Literature**　Marguerite Blessington, *Grace Cassidy*; Thomas Carlyle, *Sartor Resartus*; Charles Lamb, *Last Essays of Elia*; Charles Lyell, *Principles of Geology*; George Sand, *Lelia*.

**World Music**　Frédéric Chopin, *Four Mazurkas, Opus 17*; Heinrich Marschner, *Hans Heiling*; Felix Mendelssohn, *Italian Symphony—Beautiful Melusine Overture*; Richard Wagner, *Die Feen*.

**Miscellaneous**　The Kiev Philharmonic Society and the Warsaw Grand Opera are founded; François Fétis publishes Volume I of his *Universal Biography of Musicians and Music*; births include Pedro de Alarcón, Alexander Borodin, Johannes Brahms, Edward Burne-Jones, Henri Chapu, and Launt Thompson; deaths include Charles Chenedollé, Pierre-Narcisse Guérin, and Ferdinand Hérold.

## American Art and Literature Highlights

**Births/Deaths**　Births include art figures Charles Calverley, William Dana, Elizabet Ney, and William T. Richards and literary figures Mary Abigail Dodge (Gail Hamilton), David Ross Locke (Petroleum V. Nasby), and Edmund Clarence Stedman; deaths include sculptor William Rush.

**Art Works**　George Catlin, *The Dying Buffalo*; Thomas Cole, *The Titan's Goblet—Manfred*; Thomas Doughty, *Mill Pond and Mills in Lowell—Landscape with Stream and Mountains*; Horatio Greenough, *Saint John and the Angel*; Samuel F. B. Morse, *The Exhibition Gallery of the Louvre*; John Quidor, *The Wall Street Gate*; William Strickland, *U.S. Naval Home, Philadelphia*.

**Literature**　*Autobiography of Black Hawk*; Richard H. Dana, Sr., *Poems II*; Asa Greene, *Life and Adventures of Dr. Dodimus Duckworth, A.N.Q.*; Grenville Mellen, *The Martyr's Triumph and Other Poems*; Penina Moïse, *Fancy's Sketch Book*; John Neal, *The Down-Easters*; Seba Smith, *Life and Writings of Major Jack Downing of Downingville*; John G. Whittier, *Justice and Expediency*.

## Music

**F. Births**　Henry Clay Barnabee (actor/bass-baritone) November 14 (?); Daniel Bryant (minstrel performer); Benjamin Russel Hanby (composer) July 22; Henry S. Perkins (educator/composer) March 20; Adelaide Phillips (contralto); Grenville Dean Wilson (composer) January 26.

**G. Deaths**　William Marcellus Goodrich (organ builder) September 15; Joel Harmon, Jr. (educator/compiler); Charles Taws (Scottish-born piano and organ maker?); Thomas V. Wiesenthal (composer) March 21.

**H. Debuts**

United States: Mary Anne Paton (Scottish soprano—New York), Joseph Wood (British tenor—New York).

**K. Biographical**　William Knabe (German piano maker) emigrates to the United States and settles in Baltimore; the Montressor Company presents authentic Italian opera in Philadelphia; Italian impresario Rivafinoli tries another unsuccessful venture into Italian opera in New York.

**L. Musical Beginnings**

**Performing Groups**　Boston Academy Orchestra.

**Festivals**　Cincinnati Music Festival.

**Other**　Italian Opera House (New York); C. J. Martin and Co., Guitar Makers (New York); Henry Pilcher, Organ Builder (and Sons, 1856—Newark, New Jersey).

**M. Music Publications**

Bryan, Samuel J., *A Plain and Easy Catechism . . . with several verses and hymns*
Leavitt, Joshua, *Companion to the Christian Lyre*
Mason, Lowell, *Sabbath School Songs—Sacred Melodies* (with G. Webb)
Moore, Henry E., *Merrimack Collection of Instrumental and Martial Musick*
Zeuner, Charles, *The Ancient Lyre—The New Village Harmony: A Musical Manual for Sabbath Schools*

**N. Musical Compositions**

**Choral/Vocal**　Thomas H. Bayly, *Long, Long Ago* (song).

# 1834

☀

## Historical Highlights

The Whig Party is formed by anti-Jackson forces; the Anti-Abolitionist Riots take place in the Northern states; the first practical reaper is patented by Cyrus McCormick; the University of Louisville (Kentucky) is founded; Brooklyn, New York, is chartered; several German states take the first step toward unity with the formation of the Zollverein.

## World Cultural Highlights

**World Art**   Alexandre Decamps, *Defeat of the Cimbri*; Eugène Delacroix, *The Women of Algiers*; Joseph Turner, *The Burning of Parliament*; Emil Wolff, *Hebe and Ganymed*.

**World Literature**   Honoré de Balzac, *Le Père Goriot*; Edward Bulwer-Lytton, *The Last Days of Pompeii*; Alexander Pushkin, *The Queen of Spades*; Charles Sainte-Beuve, *Volupté*.

**World Music**   Hector Berlioz, *Harold in Italy*; Felix Mendelssohn, *Songs Without Words, Opus 19*; Niccolò Paganini, *Viola Concerto*; Robert Schumann, *Etudes Symphoniques*; Lady Jane Scott, *Annie Laurie*.

**Miscellaneous**   The Stuttgart Congress of Physicists decide on 440 vps for the tone "A" in the treble clef; births include Frédéric Bartholdi, Edgar Degas, Jan Neruda, and Amilcare Ponchielli; deaths include François Boieldieu, Samuel Taylor Coleridge, and Charles Lamb.

## American Art and Literature Highlights

**Births/Deaths**   Births include artist James M. Whistler and literary figures Charles F. Browne (Artemus Ward), Richard Realf, Frank R. Stockton, and George Upton; deaths include sculptor John H. I. Browere, artist Eliab Metcalf, and dramatist John A. Stone.

**Art Works**   George L. Brown, *Leatherstocking Kills the Panther*; George Catlin, *Little Spaniard, a Warrior*; Thomas Doughty, *The Anglers*; Robert B. Hughes, *John Trumbull*; Henry Inman, *Self-Portrait*; William Page, *The Young Merchants* (?); Ammi Phillips, *The Boy in Red*.

**Literature**   William A. Caruthers, *The Kentuckian in New York*; Caroline Gilman, *Recollections of a New England House-Keeper*; Albert Pike, *Prose Sketches and Poems, Written in the Western Country*; Susan R. Sedgwick, *Allen Prescott*; Seba Smith, *Select Letters of Major Jack Downing*; William L. Stone, *Tales and Sketches I, II*; Phillis Wheatley, *Memoir and Poems of Phillis Wheatley*.

## Music

**F. Births**   Charles R. Adams (tenor) February 9; Hart P. Danks (composer/conductor) April 6; Henry Lee Higginson (patron of the arts) November 18; Horatio R. Palmer (composer/educator) April 26; Philip Phillips (hymn singer/composer) August 13; Eben Tourjée (organist/conductor, educator) June 1; George P. Upton (music critic/author) October 25.

**G. Deaths**   François Mallet (French-born educator/composer).

**K. Biographical**   Alfred Badger, flute maker, is apprenticed to Ball and Douglas; Henry Russell (British singer/songwriter) begins an eight-year stay in Canada and the United States.

**L. Musical Beginnings**

**Performing Groups**   Mozart Sacred Society (Newark).

**Educational**   Wyeth Music School (Chicago—first known).

**Other**   Nathan Brainard Music Store (Cleveland); William E. Millett and Sons, Music Store and Publisher (New York).

**M. Music Publications**

Mason, Lowell, *Manual of the Boston Academy of Music*

Mason, Lowell, and Babcock, R., Jr., *Union Hymns*
Mason, Timothy B., *The Ohio Sacred Harp*
Merrill, A. and Brown, W.C., *The Wesleyan Harp*
Porter, William, *The Musical Cyclopedia*

**N. Musical Compositions**

**Choral/Vocal**   Anonymous, *Zip Coon (Turkey in the Straw)*.

**Concertos**   Anthony P. Heinrich, *Concerto for the Kent Bugle*.

**Orchestra/Band**   Anthony P. Heinrich, *Treaty of William Penn with the Indians* (concerto grosso)—*The Tower of Babel, or The Languages Confounded*—*Schiller*—*The Indian War Council*—*Complaint of Logan the Mingo Chief*—*The Mocking Bird to the Nightingale*.

**Piano/Organ**   Christopher Meineke, *Funeral March for General Lafayette*; Charles Thibault, *Variations, Le tournoi, Opus 24*.

# 1835

❀

## Historical Highlights

An assassin's gun misfires and Andrew Jackson's life is spared; the Liberty Bell cracks during Justice Marshall's funeral; the Second Seminole War is fought in Florida; the revolver is patented by Samuel Colt; Philadelphia passes the first 10-hour labor law; the Texas Revolution against the Mexicans begins; Halley's Comet makes its scheduled appearance.

## World Cultural Highlights

**World Art**   John Constable, *The Valley Farm*; Jean-Baptiste Corot, *Hagar in the Desert*; Wilhelm von Kaulbach, *The Battle of the Huns*; Antoine-Auguste Préault, *Slaughter*.

**World Literature**   Hans Christian Andersen, *Fairy Tales for Children I*; Georg Büchner, *Dantons Tod*; Nikolai Gogol, *Taras Bulba*; Alfred de Musset, *Lorenzaccio*.

**World Music**   Vincenzo Bellini, *I puritani*; Gaetano Donizetti, *Lucia di Lammermoor*; Robert Schumann, *Carnaval*; Richard Wagner, *Das Liebesverbot* —*Columbus Overture*.

**Miscellaneous**   Music Conservatories open in Geneva, Ghent, Lisbon, and Metz; births include Giosuè Carducci, Vitezslav Hálek, and Camille Saint-Saëns; deaths include Vincenzo Bellini, Kazimierz Brodzinski, Antoine-Jean Gros, August Platen, and William Motherwell.

## American Art and Literature Highlights

**Births/Deaths**   Births include art figures Stanley Haseltine, John La Farge, Larkin Mead, and literary figures Samuel L. Clemens (Mark Twain), Augusta Jane Evans, Harriet E. Spofford, William O. Stoddard, and Celia Thaxter; deaths include artist Simon Fitch and poet Henry Knight.

**Art Works**   Washington Allston, *The Evening Hymn*; George Catlin, *Ball Play of the Women, Prairie du Chien*; Thomas Cole, *The Tornado*; Thomas Doughty, *In Nature's Wonderland*; Asher B. Durand, *Wrath of Peter Stuyvesant*; Thomas Eakins, *The Swimming Hole*; Samuel F. B. Morse, *Niagara Falls from Table Rock*; William Mount, *Bargaining for a Horse*.

**Literature**   Robert M. Bird, *The Hawks of Hawk-Hollow*; Joseph R. Drake, *The Culprit Fay and Other Poems*; William D. Gallagher, *Erato I, II*; Charles F. Hoffman, *A Winter in the West*; Washington Irving, *A Tour of the Prairies*; Cornelius A. Logan, *The Wag of Maine*; A. B. Longstreet, *Georgia Scenes, Characters and Incidents*; William G. Simms, *The Yemassee*.

## Music

**F. Births**   Andrew Carnegie (patron of the arts) November 25; William G. Fischer (hymn composer/conductor) October 14; George Sherburn Hutchings (organ builder) December 9; Theodore F. Seward (music educator) January 25.

**G. Deaths**    Amzi Chapin (singing master) February 19; Georgina Oldmixon (British-born soprano) February 3; John Osborne (piano maker) May 27.

**H. Debuts**

**United States**    Charlotte Cushman (contralto—Boston).

**I. New Positions**

**Conductors**: Francis Schenig (US Marine Band—to 1836).

**J. Honors**    Lowell Mason (honorary doctorate, New York University).

**K. Biographical**    Louis Moreau Gottschalk begins music lessons with François Letellier in New Orleans; A. U. Hayter (British organist) comes to the United States; Henry Christian Timm (German pianist/organist) emigrates to the United States and settles in New York.

**L. Musical Beginnings**

**Performing Groups**    Boston Brass Band; Old Settler's Harmonic Society (Chicago Harmonic Society); Philadelphia Männerchor (to 1962).

**Educational**    Music Vale Academy; Whittlesey's Music School (Salem).

**Other**    Oliver Ditson and Co., Publishers (Boston); Fiot and Meignen, Publishers; Knabe and Gaehle, Piano Makers (Baltimore); St. Charles Theater (New Orleans); St. James Hall (Buffalo).

**M. Music Publications**

Mason, Lowell, *Boston Academy Collection of Church Music*
Mason, L. T., *The Sacred Harp, or, Eclectic Harmony*
Moore, Henry E., *New Hampshire Collection*
Shaw, Oliver, *Social Sacred Melodies*
Walker, William, *The Southern Harmony and Musical Companion*

**N. Musical Compositions**

**Choral/Vocal**    John Hill Hewitt, *The Knight of the Raven Black Plume* (song).

**Orchestra/Band**    Anthony P. Heinrich, *The Jäger's Adieu*.

**Piano/Organ**    Julius Metz, *Alliance Waltz—Tyrolean Waltz with Variations*; Peter K. Moran, *Variations on "Coal Black Rose."*

**Symphonies**    Anthony P. Heinrich, *Gran sinfonia eroica*.

# 1836

☀

## Historical Highlights

Martin Van Buren becomes the eighth president; Arkansas is admitted as the 25th state; a panic follows Jackson's publication of his *Specie Circular*; work begins on the Washington Monument; Cleveland, Ohio, is incorporated; the Texans lose at the battle of the Alamo but defeat the Mexicans at San Jacinto; the "Great Trek" of the Boers out of South Africa begins.

## World Cultural Highlights

**World Art**    Jean-Baptiste Corot, *Diana and Actaeon*; Ernest Meissonier, *The Errand Boy*; Friedrich Overbeck, *Marriage of the Virgin*; François Rude, *La Marseillaise* (Arc de Triomphe).

**World Literature**    Georg Büchner, *Woyzeck;* Charles Dickens, *The Pickwick Papers*; Nikolai Gogol, *The Inspector General*; Antonio Garcia Gutiérrez, *Il Trovador*; Alphonse de Lamartine, *Jocelyn*.

**World Music**    Frédéric Chopin, *Twelve Etudes, Opus 25*; Mikhail Glinka, *A Life for the Tsar*; Franz Liszt, *Années de Pèlerinage, Year I*; Giacomo Meyerbeer, *Les Huguenots*; Richard Wagner, *Polonia Overture*.

**Miscellaneous**   The Huddersfield Choral Society is founded in England; births include Lawrence Alma-Tadema, Léo Delibes, Ignace Fantin-Latour, Edward J. Poynter, and James Tissot; deaths include George Colman, Jr., Christian Grabbe, Rouget de Lisle, and Carle Vernet.

## American Art and Literature Highlights

**Births/Deaths**   Births include art figures Winslow Homer, Homer Dodge Martin, Elihu Vedder, and literary figures Thomas Bailey Aldrich, Bret Harte, Robert Newell (Orpheus C. Kerr), and Mary A. Townsend; deaths include artist Ezra Ames, author Hannah Crocker, and poet Robert Dinsmore.

**Art Works**   George Catlin, *Big Sail, a Chief—Sioux Indians Pursuing a Stag in Their Canoe*; Thomas Cole, *The Course of Empire* (Series)—*The Oxbow*; Joseph H. Davis, *James and Sarah Tuttle*; William S. Mount, *Farmer's Nooning*; John Neagle, *The Studious Artist*; John Trumbull, *Last Family to Perish in the Deluge*.

**Literature**   Elizabeth M. Chandler, *Essays, Philosophical and Moral*; William Dunlap, *Thirty Years Ago: or, Memoirs of a Water Drinker*; Ralph Waldo Emerson, *Nature*; Richard Hildreth, *The Slave*; Oliver Wendell Holmes, *Poems*; Washington Irving, *Astoria*; William H. McGuffey, *Eclectic Reader I, II*; Nathaniel B. Tucker, *The Partisan Leader*; John Greenleaf Whittier, *Mogg Megone*.

## Music

**F. Births**   John R. G. Hassard (critic); Elise Hensler (soprano); Charles Jerome Hopkins (composer/pianist) April 4; Augustus D. Juilliard (music patron) April 19; Rigdon McCoy McIntosh (compiler); Thomas P. Ryder (organist) June 29; Myron Whitney (bassist) September 5; Benjamin E. Woolf (music critic/composer) February 16.

**G. Deaths**   Supply Belcher (music dealer/publisher) June 9; Johann Gottlieb Graupner (German-born composer/publisher) April 16; Daniel Read (composer/compiler) December 4.

**H. Debuts**

**United States**   Henry Russell (British singer—New York), Daniel Schlesinger (German pianist—New York), Henry Christian Timm (German pianist—New York).

**I. New Positions**

**Conductors**   Raphael R. Triay (US Marine Band—to 1843).

**Other**   William Henry Fry (music critic, *Philadelphia National Gazette*—to 1841).

**K. Biographical**   Charles Balmer (German conductor/composer) emigrates to the United States, finally settling in St. Louis in 1839; Louis Moreau Gottschalk, age 7, is called to play in the New Orleans Cathedral; Henry Wellington Greatorex (British composer/organist) emigrates to the United States and settles in Charleston, South Carolina; Uri K. Hill goes to Europe to study with Ludwig Spohr; George Loder (Australian conductor/composer) comes to the United States and settles in Baltimore; Daniel Schlesinger (German pianist) settles in the United States.

**L. Musical Beginnings**

**Performing Groups**   Ashley Slave Band (Arkansas); Boston Academy Orchestra; Dayton Philharmonic Society I; Old Settler's Harmonic Society (Chicago); Portland Sacred Music Society (Maine).

**Other**   S. Brainard's Son, Publisher (Cleveland); Lion Theater (Melodeon—Boston); J. B. Lippincott and Co. (Philadelphia); Osbourn and Strail Musical Supplies (Chicago).

**M. Music Publications**

Chapman, Maria W., *Songs of the Free and Hymns of Christian Freedom*
Mason, Lowell, *Boston Academy's Collection of Choruses*
Steffy, John W., *The Valley Harmonist*
Wolle, Peter, *Moravian Tune Book*

**N. Musical Compositions**

**Choral/Vocal**   Charles E. Horn, *The Remission of Sin* (oratorio).

# 1837

☀

## Historical Highlights

Michigan enters the Union as the 26th state; the Second Seminole War ends in Florida; the Chesapeake and Ohio Railroad is chartered; Atlanta, Georgia, is founded; W. Crompton patents the power loom; the American and Foreign Bible Society is founded; Queen Victoria ascends the British throne; several rebellions against British rule fail in Canada.

## World Cultural Highlights

**World Art**   Alfred Edward Chalon, *John Knox, the Reprover*; Thomas Cole, *Departure and Return*; Eugène Delacroix, *Battle of Taillebourg*; George Watts, *A Wounded Heron.*

**World Literature**   Honoré de Balzac, *Illusions Perdues*; Louis Bertrand, *Gaspard de la Nuit*; Charles Dickens, *Oliver Twist*; Joseph von Eichendorff, *Poems*; Alphonse de Lamartine, *Chute d'un Ange.*

**World Music**   Hector Berlioz, *Requiem*; Frédéric Chopin, *Sonata, Opus 35, "Funeral March"*; Felix Mendelssohn, *Piano Concerto No. 2*; Robert Schumann, *Davidsbündlertänze*; Ludwig Spohr, *Symphony No. 5, "Lenore."*

**Miscellaneous**   The Royal College of Art is founded in London; births include Mily Balakirev, Alphonse Legros, Hans von Maurées, Algernon Swinburne, and Emil Waldteufel; deaths include John Constable, John Field, François Gérard, Giacomo Leopardi, and Alexander Pushkin.

## American Art and Literature Highlights

**Births/Deaths**   Births include artist Alfred Bricher and literary figures John Burroughs, Edward Eggleston, and William Dean Howells; deaths include literary figures Thomas G. Fessenden, Asa Greene, Abiel Holmes, and Tabitha Gilman Tenney.

**Art Works**   Thomas Cole, *The Departure—The Return—In the Catskills, Early Autumn*; Horatio Greenough, *The Rescue* (marble); George Harvey, *View on the Hudson* (?); Alfred Miller, *Fort Laramie—The Trapper's Bride*; Samuel F. B. Morse, *The Muse—Susan Walker Morse*; William S. Mount, *The Long Story*; Rembrandt Peale, *Day Dreams*; Robert W. Weir, *Saint Nicholas* (?).

**Literature**   Robert M. Bird, *Nick of the Woods: or, the Jibbenainosay*; James F. Cooper, *Gleanings in Europe*; Ralph W. Emerson, *The American Scholar*; William D. Gallagher, *Erato III*; Nathaniel Hawthorne, *Twice-Told Tales*; Washington Irving, *The Adventures of Captain Bonneville*; Epes Sargent, *Velasco*; William Ware, *Zenobia, or, The Fall of Palmyra*; John G. Whittier, *Poems Written During the Progress of the Abolition Question*; Hubbard Winslow, *Virtue and Happiness.*

## Music

**F. Births**   Benjamin J. Lang (pianist/conductor/composer) December 28; Ernest Guiraud (composer) June 23; William Shakespeare Hays (song composer) July 19; Charles H. Jarvis (pianist) December 20; William S. B. Mathews (organist) May 8; Tony Pastor (singer/impresario) May 28; Smith Newhall Penfield (organist/composer) April 4; John R. Sweney (composer/hymnist/conductor) December 31; Joseph E. Winner (composer/publisher).

**G. Deaths**   Peter Albrecht Von Hagen, Jr. (violinist/composer) September 12.

**H. Debuts**

**United States**   Madame Maria Caradori-Allan (Italian soprano—New York).

**I. New Positions**

**Conductors**   Daniel Schlesinger (New York Concordia Society).

**Other**   Pierre Davis (manager, Théâtre d'Orléans, New Orleans—to 1853).

**K. Biographical**   Anthony Philip Heinrich decides to settle in New York; George Jardine (British organ builder) emigrates to the United States and settles in New York; Lowell Mason makes his first visit to Europe to study their educational techniques; William Robyn (German conductor/cellist/composer) emigrates to the United States. and settles in St. Louis; Gustav Schirmer (German publisher) comes to the United States and settles in New York.

**L. Musical Beginnings**

**Performing Groups**   Cleveland Harmonic Society; Cleveland Mozart Society; Harvard Musical Association (Pierian Sodality); Newark Amateur Glee Co.; Philadelphia Philharmonic Society.

**Other**   Horn's Music Store (New York); Little, Brown and Co., Publishers (Boston); Tiffany, Young and Ellis Co. (New York).

**M. Music Publications**

Arnold, S. and Colman, E., *The Family Choir*
Caldwell, William, *The Union Harmony*
Hastings, Thomas, *The Manhattan Collection*
Mason, Lowell, *The Sabbath School Harp—The Odeon: A Collection of Secular Melodies* (with G. Webb)
Whittemore, Thomas, *Songs of Zion*

**N. Musical Compositions**

**Choral/Vocal**   Henry Russell, *Woodman, Spare That Tree* (song); George James Webb, *Webb (Stand Up! Stand Up for Jesus!)*.

**Orchestra/Band**   Anthony P. Heinrich, *Pocahontas* (romantic fantasy)—*The Hunters of Kentucky*.

**Piano/Organ**   Anthony P. Heinrich, *Elegia Impromtu*.

**Symphonies**   Anthony P. Heinrich, *The Columbiad, "Grand American National Chivalrous Symphony"—Bohemia ("Sinfonia Romantica")*.

# 1838

❀

## Historical Highlights

The Underground Railway for the help of runaway slaves is formed in opposition to the Fugitive Slave Law; the Cherokee Indians are forced to move to a reservation in Oklahoma, the so-called Trail of Tears; the Iowa Territory is formed; Samuel Morse develops his famous Code; steamship travel between the Old and New Worlds begins.

## World Cultural Highlights

**World Art**   Eugène Delacroix, *The Capture of Constantinople*; Wilhelm von Kaulbach, *Destruction of Jerusalem*; Ary Scheffer, *Franz Liszt*; Bertel Thorvaldsen, *Christ and the Apostles*.

**World Literature**   Elizabeth Browning, *The Seraphim and Other Poems*; Victor Hugo, *Ruy Blas*; Karl Immermann, *Münchhausen I, II*; Bernhard Malmström, *Ariadne*.

**World Music**   Hector Berlioz, *Benvenuto Cellini*; Franz Liszt, *Grand Galop Chromatique—Etudes d'Exécution Transcendante d'après Paganini*; Robert Schumann, *Kreisleriana—Kinderszenen*.

**Miscellaneous**   The London National Gallery opens; the London Promenade Concerts begin; the Besson Instrument Co. is founded in Paris; births include Georges Bizet, Charles Carolus-Durand, Aimé-Jules Dalou, and David Gray; deaths include Adalbert von Chamisso and Johann Maelzel.

## American Art and Literature Highlights

**Births/Deaths**   Births include art figures David Neal, Walter Shirlaw, Edward Valentine, and literary figures Augustin Daly, John M. Hay, Abram J. Ryan, Horace E. Scudder, Francis H. Smith, and Albion W. Tourgée; deaths include literary figures Lorenzo da Ponte, Anne McVickar Grant, and Peter Irving.

**Art Works**   John J. Audubon, *The Birds of America* (four volumes published); Thomas Cole, *Dream of Arcadia—Schroon Mountain, Adirondacks*; Charles Deas, *Turkey Shooting*; Horatio Greenough, *Abdiel*; Christian Mayr, *Kitchen Ball at White Sulphur Springs*; William S. Mount, *The Painter's Triumph*; Hiram Powers, *Eve*; John Quidor, *Battle Scene from Knickerbocker's History of New York*.

**Literature**   Caroline Gilman, *Recollection of a Southern Matron*; John P. Kennedy, *Rob of the Bowl*; Eliza B. Lee, *Sketches of a New England Village*; George P. Morris, *The Deserted Bride and Other Poems*; Joseph C. Neal, *Charcoal Sketches*; Frances S. Osgood, *A Wreath of Wild Flowers from New England*; Edgar Allen Poe, *Narrative of Arthur Gordon Pym*; Jones Very, *Essays and Poems*; William Ware, *Aurelian*; John Greenleaf Whittier, *Poems*.

## Music

**F. Births**   Philip P. Bliss (singer/hymnwriter) July 9; David Braham (song composer); James R. Fairlamb (organist/composer) January 23; Alice C. Fletcher (ethnomusicologist) March 16; William J. Kirkpatrick (composer/compiler) February 27; Alfred H. Pease (composer/pianist) May 6; David W. Reeves (bandmaster/cornetist) February 14; Eugene Thayer (organist/composer) December 11; David D. Wood (organist/composer) March 2.

**G. Deaths**   Benjamin Dearborn (singing teacher) February 22; Asa Hopkins (woodwind maker) October 27; Jonathan Huntington (composer/tenor) July 29; Jeremiah Ingalls (composer/compiler) April 6; Daniel Schlesinger (German-born pianist) January 8.

**H. Debuts**

**United States**   Edward Seguin (British bass—New York), John Wilson (Scottish tenor—tour).

**I. New Positions**

**Conductors**   Eugène-Prosper Prévost (Théâtre d'Orléans—to 1859).

**Educational**   Lowell Mason (superintendent of music, Boston Schools); William Robyn (St. Louis University—to 1852).

**Other**   Thomas J. Bowers (organ, St. Thomas' African Episcopal Church, Philadelphia).

**K. Biographical**   Grafulla (Spanish bandmaster/composer) comes to the United States and settles in New York; John Hill Hewitt has a book of his poetry published; Edward Hodges leaves Canada and settles in New York; Francis Johnson's Colored Band plays for Queen Victoria during their European tour; Eugène-Prosper Prévost (French conductor) emigrates to the United States and settles in New Orleans; Arthur and Anne Seguin (British bass and soprano) come to the United States and form their own opera company in New York; Jane Shirreff (British soprano) and John Wilson (Scottish tenor) begin two years of concertizing in the United States to great acclaim; vocal music becomes a part of public school curriculum in Boston.

**L. Musical Beginnings**

**Performing Groups**   English Opera Co. (by the Seguins—to 1847); St. Louis Philharmonic Orchestra (1).

**Other**   J. Lathrop Allen Instrument Shop (Sturbridge, Massachusetts); *Parlour Review and Journal of Music, Literature and the Fine Arts*; St. Louis Musical Fund Society.

**M. Music Publications**

Jackson, John B., *Knoxville Harmony*
Mason, Lowell, *The Boston Glee Book*
Pond, Sylvanus, *Union Melodies*

**N. Musical Compositions**

**Choral/Vocal**   Anonymous, *She Wore a Yellow Ribbon*; Edward Harper, *Jim Along Josey*; John H. Hewitt, *Flora's Festival* (juvenile cantata); Henry Russell, *A Life on the Ocean Wave* (song); James E. Spilman, *Flow Gently, Sweet Afton*.

**Operas**   William Henry Fry, *Cristiani e pagani* (unfinished opera).

**Orchestra/Band**   William Henry Fry, *Overture, Aurelia the Vestal*.

# 1839

❀

## Historical Highlights

The United States settles a dispute with Canada over the Canadian-Maine boundary; Fort Sutter (Sacramento), California, is founded; the process of vulcanization is discovered by Charles Goodyear; the University of Missouri and Boston University are founded; the Opium War takes place between China and Great Britain.

## World Cultural Highlights

**World Art**  Eugène Delacroix, *Jewish Wedding in Morocco*; Charles Eastlake, *Christ Blessing the Children*; John Martin, *The Coronation of Queen Victoria*; Joseph Turner, *The Fighting Temeraire*.

**World Literature**  Edward Bulwer-Lytton, *Richelieu*; Charles Dickens, *Nicholas Nickleby*; Jeremias Gotthelf, *Leiden und Freuden eines Schulmeisters*; Juliusz Slowacki, *Mazeppa*.

**World Music**  Hector Berlioz, *Romeo and Juliet*; Franz Liszt, *Piano Concerto No. 2—Années de Pèlerinage, Year II*; Felix Mendelssohn, *Ruy Blas Overture*; Robert Schumann, *Faschingsschwank aus Wien*.

**Miscellaneous**  The North German Music Festivals begin in Lübeck; births include Paul Cézanne, Modest Mussorgsky, Karl A. Oesterley, Joseph Rheinberger and Alfred Sisley; deaths include Joseph Koch, Karl Nicander, Ferdinando Paër, Winthrop Praed and Fernando Sor.

## American Art and Literature Highlights

**Births/Deaths**  Births include sculptors George Bissell and Franklin Simmons, and literary figures Thomas Cooper De Leon, George C. Eggleston, James A. Herne, Cincinnatus Miller, and James Ryder Randall; deaths include artist/playwright William Dunlap amd poet William Leggett.

**Art Works**  J. Maze Burbank, *Religious Camp Meeting*; Thomas Cole, *Crawford Notch, White Mountains*; Thomas Crawford, *Orpheus—Cerberus*; Charles Deas, *The Devil and Tom Walker*; Asher B. Durand, *Sunday Morning*; Hiram Powers, *Proserpine*; John Quidor, *Antony van Corlear Brought to Peter Stuyvesant—Rip Van Winkle at Vedder's Tavern*; Joshua Shaw, *On the Susquehanna*.

**Literature**  Caroline Gilman, *Tales and Ballads*; Charles Hoffman, *Wild Scenes in the Forest and Prairie*; Caroline Kirkland, *A New Home—Who'll Follow?*; Henry Wadsworth Longfellow, *Voices of the Night*; Cornelius Mathews, *Behemoth: A Legend of the Mound-Builders*; Edgar Allen Poe, *Tales of the Grotesque and Arabesque*; Daniel Thompson, *The Green Mountain Boys*.

## Music

**F. Births**  Dudley Buck (organist/composer) March 10; E. A. Hoffman (hymnwriter) May 4; John Knowles Paine (composer/educator) January 9; Almon K. Virgil (music educator) August 13.

**H. Debuts**

**United States**  Elizabeth Poole (British mezzo-soprano), The Rainer Family (New York).

**I. New Positions**

**Educational**  A. N. Johnson (music, Boston Public Schools—to c.1855).

**Other**  Edward Hodges (organ, Trinity Parish Church, New York—to 1859).

**K. Biographical**  Charles Grobe (German composer/pianist) emigrates to the United States; the Hutchinson Family choral group makes their first public appearance; the Swiss Rainer Family choral group begins a four-year tour of the United States; George Frederick Root tries teaching music in Boston; Hermann L. Schreiner (German publisher) comes to the United States; Jane Sloman (British pianist/composer) comes to the United States.

**L. Musical Beginnings**

**Other**  George Jadine and Son, Organs (New York); *The Musical Magazine, or Repository of*

*Musical Science, Literature and Intelligence* (to 1842); W. C. Peters Music Store; Nathaniel Philips, Music Publisher (St. Louis); George Reed Music Store (Boston—G. P. Reed and Co., 1850).

**M. Music Publications**

Mason, Lowell, *The Modern Psalmist—The Boston Anthem Book*
Paine, David, *Portland Sacred Music Society's Collection of Church Music*

**N. Musical Compositions**

**Choral/Vocal**   Charles E. Horn, *Ode to Music*; Joseph P. Knight, *Rocked in the Cradle of the Deep*.

**Piano/Organ**   G. H. Draper, *The St. Louis Grand March*.

# 1840

✿

## Historical Highlights

The US population reaches 17,069,000; William Henry Harrison is elected the ninth president; Congress passes the 10-hour day for all government employees; Congress recognizes the new Republic of Texas; the Cumberland Highway is finished; Great Britain sets up the first postal system and the first stamp, the "Penny Black"; the Act of Union combines Canada into one entity.

## World Cultural Highlights

**World Art**   Augustus Callcott, *Milton Dictating to His Daughter*; Joseph Dannhauser, *Liszt at the Piano*; John Martin, *The Eve of the Deluge*; Joseph Turner, *Yacht Approaching the Coast*.

**World Literature**   Marguerite Blessington, *The Idler in Italy*; Charles Dickens, *The Old Curiosity Shop*; Leigh Hunt, *A Legend of Florence*; William Thackeray, *Paris Sketch Book*.

**World Music**   Gaetano Donizetti, *La fille du régiment*; Felix Mendelssohn, *Symphony No. 2*; Robert Schumann, *Dichterliebe—Frauenliebe und -leben*; Richard Wagner, *Rienzi—A Faust Overture*.

**Miscellaneous**   The National Conservatory of Budapest opens; the Saxophone is introduced; births include Alphonse Daudet, Thomas Hardy, Thomas Hovenden, Claude Monet, Auguste Rodin, Peter Tchaikovsky, and Émile Zola; deaths include Fanny Burney, Casper Friedrich, and Niccolò Paganini.

## American Art and Literature

**Births/Deaths**   Births include artists William Bunce, Charles H. Moore, Alfred Thompson, and literary figures Edward S. Ellis, Charles W. Peck, and Constance Fenimore Woolson; deaths include literary figures Charles Follen, Hannah Webster Foster, and John Wesley Jarvis.

**Art Works**   George C. Bingham, *The Dull Story*; Thomas Cole, *The Voyage of Life Series—The Architect's Dream*; George Hollingsworth, *The Hollingsworth Family*; Henry Inman, *Picnic in the Catskill Mountains* (?); Fitz Hugh Lane, *Norwich from the West Side of the River*; Alfred Miller, *Fur Trapper's Rendezvous*; Bass Otis, *Self-Portrait*; Robert Salmon, *Rainford's Island, Boston Harbor*.

**Literature**   Amos B. Alcott, *Orphic Sayings*; Orestes A. Brownson, *Charles Elwood: or, The Infidel Converted*; James F. Cooper, *The Pathfinder*; Richard Dana, Jr., *Two Years before the Mast*; Charles F. Hoffman, *Greyslaer: A Romance of the Mohawk*; Washington Irving, *Oliver Goldsmith*; Eliza B. Lee, *Delusion, or, The Witch of New England*; Cornelius Mathews, *The Politicians*; George P. Morris, *Poems*; John Pierpont, *Airs of Palestine and Other Poems*; Nathaniel Willis, *Loiterings of Travel*.

## Music

**F. Births**   William Candidus (tenor) July 25; William Horatio Clarke (organ builder) March 8; Isabella Stewart Gardner (patron of the arts) April 14; Aldine S. Kieffer (publisher/compiler)

August 1; Barrett Poznanski (violinist) December 11; Ira D. Sankey (clergyman/composer) August 28; George E. Whiting (organist/composer) September 14.

**H. Debuts**

**United States**   John Braham (British tenor—tour); Fanny Elssler (Austrian ballerina).

**I. New Positions**

**Conductors**   Pierre Joseph Varney (French Opera Co., New Orleans—to 1850).

**Educational**   A. N. Johnson (Boston Academy of Music—to 1849).

**Other**   William B. Bradbury (organ, Baptist Tabernacle, Boston); A. N. Johnson (organ, Park Street Church, Boston—to 1858); Samuel P. Tuckerman (organ, St. Paul's Church, Boston—to 1849).

**K. Biographical**   John Braham (British tenor) visits the United States; John Daniel (Scottish composer) comes to the United States.

**L. Musical Beginnings**

**Performing Groups**   St. Louis Sacred Music Society.

**Educational**   National Music Convention.

**Other**   Cast-Iron Piano Frame (patent by Jonas Chickering); J. and C. Fischer, Pianos (New York); George A. Prince and Co., Reed Organ Makers (Buffalo?).

**M. Music Publications** Thomas Hastings, *The Sacred Lyre*.

**N. Musical Compositions**

**Choral/Vocal**   Henry Russell, *The Old Arm Chair* (song—words by Eliza Cook).

**Operas**   Charles E. Horn, *Ahmed al Ramel, or The Pilgrim of Love*.

# 1841

✻

## Historical Highlights

President William Henry Harrison dies and John Tyler becomes the tenth president; Tyler's cabinet resigns en masse after the Whigs denounce him; Brook Farm is founded in Massachusetts; Fordham University is founded; the British seize Hong Kong and make it a British protectorate; New Zealand also becomes a British colony; David Livingstone begins his exploration of the African continent.

## World Cultural Highlights

**World Art**   Paul Delaroche, *Apotheosis of Art*; Charles Eastlake, *Christ Weeping over Jerusalem*; Carl Spitzweg, *The Sunday Walk*; Joseph Turner, *Peace: Burial at Sea*.

**World Literature**   Marguerite Blessington, *The Idler in France*; Robert Browning, *Pippa Passes*; Mikhail Lermontov, *The Demon*; Frederick Marryat, *Masterman Ready*.

**World Music**   Hector Berlioz, *Nuits d'été*; Niels Gade, *Symphony 1*; Gioacchino Rossini, *Stabat Mater*; Robert Schumann, *Symphonies No. 1, 4*; Richard Wagner, *The Flying Dutchman*.

**Miscellaneous**   *Punch* begins publication; Alphonse Leduc Publishing Co. opens; the Royal Saxon Opera House opens in Dresden; births include Frédéric Bazille, Emanuel Chabrier, Antonín Dvořák, and Pierre-Auguste Renoir; deaths include Louis Bertrand, J. H. von Dannecker, and David Wilkie.

## American Art and Literature Highlights

**Births/Deaths**   Births include Edward L. Henry, Henry Mosler, John F. Weir, and literary figures Charles Heber Clark, Edward Rowland Sill, and George A. Townsend; deaths include literary figures William Austin, Willis Gaylord Clark, James A. Hillhouse, Ellen Sturgis Hooper, and Grenville Mellen.

**Art Works**   James G. Clonney, *Militia Training*; Thomas Doughty, *Landscape with a House*; Horatio Greenough, *Venus Victrix*; Daniel Huntington, *Mercy's Dream*; Chauncey Ives, *Noah Webster*; John C. King, *Reverend Francis Greenwood*; William S. Mount, *Cider Making*.

**Literature**   Washington Allston, *Monaldi*; James F. Cooper, *The Deerslayer*; Richard Dana, Jr., *The Seaman's Friend*; Ralph W. Emerson, *Essays I*; Joseph Ingraham, *The Quadroone*; John B. Jones, *Wild Western Scenes*; Henry W. Longfellow, *Ballads and Other Poems*; James R. Lowell, *Poems I: A Year of Life*; Frances S. Osgood, *The Poetry of Flowers and Flowers of Poetry*.

## Music

**F. Births**   Annie Louise Cary (contralto?) October 22; Stephen A. Emery (composer/conductor) October 4; Henry E. Moore (composer/educator); John Paul Morgan (organist/composer/conductor) February 13; John Stark (music publisher) April 11; Samuel P. Warren (organist/composer) February 18.

**I. New Positions**

**Educational**   Benjamin Franklin Baker (public school music, Boston); John Hill Hewitt (music, Chesapeake Female College, Richmond, Virginia—to 1850).

**Other**   William B. Bradbury (organ, Baptist Tabernacle, New York).

**K. Biographical**   Francis Scala (Italian bandmaster/composer) enlists on a US frigate that takes him to the United States, where he switches to the Marines; William V. Wallace (Irish composer) arrives in New Orleans from South America and befriends Louis Moreau Gottschalk; Elbridge G. Wright moves to Boston and sets up his instrument shop.

**L. Musical Beginnings**

**Other**   Austin Lyceum (Texas); Boston (American) Musical Convention.

**M. Music Publications**

Bradbury, William B., *The Young Choir*
Mason, Lowell, *Carmina Sacra*
Pond, Sylvanus, *The United States Psalmody*
Traetta, Filippo, *Rudiments of Singing I*

**N. Musical Compositions**

**Choral/Vocal**   Anthony P. Heinrich, *The Jubilee* (chorus and orchestra); Henry Russell, *The Gambler's Wife—My Mother's Bible* (songs).

**Operas**   William Henry Fry, *Aurelia the Vestal*.

# 1842

❀

## Historical Highlights

Massachusetts limits the number of hours that a child may work to 10 hours a day; Dorr's Rebellion in Rhode Island leads to universal male suffrage; the Webster-Ashburton Treaty settles the northeastern Canada-US boundary dispute; the Opium War comes to an end in China; the British Mining Act forbids women and children to work in the mines.

## World Cultural Highlights

**World Art**   Jean-Auguste Ingres, *Cherubini and the Muse of Poetry*; Théodore Rousseau, *Under the Birches in the Evening*; Joseph Turner, *Steamer in a Snow Storm*.

**World Literature**   Charles Dickens, *American Notes*; Nikolai Gogol, *Dead Souls*; Thomas Macaulay, *Lays of Ancient Rome*; Aubrey de Vere, *The Waldenses and Other Poems*.

**World Music**    Franz Berwald, *Symphonies No. 1, 2*; Mikhail Glinka, *Russlan and Ludmilla*; Felix Mendelssohn, *"Scotch" Symphony (No. 3)*; Giuseppe Verdi, *Nabucco*.

**Miscellaneous**    The Vienna Philharmonic Orchestra is founded; Escudier Publishing House opens in Paris; births include Giovanni Boldini, François Coppée, Stéphane Mallarmé, Jules Massenet, and Arthur Sullivan; deaths include Clemens Brentano, Luigi Cherubini, Stendhal, and Louise Vigée-Lebrun.

## American Art and Literature Highlights

**Births/Deaths**    Births include literary figures Charles F. Adams, Ambrose G. Bierce, Edwin L. Bynner, John Habberton, William James, Sidney Lanier, and Steele MacKaye; deaths include artist Jacob Eichholtz and literary figures William E. Channing, Sr., McDonald Clarke, and Samuel Woodworth.

**Art Works**    John J. Audubon, *The American Porcupine*; Thomas Cole, *The Voyage of Life Series* (?); Thomas Crawford, *Hebe and Ganymede*; Jeremiah Hardy, *Catharine Hardy and Her Daughter*; Emanuel Leutze, *Return of Columbus in Chains to Cadiz*; Robert Mills, *Treasury Building, Washington, DC*; Hiram Powers, *Eve Tempted*; John Vanderlyn, *The Return of Columbus*.

**Literature**    William C. Bryant, *The Fountain and Other Poems*; Nathaniel Hawthorne, *Biographical Stories for Children*; Henry Wadsworth Longfellow, *Poems on Slavery*; Cornelius Mathews, *The Career of Puffer Hopkins*; Edgar Allen Poe, *The Masque of the Red Death*; Elizabeth O. Smith, *The Western Captive*; Walt Whitman, *Franklin Evans; or, The Inebriate*.

## Music

**F. Births**    George C. Dobson (banjoist) April; Clara Louise Kellogg (soprano/impresario) July 9; Billy Kersands (minstrel performer); James Monroe Trotter (music historian) November 8; Samuel B. Whitney (organist/composer) June 4.

**G. Deaths**    Alpheus Babcock (piano maker) April 3; Lucius Chapin (singing master) December 24; Timothy Swan (composer/compiler) July 23.

**H. Debuts**

**United States**    Max Bohrer (German cellist—tour).

**I. New Positions**

**Other**    Samuel P. Jackson (organ, St. Bartholomew's, New York—to 1861).

**K. Biographical**    J. Lathrop Allen moves his instrument business to Boston; Louis Moreau Gottschalk, age 13, is sent to Paris for further music study but is refused admittance by the conservatory because he is an American and "no American can be good enough for the Conservatory of Paris"; Simon Hasslet (German composer/conductor) moves to the United States and settles in Philadelphia; Theodore von La Hache (German composer/pianist) emigrates to the United States and settles in New Orleans; Lauro Rossi and his wife join the New Orleans Opera Company.

**L. Musical Beginnings**

**Performing Groups**    Aeolian Vocalists (The Hutchinson Family); Chicago Musical Society; Cleveland Sacred Music Society; Philharmonic Symphony Society of New York III.

**Other**    Elias Howe Music Shop (Providence—moves to Boston in 1843); Werlein Music Store (Vicksburg, Mississippi).

**M. Music Publications**

Day, H. W., *Revival Hymns*
Hastings, Thomas, *Sacred Songs for Family and Social Worship*
Moore, John W., *Sacred Minstrel*
Woodbury, I. and Baker, B., *The Boston Musical Education Society's Collection of Church Music*

**N. Musical Compositions**

**Choral/Vocal**    Anthony P. Heinrich, *Oratorio of the Pilgrim Fathers (?)*.

**Operas**   Charles E. Horn, *The Maid of Saxony*; Eugène-Prosper Prévost, *Esmeralda*.

**Piano/Organ**   Charles Grobe, *Mnemosyne, Opus 14* (piano, after Liszt's Opus 8); Léopold Meignen, *Introduction and Variations, "Tho' You Leave Me Now in Sorrow."*

# 1843

☀

## Historical Highlights

J. C. Fremont explores the Oregon and New Mexico Territories; Santa Ana, Mexican president, warns the United States against the annexation of Texas; Dorothea Dix begins a campaign against poor prison and asylum conditions in the country; Atlanta, Georgia, is founded; Louis Napoléon becomes head of the French Republic; Isabella II becomes Queen of Spain when the dictatorship is overthrown.

## World Cultural Highlights

**World Art**   Théodore Chassériau, *The Two Sisters*; Jean-Baptiste Corot, *Destruction of Sodom*; Charles Gleyre, *St. John and the Apocalypse*; Joseph Turner, *The Sun of Venice Going to Sea*.

**World Literature**   Berthold Auerbach, *Schwarzwälder Dorfgeschichten*; Charles Dickens, *A Christmas Carol*; Antonio Gutiérrez, *Simón Bocanegra*; Friedrich Hebbel, *Maria Magdalena*.

**World Music**   Michael Balfe, *The Bohemian Girl*; Gaetano Donizetti, *Don Pasquale*; Neils Gade, *Symphony 2*; Felix Mendelssohn, *A Midsummer Night's Dream*; Giuseppe Verdi, *I Lombardi*.

**Miscellaneous**   The Leipzig Conservatory of Music is founded; Copenhagen's Tivoli Gardens opens; births include Edvard Grieg, Alexandre Regnault, Hans Richter, and Charles van der Stappen; deaths include Casimir Delavigne, Johann Hölderlein, Friedrich La Motte-Fouqué, and Robert Southey.

## American Art and Literature Highlights

**Births/Deaths**   Births include art figures James Champney, Edward Kemeys, Henry Walker, and literary figures Bartley Campbell, Prentiss Ingraham, Henry James, Jr., Frank H. Murdoch, and Charles W. Stoddard; deaths include artists Washington Allston, John Trumbull, and literary figures Thomas Branagan, Francis Scott Key, and Noah Webster.

**Art Works**   Washington Alston, *Belshazzar's Feast*; Henry K. Browne, *Indian Boy*; Thomas Cole, *River in the Catskills*; Thomas Crawford, *The Genius of Mirth*; John Neagle, *Henry Clay*; William Page, *Cupid and Psyche*; Hiram Powers, *The Greek Slave* (?); Peter Rothermel, *Discovery of the Mississippi by DeSoto*; John M. Stanley, *International Indian Council*; John Vanderlyn, *Niagara* (?).

**Literature**   William Channing II, *Poems I*; James F. Cooper, *Wyandotté*; Thomas D. English, *Ben Bolt*; Theodore S. Fay, *Hoboken*; Joseph C. Neal, *In Town and About*; Thomas L. Nichols, *Ellen Ramsay*; William H. Smith, *The Drunkard: or, The Fallen Saved*; William T. Thompson, *Major Jones's Courtship*; John Greenleaf Whittier, *Lays of My Home and Other Poems*; Nathaniel Willis, *Poems of Passion*.

## Music

**F. Births**   John C. Fillmore (music educator) February 4; Adolph Neuendorff (conductor/impresario/composer) June 13; William Sudds (bandmaster/composer) March 5; Manuel Gregorio Tavárez (composer/educator) November 28.

**G. Deaths**   Gaetano Carusi (Italian-born musician/composer/conductor) June 17.

**H. Debuts**

**United States**   Alexandre-Joseph Artôt (Belgian violinist—tour), Ole Bull (Norwegian violinist—New York), Jeanne Anaïs Castellan (French soprano—New York), Laure Cinti-Damoreau (French soprano—tour), Henri Vieuxtemps (Belgian violinist—tour).

**I. New Positions**

**Conductors**　David Hiram Chandler (Portland Band—to 1860); Antonio Pons (US Marine Band—to 1844).

**K. Biographical**　George Frederick Bristow begins playing violin in the New York Philharmonic Orchestra; Ole Bull (Norwegian violinist) concertizes in the United States from November until December of 1845; Alexander Thayer graduates with a BA degree from Harvard; Henri Vieuxtemps (Belgian violinist) makes the first of three concert tours of the United States; the Virginia Minstrels travel to England, the first American minstrel group to go abroad.

**L. Musical Beginnings**

**Performing Groups**　Christy's Minstrels; Sanford's Minstrels; Virginia Serenaders (Minstrels).

**Other**　*World of Music.*

**M. Music Publications**

*The New York Sacred Music Society's Collection of Church Music*
Bradbury, William, *The School Singer*
Himes, Joshua V., *The Millennial Harp*
Loder, George, *The New York Glee Book*
Plimpton, Job, *The Washington Choir* (collection of temperance music)
Tractta, Filippo, *Rudiments of the Art of Singing II, III*
Young, Isaac, *A Short Abridgement of the Rules of Music*

**N. Musical Compositions**

**Choral/Vocal**　E. P. Christy, *Farewell (Good Night) Ladies*; Dan Emmett, *Old Dan Tucker—De Boatman's Dance—My Old Aunt Sally*; Henry Russell, *The Indian Hunter*; Thomas à Becket, *Columbia, the Gem of the Ocean.*

**Piano/Organ**　Christopher Meineke, *The Harlem Waltz.*

# 1844

❀

## Historical Highlights

James Polk is elected the 11th president; the first telegraph message, "What hath God wrought?" is sent from Washington, DC to Baltimore; the Universities of Mississippi and Notre Dame are chartered; the Young Men's Christian Association (YMCA) is founded in London; the Dominican Republic gains its independence from Haiti.

## World Cultural Highlights

**World Art**　Théodore Chassériau, *Etchings for Othello*; Edwin Landseer, *The Challenge*; Jean-François Millet, *The Milkmaid*; Joseph Turner, *Rain, Steam and Speed.*

**World Literature**　Honoré de Balzac, *Modeste Mignon*; Charles Dickens, *Martin Chuzzlewit*; Alexandre Dumas, père, *Three Musketeers*; William Thackeray, *Barry Lyndon.*

**World Music**　Hector Berlioz, *Roman Carnival Overture*; Frédéric Chopin, *Piano Sonata in B Minor*; Felix Mendelssohn, *Violin Concerto*; Giuseppe Verdi, *Ernani.*

**Miscellaneous**　Johann Strauss, Jr., forms his own orchestra; births include Anatole France, Friedrich Nietzsche, Ilya Repin, Nicholas Rimsky-Korsakov, Henri Rousseau, Pablo de Sarasate, Paul Verlaine, and Charles Widor; deaths include Thomas Campbell, Sándor Kisfaludy, and Bertel Thorvaldsen.

## American Art and Literature Highlights

**Births/Deaths**　Births include art figures Mary Cassatt, Thomas Eakins, Martin Millmore, Olin Levi Warner, and literary figures George Washington Cable, Charles King, and Elizabeth Stuart

Ward; deaths include literary figures Sumner Lincoln Fairfield, Margaret B. Smith, William L. Stone, Caroline M. Warren, and artist Robert W. Salmon.

**Art Works**   George Bingham, *The Mill Boy*; James G. Clonney, *In the Cornfield*; Thomas Cole, *The Old Mill at Sunset*; Francis W. Edmonds, *The Image Peddler*; Richard S. Greenough, *William H. Prescott*; George Harvey, *The Apostle Oak*; Thomas Hicks, *Calculating*; Fitz Hugh Lane, *View of Gloucester from Dolliver's Neck;* Hiram Powers, *Proserpine*; Richard Woodville, *Soldier's Experience*.

**Literature**   William C. Bryant, *The White-Footed Doe and Other Poems*; Charles J. Cannon, *Mora Carmody*; Christopher Cranch, *Poems*; Ralph W. Emerson, *Essays II*; George Lippard, *The Monks of Monk Hall*; James R. Lowell, *Poems II*; Clement C. Moore, *Poems*; Susan R. Sedgwick, *Alida: or, Town and Country*; John G. Whittier, *Miscellaneous Poems*; Nathaniel Willis, *Pencillings by the Way*.

# Music

**F. Births**   Alfred Arthur (tenor/conductor) October 8; Otis Bardwell Boise (organist) August 13; Amy Fay (pianist) May 21; Edward "Ned" Harrigan (lyricist/performer) October 26; George Osgood (tenor/educator) April 3; Carlyle Petersilea (pianist/educator) January 18; Thomas H. Rollinson (bandmaster/composer) January 4.

**G. Deaths**   Uri Keeler Hill (composer/compiler) November 9; Oliver Holden (composer/compiler) September 4; Francis Johnson (cornetist/bandmaster) April 6; Elisha J. King (composer) August 31; John Meacham, Jr. (piano maker) December 8; Asahel Nettleton (evangelist/compiler) May 6; Oliver Holden (musician/clergyman) September 4; John Rowe Parker (music dealer/publisher) December 29; Johann Christian Till (Moravian organist) November 19.

**H. Debuts**

**United States**   Henry Phillips (British bass-baritone—tour).

**Other**   Louis Moreau Gottschalk (pianist—Paris).

**I. New Positions**

**Educational**   Joseph Lucchesi (US Marine Band—to 1846); George F. Root (voice, Abbott's School for Young Ladies, New York).

**Other**   Margaret Fuller (critic, *New York Tribune*—to 1846).

**K. Biographical**   Salvatore Patti (Italian tenor/manager) comes to the United States and settles in New York; Pittsburgh introduces music into its public school curriculum; George Frederick Root moves to New York; Lauro Rossi quits the New Orleans Opera Co. and returns to Italy; Henry Russell returns permanently to England.

**L. Musical Beginnings**

**Performing Groups**   Baker Family Singers (vocal quartet); Kitchen Minstrels.

**Educational**   Musical Institute of New York (becomes Harmonic Society in 1849).

**Other**   Couse Music Store (first music store in Detroit); Palmo's Opera House (New York).

**M. Music Publications**

Howe, Elias, *First Part of the Musician's Companion*
Johnson, A. N., *Instructions in Thorough-bass*
Mason, Lowell, *The Vocalist*
Tuckerman, Samuel, *Episcopal Harp*
White, B. F. and King, E. J., *The Sacred Harp*

**N. Musical Compositions**

**Chamber Music**   George F. Bristow, *Duetto Concertante, Opus 1* (violin and piano).

**Choral/Vocal**   Anonymous, *The Ole Grey Goose Is Dead (Go Tell Aunt Rhody)—Skip to My Lou, My Darling*; Stephen Foster, *Open Thy Lattice, Love* (song); Cool White, *Lubly Fan (Buffalo Gals)* (song).

# 1845

❄

## Historical Highlights

Florida and Texas enter the Union as the 27th and 28th states, respectively; Mexico snubs the envoys sent to settle the Texas and California questions; the US Naval Academy opens in Annapolis, Maryland; Baylor University is founded in Texas; over a million people die in the potato blight famine in Ireland; the first underwater cable is laid across the English Channel.

## World Cultural Highlights

**World Art**    Jean-Baptiste Corot, *Homer and the Shepherds*; David Cox, *Sun, Wind and Rain*; Adolph Menzel, *Room with a Balcony*; Joseph Turner, *Sun Setting over a Lake*.

**World Literature**    Honoré de Balzac, *Les Paysans*; Charles Dickens, *The Cricket on the Hearth*; Alexandre Dumas, père, *The Count of Monte Cristo*; Prosper Mérimée, *Carmen*.

**World Music**    Franz Berwald, *Symphonies No. 3, 4*; Felix Mendelssohn, *Athalie Music*; Robert Schumann, *Piano Concerto*; Giuseppe Verdi, *Giovanna d'Arco*; Richard Wagner, *Tannhäuser*.

**Miscellaneous**    The Black Obelisk of Shalmaneser is discovered; the Beethoven Memorial is unveiled; births include Leopold Auer, Karl Begas, Jr., Sarah Bernhardt, and Gabriel Fauré; deaths include János Bacsányi, Louis-Léopold Boilly, Thomas Hood, August von Schlegel, and Henrik Wergeland.

## American Art and Literture Highlights

**Births/Deaths**    Births include art figures Maria Dewing, Edmonia Lewis, and literary figures Will Carleton, Edward Harrigan, John Ames Mitchell, and John B. Tabb; deaths include artists Henry Sargent, Isaac Sheffield, and literary figures Thomas Andros, Maria Brooks, and James McHenry.

**Art Works**    George C. Bingham, *Fur Traders Descending the Missouri*; Harry K. Brown, *La Grazia*; Otis A. Bullard, *Barn Scene in Genesee County*; Thomas Cole, *View Across Frenchman's Bay after a Squall;* Charles Deas, *The Death Struggle*; Robert S. Duncanson, *Drunkard's Plight*; William S. Mount, *Eel Spearing at Setauket*; John M. Stanley, *Buffalo Hunt on the Southwestern Prairies*.

**Literature**    Lydia M. Child, *Letters from New York*; Thomas Chivers, *The Lost Pleiad and Other Poems*; James F. Cooper, *Satanstoe*; Dorothea Dix, *Remarks on Prisons and Prison Discipline*; Frederick Douglass, *Life of Frederick Douglass, an American Slave*; Sylvester Judd, *Margaret: A Tale of the Real and Ideal*; Edgar Allan Poe, *The Raven and Other Poems*; William T. Thompson, *Major Jones's Chronicles of Pineville*; Amelia Welby, *Poems*; Nathaniel Willis, *Dashes at Life with a Free Pencil*.

## Music

**F. Births**    Nellie E. Brown (soprano); Emmons Howard (organ builder) October 1; John Nelson Pattison (pianist?) October 22; Ernst Perabo (pianist) November 14; Jule Edson Perkins (bassist) March 19; Emma Thursby (soprano) February 21.

**G. Deaths**    Lewis Edson, Jr. (singing master/poet) May 23; Alexander Juhan (violinist/conductor/composer); Johann Christoph Mueller (flutist/violinist); Sophia Henrietta Hewitt Ostinelli (pianist) September 3.

**H. Debuts**

**United States**    Clara M. Brinkerhoff (New York), Leopold von Meyer (Austrian pianist—New York), John Templeton (Scottish tenor—tour), Hermann Wollenhaupt (German pianist—tour).

**K. Biographical**    William Boucher (German instrument maker) emigrates to the United States and settles in Baltimore; William Henry Fry writes the first known American opera, *Leonora*; Thomas Ryan (Irish violist/clarinettist) emigrates to the United States and settles in Boston;

Theodore Thomas's family comes to the United States; Hermann Adolf Wollenhaupt (German pianist/composer) comes to the United States and settles in New York.

**L. Musical Beginnings**

**Performing Groups**   Alleghanians (vocal quartet); Boston Chamber Music Concerts; St. Louis Musical Society Polyhymnia.

**Other**   Calliope; Southern Musical Convention; William Benjamin Simmons, Organ Maker; Horace Waters Music Store (New York); Winner Brothers Music Store (Philadelphia).

**M. Music Publications**

Bradbury, William, *Young Melodies—Musical Gems for School and Home*
Hastings, Thomas, *Indian Melodies*
Mason, Lowell and Webb, G., *The Psaltery*
Woodbury, Isaac B., *The Choral*

**N. Musical Compositions**

**Choral/Vocal**   Anthony P. Heinrich, *The Warrior's March* (chorus and orchestra); John H. Hewitt, *Jephtha* (oratorio)—*The Fairy Bridal* (cantata after Shakespeare).

**Operas**   William Henry Fry, *Leonora*; Eugène-Prosper Prévost, *La chaste Suzanne*.

**Orchestra/Band**   George F. Bristow, *Overture in E-Flat Major, Opus 3*; Anthony P. Heinrich, *Boadicèa* (concert overture).

**Piano/Organ**   George F. Bristow, *Grand Waltz de Bravura, Opus 6*; Louis Moreau Gottschalk, *Bamboula*; Charles Grobe, *United States Grand Waltz, Opus 43*.

**Symphonies**   George F. Bristow, *Symphony No. 1 in E-Flat Major*; Léopold Meignen, *Symphonie Militaire*.

# 1846

☀

## Historical Highlights

The Mexican War begins; the United States and Canada agree on the 49th parallel as the border of the Oregon Territory; Iowa becomes the 29th state; Milwaukee, Wisconsin, is incorporated; the Pennsylvania Railroad is chartered; patents include the pneumatic tire and the sewing machine; the planet Neptune is discovered; Mesopotamian cuneiform writing is finally deciphered.

## World Cultural Highlights

**World Art**   Eugène Delacroix, *Abduction of Rebecca*; Edwin Landseer, *The Stag at Bay*; John Millais, *Pizarro and the Incas*; Jean-François Millet, *Oedipus Unbound*.

**World Literature**   Robert Browning, *Bells and Pomegranates*; Feodor Dostoveysky, *Poor Folk*; Dmitri Grigorovich, *The Village*; Eduard Mörike, *Idylle vom Bodensee*.

**World Music**   Hector Berlioz, *The Damnation of Faust*; Felix Mendelssohn, *Elijah*; Robert Schumann, *Symphony 2 in C*; Franz von Suppé, *Poet and Peasant*; Giuseppe Verdi, *Attila*.

**Miscellaneous**   The Oslo Philharmonic Society and the Munich Conservatory of Music open; Eugène Albert, Woodwind Maker, opens in Brussels; births include Holger Drachmann, Alfred Graves, and Henryk Sienkiewicz; deaths include George Darley, Benjamin Haydon, and Étienne Senancour.

## American Art and Literature Highlights

**Births/Deaths**   Births include artists Francis Millet, Frederic Vinton, and literary figures Anna Katharine Green, Julian Hawthorne, Lloyd Mifflin, and Edward Noyes Westcott; deaths include John Brewster, Jr., Henry Inman, and literary figures William A. Caruthers, Theodore Dwight, Sr., and Sarah Wentworth Morton.

**Art Works**    George Bingham, *Jolly Flatboatmen I*; Henry Brown, *Aboriginal Hunter*; Frederic Church, *Hooker and Company Journeying through the Wilderness*; Thomas Cole, *The Pic-Nic*; Charles Deas, *The Voyagers*; Edward Hicks, *Noah's Ark*; Charles Ingham, *Flower Girl*; George Inness, *The Afternoon*; William Ranney, *Hunting Wild Horses*; John Stanley, *Black Knife, Apache Warrior*.

**Literature**    James F. Cooper, *The Redskins*; Ralph Waldo Emerson, *Poems*; Nathaniel Hawthorne, *Mosses from an Old Manse*; Herman Melville, *Typee*; Frances S. Osgood, *The Cries of New York*; William G. Simms, *Areytos, or Songs and Ballads of the South*; Ann S. Stephens, *The Diamond Necklace and Other Tales*; John Greenleaf Whittier, *Voices of Freedom*.

## Music

**F. Births**    Homer Bartlett (composer/organist) December 28; William H. Dana (composer/pedagogue) June 10; William Wallace Gilchrist (composer) January 8; Silas G. Pratt (composer/author) August 4; Frederick W. Root (organist/composer) June 13; George C. Stebbins (hymn composer) February 26.

**H. Debuts**

**United States**    Henri Herz (Austrian pianist—New York), William Mason (pianist—Boston), Ernesto Camille Sivori (Italian violinist—United States).

**I. New Positions**

**Conductors**    Raphael R. Triay (US Marine Band—to 1855).

**Other**    William Henry Fry (European correspondant, *New York Tribune*)

**K. Biographical**    Stephen Foster moves to Cincinnati to be bookkeeper for his brother's business; August Martin Gemünder (German violin maker) comes to the United States and opens a shop in Springfield, Massachusetts; Louis Moreau Gottschalk has his first piece published and suffers from typhoid fever; Matthias Keller (German violinist/composer) comes to the United States and plays violin in various Philadelphia theaters; Alexander Thayer receives his MA degree from Harvard.

**L. Musical Beginnings**

**Performing Groups**    Chicago Choral Union; Eintracht (Newark German singing society); New Orleans Serenaders; St. Louis Oratorio Society; White's Serenaders.

**Other**    Alfred Badger Flute Shop (New York); Baker and Scribner, Publishers (New York); Brainard and Mould Music Salon and Fancy Goods and Confectionary (Chicago); Carhart and Needham, Reed Organ Makers (New York); Estey Organ Co. (Brattleboro, Vermont); Stephen T. Gordon Publishing Co. (Hartford, Connecticut); Hall, Labagh and Co., Organ Builders (New York); Kerksieg and Bruesing Co., Music Publishers (New York) (G. Schirmer); Peters (Field) and Co., Publisher (Cincinnati, Ohio).

**M. Music Publications**

Aikin, Jesse B., *The Christian Minstrel*
Hood, George, *A History of Music in New England with Biographical Sketches . . .*
Johnson, S. and Longfellow, S., *Book of Hymns for Public and Private Devotion*
Root, George F., *The Young Ladies' Choir*
Walker, William, *Southern and Western Pocket Harmonist*

**N. Musical Compositions**

**Choral/Vocal**    Anonymous, *Green Grow the Lilacs—The Rose of Alabama* (words by S. S. Steele); Dan Emmett, *De Blue Tail Fly (Jimmy Crack Corn)*; Stephen Foster, *There's a Good Time Coming*; Edward L. White, *The Bridge of Sighs* (words by T. Hood).

**Operas**    Eugène-Prosper Prévost, *Adolphe et Clari*.

**Orchestra/Band**    E. K. Eaton, *Twelve Pieces of Harmony for Military Brass Bands*; Anthony P. Heinrich, *To the Spirit of Beethoven* ("monumental symphony").

**Piano/Organ**    Louis Moreau Gottschalk, *La savane* (Creole song for piano); Theodore La Hache, *Fantasia and Variations on "The Rose of Alabama," Opus 2*.

# 1847

❀

## Historical Highlights

Adhesive postage stamps are approved by Congress; the *Chicago Tribune* begins publication; the American Medical Association is founded; the abolitionist newspaper *North Star* begins publication; the Irish begin a giant migration to the United States following the great potato famine at home; the country of Liberia, founded by freed American slaves, becomes the first republic in Africa.

## World Cultural Highlights

**World Art**   Gustave Courbet, *Man with a Pipe*; Thomas Couture, *Romans of the Decadence*; François Rude, *The Awakening of Napoleon*; George Watts, *King Alfred and the Saxons*.

**World Literature**   Charlotte Brontë, *Jane Eyre*; Emily Brontë, *Wuthering Heights*; Leigh Hunt, *Men, Women and Books*; Alfred, Lord Tennyson, *The Princess*; William Thackeray, *Vanity Fair*.

**World Music**   Frédéric Chopin, *Three Waltzes, Opus 64*; Friedrich von Flotow, *Martha*; Niels Gade, *Symphony No. 3*; Ludwig Spohr, *Symphony No. 8*; Giuseppe Verdi, *Macbeth—Jerusalem*.

**Miscellaneous**   Durand et Cie. is founded in Paris; the Imperial Conservatory is founded in Rio de Janeiro; births include Giuseppe Giacosa, Adolf von Hildebrand, and Max Liebermann; deaths include Athanasios Christopoulos, William Collins, Frans Franzen, and Felix and Fanny Mendelssohn.

## American Art and Literature Highlights

**Births/Deaths**   Births include art figures Ralph Blakelock, Vinnie Ream, Albert Ryder, Ross Turner, and literary figures Mary Hartwell Catherwood, Mary Hallock Foote, Archibald C. Gunter, Arthur S. Hardy, Julia A. Moore, and Joseph Pulitzer; deaths include literary figures Nathaniel Harrington Bannister, Alexander Hill Everett, Joseph Clay Neal, and Richard Henry Wilde.

**Art Works**   George C. Bingham, *Raftsmen Playing Cards*; James G. Clonney, *Mexican News*; Thomas Cole, *The Dead Rising from Their Tombs*; Charles Deas, *Warrior on the Edge of a Precipice*; Thomas Doughty, *Mount Desert Lighthouse*; William S. Mount, *The Power of Music*; William Ranney, *First News of the Battle of Lexington*; Robert W. Weir, *Embarkation of the Pilgrims*.

**Literature**   William Channing II, *Poems II*; Philip P. Cooke, *Froissart Ballads and Other Poems*; Ralph Waldo Emerson, *Poems I*; Fitz-Greene Halleck, *Poetical Works*; Henry Wadsworth Longfellow, *Evangeline*; Herman Melville, *Omoo*; Anna Cora Mowatt, *Armand, the Child of the People*; Epes Sargent, *Songs of the Sea with Other Poems*; William W. Story, *Poems*.

## Music

**F. Births**   Charles D. Blake (composer) September 13; Albert Ross Parsons (pianist/composer/author) September 16; Walton Perkins (pianist/educator) November 16; Leander S. Sherman (publisher) April 28; Will L. Thompson (composer/publisher) November 7; Gus Williams (singer/composer/actor) July 19.

**H. Debuts**

**United States**   Eliza Biscaccianti (New York), Anna Bishop (British soprano—New York), Robert Bochsa (French harpist—tour), Giovanni Bottesini (Italian double bassist—New Orleans), Richard Hoffman (British pianist—New York), Eliza Ostinelli (New York), Caroline Richings (as pianist—Philadelphia), Teresa Truffi (Italian soprano—New York).

**I. New Positions**

**Conductors**   Charles Edward Horn (Boston Handel and Haydn Society).

**Other**   William Henry Fry (editor, *Philadelphia Ledger*).

**K. Biographical**   Anna Bishop (British soprano) comes to the United States with Nicholas Bochsa; William B. Bradbury begins two years' study in Leipzig and travels in Europe; Wulf Fries (German cellist) settles in Boston; George Gemünder (German violin maker) comes to the United States and joins his brother in Boston; the Havana Opera Co. arrives for a season in New York; Richard Hoffman (British pianist/composer) emigrates to the United States and settles in New York.

**L. Musical Beginnings**

**Performing Groups**   Deutsche Liederkranz (New York); Mormon Tabernacle Choir (Salt Lake City, Utah).

**Other**   Adelphi Theater (Boston); *The American Musical Times*; Astor Place Opera House (New York—to 1852); Boston Musical Fund Society (to 1856); William Hall and Son; Newark Concert Hall.

**M. Music Publications**

Aikin, Jesse B., *The Juvenile Minstrel*
Fillmore, Augustus, *The Christian Psalmist*
Haskell, Russel, *A Musical Expositor*
Mason, Lowell, *The Choralist*
Woodbury, I. and Baker, B., *The New England Glee Book*

**N. Musical Compositions**

**Choral/Vocal**   Stephen Foster, *Lou'siana Belle—What Must a Fairy's Dream Be—The White House Chairs*; J. Howard and F. German, *Mary Blane*.

**Orchestra/Band**   Charles Balmer, *St. Louis Fireman's Parade March*; Anthony P. Heinrich, *The Ornithological Combat of Kings*.

**Piano/Organ**   Louis Moreau Gottschalk, *La mélancolie—La moissonneuse*; Charles Grobe, *The Battle of Buena Vista, Opus 101*; Isaac Woodbury, *Variations on the Celebrated Air, "The Watcher."*

# 1848

❀

## Historical Highlights

The Treaty of Guadalupe-Hidalgo ends the Mexican War with most of the southwestern territory ceded to the United States; Zachary Taylor is elected the 12th president; Wisconsin becomes the 30th state; the California Gold Rush begins; Tulsa Trading Post is founded in Oklahoma; the "Year of Revolutions" in Europe; Louis Napoleon becomes President of the Second French Republic.

## World Cultural Highlights

**World Art**   Rosa Bonheur, *Plowing in the Nivernais*; George Cruikshank, *The Drunkard's Children*; Edwin Landseer, *A Random Shot*; Jean-François Millet, *The Winnower*.

**World Literature**   Alexandre Dumas, fils, *La Dame aux Camélias*; Elizabeth Gaskell, *Mary Barton*; Charles Kingsley, *Yeast*; Karl Marx and Friedrich Engels, *Communist Manifesto*.

**World Music**   Hector Berlioz, *Mort d'Ophélie*; Mikhail Glinka, *Kamarinskaya*; Franz Liszt, *Piano Concerto 1—St. Cecilia Mass*; Robert Schumann, *Manfred, Incidental Music—Genoveva*.

**Miscellaneous**   The Pre-Raphaelite Brotherhood is formed in London; the Royal Irish Academy of Music opens; births include Jules Bastien-Lepage, Édouard Detaille, Charles Hubert Parry, and

Fritz von Uhde; deaths include Emily Brontë, Gaetano Donizetti, Frederick Marryat, and Steen Blicher.

## American Art and Literature Highlights

**Births/Deaths**   Births include art figures Frank Duveneck, William Harnett, Joseph Pickett, Augustus Saint-Gaudens, Louis C. Tiffany, and literary figures Frances C. Baylor, Sarah Barnwell Elliott, Joel Chandler Harris, James Otis Kaler, and Eben E. Rexford; deaths include artists Thomas Cole, Benjamin Tanner, and author William J. Snelling.

**Art Works**   James Bard, *The Alida*; Asher Durand, *Dover Plain, New York*; Henry Gray, *Wages of War*; Edward Hicks, *The Peaceable Kingdom*; Daniel Huntington, *Trout Brook*; Emanuel Leutze, *Storming of the Teocalli by Cortez and His Troops*; William S. Mount, *Farmer Whetting His Scythe*; Hiram Powers, *Fisher Boy*; Richard Woodville, *War News from Mexico—Politics in an Oyster House*.

**Literature**   Oliver Bunce, *The Morning of Life*; George W. Cutter, *Buena Vista and Other Poems*; Charles G. Eastman, *Poems*; Eliza Leslie, *Amelia, or a Young Lady of Vicissitudes*; Sarah Anna Lewis, *Child of the Sea and Other Poems*; James R. Lowell, *The Vision of Sir Launfal—The Bigelow Papers*; Joseph C. Neal, *Charcoal Sketches II*; Edwin Percy Whipple, *Essays and Reviews I*.

## Music

**F. Births**   William F. Apthorp (music critic) October 24; Edward M. Bowman (organist); Louis Charles Elson (music historian) April 17; Al G. Field (minstrel/impresario) November 7; Frederick G. Gleason (organist/composer) December 18; Howard E. Parkhurst (organist); Theodore Presser (publisher/philanthropist) July 3; Arthur W. Tams (manager/singer/collector) October 7; "Uncle" Jimmy Thompson (country fiddler); Alwina Valleria (soprano) October 12; Thomas P. Westendorf (composer) February 23.

**G. Deaths**   Charles Albrecht (piano maker) June 28; Timothy Olmstead (bandmaster/composer); Oliver Shaw (organist/tenor/composer) December 31.

**H. Debuts**

**United States**   Clara M. Brinkerhoff (soprano—New York), Otto Dresel (German pianist—New York), Salvatore Marchesi (Italian baritone—New York), Caterina Barilli Patti (Italian soprano—New York), Maurice Strakosch (Czech pianist—New York).

**I. New Positions**

**Conductors**   Max Maretzek (Italian Opera Co., New York).

**Other**   Henry Christian Timm (president, New York Philharmonic Society—to 1863).

**K. Biographical**   Theodore Eisfeld (German conductor/violinist) arrives in New York; Justin Holland settles in Cleveland and begins teaching guitar; George John Huss (German organist/conductor) comes to the United States and settles in New Jersey; Hermann Kotzschmar (German composer), in the United States with the Saxonia Band, decides to stay; Charles and Jacob Kunkel (German pianists/publishers) come to the United States and settle in Cincinnati; J. C. D. Parker graduates with law degree from Harvard, begins music study in Leipzig; Eduard Reményi flees to the United States following his revolutionary activities; Maurice Strakosch (Czech pianist/impresario) arrives in New York; Gustave Stoeckel (German organist) comes to Norfolk as a private teacher; Alexander Thayer receives an L.L.B. degree from Harvard; Albert Weber (German piano maker) emigrates to the United States; Carl Zerrahn (German conductor) settles in Boston.

**L. Musical Beginnings**

**Performing Groups**   Buffalo Liedertafel; Harrington Minstrels; Maretzek Opera Co. (New York); New York Germania Musical Society.

**Other**   Balmer and Weber Music House (St. Louis); Breusing and Kearsing Music House (New York); S. S. Griggs and Co. Publishers (Chicago); Lee and Walker, Music Publishers (Philadelphia); William Nunns and Co., Piano Makers (New York).

**M. Music Publications**

Hauser, William, *The Hesperian Harp*
Hendrickson, George, *The Union Harmony*
Jackson, Samuel, *Sacred Harmony*
Mason, L. and Webb, G., *The National Psalmist*
Swann, W. H. and M. L., *The Harp of Columbia*
Woodbury, I. and Baker, B., *The Timbrel*

**N. Musical Compositions**

**Choral/Vocal**　Thomas D. English and N. Kneass, *Sweet Alice (Ben Bolt)*; Stephen Foster, *Away Down South—Oh! Susanna—Old Uncle Ned—Stay, Summer Breath*; John H. Hewitt, *The Revellers* (juvenile cantata); Charles E. Horn, *Daniel's Prediction* (oratorio); James M. Hubbard, *My Last Cigar ('Twas Off the Blue Canaries)*.

**Symphonies**　George F. Bristow, *Sinfonia in E-Flat Major, Opus 10.*

# 1849

☀

## Historical Highlights

The Department of the Interior is created by Congress; Memphis, Tennessee, is incorporated; patents include the safety pin and the breech-loading cannon; Loyola University and Eastern Michigan University are founded; Elizabeth Blackwell becomes the first woman to receive an MD degree; Hungary, under Kossuth, tries for independence but is crushed by Russia and Austria.

## World Cultural Highlights

**World Art**　Gustave Courbet, *The Stonebreakers*; Jean-Auguste Ingres, *The Golden Age*; Dante Rossetti, *Girlhood of the Virgin*; George Watts, *Life's Illusions*.

**World Literature**　Matthew Arnold, *The Strayed Reveller*; Thomas De Quincey, *The English Mail Coach*; Charles Kingsley, *Alton Locke*; Augustin Scribe and Gabriel Legouvé, *Adrienne Lecouvreur*.

**World Music**　Hector Berlioz, *Te Deum*; Anton Bruckner, *Requiem in D Minor*; Franz Liszt, *Todtentanz*; Otto Nicolai, *The Merry Wives of Windsor*; Giuseppe Verdi, *Luisa Miller*.

**Miscellaneous**　The Brisbane School of the Arts (Australia) and National Conservatory (Santiago, Chile) open; the Norwegian Choral Festivals begin; births include Marguerite Blessington, Eugène Carrière, Alexander Kielland, Hugo Riemann, and August Strindberg; deaths include Anne Brontë, Frédéric Chopin, Maria Edgeworth, and Otto Nicolai.

## American Art and Literature Highlights

**Births/Deaths**　Births include artists William Chase, Abbott Thayer, Dwight Tryon, and literary figures Thomas A. Janvier, Sarah Orne Jewett, Emma Lazarus, James Whitcomb Riley, and Ruth Stuart; deaths include Edward Hicks, Eunice Pinney, and author Edgar Allan Poe.

**Art Works**　George Bingham, *Watching the Cargo*; Frederic Church, *Haying Near New Haven*; Thomas Cole, *The Good Shepherd*; Asher Durand, *Kindred Spirits*; Richard Greenough, *Cornelia Van Rensselaer*; Edward Hicks, *Cornell Farm*; George Inness, *Wood Chopper*; William Ranney, *Duck Hunting, Hackensack Meadows*; Robert W. Weir, *Microscope*; Richard Woodville, *Old '76 and Young '48.*

**Literature**　James F. Cooper, *The Sea Lions*; Ralph Waldo Emerson, *Representative Men*; Henry Wadsworth Longfellow, *Kavanagh*; Francis Parkman, *The California and Oregon Trail*; E. D. E. N. Southworth, *Retribution*; Henry D. Thoreau, *Civil Disobedience—A Week on the Concord and Merrimac Rivers*; John Greenleaf Whittier, *Margaret Smith's Journals.*

## Music

**F. Births**   Blind Tom Bethune (pianist/composer) May 25; Maurice Grau (impresario); Emma Osgood (soprano); Hilborne L. Roosevelt (organ builder) December 21; Marie Selika (soprano) (?).

**G. Deaths**   James Hemmenway (bandmaster/composer) July 29; Charles Edward Horn (British-born conductor/composer) October 21.

**H. Debuts**

**United States**   Ernst Lübeck (Dutch pianist—tour), Giuletta Perrini (Italian soprano—New York), John Rogers Thomas (Welsh baritone—New York).

**I. New Positions**

**Conductors**   Hermann Kotzschmar (Union Street Theater, Portland, Maine).

**K. Biographical**   The Baker Family, from New Hampshire, performs at the White House; Hans Balatka (Czech composer/conductor) emigrates to the United States and arrives in Milwaukee; Carl Barus (German conductor/composer) comes to the United States; Carl Bergmann (German cellist/conductor) emigrates to New York; Patrick S. Gilmore (Irish bandmaster/composer) comes to the United States and settles in Boston; John Rogers Thomas (Welsh baritone/composer) comes to the United States and goes to New York; Isaac Baker Woodbury leaves Boston and settles in New York; Jacob Zech (German piano maker) comes to New York.

**L. Musical Beginnings**

**Performing Groups**   Artists' Union Opera Co. (New York); Chicago Mozart Society; Cincinnati Männerchor; Detroit Harmonie; German Saengerbund of North America; Mendelssohn Quintette Club (Boston—to 1895); Sacred Harmonic Society (New York).

**Other**   American Musical Fund Society (Philadelphia); Atwill and Co. of San Francisco; Mason and Colburn Co. (Cincinnati).

**M. Music Publications**

Ball, E., *Manual of the Sacred Choir*
Hastings, T. and Bradbury, W., *The Mendelssohn Collection*
Jones, Lazarus J., *The Southern Minstrel*

**N. Musical Compositions**

**Chamber Music**   George F. Bristow, *String Quartet in F Major, Opus 1—String Quartet in G Minor, Opus 2—Violin Sonata in G Major, Opus 12*.

**Choral/Vocal**   George F. Bristow, *Eleutheria* (cantata); Stephen Foster, *My Brudder Gum—Nelly Bly—Nelly Was a Lady—Summer Longings*; Isaac Woodbury, *Lays of New England* (song cycle).

**Orchestra/Band**   George F. Bristow, *Captain Raynor's Quickstep—Serenade Waltz*; Christopher Meineke, *President Taylor's Inauguration March*; J. W. Postlewaite, *St. Louis Quick Step*.

**Piano/Organ**   Louis Moreau Gottschalk, *Le Mancenillier*; Charles Thibault, *Locomotion Polka, Opus 31*; Isaac Woodbury, *Jeannette and Jeannot Quick Step*.

# 1850

☼

## Historical Highlights

The census shows a population of 31,443,000; Millard Fillmore becomes the 13th president; California becomes the 31st state; Los Angeles is incorporated; Rochester and Utah Universities are founded; the Compromise of 1850 settles the slavery question in new territories; in the Peace of Berlin, Prussia and Denmark settle their problems over the Schleswig-Holstein controversy.

## World Cultural Highlights

**World Art**   Jean-Baptiste Corot, *Une Matinée*; Eugène Delacroix, *Arab Attacked by a Lion*; John Millais, *Christ in His Parents' Home*; Dante Rossetti, *The Annunciation*.

**World Literature**   Grace Aguilar, *Vale of Cedars*; Elizabeth Browning, *Sonnets from the Portuguese*; Charles Dickens, *David Copperfield*; Sydney Dobell, *The Roman*.

**World Music**   Franz Liszt, *Prometheus—Heroïde Funèbre*; Camille Saint-Saëns, *Symphony in A*; Robert Schumann, *Rhenish Symphony*; Ludwig Spohr, *Symphony No. 9*; Richard Wagner, *Lohengrin*.

**Miscellaneous**   The Stern Conservatory opens in Berlin; the Bach Gesellschaft is formed; births include Henri Chantavoine, Max Kalbeck, Guy de Maupassant, and Robert Louis Stevenson; deaths include Honoré de Balzac, Nikolaus Lenau, Jane Porter, Gottfried Schadow, and William Wordsworth.

## American Art and Literature Highlights

**Births/Deaths**   Births include art figures Daniel French, Charles Turner, and literary figures Edward Bellamy, Eugene Field, Lafcadio Hearn, Mary N. Murtree, John L. Stoddard, and Ella Wheeler Wilcox; deaths include literary figures Philip Pendleton Cooke, Sarah Margaret Fuller, Henry Clay Lewis, and Frances Sargent Osgood.

**Art Works**   George Bingham, *Shooting for the Beef*; William Brown, *Landscape with Two Indians*; Ernst Fischer, *Country Life*; William Jewett, *The Promised Land—the Grayson Family*; Fitz Hugh Lane, *Ships in Ice off Ten Pound Island, Gloucester—U.S. Frigate "President" Engaging the British Squadron*; William Ranney, *Duck Shooting*; Joseph W. Stock, *Fisherman with His Dog*.

**Literature**   *Poems of Alice and Phoebe Cary*; Joseph Cobb, *The Creole*; Nathaniel Hawthorne, *The Scarlet Letter*; Hannah F. Lee, *Sketches and Stories from Life*; Herman Melville, *White-Jacket*; John G. Saxe, *Humorous and Satirical Poems*; Bayard Taylor, *El Dorado*; Charles Testut, *Portraits Littéraires de la Nouvelle-Orléans*; John Greenleaf Whittier, *Songs of Labor and Other Poems*.

## Music

**F. Births**   Emma Abbott (soprano) December 9; Melville Clark (organ-piano builder); Julia Gaylord (soprano); Jules Jorden (conductor/composer) November 10; Sam Lucas (minstrel performer); John Orth (organist/composer) December 2; Alfred H. Pease (pianist/composer); Joseph P. Skelly (songwriter) June 29; Emma Steiner (composer/conductor); Antoinette Sterling (contralto) January 23; Jeannette Thurber (art patron) January 29; Daniel Brink Towner (bass/composer/educator) March 5.

**G. Deaths**   Eliakim Doolittle (singing master).

**H. Debuts**

**United States**   Giovanni Belletti (Italian baritone—tour), Angeolina Bosio (Italian soprano—New York), Miska Hauer (Austrian violinist—tour), Jenny Lind (Swedish soprano—New York), Ignacio Marini (Italian bass—New York), Amalia Patti (Italian soprano), Maria Dolores Nau (soprano), Teresa Parodi (Italian soprano—New York), Eduard Reményi (Hungarian violinist—New York), Lorenzo Salvi (Italian tenor—New York), Pablo de Sarasate (Spanish violinist—tour), Signora Steffanone (Italian soprano—New York).

**I. New Positions**

**Conductors**   Hans Balatka (Milwaukee Musical Society—to 1860); William B. Bradbury (choir, Broadway Tabernacle, New York—to 1854).

**Educational**   Benjamin Franklin Baker (principal, Boston Music School).

**Other**   Theodore von La Hache (first organist, St. Theresa of Avila, New Orleans); Isaac Baker Woodbury (editor, *American Monthly Musical Review*—to 1853).

**K. Biographical**   J. Lathrop Allen designs an efficient rotary valve for brass instruments; Thomas Appleton moves his organ business to Reading, Pennsylvania; Julius Dyhrenfurth leads the first opera in Chicago (Bellini's *La Sonnambula*) in July and first symphony concert in October; Jenny Lind appears under the auspices of P. T. Barnum; George F. Root goes to Paris for further music study; Adam A. Stein (German organ builder) is brought to the United States; Heinrich E. Steinway

(German piano builder) moves to New York; William F. Sudds (British-born composer) is brought to the United States at age seven; Philip Werlein moves to New Orleans and begins working in Ashbrand's Music Store.

**L. Musical Beginnings**

**Performing Groups**  Balatka String Quartet; Chicago Philharmonic Society; Cleveland Mendelssohn Society; Ordway's Aeolian Vocalists (minstrel group); Washington Philharmonic Society (DC); Worcester Festival Association.

**Other**  Chicago Tremont Music Hall; *Choral Advocate and Singing-class Journal* (to 1873); Clough and Warren Organ Co. (Detroit); *The Dulcimer*; *Musical World and New York Musical Times*; *The New York Musical Review and Choral Advocate*; M. J. Paillard and Co. (New York); Pillow and Drew Music Store (first in Portland, Oregon); J. Sage and Sons, Piano and Music Store (Buffalo).

**M. Music Publications**

Bradbury, William B., *The Alpine Glee Singer—Sabbath-School Melodies*
Hastings, Thomas, *Devotional Hymns and Religious Poems*
Mason, Lowell, *Cantica Laudis*
Willis, Richard S., *Church Chorals and Choir Studies*
Woodbury, Isaac, *The Dulcimer*

**N. Musical Compositions**

**Choral/Vocal**  Stephen Foster, *Camptown Races*; Thomas Oliphant and Teodoro Cottrau, *Santa Lucia*; Sylvanus Pond, *Franklin Square*; Richard S. Willis, *Carol (It Came Upon a Midnight Clear)*.

**Piano/Organ**  George F. Bristow, *Andante and Polonaise, Opus 18*; Louis Moreau Gottschalk, *Le Bananier: Chanson des Negres*; Isaac Woodbury, *Elfin Quick Step—Sweet Memories Waltz—The Willow Wood Quick Step*.

**Symphonies**  C. C. Perkins, *Grand Symphony* (premiere date).

# 1851

☼

## Historical Highlights

The Illinois Central Railroad is chartered; the first American YMCA opens in Boston; Des Moines, Iowa, and Portland, Oregon, are chartered; Isaac Singer patents the sewing machine; the clipper ship *Flying Cloud* is launched; Louis Napoléon launches a coup-d'etat in France, paving the way for a new empire; the London International Industrial Exposition is the first held.

## World Cultural Highlights

**World Art**  Jean-Baptiste Corot, *Dance of the Nymphs*; Gustave Courbet, *The Village Damsels*; Edwin Landseer, *Monarch of the Glen*; John Millais, *Christ in the Carpenter's Shop*.

**World Literature**  Alexandre Dumas, père, *Diane de Lys*; Friedrich Hebbel, *Julia*; Auguste Hoffmann, *Liebeslieder*; Gottfried Keller, *Der Grüne Heinrich*; Wilhelm Müller, *Lorelei*.

**World Music**  Mikhail Glinka, *Summer Night in Madrid*; Franz Liszt, *Twelve Transcendental Etudes—Mazeppa*; Ambroise Thomas, *Raymond*; Giuseppe Verdi, *Rigoletto*.

**Miscellaneous**  The Cologne Conservatory of Music is founded; births include Vincent d'Indy and Mrs. Humphrey Ward; deaths include Tomaso Albinoni, Joanna Baillie, Alexei Egorov, Harriet Lee, Albert Lortzing, Mary Wollstonecraft Shelley, Gaspare Spontini, and Joseph Turner.

## American Art and Literature Highlights

**Births/Deaths**  Births include art figures John J. Boyle, Thomas W. Dewing, Samuel A. Robb,

Frederick J. Sykes, and literary figures Kate O'Flaherty Chopin and Grace King; deaths include artists John James Audubon, Thomas Birch, and literary figures James Fenimore Cooper, Frederic Stanhope Hill, and Mordecai M. Noah.

**Art Works**   Thomas Crawford, *Babes in the Wood*; Seth Eastman, *Ball Play on the Prairie* (?); John A. Jackson, *Daniel Webster*; Emanuel Leutze, *Washington Crossing the Delaware*; Alfred Miller, *Indian Scout*; William Rinehart, *The Smokers*; Richard C. Woodville, *Waiting for the Stage*.

**Literature**   Joseph Cobb, *Mississippi Scenes*; George Curtis, *Nile Notes of a Howadji*; Nathaniel Hawthorne, *The House of the Seven Gables*; Henry Wadsworth Longfellow, *The Golden Legend*; Herman Melville, *Moby Dick*; Henry T. Tuckerman, *Poems*; Frances and Metta Victor, *Poems of Sentiment and Imagination*.

## Music—The Vernacular/Commercial Scene

**B. Deaths**   Master Juba Lane (dancer/minstrel).

**E. Representative Works**

**Songs**   Anonymous, *The Arkansas Traveler*; Stephen Foster, *Old Folks at Home—Ring De Banjo*; George P. Knauff, *Wait for the Wagon*.

## Music—The Cultivated/Art Music Scene

**F. Births**   Theodore Baker (lexicographer) June 3; W. C. Brownell (music critic/author) August 30; Hiram Clarence Eddy (organist) June 23; Minnie Hauk (mezzo-soprano) November 16; Albert A. Stanley (organist/teacher) May 25; Charles A. Tindley (pastor/hymn writer) July 7; Frank Rush Webb (organist/bandmaster) October 8.

**G. Deaths**   Edward L. White (composer/educator); George Willig (German-born publisher) December 30.

**H. Debuts**

**United States**   Marietta Alboni (Italian contralto—New York), Frederick Brandeis (Austrian pianist—New York), Elizabeth Greenfield (the "Black Swan"—Buffalo), Catherine Hayes (Irish soprano—New York), Sophie Anne Thillon (British soprano—San Francisco).

**I. New Positions**

**Conductors**   George F. Bristow (New York Harmonic Society—to 1862).

**Other**   Hermann Kotzschmar (organ, First Unitarian Church, Portland, Maine—to 1898); Richard Grant White (music critic, *Morning Courier and New York Inquirer*—to 1857).

**K. Biographical**   Carl Jonas Almquist (Swedish composer), fleeing a charge of murder, comes to the United States (to 1865); Louis Moreau Gottschalk experiences exceptional fame in Switzerland and goes to Spain; James C. D. Parker goes to Leipzig for further music study.

**L. Musical Beginnings**

**Performing Groups**   Milwaukee Musikverein; Washington Sängerbund (DC).

**Educational**   Boston Music School.

**Other**   Haines Brothers Piano Co. (East Rochester); Hempsted Music Store and Publisher (Milwaukee); William A. Johnson, Organ Builder (Westfield, Massachusetts); George Kilgen Organ Co. (New York); W. C. Peters and Sons, Music Publishers (Cincinnati); Peters, Cragg and Co. (Louisville); John L. Peters and Brother, Music Publishers (St. Louis); Anson D. F. Randolph, Publisher (New York).

**M. Music Publications**

Beecher, Henry Ward, *Plymouth Collection*
Funk, Joseph, *Harmonia Sacra*
Greatorex, Henry W., *Collection of Sacred Music*
Hastings, Thomas, *Songs of Zion*
Jones, Darius, *Plymouth Collection of Hymns and Tunes*

Mason, Lowell, *The Glee Hive*
Woodbury, Isaac, *Liber Musicus*

**N. Musical Compositions**

**Choral/Vocal**   Theodore La Hache, *Grand Jubilee Mass*; Isaac Woodbury, *The Cantata of Washington*.

**Piano/Organ**   Louis Moreau Gottschalk, *Danses des ombres—Fantasy on "God Save the Queen"—Souvenirs d'Andalousie*; William Iucho, *Variations on "The Arkansas Traveller."*

# 1852

☀

## Historical Highlights

Franklin Pierce is elected the 14th president; Wells Fargo and Co. opens offices in San Francisco; Massachusetts passes the first compulsory school attendance law; the Studebaker Auto Co. is founded in South Bend, Indiana; E. G. Otis introduces the safety elevator; Louis Napoléon declares himself emperor of the Second French Empire; the Second Burmese War takes place in southeast Asia.

## World Cultural Highlights

**World Art**   Anselm Feuerbach, *Hafiz at the Well*; Adolf von Menzel, *Flute Concert at Sans Souci*; John Millais, *Ophelia*; François Rude, *Jeanne d'Arc*.

**World Literature**   Dion Boucicault, *The Corsican Brothers*; Alexandre Dumas, fils, *La Dame aux Camélias* (stage version); Charles de Lisle, *Poèmes antiques*; Charles Reade, *Masks and Faces*.

**World Music**   Daniel Auber, *Marco Spada*; Johannes Brahms, *Piano Sonata No. 2*; Niels Gade, *Symphony No. 5*; Franz Liszt, *Hungarian Fantasy*; Robert Schumann, *Requiem*.

**Miscellaneous**   Melbourne Philharmonic Society is founded in Australia; births include Charles Bourget, Alfredo Oriani, and Charles Villiers Stanford; deaths include Esteban Echeverria, Nikolai Gogol, Thomas Moore, Ernest Raupach, and Vasili Zhukovski.

## American Art and Literature Highlights

**Births/Deaths**   Births include literary figures Mary E. Wilkins Freeman, Robert Grant, Edwin C. Markham, Brander Matthews, Henry van Dyke, and art figures Chester Loomis, Theodore Robinson, and Julian Alden Weir; deaths include art figures John Frazee, Horatio Greenough, John Vanderlyn, and literary figures John Howard Payne, Elizabeth Phelps, and Amelia Ball Welby.

**Art Works**   George Bingham, *Daniel Boone Escorting Settlers*; Frederic Church, *Grand Manan Island, Bay of Fundy*; John F. Kensett, *A Cascade in the Forest*; Thomas Rossiter, *Rebecca at the Well*; William W. Story, *Arcadian Shepherd Boy*; Richard C. Woodville, *The Sailor's Wedding*.

**Literature**   William C. Bryant, *Letters of a Traveller*; George W. Curtis, *The Howadji in Syria*; Nathaniel Hawthorne, *The Blithedale Romance—The Snow-Image and Other Twice-Told Tales*; Herman Melville, *Pierre: or, the Ambiguities*; Richard H. Stoddard, *Poems*; Harriet Beecher Stowe, *Uncle Tom's Cabin*.

## Music—The Vernacular/Commercial Scene

**A. Births**   Willard Spenser (composer).

**D. Publications**   E. K. Eaton, *Eaton's Series of National and Popular Songs I*.

**E. Representative Works**

**Songs**   Anonymous, *Row, Row, Row Your Boat*; Stephen Foster, *Massa's in de Cold, Cold Ground*; S. M. Grannis and C. A. Mason, *Do They Miss Me at Home?*

## Music—The Cultivated/Art Music Scene

**F. Births**    Benjamin Ives Gilman (ethnomusicologist) February 19.

**G. Deaths**    George Catlin (music instrument maker) May 1; Edward Seguin (British-born bass/impresario) December 13.

**H. Debuts**

**United States**    Alfred Jaëll (Austrian pianist—tour), Caroline Richings (as soprano), Henriette Sontag (German soprano—tour), Camilla Urso (French violinist, age 10—New York).

**I. New Positions**

**Conductors**    Carl Bergmann (Boston Handel and Haydn Society—to 1854); Theodore Eisfeld (New York Philharmonic Orchestra—to 1865); Patrick S. Gilmore (Suffolk Brass Band).

**Educational**    Armand Edward Blackmar (music, Centenary College, Mississippi).

**Other**    William Henry Fry (music critic, *New York Tribune* (to 1863); Richard S. Willis (editor, *Musical Times* and *Musical World*—to 1860).

**K. Biographical**    First Normal Institute of Music held in New York City; Ole Bull founds a colony for Norwegian immigrants in Pennsylvania; Otto Dresel (German pianist) comes to Boston, Louis Grunewald (German publisher/impresario) emigrates to the United States and settles in New Orleans; August and George Gemunder move their violin business from Boston to New York; Jenny Lind marries the American conductor Otto Goldschmidt; Adelaide Phillips goes to Europe for further study.

**L. Musical Beginnings**

**Performing Groups**    Chattahoochie Musical Convention; Chicago Männergesang-Verein; Cleveland St. Cecilia Society; San Francisco Philharmonic Society.

**Other**    Joseph Atwill and Co., Music Publishers (San Francisco); Boston Music Hall (Aquarius Theater); *Dwight's Journal of Music* (to 1881); Novello's Sacred Music Store (N.Y. branch of Novello and Co., London); Stieff Piano Co. (Baltimore); Weber Piano Workshop (New York).

**M. Music Publications**

Mason, Lowell, *The New Carmina Sacra—Mason's Handbook of Psalmody*
Moore, John W., *Complete Encyclopedia of Music, Elementary, Technical, Historical, Biographical, Vocal and Instrumental*
Southard, Lucien, *Union Glee Book*

**N. Musical Compositions**

**Choral/Vocal**    Theodore La Hache, *Grand Dedication Cantata*; George F. Root, *The Flower Queen* (cantata); H. S. Thompson, *Lily Dale*; Isaac Woodbury, *Uncle Tom's Lament for Eva* (song).

**Piano/Organ**    George F. Bristow, *A Life on the Ocean Wave, Opus 21*.

**Symphonies**    William Henry Fry, *"The Breaking Heart" Symphony*.

# 1853

❋

## Historical Highlights

The Gadsden Purchase of land from Mexico takes place; Washington Territory is formed from the Oregon Territory; the New York Central Railroad is chartered; the character of "Uncle Sam" first appears in political cartoons; Commodore Perry opens Japan to world trade; Turkey and Russia begin the Crimean War; England becomes the first nation to require smallpox vaccinations.

## World Cultural Highlights

**World Art**    Rosa Bonheur, *The Horse Fair*; Gustave Courbet, *The Bathers*; John Martin, *The*

*Great Day of His Wrath*; John Millais, *The Proscribed Royalist—The Order of Release*.

**World Literature** Charles Dickens, *Bleak House*; Alexandre Dumas, père, *Ange Pitou*; Elizabeth Gaskell, *Cranford*; Charles Kingsley, *Hypatia*; John Ruskin, *The Stones of Venice*.

**World Music** Franz Liszt, *B Minor Piano Sonata—Festklänge*; Robert Schumann, *Introduction and Allegro, Opus 131—Overture to Faust*; Giuseppe Verdi's, *Il trovatore—La Traviata*.

**Miscellaneous** The Bechstein Piano Co. opens in Berlin, the Blüthner Piano Co. in Leipzig and Schiedmayer Piano Co. in Stuttgart; births include René Bazin, Ferdinand Hodler, and Vincent van Gogh; deaths include Pierre Fontaine, Tommaso Grossi, and Johann Tieck.

## American Art and Literature Highlights

**Births/Deaths** Births include art figures William Couper, John Haberle, John M. Hamilton, Robert Will Hicok Low, J. Francis Murphy, William L. Picknell, Frederic W. Ruckstull, John Twachtmann, and literary figures Henry C. DeMille, Edgar W. Howe, and Irwin Russell; deaths include artist Sarah Goodridge, novelist Sylvester Judd, and dramatist Cornelius Ambrosius.

**Art Works** George H. Durrie, *Going to Church*; John W. Ehninger, *The Yankee Peddler*; Sanford Gifford, *Summer Afternoon*; Thomas Le Clear, *Buffalo Newsboy*; William S. Mount, *The Herald in the Country*; Willliam T. Ranney, *Advice on the Prairie*; Charles Wimar, *Indians Pursued by American Dragoons*.

**Literature** George Curtis, *Potiphar Papers*; Nathaniel Hawthorne, *Tanglewood Tales*; George Lippard, *New York: Its Upper Ten and Lower Million*; James Whitfield, *American and Other Poems*; Sarah H. Whitman, *Hours of Life and Other Poems*; John Greenleaf Whittier, *The Chapel of the Hermits and Other Poems*; Sara P. Willis, *Fern Leaves from Fanny's Portfolio*.

## Music—The Vernacular/Commercial Scene

**A. Births** John "Honey" Stromberg (composer).

**C. Biographical**

**Performing Groups** Buckley's Serenaders; Continental Vocalists (male quartet).

**D. Publications** E. K. Eaton, *Eaton's Series of National and Popular Songs II*.

**E. Representative Works**

**Songs** Anonymous, *Sweet Betsy from Pike* (first printing); H. T. Bryant, *Drink It Down, Drink It Down (Balm of Gilead, 1861)*; Dan Emmett, *Jordan Is a Hard Road to Travel*; Stephen Foster, *My Old Kentucky Home—Old Dog Tray*; George F. Root, *The Hazel Dell*.

## Music—The Cultivated/Art Music Scene

**F. Births** Monroe Althouse (composer/conductor) May 26; Henry M. Dunham (organist/composer) July 29; Arthur Foote (composer/pianist) March 5; Percy Goetschius (theorist/educator) August 30; Henry G. Hanchett (organist/pedagogue) August 29; Edwin Arthur Jones (composer/violinist) June 28; Charles H. Morse (organist/educator) January 5; James W. Pepper (instrument maker/publisher).

**G. Deaths** Jonas Chickering (piano builder) December 8; Nahum Mitchell (composer) September; Charles Thibault (French composer/pianist?).

**H. Debuts**

**United States** August Gockel (German pianist—tour), Louis Moreau Gottschalk (pianist—New York); Signor Rocco (bass?).

**I. New Positions**

**Conductors** Charles Boudousquié (Théâtre d'Orléans—to 1859); David C. Hall (Boston Brass Band); Patrick S. Gilmore (Boston Brigade Band).

**Educational** Luther Whiting Mason (music, Louisville School System).

**K. Biographical** Richard Arnold (German violinist) emigrates to the United States; Stephen

Foster leaves his wife and family and moves to New York; Louis Jullien (French conductor) comes to the United States and begins his "Monster Concerts for the Masses" in New York; Frederic and Eduard Mollenhauer (German violinists), with Julien's orchestra, stay in the United States and settle in New York; Philip Werlein buys a partnership in Ashbrand's Store, which soon becomes his own; Rudolph Wurlitzer (German instrument dealer and maker) comes to the United States and settles in Cincinnati.

## L. Musical Beginnings

**Performing Groups**   Buffalo Liederkraenzchen; Philharmonic Society of the Friends of Art (New Orleans).

**Educational**   New York Normal Music Institute.

**Other**   Berry and Gordon, Music Publishers (New York); *The Brass Band Journal* (to 1855); Metropolitan Theater (San Francisco); Miller and Beecham, Music Publishers (Baltimore); William Scharfenberg Music House (New York); Steinway and Sons, Piano Makers (New York); P. F. Werlein, Music Publisher (New Orleans).

## M. Music Publications

Aikin, Jesse B., *Harmonia Ecclesiae*
Emerson, Luther O., *The Romberg Collection*
Gould, Nathaniel D., *History of Church Music in America*
Johnson, A. W., *The Western Psalmodist*
Mason, Lowell, *Musical Letters from Abroad*
Myers, Levi C., *Manual of Sacred Music*
Richardson, Nathan, *Modern School for Piano*
Woodbury, Isaac, *Cottage Glees—The Harp of the South*
Woodbury, I. and Benjamin, L., *The New York Normal School Song Book*
Woodbury, I. and Mattison, H., *The Lute of Zion*

## N. Musical Compositions

**Choral/Vocal**   George F. Root, *Daniel* (cantata).

**Orchestra/Band**   William Henry Fry, *Metropolitan Hall March* (band); Anthony P. Heinrich, *The Wildwood Troubadour* (autobiographical "symphony").

**Piano/Organ**   Louis Moreau Gottschalk, *National Glory*; Charles Grobe, *Variations on "My Old Kentucky Home," Opus 385—Ladies' Pets: A Series of Beautiful Waltzes, Marches, Polkas.*

**Symphonies**   George F. Bristow, *Jullien Sinfonia in D Minor, Opus 24*; William Henry Fry, *Santa Claus, A Christmas Symphony—"A Day in the Country" Symphony.*

# 1854

❋

## Historical Highlights

The Republican Party is born in Wisconsin; the Kansas-Nebraska Act goes into effect while the Missouri Compromise is repealed; the Ostend Manifesto on the buying or the taking of Cuba is made public; the first black university, the Ashmun Institute, is founded; the Crimean War expands, with France and England declaring war on Russia (the Charge of the Light Brigade occurs this year).

## World Cultural Highlights

**World Art**   Antoine-Louis Barye, *War, Peace, Force, Order*; Gustave Courbet, *Women Sifting Grain*; Jean François Millet, *The Reaper*; Ferdinand Waldmüller, *The Vienna Woods*.

**World Literature**   Charles Dickens, *Hard Times;* Heinrich Heine, *Neueste Gedichte*; Coventry Patmore, *The Betrothal*; William Thackeray, *The Rose and the Ring*; Leo Tolstoy, *The Cossacks*.

**World Music**    Hector Berlioz, *L'enfance du Christ*; Johannes Brahms, *Piano Concerto No. 1*; Franz Liszt, *A Faust Symphony*; Anton Rubinstein, *Ocean Symphony*; Richard Wagner, *Das Rheingold*.

**Miscellaneous**    *Le Figaro* begins publication in France; births include Leos Janáček, Jean Rimbaud, and Oscar Wilde; deaths include Karl Begas, Albert Bitzius, Jean-Jacques Chalon, Jeremias Gotthelf, John "Mad" Martin, and Friedrich von Schelling.

## American Art and Literature Highlights

**Births/Deaths**    Births include art figures Lovell B. Harrison, John Frederick Peto, and literary figures Maud Howe Elliott, Charles L. Moore, Frank Munsey, and Edith Matilda Thomas; deaths include literary figures Robert Montgomery Bird, James Athearn Jones, Emily Cubbuck Judson (Fanny Forester), Anne Newport Royall, Richard Penn Smith, and George Watterston.

**Art Works**    James Hamilton, *Capture of the "Serapis" by John Paul Jones*; William M. Hunt, *The Little Gleaner*; Chauncey Ives, *Pandora*; William S. Mount, *Long Island Farmhouses* (?); Lily M. Spencer, *The Young Husband: First Marketing*; Arthur Tait, *Arguing the Point: Settling the Presidency*; James F. Wilkins, *Leaving the Old Homestead*.

**Literature**    Timothy Arthur, *Ten Nights in a Barroom and What I Saw There*; John E. Cooke, *Leather Stocking and Silk*; Alonzo Delano, *Life on the Plains*; Caroline Lee Hentz, *The Planter's Northern Bride*; Lucy Larcom, *Similitudes from Ocean and Prairie*; Anna Cora Mowatt, *Fashion: or, Life in New York*; William G. Simms, *The Scout*; Mary V. Terhune, *Alone*; Henry Thoreau, *Walden*.

## Music—The Vernacular/Commercial Scene

**A. Births**    James A. Bland (minstrel performer/writer) October 22; Eddie Foy (singer/dancer) March 9; John J. McNally (lyricist/librettist); Francis Wilson (singer/actor) February 7.

**C. Biographical**

**Performing Groups**    Bryant and Mallory's Minstrels.

**E. Representative Works**

**Songs**    Stephen Foster, *Jeannie with the Light Brown Hair—Hard Times Come Again No More*; G. F. Root, *There's Music in the Air*; Henry Clay Work, *We Are Coming, Sister Mary*.

## Music—The Cultivated/Art Music Scene

**F. Births**    Alfredo Barili (pianist/composer) August 2; George Chadwick (composer/teacher) November 13; Maurice Devries (baritone); George Eastman (art patron) June 12; Henry T. Finck (music critic) September 22; Adolph M. Foerster (composer/educator) February 2; Philip Hale (music critic) March 5; Henry Edward Krehbiel (critic) March 10; Julie Rivé-King (pianist) October 30; William Hall Sherwood (pianist/pedagogue) January 31; John Philip Sousa (bandmaster/composer) November 6.

**G. Deaths**    Bartholomew Brown (hymn writer); James P. Carrell (composer/compiler) October 28.

**H. Debuts**

**United States**    Louis François Drouet (French flutist—tour), Francesco Graziani (Italian baritone), Giulia Grisi (Italian soprano—tour), William Harrison (British tenor—tour), Giovanni Mario (Italian tenor—New York), Louisa Pyne (British soprano—New York), Gustav Satter (tour).

**Other**    Adelaide Phillips (contralto—Milan).

**I. New Positions**

**Conductors**    Carl Zerrahn (Boston Handel and Haydn Society—to 1896).

**Other**    George F. Bristow (Music supervisor, N.Y. Public Schools); Dan Emmett (musical director, Lea's Female Opera Troupe); Gustav Schirmer (manager, Kerksieg and Bruesing Co.).

**K. Biographical**   Louis Moreau Gottschalk goes to Cuba and suffers from malaria; Elizabeth Taylor Greenfield sings for Queen Victoria in Buckingham Palace; Theodore Hagen (German conductor/author) and Karl Merz (German composer/author) come to the United States; Nashville receives its first opera performance from Arditi's Italian Opera Company; Adolph Neuendorff (German conductor/composer) moves to the United States; Antonio Sousa (bandmaster) enlists in the US Marine Band; Morris Steinert (German music dealer) arrives in the United States; Carl Wolfsohn (German pianist/educator) comes to the United States and settles in Philadelphia; Carl Zerrahn (German flutist) stays in the United States when the Germania Musical Society orchestra disbands.

**L. Musical Beginnings**

**Performing Groups**   Cleveland Gesangverein; Indianapolis Männerchor; Männersangverein Arion (New York); Philadelphia Arion (to 1969); Pittsburgh Orchestral Society (two seasons only); Teutonia Männerchor (Pittsburgh).

**Educational**   Lyons Musical Academy (Lyons, New York); New York Academy of Music.

**Other**   Boston Music Store (Detroit); (New) Boston Theater; Bradbury's Piano-Forte Warehouse (New York); John Church Co. (Cincinnati); Faulds, Stone and Morse, Music Publishers (Louisville, Kentucky); Mason and Hamlin Organ Co. (Boston); *The Pioneer*; Richardson Music Exchange (Boston); Joseph P. Shaw Music House and Publishing Co. (Rochester).

**M. Music Publications**

Gillham, W. B., *Aeolian Lyrist*
Hastings, Thomas, *The History of Forty Choirs*
Mason, Lowell, *Musical Notation in a Nutshell—The Hallelujah*
Woodbury, Isaac, *The Columbian Glee Book—The Cythara*

**N. Musical Compositions**

**Choral/Vocal**   George F. Root, *The Pilgrim Fathers* (cantata).

**Orchestra/Band**   Henry F. Williams, *Parisien Waltzes*.

**Piano/Organ**   Louis Moreau Gottschalk, *The Banjo—Cocoyé—The Last Hope—Marche funèbre, Opus 61*; William Iucho, *Souvenirs of Kentucky: Grand Fantasie, Opus 108*.

**Symphonies**   William Henry Fry, *"Childe Harold" Symphony—"Niagara" Symphony—Sacred Symphony, Hagar in the Wilderness*.

# 1855

❀

## Historical Highlights

The Pennsylvania Rock Oil Co. becomes the first company to exploit the new resource; Northwestern University is founded in Evanston, Illinois; registered mail is introduced; Congress establishes the Court of Claims; plans are laid to introduce camels into the American west; Cyrus Field lays the first successful cable from Nova Scotia to Newfoundland.

## World Cultural Highlights

**World Art**   Gustave Courbet, *The Painter's Studio*; Ernest Meissonier, *The Gamblers*; Charles Méryon, *L'Apsis de Notre Dame*.

**World Literature**   Pedro de Alarcón, *El Final de Norma*; Robert Browning, *Men and Women*; Paul von Heyse, *Novellen*; Ivan Turgenev, *A Month in the Country*.

**World Music**   Georges Bizet, *Symphony in C Major*; Charles Gounod, *St. Cecilia Mass*; Franz Liszt, *Graner Mass—Prelude and Fugue on B-A-C-H*; Giuseppe Verdi, *Sicilian Vespers*.

**Miscellaneous**   The Neue Akademie der Tonkunst opens in Berlin; births include Ernest

Chausson, Anatole Liadov, Arthur Nikisch, Arthur Pinero, and Émile Verhaeren; deaths include Charlotte Brontë, Wilhelm von Kobell, Adam Mickiewicz, and François Rude.

## American Art and Literature Highlights

**Births/Deaths**   Births include art figures Emma F. Brigham, George De Forest Bush, George Cope, Charles M. Niehaus, and literary figures Harry S. Edwards, William Gillette, Agnes Repplier, Edgar E. Saltus, Frederic J. Stimson, Edward W. Townsend, and George E. Woodberry; deaths include artists Joseph Stock, Richard Woodville, and literary figures Joseph Hart and Sarah S. B. Keating Wood.

**Art Works**   George Bingham, *Verdict of the People*; Frederic Church, *The Andes of Ecuador*; James Clonney, *What a Catch!*; Asher B. Durand, *Landscape with Birches*; George Inness, *The Lackawanna Valley*; Chauncey Ives, *Undine Receiving Her Soul*; John F. Kensett, *Bish-Bash, South Egremont, Massachusetts*; Fitz Hugh Lane, *Casting from Hospital Island*.

**Literature**   John Bartlett, *Familiar Quotations*; Frederick Douglass, *My Bondage and My Freedom*; Augustine Duganne, *Poetical Works*; Charles Leland, *Meister Karl's Sketch-Book*; Henry W. Longfellow, *Hiawatha*; Herman Melville, *Israel Potter: His Fifty Years of Exile*; Ann Sophia Stephens, *The Old Homestead*; Walt Whitman, *Leaves of Grass*; Augusta Wilson, *Inez: A Tale of the Alamo*.

## Music — The Vernacular/Commercial Scene

**A. Births**   Julian Edwards (composer/conductor) December 11; Adam Geibel (songwriter); Tony Hart (composer/performer) July 25; Samuel S. Stewart (banjo maker/publisher) January 8.

**C. Biographical**

**Performing Groups**   Old Folks Concert Troupe (Boston).

**D. Publications**   *Put's Original California Songster*.

**E. Representative Works**

**Songs**   Stephen Foster, *Come Where My Love Lies Dreaming*; George F. Root, *Rosalie, the Prairie Flower*; Henry Tucker, *Star of the Evening*; Septimus Winner, *Listen to the Mocking Bird* (song); Richard S. Willis, *The Lone Fish (Meat) Ball*; Henry Clay Work, *Lilly-willy-woken* (song).

## Music — The Cultivated/Art Music Scene

**F. Births**   William J. Henderson (music critic) December 4; Henry C. Heyman (violinist) January 13; Emil Mollenhauer (violinist/conductor) August 4; Edward B. Perry (pianist/educator) February 14; John White (organist/composer) March 12.

**G. Deaths**   John Cole (composer/publisher) August 17.

**H. Debuts**

**United States**   Pasquale Brignoli (Italian tenor—New York), Anna Caroline de la Grange (French soprano—New York), Constance Nantier-Didiée (French mezzo—tour), Adelaide Phillipps (contralto—New York), Sigismund Thalberg (German pianist—tour), Mme. F. Vestrali (New York).

**I. New Positions**

**Conductors**   Carl Bergmann (New York Philharmonic Society—to 1876); Patrick S. Gilmore (Salem Brass Band); Francis Scala (US Marine Band—to 1871); Carl Zerrahn (Boston Philharmonic Society—to 1863).

**Educational**   Horatio R. Palmer (Rushford Academy, New York—to 1865); Gustave J. Stoeckel (Yale—to 1896).

**Other**   Isaac Baker Woodbury (editor, *New York Musical Pioneer*—to 1858).

**J. Honors and Awards**

**Honors**   Lowell Mason (doctorate, NYU).

**K. Biographical**   Dudley Buck enters Trinity College and begins piano study with W. J. Babcock; James Butterfield (British composer/violinist) comes to the United States; Benjamin J. Lang goes to Berlin and studies piano with Liszt; William Mason, after a concert tour of various American cities, settles in New York; Henry Clay Work moves to Chicago and begins working as a printer.

**L. Musical Beginnings**

**Performing Groups**   Christopher Bach Orchestra (Milwaukee); Boston Philharmonic Society II (to 1863); Buffalo Saengerbund; Classical Music Society of New Orleans; Detroit Philharmonic Society; Philadelphia Harmonie (male chorus); Stein and Buchheister Orchestra (Detroit).

**Educational**   Yale University music classes.

**Other**   American Steam Music Co. (calliopes); Berteling Woodwind Co. (Boston/New York); Board of Music Trade; Higgins Brothers, Music Publishers (Chicago); Mason and Thomas Chamber Music Soirées (New York); Mason Brothers, Music Publishers (Boston); Votteler Organ Co. (Holtkamp Organ Co.—Cleveland).

**M. Music Publications**

Baker, Benjamin, *Baker's Church Music*
Bradbury, William B., *The New York Glee and Chorus Book*
Everett, L. C. and A. B., *The Progressive Church Vocalist*
McCurry, John G., *The Social Harp*
Parker, J. C. D., *Manual of Harmony*
Root, G. F. and Mason, *Young Men's Singing Book*
Southard, Lucien, *A Course in Harmony*
Woodbury, Isaac, *The Casket*

**N. Musical Compositions**

**Choral/Vocal**   George F. Bristow, *Morning Service, Opus 19*; F. T. S. Darley, *The Cities of the Plain* (oratorio premiere); Theodore La Hache, *St. Anthony Mass—St. Patrick Mass, Opus 141—St. Theresa Mass*; C. C. Perkins, *Pilgrim's Cantata* (premiere).

**Operas**   George F. Bristow, *Rip Van Winkle*.

**Piano/Organ**   Louis Moreau Gottschalk, *Printemps d'amour*; Ureli Corelli Hill, *The Kentucky Characteristic Grand March*; Jerome Hopkins, *Rip Van Winkle Polka*.

# 1856

❄

## Historical Highlights

James Buchanan is elected the 15th president; first convention of the new Republican Party takes place; the Potawatomie Massacre coins the phrase "Bloody Kansas"; the Western Union Company is founded; Dallas, Texas, is incorporated; the Crimean War ends; the Congress of Berlin settles the Eastern question and many points of international law; the Bessemer Process revolutionizes the steel industry.

## World Cultural Highlights

**World Art**   Gustave Courbet, *Girls on the Bank of the Seine*; Eugène Delacroix, *The Sultan of Morocco*; Arthur Hughes, *The Eve of St. Agnes*; John Millais, *The Blind Girl*.

**World Literature**   Sergei Aksakov, *Chronicles of a Russian Family*; Heinrich Heine, *Last Poems*; Victor Hugo, *Les Contemplations*; Henrik Ibsen, *The Banquet at Solhaug*.

**World Music**   Johannes Brahms, *Variations, Opus 21, No. 1, 2*; Franz Liszt, *Dante Symphony— Piano Concerto No. 1*; Camille Saint-Saëns, *Symphony in F, "Urbs Roma"*; Richard Wagner, *Die Walküre*.

**Miscellaneous**   The Dresden Conservatory of Music opens; births include H. Rider Haggard, Arthur Rimbaud, George Bernard Shaw, and Sergei Taneiev; deaths include Adolphe Adam, Paul Delaroche, Heinrich Heine, Robert Schumann, and Richard Westmacott.

## American Art and Literature Highlights

**Births/Deaths**   Births include art figures John Alexander, Jefferson Chalfant, Kenyon Cox, John Singer Sargent, and literary figures L. Frank Baum, Henry Carleton, Sarah McLean, Lizette Woodworth Reese, Mabel Loomis Todd, and Kate Douglas Wiggin; deaths include artists John Bard, Thomas Doughty, and literary figures Joseph M. Field, Caroline Lee Hentz, Nicholas M. Hentz, and James G. Percival.

**Art Works**   Thomas Crawford, *Indian Chief Contemplating the Progress of Civilization*; Fitz Hugh Lane, *Off Mount Desert Island*; Louis Maurer, *Preparing for Market*; William Mount, *The Banjo Player*; Charles C. Nahl, *Saturday Evening in the Mines*; Erastus Palmer, *The Indian Girl (Dawn of Christianity)*; John Quidor, *Wolfert's Will*; Randolph Rogers, *Nydia, the Blind Flower Girl of Pompeii*.

**Literature**   Frederick Cozzens, *The Sparrowgrass Papers*; George Curtis, *Prue and I*; Ralph Waldo Emerson, *English Traits*; William W. Lord, *André*; Herman Melville, *The Confidence-Man—The Piazza Tales*; Margaret Preston, *Silverwood*; Mayne Reid, *The Quadroon*; Harriet Beecher Stowe, *Dred: A Tale of the Great Dismal Swamp*; John Greenleaf Whittier, *The Panorama and Other Poems*.

## Music—The Vernacular/Commercial Scene

**A. Births**   Lew Dockstader (minstrel performer) August 7; Orville H. Gibson (mandolin-guitar maker); William J. Scanlan (actor/composer) February 14.

**E. Representative Works**

**Songs**   Hart P. Danks, *Anna Lee*; Benjamin R. Hanby, *Darling Nellie Gray*; Richard J. McGowan, *Root, Hog, or Die*.

## Music—The Cultivated/Art Music Scene

**F. Births**   Franz Xavier Arens (German composer) October 28; Johann Beck (conductor/composer) September 12; Arthur H. Bird (pianist/composer) July 23; John H. Brewer (organist/composer) January 18; Charles H. Gabriel (composer) August 18; Daniel Guggenheim (art patron) July 9; Marie Litta (soprano) July 7; Willard Patton (tenor/composer) May 26; Mary Elizabeth Salter (soprano/composer) March 15; Alice J. Shaw (concert whistler); George Templeton Strong (composer/artist) May 26.

**G. Deaths**   Stephen Jenks (composer/compiler) June 3.

**H. Debuts**

**United States**   Charles R. Adams (tenor—Boston), Mlle. Johansen (soprano—New York).

**I. New Positions**

**Educational**   Luther Whiting Mason (music, Cincinnati School System).

**K. Biographical**   David Braham (British composer/conductor), Sebastian Bach Mills (British pianist), and Heinrich Mollenhauer (German cellist) come to New York; Julius Eichberg (German violinist/composer) leaves Switzerland and comes to the United States, eventually settling in New York; Louis Moreau Gottschalk suffers a fiasco in Canada, and begins teaching in New York; Anthony Philip Heinrich begins a three-year stay in Europe; George Lee and William Walker buy out George Willig's music business; Frédéric L. Ritter (Belgian conductor) comes to the United States and settles in Cincinnati; Sigismond Thalberg (Swiss pianist/composer) begins a two-year concert tour of the United States.

**L. Musical Beginnings**

**Performing Groups**   Cincinnati Cecilia Society; Cincinnati Harmonic Society; Cincinnati

Philharmonic Orchestra; Germania Concert Society (San Francisco); Germania Orchestra (Philadelphia—to 1895).

**Other**    American-Music Association (New York); Decker and Son, Pianos (Albany); Wurlitzer Organ Co. (Cincinnati); *Western Journal of Music* (Chicago); Jacob Zech, Piano Maker (San Francisco).

**M. Music Publications**

Everett, L. C. and A. B., *The New Thesaurus Musicus: or, The United States Collection of Church Music*
Hastings, Thomas, *Sacred Praise—The Selah*
Willis, Richard S., *Our Church Music*
Woodbury, Isaac, *The Anthem Dulcimer—The Song Crown*

**N. Musical Compositions**

**Choral/Vocal**    Benjamin F. Baker, *The Storm King* (cantata), William Henry Fry, *Stabat Mater* (oratorio); Leopold Meignen, *The Deluge* (cantata).

**Orchestra/Band**    George F. Bristow, *Overture, Winter's Tale.*

**Piano/Organ**    Louis Moreau Gottschalk, *Manchega* (concert etude); Charles Grobe, *Grobe's Parlour Music: Lessons for Ladies* (13 piano pieces).

# 1857

❀

## Historical Highlights

A financial panic takes place in the United States; the Dred Scott decision is handed down by the Supreme Court; Michigan State College becomes the first Land Grant College; Omaha, Nebraska and Minneapolis, Minnesota, are incorporated; the Sepoy Rebellion against British rule takes place in India; Garibaldi, in an attempt to unify the Italian states, forms the Italian National Association.

## World Cultural Highlights

**World Art**    Antoine-Louis Barye, *Napoleon Dominating History and the Arts*; Gustave Courbet, *The Hunting Party*; Ernest Meissonier, *The Blacksmith*; John Millais, *The Escape of the Heretic*.

**World Literature**    Charles Baudelaire, *Les Fleurs du Mal;* Elizabeth Barrett Browning, *Aurora Leigh*; Charles Dickens, *Little Dorrit*; Gustave Flaubert, *Madame Bovary*; Thomas Hughes, *Tom Brown's Schooldays*.

**World Music**    Johannes Brahms, *Serenade No. 1 for Orchestra*; Franz Liszt, *The Battle of the Huns—Die Ideale*; Giuseppe Verdi, *Simon Boccanegra*; Richard Wagner, *Wesendonk Songs*.

**Miscellaneous**    The Imperial Academy of Music and National Opera of Rio de Janeiro are founded; births include Joseph Conrad, Edward Elgar, Max Klinger, and Hendrik von Pontoppidan; deaths include Johan Dahl, Joseph von Eichendorff, Mikhail Glinka, Alfred de Musset, and Marie Joseph Sue.

## American Art and Literature Highlights

**Births/Deaths**    Births include art figures Robert Blum, Bruce Crane, Arthur Dow, Charles Eaton, Edward C. Potter, and literary figures Gertrude Atherton, Alice Brown, Samuel M. Crothers, Frank H. Cushing, Margaret Deland, Emerson Hough, James G. Huneker, Thomas W. Lawson, Frank L. Stanton, and Ida M. Tarbell; deaths include sculptor Thomas Crawford and artist William T. Ranney.

**Art Works**    George Bingham, *Jolly Flatboatmen in Port*; Frederic Church, *Niagara*; Jasper Cropsey, *Indian Summer in the White Mountains*; George Durrie, *East Rock*; Thomas Hotchkiss, *Mount Washington, NH*; William M. Hunt, *The Belated Kid*; T. H. Matteson, *Erastus Dow in His*

*Studio*; Christian Schussele, *Men of Progress*; Aaron Shattuck, *The Pool*; James Whistler, *At the Piano*.

**Literature**    Paul H. Hayne, *Avolio and Other Poems*; Josiah Holland, *The Bay-Path*; Mirabeau Lamar, *Verse Memorials*; Fitz Hugh Ludlow, *The Hasheesh Eater*; Alexander Meek, *Songs and Poems of the South*; Catharine Sedgwick, *Married or Single?*; Austin Steward, *Twenty-two Years a Slave and Forty Years a Freeman*; Richard H. Stoddard, *Songs of the Summer*.

## Music—The Vernacular/Commercial Scene

**A. Births**    Edwin E. Bagley (march composer); Henry W. Petrie (singer/writer) March 4.

**B. Deaths**    Edgar Smith (lyricist) December 9.

**C. Biographical**

**Performing Groups**    Bryant's Minstrels.

**New Beginnings**    New Orleans Mardi Gras.

**E. Representative Works**

**Songs**    W. S. Hays, *Evangeline*; Judson Hutchinson and Longstreet, *Mrs. Lofty and I*; J. S. Pierpont, *Jingle Bells*; H. D. L. and J. P. Webster, *Lorena*.

## Music—The Cultivated/Art Music Scene

**F. Births**    David Bispham (baritone) January 5; Benjamin Cutter (violinist/theorist) September 6; Sam Franko (violinist/conductor) January 20; Charles Hedmont (tenor) October 24; James G. Huneker (music author) January 31; Clayton Johns (composer/pianist) November 24; Edgar Stillman Kelley (organist/composer) April 14; Gustav Kobbé (writer on music) March; Carl V. Lachmund (pianist/composer/conductor) March 27; Lillian Nordica (soprano) December 12; Henry B. Pasmore (singer/composer) June 27; Waldo Selden Pratt (music historian/hymnologist) November 10; Henry Schoenefeld (composer/conductor) October 4; Mary Knight Wood (pianist/composer) April 7.

**G. Deaths**    Johann Christian Bechler (composer); Ananias Davisson (composer) October 21; Charles Zeuner (German-born composer/organist) November 7.

**H. Debuts**

**United States**    Karl Johann Formes (German bass—New York), Erminia Frezzolini (Italian sopra-no—New York), Marietta Gazzaniga (New York).

**I. New Positions**

**Conductors**    C. M. Cady (Chicago Musical Union); Theodore Eisler (Brooklyn Philharmonic Orchestra).

**Educational**    Maurice Strakosch (director, NY Academy of Music).

**K. Biographical**    Karl Anschütz (German conductor) comes to the United States; Theodore Berteling moves his instrument business to New York; Dudley Buck leaves for music study in Leipzig; Caryl Florio (British organist/composer) comes to the United States and settles in New York; Robert Goldbeck (German pianist/composer) comes to the United States and settles in New York; Louis Moreau Gottschalk sends his pregnant girlfriend, Ada Clara, to Paris and goes to South America with Adelina Patti and her husband; Henri Vieuxtemps joins Sigismond Thalberg on a second US concert tour.

**L. Musical Beginnings**

**Performing Groups**    Brooklyn Philharmonic Society; Chicago Musical Union; Ullman and Strakosch Opera Co. (by merger).

**Educational**    American Academy of Music (Philadelphia); Baltimore Academy of Music (Peabody Conservatory).

**Other**    Keller's Patent Steam Violin Manufactory (Philadelphia); W. W. Kimball Co., Music

Publishers (Chicago); George Steck and Co., Piano Makers (New York); John F. Stratton Brass Instrument Factory (New York); J. J. Whittemore Music Store (Detroit).

**M. Music Publications**

Brown, Francis H., *Institute Chorus Book*
Emerson, Luther O., *The Golden Wreath*
Woodbury, Isaac, *The Thanksgiving*

**N. Musical Compositions**

**Choral/Vocal**  Eugène-Prosper Prévost, *Requiem*; George F. Root, *The Haymakers* (cantata).

**Orchestra/Band**  William Henry Fry, *Overture, The World's Own*.

**Piano/Organ**  Louis Moreau Gottschalk, *Souvenir de Puerto Rico—Danza*; Charles Grobe, *Melodies of the Day* (one hundred sets of variations).

**Symphonies**  Johann Beck, *Symphony No. 1, "Sindbad," Opus 1* (unfinished).

# 1858

☀

## Historical Highlights

Minnesota enters the Union as the 32nd state; Lincoln and Douglas cover the state of Illinois with their debates; Denver, Colorado, is founded; stagecoach service begins between St. Louis and San Francisco; the Squibb Pharmaceutical Lab is founded; the first American YWCA opens in New York; the Sepoy Rebellion ends in India, which is made a British Crown Colony; Cyrus Field lays the first Atlantic Cable, which breaks after a short time.

## World Cultural Highlights

**World Art**  Charles Daubigny, *Le Printemps*; Eugène Delacroix, *Fording a Stream in Morocco*; William Frith, *Derby Day*; Edwin Landseer, *Trafalgar Square Lions*; Adolf von Menzel, *Bon Soir, Messieurs*.

**World Literature**  Wilhelm Busch, *Max und Moritz*; George Eliot, *Scenes from Clerical Life*; Octave Feuillet, *Roman d'un jeune homme pauvre*; Ivan Turgenev, *A Nest of Gentlefolk*.

**World Music**  Hector Berlioz, *Les Troyens*; Charles Gounod, *Le Médecin malgré lui*; Jacques Offenbach, *Orpheus in the Underworld*; Camille Saint-Saëns, *Piano Concerto No. 1*.

**Miscellaneous**  The Hallé Orchestra is founded in Manchester; the Vienna Music Academy opens; births include Lovis Corinth, Remy de Goncourt, Selma Lagerlöf, Giacomo Puccini, and Edith Somerville; deaths include Anton Diabelli and Ary Scheffer.

## American Art and Literature Highlights

**Births/Deaths**  Births include art figures Herbert Adams, Willard Metcalf, Charles Ulrich, Robert W. Vonnoh, and literary figures Charles W. Chestnutt, William N. Harben, and John T. Moore; deaths include sculptors Hezekiah Auger, Edward Bartholomew, and literary figures James Nelson Barker, Thomas H. Chivers, Joseph B. Cobb, Robert Taylor Conrad, Robert Hare, and William Trotter Porter.

**Art Works**  Albert Bierstadt, *Yosemite Valley—Indians near Fort Laramie*; Albertus Browere, *Gold Mining in California*; George Durrie, *Winter Scene in New Haven*; Harriet Hosmer, *Zenobia*; Frank Mayer, *Independence: Squire Jack Porter*; William H. Rinehart, *Morning—Evening*; John Stanley, *Disputed Shot*; William W. Story, *Cleopatra*; Jerome Thompson, *"Pick Nick" near Mount Mansfield*.

**Literature**  William W. Brown, *The Escape*; Joseph B. Cobb, *Leisure Labors*; Samuel Hammett, *Piney Woods Tavern, or Sam Slick in Texas*; Oliver Wendell Holmes, *The Autocrat of the Breakfast*

*Table*; Henry Wadsworth Longfellow, *The Courtship of Miles Standish*; John Gorhan Palfrey, *History of New England I*; William T. Thompson, *Scenes of Georgia*; Thomas Ward, *Flora, or, The Gypsy's Frolic*.

## Music—The Vernacular/Commercial Scene

**A. Births**    Paul Dresser (songwriter) April 22; William De Wolf Hopper (singer/actor) March 30; Henry Woolson Morse (composer/lyricist) February 24; Chauncey Olcott (singer/composer) June 21; E. T. Paull (bandmaster/composer).

**C. Biographical**

**Miscellaneous**    Dan Emmett becomes composer for Bryant's Minstrels; Elias Howe publishes *The Complete Ball-Room Hand Book*.

**D. Publications**    *Put's Golden Songster*.

**E. Representative Works**

**Songs**    Anonymous (J. K.), *The Yellow Rose of Texas (Song of the Texas Rangers)*; J. Warner, *Down in Alabam' (The Old Gray Mare)*.

## Music—The Cultivated/Art Music Scene

**F. Births**    Herman Bellstedt (bandmaster/cornetist) February 21; Frank W. Burdett (publisher) October 29; Herman Devries (bass) December 25; Robert Browne Hall (bandmaster/composer) June 30; Charles B. Hawley (composer) February 14; Frank Holton (brass-instrument maker) March 10; Peter C. Lutkin (organist/composer) March 27; Frank Lynes (composer/organist) May 16; Eugène E. Oudin (baritone) February 24; Harry Rowe Shelley (organist/composer) June 2; A. J. Showalter (publisher/hymnist) May 1; Carl Stoeckel (art patron) December 7; Frank Van der Stucken (conductor/composer) October 15; Marie Van Zandt (soprano) October 8; Frederick Zech, Jr. (composer/pianist/conductor) May 10.

**G. Deaths**    Henry W. Greatorex (organist/composer) September 10; Abraham Prescott (stringed-instrument maker) May 6; Isaac Baker Woodbury (composer/organist/author) October 26; John Wyeth (publisher) January 23.

**H. Debuts**

**United States**    Benjamin J. Lang (pianist—Boston), Arthur Napoleão (Portugese pianist—tour), Maria Piccolomini (Italian soprano—New York), Myron Whitney, Sr. (bass—Boston).

**I. New Positions**

**Conductors**    Patrick S. Gilmore (Gilmore Band); Felipe Gutiérrez (y) Espinosa (maestro de capilla, San Juan Cathedral, Puerto Rico).

**Other**    George John Huss (organ, University Place Presbyterian Church, New York—to 1868).

**J. Honors and Awards**

**Honors**    Thomas Hastings (doctorate, New York University).

**K. Biographical**    Carlo Alberto Cappa (Italian bandmaster) leaves the United States Navy and settles in New York; John Knowles Paine begins three years of further music study in Germany.

**L. Musical Beginnings**

**Performing Groups**    Chicago Mendelssohn Society; Gilmore's Band; Mendelssohn Quintet; Milwaukee Liedertafel; New Haven Mendelssohn Society (Connecticut).

**Festivals**    Worcester Music Festival (Massachusetts—oldest in continuous existence?)

**Other**    Matthias Gray Co., Music Publishers (San Francisco); Louis Grunewald, Music Dealer and Publisher (New Orleans); Kimball Music Store (Chicago); Root and Cady, Publishers (Chicago); Russell and Tolman, Music Instruments and Publishing (by merger); San Antonio Opera House.

**M. Music Publications**

Bradbury, William, *The Jubilee*

Dadmun, John W., *Revival Melodies*
Hastings, Thomas, *Church Melodies*
Park, E. A. and Phelps, A., *The Sabbath Day Hymn Book*
Sunday School Union, *Union Prayer Meeting Hymns*
Tuckerman, Samuel, *A Collection of Cathedral Chants*

**N. Musical Compositions**

**Chamber Music**   Jerome Hopkins, *Piano Trio*.

**Choral/Vocal**   Theodore La Hache, *Union Mass*.

**Piano/Organ**   Theodore La Hache, *Grand Etude de Salon*.

**Symphonies**   George F. Bristow, *Symphony No. 3 in F-Sharp Minor, Opus 26*.

# 1859

❀

## Historical Highlights

Edwin Drake is responsible for drilling the first oil well in Titusville, Pennsylvania; a new gold rush starts in Colorado and in Nevada with the discovery of the Comstock Lode; Oregon becomes the 33rd state; the Pawnee War takes place in the Nebraska Territory; John Brown makes his raid on Harper's Ferry; Prussia forms the German National Association in an attempt at German unification; work begins on the Suez Canal in Egypt.

## World Cultural Highlights

**World Art**   Jean-Baptiste Corot, *Macbeth*; Henri Fantin-Latour, *The Two Sisters*; Jean-François Millet, *The Angelus*; William Page, *Venus*; R. Spencer Stanhope, *Thoughts of the Past*.

**World Literature**   Charles Darwin, *The Origin of Species*; Charles Dickens, *A Tale of Two Cities*; George Eliot, *Adam Bede*; Alfred Lord Tennyson, *Idylls of the King*.

**World Music**   Johannes Brahms, *Serenade No. 2—Marienlieder*; Charles Gounod, *Faust—Ave Maria* (on Bach's *Prelude No. 1*); Giuseppe Verdi, *Un Ballo in Maschera*; Richard Wagner, *Tristan und Isolde*.

**Miscellaneous**   The Imperial Russian Music Society founded in St. Petersburg; births include Arthur Conan Doyle, E. A. Housman, Mikhail Ippolitov-Ivanov, Karl Muck, and Georges Seurat; deaths include Bettina von Arnim, Leigh Hunt, Thomas Macaulay, Ludwig Spohr, and Alexis de Tocqueville.

## American Art and Literature Highlights

**Births/Deaths**   Births include artists Childe Hassam, William Lathrop, Henry R. Poor, Maurice Prendergast, Henry O. Tanner, and literary figures Irving Addison Bacheller, Katharine Lee Bates, David Belasco, and George P. Hopkins; deaths in the literary field include Delia Salter Bacon, Rufus Dawes, Washington Irving, James Matthews Legaré, John A. McClung, and historian William H. Prescott.

**Art Works**   Albert Bierstadt, *Thunderstorm in the Rockies*; Frederic Church, *Heart of the Andes*; Asher Durand, *The Catskills*; Eastman Johnson, *The Old Kentucky Home*; Alfred Miller, *The Indian Lodge*; Erastus Palmer, *The White Captive*; John Rogers, *Checker Players*; Jerome Thompson, *The Haymakers*; James Whistler, *Black Lion Wharf*; Charles Wimar, *Indians Approaching Fort Benton*.

**Literature**   John T. Adams, *The White Chief among the Red Men*; Dion Boucicault, *The Octaroon*; William C. Bryant, *Letters from Spain*; Joseph Ingraham, *The Pillar of Fire*; Washington Irving, *Life of Washington*; John B. Jones, *Wild Southern Scenes*; William Simms, *The Cassique of Kiawah*; E. D. E. N. Southworth, *The Hidden Hand*; Henry Timrod, *Poems I*; Nathaniel Willis, *The Convalescent*.

## Music—The Vernacular/Commercial Scene

**A. Births**    Jefferson De Angelis (singer/actor) November 30; Reginald De Koven (composer) April 3; Henry E. Dixey (singer/actor) January 6.

**E. Representative Works**

**Songs**    Dan Bryant, *Bryant's Essence of Old Virginny*; Dan Emmett, *Dixie—Turkey in the Straw—Johnny Roach*.

## Music—The Cultivated/Art Music Scene

**F. Births**    Charles H. Farnsworth (organist) November 29; Charles F. Lummis (ethnomusicologist) March 1; Emma Nevada (soprano) February 7; Henry W. Savage (impresario) March 21; Winthrop S. Sterling (organist) November 28; Richard Henry Warren (organist/composer) September 17.

**G. Deaths**    F. W. Allen (violin maker); Allen D. Carden (teacher/compiler) March 29; Denis-Germain Etienne (French-born pianist/conductor) January 17; Samuel Worcester (compiler) April 20.

**H. Debuts**

**United States**    Sebastian Bach Mills (British pianist—New York), Adelina Patti (Italian soprano—New York).

**I. New Positions**

**Conductors**    Julius Eichberg (Museum Concerts, Boston).

**Other**    Benjamin J. Lang (organ, Boston Handel and Haydn Society—to 1895).

**K. Biographical**    The Oliver Ditson Co. takes over publication of *Dwight's Journal*, leaving Dwight as editor; Adelina Patti makes her stage debut in New York; Eduard Sobolewski (German conductor/composer) comes to the United States and settles in Milwaukee.

**L. Musical Beginnings**

**Performing Groups**    Arion Men's Chorus (Newark); French Opera Co. of New Orleans; Richings Grand Opera Co.

**Educational**    Tourjée Musical Institute (Rhode Island).

**Other**    John Albert Violin Shop (Philadelphia); French Opera House (New Orleans); Mathias Gray Music Store (San Francisco); Metropolitan Music Association; Odell Brothers Organ Co. (New York); *Peter's Sax-Horn Journal*; *Southern Musical Advocate and Singer's Friend*.

**M. Music Publications**

Aikin, Jesse B., *The Sabbath School Minstrel*
Bradbury, William B., *Cottage Melodies*
Grobe, Charles, *New Method for the Pianoforte*
Manly, Basil, Jr., *Baptist Chorals: A Hymn and Tune Book*
Perkins, William O., *Choral Harmony*
Richardson, Nathan, *New Method for the Pianoforte*
Schaff, Philip, *Deutsches Gesangbuch* (German Reformed Church)

**N. Musical Compositions**

**Chamber Music**    John Knowles Paine, *String Quartet in D Major, Opus 5*.

**Choral/Vocal**    Theodore La Hache, *Schiller Cantata* (male voices); Harrison Millard, *Viva La America* (song).

**Orchestra/Band**    Louis Moreau Gottschalk, *A Night in the Tropics* (orchestral fantasy).

**Piano/Organ**    Louis Moreau Gottschalk, *Souvenir de la Havane* (grand caprice)—*Ojos criollos* (four hands); Charles E. J. Hopkins, *The Wild Demon, Opus 11*; John Knowles Paine, *Prelude and Fugue in G Minor* (organ)—*Piano Sonata No. 1 in A Minor, Opus 1*.

# 1860

## Historical Highlights

The census shows a population of 31,443,000 in the United States; Abraham Lincoln is elected the 16th president; the first and last convention of the Constitutional Union Party is held; Pony Express service begins between St. Joseph, Missouri, and Sacramento, California; ten years of strife begin in New Zealand with the Second Maori War; the first continuous current dynamo is invented by Picinotti; Vladivostok in Siberia is founded.

## World Cultural Highlights

**World Art**   Edgar Degas, *Spartan Girls and Boys Exercising*; William Hunt, *The Boy Jesus in the Temple*; Edouard Manet, *The Spanish Guitar Player*; Jean-François Millet, *Woman Carrying Water*.

**World Literature**   Elizabeth Barrett Browning, *Poems Before Congress*; Wilkie Collins, *Woman in White*; George Eliot, *The Mill on the Floss*; Algernon Swinburne, *The Queen Mother*.

**World Music**   Johannes Brahms, *String Sextet No. 1*; Franz Liszt, *Two Episodes from Lenau's Faust*; Bedrich Smetana, *Wallingstein's Camp*; Johann Strauss, *Perpetual Motion*.

**Miscellaneous**   Istituto Musicale of Florence opens; the Boulogne Philharmonic Society is founded; births include Isaac Albéniz, James Barrie, Anton Chekhov, Gustav Mahler, and Hugo Wolf; deaths include Konstantin Aksakov, Alfred Chalon, Johannes Riepenhausen, and Arthur Schopenhauer.

## American Art and Literature Highlights

**Births/Deaths**   Births include art figures Thomas Clarke, Benjamin Clinedinst, Julius Gari Melchers, Lorado Taft, and literary figures Abraham Cahan, Hamlin Garland, Charlotte P. Gilman, Charles H. Hoyt, Harriet Monroe, and Owen Wister; deaths include artists Charles Fraser, Rembrandt Peale, and literary figures Charles G. Eastman, Samuel G. Goodrich, Joseph Ingraham, and James K. Paulding.

**Art Works**   David Blythe, *The Postoffice*; Frederic Church, *Twilight in the Wilderness*; Martin Heade, *Approaching Storm, Beach near Newport*; Eastman Johnson, *Corn Husking*; Fitz Hugh Lane, *Ship "Starlight" in the Fog*; Flora Palmer, *A Midnight Race on the Mississippi*; John Quidor, *Peter Stuyvesant Watching Festivities on the Battery*; William Rimmer, *Falling Gladiator* (cast, 1900).

**Literature**   Dion Boucicault, *The Colleen Bawn*; Ralph Waldo Emerson, *The Conduct of Life*; Nathaniel Hawthorne, *The Marble Faun*; Oliver Wendell Holmes, *The Professor at the Breakfast Table*; W. H. Howells and J. J. Piatt, *Poems of Two Friends*; Edmund C. Stedman, *Poems Lyrical and Idyllic*; Frederick G. Tuckerman, *Poems*; John Greenleaf Whittier, *Home Ballads, Poems and Lyrics*.

## Music — The Vernacular/Commercial Scene

**A. Births**   Edgar O. Silver (publisher); Harry B. Smith (lyricist) December 28.

**B. Deaths**   Joel Walker Sweeney (banjo/singer).

**D. Publications**   *Father Kemp's Old Folk's Concert Tunes*.

**E. Representative Works**

**Songs**   Anonymous, *Go Down, Moses* (traditional spiritual); Stephen Foster, *Old Black Joe;* Frances Kyle, *Seeing Nellie Home (Aunt Dinah's Quilting Party)*; John R. Thomas/Enoch, *"Tis But a Little Faded Flower"*; H. S. Thompson, *Annie Lisle (Far Above Cayuga's Waters)*.

## Music — The Cultivated/Art Music Scene

**F. Births**   Jessie Bartlett Davis (contralto/actress) August; William Foden (guitarist/composer) March 23; Céleste de Longpré Heckscher (composer) February 23; Dora Henninges (mezzo-soprano) August 2; Lillian Henschel (soprano) January 17; Arthur E. Johnstone (composer/educator) May 13; Alfred G. Robyn (pianist/organist/composer) April 29.

**G. Deaths**   Paul Emile Johns (Polish-born pianist/composer) August 10; Truman S. Wetmore (psalmist) July 21.

**H. Debuts**

**United States**   Pauline Colson (New York), Achille Errani (Italian tenor—New York), Inez Fabbri (Austrian soprano—New York), Giovanni Sbriglia (Italian tenor—New York).

**I. New Positions**

**Conductors**   Hans Balatka (Chicago Philharmonic Society—to 1868); Eduard Sobolewski (St. Louis Philharmonic Society II—to 1866).

**Other**   Joseph Rosenthal (organ, Calvary Church, New York); George W. Warren (organ, Holy Trinity Church, Brooklyn—to 1870).

**K. Biographical**   Minnie Hauk moves with her family to New Orleans; Francis Scala leads the Marine Band in a White House concert honoring the Prince of Wales.

**L. Musical Beginnings**

**Performing Groups**   Amateur Musical Society (Hawaii); Bridge House Concerts (first chamber music series in Chicago); Chicago Philharmonic Orchestra (reorganized—to 1868); Denver Sax Horn Band; Dodsworth Band (Washington, DC); Newark Harmonic Society II; Oberlin Musical Union; St. Louis Philharmonic Society II; San Francisco Oratorio Society; Seventh Regiment Band (New York).

**Other**   Blackmar Brothers Music Store and Publishing House (New Orleans); *Boston Musical Times*; Elias Howe Music Publishing Co. (Boston).

**M. Music Publications**

Emerson, Luther O., *The Golden Harp—The Sabbath Harmony*
Longfellow, Samuel, *A Book of Hymns and Tunes*
Mason, Lowell, *The People's Tune Book*
Oliver, Henry, *Oliver's Collection of Hymn and Psalm Tunes*
Perkins, Henry S., *Nightingale*

**N. Musical Compositions**

**Choral/Vocal**   William B. Bradbury, *Sweet Hour of Prayer*; George F. Bristow, *Gloria Patri, Opus 31*; George F. Root, *Belshazzar's Feast* (cantata).

**Operas**   Louis Moreau Gottschalk, *Escenas campestres* (chamber opera).

**Orchestra/Band**   William Henry Fry, *Overture, Evangeline*.

**Piano/Organ**   Charles Grobe, *Variations on "Dixie's Land," Opus 1250—Beauties of Beethoven* (six sets of variations); George John Huss, *Le Papillon—Impromtu*; John Knowles Paine, *Fantasia and Fugue in E Minor, Opus 2/1—Concert Variations on the Austrian Hymn, Opus 3/1*.

# 1861

☀

## Historical Highlights

The US Civil War begins—the Battle of Bull Run takes place; West Virginia secedes from Virginia and stays with the Union; Kansas becomes the 34th state; Yale University gives the first Ph.D. degree in America; Vassar College is chartered; Czar Alexander II emancipates the Russian serfs; Italian unification begins as Victor Emmanuel II of Sardinia is crowned.

## World Cultural Highlights

**World Art**   Jean-Baptiste Carpeaux, *Ugolino and His Sons*; Gustave Courbet, *The Stag Fight*;

Eugène Delacroix, *The Lion Hunt*; Gustave Doré, *Dante's Inferno*; Joseph Paton, *Luther at Erfurt*.

**World Literature**   Charles Dickens, *Great Expectations*; Feodor Dostoyevsky, *The House of the Dead*; George Eliot, *Silas Marner*; Charles Reade, *The Cloister and the Hearth*; Alexei Tolstoy, *Don Juan*.

**World Music**   Johannes Brahms, *Variations and Fugue on a Theme by Handel—Piano Quartets No. 1, 2*; Antonín Dvořàk, *String Quintet, Opus 1*; Joseph Joachim Raff, *Symphony No. 1*.

**Miscellaneous**   The London Royal Academy of Music opens; Jurgensen Music Publishers opens in Moscow; births include Émile Bourdelle, Aristide Maillol, Ernestine Schumann-Heink, and Rabindranath Tagore; deaths include Elizabeth Barrett Browning, Ivan Nikitin, and Augustin Scribe.

## American Art and Literature Highlights

**Births/Deaths**   Births include art figures Cyrus Dallin, Frederic Remington, Charles Schreyvogel, Frederick Waugh, and literary figures Richard E. Burton, William Easton, Louise Imogen Guiney, Henry Harland (Sidney Luska), Charles B. Loomis, Albert B. Paine, and Morgan A. Robertson; deaths include art figures Benjamin Akers, Bass Otis, Samuel L. Waldo, and poet Theodore Winthrop.

**Art Works**   Frederic Church, *The Icebergs*; Henry P. Gray, *Judgment of Paris*; Winslow Homer, *Bivouac Fire on the Potomac*; Daniel Huntington, *Katrina von Tassel and Ichabod Crane*; George Inness, *Delaware Water Gap*; Emanuel Leutze, *Westward the Course of the Empire Takes Its Way*; Willliam Rimmer, *The Dying Centaur* (cast 1871); William W. Story, *Libyan Sibyl*.

**Literature**   Thomas Aldrich, *Pampinea*; Jane Andrews, *The Seven Little Sisters . . .* ; Rebecca H. Davis, *Life in the Iron Mills*; Charles Gayler, *The Magic Marriage*; Lucretia and Edward Hale, *Struggle for Life*; Oliver W. Holmes, *Elsie Venner*; Harriet Jacobs, *Incidents in the Life of a Slave Girl; Written by Herself*; Frederick Olmsted, *The Cotton Kingdom*; Theodore Winthrop, *Cecil Dreeme*.

## Music—The Vernacular/Commercial Scene

**A. Births**   Monroe H. Rosenfeld (songwriter/journalist); Lillian Russell (actress/soprano) December 4; James Thornton (composer/lyricist) December 5.

**J. Representative Works**

**Songs**   Harry McCarthy, *The Bonnie Blue Flag*; George R. Poulton and W. W. Fosdick, *Aura Lee*; James R. Randall (words), *Maryland, My Maryland*; George F. Root, *The Vacant Chair*; Henry Clay Work, *Songs: Beautiful Rose—Brave Boys Are They—Lost on the Lady Elgin—Nellie Lost and Found—Our Captain's Last Words—Little Hallie*.

## Music—The Cultivated/Art Music Scene

**F. Births**   Gustave L. Becker (pianist/educator) May 22; Frances M. Clark (music educator) May 27; William Arms Fisher (editor/publisher) April 27; Nahan Franko (violinist/conductor) July 23; Gertrude Griswold (soprano); Edward MacDowell (pianist/composer) December 18; Thomas W. Surette (music educator) September 7; Arthur B. Whiting (pianist/composer) June 20; Huntington Woodman (organist/composer) January 18.

**G. Deaths**   Christian H. Eisenbrandt (German-born instrument maker) March 10; Peter Erben (organist/publisher) April 30; Edward "Ned" Kendall (bandmaster/keyed bugle) October 26; Horace Meacham (piano builder).

**H. Debuts**

**United States**   William Castle (tenor—New York), Isabella Hinkley (New York), Clara Louise Kellogg (soprano—New York), Carlotta Patti (Italian soprano—New York).

**I. New Positions**

**Educational**   Carl Anschutz (National Music Institute, New York); Karl Merz (music director,

Oxford Female College, Ohio—to 1882); John Knowles Paine (organist/instructor, Harvard); Eben Tourjée (music director, East Greenwich Seminary).

**Other**    Homer Bartlett (organ, Madison Avenue Baptist Church, New York); Samuel P. Jackson (organ, Church of the Ascension, New York—to 1875).

**K. Biographical**    Louis Moreau Gottschalk, upon the outbreak of the Civil War, leaves the West Indies and returns to the United States and the Union cause; John Knowles Paine returns from European study and settles in Boston; Gustav Schirmer buys out Breusing and Kearsing (Beer and Schirmer, incorporated in 1866); John Philip Sousa receives his first music instruction; Maurice Strakosch returns to Europe.

**L. Musical Beginnings**

**Performing Groups**    Biscacciante Opera Co. (San Francisco); Denver City Band; Yale Glee Club.

**Educational**    Brooklyn Academy of Music; Orpheon Free Schools (New York).

**Other**    American Cabinet Organ; Bradbury Publishers (New York); Harrison and Harrison, Organ Builders; Schreiner Music Store and Publishing Co. (Savannah, Georgia).

**M. Music Publications**

Bradbury, William B., *The Golden Shower—The Golden Chain of Sabbath School Melodies*
Parker, J. C. D., *Sacred Choruses: Selected . . . from the Works of Selected Composers*
Perkins, William O., *Atlantic Glee Book—Union Star Glee Book*

**N. Musical Compositions**

**Choral/Vocal**    George Frederick Bristow, *Praise to God* (cantata).

**Operas**    Edward Mollenhauer, *The Corsican Bride*.

**Orchestra/Band**    George Frederick Bristow, *Overture, Columbus, Opus 32*.

**Piano/Organ**    Blind Tom Bethune, *The Battle of Manassas*; George Frederick Bristow, *Souvenir de Mount Vernon, Opus 29;* Charles Grobe, *Music of the Union, Opus 1348*; Theodore La Hache, *Grand Parade March*; Edward Mack, *General McClellan's Grand March*; John Knowles Paine, *Concert Variations on the Star-Spangled Banner, Opus 3/2*.

# 1862

❀

## Historical Highlights

The Battles of Antietam, Shiloh, and the second Bull Run take place; the first battle between iron-clad boats takes place between the *Monitor* and the *Merrimac*; slavery is abolished in the District of Columbia; the Congressional Medal of Honor is created; Great Northern and Union Pacific Railroads are formed; Otto von Bismarck becomes Chancellor of Prussia; the Gatling gun is introduced.

## World Cultural Highlights

**World Art**    Honoré Daumier, *The Third-Class Carriage*; Jean-Auguste Ingres, *Bain Turque*; Wilhelm von Kaulbach, *Battle of Salamis*; Édouard Manet, *The Old Musician*.

**World Literature**    Gustave Flaubert, *Salammbô*; Victor Hugo, *Les Misérables*; Charles de Lisle, *Poèmes Barbares*; William Thackeray, *The Adventures of Philip*; Ivan Turgenev, *Fathers and Sons*.

**World Music**    Hector Berlioz, *Béatrice et Bénédict*; César Franck, *Grande Pièce Symphonique, Opus 17*; Charles Gounod, *La reine de Saba*; Giuseppe Verdi, *La forza del destino—Hymn of the Nations*.

**Miscellaneous**    The Prague National Opera House and the St. Petersburg Conservatory of Music open; births include Claude Debussy, Frederick Delius, Gerhart Hauptmann, Gustav Klimt, and Maurice Maeterlinck; deaths include Ludwig Fulda, Jacques Halévy, and Johann Uhland.

## American Art and Literature Highlights

**Births/Deaths**　Births include art figures George Brewster, Edgar Cameron, Arthur Davies, Charles Grafly, Robert Reid, Edmund Tarbell, and literary figures Frank Doubleday, Laura Jean Libbey, Langdon E. Mitchell, William S. Porter (O. Henry), and Edith Wharton; deaths include artists Charles Bird King, Karl Wimar, and literary figures James Heath, Fitz Hugh O'Brien, and Henry David Thoreau.

**Art Works**　Albert Bierstadt, *Attack on a Union Picket Post—Guerilla Warfare*; Sanford Gifford, *Kauterskill Falls*; Winslow Homer, *The Sharpshooter*; William Hunt, *The Drummer Boy* (?); Fitz Hugh Lane, *Owl's Head, Penobscot Bay, Maine*; Honer D. Martin, *Iron Mine, Port Henry, N.Y.* (?); Emma Stebbins, *Angel of the Waters*; James Whistler, *The White Girl (Symphony in White)*.

**Literature**　Charles F. Browne, *Artemus Ward: His Book*; Rebecca Davis, *Margaret Howth*; Oliver Wendell Holmes, *Songs in Many Keys*; James Russell Lowell, *Bigelow Papers, Series II*; Robert Newell, *The Orpheus C. Kerr Papers I*; Thomas B. Read, *The Wagoner of the Alleghanies*; Harriet Beecher Stowe, *Agnes of Sorrento*; James B. Taylor, *The Poet's Journal*.

## Music—The Vernacular/Commercial Scene

**A. Births**　Carrie Jacobs Bond (songwriter) August 11; May Irwin (singer/actress) June 27; Robert A. King (composer/lyricist) September 20.

**B. Deaths**　Edwin P. Christy (minstrel/impresario).

**E. Representative Works**

**Musicals**　Julius Eichberg and B. E. Woolf, *The Doctor of Alcantara*.

**Songs**　George Christy, *The Essense of Kentucky*; Foster and Gibbons, *We Are Coming, Father Abraham*; Will S. Hay, *The Drummer Boy of Shiloh*; George F. Root, *The Battle Cry of Freedom—Just before the Battle, Mother*; Septimus Winner, *Give Us Back Our Old Commander*; Henry Clay Work, *Songs: Kingdom Coming—Uncle Joe's "Hail Columbia!"—The First Love Dream—The Girls at Home—God Save the Nation—Grafted into the Army—We'll Go Down Ourselves*.

## Music—The Cultivated/Art Music Scene

**F. Births**　Perry Averill (baritone) June 11; Samuel Baldwin (organist) January 25; Austin Martin Gemunder (violin maker) May 4; Henry Holden Huss (pianist/composer) June 21; Ernest Richard Kroeger (organist/composer) August 10; Zélie de Lussan (soprano) December 21; Ethelbert Nevin (composer) November 25; Edmund Severn (composer/educator) December 10.

**G. Deaths**　Joseph Funk (composer/compiler) December 24; Charles M. Stieff (German-born piano maker) January 1.

**H. Debuts**

**United States**　Nikodem Biernacki (Polish violinist—tour), Teresa Carreño (Venezuelan pianist, age 8—New York), Benjamin J. Lang (as conductor—Boston), Genevieve Ward (soprano—New York).

**I. New Positions**

**Conductors**　Frédéric L. Ritter (Sacred Harmonic Society, New York); Theodore Thomas (Brooklyn Philharmonic Society—to 1891).

**Educational**　John Knowles Paine (first music professor at an American University, Harvard—to 1905).

**Other**　Dudley Buck (organ, St. James Church, Chicago); Frederick W. Root (organ, Swedenborgian Church, Chicago).

**K. Biographical**　William B. Bradbury writes one of the most popular children's hymns of all time, *Jesus Loves Me, This I Know*; Dudley Buck returns to the United States and begins teaching in Hartford, Connecticut; Louis Moreau Gottschalk makes his second concert tour of the United States; Carlyle Petersilea moves to Leipzig, Germany.

**L. Musical Beginnings**

**Performing Groups**   Continental Singing Society (Buffalo).

**Educational**   Harvard Music School.

**Other**   Baldwin Piano Co. (Cincinnati); Decker Brothers, Pianos (New York); Charles Grobe Musical and Educational Agency; Hall and Quinby Brass Instrument Factory (Boston); Salt Lake City Theater.

**M. Music Publications**

*Evangelisches Gesangbuch* (German Evangelical Church).

Bradbury, William, *Oriola*

Hart, H. C., *Col. H. C. Hart's New and Improved Instructor for the Drum*

Hastings, Thomas, *The Songs of the Church*

Kittredge, Walter, *The Union Song Book*

**N. Musical Compositions**

**Choral/Vocal**   Jerome Hopkins, *Victory Te Deum*; Theodore La Hache, *The Volunteer's Farewell* (song); John Knowles Paine, *Hymn for Harvard Commencement*; George Frederick Root, *The Christian Graces* (cantata).

**Operas**   Julius Eichberg, *The Doctor of Alcantara*; John Knowles Paine, *Il pesceballo*.

**Orchestra/Band**   William Henry Fry, *Overture, Macbeth*.

**Piano/Organ**   Louis Moreau Gottschalk, *The Union*.

# 1863

❋

## Historical Highlights

The Battle of Gettysburg occurs in July—President Lincoln gives his Gettysburg Address in November; the Emancipation Proclamation is made public; West Virginia becomes the 35th state; draft riots occur in New York; Congress passes the National Bank Act; Thanksgiving is made a national holiday; the French attempt to set up a French empire in Mexico; London's first subway opens.

## World Cultural Highlights

**World Art**   Gustave Courbet, *The Trellis*; Honoré Daumier, *Crispin and Scapin*; Édouard Manet, *Déjeuner sur l'Herbe*; Jean-François Millet, *Man with the Hoe*; Dante Rossetti, *Beata Beatrix*.

**World Literature**   John Brown, *Marjorie Fleming*; Charles Dickens, *Our Mutual Friend*; Elizabeth Gaskell, *Sylvia's Lovers*; Jules Verne, *Five Weeks in a Balloon*.

**World Music**   Georges Bizet, *The Pearl Fishers*; Johannes Brahms, *Variations on a Theme of Paganini*; Giacomo Meyerbeer, *L'Africaine*; Gioacchino Rossini, *Petite Messe Solennelle*.

**Miscellaneous**   John Curwen and Sons, Ltd., begin publishing music in London; births include Gabriele d'Annunzio, Anthony Hawkins, Edvard Munch, Lucien Pissarro, and Felix Weingartner; deaths include Eugène Delacroix, Christian Hebbel, William Thackeray, and Alfred de Vigny.

## American Art and Literature Highlights

**Births/Deaths**   Births include art figures Cecilia Beaux, Frederick MacMonnies, and literary figures Eleanor Atkinson, Elaine Goodale, Amélie Rives, George Santayana, and Gene Stratton Porter; deaths include art figures George Durrie, Alvan Fisher, Alexander Galt, Anne Hall, Charles Ingham, and literary figures Charlotte Barnes, George L. Duyckinck, William J. Grayson, and Clement C. Moore.

**Art Works**   Albert Bierstadt, *The Bombardment of Fort Sumter*; Constantine Brumidi, *Apotheosis of Washington, U.S. Capitol*; Richard Greenough, *Carthaginian Girl*; Alexander and Moritz Kann, *The Emancipation Proclamation*; Larkin Mead, *Echo* (?); John Rogers, *Union Refugees*; William

W. Story, *Saul*; Elihu Vedder, *Questioner of the Sphinx*; John Quincy Adams Ward, *Freedman*.

**Literature**   Thomas Aldrich, *Poems*; Nathaniel Hawthorne, *Our Old Home*; Thomas Higginson, *Out-Door Papers*; Henry Wadsworth Longfellow, *Tales of a Wayside Inn I*; Robert Newell, *The Orpheus C. Kerr Papers II*; Harriet E. Spofford, *The Amber Gods and Other Stories*; John Greenleaf Whittier, *In War Time and Other Poems*; Theodore Winthrop, *The Canoe and the Saddle*.

## Music—The Vernacular/Commercial Scene

**A. Births**   Sam Bernard (singer/actor) June 3; Bob Cole (lyricist/composer); Gussie L. Davis (songwriter).

**E. Representative Works**

**Songs**   Anonymous, *Johnny Schmoker*; Patrick S. Gilmore, *When Johnny Comes Marching Home*; John H. Hewitt, *All Quiet along the Potomac Tonight*; Walter Kittredge, *Tenting on the Old Camp Ground*; Henry Clay Work, *Songs: Babylon Is Fallen!—Days When We Were Young—Grandmother Told Me So—Little Major—Sleeping for the Flag—Song of a Thousand Years—Watching for Pa*.

## Music—The Cultivated/Art Music Scene

**F. Births**   Richard Aldrich (music critic) July 31; Gilbert R. Combs (organist) January 5; Charles Dennée (pianist/pedagogue) September 1; Helen Hood (composer) June 28; Emma Juch (soprano) July 4; Horatio Parker (composer/church musician) September 15; Frances Saville (soprano) January 6; Fannie Bloomfield Zeisler (pianist) July 16.

**G. Deaths**   Hermann Adolf Wollenhaupt (German-born pianist) September 18.

**I. New Positions**

**Other**   George P. Upton (music critic, *Chicago Tribune*—to 1881); Henry C. Watson (music critic, *New York Tribune*—to 1867); Henry Clay Work (editor, *The Song Messenger*).

**K. Biographical**   Boston's "Great Organ" is installed in the Music Hall by Walcker and Sons of Stuttgart (official inauguration November 2); Hugo Sohmer (German piano maker) comes to New York and begins working in the Schuetz and Luedolf Piano Factory.

**L. Musical Beginnings**

**Performing Groups**   Buffalo St. Cecilia Society; New York Mendelssohn Society (to 1872).

**Other**   Albrecht and Co., Piano Makers (Philadelphia); Boston Musician's Union; Mathushek Piano Co. (New York); Henry Miller and Sons Piano Co. (Boston); Musical Mutual Protective Union of New York; Philadelphia Musical Association; Philip Phillips and Co., Pianos and Publishing (Cincinnati); *Song Messenger of the North-West*.

**M. Music Publications**

Bradbury, William B., *Pilgrim's Songs*
Butterfield, James, *Star of the West*
Emerson, Luther O., *The Harp of Judah*
Peters, W. C., ed., *Peter's Catholic Harp*
Waters, Horace, *The Athenaeum Collection—Water's Golden Harp*

**N. Musical Compositions**

**Operas**   John H. Hewitt, *King Linkum the First—The Vivandiere*.

**Piano/Organ**   Louis Moreau Gottschalk, *La gallina* (four hands).

# 1864

⚙

## Historical Highlights

Sherman's march to the sea takes place in Georgia; Ulysses S. Grant is appointed Supreme Commander of the Union Army; Abraham Lincoln is re-elected president; Nevada becomes the

36th state; railroad sleeping cars are introduced by Pullman; "In God We Trust" first appears on US coins; the Charlottetown Conference debates the Unification of Canada; the International Red Cross is founded.

## World Cultural Highlights

**World Art**   Henri Fantin-Latour, *Hommage à Delacroix*; Édouard Manet, *Battle of the Kearsarge and the Alabama*; Gustave Moreau, *Oedipus and the Sphinx*; Auguste Rodin, *Man with the Broken Nose*.

**World Literature**   Robert Browning, *Dramatis Personae*; Alexis Kivi, *Kullervo*; John Marston, *Donna Diana*; Alfred, Lord Tennyson, *Enoch Arden*; Jules Verne, *Journey to the Center of the Earth*.

**World Music**   Johannes Brahms, *Piano Quintet—String Sextet No. 2*; Anton Bruckner, *Symphony in D Minor, "Die Nullte"*; Edvard Grieg, *Symphony in C Minor*; Franz von Suppé, *Pique Dame*.

**Miscellaneous**   The Moscow Philharmonic Orchestra and the Bucharest Conservatory of Music are founded; births include Richard Strauss, Henri Toulouse-Latrec, Frank Wedekind, and Israel Zangwill; deaths include William Dyce, Walter Landor, Giacomo Meyerbeer, and Robert Surtees.

## American Art and Literature Highlights

**Births/Deaths**   Births include artists Henry Dearth, Louis Eilshemius, Charles M. Russell, Alfred Stieglitz, Charles H. Woodbury, and literary figures Richard Harding Davis, Thomas Dixon, and Richard Hovey; deaths include artists James Frothingham, Rubens Peale, and literary figures Joseph Baldwin, Nathaniel Hawthorne, Caroline Kirkland, Eliza Buckminster Lee, and George Pope Morris.

**Art Works**   Sanford Gifford, *Twilight in the Adirondacks*; Martin Heade, *Orchids and Hummingbird*; Rubens Peale, *Ruffed Grouse in Underbrush*; John Rogers, *"Wounded to the Rear"—One Last Shot*; William W. Story, *Medea*; Elihu Vedder, *The Lair of the Sea Serpent—The Lost Mind*; John Quincy Adams Ward, *The Indian Hunter*; James M. Whistler, *The Golden Screen*.

**Literature**   William C. Bryant, *Thirty Poems*; Oliver Wendell Holmes, *Soundings from the Atlantic*; Richard M. Johnston, *Georgia Sketches*; Abraham Lincoln, *Second Inaugural Address*; David C. Locke, *The Nasby Papers*; James Russell Lowell, *Fireside Travels*; Epes Sargent, *Peculiar: A Tale of the Great Transition*; Henry D. Thoreau, *The Maine Woods* (posthumous); Walt Whitman, *Drum-Taps*.

## Music—The Vernacular/Commercial Scene

**A. Births**   Blind Boone (ragtime composer/pianist) May 17.

**B. Deaths**   Frederick Buckley (composer/impresario) October; Stephen Foster (songwriter) January 13.

**E. Representative Works**

**Songs**   Mrs. C. C. Barnard, *Take Back the Heart You Gave*; S. H. H. Byers, *Sherman's March to the Sea*; Stephen Foster, *Beautiful Dreamer*; Johnny Reb, *Goober Peas*; George F. Root, *Tramp! Tramp! Tramp!*; Septimus Winner, *Der Deitcher's Dog ("Where ish mine little dog gone")*; H. C. Work, *Songs: Columbia's Guardian Angels—Father, Dear Father, Come Home with Me Now—Corporal Schnapps—The Picture on the Wall—Wake, Nicodemus!—Washington and Lincoln*.

## Music—The Cultivated/Art Music Scene

**F. Births**   Flora Batson (soprano) April 16; Elizabeth Sprague Coolidge (art patron) October 30; Eleanor E. Freer (composer) May 14; Philip Goepp (organist/composer) June 23; William Sherman Haynes (flute maker) July 27; Sidney Homer (composer) December 9; Jean Paul Kürsteiner (pianist/pedagogue) July 8; Ella Russell (soprano) March 30; Gustave Schirmer II (publisher) February 18; Thomas Tapper (music educator) January 28; Hale A. VanderCook (bandmaster/composer/educator) September 3; James D. Vaughan (publisher/composer) December 14; Benjamin L. Whelpley (pianist/organist) October 23.

**G. Deaths**  Nathan Adams (brass instrument maker) March 16; John Firth (piano maker) September 10; William Henry Fry (composer) December 21; Nathaniel Duren Gould (singing master/compiler) May 28; Charles F. Hupfield (German-born violinist/conductor) June 15; Job Plimpton (composer/organ builder).

**H. Debuts**

**United States**  Alfred H. Pease (pianist—New York), Giorgio Stigelli (German tenor—tour), Arthur W. Tams (baritone—Philadelphia), Jennie Van Zandt (soprano—New York).

**I. New Positions**

**Conductors**  Theodore Thomas (New York Symphony Orchestra—to 1878).

**Other**  Luther Whiting Mason (music, Boston Primary Schools); James C. D. Parker (organ, Trinity Church, Boston—to 1891); Samuel Tuckerman (organ, Trinity Church, New York).

**K. Biographical**  Emma Albani moves with her family to New York; J. Lathrop Allen decides to move his brass shop to New York; Fanny J. Crosby dedicates her poetic talents to the writing of hymns; Achille Errani begins teaching voice in New York; the Harvard Musical Association begins sponsoring symphony concerts in Boston; Franz Schwarzer (Austrian zither maker) emigrates to the United States and decides to settle in Washington, Missouri; Charles F. Zimmermann (German instrument maker) emigrates to the United States and settles in Philadelphia.

**L. Musical Beginnings**

**Performing Groups**  Portland Mechanics Band (Oregon).

**Educational**  Musical Institute of Providence (Providence Conservatory of Music); Yale University Fine Arts Department (first in the United States).

**Other**  J. Fischer and Brother (Carl J.), Music Publisher (Dayton, Ohio); Gilmore, Graves and Co., Brass Instruments (Boston); Irving Hall Symphonic Soirées (by Theodore Thomas); Kranich and Bach Piano Co. (New York); Lyon and Healy Co. (Chicago), *Orpheonist and Philharmonic Journal*; Music Hall (Academy of Music, Milwaukee); *Western Musical World (Brainard's Musical World)*.

**M. Music Publications**

Bradbury, William B., *Bradbury's Devotional—Devotional Hymn and Tune Book—The Golden Censer*

Hodges, Edward, *Trinity Collection of Church Music*

Hood, George, *Musical Manual Designed as a Text-book for Classes or Private Pupils . . .*

Robinson, Charles S., *Songs for the Sanctuary*

Root, George F., *The Musical Curriculum*

Tuckerman, Samuel, *Trinity Collection of Church Music*

**N. Musical Compositions**

**Choral/Vocal**  William B. Bradbury, *He Leadeth Me* (hymn); William Henry Fry, *Mass in E-flat Major—Kyrie Eleison*; Theodore La Hache, *Mass for Peace*.

**Operas**  Julius Eichberg, *A Night in Rome* (operetta); William Henry Fry, *Notre Dame de Paris* (opera).

**Piano/Organ**  Louis Moreau Gottschalk, *The Dying Poet—The Maiden's Blush* (grande valse de concert); John Knowles Paine, *Two Preludes, Opus 19, for Organ*; Eliza Pattiani, *May Breeze: Variations Brillante*.

# 1865

❄

## Historical Highlights

The Civil War ends; President Lincoln is assassinated and Andrew Johnson becomes the 17th president; the 13th Amendment ends slavery in the United States and all its territories; the Southern Pacific Railroad is chartered; work begins on a transcontinental line; Purdue and Cornell

Universities are founded; the War of the Triple Alliance (Argentina, Brazil, and Uruguay against Paraguay) begins.

## World Cultural Highlights

**World Art**    Jean-Baptiste Corot, *La Zingara*; Gustave Doré, *Bible Illustrations*; Édouard Manet, *Olympia*; William Orchardson, *Challenged*.

**World Literature**    Lewis Carroll, *Alice's Adventures in Wonderland*; Mary E. Dodge, *Hans Brinker*; Elizabeth Gaskell, *Wives and Daughters*; Cardinal Newman, *The Dream of Gerontius*.

**World Music**    Johannes Brahms, *"Horn" Trio, Opus 40*; Antonín Dvořák, *Symphony No. 1, 2*; Edvard Grieg, *I Love Thee*; Jacques Offenbach, *La belle Hélène*; Franz von Suppé, *Die Schöne Galatea*.

**Miscellaneous**    Hawkes and Co. Publishers founded in Germany; the Augsburg State Orchestra is founded; births include Paul Dukas, Emmuska Orczy, Jean Sibelius, and William Yeats; deaths include Elizabeth Gaskell, Bernhard Malmström, Ferdinand Waldmüller, and W. Vincent Wallace.

## American Art and Literature Highlights

**Births/Deaths**    Births include art figures Paul Bartlett, Philip L. Hale, Robert Henri, Henry Kitson, and literary figures Irving Babbitt, Madison J. Cawein, Holman F. Day, Clyde Fitch, Paul Leicester Ford, Grace L. Hill, Elizabeth Robins, and Lloyd P. Smith; deaths include artists David Blythe, Fitz Hugh Lane, John Neagle, Ammi Phillips, and literary figures Jeremiah Clemens, George Washington Cotter, Hannah F. Gould, Samuel Hammett (Philip Paxton), Hannah F. Lee, and Lydia H. H. Sigourney.

**Art Works**    William H. Beard, *Susanna and the Elders*; David Blythe, *Dry Goods and Notions— The Battle of Gettysburg*; Martin Heade, *Spring Showers, Connecticut Valley*; Harriet Hosmer, *Sleeping Faun*; George Inness, *The Delaware Valley*; William Richards, *Neglected Corner of a Wheat Field*; James Smillie, *Kaaterskill Cove*; John Quincy Adams Ward, *Emancipation Group* (cast 1873).

**Literature**    Charles F. Browne, *Artemus Ward: His Travels*; Mary E. Dodge, *Hans Brinker, or The Silver Skates*; Edward E. Hale, *The Man Without a Country*; Oliver Wendell Holmes, *Humorous Poems*; Robert Newell, *The Orpheus C. Kerr Papers III*; Henry W. Shaw, *Josh Billings: His Sayings*; Samuel Ward, *Lyrical Reactions*; John Greenleaf Whittier, *National Lyrics*.

## Music — The Vernacular/Commercial Scene

**A. Births**    Will Marion Cook (composer); Charles K. Harris (songwriter/publisher) May 1; Raymond Hitchcock (singer/actor) October 22; William Jerome (lyricist) September 30; Fay Templeton (singer/actress) December 25.

**C. Biographical**

**Performing Groups**    Brooker and Clayton's Georgia Minstrels.

**E. Representative Works**

**Songs**    Anonymous, *Johnny Is My Darling—Go Tell It on the Mountain* (traditional spiritual)— *Roll, Jordon, Roll—Nobody Knows De Trouble I've Seen—Were You There When They Crucified My Lord?*; J. B. Murphy, *Nicodemus Johnson*; William S. Pitts, *The Little Brown Church in the Vale*; Septimus Winner, *Ellie Rhee (Carry Me Back to Tennessee)*; H. C. Work, *Songs: Marching Through Georgia—Now, Moses!—Ring the Bell—Watchman!—The Ship That Never Return'd—Tis Finished! or Sing Hallelujah*.

## Music — The Cultivated/Art Music Scene

**F. Births**    Maurice Arnold (violinist/composer) January 19; Charles Barnhouse (music publisher) March 20; William Crane Carl (organist) March 2; Charles W. Clark (baritone) October 15; Earl Ross Drake (violinist/composer) November 26; Emma Eames (soprano) August 13; Clarence Grant

Hamilton (organist/educator) June 9; Harvey Worthingotn Loomis (composer) February 5; Edward B. Marks (publisher) November 28; Frank J. Metcalf (hymnologist) April 4; William L. Phelps (music critic) January 2; Gustav Saenger (editor/arranger) May 31; Sibyl Sanderson (soprano) December 7; Ernest C. Schirmer (publisher) March 15; Henry Dike Sleeper (organist/composer) October 9.

**H. Debuts**

**United States**   Alfredo Barili (age 11—New York), Rose Hersee (British soprano—tour), Frantz Jehin-Prume (Belgian violinist—tour), Jules Levy (British cornetist—Boston), Euphrosyne Parepa-Rosa (Scottish soprano—New York), Ernst Perabo (pianist—tour).

**I. New Positions**

**Conductors**   Simon Hassler (orchestra, Walnut Street Theater, Philadelphia—to 1872).

**K. Biographical**   Louis Moreau Gottschalk, in trouble over a young lady in California, flees the country and ends up in Brazil; Frederick E. Kitziger (German composer) comes to the United States and settles in New Orleans; Ernst Perabo (German pianist/composer) settles in the United States.

**L. Musical Beginnings**

**Performing Groups**   Chicago Männerchor; Germania Men's Chorus (Newark); Harvard Musical Association Concert Series; New York Summer Garden Concerts (to 1891).

**Educational**   (Frederic) Mollenhauer Studio of Music (Brooklyn); Oberlin College Conservatory of Music; Orpheon Free School (by C. J. Hopkins).

**Other**   Crosby Opera House (Chicago); Tony Pastor's Opera House (New York); Moses Slater, Brass Instruments (New York); Welte Musical Instrument Co. New York Branch.

**M. Music Publications**

Emerson, Luther O., *Merry Chimes*
Fillmore, Augustus D., *The Harp of Zion*
Formes, Karl J., *Method of Singing*
Phillips, Philip, *Hallowed Songs*

**N. Musical Compositions**

**Choral/Vocal**   George Frederick Bristow, *Evening Service, Opus 36*; Robert Lowry, *Shall We Gather at the River* (hymn); Edward Mack, *Dirge for President Lincoln*; John Knowles Paine, *Mass in D Major, Opus 10*.

**Operas**   Julius Eichberg, *The Rose of Tyrol* (operetta).

**Piano/Organ**   George F. Bristow, *Eroica, Opus 38*; Edward Mack, *President Lincoln's Funeral March*; John Knowles Paine, *Funeral March in Memory of President Lincoln, Opus 9*.

# 1866

☀

## Historical Highlights

Congress passes the Civil Rights Act over President Johnson's veto; Ulysses S. Grant becomes the first American general; the "nickel" is approved for coining by the Treasury Department; The Grand Army of the Republic (GAR) is founded; Cyrus Field succeeds in laying a lasting Atlantic cable; Alfred Nobel invents dynamite; the Seven Weeks War between Prussia and Austria occurs.

## World Cultural Highlights

**World Art**   Honoré Daumier, *Don Quixote and the Windmills*; Frederic Leighton, *The Syracusan Bride*; Édouard Manet, *The Fifer*; Claude Monet, *Camille*; Dante Rosetti, *Monna Vanna*.

**World Literature**   Feodor Dostoyevsky, *Crime and Punishment*; Victor Hugo, *The Toilers of the Sea*; Alexei Tolstoy, *The Death of Ivan the Terrible*; Leo Tolstoy, *War and Peace*.

**World Music**    Anton Bruckner, *Symphony No. 1*; Franz Liszt, *Christus*; Franz von Suppé, *Light Cavalry*; Peter Tchaikovsky, *Symphony No. 1, "Winter Dreams"*; Ambroise Thomas, *Mignon*.

**Miscellaneous**    The Moscow Conservatory of Music and the Concert Society of Madrid are founded; births include Tristan Bernard, Ferruccio Busoni, Vasili Kandinsky, and Erik Satie; deaths include Carl Almqvist, Roger de Beauvoir, Paul Ernst, Thomas Peacock, and Friedrich Rückert.

## American Art and Literature Highlights

**Births/Deaths**    Births include art figures Jules Guerin, William Leigh, Louis Loeb, Robert MacCameron, Herman A. MacNeil, and literary figures George Ade, Dora Read Goodale, Philander C. Johnson, Richard Le Gallienne, George B. McCutcheon, Willliam Patten (Burt Standish), and Edward L. White; deaths include Maria Susanna Cummins, John B. Jones, John Pierpont, and Frederick W. Thomas.

**Art Works**    Frederic Church, *Rainy Season in the Tropics*; Samuel Colman, *Storm King on the Hudson*; Thomas Hicks, *The Musical: Barber Shop, Trenton Falls, NY*; Winslow Homer, *The Prisoners from the Front*; Harriet Hosmer, *Waking Faun*; John La Farge, *The Greek Love Token*; William W. Story, *Delilah*; John F. Weir, *The Gun Foundry*; James M. Whistler, *Valparaiso Harbor*.

**Literature**    George Arnold, *A Sea-Shore Idyl and Other Poems*; Charles Barras, *The Black Crook*; Henry Brownell, *War-Lyrics and Other Poems*; John Esten Cooke, *Surrey of Eagle's Nest*; Julia Ward Howe, *Later Lyrics*; Herman Melville, *Battle-Pieces and Aspects of the War*; John J. Piatt, *Poems in Sunshine and Firelight*; Edna Dean Proctor, *Poems*; John Greenleaf Whittier, *Snow-Bound*.

## Music—The Vernacular/Commercial Scene

**A. Births**    Henry Blossom (lyricist) May 6.

**E. Representative Works**

**Musicals**    Various composers, *The Black Crook*.

**Songs**    James A. Butterfield, *When You and I Were Young, Maggie*; Claribel (Charlotte Barnard), *Come Back to Erin*; Hattie Fox and A. D. Walridge, *Now I Lay Me Down to Sleep*; W. S. Hays, *Write Me a Letter from Home—We Parted by the River*; Billy Newcomb, *The Big Sunflower*; H. C. Work, *Songs: Lillie of the Snowstorm, or Please Father, Let Us In—When the "Evening Star" Went Down—Who Shall Rule This American Nation?*

## Music—The Cultivated/Art Music Scene

**F. Births**    Clarence C. Birchard (music publisher) July 13; Henry T. Burleigh (composer/singer) December 2; Ebenezer Child (composer/compiler); Rosetter Gleason Cole (organist/composer) February 5; Arthur Mansfield Curry (composer/pedagogue) January 27; Clara Anna Korn (composer/educator) January 30; David Mannes (violinist/conductor) February 16; Carl E. Seashore (musician/psychologist) January 28; Ernest M. Skinner (organ builder) January 15; Henry B. Tremaine (piano maker) July 20.

**H. Debuts**

**United States**    Minnie Hauk (soprano, age 14, Brooklyn), Carl August Rosa (German violinist—tour).

**I. New Positions**

**Conductors**    David W. Reeves (American Band of Providence—to 1900); Carl Zerrahn (Harvard Musical Association).

**Other**    Alexander Thayer (American Consul, Trieste—to 1882).

**K. Biographical**    Annie Louise Cary goes to Milan for further voice study with Giovanni Corsi; Theodore Eisfeld decides to return to his native Germany; Gustav Schirmer becomes sole owner of his publishing firm; Arthur P. Schmidt (German publisher) comes to the United States and settles in Boston; Theodore Thomas becomes sole conductor of the Brooklyn Philharmonic.

**L. Musical Beginnings**

**Performing Groups**   Louisville Philharmonic Society (Kentucky); Mendelssohn Glee Club of New York; New Orleans Harmonic Association; Portland Philharmonic Music Society (Oregon).

**Other**   Continental Theater (Boston); Greenlaw Opera House (Memphis); La Hache and Doll Piano Store (New Orleans); St. Paul Opera House; Steinway Hall (New York); Summer Terrace Garden Concerts (New York).

**M. Music Publications**

Bristow, G. and Nash, F. H., *Cantara, or Teacher of Singing*
Emerson, Luther O., *Jubilate*
McIntosh, Rigdon M., *Richmond Collection of Sacred Music*
Phillips, Philip, *The Singing Pilgrim, or Pilgrim's Progress Illustrated in Song*

**N. Musical Compositions**

**Choral/Vocal**   George Frederick Bristow, *Daniel* (oratorio); Caryl Florio, *Piano Trio in D Major*; Theodore La Hache, *The Conquered Banner* (song); J. P. Webster, *The Great Rebellion* (cantata).

**Orchestra/Band**   Caryl Florio, *The Ice Witch* (incidental music)—*Clairvoyance* (incidental music).

**Piano/Organ**   Dudley Buck, *Grand Sonata in E-Flat Major for Organ*; Charles Grobe, *Variations on "Come Home, Father!," Opus 1805*; John Knowles Paine, *Four Character Pieces, Opus 11*; Silas G. Pratt, *Shakespearian Grand March*; Jane Sloman, *La Favorite: Etude Mazurka*.

# 1867

❀

## Historical Highlights

"Seward's Folly"—the United States buys Alaska from Russia; Nebraska becomes the 37th state; John D. Rockefeller forms the Standard Oil Co.; first cattle drive along the Chisholm Trail takes place; Johns Hopkins University is founded; Joseph I becomes Emperor of a new Austrian-Hungarian Empire; the French Empire in Mexico ends; Canada becomes a state in the British Commonwealth.

## World Cultural Highlights

**World Art**   Lawrence Alma-Tadema, *Tarquinius Superbus*; Édouard Manet, *The Execution of Emperor Maximilian*; John Millais, *Jephthah*; Claude Monet, *Ladies in a Garden*; Pierre-Auguste Renoir, *Diana*.

**World Literature**   Michel Carré, *Mignon*; Henrik Ibsen, *Peer Gynt*; Karl Marx, *Das Kapital*; Ivan Turgenev, *Smoke*; Émile Zola, *Thérèse Raquin*.

**World Music**   Georges Bizet, *The Fair Maid of Perth*; Anton Bruckner, *Mass in F Minor*; Edvard Grieg, *Lyric Pieces I*; Modest Moussorgsky, *A Night on Bald Mountain*; Johann Strauss, *Blue Danube Waltz*.

**Miscellaneous**   The Norwegian Academy of Music and the Music Academy of Buda open; births include Pierre Bonnard, John Galsworthy, Emil Nolde, and Arturo Toscanini; deaths include Charles Baudelaire, Serafín Estébanez Calderon, and Alexander Scott.

## American Art and Literature Highlights

**Births/Deaths**   Births include art figures Gutzon Borglum, George Luks, Bela Pratt, and literary figures Lilian Bell, Finley P. Dunne, and Laura Wilder; deaths include artists James Clonney, Charles Deas, and literary figures Alfred Arrington (Charles Summerfield), Charles Browne (Artemus Ward), Fitz-Greene Halleck, Catharine M. Sedgwick, Susan R. Sedgwick, Henry Timrod, and Nathaniel P. Willis.

**Art Works**   Albert Bierstadt, *The Domes of Yosemite*; Edward L. Henry, *The 9:45 Accommodation, Stratford, CT*; Edmonia Lewis, *Forever Free—Abraham Lincoln* (marble); Homer D. Martin, *A North Woods Lake*; Charles C. Nahl, *Indian Servant with Dogs*; Augustus Saint-Gaudens, *Bernard Saint-Gaudens*; Emma Stebbins, *Columbus* (Brooklyn Center); John F. Weir, *Forging the Shaft*.

**Literature**   Horatio Alger, *Ragged Dick*; Charles F. Browne, *Artemus Ward in London*; John E. Cooke, *Wearing of the Gray*; Ralph W. Emerson, *May-Day and Other Pieces*; Martha Finley, *Elsie Dinsmore*; George W. Harris, *Sut Lovingood Yarns*; Oliver Wendell Holmes, *The Guardian Angel*; Sidney Lanier, *Tiger Lilies*; John Greenleaf Whittier, *The Tent of the Beach and Other Poems*.

## Music—The Vernacular/Commercial Scene

**A. Births**   John W. Bratton (composer/impresario) January 21; Anne Caldwell (lyricist) August 30; Joseph Cawthorn (singer/actor) March 29; Lew Fields (singer/impresario/comedian) January 1; John E. Howard (composer/lyricist) February 12; John Avery Lomax (folk music collector) September 23; Joe Weber (singer/impresario/comedian) August 11.

**B. Deaths**   Benjamin Russell Hanby (songwriter) March 16.

**E. Representative Works**

**Musicals**   Various composers and J. Mortimer, *The White Faun*.

**Songs**   Henry Clay Work, *Songs: Come Back to the Farm—Dad's a Millionaire*.

## Music—The Cultivated/Art Music Scene

**F. Births**   Amy (Mrs. H. H. A.) Beach (pianist/composer) September 5; Robert Blass (bass) October 27; Herbert L. Clarke (cornetist/bandmaster) September 12; Patrick Conway (bandmaster/conductor) July 4; Frances Densmore (ethnomusicologist) May 21; Charles W. Douglas (organist/composer) February 15; Emma Azalia Hackley (soprano) June 29; William Wade Hinshaw (baritone/impresario) November 3; Margaret Ruthven Lang (composer) November 27; Henry Taylor Parker (music/drama critic) April 29; Maud Powell (violinist) August 22; Vincent F. Safranek (bandmaster/composer) March 24; Roland F. Seitz (bandmaster/composer/publisher) June 14; John W. Thompson (organist/composer) December 21; Edyth Walker (mezzo-soprano) March 27; Gertrude Clark Whittall (art patron) October 7; Harry Evan Williams (tenor) September 7.

**H. Debuts**

**United States**   William Candidus (tenor—New York), Bernhard Listemann (German violinist—New York).

**Other**   Annie Louise Cary (Copenhagen, Denmark).

**I. New Positions**

**Conductors**   George F. Bristow (New York Mendelssohn Society—to 1871); Adolph Neuendorff (Stadt Theater, New York—to 1871).

**Educational**   Clara Bauer (director, Cincinnati Conservatory—to 1912); Julius Eichberg (director, Boston Conservatory); Stephen A. Emery (theory, New England Conservatory); Frédéric L. Ritter (Vassar College); Eben Tourjée (director, New England Conservatory—to 1891); Carl Zerrahn (theory, New England Conservatory—to 1898); Florenz Ziegfeld, Sr. (director, Chicago Academy).

**Other**   Samuel P. Warren (organ, Grace Episcopal, New York—to 1894).

**K. Biographical**   Emma Juch moves back to the United States; Clara Kellogg makes her European opera debut in London; Gustave Kerker (German composer/conductor) comes with his family to the United States and settles in Louisville, Kentucky; Emil Liebling (German composer/pianist) and Bernard Listemann (German violinist/conductor) come to the United States; Heinrich Maylath (Austrian pianist) comes to the United States and teaches in New York.

**L. Musical Beginnings**

**Performing Groups**   Beethoven Männerchor (San Antonio); Chandler's Band (Portland, Maine);

Denver Musical Union; Hyers Sisters (vocal duo); Knoxville Philharmonic Society (Tennessee—to 1885); New York Trio; San Jose Symphonic Society.

**Educational**   Boston Conservatory of Music; Chicago Academy of Music (Chicago Musical College); Cincinnati Conservatory of Music; New England Conservatory of Music.

**Other**   Bigelow and Main, Music Publishers (New York); Pence Opera House (Minneapolis); Schreiber Cornet Co. (New York); Smith, White and Perry, Publishers (Boston); Turner and Steere Organ Co. (Westfield, Massachusetts).

## M. Music Publications

Allen, W. F. et al., *Slave Songs of the United States*
Bradbury, William B., *Fresh Laurels for Sabbath School*
Mason, William G., *A Method for Piano*
Palmer, Horatio, *The Song Queen—Revival and Camp Meeting Minstrel ("The Perkinpine Songster")*
Robyn, Henry, *Thorough Description of the Braille System for the Reading and Writing of Music*
Seward, Theodore, ed , *The Temple Choir*
Swann, M. L., *The New Harp of Columbia*
Tuckerman, Henry T., *Book of the Artists*
Walker, William, *Christian Harmony*

## N. Musical Compositions

**Choral/Vocal**   Joseph P. Webster, *In the Sweet By and By* (song).

**Orchestra/Band**   Silas G. Pratt, *Orchestral Galop*; Frédéric L. Ritter, *Overture to Othello* (premiere).

**Piano/Organ**   Homer Bartlett, *Grande Polka de Concert*; George F. Bristow, *Raindrops, Opus 43*; Charles Grobe, *Buds and Blossoms* (150 sets of variations); Joseph Noll, *The Black Crook Waltzes*; Silas G. Pratt, *Grand March Heroïque*.

# 1868

### ☀

## Historical Highlights

The impeachment of President Andrew Johnson fails by one vote; Ulysses S. Grant is elected the 18th president; the 14th Amendment on the apportionment of Representatives is ratified; dining car service begins on the rail lines; the Burlingame Treaty opens the country to immigration of cheap labor from the Orient; Cuba attempts independence in a war with Spain.

## World Cultural Highlights

**World Art**   Edgar Degas, *L'Orchestre*; Jean Falguière, *The Christian Martyr*; Claude Monet, *The River*; Pierre-Auguste Renoir, *The Skaters*; George Watts, *The Meeting of Jacob and Esau*.

**World Literature**   Charles Aïdé, *The Marstons*; Alphonse Daudet, *La Petit Chose*; Feodor Dostoyevsky, *The Idiot*; Alexei Tolstoy, *Czar Feodor Ivanovich*; Albert Wolff, *Judith*.

**World Music**   Johannes Brahms, *German Requiem*; Edvard Grieg, *Piano Concerto*; Johann Strauss, *Tales from the Vienna Woods*; Richard Wagner, *Die Meistersinger von Nürnberg*.

**Miscellaneous**   The Royal Danish Music Conservatory opens in Copenhagen; births include Paul Claudel, Maxim Gorky, Wladyslaw Reymont, Edmond Rostand, and Édouard Vuillard; deaths include Franz Berwald, Robert Griepenkerl, Charles Meryon, and Gioacchino Rossini.

## American Art and Literature Highlights

**Births/Deaths**   Births include art figures Solon Borglum, Leon Dabo, Alfred Maurer, and literary figures Mary Austin, W. E. B. DuBois, Norman Hapgood, Charlotte B. Parker, Eleanor H. Porter, Mary Watts, and William A. White; deaths include artists Charles Jarvis, Emanuel Leutze, William

S. Mount, and literary figures Albert Greene, Adah Isaacs Menken, Seba Smith, and Daniel P. Thompson.

**Art Works**    Albert Bierstadt, *Among the Sierra Nevada Mountains*; Martin J. Heade, *Storm Approaching Narragansett Bay*; Edward L. Henry, *Philadelphia Interior*; Eastman Johnson, *The Boyhood of Lincoln*; John La Farge, *Paradise Valley, Newport*; Edmonia Lewis, *Scenes from "Hiawatha"*; John Rogers, *Council of War*; John M. Stanley, *Trial of Red Jacket*; Emma Stebbins, *The Infant Samuel*.

**Literature**    Louisa May Alcott, *Little Women*; Daniel Brinton, *Myths of the Americas*; John E. Cooke, *Fairfax*; Rebecca Davis, *Waiting for the Verdict*; Martha Finley, *Elsie's Holiday at Roselands*; Cincinnatus Miller, *Specimens*; Henry Shaw, *Josh Billings on Ice and Other Things*; Edward Sill, *The Hermitage and Other Poems*; Frances M. Whitcher, *Widow Spriggins, Mary Elmer and Other Sketches*.

## Music — The Vernacular/Commercial Scene

**A. Births**    "Fiddlin'" John Carson (country fiddler) March 23; Scott Joplin (ragtime composer/pianist) November 24 (?); Vess L. Ossman (ragtime banjoist) August 21; Jerome H. Remick (publisher) November 15; Ren Shields (composer/lyricist) February 22.

**C. Biographical**

**Performing Groups**    Emerson, Allen and Manning's Minstrels.

**E. Representative Works**

**Musicals**    Various composers and G. L. Fox, *Humpty Dumpty*; Various composers, *Ixion, or, The Man at the Wheel*.

**Songs**    Alfred Lee and G. Leybourne, *The Man on the Flying Trapeze*; Charles E. Pratt and W. H. Lingard, *Walking Down Broadway*; Septimus Winner, *Whispering Hope—Ten Little Indians*; Henry C. Work, *Songs: Agnes by the River—Our Last Grand Camping Ground—Song of the Red Men*.

## Music — The Cultivated/Art Music Scene

**F. Births**    Henry F. Gilbert (composer) September 26; Alice Nielsen (soprano?) June 7; Wallace C. Sabine (acoustician) June 13; Oscar Saenger (singer/educator) January 5; Charles Sanford Skilton (composer) August 16; Ellison Van Hoose (tenor) August 18.

**G. Deaths**    William B. Bradbury (composer/organist) January 7; William Darracott, Jr. (violin maker).

**H. Debuts**

**United States**    Ferdinand von Inten (German pianist—New York).

**I. New Positions**

**Educational**    Lucien Southard (director, Peabody Conservatory—to 1871).

**Other**    John R. Hassard (music critic, *New York Tribune*—to 1884); Theodore Seward (editor, *New York Musical Gazette*).

**K. Biographical**    Minnie Hauk is given a grant to go to Europe, where she debuts in London and Paris; Silas Pratt goes to Europe to study music in Berlin; John Philip Sousa, age 13, enlists in the Marine Band, but studies music privately with George F. Benkert; Bernhard Ziehn (German theorist) comes to the United States and settles in Chicago.

**L. Musical Beginnings**

**Performing Groups**    Chicago Oratorio Society; Salem (Massachusetts) Oratorio Society; Theodore Thomas Symphony Orchestra.

**Educational**    Goldbeck Conservatory of Music (Chicago).

**Other**    Charles F. Albert Violin Shop (Philadelphia); Grand (Pike's) Opera House (New York); Kunkel Brothers, Music Publishers (St. Louis); *The Musical Independent*; *New York Philharmonic Journal*; *Weekly Comic and Sentimental Singers Journal*.

**M. Music Publications**

Hillman, Joseph, *The Revivalist*

Mathews, W. S. B., *An Outline of Musical Form*

Perkins, Henry S., *College Hymn and Tune Book—Perkins' Vocal Method*

**N. Musical Compositions**

**Choral/Vocal**   Horatio Palmer, *Yield Not to Temptation* (hymn).

**Concertos**   Louis Moreau Gottschalk, *Grand Tarantelle for Piano and Orchestra*.

**Operas**   Julius Eichberg, *The Two Cadis* (operetta); Karl Merz, *The Runaway Flirt* (operetta).

**Piano/Organ**   Dudley Buck, *Concert Variations on "The Star-Spangled Banner," Opus 23* (organ); Louis Moreau Gottschalk, *Morte!, Opus 50—Marche solennelle*; Edward Mack, *General Grant's Grand March*.

**Symphonies**   Louis Moreau Gottschalk, *Symphony No. 2, "A Montevideo."*

# 1869

❀

## Historical Highlights

The transcontinental railroad is completed at Promontory Point in Utah; Black Friday on Wall Street begins a panic; the American Women Suffrage Association is founded; the Knights of Labor is founded in Philadelphia; the University of Nebraska is founded; the Suez Canal is opened; the British Parliament abolishes mandatory imprisonment for debt; France is given a parliamentary government.

## World Cultural Highlights

**World Art**   Eugène Boudin, *On the Beach at Deauville*; Jean-Baptiste Carpeaux, *The Dance*; Frederic Leighton, *Electra at Agamemnon's Tomb*; Édouard Manet, *The Balcony*; Alexandre Regnault, *Judith*.

**World Literature**   Richard Blackmore, *Lorna Doone*; Robert Browning, *The Ring and the Book*; Victor Hugo, *L'Homme qui rit*; Aubrey de Vere, *Irish Odes*; Paul Verlaine, *Fêtes Galantes*.

**World Music**   Johannes Brahms, *Liebeslieder Waltzes—Alto Rhapsody*; Modest Moussorgsky, *Boris Goudunov*; Peter Tchaikovsky, *Fantasy-Overture, Romeo and Juliet*; Richard Wagner, *Siegfried*.

**Miscellaneous**   The Vienna Staatsoper is founded; the Durand Publishing House opens in Paris; births include Bo Hjalmar Bergman, André Gide, Henri Matisse, and Hans Pfitzner; deaths include Hector Berlioz, Alphonse de Lamartine, Robert Lauder, and Charles Saint-Beuve.

## American Art and Literature Highlights

**Births/Deaths**   Births include architect Frank Lloyd Wright and literary figures Henry W. Boynton, Marion Cook, Olive Dargan (Fielding Burke), Chester Bailey Fernald, Hutchins Hapgood, Edgar Lee Masters, William V. Moody, Edwin Arlington Robinson, George Sterling, and Booth Tarkington; deaths include artist Thomas Hotchkiss and literary figures Frederick Cozzens and Henry A. Wise.

**Art Works**   Joseph Becker, *Snow Sheds, Central Pacific Railroad, Sierra Nevada Mountains*; G. P. A. Healy et al., *The Arch of Titus*; John Jackson, *Eve Mourning Over the Dead Body of Abel*; John F. Kensett, *Marine Off Big Rock*; Thomas Moran, *Spirit of the Indian*; Thomas B. Read, *A Painter's Dream*; William Rinehart, *Children Sleeping* (marble); Lilly M. Spencer, *We Both Must Fade*.

**Literature**   Mary E. Dodge, *A Few Friends and How They Amused Themselves*; Henry James, *Pyramus and Thisbe*; Lucy Larcom, *Poems*; James Russell Lowell, *Under the Willows and Other Poems*; Cincinnatus Miller, *Joaquin et al.*; E. D. E. N. Southworth, *The Fatal Marriage*; Mark Twain, *The Innocents Abroad*; John Greenleaf Whittier, *Among the Hills and Other Poems*.

## Music—The Vernacular/Commercial Scene

**A. Births**   Marie Dressler (singer/actress) November 9; Frederick Allen "Kerry" Mills (composer/publisher) February 1; Rida Johnson Young (lyricist) February 28; Florenz Ziegfeld (impresario) March 21.

**C. Biographical**

**Miscellaneous**   Anna Held (French-born Polish singer) comes to the United States.

**E. Representative Works**

**Musicals**   Various composers, *Hiccory Diccory Dock.*

**Songs**   Billy Reeves, *Shew, Fly, Don't Bother Me*; Joseph Winner, *Little Brown Jug*; Henry Tucker and G. Cooper, *Sweet Genevieve*; Will S. Hays, *She's the Sweetest of Them All*; Henry Clay Work, *Songs: The Buckskin Bag of Gold—Crossing the Grand Sierras—No Letters from Home.*

## Music—The Cultivated/Art Music Scene

**F. Births**   John T. Austin (organ builder) May 16; Harry L. Freeman (composer) October 9; Victor Harris (conductor/composer/pianist) April 27; Sissieretta Jones (soprano) January 5; Clara Damrosch Mannes (pianist/educator) December 12; Caro Roma (soprano/composer) September 10; Patty Stair (organist/composer) November 12; George W. Stebbins (organist/composer) June 16; William F. Zech (violinist/conductor) July 22.

**G. Deaths**   Louis Moreau Gottschalk (pianist/composer) December 18; Theodore von La Hache (German-born pianist/composer) November 21; George Peabody (art patron) November 4; Marcus Lafayette Swan (composer/hymnist?).

**H. Debuts**

**United States**   Nahan Franko (violinist—New York), Sam Franko (violinist—New York), Anna Mehlig (pianist—Farmington, Connecticut), Walton Perkins (pianist—New York).

**Other**   Jule Edson Perkins (bass—Italy).

**I. New Positions**

**Conductors**   Hermann Kotzschmar (Haydn Society of Portland, Maine).

**Educational**   Fenlon B. Rice (Oberlin College).

**Other**   George E. Whiting (organ, King's Chapel, Boston—to 1874).

**J. Honors and Awards**

**Honors**   John Knowles Paine (MA, Harvard); Eben Tourjée (PhD, Wesleyan University).

**K. Biographical**   William Foster Apthorp graduates from Harvard; Dudley Buck moves to Chicago as organist until the Great Chicago Fire; Patrick Gilmore stages his mammoth National Peace Jubilee in Boston; Edward MacDowell begins piano lessons from Juan Buitrago; Theodore Thomas takes his orchestra on its first national tour.

**L. Musical Beginnings**

**Performing Groups**   Buffalo Beethoven Musical Society; Grand Army of the Republic Band; Parepa-Rosa English Opera Co.; Portland Rossini Club (Maine—first women's musical organization in the United States); Washington Choral Society.

**Educational**   Philadelphia Musical Academy; Wyman Music School (Claremont, New York).

**Other**   Boston Musical Instrument Co.; John Church and Co.; Concordia Publishing House (St. Louis); *The Folio: A Journal of Music, Art and Literature*; Detroit Opera House; German Opera Theater (San Francisco); Benjamin Hitchcock Music Store (New York); Hoffman's Music Store (Leavenworth, Kansas); Hutchings, Plaisted and Co.

**M. Music Publications**

Butterfield, James A., *Butterfield's Anthems*
Knapp, Phebe Palmer, *Notes of Joy*

Listemann, Bernhard, *Modern Method of Violin Playing*
Mason, Lowell, *Carmina Sacra Enlarged: The American Tune Book*
Perkins, William O., *Starry Crown*
Seller, Emma, *Voice in Singing*

**N. Musical Compositions**

**Operas**  James Fairlamb, *Valérie, or Treasured Tokens*; Caryl Florio, *Les tours de Mercure* (operetta); Louis Moreau Gottschalk, *Charles IX—Isaura de Salerno*.

**Orchestra/Band**  Charles Converse, *American Overture on Hail, Columbia*.

**Piano/Organ**  Louis Moreau Gottschalk, *The Dying Swan*; George John Huss, *Capricietto alla Militaire*.

# 1870

❀

## Historical Highlights

The census shows a US population of 39,818,000, an increase of 26% over ten years; the 15th Amendment on the right to vote is ratified; the Department of Justice and the US Weather Bureau are formed; Ohio State University is founded; the Franco-Prussian War begins; Napoleon III is deposed and the Third French Republic is formed.

## World Cultural Highlights

**World Art**  Paul Cézanne, *The Black Clock*; Henri Chapu, *Jeanne d'Arc*; Gustave Courbet, *The Wave*; Jean Falguière, *Victor in the Cockfight*; Alexandre Regnault, *Salome*.

**World Literature**  Benjamin Disraeli, *Lothair*; Alexis Kivi, *The Seven Brothers*; Alexei Tolstoy, *Czar Boris*; Jules Verne, *Twenty Thousand Leagues Under the Sea*; Émile Zola, *La Débacle*.

**World Music**  Max Bruch, *Symphonies No. 1, 2*; Léo Delibes, *Coppélia*; Camille Saint-Saëns, *Introduction and Rondo Capriccioso*; Bedřich Smetana, *Bartered Bride*; Richard Wagner, *Siegfried Idyll*.

**Miscellaneous**  The Salzburg Mozarteum opens; the Zagreb Opera Co. is founded; the Brighton Festivals begin in England; births include Ernst Barlach, Ivan Bunin, Maurice Denis, and Franz Lehár; deaths include Charles Dickens, Alexandre Dumas, père, Jules de Goncourt and Prosper Mérimée.

## American Art and Literature Highlights

**Births/Deaths**  Births include art figures Hugh Breckenridge, A. Stirling Calder, William Glackens, John Maris, Maxfield Parrish, and literary figures Mary Johnston, Paul Kester, Robert M. Lovett, and Alice Caldwell Rice; deaths include literary figures John Pendleton Kennedy (Mark Littleton), Fitz-Hugh Ludlow, Anna Cora Mowatt, James M. Whitfield, Emma Hart Willard, and Harriet Wilson.

**Art Works**  Peter John Hennessy, *Mon Brave*; Daniel Huntington, *The Field Family in a Garden*; Eastman Johnson, *The Shelter*; John F. Kensett, *Thunderstorm over Lake George*; Homer D. Martin, *Lake Sanford, Adirondacks, Spring*; Andrew Melrose, *Morning in the Andes*; William Rinehart, *Antigone*; Peter Rothermel, *Battle of Gettysburg* (?); Thomas Wood, *The Village Post Office*.

**Literature**  Louisa May Alcott, *The Old-Fashioned Girl*; Thomas Aldrich, *Story of a Bad Boy*; Charles Gayler, *Fritz: Our Cousin-German*; Bret Harte, *The Luck of Roaring Camp and Other Stories*; Helen Hunt Jackson, *Verses by H. H.*; James Russell Lowell, *Among My Books I*; Cincinnatus Miller, *Pacific Poems*; Margaret Preston, *Old Songs and New*; John Greenleaf Whittier, *Ballads of New England*.

## Music—The Vernacular/Commercial Scene

**A. Births**  Marie Cahill (singer/actress) (?) February 7; Glen MacDonough (lyricist); Uncle

Dave Macon (singer) October 7; Dave Montgomery (singer/actor) April 21; Joseph W. Stern (composer) January 11; Lynn Udal (songwriter) February 4.

**E. Representative Works**

**Musicals**     Various composers, *The Twelve Temptations*.

**Songs**     Anonymous, *Frankie and Johnny*; Hart Pease Danks and W. Gardner, *Don't Be Angry with Me, Darling*; Henry Clay Work, *Georgie Sails Tomorrow!*

## Music—The Cultivated/Art Music Scene

**F. Births**     Joseph C. Breil (composer) June 28; Howard Brockway (pianist/composer) November 22; Mme. Charles Cahier (contralto) January 8; Louis Coerne (composer) February 27; Henry Eichheim (violinist/conductor/composer) January 3; Mabel Wood Hill (composer) March 12; Lucius Hosmer (composer) August 14; Harry Benjamin Jepson (organist/composer) August 16; Arthur Pryor (trombonist/bandmaster) September 22; Leon Rains (bassist) October 1; Francis Rogers (baritone) April 14; Rose Laura Sutro (pianist) September 15; William T. Upton (pianist/musicologist) December 17; Hermann Wetzler (organist/conductor/composer) September 8.

**G. Deaths**     Carl Anschütz (German bassist/conductor) January 13.

**H. Debuts**

**United States**     Annie Cary (contralto—New York), Marie Krebs (German pianist), Christine Nilsson (Swedish soprano—New York).

**I. New Positions**

Others George W. Warren (organ, St. Thomas Church, Manhattan—to 1902).

**K. Biographical**     Inez Fabbri and her husband return to the United States to stay; Arthur Foote enters Harvard; Henry C. Heyman studies in Leipzig; Minnie Hauk makes her Vienna debut; Gustav Hinrichs (German conductor) comes to the United States; Ethelbert Nevin begins piano lessons at the Pittsburgh Conservatory; Horace Nicholl (British organist/composer) emigrates to the United States and settles in Pittsburgh; Richard Zechwer (German pianist) emigrates to the United States and settles in Philadelphia.

**L. Musical Beginnings**

**Performing Groups**     Denver German Männerchor; Ladies Morning Musicale (Buffalo).

**Other**     John Church and Co. (buys out O. Ditson's midwest holdings); Coates Opera House (Kansas City); Horton Hall Theater (San Diego); Merced Theater (Los Angeles); *Musical Million and Fireside Friend* (to 1914); Patent Note Publishing Co.

**M. Music Publications:**

Baker, Benjamin F., *Thorough-Bass and Harmony*
Bliss, P. P., *The Charm*
Butterfield, James A., *Butterfield's Collection of Sacred Music*
Parker, James C. D., *Theoretical and Practical Harmony*
Perkins, William O., *Laurel Wreath*
Ritter, Frédéric, *A History of Music in the Form of Lectures I*
Tourjée, Eben, *The New England Conservatory's Pianoforte Method*

**N. Musical Compositions**

**Chamber Music**     Caryl Florio, *Piano Quintet*.

**Choral/Vocal**     P. P. Bliss, *Hold the Fort* (sacred song).

**Orchestra/Band**     Dudley Buck, *Culprit Fay Overture, Opus 44*; Jerome Hopkins, *Serenade in E Major*; Silas G. Pratt, *Symphonic Sketch, "Magdalena's Lament."*

**Piano/Organ**     Caryl Florio, *Marche des Fées*; Richard Hoffman, *In Memoriam L. M. G.*; Silas G. Pratt, *Shadow Thoughts: Three Impromptus*.

# 1871

❁

## Historical Highlights

The Great Chicago Fire destroys much of the city; the Treaty of Washington settles the fishing rights between the United States and Canada; the Civil Service Commission is established; the Franco-Prussian War ends and the German Empire is proclaimed; the British Parliament legalizes labor unions; Henry Stanley finds David Livingstone in Africa; the first luxury liner, the *S.S. Oceanic,* is launched.

## World Cultural Highlights

**World Art**   Reinhold Begas, *Schiller Memorial* (Berlin); Edgar Degas, *Father Listening to Pagans;* Édouard Manet, *Le Repos;* John Millais, *Chill October;* Dante Rossetti, *The Dream of Dante.*

**World Literature**   Edward Lear, *Nonsense Songs and Stories,* Arthur Rimbaud, *Les Illuminations;* Algernon Swinburne, *Songs before Sunrise.*

**World Music**   Johannes Brahms, *Schicksalslied—Triumphslied;* César Franck, *Panis Angelicus;* Niels Gade, *Symphony No. 8;* Camille Saint-Saëns, *Le Rouet d'Omphale;* Giuseppe Verdi, *Aida.*

**Miscellaneous**   Royal Albert Hall opens in London; the Oslo Philharmonic Orchestra is founded; births include Leonid Andreyev, Frantisek Kupka, Willem Mengelberg, Marcel Proust, Georges Rouault, and John M. Synge; deaths include Émile Deschamps, François Fétis, George Hayter, and Alexandre Regnault.

## American Art and Literature Highlights

**Births/Deaths**   Births include art figures Victor Brenner, Lyonel Feininger, and John Sloan, and literary figures Samuel H. Adams, Winston Churchill, Stephen Crane, Thomas Daly, Theodore Dreiser, James Forbes, William MacLeod Raine, Lola Ridge, and Jesse L. Williams; deaths include artist Thomas Rossiter and literary figures Henry Brackenridge, Alice and Phoebe Cary, Charles Scribner, George Ticknor, and Henry Theodore Tuckerman.

**Art Works**   Jasper Cropsey, *Mountain Lake;* Frank Duveneck, *The Old Professor;* Thomas Eakins, *Max Schmidt in a Single Scull;* Winslow Homer, *The Country School;* Eastman Johnson, *The Old Stagecoach;* Edward Kemeys, *Hudson Bay Wolves;* Vinnie Ream, *Abraham Lincoln;* William Rimmer, *Fighting Lions;* William Wetmore Story, *Salome;* William A. Walker, *The Newsboy.*

**Literature**   Louisa May Alcott, *Little Men;* Edward Eggleston, *The Hoosier Schoolmaster;* William D. Howells, *Suburban Sketches;* Emma Lazarus, *Admetus and Other Poems;* James Russell Lowell, *My Study Windows;* Cincinnatus Miller, *Songs of the Sierras;* Harriet Spofford, *New England Legends;* Richard H. Stoddard, *Book of the East and Other Poems;* Walt Whitman, *Passage to India.*

## Music—The Vernacular/Commercial Scene

**A. Births**   Alfred Bryan (lyricist); Richard Carle (singer/actor) July 7; Benjamin R. Harney (ragtime pianist/writer) April 30; Frederick K. Logan (composer) October 15; Neil Moret (composer/lyricist); Blanche Ring (actress/singer) April 24.

**C. Biographical**

**Miscellaneous**   The Jubilee Singers from Fisk University tour the East Coast.

**E. Representative Works**

**Songs**   Anonymous, *Goodbye, Liza Jane;* William Gooch and H. Birch, *Reuben and Rachel;* W.

S. Hays, *The Little Old Log Cabin in the Lane—No. 29;* Henry Clay Work, *Joy in Heaven! or The Returning Wanderer's Welcome—Take Them Away! They'll Drive Me Crazy.*

## Music—The Cultivated/Art Music Scene

**F. Births**   Frederick S. Converse (composer/administrator) January 5; Arthur Fickénscher (pianist/composer) March 9; Olive Fremstad (soprano) March 14; John Wallace Goodrich (organist/conductor) May 27; Henry Hadley (composer/conductor) December 20; Louise Homer (contralto) April 30; Arthur Nevin (composer/conductor) April 27; Antonio Paoli (Puerto Rican tenor) April 14; Franklin Peale Patterson (composer) January 5; Bertram Shapleigh (composer/pianist) January 15; Blanche W. Walton (patron of the arts) November 15; Henry W. Wehrmann, Jr. (violinist/composer); Clarence Whitehill (bass-baritone) November 5; Howard Eugene Wurlitzer (instrument maker/dealer) September 5.

**G. Deaths**   George E. Blake (publisher) February 24; Silas Brainard (music publisher) April 8; Thomas E. Chickering (piano builder) February 14; Theodore Hagen (German-born educator/author) December 27; Sylvanus Billings Pond (composer/publisher) March 12; Heinrich E. Steinway (German-born piano maker) February 7; William Whiteley (instrument maker) March 25; Peter Wolle (Moravian composer) November 14.

**H. Debuts**

**United States**   Leopold Damrosch (German conductor—New York), Tom Karl (Irish tenor—New York), Francis Korbay (Hungarian tenor—New York), Janet Patey (Scottish contralto—tour), Clara Kathleen Rogers (British soprano—New York), Hermine Rudersdorff (Ukrainian soprano—Boston), Theodor Wachtel (German tenor—New York).

**Other**   Alwina Valleria (soprano—London).

**I. New Positions**

**Conductors**   Leopold Damrosch (German conductor—New York Männergesangverein Arion—to 1883); Henry Fries (US Marine Band—to 1873); B. J. Lang (Boston Apollo Club).

**Educational**   Dudley Buck (New England Conservatory); Wulf Fries (Petersilea's Music School); Asger Hamerik (director, Peabody Conservatory); J. C. D. Parker (New England Conservatory—to 1897); Fenlon B. Rice (director, Oberlin Conservatory—to 1901); Grenville Dean Wilson (music head, Rockland Institute, Nyack).

**Other**   Silas Pratt (organ, Church of the Messiah, Chicago); Ebenezer Prout (editor, *Monthly Musical Record*).

**K. Biographical**   Leopold Damrosch (German violinist/conductor) comes to the United States as conductor in New York, with Frank and Walter Damrosch following their brother soon afterward; Dudley Buck, following the Great Chicago Fire, moves to Boston; Silas G. Pratt returns to the United States from study in Europe; Clara Kathleen Rogers (British soprano) comes to the United States with the Parepa-Rosa Co. and decides to stay; Root and Cady lose their publishing business as a result of the Chicago fire; Ira Sankey joins D. L. Moody in evangelism; William H. Sherwood begins five years of music study in Europe.

**L. Musical Beginnings**

**Performing Groups**   Boston Apollo Club; Buffalo Choral Union; Fisk Jubilee Singers (Nashville, Tennessee); Indianapolis Philharmonic Orchestra; Los Angeles Musical Association.

**Educational**   Beethoven Conservatory of Music (St. Louis, Missouri); Cleveland Conservatory of Music; Illinois College Conservatory of Music (Jacksonville, Florida); Minneapolis Academy of Music; Petersilea Academy of Music (Boston).

**Other**   Church's Musical Visitor; Conover Brothers Music Store and Publishers (Kansas City, Missouri); Grand Opera House (Milwaukee, Wisconsin); Musicians' National Protective Association; Packard Piano and Organ Co. (Fort Wayne, Indiana); Providence Opera House (Rhode Island); Sherman and Hyde, Music Store and Publisher (Sherman, Clay and Co.).

**M. Music Publications**

Mason, Lowell, *The Pestalozzian Music Teacher*
Perkins, Henry S., *Song Echo*
Perkins, William O., *Orpheon*
Squire, Albert, *Squire's Cornet Band Olio*

**N. Musical Compositions**

**Operas**  James A. Butterfield, *Belshazzar;* Silas G. Pratt, *Antonio (Lucille);* Eugène-Prosper Prévost, *Blanche et Renée.*

**Piano/Organ**  Dudley Buck, *Variations on "Annie Laurie," Opus 51* (organ).

**Symphonies**  Silas G. Pratt, *Symphony No. 1.*

# 1872

❀

## Historical Highlights

President Ulysses S. Grant is re-elected; the Crédit Mobilier scandal breaks out; Congress passes the Amnesty Act pardoning all Confederate leaders; Montgomery Ward opens his first store in Chicago; Arbor Day is first celebrated in Nebraska; Yellowstone National Park is created; Porfirio Díaz becomes president of the Mexican Republic; the Carlists are defeated in the Spanish Civil War.

## World Cultural Highlights

**World Art**  Arnold Böcklin, *The Battle of the Centaurs;* Max Liebermann, *Women Plucking Geese;* Claude Monet, *Impression: Sunrise;* Pierre-Auguste Renoir, *Pont Neuf.*

**World Literature**  Samuel Butler, *Erewhon;* Lewis Carroll, *Through the Looking Glass;* Alphonse Daudet, *L'Arlésienne;* George Eliot, *Middlemarch;* Victor Hugo, *L'Année Terrible.*

**World Music**  Anton Bruckner, *Symphony No. 2,* Modest Moussorgsky, *The Nursery;* Joseph Joachim Raff, *Symphony No. 5, "Lenore";* Peter Tchaikovsky, *Symphony No. 2, "Little Russian."*

**Miscellaneous**  Bösendorfer Saal opens in Vienna; the Trinity College of Music opens in London; births include Félix Bataille, Sergei Diaghilev, Piet Mondrian, and Ralph Vaughan Williams; deaths include Julius Schnorr von Carolsfeld, Théophile Gautier, and Franz Grillparzer.

## American Art and Literature Highlights

**Births/Deaths**  Births include sculptors Frederick Sievers, Bessie Vonnoh, and literary figures Paul Laurence Dunbar, Leonora Speyer, Albert P. Terhune, and Harold Bell Wright; deaths include art figures George Catlin, John Kensett, Samuel F. B. Morse, John Mix Stanley, Thomas Sully, and literary figures Henry H. Brownell, Frank H. Murdoch, Thomas B. Read, and Sara P. Willis (Fanny Fern).

**Art Works**  Ralph Blakelock, *Peace Among the Nations* (?); Samuel Colman, Jr., *Ships of the Plains;* Frank Duveneck, *Whistling Boy;* Winslow Homer, *Snap the Whip;* Thomas W. Hood, *Yankee Peddler;* Charles Nahl, *Sunday Morning in the Mines;* William Rimmer, *Flight and Pursuit;* William Rinehart, *Clytie;* James M. Whistler, *The Artist's Mother;* T. Worthington Whittredge, *Home by the Sea.*

**Literature**  Edward Eggleston, *The End of the World;* Oliver Wendell Holmes, *The Poet at the Breakfast Table;* William D. Howells, *Their Wedding Journey;* Helen Hunt Jackson, *Bits of Travel;* Frank H. Murdoch, *Davy Crockett;* Albert Pike, *Hymns to the Gods and Other Poems;* Bayard Taylor, *The Masque of the Gods;* Celia Thaxter, *Poems;* Mark Twain, *Roughing It.*

## Music—The Vernacular/Commercial Scene

**A. Births**  Thurland Chattaway (composer/lyricist) April 8; Bill Johnson (bass) (?) August 10; A. Baldwin Sloane (composer) August 28; Harry Von Tilzer (songwriter/publisher) July 8.

**E. Representative Works**

**Musicals**   Various composers, *Leo and Lotos*.

**Songs**   T. Brigham Bishop and G. Cooper, *Pretty as a Picture;* Hart Pease Danks and Eben Rexford, *Silver Threads Among the Gold—Pauline;* William J. Scanlan, *Jim Fisk* (?); Henry Clay Work, *Traveling Homeward*.

## Music—The Cultivated/Art Music Scene

**F. Births**   Bentley D. Ackley (hymn writer/editor) September 27; Suzanne Adams (soprano) November 28; Henry P. Eames (pianist/educator) September 12; Arthur Farwell (composer/critic) April 23; Hallett Gilberté (composer) March 14; Rubin Goldmark (composer) August 15; Edward Burlingame Hill (composer) September 9; Rupert Hughes (writer on music) January 31; Caspar Koch (organist) November 25; Edward Schneider (pianist/composer) October 3; Ottilie Sutro (pianist) January 4; Frank E. Ward (organist/pianist/composer) October 7.

**G. Deaths**   Thomas Appleton (organ builder) July 11; Lewis Carusi (horn and dance instructor); Thomas Hastings (composer/hymnist) May 15; Lowell Mason (organist/composer/educator) August 11; Eugène-Prosper Prévost (French conductor/composer) August 19; Eduard Sobolewski (German-born violinist/conductor) May 17.

**H. Debuts**

**United States**   Pauline Lucca (Austrian soprano—New York), Minna Peschka-Leutner (Austrian soprano—Boston), Anton Rubinstein (Russian pianist—tour), Charles Santley (British baritone—New York), Émile Sauret (French violinist—tour), Henri Wieniawski (Polish violinist—tour).

**I. New Positions**

**Conductors**   Simon Hassler (Chesnut Street Theater, Philadelphia—to 1882); Adolph Neuendorff (Germania Theater, New York); Silas Pratt (Chicago Apollo Club).

**Other**   William Horatio Clarke (music superintendent, Dayton Public Schools).

**J. Honors and Awards**

**Honors**   William Mason (PhD, Yale).

**K. Biographical**   Emma Abbott goes to Europe to study voice in Milan and Paris; Herman Bellstedt's family settles in Cincinnati; Teresa Carreño marries her first husband, violinist Émile Sauret; S. Austen Pearce (British organist) emigrates to the United States and settles in New York; Anton Rubinstein begins a 215-concert tour of the United States with Henri Wieniawski; Johann Strauss, Jr., visits the United States and conducts several "monster concerts" in Boston and New York.

**L. Musical Beginnings**

**Performing Groups**   Apollo Club of Chicago; Cincinnati Symphony Orchestra; Philadelphia Orpheus Club; San Diego Philharmonic Society; Willimantic Brass Band (Massachusetts).

**Festivals**   World Peace Jubilee and International Musical Festival.

**Educational**   Boston University College of Music; National College of Music (Boston, one year only); St. Louis Conservatory of Music.

**Other**   Carl Fischer Publishing Co. (New York); Germania Theater (New York); Ruebush, Kieffer and Co., Music Publishers; E. Schuberth, Music Publisher (New York); Schwarzer Zither Factory (Washington, Missouri); Sohmer and Co., Piano Manufacturers (New York); Staub's Opera House (Knoxville, Tennessee); Turnverein Hall (Los Angeles); Rudolph Wurlitzer and Brother (Cincinnati—incorporated 1890).

**M. Music Publications**

Bliss, P. P., *The Tree*
Perkins, Henry S., *Advance*
Perkins, William O., *Church Welcome*

Root, George F., *The Normal Musical Handbook*
Seward, Theodore, ed., *The Coronation*

**N. Musical Compositions**

**Chamber Music**   Caryl Florio, *Reverie and Scherzo* (two clarinets and strings).

**Choral/Vocal**   George Frederick Bristow, *The Pioneer* (secular cantata); Dudley Buck, *The Forty-Sixth Psalm—Festival Hymn, Opus 57;* Julius Eichberg, *To Thee, O Country Great and Free* (chorus); Caryl Florio, *Song of the Elements* (cantata); Robert Lowry, *I Need Thee Every Hour* (sacred song); Horace Nicholl, *Mass in E-Flat Major, Opus 1;* John Knowles Paine, *St. Peter, Opus 20* (oratorio); George E. Whiting, *Mass in C Minor.*

**Concertos**   Jerome Hopkins, *Concerto for Piano and Orchestra.*

**Operas**   John H. Hewitt, *The Musical Enthusiast* (operetta).

**Orchestra/Band**   John Philip Sousa, *Moonlight on the Potomac Waltzes.*

**Symphonies**   George Frederick Bristow, *Symphony No. 4, "Arcadian," Opus 50.*

# 1873

❀

## Historical Highlights

A financial panic ushers in a six-year depression; Jesse James pulls his first train robbery; San Francisco introduces the cable car; penny postcards are introduced to the public; P. T. Barnum's Greatest Show on Earth opens; Texas Christian University is founded; Zanzibar closes its slave markets and halts all slave trade in its territory.

## World Cultural Highlights

**World Art**   Paul Cézanne, *The Straw Hat;* Edgar Degas, *The Cotton Market, New Orleans,* George Inness, *The Monk;* Édouard Manet, *The Railway;* Claude Monet, *The Poppy Fields.*

**World Literature**   Thomas Aldrich, *Marjorie Daw;* Thomas Hardy, *A Pair of Blue Eyes;* Arthur Rimbaud, *Une Saison en Enfer;* Jules Verne, *Around the World in Eighty Days.*

**World Music**   Johannes Brahms, *Variations on a Theme by Haydn—String Quartets No. 1, 2;* Anton Bruckner, *Symphony No. 3;* Antonín Dvořák, *Symphony No. 3;* Edouard Lalo, *Symphonie Espagnole.*

**Miscellaneous**   The Bristol Music Festivals begin in England; the English Opera Co. and the Finnish National Opera Co. are both founded; births include Feodor Chaliapin, Enrico Caruso, and Sergei Rachmaninoff; deaths include Edward Bulwer-Lytton, Edwin Landseer, and Alessandro Manzoni.

## American Art and Literature Highlights

**Births/Deaths**   Births include literary figures Willa Cather, Felipe Chacón, Dane Coolidge, Benjamin DeCasseres, William Irwin, George Cabot Lodge, Anne Douglas Sedgwick, and William E. Woodward; deaths include art figures William Jewett, Hiram Powers, and literary figures Charles Barras, Caroline Chesebro', Lewis G. Clark, Frederick Tuckerman, and Thomas Ward (Flaccus).

**Art Works**   Thomas Eakins, *The Biglen Brothers Racing;* Winslow Homer, *The Berry Pickers—Gathering Autumn Leaves;* Thomas W. Hood, *The Village Post Office;* George Inness, *The Monk;* Chauncey B. Ives, *Ivo and Bacchus;* Hiram Powers, *The Last of the Tribe;* Francis A. Silva, *Calm at Sunset.*

**Literature**   Thomas Aldrich, *Marjorie Daw;* Will Carleton, *Farm Ballads;* Augustin Daly, *Roughing It;* William D. Howells, *A Chance Acquaintance;* Cincinnatus Miller, *Songs of the*

*Sunlands*; Henry Peterson, *Pemberton*; Celia Thaxter, *Among the Isles of Shoals*; Mark Twain and C. Warner, *The Gilded Age*; Walt Whitman, *Memoranda During the War*; Constance F. Woolson, *The Old Stone House*.

## Music—The Vernacular/Commercial Scene

**A. Births**    J. Keirn Brennan (lyricist) November 24; William C. Handy (trumpeter/composer) November 16; Otto Harbach (librettist/lyricist) August 18; Max Hoffmann (ragtime composer) December 8; J. Rosamond Johnson (composer/lyricist) August 11; Papa Jack Laine (percussionist/bandleader) September 21; Theodore Morse (songwriter/publisher) April 13; Fred Stone (singer/actor) August 19; Tom Turpin (ragtime pianist); George Walker (minstrel).

**E. Representative Works**

**Songs**    Anonymous, *John Henry*; David Braham and Ned Harrigan, *The Mulligan Guard*; William S. Hays, *Mollie Darling*; Dan Kelly (?), *Home, Home on the Range*.

## Music—The Cultivated/Art Music Scene

**F. Births**    Clarence Dickinson (organist) May 7; Peter W. Dykema (music educator) November 25; Arthur Elson (writer on music) November 18; Franz Listemann (cellist) December 17; Daniel G. Mason (composer/educator) November 20; Mary Carr Moore (composer/educator) August 6; Jane Osborn-Hannah (soprano) July 8; Adrienne Osborne (contralto) December 2; Anita Rio (soprano) July 30; Oscar G. T. Sonneck (musicologist/editor) October 6; T. Carl Whitmer (organist/composer) June 24; Herbert Witherspoon (bassist/administrator) July 21; John W. Work (tenor/conductor/composer) August 6; Rudolph Henry Wurlitzer (violinist/violin maker) December 30.

**G. Deaths**    A. U. Hayter (British-born organist) July 28; Joshua Leavitt (hymnbook compiler) January 16; Sylvester Main (publisher) October 5; Léopold Meignen (French-born composer/publisher).

**H. Debuts**

**United States**    Italo Campanini (Italian tenor—New York), Arabella Goddard (British pianist—tour), Joseph Maas (British tenor—tour), Mathilde Mallinger (Croatian soprano), Victor Maurel (French baritone—New York), Ilma de Murska (Croatian soprano—tour), Emma Osgood (soprano—Boston), Enrico Tamberlik (Italian tenor—New York).

**Other**    Antoinette Sterling (contralto—London).

**I. New Positions**

**Conductors**    Patrick S. Gilmore (22nd Regiment Band, New York); Louis Schneider (US Marine Band—to 1880); Theodore Thomas (Cincinnati Festivals—to 1894); Carl Wolfsohn (Chicago Beethoven Society Choir).

**Educational**    Eben Tourjée (dean, College of Music, Boston University).

**Other**    John Sullivan Dwight (president, Harvard Musical Association—to 1893).

**K. Biographical**    Poet Sidney Lanier becomes first flutist with the Peabody Orchestra; John Knowles Paine becomes an assistant professor of music at Harvard University; Antoinette Sterling decides to return to Europe to live.

**L. Musical Beginnings**

**Performing Groups**    Beethoven String Quartet (Boston); Cincinnati Beethoven Society; Cleveland Vocal Society; English Opera Co. (by Clara Kellogg); Mozart Association of Richmond (Virginia); Oratorio Society of New York; Orpheus Society of Springfield, Massachusetts; Pittsburgh Germania Orchestra; St. Cecilia Society of America.

**Festivals**    Cincinnati May Festival.

**Educational**    Northwestern University Conservatory of Music

**Other**    Grand Opera House (Little Rock, Arkansas); *The Kansas Folio: A Repertoire of Music, Art and Literature*; Macauley's Theater (Louisville, Kentucky).

**M. Music Publications**

Bliss, P. P., *Sunshine for Sunday School*
Dana, William H., *Practical Thorough-Bass*
Grider, Rufus, *Historical Notes on Music in Bethlehem, Pennsylvania, from 1741 to 1871*
Knapp, Phebe Palmer, *Bible School Songs*
Root, Frederick W., *F. W. Root's School of Singing*
Sankey, Ira, *Sacred Songs and Solos*
Walker, William, *Fruits and Flowers*

**N. Musical Compositions**

**Chamber Music**   Sidney Lanier, *Fieldlarks and Blackbirds—Danse des Moucherons* (flute and piano).

**Choral/Vocal**   George Frederick Bristow, *Morning Service, Opus 51*; J. P. Webster, *The Beatitudes* (cantata); George E. Whiting, *Prologue to "The Golden Legend."*

**Orchestra/Band**   Ernest Guiraud, *Gretna Green* (band); Silas G. Pratt, *Homage to Chicago March*; John Philip Sousa, *March, Review—Salutation March*.

**Piano/Organ**   John Knowles Paine, *Ten Sketches: In the Country, Opus 26*.

# 1874

✸

## Historical Highlights

The first electrically powered streetcar begins running in New York; the Republican elephant first appears in a Nast cartoon; J. F. Glidden invents the "revolution in ranching," barbed wire; the Women's Christian Temperance League is formed; Benjamin Disraeli becomes Prime Minister of England; the British Parliament passes the Factory Act limiting the work week to 56½ hours.

## World Cultural Highlights

**World Art**   Thomas Barker, *Charge of the Light Brigade*; Édouard Manet, *Boating at Argenteuil*; Pierre-Auguste Renoir, *The Loge*; Dante Rossetti, *Proserpine in Hades*.

**World Literature**   Pedro de Alarcón, *The Three-Cornered Hat*; François Coppée, *Le Cahier Rouge*; Thomas Hardy, *Far from the Madding Crowd*; Paul Verlaine, *Romances sans Paroles*.

**World Music**   Anton Bruckner, *Symphony No. 4*; Modest Moussorgsky, *Pictures at an Exhibition*; Johann Strauss, *Die Fledermaus*; Giuseppe Verdi, *Requiem*; Richard Wagner, *Götterdämmerung*.

**Miscellaneous**   Ernst Eulenburg begins publishing music in Leipzig; the Munich Akademie der Tonkunst opens; births include Hugo von Hofmannsthal, Gustav Holst, W. Somerset Maugham, and Arnold Schönberg; deaths include Sidney Dobell, Vitezslav Hálek, and Wilhelm von Kaulbach.

## American Art and Literature Highlights

**Births/Deaths**   Births include artists Romaine Brooks, Frederick Frieseke, and literary figures Clarence S. Day, Jr., Robert Frost, Zona Gale, Ellen Glasgow, Amy Lowell, Gertrude Stein, Trumbull Stickney, and Mary Vorse; deaths include art figures James Ellsworth, William H. Rinehart, Edward Troye, and literary figures Lydia Baxter, Victor Séjour, and Francis Orray Ticknor.

**Art Works**   Thomas Eakins, *Starting Out after Rail*; Thomas Gould, *Westwind* (?); Henry Gray, *Birth of Our Flag*; William Harnett, *Paint Tubes and Grapes*; William Hunt, *The Ball Players*; Charles H. Moore, *Sawmill at West Boxford*; Thomas Moran, *Chasm of the Colorado*; William T. Richards, *Lake Squam from Red Hill*; Thomas Shirlaw, *Toning the Bell*; T. Worthington Whittredge, *Camp Meeting*.

**Literature**   Ambrose Bierce, *Cobwebs from an Empty Skull*; William C. Bryant, *Among the Trees*;

Mary E. Dodge, *Rhymes and Jingles*; Edward Eggleston, *The Circuit Rider*; Oliver Wendell Holmes, *Songs of Many Seasons*; Henry Wadsworth Longfellow, *Tales of a Wayside Inn III*; Bayard Taylor, *The Prophet, a Tragedy*; Mary Townsend, *The Captain's Story and Other Verse*.

## Music—The Vernacular/Commercial Scene

**A. Births**    George Botsford (composer) February 24; Lulu Glaser (singer/dancer) June 2; Abe Holzmann (ragtime composer) August 19; George Pullen Jackson (folksong historian) August 20; Andrew B. Sterling (lyricist) August 26; Egbert (Bert) Williams (minstrel/writer) November 12.

**E. Representative Works**

**Musicals**    Edward E. Rice and J. C. Goodwin, *Evangeline*.

**Songs**    David Braham and Ned Harrigan, *The Skidmore Guard—Patrick's Day Parade*; Rollin Howard, *You Never Miss the Water Till the Well Runs Dry*; Will L. Thompson, *Gathering Shells from the Sea-Shore—Drifting with the Tide*; Charles A. White, *Ise Gwine Back to Dixie*.

## Music—The Cultivated/Art Music Scene

**F. Births**    Lilian E. Blauvelt (soprano) March 16; G. Clara Clemens (contralto) June 8; Emilio de Gogorza (baritone) May 29; Glenn Dillard Gunn (music critic/conductor) October 2; Charles E. Ives (composer) October 20; Leonard Liebling (pianist/critic) February 7; Riccardo Martin (tenor) November 18; Arne Oldberg (pianist/composer) July 12; Minnie Saltzmann-Stevens (soprano) March 17; Oley Speaks (composer/baritone) June 28; Anice Terhune (pianist/composer) October 27.

**G. Deaths**    Thomas Hall (organ builder) May 23; William Hall (piano maker) May 3; Emilius N. Scherr (Danish-born instrument maker) August 14.

**H. Debuts**

**United States**    Emma Albani (soprano—New York), Nellie E. Brown (soprano—Boston), Emmy Fursch-Madi (French soprano—New York), Giovanni Tagliapietra (Italian baritone—New York).

**I. New Positions**

**Conductors**    William W. Gilchrist (Mendelssohn Glee Club, Philadelphia—to 1914); B. J. Lang (Cecilia Society of Boston—to 1807).

**Other**    Henry E. Krehbiel (music critic, *Cincinnati Gazette*—to 1880).

**K. Biographical**    Theodore Baker goes to Germany for advanced music study in Leipzig.

**L. Musical Beginnings**

**Performing Groups**    Cecilia Society of Boston; Dayton Philharmonic Society II; Handel Chorus of Springfield, Massachusetts; Mendelssohn Glee Club of Philadelphia; Philharmonic Club of Boston; San Diego Silver Cornet Band.

**Festivals**    Chautauqua Summer Music Festival.

**Educational**    Chautauqua Institution (New York); Detroit Conservatory of Music; Milwaukee College of Music; Olivet Conservatory of Music (Michigan).

**Other**    William Lewis and Son, Violin dealers (Chicago): Sustaining Pedal for the Piano (by H. G. Hanchett).

**M. Music Publications**

Bliss, Philip P., *Gospel Songs for Gospel Meetings*
Holland, Justin, *Holland's Comprehensive Method for the Guitar*
Palmer, Horatio, *The Song Monarch*
Perkins, Henry S., *Convention Choruses*
Ritter, Frédéric L., *A History of Music in the Form of Lectures II*
Seward, Theodore, ed., *The Vineyard of Song*

**N. Musical Compositions**

**Chamber Music**    Sidney Lanier, *Wind-song* (flute); John Knowles Paine, *Piano Trio in D Minor, Opus 22*.

**Choral/Vocal**   Dudley Buck, *The Legend of Don Munio* (secular cantata); Ira Sankey, *The Ninety and Nine* (hymn); George E. Whiting, *Mass in F Minor*.

**Operas**   Silas G. Pratt, *Antonio*.

**Orchestra/Band**   John Philip Sousa, *La Reine d'Amour Waltzes*.

**Piano/Organ**   Silas G. Pratt, *Fantasie Caprice—Grand Polonaise I*.

# 1875

✦

## Historical Highlights

The Civil Rights Act forbids racial discrimination in public facilities; Congress passes the Specie Resumption Act permitting paper money to be redeemed on demand; Hebrew Union College (New York) and Brigham Young University (Utah) are founded; Verney Cameron becomes the first white man to cross Africa east to west; Captain M. Webb becomes the first person to swim the English Channel.

## World Cultural Highlights

**World Art**   Édouard Manet, *Washing Day*; Camille Pissarro, *Climbing Path at L'Hermitage*; Pierre-Auguste Renoir, *Two Little Circus Girls*.

**World Literature**   Ventura Aguilera, *La Arcadia Moderne*; Pedro de Alarcón, *Amores y Amoriós*; Holger Drachmann, *Muffled Melodies*; Paul von Heyse, *Im Paradiese*.

**World Music**   Georges Bizet, *Carmen*; Antonín Dvořák, *Serenade for Strings*; Edvard Grieg, *Peer Gynt*; Gilbert and Sullivan, *Trial by Jury*; Peter Tchaikovsky, *Piano Concerto No. 1*.

**Miscellaneous**   The Liszt Academy of Music opens in Hungary; births include Thomas Mann, Maurice Ravel, Rainer Maria Rilke, and Jacques Villon; deaths include Hans Christian Andersen, Georges Bizet, Jean-Baptiste Corot, Charles Kingsley, Edward Mörike, and Alexei Tolstoy.

## American Art and Literature Highlights

**Births/Deaths**   Births include artists Spencer Nichols, H. Lyman Saÿen, and literary figures Edgar Rice Burroughs, Edith Delano, Wallace Irwin, Percy MacKaye, Joel E. Spingarn, and Ridgely Torrence; deaths include sculptor Horatio Stone, artist Seth Eastman, William O. Stone, and literary figures William B. Bernard, John Ross Browne, and Charles Sprague.

**Art Works**   William M. Chase, *Pablo de Sarasate*; Thomas Eakins, *The Gross Clinic*; Daniel French, *The Minute Man (Concord, Massachusetts);* Martin Heade, *Fighting Hummingbirds with Two Orchids*; Thomas Hicks, *Dropped in to Hear the News*; Eastman Johnson, *The Cranberry Pickers*; J. Alden Weir, *A Brittany Interior*; James M. Whistler, *Nocturne in Black and Gold: The Falling Rocket*.

**Literature**   Louisa May Alcott, *Eight Cousins*; Will Carleton, *City Ballads*; Ralph Waldo Emerson, *Letters and Social Aims*; Bret Harte, *Tales of the Argonauts*; Josiah Holland, *Sevenoaks*; William D. Howells, *A Foregone Conclusion*; Cincinnatus Miller, *The Ship in the Desert*; Nora Perry, *After the Ball and Other Poems*; Maurice Thompson, *Hoosier Mosaics*; Elizabeth Ward, *Poetic Studies*.

## Music—The Vernacular/Commercial Scene

**A. Births**   Natalie Curtis (folksong collector) April 26; William H. Krell (ragtime composer); Eddie Leonard (minstrel); Lee Shubert (impresario); Robert B. Smith (lyricist) June 4.

**B. Deaths**   Daniel Bryant (minstrel performer) April 10; William J. Hays, Sr. (songwriter); Joseph P. Webster (composer/performer) January 18.

**E. Representative Works**

**Musicals**   Various composers, *Around the World in Eighty Days* (Kiralfy version).

**Songs**   George N. Brown and A. W. French, *Barney, Take Me Home Again*; Henry Clay Work, *Grandfather's Clock*.

## Music—The Cultivated/Art Music Scene

**F. Births**   James F. Cooke (author/composer) November 14; Pearl G. Curran (composer) June 25; Putnam Griswold (bass-baritone) December 23; Josephine Jacoby (contralto); Fred Jewell (composer/bandmaster/publisher) May 28; Ethel Newcomb (pianist) October 30; Arthur H. Ryder (organist) April 30; Camille Zechwer (pianist/composer) June 26.

**G. Deaths**   Asa B. Everett (hymn composer) September; Ureli Corelli Hill (violinist/conductor) September 2; Jule Edson Perkins (bassist) February 25; Samuel Priestly Taylor (British-born organist) July 15.

**H. Debuts**

**United States**   Hans von Bülow (German pianist—Boston), Maud Morgan (harpist—New York), Eugenie Pappenheim (Austrian soprano—New York), Julie Rivé-King (pianist—New York), Antoinette Sterling (contralto—New York), Therese Tietjens (soprano—New York), Fanny Bloomfield Zeisler (pianist—Chicago).

**I. New Positions**

**Educational**   Hugh A. Clarke (University of Pennsylvania).

**K. Biographical**   Dudley Buck becomes assistant conductor of the Theodore Thomas Orchestra; Teresa Carreño marries her second husband, baritone Giovanni Tagliapietra; Oliver Ditson buys out Lee and Walker's music publishing business; Arthur W. Foote receives the first M.A. in music given by an American University, Harvard; John Knowles Paine becomes a full professor at Harvard, the first musician to achieve that rank; Silas G. Pratt returns to Germany and studies piano with Liszt; Henry Schoenefeld begins study in the Leipzig Conservatory; John Philip Sousa is discharged from the Marine Band and begins teaching privately.

**L. Musical Beginnings**

**Performing Groups**   Charleston Musical Association (South Carolina); Harmonie Cornet Band (San Diego); Philadelphia Cecilia Club; Springfield Orchestral Club (Massachusetts).

**Educational**   Hershey School of Musical Art (Chicago); University of Pennsylvania Music Department; University of Washington Music Department.

**Other**   A. B. Chase Co. (Ohio); Conn-Dupont Co. (Elkhart, Indiana); M. P. Möller, Organ Builder (Erie, Pennsylvania); *The Music Trade Review*; Root and Sons Music Co. (Chicago); Will Thompson, Music Publisher (East Liverpool, Ohio); Whitney's Grand Opera House (Detroit, Michigan).

**M. Music Publications**

Dana, William H., *Orchestration*
Merz, Karl, *Musical Hints for the Million*
Patton, George F., *A Practical Guide to the Arrangement of Band Music*
Perkins, William O., *Shining River—Perkins' Singing School*
Robinson, Charles, *Psalms and Hymns*
Sankey, Ira, *Gospel Hymns and Sacred Songs*

**N. Musical Compositions**

**Chamber Music**   John Knowles Paine, *Violin Sonata in B Minor, Opus 24*.

**Choral/Vocal**   Leopold Damrosch, *Ruth and Naomi* (oratorio premiere); Jerome Hopkins, *Vesper Service;* Robert Lowry, *Low in the Grave He Lay* (sacred song).

**Concertos**   Caryl Florio, *Piano Concerto in A-Flat Major*; Alfred H. Pease, *Piano Concerto*.

**Operas**   James A. Butterfield, *Ruth, the Gleaner*.

**Orchestra/Band**   Dudley Buck, *Romanza for Four Horns and Orchestra, Opus 71*; John Philip

Sousa, *The Phoenix* (incidental music).

**Piano/Organ**  Charles Grobe, *Centennial Memorial March, 1776–1876*; Edward Mack, *Centennial March Series: Agricultural—Centennial—Horticultural—Machinery—Memorial*; Silas G. Pratt, *Grand Valse Etude*.

**Symphonies**  John Knowles Paine, *Symphony No. 1 in C Minor, Opus 23*; Silas G. Pratt, *Symphony No. 2, "The Prodigal Son."*

# 1876

☀

## Historical Highlights

Rutherford B. Hayes is elected the 19th president; Colorado enters the Union as the 38th state; the Battle of Little Big Horn results in the death of General Custer and his troops; Alexander Graham Bell patents the telephone—first message sent on March 10; the International American Centennial Exposition takes place; the American Library Association is founded.

## World Cultural Highlights

**World Art**  Edgar Degas, *The Absinthe Drinkers*; Gustave Moreau, *L'Apparition*; Edward Poynter, *Atalanta's Race*; Pierre-Auguste Renoir, *The Swing*; Alfred Sisley, *The Flood at Port-Marly*.

**World Literature**  Lewis Carroll, *The Hunting of the Snark*; George Eliot, *Daniel Deronda*; Stéphane Mallarmé, *L'Après-midi d'un Faune*; Alfred Lord Tennyson, *Harold*; Ivan Turgenev, *Virgin Soil*.

**World Music**  Johannes Brahms, *Symphony No. 1*; Anton Bruckner, *Symphony No. 5*; Bedřich Smetana, *String Quartet, "From My Life"*; Peter Tchaikovsky, *Swan Lake—Francesca da Rimini*.

**Miscellaneous**  The Bayreuth Wagner Festivals begin; the Zurich Music School opens; births include Constantin Brancusi, Pablo Casals, Raymond Duchamp-Villon, Maurice de Vlaminck, and Bruno Walter; deaths include Louis Colet, Charles Coussemaker, Frederik Paludan-Müller, and George Sand.

## American Art and Literature Highlights

**Births/Deaths**  Births include art figures James Fraser, Anna Huntington, Everett Shinn, and literary figures Sherwood Anderson, Irvin S. Cobb, William E. Leonard, Jack London, and Mary Roberts Rinehart; deaths include literary figures Orestes A. Brownson, Horace Bushnell, Samuel B. H. Judah, and John Neal.

**Art Works**  John G. Brown, *Country Gallants*; Thomas Eakins, *The Chess Players*; Erastus Field, *Historical Monument of the American Republic*; Winslow Homer, *Breezing Up*; Chauncey Ives, *Egeria*; John La Farge, *Interior, Trinity Church, Boston*; Edmonia Lewis, *The Death of Cleopatra*; Frank B. Mayer, *Francis St., Annapolis*; John Roger, *Weighing the Baby*; Frederick J. Sykes, *Seascape*.

**Literature**  Louisa May Alcott, *Silver Pitchers and Independence*; William C. Bryant, *The Flood of Years*; Edward E. Hale, *Philip Nolan's Friends*; Helen Jackson, *Mercy Philbrick's Choice*; Henry James, *Roderick Hudson*; James Russell Lowell, *Among My Books II*; Henry Morford, *The Spur of Monmouth*; Mark Twain, *The Adventures of Tom Sawyer*; Ella Wilcox, *Poems of Passion*.

## Music—The Vernacular/Commercial Scene

**A. Births**  Will D. Cobb (lyricist) July 6; Charles Hunter (ragtime composer) May 16; Tony Jackson (ragtime piano) June 5; Charles L. Johnson (ragtime pianist/composer) December 3; Victor

Moore (singer/actor) February 24; Sam Schubert (impresario); William H. Tyers (ragtime composer) March 27.

**E. Representative Works**

**Musicals**   Max Maretzek, *Baba*.

**Songs**   Daniel McCarthy, *The Hat Me Father Wore*; John R. Thomas and G. Cooper, *The Rose of Killarney*; Thomas P. Westendorf, *I'll Take You Home Again, Kathleen*; Henry Clay Work, *Songs: The Mystic Veil—Sweet Echo Dell—Touch the Sleeping Strings—Used-up Joe*.

## Music—The Cultivated/Art Music Scene

**F. Births**   Frederic Ayres (composer) March 17; Mary Louise Curtis Bok (patron of the arts) August 6; John Alden Carpenter (composer) February 28; Horatio Connell (baritone) March 15; Ralph Kinder (organist/composer) January 27; Carl Ruggles (composer) March 11; Ernest Schelling (composer/conductor) July 26; Walter Stockhoff (composer) November 12.

**G. Deaths**   Carl Bergmann (German-born conductor/cellist) August 16; Philip Paul Bliss (hymn writer) December 29; Elizabeth Taylor Greenfield (singer); William B. Simmons (organ builder) October 31.

**H. Debuts**

**United States**   Anna del Belocca (contralto—New York), Anna Essipova (Russian pianist—tour), Amy Fay (pianist—New York), Lillian Henschel (soprano—Boston), Lillian Nordica (soprano—Boston), Jeannie Winston (soprano—San Francisco).

**Other**   Emma Abbott (soprano—London), Marie Litta (soprano—London).

**I. New Positions**

**Conductors**   George Matzka (New York Philharmonic Orchestra).

**Educational**   George W. Chadwick (theory, Olivet College, Michigan); Henry Dunham (New England Conservatory—to 1929); Frederic G. Gleason (Hershey Music School, Chicago); Eban Tourjée (President, Music Teachers National Association [MTNA]); George E. Whiting (organ, New England Conservatory—to 1898); Richard Zeckwer (director, Philadelphia Musical Academy—to 1917).

**Other**   William Foster Apthorp (critic, *Atlantic Monthly*); Arthur Foote (organ, Church of the Disciples, Boston—to 1878); George E. Whiting (organ, Church of the Immaculate Conception, Boston—to 1910).

**K. Biographical**   Carl Bergmann, in ill health, resigns as conductor of the New York Philharmonic Orchestra; Ole Bull reconciles with his wife and returns to the United States; George Chadwick quits his father's business to begin teaching music; Francesco Fanciulli (Italian bandmaster/composer) comes to the United States and settles in New York; Adolph Forster settles in Pittsburgh as teacher and conductor; Percy Goetschius begins teaching theory at the Stuttgart Conservatory; Victor Herbert enters the Stuttgart Conservatory; Edgar Stillman Kelley begins four years of study in Germany; Alessandro Liberati (Italian cornetist/bandmaster) leaves Canada for Detroit; Otto Lohse (German conductor/composer) comes to the United States; Edward MacDowell enters the Paris Conservatory on a scholarship; Jacques Offenbach (French composer) visits the United States; Steinway and Sons exhibit their pianos at the Centennial Exhibition in Philadelphia; George Werrenrath (Danish tenor) comes to the United States.

**L. Musical Beginnings**

**Performing Groups**   San Francisco Loring Club.

**Educational**   Jubilee Hall (Fisk University); Music Teachers National Association (MTNA).

**Other**   Evans Hall (Fort Worth, Texas); J. W. Pepper, Music Publisher (Philadelphia); Arthur P. Schmidt Co., Music Publishers (Boston); Adam and Oliver Shattinger, Music Publishers (St. Louis); Tremaine Brothers (Tremaine Piano Co.—New York); Wade's (Grand) Opera House (San Francisco); Wilcox and White, Organ Makers (Connecticut).

**M. Music Publications**

Aikin, J., Allen, C., and Main, H., *The Imperial Harmony*
Dana, William H., *Instrumentation for Military Bands*
Holland, Justin, *Holland's Modern Method for the Guitar*
Moore, John W., *A Dictionary of Musical Information . . .*
Palmer, Horatio, *Palmer's Theory of Music*
Ritter, Fanny R., *Woman as a Musician: An Art-Historical Study*
Willis, Richard Storrs, *Waif of Song*

**N. Musical Compositions**

**Choral/Vocal**    Dudley Buck, *The Centennial Meditation of Columbia* (secular cantata); John Knowles Paine, *Centennial Hymn, Opus 27*; Silas G. Pratt, *Centennial Hymn*; Otto Singer, *Landing of the Pilgrim Fathers* (cantata).

**Orchestra/Band**    Horace Nicholl, *Orchestral Suite in A Major, Opus 3*; John Knowles Paine, *Overture, As You Like It, Opus 28—The Tempest, Opus 31* (symphonic poem); Silas G. Pratt, *Anniversary Overture*; John Philip Sousa, *The Honored Dead March—Revival March—Sounds from the Revivals* (fantasy for band).

**Piano/Organ**    Edward MacDowell, *Eight Chansons Fugitives, Opus 2—Three Petits morceaux, Opus 4    Suite, Opus 5*; John Knowles Paine, *Four Character Pieces, Opus 25*.

# 1877

❀

## Historical Highlights

Congress passes the Desert Land Act providing for up to 640 acres of land at 25 cents an acre; the Bell Telephone Co. is founded; Thomas Edison patents the phonograph; the Nez Perce Indian War takes place in the Pacific Northwest; the United Labor Party begins a short career; Romania gains its independence; Emile Berliner introduces the microphone; the two moons of Mars are discovered.

## World Cultural Highlights

**World Art**    Edward Burne-Jones, *The Mirror of Venus*; Edgar Degas, *Dancers at the Bar*; Édouard Manet, *Nana*; Claude Monet, *Gare Saint-Lazare*; Alfred Sisley, *The Bridge at Sèvres*.

**World Literature**    Michel Carré, *Paul et Virginie*; Alphonse Daudet, *The Nabob*; Henrik Ibsen, *Pillars of Society*; Leo Tolstoy, *Anna Karenina*; Émile Zola, *The Drunkard*.

**World Music**    Johannes Brahms, *Symphony No. 2*; Modest Moussorgsky, *Songs and Dances of Death*; Camille Saint-Saëns, *Samson and Delilah*; Peter Tchaikovsky, *Symphony No. 4 in F Minor*.

**Miscellaneous**    The Salzburg Festivals begin; the Romanian Opera Co. is formed; births include Ernst von Dohnányi, Kees van Dongen, Raoul Dufy, Mary Garden, George Kolbe, and Jean Tharaud; deaths include Friedrich von Hackländer, Ludwig Köchel, and Johan Runeberg.

## American Art and Literature Highlights

**Births/Deaths**    Births include art figures Marsden Hartley, Herbert Haseltine, Albert Laessle, Jacob Lawrence, Lee Lawrie, Gertrude Whitney, Mahonri Young, and literary figures Edwina S. Babcock, Rex Beach, Lloyd C. Douglas, Gordon H. Gerould, and Reginald W. Kauffman; deaths include sculptor Joel T. Hart and literary figures Charles Briggs, William Hosmer, and Joseph S. Jones.

**Art Works**    Thomas Eakins, *William Rush Carving the Allegorical Figure of the Schuylkill River I*; George Fuller, *Dandelion Girl*; William M. Hunt, *The Bathers*; John La Farge, *Murals, St. Thomas' Cathedral, New York*; William T. Richards, *Cove on Conanicut Island*; John Rogers,

*Checkers Up at the Farm*; John S. Sargent, *Carolus-Duran*; Thomas W. Whittredge, *On the Plains, Colorado*.

**Literature**   Thomas Aldrich, *Flower and Thorn*; William C. Bryant, *A Lifetime*; Augustin Daly, *The Dark City*; John Habberton, *Other People's Children*; Julian Hawthorne, *Garth*; Helen Jackson, *Hetty's Strange History*; Henry James, *The American*; Sarah Orne Jewett, *Deephaven*; Sidney Lanier, *Poems*; Cincinnatus Miller, *The Baroness of New York*; Susan B. Warner, *Diana*.

## Music—The Vernacular/Commercial Scene

**A. Births**   Charles "Buddy" Bolden (cornetist/bandleader) September 6; Joseph F. Lamb (ragtime composer) December 6; Edward Madden (lyricist) July 17.

**C. Biographical**

**Performing Groups**   Primrose and West Co. (minstrels).

**E. Representative Works**

**Musicals**   David Braham, *Old Lavender*.

**Songs**   Percy French, *Abdulla Bulbul Ameer*; Annie F. Harrison, *In the Gloaming*; William S. Hays, *Early in the Morning—Roll Out! Heave Dat Cotton*; Arthur de Lulli, *The Celebrated Chop Waltz (Chopsticks)*; Robert Lowry, *Where Is My Wandering Boy Tonight*; F. W. Wellman, Jr. and C. A. Burke, *Branigan's Band*; Henry Clay Work, *Crying for Bread—Farewell, My Loved One! —The Fire Bells Are Ringing—King Bibler's Army—Mac O'Macorkity—Phantom Footsteps—Shadows on the Floor—Tie the Knot Tightly*.

## Music—The Cultivated/Art Music Scene

**F. Births**   Morton Adkins (baritone) October 31; Russell Alexander (band composer) February 26; John Parsons Beach (composer/pianist) October 11; Angela Diller (pianist/pedagogue) August 1; Ernest N. Doring (violin expert) May 29; Isadora Duncan (ballerina) May 26; John Lawrence Erb (pedagogue/author) February 5; Blair Fairchild (composer) June 23; Edwin A. Fleisher (art patron) July 11; Weston S. Gales (organist/conductor) November 5; Katherine Heyman (pianist); Corinne Rider-Kelsey (soprano) February 24; Oscar Seagle (baritone) October 31; David Stanley Smith (conductor/composer) July 6; N. Clark Smith (conductor/composer) July 31; Marcia Van Dresser (soprano) December 4; Harriet Ware (pianist/composer) August 26.

**H. Debuts**

**United States**   Emma Abbott (soprano—New York), Marie Hippolyte Rôze (French soprano—tour), Josef Heinrich Wiegand (German bass—tour).

**I. New Positions**

**Educational**   Edward Schultze (director, Syracuse University Music Department).

**Other**   Dudley Buck (organ, Holy Trinity, New York—to 1901).

**K. Biographical**   Charles R. Adams returns to the United States after several years singing in Europe; Annie Louise Cary becomes the first American woman to sing a Wagner role in the United States; George Chadwick leaves for Europe to study music with Haupt and Jadassohn; Gustav Dannreuther (German violinist) comes to the United States; Louis Elson leaves Leipzig and returns to the United States; Henry C. Heyman returns to San Francisco from study in Germany.

**L. Musical Beginnings**

**Performing Groups**   Balatka Quintet Club (St. Louis); Nyack Symphonic Society (New York); Schubert String Quartet.

**Educational**   Morgan Conservatory of Music (Oakland, California); Philadelphia Conservatory of Music; Syracuse University Music Department.

**Other**   *Caecilia* (begun in Germany in 1874); Central City Opera House (Colorado); Ladies (Indiana) Matinee Musicale (Indianapolis); *J. W. Pepper's Musical Times and Band Journal (Musical Times)*; Tivoli Opera House (San Francisco).

**M. Music Publications**

Buck, Dudley, *Illustrations in Choir Accompaniment*
Hewitt, John Hill, *Shadows on the Wall; or, Glimpses of the Past*
James, Henry Fillmore, *Songs of Gratitude*
Johnson, A. N., *Chorus Choir Instruction Book*
Offenbach, Jacques, *Offenbach en Amérique*
Pearce, S. Austen, *Columbia College Chapel Music*

**N. Musical Compositions**

**Chamber Music** Johann H. Beck, *Elegiac Song, Opus 4, No. 1—String Quartet No. 1*; Caryl Florio, *String Quartet No. 1.*

**Choral/Vocal** Charles E. Hopkins, *Samuel* (oratorio); J. C. D. Parker, *Redemption Hymn*; George E. Whiting, *Dream Pictures*.

**Concertos** John Knowles Paine, *Duo Concertante, Opus 33* (violin, cello, and orchestra).

**Operas** Frederick Gleason, *Otho Visconti*; Karl Merz, *Last Will and Testament* (operetta).

**Orchestra/Band** Silas G. Pratt, *Canon for String Orchestra—Variations on "Sweet Bye and Bye"*; John Philip Sousa, *Across the Danube March—Sardanapolis Waltzes—The Rivals Overture—The Blending of the Blue and Gray* (fantasy for band).

**Piano/Organ** Dudley Buck, *Organ Sonata No. 2 in G Minor, Opus 77—Variations on "The Last Rose of Summer," Opus 59* (organ); George John Huss, *Studies of Seconds—Six Etudes Speciales*.

# 1878

☀

## Historical Highlights

New Haven, Connecticut, receives the first telephone exchange in the country and lists 50 names; Congress passes the Bland-Allison Act on the coining of silver; Tombstone, Arizona, founded as the result of a new gold strike; Joseph Pulitzer buys the *St. Louis Post-Dispatch*; the Congress of Berlin divides the Turkish Ottoman Empire among the European powers.

## World Cultural Highlights

**World Art** Jules Bastien-Lepage, *The Haymakers*; Hans von Marées, *The Ages of Man*; Ernest Meissonier, *Cuirassiers of 1805*; Pierre-Auguste Rodin, *The Walking Man*.

**World Literature** Rudolf Baumbach, *Lieder eines Fahrenden Gesellen*; Holger Drachmann, *On a Sailor's Word*; Thomas Hardy, *Return of the Native*; José Hernández, *La Vuelta de Martin Fierro*.

**World Music** Johannes Brahms, *Violin Concerto*; Antonín Dvořák, *Slavonic Dances I*; Gilbert and Sullivan, *H.M.S. Pinafore*; Peter Tchaikovsky, *Eugene Onegin—Violin Concerto*.

**Miscellaneous** Theodor Steingräber Publishing House opens; the Dresden Opera House opens; births include Émile Cammaerts, Kazimir Malevich, John Masefield and Ferenc Molnár; deaths include George Cruikshank, Charles-François Daubigny, and Richard Upjohn.

## American Art and Literature Highlights

**Births/Deaths** Births include sculptor Abastemia St. Leger Eberle and literary figures Louis Anspacher, Walter Arensberg, Grace W. Conkling, James Oliver Curwood, William C. De Mille, Carl Sandburg, and Upton Sinclair (novelist); deaths include artists James Hamilton, George Harvey, and literary figures Hew Ainslie, William Cullen Bryant, Evert A. Duyckinck, Richard Realf, and Bayard Taylor.

**Art Works** Alfred T. Bricher, *Morning at Grand Manan*; William M. Chase, *Chrysanthemums*; George Fuller, *The Tomato Patch*; William Harnett, *Music and Literature*; William M. Hunt,

*Anahita, Flight of Night* (?); George Inness, *The Coming Storm*; William Keith, *California Pines*; Edward Kemeys, *Bison and Wolves*; John S. Sargent, *The Oyster Gatherers*; John Twachtman, *Venice Landscape*.

**Literature**   Edward Bellamy, *Six to One: A Nantucket Idyl*; Edward Eggleston, *Roxy*; Ralph Waldo Emerson, *Fortune of the Republic*; Bronson Howard, *The Banker's Daughter*; Henry James, *The Europeans*; John B. O'Reilly, *Songs, Legends and Ballads*; Bayard Taylor, *Prince Deukalion*; Charles D. Warner, *Being a Boy*; John Greenleaf Whittier, *The Vision of Echard and Other Poems*.

## Music—The Vernacular/Commercial Scene

**A. Births**   Ernest R. Ball (composer) July 21; Joe Howard (singer/composer) February 12; Alphonse Picou (clarinetist) October 19; George M. Cohan (composer/actor/producer) July 3 (?); Eva Tanguay (singer/dancer); Albert Von Tilzer (songwriter/publisher) March 29.

**B. Deaths**   Billy Whitlock (minstrel/banjoist/songwriter).

**C. Biographical**

**Performing Groups**   Haverly's Mastodon Minstrels (disbanded in 1896).

**New Beginnings**   S. S. Stewart's Banjo School (Philadelphia).

**E. Representative Works**

**Musicals**   David Braham and Harrigan and Hart, *The Mulligan Guards' Picnic—The Lorgaire— The Mulligan Guards' Christmas*; Joseph K. Emmet, *Fritz, Our Cousin German*.

**Songs**   James Bland, *Carry Me Back to Old Virginny—In the Evening by the Moonlight*; David Braham and Ned Harrigan, *Sweet Mary Ann—The Skidmore Fancy Ball*; Joseph K. Emmett, *Emmett's Lullaby*; Harry Kennedy, *A Flower from Mother's Grave*; Queen Liliuokalani, *Aloha Oe*; Charles A. White, *When the Leaves Begin to Turn*; Henry Clay Work, *Songs: Pity Me, Loo! (California Bird Song)—Sequel to Grandfather's Clock*.

## Music—The Cultivated/Art Music Scene

**F. Births**   Louis Bernstein (publisher) March 13; Eleonora de Cisneros (mezzo-soprano) November 1; Augusta Cottlow (pianist) April 2; Mabel Wheeler Daniels (composer) November 27; Rita Fornia (soprano) July 17; Heinrich Gebhard (pianist/composer) June 25; Lawrence Gilman (music critic) July 5; Edwin Franko Goldman (bandmaster/composer) January 1; Otto Kinkeldey (musicologist) November 27; Thurlow Lieurance (composer) March 21; Albert Mildenberg (composer) January 13; Albert Riemenschneider (organist/conductor) August 31.

**G. Deaths**   Samuel Graves (instrument maker) November 18.

**H. Debuts**

**United States**   A. J. (Signor) Foli (British bassist—tour), Etelka Gerster (Hungarian soprano— New York), Marie Litta (soprano—Chicago), Zélie de Lussan (soprano—New York), Giuseppe del Puente (Italian baritone—New York), Franz Rummel (British pianist—tour), Zélia Trebelli (French mezzo-soprano—tour), August Wilhelmj (German violinist—tour).

**I. New Positions**

**Other**   Heinrich Conried (manager, Germania Theater, New York); Arthur Foote (organ, choir, First Unitarian Church, Boston—to 1910); Ernest R. Kroeger (organ, Trinity Episcopal Church, St. Louis—to 1885); W. S. B. Mathews (music critic, *Chicago Tribune*—to 1886); Harry Rowe Shelley (organ, Fifth Avenue Baptist Church, New York—to 1936).

**J. Honors and Awards**

**Honors**   William W. Gilchrist (Abt Society Prize).

**K. Biographical**   George W. Chadwick enrolls in Leipzig Conservatory; Minnie Hauk returns to the United States and sings the title role in the first American performance of Bizet's *Carmen;* Bruno Oscar Klein (German pianist/composer) comes to the United States; Ethelbert Nevin enters the University of Pittsburgh; Waldo S. Pratt receives a BA degree from Williams College; Eduard

Reményi (Hungarian violinist), becoming a resident of the United States, becomes the first violinist to perform at the White House; Julie Rivé-King marries her former tour manager, Frank King; Clara K. Rogers marries American lawyer Henry M. Rogers and gives up her operatic career; John Philip Sousa begins work with Philadelphia publisher J. M. Stoddart.

**L. Musical Beginnings**

**Performing Groups**　Emma Abbott Opera Co.; Los Angeles Philharmonic Society; Milwaukee Liederkranz; New York Symphony (by Damrosch); Oratorio Society of Newark; Philharmonic Quintet Club (St. Louis).

**Educational**　Cincinnati College of Music; Milwaukee Conservatory of Music; New York College of Music (absorbed by New York University in 1968).

**Other**　*Boston Musical Record*; Cincinnati Music Hall; J. W. Jenkins Music Co. (Kansas City, Missouri); *Kunkel's Music Review* (to 1906); *Musical Critic and Trade Review*; Mechanical Orguinette Co. (Aeolian Organ Co.).

**M. Music Publications**

Hauser, W. and Turner, B., *The Olive Leaf*
Mason, William, *Pianoforte Technics*
Moore, John W., *The Sentimental Songbook*
The Stoughton Musical Society's Collection of Sacred Music
Trotter, James M., *Music and Some Highly Musical People: Containing . . . Sketches of the Lives of Remarkable Musicians of the Colored Race*
Zimmermann, Charles, *Zimmermann's Directory of Music in General*

**N. Musical Compositions**

**Chamber Music**　George W. Chadwick, *String Quartet No. 1 in G Minor* — *String Quartet No. 2 in C Major*; Caryl Florio, *String Quartet No. 2* (orchestrated as *Symphony No. 2*).

**Choral/Vocal**　Dudley Buck, *The Nun of Nidaros* (cantata); George Frederick Root, *The Song Tournament* (cantata); Otto Singer, *Festival Ode*.

**Operas**　Jerome Hopkins, *Dumb Love*; Edward Mollenhauer, *Manhattan Beach, or, Love Among the Breakers*.

**Orchestra/Band**　Dudley Buck, *Marmion Overture*; Caryl Florio, *Marche Triomphale*; Horace Nicholl, *Tartarus, Opus 11* (symphonic poem); John Philip Sousa, *Esprit de Corps March*.

**Piano/Organ**　Arthur H. Bird, *French Overture* (four hands); Silas G. Pratt, *Grand Polonaise II*.

**Symphonies**　Caryl Florio (see String Quartets); Adolph Neuendorff, *Symphony No. 1*.

# 1879

❉

## Historical Highlights

The first Woolworth store opens in Lancaster, Pennsylvania; the first incandescent light bulb is demonstrated; the Archeological Institute of America is founded; Radcliffe College is founded; the War of the Pacific ends with Chile defeating Bolivia and Peru; the Belgian Congo is reorganized in Africa as the Congo Free State; the British fight the Zulu War in the Transvaal in South Africa.

## World Cultural Highlights

**World Art**　Jules Bastien-Lepage, *Sarah Bernhardt*; Benjamin Constant, *Favorite of the Emir*; Edgar Degas, *Awaiting the Cue*; Édouard Manet, *In a Boat*; Camille Pissarro, *Le Fond de l'Hermitage*.

**World Literature**　Robert Browning, *Dramatic Idylls I*; Feodor Dostoyevsky, *The Brothers Karamozov*; Giuseppe Giacosa, *The Husband in Love with His Wife*; Henrik Ibsen, *The Doll's House*.

**World Music**　Johannes Brahms, *Two Rhapsodies, Opus 79*; Antonín Dvořák, *Czech Suite*; Cesar Franck, *Beatitudes*; Gilbert and Sullivan, *The Pirates of Penzance*; Bedrich Smetana, *My Country*.

**Miscellaneous**　The Opéra de Monte Carlo and the Geneva Opera Co. are founded; births include Thomas Beecham, Vanessa Bell, René Dumesnil, E. M. Forster, John Ireland, and Paul Klee; deaths include Thomas Couture, Honoré Daumier, Antoine Preault, and Emil Wolf.

## American Art and Literature Highlights

**Births/Deaths**　Births include art figures Gifford Beall, Edward McCartan, Robert Spencer, and literary figures James B. Cabell, Dorothy C. Fisher, Katherine F. Gerould, Vachel Lindsay, and Wallace Stevens; deaths include art figures George Bingham, William Morris Hunt, William Rimmer, Christian Schussele, and literary figures Ethel Lynn Beers, Richard Henry Dana, Sr., and Sarah Josepha Hale.

**Art Works**　John G. Brown, *Longshoremen's Noon*; Frank Duveneck, *The Blacksmith* (?); Thomas Eakins, *The Fairman Rogers Four-in-Hand*; Jeremiah Hardy, *The Artist's Rose Garden*; William Harnett, *The Artist's Card Rack*; William Keith, *Evening Glow*; Thomas Moran, *The Mirage, Teton Chain, Idaho*; John Twachtman, *New York Harbor*; Elihu Vedder, *In Memoriam*; Olin L. Warner, *Twilight*.

**Literature**　Ethel L. Beers, *All Quiet along the Potomac*; John Burroughs, *Locusts and Wild Honey*; George W. Cable, *Old Creole Days*; Henry George, *Progress and Poverty*; William D. Howells, *The Lady of the Aroostook*; Henry James, *Daisy Miller*; Sarah O. Jewett, *Old Friends and New*; Abram J. Ryan, *Father Ryan's Poems*; Frank R. Stockton, *Rudder Grange*; Celia Thaxter, *Drift-Weed*; Francis Ticknor, *Poems*; Albion Tourgée, *A Fool's Errand*; Sarah Helen Whitman, *Poems*.

## Music—The Vernacular/Commercial Scene

**A. Births**　Harry Armstrong (singer/composer) July 22; Harry Creamer (lyricist) June 21; Gus Edwards (singer/composer) August 18; Ernie Erdman (songwriter) October 23; Silvio Hein (composer) March 15; Raymond Hubbell (composer) June 1; Jack Norworth (composer/lyricist) January 5; Chris Smith (composer) October 12; Harry H. Williams (lyricist) August 29.

**C. Biographical**

**New Beginnings**　Daly's Theater (New York).

**E. Representative Works**

**Musicals**　David Braham and Ned Harrigan, *The Mulligan Guards' Ball—Sweet Mary Ann—The Mulligan Guards' Chowder*; Joseph K. Emmett, *Fritz in Ireland*; Gustave A. Kerker, *The Cadets*; Max Maretzek, *Sleepy Hollow*; Edward E. Rice, *Hiawatha*; Nate Salsbury, *The Brook*; Various composers, *Enchantment—A Pullman Palace Car*.

**Songs**　James Bland, *Oh, Dem Golden Slippers—In the Morning by the Bright Light*; David Braham and Ned Harrigan, *The Babies on Our Block*; Henry Clay Work, *Songs: Come to Me, Sunbeam! I'm Dying—The Old Village Doctor, or Come, Take Your Medicine*.

## Music—The Cultivated/Art Music Scene

**F. Births**　Franz Bornschein (composer) February 10; John Erskine (pianist/educator) October 5; Maud Fay (soprano) April 18; Frank La Forge (pianist/composer) October 22; Mayhew Lake (composer/conductor/editor) October 25; Benjamin Lambord (organist/conductor/composer) June 10; Eastwood Lane (composer) May 22; Francis Maclennan (tenor) January 7; Verne Q. Powell (woodwind maker) April 7.

**G. Deaths**　Charles Grobe (German-born composer/teacher) October 20; Albert Weber (German piano maker) June 25; Benjamin Franklin White (composer/compiler/teacher) December 5.

**H. Debuts**

**United States**　Timothée Adamowski (Polish violinist—Boston), Mathilde Bauermeister (German soprano—tour), Henry G. Hanchett (pianist—New York), Rafael Joseffy (Hungarian pianist—New

York), Marie Litta (soprano—Boston), Marie Marimon (New York), Melitta Otto (German soprano—New York), Adriano Pantaleoni (Italian baritone), Alwina Valleria (soprano—New York).

**Other**   Hope Glenn (contralto—Malta), Lillian Nordica (soprano—Milan), Marie Van Zandt (soprano—Turin).

**I. New Positions**

**Educational**   Carl Christian Müller (theory, New York College of Music); John Frederick Rudolphsen (Cincinnati Conservatory of Music).

**K. Biographical**   Timothée Adamowski (Polish violinist) makes his first concert tour of the United States and decides to settle in Boston; Charles Adams begins private voice teaching in Boston; Rudolf Bial (German conductor/violinist) comes to the United States; Gilbert and Sullivan come to the United States and put on "authorized" performances of their works in New York; Rafael Joseffy (Hungarian pianist) settles in the United States; Edward MacDowell leaves the Paris Conservatory and enters Frankfurt Conservatory to study with Raff; Ethelbert Nevin leaves college after one year and enters the family business; Henry Schoenefeld begins teaching in Chicago; John Philip Sousa marries singer Jane von Middlesworth Bellis; Alwina Valleria makes her Covent Garden debut in addition to her US debut.

**L. Musical Beginnings**

**Performing Groups**   Boston Ideal Opera Co.; Boston Philharmonic Society III (to 1883); Mozart Club of Pittsburgh; University of Michigan Choral Union.

**Festivals**   Pittsburgh Music Festival.

**Educational**   Balatka Academy of Musical Art (Chicago); Central Music Hall (Chicago); Denver University School of Music; University of Michigan School of Music; Virgil School of Music, Peoria, Illinois.

**Other**   *Music Trade Journal*; Schroeder and Gunther, Music Publishers (New York); Squire's Opera House (Seattle); Tivoli Theater III (San Francisco).

**M. Music Publications**

Cheney, Simeon P., *The American Singing Book . . . Containing Biographies of Forty of the Leading Composers—Brother Cheney's Collection of Old Folks Concert Music . . .*
Perkins, Henry S., *Perkins' Class and Choir*
Perkins, William O., *The Temple*
Whiting, George E., *The Organist*

**N. Musical Compositions**

**Chamber Music**   Caryl Florio, *Allegro de Concert* (saxophone quartet).

**Choral/Vocal**   Dudley Buck, *Scenes from "The Golden Legend"* (Cincinnati Festival Prize).

**Concertos**   Caryl Florio, *Introduction, Theme and Variations* (alto sax and orchestra).

**Operas**   James A. Butterfield, *The Race for a Wife*; Caryl Florio, *Gulda*; John Philip Sousa, *Katherine* (operetta).

**Orchestra/Band**   Dudley Buck, *Festival Overture on "The Star-Spangled Banner"*; George W. Chadwick, *Overture, Rip Van Winkle*; Silas G. Pratt, *Serenade for String Orchestra*; John Philip Sousa, *Globe and Eagle March—March, on the Tramp—Resumption March.*

**Piano/Organ**   Silas G. Pratt, *Caprice Fantastique—Nocturne Impromtu.*

# 1880

❁

## Historical Highlights

The census shows a population of 50,189,000, a 26% increase in ten years—New York passes the one million mark; James A. Garfield is elected the 20th president; Cleveland, Ohio, becomes the first city to be lit by electricity; the first Salvation Army branch opens in Pennsylvania; the British Parliament votes compulsory and free education for children to the age of ten; the Irish rebel against British rule.

## World Cultural Highlights

**World Art**    Arnold Böcklin, *The Isle of the Dead*; Paul Gauguin, *The Yellow Christ*; Claude Monet, *Banks of the Seine*; Pierre-Auguste Rodin, *The Thinker*; George Watts, *Watchman, What of the Night?*

**World Literature**    Henri Chantavoine, *Satires Contemporaines*; Benjamin Disraeli, *Endymion*; Algernon Swinburne, *Songs of the Springtides*; Giovanni Verga, *Under the Shadow of Etna*; Émile Zola, *Nana*.

**World Music**    Johannes Brahms, *Academic Festival Overture*; Gustav Mahler, *Das Klagende Lied*; Jacques Offenbach, *The Tales of Hoffmann*; Peter Tchaikovsky, *1812 Festival Overture*.

**Miscellaneous**    The Birmingham Musical Association in England and the Naples Orchestral Society are founded; births include Guillaume Apollinaire, Ernest Bloch, André Derain, and Alfred Noyes; deaths include Ole Bull, George Eliot, Gustave Flaubert, Jacques Offenbach, and Henri Wieniawski.

## American Art and Literature Highlights

**Births/Deaths**    Births include art figures Arthur Dove, Jacob Epstein, Walt Kuhn, Abraham Walkowitz, and literary figures Joseph Hergesheimer, Peter B. Kyne, Louis V. Ledoux, Henry L. Mencken, Kathleen Norris, Channing Pollock, and Carl Van Vechten; deaths include artists Constantino Brumidi, Sanford R. Gifford, and literary figures Lydia M. Child, Epes Sargent, and Jones Very.

**Art Works**    William H. Beard, *The Bulls and Bears of Wall Street*; Albertus Browere, *Rip Van Winkle Chased from His Home*; William M. Chase, *In the Studio*; Eastman Johnson, *The Cranberry Harvest*; Albert P. Ryder, *Mending the Harness*; Frank Simmons, *Penelope* (?); William A. Walker, *Card Players on the Steamboat*; A. M. Willard, *The Spirit of '76*.

**Literature**    George W. Cable, *The Grandissimes*; Philander Deming, *Adirondack Stories*; Joel Chandler Harris, *Uncle Remus: His Songs and Sayings*; Oliver Wendell Holmes, *The Iron Gate and Other Poems*; Charles de Kay, *Hesperus and Other Poems*; Steele MacKaye, *Hazel Kirke*; Albion W. Tourgée, *Bricks Without Straw*; Mark Twain, *A Tramp Abroad*; Lew Wallace, *Ben Hur*.

## Music — The Vernacular/Commercial Scene

**A. Births**    Nora Bayes (singer); Dorothy Donnelly (lyricist) January 28; Big Eye Louis Nelson (1885?—clarinetist) January 28; J. J. Shubert (impresario) August 15.

**C. Biographical**

**Performing Groups**    Excelsior Brass Band (New Orleans—to 1931).

**New Beginnings**    Fairbanks and Cole, Banjo Makers (Boston).

**E. Representative Works**

**Musicals**    David Braham and Ned Harrigan, *The Mulligan Guards' Surprise—The Mulligan Guards' Nominee*; Alfred Cellier and B. Rowe, *Charity Begins at Home—The Sultan of Mocha*.

**Songs**    Anonymous, *The Old Chisholm Trail* (?); James Bland, *Hand Me Down My Walking Cane—De Golden Wedding*; David Braham and Ned Harrigan, *Whist! The Boogie Man*; William S. Hays, *Walk in de Middle of de Road*; Harry Kennedy, *Cradle's Empty, Baby's Gone*; Godfrey Marks, *Sailing, Sailing Over the Bounding Main*; D. S. McCosh, *Hear Dem Bells*.

## Music — The Cultivated/Art Music Scene

**F. Births**    Richard Buhlig (pianist) December 21; Eric De Lamarter (organist/conductor) February 18; Albert von Doenhoff (pianist) March 16; Henry S. Drinker (music dilettante) September 15; John Homer Grunn (pianist/composer) May 5; A. A. Harding (bandmaster) February 10; Estelle Liebling (soprano) April 21; Homer Rodeheaver (singing evangelist/publisher) October 4; Alexander Russell (organist/pianist) October 2; Arthur Shepherd (composer/conductor) February 19; Theodore Stearns (composer/conductor) January 10; Carl Van Vechten (critic/author) June 17; Clarence C. White (violinist/composer) August 10; Florence Wickham (contralto/composer); Frederick J. Work (composer/educator) August 11.

**G. Deaths**   Adolph Baumbach (German-born pianist/composer); Claudio Grafulla (Spanish-born bandmaster/composer) December 2; William Hauser (composer/hymnist) December 29.

**H. Debuts**

**United States**   Castelmary (French baritone—New York), Árpád Doppler (Hungarian pianist—New York), George Henschel (German baritone—New York), Carl Valentine Lachmund (pianist—tour), Luigi Ravelli (Italian tenor—New York).

**Other**   Emma Nevada (soprano—London).

**I. New Positions**

**Conductors**   Matthew Arbuckle (9th Regiment Band—to 1882); Rudolf Bial (Thalia Theater, New York); Jules Jordan (Arion Club of Providence—to 1920); Gustave Kerker (H. V. B. Mann Opera Co.—to 1883); Joseph Otten (St. Louis Choral Symphony Society—to 1894); John Philip Sousa (US Marine Band—to 1892); Theodore Thomas (New York Philharmonic Orchestra—to 1891).

**Educational**   Otto Bendix (piano, New England Conservatory); Calvin B. Cady (University of Michigan—to 1888); Louis C. Elson (music history, New England Conservatory); Ilma di Murska (voice, National Conservatory, New York).

**Other**   Hugh Allen (organ, St. Saviour's, Reading); George W. Chadwick (organ, South Presbyterian Church, Boston); H. E. Krehbiel (music critic, *New York Tribune*—to 1923); Otto Floersheim (editor, *The Musical Courier*).

**J. Honors and Awards**

**Honors**   Leopold Damrosch (doctorate, Columbia).

**K. Biographical**   Otto Bendix (Danish pianist/composer) comes to the United States; George W. Chadwick returns from study in Germany and begins teaching music privately in Boston; Philip Hale is admitted to the bar; Louis Maas (German pianist) emigrates to the United States and settles in Boston; Luther Whiting Mason is invited to Japan to supervise the establishment of a school music system; Constantin Sternberg (Russian pianist/composer) emigrates to the United States; Marie Van Zandt makes her Paris Opera debut.

**L. Musical Beginnings**

**Performing Groups**   St. Louis Choral Society (Choral Symphony Society in 1890); St. Louis Symphony Orchestra.

**Educational**   Ann Arbor School of Music (part of University of Michigan, 1892); St. Louis College of Music; University of Nebraska School of Music.

**Other**   W. W. Kimball Organ Co.; *The Musical Courier; Musical Harp; Musical Herald.*

**M. Music Publications**

Clarke, Hugh A., *Harmony*
Elson, Louis C., *Curiosities of Music*
Emery, Stephen A., *Elements of Harmony*
Perkins, Henry S., *Perkins' Graded Anthems*
Seward, Theodore, *The Tonic Sol-fa Music Reader*
Staples, Samuel E., *The Ancient Psalmody and Hymnology of New England*
Upton, George P., *Women in Music*

**N. Musical Compositions**

**Chamber Music**   Johann H. Beck, *String Quartet No. 4*; Edwin A. Jones, *String Quartet No. 1, Opus 13.*

**Choral/Vocal**   George Frederick Bristow, *The Great Republic, Ode to the American Union* (secular cantata); Dudley Buck, *Midnight Service for New Year's Eve*; George F. Root, *Under the Palms* (cantata); John R. Sweeney, *Tell Me the Story of Jesus* (hymn).

**Operas**   Dudley Buck, *Deseret, or, A Saint's Affliction*; James A. Butterfield, *Window Glass*; Adolph Neuendorff, *Der Rattenfänger von Hameln*.

**Orchestra/Band**   David W. Reeves, *Second Regimental Connecticut N. G. March*; John Philip Sousa, *Our Flirtation* (incidental music)—*Paroles d'Amour Waltzes—In Parlor and Street* (fantasy for band).

**Symphonies**   Asger Hamerik, *Symphonie Poétique in F Major, Opus 26*; Adolph Neuendorff, *Symphony No. 2*; E. C. Phelps, *Hiawatha Symphony*.

# 1881

☀

## Historical Highlights

President James Garfield is assassinated and Chester Arthur becomes the 21st president; Clara Barton founds the Red Cross; the Federation of Organized Trades and Labor Unions is organized; Tuskegee Institute is founded; Alexander II of Russia is assassinated and Alexander III becomes czar; France takes over Tunis in North Africa as a protectorate; Louis Pasteur isolates the rabies virus.

## World Cultural Highlights

**World Art**   Max Liebermann, *The Cobbler's Shop*; Édouard Manet, *Emmanuel Chabrier*; Pierre-Auguste Renoir, *Luncheon of the Boating Party*; Ilya Repin, *Modest Moussousky*; Auguste Rodin, *Adam*.

**World Literature**   Carlo Collodi, *Pinocchio*; Henrik Ibsen, *Ghosts*; Guy de Maupassant, *La Maison Tellier*; Dante Rossetti, *The House of Life*; Johanna Spyri, *Heidi*; Paul Verlaine, *Sagesse*.

**World Music**   Johannes Brahms, *Piano Concerto No. 2—Tragic Overture*; Anton Bruckner, *Symphony No. 6 in A*; Edvard Grieg, *Norwegian Dances, Opus 35*; Giuseppe Verdi, *Simon Boccanegra*.

**Miscellaneous**   The Concerts Lamoureux begin in Paris; the Scharwenka Conservatory (Berlin) and the Kraków Conservatory open; births include Béla Bartók, Georges Braque, Pablo Picasso, and Stefan Zweig; deaths include Benjamin Disraeli, Feodor Dostoyevsky, and Modest Moussorgsky.

## American Art and Literature Highlights

**Births/Deaths**   Births include sculptor Morton Schamberg, artist Max Weber and literary figures Edgar Guest, Alice Corbin Henderson, Clarence B. Kelland, William M. McFee, Charles G. Norris, and Thomas S. Stribling; deaths include art figures Thomas Gould, John Quidor, and literary figures Eliza Ann Dupuy, Sidney Lanier, Henry Morford, Alfred B. Street, and William Ross Wallace.

**Art Works**   Thomas Eakins, *Pathetic Song*; Thomas Hovenden, *Sunday Morning*; Eastman Johnson, *The Funding Bill*; Edward May, *Edith Newbold Jones (Wharton)*; John F. Peto, *Old Souvenirs*; Augustus Saint-Gaudens, *The Admiral David Farragut Monument*; William A. Walker, *Cotton Plantation on the Mississippi*; Alexander H. Wyant, *An Old Clearing*.

**Literature**   Edward Eggleston, *The Hoosier Schoolboy*; James T. Fields, *Ballads and Poems*; William D. Howells, *A Fearful Responsibility*; Henry James, *The Portrait of a Lady*; Sarah Orne Jewett, *Country By-Ways*; Harriet M. Lothrop, *Five Little Peppers and How They Grew*; Cincinnatus Miller, *The Danites in the Sierras*; John Piatt, *Idyls and Lyrics of the Ohio Valley*; Harriet Spofford, *Poems*.

## Music—The Vernacular/Commercial Scene

**A. Births**   James Tim Brymn (composer/bandleader) October 5; Louis Chauvin (ragtime pianist/composer) March 13; Axel W. Christensen (pianist) March 23; James Reese Europe (band-leader/songwriter) February 22; Ted Snyder (composer) August 15.

**C. Biographical**

**New Beginnings**   New Theater Comique (New York); Tony Pastor's Music Hall (New York).

**D. Publications**   J. B. T. Marsh, *The Story of the Jubilee Singers, with Their Songs*.

**E. Representative Works**

**Musicals**   David Braham and Ned Harrigan, *The Major—The Mulligans' Silver Wedding*; Henry Woolson Morse, *Cinderella at School*; William J. Scanlan, *Friend and Foe*.

**Songs**   James Bland, *Oh, Lucinda!—The Colored Hop*; David Braham and Med Harrigan, *Paddy Duffy's Cart*; William D. Hendrickson, *The Spanish Cavalier*; Paul Lacombe, *Estudiantina*; Joseph P. Skelly, *Are You Going to the Ball This Evening?*

## Music—The Cultivated/Art Music Scene

**F. Births**   Charles Wakefield Cadman (composer) December 24; Fannie Dillon (pianist/compos-er) March 16; Henry Fillmore, Jr. (bandmaster/composer) December 3; Harvey B. Gaul (organ-ist/composer) April 11; Arthur M. Hartmann (violinist/composer) July 22; Arthur Judson (concert manager) February 17; José Quintón (composer) February 1; Lewis Richards (harpsichordist) April 11; Yvonne de Tréville (soprano) August 25; William C. White (bandmaster/composer) September 29.

**G. Deaths**   Rudolf Bial (German-born conductor) November 23; John Daniel (Scottish-born educa-tor/composer) June 21; Lucien H. Southard (composer) January 10.

**H. Debuts**

**United States**   Carl Baermann (German pianist—Boston), Josef Bayer (Austrian conductor—New York), Leandro Campanari (Italian violinist—Boston), Emma Juch (soprano/impresario—New York), Adele Margulies (Austrian pianist—New York), Nicolini (French tenor—tour).

**Other**   Gertrude Griswold (soprano—Paris).

**I. New Positions**

**Conductors**   George Henschel (Boston Symphony Orchestra—to 1904).

**Other**   William F. Apthorp (music critic, *Boston Evening Transcript*); John H. Brewer (organ, Lafayette Avenue Presbyterian Church, Brooklyn—to 1931); Henry T. Finck (music critic, *New York Evening Post*); Frederick E. Kitziger (organ, Touro Synagogue, New Orleans); Theodore Seward (editor, *Tonic Sol-fa Advocate*); Eugene Thayer (organ, Fifth Avenue Presbyterian Church, New York).

**J. Honors and Awards**

**Honors**   Edward M. Bowman (first American in the London Royal College of Organists); George Frederick Root (PhD, University of Chicago).

**K. Biographical**   Frederick Archer (British organist/composer), Carl Baermann (German pianist/composer), Leandro Campanari (Italian violinist/conductor), Eduard Herrmann (German violinist/conductor), and Will Rossiter (British composer/publisher) all come to the United States; Lillian Bailey marries conductor George Henschel; Albino Gorno (Italian pianist), on tour with Adelina Patti, decides to stay in the United States; Charles Martin Loeffler (Alsatian composer) comes to the United States from Paris and joins Damrosch's orchestra; Edward MacDowell teach-es piano at Darmstadt Conservatory; Horatio Parker enters the Royal Conservatory in Munich for further music study; Waldo S. Pratt receives an MA degree from Williams College; Bertha Feiring Tapper (Norwegian pianist) comes to the United States.

**L. Musical Beginnings**

**Performing Groups**   Boston Symphony Orchestra; Church Choral Union (New York); Cleveland Philharmonic Society; Hosmer Hall Choral Union (Hartford); Little's Brass Band and Co. (Springfield, Massachusetts); Providence Arion Club (Rhode Island); St. Louis Musical Union.

**Other**   *Chicago Musical Times*; Cincinnati Musicians' Protective Union; Harms Music Publishing Co. (New York); *Perry's Musical Magazine*; Tabor (Grand) Opera House (Denver); *Tonic Sol-Fa Advocate* (to 1886).

### M. Music Publications

Fay, Amy, *Music Study in Germany*
Gottschalk, Louis M., *Notes of a Pianist*
McIntosh, Rigdon M., *Light and Life: A Collection of New Hymns and Tunes* . . .
Merz, Karl, *Elements of Harmony and Counterpoint*
Perkins, Henry S., *Good Templar*
Sherwin, William F., *Heart and Voice*
Ziehn, Bernhard, *System of Exercises for Pianoforte and a New Method of Instruction for Beginners*

### N. Musical Compositions

**Chamber Music**   Arthur Foote, *Three Pieces, Opus 1, for Cello and Piano*.

**Choral/Vocal**   Dudley Buck, *King Olaf's Christmas* (secular cantata); George W. Chadwick, *The Viking's Last Voyage*; Edward MacDowell, *Five Songs, Opus 11, 12*; Ethelbert Nevin, *The Milkmaid's Song*.

**Concertos**   Frederick Zech, Jr., *Concerto No. 1 for Piano and Orchestra*.

**Operas**   John Philip Sousa, *Florine* (unfinished operetta).

**Orchestra/Band**   Edwin A. Jones, *Dedication March*; John Knowles Paine, *Oedipus Tyrannus* (incidental music); Silas A. Pratt, *Overture to Zenobia*; John Philip Sousa, *Marches—Guide Right—In Memoriam (President Garfield's Funeral March)—President Garfield's Inauguration March—Right Forward—Yorktown Centennial—Wolverine March*.

**Piano/Organ**   Edward MacDowell, *First Modern Suite in E Minor, Opus 10—Prelude and Fugue in D Minor, Opus 13* (piano); Silas A. Pratt, *Meditation Religieuse, Opus 12*.

# 1882

✻

## Historical Highlights

The New York Central Labor Union begins the observance of Labor Day; Chinese Exclusion Act passed by Congress; Dow Jones and Co. is formed; the famous feud between the Hatfields and the McCoys begins and continues to 1896; Germany, Italy, and the Austro-Hungarian Empire form the Triple Alliance; Great Britain takes over Egypt as a protectorate.

## World Cultural Highlights

**World Art**   Benjamin Constant, *The Day After Victory*; James Ensor, *Woman Eating Oysters*; Édouard Manet, *The Bar at the Folies Bergere*; Georges Seurat, *Farm Women at Work*.

**World Literature**   Charles Aïdé, *Songs Without Music*; Robert Buchanan, *Ballads of Life, Love and Humor*; Henrik Ibsen, *An Enemy of the People*; Robert Louis Stevenson, *New Arabian Nights*.

**World Music**   Antonín Dvořák, *In Nature's Realm*; Cesar Franck, *Le Chasseur Maudit*; Edouard Lalo, *Namouna*; Gilbert and Sullivan, *Iolanthe*; Richard Wagner, *Parsifal*.

**Miscellaneous**   The Berlin Philharmonic Orchestra is formed; the Sibelius Academy is founded as the Helsinki College of Music; births include James Joyce, Wyndham Lewis, Elie Nadelman, and Igor Stravinsky; deaths include Thomas Barker, Joseph Joachim Raff, Dante Rossetti, and James Thomson.

## American Art and Literature Highlights

**Births/Deaths**   Births include art figures George W. Bellows, Arthur Carles, Edward Hopper,

Rockwell Kent, and literary figures Jesse Redmon Fauset, Susan Glaspell, Avery Hopwood, Olive Prouty, and Margaret Wilson; deaths include artist Thomas LeClear and literary figures Richard Henry Dana, Jr., Ralph Waldo Emerson, Henry James (Sr.), and Henry Wadsworth Longfellow.

**Art Works**  Thomas Anshutz, *Steelworkers' Noontime* (?); William Beard, *The Lost Balloon*; Ralph Blakelock, *Moonlight*; William Bradford, *Icebergs in the Arctic*; John Greenough, *Circe*; George Inness, *June*; Homer D. Martin, *Newport Landscape*; Thomas Moran, *Cliffs of the Upper Colorado River, Wyoming*; John Singer Sargent, *El Jaleo—The Daughters of Edward Boit*.

**Literature**  Mary Ames, *Poems of Life and Nature*; Eugene Field, *The Tribune Primer*; Paul H. Hayne, *Complete Poems*; William D. Howells, *A Modern Instance*; Charles Lewis, *Brother Gardner's Lime Kiln Club*; Silas W. Mitchell, *The Hill of Stones*; Mary A. Townsend, *Down the Bayou and Other Poems*; Mark Twain, *The Prince and the Pauper*; Walt Whitman, *Specimen Days and Collect*.

## Music—The Vernacular/Commercial Scene

**A. Births**  Henry Burr (singer) January 15; Joe Jordan (pianist/writer) February 11; Ballard MacDonald (lyricist) October 15; Geoffrey O'Hara (composer) February 2; Egbert Van Alstyne (composer) March 5.

**B. Deaths**  Henry Tucker (composer/singer) February 10.

**C. Biographical**

**Miscellaneous**  Ludwig Englander (Austrian composer/conductor) comes to the United States.

**D. Publications**  *Stewart's Banjo and Guitar Journal*.

**E. Representative Works**

**Musicals**  David Braham and Ned Harrigan, *McSorley's Inflation—Squatter Sovereignty*; Joseph K. Emmett, *Fritz Among the Gypsies*; John P. Sousa and W. J. Vance, *The Smugglers*; Willard Spenser, *The Little Tycoon*.

**Songs**  Joseph K. Emmett, *Sweet Violets*; David Braham and Ned Harrigan, *The Widow Nolan's Goat—When the Clock in the Tower Strikes Twelve*; Henry Clay Work, *Songs: Don't Be Cruel to the Motherless Darlings—The Parrot and the Billy Goat—The Monkey and the Mule—When You Get Home, Remember Me—Where's My Billy Goat Gone To?*

## Music—The Cultivated/Art Music Scene

**F. Births**  Seth Bingham (organist/composer) April 16; R. Nathaniel Dett (composer/pianist/conductor) October 11; Carl Eppert (composer) November 5; Geraldine Farrar (soprano) February 28; Donald Ferguson (music educator) May 11; Karl Gehrkens (music educator) April 19, Mary Howe (composer/pianist) April 4; Ralph Lyford (conductor/composer) February 22; John Powell (pianist/composer) September 6; Olga Samaroff (pianist) August 8; Carl H. Tollefsen (violinist/teacher) August 15; Michael Zadora (pianist/composer) June 14.

**G. Deaths**  Augusta Browne (Irish-born composer/author) January 11; George Hood (clergyman/composer/author) September 24; George Jardine (British-born organ builder) February 13; Alfred H. Pease (composer/pianist) July 12 (?); Adelaide Phillips (contralto); Caroline Richings-Bernard (soprano/ pianist/impresario) January 14; Hermine Rudersdorff (Ukrainian-born soprano) February 26.

**H. Debuts**

**United States**  Amalie Materna (German soprano—Cincinnati), Robert Philipp (German tenor—tour), Sofia Scalchi (Italian mezzo-soprano—New York).

**I. New Positions**

**Conductors**  Simon Hassler (Chestnut Street Opera House, Philadelphia—to 1899); Theodore Thomas (Philadelphia Symphony Orchestra—to 1891).

**Educational**  George W. Chadwick (theory/composition, New England Conservatory—director in 1897); Carl Faelton (piano, Peabody Conservatory—to 1885); William W. Gilchrist (voice, Philadelphia Musical Academy); Waldo S. Pratt (hymnology, Hartford Theological Seminary—to 1925).

**Other**    William C. Carl (organ, First Presbyterian Church, Newark, New Jersey).

**K. Biographical**    Theodore Baker receives a doctorate from Leipzig University; Annie Louise Cary retires from the operatic stage; Carl Faelton (German pianist/pedagogue) emigrates to the United States; Edward MacDowell, at Liszt's invitation, plays his *Piano Concerto No. 1* in Zurich; Lillian Nordica also decides to retire from the operatic stage; Ernest Schelling begins three years of study at the Paris Conservatory.

**L. Musical Beginnings**

**Performing Groups**    Bethlehem Choral Union (Pennsylvania); Denver Chorus Club; Little Rock Männerchor; Mendelssohn Quintette Club (St. Louis); Oratorio Society of Baltimore; St. Paul Schubert Club.

**Festivals**    Messiah Festival (Lindsborg, Kansas).

**Educational**    American Association of University Women Education Foundation; Prang Educational Co. (Boston).

**Other**    Mason and Hamlin Piano Co. (Boston); *Music and Drama*; John Stark and Son, Music and Pianos (Sedalia, Missouri).

**M. Music Publications**

Buck, Dudley, *The Influence of the Organ in History*
Eddy, Clarence, *The Church and Concert Organist I*
Emery, Stephen A., *Foundation Studies in Pianoforte Playing*
Goetschius, Percy, *The Material Used in Musical Composition—The Theory and Practice of Tone-Relations*
Hanchett, Henry G., *Teaching as a Science*
Perkins, William O., *Choral Choir*
Showalter, Anthony J., *Harmony and Composition*

**N. Musical Compositions**

**Choral/Vocal**    Frederick Gilchrist, *Psalm 46* (Cincinnati Festival Prize); William J. Kirkpatrick, *Jesus Saves—'Tis So Sweet to Trust in Jesus—Redeemed, How I Love to Proclaim It* (hymns); James McGranahan, *Hallelujah for the Cross* (hymn); John Knowles Paine, *The Realm of Fancy, Opus 36—Phoebus, Arise!* (cantatas); Horatio Parker, *Five Songs, Opus 2*; George F. Root, *David, the Shepherd Boy* (cantata); Samuel A. Ward, *Maderna* (hymn tune for *America the Beautiful*).

**Concertos**    Edward MacDowell, *Piano Concerto No. 1 in A Minor*.

**Operas**    Charles D. Blake, *The Light-Keeper's Daughter*; Caryl Florio, *Uncle Tom's Cabin*; Jerome Hopkins, *Taffy and Old Munch*; Karl Merz, *Katie Dean* (operetta); Adolph Neuendorff, *Don Quixote*; Willard Patton, *The Gallant Garroter* (operetta); Silas G. Pratt, *Zenobia, Queen of Palmyra*.

**Orchestra/Band**    Arthur H. Bird, *Serenade for Strings—Suite in E Major for Strings, Opus 1*; Patrick S. Gilmore, *Famous Twenty-Second Regiment March*; John Philip Sousa, *Congress Hall March*; Frank Van der Stucken, *The Tempest* (incidental music).

**Piano/Organ**    Arthur H. Bird, *Three Pieces for Piano, Opus 2—Four Sonatas for Organ*; Edward MacDowell, *Second Modern Suite in A Minor, Opus 14—Serenade, Opus 16*.

**Symphonies**    George W. Chadwick, *Symphony No. 1*; Louis Maas, *Symphony, "On the Prairies."*

# 1883

☀

## Historical Highlights

The Brooklyn Bridge opens in New York; the second Civil Service Commission is set up by the Pendleton Act; William "Buffalo Bill" Cody takes his Wild West Show to Eastern audiences; vaudeville begins at the Gaiety Theater in Boston; the volcano Krakatoa erupts mightily, causing great loss of life in the immediate South Pacific vicinity and weather problems on a worldwide scale.

## World Cultural Highlights

**World Art**    Arnold Böcklin, *Odysseus and Calypso*; George Inness, *Sunset in the Woods*; Édouard Manet, *White Lilacs and Roses*; William Orchardson, *Voltaire*; Pierre Renoir, *By the Seashore*.

**World Literature**    Victor Hugo, *The Legend of the Ages*; Friedrich Nietzsche, *Also Sprach Zarathustra*; Robert Louis Stevenson, *Treasure Island*; Émile Zola, *Au Bonheur des Dames*.

**World Music**    Johannes Brahms, *Symphony No. 3*; Anton Bruckner, *Symphony No. 7*; Emmanuel Chabrier, *España Rhapsody*; Leo Delibes, *Lakmé*; Gustav Mahler, *Songs of a Wayfarer*.

**Miscellaneous**    The Amsterdam Concertgebouw Society is formed; the Adelaide College of Music opens in Australia; births include Franz Kafka, José Orozco, Alexei Tolstoy, Maurice Utrillo, and Anton Webern; deaths include Oscar Begas, Édouard Manet, Ivan Turgenev, and Richard Wagner.

## American Art and Literature Highlights

**Births/Deaths**    Births include art figures Charles Demuth, Ivan Mestrovic, Charles Sheeler, and literary figures Badger Clark, Max Eastman, Martin Flavin, Ruth Wright Kauffman, Clarence E. Mulford, William Carlos Williams, and Austin Tappan Wright; deaths include art figures Albert Bellows, William Brown Clark Mills, and novelist Thomas Mayne Reid.

**Art Works**    Ralph A. Blakelock, *Hawley Valley*; Thomas Eakins, *The Swimming Hole*; Childe Hassam, *The Beach at Dunkirk*; Winslow Homer, *Inside the Bar, Tynemouth*; Edward Kemeys, *Still Hunt*; Thomas Moran, *The Tower of Cortes*; William A. Walker, *The Levee at New Orleans*; John Quincy Adams Ward, *George Washington* (New York); Worthington Whittredge, *Old Homestead by the Sea*.

**Literature**    Joel Chandler Harris, *Nights with Uncle Remus*; Nathaniel Hawthorne, *Dr. Grimshawe's Secret*; Oliver Wendell Holmes, *Pages from an Old Volume of Life*; William D. Howells, *A Woman's Reasons*; Katherine S. MacDowell, *Dialect Tales*; James Whitcomb Riley, *The Old Swimmin' Hole and 'Leven More Poems*; Mark Twain, *Life on the Mississippi*; John Greenleaf Whittier, *The Bay of Seven Islands and Other Poems*.

## Music—The Vernacular/Commercial Scene

**A. Births**    Harry Alford (composer); Eubie Blake (pianist/composer) February 7; Gus Cannon (banjoist) September 12; Vernon Dalhart (singer) April 6; Cecil Mack (lyricist); Mamie Smith (singer) May 26; Dave Stamper (composer) November 10.

**C. Biographical**

**New Beginnings**    Gretsch Guitar Co. (Brooklyn).

**D. Publications**    S. S. Stewart, *The Complete American Banjo School*.

**E. Representative Works**

**Musicals**    David Braham and Ned Harrigan, *Cordelia's Aspirations—The Muddy Day*; Ludwig Englander, *Der Prinz Gemahl (The Prince Consort)*; Edward E. Rice, *Pop*; William J. Scanlan, *The Irish Minstrel*.

**Songs**    Paul Allen, *New Coon in Town*; Anonymous, *There Is a Tavern in the Town—Polly Wolly Doodle*; David Braham and Ned Harrigan, *My Dad's Dinner Pail*; Frank Howard, *When the Robins Nest Again*; Pat Rooney, *Is That You, Mr. Riley?*; Joseph P. Skelley, *Strolling on the Brooklyn Bridge*; Charles A. White, *Marguerite*; Henry Clay Work, *Songs: Come, Pretty Schoolgirl—The Lost Letter—The Silver Horn*.

## Music—The Cultivated/Art Music Scene

**F. Births**    Paul H. Allen (composer) November 28; Melville Antone Clark (harpsichord builder) September 12; Bainbridge Crist (composer) February 13; Archibald Davison (conductor/educator) October 22; Carl Deis (organist/composer) March 7; Hazel Harrison (pianist) May 12; Judge Jackson (composer/compiler) March 12; Edwin Arthur Kraft (organist) January 8; Reinald Werrenrath (baritone) August 7.

**G. Deaths**    Matthew Arbuckle (cornetist/bandmaster) May 23; Marie Litta (soprano); Heinrich Maylath (Austrian-born pianist) December 31; Ernst T. Seltmann (German-born brass instrument maker) June 27; Manuel Gregorio Tavárez (composer/educator) July 1.

**H. Debuts**

**United States**    Amy Beach (pianist—Boston), Ricardo Castro (Mexican pianist—New Orleans), Helen Hopekirk (Scottish pianist—Boston), Antoine de Kontski (Polish pianist—tour), Ovide Musin (Belgian violinist—New York).

**Metropolitan Opera**    Cleofonte Campanini (Italian conductor), Italo Campanini (Italian tenor), Joseph Capoul (French tenor), Baldassare Corsini (Italian bass), Emmy Fürsch-Madi (French soprano), Amadeo Grazzi (Italian tenor), Luigi Guadagnini (Italian baritone), Giuseppe Kaschmann (Italian baritone), Emily and Louise Lablache (Italian mezzo-sopranos), Giovanni Mirabella (Italian bass), Christine Nilsson (Swedish soprano), Franco Novara (Italian bass), Giuseppe del Puente (Italian baritone), Sofia Scalchi (Italian mezzo-soprano), Marcella Sembrich (Polish soprano), Roberto Stagno (Italian tenor), Zélia Trebelli (French mezzo-soprano), Alwina Valleria (soprano).

**I. New Positions**

**Conductors**    Gustave Kerker (Thalia Theater, New York—to 1984).

**Educational**    Charles Dennée (piano, New England Conservatory—to 1897); Peter C. Lutkin (organ/piano, Northwestern University); Henry Schradieck (Cincinnati College of Music—to 1889).

**Other**    Henry Abbey (manager, Metropolitan Opera).

**J. Honors and Awards**

**Honors**    Henry K. Oliver (PhD, Dartmouth).

**K. Biographical**    Emma Albani returns to the United States; Anna Bishop gives her farewell concert in New York; Max Bruch (German composer) visits the United States and conducts his own works; Walter Damrosch takes the New York Symphony Orchestra on a tour of the western United States; Mary Garden comes to the United States with her family; Henry Charles Lahee (British writer on music) comes to the United States and settles in Boston; Ethelbert Nevin begins private music teaching in Pittsburgh; Arthur Whiting goes to Germany to study at the Munich Conservatory.

**L. Musical Beginnings**

**Performing Groups**    Apollo Club of Portland (Oregon); Boston Bach Club; Little Rock Aesthetic Club; Little Rock Musical Coterie; Metropolitan Opera Co. (New York); Newark Harmonie Society.

**Educational**    Los Angeles Conservatory of Music; University of Southern California School of the Performing Arts.

**Other**    Buffalo Music Hall; Dallas Opera House; *Echo: A Music Journal*; Everett Piano Co. (Boston); E. O. Excell and Co., Publishers; Fort Worth Opera House; Fred Gretsch Manufacturing Co. (Brooklyn); Emmons Howard, Organ Builder (Westfield, Massachusetts); *The Keynote*; Metropolitan Opera House (New York); Theodore Presser Co., Music Publisher (Philadelphia); Springfield Tonic Sol-Fa Association (Massachusetts); Weber Hall (Chicago).

**M. Music Publications**

*The Baptist Hymnal*
Fillmore, John C., *Pianoforte Music: Its History* . . .
Palmer, Horatio, *The Common Sense Music Reader*
Perkins, Henry S., *The Choir*
Ritter, Frédéric, *Music in America*
Taylor, Marshall, *A Collection of Revival Hymns and Plantation Melodies*

**N. Musical Compositions**

**Chamber Music**    Arthur Foote, *String Quartet No. 1 in G Minor, Opus 4—Piano Trio No. 1 in C Minor, Opus 5*; Horace Nicholl, *Violin Sonata in A Major, Opus 13*.

**Choral/Vocal** James McGranahan, *Showers of Blessing* (hymn); Arthur H. Messiter, *Marion (Rejoice, Ye Pure in Heart)* (hymn); John Knowles Paine, *The Nativity, Opus 38* (cantata); Horatio Parker, *The Lord Is My Shepherd, Opus 3* (treble voices); J. C. D. Parker, *The Blind King* (male voices and orchestra); George F. Root, *The Choicest Gift* (cantata).

**Operas** John Philip Sousa, *Désirée* (operetta); Frank Van der Stucken, *Vlasda*.

**Orchestra/Band** George W. Chadwick, *Overture, Thalia*; Horatio Parker, *Concert Overture in E-flat Major*; John Philip Sousa, *Marches—Bonnie Annie Laurie—Mother Goose—Pet of the Petticoats—Right-Left March—Transit of Venus*; Frank Van der Stucken, *Prologue to William Ratcliffe*.

**Piano/Organ** Arthur H. Bird, *Sonata—Gavotte, Album Leaf and Lullaby, Opus 3—Six Sketches*; Edward MacDowell, *Two Fantasie Pieces, Opus 17*.

**Symphonies** Asger Hamerik, *Symphonie Tragique in C Minor, Opus 32*; Louis Maas, *Symphony No. 2, "American," Opus 15* (premiere); Frederick Zech, Jr., *Symphony No. 1*.

# 1884

❊

## Historical Highlights

Grover Cleveland is elected the 22nd president; the American Historical Association is established; the National Cash Register Co. is founded; L. E. Waterman introduces the first practical fountain pen; first modern bicycle makes its appearance in England; Berlin West German Conference meets; Germany annexes several Southwest African states; Hiram Maxim invents the machine gun.

## World Cultural Highlights

**World Art** Pierre de Chavannes, *Humanistic and Christian Inspiration*; Pierre-Auguste Renoir, *The Girl with the Straw Hat*; Auguste Rodin, *The Burghers of Calais*; Georges Seurat, *Une Baignade, Asières*.

**World Literature** Alphonse Daudet, *Sappho*; Henrik Ibsen, *The Wild Duck*; Alfred Lord Tennyson, *Becket*; Giovanni Verga, *Cavalleria Rusticana*; Paul Verlaine, *Les Poétes Maudits*.

**World Music** Claude Debussy, *L'Enfant Prodigue*; Antonín Dvořák, *From Bohemia's Forests*; Cesar Franck, *Prelude, Chorale and Fugue—Les Djinns*; Richard Strauss, *Horn Concerto No. 1*.

**Miscellaneous** The Amsterdam Conservatory of Music and the Bavarian Music Conservatory open; births include Max Beckman, Lion Ichtwanger, Amedeo Modigliani, and Sean O'Casey; deaths include Jules Bastien-Lepage, Charles Calverley, Charles Reade, and Bedřich Smetana.

## American Art and Literature Highlights

**Births/Deaths** Births include artists José de Creeft, George Ennis, and literary figures Earl Derr Biggers, Fannie S. Gifford, Cornelia L. Meigs, Damon Runyon, and Sara Teasdale; deaths include literary figures William W. Brown, William Channing, Augustine Duganne, and Samuel Ward.

**Art Works** Cyrus E. Dallin, *Indian Chief*; Daniel C. French, *John Harvard* (Harvard Yard); George Fuller, *Fedalma*; Winslow Homer, *The Life Line*; George Inness, *Brush Burning*; Louis Moeller, *Another Investment*; Albert P. Ryder, *Toilers of the Sea*; John Singer Sargent, *Portrait of Madame X*; John Twachtman, *The Mouth of the Seine*; Charles F. Ulrich, *In the Land of Promise*.

**Literature** Henry Adams, *Esther*; George W. Cable, *The Creoles of New Orleans*; Louise Guiney, *Poems at the Start*; Joel Chandler Harris, *Mungo and Other Sketches*; Helen Hunt Jackson, *Ramona*; Sarah Orne Jewett, *A Country Doctor*; Mary Murfree, *In the Tennessee Mountains*; Henry Timrod, *Kathie Poems*; Mark Twain, *Adventures of Huckleberry Finn*; Elizabeth Ward, *Songs of the Silent World*.

## Music — The Vernacular/Commercial Scene

**A. Births**    Joseph A. Burke (composer) March 18; Oscar "Papa" Celestin (trumpeter/bandleader) January 1; Burt Kalmar (lyricist) February 10; George W. Meyer (composer) January 1; Irving Mills (impresario/publisher) January 16; Lewis F. Muir (pianist/composer); Al Piantadosi (songwriter) July 18; Riley Puckett (singer/guitarist) May 7; Sophie Tucker (singer) January 13.

**B. Deaths**    Henry Clay Work (composer) June 8.

**E. Representative Works**

**Musicals**    David Braham and Ned Harrigan, *Investigation—Dan's Tribulations*; Joseph K. Emmet, *Fritz, the Bohemian*; Ludwig Englander, *1776*; H. Woolson Morse and J. C. Goodwin, *Madam Piper*; Edward E. Rice, *Adonis*.

**Songs**    G. Clifton Bingham and J. L. Molloy, *Love's Old Sweet Song*; Robert A. King, *While Strolling Through the Park One Day*; Jennie Lindsay, *Always Take Mother's Advice*; Percy Montrose, *Oh, My Darling Clementine*; Hubbard Smith and E. Field, *Listen to My Tale of Woe*; Henry Clay Work, *Drop the Pink Curtains*; Banks Winter, *White Wings*.

## Music — The Cultivated/Art Music Scene

**F. Births**    Florence Austin (violinist) March 11; Ruth Lynda Deyo (pianist) April 20; Rafaelo Diaz (tenor); Florence Eastman (soprano) October 24; Albert Elkus (composer/educator) April 30; Alma Gluck (soprano) May 11; Edwin Grasse (violinist/composer) August 13; Charles T. Griffes (composer) September 17; Louis Gruenberg (composer) August 3; Edwin Hughes (pianist) August 15; Marie Sundelius (soprano) February 4; Wintter Watts (composer) March 14; Emerson Whithorne (pianist/composer) September 6; John M. Williams (pianist/pedagogue) January 1.

**G. Deaths**    Pasquale Brignoli (Italian-born tenor) October 30.

**H. Debuts**

**United States**    Leopold Godowsky (Polish pianist—Boston), Victor Küzdö (Hungarian violinist—tour), Michael Maybrick (British baritone—tour), Emma Nevada (soprano—New York), Emil Scaria (Austrian bass—tour), Hermann Winkelmann (German tenor—New York).

**Metropolitan Opera**    Marianne Brandt (Austrian soprano), Leopold Damrosch (German conductor), Marie Hanfstängel (German soprano), Anton Schott (German tenor), Frau Seidl-Krauss (German soprano), Joseph Staudigl, Jr. (Austrian baritone).

**I. New Positions**

**Conductors**    Wilhelm Gericke (Boston Symphony Orchestra—to 1889); Gustave Kerker (Bijou Opera House, New York); Frank Van der Stucken (Arion Society of New York).

**Educational**    John C. Fillmore (director, Milwaukee School of Music); William F. Sherwin (choral music, New England Conservatory).

**Other**    Frederick Gleason (music critic, *Chicago Tribune*); Smith Newhall Penfield (president, MTNA).

**K. Biographical**    Giuseppe Campanari (Italian cellist/baritone) comes to the United States; Frederick Delius, at his father's instigation, leaves England for his Florida orange plantation but meets the Jacksonville organist, Thomas Ward; Edward MacDowell returns to the United States long enough to marry Marian Nevins and goes back to Frankfurt; Ethelbert Nevin begins two years of music study in Berlin.

**L. Musical Beginnings**

**Performing Groups**    Beethoven (Dannreuther) String Quartet (New York); Boston Orchestral Club; Treble Clef Club (Philadelphia—to 1934).

**Educational**    American College of Musicians; Charleston Conservatory of Music (South Carolina); Chicago Conservatory of Music; Milwaukee School of Music; University of Kansas Music Department.

**Other**    Albaugh's Opera House (Washington, DC); *American (Music Journal)*; Child's Grand

Opera House (Los Angeles); Henry Distin, Instrument Maker (Philadelphia); John Friedrich and Brother, Violin Makers (New York); Frye's Opera House (Seattle); Kunkel's Popular Concerts (St. Louis); Krueger Auditorium (Newark); Ludden and Bates (Savannah, Georgia); A. J. Showalter, Music Publisher.

**M. Music Publications**

Dana, William H., *Practical Harmony*
Krehbiel, Henry E., *Notes on the Cultivation of Choral Music and the Oratorio Society of New York*
Palmer, Horatio, *The Choral Union*

**N. Musical Compositions**

**Choral/Vocal**   Victor Herbert, *Blümlein an Herzen, Opus 4* (song)—*Der Schönheit Krone, Opus 5* (male voices); Horatio Parker, *Mountain Shepherd's Song, Opus 1* (male voices)—*Ballade of a Knight and His Daughter*; Monroe Rosenfeld, *Climbing Up the Golden Stairs* (song).

**Concertos**   Victor Herbert, *Suite, Opus 3, for Cello and Orchestra.*

**Orchestra/Band**   Arthur H. Bird, *Concert Overture in D Major—Eine Carneval Szene, Opus 5—Little Suite I*; Henry H. Huss, *Forest Idylls*; Edgar Stillman Kelley, *Music to MacBeth, Opus 7*; Horatio Parker, *Overture, Regulus, Opus 5—Venetian Overture, Opus 12—Scherzo in G Minor for Orchestra, Opus 13.*

**Piano/Organ**   George Frederick Bristow, *La Vivandiere, Opus 51*; Edward MacDowell, *Two Pieces, Opus 18—Wald Idyllen, Opus 19*; John Knowles Paine, *Three Pieces, Opus 41.*

# 1885

☼

## Historical Highlights

The Washington Monument is dedicated; the Great Lakes are connected by the opening of the Locks at Sault-Ste. Marie; American Telephone and Telegraph Co. is incorporated; Stanford University is founded in California; streetcar service begins in Baltimore; Louis Pasteur gives the first successful rabies inoculation; Belgium takes over the Congo region of Africa.

## World Cultural Highlights

**World Art**   Paul Cézanne, *Mont St. Victoire*; Benjamin Constant, *Vengeance of the Cherif*; Edgar Degas, *Jockeys*; Alfred Sisley, *Small Meadows in Spring*; Vincent Van Gogh, *The Potato Eaters*.

**World Literature**   Alphonse Daudet, *Tartarin on the Alps*; H. Rider Haggard, *King Solomon's Mines*; George Meredith, *Diana of the Crossways*; Robert Louis Stevenson, *A Child's Garden of Verse*.

**World Music**   Johannes Brahms, *Symphony No. 4*; Antonín Dvořák, *Symphony No. 7*; César Franck, *Symphonic Variations*; Gilbert and Sullivan, *The Mikado*; Johann Strauss, *The Gypsy Baron*.

**Miscellaneous**   The Belaiev Publishing House opens in St. Petersburg, Russia; the Melbourne Academy of Music opens in Australia; births include Otto Klemperer, David Lawrence, Jules Romain, and Edgard Varèse; deaths include Per Atterbom, Carl Cauer, Victor Hugo, and Carl Spitzweg.

## American Art and Literature Highlights

**Births/Deaths**   Births include sculptors Paul Manship, Hugh Robus, John Storrs, and literary figures Thomas B. Costain, DuBose Heyward, Frances Parkinson Keyes, Ring Lardner, Sinclair Lewis, Ezra Pound, Carl Van Doren, and Elinor Wylie; deaths include artists William Page, Benjamin Reinhardt, and literary figures Martin R. Delaney, Helen Hunt Jackson, and Henry W. Shaw (Josh Billings).

**Art Works**   Ralph Blakelock, *Moonlight, Indian Encampment*; William Harnett, *After the Hunt*;

Winslow Homer, *The Fog Warning*; John La Farge, *Murals, Church of the Incarnation, N.Y.*; John F. Peto, *The Poor Man's Store*; Charles Russell, *Breaking Camp*; Albert P. Ryder, *Jonah* (?); Charles F. Ulrich, *The Village Print Shop* (?); Elihu Vedder, *The Cup of Death*; John Q. A. Ward, *Pilgrim*.

**Literature**    Amelia Barr, *Jan Vedder's Wife*; George W. Cable, *The Silent South*; William C. Faulkner, *The White Rose of Memphis*; Louise Guiney, *Goose Quill Papers*; Oliver W. Holmes, *A Mortal Antipathy*; William D. Howells, *The Rise of Silas Lapham*; Henry F. Keenan, *The Money-Makers*; Mary N. Murfree, *Prophet of the Great Smoky Mountains*; William W. Story, *Fiametta: A Summer Idyll*.

## Music—The Vernacular/Commercial Scene

**A. Births**    Gene Buck (songwriter/lyricist) August 8; Lucie E. Campbell (composer) April 30; Jerome Kern (composer) January 27; Leadbelly (Huddie Ledbetter) (singer/guitarist) January 21; Edgar Leslie (lyricist) December 31; Sam M. Lewis (lyricist) October 25; Joseph McCarthy (lyricist) September 27; James Monaco (composer) January 13; Joseph "King" Oliver (cornetist/bandleader) May 11; James Scott (ragtime pianist/composer) February 12; Herbert Stothart (composer) September 11.

**C. Biographical**

**Performing Groups**    Onward Brass Band I (New Orleans—to 1930).

**New Beginnings**    Bijou Theater (Boston).

**E. Representative Works**

**Musicals**    David Braham, *The Investigation*; Harrigan and Hart, *Old Lavender*; William J. Scanlan, *Shane na Lawn*.

**Songs**    Anonymous, *The Big Rock Candy Mountain*; David Braham and Ned Harrigan, *Poverty's Tears Ebb and Flow*; John J. Handley, *Sleep, Baby, Sleep (Irene's Lullaby)*; William J. Scanlan, *Remember, Boy, You're Irish*.

**Other**    F. W. Meacham, *American Patrol*.

## Music—The Cultivated/Art Music Scene

**F. Births**    Cecil Burleigh (composer/violinist) April 17; Hugh F. MacColl (composer/organist) February 22; Francis Macmillen (violinist) October 14; Mana-Zucca (composer/pianist); Lucille Marcel (soprano); Wallingford Riegger (composer) April 29; Sigmund Spaeth (writer on music) April 10; Deems Taylor (composer/critic) December 22.

**G. Deaths**    Thomas J. Bowers (organist/tenor) October 3; Leopold Damrosch (German-born conductor) February 15; Samuel P. Jackson (organist/composer) July 27; Henry F. Miller (piano maker) August 14; Frederic Mollenhauer (German-born violinist/conductor) April 14; Henry K. Oliver (organist/composer) August 12; Chabrier Peloubet (woodwind and reed organ maker) October 30; Philip P. Werlein (German-born dealer/publisher) April 17.

**H. Debuts**

**United States**    Flora Batson (soprano—New York), Alma Fohstrom (Finnish soprano—tour), August Hyllested (Swedish pianist—tour), Félia Litvinne (Russian soprano—New York), Maud Powell (violinist—Orange, New Jersey), Sophie Traubman (soprano—New York), Edmond-Alphonse Vergnet (French tenor).

**Metropolitan Opera**    Max Alvary (German tenor), Walter Damrosch (German conductor), Emil F. Fischer (German bass), Lilli Lehmann (German soprano), John R. Lund (German conductor), Amalie Materna (Austrian soprano), Anton Seidl (Hungarian conductor).

**I. New Positions**

**Conductors**    Walter Damrosch (New York Symphony Orchestra); Anton Seidl (Metropolitan Opera).

**Educational**    Jacques-Joseph Bouhy (director, New York Conservatory—to 1889); Carl Faelten (New England Conservatory—to 1897); Emil Oberhoffer (Manhattan College).

**Other**   Richard Aldrich (music critic, *Providence Journal*); Ernest R. Kroeger (organ, Church of the Messiah, St. Louis—to 1921).

**K. Biographical**   Richard Aldrich graduates from Harvard; Amy Marcy Cheney marries a doctor, Henry Harris Aubrey Beach; Frederick Delius abandons his Florida orange farm and begins music teaching in Jacksonville; Ferruccio Giannini (Italian tenor) comes to the United States; Franz Kneisel (Romanian violinist) comes to the United States as concertmaster of the Boston Symphony Orchestra; Lillian Nordica, following her husband's death, redebuts in Boston; Emil Oberhoffer (German conductor) comes to New York; Horatio Parker returns from Europe and begins teaching in the Cathedral School in New York; Daniel B. Towner joins the D. L. Moody evangelistic team.

**L. Musical Beginnings**

**Performing Groups**   American (National) Opera Co. (New York); Boston Pops Orchestra; San Diego City Guard Band.

**Educational**   Arizona State University School of Music; Cleveland School of Music; Combs School of Music (Philadelphia); Fisk University Music Department; National Conservatory of Music (New York); Newark College of Music; Northwestern Conservatory of Music (Minneapolis).

**Other**   Autoharp (by C. F. Zimmermann); Boston Music Co.; Boston Promenade Concerts; Chestnut Street Opera House (Philadelphia); Estey Piano Co. (Vermont); Leach's Opera House (San Diego); Listemann Concert Co. (Boston); *The Metronome* (to 1961); Musicians Mutual Benefit Association (St. Louis); Silver Burdett Co, Music Publishers (Boston); John Stark and Son Music Store (Sedalia, Missouri); M. Witmark and Sons, Publishers (New York).

**M. Music Publications**

Eddy, Clarence, *The Church and Concert Organist II*
Paine, John K., *Lecture Notes*
Tufts, J. and Holt, H., *The Normal Music Course: A Series of Exercises, Studies and Songs, Defining and Illustrating the Art of Sight Singing*

**N. Musical Compositions**

**Chamber Music**   George W. Chadwick, *String Quartet No. 3 in D Major*; Arthur Foote, *Three Characteristic Pieces, Opus 9* (violin and piano); Horatio Parker, *String Quartet in F Major, Opus 11*.

**Choral/Vocal**   George Frederick Bristow, *Mass in C Major, Opus 57*; Dudley Buck, *The Voyage of Columbus* (cantata); Arthur Foote, *The Farewell of Hiawatha, Opus 11* (male chorus and orchestra); William W. Gilchrist, *Eight Songs*; Horatio Parker, *König Trojan, Opus 8* (baritone, chorus, and orchestra); George F. Root, *Santa Claus' Mistake* (cantata).

**Concertos**   Arthur H. Bird, *Melody and Spanish Dance, Opus 9* (violin and chamber orchestra); Henry Huss, *Rhapsody for Piano and Orchestra*; E. C. Phelps, *American Legend* (violin and orchestra).

**Operas**   Frederick Gleason, *Montezuma*; John Philip Sousa, *The Queen of Hearts* (operetta).

**Orchestra/Band**   Johann H. Beck, *Scherzo No. 1 for Orchestra* (revised 1895); Arthur H. Bird, *Little Suite II, Opus 6*; Edward MacDowell, *Hamlet—Ophelia* (symphonic poems); Horace Nicholl, *Hamlet, Opus 14* ("psychic sketch"); Silas G. Pratt, *The Prodigal Son*; John Philip Sousa, *Marches—Mikado—Mother Hubbard—Sound Off—Triumph of Time*; Templeton Strong, *Undine* (symphonic poem).

**Piano/Organ**   George Frederick Bristow, *Dreamland, Opus 59*; George W. Chadwick, *Ten Canonic Studies for Organ*; Henry H. Huss, *Ballade in F Major*; Edward MacDowell, *Three Poesien, Opus 20* (four hands); H. H. Thiele, *The Telephone Galop*.

**Symphonies**   Arthur H. Bird, *Symphony in A Major, Opus 8*; Asger Hamerik, *Symphonie Lyrique in E Major, Opus 33*; Horatio Parker, *Symphony in C Minor, Opus 7*.

# 1886

❀

## Historical Highlights

Samuel Gompers becomes the first president of the reorganized American Federation of Labor; the Haymarket Square Riots take place in Chicago; France's gift to the American people, the Statue of Liberty, is officially unveiled; Congress passes the Presidential Succession Act; Apache leader Geronimo is captured in the Arizona territory; Vancouver, British Columbia, is incorporated.

## World Cultural Highlights

**World Art**   Edward Burne-Jones, *The Depths of the Sea*; Auguste Rodin, *The Kiss*; Henri Rousseau, *Un Soir de Carnaval*; Georges Seurat, *Sunday Afternoon, Grande Jatte*; Hamo Thornycroft, *A Sower*.

**World Literature**   Arthur Rimbaud, *Les Illuminations*; Robert Louis Stevenson, *Dr. Jekyll and Mr. Hyde*; Alfred Lord Tennyson, *Locksley Hall Sixty Years After*; Leo Tolstoy, *The Power of Darkness*.

**World Music**   César Franck, *Violin Sonata in A*; Alexander Glazunov, *Symphony No. 2*; Vincent d'Indy, *Symphony on a French Mountain Air*; Camille Saint-Saëns, *Symphony No. 3, "Organ."*

**Miscellaneous**   The Toronto Royal Conservatory of Music opens; births include Wilhelm Fürtwängler, Nikolai Gumilyov, Oscar Kokoschka, Antoine Pevsner, Diego Rivera, and Arthur Rubinstein; deaths include William Barnes, Franz Liszt, and Amilcare Ponchielli.

## American Art and Literature Highlights

**Births/Deaths**   Births include artists Bernard Karfiol, Morgan Russell, and literary figures Zoë Akins, William Rose Benét, Hilda Doolittle, Alfred Joyce Kilmer, Wilbur D. Steele, and Rex Stout; deaths include artists Henry K. Brown, Asher Durand, Jerome Thompson, and literary figures Mary B. Chesnut, Emily Dickinson, Paul H. Hayne, E. Z. C. Judson (Ned Buntline), and Ann Sophia Stephens.

**Art Works**   William M. Harnett, *The Old Violin*; Childe Hassam, *Boston Common at Twilight*; Winslow Homer, *Eight Bells*; Chauncey B. Ives, *The Willing Captive*; Julius Melchers, *The Sermon*; Augustus Saint-Gaudens, *Standing Lincoln* (cast 1912); John Singer Sargent, *Carnation, Lily, Lily, Rose*; William A. Walker, *The Bombardment of Ft. Sumter*; John Quincy Adams Ward, *President Garfield*.

**Literature**   Louisa May Alcott, *Jo's Boys*; Frances Hodgson Burnett, *Little Lord Fauntleroy*; Helen H. Jackson, *Sonnets and Lyrics*; Henry James, *The Bostonians*; Sarah Orne Jewett, *A White Heron and Other Stories*; James Russell Lowell, *Democracy and Other Addresses*; Frank Moore, *Songs and Ballads of the Southern People*; Celia Thaxter, *Idylls and Pastorals*.

## Music—The Vernacular/Commercial Scene

**A. Births**   Shelton Brooks (songwriter) May 4; L. Wolfe Gilbert (songwriter) August 31; Al Jolson (singer/actor) May 26; Gus Kahn (lyricist) November 6; Edward "Kid" Ory (trombonist/bandleader) December 25; Charles Henry Pace (composer/publisher) August 4; Gertrude "Ma" Rainey (singer) April 26.

**C. Biographical**

**Performing Groups**   Al G. Field's Minstrels (to 1928).

**D. Publications**   F. O. Jones, ed., *A Handbook of American Music and Musicians, Containing Biographies of American Musicians, and Histories of the Principal Musical Institutions, Firms and Societies*.

**E. Representative Works**

**Musicals**   David Braham and Ned Harrigan, *The O'Reagans*.

**Songs**   Gussie Davis, *The Lighthouse by the Sea*; Paul Dresser, *The Letter That Never Came*; Edward Jakobowski, *What the Dickie-Birds Say*; Monroe Rosenfeld, *Johnny Get Your Gun*.

## Music—The Cultivated/Art Music Scene

**F. Births**   Edward Ballantine (composer) August 6; John J. Becker (composer) January 22; Olin Downes (music critic) January 27; Fay Foster (pianist/composer) November 8; George Foote (composer) February 19; Mabel Garrison (soprano) April 24; Charles Seeger (musicologist) December 14; Nicolai Sokoloff (conductor) May 28.

**G. Deaths**   Charlotte Cushman (contralto) February 18; John Gordon McCurry (composer/compiler) December 4; Hilborne L. Roosevelt (organ builder) December 30.

**H. Debuts**

**United States**   Pauline Allemand (New York), Adele Aus der Ohe (German pianist—tour), Ethelbert Nevin (as pianist—Boston), Eugène E. Oudin (baritone—New York), August Spanuth (German pianist—tour), Giulia Valda (soprano—New York), Cornelie Van Zanten (Dutch soprano—tour), Benjamin Whelpley (pianist—Boston).

**Metropolitan Opera**   Max Heinrich (German baritone), Georgine Neuendorff (Austrian soprano), Albert Niemann (German tenor), Gisela Staudigl (Austrian contralto).

**I. New Positions**

**Other**   Louis C. Elson (music editor, *Boston Daily Advertiser*—to 1920); Richard II. Warren (organ, St. Bartholomew's, New York—to 1905).

**K. Biographical**   Frederick Delius leaves the orange groves of Florida and moves to Leipzig where he enters the Conservatory; Henry Gilbert enrolls in New England Conservatory; Victor Herbert (Irish cellist/composer/conductor) and his new wife come to the United States to work at the Metropolitan Opera; Hugo Kaun (German composer) emigrates to the United States and settles in Milwaukee; Humphrey John Stewart (British organist/composer) emigrates to the United States and settles in San Francisco; Alwina Valleria retires from the stage; Max Zach (Russian violist/conductor) comes to the United States and begins playing in the Boston Symphony Orchestra.

**L. Musical Beginnings**

**Performing Groups**   Austin Musical Union (Texas); Dayton Young Men's Christian Association Orchestra; Eurydice Chorus of Philadelphia (to 1918); Kneisel String Quartet (Boston).

**Festivals**   Norfolk Choral Festival.

**Educational**   American Conservatory of Music (Chicago); Illinois Music Teachers Association; Metropolitan Conservatory (College, 1891) of Music (American Institute of Applied Music in 1900, New York); Minneapolis School of Fine Arts; University of Oregon School of Music.

**Other**   American Academy and Institute of Fine Arts; American Publisher's Copyright League; Friday Morning Music Club (Washington, DC); Grand Opera House (San Antonio); Nellie Brown Mitchell Concert Co.; National League of Musicians.

**M. Music Publications**

Christiani, Adolf, *Principles of Musical Expression in Piano Playing*
Parsons, Albert R., *The Science of Pianoforte Practice*
Upton, George P., *The Standard Operas*
Warrington, James, *Hymns and Tunes for the Children of the Church*

## N. Musical Compositions

**Chamber Music**   Johann H. Beck, *String Sextet in D Minor*; Arthur Foote, *Three Pieces, Opus 9* (violin and piano).

**Choral/Vocal**   Amy (Mrs. H. H. A.) Beach, *Four Songs, Opus 1*; Dudley Buck, *The Light of Asia* (secular cantata); George W. Chadwick, *Dedication Ode*; Horatio Parker, *Three Love Songs, Opus 10—Idylle, Opus 15* (cantata after Goethe); George F. Root, *Faith Triumphant* (cantata).

**Concertos**   Arthur H. Bird, *Introduction and Fugue in D Minor, Opus 16* (organ and orchestra);

Caryl Florio, *Concerto in A-Flat Major for Piano and Orchestra*; Edward MacDowell, *Concerto No. 2 in D Minor for Piano and Orchestra*.

**Orchestra/Band**  Arthur H. Bird, *Volksfest—Rübezahl* (ballets); George W. Chadwick, *Overture, The Miller's Daughter*; Arthur Foote, *In the Mountains, Opus 14* (revised 1910); Edwin A. Jones, *Suite Ancienne, Opus 17*; Edward MacDowell, *Lancelot and Elaine, Opus 25* (symphonic poem); John Philip Sousa, *The Gladiator March—The Rifle Regiment March—Overture, Tally-Ho—Overture, Vautour—Presidential Polonaise—Sandalphon Waltzes—La Reine de la Mer Waltzes*; Arthur B. Whiting, *Concert Overture*.

**Piano/Organ**  Arthur H. Bird, *Eight Sketches, Opus 15*; Dudley Buck, *Grand Sonata No. 1 in E-Flat Major, Opus 22, for Organ*; Edward MacDowell, *Four Pieces, Opus 24*; Horatio Parker, *Five Characteristic Pieces, Opus 9*; Septimus Winner, *The Gettysburg March*; Isadore Witmark, *President Cleveland's Wedding March*.

**Symphonies**  George W. Chadwick, *Symphony No. 2 in B-Flat Major*.

# 1887

☼

## Historical Highlights

A busy Congress passes the Dawes Severalty Act, Electoral Count Act, Hatch Act and the Interstate Commerce Act; free mail delivery begins in the larger cities and towns; the first World Colonial Conference opens in London; internal combustion cars are produced by both Gottlieb Daimler and Karl Benz; newly formed French Indo-China is a combination of Cambodia, Laos, and Vietnam.

## World Cultural Highlights

**World Art**  Pierre de Chavannes, *Allegory: Arts and Sciences*; Max Klinger, *The Judgment of Paris*; Max Liebermann, *The Flax Spinners*; Hans von Marées, *The Hesperides*; Pierre Renoir, *The Bathers*.

**World Literature**  Arthur Conan Doyle, *A Study in Scarlet*; Thomas Hardy, *The Woodlanders*; Victorien Sardou, *La Tosca*; August Strindberg, *Der Vater*; Oscar Wilde, *The Canterbury Ghost*.

**World Music**  Alexander Borodin, *Prince Igor—Symphony No. 3*; Johannes Brahms, *Double Concerto for Violin and Cello*; Claude Debussy, *Printemps*; Nicholas Rimsky-Korsakov, *Capriccio Espagnol*.

**Miscellaneous**  The Yamaha Company opens in Japan, as does the Tokyo Music School; the London College of Music opens; births include Rupert Brooke, Marc Chagall, Edith Sitwell, and Heitor Villa-Lobos; deaths include Alexander Borodin, Jenny Lind, and Hans von Marées.

## American Art and Literature Highlights

**Births/Deaths**  Births include art figures James Chapin, Malvina Hoffman, Georgia O'Keeffe, Marguerite and William Zorach, and literary figures Mary Ellen Chase, Edna Ferber, James N. Hall, Robinson Jeffers, Marianne Moore, and Alexander Woollcott; deaths include literary figures Albertus de Browere, Sylvanus Cobb, Jr., Emma Lazarus, John G. Saxe, and Edward Rowland Sill.

**Art Works**  Paul W. Bartlett, *Bohemian Bear Tamer*; Robert F. Blum, *Venetian Lace Makers*; George Cope, *Fisherman's Accoutrements*; William Harnett, *The Magic Flute*; Childe Hassam, *Grand Prix Day*; George Inness, *September Afternoon*; John F. Peto, *Ordinary Objects in the Artist's Creative Mind*; Theodore Robinson, *At the Piano*; Albert Ryder, *The Flying Dutchman*; Olin Warner, *Diana*.

**Literature**  Katharine Bates, *College Beautiful and Other Poems*; Edward Bellamy, *Looking Backward: 2000–1887*; Mary E. W. Freeman, *A Humble Romance and Other Stories*; Louise Guiney, *The White Sail and Other Poems*; Joel Chandler Harris, *Free Joe and Other Georgian Sketches*; Henry James, *What Maisie Knew*; Thomas Page, *In Ole Virginia*; James Whitcomb Riley, *Afterwhiles*.

## Music—The Vernacular/Commercial Scene

**A. Births**  Lovie Austin (pianist) September 19; Nat D. Ayer (pianist/composer) September 30; Euday Bowman (pianist/composer) November 9; Louis A. Hirsch (composer) November 28; Howard E. Johnson (lyricist) June 2; James Lamb (ragtime pianist/composer); Charley Patton (singer/guitarist); E. K. Robertson (country fiddler) November 20; Julia Sanderson (singer/actress) August 20; Percy Wenrich (songwriter/pianist) January 23.

**E. Representative Works**

**Musicals**  David Braham and Ned Harrigan, *Pete*; David Braham and E. E. Rice, *The Corsair*; Edward Darling and A. C. Wheeler, *Big Pony*.

**Songs**  Effie I. Crockett, *Rock-a-Bye, Baby*; Paul Dresser, *The Outcast Unknown*; Will Fox and J. F. Mitchell, *Twelve Months Ago Tonight*; Charles Graham, *If the Waters Could Speak as They Flow*; Felix McGlennon, *Comrades*; Hubbard T. Smith and S. M. Peck, *If You Love Me Darling, Tell Me with Your Eyes*.

## Music—The Cultivated/Art Music Scene

**F. Births**  Alfred H. Ackley (evangelist/hymn writer) January 21; Edward S. Barnes (organist/composer) September 14; Marion Bauer (composer/author) August 15; Richard Bonelli (baritone) February 6; Clara Edwards (composer/pianist) March 18; Walter Golde (pianist/composer) January 4; William Gustafsson (bassist) November 23; Roland Hayes (tenor) June 3; Felice Lyne (soprano) September 1; Louis Persinger (violinist/pianist) February 11, Lily Strickland (pianist/composer) January 28; Oscar Thompson (music critic/author) October 10; David M. Williams (organist/composer) February 20; John Finley Williamson (conductor/educator) June 23.

**G. Deaths**  Justin Holland (composer/guitarist) March 24; Thomas P. Ryder (organist) December 2; George James Webb (British-born composer/conductor) October 7.

**H. Debuts**

**United States**  Victor Herbert (German cellist—New York); Arthur Hartmann (violinist—Philadelphia); Josef Hofmann (Polish pianist, age 11—New York); Lawrence Kellie (British tenor—New York); Barton M'Guckin (Irish tenor—tour); Sophie Sedlmair (German soprano—New York); Teresina Tua (Italian violinist—New York).

**Metropolitan Opera**  Johannes Elmblad (Swedish bass), Adelina Patti (Italian soprano).

**I. New Positions**

**Other**  William James Henderson (music critic, *The New York Times*—to 1902); John White (organ, Church of the Ascension, New York—to 1896).

**K. Biographical**  Carl Busch (Danish composer/conductor) emigrates to the United States and settles in Kansas City, Missouri; Karl Fiqué (German organist/composer) emigrates to the United States and settles in Brooklyn; Victor Herbert performs his own *Cello Concerto* with the New York Philharmonic Orchestra; Clara Kellogg marries her manager and retires from the operatic stage; Charles Martin Loeffler becomes an American citizen; Emma Nevada and Lillian Nordica make their Covent Garden debuts; William H. Santelmann (German violinist/bandmaster) comes to the United States.

**L. Musical Beginnings**

**Performing Groups**  Bostonian's Light Opera Group; Buffalo Orchestral Association; Dallas Philharmonic Society; Denver Municipal Band; Germania Band (Reading, Pennsylvania); Innes Band of New York.

**Educational**  Denver Music Conservatory.

**Other**  American Gramophone Co. (Washington, DC); Carl G. Becker, Violin Maker (Chicago); Louis Opera House (San Diego); Marston Club (women's music club, Portland, Maine); George Southwell, Music Publisher (Kansas City).

**M. Music Publications**

*George F. Bristow's New and Improved Method for the Reed or Cabinet Organ*

Eddy, Clarence, *The Organ in Church*
Fillmore, John C., *New Lessons in Harmony*
Krane, Julia E., *Music Teacher's Manual*
Showalter, A. J., *Rudiments of Music*
Upton, George P., *The Standard Oratorios*
Ziehn, Bernhard, *Harmonie und Modulationslehre*

## N. Musical Compositions

**Chamber Music**   Arthur H. Bird, *Nonet for Woodwinds*; Edwin A. Jones, *String Quartet No. 2*.

**Choral/Vocal**   Amy Beach, *Three Songs on Burns, Opus 12*; Charles Converse, *God with Us* (American hymn); Caryl Florio, *The Crown of the Year* (cantata); Asger Hamerik, *Requiem in C Minor, Opus 34*; James McGranahan, *I Will Sing of My Redeemer* (hymn); George F. Root, *The Pillar of Fire* (cantata); John R. Sweeney, *There Is Sunshine in My Soul Today* (hymn); Daniel Towner, *Trust and Obey* (hymn).

**Concertos**   Arthur H. Bird, *Oriental Scene and Caprice, Opus 17* (flute and chamber orchestra); Dudley Buck, *Canzonetta and Bolero* (violin and orchestra); Edward MacDowell, *Romanze for Cello and Orchestra, Opus 35*.

**Operas**   Edgar S. Kelley, *Pompeiian Picnic, Opus 9* (operetta); Adolph Neuendorff, *Prince Waldmeister*; Silas G. Pratt, *Lucille*.

**Orchestra/Band**   George W. Chadwick, *Overture, Melpomene*; Victor Herbert, *Honeymoon*; Edward MacDowell, *Lamia, Opus 29* (symphonic poem); John Philip Sousa, *The Occidental March*.

**Piano/Organ**   Arthur H. Bird, *Ten Pieces, Opus 20, 21—American Melodies, Opus 23* (four hands); Dudley Buck, *Grand Sonata No. 2 for Organ*; Edward MacDowell, *Idyllen: Six Little Pieces, Opus 28—Six Poems after Heine, Opus 31—Etude de Concert, Opus 36*.

**Symphonies**   Caryl Florio, *Symphony No. 1 in G Major—Symphony No. 2 in C Major*.

# 1888

☀

## Historical Highlights

Benjamin Harrison is elected as the 23rd president despite having lost in the popular vote; Charles M. Hall introduces a cheaper method for the commercial production of aluminum; the Kodak camera first appears on the market; *National Geographic Magazine* begins publication; the neutrality of the Suez Canal is guaranteed by the European powers; France annexes Tahiti.

## World Cultural Highlights

**World Art**   Paul Gauguin, *Vision After the Sermon*; Pierre-Auguste Renoir, *After the Bath*; Henri de Toulouse-Latrec, *Circus Fernando Ringmaster*; Vincent Van Gogh, *L'Arlesienne*.

**World Literature**   Thomas Hardy, *Tess of the d'Urbervilles*; Rudyard Kipling, *The Phantom Rickshaw*; Robert Louis Stevenson, *The Master of Ballantrae*; August Strindberg, *Miss Julie*.

**World Music**   César Franck, *Symphony in D Minor*; Gustav Mahler, *Symphony No. 1*; Nicholas Rimsky-Korsakov, *Scheherazade*; Richard Strauss, *Don Juan*; Peter Tchaikovsky, *Symphony No. 5*.

**Miscellaneous**   The German Theatre opens in Prague and the Teatro Costanzi in Rome; the Amsterdam Concertgebouw is built; births include Josef Albers, Giorgio di Chirico, Katherine Mansfield, and Fritz Reiner; deaths include Charles Alkan, Matthew Arnold, Antoine Étex, and Edward Lear.

## American Art and Literature Highlights

**Births/Deaths**   Births include artists Horace Pippin, Henry V. Poor, and literary figures Maxwell

Anderson, Raymond Chandler, T. S. Eliot, Eugene O'Neill, Anne Parrish, John Crowe Ransom, Lew Sarett, and Alan Seeger; deaths include literary figures Louisa May Alcott, David Ross Locke (Petroleum V. Nasby), and Caroline S. Tappan.

**Art Works**   Albert Bierstadt, *Last of the Buffalo*; John J. Boyle, *Stone Age in America*; George Brush, *The Moose Hunt*; Jefferson Chalfant, *The Old Violin*; Daniel French, *Thomas Gallaudet Memorial*; William Harnett, *Music and Good Luck*; John La Farge, *Murals, Church of the Ascension, New York*; Alexander Pope, *Emblems of the Civil War*; Robert W. Vonnoh, *Poppies*; J. Alden Weir, *Idle Hours*.

**Literature**   Edward Eggleston, *The Graysons*; Oliver Wendell Holmes, *Before the Curfew and Other Poems*; Henry James, *Partial Portraits*; Herman Melville, *John Marr and Other Sailors*; James Whitcomb Riley, *Pipes o' Pan at Zekesbury*; Amélie Rives, *The Quick or the Dead*; Elizabeth Seaman, *Ten Days in a Madhouse*; John Greenleaf Whittier, *Narrative and Legendary Poems*.

## Music — The Vernacular/Commercial Scene

**A. Births**   Harry Archer (composer) February 21; May Aufderheide (ragtime composer) May 21; Irving Berlin (composer) May 11; Bobby Clark (singer/composer) June 16; Artie Matthews (ragtime composer) November 15; Sidney B. Mitchell (lyricist) June 15; Abe Olman (songwriter) December 20; Roy Webb (composer) October 3; Pete Wendling (pianist/composer) June 6.

**C. Biographical**

**Performing Groups**   Papa Laine's Ragtime Band.

**Miscellaneous**   Gustav Luders (German composer) comes to the United States.

**D. Publications**   S. S. Stewart, *The Banjo: A Dissertation*.

**E. Representative Works**

**Musicals**   David Braham, *Waddy Googan*; Gustave A. Kerker, *The Pearl of Pekin*; Reginald De Koven and Henry B. Smith, *The Begum*; Julius J. Lyons and A. Nowack, *The Lady or the Tiger?*

**Songs**   Anonymous, *Drill, Ye Tarriers, Drill*; Sam Devere, *The Whistling Coon*; Paul Dresser, *The Convict and the Bird*; Monroe H. Rosenfeld, *With All Her Faults, I Love Her Still*; Joseph J. Sullivan, *Where Did You Get That Hat?*

## Music — The Cultivated/Art Music Scene

**F. Births**   Louis d'Angelo (baritone) May 6; Philip Greeley Clapp (composer) August 4; Lucile Crews (composer) August 23; Felix Deyo (composer/pianist) April 21; George S. Dickinson (music educator) February 9; Sophie Drinker (writer on music) August 24; Alice Gentle (mezzo-soprano) June 30; Lillian Grenville (soprano) November 20; John Hays Hammond, Jr. (organ builder) April 13; Sol Hurok (manager/impresario) April 9; Hall Johnson (conductor/composer) March 12; Ernst C. Krohn (musicologist) December 23; George Meader (tenor) July 6; Florence Bea Price (composer) April 9; Oscar Rasbach (composer) August 2; Rudolph E. Reuter (pianist) September 21; Albert Spalding (violinist) August 15; Burnet Corwin Tuthill (composer/conductor) November 16.

**G. Deaths**   Oliver Ditson (publisher) December 21; Edmund Neupert (Norwegian pianist/pedagogue) June 22; Anne Seguin (British-born soprano) August; William F. Sherwin (composer) April 14.

**H. Debuts**

**United States**   Joseph V. Capoul (French tenor—New York), Sissieretta Jones (soprano—New York), Fritz Kreisler (Austrian violinist—Boston), Leonard Labatt (Swedish tenor—tour), Edward Lloyd (British tenor—Cincinnati), Fanny Moren-Olden (New York), Moritz Rosenthal (Austrian pianist—Boston), Eva Tetrazzini (soprano—New York).

**Metropolitan Opera**   Alma Fohstrom (Finnish soprano), Sophie Traubman (soprano), Joseph Beck (baritone), Alois Grienauer (baritone), Félice Kaschowska (soprano), Emmy Miron (mezzo-soprano), Albert Mittelhauser (tenor), Ludwig Mödlinger (bass), Karl Moran (tenor), Fanny Moran-

Olden (German soprano), Julius Perotti (tenor), Wilhelm Sedlmayer (tenor), Emil Steger (baritone). **Other** Sibyl Sanderson (The Hague, Holland).

**I. New Positions**

**Educational** Charles H. Farnsworth (director of music, Colorado University); James Huneker (piano, National Conservatory, New York); Rafael Joseffy (National Conservatory, New York—to 1906); Horatio R. Palmer (music director, Chatauqua—to 1901); Silas G. Pratt (Metropolitan School, New York); Albert A. Stanley (University of Michigan).

**Other** Louis Charles Elson (critic, *Boston Advertiser*—to 1920); Henry Houseley (organ, Episcopal Cathedral of St. John in the Wilderness, Denver—to 1925); Horatio Parker (organ, Holy Trinity Church, New York—to 1893); Thomas H. Rollinson (band department, Oliver Ditson Co.).

**K. Biographical** F. Melius Christiansen (Norwegian conductor/composer) comes to the United States and settles in San Francisco for two years; Julian Edwards (British conductor/composer) emigrates to the United States and becomes an operetta conductor; Edward MacDowell returns permanently to the United States and settles in Boston; Ethelbert Nevin marries Anne Paul and moves to Boston; Silas G. Pratt leaves Chicago for New York.

**L. Musical Beginnings**

**Performing Groups** Adamowski String Quartet; Beethoven Club (Memphis); Fadette Ladies' Orchestra of Boston; Hinrichs Opera Co. (Philadelphia); Mozart Musical and Literary Society (Dayton, Ohio).

**Educational** Artist-Artisan Institute (New York); Des Moines Musical College; University of Utah Music Department.

**Other** Aeolian Organ and Music Co. (New York); Bijou Theater (Knoxville, Tennessee); Boston Manuscript Club; Dayton Mozart Musical and Literary Society; Ellis Club (Los Angeles); Grand Opera House (Philadelphia); Harlem Opera House (New York); Carmen Primavera, Violin Maker (Philadelphia); Clayton F. Summy Co., Music Publishers (Chicago).

**M. Music Publications**

Clappé, Arthur A., *The Band Teacher's Assistant*
Clarke, Hugh, *Manual of Orchestration*
Elson, Louis C., *The History of German Song*
Faelten, Carl, *The Conservatory Course for Pianoforte*
Fillmore, John C., *Lessons in Musical History*
Goodrich, Alfred, *The Art of Song*
Mathews, W. S. B., *How to Understand Music*
Seward, Theodore, *A Revolution in Music Teaching*
Showalter, A. J., *Class, Choir and Congregation*
Tufts, John W., *Aeolean Collection: Part Songs for Female Voices*
Upton, George P., *The Standard Cantatas*

**N. Musical Compositions**

**Chamber Music** George W. Chadwick, *Piano Quintet in E-Flat Major*.

**Choral/Vocal** Rosetter G. Cole, *The Passing of Summer* (cantata); Arthur Foote, *The Wreck of the Hesperus, Opus 17*; William Gilchrist, *Prayer and Praise—Legend of the Bended Spear*; Victor Herbert, *Three Songs, Opus 15*; Charles Ives, *Psalm XLII*; Edward MacDowell, *Three Songs, Opus 33*; John Knowles Paine, *Song of Promise, Opus 43* (cantata); Horatio Parker, *Normannenzug, Opus 16* (cantata); Silas G. Pratt, *The Musical Metempsychosis* (musical entertainment); George F. Root, *The Coming of the Flowers* (cantata)—*Snow White and the Seven Dwarfs* (children's cantata).

**Concertos** Horace Nicholl, *Piano Concerto in D Minor, Opus 10*; Arthur B. Whiting, *Concerto in D Minor for Piano and Orchestra—Suite for Four Horns and Strings, Opus 6*.

**Operas** John Philip Sousa, *The Wolf* (operetta).

**Orchestra/Band**    Arthur H. Bird, *Two Episodes for Orchestra—Two Poems, Opus 25—Two Pieces, Opus 28, for Strings*; John Knowles Paine, *An Island Fantasy, Opus 44* (symphonic poem); John Philip Sousa, *Marches—Ben Bolt—The Crusader—National Fencibles—Semper Fidelis*.

**Piano/Organ**    Arthur H. Bird, *Four Pieces, Opus 26*; Dudley Buck, *Variations on "Old Folks at Home"* (organ); Charles Kunkel, *Alpine Storm*; Edward MacDowell, *Les Orientales, Opus 37—Marionetten, Opus 38*.

# 1889
⚙

## Historical Highlights

North and South Dakota, Montana, and Washington become the 39th–42nd states; the Oklahoma Territory opens; Oklahoma City is built up overnight; the Mayo Clinic is founded in Minnesota; the great Johnstown Flood takes place in Ohio; the first International American Conference is held; Japan receives a Parliamentary government; the Eiffel Tower is built for the Paris Exposition.

## World Cultural Highlights

**World Art**    Max Liebermann, *Mending the Nets*; Frederick Macmonnies, *Diana*; Pierre-Auguste Renoir, *Girl with Daisies*; Auguste Rodin, *The Thinker*; Vincent Van Gogh, *The Starry Night*.

**World Literature**    Maurice Maeterlinck, *La Princesse Madeleine*; Friedrich Nietzsche, *Götzendämmerung*; William Yeats, *The Wanderings of Oisin and Other Poems*.

**World Music**    Claude Debussy, *Petite Suite*; Antonín Dvořák, *Symphony No. 8*; Richard Strauss, *Death and Transfiguration*; Peter Tchaikovsky, *Sleeping Beauty*; Hugo Wolf, *Spanisches Liederbuch*.

**Miscellaneous**    The Coblenz Music Conservatory opens; births include Willi Baumeister, Adrian Boult, Tristan Derème, and Arnold Toynbee; deaths include Robert Browning, Champfleury, Eliza Cook, Gerard M. Hopkins, and Frederick A. Ousley.

## American Art and Literature Highlights

**Births/Deaths**    Births include artist Thomas Hart Benton and literary figures George Abbott, Robert Benchley, Erle Stanley Gardner, Fannie Hurst, George S. Kaufman, Howard Lindsay, and Ben Ames Williams; deaths include artists John Ehninger, Robert Weir, author William C. Faulkner, and dramatist Cornelius Mathews.

**Art Works**    Cyrus E. Dallin, *The Signal of Peace*; Edwin R. Elmer, *Mourning Picture* (?); Thomas Eakins, *The Wrestlers*; William Harnett, *Old Cupboard Door*; Childe Hassam, *Winter Nightfall in the City*; George Inness, *Niagara*; Homer D. Martin, *Wild Coast, Newport*; Julius Stewart, *The Hunt Supper*; Abbott H. Thayer, *Angel* (?); Olin Levi Warner, *Joseph, Chief of the Nez Perce*.

**Literature**    Katharine Bates, *Rose and Thorn*; George W. Cable, *Strange True Stories of Louisiana*; Eugene Field, *A Little Book of Western Verse*; Blanche Howard, *The Open Door*; Lucy Larcom, *A New England Girlhood*; Theodore Roosevelt, *The Winning of the West*; Mark Twain, *A Connecticut Yankee in King Arthur's Court*; Charles Webb, *Vagrom Verses*.

## Music—The Vernacular/Commercial Scene

**A. Births**    Elsie Janis (singer/actress) March 16; William "Bunk" Johnson (trumpeter) December 27; Lonnie Johnson (blues singer/guitarist) February 8; Dominick La Rocca (cornetist); Louis Silver (composer/pianist) September 6; Noble Sissle (singer/lyricist) July 10; Spencer Williams (composer) October 14; Joe Young (singer/lyricist) July 4.

**D. Publications**    Nicholas Smith, *Stories of the Great National Songs*.

**E. Representative Works**

**Musicals**   Gustave A. Kerker, *Castles in the Air*; Reginald De Koven and H. B. Smith, *Don Quixote*.

**Songs**   Harry Dacre, *Playmates*; Joseph Flynn, *Down Went McGinty*; John W. Kelly, *Slide, Kelly, Slide*; Reginald De Koven and H. B. Smith, *Oh, Promise Me*.

## Music—The Cultivated/Art Music Scene

**F. Births**   Anna Case (soprano) October 29; Eugene MacDonald Bonner (composer); Samuel Chotzinoff (pianist/critic) July 4; Harold Flammer (music publisher) September 19; Charles Hackett (tenor) November 4; Ethel G. Hier (pianist/composer) June 25; Clarence Loomis (pianist/composer) December 13; David Saperton (pianist) October 29; Frederick P. Search (cellist/conductor) July 22; Alexander Smallens (conductor) January 1; John S. Thompson (pianist/educator) March 8; Max Wald (composer) July 14.

**G. Deaths**   Benjamin Franklin Baker (composer) March 11; Louis Maas (German-born pianist) September 17; John W. Moore (musicologist/lexicographer) March 23; Eugene Thayer (organist/composer) June 27; Jacob Zech (German-born piano maker) September 13.

**H. Debuts**

**United States**   Eugène d'Albert (Scottish pianist—tour), Selma Kronold (Polish soprano—New York), Francesco Tamagno (Italian tenor—Chicago).

**Metropolitan Opera**   Paul Kalisch (German tenor), Theodor Reichmann (German baritone).

**Other**   Emma Eames (soprano—Paris Opera), Sibyl Sanderson (soprano—Paris).

**I. New Positions**

**Conductors**   Emil Mollenhauer (Boston [German] Band); Arthur Nikisch (Boston Symphony Orchestra—to 1893).

**Educational**   Wulf Fries (Boston Conservatory); William H. Sherwood (piano head, Chicago Conservatory—to 1896).

**Other**   Richard Aldrich (music critic, *Washington Evening Star*); Reginald DeKoven (music critic, *Chicago Evening Post*); Theodore Seward (editor, *Universal Song*).

**K. Biographical**   Joseph Adamowski (Polish cellist) joins his brother in the United States; John Turnell Austin (British organ builder) emigrates to the United States, works in Detroit; Frederick Converse enters Harvard University; Henry Gilbert begins three years of music composition study with MacDowell; Anton Seidl conducts the first performance of Wagner's *Ring Cycle* in the United States; Charles Sanford Skilton graduates with a BA degree from Yale and begins studying music composition with Dudley Buck.

**L. Musical Beginnings**

**Performing Groups**   Boston Festival Orchestra; Brooklyn Symphony Orchestra; Church Choral Society of New York; Euterpe Choral Society of New York; Nahan Franko Orchestra; Emma Juch Opera Co.; Kansas City Apollo Club; Liberati's Grand Military Band; Newark Orpheus Club; Norwegian Male Chorus (Seattle); Treble Clef (Lyric Club—Los Angeles women's club).

**Other**   Chicago Auditorium Theater; Columbia Phonograph Co. (Washington, DC); Hamilton Organ Co. (Chicago); Hampden County Musical Association (Massachusetts); New York Manuscript Society (Society of American Musicians and Composers, 1899); Vega Co., Stringed Instrument Makers (Boston).

**M. Music Publications**

Finck, Henry T., *Chopin and Other Musical Essays*
Goodrich, Alfred, *Complete Musical Analysis*
Henderson, William J., *The Story of Music*
Mathews, William, *A Hundred Years of Music in America*
Pearce, S. Austen, *Pocket Dictionary of Musical Terms*

Upton, George P., *The Standard Symphonies*
Virgil, A. K., *The Virgil Clavier Method: Foundation Exercises I*

**N. Musical Compositions**

**Chamber Music**   Arthur H. Bird, *Suite in D Major, for Ten Wind Instruments*; Arthur Foote, *Violin Sonata in G Minor, Opus 20*; Charles M. Loeffler, *String Quartet in A Minor*.

**Choral/Vocal**   Amy Beach, *Three Songs, Opus 11*; Frederick Gleason, *Auditorium Festival Ode* (cantata); Victor Herbert, *Eight Songs, Opus 10, 13, 14*; Henry H. Huss, *Festival Sanctus*; Margaret R. Lang, *Ojalá* (song); Ethelbert Nevin, *Five Songs, Opus 5*; George F. Root, *Bethlehem—The Building of the Temple* (cantatas); John White, *Missa Solemnis*.

**Concertos**   Henry H. Huss, *Romance and Polonaise*.

**Operas**   Dudley Buck, *Serapis*; Henry Hadley, *Happy Jack* (operetta); Willard Patton, *La Fiesta* (operetta); Thomas Surette, *Priscilla, or The Pilgrim's Proxy* (operetta).

**Orchestra/Band**   Johann H. Beck, *Scherzo No. 2 for Orchestra*; George F. Bristow, *Overture, Jibbenainosay, Opus 64*; Victor Herbert, *Serenade for Strings, Opus 12*; John Philip Sousa, *Marches—The Picador—Quilting Party—The Thunderer—Washington Post*.

**Piano/Organ**   Amy Beach, *Valse-caprice for Piano, Opus 4*; Arthur H. Bird, *Theme and Variations, Opus 27—Four Romances, Opus 29*; Henry H. Huss, *Three Bagatelles*; Horace Nicholl, *Eight Character Pieces, Opus 23* (four hands).

**Symphonies**   Anger Hamerik, *Symphonie Majesteuse in C Major, Opus 35*; Horace Nicholl, *Symphony No. 2 in C Major, Opus 12* (first performance).

# 1890

❋

## Historical Highlights

The census shows a population of 62,980,000; Idaho and Wyoming become the 43rd and 44th states, respectively; the last major Indian war, Ghost Dance, takes place; Sitting Bull, chief of the Sioux Indians, is killed in South Dakota; Sequoia and Yosemite National Parks are formed; Congress passes the Sherman Antitrust Act and Sherman Silver Purchase Act; Otto von Bismarck resigns as German chancellor.

## World Cultural Highlights

**World Art**   Frederic Leighton, *Psyche's Bath*; Edward Poynter, *The Queen of Sheba Visiting Solomon*; Pierre-Auguste Renoir, *Girl Wiping Her Feet*; Georges Seurat, *Le Chahut*.

**World Literature**   Anatole France, *Thaïs*; Henrik Ibsen, *Hedda Gabler*; Maurice Maeterlinck, *The Intruder*; Leo Tolstoy, *The Kreutzer Sonata*; Oscar Wilde, *The Picture of Dorian Gray*.

**World Music**   Johannes Brahms, *String Quintet No. 2*; Ernest Chausson, *Symphony in B-flat Major*; Antonín Dvořák, *Requiem*; Alexander Glazunov, *Symphony No. 3*; Nicolas Rimsky-Korsakov, *Mlada*.

**Miscellaneous**   The Société Nationale des Beaux-Arts is formed in Paris; the Royal Scottish Academy of Music is founded; births include Naum Gabo, Jacques Ibert, Boris Pasternak, and Franz Werfel; deaths include César Franck, Niels Gade, Vincent Van Gogh (by suicide), and John Newman.

## American Art and Literature Highlights

**Births/Deaths**   Births include art figures Robert Laurent, Stanton Macdonald-Wright, Man Ray, Mark Tobey, and literary figures Katherine G. Biddle, Marc Connelly, H. P. Lovecraft, Christopher Morley, Katherine Anne Porter, and Margaret Widdemer; deaths include artist Thomas Hicks and literary figures George Henry Boker, Dion Boucicault, Oliver Bell Bunce, and John Boyle O'Reilly.

**Art Works**   John G. Brown, *Tuckered Out—The Shoeshine Boy*; Arthur B. Davies, *Erie Canal*; Thomas Eakins, *The Bohemian*; Henry F. Farny, *Indian Camp*; William Harnett, *The Faithful Colt*; Thomas Hovenden, *Breaking Home Ties*; John F. Peto, *Still Life with Lanterns* (?); Frederic Remington, *The Buffalo Hunt*; Edmund Stewardson, *The Bather*; John Twachtman, *Along the River, Winter* (?).

**Literature**   Katharine Bates, *Sunshine and Other Verses for Children*; Emily Dickinson, *Poems I*; Eugene Field, *A Little Book of Profitable Tales*; Clyde Fitch, *Beau Brummell*; James A. Herne, *Margaret Fleming*; Henry James, *The Tragic Muse*; Silas W. Mitchell, *A Psalm of Deaths and Other Poems*; Richard Stoddard, *The Lion's Cub: With Other Verse*; Lydia L. A. Very, *Poems and Prose Writings*.

## Music — The Vernacular/Commercial Scene

**A. Births**   Freddie Keppard (cornetist/bandleader) February 27; Fate Marable (pianist/band-leader), December 2; Jelly Roll Morton (pianist/composer) October 20; Paul Pratt (ragtime pianist) November 1; Victor Schertzinger (composer) April 8; Harry Tierney (songwriter) May 21; Paul Whiteman (bandleader) March 28.

**B. Deaths**   Horace Weston (folk banjo) May 22.

**D. Publications**   Alfred A. Farland, *Banjo Method*.

**E. Representative Works**

**Musicals**   David Braham and Ned Harrigan, *Reilly and the 400*; Joseph K. Emmett, *Fritz in a Madhouse*; Gustave Kerker, *Castles in the Air*; Reginald De Koven and H. B. Smith, *Robin Hood*; Woolson Morse, *The Merry Monarch*.

**Songs**   David Braham and Ned Harrigan, *Maggie Murphy's Home*; John W. Kelly, *Throw Him Down McCloskey*; Charles Lawler and J. Thornton, *The Irish Jubilee*; Woolson Morse and J. C. Goodwin, *Love Will Find a Way*; Michael Nolan, *Little Annie Rooney*; James Thornton, *Remember Poor Mother at Home*.

## Music — The Cultivated/Art Music Scene

**F. Births**   Joseph W. Clokey (organist/composer) August 28; Carl Hugo Grimm (organist/com-poser) October 31; John Tasker Howard (writer/composer) November 30; Philip James (compos-er/conductor) May 17; Walter Kramer (critic/publisher/composer) September 23; Kathleen Lockhart Manning (composer) October 24; Harold C. Morris (pianist/composer) March 17; Lee Pattison (pianist) July 22; Paul Rosenfeld (critic/author) May 4; Gustave Schirmer III (publisher) December 29; Edwin John Stringham (composer/educator) July 11; Powell Weaver (organist/pianist/composer) June 10; George A. Wedge (organist/author) January 15.

**G. Deaths**   John W. Dadmun (hymn composer) May 6; Otto Dresel (pianist/conductor) July 26; Stephen T. Gordon (music publisher); John Hill Hewitt (poet/composer) October 7; Benjamin Franklin Quinby (brass instrument maker) July 9; Samuel Parkman Tuckerman (organist/compos-er) June 30.

**H. Debuts**

**United States**   Andrew Black (Scottish baritone—tour), Marie Goetze (German contralto—New York), Gerhard Stehmann (St. Louis).

**Metropolitan Opera**   Andreas Dippel (German tenor), Heinrich Gudehus (German tenor), Antonia Mielke (German soprano), Francesco Tamagno (Italian tenor), Heinrich Vogl (German tenor).

**I. New Positions**

**Conductors**   Henry T. Gleck (Harlem Philharmonic Society).

**Educational**   Carl Faelten (director, New England Conservatory); Leopold Godowsky (New York College of Music—to 1895); Percy Goetschius (professor of music history/theory, Syracuse University—to 1892); Constantin Sternberg (director, Sternberg School of Music—to 1924).

**Other**   George W. Chadwick (director, Springfield Festival); Philip Hale (music critic, *Boston Post*).

### J. Honors and Awards

**Honors**   John Knowles Paine (PhD, Yale).

**K. Biographical**   Louis Coerne goes to Munich for two years to study with Rheinberger; Alma Gluck's family leaves Romania for the United States; Percy Goetschius returns to the United States; Hugo Leichtentritt (Polish musicologist/critic) comes to the United States; Adolf Philipp (German composer/singer) is brought to the United States to sing operetta in the Amberg Theater in New York; Gustav Strube (German composer/conductor) comes to the United States and joins the Boston Symphony Orchestra.

### L. Musical Beginnings

**Performing Groups**   Denver Choral Society; Harlem Philharmonic Society; San Francisco Musical Club.

**Educational**   Hartford School of Music (Conservatory); North Texas State University School of Music; Sternberg School of Music (Philadelphia).

**Other**   Legg Brothers Music Store and Publications (Kansas City), Lorenz Publishing Co. (Dayton, Ohio); Marquam Grand Theater (Portland, Oregon); *Music Trades*; *Organ*; Frederick A. Stokes Co., Publisher (New York); James D. Vaughan, Gospel Publisher; Virgil Practice Clavier Co. (New York).

### M. Music Publications

*Hymns and Tunes for Public and Private Worship and Sunday School Songs* (Mennonite)
Apthorp, W. F. and Champlin, J. D., eds., *Cyclopedia of Music and Musicians*
Elson, Louis C., *The Theory of Music*
Mathews, William, *Primer of Musical Forms*
Sousa, John P., *National, Patriotic and Typical Airs of All Countries*
Vaughan, James D., *Gospel Chimes*

### N. Musical Compositions

**Chamber Music**   Arthur Foote, *Piano Quartet in C Major, Opus 23*; Ottakar Novácek, *String Quartet No. 1*.

**Choral/Vocal**   Amy Beach, *Mass in E-Flat Major, Opus 5—Songs of the Sea: A Canadian Boat Song, Opus 10*; Victor Herbert, *Die Versunkenen, Opus 20* (song); Henry H. Huss, *Ave Maria, Opus 4*; Edwin A. Jones, *Easter Concert, Opus 28* (oratorio); William Kirkpatrick, *He Hideth My Soul* (hymn); Edward MacDowell, *Six Love Songs, Opus 40*; Horatio Parker, *The Kobolds, Opus 21* (cantata)—*Magnificat in E-Flat Major*; J. C. D. Parker, *St. John* (cantata); George F. Root, *Florens, the Pilgrim* (cantata)—*Jacob and Esau* (cantata).

**Concertos**   Arthur H. Bird, *Romance for Violin and Chamber Orchestra*; Richard Burmeister, *Piano Concerto* (premiere); Charles M. Loeffler, *Les Veillées de l'Ukraine* (violin and orchestra).

**Operas**   Gustav Hinrichs, *Onti-Ora*; Humphrey Stewart, *His Majesty*.

**Orchestra/Band**   Arthur H. Bird, *Little Suite III, "Souvenirs of Summer Saturdays," Opus 32*; Carl Busch, *Orchestral Suite No. 1*; Arthur Foote, *Francesca da Rimini, Opus 24* (symphonic prologue); Horatio Parker, *Overture, Count Robert of Paris, Opus 24b*; Henry Schoenefeld, *Suite caractéristique* (strings); John Philip Sousa, *Marches—Corcoran Cadets—High School Cadets—Loyal Legion*.

**Piano/Organ**   Arthur H. Bird, *Seven Pieces, Opus 31, 33*; George F. Bristow, *Marche-Caprice, Opus 51*; Edward MacDowell, *Twelve Etudes, Opus 39*; Ethelbert Nevin, *Three Duets, Opus 4—Four Pieces, Opus 7*; Horatio Parker, *Four Organ Compositions, Opus 17—Four Sketches, Opus 19*.

# 1891

❄

## Historical Highlights

The US Court of Appeals is formed; protesting farmers in Ohio, unhappy with regular politics, form the Populist Party; the International Copyright Law is passed by Congress; William Morrison develops the electric car; Yellowstone National Park is established; the United States of Brazil is formed in South America; work begins on the Trans-Siberian railroad (finished in 1917).

## World Cultural Highlights

**World Art**   Philip Calderon, *Renunciation of St. Elizabeth*; Paul Cézanne, *The Card Players*; Paul Gauguin, *Hail Mary*; Claude Monet, *Haystacks*; Henri de Toulouse-Latrec, *At the Moulin Rouge*.

**World Literature**   James Barrie, *The Little Minister*; Arthur Conan Doyle, *The Adventures of Sherlock Holmes*; Rudyard Kipling, *The Light That Failed*; George du Maurier, *Peter Ibbetson*.

**World Music**   Johannes Brahms, *Clarinet Quintet*; Antonín Dvořák, *Carnaval Overture*; Pietro Mascagni, *L'amico Fritz*; Alexander Scriabin, *Symphony No. 1*; Hugo Wolf, *Italienisches Liederbuch*.

**Miscellaneous**   The Vancouver Opera House, the Zurich Opera Co. and House are opened; births include Jean Cocteau, Max Ernst, Pär Lagerkvist, Jacques Lipchitz, and Sergei Prokofiev; deaths include Pedro de Alarcón, Léo Delibes, Ernest Meissonier, Arthur Rimbaud, and Georges Seurat.

## American Art and Literature Highlights

**Births/Deaths**   Births include artists Edwin and Preston Dickinson, Karl Knaths, and literary figures Margaret Banning, Sidney Howard, Zora Neale Hurston, Henry Miller, and Anne Nichols; deaths include artist Jervis McEntee and literary figures James Russell Lowell, Herman Melville, and Albert Pike.

**Art Works**   Daniel French, *Angel of Death and the Sculptor*; Winslow Homer, *Huntsman and Dogs*; George Inness, *Early Autumn, Montclair*; John La Farge, *Maua, Our Boatman*; Albert Ryder, *Siegfried and the Rhinemaidens*; Augustus Saint-Gaudens, *Adams Memorial*; Frederick J. Sykes, *In the Catskills*; Edmund Tarbell, *In the Orchard*; Abbott Thayer, *Virgin Enthroned*; Julian A. Weir, *The Open Book*.

**Literature**   Katharine Bates, *Hermit Island*; Richard Davis, *Gallegher and Other Stories*; Emily Dickinson, *Poems II*; Edward Eggleston, *The Faith Doctor*; Mary Wilkins Freeman, *A New England Nun and Other Stories*; Hamlin Garland, *Main-Travelled Roads*; William D. Howells, *Criticism and Fiction*; Thomas A. Janvier, *Stories of Old New Spain*; Walt Whitman, *Good-bye, My Fancy*.

## Music—The Vernacular/Commercial Scene

**A. Births**   Fannie Brice (singer/actress) October 29; A. P. Carter (singer) April 15; Grant Clarke (lyricist) May 14; Con Conrad (composer) June 18; Al Dubin (lyricist) June 10; James P. Johnson (pianist/composer) February 1; Cole Porter (composer) June 9; Blossom Seeley (singer/dancer) July 16; Richard Whiting (composer) November 12.

**B. Deaths**   Charley White (minstrel/manager) January 4; Cool White (minstrel) April 23.

**D. Publications**   George Root, *The Story of a Musical Life: An Autobiography*.

**E. Representative Works**

**Musicals**   David Braham and Ned Harrigan, *The Last of the Hogans*; Percy Gaunt, *A Trip to Chinatown*; Adam Itzel and H. B. Smith, *The Tar and the Tartar*; George H. Jessop and H. Townsend, *Mavourneen*; Woolson Morse and J. C. Goodwin, *Wang*.

**Songs**   Anonymous, *Ta-ra-ra-boom-de-É*; Harry Bulger and J. S. Matthews, *Hey, Rube!*; Paul Dresser, *The Pardon That Came Too Late*; Charles Graham, *The Picture That's Turned to the Wall*;

Charles K. Harris, *Kiss and Let's Make Up*; Woolson Morse and J. C. Goodwin, *Ask the Man in the Moon—A Pretty Girl*; William J. Scanlan, *Molly O!*

## Music—The Cultivated/Art Music Scene

**F. Births**  Richard F. Donovan (organist/conductor) November 29; Samuel Gardner (Russian-born violinist/composer) August 25; Frederick Jacobi (composer/conductor) May 4; Karl L. King (bandmaster/composer) February 21; Florence Macbeth (soprano) January 12; Joseph Maddy (music educator) October 14; Guy Maier (pianist/educator) August 15; Timothy Spelman (composer) January 21; John Charles Thomas (baritone) September 6; Adolph Weiss (composer/bassoonist) September 12.

**G. Deaths**  Emma Abbott (soprano/impresario) January 5; Joseph Atwill (music publisher); Harvey B. Dodsworth (bandmaster/publisher); Stephen A. Emery (composer) April 15; John Henry Hopkins (clergyman/hymn writer) August 13; Frédéric L. Ritter (German-born conductor/composer) July 4; Eben Tourjée (organist/conductor/educator) April 12.

**H. Debuts**

**United States**  Joseph Breil (tenor—New York), Adolf Brodsky (violinist—New York), Ferruccio Busoni (Italian pianist—New York), Emma Eames (soprano—Chicago), Arthur Friedheim (German pianist—New York), Ferruccio Giannini (Italian tenor—Boston), Vladimir de Pachmann (Russian pianist—tour), Ignace Jan Paderewski (Polish pianist—New York), Franz Xavier Scharwenka (Polish pianist—New York), Marie Van Zandt (Chicago).

**Metropolitan Opera**  Emma Albani (British soprano), Mathilde Bauermeister (German soprano), Edouard De Reske (Polish bass), Jean De Reske (Polish tenor), Emma Eames (soprano), Minnie Hauk (soprano), Selma Kronold (Polish soprano), Lillian Nordica (soprano), Marie Van Zandt (soprano).

**Other**  David Bispham (baritone—London).

**I. New Positions**

**Conductors**  Anton Seidl (New York Philharmonic Orchestra—to 1898); Theodore Thomas (Chicago Symphony Orchestra—to 1904).

**Educational**  Ferruccio Busoni (piano, New England Conservatory—to 1894); Henry Charles Lahee (secretary, New England Conservatory); Henry S. Perkins (director, Chicago National College of Music—to 1914).

**Other**  Richard Aldrich (music critic, *New York Tribune*—to 1901); Maurice Grau (manager, Metropolitan Opera—to 1903); Philip Hale (music critic, *Boston Journal*—to 1903); James G. Huneker (music critic, *New York Recorder*).

**K. Biographical**  Theodore Baker returns to the United States and goes to work for G. Schirmer; Adolf Brodsky (Russian violinist) comes to the United States and becomes concertmaster of the New York Symphony Orchestra; Platon Brounoff (Russian composer/conductor) comes to the United States; Ferruccio Busoni begins a three-year stay in the United States; Emma Eames makes her Covent Garden debut; Leopold Godowsky becomes an American citizen; Philip Goepp quits law practice and devotes himself to music; Bruno Huhn (British pianist/conductor) comes to the United States; Hugo Leichtentritt and Daniel G. Mason enter Harvard; Ethelbert Nevin moves to Paris; Carl E. Seashore graduates with a BA degree from Gustavus Adolphus College; Charles S. Skilton goes to Berlin for further music study; Peter Tchaikovsky visits the United States and conducts at the opening of Carnegie Hall.

**L. Musical Beginnings**

**Performing Groups**  Amphion Glee Club (Washington, DC); Chicago Symphony Orchestra; Cleveland Singer's Club.

**Festivals**  Fiesta San Jacinto (San Antonio).

**Educational**  Scharwenka Conservatory, New York Branch; Strassberger's Conservatory of Music (St. Louis); University of Kansas School of Fine Arts; University of Washington School of

Music; Virgil Practice Clavier School (New York).

**Other**  Carnegie Hall (New York); Ladies Musical Club (Seattle); *Music* (to 1902); *The Musical Messenger: A Monthly Magazine* (Cincinnati—to 1917).

### M. Music Publications

Aikin, Jesse B., *The True Principles of the Science of Music*
*The Church Hymnary* (Dutch Reformed)
Elson, Louis C., *European Reminiscences, Musical and Otherwise*
Henderson, William J., *Preludes and Studies*
Krehbiel, Henry E., *Studies in the Wagnerian Drama*
Mathews, W. S. B., *A Popular History of the Art of Music*
Ritter, Frédéric, *Music in Its Relation to Intellectual Life*
Tapper, Thomas, *The Music Life*

### N. Musical Compositions

**Chamber Music**  Charles Martin Loeffler, *String Sextet* (?); Ethelbert Nevin, *Melody and Habanera, Opus 8* (violin and piano); Arthur B. Whiting, *Violin Sonata*.

**Choral/Vocal**  Homer Bartlett, *The Last Chieftain* (cantata); Amy Beach, *Festival Jubilate, Opus 17—Three Songs, Opus 2—Four Songs, Opus 14*; Arthur H. Bird, *Frau Holde, Opus 30* (song cycle); J. F. Bridges, *The Repentance of Nineveh* (oratorio); Dudley Buck, *Bugle Song—The Story of the Cross* (cantata); George W. Chadwick, *The Pilgrims—Phoenix Expirans* (cantatas); Caryl Florio, *The Night at Bethlehem* (cantata); Arthur Foote, *The Skeleton in Armor, Opus 28*; Victor Herbert, *Der Gefangene (The Captive)* (cantata); Edward MacDowell, *Two Northern Songs, Opus 43*; Ethelbert Nevin, *Five Songs, Opus 12*; Horatio Parker, *Dream King and His Love* (National Conservatory Prize)—*Twelve Songs, Opus 22, 23, 24—Te Deum in A Major*; Silas G. Pratt, *The Inca's Farewell* (cantata).

**Concertos**  Arthur H. Bird, *Variations on an American Folksong, Opus 34* (flute and orchestra); Victor Herbert, *Fantasy on a Schubert Theme for Cello and Orchestra*; Harry B. Shelley, *Concerto for Violin and Orchestra*.

**Orchestra/Band**  Arthur Foote, *Serenade, Opus 25* (strings); Edgar S. Kelley, *Prometheus Bound, Opus 16* (incidental music); Edward MacDowell, *Suite No. 1 in A Minor, Opus 42*; F. W. Meacham, *American Patrol*.

**Piano/Organ**  Arthur H. Bird, *Album Leaf and Scherzando, Opus 35*; Charles Ives, *Variations on "America"* (organ); Edgar S. Kelley, *Three Pieces, Opus 2* (arranged for string orchestra, 1912); Ethelbert Nevin, *Water Scenes, Opus 13*; Horatio Parker, *Six Lyrics for Piano, Opus 25—Eight Organ Pieces, Opus 20, 28*.

**Symphonies**  William W. Gilchrist, *Symphony No. 1 in C Major*; Asger Hamerik, *Symphonie Sérieuse in G Minor, Opus 36*.

# 1892

☀

## Historical Highlights

Grover Cleveland is elected for a second nonconsecutive term, making him the 24th as well as the 22nd president; Charles Duryea and Henry Ford both enter the auto manufacturing business; the adding machine is patented by W. S. Burroughs; the General Electric Co. is incorporated; Rudolph Diesel patents the diesel engine; William Gladstone begins his last term as British Prime Minister.

## World Cultural Highlights

**World Art**  Thomas Clarke, *Night Market, Morocco*; Georges Rouault, *Job and His Friends*; Henri de Toulouse-Lautrec, *At the Moulin Rouge, 1892*; George Watts, *Sic Transit*.

**World Literature**   Henrik Ibsen, *The Master Builder*; Rudyard Kipling, *The Naulakha*; Maurice Maeterlinck, *Pelléas et Mélisande*; Oscar Wilde, *Lady Windermere's Fan*; Émile Zola, *La Débacle*.

**World Music**   Johannes Brahms, *Piano Works, Opus 117–119*; Antonín Dvořák, *Othello*; Ruggiero Leoncavallo, *I Pagliacci*; Jean Sibelius, *En Saga—Kullervo*; Peter Tchaikovsky, *The Nutcracker*.

**Miscellaneous**   The Barcewicz (Warsaw), the Bohemian (Prague), and the Parent (Paris) String Quartets are formed; births include Richard Aldington, Arthur Honegger, Darius Milhaud, Osbert Sitwell, and J. R. R. Tolkien; deaths include Friedrich von Bodenstedt, Alfred Lord Tennyson, and Albert Wolff.

## American Art and Literature Highlights

**Births/Deaths**   Births include artists Robert Coffin, Louis Lozowick, Grant Wood, and literary figures Pearl Buck, James M. Cain, Frederick Fause (Max Brand), Will James, Archibald MacLeish, Edna St. Vincent Millay, and Ruth Suckow; deaths include art figures William Harnett, Randolph Rogers, and literary figures Christopher Cranch, Thomas Parsons, Walt Whitman, and John Greenleaf Whittier.

**Art Works**   George Barnard, *Brotherly Love*; William Chase, *Pulling for Shore*; Irving Couse, *The Captive*; Thomas Eakins, *Concert Singer*; Daniel French, *Republic*; John Haberle, *The Bachelor's Drawer* (?); William Harnett, *Old Models*; George Inness, *A Pool in the Woods*; Homer D. Martin, *Honfleur Light*; Thomas Moran, *Mist in Kanab Canyon, Utah*; Augustus Saint-Gaudens, *Diana*.

**Literature**   Eugene Field, *With Trumpet and Drum*; Sam Walter Foss, *Back Country Poems*; Hamlin Garland, *Jason Edwards*; Joel Chandler Harris, *Uncle Remus and His Friends*; Constance Harrison, *A Daughter of the South*; Lucy Larcom, *The Unseen Friend*; Edna D. Proctor, *Songs of the Ancient People*; Agnes Repplier, *Essays in Miniature*; Mark Twain, *The American Claimant*.

## Music—The Vernacular/Commercial Scene

**A. Births**   Fred E. Ahlert (composer) September 19; Eddie Cantor (singer/actor) January 31; Harry Carroll (composer) November 28; Mort Dixon (lyricist) March 20; Johnny Dodds (clarinet) April 12; Jack Donohue (singer/dancer); Pops Foster (string bass) May 18; James Hanley (composer/lyricist) February 17; Ted Lewis (clarinetist/bandleader) June 6; Lillian Lorraine (singer/actress) January 1; John Jacob Niles (folk singer/collector) April 28; Charlie Poole (banjo/bandleader) March 22; Speckled Red (singer/pianist) October 23; J. Russel Robinson (pianist/composer) July 8; V. O. Stamps (publisher) September 18; Jimmie Tarlton (singer) May 8; Roy Turk (lyricist) September 20; Peggy Wood (singer/actress) February 9; Jack Yellen (lyricist) July 6 (in Poland).

**C. Biographical**

**Performing Groups**   Reliance Brass Band (New Orleans—to 1918).

**New Beginnings**   Union Gospel Tabernacle (Nashville).

**Miscellaneous**   Jean Schwartz (Hungarian composer) comes to the United States.

**E. Representative Works**

**Musicals**   Reginald de Koven and H. B. Smith, *The Fencing Master*; Julian Edwards and H. B. Smith, *Jupiter*; William W. Furst and C. A. Byrne, *The Isle of Champagne*; Edgar S. Kelley and C. M. S. McLellan, *Puritania*.

**Songs**   Harry Dacre, *A Bicycle Built for Two*; Percy Gaunt, *Push Dem Clouds Away*; Fred Gilbert, *The Man That Broke the Bank at Monte Carlo*; Charles K. Harris and H. Kennedy, *Molly and I and the Baby—After the Ball*; Hattie Starr, *Somebody Loves Me*; R. M. Stults, *The Sweetest Story Ever Told*; James Thornton and Harding, *My Sweetheart's the Man in the Moon*.

## Music—The Cultivated/Art Music Scene

**F. Births**   Howard Barlow (conductor) May 1; Samuel Barlow (composer/author) June 1; Sophie Braslau (contralto) August 16; Mario Chamlee (tenor) May 29; Frederic Fradkin (violinist) April 2;

Harold Gleason (organist/musicologist) April 26; Ferde Grofé (composer/arranger) March 27; David Guion (composer) December 15; Charles Haubiel (pianist/composer) January 30; Frances McCollin (composer/conductor) October 24; Radiana Pazmor (contralto) May 12; Carmela Ponselle (mezzo-soprano) June 7; John Donald Robb (composer) June 12.

**G. Deaths**   Alfred Badger (flute maker) November 8; Patrick S. Gilmore (Irish-born bandmaster) September 24; A. N. Johnson (theoretician/publisher) January 1; Henry Christian Timm (German-born conductor/pianist) September 5; James Monroe Trotter (music historian) February 2; Charles A. White (composer/publisher) January 13.

**H. Debuts**

**United States**   Olive Fremstad (soprano—Boston), Martha Leffler-Burckhard (German soprano—tour), José Vianna da Motta (Portuguese pianist—tour).

**Metropolitan Opera**   Luigi Arditi (Italian conductor), Jean Lassalle (French baritone).

**Other**   Frances Saville (soprano—Brussels).

**I. New Positions**

**Conductors**   Francesco Fanciulli (US Marine Band—to 1897); Emil Mollenhauer (Boston Festival Orchestra—to 1914); David W. Reeves (Gilmore Band).

**Educational**   Franz X. Arens (president, Indianapolis College of Music—to 1896); Antonín Dvořák (director, National Conservatory of Music, New York—to 1895); Percy Goetschius (New England Conservatory—to 1896); Martin Röder (voice, New England Conservatory).

**Other**   Theodore Baker (literary editor, G. Schirmer); William Crane Carl (organ, First Presbyterian Church, New York—to 1936); Heinrich Conried (manager, Irving Place Theater, New York).

**K. Biographical**   George Ashdown Audsley (Scottish organist/architect) emigrates to the United States; David Bispham makes his Covent Garden debut; Henry Burleigh enters the National Conservatory in New York; Teresa Carreño marries again, this time to Eugen d'Albert; Giuseppe Ferrata (Italian pianist/composer) emigrates to the United States and settles in New Orleans; Paolo Gallico (Italian pianist/composer) emigrates to the United States and settles in New York; the Metropolitan Opera House is destroyed by fire; Arthur Pryor becomes trombone soloist in Sousa's band; Arthur Shepherd, age 12, is sent to Boston to study at the New England Conservatory; Martinus Sieveking (Dutch pianist) settles in the United States; John Philip Sousa resigns from the Marines to form his own band.

**L. Musical Beginnings**

**Performing Groups**   Lehman String Quartet; Orpheus Club of Oakland (California); People's Choral Union and Singing Classes (New York); Sousa Band; Syracuse Symphony Orchestra Society; Utah Symphony Orchestra (I) (Salt Lake City—to 1930).

**Educational**   Albany College (Lewis and Clark College) Music Department (Oregon); *School Music Review*.

**Other**   Boosey and Co. (Boosey and Hawkes in 1930), New York; Fisher Opera House (San Diego); Charles K. Harris, Music Publisher (New York); Hope Publishing Co. (Chicago); Manuscript Music Society (Philadelphia); Joseph Meyerhoff Symphony Hall (Baltimore); Schirmer's Library of Musical Classics.

**M. Music Publications**

Cheney, Simeon P., *Wood Notes Wild: Notations of Bird Music* (posthumous publication)
Clarke, Hugh A., *Theory Explained*
Elson, Louis C., *The Realm of Music*
Florio, Caryl, *A Textbook of Practical Harmony*
Root, George F., *Root's Harmony and Composition*

**N. Musical Compositions**

**Chamber Music**   Rosetter Gleason Cole, *Violin Sonata in D Major, Opus 8*.

**Choral/Vocal**    Amy Beach, *Eilende Wolken, Segler die Lüfte* (alto and orchestra); Dudley Buck, *Communion Service in C Major—The Story of the Cross—The Triumph of David* (cantatas); George W. Chadwick, *Ode for the Opening of the Chicago World's Fair* (chorus); William Kirkpatrick, *Lord, I'm Coming Home* (gospel song); Ethelbert Nevin, *Three Songs, Opus 17*; John Knowles Paine, *Columbus March and Hymn*; Horatio Parker, *Six Songs, Opus 29*; Silas G. Pratt, *The Triumph of Columbus*; George F. Root, *Columbus, the Hero of Fate—Phyllis, the Farmer's Daughter* (cantatas); George W. Warren, *National Hymn (God of Our Fathers)*.

**Concertos**    Charles E. Hopkins, *Concerto for Piano Trio and Orchestra.*

**Operas**    George W. Chadwick, *The Quiet Lodging*; Julian Edwards, *Jupiter, or The Cobbler and the King*; Adolph Neuendorff, *The Minstrel.*

**Orchestra/Band**    Louis A. Coerne, *Suite in D Minor for Strings*; Victor Herbert, *Irish Rhapsody*; Charles E. Ives, *Three Marches for Band (K. 2–4)*; John Philip Sousa, *Marches—The Belle of Chicago—Homeward Bound—March of the Royal Trumpets—On Parade (The Lion Tamer)—The Triton—Songs of Grace and Songs of Glory* (fantasy for band); Frederick Zech, Jr., *Concert Overture.*

**Piano/Organ**    Amy Beach, *Four Sketches, Opus 15*; Louis A. Coerne, *Organ Concerto in E Major*; Edward MacDowell, *Sonata No. 1, Opus 45, "Tragica"*; Ethelbert Nevin, *In Arcady, Opus 16—Two Etudes, Opus 18.*

**Symphonies**    George T. Strong, *Symphony No. 3, "Sintram."*

# 1893

❀

## Historical Highlights

Another financial panic ushers in a four-year depression; Sears, Roebuck and Co. is founded; the Columbian Exposition is held in Chicago, where the ferris wheel is introduced—the Field Museum of Natural History opens as part of the Exposition; Hawaii becomes a republic—the first treaty for United States annexation is withdrawn; New Zealand becomes the first country to grant women suffrage.

## World Cultural Highlights

**World Art**    Paul Gauguin, *Annah, the Javanese Girl*; Hermann Knackfuss, *The Holy Family*; Constantin Meunier, *Longshoreman*; Edvard Munch, *The Scream*; Georges Rouault, *Ordeal of Samson.*

**World Literature**    Arthur Conan Doyle, *Memoirs of Sherlock Holmes*; Stéphane Mallarmé, *Vers et Prose*; Arthur Pinero, *The Second Mrs. Tanqueray*; Robert Louis Stevenson, *David Balfour.*

**World Music**    Antonín Dvořák, *New World Symphony*; Engelbert Humperdinck, *Hansel und Gretel*; Jean Sibelius, *Swan of Tuonela*; Peter Tchaikovsky, *Symphony No. 6, "Pathetique"*; Giuseppe Verdi, *Falstaff.*

**Miscellaneous**    The Munich Philharmonic Orchestra is formed; Queen's Hall opens in London; births include George Grosz, Joan Miró, Wilfred Owen, and Andrés Segovia; deaths include Charles Gounod, Guy de Maupassant, Aleksei Plescheyev, and Peter Ilich Tchaikovsky.

## American Art and Literature Highlights

**Births/Deaths**    Births include artists Milton Avery, Charles Burchfield, and literary figures Faith Baldwin, S. N. Behrman, Nella Larsen, Anita Loos, J. P. Marquand, Charles F. Oursler, and Dorothy Parker; deaths include artists Karl Bodmer, John Casilear, and literary figures Edwin L. Bynner, Henry C. DeMille, Lucy Larcom, and Elizabeth Oakes Smith.

**Art Works**    Herbert Adams, *Primavera*; Albert Bierstadt, *Landing of Columbus*; George Barnard,

*The Struggle of the Two Natures in Man*; Charles Grafly, *Aeneas and Anchises*; Winslow Homer, *The Fox Hunt*; George Inness, *The Home of the Heron*; Frederick MacMonnies, *Barge of State (Columbian Exposition)*; Bela L. Pratt, *The Genius of Navigation*; Henry O. Tanner, *The Banjo Lesson*.

**Literature**    Stephen Crane, *Maggie: A Girl of the Streets*; Paul L. Dunbar, *Oak and Ivy*; Henry Fuller, *The Cliff-Dwellers*; Hamlin Garland, *Prairie Folks*; Edward E. Hale, *A New England Boyhood*; William D. Howells, *The World of Chance*; Henry James, *The Real Thing and Other Tales*; Sarah Orne Jewett, *A Native of Winby and Other Stories*; Silas W. Mitchell, *The Mother and Other Tales*.

## Music — The Vernacular/Commercial Scene

**A. Births**    Milton Ager (composer) October 6; Big Bill Broonzy (singer) June 26; Perry "Mule" Bradford (pianist/composer) February 14; Lew Brown (lyricist) December 10; Bo Carter (singer) March 21; Elizabeth "Libba" Cotten (singer/guitarist); Walter Donaldson (composer/lyricist); Cliff Friend (composer) October 1; Walter "Furry" Lewis (guitarist) March 6; Charles "Lucky" Roberts (pianist/composer) August 7; Ernest "Pop" Stoneman (banjoist/harmonicist) May 25; Harry Warren (songwriter) December 24.

**B. Deaths**    James Pierpont (songwriter).

**C. Biographical**

**Performing Groups**    Forty Whites and Thirty Blacks (Primrose and West Minstrel Group).

**New Beginnings**    Colonial Theater (Boston); Empire Theater (New York).

**Miscellaneous**    Adolf Philipp leaves the Amberg company and begins producing musical comedies at the Germania Theater in New York.

**E. Representative Works**

**Musicals**    David Braham and Ned Harrigan, *The Woolen Stockings*; Reginald De Koven and G. MacDonough, *The Knickerbockers—The Algerian*; Julian Edwards, *King Rene's Daughter*; William W. Furst and C. A. Byrne, *Princess Nicotine*; May Irwin, *A Country Sport*; Carl Plueger and E. E. Rice, *1492*.

**Songs**    Gussie L. Davis and W. H. Windom, *The Fatal Wedding*; Harry and John Dillon, *Do, Do, My Huckleberry Do*; Charles Graham, *Two Little Girls in Blue*; Patty and Mildred Hill, *Good Morning to All (Happy Birthday to You)*; Edward B. Marks and W. Lorraine, *December and May*; Hattie Starr, *Little Alabama Coon*; Fred Stone, *My Ragtime Baby*; Joseph Tabrar, *Daddy Wouldn't Buy Me a Bow-Wow*; Theodore Tobani, *Hearts and Flowers*; Arthur West, *See, Saw, Margery Daw*.

## Music — The Cultivated/Art Music Scene

**F. Births**    Martha Graham (dancer) Pittsburgh; Elliot Griffes (pianist/composer) January 28; Michel Gusikoff (violinist/composer) May 15; Edwin F. Kalmus (publisher) December 15; Douglas Moore (composer) August 10; Bernard Rogers (composer) February 4.

**G. Deaths**    John S. Dwight (writer on music) September 5; Julius Eichberg (German-born violinist/composer) January 19; Gustav Schirmer (German-born publisher) August 6; Horace Waters (publisher).

**H. Debuts**

**United States**    Richard Burmeister (pianist—New York), Giuseppe Campanari (Italian baritone—New York), Benjamin Davies (British tenor—Chicago), Harry P. Greene (Irish bass-baritone—tour), Vilhelm Herold (Danish tenor—Chicago), Alberto Jonás (Spanish pianist—New York), Henri Marteau (French violinist—tour), Alice Nielsen (soprano—Oakland), Maurice Renaud (French baritone—New Orleans), Josef Slivinski (Polish pianist—New York).

**Metropolitan Opera**    Mario Ancona (Italian baritone), Sigrid Arnoldson (Swedish soprano), Enrico Bevignani (Italian conductor), Emma Calvé (French soprano), Armand Castelmary (French bass-baritone), Ruth Lynda Deyo (age 9, Chicago), Luigi Mancinelli (Italian conductor), Nellie Melba (Australian soprano), Pol Plançon (French bass), Francisco Vignas (Spanish tenor).

**Other**   Lillian Blauvelt (soprano—Brussels).

## I. New Positions

**Conductors**   Francesco Fanciulli (US Marine Band—to 1898); Victor Herbert (22nd Regiment Band); Emil Paur (Boston Symphony Orchestra—to 1898).

**Educational**   Edward Dickinson (music history, Oberlin); Ferdinand Dunkley (St. Agnes' School, Albany); Daniel B. Towner (music head, Moody Bible Institute).

**Other**   Charles E. Ives (organ, St. Thomas Episcopal Church, New Haven); Edgar S. Kelley (music critic, *San Francisco Examiner*); Horatio Parker (organ/choir, Trinity Church, Boston—to 1902).

**K. Biographical**   Amy Beach hears her *Festival Jubilate* in its premiere at the Chicago Fair; Frederick S. Converse graduates with a B.A. degree from Harvard; Antonín Dvořák discovers the Bohemian colony in Spillsville, Iowa; Arthur Farwell graduates with a degree in engineering; Otto Kahn (German-born art patron) comes to the United States; Margaret Ruthven Lang becomes the first American woman to have a work (*Dramatic Overture*) performed by a major orchestra, the Boston Symphony Orchestra; Ethelbert Nevin suffers a nervous breakdown; Emil Oberhoffer becomes an American citizen; Fritz Scheel (German violinist/conductor) emigrates to the United States; Bertram Shapleigh receives an MD degree but becomes a lecturer on the arts.

## L. Musical Beginnings

**Performing Groups**   Amphion Club (San Diego); Brooklyn Oratorio Society; Madison Choral Union (University of Wisconsin); Newark Symphony Orchestra; St. Louis Amateur Orchestra (Philharmonic Society III).

**Educational**   University of Oklahoma Department of Music.

**Other**   Gray's Armory (Cleveland); King Musical Instrument Co. (Cleveland); North Tonawanda Barrel Organ Works (DeKleist Musical Instrument Co.); Stein Organ Works (New York); Wednesday Club of Richmond (Virginia).

## M. Music Publications

Rogers, Clara K., *The Philosophy of Singing*
Sherwood, W. Henry, *The Harp of Zion*

## N. Musical Compositions

**Chamber Music**   Louis A. Coerne, *String Quartet in C Minor, Opus 19*; Arthur Foote, *String Quartet No. 2 in E Major, Opus 32*; Victor Herbert, *Mélodie for Cello and Piano*.

**Choral/Vocal**   Amy Beach, *Six Songs, Opus 19, 21*; George W. Chadwick, *The Lily Nymph* (cantata); Edward MacDowell, *Eight Songs, Opus 47*; Horatio Parker, *Hora Novissima, Opus 30* (oratorio)—*The Holy Child, Opus 37* (cantata) —*Seven Choruses for Male Voices, Opus 33, 39—Three Songs, Opus 34*; George F. Root, *The Festival of the Flowers* (cantata); Harry R. Shelley, *Vexilla regis* (cantata).

**Concertos**   Amy Beach, *Romance for Violin and Piano, Opus 23*; Arthur Foote, *Concerto for Cello and Orchestra, Opus 33*; Victor Herbert, *Fantasia for Violin and Orchestra*; Charles M. Loeffler, *Morceau fantastique* (cello and orchestra); Ethelbert Nevin, *A Book of Songs, Opus 20*.

**Operas**   Harry L. Freeman, *The Martyr*; George E. Whiting, *Lenora*.

**Orchestra/Band**   Amy Beach, *Bal masqué*; Louis Coerne, *Hiawatha*; Victor Herbert, *The Vision of Columbus*; Margaret R. Lang, *Dramatic Overture, Opus 12* (first performance)—*Witichis Overture*; Harry R. Shelley, *Carnival Overture*; John Philip Sousa, *The Last Days of Pompeii* (suite)—*The Salute of the Nations* (band fantasy)—*Marches—The Beau Ideal—Liberty Bell—Manhattan Beach*.

**Piano/Organ**   George F. Bristow, *School March, Opus 63*; Horatio Parker, *Five Sketches for Organ, Opus 32—Four Organ Pieces, Opus 36*.

**Symphonies**    George F. Bristow, *Niagara Symphony* (soloists, chorus, and orchestra); Henry Schoenefeld, *Symphony No. 1, "Rural"* (National Conservatory Prize).

# 1894

✸

## Historical Highlights

Jacob Coxey leads an army of the unemployed in a march on Washington, DC; a bitter Pullman strike spreads; a graduated income tax law is passed by Congress; Labor Day becomes an official government holiday; a Chinese Exclusion Treaty is signed with China; the first Sunday comics are printed; the United Daughters of the Confederacy is formed; the Sino-Japanese War begins.

## World Cultural Highlights

**World Art**    Claude Monet, *Rouen Cathedral, Early Morning*; Philip Steer, *Girls Running on Walberick Pier*; Édouard Vuillard, *Jardin de Paris*.

**World Literature**    Anthony Hawkins, *The Prisoner of Zenda*; Rudyard Kipling, *Jungle Book*; George du Maurier, *Trilby*; Edmund Rostand, *Les Romanesques*; George Bernard Shaw, *Arms and the Man*.

**World Music**    Anton Bruckner, *Symphony No. 9*; Claude Debussy, *Prélude à l'après-midi d'un faune*; Gabriel Fauré, *Dolly*; Gustav Mahler, *Resurrection Symphony*; Carl Nielsen, *Symphony No. 1*.

**Miscellaneous**    The Toronto Mendelssohn Choir is formed; the Heidelberg Conservatory of Music opens; births include Karl Böhm, Aldous Huxley, and J. B. Priestley; deaths include Hans von Bülow, Charles de Lisle, Christina Rossetti, Robert Louis Stevenson, and Launt Thompson.

## American Art and Literature Highlights

**Births/Deaths**    Births include artists Stuart Davis, Norman Rockwell, and literary figures E. E. Cummings, Laurence Stallings, James Thurber, Eunice Tietjens, and Mark Van Doren; deaths include art figures William Bartlett, George P. A. Healy, George Inness, Chauncey Ives, Constance Woolson, and literary figures William Gallagher, Oliver Wendell Holmes, and Celia Thaxter.

**Art Works**    Herbert Adams, *Singing Boys*; James Fraser, *End of the Trail*; John Haberle, *Grandma's Hearthstone*; Winslow Homer, *High Cliff, Coast of Maine*; George Inness, *Autumn Landscape*; Frederick MacMonnies, *Bacchante with Infant Faun*; Theodore Robinson, *On the Tow Path*; Abbott H. Thayer, *Florence Protecting the Arts* (?); John Twachtman, *Niagara Falls*.

**Literature**    Kate O'Flaherty Chopin, *Bayou Folk*; Eugene Field, *Love Songs of Childhood*; Mary Wilkins Freeman, *Pembroke*; Hamlin Garland, *Crumbling Idols*; William D. Howells, *A Traveler from Altruria*; Thomas Janvier, *In Old New York*; Agnes Repplier, *In the Dozy Hours*; Celia Thaxter, *An Island Garden*; Mark Twain, *Pudd'nhead Wilson—Tom Sawyer Abroad*.

## Music—The Vernacular/Commercial Scene

**A. Births**    Harry Akst (composer/lyricist) August 15; Roy Bargy (pianist/composer) July 31; Arthur Freed (lyricist) September 9; Herman Hupfeld (composer) February 1; Isham Jones (bandleader) January 31; Ted Koehler (lyricist) July 18; Vincent Lopez (pianist/bandleader) December 30; Jimmy McHugh (composer) July 10; Joseph Meyer (composer) March 12; Bennie Moten (pianist/bandleader) November 13; Willard Robison (singer/writer) September 18; Ada "Bricktop" Smith (singer) August 14; Bessie Smith (singer) April 15; Clara Smith (singer?); Jimmy Yancey (piano?).

**C. Biographical**

**New Beginnings**    Howley, Haviland and Co., Publishers; Whitney-Warner Co. (Jerome H. Remick Co.).

## E. Representative Works

**Musicals**    David Braham and Ned Harrigan, *Notoriety*; Gustave A. Kerker, *Prince Kam, or A Trip to Venus*; George W. Chadwick and R. A. Barnet, *Tabasco*; Julian Edwards and S. Stange, *Madeline, or, The Magic Kiss*; Reginald de Koven and H. B. Smith, *Rob Roy*; Victor Herbert and F. Neilson, *Prince Ananias*; Sydney Jones and H. Greenbank, *A Gaiety Girl*; Woolson Morse, *Dr. Syntax*; Willard Spenser, *The Princess Bonnie*; Thomas P. Thorne and C. M. Greene, *The Maid of Plymouth*; Various composers, *The Passing Show*.

**Songs**    James W. Blake and C. B. Lawler, *The Sidewalks of New York*; George Evans, *I'll Be True to My Honey Boy*; William B. Gray, *She Is More to Be Pitied Than Censured*; Joseph W. Stern and E. B. Marks, *The Little Lost Child*; Helene Mora, *Kathleen*; Felix McGlennon and M. H. Rosenfeld, *And Her Golden Hair Was Hanging Down Her Back*; Anita Owen, *Sweet Bunch of Daisies*; James Thornton, *She May Have Seen Better Days*; Philip Wingate and H. W. Petrie, *I Don't Want to Play in Your Yard — You Can't Play in Our Yard Any More*.

## Music—The Cultivated/Art Music Scene

**F. Births**    Robert Russell Bennett (composer/arranger) June 15; Frank Black (conductor) November 29; Mildred Dilling (harpist/educator) February 23; Merle S. Evans (bandmaster) December 26; Arthur Fiedler (conductor/violinist) December 17; Karl Krueger (conductor) January 19; Jacob Kwalwasser (educator) February 27; Wesley La Violette (composer/educator) January 4; Arthur Loesser (pianist/critic) August 28; Walter Piston (composer/educator) January 20; Carroll Pratt (musicologist/psychologist) April 27; Albert Stoessel (violinist/conductor/composer) October 11; Mark Wessel (composer/pianist) March 26.

**G. Deaths**    Isaac Fiske (brass instrument maker) September 17; Emmy Fürsch-Madi (French soprano) September 19; Eugène F. Oudin (baritone) November 4; John Sage (publisher) April 10; George Stevens (organ builder) August 15.

**H. Debuts**

**United States**    Marie Brema (British contralto—tour), Benno Schönberger (Austrian pianist—tour), Ottilie and Rose Sutro (duo-pianists—New York), César Thomson (Belgian violinist—New York), Eugène Ysaÿe (Belgian violinist—New York).

**Metropolitan Opera**    Giuseppe Campanari (Italian baritone), Fernando De Lucia (Italian tenor), Zélie de Lussan (soprano), Eugenia Mantelli (Italian soprano), Victor Maurel (French baritone).

**Other**    Edyth Walker (mezzo-soprano—Berlin).

**I. New Positions**

**Conductors**    Alfred Ernst (St. Louis Choral Symphony Society—to 1907).

**Educational**    Josef Hofmann (director, Curtis Institute); Alberto Jonás (University of Michigan—to 1898); Horatio Parker (theory, Yale—to 1919); Henry Schradieck (National Conservatory, New York—to 1899); William T. Upton (piano, Oberlin—to 1936); Huntington Woodman (theory, Packer Collegiate Institute—to 1941).

**Other**    Henry T. Burleigh (soloist, St. George's, New York—to 1946).

**K. Biographical**    Ferruccio Busoni leaves the United States and returns permanently to Berlin; Gaston-Marie Déthier (Belgian organist) comes to the United States; Rubin Goldmark, for health reasons, moves from New York to Colorado; H. Willard Gray (British music publisher) comes to the United States as head of Novello, Ewer and Co. in New York; Henry Hadley begins studying music in Vienna; Edward Burlingame Hill graduates with highest honors from Harvard; Hugo Leichtentritt graduates from Harvard and returns to Europe for almost 40 years; Louis Victor Saar (Dutch composer) comes to New York as accompanist at the Metropolitan Opera; Wallace A. Sabin (British organist) emigrates to the United States and settles in San Francisco; Henry Schradieck (German violinist) moves permanently to the United States.

**L. Musical Beginnings**

**Performing Groups**    American Symphony Orchestra; Apollo Club of St. Louis; Damrosch Opera

Co. (by Walter Damrosch); Musical Art Society of New York; New Haven Symphony Orchestra; Maud Powell String Quartet.

**Festivals**   Ann Arbor May Festival.

**Educational**   Lawrence College Conservatory of Music (Wisconsin); Mills College Music Department; Third Street Music School Settlement (New York); University of Wisconsin Music Department; Yale University School of Music.

**Other**   *The Cadenza: A Monthly Journal Devoted to Banjo, Mandolin and Guitar* (to 1924); Foster-Armstrong Piano Co. (Rochester); Hoffman's Music Store, Kansas City Branch; Kansas City Athenaeum; Lyric Theater, Baltimore; Joseph Stern and Co. (Edward B. Marks Co. in 1920).

**M. Music Publications**

Apthorp, William F., *Musicians and Music-Lovers*
Klauser, Karl, *Half Hours with the Best Composers*

**N. Musical Compositions**

**Chamber Music**   Horatio Parker, *String Quintet in D Minor, Opus 38—Suite in E Minor for Violin and Piano, Opus 41.*

**Choral/Vocal**   Henry H. Huss, *Cleopatra's Death*; Charles E. Ives, *Psalm 150—Psalm 67—Psalm 54—Psalm 40* (revised 1924); Horatio Parker, *Two Shakespeare Songs*; J. C. D. Parker, *The Life of Man* (oratorio); Silas G. Pratt, *America* (cantata); George F. Root, *Plough and Sickle* (cantata).

**Concertos**   Victor Herbert, *Concerto No. 1 for Cello and Orchestra, Opus 8—Eldorado* (piano and band); Helen Hopekirk, *Concertstück in D Minor* (piano and orchestra); Henry Huss, *Concerto for Piano and Orchestra*; Charles M. Loeffler, *Divertimento in A Minor, Opus 1* (violin and orchestra)—*Fantastic Concerto* (cello and orchestra).

**Operas**   George F. Bristow, *King of the Mountains* (unfinished); George W. Chadwick, *Tabasco*.

**Orchestra/Band**   George W. Chadwick, *A Pastoral Prelude*; Arthur Farwell, *The Death of Virginia, Opus 4* (symphonic poem); Victor Herbert, *Ice-Water Galop* (band); Charles E. Ives, *Circus Band March*; John Philip Sousa, *The Directorate March*.

**Piano/Organ**   Amy Beach, *Ballad, Opus 6—Three Morceaux caractéristiques, Opus 28*; George F. Bristow, *Plantation Pleasures, Opus 82*; Edele Hohnstock, *Le Diamant: Polka Brillante*; Henry H. Huss, *Three Intermezzi*; Edward MacDowell, *Twelve Virtuoso Etudes, Opus 46*; Ethelbert Nevin, *Mazurka in E-Flat Major*.

**Symphonies**   Amy Beach, *Symphony in E Minor, Opus 32, "Gaelic"*; George W. Chadwick, *Symphony No. 3 in F Major* (National Conservatory Prize).

# 1895

☀

## Historical Highlights

The first auto race takes place between Chicago and Waukegan in Illinois—the average speed is 7$\frac{1}{2}$ m.p.h.; the Boston Subway, first in the nation, opens for service; the Venezuela-British dispute offers the first test to the Monroe Doctrine in the Americas; the Duryea Motor Wagon Co. opens in Massachusetts; Marconi sends the first telegraph message on a one-mile wire; the Lumière Brothers in Paris present the first moving pictures; W. K. Roentgen discovers x-rays.

## World Cultural Highlights

**World Art**   Pierre de Chavannes, *Inspiring Muses and Genius*; Edgar Degas, *Dancer Looking at Her Foot*; Käthe Kollwitz, *Revolt of the Weavers*; Henri Rousseau, *Tiger Hunt*.

**World Literature**   Joseph Conrad, *Almayer's Folly*; Henryk Sienkiewicz, *Quo Vadis?*; H. G. Wells, *The Time Machine*; Oscar Wilde, *The Importance of Being Earnest*.

**World Music**   Antonín Dvořák, *Cello Concerto*; Mikhail Ippolitov-Ivanov, *Caucasian Sketches*; Sergei Rachmaninoff, *Symphony No. 1*; Richard Strauss, *Till Eulenspiegel's Merry Pranks*.

**Miscellaneous**   The Museo Nacional de Bellas Artes founded in Argentina; the Sheffield Music Festivals begin in England; births include Robert Graves, Paul Hindemith, and László Moholy-Nagy; deaths include John Bell, Alexandre Dumas, fils, Thomas Huxley, and Silvestro Lega.

## American Art and Literature Highlights

**Births/Deaths**   Births include artists Adolf Dehn, Abraham Rattner, and literary figures Babette Deutsch, Vardis Fisher, Robert S. Hillyer, Charles MacArthur, and Helen H. Santmyer; deaths include art figures Thomas Hovenden, Peter Rothermel, William W. Story, Leonard Volk, Charles Ward, and literary figures Hjalmar H. Boyesen, Frederick Douglass, Eugene Field, and Charles Etienne Gayarré.

**Art Works**   George De Forest Bush, *Mother and Child*; William M. Chase, *A Friendly Call*; Maria O. Dewing, *Garden in May*; Thomas Dewing, *Music*; Childe Hassam, *The White Dory*; Winslow Homer, *The Northeaster*; Edward Kemeys, *Lions, Chicago Art Museum*; Frederic Remington, *Bronco Buster*; John H. Twachtman, *Snowbound The Rapids, Yellowstone*; J. Alden Weir, *The Red Bridge*.

**Literature**   Winnifred Babcock, *The Old Jinriksha*; Stephen Crane, *The Red Badge of Courage*; Paul L. Dunbar, *Majors and Minors*; Constance Harrison, *An Errant Wooing*; Philip H. Savage, *First Poems and Fragments*; Frank Stockton, *The Adventures of Captain Horn*; Edward Townsend, *A Daughter of the Tenements*; Mary A. Townsend, *Distaff and Spindle*; Henry van Dyke, *Little Rivers*.

## Music—The Vernacular/Commercial Scene

**A. Births**   Irving Aronson (composer/bandleader) February 7; Belle Baker (singer); Irene Bordoni (singer/dancer) January 16; Irving Caesar (lyricist/composer) July 4; Edward "Zez" Confrey (pianist/bandleader) April 3; Jesse Crawford (jazz organist) December 2; Benny Davis (lyricist) August 21; Buddy de Sylva (lyricist) January 27; Cliff Edwards (singer) June 14; Sonny Greer (drummer) December 13; Oscar Hammerstein II (librettist/lyricist) July 12; Alberta Hunter (singer) April 1; Bradley Kincaid (folk singer/bandleader) July 13; Mance Lipscomb (guitarist/fiddler/singer) April 9; William McKinney (drummer/bandleader) September 17; Lizzie Miles (singer) March 31; Jimmy Noone (clarinetist/bandleader) April 23; Andy Razaf (lyricist) December 16; Leo Robin (lyricist) April 6; Harry Ruby (composer/lyricist) January 27; Nat Shilkret (composer/arranger) December 25.

**B. Deaths**   Joseph P. Skelley (Irish-born songwriter) June 23.

**C. Biographical**

**New Beginnings**   Leo Feist, Publisher; Shapiro, Bernstein and Co., Music Publishers (New York).

**E. Representative Works**

**Musicals**   Reginald De Koven and H. B. Smith, *The Tzigane*; Ludwig Englander and J. C. Goodwin, *A Daughter of the Revolution*; William W. Furst and J. C. Cheever, *Fleur-De-Lis*; Victor Herbert and H. B. Smith, *The Wizard of the Nile*; Gustave Kerker and R. F. Carroll, *Kismet*; Edward E. Rice and R. A. Barnet, *Excelsior, Jr.*

**Songs**   George M. Cohan, *Hot Tamale Alley*; Paul Dresser, *Just Tell Them That You Saw Me*; Ben Harney, *You've Been A Good Old Wagon But You Done Broke Down*; W. H. Holmes and C. W. Berkeley, *The Hand That Rocks the Cradle*; John Stromberg, *My Best Girl's a New Yorker*; James Thornton, *Don't Give Up the Old Love for the New*; Charles B. Ward and J. E. Palmer, *The Band Played On*; Safford Waters, *The Belle of Avenoo A*.

**Other**   Kerry Mills, *Rufus on Parade* (cakewalk march).

## Music—The Cultivated/Art Music Scene

**F. Births**   Eddy Brown (violinist) July 15; Ernest Charles (composer) November 21; Granville

English (composer) January 27; Laurens Hammond (electric instrumentalist) January 11; Eva Jessye (conductor/composer) January 20; William Kincaid (flutist) April 26; Albert Hay Malotte (composer) May 19; Carl McKinley (composer/organist) October 9; Moshe Paranov (conductor/pianist) October 28; Olga Rudge (violinist/musicologist) April 13; Nat Shilkret (conductor/arranger) January 1; Leo Sowerby (organist/composer) May 1; William Grant Still (composer) May 11; Paul White (composer/violinist) August 22.

**G. Deaths**  August M. L. Gemünder (German-born violin maker) September 7; Elias Howe (music publisher) July 6; Harrison Millard (composer) September 10; Thomas D. Paine (instrument maker) January 1; Philip Phillips (hymn composer/singer) June 25; George Frederick Root (composer/educator) August 6.

**H. Debuts**

**United States**  Perry Averill (baritone—Boston), Willy Burmeister (violinist—tour), Yvette Guilbert (singer—New York), Katharina Klafsky (Hungarian soprano—New York), Martin Pierre Marsick (Belgian violinist—tour), Franz Ondriczek (violinist—New York), Alfred Reisenauer (pianist), Joseph Sheehan (tenor—Boston), Minnie Tracey (soprano—Philadelphia).

**Metropolitan Opera**  Vittorio Arimondi (Italian bass), Lloyd d'Aubigne (tenor), Lola Beeth (Polish soprano), Marie Brema (British mezzo-soprano), Giuseppe Cremonini (Italian tenor), Maurice Devries (baritone), Rosa Olitzka (German contralto), Sibyl Sanderson (soprano), Frances Saville (soprano), Rosa Sucher (German soprano).

**Other**  Suzanne Adams (soprano—Paris).

**I. New Positions**

**Conductors**  Johann H. Beck (Detroit Symphony Orchestra); Horatio Parker (New Haven Symphony Orchestra—to 1918); Fritz Scheel (San Francisco Symphony Orchestra—to 1899); Frank Van der Stucken (Cincinnati Symphony Orchestra—to 1907); Max Zach (Boston Pops—to 1902).

**Educational**  Frederick Archer (organ, Carnegie Institute, Pittsburgh); Leopold Godowsky (piano head, Chicago Conservatory—to 1900); Henry Hadley (music director, St. Paul's School, Garden City, New York—to 1902); Harry B. Jepson (organist, Yale—to 1902); Peter C. Lutkin (dean, Northwestern University School of Music).

**K. Biographical**  Louise Beatty marries composer Sidney Homer; Otto Bendix moves to San Francisco where he opens his own music school; Luther O. Emerson receives a doctorate from Findlay College; Fortune Gallo (Italian opera impresario) emigrates to the United States; Zélie de Lussan makes her Covent Garden debut; Ethelbert Nevin moves his family to Italy; Carl E. Seashore receives his PhD from Yale; Frederick Stock (German violinist/conductor) moves to the United States and begins playing in the Chicago Symphony Orchestra; Antoinette Szymanowska (Polish pianist) emigrates to the United States and settles in Boston.

**L. Musical Beginnings**

**Performing Groups**  Cincinnati Orchestral Association; Pittsburgh Orchestra; San Francisco Symphony Society; Henry Savage Grand Opera Co. (Boston).

**Educational**  American School of Classical Studies (Rome); Bendix Music Conservatory (San Francisco); Northwestern University School of Music; University of Illinois School of Music.

**Other**  *The Baton: A Monthly Journal Devoted to Western Music Matters* (to 1897); Beethoven Concert Hall (San Antonio); Carnegie Music Hall (Pittsburgh); Hall, Mack Co. (Philadelphia publishing firm); Murray M. Harris Organ Factory (Los Angeles); Music Publishers Association of the United States; *The Musical Leader and Concertgoer* (Chicago—to 1967).

**M. Music Publications**

Baker, Theodore, *A Dictionary of Musical Terms*
Gow, George, *The Structure of Music*
Pratt, Waldo S., *The History of English Hymnody*

**N. Musical Compositions**

**Chamber Music**   Henry Eichheim, *String Quartet*.

**Choral/Vocal**   Amy Beach, *Four Songs, Opus 49*; Dudley Buck, *The Coming of the King* (cantata); Margaret R. Lang, *Sappho's Prayer to Aphrodite, Opus 24* (first performance); Horatio Parker, *Cáhal Mór, Opus 40* (baritone and orchestra); Harry R. Shelley, *The Inheritance Divine* (cantata); Charles S. Skilton, *Lenore* (cantata after Poe).

**Concertos**   Howard Brockway, *Cavatina* (violin and orchestra); Ottokar Novácek, *Perpetuum Mobile* (violin and orchestra).

**Orchestra/Band**   Arthur H. Bird, *Orchestral Suite No. 3*; Arthur Foote, *Suite No. 3 in D Minor for Orchestra, Opus 36*; Victor Herbert, *Badinage for Orchestra*; Edward MacDowell, *Suite No. 2 in E Minor, Opus 48, "Indian"*; John Philip Sousa, *King Cotton March*.

**Piano/Organ**   George F. Bristow, *Plantation Memories No. 2, 3*; Victor Herbert, *The Belle of Pittsburgh—Salute to America*; Edward MacDowell, *Sonata No. 2 in G Minor, Opus 50, "Eroica"*; Daniel G. Mason, *Sonata*; Ethelbert Nevin, *Maggio in Toscana*; Clara Kathleen Rogers, *Scherzo in D Major, Opus 32*.

**Symphonies**   Howard Brockway, *Symphony in D Major*.

# 1896

❁

## Historical Highlights

William McKinley is elected the 25th president; Utah enters the Union as the 45th state; Miami, Florida, is incorporated; the electric stove and the flashlight are both introduced; William Cullen Bryant gives his famous "Cross of Gold" speech; the Young Turks are formed to foster the cause of Turkish independence; Italian troops withdraw from Abyssinia after severe defeats.

## World Cultural Highlights

**World Art**   Paul Gauguin, *Nativity*; Frederic Leighton, *Clytie*; Gustave Moreau, *Jupiter and Séméle*; Pierre-Auguste Renoir, *Standing Bather*; Pierre Anders Zorn, *Nymph and Faun*.

**World Literature**   Anton Chekhov, *The Sea Gull*; A. E. Housman, *A Shropshire Lad*; William Morris, *The Well at the World's End*; Marcel Proust, *Pleasures and Regrets*; Oscar Wilde, *Salomé*.

**World Music**   Vincent d'Indy, *Istar Variations*; Gustav Mahler, *Symphony No. 3*; Giacomo Puccini, *La Bohème*; Richard Strauss, *Also Sprach Zarathustra*; Hugo Wolf, *Der Corregidor*.

**Miscellaneous**   The music publisher, Editions Salabert, opens in Paris; births include Alexander Brailowsky, A. J. Cronin, Dimitri Mitropoulos, and Liam O'Flaherty; deaths include Anton Bruckner, Frederic Leighton, George du Maurier, Henry Moore, William Morris, and Paul Verlaine.

## American Art and Literature Highlights

**Births/Deaths**   Births include art figures Louis Bouché, Allyn Cox, Morris Kantor, Frederick Kiesler, and literary figures Louis Bromfield, John Dos Passos, F. Scott Fitzgerald, Louis Ginsberg, Margaret Rawlings, Robert E. Sherwood, and Grace Zaring Stone; deaths include art figures Thomas Hinckley, George Lambdin, Charles Reinhardt, Theodore Robinson, Olin Levi Warner, and literary figures Mary Abigail Dodge (Gail Hamilton), Nora Perry, and Harriet Beecher Stowe.

**Art Works**   Cecilia Beaux, *Dorothea Francesca*; Lydia F. Emmet, *A Cabbage Patch*; Thomas Eakins, *Portrait of a Lady*; Charles Grafly, *Vultures of War*; Winslow Homer, *The Lookout—"All's Well"*; William R. Leigh, *Sophie Hunter Colston*; William O. Partridge, *Equestrian Statue, Ulysses S. Grant*; Albert Ryder, *Constance*; Henry O. Tanner, *Daniel in the Lions' Den*; Bessie Vonnoh, *Young Mother*.

**Literature**   Frances Burnett, *A Lady of Quality*; Abraham Cahan, *Yekl, a Tale of the New York Ghetto*; Emily Dickinson, *Poems III* (posthumous); Harold Frederic, *The Damnation of Theron Ware*; Sarah Orne Jewett, *Country of the Pointed Firs*; Vincent O'Sullivan, *Poems*; Lizette Reese, *A Quiet Road*; Mark Twain, *Personal Recollections of Joan of Arc*; Henry van Dyke, *Story of the Other Wise Man*.

## Music—The Vernacular/Commercial Scene

**A. Births**   Phil Baxter (composer/bandleader) September 5; Nacio Herb Brown (songwriter); Ida Cox (singer) February 25; Gary Davis (guitarist/singer) April 30; Edith Day (singer/actress) April 10; Howard Dietz (lyricist) September 8; Ruth Etting (singer/actress) November 23; Jesse "Lone Cat" Fuller (singer/guitarist) March 12; Jay Gorney (composer) December 12; Ray Henderson (composer) December 1; Sallie Martin (singer) November 20; Lew Pollack (composer/lyricist) June 16; Frank Stamps (publisher) October 7; Larry Stock (pianist/composer) December 4; Ethel Waters (singer/actress) October 31; Harry M. Woods (composer) November 4; Joe Young (lyricist).

**B. Deaths**   Allen Dodsworth (bandmaster); Percy Gaunt (composer) September 5.

**C. Biographical**

**Performing Groups**   Black Patti's Troubadours.

**New Beginnings**   *Billboard*; Weber and Field's Music Hall (New York).

**Miscellaneous**   Karl Hoschna (Bohemian composer) comes to the United States; Scott Joplin settles in Sedalia, Missouri; *Oriental America* becomes first black musical to hit Broadway.

**E. Representative Works**

**Musicals**   David Braham and Ned Harrigan, *Marty Malone*; Reginald De Koven and H. B. Smith, *The Mandarin*; Ludwig Englander and H. B. Smith, *The Caliph—Half a King*; William W. Furst and C. Fitch, *Bohemia*; Oscar Hammerstein, *Santa Maria*; Victor Herbert, *The Gold Bug*; Gustave A. Kerker and H. Morton, *An American Beauty*; Woolson Morse and J. C. Goodwin, *Lost, Strayed or Stolen*; John P. Sousa, *El Capitan*; Various composers, *In Gay New York*.

**Songs**   Anonymous, *Red River Valley*; Henry Armstrong and R. G. Husch, *Sweet Adeline*; James M. Black and K. E. Purvis, *When the Saints Go Marching In*; John W. Bratton and W. H. Ford, *I Love You in the Same Old Way*; Stanley Carter and H. Braisted, *You're Not the Only Pebble on the Beach*; Adam Geibel, *Kentucky Babe*; Ben R. Harney, *Mr. Johnson, Turn Me Loose—The Cake Walk in the Sky*; Theodore Metz and J. Hayden, *A Hot Time in the Old Town Tonight*; Ernest Hogan, *All Coons Look Alike to Me*; Maude Nugent, *Sweet Rosie O'Grady*.

## Music—The Cultivated/Art Music Scene

**F. Births**   Richard Hammond (composer) August 26; Howard Hanson (composer/conductor/educator) October 28; Glen Haydon (musicologist) December 9; Walter Helfer (composer) September 30; Richard Kountz (conductor) July 8; Queena Mario (soprano) August 21; Leroy Robertson (composer) December 21; Roger Sessions (composer) December 28; Virgil Thomson (composer/critic) November 25; Lawrence Tibbett (baritone) November 16; Jacques Wolfe (composer/pianist) April 29.

**G. Deaths**   Luther Whiting Mason (music educator) July 4; John Rogers Thomas (Welsh-born baritone/composer) April 5.

**H. Debuts**

**United States**   Jacques Bars (tenor—New York), David Ffrangcon-Davies (British baritone—tour), Carl Halir (Bohemian violinist—tour), Bronislaw Huberman (Polish violinist—tour), Bruno Huhn (British pianist—New York), Oscar Seagle (baritone—New York), Milka Ternina (Croatian soprano—Boston), Pietro Adolfo Tirindelli (Italian violinist—Cincinnati).

**Metropolitan Opera**   David Bispham (baritone), Félia Litvinne (Russian soprano), Thomas Salignac (French tenor), Adolf Wallnöfer (German baritone/tenor).

**I. New Positions**

**Conductors**   Frederick Archer (Pittsburgh Symphony Orchestra—to 1898); Carl V. Lachmund (Women's String Orchestra of New York).

**Educational**   Luigi von Kunits (violin, Pittsburgh Conservatory—to 1910); Edward MacDowell (music head, Columbia University); Frank Van der Stucken (dean, Cincinnati College of Music—to 1906).

**Other**   Walter Henry Hall (organ, St. James, New York).

## J. Honors and Awards

**Honors**   Edward MacDowell (doctorate, Princeton).

**K. Biographical**   Frederick Shepherd Converse goes to Munich to study with Rheinberger at the Royal Academy; Percy Goetschius resigns his conservatory post and begins teaching privately in Boston; William T. Upton receives his BA degree from Oberlin.

## L. Musical Beginnings

**Performing Groups**   Adamowski Trio (Boston); Indianapolis Symphony Orchestra I (to 1906); MacDowell Club of Boston; Portland Symphony Orchestra (Oregon Symphony Orchestra in 1967); Women's String Orchestra of New York.

**Other**   American Federation of Musicians (AFM); American Guild of Organists (New York); *The Etude* (to 1957); *The Musician* (to 1948); Paderewski Prize for young American Composers; Steinert Hall (Boston).

## M. Music Publications

Clarke, Hugh A., *Pronouncing Dictionary of Musical Terms*
Goepp, Philip, *Annals of Music in Philadelphia and the History of the Musical Fund Society* . . .
Krehbiel, Henry E., *How to Listen to Music*
Mathews, W. and Liebling, E., *Pronouncing and Defining Dictionary of Music*
Virgil, A. K., *The Virgil Clavier Method: Foundation Exercises II*

## N. Musical Compositions

**Chamber Music**   Amy Beach, *Violin Sonata in A Minor, Opus 34*; George W. Chadwick, *String Quartet No. 4 in E Minor*; Caryl Florio, *String Quartet No. 3* (incomplete); Charles Ives, *String Quartet No. 1, "From the Salvation Army."*

**Choral/Vocal**   Amy Beach, *Three Songs, Opus 31—Four Songs, Opus 35*; Arthur H. Bird, *Five Songs, Opus 36*; Dudley Buck, *Christ, the Victor* (cantata); Victor Herbert, *Love Song*; George F. Root, *The Star of Light* (cantata)—*Our Flag with the Stars and Stripes* (cantata).

**Concertos**   Victor Herbert, *The Veiled Prophet* (piano and band); Frederick Zech, Jr., *Concerto No. 4 for Piano and Orchestra*.

**Operas**   Julian Edwards, *Brian Boru—The Goddess of Truth*; Frederick Zech, Jr., *La Paloma, or The Cruise of the Excelsior*.

**Orchestra/Band**   John Alden Carpenter, *Strawberry Night Festival Music—Branglebrink* (incidental music); Frederick Gleason, *Edris* (symphonic poem); Margaret R. Lang, *Armida, Opus 24* (first performance); John Philip Sousa, *El Capitan March—Stars and Stripes Forever—Colonial Dames Waltzes*.

**Piano/Organ**   Edward MacDowell, *Woodland Sketches, Opus 51*; Ethelbert Nevin, *La Guitare, Maggio in Toscana* (piano suite).

# 1897

❀

## Historical Highlights

The Klondike Gold Rush takes place in Alaska; the Dingley Tariff hits a new high in protectionism; C. W. Post introduces grape nuts to the American public and W. K. Kellogg introduces corn flakes; the running of the Boston Marathon begins; the Greek-Turkish War closes with the Peace of Constantinople; the first Zionist Congress for a Jewish state in Palestine meets in Basle.

## World Cultural Highlights

**World Art**    Aimé-Jules Dalou, *The Peasant*; Paul Gauguin, *Day-Dreaming*; Emil Nolde, *Mountain Giants*; Pierre-Auguste Rodin, *Honoré de Balzac*; Henri Rousseau, *The Sleeping Gypsy*.

**World Literature**    Joseph Conrad, *The Nigger of the "Narcissus"*; Rudyard Kipling, *Captains Courageous*; Edmond Rostand, *Cyrano de Bergerac*; George Bernard Shaw, *Candide*.

**World Music**    Ferruccio Busoni, *A Comedy Overture—Violin Concerto*; Frederick Delius, *Piano Concerto—Koanga*; Paul Dukas, *The Sorcerer's Apprentice*; Richard Strauss, *Don Quixote*.

**Miscellaneous**    The Tate Gallery opens in London; Feis Ceoil, the Irish Festivals begin; Gustav Mahler begins conducting at the Vienna Opera; births include Paul Delvaux, Wanda Landowska, and Sacheverell Sitwell; deaths include Johannes Brahms, Alphonse Daudet, and Margaret Oliphant.

## American Art and Literature Highlights

**Births/Deaths**    Births include art figures Ivan Albright, John Curry, William Gropper, Reuben Nakian, and literary figures Louise Bogan, William Faulkner, Paul Gallico, Josephine Herbst, Horace McCoy, and Thornton Wilder; deaths include artists James Bard, Homer Martin, Charles Nahl, William Picknell, and authors Henry George and Margaret J. Preston.

**Art Works**    Cecilia Beaux, *Dorothea in the Woods*; Charles Grafly, *Symbol of Life*; Childe Hassam, *Ponte Santa Trinita*; John La Farge, *The Strange Thing Little Kiosai Saw in the River*; Thomas Moran, *The Teton Range*; Augustus Saint-Gaudens, *The Robert G. Shaw Memorial*; Henry O. Tanner, *The Raising of Lazarus*; Abbott H. Thayer, *Caritas*; William A. Walker, *South Georgia Shanty*.

**Literature**    Kate O'Flaherty Chopin, *A Night in Arcadie*; John W. Fox, *The Kentuckians*; Sam W. Foss, *Dreams in Homespun*; William D. Howells, *The Landlord at Lion's Head*; Henry James, *The Spoils of Poynton*; Edwin A. Robinson, *Children of the Night*; Harriet E. Spofford, *In Titian's Garden and Other Poems*; Mark Twain, *Following the Equator*; Henry van Dyke, *The Builders and Other Poems*.

## Music—The Vernacular/Commercial Scene

**A. Births**    Gus Arnheim (composer/bandleader) September 11; Sidney Bechet (clarinetist/saxophonist) May 14; Felix Bernard (pianist/composer) April 28; William Herbert Brewster, Sr. (1899?—composer) July 2; Sam Chatmon (guitarist) January 10; J. Fred Coots (composer) May 2; Fletcher Henderson (pianist/bandleader) December 18; Blind Lemon Jefferson (singer/guitarist); Abe Lyman (drummer/bandleader) August 4; Jimmie Rodgers (singer) September 8; Fred Rose (composer/publisher) August 24; Vivienne Segal (singer/actress) April 19; Willie "the Lion" Smith (pianist) November 25; Sam H. Stept (composer) September 18; Kay Swift (composer/lyricist) April 19; Sonny Boy Williamson (singer) December 5.

**C. Biographical**

**New Beginnings**    Morse Music Co. (New York).

**D. Publications**    Benjamin R. Harney, *Ben Harney's Ragtime Instructor*.

**E. Representative Works**

**Musicals**    Ludwig Englander, *A Round of Pleasure*; Victor Herbert and H. B. Smith, *The Serenade—The Idol's Eye*; Edward Holst and H. L. Ensign, *1999*; Gustave A. Kerker and H. Morton, *The Belle of New York—The Telephone Girl*; Reginald De Koven and H. B. Smith, *The Highwayman*; Chauncey Olcott and A. Pitou, *Sweet Inniscarra*; Richard Stahl and C. Hoyt, *A Contented Woman*; Various composers, *Miss Manhattan*.

**Songs**    Paul Dresser, *On the Banks of the Wabash*; John S. Fearis and J. B. Pounds, *Beautiful Isle of Somewhere*; Charles K. Harris, *I've Just Come Back to Say Goodbye—Break the News to Mother*; Reginald De Koven and H. B. Smith, *Do You Remember Love?*; Kerry Mills and C.

Shackford, *Let Bygones Be Bygones*; Henry W. Petrie and A. J. Lamb, *Asleep In the Deep*; Monroe H. Rosenfeld, *Take Back Your Gold*; Harry Von Tilzer, *I'd Leave My Happy Home for You*.

**Other**   W. H. Krell, *The Mississippi Rag* (first to be copyrighted); Kerry Mills, *At a Georgia Camp Meeting*; Tom Turpin, *Harlem Rag*.

## Music — The Cultivated/Art Music Scene

**F. Births**   J. Murray Barbour (acoustician/musicologist) March 31; Hans Barth (pianist/composer) June 25; Henry D. Cowell (composer) March 11; Frederick Jagel (tenor) January 10; Harrison Kerr (composer) October 13; Donald MacArdle (musicologist) July 3; Quinto Maganini (conductor/arranger) November 30; Rosa Ponselle (soprano) January 22; Hugh Porter (organist) September 18; Quincy Porter (composer) February 7; Lamar E. Stringfield (composer/flutist/conductor) October 10.

**G. Deaths**   Achille Errani (Italian-born tenor) January 6; Hiram Murray Higgins (publisher) July 13; Lazarus J. Jones (compiler); Adolph Neuendorff (German-born conductor/composer) December 4; Alexander Thayer (music historian) July 15; Grenville Dean Wilson (composer) September 20.

**H. Debuts**

**United States**   Maria Charlotte Geistinger (Austrian soprano — New York), Emilio de Gogorza (baritone — New York), Denis O'Sullivan (baritone — San Francisco), Raoul Pugno (Italian pianist), Corinne Rider-Kelsey (soprano — Rockford, Illinois), Ellison Van Hoose (tenor — New York).

**Metropolitan Opera**   William Mertons (baritone), Mina Schilling (soprano), Clémentine de Vère (French soprano).

**I. New Positions**

**Conductors**   Arthur Shepherd (Salt Lake City Theater).

**Educational**   Felix Borowski (music history, Chicago Music College — to 1925); George W. Chadwick (director, New England Conservatory); Frank H. Damrosch (superintendent of music, New York Public Schools); Wallace Goodrich (New England Conservatory — to 1942); Helen Hopekirk (New England Conservatory); Charles Sanford Skilton (piano, State Normal School, Trenton).

**Other**   Philip Hale (editor, *Musical Record* — to 1901); Hermann Wetzler (organ, Old Trinity Church, New York — to 1901).

**K. Biographical**   Felix Borowski (British composer/critic) comes to the United States and teaches in Chicago; John Alden Carpenter graduates from Harvard and enters his father's business; Arthur Farwell goes to Germany to study with Humperdinck and Pfitzner; Felix Fox (German pianist) comes to the United States and settles in Boston; Helen Hopekirk (Scottish pianist/composer) comes to the United States; Arthur Shepherd graduates from the New England Conservatory and moves to Salt Lake City.

**L. Musical Beginnings**

**Performing Groups**   Castle Square Opera Co. (Boston); Kansas City Oratorio Society; Philadelphia Choral Society (to 1946).

**Festivals**   Maine Music Festival (to 1926).

**Educational**   Faelten Piano School (Boston); Library of Congress Division of Music; Sherwood School of Music (Chicago).

**Other**   *The Musical Herald*; National Piano Manufacturer's Association.

**M. Music Publications**

Chadwick, George W., *Harmony: A Course of Study*
Gruenberg, Eugene, *The Violinist's Manual*
Mathews, W. S. B., *Music, Its Ideals and Methods*

### N. Musical Compositions

**Chamber Music**  Carl Busch, *String Quartet*; Arthur Foote, *Piano Quintet in A Minor, Opus 38*; Charles Ives, *Fugue in Four Keys on the Shining Shore*; Charles S. Skilton, *Violin Sonata No. 1* (MTNA Prize); Frederick Zech, Jr., *String Quartet No. 1*.

**Choral/Vocal**  Amy Beach, *Three Shakespeare Choruses, Opus 39—Three Shakespeare Songs, Opus 37*; George W. Chadwick, *Lochinvar* (baritone and orchestra); Victor Herbert, *The Fight Is Made and Won* (song)—*Anthem of Lambs*; Horatio Parker, *The Legend of St. Christopher* (oratorio); Willard Patton, *Isaiah* (oratorio).

**Concertos**  Victor Herbert, *McKinley Inauguration* (piano and band); Charles M. Loeffler, *La mort de Tintagiles, Opus 6*; Arthur B. Whiting, *Fantasia in B-flat Minor for Piano and Orchestra, Opus 11*; Camille Zeckwer, *Concerto for Piano and Orchestra*.

**Operas**  Arthur H. Bird, *Daphne, or The Pipes of Arcadia* (operetta); Louis A. Coerne, *A Woman of Marblehead*; Julian Edwards, *The Wedding Day*; Thomas W. Surette, *The Eve of Saint Agnes* (operetta).

**Orchestra/Band**  Platon Brounoff, *Overture, Russia*; Victor Herbert, *The President's March* (band and/or orchestra); Henry H. Huss, *Festival March*; Arthur Nevin, *Lorna Doone Suite*; John Philip Sousa, *The Lady of the White House Waltzes*.

**Piano/Organ**  Amy Beach, *Children's Album, Opus 36*; John Alden Carpenter, *Sonata No. 1*.

**Symphonies**  Henry Hadley, *Symphony No. 1 in D Minor, "Youth and Life," Opus 25*; Harry R. Shelley, *Symphony*.

# 1898

✺

## Historical Highlights

The Spanish-American War begins; the Treaty of Paris reimburses Spain for the territories of Guam, Hawaii, Puerto Rico, and the Philippines; the discovery of the Kensington Stone proves the early visits of the Norsemen to the New World; the Metro, Paris' subway, opens to the public; Count von Zeppelin invents the airship named after him; the Curies discover the existence of radium.

## World Cultural Highlights

**World Art**  Paul Gauguin, *The White Horse*; Auguste Rodin, *The Hand of God*.

**World Literature**  Anton Chekhov, *Uncle Vanya*; John Long, *Madame Butterfly*; Arthur Pinero, *Trelawny of the "Wells"*; H. G. Wells, *War of the Worlds*; Oscar Wilde, *Ballad of Reading Gaol*.

**World Music**  Edvard Grieg, *Symphonic Dances*; Alexander Scriabin, *Piano Concerto—Piano Sonatas No. 2, 3*; Richard Strauss, *Ein Heldenleben*; Giuseppe Verdi, *Four Sacred Pieces*.

**Miscellaneous**  The Vienna Volksoper and the Deutsche Gramophon Gesellschaft are founded; births include Bertolt Brecht, René Magritte and Erich Remarque; deaths include Edward Burne-Jones, Lewis Carroll, Pierre de Chavannes, Stéphane Mallarmé, and Gustave Moreau.

## American Art and Literature Highlights

**Births/Deaths**  Births include art figures Alexander Calder, Alexandre Hogue, Reginald Marsh and Ben Shahn; and literary figures Stephen Vincent Benét, Malcolm Cowley, Rose Franken, Henry M. Robinson, and Antoinette Scudder; deaths include artist William M. Brown and literary figures Edward Bellamy, Theodore S. Fay, Harold Frederic, Blanche Willis Howard, and Edward Noyes Westcott.

**Art Works** Herbert Adams, *Winged Victory*; Cecilia Beaux, *Man with Cat*; Ralph Blakelock, *Twilight*: Solon Borglum, *Lassoing Wild Horses*; Cyrus E. Dallin, *Medicine Man*; Thomas Eakins, *The Agnew Clinic—Taking the Count*; Daniel French, *The Hunt Memorial*; Frederic Remington, *The Scalp*; Charles Russell, *A Desperate Stand*; Henry Tanner, *The Annunciation*; Abbott Thayer, *Young Woman*.

**Literature** Gertrude Atherton, *The Californians*; Stephen Crane, *The Open Boat and Other Tales*; Finley P. Dunne, *Mr. Dooley in Peace and War*; Clyde Fitch, *The Moth and the Flame*; Mary E. Freeman, *People of Our Neighborhood*; Ellen Glasgow, *Phases of an Inferior Planet*; Henry James, *The Two Magics*; Morris Rosenfeld, *Songs of the Ghetto*; E. M. Westcott, *David Harum*.

## Music — The Vernacular/Commercial Scene

**A. Births** Lil Armstrong (pianist/singer) February 3; Louis "Satchmo" Armstrong (trumpet) (?); Sweet Emma Barrett (pianist) March 25; Warren "Baby" Dodds (drummer) December 24; Edgar Y. Harburg (lyricist/librettist) April 8; Arthur James Johnston (composer/arranger) January 10; Andy Kirk (saxophonist/bandleader) May 29; Marilyn Miller (singer/actress) September 1; Irving "Miff" Mole (bandleader); Molly Picon (singer) February 28; Granny Riddle (folksinger) November 21; Arthur Smith (fiddler) April 10; Charles Tobias (lyricist) August 15; Clarence Williams (pianist) October; Dewey P. Williams (singer) March 5; Vincent Youmans (composer) September 27.

**B. Deaths** William J. Scanlan (actor/songwriter/singer) February 18.

**C. Biographical**

**Prizes and Honors** Reginald De Koven (National Institute of Arts and Letters).

**E. Representative Works**

**Musicals** Bob Cole and B. Johnson, *Trip to Coontown*; Will M. Cook and P. Dunbar, *Clorindy, or The Origin of the Cakewalk*; Ludwig Englander, *The Little Corporal*; Victor Herbert and H. B. Smith, *The Fortune Teller*; Gustave A. Kerker and H. Morton, *The Telephone Girl—Yankee Doodle Dandy*; John P. Sousa, *The Bride Elect—The Charlatan*; John Stromberg and H. B. Smith, *Hurly Burly*; Edward W. Townsend and G. MacDonough, *The Marquis of Michigan*.

**Songs** Anonymous, *Boola, Boola (Yale School Song)*; Harry Armstrong and James J. Walker, *Goodbye, Eyes of Blue*; Frederic F. Bullard and R. Hovey, *It's Always Fair Weather When Good Fellows Get Together*; Paul Dresser, *Come Tell Me What's Your Answer, Yes or No*; Charles Horwitz and H. V. Bowers, *Because*; Monroe H. Rosenfeld and C. E. Foreman, *Gold Will Buy Most Anything but a True Girl's Heart*; Andrew B. Sterlins and H. Von Tilzer, *My Old New Hampshire Home*; Rudolf Thaler and A. Pestalozza, *Ciribiribin*; James Thornton, *When You Were Sweet Sixteen*.

## Music — The Cultivated/Art Music Scene

**F. Births** Ernst Bacon (composer/pianist) May 26; Wheeler Beckett (conductor/composer) March 7; Joseph Bentonelli (tenor) September 10; Jules Bledsoe (baritone) December 29; Louis Cheslock (violinist/composer) September 25; William Levi Dawson (composer) September 26; Herbert Elwell (composer/critic) May 10; George Gershwin (pianist/composer) September 26; Albert Goldberg (music critic) June 2; Frederick D. Hall (music educator) December 14; Roy Harris (composer) February 12; Mischa Levitzki (pianist) May 25; Grace Moore (soprano) December 5; Arthur William Poister (organist) June 13; Paul Robeson (bass-baritone) April 9; Beryl Rubinstein (pianist/composer) October 26; Alfred Wallenstein (conductor/cellist) October 7.

**G. Deaths** George F. Bristow (composer) December 13; John C. Fillmore (music educator) August 14; Charles Jerome Hopkins (composer/author) November 4; Eduard Reményi (Hungarian-born violinist) May 15; Anton Seidl (Hungarian-born conductor) March 28; Charles Zimmermann (German-born instrument maker) October 20.

**H. Debuts**

**United States**   Yeatman Griffith (Cincinnati), Leon Rains (bass—tour), Francis Rogers (baritone—Boston), Emil Sauer (German pianist—New York), Ernestine Schumann Heink (Austrian contralto—Chicago), Hildegard Hoffman (soprano), Maud MacCarthy (violinist—New York), Albert Saléza (French tenor—Chicago), Alexander Siloti (Russian pianist—New York), Yvonne de Tréville (soprano—New York), Herbert Witherspoon (bass—New York).

**Metropolitan Opera**   Herman Devries (bass), Albert Saléza (Belgian tenor), Ernest Van Dyck (Belgian tenor), Anton Van Rooy (Dutch bass-baritone), Albert Saléza (French tenor), Ernest Van Dyck (Belgian tenor).

**Other**   Louise Homer (contralto—Vichy, France), Estelle Liebling (soprano—Dresden), Clarence Whitehill (bass-baritone—Brussels).

**I. New Positions**

**Conductors**   Wilhelm Gericke (Boston Symphony Orchestra—second term—to 1906); Harley Hamilton (Los Angeles Symphony Orchestra—to 1913); Victor Herbert (Pittsburgh Orchestra—to 1904); Emil Paur (New York Philharmonic Orchestra—to 1902); Franz Schalk (Metropolitan Opera); William H. Santelmann (US Marine Band—to 1927).

**Educational**   Alberto Jonás (Detroit Conservatory—to 1904); Harold Randolph (director, Peabody Conservatory); Louis Victor Saar (National Conservatory, New York); John W. Work (Latin and history, Fisk University).

**Other**   John Freund (editor, *Musical America*—to 1924).

**J. Honors and Awards**

**Honors**   Arthur H. Bird, Dudley Buck, George W. Chadwick, Arthur W. Foote, William Wallace Gilchrist, Edgar Stillman Kelley, Ethelbert Nevin, John Knowles Paine, Horatio Parker, Harry Rowe Shelley, and Frank Van der Stucken (National Institute); Humphrey John Stewart (Clemson Medal).

**K. Biographical**   Suzanne Adams makes her Covent Garden debut; Frederick S. Converse graduates from the Royal Academy in Munich; Charles Ives graduates from Yale; Jerome Remick buys an interest in Whitney-Warner Publishing Co.; Nicolai Sokoloff (Russian violinist/conductor) is brought to United States at age 12; Arnold Volpe (Lithuanian conductor) comes to the United States and settles in New York.

**L. Musical Beginnings**

**Performing Groups**   Bethlehem Bach Choir (Pennsylvania); Euterpean Club (Fort Worth); Maurice Grau Opera Co.; Los Angeles Symphony Orchestra; Young People's Symphony Concerts (New York, by Frank Damrosch).

**Educational**   Fox-Buonameci School of Pianoforte Playing (Boston); Mu Alpha Sinfonia Fraternity; Oregon Conservatory of Music (Portland—to 1932); Phi Mu Alpha Sinfonia Fraternity; Phi Mu Gamma, Fine Arts Sorority.

**Other**   Knoxville Tuesday Morning Musical Club (Tennessee); Manhattan Opera House I; Theodore Morse, Publisher (New York); *Musical America*; National Federation of Music Clubs; National Institute of Arts and Letters; Rosenfeld Musical Press Bureau (New York).

**M. Music Publications**

Apthorp, William F., *By the Way, being a Collection of Short Essays about Music*
Clarke, Hugh A., *A System of Harmony*
Elson, Louis C., *Great Composers and Their Works*
Goetschius, Percy, *Homophonic Forms of Musical Composition*
Henderson, William J., *How Music Developed—What Is Good Music?*
Krehbiel, Henry E., *Music and Manners in the Classical Period*

Lahee, Henry C., *Famous Singers of Today and Yesterday*
Warrington, James, *Short Titles of Books Relating to or Illustrating the History and Practice of Psalmody in the United States*

**N. Musical Compositions**

**Chamber Music**    Arthur H. Bird, *Serenade for Nineteen Wind Instruments, Opus 40*; George W. Chadwick, *String Quartet No. 5 in D Minor*; Arthur Farwell, *Ballade, Opus 1, for Violin and Piano*; Victor Herbert, *Humoresque for Woodwinds*; Ottokar Nováček, *String Quartet No. 2*.

**Choral/Vocal**    Amy Beach, *Three Songs, Opus 41—Song of Welcome* (chorus and orchestra); Dudley Buck, *Paul Revere's Ride* (male chorus and orchestra); Edward MacDowell, *Four Songs, Opus 56*; Ethelbert Nevin, *The Rosary*; Harry R. Shelley, *Death and Life* (cantata).

**Concertos**    Victor Herbert, *Concerto No. 2 for Cello and Orchestra, Opus 30*.

**Operas**    Harry L. Freeman, *Zuluki*; John Knowles Paine, *Azara*.

**Orchestra/Band**    Victor Herbert, *American Fantasia for Orchestra—March of the 22nd Regiment*; Henry H. Huss, *Cleopatra's Death*; Hugo Kaun, *Festival March and Hymn*.

**Piano/Organ**    Arthur H. Bird, *Three Oriental Sketches for Organ, Opus 42*; John Alden Carpenter, *Nocturne for Piano*; Edward MacDowell, *Sea Pieces, Opus 55*; Ethelbert Nevin, *A Day in Venice, Opus 25* (piano suite).

**Symphonies**    Carl Busch, *Symphony*; Frederick Converse, *Symphony No. 1 in D Minor*; Charles Ives, *Symphony No. 1*; Hugo Kaun, *Symphony*.

# 1899

☀

## Historical Highlights

The United States makes protectorates out of Cuba, Puerto Rico, and Guam while the Philippines begin their revolt for full independence; John Hay proclaims the "Open Door Policy" in regard to our trade with China; the first Packard auto is built; Mount Rainier National Park is established by Congress; in the First Hague Conference, a permanent Court of Arbitration is set up to settle disputes between countries; Friedrich Bayer introduces aspirin.

## World Cultural Highlights

**World Art**    Edgar Degas. *Three Dancers*; James Ensor, *Artists and Masks*; Paul Gauguin, *Tahitian Women and Mangoes*; Roland Perry, *The Valkyrie*; Pierre-Auguste Renoir, *Gabrielle with a Rose*.

**World Literature**    Anton Chekhov, *The Three Sisters*; John Galsworthy, *Jocelyn*; Rudyard Kipling, *Stalky and Company*; Wladyslaw Reymont, *Promised Land*; William Yeats, *Wind Among the Reeds*.

**World Music**    Claude Debussy, *Three Nocturnes for Orchestra*; Edward Elgar, *Enigma Variations*; Arnold Schönberg, *Transfigured Night*; Jean Sibelius, *Symphony No. 1—Finlandia*.

**Miscellaneous**    The Irish Literary Theater is formed; the Havana Conservatory of Music opens; births include Noel Coward, Eugene Ormandy, Francis Poulenc, and Moses and Raphael Soyer; deaths include Rosa Bonheur, Ernest Chausson, Victor Cherbuliez, Alfred Sisley, and Johann Strauss, Jr.

## American Art and Literature Highlights

**Births/Deaths**    Births include artists Fritz Glarner, Bradley W. Tomlin, and literary figures Léonie

Fuller Adams, Archie Binns, Charles Bruce Catton, Hart Crane, Ernest Haycox, Ernest Hemingway, Emily Kimbrough, Allen Tate, and E. B. White; deaths include literary figures Horatio Alger, Jr., Augustin Daly, Frederic Beecher Perkins, Philip Henry Savage, and E. D. E. N. Southworth.

**Art Works**   Cyrus Dallin, *Medicine Man*; Thomas Eakins, *Between Rounds*; Childe Hassam, *New England Headlands*; Winslow Homer, *The Gulf Stream—After the Hurricane, Bahamas*; Frederick MacMonnies, *Horse Tamers*; Maurice Prendergast, *Umbrellas in the Rain*; Augustus Saint-Gaudens, *The Puritan*; Charles Schreyvogel, *My Bunkie*; J. Alden Weir, *The Donkey Ride*.

**Literature**   Abraham Cahan, *The Imported Bridegroom and Other Stories*; Charles Chestnutt, *Conjure Woman*; Kate O'Flaherty Chopin, *The Awakening*; Stephen Crane, *War Is Kind and Other Lines*; Finley P. Dunne, *Mr. Dooley in the Hearts of His Countrymen*; Clyde Fitch, *The Cowboy and the Lady*; Edwin Markham, *The Man with the Hoe and Other Poems*; Frank Norris, *McTeague*.

## Music—The Vernacular/Commercial Scene

**A. Births**   Hoagy Carmichael (pianist/writer) November 22; Leroy Carr (singer); Thomas A. Dorsey (singer/pianist); John Woods Duke (composer/pianist) July 30; Duke Ellington (composer/bandleader) April 29; Sleepy John Estes (singer) January 25; Charles Graham (songwriter); Billy Hill (composer) July 14; Red McKinzie (bandleader) October 14; Billy Rose (lyricist) September 6; Abner Silver (composer/lyricist) December 28; "Whispering Jack" Smith (singer).

**B. Deaths**   Gussie L. Davis (songwriter).

**C. Biographical**

**New Beginnings**   Victoria Theater (New York—by Hammerstein).

**Miscellaneous**   Ralph Blakelock suffers a nervous breakdown.

**E. Representative Works**

**Musicals**   Ludwig Englander, *The Rounders—The Man in the Moon*; Victor Herbert and H. B. Smith, *Cyrano de Bergerac—The Singing Girl*; V. Herbert and F. Daniels, *The Ameer*; Reginald De Koven and H. B. Smith, *The Three Dragoons*; Chauncey Olcott and A. Pitou, *A Romance of Athlone*; John Philip Sousa, *Chris and the Wonderful Lamp*; John Stromberg and H. B. Smith, *Whirl-i-gig*.

**Songs**   Anonymous, *She'll Be Coming 'Round the Mountain*; Paul Dresser, *On the Banks of the Wabash Far Away—In Good Old New York Town*; Julian Edwards and W. D. Cobb, *I Couldn't Stand to See My Baby Lose*; Charles Horwitz and F. V. Bowers, *Always*; Joseph E. Howard, *Hello, My Baby*; Andrew Mack, *Heart of My Heart (Story of Rose)*; Chauncey Olcott, *My Wild Irish Rose*; Joseph P. Skelly and G. Cooper, *Is Mother Thinking of Her Boy?*; Andrew B. Sterling and H. Von Tilzer, *Where the Sweet Magnolias Grow*.

**Other**   Gus W. Bernard, *Colored Aristocracy Cakewalk*; Eubie Blake, *Charleston Rag*; Charles Hunter, *Tickled to Death—Ragtime March and Two-Step*; C. L. Johnson, *Rags: Doc Brown's Cake Walk—Scandalous Thompson*; Scott Joplin, *Maple Leaf Rag—Original Rag*; Kerry Mills, *Whistling Rufus*; Tom Turpin, *Bowery Buck Rag*.

## Music—The Cultivated/Art Music Scene

**F. Births**   Otto E. Albrecht (musicologist) July 8; Paul Althouse (tenor) December 2; Claudia Cassidy (critic) November 15; Wilbur Chenoweth (pianist/composer) June 4; Werner Janssen (conductor/composer) June 1; Alton Jones (pianist) August 2; Dorothea Dix Lawrence (soprano/folklore scholar) September 22; Leopold Mannes (pianist/composer) December 26; Harl McDonald (composer) July 27; George Frederick McKay (composer) June 11; George K. Raudenbush (conductor/violinist) March 13; Gustave Reese (musicologist) November 29; Randall Thompson (composer) April 21; Helen Traubel (soprano) June 20.

**G. Deaths**   Hans Balatka (Czech-born conductor/composer) April 17; William Boucher (instrument maker) March 11; A. J. (Signor) Foli (bassist) October 20; George Gemunder (German violin maker) January 15; Felipe Gutiérrez (y) Espinosa (Puerto Rican composer) November 27; Edvard Holst (Danish-born composer) February 4; Robert Lowry (hymn writer) November 25; Rigdon McCoy McIntosh (compiler); Joseph P. Shaw (British-born publisher); Moses Slater (British-born brass instrument maker) October 11; John R. Sweney (composer-hymnist) April 10.

**H. Debuts**

**United States**  Albert Alvarez (French tenor—Boston), Clara Butt (British contralto—tour), Eleanora de Cisneros (mezzo-soprano—Chicago), Erno von Dohnányi (Hungarian pianist—New York), Heinrich Gebhard (pianist—Boston), Mark Hambourg (Russian pianist—Boston), Katherine Heyman (pianist—Boston), William W. Hinshaw (bassist—St. Louis), Blanche Marchesi (French soprano—tour), Wilma Neruda (Bohemian violinist—tour).

**Metropolitan Opera**  Suzanne Adams (soprano), Albert Alvarez (French tenor), Emilie Herzog (Swiss soprano), Emil Paur (Austrian conductor), Antonio Pini-Corsi (Italian bass), Ernestine Schumann-Heink (Austrian contralto), Antonio Scotti (Italian baritone).

**I. New Positions**

**Conductors**  Emil Mollenhauer (Boston Handel and Haydn Society—to 1927).

**Educational**  Frederick Converse (theory, New England Conservatory); Arne Oldberg (piano, Northwestern—to 1941); Emil Paur (director, National Conservatory, New York—to 1902); Henry Schradieck (South Broad St. Conservatory, Philadelphia—to 1912).

**Other**  Harry R. Shelley (organ, Fifth Avenue Baptist Church, New York); Henry W. Wehrmann, Jr. (organ, First Presbyterian Church, New Orleans).

**K. Biographical**  Geraldine Farrar goes to Paris for further voice study; Arthur Farwell returns to the United States and begins lecturing at Cornell University; William W. Hinshaw makes his operatic debut in St. Louis; Louise Homer makes her Covent Garden debut; Gaetano Merola (Italian conductor/manager) comes to the United States as an assistant conductor at the Metropolitan Opera; Oscar G. T. Sonneck returns to the United States and begins researching early American music; Frederick Stock becomes assistant to Theodore Thomas at the Chicago Symphony Orchestra.

**L. Musical Beginnings**

**Performing Groups**  Hartford Philharmonic Orchestra; Kansas City Musical Club; Litchfield County Choral Union (Connecticut); New York Women's Philharmonic Society; Norfolk Chamber Music Festival; Washington Permanent Chorus.

**Educational**  Guilmant Organ School (New York); University of Oklahoma School of Music.

**Other**  John Austin Organ Co. (Hartford); *Brainard's Musical*; *Choir: a Monthly Journal of Church Music*; Lyon and Healy Harp Co. (Chicago); Olympian Music Hall (New York); Willis Music Co. (Cincinnati); Wurlitzer Tonophone (coin-operated electric piano).

**M. Music Publications**

Clarke, Hugh A., *Music and the Comrade Arts*
Elson, Louis, *The National Music of America and Its Sources*
Henderson, William J., *The Orchestra and Orchestral Music*
Huneker, James G., *Mezzotints in Modern Music*
Lahee, Henry C., *Famous Violinists of Today and Yesterday*
Matthews, W. S. B., *A Hundred Years of Music in America*

**N. Musical Compositions**

**Choral/Vocal**  Amy Beach, *Five Songs on Burns, Opus 43*; Henry Hadley, *In Music's Praise* (cantata—Oliver Ditson Prize); Charles Ives, *The Celestial Country* (cantata)—*Psalm 100*—*Psalm 14*; Margaret R. Lang, *Te Deum, Opus 34*; Edward MacDowell, *Three Songs, Opus 58*; Ethelbert Nevin, *Songs from Vineacre, Opus 28*—*En Passant, Opus 30*—*Captive Memories, Opus 29* (song cycle); Horatio Parker, *Adstant Angelorum Chori, Opus 45*—*Six Old English Songs, Opus 47*.

**Concertos**   Amy Beach, *Concerto in C-Sharp Minor, Opus 45, for Piano and Orchestra.*

**Orchestra/Band**   Frederick Gleason, *The Song of Life* (symphonic poem); Hugo Kaun, *Overture, Der Mahler von Antwerp*; Edgar S. Kelley, *Ben Hur, Opus 17* (incidental music); Arne Oldberg, *Overture, Paolo and Francesca*; Horatio Parker, *A Northern Ballad, Opus 46*; John Philip Sousa, *Hands Across the Sea March—The Man Behind the Gun March.*

**Piano/Organ**   Arthur Farwell, *Owasco Memories, Opus 8*; Clayton Johns, *Introduction and Fugue*; Edward MacDowell, *Sonata No. 3 in D Minor, Opus 57, "Norse"*; Horace Nicholl, *Twelve Etudes Mélodiques, Opus 26*; Horatio Parker, *Three Characteristic Pieces, Opus 49.*

# 1900

❉

## Historical Highlights

The census indicates a population of 76,212,000 in 45 states; William McKinley is re-elected president, Hawaii becomes an official United States territory; Carrie Nation begins her hatchet crusade against liquor; the Paris Universal Exposition takes place.

## World Cultural Highlights

**World Art**  Pierre Bonnard, *Man and Woman*; Émile Bourdelle, *Head of Apollo*; Henri de Toulouse-Lautrec, *La Modiste*; Pablo Picasso, *Le Moulin de la Galette*; Auguste Rodin, *The Gates of Hell*.

**World Literature**  Gabriele d'Annunzio, *Il fuoco*; Joseph Conrad, *Lord Jim*; Sigmund Freud, *The Interpretation of Dreams*; George Bernard Shaw, *Caesar and Cleopatra*.

**World Music**  Gustave Charpentier, *Louise*; Edward Elgar, *Dream of Gerontius*; Gustave Mahler, *Symphony No. 4*; Jules Massenet, *Phèdre*; Giacomo Puccini, *Tosca*; Alexander Scriabin, *Symphony No. 1*.

**Miscellaneous**  The Vienna Symphony Orchestra is founded; births include Salvatore Baccaloni, James Hilton, George Seferis, Yves Tanguy, and Kurt Weill; deaths include Jean Falguière, George Grove, Wilhelm Leibl, John Ruskin, Arthur Sullivan, and Oscar Wilde.

## American Art and Literature Highlights

**Births/Deaths**  Births include art figures Julian Levi, Louise Nevelson, Jack Tworkov, and literary figures Sally Benson, Edward Dahlberg, Laura Hobson, Cyril Hume, Margaret Mitchell, William L. White, and Thomas Wolfe; deaths include artists William Beard, Frederic Church, Jasper Cropsey, William Sonntag, and literary figures Stephen Crane, Rowland E. Robinson, and Charles Dudley Warner.

**Art Works**  Solon Borglum, *On the Border of White Man's Land*; Henry Cross, *Geronimo*; Thomas Eakins, *The Thinker: Louis H. Kenton*; Winslow Homer, *West Point, Prout's Neck*; John F. Peto, *Old Reminiscences*; Maurice Prendergast, *Central Park*; Robert Reid, *Fleurs-de-lis* (?); John S. Sargent, *Wyndham Sisters*; John Twachtman, *Winter Harmony—Sailing in the Mist*; Bessie Vonnoh, *Dancing Figure*.

**Literature**  Irving Bacheller, *Eben Holden*; L. Frank Baum, *The Wonderful Wizard of Oz*; Charles Chesnutt, *The House Behind the Cedars*; Stephen Crane, *Wounds in the Rain*; Theodore Dreiser, *Sister Carrie*; Finley P. Dunne, *Mr. Dooley's Philosophy*; Ellen Glasgow, *Voice of the People*; Jack London, *Son of the Wolf*; James Whitcomb Riley, *Home Folks*; Booth Tarkington, *Monsieur Beaucaire*.

## Music—The Vernacular/Commercial Scene

**A. Births**  Alger "Texas" Alexander (singer) September 12; Boyd Atkins (saxophonist/fiddler); Gene Austin (singer) June 24; Xavier Cugat (bandleader) January 1; Peter De Rose (composer)

March 10; Ted Fiorito (composer/bandleader) December 20; Jimmy Harrison (trombonist/singer) October 17; Buell Kazee (folk singer) August 29; Tommy Ladnier (trumpeter) May 28; Dickey Lee (singer) September 21; George Lewis (clarinetist) July 13; Paul Mares (trumpeter/composer) June 15; Mabel Mercer (singer) February 3; Helen Morgan (singer); Alfred Newman (composer/conductor) March 17; Walter Page (string bassist/bandleader) February 9; Tony Parenti (clarinetist/saxophonist) August 6; Mitchell Parish (lyricist) July 10; Don Redman (composer/bandleader) July 29; Malvina Reynolds (songwriter) August 23; Arthur Schwartz (composer) November 25; Nat Simon (composer) August 6; Victor Young (composer/conductor) August 8.

**B. Deaths**   Charles Hoyt (lyricist/librettist/producer) November 20.

**C. Biographical**

**New Beginnings**   Vaudeville Managers Association.

**Miscellaneous**   Julian Edwards becomes an American citizen; Fred Fischer (German composer) comes to the United States.

**D. Publications**   Edward Le Roy Rice, *Monarchs of Minstrelsy, from "Daddy" Rice to Date*.

**E. Representative Works**

**Musicals**   Cook and Rogers, *Sons of Ham* (musical); Ludwig Englander and Smith, *The Monks of Malabar—The Belle of Bohemia*; Victor Herbert and H. B. Smith, *The Viceroy*; Gustav Luders and F. Pixley, *The Burgomaster*; A. Baldwin Sloane and G. V. Hobart, *The Giddy Throng*; Leslie Stewart, *Florodora*; John Stromberg and H. B. Smith, *Fiddle-Dee-Dee*.

**Songs**   Paul Dresser, *The Blue and the Gray*; Gus Edwards and W. D. Cobb, *I Can't Tell Why I Love You, but I Do*; J. Rosamond Johnson, *Lift Every Voice and Sing*; J. Bodewalt Lampe and G. Sidney, *Creole Belle*; W. H. Myddleton, *Down South*; John Queen and H. Cannon, *Just Because She Made Dem Goo-Goo Eyes*; Leslie Stuart and O. Hall, *Tell Me, Pretty Maiden*; James Thornton, *The Bridge of Sighs*; Harry Von Tilzer and A. J. Lamb, *A Bird in a Gilded Cage*; Ellen Wright and J. Fane, *Violets*.

**Other**   Charles Hunter, *A Tennessee Tantalizer*; Tom Turpin, *A Ragtime Nightmare*.

## Music—The Cultivated/Art Music Scene

**F. Births**   George Antheil (composer/pianist) July 8; Leon Barzin (conductor) November 27; Martha Beck (composer) January 19; Aaron Copland (composer/conductor) November 14; Richard Crooks (tenor) June 25; Maurice Eisenberg (cellist) February 24; Isadore Freed (composer) March 26; Joseph Fuchs (violinist) April 26; Florence G. Galajikian (pianist/composer) July 29; Helen Hewitt (musicologist) May 2; Otto Luening (composer/conductor) June 15; Colin McPhee (ethnomusicologist/composer) March 15; Charles O'Connell (conductor/record executive) April 22; Solomon Pinsleur (pianist/composer) September 19; Max Rosen (violinist) April 11; Alexander Steinert (conductor/pianist) September 21; Gladys Swarthout (contralto) December 25; Joseph F. Wagner (composer/conductor) January 9; Fred Waring (conductor/publisher/writer) June 9; Elinor Remick Warren (pianist/composer) February 23.

**G. Deaths**   Charles R. Adams (tenor) July 4; Jesse B. Aikin (compiler/singing master); David C. Hall (brass instrument maker) February 11; S. Austen Pearce (British-born organist) April 9; David W. Reeves (bandmaster/cornetist) March 8; John Wesley Steere (organ builder) December 11; Richard Storrs Willis (composer/author) May 7.

**H. Debuts**

**United States**   Harold Bauer (British pianist, Boston), Robert Blass (tenor—San Francisco), Ossip Gabrilowitsch (Russian pianist—New York), Louise Homer (contralto—San Francisco), Marcel Journet (French bass—San Francisco), Edwin Lemare (British organist—tour), Fritzi Scheff (Austrian soprano—San Francisco), Clarence Whitehill (bass-baritone—New York).

**Metropolitan Opera**   Hans Breuer (German tenor), Fritz Friedrichs (German— New York), Johanna Gadski (German soprano), Charles Gilibert (French bass), Louise Homer (contralto), Milka Ternina (Croatian soprano).

**Other**    Mary Garden (soprano—Paris).

**I. New Positions**

**Conductors**    Fritz Scheel (Philadelphia Orchestra—to 1907); Gustav Strube (Boston Pops—to 1902).

**Educational**    Frederick Gleason (general director, Chicago Conservatory—to 1903).

**Other**    James G. Huneker (music/art critic, *New York Sun*—to 1912); Charles Ives (organ, Central Presbyterian Church, New York); John J. McClellan (organ, Mormon Tabernacle).

**J. Honors and Awards**

**Honors**    Peter Christian Lutkin (MusD, Syracuse University).

**K. Biographical**    Ossip Gabrilowitsch makes his first American tour; Asger Hamerik, leaving Peabody, tours Europe and settles in Copenhagen; Henriot Lévy (Polish pianist/composer) emigrates to the United States; Wallingford Riegger begins serious music study when his family moves to New York; John Philip Sousa takes his band on its first European tour with huge success; Moritz Steiner donates his instrument collection to Yale University; Edouard Strauss takes his Vienna Orchestra on a tour of the United States

**L. Musical Beginnings**

**Performing Groups**    Amateur Symphony Orchestra (Denver, Colorado); Dallas Symphony Club, Honolulu Symphony Society; Longy Club (Boston); Philadelphia Orchestra.

**Festivals**    Bethlehem Bach Festival (Pennsylvania).

**Educational**    Drake School of Music (Chicago); West Side Musical College (Cleveland).

**Other**    *American Music Journal* (Cleveland—to 1907); Boston Symphony Hall; Butler Standard Theater (Kansas City); Melville Clark Piano Co.; Hall of Fame for Great Americans; Kotzschmar Club (Portland, Maine); Leedy and Cooley (Leedy Manufacturing Co., 1903); People's Symphony Concerts (New York); *The Violinist* (to 1937).

**M. Music Publications**

Baker, Theodore, *A Biographical Dictionary of Music*
Boise, Otis B., *Harmony Made Practical*
Clarke, Hugh A. *The Elements of Vocal Harmony*
Elson, Louis C., *Famous Composers and Their Works*
Finck, Henry T., *Songs and Song Writers*
Fletcher, Alice C., *Indian Story and Song from North America*
Hughes, Rupert, *Contemporary American Composers*
Messiter, Arthur, *Literature of Music* (8 volumes)

**N. Musical Compositions**

**Choral/Vocal**    Amy Beach, *Three Browning (Robert) Songs, Opus 44*; Franz Bornschein, *String Quartet*; Charles Gabriel, *The Glory Song*; Charles Ives, *Psalm 135*; Arne Oldberg, *String Quartet in C Minor*; Horatio Parker, *A Wanderer's Psalm—Three Songs, Opus 52*.

**Concertos**    Helen Hopekirk, *Concerto for Piano and Orchestra*; Charles M. Loeffler, *Divertissement espagnol* (sax and orchestra).

**Operas**    John Alden Carpenter, *The Little Dutch Girl* (pastoral play); George W. Chadwick, *Judith*; Willard Patton, *The Star of Empire*; Humphrey Stewart, *The Conspirators*.

**Orchestra/Band**    Russell Alexander, *March, Memphis, the Majestic—The Steeplechase March*; George W. Chadwick, *Overture, Adonais*; Frederick Converse, *The Festival of Pan* (symphonic poem); Arthur Farwell, *Academic Overture, "Cornell," Opus 9*; Arthur Foote, *Four Character Pieces after the Rubáiyát of Omar Khayyám, Opus 48*; Julius Fučik, *Entry of the Gladiators*; Frederick Gleason, *The Song of Life* (symphonic poem); Rubin Goldmark, *Hiawatha* (tone poem); Henry Hadley, *In Bohemia, Opus 28*; Arthur Nevin, *A Night in Yaddo Land* (masque); John Knowles Paine, *The Birds* (incidental music); Harry R. Shelley, *Santa Claus Overture*; John Philip Sousa, *Hail to the Spirit of Liberty*; Frank Van der Stucken, *Pax Triumphans* (symphonic poem).

**Piano/Organ**    Arthur Farwell, *American Indian Melodies, Opus 11*; Victor Herbert, *Six Pieces for Piano, Set I*; Edward MacDowell, *Sonata No. 4 in E Minor, "Keltic"*; Horace Nicholl, *Twelve Symphonic Preludes and Fugues, Opus 30 for Organ.*

**Symphonies**    Edgar S. Kelley, *Symphony No. 1, "Gulliver: His Voyage to Lilliput."*

# 1901

☀

## Historical Highlights

President McKinley is assassinated and Theodore Roosevelt becomes the 26th president; the first auto licenses are issued in New York; the Panama Canal becomes a step closer to reality with the signing of the Hay-Pauncefote Treaty; Queen Victoria dies and Edward VII becomes the British monarch; Marconi sends the first transatlantic wireless message.

## World Cultural Highlights

**World Art**    Paul Gauguin, *The Gold in Their Bodies*; Aristide Maillol, *Seated Woman*; Henri de Toulouse-Lautrec, *Opera Messalina*; Maurice Vlaminck, *The Dock at Bougival.*

**World Literature**    Anton Chekhov, *The Three Sisters*; Thomas Hardy, *Poems of the Past and Present*; Thomas Mann, *Buddenbrooks*; Rudyard Kipling, *Kim*; August Strindberg, *The Dance of Death.*

**World Music**    Frederick Delius, *A Village Romeo and Juliet*; Sergei Rachmaninoff, *Piano Concerto No. 2—Suite No. 2 for Two Pianos*; Arnold Schoenberg, *Gurre-Lieder*; Jean Sibelius, *Symphony No. 2.*

**Miscellaneous**    Universal Edition in Vienna begins publishing; the Warsaw Philharmonic is founded; births include Edward van Beinum, Jean Dubuffet, and Marino Marini; deaths include Arnold Böcklin, Johann Malmström, Salvatore Quasimodo, Henri de Toulouse-Latrec, and Giuseppe Verdi.

## American Art and Literature Highlights

**Births/Deaths**    Births include artists Richmond Barthé, Philip Evergood, William Johnson, and literary figures Robert Francis, Zora Neale Hurston, Oliver H. Perry La Farge, Laura Riding, and Glenway Wescott; deaths include literary figures William E. Channing II, James A. Herne, Robert Newell (Orpheus C. Kerr), James M. Thompson, Mary Van Voorhis Townsend, and Lydia Louise Very.

**Art Works**    Herbert Adams, *The Age of Enlightenment*; A. Stirling Calder, *The Man Cub*; William Glackens, *Hammerstein's Roof Garden* (?); Hermon MacNeil, *The Despotic Age*; Thomas Moran, *The Grand Canyon of the Yellowstone II*; Maurice Prendergast, *Central Park*; John Sloan, *East Entrance, City Hall, Philadelphia*; John M. Twachtman, *Fishing Boats at Gloucester.*

**Literature**    Winston Churchill, *The Crisis*; Arthur Colton, *The Delectable Mountains*; Finley P. Dunne, *Mr. Dooley's Opinions*; Edwin Lefevre, *Wall Street Stories*; Edwin C. Markham, *Lincoln and Other Poems*; George McCutcheon, *Graustark*; Frank Norris, *The Octopus*; Alice C. Rice, *Mrs. Wiggs of the Cabbage Patch*; Booker T. Washington, *Up from Slavery*; Albery A. Whitman, *The Octoroon.*

## Music—The Vernacular/Commercial Scene

**A. Births**    James "Kokomo" Arnold (singer/guitarist) February 15; Frank Churchill (composer) October 20; Hugo Friedhofer (composer) May 3; Edmond Hall (clarinetist) May 15; Horace Heidt (bandleader) May 21; Tommy Jarrell (violinist/singer) March 1; Wayne King (bandleader) February 16; Phil Napoleon (trumpeter/bandleader) September 2; Ralph Rainger (composer/pianist) October 7; Frankie Trumbauer (saxophonist) May 30; Rudy Vallee (band-leader/singer) July 28; Ned Washington (lyricist) August 15; Ray Whitley (singer) December 5.

**C. Biographical**

**Performing Groups**   Dockstader's Minstrels; Imperial Orchestra (New Orleans).

**E. Representative Works**

**Musicals**   George M. Cohan, *The Governor's Son*; Reginald de Koven and H. B. Smith, *The Little Duchess*; Ludwig Englander and G. MacDonough, *The New Yorkers*; Ludwig Englander and H. B. Smith, *The Strollers*; Gustave A. Kerker and H. Morton, *The Girl from Up There*; Gustave Luders and F. Pixley, *King Dodo*; T. Maclaglen and W. H. Lingard, *Captain Jinks of the Horse Marines*; Chauncey Olcott, *Garrett O'Magh*; Willard Spenser, *Miss Bob White*; Joe Weber and Lew Fields, *Hoity-Toity*.

**Songs**   Carrie Jacobs Bond, *I Love You Truly—Just A-Wearyin' for You*; Gus Edwards and W. Cobb, *I'll Be with You When the Roses Bloom Again*; Leo Friedman, *Coon, Coon, Coon*; Charles K. Harris, *Hello, Central, Give Me Heaven*; J. Schwartz and W. Jerome, *Any Old Place I Can Hang My Hat Is Home Sweet Home to Me*; N. Moret and J. O'Dea, *Hiawatha*; Ethelbert Nevin and F. L. Stanton, *Mighty Lak' a Rose*; H. Von Tilzer and A. Sterling, *Down Where the Cotton Blossoms Grow*; W. Wilson and J. Queen, *Ain't Dat a Shame?*

**Other**   Charles Hunter, *Cotton Bolls Rag—Queen of Love*; Scott Joplin, *Rags: The Easy Winners—Peacherine—Sunflower Slow Drag*.

## Music—The Cultivated/Art Music Scene

**F. Births**   Saul Caston (conductor/trumpeter) August 22; Olaf Christiansen (conductor) August 12; John Corigliano, Sr. (violinist) August 28; Ruth Crawford (composer/educator) July 3; Nelson Eddy (baritone) June 29; Hamilton Forrest (composer) January 8; E. Thayer Gaston (music therapist) July 4; Carroll Hollister (pianist) April 6; Dorothy James (composer) December 1; William Kroll (violinist) January 30; Harry Partch (composer/performer) June 24; Willard Rhodes (ethnomusicologist) May 12; Alexander Schreiner (organist) July 31; Tibor Serly (composer/theorist) November 25; Moses Smith (critic) March 4; Oliver Strunk (musicologist) March 22; Harry Robert Wilson (conductor/composer) May 18; John Wesley Work, Jr. (composer/conductor) June 15.

**G. Deaths**   Charles Francis Albert (violin maker); Frederick Archer (British-born organist/conductor) October 22; Joseph Fisher (German-born publisher) November 24; Lillian Henschel (soprano) November 4; William Allen Johnson (organ maker) January; Ethelbert Nevin (composer) February 17; Daniel Webster Whittle (hymnist) March 4; Benjamin E. Woolf (British-born critic/composer) February 7.

**H. Debuts**

**United States**   Florence Austin (violinist—New York), E. Azalia Hackley (Denver); Jan Kubelik (Czech violinist—New York).

**Metropolitan Opera**   Lucienne Bréval (Swiss soprano), Emilio De Marchi (Italian tenor), Marguerite MacIntyre (British soprano), Marie Mattfeld (German mezzo-soprano), Albert Reiss (German tenor), Andrés de Segurola (Spanish bass).

**Other**   Richard Buhlig (pianist—Berlin), Geraldine Farrar (soprano—Berlin), Rita Fornia (mezzo-soprano—Hamburg).

**I. New Positions**

**Conductors**   Emil Oberhoffer (Philharmonic Choral Society, Minneapolis—to 1923).

**Educational**   Rudolph Ganz (Chicago Musical College); Edward F. Schneider (Mills College—to 1936).

**Other**   Lawrence Gilman (music critic, *Harper's Weekly*—to 1913); Edwin Arthur Kraft (organ, St. Thomas's, Brooklyn—to 1904); Thomas Tapper (editor, *Music Record and Review*—to 1907).

**K. Biographical**   Rudoph Ganz (Swiss pianist/conductor) comes to the United States; Arthur Shepherd marries Hattie Hooper Jennings of Salt Lake City.

**L. Musical Beginnings**

**Performing Groups**   Boston Choral Art Society; Century Music Club (Atlanta).

**Educational**   University of California, Berkeley, Music Department.

**Other**   C. C. Birchard Co. (Boston); Brook Mays Music Co. (Dallas); Buffalo Temple of Music (New York); *The Church Music Review*; Daniels and Russell, Music Publishers (St. Louis); *International Musician*; *Musical Life* (to 1904); *Sinfonian*; Skinner Organ Co. (Boston—merges with Aeolian Co. in 1921); Victor Talking Machine Co.; Wa-Wan Press (Boston).

**M. Music Publications**

Apthorp, William Foster, *The Opera, Past and Present*
Clarke, Hugh A., *Counterpoint—Highways and Byways of Music*
Elson, Arthur, *A Critical History of the Opera*
Elson, Louis C. *Shakespeare in Music*
Kobbé, Gustav, *Opera Singers*
Lahee, Henry C., *Famous Pianists of Today and Yesterday*
Pratt, Waldo S., *Musical Ministries in the Church*
Redman, Harry N., *A Pronouncing Dictionary of Musical Terms*

**N. Musical Compositions**

**Chamber Music**   Arthur Bird, *Two Decimettes* (winds—Paderewski Prize); Edgar S. Kelley, *Piano Quintet, Opus 20*; Horace Nicholl, *String Quartet in C Major, Opus 39—Piano Trio in B Minor*.

**Choral/Vocal**   Amy Beach, *Sylvania: A Wedding Cantata*; Charles Ives, *Psalm XXV—Three Harvest Home Chorales—The Children's Hour* (song); Edward MacDowell, *Three Songs, Opus 60*; Horatio Parker, *Three Part-Songs for Male Voices, Opus 48—Four Songs, Opus 51—A Star Song, Opus 54* (Paderewski Prize)—*Greek Festival Hymn*; Arthur B. Whiting, *The Rubaiyát of Omar Khayyám, Opus 18*.

**Concertos**   Frederick Converse, *Night and Day, Two Poems after Whitman* (piano and orchestra); Victor Herbert, *Pan-American* (piano and orchestra).

**Operas**   Julian Edwards, *Dolly Varden*; Francesco Fanciulli, *Priscilla*; Harry R. Shelley, *Romeo and Juliet*.

**Orchestra/Band**   Russell Alexander, *Colossus of Columbia March—Shoot the Chutes March*; Frederick Converse, *Endymion's Narrative*; Henry Hadley, *Herod Overture, Opus 31*; Victor Herbert, *Auditorium Festival March—Suite Romantique, Opus 31—Woodland Fancies, Opus 34*; John N. Klohr, *The Billboard March*; Margaret R. Lang, *Ballade in D Minor, Opus 36* (first performed); Arthur Shepherd, *Ouverture Joyeuse, Opus 3*; David S. Smith, *Darkness and Dawn* (tone poem); John Philip Sousa, *Invincible Eagle March—The Pride of Pittsburgh March*; Gustav Strube, *Rhapsody for Orchestra*.

**Piano/Organ**   Arthur Farwell, *Dawn, Fantasy on Two Indian Themes, Opus 12—Symbolist Study No. 1, "Toward the Dream," Opus 16*; Henry H. Huss, *Menuet and Gavotte Caprieuse, Opus 18—Quatre Préludes en forme d'études, Opus 17*.

**Symphonies**   Henry Hadley, *Symphony No. 2, "The Four Seasons," Opus 30* (Paderewski Prize).

# 1902

❀

## Historical Highlights

Congress puts a limit on the number of Chinese that may enter the United States in any year; the Drago Doctrine seeks to promote protectionism of the South American countries; the American

Philosophical Association is formed; the United States pulls out of Cuba, which becomes a new republic; the Boer War ends in Africa.

## World Cultural Highlights

**World Art**    Henri Matisse, *Notre Dame*; Camille Pissarro, *Corner of the Meadow, Eragny*; Pierre-Auguste Renoir, *Reclining Bather*; Auguste Rodin, *Romeo and Juliet*.

**World Literature**    Arthur Conan Doyle, *The Hound of the Baskervilles*; Rudyard Kipling, *Just-So Stories*; Maurice Maeterlinck, *Monna Vanna*; Alfred E. Mason, *The Four Feathers*.

**World Music**    Claude Debussy, *Pelleas et Mélisande;* Frederick Delius, *Appalachia;* Gustav Mahler, *Symphony No. 5—Kindertotenlieder*; Carl Nielsen, *Symphony No. 2, "The Four Temperaments."*

**Miscellaneous**    The Nottingham Music and Drama Festivals begin; births include Eugen Jochum and Josef Krips; deaths include Hermann Allmers, Aimé Jules Dalou, James J. Tissot, and Émile Zola.

## American Art and Literature Highlights

**Births/Deaths**    Births include artists Isabel Bishop, Adolph Gottlieb, literary figures Kenneth Fearing, Langston Hughes, Ogden Nash, John Steinbeck, Jessamyn West, Philip G. Wylie, and Marya Zaturenska; deaths include artists Albert Bierstadt, Lily Spencer, John Twachtman, literary figures Edward Eggleston, Bret Harte, Frank Norris, Frank Stockton, Elizabeth B. Stoddard, and Ellen Drew Stoddard.

**Art Works**    Edwin A. Abbey, *The Quest of the Holy Grail*; George Barnard, *The Hewer*; Mary Cassatt, *The Caress*; Arthur B. Davies, *Dancing Children*; Thomas Eakins, *Self-Portrait*; Charles Grafly, *In Much Wisdom*; Robert Henri, *West Fifty-Seventh Street*; Winslow Homer, *Early Morning after a Storm at Sea*; Albert Laessle, *Turtle and Lizards*; John Twachtman, *Hemlock Pool*.

**Literature**    Finley P. Dunne, *Observations of Mr. Dooley*; Clyde Fitch, *Girl with the Green Eyes*; Hamlin Garland, *Captain of the Gray-Horse Troop*; Henry James, *The Wings of the Dove*; Robert Johnson, *Poems*; Jack London, *People of the Abyss*; George McCutcheon, *Brewster's Millions*; Myrtel Reed, *Lavender and Old Lace*; Edith Wharton, *The Valley of Decision*; Owen Wister, *The Virginian*.

## Music—The Vernacular/Commercial Scene

**A. Births**    Louis Alter (composer) June 18; Jimmy Archey (trombonist) October 12; Buster Bailey (clarinetist) July 19; Phil Charig (composer) August 31; Sam Coslow (lyricist); Jimmie Davis (singer) September 11; Al Dexter (singer) May 4; Sammy Fain (composer) June 17; Al Hoffman (songwriter) September 25; Son House (singer/guitarist) March 21; Blind Willie Johnson (singer); Bessie Jones (singer) February 8; Eddie Lang (guitarist) October 25; Guy Lombardo (bandleader) June 19; Jimmy Lunceford (bandleader) June 6; Richard Rodgers (composer) June 28; Jimmie Rushing (singer) August 26; Arthur Schutt (pianist/arranger) November 21; Joe Smith (trumpeter) June 28; William "Chick" Webb (drummer/bandleader); Peetie Wheatstraw (pianist/singer) December 21; Meredith Willson (composer/conductor) May 18.

**B. Deaths**    John "Honey" Stromberg (composer); Septimus Winner (composer) November 22.

**C. Biographical**

**New Beginnings**    Gibson Mandolin-Guitar Manufacturing Co. (Kalamazoo, Michigan); Harry Von Tilzer Music Co. (New York).

**E. Representative Works**

**Musicals**    Will R. Anderson, *The Silver Slipper*; Reginald de Koven and H. B. Smith, *Maid Marian*; Julian Edwards and S. Stange, *When Johnny Comes Marching Home*; Ludwig Englander and G. V. Hobart, *Sally in Our Alley—The Wild Rose*; Chauncey Olcott, *Old Limerick Town*; Jean Schwartz and W. Jerome, *A Chinese Honeymoon—The Wild Rose*; A. Baldwin Sloane and S. Rosenfeld, *The Mocking Bird*; John Stromberg and E. Smith, *Twirly Whirly*.

**Songs**   Hughie Cannon, *Bill Bailey, Won't You Please Come Home*; Bob Cole, *Under the Bamboo Tree*; Paul Dresser, *In Dear Old Illinois*; George Evans and Ren Shields, *In the Good Old Summertime*; Edward Teschemacher and G. d'Hardelot, *Because*; Harry Von Tilzer, *Down Where the Wurzburger Flows—On a Sunday Afternoon*.

**Other**   Scott Joplin, *Rags: The Entertainer—A Breeze from Alabama—Elite Syncopations—The Strenuous Life*; Joe Jordan, *Double Fudge Rag*; Jelly Roll Morton, *New Orleans Blues*.

## Music—The Cultivated/Art Music Scene

**F. Births**   Marian Anderson (contralto) February 17; Antonia Brico (conductor) June 26; Mark Brunswick (composer) January 6; Theodore Chanler (critic/composer) April 29; Celius Dougherty (pianist/composer) May 27; Theodore M. Finney (musicologist) March 14; Dusolina Giannini (soprano) December 19; Donald Jay Grout (musicologist) September 28; Allen Irvine McHose (theorist) May 14; A. Tillman Merritt (musicologist) February 15; William D. Revelli (bandmaster) February 12; Jesús María Sanromá (pianist) November 7; Alice Tully (mezzo-soprano/philanthropist) September 11; John Vincent (composer/educator) May 17; G. Wallace Wordworth (conductor/organist) November 6.

**G. Deaths**   Henry Stephen Cutler (organist) December 5; Wulf Fries (German-born cellist) April 29; George Kilgen (German-born organ maker); William Perkins (singer/composer) January 13; Camilla Urso (French-born violinist) January 20; George William Warren (organist) March 17; John White (organist) July 18.

**H. Debuts**

**United States**   Jaroslav Kocian (Czech violinist—New York), Francesco Navarrini (Italian bass—tour), Antonio Paoli (Puerto Rican tenor—tour), Elsa Ruegger (Swiss cellist—New York).

**Metropolitan Opera**   Georges Anthes (German tenor), Alexander von Bandrowski (Polish tenor), Alfred Hertz (German conductor), Louise Kirkby-Lunn (British mezzo-soprano), Estelle Liebling (soprano), Helen Mapleson (mezzo-soprano), Marie Maurer (mezzo-soprano), Luise Reuss-Belce (Austrian soprano).

**Other**   Francis Maclennan (tenor—London), Florence Wickham (contralto—Wiesbaden).

**I. New Positions**

**Conductors**   Walter Damrosch (New York Philharmonic Orchestra, one season); Wallace Goodrich (Boston Choral Art Society—to 1907); Victor Harris (St. Cecilia Club, New York—to 1936); Alfred Hertz (Metropolitan Opera—to 1915); R. E. Trognitz (San Diego Symphony Orchestra—to 1910).

**Educational**   Emil Oberhoffer (University of Minnesota—to 1905); Clara Kathleen Rogers (New England Conservatory); Alexander Russell (Syracuse University—to 1906); Carl E. Seashore (University of Iowa); Henry Dike Sleeper (music head, Smith College—to 1924).

**Other**   Richard Aldrich (music critic, *New York Times*—to 1923); Heinrich Conried (manager, Metropolitan Opera—to 1908); William James Henderson (music critic, *New York Sun*—to 1920); Horatio Parker (organist/choirmaster, St. Nicholas, New York—to 1910); Oscar G. Sonneck (head, music division, Library of Congress—to 1917); Caryl B. Storrs (music critic, *Minneapolis Tribune*).

**J. Honors and Awards**

**Honors**   Horatio Parker (PhD, Cambridge).

**K. Biographical**   Teresa Carreño marries her fourth husband, Arturo Tagliapetra; Edgar Stillman Kelley moves to Berlin and teaches music until 1910; Pietro Mascagni conducts his operas on a tour of the United States

**L. Musical Beginnings**

**Performing Groups**   Cleveland Grand Orchestra; Dayton Chaminade Club; Flonzaley String Quartet (New York); Fort Worth Harmony Club (Texas); Olive Mead String Quartet; San Diego

Symphony Orchestra; Tulsa Commercial Club Band; Washington (DC) Symphony Orchestra (only three seasons); Young Men's Symphony Orchestra of New York.

**Educational**   Florida State College School of Music.

**Other**   Gillis Opera House (Kansas City); Tuesday Morning Music Club (Springfield, Massachusetts); Tulsa Commercial Club Band.

## M. Music Publications

Boise, Otis B., *Music and Its Masters*
Elson, Arthur, *Orchestra Instruments and Their Use*
Goetschius, Percy, *Counterpoint*
Huneker, James G., *Melomaniacs*
Joseffy, Rafael, *School of Advanced Piano Playing*
Lahee, Henry C., *Grand Opera in America*
Mason, Daniel G., *From Grieg to Brahms*
Mathews, W. S. B., *The Great in Music*
Perry, Edward B., *Descriptive Analyses of Piano Works*
Upton, George P., *Musical Pastels—The Standard Light Operas*

## N. Musical Compositions

**Chamber Music**   Victor Herbert, *Soixante-neuf* (string quartet); Charles Ives, *Violin Sonata (KW. 4)*; Frederick Zech, Jr., *String Quartet No. 2.*

**Choral/Vocal**   Amy Beach, *A Song of Liberty—Four Songs, Opus 48*; Frederick Converse, *La Belle Dame sans Merci* (baritone and orchestra); Ethelbert Nevin, *The Quest* (oratorio).

**Concertos**   Frederick Converse, *Violin Concerto*; Horatio Parker, *Organ Concerto, Opus 55.*

**Operas**   Louis Coerne, *Zenobia.*

**Orchestra/Band**   Russell Alexander, *Embossing the Emblem March*; Charles Ives, *From the Steeples and the Mountains*; John Philip Sousa, *Imperial Edward March—Suite, Looking Up.*

**Piano/Organ**   Arthur Farwell, *The Domain of Hurakan, Opus 15* (orchestrated 1910); Henry H. Huss, *La Nuit* (orchestrated 1939); Edward MacDowell, *Fireside Tales, Opus 61—New England Idylls, Opus 62*; Arthur Nevin, *Miniature Suite*; Ethelbert Nevin, *O'er Hill and Dale*; Horace Nicholls, *Life, Opus 50* (symphonic poem for organ).

**Symphonies**   Ernest Bloch, *Symphony in C-Sharp Minor*; Charles Ives, *Symphony No. 2.*

# 1903

☀

## Historical Highlights

The Wright Brothers make their first flight at Kitty Hawk—120 feet in 12 seconds; the first cross-country auto trip takes 52 days; Canada and the United States settle their longstanding border dispute; the Canal Zone is formed in Panama by the Hay-Bunau-Varilla Treaty after President Roosevelt aids the Panamanians in gaining independence from Colombia.

## World Cultural Highlights

**World Art**   Barbara Hepworth, *Torso*; Wilhelm Lehmbruck, *Standing Youth*; Henri Matisse, *The Guitarist*; Pablo Picasso, *The Old Guitarist*; Georges Rouault, *The Bathers*.

**World Literature**   Samuel Butler, *The Way of All Flesh*; Joseph Conrad, *Typhoon and Other Stories*; Thomas Hardy, *The Dynasts*; Tristan Klingsor, *Schéhérazade*; George Bernard Shaw, *Man and Superman*.

**World Music**   Maurice Ravel, *String Quartet*; Arnold Schönberg, *Pelleas und Mélisande*; Alexander Scriabin, *Symphony No. 2*; Jean Sibelius, *Violin Concerto*; Richard Strauss, *Sinfonia Domestica*.

**Miscellaneous**    The Société Symphonique de Québec is founded; births include Kenneth Clark, Aram Khachaturian, Mark Rothko, Gregor Piatigorsky, and Graham Sutherland; deaths include George Gissing, Paul Gauguin, Gabriel Legouvé, Camille Pissarro, and Hugo Wolf.

## American Art and Literature Highlights

**Births/Deaths**    Births include artists Robert Gwathmey, Seymour Lipton, literary figures Erskine Caldwell, James Cozzens, Countee Cullen, Alexander Laing, Clare Boothe Luce, Irving Stone, and Nathan Weinstein (Nathaniel West); deaths include artists Robert Blum, James W. Champney, James M. Whistler, Thomas Wood, and literary figures Noah Brooks and Richard H. Stoddard.

**Art Works**    Daniel C. French, *Alma Mater*; Childe Hassam, *Fourmaster Schooner*; Robert Henri, *Wyoming Valley, Pennsylvania*; Maurice Prendergast, *Central Park in 1903*; Frederic Remington, *Fight for the Water Hole*; John S. Sargent, *Charles Martin Loeffler*; Charles Schreyvogel, *Custer's Demands*; Everett Shinn, *Trapeze, Winter Garden*; Abbott H. Thayer, *The Stevenson Memorial Angel*.

**Literature**    Josephine Bacon, *Poems*; W. E. B. Du Bois, *Souls of Black Folk*; Paul L. Dunbar, *Lyrics of Love and Laughter*; John W. Fox, *Little Shepherd of Kingdom Come*; Henry James, *The Ambassadors*; Jack London, *Call of the Wild*; H. L. Mencken, *Ventures into Verse*; Frank Norris, *The Pit*; Nora Smith, *Rebecca of Sunnybrook Farm*; George Sterling, *Testimony of the Suns and Other Poems*.

## Music — The Vernacular/Commercial Scene

**A. Births**    Roy Acuff (singer) September 15; Bix Beiderbecke (clarinetist) March 10; Milton Brown (singer) September 8; Frankie Carle (bandleader) March 25; Joe Garland (composer/arranger) August 15; Earl "Fatha" Hines (pianist) December 28; Claude Hopkins (pianist/bandleader) August 24; Irving Kahal (lyricist) March 5; Matty Malneck (composer) December 9; Clyde McCoy (trumpeter/bandleader) December 29; Bubber Miley (trumpeter) January 19 (?); Ben Pollack (drummer/bandleader) June 22; Jimmy Rushing (singer) August 26; Joe Venuti (violinist/bandleader) September 16; Teddy Weatherford (pianist/bandleader) October 11; Lawrence Welk (bandleader) March 11; Big Joe Williams (guitarist/singer) October 16.

**B. Deaths**    Charles Dupee Blake (composer) November 24; H. P. Danks (composer/singer) November 20.

**C. Biographical**

**New Beginnings**    *Edison Phonograph Monthly*; Majestic Theater (New York); York Music Co. (New York).

**Miscellaneous**    Monroe Rosenfeld coins the name "Tin Pan Alley" for 28th Street in New York City.

**E. Representative Works**

**Musicals**    George M. Cohan, *Running for Office*; Ludwig Englander and H. B. Smith, *The Jewel of Asia*; Henry Hadley and F. Rankin, *Nancy Brown*; Victor Herbert and G. MacDonough, *Babes in Toyland*; Victor Herbert and H. B. Smith, *Babette*; Scott Joplin, *The Guest of Honor* ("ragtime opera"); Gustave Luders, *The Prince of Pilsen*; Gustav A. Kerker and H. B. Smith, *The Blonde in Black*; Reginald De Koven and C. Klein, *The Red Feather*; Jean Schwartz and W. Jerome, *The Jersey Lily*; A. Baldwin Sloane and P. Tietjens, *The Wizard of Oz*.

**Songs**    Anonymous, *The Wreck of the Old '97*; H. Armstrong and R. H. Gerard, *Sweet Adeline*; George Evans and Ren Shields, *In the Merry Month of May*; Charles K. Harris, *Always in the Way*; Robert A. King, *Anona*; Eddie Leonard, *Ida, Sweet as Apple Cider*; T. Morse and R. Buck, *Dear Old Girl*; F. E. Tours and R. Kipling, *Mother o' Mine*; H. Von Tilzer and A. Sterling, *Under the Anheuser Bush*.

**Other**    Raymond W. Conner, *Carpet Rags*; Scott Joplin, *Rags: Palm Leaf—Something Doing—Weeping Willow*; James Scott, *The Fascinator—A Summer Breeze: March and Two Step*; Tom Turpin, *St. Louis Rag*.

## Music — The Cultivated/Art Music Scene

**F. Births**  Abram Chasins (music author) August 17; J. M. Coopersmith (musicologist) November 20; Robert Delaney (composer) July 24; Todd Duncan (baritone) February 12; Irwin Fischer (organist) July 5; Lillian Fuchs (violist/composer) November 18; Vittorio Giannini (composer) October 19; Louis Krasner (violinist) June 21; Charles Kullman (tenor) January 13; Jeanette MacDonald (soprano) June 18; Winthrop Sargeant (critic) December 10; Henry Sopkin (conductor) October 20; Donald Voorhees (conductor) July 26; Robert Weede (baritone) February 11.

**G. Deaths**  Henry Distin (British-born brass instrument maker) October 11; Frederick Gleason (organist) December 6; Frederick E. Kitziger (German-born composer) February 3; Jules Levy (British-born cornettist) November 28; Thomas Ryan (Irish-born clarinetist/violist) March 5; Sibyl Sanderson (soprano) May 15; Francis Scala (Italian-born bandmaster) April 18; Clark J. Whitney (publisher/impresario) March 2 (?); Henry Williams (violinist/composer) August 13.

**H. Debuts**

**United States**  Dan Beddoe (Welsh tenor—New York), Ada Crossley (Australian contralto—tour), Rita Fornia (mezzo-soprano—tour), Jacques Thibaud (French violinist—New York).

**Metropolitan Opera**  Julius Bayer (tenor), Paula Braendle (mezzo-soprano), Alois Burgstaller (German tenor), Enrico Caruso (Italian tenor), Minnie Egener (soprano), Mildred Elliott (soprano), Olive Fremstad (soprano—operatic debut), Otto Goritz (German baritone), Ernst Kraus (German tenor), Johanna Pöhlmann (mezzo-soprano), Arcangelo Rossi (bass), Marcia Van Dresser (soprano), Edyth Walker (mezzo-soprano), Marion Weed (soprano).

**Other**  Francis Macmillan (violinist—Brussels), Lucille Marcel (soprano—Paris), Ethel Newcomb (pianist—Vienna).

**I. New Positions**

**Conductors**  Emil Oberhoffer (Minneapolis Symphony Orchestra—to 1923); Horatio Parker (New Haven Oratorio Society—to 1914)

**Educational**  Joseph Adamowski (cello, New England Conservatory); Howard Brockway (Peabody Conservatory—to 1909); F. Melius Christiansen (music head, St. Olaf College, Minnesota); Frederick S. Converse (Harvard—to 1907); Charles S. Skilton (dean, fine arts, University of Kansas—to 1915); David Stanley Smith (Yale—to 1946).

**Other**  Amy Fay (president, Women's Philharmonic Society, New York); Heinrich Conried (manager, Metropolitan Opera—to 1908).

**K. Biographical**  William Foster Apthorp retires and goes to live in Switzerland; Charles Wakefield Cadman moves with his family to Pennsylvania and begins working in a steel mill; Charles Tomlinson Griffes goes to Berlin, where he studies composition with Englebert Humperdinck; Eugen Haile (German composer) comes to the United States; Robert Hope-Jones (British organ maker) comes to the United States and begins working with various organ firms; Charles M. Loeffler resigns from the Boston Symphony Orchestra for full-time composing and farming; Fritzi Scheff leaves the Met for appearances in Victor Herbert's operettas.

**L. Musical Beginnings**

**Performing Groups**  Minneapolis Symphony Orchestra; New Haven Oratorio Society; New York Symphony Orchestra; Arthur Pryor Band; Seattle Symphony Orchestra I.

**Educational**  Cornell University Music Department; Hinshaw School of Opera (Chicago); Mu Phi Epsilon Sorority (Cincinnati); Sigma Alpha Iota Sorority (University of Michigan); University of Minnesota School of Music.

**Other**  Aeolian Weber Piano and Pianola Co. (New York); Columbia Record Co. (New York); *Musical Review (Pacific Coast M.R., 1907)*; Wetzler Symphony Concerts (New York).

**M. Music Publications**

Burton, Frederick, *Songs of the Ojibway Indians*
Elson, Arthur, *Women's Work in Music*

Farwell, Arthur, *A Letter to American Composers*
Goldbeck, Robert, *Encyclopedia of Music Education*
Hughes, Rupert, *The Musical Guide—Love Affairs of the Great Musicians*
Lahee, Henry C., *The Organ and Its Masters*

**N. Musical Compositions**

**Chamber Music**   Arthur Farwell, *To Morfydd* (oboe and piano); Henry H. Huss, *Violin Sonata, Opus 19*; Frederick Zech, Jr., *Piano Quintet*.

**Choral/Vocal**   Amy Beach, *A Hymn of Freedom: America—Four Songs, Opus 51*; Henry Hadley, *The Princess of Ys, Opus 34* (women's voices); John Knowles Paine, *Hymn of the West*; José Quintón, *Requiem*; Harry R. Shelley, *The Pilgrims* (cantata).

**Operas**   Harry L. Freeman, *African Kraal*; William L. Howland, *Sarrona*; Albert Mildenberg, *The Wood Witch*.

**Orchestra/Band**   Russell Alexander, *The Exposition Four March—Storming El Caney Galop*; Amy Beach, *Jephthah's Daughter, Opus 53*; Howard Brockway, *Sylvan Suite*; Frederick Converse, *Euphrosyne Overture*; Henry F. Gilbert, *Americanesque*; Henry Hadley, *Oriental Suite, Opus 32*; Victor Herbert, *Suite for Orchestra, Opus 35*; Charles Ives, *Overture and March "1776"—Country Band March—An Old Song Deranged*; Albert Mildenburg, *Vathek, Opus 56* (symphonic poem); Horatio Parker, *Vathek* (symphonic poem); John Philip Sousa, *Jack Tar March*; Humphrey Stewart, *Montezuma Suite*.

**Piano/Organ**   Henry F. Gilbert, *Two Verlaine Moods, Opus 8*; Victor Herbert, *Valse lente, Under the Elms*.

# 1904

☼

## Historical Highlights

Theodore Roosevelt is elected to his first full term as president and chooses William Howard Taft as his secretary of war; the Louisiana Purchase Exposition opens in St. Louis; the New York subway begins limited operation; the Cadillac Motor Car Co. is founded; W. C. Gorgas conquers Yellow Fever in Panama, opening the way to completion of the canal.

## World Cultural Highlights

**World Art**   Marco Alonso, *Christ of the Andes*; Pablo Picasso, *The Two Sisters*; Georges Rouault, *The Tragic Clown*; Henri Rousseau, *The Wedding*; Maurice Vlaminck, *Kitchen Interior*.

**World Literature**   James Barrie, *Peter Pan*; Anton Chekhov, *The Cherry Orchard*; Joseph Conrad, *Nostromo*; Jack London, *The Sea Wolf*; John Synge, *Riders to the Sea*.

**World Music**   Ferruccio Busoni, *Piano Concerto*; Gustav Mahler, *Symphony No. 6*; Giacomo Puccini, *Madame Butterfly*; Ralph Vaughan Williams, *Songs of Travel—The House of Life*.

**Miscellaneous**   The London Symphony Orchestra and the McGill Conservatory of Music (Canada) are founded; births include Salvador Dali, Christopher Isherwood, Dmitri Kabalevsky, Willem de Kooning, and Pablo Neruda; deaths include Anton Chekhov, Antonín Dvořák, Franz von Lembach, and George Watts.

## American Art and Literature Highlights

**Births/Deaths**   Births include art figures Paul Cadmus, Arshile Gorky, Chaim Gross, Peter Hurd, Isamu Noguchi, and Clyfford Still; and literary figures James T. Farrell, Moss Hart, McKinlay Kantor, S. J. Perelman, Isaac Bashevis Singer, and Louis Zukofsky; deaths include art figures Richard Greenough, Martin Heade, Erastus Palmer, and literary figures Kate O'Flaherty Chopin, Lafcadio Hearn, and Joseph Trumbull Stickney.

**Art Works**    Gutzon Borglum, *Mares of Diomedes*; Thomas Eakins, *The Violinist*; William Glackens, *The Drive, Central Park*; Childe Hassam, *West Wind, Isles of Shoals*; Robert Henri, *Young Woman in White*; Winslow Homer, *A Summer Squall*; John F. Peto, *Old Companions*; Frederic Remington, *Emigrants*; Adolph Weinman, *Destiny of the Red Man*; Mahonri Young, *Bovet Arthur: a Laborer*.

**Literature**    William Braithwaite, *Lyrics of Life and Love*; Ellen Glasgow, *The Deliverance*; Joel Chandler Harris, *The Tar Baby*; Jack London, *The Sea-Wolf*; George McCutcheon, *Beverly of Graustark*; William Moody, *The Fire-Bringer*; Mary N. Murfree, *The Frontiersman*; Gene Stratton Porter, *Freckles*; O. Henry, *Cabbages and Kings*; Henry Van Dyke, *Music and Other Poems*.

## Music—The Vernacular/Commercial Scene

**A. Births**    Herman Autrey (trumpeter) December 4; "Count" Basie (pianist/bandleader) August 21; Cliff Carlisle (singer/writer) May 6; Bill Challis (pianist) July 8; Bing Crosby (singer) May 2; Eddie DeLange (composer/lyricist) January 12; Jimmy Dorsey (bandleader) February 29; Mississippi Fred Dowell (singer/guitarist) January 12; Mack Gordon (composer/lyricist) June 21; Phil Harris (bandleader) January 16; Moss Hart (lyricist) October 24; Coleman Hawkins (saxophonist) November 21; Glenn Miller (bandleader) March 1; Russ Morgan (trombonist/bandleader) April 28; Dick Powell (singer/actor) November 14; Adrian Rollini (saxophonist) June 28; Clarence "Pine Top" Smith (pianist) June 11; Jess Stacy (pianist) August 11; "Fats" Waller (pianist/bandleader) May 21; Mabel Wayne (composer/pianist) July 16.

**B. Deaths**    Daniel Emmett (minstrel performer/composer) June 28.

**D. Publications**    Axel Christensen, *Christensen's Rag-time Instruction Book for Piano*

**E. Representative Works**

**Musicals**    George M. Cohan, *Little Johnny Jones*; Ludwig Englander and H. B. Smith, *A Madcap Princess*; Ludwig Englander and S. Stange, *The Two Roses*; Victor Herbert and G. MacDonough, *It Happened in Nordland*; Gustave Luders, *The Sho Gun*; Gustave Luders and F. Pixley, *Woodland*; Alfred G. Robyn and H. Blossom, *The Yankee Consul*; Jean Schwartz and W. Jerome, *Piff!!! Paff!!! Pouf!!!*

**Songs**    Thomas S. Allen, *By the Watermelon Vine—Lindy Lou*; Gus Edwards and W. Cobb, *Goodbye, Little Girl, Goodbye*; George Evans and Ren Shields, *Come, Take a Trip in My Airship*; Theodore Morse and E. Madden, *Way Down in My Heart—Blue Bell*; Kerry Mills, *Meet Me in St. Louis, Louis*; Egbert A. Van Alstyne and H. Williams, *Back, Back to Baltimore*; Albert Von Tilzer and C. Mack, *Teasing*; Harry Von Tilzer and A. Sterling, *Alexander, Don't You Love Your Baby No More?*

**Other**    Scott Joplin, *Rags: The Cascades—The Chrysanthemum—The Favorite—The Sycamore*; Joe Jordan, *Pekin Rag*; James Scott, *On the Pike: March and Two Step*; Tom Turpin, *Buffalo Rag*.

## Music—The Cultivated/Art Music Scene

**F. Births**    Putnam C. Aldrich (musicologist) July 14; Martin Bernstein (author) December 14; Norman Cordon (baritone) January 20; Charles W. Fox (musicologist) July 24; Anthony Galla-Rini (accordion virtuoso) January 18; Sascha Gorodnitzki (pianist) May 24; Charles Haywood (musicologist) December 20; Julius Huehn (baritone) January 12; Herbert Inch (composer) November 25; Clarence Mader (organist) January 23; James Melton (tenor) January 2; Carl Parrish (musicologist) October 9; Jan Peerce (tenor) June 3; Max Pollikoff (violinist) March 30; Harold Spivacke (musicologist) July 18; Carl Weinrich (organist) July 2; Robert Whitney (conductor) July 9.

**G. Deaths**    George John Huss (German-born organist); Aldine S. Kieffer (publisher/composer) November 30; Franz Schwarzer (Austrian-born zither maker) February 21; Antoinette Sterling (contralto) January 9.

**H. Debuts**

**United States**    Pablo Casals (Spanish cellist—New York), Clara Clemens (contralto—Norfolk,

Connecticut), Theodore Liebhammer (Austrian baritone—tour), Francis Maclennan (tenor—tour), Agnes Nicholls (British soprano—tour), Walter H. Rothwell (British conductor—New York), Vasili Safonov (Russian conductor—New York), Luisa Tetrazzini (Italian soprano—San Francisco), Florence Wickham (contralto—tour).

**Metropolitan Opera** Aïno Ackté (Finnish soprano), Bella Alten (Polish soprano), Maria DeMacchi (soprano), Eugenio Giraldoni (Italian baritone), Roberta Glanville (soprano), Emilie Herzog (Swiss soprano), Heinrich Knote (German tenor), Taurino Parvis (Italian baritone), Edith Vail (soprano).

**Other** Mme. Charles Cahier (contralto—Nice), Riccardo Martin (tenor—Nantes), Jane Osborn-Hannah (soprano—Leipzig).

### I. New Positions

**Conductors** Emil Paur (Pittsburgh Symphony Orchestra—to 1910); Walter Henry Rothwell (Savage Opera Co.); Arnold Volpe (Volpe Symphony Orchestra—to 1914).

**Educational** Horatio Parker (music dean, Yale—to 1919); Cornelius Rybner (music head, Columbia).

**Other** Philip Hale (music/drama critic, *Boston Herald*—to 1933); Caspar Koch (city organ, Pittsburgh—to 1954); Edwin Arthur Kraft (organist, St. Matthew's, Wheeling, West Virginia—to 1907); Gustav Saenger (editor, *Musical Observer*—to 1929).

### J. Honors and Awards

**Honors** Frank Damrosch (MusD, Yale); Edward MacDowell (American Academy).

**K. Biographical** Samuel Coleridge Taylor (British composer) visits the United States; Pietro Floridia (Italian composer), Victor Kolar (Czech violinist), Walter Rothwell (British conductor), Cornelius Rybner (Danish pianist), and Kurt Schindler (German conductor) all emigrate to the United States; Alexandre Guilmant (French organist) performs at the Louisiana Purchase Exposition in St. Louis; Henry Hadley begins five years of conducting in Germany; Hazel Harrison becomes the first American-trained soloist to perform with a European orchestra, the Berlin Philharmonic Orchestra; Edward MacDowell resigns his post at Columbia—first signs of mental illness appear; Maud Powell becomes the first violinist to record for Victor Talking Machine Co.; Richard Strauss conducts his *Domestic Symphony* in New York.

### L. Musical Beginnings

**Performing Groups** Arion Singing Society of Denver; Fanciulli Band; Guido Chorus (Buffalo, New York); Victor Herbert Orchestra; Nashville Symphony Orchestra; N. Clark Smith Ladies' Orchestra (Chicago); Russian Symphony Orchestra of New York; Smith's Mandolin and Stringed Instrument Club (Chicago); Volpe Symphony Orchestra (New York).

**Educational** Cadek School of Music (Chattanooga); Kroeger School of Music (St. Louis).

**Other** American Academy of Arts and Letters; Chicago Orchestra Hall; (New) Dallas Opera House; Forest Park Theater (Little Rock); F. B. Haviland Publishing Co.; *Musical Messenger* (Chicago—to 1924); Louis Weber (Weber Brothers), Music Publishers (Kansas City, Kansas).

### M. Music Publications

Aldrich, Richard, *A Guide to Parsifal*
Elson, Louis C., *The History of American Music*
Faelten, Carl, *The Faelten System of Fundamental Pianoforte Instruction*
Gilman, Lawrence, *Phases of Modern Music*
Goetschius, Percy, *Lessons in Music Form*
Henderson, William J., *Modern Musical Drift*
Huneker, James G., *Overtones: A Book of Temperaments*
Showalter, A. J., *The Best Gospel Songs and their Composers*

### N. Musical Compositions

**Chamber Music** Frederick Converse, *String Quartet No. 2 in A Minor*; Horatio Parker, *Suite for Piano Trio, Opus 35*.

**Choral/Vocal**   Amy Beach, *The Sea-fairies* (treble voices and orchestra)—*Four Songs, Opus 56*; Victor Herbert, *Christ is Risen* (anthem)—*In the Folds of the Starry Flag* (song); Horatio Parker, *Four Songs, Opus 59*—*Office for the Holy Communion*.

**Concertos**   Arthur Farwell, *Symbolist Study No. 2, "Perhelion"* (piano and orchestra).

**Operas**   Harry L. Freeman, *The Octoroon*.

**Orchestra/Band**   Russell Alexander, *Paramour of Panama March*; Ernest Bloch, *Hiver* (symphonic poem); George Chadwick, *Cleopatra* (symphonic poem)—*Sinfonietta in D Major*—*Symphonic Sketches* (completed); Rosetter G. Cole, *Hiawatha's Wooing, Opus 20*; Frederick Converse, *The Mystic Trumpeter*; Henry F. Gilbert, *Symphonic Prelude*—*Riders to the Sea*; Charles Ives, *Thanksgiving, and/or Forefather's Day*; Horatio Parker, *The Eternal Feminine* (incidental music); Leo Schulz, *American Festival Overture*; John Philip Sousa, *The Diplomat March*—*At the King's Court* (suite); Frederick Stock, *Symphonic Variations*.

**Piano/Organ**   Amy Beach, *Variations on Balkan Themes, Opus 60*; Arthur Bird, *Concert Fantasia* (organ); Louis Campbell-Tipton, *Sonata Heroic*; Arthur Foote, *Suite in D Major for Organ*; Henry F. Gilbert, *Island of the Fay* (orchestrated 1923); Henry H. Huss, *La Nuit* (orchestrated 1941); E. T. Paull, *The Circus Parade*; Arthur Shepherd, *Prelude in B Minor* (organ)

**Symphonies**   Charles Ives, *Symphony No. 3, "The Camp Meeting."*

# 1905

❁

## Historical Highlights

The New York subway officially opens; the Rotary Clubs of America are formed; New Orleans suffers an outbreak of yellow fever; Devil's Tower National Park and Petrified Forest National Park are established; Einstein makes public his special theory of relativity. The Russo-Japanese War ends with the defeat of the Russian fleet; Bloody Sunday in St. Petersburg, Russia.

## World Cultural Highlights

**World Art**   Paul Cézanne, *Les Grandes Baigneuses*; Aristide Maillol, *The Mediterranean*; Henri Matisse, *Luxe, Calme et Volupté*; Georges Rouault, *Head of Christ*; Henri Rousseau, *Jungle with Lion*.

**World Literature**   Edward Forster, *Where Angels Fear to Tread*; Emmuska Orczy, *The Scarlet Pimpernel*; George Bernard Shaw, *Major Barbara*; H. G. Wells, *A Modern Utopia*.

**World Music**   Claude Debussy, *La Mer*; Frederick Delius, *A Mass of Life*; Gustav Mahler, *Symphony No. 7*; Alexander Scriabin, *Symphony No. 3, "The Divine Poem"*; Richard Strauss, *Salomé*.

**Miscellaneous**   The Gothenburg Symphony in Sweden and the New Symphony of London are founded; births include André Jolivet, Jean-Paul Sartre, Mikhail Sholokhov, and Michael Tippett; deaths include Adolphe Bouguereau, Adolf von Menzel, Constantin Meunier, and Jules Verne.

## American Art and Literature Highlights

**Births/Deaths**   Births include artist Barnett Newman and literary figures Viña Delmar, George Dillon, Lillian Hellman, Phyllis McGinley, John O'Hara, Kenneth Rexroth, and Robert Penn Warren; deaths include artist Arthur Tait and literary figures Mary Elizabeth Dodge, Henry Harland (Sidney Luska), Frederic L. Knowles, Albion W. Tourgée, and Lew Wallace.

**Art Works**   Childe Hassam, *Southwest Wind*; Albert Laessle, *Turning Turtle*; Ernest Lawson, *The Flatiron Building*; George B. Luks, *The Spielers*; Hermon MacNeil, *Coming of the White Man*; Frederic Remington, *Bronco Buster*; Charles M. Russell, *Buffalo Hunt*; Everett Shinn, *Fifth Avenue and 34th Street*; John Sloan, *Fifth Avenue Critics*; Julian A. Weir, *Upland Pasture* (?).

**Literature**   Charles Chesnutt, *The Colonel's Dream*; Mary B. Chesnutt, *Diary from Dixie*;

Thomas Dixon, *The Clansman*; Paul L. Dunbar, *Lyrics of Sunshine and Shadow*; Percy S. Grant, *Ad Matrem and Other Poems*; Joel Chandler Harris, *Told by Uncle Remus*; Mary Jane Holmes, *The Abandoned Farm*; Wallace Irwin, *Chinatown Ballads*; Edith Wharton, *The House of Mirth*.

## Music—The Vernacular/Commercial Scene

**A. Births**   Ivie Anderson (singer) July 10; Harold Arlen (composer) February 15; Clyde Bernhardt (trombonist/bandleader) July 11; Tiny Bradshaw (pianist/bandleader) September 23; Doc Cheatham (trumpeter) June 13; Eddie Condon (banjoist/guitarist) November 16; Arthur "Big Boy" Crudup (singer) August 24; Tommy Dorsey (trombonist/bandleader) November 19; Dorothy Fields (lyricist); Bertha Hill (singer) March 15; Meade Lewis (pianist) September 4; Ernest "Red" Nichols (bandleader/cornetist) May 8; Tex Ritter (singer/writer) January 12; Charlie Spivak (trumpeter/bandleader) February 17; Jule Styne (composer) December 31; Jack Teagarden (trombonist/singer) August 29; Bob Wills (fiddler/bandleader) March 6.

**B. Deaths**   David Braham (composer/conductor) April 11; Sam Sanford (minstrel performer) December 31.

**C. Biographical**

**Performing Groups**   Memphis Students.

**New Beginnings**   Fred Fisher, Publisher; Hippodrome Theater (New York); *Variety*.

**E. Representative Works**

**Musicals**   Victor Herbert and H. Blossom, *Mlle. Modiste*; Victor Herbert and G. Donough, *Wonderland*; Victor Herbert and H. B. Smith, *Miss Dolly Dollars*; Karl Hoschna and O. Harbach, *The Belle of the West*; Joseph E. Howard and F. Adams, *The Umpire*; Raymond Hubbell and R. B. Smith, *Fantana*; Jean Schwartz and W. Jerome, *The Ham Tree—Sergeant Brue—The White Cat*.

**Songs**   Thurland Chattaway and K. Mills, *Red Wing*; Paul Dresser, *My Gal Sal*; Gus Edwards, *In My Merry Oldsmobile*; Theodore Morse and E. Madden, *Daddy's Little Girl*; Arthur A. Penn, *Carissima*; Arthur Pryor, *The Whistler and His Dog*; Harry O. Sutton and J. Lenox, *I Don't Care*; Egbert A. Van Alstyne and H. Williams, *In the Shade of the Old Apple Tree*; Harry Von Tilzer, *Wait 'til the Sun Shines, Nellie—Down on the Farm*; Harry Von Tilzer and A. Sterling, *What You Gonna Do When the Rent Comes 'Round (Rufus Rastus Johnson Brown)*; Bert Williams and A. Rogers, *Nobody*.

**Other**   Irene Giblin, *Chicken Chowder Rag*; Scott Joplin, *Rags: Eugenia—Leola*; Joe Jordan, *J. J. J. Rag*; Joseph Lamb, *Celestine Waltzes*; Mary Baugh Watson, *Dish Rag*.

## Music—The Cultivated/Art Music Scene

**F. Births**   Marc Blitzstein (composer) March 2; Nathan Broder (musicologist) December 1; Ulric Cole (composer/pianist) September 9; Leonard Ellinwood (musicologist) February 13; Mark Hindsley (conductor/arranger) October 18; Helen Jepson (soprano) November 28; Louis Kaufman (violinist) May 10; John Kirkpatrick (pianist) March 18; Alexander McCurdy (organist) August 18; Arthur Mendel (musicologist) June 6; Undine Smith Moore (composer) August 25; John W. Schaum (pianist/pedagogue) January 27; Carleton Sprague Smith (musicologist) August 8; Herbert Weinstock (music author) November 6.

**G. Deaths**   J. Lathrop Allen (brass instrument maker); Jessie Bartlett Davis (contralto) May 14; John Nelson Pattison (pianist) July 27; William Robyn (German-born conductor/organist) March 2; Theodore Thomas (German-born conductor) January 4; Frederick Zech, Sr. (German-born piano maker) October 25.

**H. Debuts**

**United States**   Albert von Doenhoff (pianist—New York), Marie Hall (British violinist—New York), Willem Mengelberg (Dutch conductor—New York), Alice Nielsen (opera debut—New York), Giorgio Polacco (Italian conductor—San Francisco), Olga Samaroff (pianist—New York), Felix Weingartner (Austrian conductor—New York).

**Metropolitan Opera**   Lina Abarbanell (German soprano), Tony Franke (baritone), Jeanne Jomelli (soprano), Franciso Nuibo (French tenor), Giovanni Parolli (Italian tenor), Marie Rappold (soprano).

**Other**   Albert Spalding (violinist—Paris).

### I. New Positions

**Conductors**   Frederick Stock (Chicago Orchestra—to 1942); Max Zach (Boston Pops, second term—to 1907).

**Educational**   John Lawrence Erb (director, Wooster Conservatory, Ohio—to 1913); Percy Goetschius (Institute of Musical Art—to 1925); Daniel Gregory Mason (Columbia University—to 1942).

### J. Honors and Awards

**Honors**   George W. Chadwick (PhD, Tufts); Horatio Parker (American Academy); Arthur Battelle Whiting (National Institute).

### K. Biographical   Georges Barrère (French flutist) comes to the United States to play first flute with Damrosch's New York Symphony Orchestra; Louis Coerne receives the first PhD in music to be given by an American institution, Harvard; Sir Edward Elgar visits the United States and receives an honorary doctorate from Yale; Carl Engel (German musicologist) emigrates to the United States; the Kneisel Quartet moves to New York and begins work with the Institute of Musical Art; Minnie Saltzmann-Stevens goes to Paris to study voice with Jean De Reszke; Ernest Schelling returns to the United States after 23 years in Europe; Kurt Schindler (German conductor) is invited to New York to conduct at the Met; Ernestine Schumann-Heink marries her third husband, Chicago lawyer William Rapp, Jr.

### L. Musical Beginnings

**Performing Groups**   Providence Chaminade Club (Rhode Island).

**Educational**   Institute of Musical Art (Juilliard); Lachmund Conservatory (New York).

**Other**   Drake University Auditorium; Minneapolis Auditorium (Lyceum); Morse and Haviland, Music Publishers (New York); Rome Prize, American.

### M. Music Publications

Aldrich, Richard, *A Guide to the Ring of the Nibelung*
Audsley, George A., *The Art of Organ Building*
Baker, Theodore, *A Pronouncing Pocket Manual of Musical Terms*
Curtis, Natalie, *Songs of Ancient America*
Daniels, Mabel W., *An American Girl in Munich: Impressions of a Music Student*
Elson, Louis C., *Elson's Music Dictionary*
Foote, A. W. and Spaulding, W. R., *Modern Harmony in its Theory and Practice*
Hanchett, Henry G., *The Art of the Musician*
Huneker, James G., *Visionaries*
Pratt, Silas G., *The Pianist's Mental Velocity*
Sonneck, Oscar T., *A Bibliography of Early Secular American Music*

### N. Musical Compositions

**Chamber Music**   Arthur Shepherd, *Two Movements for String Quartet*.

**Choral/Vocal**   Stephen Adams, *The Holy City*; Arthur Farwell, *Folk Songs of the West and South, Opus 19*; Charles H. Gabriel, *His Eye Is on the Sparrow*; Henry F. Gilbert, *Celtic Songs* (song cycle); Victor Herbert, *An Easter Dawn*; Margaret R. Lang, *Nonsense Rhymes and Pictures* (after Lear); Charles M. Loeffler, *Four Poems, Opus 15*; Horatio Parker, *Three Sacred Songs, Opus 58— Spirit of Beauty, Opus 61* (male chorus and orchestra); Harry R. Shelley, *The Soul Triumphant* (cantata); Humphrey Stewart, *Victory Cantata*.

**Operas**   Frederick Converse, *The Pipe of Desire* (Bispham Medal); Lucius Hosmer, *The Rose of the Alhambra*; Alfred G. Robyn, *The Gypsy Girl*; John Philip Sousa, *The Freelance* (operetta).

**Orchestra/Band** Russell Alexander, *Salute to Seattle March—Song of the South March*; Ernest Bloch, *Printemps* (symphonic poem); Arthur Farwell, *Symbolist Study No. 3: After Whitman, Opus 18*; Charles T. Griffes, *Overture*; Henry Hadley, *Salome, Opus 55* (tone poem); Victor Herbert, *Spanish Rhapsody*; Horatio Parker, *The Prince of India* (incidental music); Ernst Schelling, *Fantastic Suite;* Bertram Shapleigh, *Dance of the Dervishes, Opus 53*; Gustav Strube, *Longing* (symphonic poem).

**Piano/Organ** George W. Chadwick, *Five Pieces*; Arthur Farwell, *From Mesa and Plain, Opus 20—Impressions of the Wa-Wan Ceremony of the Omaha Indians, Opus 21*; Charles Ives, *Three-page Sonata*.

# 1906

✵

## Historical Highlights

The Great San Francisco Earthquake takes 700 lives and costs over four million dollars in damage; Congress votes to send troops into Cuba to help restore order; the Pure Food and Drug Act and the Meat Inspection Act are passed by Congress; Victrolas first appear on the market; Britain's first large battleship, the *Dreadnought*, is launched.

## World Cultural Highlights

**World Art** André Derain, *Turning Road, l'Estaque*; Aristide Maillol, *Chained Action*; Henri Matisse, *The Joy of Life*; Georges Rouault, *At the Mirror*; Maurice de Vlaminck, *The Banks of the Seine*.

**World Literature** Valeri Bryusov, *Stephanos*; Joseph Conrad, *Mirror of the Sea*; William Yeats, *Deirdre*.

**World Music** Hugo Alfvén, *Symphony No. 3;* Edward Elgar, *The Kingdom*; Carl Nielsen, *Masquerade*; Albert Roussel, *Symphony No. 1, "Le Poème de la Forêt"*; Jean Sibelius, *Pohjola's Daughter*.

**Miscellaneous** The Welsh Folk Song Society is formed; the Toronto Symphony is founded; births include Samuel Beckett, John Betjeman, Antal Dorati, and Dmitri Shostakovich; deaths include Anton Arensky, Jules Breton, Paul Cézanne, Giuseppe Giacosa, and Henrik Ibsen.

## American Art and Literature Highlights

**Births/Deaths** Births include art figures Peter Blume, James Brooks, Herbert Ferber, Louis Guglielmi, and literary figures George Dillon, Ann Morrow Lindbergh, Sterling North, Clifford Odets, and Jessamyn West; deaths include artists Daniel Huntington, Eastman Johnson, and literary figures Paul L. Dunbar, Daniel Henderson, and Fanny Herring.

**Art Works** Arthur B. Davies, *The Unicorns*; Thomas Eakins, *William Rush Carving His Allegorical Figure of the Schuylkill River II*; Childe Hassam, *Church at Old Lyme*; Edward L. Henry, *Carriage Ride on a Country Lane*; Gary Melchers, *Mother and Child*; Frederic Remington, *Howl of the Weather*; Everett Shinn, *Theater Box*; John Sloan, *Roof, Summer Night*; Julian A. Weir, *A Gentlewoman*.

**Literature** Finley P. Dunne, *Dissertations by Mr. Dooley*; Joel Chandler Harris, *Uncle Remus and Br'er Rabbit*; Philander C. Johnson, *Senator Sorgham's Primer of Politics*; Jack London, *White Fang*; Edna Dean Proctor, *Songs of America*; Robert C. Rogers, *The Rosary and Other Poems*; Edwin M. Royle, *Squaw Man*; Upton Sinclair, *The Jungle*; Owen Wister, *Lady Baltimore*.

## Music—The Vernacular/Commercial Scene

**A. Births** Harold Adamson (lyricist) December 10; Josephine Baker (singer) June 30; Barney Bigard (clarinetist) March 3; Wild Bill Davison (cornetist) January 5; Eddie Durham (trombonist/arranger) August 19; Bud Freeman (saxophonist) April 4; Hildegarde (singer); Charles W. Hunter (pianist/composer) January 23; Kay Kyser (bandleader) June 18; Freddy Martin (saxophonist/bandleader) December 9; Little Brother Montgomery (pianist) April 18; Ozzie Nelson (bandleader/writer) March 20; "Pee Wee" Russell (clarinetist) March 27; Willie Mae Ford Smith (singer); "Muggsy" Spanier (cornetist) November 9; Victoria Spivey (pianist/singer) October 15; Al Stillman (lyricist) June 26; Joe Sullivan (pianist/writer) November 4; Roosevelt Sykes (pianist/singer); Frank Teschemacher (clarinetist/saxophonist) March 13.

**B. Deaths**    Paul Dresser (composer) January 30; Charles Hunter (ragtime composer/pianist) January 23.

**C. Biographical**

**New Beginnings**    Amsterdam Musical Association (New York); Gus Edwards Publishing Co. (New York); Gotham-Attucks Music Publishers (New York); Majestic Theater (Chicago); United States Amusement Co.

**E. Representative Works**

**Musicals**    B. H. Burt and S. Hein, *Marrying Mary*; George M. Cohan, *George Washington, Jr.—Forty-Five Minutes from Broadway*; Ludwig Englander and H. B. Smith, *The Rich Mr. Hoggenheimer*; Victor Herbert and H. Blossom, *The Red Mill—Dream City—The Magic Knight*; Max Hoffman and H. B. Smith, *A Parisian Model*; Karl Hoschna and C. Douglas, *The Girl from Broadway*; Gustave Kerker and R. Burnside, *The Tourists*; John Philip Sousa and H. B. Smith, *The Freelance*.

**Songs**    Ernest R. Ball and D. Reed, *Love Me and the World Is Mine*; Will D. Cobb and R. Shields, *Waltz Me Around Again, Willie— 'Round, 'Round, 'Round*; Jean Schwartz and W. Jerome, *Chinatown, My Chinatown*; Maxwell Silver and Ed Rose, *He Walked Right In, Turned Around and Walked Right Out Again*; Alfred H. Miles, R. Lovell, and C. A. Zimmerman, *Anchors Aweigh*; Egbert A. Van Alstyne and H. Williams, *Cheyenne*.

**Other**    Geraldine Dobyns, *Possum Rag*; Irene Giblin, *Sleepy Lou Rag*; Charles L. Johnson, *Rags: Dill Pickles—Iola*; Joseph Lamb, *Florentine Waltzes*; Jelly Roll Morton, *King Porter Stomp*; Adaline Shepherd, *Pickles and Peppers*.

## Music—The Cultivated/Art Music Scene

**F. Births**    Gilbert Chase (music historian/critic) September 4; Paul Creston (composer) October 10; Ross Lee Finney (composer) December 23; Avery Fisher (art patron) March 4; Alfred Frankenstein (critic) October 5; Miriam Gideon (composer) October 23; Elizabeth A. Green (violinist) August 21; Hunter Johnson (composer) April 14; Arthur Kreutz (composer/violinist) July 25; Oscar Levant (pianist/author) December 27; Normand Lockwood (composer/educator) March 19; Joseph Machlis (musicologist) August 11; William J. Mitchell (musicologist) November 21; Robert L. Sanders (composer) July 2; David Sheinfeld (composer/violinist) September 20; Cecil Smith (critic) July 12; Louise Talma (composer) October 31; Homer Ulrich (musicologist) March 27; David Van Vactor (composer/conductor) May 8.

**G. Deaths**    Flora Batson (soprano) December 1; John Knowles Paine (composer) April 25.

**H. Debuts**

**United States**    Amadeo Bassi (Italian tenor—New York), Alessandro Bonci (Italian tenor—New York), Eleanora de Cisneros (soprano—New York), Florencio Constantino (Spanish tenor—New Orleans), Charles Dalmorès (French tenor—New York), Ruth Deyo (pianist—New York), Pauline Donalda (Canadian soprano—New York), Josef Lhévinne (Russian pianist—New York), Francis MacMillan (violinist—New York), Riccardo Martin (tenor—New Orleans), Maurice Renaud (French baritone—New York), Artur Rubinstein (Polish pianist—tour).

**Metropolitan Opera**    Bessie Abott (soprano), Carl Burrian (Czech tenor), Lina Cavalieri (Italian soprano), Geraldine Farrar (soprano), Vittorio Navarini (Italian bass), Charles Rousselière (French tenor), Riccardo Stracciari (Italian baritone).

**Other**   Maud Fay (soprano—Munich), Lillian Grenville (Nice).

**I. New Positions**

**Conductors**   Cleofonte Campanini (Manhattan Opera House—to 1909); Karl Muck (Boston Symphony Orchestra—first term to 1908); Vasili Safonov (New York Philharmonic Orchestra—to 1909).

**Educational**   Silas G. Pratt (Pratt); Louis Victor Saar (Cincinnati Conservatory—to 1917); Vasili Safonov (director, National Conservatory, New York—to 1909); Sigismond Stojowski (piano head, Institute of Music Art, New York—to 1912).

**Other**   E. Olin Downes (music critic, *Boston Post*—to 1924); Wallace A. Sabin (organ, First Church of Christ, Scientist, San Francisco—to 1937).

**K. Biographical**   John Alden Carpenter studies composition with Elgar; Cleofonte Campanini (Italian conductor), Edouard Déthier (Belgian violinist), Sol Hurok (Russian impresario), and Sigismond Stojowski (Polish pianist) come to the United States; Rudolf Friml (Czech composer/pianist) decides to settle in the United States; Richard Hageman (Dutch composer) travels to New York as accompanist for Yvette Guilbert and decides to stay; Ruggiero Leoncavallo conducts the La Scala Orchestra in their opening in New York; Camille Saint-Saëns visits the United States; Alexander Scriabin performs his own work in New York.

**L. Musical Beginnings**

**Performing Groups**   Chicago Musical Arts Society; Manhattan Opera Company and House; New Orleans Philharmonic Society.

**Educational**   Germantown Conservatory of Music (Philadelphia); Greenwich House Music School (New York); Kansas City Conservatory of Music; Pratt Institute of Music and Art (Pittsburgh).

**Other**   Sam Fox, Music Publisher (Cleveland); H. W. Gray Company, Inc.; Los Angeles Auditorium (Philharmonic Auditorium, 1920); Presser Home for Retired Music Teachers (Philadelphia); Shubert Theatre (Kansas City).

**M. Music Publications**

Henderson, William J. *The Art of the Singer*
Kobbé, Gustav, *Famous American Songs—How to Appreciate Music*
Mason, Daniel G., *The Romantic Composers*
Sankey, Ira, *Story of the Gospel Hymns*

**N. Musical Compositions**

**Chamber Music**   Victor Herbert, *Romance for Cello*; Charles Ives, *Hallowe'en* (string quartet and piano); David S. Smith, *String Quartet No. 1 in E Minor*; Frederick Zech, Jr., *Flute Sonata*.

**Choral/Vocal**   Charles W. Cadman, *At Dawning* (song); Frederick Converse, *Job* (oratorio); Victor Herbert, *In the Sweet Bye and Bye* (song); Margaret Lang, *The Lonely Rose* (cantata); Daniel G. Mason, *Four Love Songs, Opus 4*; Horatio Parker, *The Shepherd's Vision, Opus 63* (cantata).

**Concertos**   Henry H. Huss, *Violin Concerto in C Minor, Opus 12*; Ernest Schelling, *Suite Fantastique* (piano and orchestra).

**Operas**   Harry L. Freeman, *Valdo*; Henry F. Gilbert, *Uncle Remus* (contains *Comedy Overture on Negro Themes*); Henry Hadley, *Merlin and Vivian, Opus 52*.

**Orchestra/Band**   E. E. Bagley, *National Emblem March*; Charles W. Cadman, *Jeanne d'Arc* (incidental music); George W. Chadwick, *Euterpe Overture*; Arthur Farwell, *Symbolist Study No. 4—Symbolist Study No. 5*; Victor Herbert, *Western Overture*; Charles Ives, *The Pond—Set for Theater Orchestra—The Unanswered Question—Central Park in the Dark—All the Way Around and Back*; Charles M. Loeffler, *A Pagan Poem* (based on 1901 chamber work); John P. Sousa, *Free Lance March*; Humphrey Stewart, *Scenes in California*.

**Piano/Organ**   Charles W. Cadman, *Prairie Sketches* (orchestrated 1923); John Powell, *In the South, Opus 16—Variations and Double Fugue*.

**Symphonies**   Henry Hadley, *Symphony No. 3 in B Minor*; Frederick Zech, *Symphony No. 5*.

# 1907

✦

## Historical Highlights

Financial panic occurs in the United States; Oklahoma is admitted to the Union as the 46th state; President Roosevelt sends the "Great White Fleet" on a world cruise; the United Press News Agency begins operation; Mother's Day is first observed in Philadelphia; the Triple Alliance and the Triple Entente are formed by the European powers; Mahatma Gandhi begins his civil disobedience crusade.

## World Cultural Highlights

**World Art**   Gustav Klimt, *The Kiss*; Claude Monet, *Water Lilies at Giverny*; Pablo Picasso, *Les Demoiselles d'Avignon*; Edward Poynter, *Lesbia and Sparrow*; Henri Rousseau, *The Snake Charmer*.

**World Literature**   Joseph Conrad, *The Secret Agent*; Maxim Gorky, *Mother*; James Joyce, *Chamber Music*; Maurice Maeterlinck, *Ariane et Barbe-Bleue*; John Synge, *Playboy of the Western World*.

**World Music**   Gustav Mahler, *Symphony No. 8*, *"Symphony of a Thousand"*; Serge Rachmaninoff, *Symphony No. 2—Isle of the Dead*; Maurice Ravel, *Rhapsodie Espagnole*; Jean Sibelius, *Symphony No. 3*.

**Miscellaneous**   The Kiel Opera and Opera House and the Blüthner Orchestra of Berlin are founded; births include W. H. Auden, Ilya Bolotowsky, Christopher Fry, Daphne du Maurier, and Willem von Otterloo; deaths include Giosuè Carducci, Edvard Grieg, and Joris-Karl Huysmans.

## American Art and Literature Highlights

**Births/Deaths**   Births include art figures Aaron Bohrod, Irene Pereira, Fairfield Porter, Theodore Roszak, and literary figures Rachel Carson, Mary C. Chase, Helen MacInnes, James A. Michener, and H. Allen Smith; deaths include art figures Edward Kemeys, Elizabet Ney, John F. Peto, Augustus Saint-Gaudens, poet Thomas B. Aldrich, and novelist Archibald Gunter.

**Art Works**   George Bellows, *Forty-Two Kids*; Rockwell Kent, *Winter, A View of Monhegan, Maine*; Ernest Lawson, *Winter on the River*; George B. Luks, *Woman with Macaws*; Maurice Prendergast, *April Snow, Salem*; Frederic Remington, *Cavalry Charge on the Southern Plains*; Augustus Saint-Gaudens, *Abraham Lincoln*; John Sloan, *Wake of the Ferry*; Dwight W. Tryon, *Before Sunrise*.

**Literature**   George Ade, *Father and the Boys*; James B. Cabell, *Gallantry*; Thomas Dixon, *The Traitor*; Henry James, *The American Scene*; Jack London, *The Iron Heel*; Robert M. Lovett, *A Winged Victory*; Mary N. Murfree, *The Windfall*; Edwin M. Royle, *The Struggle Everlasting*; George S. Viereck, *Nineveh and Other Poems*; Harold B. Wright, *Shepherd of the Hills*.

## Music—The Vernacular/Commercial Scene

**A. Births**   Gene Autry (singer/actor) September 29; Mildred Bailey (singer) February 27; "Puddinghead" Battle (trumpeter/arranger) October 3; Connee Boswell (singer) December 3; Lawrence Brown (trombonist) August 3; Cab Calloway (bandleader) December 25; Benny Carter (saxophonist/bandleader) August 8; Cousin Joe (ukelele player/pianist) December 20; Ralph Freed (writer) May 1; Leigh Harline (composer) March 26; Edward Heyman (lyricist) March 14; Johnny Hodges (saxophonist) July 25; Pee Wee Hunt (trombonist/bandleader) May 10; Enoch Light (bandleader) August 18; Roberta Martin (singer/writer) February 12; Jimmy McPartland (trumpeter/bandleader) March 15; Benny Morton (trombonist) January 31; Tony Pastor (saxophonist/bandleader) October 26; Rex Stewart (cornetist) February 22; Joe Turner (pianist) November 3; Paul Francis Webster (lyricist) December 20; Alec Wilder (composer/arranger) February 16.

**B. Deaths**  William Shakespeare Hays (writer) July 22.

**C. Biographical**

**New Beginnings**  Proctor Amusement Co.; Ziegfeld Follies (to 1931).

**E. Representative Works**

**Musicals**  George M. Cohan, *The Honeymooners—The Talk of New York*; Bob Cole and Rosamond Johnson, *The Shoo Fly Regiment*; L. Englander, S. Rosenfeld, and J. C. Harvey, *The Gay White Way*; Victor Herbert, *The Tattooed Man*; J. E. Howard, W. Hough, and F. Adams, *The Time, the Place and the Girl*; Gustave Kerker, *Fascinating Flora—The White Hen*; Franz Lehár, *The Merry Widow* (US premiere).

**Songs**  Anonymous, *Bell Bottom Trousers*; Benjamin H. Burt, *Much Obliged to You*; George M. Cohan, *Harrigan*; W. M. Cook and A. Rogers, *Bon Bon Buddy*; Gus Edwards, *School Days*; Frederick A. Mills, *Red Wing*; E. Teschemacher and E. J. Margetson, *Tommy Lad*; E. A. Van Alstyne and H. Williams, *There Never Was a Girl Like You—I'm Afraid to Go Home in the Dark*; A. Von Tilzer and J. Norworth, *Honey Boy*.

**Other**  Imogen Giles, *Red Peppers Rag*; Scott Joplin, *Rags: Rose Leaf—Gladiolus—Heliotrope Bouquet—Lily Queen—Nonpareil—Searchlight*; Julia L. Niebergall, *Hoosier Rag*; James Scott, *Kansas City Rag*.

## Music—The Cultivated/Art Music Scene

**F. Births**  Josef Alexander (composer) May 15; Albert Ammons (pianist/composer) September 23; Winifred Cecil (soprano) August 31; John Challis (harpsichord maker) January 9; Ellabelle Davis (soprano) March 17; Arnold Elson (composer) September 30; David Ewen (music author) November 26; Walter Hinrichsen (publisher) Sept 23; Theodate Johnson (soprano/publisher) August 13; Edwin McArthur (conductor) September 24; Lina Pagliughi (soprano) May 27; Burrill Phillips (composer) November 9; Howard Swanson (composer) August 18; Marion Talley (soprano) December 20; Howard Taubman (music/drama critic) July 4.

**G. Deaths**  Maurice Grau (Bohemian-born impresario) March 14; Francis F. Hagen (Moravian composer) July 7; Robert Browne Hall (cornetist/bandmaster) June 8; James McGranahan (hymnist) July 7; Horatio R. Palmer (educator/composer) November 15; Fritz Scheel (German-born violinist/conductor) March 13; Gustave Schirmer II (publisher) July 15; Gustave Stoeckel (German-born organist) May 14; William B. Tremaine (piano maker); Carl Wolfsohn (German-born pianist) July 30.

**H. Debuts**

**United States**  Ramón Blanchart (Spanish baritone—New York), Richard Buhlig (pianist—New York), Feodor Chaliapin (Russian bass—New York), Armand Crabbé (Belgian baritone—New York), Adamo Didur (Polish bass—New York), Mary Garden (soprano—New York), Jeanne Gerville-Réache (French contralto—New York), Katharine Goodson (British pianist—Boston), Francisco Signorini (Italian tenor—San Francisco), Giovanni Zenatello (Italian tenor—New York), Alice Zepilli (New York).

**Metropolitan Opera**  Alessandro Bonci (Italian tenor), Feodor Chaliapin (Russian bass), Rita Fornia (soprano), Frieda Langendorff (German soprano), Riccardo Martin (tenor).

**Other**  Kathleen Howard (contralto—Metz), John Powell (pianist—Berlin).

**I. New Positions**

**Conductors**  Carl Pohlig (Philadelphia Symphony Orchestra—to 1912); Max Zach (St. Louis Symphony Orchestra—to 1921).

**Educational**  Samuel Baldwin (City College of New York); Gustav Dannreuther (violin, Vassar); Karl Gehrkens (Oberlin—to 1942); Charles Tomlinson Griffes (director of music, Hackley School); Albert Austin Harding (University of Illinois—to 1948); Walton Perkins (president, Chicago Conservatory—to 1920).

**Other**   Edwin Arthur Kraft (organ, Trinity Cathedral, Cleveland—to 1959); Kurt Schindler (editor/critic, G. Schirmer); Pietro Yon (organist, St. Francis-Xavier, New York—to 1919).

**K. Biographical**   Hans Barth moves to the United States with his family; Sir Edward Elgar conducts his oratorios *The Apostles* and *The Kingdom* in New York; Scott Joplin moves to New York; Leo Ornstein (Russian pianist/composer) emigrates to the United States; Giacomo Puccini attends the Metropolitan Opera premiere of his *Madame Butterfly*; Carl Ruggles moves to Winona, Minnesota, and founds the Winona Symphony Orchestra; Emerson Whithorne marries pianist Ethel Leginska (divorced 1916); Pietro Yon (Italian organist/composer) emigrates to the United States.

**L. Musical Beginnings**

**Performing Groups**   Choral Club of Hartford.

**Other**   Hope-Jones Organ Co. (Tonawanda, New York); Charles L. Johnson, Music Publisher (Kansas City); MacDowell Colony (New Hampshire); Moore Theater (Seattle); *The Musical Observer* (to 1931); National Wa-Wan Society of America.

**M. Music Publications**

Carl, William C., *Master-Studies for the Organ*
Curtis, Natalie, *The Indians' Book*
Elson, Arthur, *Music Club Programs from All Nations*
Elson, Louis C., *Elson's Pocket Music Dictionary*
Gilman, Lawrence, *Stories of Symphonic Music—The Music of Tomorrow and Other Studies*
Pratt, Waldo S., *The History of Music*
Sonneck, Oscar T., *Early Concert Life in America (1731–1800)*

**N. Musical Compositions**

**Chamber Music**   Amy Beach, *Piano Quintet in F-Sharp Minor, Opus 67*; Edgar S. Kelley, *String Quartet, Opus 25*; John Powell, *String Quartet No. 1*.

**Choral/Vocal**   Amy Beach, *The Chambered Nautilus*; Charles W. Cadman, *Four American Indian Songs*; Julian Edwards, *Lazarus* (cantata); William W. Gilchrist, *An Easter Idyll*; Victor Herbert, *If Love Were What the Rose Is—Love Laid His Sleepless Head—The Friars* (songs); Edward B. Hill, *Nuns of the Perpetual Adoration* (cantata); Henry H. Huss, *Four Songs, Opus 22*; Margaret R. Lang, *More Nonsense Rhymes and Pictures* (after Lear); Horatio Parker, *Crépuscule, Opus 62* (mezzo-soprano and orchestra)—*King Gorm the Grim, Opus 64*; Bertram Shapleigh, *The Raven, Opus 50* (after Poe); Arthur Shepherd, *The Lord Hath Brought Again Zion*; Oley Speaks, *On the Road to Mandalay*; George Stebbins, *Have Thine Own Way, Lord*; Humphrey Stewart, *Mass in D Minor*.

**Concertos**   Frederick Zech, Jr., *Cello Concerto*.

**Operas**   Julian Edwards, *The Patriot*; Alfred G. Robyn, *The Yankee Tourist*.

**Orchestra/Band**   Russell Alexander, *The Comedy Club March—La Reine March*; Arthur Foote, *Suite in E Major for Strings, Opus 63*; Charles T. Griffes, *Symphonische Phantasie*; Charles Ives, *Emerson Overture*; Emil Paur, *An Easter Idyll*; John Philip Sousa, *Powhattan's Daughter March*.

**Piano/Organ**   Amy Beach, *Eskimos, Four Characteristic Pieces, Opus 64*; John Powell, *At the Fair* (piano suite)—*Sonate Noble, Opus 21*; Arthur Shepherd, *Sonata No. 1 in F Minor, Opus 4*.

# 1908

❄

### Historical Highlights

William Howard Taft is elected the 27th president; the New York Singer Building becomes the city's first skyscraper; the Hudson River Tunnel is opened for use in New York; the model T Ford is introduced; the *Christian Science Monitor* begins publication; the first boy scout troop is formed in England; Bulgaria declares its independence from Turkish authority.

## World Cultural Highlights

**World Art**   Emile Bourdelle, *Beethoven in the Wind;* Constantin Brancusi, *The Kiss*; Georges Braque, *The Houses of l'Estaque*; Henri Matisse, *The Girl with the Green Eyes*; Maurice de Vlaminck, *The Red Trees*.

**World Literature**   Leonid Andreyev, *The Black Maskers*; Valeri Bryusov, *The Fiery Angel*; E. M. Forster, *A Room with a View*; Anatole France, *Penguin Island*; Maurice Maeterlinck, *The Bluebird*.

**World Music**   Claude Debussy, *Iberia*; Edward Elgar, *Symphony No. 1*; Gustav Mahler, *Das Lied von der Erde*; Maurice Ravel, *Mother Goose Suite—Gaspard de la Nuit*; Igor Stravinsky, *Fireworks*.

**Miscellaneous**   The New Royal Opera Co. (Berlin) and the Sofia National Opera are founded; births include Herbert von Karajan, Olivier Messiaen, and Victor Vasarely; deaths include François Coppée, Holger Drachmann, Nicolai Rimsky-Korsakov, Pablo Sarasate, and Victorien Sardou.

## American Art and Literature Highlights

**Births/Deaths**   Births include artist Lee Krasner and literary figures Martha Gellhorn, Frederic Prokosch, Theodore Roethke, William Saroyan, and Richard Wright; deaths include sculptor Harriet Hosmer and literary figures Ernest F. Fenollosa, Joel Chandler Harris, Bronson Howard, Donald G. Mitchell, Ellen Louise Moulton, and Edmund Clarence Stedman.

**Art Works**   George Bellows, *Up the Hudson*; Arthur G. Dove, *The Lobster*; William Glackens, *The Shoppers*; Marsden Hartley, *Storm Clouds, Maine*; Frederic Remington, *His First Lesson*; John S. Sargent, *The Black Brook*; Charles Schreyvogel, *Summit Springs Rescue, 1869*; Everett Shinn, *A Winter's Night, Broadway*; John Sloan, *South Beach Bathers*; Edmund Tarbell, *Josephine and Mercie*.

**Literature**   Winston Churchill, *Mr. Crewe's Career*; John W. Fox, *The Trail of the Lonesome Pine*; Robert Herrick, *The Master of the Inn*; William Hurlbut, *The Fighting Hope*; Jack London, *Martin Eden*; Percy MacKaye, *The Scarecrow*; L. M. Montgomery, *Anne of Green Gables*; David G. Phillips, *The Worth of a Woman*; Ezra Pound, *A Lume Spento;* Elizabeth Ward, *Though Life Do Us Part*.

## Music—The Vernacular/Commercial Scene

**A. Births**   Henry "Red" Allen (trumpeter) January 7; Leroy Anderson (composer) June 29; Billy Banks (singer); Bunny Berigan (trumpeter) November 2; "Chu" Berry (saxophonist) September 13; Johnny Burke (composer/lyricist) October 3; Russ Columbo (singer/composer) January 14; Percy Faith (conductor/arranger) April 7; Johnny Green (composer) October 10; Stuart Hamblen (singer/writer) October 20; Lennie Hayton (pianist) February 13; Louis Jordan (saxophonist/singer) July 8; John Kirby (string bassist/bandleader) December 31; Joshua Logan (lyricist) October 5; Red Norvo (drummer) March 31; "Hot Lips" Page (trumpeter) January 27; Sammy Price (pianist); Harold Rome (composer/lyricist) May 27; Jabbo Smith (trumpeter/trombonist) December 24; Dave Tough (drummer) April 26; Josh White (singer/guitarist) February 11; "Cootie" Williams (trumpeter/bandleader) July 24.

**B. Deaths**   Louis Chauvin (ragtime pianist/writer) March 26; Tony Pastor (singer/impresario) August 16.

**C. Biographical**

**Performing Groups**   Original Creole Band.

**New Beginnings**   Pace-Handy Co., Music Publishers; Ted Snyder Music Co.

**D. Publications**   Scott Joplin, *School of Ragtime—Six Exercises for Piano*.

**E. Representative Works**:

**Musicals**   George M. Cohan, *The Yankee Prince—Fifty Miles from Boston*; Victor Herbert, *Little*

*Nemo*—(*The Rose of*) *Algeria*; Karl Hoschna and O. Harbach, *The Three Twins*; Joseph E. Howard, W. Hough, and F. Adams, *A Stubborn Cinderella*; Gustave Luders, F. Pixley, *Marcello*.

**Songs**   Charles N. Daniels, A. H. Brown, and Seymour Rice, *You Tell Me Your Dream*; Edmund L. Gruber, *The Caissons Go Rolling Along*; Karl Hoschna and O. Harbach, *Cuddle Up a Little Closer, Lovey Mine*; Kerry Mills and A. J. Lamb, *Any Old Port in a Storm*; Theodore Morse and E. Madden, *Down in Jungle Town*; Jack Norworth and N. Bayes, *Shine On, Harvest Moon*; Anita Owen, *Daisies Won't Tell*; W. C. Powell, *Sweet Violets*; Albert Von Tilzer, *Take Me Out to the Ball Game*.

**Other**   May Aufderheide, *Dusty Rag*; Scott Joplin, *Rags: Fig Leaf—Pine Apple—Sugar Cane*; James Lamb, *Sensation Rag*; Jelly Roll Morton, *Frag-i-more Rag*.

## Music—The Cultivated/Art Music Scene

**F. Births**   Webster Aitken (pianist) June 17; Roberta Bitgood (composer) January 15; Radie Britain (composer) March 17; Armen Carapetyan (musicologist) October 11; Elliott Carter (composer) December 11; Henry L. Clarke (musicologist/composer) March 9; Louise E. Cuyler (musicologist) March 14; John Green (pianist/conductor) October 10; H. Earle Johnson (critic) May; Irving Kolodin (critic) February 22; Sylvia Marlowe (harpsichordist) September 26; Benno Rabinof (violinist) October 11; Halsey Stevens (composer/musicologist) December 3; Gerald Strang (composer) February 13; James Sykes (pianist) July 10; John Verrall (composer) June 17; Beveridge Webster (pianist) May 13; Paul Yoder (composer) October 8.

**G. Deaths**   Blind Tom Bethune (pianist/composer) June 13; James R. Fairlamb (organist) April 16; Robert Goldbeck (German-born pianist/composer) May 16; Edward MacDowell (composer/pianist) January 23; William Mason (pianist/composer) July 14; Ira Sankey (evangelist/hymnist) August 13; John Wheeler Tufts (organist/educator) March 18.

**H. Debuts**

**United States**   Hans Barth (German pianist—New York), Hector Dufranne (Belgian bass-baritone—New York), Misha Elman (Russian violinist—New York), Gustave Huberdeau (French bass—New York), Maria Labia (Italian soprano—New York), Hans Letz (German violinist—New York), Jean Périer (French baritone—New York), Mario Sammarco (Italian baritone—New York), Albert Spalding (violinist—New York), Luisa Tetrazzini (Italian soprano—New York), Félix Vieuille (French bass—New York), Ludwig Wüllner (German vocalist—tour).

**Metropolitan Opera**   Frances Alda (New Zealand soprano), Pasquale Amato (Italian baritone), Angelo Bada (Italian tenor), Emmy Destinn (Czech soprano), Adamo Didur (Polish bass), Fritz Feinhals (German baritone), Maria Gay (Spanish mezzo-soprano), Martha Leffler-Burckard (German soprano), Gustav Mahler (Austrian conductor), Berta Morena (German soprano), Jean Noté (Belgian baritone), Giulio Rossi (Italian bass), Erik Schmedes (Danish tenor), Matja von Niessen-Stone (Russian soprano), Herbert Witherspoon (bass).

**I. New Positions**

**Conductors**   Max Fiedler (Boston Symphony Orchestra—to 1912); Michael Kegrizi (Seattle Symphony Orchestra); Walter Henry Rothwell (St. Paul Symphony Orchestra—to 1908); Arturo Toscanini (Metropolitan Opera—to 1915).

**Educational**   Timothée Adamowski (New England Conservatory—to 1933); Seth Bingham (Yale—to 1919); Edward Burlingame Hill (Harvard—to 1940).

**Other**   Charles Wakefield Cadman (music editor/critic, *Pittsburgh Dispatch*); James F. Cooke (editor, *Etude*—to 1949); Giulio Gatti-Casazza (manager, Metropolitan Opera).

**J. Honors and Awards**

**Honors**   Frederick S. Converse, Victor Herbert, and Martin Loeffler (National Institute); Julia Ward Howe (American Academy).

**K. Biographical**   Bentley D. Ackley becomes secretary and pianist to evangelist Billy Sunday; Heinrich Hammer (German violinist/conductor) comes to the United States; Charles E. Ives marries Harmony Twichell and goes into insurance partnership with his friend to form Myrick and Ives; the Albert Schatz Collection of Original Opera Libretti goes to the Library of Congress.

## L. Musical Beginnings

**Performing Groups**   Buffalo Philharmonic Society II; Maud Powell Trio; Seattle Symphnoy Orchestra.

**Educational**   Belgian School of Violin (New York, by Ovide Musin); Brooklyn Academy of Music New Building; Philadelphia Settlement Music School; *School Music Monthly.*

**Other**   American Piano Co. (consolidation of Knabe, Chickering, and Foster-Armstrong Co.); Hammerstein Opera House (Philadelphia); National Association of Organists.

## M. Music Publications

Coerne, Louis A. *The Evolution of Modern Orchestration*
Hamilton, Clarence, *Outlines of Music History*
Hofmann, Josef, *Piano Playing*
Hubard, W. L., ed., *The American History and Encyclopedia of Music I*
Krehbiel, Henry E., *Chapters of Opera*
Mason, Daniel G., *The Orchestral Instruments*
Pratt, Waldo S., *Class Notes in Music History*
Sonneck, Oscar T., *Dramatic Music: Catalogue of Full Scores in . . . the Library of Congress*
Upton, George P., *Musical Memories: . . . Celebrities of the Half Century, 1850–1900*

## N. Musical Compositions

**Chamber Music**   Arthur Foote, *Piano Trio No. 2 in B-Flat Major, Opus 65*; Charles Ives, *Violin Sonata No. 1*; Daniel G. Mason, *Violin Sonata.*

**Choral/Vocal**   Amy Beach, *Two Mother Songs, Opus 69*; Johann H. Beck, *Meeresabend*; George W. Chadwick, *Noel*; Arthur Farwell, *Three Indian Songs, Opus 32*; Mary E. Salter, *Outdoor Sketches.*

**Operas**   Deems Taylor, *Cap'n Kidd and Co.*

**Orchestra/Band**   Russell Alexander, *Marches—Baltimore's Boast—The Cantonians—The Southerner—Bastinado Galop*; Philip G. Clapp, *Norge* (tone poem); A. T. Davison, *Hero and Leander* (symphonic poem); Blair Fairchild, *East and West*; Henry F. Gilbert, *Dance in the Place Congo* (?); Victor Herbert, *The Jester's Serenade—Wedding Music*; Arne Oldberg, *Paolo and Francesca* (symphonic poem); Bertram Shapleigh, *Ramayana Suite, Opus 45—Gur Amir Suite, Opus 51*; John Philip Sousa, *Fairest of the Fair.*

**Piano/Organ**   Louis Campbell-Tipton, *Two Legends*; George W. Chadwick, *Theme, Variations and Fugue* (organ); Charles Ives, *The Anti-abolitionist Riots*; Horatio Parker, *Organ Sonata in E-Flat Major—Five Short Pieces for Organ, Opus 68*; Arthur Shepherd, *Nocturne in B Minor*; Emerson Whithorne, *The Gate of Memory.*

# 1909

✦

## Historical Highlights

Henry Ford introduces the assembly line into his plant; higher protective tariffs are set by the Payne-Aldrich Tariff; the National Conservation Association is founded, as is the National Association for the Advancement of Colored People (NAACP); Robert Peary and his party of explorers become the first people to reach the North Pole; the British Parliament forms the Union of South Africa.

## World Cultural Highlights

**World Art**   Umberto Boccioni, *Riot in the Gallery*; Émile Bourdelle, *Héraclès Archer*; Emil Nolde, *Pentecost: The Last Supper*; Pablo Picasso, *Harlequin*; Auguste Rodin, *Head of Mahler.*

**World Literature**   Guillaume Apollinaire, *L'Enchanteur Pourrissent*; Sem Benelli, *L'Amore dei Tre Re*; Ferenc Molnár, *Liliom*; August Strindberg, *The Great Highway*; H. G. Wells, *Tono-Bungay*.

**World Music**   Isaac Albéniz, *Iberia*; Gustav Mahler, *Symphony No. 9*; Arnold Schönberg, *Five Pieces for Orchestra*; Richard Strauss, *Elektra*; Ralph Vaughan Williams, *Sea Symphony (No. 1)*.

**Miscellaneous**   The Ballet Russe is founded by Diaghilev; the Beecham Orchestra is founded in London; births include Eric Ambler, Victor Borge, and Vagn Holmboe; deaths include Isaac Albéniz, Catulle Mendès, George Meredith, Alfredo Oriani, Algernon Swinburne, and John Synge.

## American Art and Literature Highlights

**Births/Deaths**   Births include artists Marion Greenwood, John Koch, Loren MacIver, and literary figures James Agee, Nelson Algren, Gladys Schmitt, Wallace E. Stegner, and Eudora Welty; deaths include artists Frederic Remington, Walter Shirlaw, and literary figures Martha Finley (Farquharson), Clyde Fitch, Edward Everett Hale, Sarah Orne Jewett, George Cabot Lodge, and John Banister Tabb.

**Art Works**   George Bellows, *Stag at Sharkey's—Both Members of This Club*; Arthur B. Davies, *The Dream (?)*; Daniel C. French, *Mourning Victory*; Marsden Hartley, *The Mountains*; Winslow Homer, *Right and Left*; Rockwell Kent, *Snow Fields*; William M. Paxton, *Tea Leaves*; Joseph Pennell, *The Things that Tower: Collieries*; Frederick Remington, *Indian Warfare*.

**Literature**   Amelia E. Barr, *The House on Cherry Street*; Hamlin Garland, *The Moccasin Ranch*; Susan Glaspell, *The Glory of the Conquered*; William V. Moody, *The Faith Healer*; Gene Stratton Porter, *A Girl of the Limberlost*; Ezra Pound, *Personae*; George Sterling, *The Wine of Wizardry and Other Poems*; Henry van Dyke, *Le Génie de L'Amérique*; William C. Williams, *Poems*.

## Music—The Vernacular/Commercial Scene

**A. Births**   Ray Bauduc (drummer) June 18; Cleo Brown (pianist/singer) December 8; Maybelle Carter (singer) May 10; Larry Clinton (bandleader/arranger) August 17; Skinnay Ennis (singer/bandleader) August 13; Benny Goodman (clarinetist/bandleader) May 30; Lionel Hampton (drummer/bandleader) April 12; Burl Ives (folksinger) June 14; Gene Krupa (drummer/bandleader) January 15; Jerry Livingston (composer) March 25; Johnny Marks (songwriter) November 10; Jay "Hootie" McShann (pianist/bandleader) January 12; Johnny Mercer (lyricist/composer) November 18; Ethel Merman (singer) January 16; Kate Smith (singer) May 1; Stuff Smith (violinist) August 14; Art Tatum (pianist) October 13; Claude Thornhill (bandleader) August 10; William "Chick" Webb (drummer/bandleader) February 10; Ben Webster (saxophonist) March 27; Lester Young (saxophonist) August 27.

**B. Deaths**   Ernest Hogan (singer/writer) May 20.

**E. Representative Works**

**Musicals**   Bob Cole and J. R. Johnson, *The Red Moon*; George M. Cohan, *The Man Who Owns Broadway*; Victor Herbert and H. B. Smith, *Old Dutch*; Gustave Luders, *The Fair Co-ed*; Glen MacDonough and Raymond Hubbell, *The Midnight Sons*; Jean Schwartz, W. Jerome, and J. J. McNally, *In Hayti*; Oscar Straus, *The Chocolate Soldier* (United States premiere).

**Songs**   Billy Clark and H. Armstrong, *I Love My Wife, But Oh You Kid*; Carrie Jacobs Bond, *A Perfect Day*; Gus Edwards and E. Madden, *By the Light of the Silvery Moon*; Leo Friedman and B. S. Whitson, *Meet Me Tonight in Dreamland*; W. C. Handy, *Memphis Blues*; Joseph E. Howard and H. Orlob, *I Wonder Who's Kissing Her Now?*; Eddie Newton and T. L. Seibert, *Casey Jones*; A. Baldwin Sloane and E. Smith, *Heaven Will Protect the Working Girl*; Albert Von Tilzer and J. McCree, *Carrie*; Percy Wenrich, *Put on Your Old Grey Bonnet*.

**Other**   May Aufderheide, *The Thriller—Richmond Rag*; Axel Christensen, *The Cauldron Rag*; Scott Joplin, *Rags: Country Club—Euphonic Sounds—Paragon—Wall Street*; Joseph Lamb, *Ethiopia Rag—Excelsior Rag*; Henry Lodge, *Temptation Rag*; Paul Pratt, *Vanity Rag*; James Scott, *Rags: Grace and Beauty—Great Scott—Sunburst—Ragtime Betty*; Percy Wenrich, *Cotton Babes Rag*.

## Music—The Cultivated/Art Music Scene

**F. Births**    Rose Bampton (soprano) November 28; Alexander Broude (publisher) January 1; Agnes DeMille (choreographer); Anthony Donato (composer/violinist) March 8; Edwin Gerschefski (composer/pianist) June 19; Josef Gingold (violinist/pedagogue) October 28; Mack Harrell (baritone) October 8; Margaret Harshaw (mezzo-soprano) May 12; Charles Holland (tenor) December 27; Milton Katims (conductor) June 24; Vera Brodsky Lawrence (pianist/music historian) July 1; Norman Lloyd (theorist) November 8; W. Thomas Marrocco (musicologist) December 5; Paul Nordoff (composer/therapist) June 4; Arnold Shaw (composer/author) June 28; Elie Siegmeister (composer) January 15; Milton Steinhardt (musicologist) November 13.

**G. Deaths**    Dudley Buck (composer/organist) October 6; Inez Fabbri (Austrian-born soprano) August 30; Richard Hoffman (British-born pianist/composer) August 17; Phebe Palmer Knapp (hymnist) July 10; Hermann Kotzschmar (German-born organist) April 12; Benjamin J. Lang (pianist/composer) April 3; Fritz Listemann (German-born violinist) December 28; Will L. Thompson (composer/publisher) September 20; Carl Zerrahn (German-born flutist) December 29.

**H. Debuts**

**United States**    Eugenia Bronskaja (Russian soprano), Nazzareno De Angelis (Italian bass—New York), Gervase Elwes (British tenor—tour), Albert Huberty (Belgian tenor), Tilly Koenen (Dutch soprano—tour), John McCormack (Irish tenor—New York), Joseph Malkin (Russian cellist—New York), Jeanne Maubourg (Belgian mezzo-soprano—New York), Carmen Melis (Italian soprano—New York), Yolanda Mérö (Hungarian pianist—New York), Sergei Rachmaninoff (Russian pianist—Northampton, Massachusetts).

**Metropolitan Opera**    Edmond Clément (French tenor), Dinh Gilly (Algerian-born baritone), Alma Gluck (Romanian soprano), Carl Jörn (Latvian tenor), Lydia Lipkovska (Russian soprano), Alice Nielsen (soprano), Leon Rains (bass), Leo Slezak (Austrian tenor), Clarence Whitehill (bass-baritone), Florence Wickham (contralto).

**Other**    Minnie Saltzmann-Stevens (soprano—London).

**I. New Positions**

**Conductors**    Henry K. Hadley (Seattle Symphony Orchestra—to 1911); Gustav Mahler (New York Philharmonic Orchestra—to 1911); Leopold Stokowski (Cincinnati Orchestra Association—to 1912).

**Educational**    Giuseppe Ferrata (Newcomb College, New Orleans—to 1928); T. Carl Whitmer (music, Pennsylvania College for Women—to 1916).

**Other**    Carl Engel (music editor, Boston Music Co.—to 1922); Arthur Farwell (critic, *Musical America*—to 1914); Arthur Foote (president, American Guild of Organists).

**J. Honors and Awards**

**Honors**    George W. Chadwick (American Academy); Paul Manship (Rome Prize).

**K. Biographical**    Charles W. Cadman spends a summer with the Omaha Indians; John Alden Carpenter becomes vice president of his father's firm in Park Ridge, Illinois; G. Clara Clemens marries Ossip Gabrilowitsch; Victor Maurel (French baritone) and Sigmund Romberg (Hungarian composer) come to the United States; Sergei Rachmaninoff (Russian pianist/composer) makes his first American concert tour; Carlos Salzedo moves to New York and joins the Met orchestra; Arthur Shepherd leaves Salt Lake City for Boston.

**L. Musical Beginnings**

**Performing Groups**    Boston Opera Co.; International Grand Opera Co. of Chicago; MacDowell Chorus (Schola Cantorum); Memphis Symphony Orchestra I; Musical Association of San Francisco; Philadelphia Little Symphony; Pittsburgh Mendelssohn Choir; Tollefsen Trio (New York).

**Festivals**    Atlanta Music Festival Association; Chicago North Shore Festival.

**Educational**    Delta Omicron International Music Fraternity (Cincinnati Conservatory); Tulane University Music Department; VanderCook's College of Music (Chicago).

**Other**   Boston Opera House; Carl Fischer, Boston Branch; Gamble Hinged Music Co. (Chicago); William Moennig and Son (Philadelphia).

## M. Music Publications

Burton, Frederick, *American Primitive Music*
Finck, Henry T., *Success in Music and How It Is Won*
Foote, Arthur, *Some Practical Things in Piano-Playing*
Gilman, Lawrence, *Aspects of Modern Opera*
Hofmann, Josef, *Piano Questions Answered*
Johns, Clayton, *The Essentials of Pianoforte Playing*
Krehbiel, Henry E., *A Book of Operas*
Mason, Daniel G., *A Guide to Music*

## N. Musical Compositions

**Chamber Music**   Philip G. Clapp, *String Quartet in C Minor* (revised 1924, 1936)—*Violin Sonata*; Blair Fairchild, *String Quartet No. 1*; Rubin Goldmark, *Piano Quintet* (Paderewski Prize).

**Choral/Vocal**   Charles W. Cadman, *The Vision of Sir Launfal* (male voices); George Chadwick, *Four Irish Songs—Joshua* (voice and orchestra); Henry F. Gilbert, *Fish Wharf Rhapsody*; William W. Gilchrist, *The Lamb of God*; Victor Herbert, *Love's Oracle* (song); Arthur Shepherd, *Five Songs on Poems of James Russell Lowell, Opus 7*.

**Operas**   Harry L. Freeman, *The Tryst*; Henry Hadley, *Safié, Opus 63*; John Philip Sousa, *The American Maid* (operetta).

**Orchestra/Band**   Russell Alexander, *Hampton Roads March—Pall Mall Famous March*; Joseph C. Breil, *The Climax* (incidental music); John Alden Carpenter, *Suite for Orchestra*; George W. Chadwick, *Suite Symphonique in E-Flat Major*; Henry Hadley, *The Culprit Fay, Opus 62* (National Music Clubs Prize); Charles Ives, *Washington's Birthday*; Arne Oldberg, *Academic Overture*; John P. Sousa, *The Glory of the Yankee Navy*.

**Piano/Organ**   Charles Ives, *Sonata No. 1—Some Southpaw Pitching*; Arne Oldberg, *Sonata, Opus 28*; Clara Gottschalk Peterson, *Staccato Polka*.

**Symphonies**   Emil Paur, *Symphony in A, "In der Natur"*; Gustav Strube, *Symphony in B Minor*.

# 1910

☼

## Historical Highlights

The census shows a United States population of 92,228,000 in 46 states; Halley's comet makes its scheduled appearance; Glacier National Park is established; the Boy Scouts of America organization is incorporated; Kent State University is founded in Ohio; a Mexican revolution leads to the founding of a new Republic of Mexico.

## World Cultural Highlights

**World Art**   Umberto Boccioni, *The City Rises*; Émile Bourdelle, *Rodin at Work*; Giorgio de Chirico, *Enigma of an Autumn Afternoon*; Wilhelm Lehmbruck, *Standing Woman*; Amedeo Modigliani, *The Cellist*.

**World Literature**   Sigmund Freud, *Five Lectures on Psychoanalysis*; John Galsworthy, *Justice,* Ferenc Molnár, *The Guardsman*; Edmond Rostand, *Chantecler*; John Synge, *Deirdre of the Sorrows*.

**World Music**   Giacomo Puccini, *The Girl of the Golden West*; Richard Strauss, *Der Rosenkavalier*; Igor Stravinsky, *The Firebird*; Ralph Vaughan Williams, *Fantasia on a Theme of Thomas Tallis*.

**Miscellaneous**   The Berlin Deutsche Oper opens; the Barcelona and Havana symphonies are founded; births include Manfred Bukofzer, Jean Genêt, and Jean Martinon; deaths include Mily Balakirev, Björnstjerne Björnson, William H. Hunt, William Orchardson, Henri Rousseau, and Leo Tolstoy.

## American Art and Literature Highlights

**Births/Deaths**  Births include artists Paul Feeley, Morris Graves, Franz Kline, and literary figures Abe Burrows, Robert Fitzgerald, Josephina Niggli, and Winfield T. Scott; deaths include art figures Winslow Homer, John La Farge, Larkin Mead, John Quincy Adams Ward, and literary figures Samuel Clemens, Julia Ward Howe, William James, William V. Moody, and William S. Porter (O. Henry).

**Art Works**  George Bellows, *A Morning Snow—Hudson River*; Cyrus E. Dallin, *The Scout*; Thomas Dewing, *Lady in White*; A. St. Leger Eberle, *Windy Doorstep*; Childe Hassam, *Road to the Land of Nod*; Robert Reid, *Violet Kimona*; Frederic Remington, *The Stampede*; Albert Ryder, *Death on a Pale Horse*; Everett Shinn, *Dancer in White*; Max Weber, *Composition with Three Figures*.

**Literature**  Irving Babbitt, *The New Laokoön*; Josephine Bacon, *Biography of a Boy*; Winston Churchill, *A Modern Chronicle*; Finley P. Dunne, *Mr. Dooley Says*; Strickland Gillilan, *Including Finnigin*; Hutchins Hapgood, *Types from City Streets*; Charles Klein, *The Gamblers*; Stephen Leacock, *Literary Lapses*; Ezra Pound, *The Spirit of Romance*; Edwin A. Robinson, *The Town Down the River*.

## Music — The Vernacular/Commercial Scene

**A. Births**  Lou Busch (pianist/composer) July 18; Sidney "Big Sid" Catlett (drummer) January 17; Spade Cooley (fiddler/bandleader) December 17; Eddy Duchin (pianist/bandleader) April 10; Red Foley (singer/writer) June 17; Clyde Hart (pianist); Milt Hinton (string bassist) June 23; Howlin' Wolf (singer/performer) June 10; Gordon Jenkins (conductor/arranger) May 12; Albert "Bud" Johnson (saxophonist); Dick Jurgens (trumpeter/bandleader) January 8; Sammy Kaye (bandleader) March 13; John Jacob Loeb (composer) February 18; Frank Loesser (composer/librettist) June 29; Joseph Myrow (songwriter) February 28; Alex North (composer) December 4; Sy Oliver (composer/arranger) December 17; Eleanor Powell (singer/dancer) November 21; Earl Robinson (composer) July 2; Raymond Scott (pianist/arranger) September 10; Artie Shaw (clarinetist/bandleader) May 23; Ethel Smith (organist) November 22; T-Bone Walker (guitarist/singer) May 28; Mary Lou Williams (pianist) May 8; Hugo Winterhalter (conductor) August 15.

**C. Biographical**

**Performing Groups**  Frank Christian's Ragtime Band (New Orleans); Coltrane Quartet.

**New Beginnings**  Morse Music Co. (sold to Leo Feist in 1915); Music Publishers Protective Association (against payola excesses); Pace Music House (Chicago).

**D. Publications**  John Avery Lomax, *Cowboy Songs and Other Frontier Ballads*.

**E. Representative Works**

**Musicals**  Victor Herbert and R. J. Young, *Naughty Marietta*; Max Hoffmann, *The Young Turk*; Karl Hoschna and O. Harbach, *Bright Eyes—Madame Sherry*; Joe Howard and C. Davis, *The Sweetest Girl in Paris*; Raymond Hubbell and G. Macdonough, *The Jolly Bachelors—The Bachelor Belles*; Jean Schwartz and W. Jerome, *Up and Down Broadway*; A. Baldwin Sloane and E. Smith, *Tillie's Nightmare*.

**Songs**  Ernest Ball and Chauncey Olcott, *Mother Machree*; Shelton Brooks, *Some of These Days*; Fred Fisher and A. Bryan, *Come, Josephine, in My Flying Machine*; Leo Friedman and B. S. Whitson, *Let Me Call You Sweetheart*; J. Jordan and W. M. Cook, *Lovey Joe*; Dermot MacMurrough and J. V. Rowe, *Macushla*; Cole Porter, *Bridget*; Tell Taylor, *Down by the Old Mill Stream*; Albert Von Tilzer and J. McCree, *Put Your Arms Around Me, Honey*; W. R. Williams, *I'd Love to Live in Loveland (With a Girl Like You)*.

**Other**  May Aufderheide, *Totally Different Rag—Blue Ribbon Rag*; George Botsford, *Grizzly Bear Rag—Chatterbox Rag*; Joseph Daly, *The Chicken Reel*; Albert Gumble, *The Chanticleer Rag*;

Scott Joplin, *Stoptime Rag;* Joseph F. Lamb, *Champagne Rag*; Leighton Brothers and Ron Shields, *Steamboat Bill*; Paul Pratt, *Walhalla Rag*; James Scott, *Hilarity Rag—Ophelia Rag—Hearts Longing Waltzes*; Percy Wenrich, *Egyptian Rag*.

## Music—The Cultivated/Art Music Scene

**F. Births**   Samuel Barber (composer) March 9; David D. Boyden (musicologist) December 10; J. Walter Cassel (baritone) May 15; Arthur Cohn (composer/conductor) November 6; William D. Denny (composer/violist) July 2; Lehman Engel (composer/conductor) September 14; Richard Franko Goldman (bandmaster) December 7; Parks Grant (composer) January 4; Charles Jones (composer) June 21; Edward Kilenyi, Jr. (pianist) May 7; Dorothy Maynor (soprano) September 3; Henry Pleasants (music author) May 12; H. Owen Reed (composer) June 17; Renold Schilke (brass instrument maker) June 30; William Schuman (composer/administrator) August 4; Leonard Shure (pianist) April 10; Izler Solomon (conductor) January 11; Leon Stein (composer/writer) September 18.

**G. Deaths**   Julian Edwards (British-born composer/conductor) September 5; Charles Gilibert (French-born baritone) October 11; George D. Russell (dealer/publisher) February 3; Myron Whitney (bassist) September 19; David D. Wood (organist) March 27.

**H. Debuts**

**United States**   Adolphe Borchard (French pianist), Lillian Grenville (soprano—Chicago), Orville Harrold (tenor—New York), Liza Lehmann (British soprano—tour), Kathleen Parlow (Canadian violinist—New York), Marie Sundelius (soprano—Boston).

**Metropolitan Opera**   Max Bendix (conductor), Marie Delna (French contralto), William W. Hinshaw (baritone), Walter Hyde (British tenor), Hermann Jadlowker (Latvian tenor), John McCormack (Irish tenor), Jane Osborn-Hannah (soprano), Maurice Renaud (French baritone), Léon Rothier (French bass), Dmitri Smirnov (Russian tenor), Lucie Weidt (German soprano).

**Other**   George Meader (tenor—Leipzig).

**I. New Positions**

**Conductors**   Cleofonte Campanini (Chicago Grand Opera Co.—to 1919).

**Educational**   George Boyle (piano, Peabody—to 1922); Louis A. Coerne (music head, University of Wisconsin—to 1915); Arthur Shepherd (New England Conservatory—to 1920).

**Other**   Andreas Dippel (manager, Chicago Opera); Harvey Gaul (organ, Calvary Church, Pittsburgh); Glenn D. Gunn (music critic, *Chicago Tribune*—to 1915); A. Walter Kramer (staff, *Musical America*—to 1922); Alexander Russell (organ activities, Wanamaker's, New York).

**J. Honors and Awards**

**Honors**   Howard Brockway and David Stanley Smith (National Institute).

**K. Biographical**   Frances Alda marries impresario Giulio Gatti-Casazza; George F. Boyle (Australian pianist/composer) comes to the United States; Arthur Farwell moves to New York and becomes supervisor of municipal music concerts; George Gershwin's family buys a new piano, which young George masters in a short time; Gustave Langenus (Belgian clarinetist) comes to the United States and begins playing in the New York Philharmonic Orchestra; John P. Sousa takes his band on a world tour.

**L. Musical Beginnings**

**Performing Groups**   Barrère Ensemble (Little Symphony in 1914); Chicago-Philadelphia Opera Co.; Cleveland Symphony Orchestra; Indianapolis Symphony Orchestra II (to 1914); Pittsburgh Orchestra Association; San Carlo Opera Co. (New York).

**Festivals**   MacDowell Festivals (Peterborough, New Hampshire).

**Educational**   Boston School of Music; Indiana University Music Department (School of Music, 1921).

**Other**   Clef Club (black musicians' association); Rodeheaver-Ackley Publishing Co. (Chicago); Wurlitzer Hope-Jones Unit Orchestra ("Mighty Wurlitzer").

**M. Music Publications**

Cooke, James F., *The Standard History of Music*
Earhart, Will, *Art Songs for High Schools*
Elson, Louis, *Mistakes and Disputed Points in Music*
Hamilton, Clarence, *Piano Teaching*
Hoffman, Richard, *Some Musical Recollections of Fifty Years*
Hubbard, William, ed., *The American History and Encyclopedia of Music*
Upton, George P., *Standard Musical Biographies*

**N. Musical Compositions**

**Chamber Music**   Charles E. Ives, *Violin Sonata No. 2*; Fritz Kreisler, *Liebesfreud—Liebeslied*; Frederick Search, *String Quartet No. 1*.

**Choral/Vocal**   Amy Beach, *Three Songs, Opus 71*; Charles Wakefield Cadman, *Sayonara* (song cycle); Philip G. Clapp, *Song of Youth*; Arthur Farwell, *Hymn to Liberty, Opus 35*; Horatio Parker, *Seven Songs, Opus 70*; Bertram Shapleigh, *Vedic Hymn, Opus 56*; Oley Speaks, *Morning* (song); Humphrey Stewart, *Christmas Cantata—St. Anthony Mass*.

**Concertos**   Victor Herbert, *L'Encore* (flute, clarinet, and orchestra); John Powell, *Violin Concerto*.

**Operas**   Joseph C. Breil, *Love Laughs at Locksmiths* (operetta); Frederick Converse, *Sacrifice*; Arthur Nevin, *Poia*; Horatio Parker, *Mona, Opus 71* (Metropolitan Opera Association Prize); Roger Sessions, *Lancelot and Elaine*.

**Orchestra/Band**   John J. Becker, *The Season of Pan* (ballet); Victor Herbert, *Aschenbrödel March*; Henry F. Gilbert, *Strife*; William W. Gilchrist, *Symphonic Poem in G Minor* (?); Karl King, *Emblem of Freedom March*; Bertram Shapleigh, *Mirage, Opus 57* (tone poem); John P. Sousa, *The Federal March*; Gustav Strube, *Overture, Puck*.

**Piano/Organ**   Frederick Ayres, *Two Fugues, Opus 9*; John J. Becker, *Sonata, "The Modern Man I Sing"*; Arthur Bird, *Four Pieces for Piano*; Leo Ornstein, *Impressions of Notre Dame*; Horatio Parker, *Four Organ Compositions, Opus 66*.

**Symphonies**   Paul H. Allen, *Symphony No. 6 in D Major, "Pilgrim"* (Paderewski Prize); Philip G. Clapp, *Symphony No. 1 in E Major*; Arne Oldberg, *Symphony in F Minor, Opus 23*; David S. Smith, *Symphony No. 1 in F Minor*.

# 1911

☀

## Historical Highlights

The first transcontinental flight across the United States takes 82 hours, 4 minutes; the Standard Oil Co. and the American Tobacco Co. are broken up by the Supreme Court; air conditioning is invented and so is the self-starter for automobile engines; Roald Amundsen becomes the first person to reach the South Pole; Parliament curtails the power of the British House of Lords.

## World Cultural Highlights

**World Art**   Umberto Boccioni, *States of Mind*; Marc Chagall, *I and the Village*; Wilhelm Lehmbruck, *Kneeling Woman*; Henri Matisse, *The Red Studio*; Aston Webb, *Admiralty Arch, London*.

**World Literature**   Guillaume Apollinaire, *Le Bestiaire*; E. M. Forster, *Celestial Omnibus*: John Galsworthy, *The Patrician*; Hugo von Hofmannsthal, *Jedermann*; George Moore, *Hail and Farewell—Ave*.

**World Music**   Béla Bartók, *Bluebeard's Castle*; Reinhold Glière, *Ilya Morometz Symphony (No. 3)*; Carl Nielsen, *Sinfonia Espansiva*; Jean Sibelius, *Symphony No. 4*; Igor Stravinsky, *Petrouchka*.

**Miscellaneous**   The Finnish Opera Co. is founded in Helsinki and the Bonn Symphony Orchestra in Germany; births include Czeslav Milosz, Allan Pettersson, Terence Rattigan, and Henri Troyat; deaths include Reinhold Begas, Mikolajus Ciurlionis, Odysseus Elytis, Alphonse Legros, and Gustav Mahler.

## American Art and Literature

**Births/Deaths**   Births include art figures Will Barnet, Louise Bourgeois, Gertrude Greene, and literary figures Elizabeth Bishop, Sam Levinson, Kenneth Patchen, Tennessee Williams, and Audrey Wurdemann; deaths include art figures Edwin Abbey, Thomas Ball, William Keith, Frederic Vinton, and literary figures Elizabeth Akers, George Eggleston, Charles B. Loomis, and Denman Thompson.

**Art Works**   Man Ray, *Five Figures*; Paul Manship, *Duck Girl*; John Marin, *Series: The Woolworth Building—Movement, Fifth Avenue*; Kenneth H. Miller, *Recumbent Figure*; Bela Pratt, *Art—Science*; John Singer Sargent, *Under the Rialto*; John Sloan, *Woman's Work*; Lorado Taft, *Black Hawk*; Max Weber, *Decoration with Seated Figure—Summer*.

**Literature**   Mary Austin, *The Arrow Maker*; Irving A. Bacheller, *Keeping Up with Lizzie*; Katharine Lee Bates, *America the Beautiful and Other Poems*; Theodore Dreiser, *Jennie Gerhardt*; Finley P. Dunne, *New Dooley Book*; Alfred J. Kilmer, *Summer of Love*; John Muir, *My First Summer in the Sierras*; Sara Teasdale, *Helen of Troy and Other Poems*; Edith Wharton, *Ethan Frome*.

## Music—The Vernacular/Commercial Scene

**A. Births**   Blue Barron (trombonist/bandleader) March 22; Buck Clayton (trumpeter/arranger) November 12; Roy Eldridge (trumpeter) January 30; Jane Froman (singer) November 10; Stanley Hicks (folk singer/instrument maker) October 13; Mahalia Jackson (singer) October 26; Jo Jones (drummer) October 7; Spike Jones (musical satirist) December 14; Stan Kenton (bandleader) December 15; Mitch Miller (singer/conductor) July 4; Bill Monroe (mandolin player/bandleader) September 13; Louis Prima (trumpeter) December 7; Alvino Rey (guitarist) July 1; Roy Rogers (singer/actor) November 5; Maxine Sullivan (singer) May 13; Sonny Terry (singer/harmonica) October 24; J. "Big Joe" Turner (singer) May 18.

**B. Deaths**   James Bland (minstrel performer) May 5; Bob Cole (lyricist); Edward "Ned" Harrigan (lyricist) June 6; Karl Hoschna (composer) December 23; George Walker (minstrel performer).

**C. Biographical**

**Performing Groups**   Kid Ory Band (New Orleans).

**New Beginnings**   National Vaudeville Artists; Winter Garden (New York).

**Miscellaneous**   Ivan Caryll (Belgian composer) comes to the United States.

**E. Representative Works**

**Musicals**   Ivan Caryll and C. M. S. McLellan, *The Pink Lady*; George M. Cohan, *The Little Millionaire*; Reginald De Koven, *The Wedding Trip*; Victor Herbert, *The Duchess—The Enchantress—When Sweet Sixteen*; Louis A. Hirsch and E. Eysler, *Vera Violetta*; Karl Hoschna and O. Harbach, *The Fascinating Widow—The Girl of My Dreams*; Cole Porter, *Cora*.

**Songs**   Nat Ayer and A. S. Brown, *Oh You Beautiful Doll*; Irving Berlin, *Alexander's Ragtime Band*; W. A. Dillon and H. Von Tilzer, *I Want a Girl Just Like the Girl That Married Dear Old Dad*; Meade Minnigerode and G. S. Pomeroy, *The Whiffenpoof Song*; Jelly Roll Morton, *Grandpa's Spells*; Lewis F. Muir, *Waiting for the Robert E. Lee*; Egbert A. Van Alstyne and H. Williams, *Good Night, Ladies*.

**Other**   May Aufderheide, *Novelty Rag*; Irving Berlin, *Ragtime Violin*; Charlotte Blake, *That Tired Rag*; Julia Lee Niebergall, *Horseshoe Rag*; James Scott, *Princess Rag—Quality Rag—Ragtime Oriole*; Ted Snyder, *That Mysterious Rag*; Percy Wenrich, *Skeleton Rag—Sunflower Rag*; Gladys Yelvington, *Piffle Rag*.

## Music—The Cultivated/Art Music Scene

**F. Births**   Jeanne Behrend (pianist/composer) May 11; Shura Cherkassky (pianist) October 7; Oliver Daniel (musicologist) November 24; Edward O. D. Downes (musicologist) August 12; Weldon Hart (composer) September 19; Bernard Herrmann (composer/conductor) June 29; Alan Hovhaness (composer) March 8; Ralph Kirkpatrick (harpsichordist) June 10; Robert McBride (composer) February 20; Howard Mitchell (cellist/conductor) March 11; Lionel Nowak (pianist/composer); Walter Rubsamen (musicologist) July 21; Julia Smith (composer/pianist) January 25; George Tremblay (pianist/composer) January 14; Leonard Warren (baritone) April 21.

**G. Deaths**   Edwin Arthur Jones (composer/violinist) January 9; Bruno Oscar Klein (German-born pianist/composer) June 22; Emma Osgood (soprano) November 8; Madeline Schiller (British-born pianist) July 3; William Hall Sherwood (pianist/composer) January 7.

**H. Debuts**

**United States**   George Baklanov (Russian baritone—Boston), Leonard Borwick (British pianist—tour), Rafaelo Diaz (tenor—Boston), Jenny Dufau (French soprano—Chicago), Fredric Fradkin (violinist—New York), Ludwig Hess (German tenor—tour), Leo Ornstein (pianist—New York), Minnie Saltzmann-Stevens (soprano—Chicago), Arthur Shattuck (pianist—New York), Maggie Teyte (British soprano—Chicago), Efrem Zimbalist (Russian violinist—Boston).

**Metropolitan Opera**   Amedeo Bassi (Italian tenor), Putnam Griswold (bass-baritone), Heinrich Hensel (German tenor), Margarete Matzenauer (Hungarian soprano), Luisa Tetrazzini (Italian soprano), Hermann Weil (German baritone).

**Other**   Felice Lyne (soprano—London), George Meader (tenor—Leipzig).

**I. New Positions**

**Conductors**   Carl Busch (Kansas City Symphony Orchestra—to 1918); Henry K. Hadley (San Francisco Symphony Orchestra—to 1915); Josef Stransky (New York Philharmonic Orchestra—to 1923).

**Educational**   Felix Deyo (Brooklyn Conservatory—to 1939); Harry L. Freeman (director, Freeman School of Music); Edgar Stillman Kelley (theory/composition, Cincinnati Conservatory—to 1934).

**Other**   Leonard Liebling (editor-in-chief, *Musical Courier*).

**J. Honors and Awards**

**Honors**   Franz Kneisel (doctorate, Yale).

**K. Biographical**   Jean-Baptiste Beck (French musicologist) comes to the United States; Misha Elman (Ukranian violinist) decides to settle in the United States; Emilio de Gogorza marries soprano Emma Eames; Paolo Martucci (Italian pianist) comes to the United States; Tibor Serly, age 10, becomes an American citizen; William Grant Still leaves Arkansas for science study at Wilberforce College; Ermanno Wolf-Ferrari visits the United States; Efrem Zimbalist (Russian violinist), following his debut, decides to stay in the United States.

**L. Musical Beginnings**

**Performing Groups**   Austin Symphony Orchestra (Texas); Goldman Band (New York); Indianapolis Orchestral Association; Kansas City Symphony Orchestra (to 1918); San Francisco Symphony Orchestra.

**Educational**   Freeman School of Music; University of California, Los Angeles, Music Department; United States Army Music School.

**Other**   Carnegie Corporation of New York; Knabe Brothers Co. (New York); Musicians Club of New York; *Pacific Coast Musician* (to 1948); Ricordi, New York branch; Savoy Theater (San Diego).

**M. Music Publications**

Clappé, Arthur A., *The Wind-band and Its Instruments*

Dickinson, Edward, *The Education of the Music Lover*
Dolge, Alfred, *Pianos and Their Makers*
Erb, John L., *Elements of Harmony—Hymns and Church Music*
Hamilton, Clarence, *Sound and Its Relation to Music*
Krehbiel, Henry E., *The Pianoforte and Its Music*
Laurendeau, Louis P., *Practical Band Arranger*
Parkhurst, Howard E., *Complete Method for the Modern Organ*
Ziehn, Bernhard, *Five- and Six-Part Harmonies*

**N. Musical Compositions**

**Chamber Music** John Alden Carpenter, *Violin Sonata*; Blair Fairchild, *String Quartet No. 2*; Arthur Foote, *String Quartet No. 3 in D Major, Opus 70*; Charles Ives, *Pianist Trio*; Daniel G. Mason, *Pianist Quartet, Opus 7*.

**Choral/Vocal** Carrie Jacobs Bond, *Half Minute Songs*; Henry Hadley, *The Nightingale and the Rose, Opus 54* (women's voices); Horatio Parker, *A Song of the Times, Opus 73—School Songs, Opus 66*.

**Operas** Paul Hastings Allen, *O Munasterio*; Victor Herbert, *Natouma*; Scott Joplin, *Treemonisha*; Mary Carr Moore, *Narcissa* (Bispham Medal); Arthur F. Nevin, *Twilight*, Harry R. Shelley, *Old Black Joe*.

**Orchestra/Band** George W. Chadwick, *Everywoman* (incidental music); Arthur M. Curry, *Atala* (symphonic poem); Henry F. Gilbert, *The Intimate Story of Indian Tribal Life* (21 miniatures)—*Three American Dances*; Edwin Franko Goldman, *The Pride of America March*; William H. Humiston, *Suite in F-Sharp Minor*; Charles Ives, *Set No. 1 for Small Orchestra* (completed)—*The Gong on the Hook and Ladder*; Karl King, *Robinson's Grand Entry March*; Arthur Nevin, *Springs of Saratoga*; Horatio Parker, *Collegiate Overture, Opus 72*.

**Piano/Organ** R. Nathaniel Dett, *Magnolia Suite*; Leo Ornstein, *Wild Men's Dance*.

**Symphonies** Henry Hadley, *Symphony No. 4, "North, East, South and West."*

# 1912

❀

## Historical Highlights

Woodrow Wilson is elected the 28th president when Theodore Roosevelt, at odds with his old friend Taft, forms the Bull Moose Party; New Mexico and Arizona become the 47th and 48th states, respectively; Alaska is organized as a United States Territory; all Federal employees are given an eight-hour workday by law; the "unsinkable" Titanic sinks on its maiden voyage with over 1,500 people aboard.

## World Cultural Highlights

**World Art** Émile Bourdelle, *Apollo and His Thought*; Wassily Kandinsky, *Montmartre: Le Passage Cottin*; Piet Mondrian, *Simultaneous Windows*; Marcel Duchamp, *Nude Descending a Staircase No. 2*.

**World Literature** Rupert Brooke, *Poems*; George Moore, *Hail and Farewell—Salve*; Romain Rolland, *Jean Christophe*; George Bernard Shaw, *Pygmalion*; Rabindranath Tagore, *Gitanjali*.

**World Music** Claude Debussy, *Jeux*; Serge Prokofiev, *Sarcasms*; Maurice Ravel, *Daphnis and Chloe*; Arnold Schoenberg, *Pierrot Lunaire*; Richard Strauss, *Ariadne auf Naxos*.

**Miscellaneous** The Berlin Opera House opens; the Pro Arte String Quartet formed in Belgium; births include Igor Markevitch, György Sándor, and Georg Solti; deaths include Lawrence Alma-Tadema, Édouard Detaille, Samuel Coleridge Taylor, Jules Massenet, and August Strindberg.

## American Art and Literature Highlights

**Births/Deaths**    Births include art figures William Baziotes, Morris Louis, Jackson Pollack, Tony Smith, and literary figures John Cheever, Garson Kanin, Mary McCarthy, and Eleanor May Sarton; deaths include art figures Thomas Anshutz, Louis Potter, Charles Schreyvogel, and literary figures Will Carleton, James Otis Kaler, Robert Cameron Rogers, and Margaret E. Sangster.

**Art Works**    Alexander Archipenko, *Walking—Woman*; Arthur B. Carles, *Interior with Woman at Piano*; Robert Henri, *Blind Spanish Singer*; Malvina Hoffman, *Bacchanale Russe*; John Marin, *Movement, Fifth Avenue*; Louis Maurer, *September Morn*; Maurice Prendergast, *Summer, New England*; Charles Russell, *Lewis and Clark Meeting the Flathead Indians*.

**Literature**    George Ade, *Knocking the Neighbors*; Louis Anspacher, *The Glass House*; Mart Antin, *The Promised Land*; Eleanor Atkinson, *Greyfriar's Bobby*; Irvin Cobb, *Back Home*; Theodore Dreiser, *The Financier*; Amy Lowell, *Dome of Many-Colored Glass*; J. Hartley Manners, *Peg o' My Heart*; Christopher Morley, *The Eighth Sin*; Ezra Pound, *Ripostes*; George Viereck, *Candle and the Flame*.

## Music—The Vernacular/Commercial Scene

**A. Births**    Kenny Baker (singer) September 30; Dave Barbour (guitarist/writer) May 28; Les Brown (bandleader) March 14; Perry Como (singer) May 18; Buddy Clark (singer) July 26; Mack David (lyricist/composer) July 5; Gil Evans (arranger/pianist) May 13; Rex Griffin (singer/composer) August 12; Woody Guthrie (folksinger) July 14; Sam "Lightnin" Hopkins (singer/guitarist) March 15; Gene Kelly (dancer/actor) August 21; Burton Lane (composer) February 2; Jack Lawrence (composer) April 7; Tony Martin (singer) December 22; Vaughn Monroe (singer/bandleader) October 7; David Raksin (composer) August 4; Paul Weston (composer/arranger) March 12; Teddy Wilson (pianist) November 24.

**B. Deaths**    William G. Fischer (hymnist) August 12.

**C. Biographical**

**Performing Groups**    Original Creole Orchestra (Los Angeles).

**New Beginnings**    Waterson, Berlin and Snyder, Publishers (New York).

**Miscellaneous**    James Reese Europe leads the first black jazz orchestra to appear in Carnegie Hall; the Shuberts begin their annual presentations of The Passing Show.

**D. Publications**    Will Marion Cook, *Collection of Negro Songs*.

**E. Representative Works**

**Musicals**    Ivan Caryll and C. M. S. McLellan, *Oh, Oh, Delphine*; Rudolf Friml and H. Atteridge, *The Firefly*; John L. Golden and J. Cawthorn, *The Sunshine Girl*; Victor Herbert, *The Lady of the Slipper*; Karl Hoschna and B. H. Burt, *The Wall Street Girl*; Raymond Hubbell and H. Blossom, *The Man from Cook's*; Gustave A. Kerker, *Two Little Brides*; Jerome Kern, *The Red Petticoat*; Gustave Luders and F. Pixley, *The Gypsy*; Cole Porter, *The Pot of Gold—The Villain Still Pursued Her*.

**Songs**    Maurice Abrahams, *Ragtime Cowboy Joe—Hitchy-Koo*; Ernest Ball and C. Olcott, *When Irish Eyes Are Smiling*; Ernie Burnett and G. Norton, *My Melancholy Baby*; L. Wolfe Gilbert, *Waitin' for the Robert E. Lee*; Charles Glover and C. M. Spencer, *The Rose of Tralee*; Jack Judge and H. H. Williams, *It's a Long Way to Tipperary*; Edward Madden and P. Wenrich, *Moonlight Bay*; F. Dudleigh Vernor, *The Sweetheart of Sigma Chi*; Harry Von Tilzer, *In the Evening by the Moonlight*; H. Von Tilzer and W. Jerome, *And the Green Grass Grew All Around*.

**Other**    Eubie Blake, *Classical Rag*; George Botsford, *Eskimo Rag*; Scott Joplin, *Scott Joplin's New Rag*; Nick La Rocca, *Tiger Rag—Sensation Rag*; Julia Lee Niebergall, *Rad Rambler Rag*; J. Russell Robinson, *That Eccentric Rag*.

## Music—The Cultivated/Art Music Scene

**F. Births**    Wayne Barlow (composer) September 12; Arthur Berger (composer) May 15; Raynor Brown (composer/organist) February 23; John Cage (composer) September 5; Claire Coci (organist) March 15; Virgil Fox (organist) May 3; Don Gillis (composer) June 17; Carleen M. Hutchins (string instrument maker) May 24; Robert Lawrence (conductor/critic) March 18; Ray Lev (pianist) May 8; Conlon Nancarrow (composer) October 27; William S. Newman (musicologist) April 6.

**G. Deaths**  Otis Bardwell Boise (organist) December 2; William H. Clarke (organ builder) December 11; W. S. B. Mathews (organist) April 1; John F. Stratton (instrument maker) October 23; Bernhard Ziehn (theorist) September 8.

**H. Debuts**

**United States**  Wilhelm Backhaus (German pianist—New York), Gottfried Galston (Austrian soprano—tour), Mabel Garrison (soprano—Boston), Elena Gerhardt (German mezzo-soprano—tour), Lucille Marcel (soprano—Boston), Vanni Marcoux (French bass-baritone—Boston), Louis Persinger (violinist—Philadelphia), John Powell (pianist—New York), Titta Ruffo (Italian baritone—Philadelphia), Friedrich Schorr (Hungarian baritone—Chicago), Jacques Urlus (Dutch tenor—Boston), Alfred Wallenstein (cellist—Los Angeles).

**Metropolitan Opera**  Lucrezia Bori (Spanish soprano), Frieda Hempel (German soprano), Giorgio Polacco (Italian conductor).

**Other**  Louis Gruenberg (pianist—Berlin), Edward Johnson (tenor—Padua).

**I. New Positions**

**Conductors**  Louis Koemmenich (Oratorio Society of New York—to 1917); Ernst Kunwald (Cincinnati Symphony Orchestra—to 1917); Karl Muck (Boston Symphony Orchestra, second term—to 1918); Giorgio Polacco (Metropolitan Opera—to 1917); Erno Rapee (Hungarian Opera Co., New York); Leopold Stokowski (Philadelphia Orchestra—to 1938).

**Educational**  Edward Ballantine (Harvard—to 1947); Clarence Dickinson (sacred music, Union Theological Seminary); Clayton Johns (New England Conservatory—to 1916); Henry Schradieck (American Institute of Applied Music, New York); Charles Seeger (music chair, Berkeley—to 1919).

**Other**  Seth Bingham (organ, Madison Avenue Presbyterian Church, New York—to 1951); T. Tertius Noble (organ, St. Thomas' Episcopal Church, New York—to 1947); Powell Weaver (organ, Grand Avenue Temple, Kansas City—to 1937).

**J. Honors and Awards**

**Honors**  Frederick Stock (National Institute).

**K. Biographical**  Hans Barth becomes an American citizen; Alberto Bimboni (Italian pianist/composer) comes to the United States; Henry Cowell shocks the San Francisco Music Club with his tone-clusters at the piano; George Gershwin receives his first music lessons; Charles Ives moves his family to their new farm in West Redding, Connecticut; Arthur Nikisch directs the London Symphony Orchestra on their first visit to the United States; Walter Piston begins art study in Massachusetts; Erno Rapee (Hungarian conductor) comes to the United States; Max de Schauensee (Italian tenor/critic) comes to the United States and studies at Curtis; Alexander Schreiner (German organist) moves with his folks to the United States.

**L. Musical Beginnings**

**Performing Groups**  Cathedral Choir of Men and Boys, Cathedral of St. Peter and St. Paul, Washington, DC; Lambord Choral Society (Modern Music Society, 1914); New York Military (Goldman) Band; Oratorio Society of Los Angeles; St. Olaf College Choir (Minnesota); Schubert Club of Kansas City; Seattle Musical Arts Society.

**Educational**  Cleveland Music School Settlement; Music School Settlement for Colored Children (New York); Phi Beta Fraternity (Northwestern University); Vocal Normal School (Chicago).

**Other**  Art Publication Society (St. Louis); Bosse Music Book Publishers (New York); *Harvard Musical Review*; James D. Vaughan Co. (Lawrenceburg, Tennessee).

**M. Music Publications**

Boyd, Charles N., *Lectures on Church Music*
Clarke, Herbert L., *Technical Studies for the Cornet*

Elson, Louis C., *Modern Music and Musicians*
Gunn, Glenn D., *A Course on the History and Aesthetics of Music*
Hughes, Rupert, *Music Lovers' Encyclopedia*
Lahee, Henry C., *The Grand Opera Singers of Today*
Ziehn, Bernhard, *Canonical Studies: A New Technic in Composition*

**N. Musical Compositions**

**Chamber Music**    Percy Grainger, *Handel in the Strand* (trio, orchestrated 1932); Louis Gruenberg, *Violin Sonata No. 1.*

**Choral/Vocal**    Carrie Jacobs Bond, *The Sandman*; Victor Herbert, *Love's Hour*; Charles Ives, *Lincoln, the Great Commoner*; C. A. Miles, *I Come to the Garden Alone* (gospel hymn); Horatio Parker, *Seven Greek Pastoral Scenes, Opus 74* (women's voices); Bertram Shapleigh, *The Fir Tree and the Brook, Opus 54—The Tale of the Dismal Swamp, Opus 55.*

**Concertos**    Felix Borowski, *Piano Concerto.*

**Operas**    Charles W. Cadman, *The Land of the Misty Water (Ramala)*; Harry L. Freeman, *The Prophecy*; Louis Gruenberg, *The Witch of Brocken* (operetta); Albert Mildenberg, *Love's Locksmith*; Mary Carr Moore, *The Leper*; Alfred G. Robyn, *All for the Ladies.*

**Orchestra/Band**    John J. Becker, *Two Orchestral Sketches (Cossack Sketches)*; Joseph C. Breil, *Queen Elizabeth* (film music); Philip G. Clapp, *Summer* (symphonic poem); Arthur Farwell, *Symbolist Study No. 6, "Mountain Vision," Opus 37—Joseph and His Brethren, Opus 38* (incidental music); Arthur Foote, *Four Character Pieces after Omar Khayyám*; Henry F. Gilbert, *Negro Rhapsody*; Victor Herbert, *The Lambs' Star Gambol*; Charles Ives, *Robert Browning Overture— First Orchestral Set (Three Places in New England)—Decoration Day—Matthew Arnold Overture*; Silas G. Pratt, *A Tragedy of the Deep* (symphonic poem); Wallingford Riegger, *Overture, the Beggarman*; David S. Smith, *Prince Hal Overture, Opus 31* (?); Deems Taylor, *The Siren Song, Opus 2* (symphonic poem); Emerson Whithorne, *The Rain.*

**Piano/Organ**    John J. Becker, *The Mountains* (?); Arthur Bird, *Three Miniature Poems (after Longfellow)*; John Alden Carpenter, *Polonaise Américaine*; R. Nathaniel Dett, *In the Bottoms Suite*; Henry F. Gilbert, *Indian Scenes*; Charles T. Griffes, *The Pleasure Dome of Kubla Khan* (orchestrated, 1917); Henry H. Huss, *Six Pieces for Pianoforte, Opus 23*; Daniel G. Mason, *Passacaglia and Fugue, Opus 10.*

**Symphonies**    John J. Becker, *Symphony No. 1, "Etude primitive."*

# 1913

☀

## Historical Highlights

The 16th Amendment establishing a federal income tax and the 17th Amendment providing for the direct election of senators are ratified; the Woolworth Building in New York is the newest, tallest skyscraper; the Federal Reserve Act is passed; the Rockefeller Foundation is founded; Albert Schweitzer opens a hospital in the French Congo.

## World Cultural Highlights

**World Art**    Marc Chagall, *The Musicians*; Christian Eriksson, *The Little Mermaid*; Fernand Léger, *Contrast of Forms*; Franz Marc, *Tower of Blue Horse*; Georges Rouault, *Three Judges.*

**World Literature**    Joseph Conrad, *Chance*; Maxim Gorky, *My Childhood*; D. H. Lawrence, *Sons and Lovers*; Jack London, *John Barleycorn*; Thomas Mann, *Death in Venice.*

**World Music**    Edward Elgar, *Falstaff*; Sergei Rachmaninoff, *The Bells*; Igor Stravinsky, *Le Sacre du Printemps*; Ralph Vaughan Williams, *London Symphony*; Anton Webern, *Five Pieces for Orchestra.*

**Miscellaneous**  The Lisbon Philharmonic Orchestra is founded; the London School of Dalcroze Eurythmics opens; births include Gina Bachauer, Benjamin Britten, Albert Camus, Tikhon Khrennikov, and Witold Lutoslawski.

## American Art and Literature

**Births/Deaths**  Births include art figures Peter Agostini, Philip Guston, Ibram Lassaw, Ad Reinhardt, and literary figures Robert Hayden, William Inge, Muriel Rukeyser, Karl Jay Shapiro, and Irwin Shaw; deaths include artist Julie Kempson, sculptor Franklin Simmons, and literary figures Julia Caroline Dorr, Thomas Janvier, Cincinnatus Miller, and Jane Marsh Parker.

**Art Works**  George Bellows, *The Cliff Dwellers*; Lovis Corinth, *Ariadne auf Naxos*; Stuart Davis, *Ebb Tide—Provincetown*; Lyonel Feininger, *Bridge I*; Childe Hassam, *Sunny Blue Sea*; Robert Henri, *Himself—Herself*; Ernest Lawson, *Spring Night, Harlem River*; Frederick MacMonnies, *Truth and Inspiration*; Paul Manship, *Centaur and Dryad*; Morgan Russell, *Synchromie en vert*.

**Literature**  Frances Allen, *The Invaders*; William R. Benét, *Merchants from Cathay*; Willa Cather, *O Pioneers!*; John W. Fox, *The Heart of the Hills*; Robert Frost, *A Boy's Will*; Ellen Glasgow, *Virginia*; Henry James, *A Small Boy and Others*; Vachel Lindsay, *General William Booth Enters into Heaven and Other Poems*; Eleanor Porter, *Pollyanna*; Gene Stratton Porter, *Laddie*.

## Music—The Vernacular/Commercial Scene

**A. Births**  Charlie Barnet (saxophonist/bandleader) October 26; Earl Bostic (saxophonist/band leader) April 25; Sammy Cahn (lyricist) June 18; Carmen Cavallero (pianist/bandleader); Bob Crosby (bandleader) August 25; Woody Herman (clarinetist/bandleader) May 16; Roscoe Holcomb (folk singer/guitarist); Helen Humes (singer) June 23; Grandpa Jones (singer/banjo) October 20; Frankie Laine (singer) March 30; Frances Langford (singer) April 4; Mary Martin (singer/actress) December 1; Rose Murphy (singer/pianist); Frank Proffitt (banjo maker); Jimmy Van Heusen (composer/publisher) January 26.

**B. Deaths**  Gustav Luders (German-born composer) January; Ren Shields (composer/lyricist).

**C. Biographical**

**New Beginnings**  Palace Theater (New York); Shubert Alley (New York); Tempo Club (entertainment agency for blacks).

**E. Representative Works**

**Musicals**  Ivan Caryl and C. M. S. McLellan, *The Little Café*; Reginald de Koven and H. B. Smith, *Her Little Highness*; Rudolf Friml and O. Harbach, *High Jinks*; Victor Herbert, *The Madcap Duchess;* Victor Herbert and H. B. Smith, *Sweethearts*; Gustave Luders and A. Hopwood, *Somewhere Else*; Chauncey Olcott and G. Graff, *The Isle o' Dreams*; Cole Porter, *The Kaleidoscope*; Jean Schwartz, *The Honeymoon Express*; Jean Schwartz and H. Atteridge, *The Passing Show II*; John Philip Sousa and L. Liebling, *The American Maid*.

**Songs**  Maurice Abrahams and G. Clarke, *Get Out and Get Under*; Irving Berlin, *That International Rag*; John W. Bratton, *The Teddy Bear's Picnic*; Zo Elliott and S. King, *There's a Long, Long Trail*; Fred Fisher and A. Bryan, *Peg O' My Heart*; Ballard MacDonald and H. Carroll, *The Trail of the Lonesome Pine*; James Monaco and J. McCarthy, *You Made Me Love You*; Chris Smith and J. Burris, *Ballin' the Jack*.

**Other**  George Botsford, *Buckeye Rag—Incandescent Rag—Universal Rag*; Irene Cozad, *Eatin' Time Rag*; Joseph Lamb, *American Beauty Rag*; Lucky Roberts, *Junk Man Rag—Pork and Beans*; Wilbur Sweatman, *Down Home Rag*; Harry Tierney, *Lousiana Rag*; Percy Wenrich, *Whipped Cream*.

## Music—The Cultivated/Art Music Scene

**F. Births**  John Barrows (horn virtuoso) February 12; Margaret Bonds (composer/pianist) March 3; Henry Brant (composer) September 15; Peggy Stuart Coolidge (composer/pianist) July 19;

Norman Dello Joio (composer) January 24; Vincent H. Duckles (musicologist) September 21; John Edmunds (composer) June 10; Alvin Etler (composer) February 19; Vivian Fine (composer) September 28; Grant Fletcher (composer/conductor) October 25; Morton Gould (composer/conductor) December 10; Clare Grundman (composer/arranger) May 11; Everett Burton Helm (composer/writer) July 17; Richard Hoppin (musicologist) February 22; Thor Johnson (conductor) June 10; Kent Kennan (composer) April 18; Martha Lipton (mezzo-soprano) April 6; Jerome Moross (composer); Gardner Read (composer/author) January 2; William Schwann (discographer/publisher) May 13; Risë Stevens (mezzo-soprano) June 11; Richard Tucker (tenor) August 28.

**G. Deaths**   William Foster Apthorp (critic) February 19; George Sherburn Hutchings (organ builder) June 1; Frank Lynes (organist) June 24; Hugo Sohmer (German-born pianist maker) October.

**H. Debuts**

**United States**   Julia Claussen (Swedish mezzo-soprano—Chicago), Julia Culp (Dutch contralto—New York), Carl Flesch (Hungarian violinist—New York), Samuel Gardner (violinist—New York), Beatrice Harrison (British cellist—tour), Ethel Leginska (British pianist—New York), Pavel Ludikar (Czech bass-baritone—Boston), José Mardones (Spanish bass—Boston), Lucien Muratore (French tenor—Chicago), Max von Pauer (Austrian pianist—tour), Rosa Raisa (Polish soprano—Chicago), Paul Reimers (German tenor—New York).

**Metropolitan Opera**   Paul Althouse (tenor—first American-trained singer at the Met), Luca Botta (Italian tenor), Carl Braun (German bass), Giovanni Martinelli (Italian tenor—Philadelphia debut earlier), Jacques Urlus (Dutch tenor).

**Other**   Arthur Loesser (pianist—Berlin), Florence Macbeth (soprano—Braunschweig).

**I. New Positions**

**Conductors**   Julian Paul Blitz (Houston Symphony Orchestra—to 1916); Adolph Tandler (Los Angeles Symphony Orchestra—to 1920); Ole Windingstad (Scandinavian Symphony Orchestra, New York).

**Educational**   Herman Bellstedt (Cincinnati Conservatory); Peter Dykema (University of Wisconsin—to 1924); Donald Ferguson (University of Minnesota—to 1950); Gustav Strube (theory, Peabody Institute—to 1946).

**Other**   Cleofonte Campanini (general manager, Chicago Grand Opera Co.); Mayhew Lake (editor-in-chief, band and orchestra music, Carl Fischer); Bernard Rogers (critic, *Musical America*—to 1922).

**J. Honors and Awards**

**Honors**   Ernest Schelling (National Institute).

**K. Biographical**   Max Altglass (Polish tenor) moves to the United States; Giuseppe Bamboschek (Italian conductor) comes to the United States; Jacques Gordon (Russian violinist/educator) emigrates to the United States; Ethel Leginska (British pianist/composer) comes to the United States; T. Tertius Noble (British organist/composer) emigrates to the United States; John Charles Thomas begins appearing in musical comedy on the New York stage; Ole Windingstad (Norwegian conductor/composer) settles in New York.

**L. Musical Beginnings**

**Performing Groups**   Century Opera Co. (New York); Fort Worth Symphony Orchestra; Houston Symphony Orchestra; Kortschak (Berkshire) String Quartet (Chicago); Scandinavian Symphony Orchestra of New York; Trio de Lutèce (by Carlos Salzedo).

**Educational**   Baldwin-Wallace College Conservatory of Music (by merger); Dossenbach-Klingenberg School of Music (Rochester, New York) (DKG Institute of Musical Art); Howard University Music Department; Music Education School (Portland, Oregon); Temple University School of Music.

**Other**   Civic Music Association of Chicago; Clark Harp Manufacturing Co. (Syracuse, New

York); *The Clef: The Music Journal of the West, Northwest and Southwest* (to 1920); Municipal Auditorium (Symphony Hall, Springfield, Massachusetts); Society of the Friends of Music (New York).

## M. Music Publications

Barnabee, Henry, *My Wanderings*
Densmore, Frances, *Chippewa Music*
Dolge, Alfred, *Pianos and Their Makers II*
Elson, Arthur, *The Musician's Guide*
Goetschius, P. and Tapper, Thomas, *Essentials of Music History*
Langenus, Gustave, *Modern Clarinet Playing*
Parkhurst, Howard E., *The Church Organist*
Spaeth, Sigmund, *Milton's Knowledge of Music*

## N. Musical Compositions

**Chamber Music**   Charles W. Cadman, *Piano Trio in D Major*; Charles Ives, *String Quartet No. 2*; José Quintón, *String Quartet in D Major*; Charles Seeger, *String Quartet—Violin Sonata*.

**Choral/Vocal**   George Bernard, *The Old Rugged Cross*; John Alden Carpenter, *Gitanjali* (song cycle), Mabel Wheeler Daniels, *The Desolate City*; Blair Fairchild, *Six Psalms*; Victor Herbert, *The Hail of the Friendly Sons* (male chorus); Henry H Hugg, *Nocturne*; Philip James, *Te Deum in C Major*; Margaret R. Lang, *The Night of the Star, Opus 52* (cantata)—*Wind, Opus 53* (female choir); Arthur Nevin, *The Djinns* (cantata); Horatio Parker, *The Leap of Roushan Beg* (tenor, male chorus and orchestra); Arthur Shepherd, *The City in the Sea* (cantata).

**Concertos**   Ernest Schelling, *Impressions from an Artist's Life* (piano and orchestra); Leo Sowerby, *Violin Concerto in G Major*.

**Operas**   Paul Hastings Allen, *Milda*; Walter Damrosch, *Cyrano de Bergerac*; Louis Gruenberg, *The Bride of the Gods*; Victor Herbert, *Madeleine*, Charles M. Loeffler, *The Passion of Hilarion*.

**Orchestra/Band**   Russell Alexander, *The Conquest March—Patriots of the Potomac March*; Marion F. Bauer, *Up the Ocklawaha* (symphonic poem); Ernest Bloch, *Three Jewish Poems*; Gena Branscombe, *Festival Prelude*; George W. Chadwick, *Aphrodite* (symphonic poem); Henry Hadley, *Lucifer* (tone poem); Victor Herbert, *Danse Baroque*; William H. Humiston, *Southern Fantasie*; Karl King, *Barnum and Bailey's Favorite*; José Quintón, *Concert Overture*; John Philip Sousa, *From Maine to Oregon March*; Gustav Strube, *Echo—Narcissus—Loreley* (symphonic poems).

**Piano/Organ**   Marion Bauer, *In the Country* (suite); John Alden Carpenter, *Impromptu*; Rossetter G. Cole, *From a Lover's Notebook, Opus 13*; Eastwood Lane, *In Sleepy Hollow*; Leo Ornstein, *Dwarf Suite—Sonata*; John Powell, *Sonata No. 3, "Teutonica."*

**Symphonies**   Charles Ives, *The Fourth of July (Holidays Symphony* compiled); Edgar S. Kelley, *Symphony No. 2, Opus 33, "New England"*; Frederick Search, *Symphony No. 1*.

# 1914

☼

## Historical Highlights

Transcontinental telephone service from New York to San Francisco is inaugurated; Henry Ford introduces the profit-sharing plan and the eight-hour day into his plant; the Army Air Service is formed; the Federal Trade Commission is established; the Panama Canal is finished; World War I begins following the assassination of Archduke Ferdinand and his wife in Sarajevo.

## World Cultural Highlights

**World Art**   Émile Bourdelle, *The Dying Centaur*; Georges Braque, *Music*; Giorgio de Chirico, *Gare Montparnasse*; Franz Marc, *Deer in Forest*; Pierre Renoir, *The Judgment of Paris*.

**World Literature**   Thomas Hardy, *Satires of Circumstance, Lyrics and Reveries*; James Joyce, *Dubliners*; Max Weber, *Cubist Poems*; William Butler Yeats, *Responsibilities*.

**World Music**   Frederick Delius, *North Country Sketches*; Gustav Holst, *The Planets*; Serge Prokofiev, *Scythian Suite*; Jean Sibelius, *The Oceanides*; Igor Stravinsky, *Le Rossignol*.

**Miscellaneous**   The Cape Town Symphony Orchestra founded in South Africa; births include Carlo Maria Giulini, Rafael Kubelik, Andrzej Panufnik, Sviatoslav Richter, and Dylan Thomas; deaths include Paul von Heyse, Anatol Liadov, Frédéric Mistral, and Theodore Watts-Dunton.

## American Art and Literature

**Births/Deaths**   Births include art figures Romare Bearden, Mauricio Lasansky, Walter Stuempfig, and literary figures John Berryman, William Burroughs, Ralph Ellison, John Hersey, David Ignatow, and Weldon Kees; deaths include art figures Vinnie Hoxie, Peter Moran, Vinnie Ream, and literary figures Madison Cawein, Adelaide Crapsey, Silas Weir Mitchell, and George Alfred Townsend.

**Art Works**   William Glackens, *At the Beach*; Marsden Hartley, *The Portrait of a German Officer*; Stanton MacDonald-Wright, *Abstraction on Spectrum*; Paul Manship, *Indian Pranghorn Antelope*; John Marin, *Sunset*; Morgan Russell, *Synchrony in Orange: To Form*; John Sloan, *Backyards, Greenwich Village*; Maurice Sterne, *Bali Bazaar*; Anne Whitney, *The Titanic Memorial*.

**Literature**   Edgar R. Burroughs, *Tarzan of the Apes*; Theodore Dreiser, *The Titan*; Robert Frost, *North of Boston*; Alfred J. Kilmer, *Trees and Other Poems*; Vachel Lindsay, *The Congo and Other Poems*; Jack London, *Valley of the Moon*; Amy Lowell, *Sword Blades and Poppy Seed*; Kathleen Norris, *Saturday's Child*; Wilbur Steele, *Storm*; Booth Tarkington, *Penrod*.

## Music — The Vernacular/Commercial Scene

**A. Births**   Bob Atcher (singer) May 11; Tex Beneke (saxophonist/singer) February 12; Ralph Blane (composer/lyricist) July 26; Eddie Boyd (guitarist/singer) November 25; Kitty Carlisle (singer) September 3; Kenny Clarke (drummer/bandleader) January 9; Carmen Dragon (conductor/arranger) July 28; Alfred Drake (singer) October 7; Billy Eckstine (singer/trumpeter) July 8; Ziggy Elman (trumpeter) May 26; Lester Flatt (singer/guitarist) June 28; Erskine Hawkins (trumpeter/bandleader) July 26; Lee Hays (folksinger); Eddie Howard (singer/bandleader) September 12; Ivory Joe Hunter (pianist/singer/writer) October 10; "Pee Wee" King (bandleader) February 18; Hugh Martin (composer) August 11; Sun Ra (keyboards) May; Eddie Sauter (arranger/composer) December 2; Hank Snow (singer) May 9; Floyd Tillman (singer/writer) December 8; Ernest Tubb (singer/writer) February 9; Jimmy Wakely (singer) February 16; Robert Wright (composer) September 25.

**C. Biographical**

**New Beginnings**   *Rag Time Review*.

**Miscellaneous**   James Reese Europe signs the first recording contract (by Victor) to be given to a black group; George Gershwin drops school and goes to work for Jerome Remick and Co.; Max Steiner (Austrian composer) comes to the United States.

**D. Publications**   Henry E. Krehbiel, *Afro-American Folksongs*.

**E. Representative Works**

**Musicals**   Ernest R. Ball and J. K. Brennan, *The Heart of Paddy Whack*; Irving Berlin and H. B. Smith, *Watch Your Step*; Ivan Caryll, A. Caldwell, and J. O'Dea, *Chin Chin*; George M. Cohan, *Hello, Broadway!*; Victor Herbert and R. B. Smith, *The Debutante*; V. Herbert and H. Blossom. *The Only Girl*; Jerome Kern and H. Reynolds, *The Girl from Utah*; Cole Porter, *We're All Dressed Up and Don't Know Huerto Go—Paranoia*; Sigmund Romberg and H. Atteridge, *Passing Show III*; Ted Snyder and B. Kalmar, *One Girl in a Million*.

**Songs**   Harold Atteridge and H. Carroll, *By the Beautiful Sea*; Ernest R. Ball and J. K. Brennan, *A Little Bit of Heaven*; Arthur Fields and W. Donovan, *The Aba Daba Honeymoon*; W. C. Handy, *St. Louis Blues*; Abe Olman, *Down Among the Sheltering Palms*; Caro Roma and W. H. Gardner, *Can't*

*Yo' Heah Me Callin', Caroline?*; James R. Shannon, *Too-ra-loo-ra-loo-ral, That's an Irish Lullaby*; Percy Wenrich and J. F. Mahoney, *When You Wore a Tulip*.

**Other**   Maurice Abrahams, *The Twentieth Century Rag*; Eubie Blake, *Chevy Chase Rag—Fizz Water Rag*; Euday L. Bowman, *Twelfth Street Rag*; Joseph C. Breil, *The Birth of a Nation* (film music); Duke Ellington, *Soda Fountain Rag*; James R. Europe, *Castle House Rag, Castle Walk*; James P. Johnson, *Caprice Rag*; Frederick K. Logan and J. R. Shannon, *Missouri Waltz* (words, 1916); Paul Pratt, *Hot House Rag*; James Scott, *Climax Rag—Suffragette Waltz*.

## Music—The Cultivated/Art Music Scene

**F. Births**   Larry Adler (harmonica virtuoso) February 10; Leo L. Beranek (acoustician) September 15; Norman Cazden (composer/musicologist) September 23; Catharine Crozier (organist) January 18; Cecil Effinger (composer) July 22; Philip F. Farkas (horn virtuoso) March 5; Frederick Fennell (bandmaster) July 2; Irving G. Fine (composer) December 3; Roger Goeb (composer) October 9; Edmund Haines (composer), George Kleinsinger (composer) February 13; Gail Kubik (composer) September 5; Charles Mills (composer) January 8; Robert Ottman (theorist/pedagogue) May 3; Ruth Possell (violinist) September 6; William Strickland (conductor) January 25; Rosalyn Tureck (pianist) December 14; Roger Wagner (conductor) January 16.

**G. Deaths**   Putnam Griswold (bass-baritone) February 26; Robert Hope-Jones (British-born organ builder) September 13; Emil Liebling (German-born pianist/composer) January 20; Eduard Mollenhauer (German-born violinist) May 7; Lillian Nordica (soprano) May 10; Henry S. Perkins (educator/composer) January 20; Pol Plançon (French-born bass) August 11; Rudolph Wurlitzer (German-born organ maker) January 14.

**H. Debuts**

**United States**   Clarence Adler (pianist—New York), Carl Friedberg (German pianist—tour), George H. Fryer (British pianist—tour), Louis Graveure (British baritone—New York), Kathleen Howard (contralto—New York), Florence Macbeth (soprano—Chicago), Otakar Marák (Czech tenor).

**Metropolitan Opera**   Rudolf Berger (Czech tenor), Luca Botta (Italian tenor), Sophie Braslau (contralto), Edoardo Ferrari-Fontana (Italian tenor), Mabel Garrison (soprano), Elisabeth Schumann (German soprano).

**Other**   Albert Stoessel (violinist—Berlin).

**I. New Positions**

**Conductors**   Weston Gales (Detroit Symphony Orchestra—to 1918); Nicolai Sokoloff (San Francisco Philharmonic Orchestra—to 1918).

**Educational**   John Lawrence Erb (director, University of Illinois School of Music—to 1921); Caspar Koch (Carnegie Institute of Technology—to 1941).

**Other**   Eric De Lamarter (organ, Fourth Presbyterian Church, Chicago); Harvey B. Gaul (music critic, *Pittsburgh Post-Gazette*); Otto Kinkeldey (music, New York Public Library—to 1923).

**K. Biographical**   Vincent Bach (Austrian instrument maker) moves to the United States, begins playing in the Boston Symphony Orchestra; Lorenzo Camilieri (Greek conductor/composer) settles in New York; Aurelio Giorni (Italian pianist) emigrates to the United States; Percy Grainger (Australian pianist/composer) moves to the United States; Sandor Harmati (Hungarian violinist) comes to the United States and settles in New York; Sol Hurok becomes an American citizen; Maud Karpeles visits the United States to collect American songs of British origin; Hans Kindler (Dutch conductor) comes to the United States and joins the Philadelphia Orchestra as a cellist; Wallingford Riegger goes to Germany as assistant conductor at the Würzburg Stadttheater; Lazar Weiner (Russian pianist/composer) comes to the United States.

**L. Musical Beginnings**

**Performing Groups**   Baltimore Symphony Orchestra; Barrère Little Symphony; Des Moines Eisteddfod Association; Detroit Symphony Orchestra; Eintracht Orchestra (Newark Symphony

Orchestra); New York Chamber Music Society; Oratorio Society of Utah; People's Chorus of San Diego; Standard Grand Opera Co. of Seattle.

**Educational**   Cornish Institute of the Performing and Visual Arts (Seattle); Detroit Institute of Musical Arts; Horner Institute of Fine Arts (Kansas City); Losey's Military Band School (Erie, Pennsylvania); *Music Educator's Journal*.

**Other**   American Society of Composers, Authors and Publishers (ASCAP); Lewisohn Stadium, City College, New York; Society of St. Gregory of America.

## M. Music Publications

Cooke, James F., *Great Pianists on Piano Playing*
Earhart, Will, *Music in the Public Schools*
Gehrkens, Karl, *Music Notation and Terminology*
Gilman, Lawrence, *Nature in Music and Other Studies*
Hughes, Rupert, *American Music*
Parkhurst, Howard E., *Rambles in Music-Land; Essays . . .*
Rogers, Francis, *Some Famous Singers of the Nineteenth Century*
Tapper, Thomas, *The Education of the Music Teacher*

## N. Musical Compositions

**Chamber Music**   Frederick Ayres, *Piano Trio, Opus 13—Violin Sonata No. 1, Opus 15*; Cecil Burleigh, *Four Rocky Mountain Sketches, Opus 11* (violin and piano)—*Violin Sonata, Opus 22, "The Ascension"*; Arthur Farwell, *Fugue Fantasy, Opus 44* (string quartet); Charles Ives, *Violin Sonata No. 3*; Emerson Whithorne, *Greek Impressions* (string quartet).

**Choral/Vocal**   Marion Bauer, *Orientale* (soprano and orchestra); Amy Beach, *Eight Songs, Opus 72, 73, 75, and 76*; Harry T. Burleigh, *Saracen Songs* (cycle); Charles W. Cadman, *From Wigwam and Teepee* (song cycle); Frederick Converse, *The Peace Pipe* (oratorio); Arthur Farwell, *Three Poems by Shelley, Opus 43*; Arthur Foote, *In the Gateway of Ispahan* (treble voices and orchestra); Henry F. Gilbert, *To Thee, America* (chorus and orchestra); Charles T. Griffes, *Three Tone-Images, Opus 3*; Henry Hadley, *The Golden Prince* (cantata); Charles Ives, *Quarter-tone Chorale—General William Booth Enters into Heaven*; Charles Seeger, *Derdra*; Oley Speaks, *Sylvia* (song); Deems Taylor, *The Chambered Nautilus, Opus 7* (cantata)—*The Highwayman, Opus 8* (cantata).

**Concertos**   Louis Gruenberg, *Piano Concerto No. 1*; Daniel G. Mason, *Prelude and Fugue, Opus 12* (piano and orchestra); Francis Pauly, *Piano Concerto in E-Flat*; T. Carl Whitmer, *Poem of Life* (piano and orchestra)

**Operas**   Harry L. Freeman, *Voodoo*; Mary Carr Moore, *Memories*; Horatio Parker, *Fairyland, Opus 77* (National Federation of Music Clubs Prize); David S. Smith, *Merrymount*; Gustav Strube, *The Captive*; Frederick Zech, Jr., *Wa-Kin-Yon, the Red Man*.

**Orchestra/Band**   Frederick Ayres, *Overture, Over the Plains, Opus 14*; Edward Ballantine, *Prelude to the Delectable Forest*; Carl Busch, *Minnehaha's Vision*; Charles Cadman, *Thunderbird Suite*; John Alden Carpenter, *Adventures in a Perambulator*; Rossetter G. Cole, *Symphonic Prelude, Opus 28*; Bainbridge Crist, *Egyptian Impressions*; Eric Delamarter, *The Faun Overture*; Henry F. Gilbert, *Indian Sketches*; Edward B. Hill, *Pan the Star* (ballet); A. Walter Kramer, *Two Symphonic Sketches*; Arthur F. Nevin, *Love Dreams Suite*; Dane Rudhyar, *Poèmes Ironiques*; Rubin Goldmark, *Samson* (tone poem); John Philip Sousa, *The Lambs' Gambol Overture—The Lambs' March— Columbia's Pride March*; Carl Venth, *Symphonic Prelude to an Indian Drama*.

**Piano/Organ**   Harry T. Burleigh, *From the Southland*; Rossetter G. Cole, *Meditation, Opus 29— Rhapsody, Opus 30* (both organ); Henry F. Gilbert, *Negro Dances*; Charles T. Griffes, *Three Tone Picture, Opus 5*; Leo Ornstein, *Three Moods: Anger, Grief, Joy*.

**Symphonies**   Philip G. Clapp, *Symphony No. 2 in E Minor*; Daniel G. Mason, *Symphony No. 1, Opus 11*; Lazare Saminsky, *Symphony No. 1*.

# 1915

❋

## Historical Highlights

The United States warns Germany concerning her unrestricted submarine warfare against neutral shipping; the US Coast Guard is formed; troops are sent to help quell uprisings in Haiti; the *Lusitania* is sunk off the coast of Ireland; poison gas is used for the first time in modern warfare; Hugo Junkers develops the first fighter airplane.

## World Cultural Highlights

**World Art** Constantin Brancusi, *Le Nouveau-Né*; Marc Chagall, *The Birthday*; Giorgio de Chirico, *The Seer*; Raoul Dufy, *Homage à Mozart*; Henri Matisse, *Goldfish*; Pierre Renoir, *Nude Resting*.

**World Literature** Joseph Conrad, *Victory*; D. H. Lawrence, *The Rainbow*; W. Somerset Maugham, *Of Human Bondage*; Rafael Sabatini, *The Sea Hawk*; Edith Sitwell, *The Mother and Other Poems*.

**World Music** Alban Berg, *Three Pieces for Orchestra, Opus 6*; Manuel de Falla, *Nights in the Gardens of Spain*; Jean Sibelius, *Symphony No. 5*; Richard Strauss, *Alpensinfonie*.

**Miscellaneous** The Institut Jaques-Dalcroze opens in Geneva and the Osaka Music School in Japan; births include George Grove, Karl Münchinger, and Knut Nystedt; deaths include Rupert Brook, Remy de Gourmont, Alexander Scriabin, and Sergei Taneyev.

## American Art and Literature

**Births/Deaths** Births include art figures Jack Levine, Richard Lippold, Robert Motherwell, Gabor Peterdi, and literary figures Saul Bellow, Arthur Miller, Theodore H. White, and Herman Wouk; deaths include art figures Karl Bitter, Enoch Perry, Jr., Ross Turner, Anne Whitney, and literary figures Charles Clark, Philander Deming, Francis H. Smith, and Anna Warner (Amy Lothrop).

**Art Works** A. Stirling Calder, *Fountain of Energy*; Lyonel Feininger, *Self-Portrait*; Gaston Lachaise, *Dancing Woman*; Stanton Macdonald-Wright, *Conception Synchromy*; Paul Manship, *Salome*; Man Ray, *The Dance*; Charles Russell, *When Law Dulls the Edge of Chance*; Morgan Russell, *Synchromie Cosmique*; Joseph Stella, *Battle of Light, Coney Island* (?); Max Weber, *Chinese Restaurant*.

**Literature** Eleanor Atkinson, *Johnny Appleseed*; Irvin Cobb, *Old Judge Priest*; Theodore Dreiser, *The "Genius"*; Ring Lardner, *You Know Me, Al*; Sinclair Lewis, *Trail of the Hawk*; Edwin Markham, *The Shoes of Happiness and Other Poems*; Edgar Lee Masters, *Spoon River Anthology*; Agnes Repplier, *Counter-Currents*; Sara Teasdale, *Rivers to the Sea*; Harry L. Wilson, *Ruggles of Red Gap*.

## Music — The Vernacular/Commercial Scene

**A. Births** David Akeman ("Stringbean"—comedian/banjo player) June 17; Laverne Andrews (singer) July 6; Harold Barlow (bandleader/composer) May 15; Betty Comden (lyricist) May 3; Billy Daniels (singer) September 12; Willie Dixon (singer/writer) July 1; Harry "Sweets" Edison (trumpeter) October 10; Ray Evans (lyricist) February 4; George "Chet" Forrest (composer) July 31; Jerry Gray (bandleader) July 3; Adolph Green (lyricist) December 2; Bobby Hackett (cornetist/guitarist) January 31; Eddie Heywood (pianist/arranger) December 4; Billie Holiday (singer) April 7; Buddy Johnson (pianist/bandleader) January 10; Jay Livingston (composer/lyricist) March 28; Alan Lomax (folk-scholar) January 15; Brownie McGhee (guitarist/writer) November 30;

Memphis Slim (pianist/singer) September 3; Muddy Waters (singer) April 4; Turk Murphy (trombonist) December 16; Les Paul (guitarist) June 9; Shirley Ross (singer/actress); Frank Sinatra (singer/actor) December 12; Billy Strayhorn (pianist/composer) November 29; Buddy Tate (saxophonist) February 22.

**B. Deaths** Billy Kersands (minstrel performer) June; Gus Williams (singer/composer) January 16.

**C. Biographical**

**Performing Groups** Creole Jazz Band (by "King" Oliver); Dixie Duo (Eubie Blake and Noble Sissle); Ted Lewis Big Band; Louisiana Five.

**D. Publications** John W. Work, *Folk Songs of the American Negro*.

**E. Representative Works**

**Musicals** Irving Berlin, *Stop! Look! Listen!*; Rudolf Friml and O. Harbach, *The Peasant Girl*; Victor Herbert, *The Princess Pat*; Jerome Kern and E. Janis, *Miss Information—Very Good, Eddie*; Jerome Kern and S. Greene, *Nobody Home*; Sigmund Romberg and H. Reynolds, *The Blue Paradise*; S. Romberg and O. Harbach, *Katinka*.

**Songs** George Asaf and F. Powell, *Pack Up Your Troubles in Your Old Kit Bag and Smile, Smile, Smile*; Johnny S. Black, *Paper Doll*; Theodore Morse, *M-O-T-H-E-R*; Ivor Novello and L. G. Ford, *Keep the Home Fires Burning*; G. H. Stover and H. Kailimai, *On the Beach at Waikiki*; Egbert A. Van Alstyne and G. Kahn, *Memories*; Harry Von Tilzer and A. Sterling, *Close to My Heart*; Richard Whiting and D. Radford, *It's Tulip Time in Holland*.

**Other** Felix Arndt, *Nola*; W. C. Handy, *Joe Turner Blues*; Joseph Lamb, *Cleopatra Rag—Reindeer Rag—The Ragtime Nightingale*; Artie Matthews, *Weary Blues*; Kerry Mills, *Kerry Mills Cake Walk*; Jelly Roll Morton, *Jelly Roll Blues*; Lucky Roberts, *Helter Skelter—Shy and Sly*; James Scott, *Evergreen Rag*.

## Music—The Cultivated/Art Music Scene

**F. Births** Victor Alessandro (conductor) November 27; Julius Baker (flutist) September 23; Richard Bales (composer/conductor) February 3; Esther Ballou (composer/pianist) July 17; Igor Buketoff (conductor) May 29; David Diamond (composer) July 9; Dean Dixon (conductor) January 10; Paul Hume (critic) December 13; Newell Jenkins (musicologist/conductor) February 8; Homer Keller (composer) February 17; Dai-Keong Lee (composer) September 2; Robert Palmer (composer) June 2; George Perle (composer/theorist) May 6; Vincent Persichetti (composer/theorist) June 6; Harold C. Schonberg (critic) November 29; Alan Shulman (cellist/composer) June 4; Felix Slatkin (conductor) December 22; Earl Wild (pianist) November 26.

**G. Deaths** Russell Alexander (composer) October 2; Fanny J. Crosby (poet/hymnist) February 12; William H. Doane (hymnist) December 24; Luther O. Emerson (composer/conductor) September 29; Francesco Fanciulli (bandmaster) July 17; Louis Grunewald (German-born impresario/publisher) March 1; Charles B. Hawley (organist) December 29; Benjamin Lambord (organist/conductor) June 7; Bertha Feiring Tapper (Norwegian-born pianist) September 2; Samuel Prowse Warren (organist) October 7; James Warrington (British-born bibliographer) October 3.

**H. Debuts**

**United States** Richard Bonelli (baritone—Brooklyn), Eddy Brown (violinist—New York), Florence Easton (British soprano—Chicago), Povla Frijsh (Danish soprano—New York), Eva Gauthier (Canadian mezzo-soprano—New York), Percy Grainger (Australian pianist—New York), William Kroll (violinist—New York), Guiomar Novaës (Brazilian pianist—New York), Egon Pollak (Austrian conductor—Chicago), Conchita Supervia (Spanish mezzo-soprano—Chicago).

**Metropolitan Opera** Gaetano Bavagnoli (Italian conductor), Arthur Bodanzky (Austrian conductor), Giuseppe De Luca (Italian baritone), Marie-Louise Edvina (Canadian soprano), Melanie Kurt (Austrian soprano), Henri Scott (bass), Luisa Villani (soprano).

**Other** Charles Hackett (tenor—Pavia), Max Rosen (violinist—Dresden).

## I. New Positions

**Conductors**  Arthur Bodanzky (Metropolitan Opera); Alfred Hertz (San Francisco Symphony Orchestra—to 1930).

**Educational**  Louis A. Coerne (Connecticut College for Women—to 1922); Arthur M. Curry (New England Conservatory—to 1939).

**Other**  Lawrence Gilman (music/drama critic, *North American Review*—to 1923); Arthur Judson (manager, Philadelphia Orchestra—to 1936); Oscar Sonneck (editor, *The Musical Quarterly*—to 1929); Humphrey John Stewart (municipal organist, San Diego).

## J. Honors and Awards

**Honors**  Franz Kneisel (PhD, Princeton); Ernest R. Kroeger (National Institute).

## K. Biographical  Nicholas Bessaraboff (Russian instrumental expert) is sent to the United States by his government to help facilitate shipment of war supplies; Amy Beach moves to New York; Lucien Calliet (French conductor/arranger), after touring the United States with a French band, decides to emigrate to the United States; Anis Fuleihan (Cypriot conductor) comes to the United States, Camille Saint-Saëns visits the United States and represents France at the Panama-Pacific Exposition; Leopold Stokowski becomes an American citizen; Arturo Toscanini resigns his conducting position at the Met and returns to Italy; Edgard Varèse (French composer) comes to the United States

## L. Musical Beginnings

**Performing Groups**  American Symphony Orchestra; Atlanta Music Club; Cleveland Musical Arts Association; Denver Grand Opera Co.; Fillmore Band; Little Symphony of New York; Musicians Club of Richmond, Virginia; Palestrina Choir of Philadelphia (to 1948).

**Festivals**  Newark Music Festival (to 1930).

**Educational**  Concord Summer School of Music; Denishawn School of Dancing and Related Arts (New York); Louisiana State University Music Department; Louisville Conservatory of Music, Neighborhood Music School (New Haven).

**Other**  *The Catholic Choirmaster*; Exposition (Civic) Auditorium (San Francisco); Arthur Judson Concert Management (New York); *The Musical Quarterly*; *Music and Musicians*; Ravinia Park Concerts (Chicago).

## M. Music Publications

Dickinson, Edward, *Music and Higher Education*
Elson, Arthur, *The Book of Musical Knowledge*
Fletcher, Alice C., *Indian Games and Dances*
Gabriel, Charles, *Gospel Songs and Their Writers*
Goetschius, Percy, *The Larger Forms of Musical Composition*
Huneker, James G., *The Development of the Piano*
Mason, Daniel G., *The Art of Music*
Skinner, Ernest M., *The Modern Organ*
Sonneck, Oscar G. T., *Early Opera in America*
Surette, Thomas, *Course of Study on the Development of Symphonic Music*
Upton, George P., *The Song*
Van Vechten, Carl, *Music after the Great War*

## N. Musical Compositions

**Chamber Music**  Seth Bingham, *Suite for Nine Wind Instruments*; Cecil Burleigh, *Six Nature Studies, Opus 23*; Rubin Goldmark, *Call of the Plains* (violin and piano); Victor Herbert, *The Three Solitaires* (three trumpets and piano); Frederick Search, *String Quartet No. 2*; Charles S. Skilton, *Two Indian Dances* (orchestrated 1916).

**Choral/Vocal**  Charles Alexander, *Out of the Ivory Palaces*; Harry T. Burleigh, *Five Songs on Poems of Laurence Hope—Passionale* (song cycle) —*The Young Warrior*; Henry F. Gilbert, *Hymn to*

*America*; Charles Ives, *Majority* (song); Charles M. Loeffler, *Hora mystica* (men's chorus and orchestra); Daniel G. Mason, *Six Love Songs, Opus 15*; Horatio Parker, *Morven and the Grail, Opus 79* (oratorio); Harry R. Shelley, *Lochinvar's Ride* (cantata); Arthur Shepherd, *Song of the Sea Wind* (treble voices); David S. Smith, *Rhapsody of St. Bernard, Opus 38*.

**Concertos**　Felix Borowski, *Allegro de Concert* (organ and orchestra); Cecil Burleigh, *Violin Concerto No. 1, Opus 25*; John Alden Carpenter, *Piano Concertino*; Victor Herbert, *Whispering Willows* (piano and orchestra); A. Walter Kramer, *Symphonic Rhapsody* (violin and orchestra); Clarence Loomis, *Piano Concerto*; Frederick Stock, *Violin Concerto*.

**Operas**　George W. Chadwick, *The Padrone*; Bainbridge Crist, *Le Pied de la Momie*; Henry F. Gilbert, *Fantasy in Delft*; Henry Hadley, *Azora, the Daughter of Montezuma*; John Philip Sousa, *The Irish Dragoon* (operetta).

**Orchestra/Band**　George W. Chadwick, *Tam O'Shanter* (symphonic ballad); Arthur Farwell, *Caliban, Opus 47* (incidental music); Edward B. Hill, *The Parting of Lancelot and Guinevere* (tone poem); Charles Ives, *Second Orchestral Set—Tone Roads et al.*; Frederick Jacobi, *The Pied Piper* (symphonic poem); Leo Ornstein, *The Fog* (symphonic poem); Charles Seeger, *Parthema*; Arthur Shepherd, *Overture, The Festival of Youth*; John Philip Sousa, *Pathfinder of Panama March—New York Hippodrome March*.

**Piano/Organ**　Charles W. Cadman, *Sonata in A Major*; Charles T. Griffes, *Roman Sketches, Opus 7 (The White Peacock* is orchestrated, 1919)—*Fantasy Pieces, Opus 6*; Charles Ives, *Sonata No. 2, "Concord."*

# 1916

☀

## Historical Highlights

Woodrow Wilson is re-elected president; General Pershing fails to track down Pancho Villa in Mexico; General Motors is incorporated in Delaware; Congress passes the Federal Farm Loan Act to aid the farmers; Lassen Volcanic National Park is created; David Lloyd George becomes British prime minister; the monk Rasputin is assassinated in Moscow.

## World Cultural Highlights

**World Art**　Giorgio de Chirico, *The Jewish Angel*; Robert Delauney, *The Flamenco Singer*; Wilhelm Lehmbruck, *The Fallen*; Henri Matisse, *Bathers by a River*; Pierre Renoir, *Venus*.

**World Literature**　Vicente Blasco Ibáñez, *The Four Horsemen of the Apocalypse*; James Joyce, *Portrait of the Artist as a Young Man*; Edward Thomas, *Poems*.

**World Music**　Béla Bartók, *The Wooden Prince*; Leos Janáček, *The Diary of One Who Vanished*; Carl Nielsen, *Symphony No. 4, "Inextinguishable"*; Sergei Prokofiev, *The Gambler*.

**Miscellaneous**　The City of Birmingham Symphony is founded in England; the Philippines Conservatory of Music is founded; births include Kenneth Armitage and Peter Fingesten; deaths include Karl Begas, Umberto Boccioni, Hans Richter, Henryk Sienkiewicz, and Émile Verhaeren.

## American Art and Literature

**Births/Deaths**　Births include artists Elmer Bischoff, Richard Pousette-Dart, and literary figures John Ciardi, John Killens, Harold Robbins, Anya Seton, Peter Viereck, Irving Wallace, and Frank Yerby; deaths include William M. Chase, Thomas Eakins, Henry Ranger, and literary figures Edward Ellis, Henry James, Jr., Jack London, James Whitcomb Riley, Alan Seeger, and Jean Webster.

**Art Works**　Paul Bartlett, *Democracy Protecting the Arts of Peace*; Arthur B. Davies, *Day of Good Fortune*; Stanton MacDonald-Wright, *Synchromy in Green and Orange*; Paul Manship, *Dancer and Gazelles*; Man Ray, *The Rope Dancer Accompanies Herself with Her Shadows*;

Morton Schambert, *Mechanical Abstraction*; John Sloan, *Purple Rocks and Green Sea*.

**Literature**  Amelia Burr, *Life and Living*; Robert Frost, *Mountain Interval*; Susan Glaspell, *Trifles*; Edgar Guest, *A Heap O' Livin'*; Alfred J. Kilmer, *Main Street and Other Poems*; Amy Lowell, *Men, Women and Ghosts*; Edgar Lee Masters, *Songs and Satires*; H. L. Mencken, *A Book of Burlesques*; Ezra Pound, *Lustra*; Edwin A. Robinson, *The Man Against the Sky*; Carl Sandburg, *Chicago Poems*.

## Music—The Vernacular/Commercial Scene

**A. Births**  James Woodie Alexander (singer) January 21; Cat Anderson (trumpeter) September 12; Charlie Christian (guitarist) July 29; Ray Conniff (trombonist/arranger) November 6; Bill Doggett (pianist/organist) February 6; Slim Gaillard (singer/writer) January 4; Tiny Grimes (guitarist) July 7; Dick Haymes (singer) September 13; Ina Ray Hutton (bandleader) March 13; Harry James (trumpeter/bandleader) March 15; Billy May (trumpeter/arranger) November 10; T. Texas Tyler (singer) June 20; Charlie Ventura (saxophonist) December 2; Helen Ward (singer) September 19; John L. "Sonny Boy" Williamson (singer).

**B. Deaths**  Billy Johnson (minstrel performer/writer); Sam Lucas (minstrel performer).

**C. Biographical**

**Performing Groups**  Original Dixieland Jazz Band.

**New Beginnings**  Brunswick Record Co. (Dubuque); Emerson Record Co.; Paramount Records (New York); Vocalion Records (New York).

**E. Representative Works**

**Musicals**  Irving Berlin, *The Century Girl*; Earl Carroll, *So Long, Letty*; George M. Cohan, *The Cohan Revue*; Cole Porter, *See America First*; Sigmund Romberg, H. Atteridge, and E. Smith, *Robinson Crusoe, Jr.*; Harry Tierney and R. B. Smith, *Follow Me*.

**Songs**  Eubie Blake and C. Morgan, *Bugle Call Rag*; Nat D. Ayer and C. Grey, *If You Were the Only Girl in the World*; W. C. Handy, *Beale Street Blues*; Raymond Hubbell and J. L. Golden, *Poor Butterfly*; Ada de Lachau, *Li'l Liza Jane*; Albert Von Tilzer and C. McCarron, *Oh! How She Could Yacki, Hacki, Wicki, Wacki, Woo!*; Harry A. Tierney, *M-i-s-s-i-s-s-i-p-p-i*; Egbert A. Van Alstyne, *Pretty Baby*; Spencer Williams and D. Peyton, *I Ain't Got Nobody*.

**Other**  George Botsford, *Boomerang Rag*; Joseph C. Breil, *Intolerance* (film music); Victor Herbert, *The Fall of a Nation* (film music); James P. Johnson, *Daintiness Rag*; Joseph Lamb, *Patricia Rag—Top Liner Rag*; Paul Pratt, *Springtime Rag*; Victor Schertzinger, *Civilization* (film music); James Scott, *Honey Moon Rag—Prosperity Rag*; Peter Wendling, *Chromatic Rag*.

## Music—The Cultivated/Art Music Scene

**F. Births**  Milton Babbitt (composer) May 10; Robert S. Baker (organist) July 7; Philip Bezanson (composer) January 6; Gordon Binkerd (composer) May 22; Helen Boatwright (soprano) November 17; Emerson Buckley (conductor) April 14; Bernard Greenhouse (cellist) January 3; David Hall (music author) December 16; Scott Huston (composer) October 10; William M. Judd (concert manager) August 8; Robert Kelly (composer) September 26; Ellis Kohs (composer) May 12; Irving Lowens (musicologist/critic) August 19; David McAllester (ethnomusicologist) August 6; Yehudi Menuhin (violinist) April 22; James Pease (bass-baritone) January 9; Leonard Ratner (musicologist) July 30; Albert Seay (musicologist) November 6; Robert Shaw (conductor) April 30; Eleanor Steber (soprano) July 17; Leonard Stein (musicologist) December 1; Robert M. Stevenson (musicologist) July 2; Abraham Veinus (musicologist) February 12; Ben Weber (composer) July 23.

**G. Deaths**  William Henry Dana (composer/pedagogue) February 18; Earl R. Drake (violinist) May 6; William Wallace Gilchrist (composer) December 20; Benjamin Hitchcock (publisher) April 14; Tom Karl (Irish-born tenor) March 19; Clara Kellogg (soprano/impresario) May 13; J. C. D. Parker (organist) November 27; Howard E. Parkhurst (organist); Silas G. Pratt (composer/pianist) October 30; Frederick W. Root (organist/composer) November 8.

**H. Debuts**

**United States** Ernest Ansermet (Swiss conductor), Mario Chamlee (tenor—New York), Giulio Crimi (Italian tenor—Chicago), Amelita Galli-Curci (Italian soprano—Chicago), Virgilio Lazzari (Italian bass—St. Louis), Mischa Levitzki (pianist—New York), Isolde Menges (British violinist—New York), Beryl Rubinstein (pianist—New York).

**Metropolitan Opera** Maria Barrientos (Spanish soprano), Paul Eisler (Austrian conductor), Maude Fay (soprano), Kathleen Howard (Canadian contralto), Claudia Muzio (Italian soprano), Gennaro Papi (Italian conductor), Marie Sundelius (soprano).

**I. New Positions**

**Conductors** Gennaro Papi (Metropolitan Opera—to 1926); Gustav Strube (Baltimore Symphony Orchestra—to 1930).

**Educational** Felix Borowski (president, Chicago Musical College); Howard Hanson (College of the Pacific—to 1921); Gustav Strube (director, Peabody—to 1946).

**Other** Nat Shilkret (music director, Victor Talking Machine Co.); T. Carl Whitmer (organ, choir, Sixth Presbyterian Church, Pittsburgh—to 1932).

**J. Honors and Awards**

**Honors** Edward Burlingame Hill (National Institute).

**K. Biographical** Ernest Bloch (Swiss composer) comes to the United States as conductor for the Maud Allen Dance Co. and decides to stay; Charles Hackett makes his debut at La Scala; Pierre Monteux resigns his commission from the French army and tours the United States with the Ballets Russes; Walter Piston graduates from Massachusetts Normal Art School; Dane Rudhyar (French composer) emigrates to the United States; Gustave Frederic Soderlund (Swedish composer) moves to the United States; William Grant Still begins working for W. C. Handy in Memphis.

**L. Musical Beginnings**

**Performing Groups** Dessoff Madrigal Singers (New York); Henry Fillmore Band; Mendelssohn Choir of Indianapolis; Lee Pattison-Guy Maier Two-piano Team; People's Chorus of New York; Fred Waring's Pennsylvanians.

**Educational** Innes School of Music (Denver); Lambda Phi Delta (Northwestern University); Longy School of Music (Boston); Mannes College of Music (New York).

**Other** Maverick Sunday Concerts (Woodstock, New York); National Bureau for the Advancement of Music; Presser Foundation; Syria Mosque (Pittsburgh).

**M. Music Publications**

Burleigh, Harry T., *Jubilee Songs of the United States of America*
Christiansen, Fredrik, *Practical Modulation*
Cole, Rosetter G., *Choral and Church Music*
Goldman, Edwin F., *Band Guide and Aid to Teachers*
Langenus, Gustave, *Complete Method for the Boehm Clarinet*
Mason, Daniel, *Great Modern Composers*
Miller, Dayton, *The Science of Musical Sounds*
Seeger, C. and Stricklen, E., *Harmonic Structure and Elementary Composition*
Sonneck, Oscar G. T., *Suum Cuique: Essays on Music*
VanderCook, Hale A., *A Course in Band and Orchestra Directing*

**N. Musical Compositions**

**Chamber Music** Frederick Ayres, *String Quartet*; Amy Beach, *Theme and Variations, Opus 80* (flute and string quartet); Seth Bingham, *String Quartet*; Ernest Bloch, *String Quartet No. 1*; Cecil Burleigh, *Four Prairie Sketches, Opus 13* (violin and piano); Charles Ives, *Violin Sonata No. 4, "Children's Day at the Camp Meeting"*; Leo Sowerby, *Woodwind Quintet*.

**Choral/Vocal** Amy Beach, *Two Songs, Opus 77*; John Parsons Beach, *Pippa's Holiday*; Ernest

Bloch, *Israel* (voices and orchestra); Franz C. Bornscheim, *Onawa* (N.J. Choral Society Prize); John Alden Carpenter, *Water-Colors* (four Chinese songs); R. Nathaniel Dett, *Music in the Mine* (oratorio); Charles T. Griffes, *Three Poems, Opus 9*; Victor Herbert, *The Orange White Blue* (song); Margaret R. Lang, *The Heavenly Noël, Opus 57* (female choir and orchestra); Horatio Parker, *An Allegory of War and Peace, Opus 81* (chorus and band); Mary E. Salter, *Five Songs, Opus 34*; Charles S. Skilton, *Perviglium Veneris* (cantata); Deems Taylor, *The City of Joy, Opus 9* (song cycle).

**Concertos**   Ernest Bloch, *Schelomo* (cello and orchestra); Ernest Schelling, *Violin Concerto*; Arthur Shepherd, *Fantasie Humoreske for Piano and Orchestra*; Leo Sowerby, *Piano Concerto No. 1*.

**Operas**   Paul Hastings Allen, *Last of the Mohicans*; Hans Barth, *Miragia* (operetta); George W. Chadwick, *Love's Sacrifice* (operetta); Harry L. Freeman, *Athalia*; Charles T. Griffes, *The Kairn of Koridwen* (dance drama); Henry Hadley, *Bianca* (opera—Hinshaw Prize); Gustav Strube, *Ramona*.

**Orchestra/Band**   Seth Bingham, *Wall Street Fantasy*; Franz C. Bornschein, *The Phantom Canoe*; Carl Busch, *Song of Chibiabos*; Eric Delamarter, *Masquerade Overture*; Howard Hanson, *Symphonic Prelude, Opus 6*; Horatio Parker, *Cupid and Psyche* (masque); David Stanley Smith, *Impressions, Opus 40*; John Philip Sousa, *Marches—America First—Boy Scouts of America— March of the Pan Americans*; Leo Sowerby, *Comes Autumn Time*; Edwin John Stringham, *The Phantom* (symphonic poem).

**Piano/Organ**   Percy Grainger, *Suite "In a Nutshell"*; Victor Herbert, *The World's Progress*; Colin McPhee, *Four Sketches, Opus 1*; Horatio Parker, *Introduction and Fugue in E Minor* (organ).

**Symphonies**   Arcady Dubensky, *Symphony in G Minor*; Charles Ives, *Symphony No. 4*.

# 1917

✤

## Historical Highlights

Congress declares war on Germany in April and passes the Selective Service Act, the Espionage Act, and Trading with the Enemy Act; Puerto Rico becomes a United States territory; the International Association of Lions Clubs is founded; Germany begins unrestricted submarine warfare; the Bolshevik Revolution in Russia forces Nicholas II to abdicate and Lenin and Trotsky seize power.

## World Cultural Highlights

**World Art**   Pierre Bonnard, *Nude at the Fireplace*; Carlo Carra, *Enchanted Room;* Marc Chagall, *The Grey House*; Amedeo Modigliani, *Girl with Braids*; Georges Rouault, *The Three Clowns*.

**World Literature**   Carl Jung, *Psychology of the Unconscious*; Paul Valéry, *La jeune Parque*.

**World Music**   Sergei Prokofiev, *Classical Symphony*; Ottorino Respighi, *The Fountains of Rome*; Erik Satie, *Parade*; Igor Stravinsky, *Les Noces*; Heitor Villa-Lobos, *Amazonas—Uirapuru*.

**Miscellaneous**   The Salzburg Music Festivals begin; the George Enescu Symphony is founded in Bucharest; births include Heinrich Böll, Anthony Burgess, and Dinu Lipatti; deaths include Jane Barlow, Edgar Degas, Auguste Rodin, and Edward Thomas.

## American Art and Literature Highlights

**Births/Deaths**   Births include Robert Goodnough, David Hare, Jacob Lawrence, Andrew Wyeth, and literary figures Robert Anderson, Louis Auchincloss, Gwendolyn Brooks, Carson McCullers, Robert Traill Lowell, and Peter H. Taylor; deaths include art figures Moses Ezekiel, Bela Pratt, Albert Ryder, and literary figures Samuel Greenberg, Ruth Stuart, and William Winter.

**Art Works**   George Bellows, *Dance in a Madhouse*; Charles Burchfield, *Church Bells Ringing, Rainy Winter Night*; Charles Demuth, *Vaudeville Musicians*; Arthur Dove, *Sentimental Music*;

Gaston Lachaise, *La Force Eternelle*; Elie Nadelman, *Sur la Plage*; John Sloan, *Gloucester Trolley*; Joseph Stella, *The Brooklyn Bridge*; Abraham Walkowitz, *New York*; Max Weber, *Seated Woman*.

**Literature**   Hamlin Garland, *A Son of the Middle Border*; Vachel Lindsay, *The Chinese Nightingale and Other Poems*; Edna St. Vincent Millay, *Renascence and Other Poems*; Ernest Poole, *His Family* (Pulitzer Prize); Edwin A. Robinson, *Merlin*; Upton Sinclair, *King Coal*; Booth Tarkington, *Seventeen*; Sara Teasdale, *Love Songs* (Pulitzer Prize); Jessie Williams, *Why Marry?* (Pulitzer Prize).

## Music—The Vernacular/Commercial Scene

**A. Births**   Billy Butterfield (trumpeter) January 14; Nat "King" Cole (singer) March 17; Tadd Dameron (composer/pianist) February 21; Dennis Day (singer) May 21; Bill Finnegan (arranger/bandleader) April 3; John "Dizzy" Gillespie (trumpeter/bandleader) October 21; Johnny Guarnieri (pianist) March 23; Jimmy Hamilton (clarinetist) May 25; Lena Horne (singer) June 30; Howard Keel (singer) April 13; John Latouche (lyricist) November 13; Dean Martin (singer) June 7; Leon McAuliffe (guitarist) March 1; Thelonious Monk (pianist/composer) October 10; Kenneth Morris (composer/pianist) August 28; John Raitt (singer) January 29; Buddy Rich (drummer/bandleader) September 30; Charlie Shavers (trumpeter/arranger) August 3; Dinah Shore (singer) March 1; Sylvia Syms (singer) December 2; Rufus Thomas (singer/writer) March 28; Merle Travis (singer/writer) November 29; Eddie "Cleanhead" Vinson (saxophonist/singer) December 18.

**B. Deaths**   Scott Joplin (ragtime pianist/composer) April 1.

**C. Biographical**

**Performing Groups**   Deep River Orchestra (by W. Robison); Kentucky Jazz Band (Fate Marable); Original Memphis Five; Tony Parenti Band (New Orleans); Tuxedo Brass Band (New Orleans).

**New Beginnings**   Gennett Record Co. (Richmond, Indiana).

**Miscellaneous**   Jelly Roll Morton goes to Los Angeles.

**D. Publications**   J. McGill, *Folk Songs of the Kentucky Mountains*; Sharp and Campbell, *English Folksongs from the Southern Appalachians*.

**E. Representative Works**

**Musicals**   Ivan Caryll, *Jack O'Lantern*; Rudolph Friml and O.Harbach, *Kitty Darlin'*; Victor Herbert and H. Blossom, *Eileen*; Louis A. Hirsch and O. Harbach, *Going Up*; Jerome Kern and P. G. Wodehouse, *Leave It to Jane—Oh, Boy—Have a Heart*; Sigmund Romberg and R. J. Young, *Maytime*; Egbert A. Van Alstyne and G. Kahn, *Good Night, Paul*.

**Songs**   A. Emmett Adams and D. Furber, *The Bells of St. Mary's*; Billy Baskette, C. Reisner, and B. Davis, *Good-bye Broadway, Hello France*; Shelton Brooks, *Darktown Strutters' Ball*; Harry T. Burleigh, *Little Mother of Mine*; J. Will Callahan and L. S. Roberts, *Smiles*; George M. Cohan, *Over There*; Harry DeCosta, *Tiger Rag*; James Hanley, *Back Home Again in Indiana*; Joseph McCarthy and F. Fisher, *They Go Wild, Simply Wild Over Me*; George W. Meyer, E. Leslie, and E. R. Goetz, *For Me and My Gal*; Theodore Morese and D. A. Estrom, *Hail, Hail, the Gang's All Here*; Shamus O'Connor and J. J. Stamford, *MacNamara's Band*; Ed Rose and Abe Olman, *Oh, Johnny, Oh!*

**Other**   James P. Johnson, *Harlem Strut*; Nick La Rocca, *Skeleton Jangle—At the Jazz Band Ball—Reisenweber Rag*; James Scott, *Efficiency Rag*; Leo Sowerby, *Money Musk*.

## Music—The Cultivated/Art Music Scene

**F. Births**   John Barnett (conductor) September 3; Edward T. Cone (critic/pianist) May 4; Dorothy DeLay (violinist/educator) March 31; Robert Erickson (composer) March 7; Elliot Forbes (musicologist/conductor) August 30; Sidney Foster (pianist) May 23; Lou Harrison (composer) May 14; Walter Hendl (conductor) January 12; Richard Hervig (composer) November 24; Ulysses Kay (composer) January 7; Dorothy Kirsten (soprano) July 6; William Latham (composer/educator) January 4;

Norman Luboff (conductor/arranger) May 14; Francis Madeira (pianist/conductor) February 21; Robert Merrill (baritone) June 4; Thomas Scherman (conductor) February 12; Oscar Shumsky (violinist/conductor) March 23; Nell Tangeman (mezzo-soprano) December 23; John M. Ward (musicologist) July 6; Robert Ward (composer) September 13; William J. Weichlein (musicologist) May 9; Richard Yardumian (composer) April 5.

**G. Deaths**　Teresa Carreño (Venezuelan-born pianist) June 12; Melville Clark (organ builder) November 5; Bernhard Listemann (German-born violinist) February 11.

**H. Debuts**

**United States**　Joseph Bonnet (British organist—New York), Maurice Dambois (Belgian cellist—New York), Roland Hayes (tenor—Boston), Jascha Heifetz (Russian violinist—New York), Edwin Hughes (pianist—New York), Forrest Lamont (tenor—Chicago), Geneviève Vix (French soprano—Chicago).

**Metropolitan Opera**　Louis d'Angelo (baritone), Julia Claussen (Swedish mezzo-soprano), Florence Easton (British soprano), Morgan Kingston (British tenor), José Mardones (Spanish bass), Pierre Monteux (French conductor).

**I. New Positions**

**Conductors**　Arthur Dunham (Chicago Philharmonic Orchestra); Pierre Monteux (Met).

**Educational**　John J. Becker (director of music, Notre Dame—to 1927); Richard Buhlig (Institute of Musical Art, New York); Alexander Russell (Princeton—to 1935); Louis Victor Saar (Chicago Musical College—to 1934); Roger Sessions (Smith College—to 1921); Camille Zeckwer (director, Philadelphia Musical Academy).

**Other**　Carl Deis (music editor, G. Schirmer—to 1953); Edwin Lemare (municipal organ, San Francisco—to 1921); Oscar G. T. Sonneck (director of publications, G. Schirmer).

**J. Honors and Awards**

**Honors**　Harry T. Burleigh (Spingarn Medal); Edgar S. Kelley (PhD, Cincinnati).

**K. Biographical**　The Boston Symphony Orchestra makes its first recordings; Charles W. Cadman decides to move to Los Angeles; Wallingford Riegger returns to the United States following America's entry in the war; Carl Ruggles moves to New York in hopes of the Metropolitan Opera performing his opera; Roger Sessions graduates from Yale.

**L. Musical Beginnings**

**Performing Groups**　Budapest String Quartet; Philadelphia Chamber Music Association; Portland Opera Co. (Oregon).

**Educational**　Manhattan School of Music (New York); Ada Clement Music School (San Francisco Conservatory of Music); Southern Methodist University Music Department.

**Other**　Harold Flammer, Inc., Music Publisher (New York); National Music Publishers' Association (NMPA); Portland Civic Auditorium (Oregon); Pulitzer Prize Music Scholarship; Reuter Organ Co. (Trenton, Illinois).

**M. Music Publications**

Bacon, Ernst, *Our Musical Idiom*
Dickinson, Clarence, *Excursions in Musical History*
Eddy, Clarence, *A Method for Pipe Organ*
Elson, Arthur, *Pioneer School Music Course*
Huneker, James G., *The Philharmonic Society of New York*
Krehbiel, Henry E., *A Second Book of Operas*
Metcalf, Frank, *American Psalmody*
Parsons, Albert R., *The Virtuoso Handling of the Pianoforte*
Sternberg, Constantin, *Ethics and Esthetics of Piano Playing*
Surette, Thomas, *Music and Life*
Van Vechten, Carl, *Interpreters and Interpretations*

**N. Musical Compositions**

**Chamber Music**   John Parsons Beach, *Naïve Landscape*; Leo Sowerby, *Serenade for String Quartet*; Emerson Whithorne, *String Quartet No. 1, "Greek Impressions."*

**Choral/Vocal**   Amy Beach, *Three Songs, Opus 78*; Rossetter G. Cole, *The Broken Troth, Opus 32* (cantata); Mabel Wheeler Daniels, *Peace with a Sword*; Charles T. Griffes, *Five Poems of Ancient China and Japan, Opus 10*; Henry Hadley, *Ode to Music*; Victor Herbert, *Can't You Hear Your Country Calling* (song); Daniel G. Mason, *Russians, Opus 18* (song cycle); Frances McCollin, *The Singing Leaves* (cantata); Leo Sowerby, *A Liturgy of Hope*; Pietro A. Yon, *Gesù Bambino* (Christmas song).

**Concertos**   John Alden Carpenter, *Concertino for Piano and Orchestra*; Ralph Lyford, *Piano Concerto*; John Powell, *Rapsodie Nègre* (piano and orchestra); Leo Sowerby, *Cello Concerto No. 1.*

**Operas**   Paul Hastings Allen, *Il filtro*; Seth Bingham, *La charelzenn*; Eugene M. Bonner, *Barbara Fritchie*; Reginald De Koven, *The Canterbury Pilgrims*; Carl Eppert, *Kentuckee*; Edgar S. Kelley, *The Pilgrim's Progress, Opus 37* (musical miracle play); Mary Carr Moore, *Harmony.*

**Orchestra/Band**   Edward Ballantine, *The Eve of St. Agnes*; Johann H. Beck, *Aus meinem Leben* (tone poem); Alfred Brune, *Overture, A Twilight Picture*; Cecil Burleigh, *Mountain Pictures*; John Alden Carpenter, *The Birthday of the Infanta* (ballet); Louis A. Coerne, *The Trojan Women* (incidental music); Arthur Farwell, *The Evergreen Tree, Opus 50* (Christmas masque); Samuel Gardner, *New Russia* (symphonic poem); Howard Hanson, *Symphonic Legend, Opus 8*; Edward Burlingame Hill, *Stevensonia Suite I*; Frederick Jacobi, *A California Suite*; Carl McKinley, *Indian Summer Idyll*; John Philip Sousa, *Marches: United States Field Artillery—Wisconsin Forward Forever—The White Rose—The Naval Reserve—Liberty Loan*; Leo Sowerby, *A Set of Four*; Hermann H. Wetzler, *As You Like It* (incidental music).

**Piano/Organ**   Henry Cowell, *The Tides of Manaunaun*; Victor Herbert, *Rosemary* (piano); Margaret Ruthven Lang, *The Spirit of the Old House, Opus 58*; Leo Ornstein, *Impressions of Chinatown* (also for orchestra).

**Symphonies**   John Alden Carpenter, *Symphony No. 1, "Sermons in Stones"*; Philip Clapp, *Symphony No. 3 in E-Flat Major*; Roger Sessions, *Symphony in D Major*; David Stanley Smith, *Symphony No. 2 in D Major.*

# 1918

☀

## Historical Highlights

World War I comes to an end with the Armistice on November 11; President Wilson presents his Fourteen Points for Peace; the first air mail service begins; the Browning automatic rifle is invented; many Socialists are jailed under the new Sedition Act; Austria, Czechoslovakia, Hungary, and Poland are all made independent states.

## World Cultural Highlights

**World Art**   Pierre Bonnard, *Le Jardin Sauvage*; Robert Delaunay, *Igor Stravinsky*; Max Liebemann, *Richard Strauss*; Henri Matisse, *Odalisques*; Amedeo Modigliani, *The Peasant Boy.*

**World Literature**   Rupert Brookes, *Collected Poems*; Émile Cammaerts, *Messines and Other Poems*; James Joyce, *Exiles*; Wyndham Lewis, *Tarr.*

**World Music**   Frederick Delius, *A Song before Sunrise*; Leos Janáček, *Taras Bulba*; Giacomo Puccini, *Gianni Schicchi*; Igor Stravinsky, *L'Histoire du Soldat—Ragtime for Eleven Instruments.*

**Miscellaneous**   L'Orchestre de la Suisse Romande and the Rotterdam Symphony are founded; births include Louis Dudek, Birgit Nilsson, and Alexander Solzhenitsyn; deaths include Guillaume Apollinaire, Henri Chantavoine, Claude Debussy, Gustav Klimt, and Edmond Rostand.

## American Art and Literature

**Births/Deaths**  Births include art figures Sidney Gordin, Stephen Greene, Roy Gussow, and literary figures Louis Coxe, Allen Drury, George Elliott, and Edwin G. O'Connor; deaths include art figures Henry Dearth, John Mooney, Joseph Pickett, H. Lyman Saÿen, Morton Schamberg, Charles Turner, and literary figures Charles F. Adams, Henry B. Adams, Alfred Joyce Kilmer, and John Ames Mitchell.

**Art Works**  Alexander Calder, *George Washington with Wisdom and Justice*; Childe Hassam, *Inner Harbor, Gloucester*; Robert Henri, *Pepita of Santa Fe*; Albert Laessle, *Victory Eagle*; George B. Luks, *Armistice Night*; Elie Nadelman, *Dancer*; Maurice Prendergast, *Autumn Festival*; John S. Sargent, *Gassed*; Edmund C. Tarbell, *Mother, Mercie and Mary M*; Max Weber, *Feast of Passover*.

**Literature**  Conrad Aiken, *The Charnel Rose*; Stephen V. Benét, *Young Adventure*; Willa Cather, *My Antonia*; Edgar Lee Masters, *Toward the Gulf*; Christopher Morley, *Shandygaff*; Lola Ridge, *The Ghetto and Other Poems*; Carl Sandburg, *Cornhuskers* (Pulitzer Prize); Booth Tarkington, *The Magnificent Ambersons* (Pulitzer Prize); Margaret Widdemer, *The Old Road to Paradise* (Pulitzer Prize).

## Music—The Vernacular/Commercial Scene

**A. Births**  Maxine Andrews (singer) January 3; Eddy Arnold (singer) May 15; Pearl Bailey (singer) March 29; Jimmy Blanton (stringbass) October; Stoney T. Cooper (folksinger) October 16; Sam Donahue (saxophonist/arranger) March 8; Les Elgart (trumpeter/bandleader); Ella Fitzgerald (singer) April 25; Helen Forrest (singer) April 12; Betty Grable (singer/actress) December 18; Henry D. Haynes (Homer and Jethro) July 27; Skitch Henderson (pianist/conductor) January 27; Bob Hilliard (composer/lyricist) January 28; Cisco Houston (folksinger) August 18; Ianie Hunter (folksinger) June 7; Elmore James (guitarist) January 27; Hank Jones (pianist) July 31; Alan Jay Lerner (lyricist/librettist) August 31; Jerome Robbins (dancer/choreographer) October 11.

**B. Deaths**  Orville Gibson (mandolin/guitarmaker) August 19; Anna Held (Polish-born singer/actress) August 13.

**C. Biographical**

**Performing Groups**  Vincent Lopez Big Band; Bennie Moten Trio; New York (Southern) Syncopated Orchestra; Original New Orlean Jazz Band (New York); Paul Whiteman Dance Band.

**New Beginnings**  Claxtonola Records (Iowa City); Douglas Casino (Cotton Club, New York); Okeh Records (New York).

**Miscellaneous**  "King" Oliver goes to Chicago for a 10-year stay; Luis Russell (Panamanian pianist/bandleader) comes to the United States.

**D. Publications**  Natalie Curtis, *The Hampton Series of Negro Folk Songs*.

**E. Representative Works**

**Musicals**  Irving Berlin, *Yip, Yip, Yaphank* (army revue); Ivan Caryll and P. G. Wodehouse, *The Girl Behind the Gun*; George M. Cohan, *The Cohan Revue II*; Rudolf Friml and C. Cushing, *Gloriana*; Rudolf Friml and R. J. Young, *Sometime*; Louis A. Hirsch, *The Rainbow Girl*; Raymond Hubbell and G. MacDonough, *The Kiss Burglar*; Jerome Kern, *Rock-a-Bye Baby*; J. Kern and P. G. Wodehouse, *Oh, Lady! Lady!*

**Songs**  Irving Berlin, *God Bless America* (chorus only); Walter Donaldson, *The Daughter of Rosie O'Grady*; Eddie Green, *A Good Man Is Hard to Find*; Robert A. King and B. MacDonald, *Beautiful Ohio*; J. Turner Layton and H. Creamer, *After You've Gone*; Rodgers and Hart, *Fly with Me*; Jean Schwartz and S. Lewis and J. Young, *Rock-a-Bye Your Baby with a Dixie Melody*; Geoffrey O'Hara, *K-K-K-Katy*; Harry Ruby and E. Leslie, *Come On, Papa*; Egbert A. Van Alstyne and T. Jackson, *Pretty Baby*; Richard A. Whiting, *Till We Meet Again*; Leo Wood, *Somebody Stole My Gal*.

**Other**  George L. Cobb, *Russian Rag*; Nick La Rocca, *Fidgety Feet*; James Scott, *Dixie Dimples Rag*.

## Music—The Cultivated/Art Music Scene

**F. Births**  Leonard Bernstein (composer/conductor) August 25; Howard Boatwright (composer/violinist) March 16; Carol Brice (contralto) April 16; Barry Brooke (musicologist) November 1; Ellen Faull (soprano) October 14; Carroll Glenn (violinist) October 28; Herbert Kupferberg (critic/composer) January 20; Jan La Rue (musicologist) July 31; Eugene List (pianist) July 6; Jean Madeira (mezzo-soprano) November 14; Leonard B. Meyer (musicologist) January 12; Ruggiero Ricci (violinist) July 24; George Rochberg (composer) July 5; Leonard Rose (cellist) July 27; Howard Shanet (conductor/author) November 9; Benjamin Suchoff (musicologist) January 19; Blanche Thebom (mezzo-soprano) September 19; Albert Weisser (musicologist) January 11; Frank Wigglesworth (composer) March 3.

**G. Deaths**  Richard Arnold (German-born violinist) June 21; Charles Converse (composer) October 18; Henry G. Hanchett (organist) August 19; Ferdinand Inten (German-born pianist) January 16; Gustav Kobbé (music author) July 27; Albert Mildenberg (composer) July 3; Monroe Rosenfeld (composer/publisher) December 13; Henry Schradieck (German-born violinist) March 25; Alice J. Shaw (concert whistler) April 22; Evan Williams (tenor) May 24.

**H. Debuts**

**United States**  Alfred Cortot (French pianist—New York), Alexandro Dolci (Italian tenor—Chicago), Yvonne Gall (French soprano—Chicago), Queena Mario (soprano—New York), Max Rosen (violinist—New York), Toscha Seidel (Russian violinist—New York).

**Metropolitan Opera**  Giulio Crimi (Italian tenor), Rafaelo Diaz (tenor), Alice Gentle (mezzo-soprano), Charles Hackett (tenor), Hippolito Lazaro (Spanish tenor), Rosa Ponselle (soprano).

**Other**  Samuel Dushkin (violinist—Europe).

**I. New Positions**

**Conductors**  Eric De Lamarter (Chicago Civic Orchestra—to 1936); Carl Denton (Portland [Oregon] Symphony Orchestra—to 1925); Ossip Gabrilowitsch (Detroit Symphony Orchestra); Henri Rabaud (Boston Symphony Orchestra—to 1919); David S. Smith (Horatio Parker Choir, New Haven); Nicolai Sokoloff (Cleveland Orchestra—to 1933); Eugène Ysaÿe (Cincinnati Symphony Orchestra—to 1922).

**J. Honors and Awards**

**Honors**  John Alden Carpenter (National Institute).

**K. Biographical**  Leopold Auer (Hungarian violinist) decides to settle permanently in the United States; George Bundy buys the American distributorship for Selmer instruments; Percy Grainger, Helen Hopekirk, Margarete Matzenauer, and John McCormack become naturalized American citizens; Frank Holton (brass instrument builder) decides to move his business to Elkhorn, Wisconsin; Charles Ives suffers a massive heart attack and is compelled by his doctors to curtail his business and musical activities; Charles Koechlin (French composer) makes a lecture tour of the United States; Sergei Prokofiev conducts and performs in a tour of the United States; Sergei Rachmaninoff moves his family to the United States; E. Robert Schmitz (French pianist) comes to the United States.

**L. Musical Beginnings**

**Performing Groups**  Beethoven Association of New York; Cleveland Chamber Music Society; Cleveland Orchestra; Washington (D.C.) Community Opera (National Opera Association).

**Festivals**  Coolidge Chamber Music Festival (Pittsfield, Massachusetts).

**Educational**  Ellison-White Conservatory (Portland School of Music—to 1959); Hruby Conservatory of Music (Cleveland); Pi Kappa Lambda, Music Honor Society.

**Other**  *The American Organist* (to 1970); Belwin, Inc., Music Publishers (New York); Lewisohn Stadium Concerts (New York); South Mountain Concerts (Pittsfield, Massachusetts).

**M. Music Publications**

Downes, E. Olin, *The Lure of Music*
Earhart, Will, *Music in Secondary Schools*
Elson, Louis C., *Children in Music—Women in Music*
Fisher, William A., *Notes on Music in Old Boston*

Hanchett, Henry G., *An Introduction to the Theory of Music*
Van Vechten, Carl, *The Music of Spain*

**N. Musical Compositions**

**Chamber Music**   Arthur Foote, *Nocturne and Scherzo* (flute and piano—orchestrated 1922 as *Night Piece*); Samuel Gardner, *String Quartet No. 1 in D Minor* (Pulitzer Prize)—*Piano Quintet, "To a Soldier"*; Henry H. Huss, *String Quartet No. 3 in B Minor*; Bernard Rogers, *String Quartet No. 1*; Carl Ruggles, *Mood* (violin and piano); Carlos Salzedo, *Five Poetical Studies for Harp*; David Stanley Smith, *Oboe Sonata, Opus 43*.

**Choral/Vocal**   Victor Herbert, *All Hail to You, Marines!*, A Patriotic Song; Leo Ornstein, *Ten Poems of 1917*; Horatio Parker, *The Dream of Mary, Opus 82*; Dane Rudhyar, *Trois Chansons de Bilitis*; Arthur Shepherd, *O Jesus, Who Art Gone Before* (chorus); Charles S. Skilton, *The Witch's Daughter* (cantata after Whittier)—*Electra* (incidental music—female voices and orchestra).

**Concertos**   Charles T. Griffes, *Poem for Flute and Orchestra*; Carlos Salzedo, *The Enchanted Isle* (harp and orchestra).

**Operas**   Charles W. Cadman, *Shanewis or The Robin Woman*; Henry Hadley, *Cleopatra's Night*; Arthur Nevin, *A Daughter of the Forest*; Horatio Parker, *The Dream of Mary* (morality play).

**Orchestra/Band**   Seth Bingham, *Passacaglia for Orchestra*; Rossetter Gleason Cole, *Overture, Pioneer, Opus 35*; A. T. Davison, *Tragic Overture*; Charles T. Griffes, *Notturno for Orchestra*; Howard Hanson, *Symphonic Rhapsody, Opus 14*; Charles Ives, *Set No. 3 for Small Orchestra*; Bernard Rogers, *To the Fallen*; Leo Schulz, *American Rhapsody*; Arthur Shepherd, *March Solenelle*; Charles S. Skilton, *Electra* (incidental music); John Philip Sousa, *Marches—Anchor and Star—The Chantyman's—Flags of Freedom—Sabre and Spurs—Solid Men to the Front—USAAC The Victory Chest—The Volunteers—Wedding March*; Frederick Stock, *Overture to a Romantic Comedy*.

**Piano/Organ**   Charles Tomlinson Griffes, *Sonata*; Howard Hanson, *Sonata, Opus 11*; Victor Herbert, *The Finest*; Dane Rudhyar, *Mosaics*; Randall Thompson, *Indianola Variations* (two pianos); Adolph Weiss, *Fantasie*.

**Symphonies**   Henry Cowell, *Symphony No. 1 in B Minor*; Lazare Saminsky, *Symphony No. 2*.

# 1919

⚙

## Historical Highlights

President Wilson, while on a tour promoting the League of Nations, suffers a stroke; Congress rejects the League of Nations; Prohibition is ratified; the American Legion is formed as is the American Communist Party; Grand Canyon National Park is established; the Treaty of Versailles officially ends World War I hostilities.

## World Cultural Highlights

**World Art**   Constantin Brancusi, *Bird in Space*; Paul Klee, *Dream Birds*; Fernand Léger, *The City*; Henri Matisse, *The Artist and His Model*; Amedeo Modigliani, *Reclining Nude*.

**World Literature**   Joseph Conrad, *The Arrow of God*; Hermann Hesse, *Demian*; Maurice Maeterlinck, *Le Bourgmestre de Stilmonde*; William Butler Yeats, *The Wild Swans at Coole*.

**World Music**   Béla Bartók, *The Miraculous Mandarin*; Darius Milhaud, *Le Boeuf sur le Toit*; Serge Prokofiev, *The Love of Three Oranges*; Richard Strauss, *Die Frau ohne Schatten*.

**Miscellaneous**   The Belgrade and Bratislava National Operas and Oslo Philharmonic are founded; births include Boris Christoff, Doris Lessing, and Iris Murdoch; deaths include Leonid Andreyev, Amelia Barr, Wilhelm Lehmbruck, Ruggiero Leoncavallo, Edward Poynter, and Pierre-Auguste Renoir.

## American Art and Literature

**Births/Deaths**   Births include art figures William Copley, Lester Johnson, Jason Seley, and literary figures Robert E. Duncan, William Meredith, J. D. Salinger, Max Shulman, and May Swenson; deaths include art figures Ralph Blakelock, Kenyon Cox, Frank Duveneck, Julius Stewart, J. Alden Weir, and literary figures L. Frank Baum, Sarah Morgan Piatt, and Ella Wheeler Wilcox.

**Art Works**   Milton Avery, *Spring Orchard*; George Bellows, *Children on the Porch*; Stuart Davis, *Setting Sun, Tioga, Pennsylvania*; Charles Demuth, *Acrobats*; Childe Hassam, *Fifth Avenue*; Gaston Lachaise, *Walking Woman*; Man Ray, *Lampshade*; Georgia O'Keeffe, *Over Blue*; Joseph Stella, *The Tree In My Life*; Abbott H. Thayer, *Girl Arranging Her Hair*; Grant Wood, *Psyche* (bronze).

**Literature**   Sherwood Anderson, *Winesburg, Ohio*; James B. Cabell, *Jurgen: A Comedy of Justice*; Irwin Cobb, *The Life of the Party*; Finley P. Dunne, *Mr. Dooley on Making a Will*; Ellen Glasgow, *The Builders*; Joseph Hergesheimer, *Java Head*; Christopher Morley, *The Haunted Book Shop*; Albert Terhune, *Lad, a Dog*; Ben Ames Williams, *All the Brothers Were Valiant*.

## Music—The Vernacular/Commercial Scene

**A. Births**   Art Blakey (drummer/bandleader) October 11; Gene DePaul (composer) June 17; Tennessee Ernie Ford (singer) February 13; Liberace (pianist) May 16; Buddy Morrow (trombonist/bandleader) February 8; Anita O'Day (singer) October 18; Pete Seeger (folksinger/writer) May 3; David Seville (songwriter) January 27; "Lennie" Tristano (pianist) March 19; Kitty Wells (singer) August 30.

**B. Deaths**   Henry Blossom (lyricist) March 23; James R. Europe (arranger/bandleader) May 10.

**C. Biographical**

**Performing Groups**   Clyde McCoy Band.

**New Beginnings**   Irving Berlin Music, Inc. (New York); George White Scandals begin.

**Miscellaneous**   Cole Porter studies briefly with Vincent d'Indy in Paris and marries Linda Lee Thomas.

**E. Representative Works**

**Musicals**   Irving Berlin et al., *Ziegfeld Follies of 1919*; Robert H. Bowers and H. B. Smith, *A Lonely Romeo*; Harry Carroll and H. Atteridge, *The Little Blue Devil*; Ivan Caryl and H. B. Smith, *The Canary*; Rudolf Friml and O. Harbach, *The Little Whopper—Tumble in*; George Gershwin, *La, La, Lucille*; Victor Herbert and H. B. Smith, *Angel Face—The Velvet Lady*; Fritz Kreisler and W. LeBaron, *Apple Blossoms*; Cole Porter, *Hitchy-Koo*; Harry A. Tierney and J. McCarthy, *Irene*.

**Songs**   Ernest R. Ball and J. K. Brennan, *Let the Rest of the World Go By*; Irving Berlin, *A Pretty Girl Is Like a Melody*; Felix Bernard and F. Fisher, *Dardanella*; Walter Donaldson, S. Lewis, and J. Young, *How You Gonna Keep 'Em Down on the Farm*; George Gershwin and I. Caesar, *Swanee*; Charles L. Johnson, *Sweet and Low*; Jean Kenbrovin and J. W. Kellette, *I'm Forever Blowing Bubbles*; Eugene Lockhart and E. Seitz, *The World Is Waiting for the Sunrise*; Harry Tierney and J. McCarthy, *Alice Blue Gown*; Clarence Williams and C. Warfield, *Baby, Won't You Please Come Home*.

**Other**   Victor Herbert, *Indian Summer* (words in 1939 by Al Dubin); Joseph F. Lamb, *Bohemia Rag—Alabama Rag*; Jelly Roll Morton, *Kansas City Stomp—The Pearls*; James Scott, *New Era Rag—Peace and Plenty Rag—Troubadour Rag*.

## Music—The Cultivated/Art Music Scene

**F. Births**   Merce Cunningham (dancer/choreographer) April 16; William Patrick Foster (bandmaster/composer) August 25; Arthur Gold (pianist) February 6; Noah Greenberg (musicologist/conductor) April 9; Mason Jones (horn virtuoso) June 16; Irene Jordan (soprano) April 25; Hershy Kay (composer) November 17; Leon Kirchner (composer/pianist) January 24; George London (baritone) May 5; Patricia Neway (soprano) September 30; Jonathan Sternberg (composer) July 27.

**G. Deaths**    Frank W. Burdett (publisher) November 5; Cleofonte Campanini (Italian-born violinist/conductor) December 19; Andrew Carnegie (patron of the arts) August 11; Richard Epstein (Austrian-born pianist) August 1; James Reese Europe (conductor/composer) May 10; Oscar Hammerstein I (Polish-born impresario) August 1; Henry L. Higginson (art patron) November 15; Horatio Parker (composer) March 30; James W. Pepper (instrument maker/publisher) July 28; Wallace C. Sabine (acoustician) January 10; Daniel B. Towner (bass/educator) October 3; George P. Upton (critic) May 19; Marie Van Zandt (soprano) December 31.

**H. Debuts**

**United States**    Leopold Auer (Russian violinist—New York), Winifred Christie (British pianist—New York), John Corigliano, Sr. (violinist—New York), Anis Fuleihan (Cypriot pianist—New York), Edward Johnson (Canadian tenor—Chicago), George Meader (tenor), Benno Moiseiwitsch (Russian pianist—New York), Tito Schipa (Italian tenor—Chicago), Elie Robert Schmitz (French pianist—tour).

**Metropolitan Opera**    Giuseppe Bamboschek (Italian conductor), Gabriella Besanzoni (Italian contralto), Orville Harrold (tenor), Reinald Werrenrath (baritone), Albert Wolff (French conductor), Renato Zanelli (Chilean baritone).

**I. New Positions**

**Conductors**    Walter Henry Rothwell (Los Angeles Philharmonic Orchestra—to 1927); Pierre Monteux (Boston Symphony Orchestra—to 1924); Alexander Smallens (Chicago Opera—to 1923); David S. Smith (New Haven Symphony Orchestra).

**Educational**    Seth Bingham (Columbia—to 1954); Franz Bornshein (Peabody Institute—to 1948); Philip G. Clapp (music head, University of Iowa); Wallingford Riegger (Drake University—to 1922); Rosario Scalero (Mannes School—to 1928).

**Other**    James G. Huneker (music critic, *New York World*—to 1921)

**J. Honors and Awards**

**Honors**    Charles Martin Loeffler (Legion of Honor, American Academy Gold Medal).

**K. Biographical**    George Antheil goes to New York in order to study with Ernst Bloch; Jacques Barzun (French-born critic/historian) comes to the United States; Ossip Gabrilowitsch (Russian-born conductor/pianist) settles in the United States; Karl Muck, a victim of prewar prejudice, is deported from the United States and enters a sanatorium in Austria; Walter Piston enters Harvard as a special student in music; Rosario Scalero (Italian composer) decides to emigrate to the United States; Ernest Schelling injures his hands in an auto accident; Arthur Shepherd divorces his wife and gains custody of his two sons; Virgil Thomson enters Harvard.

**L. Musical Beginnings**

**Performing Groups**    Chicago Civic Orchestra; Los Angeles Philharmonic Orchestra; (Musicians') New Symphony Orchestra of New York; St. Louis Municipal Opera Association; San Diego Philharmonic Chorus; San Diego Civic Grand Opera Association; Scotti Grand Opera Co.

**Educational**    Baylor University College of Fine Arts; Kappa Kappa Psi Fraternity (Oklahoma State University); New Orleans Conservatory; University of Iowa Music Department; University of North Carolina, Chapel Hill, Music Department.

**Other**    Vincent Bach, Mouthpiece Maker (New York); Detroit Orchestra Hall; Harcourt, Brace and Co., Publishers; Jack Mills, Inc. (Mills Music Publishers—New York); National Association of Harpists; National Association of Negro Musicians (NANM); National Association of Music Merchants (NAMM); St. Louis Municipal Opera Theater; San Francisco Community Music Center; Society for the Publication of American Music (New York).

**M. Music Publications**

Carl, William C., *Historical Organ Collection*
Cowell, Henry, *New Musical Resources* (published 1930)
Foote, Arthur W., *Modulation and Related Harmonic Questions*

Gehrkens, Karl, *An Introduction to School Music Teaching*
Kobbé, Gustav, *Kobbé's Complete Opera Book* (posthumous publication)
Krehbiel, Henry E., *More Chapters of Opera*
Seashore, Carl E., *The Psychology of Musical Talent—Measures of Musical Talent*
Sharp, Cecil, *Folk Songs of English Origins collected in the Appalachian Mountains*

**N. Musical Compositions**

**Chamber Music**   Henry Cowell, *Quartet Euphometric*; Samuel Gardner, *Variations for String Quartet*; Henry Hadley, *Pianist Quintet, Opus 50*; Charles Ives, *Chromâtimemelôdtune*; Daniel G. Mason, *String Quartet on Negro Themes, Opus 19*; John Powell, *Sonata Virginianesque* (violin and piano); Leo Sowerby, *Trio* (flute, viola, piano).

**Choral/Vocal**   John J. Becker, *Four Songs for Soprano and String Quartet*; Rubin Goldmark, *Requiem* (on Lincoln's "Gettysburg Address"); Henry Hadley, *The New Earth, Opus 85* (soloists, chorus, and orchestra); Victor Herbert, *Farewell, Molly* (songs); Harrison Kerr, *America's Creed*; Horatio Parker, *A.D. 1919* (cantata); James H. Rogers, *In Memoriam* (song cycle); Carl Ruggles, *Toys* (song); David S. Smith, *Four and Twenty Little Songs*; Wintter Watts, *Vignettes of Italy* (song cycle).

**Concertos**   Ernest Bloch, *Suite for Viola and Orchestra*; Cecil Burleigh, *Violin Concerto No. 2, Opus 43*; Carl Busch, *Cello Concerto—Violin Concerto*; Victor Herbert, *An American Idyll* (piano and orchestra); Mana Zucca, *Piano Concerto, Opus 49*.

**Operas**   John Adam Hugo, *The Temple Dancer*.

**Orchestra/Band**   Felix Borowski, *Elegie Symphonique*; George W. Chadwick, *Angel of Death* (symphonic poem); Rossetter G. Cole, *Pioneer Overture*; Michael Dvorsky (Josef Hofmann), *Haunted Castle*; Charles T. Griffes, *Bacchanale*; Louis Gruenberg, *The Hill of Dreams, Opus 10* (Flagler Prize); Henry Hadley, *Othello Overture, Opus 96*; Howard Hanson, *California Forest Play of 1920* (ballet)—*Before the Dawn* (Rome Prize); Frederick Jacobi, *The Eve of St. Agnes* (symphonic poem); Edgar S. Kelley, *Alice in Wonderland Suite*; Arthur Shepherd, *Overture to a Drama*; John Philip Sousa, *The Golden Star March—Bullets and Bayonets March*; Frederick Stock, *March and Hymn to Democracy*; Deems Taylor, *Through the Looking Glass, Opus 12*; Wintter Watts, *Young Blood* (symphonic poem—Loeb Prize); Adolf Weidig, *Concert Overture, Opus 65*; Emerson Whithorne, *Adventures of a Samurai*; T. Carl Whitmer, *A Syrian Night*.

**Piano/Organ**   Charles Tomlinson Griffes, *Three Preludes*; Elliot Griffis, *Sonata*; Howard Hanson, *Three Miniatures, Opus 12—Scandinavian Suite, Opus 13*; Eastwood Lane, *Five American Dances* (piano); Dane Rudhyar, *Dithyrambs* (also for orchestra); Charles S. Skilton, *Three Indian Sketches*.

**Symphonies**   Philip G. Clapp, *Symphony No. 4 in A Major*; Louis Gruenberg, *Symphony No. 1* (revised 1930—RCA Victor Prize).

# 1920

✿

## Historical Highlights

The census shows a population of 106,022,000, a 15% increase in ten years; Warren G. Harding is elected the 19th president; the Nineteenth Amendment gives suffrage to women; prohibition begins; transcontinental air mail service is inaugurated; the League of Nations convenes in Geneva without the United States after Congress rejects the League.

## World Cultural Highlights

**World Art**   Max Ernst, *Here Everything Is Floating*; Paul Klee, *They're Biting*; Otto Mueller, *Three Girls in the Woods*; Stanley Spencer, *Christ on the Cross*.

**World Literature**   Federico García Lorca, *The Butterfly's Curse*; Jaroslav Hasek, *Good Soldier Schweik*; George Bernard Shaw, *Heartbreak House*; H. G. Wells, *The Outline of History*.

**World Music**   Carlos Chávez, *Symphony No. 1*; Arthur Honegger, *Pastorale d'Été*; Maurice Ravel, *La Valse*; Igor Stravinsky, *Symphonies of Wind Instruments*; Joaquin Turina, *Danzas Fantasticas*.

**Miscellaneous**   The Moscow State and Zagreb Philharmonics are founded; births include Guido Cantelli, Bruno Maderna, and Arturo Michelangeli; deaths include Max Bruch, Benito Pérez Galdós, Max Klinger, and Amedeo Modigliani.

## American Art and Literature

**Births/Deaths**   Births include art figures Honoré Sharrer, Wayne Thiebaud, George Tooker, and literary figures Amy Clampitt, Laurence Ferlinghetti, Ketti Frings, Howard Nemerov, and Mario Puzo; deaths include art figures George Bissel, Thomas Clarke, Samuel Colman, Jr., Henry Mosler, and literary figures Louise Imogen Guiney, William Dean Howells, Julia Moore, and Eleanor H. Porter.

**Art Works**   George Bellows, *Gramercy Park*; Charles Burchfield, *February Thaw*; Lyonel Feininger, *Ascending Balloon*; Stanton MacDonald-Wright, *Canyon Synchromy;* Man Ray, *Eighth Street*; Paul Manship, *Diana*; John Marin, *Lower Manhattan*; Piet Mondrian, *A Composition in Red, Yellow and Blue*; Charles Sheeler, *Church Street El*; Joseph Stella, *The Bridge*.

**Literature**   Sherwood Anderson, *Poor White*; Stephen V. Benét, *Heavens and Earth*; F. Scott Fitzgerald, *This Side of Paradise*; Zona Gale, *Miss Lulu Bett* (Pulitzer Prize); Sinclair Lewis, *Main Street*; Eugene O'Neill, *Beyond the Horizon* (Pulitzer Prize); Carl Sandburg, *Smoke and Steel*; Sara Teasdale, *Flame and Shadow*; Edith Wharton, *The Age of Innocence* (Pulitzer Prize).

## Music—The Vernacular/Commercial Scene

**A. Births**   Chico Alvarez (trumpeter) February 3; Patti Andrews (singer) February 16; Oscar Brand (folksinger) February 7; Dave Brubeck (pianist/bandleader) December 6; Boudleaux Bryant (singer/writer); Johnny Desmond (singer) November 14; "Little Jimmy" Dickens (singer/writer) December 19; Jimmy Forrest (saxophonist/bandleader) January 24; Georgia Gibbs (singer) August 17; Paul Gonsalves (saxophonist) July 12; John Lee Hooker (guitarist/singer) August 22; Yusef Lateef (saxophonist/composer) October 9; Peggy Lee (singer) May 26; John Lewis (pianist/composer) May 3; Shelly Manne (drummer/bandleader) June 11; Percy Mayfield (singer/writer) August 12; Charlie "Bird" Parker (saxophonist) August 29; Hazel Scott (pianist/singer) June 11; Jo Stafford (singer) November 12; Clark Terry (trumpeter) December 14.

**C. Biographical**

**Performing Groups**   Coon-Sanders Novelty Orchestra (Nighthawk, 1924); Eureka Brass Band (New Orleans—to 1975); King Oliver's Creole Jazz Band.

**New Beginnings**   Arto Records (New York); Cardinal Record Co. (New York).

**D. Publications**   Natalie Curtis, *Songs and Tales from the Dark Continent*.

**E. Representative Works**

**Musicals**   Irving Berlin et al., *Ziegfield Follies of 1920*; Ivan Caryll, *Tip Top—Kissing Time*; Donaldson and Clark, *Silks and Satins*; George Gershwin, *George White Scandals*; Victor Herbert, *The Girl in the Spotlight*; Louis A. Hirsch and O. Harbach, *Mary*; Jerome Kern and P. G. Wodehouse, *Sally*; Herbert Stothart and O. Harbach and O. Hammerstein, *Tickle Me—Jimmie*.

**Songs**   Harry Akst, *Home Again Blues*; Irving Berlin, *After You Got What You Want, You Don't Want It*; Con Conrad and J. R. Robinson, *Margie*; Jerome Kern and B. DeSylva, *Look for the Silver Lining*; Al Jolson, B. DeSylva, and V. Rose, *Avalon*; Ted Lewis, A. B. Sterling, and B. Munro, *When My Baby Smiles At Me*; John and Malvin Schonberger, *Whispering*; Albert Von Tilzer and N. Fleeson, *I'll Be With You in Apple Blossom Time*; Richard A. Whiting and R. Egan, *Japanese Sandman*.

**Other**   W. C. Handy, *Aunt Hagar's Blues*; Jerome Kern, *Left-All-Alone-Again Blues*; Nick La

Rocca, *Toddlin' Blues—Ramblin' Blues*; Lucky Roberts, *Railroad Blues*; James Scott, *Pegasus: A Classic Rag—Modesty Rag—The Shimmie Shake*; Clarence Williams, *Sugar Blues*.

## Music—The Cultivated/Art Music Scene

**F. Births**   William Austin (musicologist) January 18; Paul Des Marais (composer) June 23; Eileen Farrell (soprano) February 13; Robert Fizdale (pianist) April 12; Paul Franke (tenor) December 23; Frank Hubbard (harpsichord maker) May 15; Earl Kim (composer) January 6; John La Montaine (composer) March 17; John Lessard (composer) July 3; Edward Lippman (musicologist) May 24; David Lloyd (tenor) February 29; Robert Mann (violinist/conductor) July 19; William Masselos (pianist) August 11; Louis Mennini (composer) November 18; Hephzibah Menuhin (pianist) May 20; Nan Merriman (mezzo-soprano) April 28; Robert Moevs (composer/educator) December 2; Hall Overton (composer) February 23; Frederik Prausnitz (conductor) August 26; Harold Shapiro (pianist/composer) April 29; Eileen Southern (musicologist) February 19; Isaac Stern (violinist) July 21; Theodor Uppman (baritone) January 12; William Warfield (baritone) January 22; Arthur Winograd (cellist/conductor) April 22.

**G. Deaths**   Eugene J. Albert (violin maker); Homer Bartlett (composer/organist) April 3; Reginald DeKoven (composer/conductor) January 16; Louis Charles Elson (music author) February 14; Caryl Florio (British-born composer) November 21; Charles Tomlinson Griffes (composer) April 8; Ernst Perabo (German-born pianist/composer) October 29; Maud Powell (violinist) January 8; William F. Sudds (British-born composer) September 25.

**H. Debuts**

**United States**   Albert Coates (British conductor—New York), Michel Gusikoff (violinist—New York), Duci Karekjarto (Yugoslavian violinist—New York), Daisy Kennedy (Australian violinist—New York), John Jacob Niles (in opera—Cincinnati), Ervin Nyiregyházi (Hungarian pianist—New York), Moshe Paranov (pianist—New York), Mishel Piastro (violinist—New York), Vasa Prihoda (Czech violinist—New York), Cyril Scott (British pianist—Philadelphia).

**Metropolitan Opera**   Mario Chamlee (tenor), Fausto Cleva (Italian conductor), Beniamino Gigli (Italian tenor), William Gustafsson (bass), Henry Hadley (conductor), Nina Morgana (soprano), Frances Peralta (soprano), Marion Telva (contralto).

**I. New Positions**

**Conductors**   Karl King (Fort Dodge Military [Municipal] Band—to 1958); David Stanley Smith (New Haven Symphony Orchestra—to 1946); Henry Wehrmann, Jr. (glee club, Tulane University—to 1934).

**Educational**   Ernest Bloch (director, Cleveland Institute—to 1925); Frederick Converse (head, theory department, New England Conservatory—to 1936); Arthur Fickénscher (University of Virginia—to 1941—first music professor); Charles Haubiel (New York Institute of Music Art—to 1930); Leo Ornstein (piano head, Philadelphia Musical Academy); David Stanley Smith (dean, Yale School of Music—to 1946).

**Other**   Arthur Elson (music critic, *Boston Advertiser*); William J. Henderson (music critic, *New York Herald*—to 1924); David M. Williams (organ, St. Bartholomew's Church, New York—to 1947).

**J. Honors and Awards**

**Honors**   Bernard Rogers (Loeb Prize); John Philip Sousa (PhD, Pennsylvania Military College).

**K. Biographical**   Richard Burgin (Polish violinist/conductor) comes to the United States as concertmaster of the Boston Symphony Orchestra; Fausto Cleva (Italian conductor), Henri Elkan (Belgian violinist/publisher), Guy Fraser Harrison (British conductor), Lazare Saminsky (Russian composer/conductor) and Bernard Wagenaar (Dutch composer) emigrate to the United States; Henry Hadley becomes assistant conductor of the New York Philharmonic Orchestra; Sandor Harmati becomes a naturalized American citizen; Werner Josten (German conductor/composer) and Nina Koshetz (Russian soprano) come to the United States on tour and decide to remain; Arthur Shepherd moves permanently to Cleveland and becomes assistant conductor of the Cleveland Orchestra; Astrid Varnay (Swedish soprano) is brought by her parents to the United States; Hugo Weisgall's (Czech composer) family emigrates to the United States, settling in Baltimore.

## L. Musical Beginnings

**Performing Groups** Boston Flute Players Club; Franco-American Musical Society (Pro-Musica—New York); Hartford Oratorio Society; Musica Sacra Society (Buffalo, New York); Nashville Symphony Orchestra II; Negro Opera Co. (by H. L. Freeman); Horatio Parker Choir (New Haven); People's Symphony Orchestra (Boston); Westminster Presbyterian Church Choir (Dayton, Ohio).

**Festivals** Cincinnati Summer Opera Festival.

**Educational** Cleveland Institute of Music; Woolcott Music Conservatory (Denver); Hartt School of Music (Hartford); Juilliard Musical Foundation (New York).

**Other** Aliénor Harpsichord Composition Awards; American Orchestral Society; Franco-American Music Society (New York); Fred Jewell Music Publishing Co.; Musical Digest.

## M. Music Publications

The Hymnal of the Reformed Church
Bellamann, Henry, A Music Teacher's Notebook
Davison, Archibald T., Protestant Church Music in America
Lake, Mayhew, The American Band Arranger
Mason, Daniel, Music as a Humanity
Rosenfeld, Paul, Musical Portraits: Interpretations of Twenty Modern Composers
Sternberg, Constantin, Tempo Rubato and Other Essays
Stoessel, Albert, The Technic of the Baton

## N. Musical Compositions

**Chamber Music** John Parsons Beach, *Poem for String Quartet*; Ernest Bloch, *Violin Sonata No. 1*; Gena Branscombe, *Violin Sonata*; Nikolai Lopatnikoff, *String Quartet No. 1*; Otto Luening, *String Quartet No. 1*; Frances McCollin, *String Quartet*; Wallingford Riegger, *Piano Trio* (Paderewski Prize—Society for Publication of American Music Prize); David S. Smith, *String Quartet No. 3 in C Major, "Gregorian."*

**Choral/Vocal** Rossetter G. Cole, *The Rock of Liberty, Opus 36* (cantata); Frederick Converse, *The Answer of the Stars*; Bainbridge Crist, *Drolleries from an Oriental Doll's House*; Henry H. Huss, *Ride of Paul Revere*; Charles M. Loeffler, *Five Irish Fantasies* (voice and orchestra); Leo Sowerby, *The Edge of Darkness* (song cycle); Deems Taylor, *Three Songs, Opus 13*; Virgil Thomson, *De Profundis*.

**Concertos** Samuel Gardner, *Violin Concerto*; Eric de Lamarter, *Organ Concerto No. 1 in E Major*; Colin McPhee, *Piano Concerto No. 1, "La mort d'Arthur"*; Daniel G. Mason, *Prelude and Fugue for Piano and Orchestra, Opus 20*; David Stanley Smith, *Fête Galante* (flute and orchestra).

**Operas** Reginald de Koven, *Rip Van Winkle*; Henry F. Gilbert, *Fantasy in Delft*; Mana Zucca, *Hypatia*; Mary Carr Moore, *The Flaming Arrow*; Timothy Spelman, *La Magnifica*.

**Orchestra/Band** John Parsons Beach, *Asolani*; Seth Bingham, *Memories of France*; Alfred Brune, *A Fairy Tale*; John Alden Carpenter, *A Pilgrim Vision* (symphonic poem); Albert I. Elkus, *Impressions from a Greek Tragedy* (Juilliard Award); Howard Hanson, *Exaltation* (symphonic poem); Victor Herbert, *Dodge Brothers March*; Edward Burlingame Hill, *Prelude to the Trojan Women—Fall of the House of Usher* (symphonic poem); Carl McKinley, *The Blue Flower* (symphonic poem—Flagler Prize); Dane Rudhyar, *Soul Fire* (tone poem); Charles S. Skilton, *Suite Primeval*; John Philip Sousa, *Comrades of the Legion—On the Campus March—Who's Who in Navy Blue*; Gustav Strube, *Four Preludes for Orchestra*; Wintter Watts, *Alice in Wonderland* (incidental music); Paul White, *Feuilles Symphoniques*; Emerson Whithorne, *Ranga* (symphonic poem).

**Piano/Organ** John Alden Carpenter, *Tango Américain*; George W. Chadwick, *Elegy in Memoriam, Horatio Parker* (organ); Nikolai Lopatnikoff, *Four Small Pieces*; Leo Ornstein, *A La*

*Mexicana*; Arthur Shepherd, *Fugue in C-Sharp Minor*; Leo Sowerby, *Requiescat in Pace* (organ); Emerson Whithorne, *The Aeroplane* (orchestrated 1925).

**Symphonies**    John J. Becker, *Symphony No. 2, "Fantasia tragica"* (revised 1937).

# 1921

❋

## Historical Highlights

Former President Taft is sworn in as Chief Justice of the Supreme Court; the Tomb of the Unknown Soldier is placed in Arlington National Cemetery; station KDKA in Pittsburgh begins regular radio programming on a commercial basis; the Quota Act limits the number of immigrants admitted to the United States; the Irish Free State is formed out of southern Ireland.

## World Cultural Highlights

**World Art**    Josef Albers, *Figure*; Max Beckmann, *The Dream*; Lovis Corinth, *Apocalypse*; Fernand Léger, *The Three Women*; Henri Matisse, *Still Life with Lemon*; Pablo Picasso, *The Three Musicians*.

**World Literature**    Federico García Lorca, *Libro de Poemas*; W. Somerset Maugham, *The Circle*; Luigi Pirandello, *Six Characters in Search of an Author*; Rafael Sabatini, *Scaramouche*.

**World Music**    Alban Berg, *Wozzeck*; Arthur Honegger, *King David*; Sergei Prokofiev, *Piano Concerto No. 3*; Albert Roussel, *Symphony No. 2*; Ralph Vaughan Williams, *A Pastoral Symphony*.

**Miscellaneous**    The Lisbon Philharmonic Orchestra is founded; the Donaueschingen Contemporary Music Festivals begin; births include Karel Appel, Malcolm Arnold, and George Matthieu; deaths include Enrico Caruso, Nikolai Gumilyov, Max Kalbeck, Francisco Pradilla, and Camille Saint-Saëns.

## American Art and Literature Highlights

**Births/Deaths**    Births include artist Calvin Burnett, sculptor Anne Truitt, and literary figures Hayden Carruth, Alex Haley, James Jones, Edward Tanner (Patrick Dennis), and Richard P. Wilbur; deaths include artists J. Francis Murphy, Abbott Thayer, William A. Walker, and literary figures John Burroughs, John Habberton, Lloyd Mifflin, and Harriet Elizabeth Spofford.

**Art Works**    Joseph Albers, *Figure*; Alexander Archipenko, *Turning Torso*; Max Beckmann, *The Dream*; George W. Bellows, *The Artist's Mother*; Cyrus E. Dallin, *Massasoit;* Stuart Davis, *Lucky Strike*; Charles Demuth, *Aucassin and Nicolette*; Edwin Dickinson, *An Anniversary*; George Grosz, *Gray Day*; Man Ray, *The Gift—Lampshade*; John Marin, *Movement: Sun, Isles and Sea*.

**Literature**    F. Scott Fitzgerald, *The Beautiful and the Damned*; Hamlin Garland, *A Daughter of the Middle Border* (Pulitzer Prize); William Hurlbut, *The Lilies of the Field*; Clarence Kelland, *Scattergood Baines*; Marianne Moore, *Poems*; Eugene O'Neill, *Desire Under the Elms*; Edwin A. Robinson, *Collected Poems* (Pulitzer Prize); Booth Tarkington, *Alice Adams* (Pulitzer Prize).

## Music — The Vernacular/Commercial Scene

**A. Births**    Richard Adler (composer) August 3; Gower Champion (dancer) June 22; Carol Channing (singer/actress) January 31; Wilma Lee Cooper (folksinger) February 7; Hal David (lyricist/composer) May 25; Tal Farlow (guitarist) June 7; Lowell Fulson (guitarist/singer) March 31; Erroll Garner (pianist) June 15; Jimmy Giuffre (clarinetist/saxophonist) April 26; Chico Hamilton (drummer/bandleader) September 21; Betty Hutton (singer/actress) February 26; Gordon MacRae (singer/actor) March 12; Bob Merrill (composer) May 17; Johnny Otis (drummer/bandleader) December 8; John Peterson (composer/publisher) November 1; Nelson Riddle (conductor/arranger) June 1; Tony Scott (clarinetist) June 17; Billy Taylor (pianist) July 24.

**B. Deaths**   Ivan Caryll (composer) November 28; Al G. Field (minstrel performer) April 3; Tony Jackson (ragtime pianist/composer) April 20.

**C. Biographical**

**Performing Groups**   California Ramblers; Abe Lyman Band (Louisiana).

**New Beginnings**   Black Swan Record Co. (New York); Brunswick Records; Music Box Theater (built by Irving Berlin).

**D. Publications**   Cecil Sharp, *Nursery Songs from the Appalachian Mountains*.

**E. Representative Works**

**Musicals**   Irving Berlin, *Music Box Revue 1921–1922*; Eubie Blake and N. Sissle, *Shuffle Along*; Rudolf Friml and O. Harbach, *June Love*; George Gershwin, *A Dangerous Maid—George White Scandals II*; Jerome Kern, *Good Morning, Dearie*; Sigmund Romberg, *Blossom Time* (based on music of Schubert)– *Love Birds*; Vincent Youmans and I. Gershwin, *Two Little Girls in Blue*.

**Songs**   Milton Ager and L. Santly, *I'm Nobody's Baby*; Irving Berlin, *All By Myself*; Eubie Blake, *Love Will Find a Way*; Con Conrad and S. Clare, *Ma! He's Making Eyes at Me*; Grant Clarke and J. Hanley, *Second Hand Rose*; George Gershwin, *Drifting Along with the Tide*; Henry Busse and Gus Wood, *Wang Wang Blues*; Robert A. King and Hughes, *I Ain't Nobody's Darling*; Herbert H. Lawson, *A New York Time*; Edward Rimbault and P. Dodridge, *How Dry I Am*; Louis Silvers and B. DeSylva, *April Showers*; Ted Snyder and H. Smith, *The Sheik of Araby*; Richard Whiting, G. Kahn, and R. Egan, *Ain't We Got Fun*.

**Other**   Irving Berlin, *School-House Blues*; Zez Confrey, *Kitten on the Keys*; Tom Delaney, *Jazz Me Blues*; James Scott, *Don't Jazz Me Rag – Victory Rag*.

## Music—The Cultivated/Art Music Scene

**F. Births**   Israel Baker (violinist) February 11; Seymour Barab (composer/cellist) January 9; Jack Beeson (composer) July 15; William Bergsma (composer) April 1; Lili Chookasian (contralto) August 1; Betty Freeman (patron of the arts) February 22; Elliott W. Galkin (critic) February 22; Margaret Hillis (conductor) October 1; Jerome Hines (bass) November 8; Andrew Imbrie (composer) April 6; Grant Johannesen (pianist) July 30; Constance Keene (pianist/pedagogue) February 9; Robert Kurka (composer) December 22; Mario Lanza (tenor) January 31; Robert McFerrin (baritone) March 19; Roger Nixon (composer) August 8; Will Ogdon (composer) April 19; Claude V. Palisca (musicologist) November 24; David Poleri (tenor) January 10; Alfred Reed (composer/conductor) January 25; Jerome W. Rosen (clarinettist/composer) July 23; Ralph Shapey (composer) March 12; Leo Smit (pianist/composer) January 12.

**G. Deaths**   David Bispham (baritone) October 2; Annie Louise Cary (contralto) April 3; Natalie Curtis (folksong collector) October 23; James G. Huneker (critic) February 9; William J. Kirkpatrick (composer) September 20; Lucille Marcel (soprano) June 22; Arthur P. Schmidt (German-born publisher) March 5; Almon K. Virgil (music educator) October 15; Max Zach (Ukranian-born violist/conductor) February 3.

**H. Debuts**

**United States**   Alfredo Casella (Italian pianist—Philadelphia), Marcel Dupré (French organist—New York), Claire Dux (German soprano—Chicago), Henri van Goudoever (Dutch cellist—New York), Paul Kochánski (Polish violinist—New York), Nina Koshetz (Russian soprano—New York), Selma Kurtz (Austrian soprano—New York), Edith Mason (soprano—Chicago), Erica Morini (violinist—New York), Elly Ney (French pianist—New York), Tino Pattiera (Italian tenor—Chicago), Lazare Saminsky (Russian conductor—Detroit), Artur Schnabel (German pianist—New York), Rosina Storchio (Italian soprano—Chicago), Emil Telmanyi (Hungarian violinist—Philadelphia), Victor Young (violinist—Chicago).

**Metropolitan Opera**   Amelita Galli-Curci (Italian soprano), Maria Jeritza (Czech soprano), George Meader (tenor), Aureliano Pertile (Italian tenor).

## I. New Positions

**Conductors**   William Berwald (Syracuse Symphony Orchestra—to 1924); Rudolph Ganz (St. Louis Symphony Orchestra—to 1927); Louis Hasselmans (French opera, Metropolitan Opera—to 1936); Willem Mengelberg (New York Philharmonic Opera—to 1930); Albert Stoessel (Oratorio Society of New York—to 1943).

**Educational**   Cecil Burleigh (University of Wisconsin—to 1955); Arthur Foote (pianist, New England Conservatory—to 1937); Harold Gleason (organ head, Eastman); Alton Jones (Juilliard—to 1971); Beryl Rubinstein (Cleveland Institute); Charles Seeger (Institute of Musical Arts, New York—to 1933); Roger Sessions (Cleveland Institute—to 1925).

**Other**   Mary Garden (artistic director, Chicago Opera); Carlos Salzedo (editor, *Eolian Review*); Deems Taylor (music critic, *New York World*—to 1925); Pietro Yon (organ, St. Francis-Xavier, New York—second term—to 1926).

## J. Honors and Awards

**Honors**   Leo Sowerby (Rome Prize).

## K. Biographical

Lorenzo Camilieri becomes a naturalized American citizen; Ruth Crawford begins music study at the American Conservatory in Chicago; Paul Kochański (Ukranian violinist) decides to emigrate to the United States; Mischa Mischakoff (Russian violinist) comes to the United States; Eugene Ormandy (Hungarian conductor) comes to the United States with a promise of a concert tour and goes to work playing violin in the Capitol Theater orchestra in New York; Christian Sinding (Norwegian composer) spends a year teaching at the Eastman School of Music; Virgil Thomson accompanies the Harvard Glee Club to Paris and decides to stay for a year's study with Nadia Boulanger; Roger Wagner (French choral conductor) is brought to the United States by his parents.

## L. Musical Beginnings

**Performing Groups**   Buffalo Symphony Society; Cleveland Messiah Civic Chorus; Denver Civic Symphony Orchestra; Denver String Quartet; Detroit Symphony Choir; Eastman Theater Orchestra (Rochester Philharmonic Orchestra); Milwaukee Civic Orchestra; Syracuse Symphony.

**Educational**   American Academy in Rome; American Conservatory at Fontainebleau; Baylor University School of Music; Cosmopolitan School of Music (Cincinnati); Diller-Quaile School of Music (New York); Eastman School of Music (merger of DKG Institute and the University of Rochester).

**Other**   American Music Guild (New York); Bispham Medal (for an opera in English by an American composer); Eastman Theater (Rochester); *Eolian Review*; International Composers' Guild (New York); New York Town Hall; E. C. Schirmer, Music Publisher (Boston); Slingerland Banjo and Drum Co. (Chicago).

## M. Music Publications

Auer, Leopold, *Violin Playing as I Teach It*
Clappé, Arthur A., *The Principles of Wind-band Transcription*
Cooke, James F., *Great Singers on the Art of Singing*
Dickinson, Clarence, *Technique and Art of Organ Playing*
Foden, William, *Foden's Grand Method for Guitarist*
Friskin, James, *The Principles of Pianoforte Practice*
Henderson, William J., *Early History of Singing*
Heyman, Katherine, *The Relation of Ultra-Modern to Archaic Music*
Pratt, Waldo S., *The Music of the Pilgrims*
Salzedo, Carlos, *Modern Study of the Harp*
Sonneck, Oscar G. T., *Miscellaneous Studies in the History of Music*

## N. Musical Compositions

**Chamber Music**   Albert I. Elkus, *Serenade for String Quartet*; Victor Herbert, *Alma Mater Song of the Catholic University of America—The Equity Star* (song); Henry H. Huss, *String Quartet in*

*B Minor, Opus 31*; David Stanley Smith, *Violin Sonata, Opus 51*; Leo Sowerby, *Cello Sonata*; Albert Stoessel, *Violin Sonata in G Major*.

**Choral/Vocal**   Bainbridge Crist, *Colored Stars* (four songs); R. Nathaniel Dett, *The Chariot Jubilee* (oratorio); Henry F. Gilbert, *Six Indian Sketches*; Charles Ives, *Charlie Rutlage* (song); Philip James, *By the Waters of Babylon—Stabat Mater Speciosa;* Oscar Rasbach, *Trees* (after Kilmer); Frederick Stock, *A Psalmodic Rhapsody*; Bernard Wagenaar, *From a Very Little Sphinx* (song cycle).

**Concertos**   Bainbridge Crist, *Abisharika* (violin and orchestra); Nikolai Lopatnikoff, *Piano Concerto No. 1, Opus 5*.

**Operas**   Paul Hastings Allen, *Cleopatra*; Avery Claflin, *The Fall of Usher*; Louis Gruenberg, *The Dumb Wife*.

**Orchestra/Band**   Charles W. Cadman, *The Rubaiyat of Omar Khayyám* (film music)—*Oriental Rhapsody (after Omar Khayyám)*; John Alden Carpenter, *Krazy Kat* (ballet); Louis Coerne, *Excalibur* (symphonic poem); Eric Delamarter, *The Giddy Puritan Overture*; Henry Eichheim, *Oriental Sketches*; Arthur Farwell, *Symphonic Poem on "March! March!," Opus 49*; Henry Hadley, *The Ocean, Opus 99* (tone poem); Richard Hammond, *Five Chinese Fairy Tales*; Henry Holden Huss, *Life's Conflicts* (symphonic poem); Karl King, *March, Invictus*; John Powell, *In Old Virginia, Opus 28*; Dane Rudhyar, *Syntony No. 1, "To the Real"—Syntony No. 2, "Surge of Fire"* (Los Angeles Philharmonic Orchestra Prize)—*The Warrior* (symphonic poem); Carl Ruggles, *Men and Angels*; Charles S. Skilton, *East and West Suite*; John P. Sousa, *Keeping Step with the Union*, Albert Stoessel, *Hispania Suite*; Edgard Varèse, *Amériques—Offrandes*.

**Piano/Organ**   George Antheil, *Airplane Sonata*; Marion Bauer, *From the New Hampshire Woods*; Charles W. Cadman, *Oriental Suite*; Victor Herbert, *A Love Sonnet*; Frederick Jacobi, *Six Pieces*; Leo Ornstein, *Arabesques*.

**Symphonies**   Leo Sowerby, *Symphony No. 1*.

# 1922

✿

## Historical Highlights

The Washington Conference on the Far East and on Disarmament begins; the Teapot Dome scandal erupts in Washington over leasing of oil deposits; WEAF, the first commercial radio station, begins broadcasting; the Lincoln Memorial is dedicated in Washington, DC; Mussolini becomes dictator in Italy; 14 Russian states form the Union of Soviet Socialist Republics (USSR).

## World Cultural Highlights

**World Art**   André Derain, *Boy with a Hat*; Paul Klee, *The Twittering Machine*; Fernand Léger, *Women in an Interior*; Henri Matisse, *The Music Lesson*; Joan Miró, *The Farm*.

**World Literature**   Bertolt Brecht, *Drums in the Night*; James Joyce, *Ulysses*; D. H. Lawrence, *Aaron's Rod*; George Bernard Shaw, *Back to Methuselah*; Virginia Wolff, *Jacob's Room*.

**World Music**   Maurice Ravel, orchestration of Moussorgsky's *Pictures at an Exhibition*; Jacques Ibert, *Escales*; Carl Nielsen, *Symphony No. 5*; Albert Roussel, *Symphony No. 3*; Edgard Varèse, *Offrandes*.

**Miscellaneous**   The Kolisch and Jerusalem String Quartets are formed; the Helsinki Folk Conservatory opens; births include Kingsley Amis, Alain Robbe-Grillet, Jules Olitski, and Jean Pierre Rampal; deaths include Félix Bataille, Wilfred Blunt, Arthur Nikisch, and Marcel Proust.

## American Art and Literature Highlights

**Births/Deaths**   Births include art figures Leonard Baskin, Richard Diebenkorn, Leon Golub, Jules Olitski, Theodoros Stamos, Richard Stankiewicz, and literary figures William Gaddis, Jack Kerouac, and Kurt Vonnegut, Jr.; deaths include art figures Solon Borglum, Anne Dow, Alexander Doyle, Charles Rumsey, and literary figures Mary Noailles Murfree and Mary Terhune (Marian Harland).

**Art Works**   George Bellows, *The White Horse;* Childe Hassam, *House on Main Street, Easthampton;* Anna H. Huntington, *Diana of the Chase;* John Marin, *Deer Isle Islets, Maine;* Hugh Robus, *The General;* Charles Sheeler, *Offices;* John Sloan, *The City from Greenwich Village;* Joseph Stella, *Skyscrapers—New York Interpreted;* Mahonri Young, *The Rigger;* William Zorach, *Floating Figure.*

**Literature**   Willa Cather, *One of Ours* (Pulitzer Prize); E. E. Cummings, *The Enormous Room;* F. Scott Fitzgerald, *Tales of the Jazz Age;* Hatcher Hughes, *Hell-Bent for Heaven* (Pulitzer Prize); Sinclair Lewis, *Babbitt;* Anne Nichols, *Abie's Irish Rose;* Eugene O'Neill, *Anna Christie* (Pulitzer Prize); Arthur Richman, *The Awful Truth;* Edith Wharton, *The Glimpses of the Moon.*

## Music—The Vernacular/Commercial Scene

**A. Births**   Ray Anthony (trumpeter/bandleader) January 20; Les Baxter (pianist/composer) March 14; Elmer Bernstein (composer/conductor) April 4; Eddie "Lockjaw" Davis (saxophonist) March 2; Tommy Edwards (singer) February 17; Alan Freed (disk jockey) December 15; Judy Garland (singer/actress) January 10; Neal Hefti (trumpeter/arranger) October 29; Al Hirt (trumpeter) November 7; Janis Paige (singer/actress) September 16; Carmen McRae (singer) April 8; Charlie Mingus (stringbassist/writer) April 22; Oscar Pettiford (string bassist/bandleader) September 30; Jean Ritchie (folksinger/writer) December 8; Kay Starr (singer) July 21; Ralph Earl Sutton (pianist) November 4.

**B. Deaths**   Lillian Russell (actress/singer) June 6; Tom Turpin (ragtime pianist/writer) August 13; Bert Williams (composer/lyricist) March 4; Harry H. Williams (lyricist) May 15.

**C. Biographical**

**Performing Groups**   New Orleans Rhythm Kings (Chicago jazz group); Cecil Scott Band I; Ted Weems Band.

**New Beginnings**   Ager, Yeller, and Bornstein, Music Publishers; Banner Record Co. (New York); Plaza Music Recording Co.

**Miscellaneous**   Vernon Duke (Vladimir Dukelsky—composer) arrives in the United States; Jelly Roll Morton leaves California for Chicago.

**E. Representative Works**

**Musicals**   Jerome Kern, *The Bunch and Judy;* Irving Berlin, *Music Box Revue 1922–1923;* George M. Cohan, *Little Nellie Kelly;* J. Fred Coots and R. Klages, *Sally, Irene and Mary;* Rudolf Friml and O. Harbach, *The Blue Kitten;* George and Ira Gershwin, *Our Nell;* Alfred Goodman and C. Wood, *The Lady in Ermine;* Victor Herbert and B. DeSylva, *Orange Blossoms;* Sigmund Romberg and C. Wood, *The Blushing Bride;* Harry A. Tierney, *Up She Goes—Glory.*

**Songs**   Walter Donaldson and G. Kahn, *My Buddy—Carolina in the Morning;* Ernie Erdman and G. Kahn, *Toot Toot Tootsie, Goodbye;* Fred Fisher, *Chicago;* Rudolf Friml and C. Cushing, *L'Amour, Toujours L'Amour;* Douglas Furber and P. Braham, *Limehouse Blues;* Arthur H. Gibbs, *Runnin' Wild;* L. Wolfe Gilbert, *Down Yonder;* W. C. Handy, *John Henry Blues;* Ray Henderson, *Georgette;* Turner Layton and H. Creamer, *Way Down Yonder in New Orleans;* Otto Rasbach and J. Kilmer, *Trees;* Fred Meinken, *Wabash Blues.*

**Other**   James Scott, *Broadway Rag;* Spencer Williams, *State Street Blues.*

## Music—The Cultivated/Art Music Scene

**F. Births**   James R. Anthony (musicologist) February 18; William Ashbrook (musicologist) January 28; Irwin Bazelon (composer) June 4; Mimi Benzell (soprano) April 6; Robert Commanday (critic) June 18; Jean Cox (tenor) January 14; Phyllis Curtin (soprano) December 3; William R. Dowd (harpsichord maker) February 28; Robert Evett (composer) November 30; William Kapell (pianist) September 20; Sylvia Kenney (musicologist) November 27; Leo Kraft (composer/pedagogue) July 24; Beatrice Laufer (composer) April 27; Cornell MacNeil (baritone) September 24; Richard Owen (composer) December 11; Regina Resnik (mezzo-soprano) August 30; Allen Dwight Sapp (composer/administrator) December 10; Abbey Simon (pianist) January 8; Francis Thorne (composer/pianist) June 23; Roy Travis (composer/theorist) June 24; George Walker (composer/pianist) June 27; Camilla Williams (soprano) October 18.

**G. Deaths**    Edwin E. Bagley (bandmaster/composer); Louis Coerne (composer) September 11; Rita Fornia (mezzo-soprano) October 27; Emma Azalia Hackley (soprano) December 13; Horace Nicholl (British-born organist) March 10; Adam A. Stein (German-born organ builder) August 6.

**H. Debuts**

**United States**    Richard Crooks (tenor—New York), Nelson Eddy (baritone—Philadelphia), Cesare Formichi (Italian baritone—Chicago), Myra Hess (British pianist—tour), Leopold Mannes (pianist—New York), Mieczyslaw Munz (Polish pianist—New York), Miron Poliakin (Russian violinist—New York), Nadia Reisenberg (Lithuanian pianist—New York), Vladimir Rosing (Russian tenor)—Rochester), Felix Salmond (British cellist—New York).

**Metropolitan Opera**    Paul Bender (German bass-baritone), Louis Hasselmans (French conductor), Edward Johnson (Canadian tenor), Queena Mario (soprano), Sigrid Onégin (German contralto), Elisabeth Rethberg (German soprano), Titta Ruffo (Italian baritone), Gustav Schützendorf (German baritone), Curt Taucher (German tenor), Armand Tokatyan (Bulgarian tenor).

**I. New Positions**

**Conductors**    Philip James (New Jersey Symphony Orchestra—to 1929); Giorgio Polacco (Chicago Civic Opera—to 1930); Fritz Reiner (Cincinnati Symphony Orchestra—to 1931).

**Educational**    William Kroll (Institute of Musical Art, New York—to 1922); Harold Morris (Juilliard—to 1939); Burnet Tuthill (general manager, Cincinnati College—to 1930); Arnold Volpe (director, Kansas City Conservatory of Music); Jaromir Weinberger (composition, Ithaca College, New York—to 1926).

**Other**    Carl Engel (head, Music Division, Library of Congress—to 1934); Glenn Dillard Gunn (music critic, *Chicago Herald and Examiner*—to 1936).

**K. Biographical**    George Antheil moves to Germany as a concert pianist; Nicolai Berezowsky (Russian violinist/composer), Margarethe Dessoff (Austrian conductor), André Kostelanetz (Russian conductor), Fritz Reiner (Hungarian conductor), Nadia Reisenberg (Lithuanian pianist), and Felix Salmond (British cellist) all come to the United States; Geraldine Farrar gives her farewell Metropolitan Opera performance; Abraham Idelssohn leaves Jerusalem for the United States; Charles Ives personally publishes his *114 Songs*; Darius Milhaud makes his first lecture-concert tour of the United States; Ralph Vaughan Williams visits the United States and conducts his works at the Norfolk Festival.

**L. Musical Beginnings**

**Performing Groups**    Eddy Brown String Quartet; Lenox String Quartet I; Philadelphia Choral Art Society; Rochester American Opera Co.; Rochester Symphony Orchestra.

**Educational**    American Academy of Teachers of Singing; Conway's Military Band School (Ithaca, New York); Glenn Dillard Gunn School of Music and Dramatic Art (Chicago); Ernest Williams School of Music (Brooklyn); Zoellner Conservatory of Music (Los Angeles).

**Other**    Hollywood Bowl Concerts (Los Angeles); Hymn Society of America (Springfield, Ohio).

**M. Music Publications**

Jonás, Alberto et al., *Master School of Modern Pianist Playing and Virtuosity*
Lahee, Henry C., *Annals of Music in America: A Chronological Record . . .*
Parker, Henry T., *Eighth-Notes*
Wedge, George A., *Advanced Ear Training*

**N. Musical Compositions**

**Chamber Music**    Marion Bauer, *Violin Sonata No. 1*; Avery Claflin, *Piano Trio*; Arthur Farwell,

*String Quartet, "The Hako," Opus 65*; Mary Howe, *Violin Sonata*; Daniel G. Mason, *Three Pieces for Flute, Harp and String Quartet, Opus 13*; John Powell, *String Quartet No. 2*; Carlos Salzedo, *Sonata for Harp and Piano*; Charles S. Skilton, *Violin Sonata No. 2 in G Minor*; Leo Sowerby, *Violin Sonata No. 1*.

**Choral/Vocal**   Charles W. Cadman, *The Sunset Trail* (cantata)—*The Willow Wind* (song cycle on Chinese themes); Paolo Gallico, *The Apocalypse* (oratorio—National Music Clubs Prize); Henry Hadley, *Resurgam, Opus 98* (oratorio)—*Christmas Cantata, Opus 91*; Victor Herbert, *Lora Lee* (male voices); Philip James, *The Nun*; Virgil Thomson, *Psalm 123*—*Psalm 133*.

**Concertos**   George Antheil, *Piano Concerto No. 1*; Eric Delamarter, *Organ Concerto No. 2 in A Major*; Bernard Rogers, *Soliloquy No. 1* (flute and strings); Leo Sowerby, *Ballad of King Estmere* (two pianos and orchestra).

**Operas**   Eleanor Freer, *Legend of the Piper*; Bernard Rogers, *Deirdre*.

**Orchestra/Band**   Edward Ballantine, *By a Lake in Russia*; Ernest Bloch, *In the Night—Four Circus Pieces—Poems of the Sea*; George W. Chadwick, *Anniversary Overture*; Blair Fairchild, *Etude Symphonique*; Rubin Goldmark, *A Negro Rhapsody*; David Guion, *Southern Nights Suite*; Victor Herbert, *Dream On—The Water Sprite* (ballet); Edward Burlingame Hill, *Stevensonia Suite II*; Wallingford Riegger, *American Polonaise (Triple Jazz), Opus 3*; Bernard Rogers, *Overture, The Faithful*; John P. Sousa, *The Dauntless Battalion March—The Gallant Seventh March*; Albert Stoessel, *Cyrano de Bergerac* (symphonic portrait); Randall Thompson, *Pierrot and Cothurnus*; Hermann H. Wetzler, *Symphonic Fantasy*; Wintter Watts, *Etchings Suite*.

**Piano/Organ**   Amy Beach, *The Fair Hills of Eire* (piano or organ)—*From Grandmother's Garden, Opus 97*; Ernest Bloch, *Four Circus Pieces*; John Alden Carpenter, *Five Pieces*; R. Nathaniel Dett, *Enchantment Suite*; Victor Herbert, *The Marion Davies March*; Sidney Homer, *Organ Sonata*; Charles Ives, *Four Transcriptions from Emerson*; Eastwood Lane, *Adirondack Sketches—Mongoliana Suite*; Leo Sowerby, *From the Northland* (orchestrated 1924—Society for Publication of American Music Prize); Humphrey Stewart, *Organ Sonata, "The Chambered Nautilus"*; Randall Thompson, *Sonata in G Minor*; Virgil Thomson, *Passacaglia for Organ*; Emerson Whithorne, *New York Days and Nights* (arranged for orchestra, 1923).

**Symphonies**   George Antheil, *Symphony No. 1, "Zingareska"*; Howard Hanson, *Symphony No. 1, "Nordic"*; Gustav Strube, *Sinfonietta*.

# 1923

❖

## Historical Highlights

Warren G. Harding dies and Calvin Coolidge becomes the 30th president; American troops are recalled from Germany; Carlsbad Caverns is made a national park; an antitoxin for scarlet fever is discovered; Adolph Hitler is jailed following the abortive "Beer Hall Putsch" in Munich; France and Belgium invade the Ruhr, seeking war reparations from the Germans.

## World Cultural Highlights

**World Art**   Marc Chagall, *Love Idyll*; Nikolaus Geiger, *Hans Pfitzner*; Pablo Picasso, *Woman in White*; Stanley Spencer, *The Resurrection*; Maurice de Vlaminck, *Village in Northern France*.

**World Literature**   Ivan Bunin, *The Village*; Aldous Huxley, *Antic Hay*; Ferenc Molnár, *The Red Mill*; Sean O'Casey, *The Shadow of a Gunman*; George Bernard Shaw, *St. Joan*.

**World Music**   Béla Bartók, *Dance Suite*; Artur Honegger, *Pacific 231*; Darius Milhaud, *La Création du Monde*; Jean Sibelius, *Symphony No. 6*; Igor Stravinsky, *Octet*; William Walton, *Façade*.

**Miscellaneous**   The Belgrade and Sarejevo Philharmonic Societies are founded, as is the Hungarian State Symphony Orchestra; births include Brendan Behan, Henryk Czyz, György Ligeti, and Wolfgang Sawallisch; deaths include Sarah Bernhardt, Louis Couperous, and Katherine Mansfield.

## American Art and Literature Highlights

**Births/Deaths**   Births include art figures Sam Francis, Ellsworth Kelly, Roy Lichtenstein, Larry Rivers, and literary figures Paddy Chayefsky, Joseph Heller, Richard Hugo, Jean Kerr, Denise Levertov, Norman Mailer, James M. Schuyler, and Upton Sinclair; deaths include sculptor Alexander M. Calder, artist Elihu Vedder, and literary figures Edna Dean Proctor and Kate Douglas Wiggin.

**Art Works**   Max Beckmann, *Charnel House*; George Bellows, *The Crucifixion*; Malvina Hoffman, *Paderewski the Artist*; Yasuo Kuniyoshi, *Boy Stealing Fruit*; Gaston Lachaise, *Woman Walking*; Louis Lozowick, *Pittsburgh—Chicago*; László Moholy-Nagy, *Space Segments*; Hugo Robus, *Walking Figure*; Charles Sheeler, *Bucks County Barn*; Max Weber, *Composition with Nude Figures* (?).

**Literature**   James B. Cabell, *The High Place*, E. E. Cummings, *Tulips Are Chimneys*; Owen Davis, *Icebound* (Pulitzer Prize); Robert Frost, *New Hampshire* (Pulitzer Prize); Edna St. Vincent Millay, *The Harp Weaver and Other Poems* (Pulitzer Prize); Lizette W. Reese, *Wild Cherry*; William C. Williams, *The Great American Novel*; Margaret Wilson, *The Able McLaughlins* (Pulitzer Prize).

## Music—The Vernacular/Commercial Scene

**A. Births**   Kenneth C. Burns (Homer and Jethro) March 10; Buddy DeFranco (clarinet) February 17; Red Garland (pianist) May 13; Dexter Gordon (saxophonist) February 27; Milt Jackson (vibes) January 1; Thaddeus Jones (cornet/bandleader) March 28; "Philly Joe" Jones (drummer) July 15; Kitty Kallen (singer) May 25; Barney Kessel (guitarist) October 17; Albert King (singer/guitarist) April 25; Charlie Mariano (saxophonist) November 12; Wes Montgomery (guitarist) March 6; "Fats" Navarro (trumpeter) September 24; Molly O'Day (singer) July 9; Tito Puente (bandleader/percussion) April 20; Tito Rodriguez (singer/bandleader) January 4; George Russell (composer/pianist) June 23; Hank Williams (singer) September 17.

**B. Deaths**   Vess L. Ossman (ragtime banjo) August 13.

**C. Biographical**

**Performing Groups**   Fletcher Henderson Jazz Band (New York); Washingtonians (Duke Ellington); Ted Weems Band I; Wolverines (Chicago jazz band).

**New Beginnings**   Maurice Abrahams Publishing Co.; Earl Carroll Vanities (to 1932).

**Miscellaneous**   Guy Lombardo's band makes its first United States appearance.

**D. Publications**   Edward "Zez" Confrey, *Modern Novelty Piano Solos*.

**E. Representative Works**

**Musicals**   Harry Archer, *Little Jessie James*; Eubie Blake, *Elsie*; George M. Cohan, *The Rise of Rosie O'Reilly*; Rudolf Friml, *Cinders*; Jerome Kern and A. Caldwell, *Stepping Stones*; Cole Porter, *Within the Quota*; Harry Ruby and B. Kalmar, *The Town Clowns*; Harry Tierney and J. McCarthy, *Kid Boots*; Vincent Youmans, O. Harbach, and O. Hammerstein, *The Wildflower*.

**Songs**   Milton Ager and J. Yellen, *Louisville Lou*; Irving Cohn, *Yes, We Have No Bananas*; Gus Arnheim, A. Lyman, and A. Freed, *I Cried For You*; Con Conrad and B. Rose, *Barney Google*; Wendell W. Hall, *It Ain't Gonna Rain No Mo'*; Ray Henderson, *That Old Gang of Mine*; Isham Jones and J. Davis, *Indiana Moon*; Eddie Leonard, *Oh, Didn't It Rain*; Cecil Mack and J. Johnson, *Charleston*; Mana Zucca and I. M. Cassel, *I Love Life*; Jack Pettis and B. Meyers, *Bugle Call Rag*; Harry Ruby, B. Kalmar, and T. Snyder, *Who's Sorry Now*; Jack B. Tenney, *Mexicali Rose*.

**Other**   George Antheil, *Jazz Sonata*; Zez Confrey, *Dizzy Fingers*; Louis Gruenberg, *Daniel Jazz*; King Oliver, *Sugar Foot Stomp—Snake Rag—Canal Street Blues*; Erno Rapee, *Robin Hood* (film music); Elmer Schoebel, *Bugle Call Rag*; John and B. Spikes, *Wolverine Blues*.

## Music—The Cultivated/Art Music Scene

**F. Births**   John Alexander (tenor) October 21; Leslie Bassett (composer) January 22; Theodore Bloomfield (conductor) June 14; Harold Blumenfeld (composer/conductor) October 15; Maria Callas (soprano) December 4; Schuyler Chapin (impresario/administrator) February 13; Robert Craft (conductor/author) October 20; Frank Erickson (composer/conductor) September 1; William Flanagan, Jr. (composer) August 14; Frank Guarrera (baritone) December 3; H. Wiley Hitchcock (musicologist) September 28; Jean Eichelberger Ivey (composer) July 3; William Kraft (composer/percussionist) September 6; Louis Lane (conductor) December 25; Donald Lybbert (composer) February 19; Frederick Marvin (pianist/musicologist) June 11; Peter Mennin (composer) May 17; Dika Newlin (musicologist) November 22; Daniel Pinkham (organist) June 5; Ned Rorem (composer) October 23; Harold Shaw (concert manager) June 11; Clifford Taylor (composer) October 20; Giorgio Tozzi (bass) January 8; Lester Trimble (composer/critic) August 29; Clifton Williams (bandmaster/composer) March 26; Franklin B. Zimmerman (musicologist) June 20.

**G. Deaths**   Arthur H. Bird (composer/pianist) December 22; Carl Fischer (German-born publisher) February 14; Alice C. Fletcher (ethnomusicologist) April 6; Gustave Kerker (German-born composer/conductor) June 29; William H. Humiston (composer) December 5; Henry Edward Krehbiel (critic) March 20; Charles Kunkel (pianist/publisher) December 3; Emil Welte (German-born instrument maker) October 25; Thomas P. Westendorf (composer) April 19; George E. Whiting (organist) October 14.

**H. Debuts**

**United States**   Claudio Arrau (Chilean pianist—New York), Shura Cherkassky (Russian pianist—Baltimore), George Enescu (Romanian violinist—New York), Dusolina Giannini (soprano—New York), Maria Ivogün (Hungarian soprano—Chicago), Alexander Kipnis (Ukranian bass—Baltimore), Wanda Landowska (Polish harpsichordist—Philadelphia), Mitja Nikisch (German pianist—New York), Graziella Pareto (Spanish soprano—Chicago), Max Pollikoff (violinist—New York), Carmela Ponselle (mezzo-soprano), Meta Seinemeyer (German soprano—tour), Helen Traubel (soprano—St. Louis), Bruno Walter (German conductor—New York).

**Metropolitan Opera**   Michael Bohnen (German bass-baritone), Miguel Fleta (Spanish tenor), Barbara Kemp (German soprano), Rudolf Laubenthal (German tenor), Giacomo Lauri-Volpi (Italian tenor), Delia Reinhardt (German soprano), Lawrence Tibbett (baritone).

**Other**   Mary Lewis (soprano—Vienna).

**I. New Positions**

**Conductors**   Howard Barlow (American National Orchestra—to 1925); Eugene Goosens (Rochester Philharmonic Orchestra—to 1931); Henry Verbrugghen (Minneapolis Symphony Orchestra—to 1931).

**Educational**   John Duke (Smith College—to 1967); Charles Haubiel (theory, NYU—to 1947); Werner Josten (Smith College, Massachusetts—to 1949); Otto Kinkeldey (music head, Cornell—to 1927); Albert Stoessel (music head, NYU—to 1930).

**Other**   Lawrence Gilman (music critic, *New York Herald Tribune*—to 1939); Leonard Liebling (music critic, *New York American*—to 1934); Gaetano Merola (general manager, San Francisco Opera—to 1953).

**J. Honors and Awards**

**Honors**   Herbert Elwell (Rome Prize); John P. Sousa (PhD, Marquette University); Wintter Watts (Prix de Rome—Pulitzer Scholarship).

**K. Biographical**   Vincent Bach, Lucien Cailliet, and Carlos Salzedo become naturalized American citizens; George Cehanovsky (Russian baritone) emigrates to the United States; Alexander Hilsberg (Polish violinist/conductor) arrives in the United States; Gustav Holst, despite an injury sustained in a fall, makes a lecture tour of the United States; Egon Kenton (Hungarian musicologist) emigrates to the United States; Boris Koutzen (Russian composer) comes to the

United States; Frédérique Joanne Petrides (Belgian conductor/violinist) comes to New York; Vladimir Rosen (Russian tenor/impresario) comes to the United States in order to head the opera section at Eastman; Fabien Sevitzky (Russian conductor) emigrates to the United States and joins the Philadelphia Orchestra; Nicolas Slonimsky (Russian author/composer) moves to the United States and begins teaching at Eastman; Virgil Thomson, graduating from Harvard, receives a fellowship to study at Juilliard; Isabelle Vengerova (Russian pianist) comes to the United States.

### L. Musical Beginnings

**Performing Groups**   American National Orchestra; Portland Symphony Orchestra (Maine); San Francisco Opera.

**Educational**   New York University Music Department.

**Other**   International Society for Contemporary Music American Section; League of Composers (New York).

### M. Music Publications

Campbell-Watson, Frank, *University Course of Music Study*
Dickinson, George, *Foretokens of the Tonal Principle*
Dykema, Peter, *School Music Handbook*
Finck, Henry T., *Musical Progress: A Series of Practical Discussions of Present Day Problems in the Tone World*
Rosenfeld, Paul, *Musical Chronicle*
Todd, H. H., *The Cokesbury Hymnal (Methodist)*
Smith, H. Augustine, *Hymns of the Living Age*
Weidig, Adolf, *Harmonic Material and Its Uses*

### N. Musical Compositions

**Chamber Music**   George Antheil, *Violin Sonata No. 1—Violin Sonata No. 2*; Ernest Bloch, *Piano Quintet No. 1 – Baal Shem* (orchestrated 1939); Herbert Elwell, *Piano Quintet*; Mary Howe, *Piano Quintet*; Otto Luening, *String Quartet No. 2*; Daniel G. Mason, *Clarinet Sonata, Opus 14*; Quincy Porter, *String Quartet No. 1*; Leo Sowerby, *String Quartet No. 1*; Gustav Strube, *String Quartet No. 1—Piano Trio—Violin Sonatas No. 1, 2*; Edgard Varèse, *Hyperprism—Octandre*; Adolph Weiss, *String Quartet No. 1*.

**Choral/Vocal**   Samuel Barber, *Seven Nursery Songs (to Sara)*; Amy Beach, *Four Songs: When Mama Sings, Opus 99*; Victor Herbert, *That Old Fashioned Garden of Mine* (song); Daniel G. Mason, *Songs of the Countryside, Opus 23* (chorus and orchestra); Carl Ruggles, *Vox clamans in deserto*; Theodore Stearns, *Snowbird* (Bispham Medal).

**Concertos**   Victor Herbert, *Cosmopolitan* (piano and orchestra); Colin McPhee, *Piano Concerto No. 2*; Leo Ornstein, *Piano Concerto*.

**Operas**   Eugene M. Bonner, *Celui Qui Espousa une Femme Muette*; Harry L. Freeman, *Vendetta*.

**Orchestra/Band**   Edward Ballantine, *From the Garden of Hellas*; Felix Borowski, *Ecce Homo* (symphonic poem); Paolo Gallico, *Euphorion*; Henry F. Gilbert, *The Island of the Fay* (symphonic poem); Edwin Franko Goldman, *On the Mall*; Howard Hanson, *Lux Aeterna, Opus 24* (symphonic poem)—*North and West* (Prize, Society for the Publication of American Music); Victor Herbert, *Overtures—Star of the North—Under the Red Robe—The Great White Way—Yolanda*; Otto Luening, *Music for Orchestra*; Leroy Robertson, *Overture in E Minor* (Endicott Prize); Ernest Schelling, *A Victory Ball*; Roger Sessions, *The Black Maskers* (incidental music); John P. Sousa, *March of the Mitten Men—Nobles of the Mystic Shrine*; Timothy M. Spelman, *Barbaresques*; Lamar Stringfield, *Indian Legend*; Carl Venth, *Pan in America* (National Federation of Music Clubs Award); Adolph Weiss, *I Segreti*; Hermann H. Wetzler, *Visionen*.

**Piano/Organ**   George Antheil, *Sonata Sauvage (No. 2)—Death of Machines (Sonata No. 3)—Sonata No. 5*; Seth Bingham, *Suite for Organ*; George W. Chadwick, *Suite in Variation Form*; Philip G. Clapp, *Sonatina*; Arthur Farwell, *Modal Invention in the Dorian Mode, Opus 68*; Horace

Nicholl, *Concert Preludes and Fugues, Opus 31*; Dane Rudhyar, *Catharsis*; Arthur Shepherd, *Prelude in E Minor for Organ*; Leo Sowerby, *From the Northland*; Randall Thompson, *Sonata in C Minor*.

**Symphonies**   Gustav Strube, *"Lanier" Symphony*.

# 1924

✸

## Historical Highlights

Calvin Coolidge is elected to his first full term as president; Congress makes all American Indians full citizens; the Dawes Plan is introduced to help Germany with war reparations; New York's Holland Tunnel is finished; Lenin dies in Russia and Stalin begins his bloodbath for control; Mussolini consolidates his control in Italy; Olympic games are held in Paris and Chamonix in France.

## World Cultural Highlights

**World Art**   Constantin Brancusi, *The Beginning of the World*; Marc Chagall, *Daughter Ida*; Charles Despiau, *Faunesse*; Juan Gris, *Violin and Fruit Dish*; Joan Miró, *Catalan Landscape*.

**World Literature**   E. M. Forster, *A Passage to India*; Thomas Mann, *The Magic Mountain*; John Masefield, *Sand Harker*; Sean O'Casey, *Juno and the Paycock*.

**World Music**   Leos Janáček, *The Cunning Little Vixen*; Sergei Prokofiev, *Symphony No. 2*; Ottorino Respighi, *The Pines of Rome*; Jean Sibelius, *Symphony No. 7*; Edgard Varèse, *Octandre*.

**Miscellaneous**   The Buenos Aires Conservatory of Music is founded as is the Munich Philharmonic; births include Anthony Caro, Neville Marriner, and Luigi Nono; deaths include Ferruccio Busoni, Joseph Conrad, Gabriel Fauré, Anatole France, and Giacomo Puccini.

## American Art and Literature Highlights

**Births/Deaths**   Births include art figures Al Brouillette, Jane Freilicher, Philip Pearlstein, George Segal, Peter Voulkos, and literary figures James Baldwin, Truman Capote, James Clavell, and Leon Uris; deaths include art figures Victor Brenner, Chester Loomis, Alexander Pope, Maurice Prendergast, and literary figures Frances E. Burnett, Laura Jean Libbey, Harriet M. Lothrop, and Gene Stratton Porter.

**Art Works**   George Bellows, *Dempsey and Firpo—Lady Jean Portrait*; A. Sterling Calder, *Swann Memorial Fountain*; Stuart Davis, *Odol*; Preston Dickinson, *Industry* (?); Lyonel Feininger, *Blue Marine*; Malvina Hoffman, *Anna Pavlova*; Gaston Lachaise, *Dolphin Fountain*; Man Ray, *Le Violon d'Ingres*; Paul Manship, *Diana and Actaeon*; Anne Whitney, *Texas War Memorial*.

**Literature**   Maxwell Anderson, *What Price Glory?*; Hilda Doolittle, *Oread, . . . and Other Poems*; William Faulkner, *The Marble Faun*; Edna Ferber, *So Big* (Pulitzer Prize); Robinson Jeffers, *Tamar and Other Poems*; Edgar Lee Masters, *The New Spoon River Anthology*; Marianne Moore, *Observations* (Dial Award); Edwin A. Robinson, *The Man Who Died Twice* (Pulitzer Prize).

## Music—The Vernacular/Commercial Scene

**A. Births**   Lee Adams (librettist/lyricist) August 14; Joe Albany (pianist) January 24; Chet Atkins (guitarist) June 20; Louie Bellson (bandleader) July 26; Clarence "Gatemouth" Brown (singer/guitarist) April 18; Doris Day (singer/actress) April 3; Paul Desmond (saxophonist) November 25; Gogi Grant (singer) September 20; Delores Gray (singer) June 7; Al Haig (pianist) July 22; Sheldon Harnick (lyricist) April 30; J. J. Johnson (trombonist/composer) January 22; Henry Mancini (composer) April 16; Sammy Nestico (arranger/composer) February 6; "Bud" Powell (pianist) September 27; Jim Reeves (singer/writer) August 20; Max Roach (drummer/composer) January 10; Leonard Rosenman (composer) September 7; Earl Scruggs (guitarist/singer) January 6; "Sonny"

Stitt (saxophonist) February 2; Sarah Vaughan (singer) March 27; Clara Ward (singer/pianist) April 21; Dinah Washington (singer) August 29; Margaret Whiting (singer) July 22.

**B. Deaths**　Lew Dockstader (minstrel performer); Louis A. Hirsch (composer) May 13; Glen MacDonough (lyricist) March 30; Theodore Morse (publisher/songwriter) May 25; E. T. Paull (bandmaster/composer); William H. Tyers (ragtime composer) April 18.

**C. Biographical**

**Performing Groups**　Mound City Blue Blowers.

**New Beginnings**　Back Stage Club (New York); Domino Records; National Barn Dance (Chicago); V. O. Stamps (Stamps-Baxter) Music Co. (Jacksonville, Texas).

**Miscellaneous**　Louis Armstrong moves to New York and Fletcher Henderson's band; Frederick Loewe (Austrian composer) comes to the United States; Old Time Fiddler's Convention takes place in Union Grove, New York.

**D. Publications**　John Jacob Niles, *Singing Soldiers*.

**E. Representative Works**

**Musicals**　Eubie Blake and Noble Sissle, *The Chocolate Dandies*; Con Conrad and W. Le Baron, *Moonlight*; Rudolf Friml, O. Harbach, and O. Hammerstein, *Rose Marie*; George and Ira Gershwin, *Lady, Be Good!—Sweet Little Devil*; Victor Herbert and R. J. Young, *The Dream Girl*; Tom Johnstone, *I'll Say She Is*; Cole Porter, *Greenwich Village Follies*; Sigmund Romberg and D. Donnelly, *The Student Prince*; Vincent Youmans, *Lollipop*.

**Songs**　Milton Ager and J. Yellen, *Bagdad—I Wonder What's Become of Sally*; Gene Austin and R. Bergere, *How Come You Do Me Like You Do*; Walter Donaldson and G. Whiting, *My Blue Heaven*; Ernie Erdman, *Nobody's Sweetheart*; George Gershwin and B. DeSylva, *Somebody Loves Me*; Isham Jones and G. Kahn, *I'll See You in My Dreams—It Had to Be You*; Ted Fiorito and G. Kahn, *Charley, My Boy*; Joseph Meyer and B. DeSylva, *California, Here I Come*; Vincent Youmans, *The Man I Love*.

**Other**　Bix Beiderbecke, *Davenport Blues*; Philip Braham, *Limehouse Blues*; Edward B. Hill, *Jazz Study No. 1*; King Oliver, *New Orleans Stomp*; Erno Rapee, *The Iron Horse* (film music); Leo Sowerby, *Syncopata*; Clarence Williams, *Gulf Coast Blues*; Spencer Williams, *Mahogany Hall Stomp*.

## Music—The Cultivated/Art Music Scene

**F. Births**　Hugh Aitken (composer) September 7; Warren Benson (composer) January 26; Thomas Beversdorf (trombone/composer) August 8; Mario di Bonaventura (conductor/publisher) February 20; Sarah Caldwell (impresario/conductor) March 6; Marilyn Costello (harpist); David Craighead (organist) January 24; Arthur B. Frackenpohl (composer) April 23; Earl George (composer/conductor) May 1; Lejaren Hiller (composer) February 23; Stanley Hollingsworth (composer) August 27; Joseph Kerman (critic) April 3; Ezra Laderman (composer) June 29; Billy Jim Layton (composer) November 14; Benjamin Lees (composer) January 8; Mildred Miller (soprano) December 16; Robert Parris (composer) May 21; Leonard Pennario (pianist) July 9; Julia Perry (composer) March 25; Alan Rich (critic) June 17; John White (musicologist) May 2; Victor Fell Yellin (musicologist) December 14.

**G. Deaths**　Monroe Althouse (composer/conductor) October 12; Johann Beck (conductor/composer) May 26; Nellie E. Brown (soprano) January; Isabella Stewart Gardner (patron of the arts) July 17; Victor Herbert (Irish-born composer/conductor) May 26; Henry C. Heyman (violinist) March 28; Edward B. Perry (pianist) June 13; A. J. Showalter (publisher/hymnist) September 24; Constantin Sternberg (Russian-born pianist) March 31; Camille Zeckwer (pianist/composer) August 7.

**H. Debuts**

**United States**　Jules Bledsoe (baritone—New York), Alexander Brailowsky (Russian pianist—New York), Antonio Cortis (Spanish tenor—Chicago), Marcel Grandjany (French harpist—New York), Fraser Gange (Scottish baritone—New York), Alton Jones (pianist—New York), Charles Kullman (tenor—New York), Georg Liebling (German pianist—New York), Yehudi Menuhin (age seven—San Francisco), Eugene Ormandy (Hungarian conductor—New York), Jesús María Sanromá (Puerto Rican pianist—Boston), Gladys Swarthout (mezzo-soprano—Chicago), John Charles Thomas (baritone—Washington, DC).

**Metropolitan Opera**    Max Altglass (Polish tenor), Karin Branzell (Swedish contralto), Toti dal Monte (Italian soprano), Nelson Eddy (baritone), Friedrich Schorr (Hungarian baritone), Tullio Serafin (Italian conductor).

**Other**    Frederick Jagel (tenor—Livorno).

## I. New Positions

**Conductors**    Guy Fraser Harrison (Eastman Theater Orchestra); Serge Koussevitzky (Boston Symphony Orchestra—to 1949); Tullio Serafin (Metropolitan Opera—to 1934); Alexander Smallens (Philadelphia Civic Opera—to 1931).

**Educational**    Carl Busch (Chicago Musical College); Saul Caston (Curtis—to 1942); Peter Dykema (Columbia—to 1939); Rubin Goldmark (head, composition, Juilliard); Howard Hanson (director, Eastman—to 1964); Ernest Hutcheson (Juilliard, dean in 1927); Paul Kochański (Juilliard—to 1934); Josef and Rosina Lhévinne (piano, Juilliard); Paul Reimers (voice, Juilliard); Francis Rogers (voice, Juilliard); Carlos Salzedo (harp, Curtis); Olga Samaroff (piano, Juilliard—to 1948); William E. Walter (director, Curtis Institute—to 1926).

**Other**    Olin Downes (music critic, *The New York Times*—to 1955); Ferdinand Dunkley (organ, Temple Sinai, New Orleans); William J. Henderson (music critic, *New York Sun*—to 1937); Edwin Lemare (municipal organ, Chattanooga—to 1929); Leonard Saminsky (music director, Temple Emanu-El, New York—to 1956); Moses Smith (music critic, *Boston American*—to 1934).

## J. Honors and Awards

**Honors**    Henry Hadley (American Academy); John Powell and Deems Taylor (National Institute).

**K. Biographical**    Ernö Balogh (Hungarian pianist), Johanna M. Beyer (German musicologist), Georg Liebling (German pianist), and Lea Luboshutz (Russian violinist) emigrate to the United States; Ernest Bloch and Toscha Seidel become American citizens; Aaron Copland returns to the United States after three years in Paris; Serge Koussevitzky (Russian conductor) comes to the United States; Walter Piston, graduating *summa cum laude* from Harvard, travels to Paris on a John Knowles Paine Fellowship and studies with Nadia Boulanger and Paul Dukas; Alexander Schreiner begins two years of organ study with Widor and Vierne in Paris; John P. Sousa joins Victor Herbert before Congress in defending composers' rights against the radio industry; Josef Stransky gives up music to becomes an art dealer.

## L. Musical Beginnings

**Performing Groups**    Adesdi Chorus (New York—Dessoff Choirs in 1930); Boston Sinfonietta; Los Angeles Grand Opera Association; Philadelphia Civic Opera Co. (to 1930); Portland Junior Symphony Orchestra (Oregon—first youth orchestra in United States); San Diego Morning Choral Club; Victor Salon Orchestra.

**Festivals**    Redlands Bowl Summer Music Festival.

**Educational**    Curtis Institute of Music (Philadelphia); Juilliard Graduate School; National Association of Schools of Music (NASM); St. Louis Institute of Music.

**Other**    Associated Glee Clubs of America; Guggenheim Foundation; *The League of Composers' Review (Modern Music)*; Lillenas Music Publishing Co.; National Music Week proclaimed; Washington (DC) Auditorium; Yaddo Artists' Colony (Saratoga Springs, New York).

## M. Music Publications

Clemens, G. Clara, *The Development of Song*
Finck, Henry T., *Musical Laughs*
Hill, Edward B., *Modern French Music*
Idelsohn, Abraham, *A History of Jewish Music*

Lhévinne, Josef, *Basic Principles in Pianoforte Playing*
Pratt, Waldo S., ed., *The New Encyclopedia of Music and Musicians*
Spaeth, Sigmund, *The Common Sense of Music*
Wedge, George, *Keyboard Harmony*

**N. Musical Compositions**

**Chamber Music**   George Antheil, *Violin Sonata No. 3—String Quartet No. 1*; Ernest Bloch, *Three Nocturnes for Piano Trio—From Jewish Life* (cello and piano)—*Méditation Hébraïque* (cello and piano)—*Violin Sonata No. 2, "Poème Mystique"*; Paolo Gallico, *Septet* (soprano, piano, horn, and string quartet); Louis Gruenberg, *Violin Sonata II*; Richard Hammond, *Oboe Sonata*; Frederick Jacobi, *String Quartet No. 1 on Indian Themes*; Tibor Serly, *String Quartet*; Gustav Strube, *Viola Sonata*.

**Choral/Vocal**   Samuel Barlow, *Three Songs from the Chinese*; Amy Beach, *Two Songs: A Mirage, Opus 100*; John J. Becker, *A Heine Song Cycle*; Mabel Wheeler Daniels, *Songs of Elfland*; Mary Carr Moore, *Beyond These Hills* (song cycle); Wallingford Riegger, *La Belle Dame sans Merci* (Coolidge Prize—first American to win); Randall Thompson, *Five Odes of Horace*; Virgil Thomson, *Psalm 135—Missa Brevis*.

**Concertos**   Gustav Strube, *Violin Concerto No. 1*.

**Operas**   Francesco DeLeone, *Algala* (Bispham Medal); Lazare Saminsky, *The Gagliarda of a Merry Plague* (opera-ballet); Humphrey Stewart, *The Hound of Heaven* (sacred music drama).

**Orchestra/Band**   John Parsons Beach, *Phantom Satyr*; Franz C. Bornschein, *The Sea God's Daughter* (symphonic poem); John Alden Carpenter, *Skyscrapers* (ballet); Henry Eichheim, *Chinese Legend* (ballet); Samuel Gardner, *Broadway* (symphonic poem); George Gershwin, *Rhapsody in Blue*; Mary Howe, *Poème*; Charles M. Loeffler, *Memories of My Childhood*; Otto Luening, *Symphonic Fantasia I*; Leopold D. Mannes, *Suite for Orchestra*; Douglas Moore, *The Pageant of P. T. Barnum*; Solomon Pinsleur, *Symphonic Ballad*; Carl Ruggles, *Men and Mountains*; John Philip Sousa, *Ancient and Honorable Artillery Company March—Black Horse Troop March—Marquette University March*; William Grant Still, *Darker America* (symphonic poem); Edwin John Stringham, *Visions*; Randall Thompson, *Symphonic Prelude, The Piper at the Gates of Dawn*; Hermann H. Wetzler, *Assisi*.

**Piano/Organ**   Amy Beach, *Two Compositions, Opus 102—Suite for Two Pianos Founded upon Old Irish Melodies, Opus 104*; John J. Becker, *Two Architectural Impressions*; Cecil Burleigh, *A Ballad of Early New England, Opus 58*; Victor Herbert, *Chant d'Amour* (organ)—*A Suite of Serenades*; Charles Ives, *Three Quarter-tone Pieces* (two pianos); Leo Ornstein, *Sonata No. 4 (?)*; Roger Sessions, *Three Chorale Preludes* (organ); Lamar Stringfield, *Nocturne*.

**Symphonies**   Aaron Copland, *Symphony for Organ and Orchestra*; Frederick Jacobi, *Symphony No. 1, "Assyrian"*; Lazare Saminsky, *Symphony No. 3, "Symphony of the Seas."*

# 1925

⚙

## Historical Highlights

The Scopes evolution trial takes place in Dayton, Tennessee; Billy Mitchell is court-martialed for criticizing the neglect of air power; the Chrysler Corporation is founded; the Charleston and cross-word puzzles become the latest national fads; Madison Square Garden opens its doors; Paul von Hindenburg becomes president of the new German Republic; an imprisoned Adolf Hitler writes *Mein Kampf*.

## World Cultural Highlights

**World Art**   Ernst Barlach, *Death*; Charles Despiau, *Eve*; Paul Klee, *A Tiny Tale of a Tiny Dwarf*; Joan Miró, *Harlequin's Carnival*; Pablo Picasso, *Three Dancers*; Georges Rouault, *The Apprentice*.

**World Literature**    Liam O'Flaherty, *The Informer*; Franz Kafka, *The Trial*; Mikhail Sholokhov, *The Don Stories*; Virginia Woolf, *Mrs. Dalloway*; William Butler Yeats, *A Vision*.

**World Music**    Leos Janáček, *The Makropoulos Affair*; Carl Nielsen, *Symphony No. 6, "Sinfonia Semplice"*; Dmitri Shostakovich, *Symphony No. 1*; Jean Sibelius, *Tapiola*.

**Miscellaneous**    The Kawai Piano Co. is founded in Japan; the Leopold Mozart Conservatory opens in Augsburg; births include Luciano Berio, Pierre Boulez, and Dietrich Fischer-Dieskau; deaths include Lovis Corinth, Pierre Louijs, Wladyslaw Reymont, and Erik Satie.

## American Art and Literature

**Births/Deaths**    Births include artist Robert Rauschenberg and literary figures William F. Buckley, Jr., Frank Gilroy, Maxine W. Kumin, Robin Moore, (Mary) Flannery O'Connor, William Styron, and Gore Vidal; deaths include art figures Paul Bartlett, George Bellows, Willard Metcalf, John Singer Sargent, Dwight Tryon, poet Amy Lowell, and author George Washington Cable.

**Art Works**    Joseph Albers, *Fugue*; Arthur B. Davies, *The Umbrian Mountains*; Charles Demuth, *Eggplants and Plums* (?); Arthur Dove, *Goin' Fishin'*; Edward Hopper, *The House by the Railroad*; Yasuo Kuniyoshi, *Strong Woman and Child*; George Luks, *The Miner*; Arnold Ronnebeck, *Brooklyn Bridge*; Ben Shahn, *Little Church* (?); John Storrs, *New York* (?)—*Gendarme Seated*.

**Literature**    Sherwood Anderson, *Dark Laughter*; F. Scott Fitzgerald, *The Great Gatsby*; DuBose Heyward, *Porgy*; Sidney Howard, *They Knew What They Wanted* (Pulitzer Prize); George Kelly, *Craig's Wife* (Pulitzer Prize); Sinclair Lewis, *Arrowsmith* (Pulitzer Prize—refused); Amy Lowell, *What's O'Clock* (Pulitzer Prize); Anne Parrish, *The Perennial Bachelor* (Harper's Prize).

## Music—The Vernacular/Commercial Scene

**A. Births**    Marie "TV Mama" Adams (singer) October 19; Gene Ammons (saxophonist/band-leader) April 14; Felice Boudleaux (songwriter) August 7; Roy James Brown (singer) September 10; Charlie Byrd (guitarist) September 16; Clifton Chenier (accordionist/singer) June 25; June Christy (singer) November 20; Al Cohn (saxophonist/composer) November 24; Sammy Davis, Jr. (singer) December 8; Bill Dixon (trumpeter/composer) October 5; Bill Haley, Jr. (singer) July 6; B. B. King (singer) September 16; James Moody (saxophonist/flutist) February 26; Donald O'Connor (singer/actor) August 30; Art Pepper (saxophonist) September 1; Oscar Peterson (pianist) August 15; Marty Robbins (singer/writer) September 26; Zoot Sims (saxophonist) October 29; Jimmy Smith (organist) December 8; Hank Thompson (singer/writer) September 3; Mel Tormé (singer) September 13; Roger Williams (pianist); Mac Wiseman (singer/guitarist) June 4.

**B. Deaths**    A. Baldwin Sloane (composer) February 21; Henry W. Petrie (singer/composer) May 25.

**C. Biographical**

**Performing Groups**    Alexander's Day Breakers (Bill Boyd's Cowboy Ramblers); Blue Devils (Walter Page Band, Oklahoma); Boswell Sisters (first recordings); Hot Five (Louis Armstrong); South Memphis Jug Band.

**New Beginnings**    Champion Records (Richmond, Indiana); Grand Ole Opry (WSM Barn Dance—Nashville).

**Miscellaneous**    Josephine Baker takes her act to Paris.

**D. Publications**    J. Johnson, *American Negro Spirituals*; Julius Mattfeld, *Folk Music of the Western Hemisphere*; Erno Rapee, *Motion Picture Moods for Pianos and Organs, Adapted to Fifty-Two Moods and Situations*.

**E. Representative Works**

**Musicals**    Irving Berlin and A. Kaufman, *The Cocoanuts*; Rudolf Friml and B. Hooker, *The Vagabond King*; George and Ira Gershwin, *Tiptoes*; G. Gershwin, O. Harbach, and O. Hammerstein, *Song of the Flame*; R. Henderson and B. DeSylva, *Big Boy*; Jerome Kern, O. Harbach, and O. Hammerstein, *Sunny*; Cole Porter, *Out O' Luck*; Rodgers and Hart, *Dearest Enemy*; Vincent Youmans, *A Night Out*; V. Youmans and O. Harbach, *No, No, Nanette*.

**Songs**  H. Akst, S. Lewis, and J. Young, *Dinah*; Irving Berlin, *Always*; B. Bernie, M. Pinkard, and K. Casey, *Sweet Georgia Brown*; B. DeSylva and J. Meyer, *If You Knew Susie Like I Know Susie*; W. Donaldson and G. Kahn, *Yes Sir, That's My Baby*; Dave Dreyer and H. Ruby, *Cecilia*; R. Henderson and B. DeSylva, *Alabamy Bound*; Ray Henderson and J. Young, *Five Foot Two, Eyes of Blue*; Richard A. Whiting, *Sleepy Time Gal*; Harry M. Woods, *Paddlin' Madelin' Home*.

**Other**  Louis Gruenberg, *Jazzberries—Jazz Suite* (orchestra); James P. Johnson, *Carolina Shout*; Jelly Roll Morton, *Black Bottom Stomp*; Erno Rapee, *What Price Glory?* (film music); Leo Sowerby, *Monotony*.

## Music—The Cultivated/Art Music Scene

**F. Births**  Adele Addison (soprano) July 24; Samuel Baron (flutist/conductor) April 25; Cathy Berberian (avant garde singer) July 4; Edith Borroff (musicologist) August 2; Will Gay Bottje (composer/flutist) June 30; Martin Chusid (musicologist) August 19; Irene Dalis (mezzo-soprano) October 8; Mattiwilda Dobbs (soprano) July 11; Charles Benton Fisk (organ builder) February 7; Armando Ghitalla (trumpeter) June 1; Charles Hamm (musicologist) April 21; Grace Hoffman (mezzo-soprano) January 14; Eugene Istomin (pianist) November 26; James King (tenor) May 22; Daniel Lewis (conductor) May 10; Robert Linn (composer) August 11; Chester Ludgin (baritone) May 20; James Lyons (critic) November 24; Americo Marino (conductor) February 5; Marilyn Mason (organist) June 29; William Mayer (composer) November 18; Kirke Mechem (composer) August 16; Patrice Munsel (soprano) May 14; Gunther Schuller (composer/conductor) November 22; Berl Senofsky (violinist) April 15; Ruth Slenczynska (pianist) January 15; Hale Smith (composer) June 29; Leland Smith (composer) August 6; Howard Smither (musicologist) November 15; Paul William Whear (composer) November 13; Ruth White (composer) September 1.

**G. Deaths**  Carl Faelten (German-born pianist) July 20; Theodore Presser (publisher/philanthropist) October 28; José Quintón (Puerto Rican pianist/composer) December 19; Alwina Valleria (soprano) February 17; John W. Work (conductor/composer) September 7.

**H. Debuts**

**United States**  Marian Anderson (contralto—New York), Florence Austral (Australian soprano—tour), Wilhelm Furtwängler (German conductor—New York), Artur Rodzinski (Polish conductor—Philadelphia), Irene Scharrer (British pianist—New York), Oscar Shumsky (violinist, age eight—Philadelphia), Alexander L. Steinert (pianist—Boston), Joseph Szigeti (Hungarian violinist—Philadelphia), Donald Tovey (British pianist), Isabelle Vengerova (Russian pianist—Detroit), Robert Whitney (conductor—Chicago).

**Metropolitan Opera**  Mario Basiola (Italian baritone), Nanny Larsén-Todsen (Swedish soprano), Maria Müller (Austrian soprano), Carmela Ponselle (mezzo-soprano).

**Other**  Joseph Bentonelli (tenor—Nice).

**I. New Positions**

**Conductors**  Willem van Hoogstraten (Portland [Oregon] Symphony Orchestra—to 1938); Karl Krueger (Seattle Symphony Orchestra—to 1932); Gennaro Papi (Chicago Civic Opera—to 1932); Joseph F. Wagner (Boston Civic Symphony Orchestra—to 1944).

**Educational**  Ernst Bacon (Eastman—to 1928); Ernest Bloch (director, San Francisco Conservatory—to 1930); Felix Borowski (Northwestern University—to 1942); Leroy Robertson (music chair, Brigham Young—to 1948); Felix Salmond (cello, Curtis—to 1942); Leo Sowerby (American Conservatory, Chicago—to 1962); Bernard Wagenaar (Juilliard—to 1968); Herbert Witherspoon (president, Chicago Musical College—to 1931).

**Other**  Samuel Chotzinoff (music critic, *New York World*—to 1931); Albert Goldberg (music critic, *Chicago Herald Examiner*—to 1936).

**J. Honors and Awards**

**Honors**  Henry Hadley (PhD, Tufts); Roland Hayes (Spingard Medal); Wallingford Riegger (PhD, Cincinnati Conservatory).

**K. Biographical**  Joseph Achron (Polish violinist/composer), Richard Dyer-Bennet (British singer), Gene Gutchë (German composer), Sergius Kagen (Russian composer/pianist), and Herman L. Schlicker (German organ builder) come to the United States; William Dawson goes to Chicago for further music study; Anis Fuleihan and Jascha Heifetz become naturalized American citizens; George Herzog (Hungarian ethnomusicologist) comes to the United States; Ottorino Respighi makes a performing/conducting tour of the United States; Igor Stravinsky makes his first conducting/performing tour of the United States; Virgil Thomson passes up several job opportunities and returns to Paris for a 15-year stay; Ernest White (Canadian organist) moves to New York.

**L. Musical Beginnings**

**Performing Groups**   American Society of Ancient Instruments (Philadelphia); Boston Civic Orchestra; Charleston Philharmonic Orchestra (South Carolina); Des Moines Civic Music Association; Haydn Male Chorus (Kansas City); New Music Society of San Francisco; Pace Jubilee Singers (Chicago); Philadelphia Chamber String Sinfonietta; Popovich Brothers Yugoslav Tamburitzen Orchestra; Women's Symphony Orchestra of Chicago.

**Educational**   Denver College of Music; Mu Beta Psi Music Fraternity; Turtle Bay Music School (New York).

**Other**   American Composer's Project; Elizabeth Sprague Coolidge Foundation; Coolidge Auditorium, Library of Congress; Fair Park Music Hall (Dallas); Guggenheim Fellowships; Mosque Theatre (Symphony Hall, Newark).

**M. Music Publications:**

Audsley, George A., *The Temple of Tone*
Auer, Leopold, *Masterworks and Their Interpretation*
Bauer, M. and Peyser, E., *How Music Grew*
Dickinson, Edward, *The Spirit of Music*
Frankenstein, Alfred, *Syncopating Saxophones*
Hamilton, Clarence, *Piano Music, Its Composers and Characteristics*
Kelley, Edgar S., *Musical Instruments*
Lahee, Henry C., *The Orchestra: A Brief Outline of Its Development in Europe and America*
Mason, Daniel G., *Artistic Ideals*
Metcalf, Frank, *American Writers and Compilers of Sacred Music*
Van Vechten, Carl, *Red: Papers on Musical Subjects*
Witherspoon, Herbert, *Singing: A Treatise for Teachers and Singers*

**N. Musical Compositions**

**Chamber Music**   Ernest Bloch, *In the Mountains, Night* (string quartet); Eugene M. Bonner, *Piano Quintet*; William Dawson, *Piano Trio*; Isadore Freed, *String Quartet No. 1*; Daniel G. Mason, *Variations on a Theme of John Powell* (string quartet); John Powell, *Violin Sonata No. 2*; Quincy Porter, *String Quartet No. 2*; Bernard Rogers, *String Quartet No. 2*; Carl Ruggles, *Portals* (13 string instruments); Ernest Schelling, *Divertimento* (piano quintet); Arthur Shepherd, *Triptych for High Voice and String Quartet*; Gustav Strube, *Cello Sonata*; Edgard Varèse, *Intégrales*; Bernard Wagenaar, *Violin Sonata* (Society for the Publication of American Music Award); Adolph Weiss, *String Quartet No. 1*; Paul White, *String Quartet*.

**Choral/Vocal**   Amy Beach, *Three Songs, Opus 117*; Howard Hanson, *The Lament for Beowulf, Opus 25*; Frederick Jacobi, *The Poet in the Desert*; Werner Josten, *Ode to St. Cecilia's Day*; Wesley La Violette, *Requiem*; Charles S. Skilton, *The Guardian Angel* (cantata); Leo Sowerby, *The Vision of Sir Launfal* (cantata); William Grant Still, *Levee Land*; Virgil Thomson, *Agnus Dei* (male chorus).

**Concertos**   Joseph Achron, *Violin Concerto No. 1, Opus 60*; Cecil Burleigh, *Violin Concerto No. 3*; George Gershwin, *Piano Concerto in F*.

**Operas**   Joseph C. Breil, *Der Asra*; Charles W. Cadman, *The Garden of Mystery*; Hamilton Forrest, *Yzdra* (Bispham Medal); Franklin Patterson, *The Echo* (Bispham Medal).

**Orchestra/Band**   George Antheil, *Ballet mécanique—A Jazz Symphonietta*; John Parsons

Beach, *New Orleans Street Cries—Mardi Gras*; Seth Bingham, *Pioneer America*; Ernest Bloch, *Concerto Grosso No. 1*; Eugene M. Bonner, *Whispers of Heavenly Death—White Nights*; Felix Borowski, *Semiramis* (symphonic poem); Charles W. Cadman, *Rappaccini's Daughter* (incidental music); Rosetter Gleason Cole, *Heroic Piece, Opus 39* (with organ); Aaron Copland, *Music for the Theater*; Richard Donovan, *Wood-Notes*; Herbert Elwell, *The Happy Hypocrite* (ballet—Eastman Publication Award); Carl Eppert, *The Pioneer*; Arthur Fickénscher, *Willowwave and Welloway*; Henry F. Gilbert, *Symphonic Piece*; Ferde Grofé, *Mississippi Suite*; Victor Herbert, *A Love Sonnet*; Philip James, *Bret Harte Overture*; Carl McKinley, *Masquerade*; Quincy Porter, *Ukrainian Suite*; John Powell, *At the Fair*; Bernard Rogers, *Prelude to Hamlet*; Roger Sessions, *Turandot* (incidental music); John P. Sousa, *The National Game March—Universal Peace March*; Deems Taylor, *Jurgen, Opus 17* (symphonic poem); Powell Weaver, *Plantation Overture*; Emerson Whithorne, *Sooner or Later* (ballet).

**Piano/Organ**  John J. Becker, *Two Chinese Miniatures*; Henry Cowell, *The Banshee*; Ruth Crawford, *Five Preludes for Piano*; Eastwood Lane, *Eastern Sea Suite*; Vittorio Ricti, *Sonatina*; Dane Rudhyar, *Three Paeans*.

**Symphonies**  Frances McCollin, *Sinfonietta I*; Harold Morris, *Symphony No. 1, "Prospice"*; Bernard Rogers, *Symphony No. 1, "Adonis."*

# 1926

❀

## Historical Highlights

R. H. Goddard launches the first practical solid-fuel rocket; the first radio network, the National Broadcasting Co. (NBC), is organized; Congress creates the Army Air Corps and establishes the Great Smokey Mountains, Mammoth Cave, and Shenandoah National Parks; Admiral Richard Byrd flies over the North Pole; Gertrude Ederle becomes the first woman to swim the English Channel.

## World Cultural Highlights

**World Art**  Marc Chagall, *Lover's Bouquet*; Vasili Kandinsky, *Several Circles*; René Magritte, *The Menaced Assassin*; Henri Matisse, *Odalisque with Tambourine*; Joan Miró, *Dog Barking at the Moon*.

**World Literature**  James Joyce, *Exiles*; Thomas Lawrence, *The Seven Pillars of Wisdom*; A. A. Milne, *Winnie the Pooh*; Sean O'Casey, *The Plough and the Stars*.

**World Music**  Béla Bartók, *Piano Concerto No. 1*; Alban Berg, *Lyric Suite*; Paul Hindemith, *Cardillac*; Leos Janáček, *Glagolitic Mass—Sinfonietta*; Zoltán Kodály, *Háry János*.

**Miscellaneous**  The NHK Symphony Orchestra of Japan is founded; births include Hans Werner Henze, Edouard van Remoortel, and Klaus Tennstedt; deaths include H. Rider Haggard, Claude Monet, Edouard van Remoortel, Rainer M. Rilke, and Israel Zangwill.

## American Art and Literature Highlights

**Births/Deaths**  Births include artist Ellen Lanyon, Robert Vickrey, and literary figures Alice Adams, A. R. Ammons, Neal Cassady, Allen Ginsberg, John C. Holmes, Alison Lurie, Frank O'Hara, William DeWitt Snodgrass, and Richard Yates; deaths include artists Thomas Moran, Charles M. Russell, Frederick Sykes, John F. Weir, and poet George Sterling.

**Art Works**  Gutzon Borglum, *The Wars of America*; Edwin Dickinson, *The Cello Player*; Lyonel Feininger, *Victory of the Sloop Maria*; Edward Hopper, *Eleven A.M.*; Robert Laurent, *The Wave*; Paul Manship, *Indian Hunter*; Georgia O'Keeffe, *Black Iris*; Abraham Rattner, *The Flying Trapeze*; Charles Sheeler, *Delmonico Building*; Max Weber, *Alone*; William Zorach, *Child with Cat*.

**Literature**    Louis Bromfield, *Early Autumn* (Pulitzer Prize); Hilda Doolittle, *Palimpsest*; Edna Ferber, *Show Boat*; Ernest Hemingway, *The Sun Also Rises*; Will James, *Smoky*; Vachel Lindsay, *The Candle in the Cabin*; Amy Lowell, *East Wind*; Eugene O'Neill, *The Great God Brown*; Thorne Smith, *Topper*; Leonora Speyer, *Fiddler's Farewell* (Pulitzer Prize); Sara Teasdale, *Dark of the Moon*.

## Music — The Vernacular/Commercial Scene

**A. Births**    Tony Bennett (singer) August 3; Chuck Berry (singer/writer) October 18; Jimmy Cleveland (trombonist) May 3; John Coltrane (saxophonist/bandleader) September 23; Ray Copeland (trumpeter) July 17; Miles Davis (trumpeter/bandleader) May 25; Blossom Dearie (singer/pianist) April 28; Lee Dorsey (singer) December 4; Buddy Greco (pianist/arranger) August 14; Guitar Slim (guitarist) December 10; Carolyn Leigh (lyricist) August 21; Julie London (singer) September 26; Max Morath (jazz pianist) October 1; Webb Pierce (singer) August 8; Ray Price (singer) January 12; Jerry Ross (singer/writer) March 9; Bobby Short (pianist/singer) September 15; Big Mama Thornton (singer) December 11; Gwen Verdon (singer/dancer) January 13.

**B. Deaths**    A. Baldwin Sloane (composer) February 21; Rida Johnson Young (lyricist) May 8.

**C. Biographical**

**Performing Groups**    Blue Jay Singers; Dark Clouds of Joy (Kansas City); McKinney's Cotton Pickers; New Orleans Wanderers; Jimmie Noone's Apex Club Orchestra; Red Hot Peppers (Chicago); Chick Webb Jazz Band.

**New Beginnings**    The National Broadcasting Company Network; *Phonograph Monthly Review*.

**Miscellaneous**    Jesse Crawford becomes organist at the Paramount Theatre, New York (to 1933).

**D. Publications**    R. Nathaniel Dett, *Religious Folk Songs of the Negro*; Charles K. Harris, *After the Ball: Forty Years of Melody*; H. O. Osgood, *So This Is Jazz*; Minnie E. Sears, *Song Index: An Index to More Than 12,000 Songs . . .* ; Sigmund Spaeth, *Read 'Em and Weep: A Treasury of American Songs . . .* ; Paul Whiteman and M.M. McBride, *Jazz*.

**E. Representative Works**

**Musicals**    R. Friml, O. Harbach, and O. Hammerstein, *The Wild Rose*; L. E. Gensler and B. DeSylva, *Queen High*; George and Ira Gershwin, *Oh, Kay!*; James F. Hanley and E. Dowling, *Honeymoon Lane*; Burt Kalman and H. B. Smith, *Countess Maritza*; Richard Rodgers, *Lido Lady*; Rodgers and Hart, *The Girl Friend—Betsy*; S. Romberg, O. Harbach, and O. Hammerstein, *The Desert Song*; Harry Ruby and B. Kalmar, *The Ramblers*; Vincent Youmans and A. Caldwell, *Oh, Please*.

**Songs**    Harry Akst and B. Davis, *Baby Face*; Joseph A. Burke and A. Dubin, *Tip-Toe Through the Tulips*; Hoagy Carmichael, *Washboard Blues*; R. Henderson and B. DeSylva, *Birth of the Blues*; R. Henderson and M. Dixon, *Bye, Bye Blackbird*; J. P. Johnson and H. Creamer, *If I Could Be with You One Hour Tonight*; Ben Ryan, *The Gang That Sang Heart of My Heart*; R. Turk and L. Handman, *Are You Lonesome Tonight?*; Harry M. Woods, *When the Red, Red Robin Comes Bob, Bob, Bobbin' Along*.

**Other**    Duke Ellington, *East St. Louis Toodle-Oo*; James P. Johnson, *Eccentricity Waltz*; Jelly Roll Morton, *Cannonball Blues*.

## Music — The Cultivated Art/Music Scene

**F. Births**    Herbert Beattie (bass) August 23; Charles Bressler (tenor) April 1; Earle Brown (composer) December 26; Barney Childs (composer) February 13; Paul Cooper (composer) May 19; John Crosby (conductor/impresario) July 12; Morton Feldman (composer) January 12; Carlisle Floyd (composer) June 11; Allen Forte (theorist) December 23; Kenneth Gaburo (composer) July 5; Herbert Handt (tenor/conductor) May 26; Lee Hoiby (composer/pianist) February 17; Ben Johnston (composer/theorist) March 15; Betsy Jolas (composer) August 5; Julius Katchen (pianist) August 15; Meyer Kupferman (clarinetist/composer) July 3; H. C. Robbins Landon (musicologist)

March 6; Evelyn Lear (soprano) January 8; Theodore Lettvin (pianist) October 29; Raymond Lewenthal (pianist) August 29; Robert Hall Lewis (composer) April 22; Ray Luke (composer) May 30; James McCracken (tenor) December 16; Nell Rankin (mezzo-soprano) January 3; Seymour Shifrin (composer/educator) February 28; William O. Smith (clarinetist) September 22; David Tudor (pianist) January 20; Paul Wolfe (violinist/composer) May 8; Robert A. Wykes (composer) May 19.

**G. Deaths**    Frederic Ayres (composer) March 17; Joseph C. Breil (composer) January 23; Henry T. Finck (critic) October 1; Frederick Neil Innes (trombonist/bandmaster) December 31; Franz Kneisel (Romanian-born violinist) March 26; Leander S. Sherman (publisher) April 5; Patty Stair (organist) April 26; Frederick Zech, Jr.(composer/conductor) October 25.

**H. Debuts**

**United States**    Lillian Fuchs (violinist—New York), Walter Gieseking (German pianist—New York), Josef Gingold (violinist—New York), Yehudi Menuhin (age nine, San Francisco), Eidé Norena (Norwegian soprano—Chicago), Solomon (British pianist—tour), Alexander Tcherepnin (Russian pianist—tour)

**Metropolitan Opera**    Vincenzo Bellezza (Italian conductor), George Cehanovsky (Russian baritone), Edytha Fleischer (German soprano), Maria Ivogün (Hungarian soprano), Mary Lewis (soprano), Pavel Ludikar (Czech bass-baritone), Lauritz Melchior (Danish tenor), Ezio Pinza (Italian bass), Marion Talley (soprano).

**Other**    John Brownlee (baritone—London); Lillian Evanti (soprano—Nice).

**I. New Positions**

**Conductors**    Antonio Modarelli (Pittsburgh Symphony Orchestra—to 1937).

**Educational**    Marion Bauer (NYU—to 1951); Martin Bernstein (NYU—to 1972); Josef Hofmann (director, Curtis Institute—to 1938); Jacob Kwalwasser (Syracuse University—to 1954); Harl McDonald (University of Pennsylvania—to 1946); Douglas Moore (Columbia—to 1962); Walter Piston (Harvard—to 1960); Wallingford Riegger (Ithaca College—to 1928).

**Other**    Amy Beach (first president, Association of American Women Composers); John K. Sherman (music critic, *Minneapolis Star*—to 1971); Pietro Yon (organ, St. Patrick's Cathedral, New York—to 1943).

**J. Honors and Awards**

**Honors**    Charles W. Cadman (PhD, USC); Charles M. Loeffler (PhD, Yale); Albert Spalding (National Institute).

**K. Biographical**    Theodore Baker retires from G. Schirmer and goes back to Germany; Edwin Gerschefski enters Yale for music study; Martha Graham presents her first independent dance concert in New York; Roy Harris begins music study with Nadia Boulanger; Josef Hofmann, Dane Rudhyar, and Hugo Weisgall become American citizens; Pierre Luboshutz (Russian pianist) and Jacob Weinberg (Russian pianist/composer) emigrate to the United States; Colin McPhee leaves his studies in Paris to return to New York; Artur Rodzinski becomes assistant to Leopold Stokowski in Philadelphia; Alexander Tcherepnin (Russian pianist/composer) tours the United States; Virgil Thomson meets Gertrude Stein; Helen Traubel refuses an opportunity to sing at the Metropolitan Opera; Adolph Weiss becomes the first American to study with Schoenberg.

**L. Musical Beginnings**

**Performing Groups**    Dayton Piano Symphony; Chicago Woman's String Quartet; Elman String Quartet (New York); Pittsburgh Symphony Orchestra.

**Festivals**    Three Choirs Festival (New York).

**Educational**    Detroit Music Settlement School; Duquesne Music Department; Jacksonville College of Music (Florida); National School Band Association; Westminster Choir College (Dayton, Ohio—New York in 1929).

**Other**    Association of American Women Composers; Elkan Publishing Co. II (Elkan-Vogel in

1928—Philadelphia); Edwin F. Kalmus, Music Publisher (New York); Walter W. Naumburg Foundation; *Phonograph Monthly Review (American Record Guide)*; Verne Q. Powell Flutes Inc. (Boston); Shea's Buffalo Theater; Kenneth Warren, Violin Dealer and Repairer (Chicago).

## M. Music Publications

Coleman, R. H., *The Modern Hymnal* (Baptist)
Davison, Archibald T., *Music Education in America*
Densmore, Frances, *The American Indians and Their Music*
Erb, John L., *Music Appreciation for the Student*
Finck, Henry T., *My Adventures in the Golden Age . . .*
Giddings, T. P. and Maddy, J. C., *Instrumental Technique for Orchestra and Band*
Hamilton, Clarence, *Epochs in Musical Progress*
Spaeth, Sigmund, *Words and Music*
VanderCook, Hale A., *Teaching the High School Band*

## N. Musical Compositions

**Chamber Music**    Frederick Ayres, *Violin Sonata No. 2—Cello Sonata*; Cecil Burleigh, *Violin Sonata, Opus 29, "From the Life of St. Paul"*; Ruth Crawford, *Violin Sonata*; Wesley La Violette, *String Quartet No. 1*; Mary Carr Moore, *String Quartet in G Minor*; Quincy Porter, *Violin Sonata No. 1*; Vittorio Rieti, *String Quartet No. 1*; Arthur Shepherd, *String Quartet in G Minor*; Virgil Thomson, *Sonata da Chiesa* (wind instruments); Bernard Wagenaar, *String Quartet No. 1*; Adolph Weiss, *String Quartet No. 2*.

**Choral/Vocal**    Louis Gruenberg, *Creation, Opus 23* (baritone and eight instruments); David S. Smith, *The Vision of Isaiah*; Gustav Strube, *Lazarus* (cantata); Virgil Thomson, *Sanctus* (male chorus); Emerson Whithorne, *Saturday's Child* (song cycle).

**Concertos**    George Antheil, *Piano Concerto No. 2*; Aaron Copland, *Piano Concerto*; Howard Hanson, *Organ Concerto, Opus 27*; Sergei Rachmaninoff, *Piano Concerto No. 4* (revised 1941); Vittorio Rieti, *Piano Concerto No. 1*; Leo Sowerby, *Medieval Poem for Organ and Orchestra*.

**Operas**    Alberto Bimboni, *Winona*; Charles W. Cadman, *The Ghost of Lollypop Bay* (operetta)—*A Witch of Salem*; Eleanor Freer, *The Chilkoot Maiden*; Ralph Lyford, *Castle Agrazant* (Bispham Medal); Deems Taylor, *The King's Henchman, Opus 19*; Carl Venth, *The Rebel*.

**Orchestra/Band**    Ernst Bacon, *Fantasy and Fugue for Orchestra*; F. E. Bigelow, *Our Director March*; Marc Blitzstein, *Sarabande for Orchestra*; Ernest Bloch, *Four Episodes for Chamber Orchestra—America: an Epic Rhapsody*; Howard Hanson, *Pan and the Priest, Opus 26* (symphonic poem); Sándor Harmati, *The Jeweled Tree* (incidental music); Victor Herbert, *A Cannibal Dance—Persian Dance and March*; Otto Luening, *Sister Beatrice* (incidental music); Daniel G. Mason, *Chanticleer Overture*; Quincy Porter, *A Midsummer Night's Dream* (incidental music)—*Orchestra Suite in C Minor*; Walllingford Riegger, *Rhapsody for Orchestra, Opus 5*; Dane Rudhyar, *Four Pentagrams*; David S. Smith, *Epic Poem, Opus 55*; John P. Sousa, *Marches—Gridiron Club—Old Ironsides—Pride of the Wolverines—Sesqui-Centennial Exposition*; Leo Sowerby, *Medieval Poem*; William Grant Still, *Suite, From the Black Belt*; Arthur B. Whiting, *The Golden Cage* (dance pageant).

**Piano/Organ**    Marian Bauer, *Sun Splendor* (two pianos—orchestrated 1934); Cecil Burleigh, *Three Mood Pictures, Opus 56—Two Sketches from the Orient, Opus 55*; Aaron Copland, *Three Moods*; Herbert Elwell, *Sonata*; George Gershwin, *Three Preludes*; Vittorio Rieti, *Piano Suite*; Roger Sessions, *Three Chorale Preludes* (organ); Charles S. Skilton, *American Indian Fantasy* (organ—orchestrated 1932); Deems Taylor, *Five Inventions—Ten Easy Pieces and a Coda for Piano*.

**Symphonies**    George Antheil, *Symphony in F Major*; Philip G. Clapp, *Symphony No. 5 in D Major—Symphony No. 6 in B Major, "Golden Gate"*; Lazare Saminsky, *Symphony No. 4*; Bernard Wagenaar, *Symphony No. 1*.

# 1927

❧

## Historical Highlights

Charles Lindbergh becomes the first to fly solo across the Atlantic—33½ hours to Paris; "The Jazz Singer" is the first sound movie to be released; work begins on the Mount Rushmore Monument; Babe Ruth sets the home run record of 60 in one season; Stalin expels Trotsky and his followers from the Russian Communist Party and assumes full control.

## World Cultural Highlights

**World Art**   Ernst Barlach, *Hovering Angel*; Constantin Brancusi, *Bird in Space*; George Braque, *The Black Rose*; Max Ernst, *The Great Forest*; Paul Klee, *Seaside Town, South of France*

**World Literature**   Elizabeth Bowen, *The Hotel*; Hermann Hesse, *Steppenwolf*; François Mauriac, *Thérèse Desqueyroux*; Virginia Woolf, *To the Lighthouse*.

**World Music**   Reinhold Glière, *The Red Poppy*; Ottorino Respighi, *Church Windows*, *Brazilian Impressions*; Dmitri Shostakovich, *Symphony No. 2*; Igor Stravinsky, *Oedipus Rex*.

**Miscellaneous**   The International Frédéric Chopin Piano Competition begins in Warsaw; births include Paul Badura-Skoda, Jean Casadesus, Günther Grass, and Mstislav Rostropovich; deaths include Juan Gris, Hugo Riemann, and Wilhelm Stenhammar.

## American Art and Literature Highlights

**Births/Deaths**   Births include art figures Allen Kaprow, Alex Katz, Edward Kienholz, Alfred Leslie, David von Schlegall, Ernest Trova, and literary figures John Ashbery, Galway Kinnell, Judith Krantz, Robert Ludlum, W. S. Merwin, and Neil Simon; deaths include artists William Dana, Maria Oakey Dewing, and literary figures James Curwood and Frank L. Stanton.

**Art Works**   George Biddle, *Cows and Sugar Cane* (?); Stuart Davis, *Egg Beater No. 1*; Charles Demuth, *My Egypt*; Lyonel Feininger, *The Steamer "Odin"*; Chaim Gross, *Mother and Child at Play*; Yasuo Kuniyoshi, *Self-Portrait as a Golfer*; Gaston Lachaise, *Standing Woman*; Reginald Marsh, *Lunch*; Elie Nadelman, *Man in a Top Hat*; Hugo Robus, *Woman Combing Her Hair— Despair*.

**Literature**   Willa Cather, *Death Comes for the Archbishop*; William Faulkner, *Mosquitoes*; Paul Green, *In Abraham's Bosom* (Pulitzer Prize); Ernest Hemingway, *Men without Women*; James W. Johnson, *God's Trombones*; Sinclair Lewis, *Elmer Gantry*; Don Marquis, *Archy and Mehitabel*; Edwin A. Robinson, *Tristram* (Pulitzer Prize); Thornton Wilder, *The Bridge of San Luis Rey* (Pulitzer Prize).

## Music—The Vernacular/Commercial Scene

**A. Births**   Lee Allen (saxophonist) July 2; Mose Allison (pianist/trumpeter) November 11; Harry Belafonte (singer) March 1; Alex Bradford (singer/writer) January 23; Chris Conner (singer) November 8; Barbara Cook (singer) October 25; Stan Getz (bandleader/saxophonist) February 2; Ferlin Husky (singer) December 3; Dick Hyman (pianist/composer) March 8; Elvin Jones (drummer) September 9; John Kander (composer) March 18; Anita Kerr (singer) October 31; Lee Konitz (saxophonist) October 13; Al Martino (singer) October 7; Giselle MacKenzie (singer) January 10; Guy Mitchell (singer) February 27; Gerry Mulligan (saxophonist/arranger) April 6; Jimmy C. Newman (singer) August 27; Patti Page (singer) November 8; Charlie Palmieri (pianist/band-leader); Junior Parker (harmonica/singer) March 3; Lee Pockriss (composer) January 20; Johnnie Ray (singer/writer) January 10; Susan Reed (singer/writer); "Doc" Severinsen (trumpeter/band-leader) July 7; Marion Williams (singer) August 29.

**B. Deaths**    Ernest R. Ball (composer) May 3; Blind Tom Boone (pianist/composer) May 17.

**C. Biographical**

**Performing Groups**    Black Bottom Stompers (Chicago); Carter Family; Casa Loma Orchestra (originally the Orange Blossoms); Chicago Footwarmers; Chickasaw Syncopators; Memphis Jug Band.

**D. Publications**    Axel Christensen, *Instruction Book for Jazz and Novelty Piano Playing*; John Jacob Niles, *Songs My Mother Never Taught Me*; Sigmund Spaeth, *Weep Some More, My Lady*.

**E. Representative Works**

**Musicals**    Irving Berlin, *Ziegfield Follies of 1927*; George M. Cohan, *The Merry Malones*; R. Friml and B. Hooker, *The White Eagle*; George and Ira Gershwin, *Funny Face*; R. Henderson and B. De Sylva, *Good News*; Raymond Hubbell, *The Girl from Cook's*; J. Kern and O. Hammerstein, *Show Boat*; Richard Rodgers, M. Hart, and H. Fields, *A Connecticut Yankee*; Harry Ruby and B. Kalmar, *The Five O'Clock Girl*; H. Tierney and J. McCarthy, *Rio Rita*; Vincent Youmans, *Hit the Deck*.

**Songs**    M. Ager and J. Yellen, *Ain't She Sweet?*; Irving Berlin, *Blue Skies*; Hoagy Carmichael, *Stardust*; Sunny Clapp, *Girl of My Dreams*; David Dreyer, *Me and My Shadow*; Sammy Fain, *Let a Smile Be Your Umbrella*; Neil Moret and G. Kahn, *Chloe*; Mary H. Morgan and H. Taylor, *Bless This House*; Horatio Nicholls and E. Leslie, *Among My Souvenirs*; Bob Nolan, *Tumbling Tumbleweeds*; Harry M. Woods, *Side by Side—I'm Looking Over a Four-Leaf Clover*.

**Other**    Duke Ellington, *Black and Tan Fantasy*; Meade Lewis, *Honky Tonk Train Blues*; King Oliver, *Doctor Jazz*; Erno Rapee, *Seventh Heaven* (film music); Clarence Williams, *Cushion Foot Stomp*.

## Music—The Cultivated/Art Music Scene

**F. Births**    Lucine Amara (soprano) March 1; Dominick Argento (composer) October 27; Bethany Beardslee (soprano) December 25; Frances Bible (mezzo-soprano) January 26; Herbert Blomstedt (conductor) July 11 (of Swedish parents); Richard Cassilly (tenor) December 14; Richard Crocker (musicologist) February 17; Emma Lou Diemer (composer) November 24; Donald Erb (composer) January 17; David Fuller (musicologist) May 1; Donald Gramm (bass-baritone) February 26; Walter S. Hartley (composer) February 21; Natalie Hinderas (pianist) June 16; Laurel Hurley (soprano) February 14; Seymour Lipkin (pianist/conductor) May 14; Salvatore Martirano (composer) January 12; Barry Morell (tenor) March 30; Lawrence K. Moss (composer) November 18; Wayne Peterson (composer) September 3; Leontyne Price (soprano) February 10; Aaron Rosand (violinist) March 15; Charles Rosen (pianist) May 5; Russell Smith (composer) April 23; Teresa Stich-Randall (soprano) December 24; Jess Thomas (tenor) August 4; Patricia Travers (violin) December 5; Norman Treigle (bass-baritone) March 6; Claire Watson (soprano) February 3; Charles Whittenberg (composer) July 6.

**G. Deaths**    Florence Austin (violinist) September 1; Isadora Duncan (ballerina) September 14; Adolph M. Foerster (composer) May 29; Jules Jordan (conductor/composer) March 5; Alessandro Liberati (Italian-born cornetist/bandmaster) November 6; Ralph Lyford (conductor/composer) September 3; Emil Mollenhauer (violinist/conductor) December 10; Walter H. Rothwell (British-born conductor) March 12; Henry W. Savage (impresario) November 29; Fannie Bloomfield Zeisler (pianist) August 20.

**H. Debuts**

**United States**    Jelly d'Arányi (Hungarian violinist—New York), Béla Bartók (Hungarian pianist—New York), Victor De Sabata (Italian conductor—New York), Robert Goldsand (Austrian pianist—New York), Hans Kindler (Dutch conductor—Philadelphia), Otto Klemperer (German conductor—New York), René Maison (Belgian tenor—Chicago), Benno Rabinof (violinist—New York), Heinrich Schlusnus (German baritone—Chicago), Robert Weede (baritone—New York).

**Metropolitan Opera**    Frederick Jagel (tenor), Walter Kirchoff (German tenor), Dorothée Manski (German soprano), Richard Mayr (Austrian bass-baritone), Grete Stückgold (German soprano).

**Other**   Lina Pagliughi (soprano—Milan), Leonard Shure (pianist—Berlin), Alice Tully (mezzo-soprano—Paris).

## I. New Positions

**Conductors**   Howard Barlow (CBS Symphony Orchestra—to 1943); Taylor Branson (United States Marine Band—to 1940); George Raudenbush (Harrisburg Symphony Orchestra—to 1950); Hugh Ross (New York Schola Cantorum—to 1971); Georg Schnéevoigt (Los Angeles Philharmonic Orchestra—to 1929); George Stoessel (Juilliard Opera and Orchestra).

**Educational**   George F. Boyle (New York Institute of Musical Art—to 1939); Jacques Barzun (Columbia); Arthur Farwell (theory/composition, Michigan State College); Alexander Hilsberg (Curtis Institute—to 1953); Otto Kinkeldey (New York Public Library—to 1930); Léa Luboshutz (Curtis); Gustave Reese (NYU); Arthur Shepherd (Western Reserve University—to 1950); Albert Stoessel (opera, Juilliard).

**Other**   Walter Damrosch (music advisor, NBC radio network); Leo Sowerby (organ, Episcopal Cathedral of St. James, Chicago—to 1962); Deems Taylor (editor, *Musical America*—to 1929).

## J. Honors and Awards

**Honors**   Louise Talma (Pleyel Award); Deems Taylor (doctorate, NYU).

**Awards**   Louis Kaufman (Loeb).

## K. Biographical

Béla Bartók makes a concert tour of the United States; William Dawson graduates with honors from the American Conservatory in Chicago; Gottfried Galston (Austrian pianist) comes to the United States and settles in St. Louis; Gian Carlo Menotti comes to the United States to study at Curtis Institute; Mischa Mischakoff, Eugene Ormandy, and Bernard Wagenaar become naturalized American citizens; Florence Price and family leave the Southland for Chicago; Hugh Ross (British conductor/organist) comes to the United States; Elie Siegmeister, graduating from Columbia University, goes to Paris to study with Nadia Boulanger for four years; Oliver Strunk spends a year studying in Berlin; Alexandre Tansman (French pianist/composer) tours the United States.

## L. Musical Beginnings

**Performing Groups**   Chamber Orchestra of Boston; Columbia Broadcasting Symphony (to 1950); Downtown Glee Club (New York); Harrisburg Symphony Orchestra (Pennsylvania); Pennsylvania Grand Opera Co. (Philadelphia).

**Educational**   Cardwell School of Music (Pittsburgh); Michigan State University Department of Music.

**Other**   Associated Music Publishers; Harry Fox Agency, Inc.; Heinz Hall for the Performing Arts (Pittsburgh); Robbins Music Corporation (New York); Shrine Auditorium (Los Angeles); Society for Contemporary Music (Philadelphia).

## M. Music Publications

Chaliapin, Feodor, *Pages from My Life*
Dickinson, George S., *The Growth and Use of Harmony*
Kwalwasser, Jacob, *Tests and Measurements in Music*
Mursell, James L., *Principles of Musical Education*
Rogers, Clara K., *Clearcut Speech in Song*
Rosenfeld, Paul, *Modern Tendencies in Music*
Russell, Charles E., *The American Orchestra and Theodore Thomas* (Pulitzer Prize)

## N. Musical Compositions

**Chamber Music**   George Antheil, *String Quartet No. 2*; John Alden Carpenter, *String Quartet*; William Dawson, *Violin Sonata*; Herbert Elwell, *Violin Sonata*; Carl Eppert, *String Quartet No. 1 in E Minor*; Arthur Farwell, *Violin Sonata, Opus 80*; Edward B. Hill, *Clarinet Sonata*; Wesley La Violette, *Piano Quintet*; Nikolai Lopatnikoff, *Violin Sonata No. 1*; Leopold D. Mannes, *String Quartet*; Daniel G. Mason, *Divertimento for Five Winds, Opus 26*; Frances McCollin, *Piano Quintet*; Leo Ornstein, *Piano Quintet*; Quincy Porter, *Piano Quintet*; David S. Smith, *Piano Quintet*.

**Choral/Vocal**   Virgil Thomson, *Capital Capitals* (male voices); Emerson Whithorne, *The Grim Troubadour* (song cycle).

**Concertos**   Harold C. Morris, *Piano Concerto*; Wallingford Riegger, *Holiday Sketches* (violin and orchestra); Emerson Whithorne, *Poem, Opus 43, for Piano and Orchestra*.

**Operas**   John J. Becker, *The City of Shagpat*; Robert Russell Bennett, *Endymion* (ballet-operetta—Juilliard Foundation Award); Eugene M. Bonner, *The Venetian Glass Nephew*; Wesley La Violette, *Shylock* (Bispham Medal); Charles S. Skilton, *Kalopin* (Bispham Medal).

**Orchestra/Band**   George Antheil, *Crucifixion*; Samuel Barlow, *Alba* (symphonic poem); Marion Bauer, *Indian Pipes*; Abraham Binder, *Holy Land Impressions—Overture, The Pioneers*; Arcady Dubensky, *From Old Russia*; Henry Eichheim, *Burma*; Arthur Farwell, *The Gods of the Mountain Suite*; Arthur Fickénscher, *The Day of Judgment—Dies Irae* (chamber orchestra); Louis Gruenberg, *The Enchanted Isle, Opus 11*; Edward B. Hill, *Lilacs* (tone poem); Herbert Inch, *Variations on a Modal Theme*; Solomon Pimsleur, *Neo-Classic Overture*; Wallingford Riegger, *Study in Sonority, Opus 7* (strings); Lazare Saminsky, *Venice*; Ernest Schelling, *Morocco*; John Philip Sousa, *Marches—The Atlantic City Pageant—Magna Carta—The Minnesota March—Riders for the Flag*; William Grant Still, *La Guiablesse* (ballet)—*Log Cabin Ballads*; Lamar Stringfield, *From the Southern Mountains* (Pulitzer Prize); Edwin John Stringham, *Springtime Overture*; Gustav Strube, *Symphonic Prologue*; Edgard Varèse, *Arcana*; Bernard Wagenaar, *Divertissement for Orchestra* (Eastman Publication Award); Wintter Watts, *The Piper* (symphonic poem); Hermann H. Wetzler, *Symphonic Dance in Basque Style*; Paul White, *Pagan Festival Overture*; Emerson Whithorne, *Fata Morgana*.

**Piano/Organ**   Amy Beach, *From Six to Twelve, Opus 119*; Marc Blitzstein, *Sonata*; Arthur Farwell, *Americana, Opus 78*; Henry F. Gilbert, *Six Pieces, Opus 19*; Henry H. Huss, *Seven Sketches, Opus 32*; Hugh F. MacColl, *Sahara Suite* (two pianos); Virgil Thomson, *Variations and Fugue on Sunday School Tunes* (organ); Adolph Weiss, *Twelve Preludes*.

**Symphonies**   Robert M. Delaney, *Don Quixote Symphony*; Edward B. Hill, *Symphony No. 1 in B Major*; Roger Sessions, *Symphony No. 1*; Arthur Shepherd, *Symphony No. 1, "Horizons" (Nature Symphony)*; Leo Sowerby, *Symphony No. 2*.

# 1928

☀

## Historical Highlights

Herbert Hoover is elected the 31st president; Admiral Richard Byrd begins a systematic exploration of Antarctica; Amelia Earhart becomes the first woman to fly the Atlantic; the first 200-inch telescope is installed at Mount Palomar Observatory in California; Mickey Mouse first appears as "Steamboat Willie"; 65 nations sign the Kellogg-Briand Pact outlawing war.

## World Cultural Highlights

**World Art**   Georges Braque, *Still Life with Jug*; Carlo Carrá, *Morning by the Sea*; Alberto Giacometti, *Observing Head*; Henri Matisse, *Seated Odalisque*; Louis Maurer, *Still Life with Fish*.

**World Literature**   Bertolt Brecht, *The Three-Penny Opera*; Aldous Huxley, *Point Counter Point*; D. H. Lawrence, *Lady Chatterley's Lover*; Virginia Woolf, *Orlando*; William Butler Yeats, *The Tower*.

**World Music**   Béla Bartók, *String Quartet No. 4*; Arnold Schoenberg, *Variations for Orchestra, Opus 31*; Dmitri Shostakovich, *The Nose*; Anton Webern, *Symphony, Opus 21*; Kurt Weill, *Three-Penny Opera*.

**Miscellaneous**   The Red Army Song and Dance Ensemble is formed; the Mexican Symphony Orchestra is founded; births include Georg Baselitz and Karlheinz Stockhausen; deaths include Nikolai Findeisen, Thomas Hardy, Vincente Ibañez, and Leos Janáček.

## American Art and Literature Highlights

**Birth/Deaths**  Births include artists Helen Frankenthaler, Al Held, Robert Indiana, Robert Irwin, Sol LeWitt, and literary figures Edward Albee, William Kennedy, Maurice Sendak, Anne Sexton, and Elie Wiesel; deaths include artists Arthur Davies, Samuel Robb, Aaron Shattuck, and literary figures William Dawson, Thomas Hardy, Avery Hopwood, George McCutcheon, and Elinor Wylie.

**Art Works**  Thomas Hart Benton, *Louisiana Rice Fields*; Alexander Calder, *The Hostess*; John S. Curry, *Baptism in Kansas*; Stuart Davis, *Eggbeater No. 4*; Charles Demuth, *I Saw the Figure 5 in Gold*; Edwin Dickinson, *Fossil Hunters*; Edward Hopper, *Manhattan Bridge Loop*; Anna Huntington, *Bulls Fighting*; Albert Laessle, *Dancing Goat*; Kenneth Miller, *The Shopper*; John Sloan, *The Lafayette*.

**Literature**  Stephen V. Benét, *John Brown's Body* (Pulitzer Prize); Louis Bromfield, *The Strange Case of Miss Annie Spragg*; Robert Frost, *West-Running Brook*; Eugene O'Neill, *Strange Interlude* (Pulitzer Prize); Julian M. Peterkin, *Scarlet Sister Mary* (Pulitzer Prize); Edna St. Vincent Millay, *The Buck in the Snow*; Carl Sandburg, *Good Morning, America*; Upton Sinclair, *Boston*.

## Music—The Vernacular/Commercial Scene

**A. Births**  Julian "Cannonball" Adderley (saxophonist) September 15; Burt Bacharach (pianist/composer) May 12; Jerry Bock (composer) November 23; Ruth Brown (singer) January 30; Rosemary Clooney (singer) May 23; Vic Damone (singer) June 12; Jimmy Dean (singer) August 10; Bo Diddley (singer) December 30; Eric Allan Dolphy (saxophonist/clarinetist) June 20; Fats Domino (singer/pianist) February 26; Art Farmer (trumpeter) August 21; Maynard Ferguson (trumpeter/band-leader) May 4; Clare Fischer (arranger/composer) October 22; Eddie Fisher (singer) August 10; Lefty Frizzell (singer) March 31; Sheila Jordan (singer); Eartha Kitt (singer) January 26; Tom Lehrer (pianist/writer) April 9; Mitch Leigh (composer); William "Bill" Russo (composer/arranger) June 25; Horace Silver (pianist/bandleader) September 2; Charles Strouse (composer) June 7.

**B. Deaths**  Nora Bayes (singer); Dorothy Donnelly (lyricist) January 3; Eddie Foy (singer/dancer) February 16; Arthur J. Lamb (lyricist) August 11; Frederick K. Logan (composer) June 11; Clarence "Pine Top" Smith (pianist/composer).

**C. Biographical**

**Performing Groups**  Gus Arnheim Big Band; Cannon's Jug Stompers; Connecticut Yankees (Rudy Vallee's band); Dixie Hummingbirds; "Fatha" Hines Big Band; Dick Jurgen's Big Band.

**New Beginnings**  Archive of American Folksong (Folk Culture—Library of Congress); Asheville Mountain Dance and Folk Festival (North Carolina); Donaldson, Douglas and Gumble, Music Publishers; Spier and Coslow Publishing Co.

**Miscellaneous**  Jelly Roll Morton moves to New York; *The Jazz Singer* becomes the first movie with sound.

**E. Representative Works**

**Musicals**  Walter Donaldson and G. Kahn, *Whoopee*; Rudolf Friml and B. Hooker, *The Three Musketeers*; George and Ira Gershwin, *Rosalie—Treasure Girl*; Ray Henderson, B. De Sylva, and L. Brown, *Hold Everything*; Jimmy McHugh and D. Fields, *Blackbirds of 1928*; Cole Porter, *Paris*; Richard Rodgers, Fields, and Hart, *Present Arms*; Sigmund Romberg and O. Hammerstein, *New Moon*; Harry Ruby and B. Kalmar, *Animal Crackers*; Fats Waller and A. Razaf, *Keep Shufflin'*; Vincent Youmans, *Rainbow*.

**Songs**  F. Ahlert and R. Turk, *I'll Get By*; Louis Alter, *Manhattan Serenade*; Phil Baxter, *I'm a Ding-Dong Daddy from Dumas*; Joseph A. Burke, *Carolina Moon*; Walter Donaldson, *Makin' Whoopee*; J. McHugh and D. Fields, *I Can't Give You Anything but Love*; M. Fisher, J. Goodwin, and L. Shay, *When You're Smiling, the Whole World Smiles with You*; J. Meyer and G. Kahn, *Crazy Rhythm*; N. Moret and R. A. Whiting, *She's Funny That Way*; Fats Waller, *Ain't Misbehavin'*; Clement Wood and J. Wolfe, *De Glory Road*; Vincent Young, *Sweet Sue*.

**Other**  Louis Gruenberg, *Six Jazz Epigrams*; Pine Top Smith, *Pine Top's Boogie Woogie*; Clarence Williams, *Organ Grinder's Blues*; Spencer Williams, *Basin Street Blues*.

## Music—The Cultivated/Art Music Scene

**F. Births**   Ruth Anderson (flutist/composer) March 21; Wallace Beery (composer/theorist) January 10; McHenry Boatwright (bass-baritone) February 29; Anshel Brusilow (violinist/conductor) August 14; James Cohn (composer/musicologist) February 12; James Dixon (conductor) April 26; Loren Driscoll (tenor) April 14; Jacob Druckman (composer) June 26; Nicolas Flagello (composer/conductor) March 15; Leon Fleisher (pianist/conductor) July 23; Gary Graffman (pianist) October 14; Robert Helps (composer/pianist) September 23; Byron Janis (pianist) March 24; Donald Johanos (conductor) February 10; Karl Korte (composer) August 25; Jacob Lateiner (pianist) May 31; Luther Whiting Mason (music educator) April 3; Seth McCoy (tenor) December 17; Russell Oberlin (countertenor) October 11; Judith Raskin (soprano) June 21; Ezra Sims (composer) January 16; Thomas Stewart (baritone) August 29; William Sydeman (composer) May 8; Robert Washburn (composer/educator) July 11; Beverly Wolff (mezzo-soprano) November 6.

**G. Deaths**   Amy Fay (pianist) February 28; Giuseppe Ferrata (Italian-born pianist) March 28; Austin M. Gemunder (violin maker) March 22; Henry F. Gilbert (composer) May 19; Eugene Gruenberg (Austrian-born violinist) November 11; Céleste de Longpré Heckscher (composer) February 18; Carl V. Lachmund (pianist/conductor) February 20; Charles F. Lummis (ethnomusicologist) November 25; Thomas Rollinson (bandmaster/composer) June 23; Oscar G. T. Sonneck (musicologist/librarian) October 30; Emma Steiner (composer/conductor) February 27; Howard Eugene Wurlitzer (instrument maker/dealer) October 30.

### H. Debuts

**United States**   Thomas Beecham (British conductor—New York), Vladimir Horowitz (Russian pianist—New York), José Iturbi (Spanish pianist—Philadelphia), Helen Jepson (soprano—Philadelphia), Wiktor Labunski (Polish pianist—New York), Frida Leider (German soprano—Chicago), Hephzibah Menuhin (pianist, age eight—San Francisco), Bernadino Molinari (Italian conductor—New York), Ruggiero Ricci (violinist, age ten—San Francisco), Andrés Segovia (Spanish guitarist—New York), Mariano Stabile (Italian baritone—Chicago).

**Metropolitan Opera**   Gertrude Kappel (German soprano), Grace Moore (soprano), Wilfred Pelletier (Canadian conductor).

### I. New Positions

**Conductors**   Arturo Toscanini (New York Philharmonic Orchestra—to 1936).

**Educational**   Leopold Auer (violin, Curtis Institute); Ernst Bacon (San Francisco Conservatory—to 1930); Herbert Elwell (Cleveland Institute—to 1945); John Erskine (president, Juilliard—to 1937); Irwin Fischer (American Conservatory, Chicago—dean in 1974); Wiktor Labunski (Nashville Conservatory—to 1931); Gustave F. Soderlund (theory, Eastman); Louise Talma (Hunter College—to 1979); Efrem Zimbalist (Curtis Institute—to 1968).

**Other**   Frank Black (music director, NBC radio network); Arthur Shepherd (music editor, *Cleveland Press*); Oscar Thompson (music critic, *New York Evening Post*—to 1934).

### J. Honors and Awards

**Honors**   George W. Chadwick (American Academy Gold Medal); Roger Sessions (Rome Prize); Louise Talma (Presser Award).

**Awards**   Louis Kaufman (Naumburg).

**K. Biographical**   Isidor Achron, Nicolai Berezowsky, André Kostelanetz, Fritz Reiner, and Fabien Sevitzky become American citizens; Franco Autori (Italian conductor), Wiktor Labunski (Polish pianist), Paul Henry Lang (Hungarian musicologist), and Joseph Schillinger (Russian theorist) all emigrate to the United States; Samuel Barber travels in Italy on a Bearns Prize; Lorene Harrison becomes the first music teacher in Anchorage, Alaska; Quincy Porter goes to Paris for a three-year stay; Maurice Ravel makes a tour of the United States; Wallingford Riegger settles permanently in New York; Isaac Stern enters San Francisco Conservatory; Gerald Strang graduates from Stanford with degrees in philosophy and languages.

## L. Musical Beginnings

**Performing Groups**  Dessoff A Capella Singers (New York); Detroit Civic Opera Co.; New Jersey Symphony Orchestra; Roth String Quartet; Santa Rosa Symphony Orchestra (California).

**Educational**  Cincinnati Institute of Fine Arts; Arthur Jordan Conservatory of Music (Indianapolis, by merger); National Music Camp (Interlochen, Michigan); National School Orchestra Association.

**Other**  Joseph H. Bearns Prize in Music; Copland-Sessions Concerts (New York); Detroit Masonic Auditorium; Famous Music Corporation (New York); Hammond Clock (Organ) Co. (Chicago); Music Appreciation Hour (Walter Damrosch on radio); Pan American Association of Composers; Southern Music (Peer-Southern in the 1940s).

## M. Music Publications

Aldrich, Richard, *Musical Discourse: From The New York Times*
Birge, Edward B., *History of Public School Music in the United States*
Borowski, Felix, *The Standard Operas*
Hamilton, Clarence, *What Every Piano Pupil Should Know*
Mason, Daniel, *The Dilemma of American Music*
Metcalf, Frank, *Stories of Hymn Tunes*
Rosenfeld, Paul, *By Way of Art*
Sousa, John Philip, *Marching Along: Recollections of Men, Women, and Music*
Strube, Gustav, *The Theory and Use of Chords*
Tweedy, Donald, *A Manual of Harmonic Technique Based on the Practice of J. S. Bach*

## N. Musical Compositions

**Chamber Music**  Samuel Barber, *Violin Sonata* (Bearns Prize); Marion Bauer, *String Quartet*; Arthur Cohn, *String Quartet No. 1, "Four Preludes"*; Boris Koutzen, *Violin Sonata*; Nikolai Lopatnikoff, *String Quartet No. 2*; Otto Luening, *String Quartet No. 3*; Hugh F. MacColl, *String Quartet No. 1*; Harold Morris, *String Quartet No. 1*; John Powell, *Violin Sonata*; Robert Sanders, *Violin Sonata*; David Stanley Smith, *Cello Sonata, Opus 69*; Adolph Weiss, *Chamber Symphony*; Emerson Whithorne, *Piano Quintet*.

**Choral/Vocal**  Marc Blitzstein, *Four Whitman Songs*; Franz C. Bornschein, *Vision of Sir Launfal*; Francis Saltus von Boskerck, *Semper Paratus* (United States Coast Guard Song); Charles W. Cadman, *The Father of Waters* (cantata); Mabel Wheeler Daniels, *The Holy Star*; Virgil Thomson, *Trois Poèmes de la Duchesse de Rohan—Les Soirées Bagnolaises*; Adolph Weiss, *Seven Songs by Dickinson* (soprano and string quartet).

**Concertos**  Joseph Achron, *Konzertanten-Kapelle, Opus 64, for Violin and Orchestra*; Samuel Barber, *Serenade* (string quartet and string orchestra); Hans Barth, *Piano Concerto, Opus 11*; Cecil Burleigh, *Violin Concerto No. 3, Opus 60*; Henry Cowell, *Piano Concerto*; Randall Thompson, *Jazz Poem* (piano and orchestra).

**Operas**  George Antheil, *Transatlantic*; Marc Blitzstein, *Triple Sec*; Charles W. Cadman, *The Belle of Havana* (operetta); Eleanor Freer, *A Christmas Tale—Preciosa, or The Spanish Student*; Sándor Harmati, *Prelude to a Melodrama* (Juilliard Foundation Prize); Mary Carr Moore, *David Rizzio*; Lazare Saminsky, *The Daughter of Jephtha*; Timothy Spelman, *The Sea Rovers*; Virgil Thomson, *Four Saints in Three Acts*; Hermann H. Wetzler, *Die Baskische Venus*.

**Orchestra/Band**  Paul Hastings Allen, *Serenade*; George Antheil, *Oedipus Rex* (incidental music); Samuel Barlow, *Ballo Sardo* (ballet); Marion Bauer, *Lament on African Themes*; Gena Branscombe, *Quebec, Symphonic Suite—Pilgrims of Destiny* (National League of American Pen Women Prize); Arcady Dubensky, *Russian Bells* (symphonic poem); John Woods Duke, *Overture in D Minor*; George Gershwin, *An American in Paris*; Charles Haubiel, *Karma: Symphonic Variations*; Douglas Moore, *Moby Dick* (symphonic poem); Robert Sanders, *Orchestra Suite*; Charles S. Skilton, *Mount Oread Overture*; John Philip Sousa, *Marches—Golden Jubilee—New Mexico March—Prince Charming—University of Nebraska March*; Lamar Stringfield, *The Seventh Queue* (ballet); Adolph Weiss, *Scherzo, American Life*.

**Piano/Organ**   Seth Bingham, *Harmonies of Florence* (organ); Abram Chasins, *Twenty-Four Preludes*; Ruth Crawford, *Four Preludes*; R. Nathaniel Dett, *The Cinnamon Grove Suite*; Herbert Elwell, *Pieces*; Roy Harris, *Sonata*; Eastwood Lane, *Sold Down the River*; Bernard Wagenaar, *Sonata*.

**Symphonies**   Philip G. Clapp, *Symphony No. 7 in A Major*; Vernon Duke, *Symphony No. 1*; Philip James, *A Sea Symphony*; Nikolai Lopatnikoff, *Symphony No. 1, Opus 12*; Solomon Pimsleur, *Symphony of Disillusionment*; Bernard Rogers, *Symphony No. 2 in A Flat Major*; Dane Rudhyar, *Symphony*; David Stanley Smith, *Symphony No. 3 in C Minor, Opus 60*; Virgil Thomson, *Symphony on a Hymn Tune*.

# 1929

✸

## Historical Highlights

Black Friday on Wall Street ushers in the stock market collapse and a worldwide depression; the St. Valentine's Day massacre takes place in Chicago; United States warships go to Shanghai to protect United States citizens; the radio program "Amos and Andy" begins broadcasting; Admiral Byrd flies over the South Pole; Leon Trotsky flees Russia for his life; penicillin is discovered by Alexander Fleming.

## World Cultural Highlights

**World Art**   Georges Braque, *The Round Table*; Salvador Dali, *Illumined Pleasures*; Paul Klee, *Fools in a Trance*; Fernand Léger, *Les Deux Danseuses*; Pablo Picasso, *Woman in an Armchair*.

**World Literature**   Jean Cocteau, *Les Enfants Terribles*; Sean O'Casey, *The Silver Tassie*; Erich Remarque, *All Quiet on the Western Front*; William Butler Yeats, *The Winding Stair*.

**World Music**   Frederick Delius, *A Song of Summer*; Dmitri Kabalevsky, *Piano Concerto No. 1*; Sergei Prokofiev, *The Prodigal Son*; Ottorino Respighi, *Roman Festivals*; William Walton, *Viola Concerto*.

**Miscellaneous**   The Symphony Orchestra of Paris is founded; the Delius Music Festival begins in London; births include Christoph von Dohnányi, Bernard Haitink, Toshiro Mayuzumi, and John Osborne; deaths include Émile-Antoine Bourdelle, Sergei Diaghilev, and Gunnar Heiberg.

## American Art and Literature Highlights

**Births/Deaths**   Births include artists Claes Oldenburg, Cy Twombly, and literary figures Marilyn French, Shirley Ann Grau, Ira Levin, Chaim Potok, Adrienne Rich, Howard Sackler, and Michael J. Shaara, Jr.; deaths include art figures Charles Grafly, Robert Henri, Robert Reid, and literary figures Katharine Lee Bates, William B. Carman, Henry B. Fuller, and Jesse L. Williams.

**Art Works**   John S. Curry, *Tornado over Kansas*; Arthur Dove, *Fog Horns*; Lyonel Feininger, *Village Street*; Edward Hopper, *Lighthouse at Two Lights*; Walt Kuhn, *The White Clown*; Ernest Lawson, *Gold Mining, Cripple Creek*; Reginald Marsh, *Second Avenue El*; Georgia O'Keeffe, *Black Cross, New Mexico*; Charles Sheeler, *The Upper Deck*; Lorado Taft, *Alma Mater*.

**Literature**   Conrad Aiken, *Selected Poems* (Pulitzer Prize); William Burnett, *Little Caesar*; Lloyd C. Douglas, *Magnificent Obsession*; William Faulkner, *The Sound and the Fury*; Ernest Hemingway, *A Farewell to Arms*; Oliver La Farge, *Laughing Boy* (Pulitzer Prize); Sinclair Lewis, *Dodsworth*; Elmer L. Rice, *Street Scene* (Pulitzer Prize); Thomas Wolfe, *Look Homeward, Angel*.

## Music—The Vernacular/Commercial Scene

**A. Births**   Johnny Ace (singer/writer) June 9; Chet Baker (trumpeter) December 23; LaVern Baker (singer) November 11; Ray Barretto (bandleader) April 29; Dick Clark (disk jockey/television host) November 30; Cy Coleman (composer/pianist) January 14; Bill Evans (pianist/composer) August 16; Clarence Fountain (singer) November 28; Jerry Goldsmith (composer/conductor) February 10; Barry Harris (pianist/composer) December 15; Wilbert Harrison (singer) January 6;

Lee Hazlewood (singer/writer) July 9; Johnny Horton (singer) April 3; Sonny James (singer) May 1; Chris Kenner (singer/writer) December 25; Dory Langdon (lyricist); Mel Lewis (drummer) May 10; Buck Owens (singer/guitarist) August 12; Joe Pass (guitarist) January 13; Jane Powell (singer) April 1; "Sonny" Rollins (saxophonist/composer) September 7; Harvey Schmidt (composer).

**B. Deaths**   Pine Top Smith (singer/pianist) March 15; Leo Wood (composer) August 2.

**C. Biographical**

**Performing Groups**   (Mills) Blue Ribbon Band; Clouds of Joy; Jimmy Lunceford Orchestra; Southernaires.

**New Beginnings**   American Record Co.; Radio Music Co.; RCA Records; Warner Brothers Music (Los Angeles).

**Miscellaneous**   Gene Buck becomes president of ASCAP (to 1941); Harry Revel (British composer) comes to the United States; Dimitri Tiomkin (Russian composer) and his wife come to the United States and settle in Hollywood where he begins a long career in movie music.

**D. Publications**   John Jacob Niles, *One Man's War*.

**E. Representative Works**

**Musicals**   Irving Berlin, *Hallelujah* (film); N. H. Brown and A. Freed, *Broadway Melody* (film); John F. Coots, *Sons O' Guns*; R. Henderson, B. De Sylva, and L. Brown, *Follow Thru—The Singing Fool* (film); George and Ira Gershwin, *Show Girl*; J. Kern and O. Hammerstein, *Sweet Adeline*; Joe Jordan, *Deep Harlem*; Cole Porter, *Wake Up and Dream—Fifty Million Frenchmen*; Andy Razaf and Fats Waller, *Connie's Hot Chocolates*; Rodgers and Hart, *Heads Up  Spring Is Here*; A. Schwartz and H. Dietz, *The Little Show*; V. Youmans and E. Eliscu, *Great Day*.

**Songs**   Milton Ager, *Happy Days Are Here Again*; Harry Akst, *Am I Blue?*; Phil Baxter, *Piccolo Pete*; Joe Burke, *Tiptoe Through the Tulips*; Hoagy Carmichael, *Rockin' Chair*; Cow Cow Davenport, *Mama Don't Allow*; Sammy Fain, *Wedding Bells Are Breaking Up That Old Gang of Mine*; Carson Robison and F. Luther, *Barnacle Bill, the Sailor*; Rodgers and Hart, *With a Song in My Heart*; Robert Saver and M. Woolsey, *When It's Springtime in the Rockies*; Fats Waller, *Honeysuckle Rose*; Richard A. Whiting and L. Robin, *Louise*; Jack Yellen, *Hard-Hearted Hannah*; Vincent Youmans, B. Rose, and E. Eliscu, *Without a Song*.

**Other**   Bennie Moten, *Moten's Blues*; Clarence Williams, *Wild Flower Rag*.

## Music—The Cultivated/Art Music Scene

**F. Births**   Joan Benson (pianist/harpsichordist) October 9; George J. Buelow (musicologist) March 31; George Crumb (composer) October 24; Stanley Drucker (clarinettist) February 4; Harold Farberman (composer/conductor) November 2; Donald Grobe (tenor) December 16; James Haar (musicologist) July 4; Janice Harsanyi (soprano) July 15; Sidney Harth (violinist/conductor) October 5; Leonard Kastle (composer/pianist) February 11; John Macurdy (bass) March 18; Robert Muczynski (composer/pianist) March 19; Ron Nelson (composer/conductor) December 14; Harvey Phillips (tuba) December 2; James K. Randall (composer) June 16; Robert Robinette (harpsichord maker) June 23; Kenneth Schermerhorn (conductor) November 20; Beverly Sills (soprano/administrator) May 25; Gerald Tarack (violinist) February 27; Paul Turok (composer) December 3; Sandra Warfield (mezzo-soprano) August 6; Yehudi Wyner (composer/conductor) June 1.

**G. Deaths**   Charles Barnhouse (publisher) November 29; Patrick Conway (conductor) June 10; Henry M. Dunham (organist) May 4; Minnie Hauk (mezzo-soprano) February 6; E. A. Hofman (hymnist) November 25; Ovide Musin (Belgian-born violinist/conductor) November 24; Walton Perkins (pianist) February 8; Cornelius Rybner (Danish-born pianist/composer) January 21; Oscar Saenger (singer/educator) April 20; Frank Van der Stucken (conductor/composer) August 16.

**H. Debuts**

**United States**   Rose Bampton (soprano—Chautauqua), Giovanni Inghilleri (Italian baritone—Chicago), Gunnar Johansen (Danish pianist—San Francisco), Nathan Milstein (Russian violinist—Philadelphia), Gregor Piatigorsky (Russian cellist—Oberlin), Emil Schipper (Austrian bass-baritone), Guido Schützendorf (Dutch bass—tour), Eva Turner (British soprano—Chicago).

**Metropolitan Opera**   Tancredi Pasero (Italian bass), Joseph Rosenstock (Polish conductor), Gladys Swarthout (mezzo-soprano).

**Other**   Webster Aitken (Vienna).

## I. New Positions

**Conductors**   Henry Hadley (Manhattan Symphony Orchestra—to 1932); Artur Rodzinski (Los Angeles Philharmonic Orchestra—to 1933).

**Educational**   John J. Becker (College of St. Thomas, Minnesota—to 1933); Louise Cuyler (University of Michigan—to 1975); Rudolph Ganz (director, Chicago Musical College—to 1954); Carl Parrish (Wells College—to 1943); Bernard Rogers (Eastman—to 1967); Cecil Smith (University of Chicago—to 1946); Joseph F. Wagner (Boston University).

**Other**   Carl Engel (editor, *Musical Quarterly*—to 1944 and president, G. Schirmer Co.); A. Walter Kramer (editor, *Musical America*—to 1936); Howard Taubman (various positions, *The New York Times*—to 1972); Lazar Weiner (music director, Central Synagogue, New York—to 1975).

## J. Honors and Awards

**Honors**   John Philip Sousa (Honorary Life President of the ABA); Frank Van der Stucken (American Academy).

**K. Biographical**   Claus Adam (Indonesian-born cellist/composer) comes with his family to the United States; Henry Cowell becomes the first American composer to be invited to lecture and perform in the USSR; Alexander Gretchaninoff (Russian composer) conducts his works while touring in the United States; Roy Harris suffers a severe spinal injury in a fall and returns to the United States for treatment; Gunnar Johansen (Danish pianist), Boris Kremenliev (Bulgarian composer/ethnomusicologist), and Gregor Piatigorsky (Russian cellist) come to the United States; John Finley Williamson moves his Westminster Choir School to Ithaca, New York.

## L. Musical Beginnings

**Performing Groups**   Cincinnati Chamber Music Society; Manhattan Symphony Orchestra; Orpheus Male Chorus (Phoenix, Arizona); Tucson Symphony Orchestra.

**Educational**   National Guild of Pianist Teachers; *The School Musician*.

**Other**   American Bandmaster's Association; Boston Esplanade Concerts; Broude Brothers Publishers (New York); Chicago Opera House; Cos Cob (Arrow) Press; Friends and Enemies of Modern Music (Hartford); Hammond Instrument Co. (Chicago); *Journal of the Acoustical Society of America*; RCA Victor Co. (merger of Radio Corporation of American and Victor); Avedis Zildjian Co. (Quincy, Massachusetts).

## M. Music Publications

Burleigh, Harry T., *Old Songs Hymnal*
Dykema, Peter, *Music Tests*
Erskine, John, *Is There a Career in Music?*
Goetschius, Percy, *Masters of the Symphony*
Rosenfeld, Paul, *An Hour with American Music*
Rubinstein, Beryl, *Outline of Piano Pedagogy*
Salzedo, Carlos, *Method for the Harp*
Spaeth, Sigmund, *They Still Sing of Love*

## N. Musical Compositions

**Chamber Music**   Amy Beach, *Movement for String Quartet, Opus 89*; John Parsons Beach, *Concert for Six Instruments*; Aaron Copland, *Vitebsk* (violin, cello, and piano); Herbert Elwell, *Divertimento for String Quartet*; Louis Gruenberg, *Piano Quintet I*; Philip James, *Organ Sonata*; Nikolai Lopatnikoff, *Cello Sonata*; Daniel G. Mason, *Fanny Blair—Folk Song Fantasy, Opus 28* (string quartet); Harold Morris, *Piano Quintet No. 1*; Arthur Nevin, *String Quartet in D Minor*; Leo Ornstein, *String Quartets No. 1*; Quincy Porter, *Violin Sonata No. 2—Clarinet Quintet*; Virgil Thomson, *Five Portraits for Four Clarinets*; Adolph Weiss, *String Quartet No. 3*.

**Choral/Vocal**  John J. Becker, *Out of the Cradle Endlessly Rocking* (cantata); Mabel Wheeler Daniels, *Exultate Deo*; William Dawson, *Out in the Fields*; Philip James, *Missa Imaginum*; Bernard Rogers, *The Raising of Lazarus* (oratorio); Timothy Spelman, *Pervigilium Veneris*.

**Concertos**  Abram Chasins, *Piano Concerto*; Wesley La Violette, *Violin Concerto No. 1*; Harold Morris, *Piano Concerto*; Tibor Serly, *Viola Concerto*; Joseph F. Wagner, *Piano Concerto*.

**Operas**  Marc Blitzstein, *Parabola and Circula*; Eleanor Freer, *Frithiof—Joan of Arc*; Wesley La Violette, *Osiris*; Clarence Loomis, *Yolanda of Cyprus*; Lamar Stringfield, *The Mountain Song*.

**Orchestra/Band**  George Antheil, *Fighting the Waves* (ballet); Ernest Bloch, *Helvetia*; Radie Britain, *Heroic Poem*; Cecil Burleigh, *Evangeline, Opus 41*; Avery Claflin, *Moby Dick Suite*; Aaron Copland, *Symphonic Ode*; Henry Eichheim, *Java*; Richard Hammond, *Fiesta—The Sea of Heaven*; Herbert Inch, *Suite for Small Orchestra*; Colin McPhee, *Sea Shanty Suite*; Walter Piston, *Suite No. 1*; John Philip Sousa, *Marches—Daughters of Texas—La Flor de Sevilla—Washington Monument—Royal Welsh Fusiliers I—University of Illinois*; Leo Sowerby, *Prairie* (symphonic poem); Lamar Stringfield, *At the Factory* (symphonic fantasy); Harriet Ware, *The Artisan* (tone poem).

**Piano/Organ**  Hans Barth, *Sonata No. 1*; Robert Russell Bennett, *Organ Sonata*; Marc Blitzstein, *Piano Percussion Music*; Harrison Kerr, *Sonata No. 1*; Dane Rudhyar, *Granites*; David S. Smith, *Sonata in A-Flat, Opus 61*; Leo Sowerby, *Florida Suite*; Timothy M. Spelman, *Sonata;* Humphrey Stewart, *Cortège Triumphal* (organ); Virgil Thomson, *Sonatas No. 1, 2*.

**Symphonies**  John J. Becker, *Symphony No. 3, "Symphonia brevis"*; Vernon Duke, *Symphony No. 2*; Edward B. Hill, *Symphony No. 2 in C Major*; Harrison Kerr, *Symphony No. 1*; Daniel G. Mason, *Symphony No. 2 in A Major, Opus 30*; Frances McCollin, *Sinfonietta II*; Vittorio Rieti, *Symphony No. 1*; Edwin John Stringham, *Symphony No. 1, "Italian"*; Randall Thompson, *Symphony No. 1*; Bernard Wagenaar, *Sinfonietta*; Emerson Whithorne, *Symphony No. 1*.

# 1930

❧

## Historical Highlights

According to the census, the United States population reaches 122,775,000; the Treasury Department forms the Bureau of Narcotics; the import tax reaches a new high via the Hawley-Smoot Tariff Bill; the Veteran's Administration is formed; the Nazis gain a majority in the German Reichstag while the last allied troops leave the Rhineland; the planet Pluto is discovered.

## World Cultural Highlights

**World Art**  Max Beckmann, *Self-Portrait with Saxophone;* Raoul Dufy, *Chateau and Horses*; Louis Maurer, *Still Life with Doily*; Piet Mondrian, *Composition in Red, Yellow and Blue*.

**World Literature**  W. H. Auden, *Poems*; Ivan Bunin, *The Well of Days*; Jean Cocteau, *La voix humaine*; Noel Coward, *Private Lives*; W. Somerset Maugham, *The Summing Up*.

**World Music**  Paul Hindemith, *Concert Music for Strings and Brass*; Arthur Honegger, *Symphony No. 1*; Dmitri Shostakovich, *The Age of Gold*; Igor Stravinsky, *Symphony of Psalms*.

**Miscellaneous**  The BBC Symphony Orchestra is founded; Boosey and Hawkes is formed by merger; births include Richard Anuszkiewic, Lazar Berman, Ted Hughes, and Harold Pinter; deaths include Arthur Conan Doyle, D. H. Lawrence, Edna O'Brien, Karl Oesterley, and Adolphe Retté.

## American Art and Literature Highlights

**Births/Deaths**  Births include artists Robert Arneson, Jasper Johns, Andy Warhol, and literary figures Harry Mathews, Joseph McElroy, and Wilfred J. J. Sheed; deaths include artists Louis Moeller, Charles Moore, William O. Partridge, and literary figures Mary E. Freeman, Bruce Friedman, and George Woodberry.

**Art Works**    Ivan Albright, *Fleeting Time, Thou Hast Left Me Old*; Charles Burchfield, *The Rainy Night*; Edward Hopper, *Early Sunday Morning*; Morris Kantor, *Haunted House*; Walt Kuhn, *A Clown with Black Wig*; Gaston Lachaise, *Torso*; Reginald Marsh, *Why Not Use the "El?"*; Alfred H. Maurer, *Two Heads with White Hair*; Charles Sheeler, *American Landscape*; Grant Wood, *American Gothic*.

**Literature**    Sholem Asch, *The Mother*; Irving Bacheller, *A Candle in the Wilderness*; Margaret Barnes, *Years of Grace* (Pulitzer Prize); Marc Connelly, *The Green Pastures* (Pulitzer Prize); Grace Crowell, *Flame in the Wind*; John Dos Passos, *The 42nd Parallel*; Edna Ferber, *Cimarron*; Susan Glaspell, *Alison's House* (Pulitzer Prize); Frances P. Keyes, *Queen Anne's Lace*.

## Music — The Vernacular/Commercial Scene

**A. Births**    Muhal Richard Abrams (pianist/composer) September 19; Pepper Adams (saxophonist) October 8; Liz Anderson (songwriter) March 13; Bill Berry (trumpeter/bandleader) September 14; Bobby Bland (singer) January 27; Clifford Brown (trumpeter) October 30; Betty Carter (singer) May 16; Ray Charles (singer/pianist) September 23; Ornette Coleman (saxophonist) March 9; Bobby Day (singer) July 1; Tommy Flanagan (pianist) March 16; Pete Fountain (clarinet) July 3; Jim Hall (guitarist); December 4; Ahmad Jamal (pianist) July 2; Joni James (singer) September 22; Julius LaRosa (singer) January 2; Little Walter (harmonica) May 1; Herbie Mann (jazz flute) April 16; Helen Merrill (singer); Odetta (singer) December 31; "Doc" Pomus (songwriter) June 27; Johnny Preston (singer) August 18; Sam Rivers (saxophonist/composer) September 25; Stephen Sondheim (composer/lyricist) March 22; Frederick C. Tillis (composer/conductor) January 5; Tiny Tim (Herbert Khaury—singer) April 12; Porter Wagoner (singer/writer) August 12; Albertina Walker (singer) August 29; Andy Williams (singer) December 3.

**B. Deaths**    Will D. Cobb (lyricist) January 20; Henry Creamer (lyricist) October 14; Jack Donohue (singer/dancer) October 1; Charles K. Harris (writer/publisher) December 22; Blind Lemon Jefferson (singer/guitarist).

**C. Biographical**

**Performing Groups**    Mills Blue Rhythm Band (Coconut Grove Orchestra); Mills Brothers (?).

**New Beginnings**    American Folksong Festival (Olive Hill, Kentucky).

**D. Publications**    Isaac Goldberg, *Tin Pan Alley: A Chronicle of the American Popular Music Racket*; James J. Johnson, *Black Manhattan*.

**E. Representative Works**

**Musicals**    Harold Arlen and J. Yellen, *You Said It*; Irving Berlin, *Putting on the Ritz* (film); Eubie Blake, *Lew Leslie's Blackbirds of 1930*; R. Henderson, B. De Sylva, and L. Brown, *Flying High*; George and Ira Gershwin, *Girl Crazy—Strike Up the Band*; Joe Jordan, *Brown Buddies*; J. McHugh and D. Fields, *The Vanderbilt Revue*; Cole Porter, *The New Yorkers*; Rodgers and Hart, *Evergreen— Simple Simon*; S. Romberg and I. Caesar, *Nina Rosa*; A. Schwartz and H. Dietz, *Three's a Crowd*; Vincent Youmans, *Smiles*.

**Songs**    Fred E. Ahlert, *Walkin' My Baby Back Home*; Hoagy Carmichael, *Georgia on My Mind*; E. Coates and J. Lawrence, *Sleepy Lagoon*; Duke Ellington, *Mood Indigo*; J. Gorney and E. Y. Harburg, *Brother, Can You Spare a Dime*; John Green, *Body and Soul*; W. King and E. Flindt, *The Waltz You Saved for Me*; Jimmy McHugh, *On the Sunny Side of the Street—Exactly Like You*; Richard Whiting and Fred Harling, *My Ideal—Beyond the Blue Horizon*.

## Music — The Cultivated/Art Music Scene

**F. Births**    Betty Allen (mezzo-soprano) March 17; David Amram (composer) November 17; Robert Ashley (composer) March 28; Larry Austin (composer) September 12; John Ness Beck (composer) November 11; Anthony di Bonaventura (pianist) November 12; David Burge (pianist/composer) March 25; Robert Ceely (composer) January 17; Rosalind Elias (mezzo-soprano) March 13; David Epstein (conductor/theorist) October 3; Richard J. Feliciano (composer) December 7; Jack S. Gottlieb (composer) October 12; Roger Hannay (composer) September 22; Paul Jacobs (pianist/harpsi-chordist) June 22; Owen Jander (musicologist) June 4; Israel Katz (ethnomusicologist) July 21; Igor Kipnis (harpsichordist) September 27; Lorin Maazel (conductor) March 6; Barry McDaniel (baritone) October 18; Bruno Nettl (ethnomusicologist) March 14; Marni Nixon (soprano) February 22; Maurice Peress (conductor/trumpeter) March 18; Roberta Peters (soprano) May 4; John Reardon (baritone) April 8; Thomas Schippers (conductor) March 9; Russell Sherman (pianist) March 25; Eric Stokes (composer) July 14; Gilbert Trythall (composer) October 28; Nancy Van der Vate (composer) December 30; John Watts (composer) July 16.

**G. Deaths**   Joseph Adamowski (Polish-born cellist) May 8; Robert Blass (bass) December 7; Karl Fiqué (German-born organist) December 7; Nahan Franko (violinist/conductor) June 7; Daniel Guggenheim (art patron) September 28; Franz Listemann (cellist) March 11; Harvey W. Loomis (composer) December 25; George Waring Stebbins (organist) February 21.

## II. Debuts

**United States**   Salvatore Baccaloni (Italian bass—Chicago), Rudolph Bockelmann (German bass-baritone—Chicago), Arthur Fiedler (conductor—Boston), Edward Habich (German bari-tone—Chicago), Carl Hartmann (German tenor—tour), Ralph Kirkpatrick (harpsichordist—Cambridge), Lotte Lehmann (German soprano—Chicago), Eugene List (pianist—Los Angeles), Hans Nissen (German bass-baritone—Chicago), George Szell (Hungarian conductor—St. Louis).

**Metropolitan Opera**   Ivar Andrésen (Norwegian bass), Hans Clemens (German tenor), Elisabeth Ohms (Dutch soprano).

## I. New Positions

**Conductors**   Leon Barzin (National Orchestral Association—to 1958); Arthur Fiedler (Boston Pops—to 1979); Guy Fraser Harrison (Rochester Civic Orchestra—to 1951); Ferdinand Schaeffer (Indianapolis Symphony Orchestra—to 1936); André Kostelanetz (conductor, CBS Radio); George Siemonn (Baltimore Symphony Orchestra—to 1935).

**Educational**   William Dawson (director, Tuskegee School of Music); Allen Irvine McHose (Eastman—to 1967); Otto Kinkeldey (second term at Cornell—to 1958); Paul Henry Lang (Vassar—to 1931); Louis Persinger (Juilliard—to 1966); Jesús María Sanromá (piano, New England Conservatory—to 1941).

**Other**   Henry Pleasants (music critic, *Philadelphia Evening Bulletin*—to 1942).

## J. Honors and Awards

**Honors**   Sascha Gorodnitzki (Schubert Memorial); Philip James (Rome Prize).

**K. Biographical**   John Cage drops his college work and spends a year traveling around Europe; Sergius Kagen becomes an American citizen; Boris Goldovsky (Russian conductor/pianist) moves to the United States; Ildebrando Pizzetti (Italian composer) visits the United States; William Schuman hears Toscanini conducting and drops his commerce classes to begin music study at Malkin Conservatory.

## L. Musical Beginnings

**Performing Groups**   Accademia dei Dilettanti di Musica (Philadelphia); Gordon String Quartet; Indianapolis Symphony Orchestra III; National Orchestra of New York.

**Educational**   International Student Music Council.

**Other**   Howard Bushnell Memorial Hall (Hartford, Connecticut); John Challis Harpsichord Co. (Michigan); Jacksonville Civic Music Association (Florida); Mann Music Center (Robin Hood Dell Concerts—Philadelphia); *Musical Review for the Blind*; National Orchestral Association; New York Musicological Society (American Musicological Society in 1934); New York Philharmonic Symphony Broadcasts.

## M. Music Publications

Campbell-Watson, Frank, *Modern Elementary Harmony*
Fisher, William, *Ye Olde New England Psalm Tunes (1620–1820) with Historical Sketches*

Johnson, Hall, *The Green Pastures Spirituals*
Pratt, Waldo S., *The Problem of Music in the Church*
Upton, William T., *Art-song in America: A Study in the Development of American Music*
Witherspoon, Herbert, *Thirty-Six Lessons in Singing for Teacher and Student*

**N. Musical Compositions**

**Chamber Music**  Hans Barth, *Quintet for Quarter-Tone Piano and Strings*; Marc Blitzstein, *String Quartet*; Arthur Cohn, *String Quartet No. 2*; Isadore Freed, *String Quartet No. 2*; Elliot Griffis, *String Quartet No. 2*; Louis Gruenberg, *Four Diversions, Opus 32* (string quartet— Coolidge Medal); Herbert Inch, *Piano Quintet*; Mary Carr Moore, *String Quartet in F Minor*; Walter Piston, *Flute Sonata*; Quincy Porter, *String Quartet No. 3*; Gustav Strube, *Wind Quintet*; Virgil Thomson, *Violin Sonata No. 1*; Emerson Whithorne, *String Quartet No. 2*.

**Choral/Vocal**  Charles Martin Loeffler, *Evocation* (women's chorus and orchestra); Elie Siegmeister, *Four Robert Frost Songs*; Charles S. Skilton, *From Forest and Stream—Mass in D Major*; Oley Speaks, *The Prayer Perfect* (song); Adolph Weiss, *The Libation Bearers*.

**Concertos**  Hans Barth, *Concerto for Quarter-Tone Piano and Strings, Opus 15*; John J. Becker, *Concerto Arabesque* (piano and orchestra); Nicolai Berezowsky, *Violin Concerto*; Ulric Cole, *Piano Concerto No. 1*; Nikolai Lopatnikoff, *Piano Concerto No. 2, Opus 15*; Gustav Strube, *Violin Concerto No. 2*; Joseph F. Wagner, *Violin Concerto No. 1*.

**Operas**  George Antheil, *Flight (Ivan the Terrible)*; Arcady Dubensky, *Downtown*; Hamilton Forrest, *Camille*; Harry L. Freeman, *Leah Kleschna*; Isadore Freed, *Homo Sum*; Eleanor Freer, *The Masque of Pandora*; Louis Gruenberg, *Jack and the Beanstalk* (Juilliard Award—Bispham Medal); Charles S. Skilton, *The Sun Bride*; Timothy Spelman, *The Sunken City*; Deems Taylor, *Peter Ibbetson, Opus 20*.

**Orchestra/Band**  George Antheil, *Capriccio*; Hans Barth, *Suite for Quarter-Tone Strings, Brass and Timpani*; Marc Blitzstein, *Cain* (ballet)—*Romantic Piece for Orchestra*; Franz C. Bornschein, *Old Louisiana* (symphonic poem); Parks Grant, *Overture, Macbeth*; David Guion, *Mother Goose Suite*; Henry Hadley, *The Streets of Pekin*; Roy Harris, *Concert Piece*; Philip James, *Song of the Night* (New York Women's Symphony Orchestra Prize); Edgar S. Kelley, *The Pit and the Pendulum Suite*; Mary Carr Moore, *Ka-mi-a-kin*; Arthur Nevin, *Symphonic Poem*; Leo Ornstein, *Lysistrata Suite*; Arthur Shepherd, *Choreographic Suite on an Exotic Theme*; Charles S. Skilton, *Autumn Night*; John Philip Sousa, *Marches—George Washington Bicentennial—Harmonica Wizard—The Legionnaires—Royal Welsh Fusiliers—Salvation Army—The Wildcats*; William Grant Still, *Sahdji* (ballet); Gustav Strube, *Americana—Sylvan Scenes*; Powell Weaver, *The Vagabond* (symphonic poem); Emerson Whithorne, *The Dream Pedlar* (symphonic poem).

**Piano/Organ**  Marion Bauer, *Four Pieces*; Aaron Copland, *Piano Variations*; Herbert Elwell, *Three Preludes*; Arthur Farwell, *In the Tetons, Opus 86—Vale of Enitharmon, Opus 91*; George F. McKay, *Organ Sonata No. 1*; Colin McPhee, *Kinesis*; Quincy Porter, *Sonata*; Roger Sessions, *Sonata No. 1*; Arthur Shepherd, *Sonata No. 2*; Leo Sowerby, *Organ Symphony in G Major*; Virgil Thomson, *Sonata No. 3*; Emerson Whithorne, *Moon Trail* (orchestrated 1933).

**Symphonies**  Philip G. Clapp, *Symphony No. 8 in C Major*; Howard Hanson, *Symphony No. 2, "Romantic"*; Colin McPhee, *Symphony No. 1*; Douglas Moore, *A Symphony of Autumn*; Vittorio Rieti, *Symphony No. 2*; Lazare Saminsky, *Symphony No. 5, "Jerusalem"*; William Grant Still, *Symphony No. 1, "Afro-American"*; Bernard Wagenaar, *Symphony No. 2*.

# 1931

☀

## Historical Highlights

*The Star Spangled Banner* is adopted as the official national anthem by Congress; New York City sees the completion of the Empire State and the Chrysler buildings; the first cyclotron is invented by Ernest O. Lawrence; the British Commonwealth of Nations is formed by the Statute of Westminster; the second Spanish Republic is set up as Alphonso XIII abdicates.

## World Cultural Highlights

**World Art**   Salvador Dali, *The Persistence of Memory*; Julio Gonzalez, *Harlequin Pierrot*; Henri Matisse, *Girl in a Yellow Dress*; Joan Miró, *Man, Woman and Child*; José Orozco, *Zapatistas*.

**World Literature**   Daphne du Maurier, *The Loving Spirit*; Virginia Woolf, *The Waves*.

**World Music**   Béla Bartók, *Piano Concerto No. 2*; Maurice Ravel, *Piano Concerto in G—Concerto for Piano, Left Hand*; Edgard Varèse, *Ionisation—Hyperprism*; William Walton, *Belshazzar's Feast*.

**Miscellaneous**   The Brussels Symphony Orchestra, Montevideo Symphony Orchestra, and Rio de Janeiro Philharmonic Orchestra are founded; births include Frank Auerbach, Alfred Brendel, John Le Carré, and Malcolm Morley; deaths include Giovanni Boldini, Thomas Caine, Vincent d'Indy, Erik Karlfeldt, Carl Nielsen, and Eugène Ysaÿe.

## American Art and Literature Highlights

**Births/Deaths**   Births include sculptor Robert Morris, artist Tom Wesselman, and literary figures Donald Bartholme, Kristin Hunter, E. L. Doctorow, Toni Morrison, George Starbuck, and Tom Wolfe, deaths include art figures Jefferson Chalfont, Benjamin Clinedienst, Daniel French, Robert Spencer, and literary figures David Belasco, Armistead Gordon, Grace King, Vachel Lindsay, and Ole E. Rölvaag.

**Art Works**   Thomas Hart Benton, *Engineer's Dream*; Peter Blume, *South of Scranton*; Stuart Davis, *Abstract Vision of New York*; Lyonel Feininger, *The Motor Boat*; John Kane, *The Monongahela Valley*; Walt Kuhn, *The Blue Clown*; Georgia O'Keeffe, *Cow's Skull, Red, White and Blue*; Horace Pippin, *End of the War: Starting Home*; Grant Wood, *The Midnight Ride of Paul Revere*.

**Literature**   Vicki Baum, *Grand Hotel*; Stephen V. Benét, *Ballads and Poems*; George Dillon, *The Flowering Stone* (Pulitzer Prize); William Faulkner, *Sanctuary*; Robert Frost, *Collected Poems* (Pulitzer Prize); G. Kaufman and M. Ryskind, *Of Thee I Sing* (Pulitzer Prize); Edna St. Vincent Millay, *Fatal Interview*; Eugene O'Neill, *Mourning Becomes Electra*; Damon Runyon, *Guys and Dolls*.

## Music—The Vernacular/Commercial Scene

**A. Births**   Nat Adderley (cornetist/composer) November 25; Rashied Ali (percussionist) July 1; David Baker (trombonist/composer) December 21; Carl Belew (singer/writer) April 21; Brook Benton (singer) September 19; Otis Blackwell (pianist/composer); Boxcar Willie (singer) September 1; Teresa Brewer (singer) May 7; Kenny Burrell (guitarist) July 31; Sonny Clark (pianist) July 21; Skeeter Davis (singer) December 30; "Ramblin'" Jack Elliott (singer/guitarist) August 1; Bob Gibson (folk singer) November 16; Tab Hunter (singer/actor) July 11; George Jones (singer/writer) September 12; Wynton Kelly (pianist) December 2; Bobbie Osborne (singer/mandolin player) December 7; Ike Turner (singer) November 26; Billy Vaughn (bandleader/arranger) April 12; Phil Woods (saxophonist) November 2.

**B. Deaths**   Bix Beiderbecke (cornetist/bandleader) August 6; Charles "Buddy" Bolden (cornetist/bandleader) November 4; Grant Clarke (lyricist/publisher) May 16; Jimmy Harrison (trombonist) July 23; John J. McNally (lyricist) March; Charlie Poole (singer) May 21; Jerome H. Remick (publisher) July 15.

**C. Biographical**

**Performing Groups**   Russ Columbo Band; Eddy Duchin Band; Kansas City Rockets; Light Crust Doughboys; Freddy Martin Big Band; Don Redman Band; Southland Troubadours.

**New Beginnings**   Thomas A. Dorsey Gospel Songs Music Publishing Co.; M. K. Jerome Publishing Co.; La Salle Music Publishers (Chicago); Songwriters' Protective Association.

**E. Representative Works**

**Musicals**   Irving Berlin, *Reaching for the Moon* (film); George and Ira Gershwin, *Of Thee I Sing!*

(Pulitzer Prize)—*Delicious* (film); Sammy Fain, *Everybody's Welcome*; J. Kern and O. Harbach, *The Cat and the Fiddle*; Rodgers and Hart, *America's Sweetheart*; S. Romberg and O. Hammerstein, *East Wind*; A. Schwartz and H. Dietz, *The Band Wagon*; H. Warren and M. Dixon, *The Laugh Parade*.

**Songs** Fred E. Ahlert, *When the Blue of the Night Meets the Dawn of the Day*; H. Arlen and T. Koehler, *I Love a Parade*; G. Arnheim, H. Tobias, and J. Lemare, *Sweet and Lovely*; C. Calloway and I. Mills, *Minnie the Moocher*; Hoagy Carmichael, *Lazy River*; J. Fred Coots, *Love Letters in the Sand*; P. De Rose and C. Tobias, *Wagon Wheels—When Your Hair Has Turned to Silver*; Gerald Marks and S. Simons, *All of Me*; R. Noble and J. Campbell, *Goodnight, Sweetheart*; Don Redman, *Chant of the Weed*; L. T. Rene and C. Muse, *When It's Sleepy Time Down South*; A. Schwartz and H. Dietz, *Dancing in the Dark*; Harry Warren, *I Found a Million Dollar Baby (in a 5 and 10 Cent Store)*.

**Other** Duke Ellington, *Creole Rhapsody*; Alfred Newman, *Indiscreet* (film music).

## Music—The Cultivated/Art Music Scene

**F. Births** Frank d'Accone (musicologist) June 13; David Baker (composer) December 21; Dalton Baldwin (pianist) December 19; Louis Ballard (composer) July 8; Martin Boykan (pianist/composer) April 12; Gloria Davy (soprano) March 29; Lucia Dlugoszewski (composer) June 16; Mignon Dunn (mezzo-soprano) June 17; Jonathan Elkus (conductor/composer) August 2; Ezio Flagello (bass) January 28; Donald Harris (composer/educator) April 7; Lilian Kallir (pianist) May 6; Alvin Lucier (composer) May 14; Donald Martino (composer) May 16; Jens Nygaard (pianist/conductor) October 26; Leslie Parnas (cellist) November 11; Joan Peyser (musicologist) June 12; Raoul Pleskow (composer/educator) October 12; Gregg Smith (conductor) August 21; Shirley Verrett (mezzo-soprano) May 31; Henry Weinberg (composer) June 7; Arthur Weisberg (conductor) April 4; Peter Westergaard (composer/theorist) May 28; Michael White (composer).

**G. Deaths** John H. Brewer (organist) November 30; George Chadwick (composer) April 4; William Gustafsen (bass) March 10; Emmons Howard (organ builder) March 18; Peter C. Lutkin (organist/conductor) December 27; Clara Kathleen Rogers (British-born pianist/composer) March 8; Emma Thursby (soprano) July 4; Adolf Weidig (German-born composer) September 23.

**H. Debuts**

**United States** Sigfrid Karg-Elert (German organist—tour), Jan Kiepura (Polish tenor—Chicago), John Kirkpatrick (pianist—New York), Nino Martini (Italian tenor—Philadelphia), Rosetta Pampanini (Italian soprano—Chicago), Risë Stevens (mezzo-soprano—New York), Richard Tauber (Austrian-born tenor—New York).

**Metropolitan Opera** Max Lorenz (German tenor), Lily Pons (French soprano), Georges Thill (French tenor).

**Other** Charles Kullman (tenor—Berlin).

**I. New Positions**

**Conductors** Vladimir Golschmann (St. Louis Symphony Orchestra—to 1957); Eugene Goossens (Cincinnati Symphony Orchestra—to 1946); Hans Kindler (National Symphony Orchestra—to 1948); Eugene Ormandy (Minneapolis Symphony Orchestra—to 1936).

**Educational** Leroy Anderson (band, Harvard—to 1935); Fraser Gange (Peabody—to 1957); John Wallace Goodrich (director, New England Conservatory—to 1942); Wiktor Labunski (Memphis College of Music—to 1937); Fritz Reiner (conducting/opera, Curtis—to 1941); Carleton Sprague Smith (music and history, Columbia—to 1967); Leon Stein (DePaul University—to 1978); Herbert Witherspoon (president, Cincinnati Conservatory of Music).

**Other** Erno Rapee (general music director, NBC); Carleton Sprague Smith (music division, New York Public Library—to 1959); Deems Taylor (music critic, *New York American*); Hugo Weisgall (music director, Har Sinai Temple Choir, Baltimore).

**J. Honors and Awards**

**Honors**   Charles Martin Loeffler (American Academy); Albert Stoessel (National Institute).

**K. Biographical**   Milton Babbitt enters the University of Pennsylvania in order to study mathematics but soon switches to the study of music; Fausto Cleva, Alexander Kipnis, and Nicolas Slonimsky all become naturalized American citizens; Ruth Crawford marries musicologist Charles Seeger; Sigrid Karg-Elert begins a year-long organ tour of the United States; Pierre Luboshutz marries pianist Genia Nemenoff; Fernando Sacconi (Italian violin maker) begins working in New York; Colin McPhee goes to Indonesia to study and work and stays till 1939; Vladimir Ussachevsky (Manchurian-born composer) comes to the United States and settles in California.

**L. Musical Beginnings**

**Performing Groups**   Albuquerque Civic Symphony Orchestra; Fort Worth Civic Music Association; National Symphony Orchestra (Washington, DC); Portland Concert Association (Maine).

**Educational**   Loyola University College of Music; Music Library Association (MLA); Pedreira Music Academy (Santurce, Puerto Rico).

**Other**   Aeolian-Skinner Organ Co. (by merger); Bruckner Society of America; G. B. Dealy Award Competition (Dallas); Galaxy Music Corporation (New York); Metropolitan Opera Broadcasts; Severance Hall (Cleveland); Society of European State Authors and Composers (SESAC, Inc.); Salzedo Harp Colony (Camden, Maine).

**M. Music Publications**

Bucharoff, Simon, *The Modern Pianist's Textbook*
Downes, Olin, *Symphonic Broadcasts*
Dykema, Peter, *Music for School Administrators*
Fisher, William A., *The Music That Washington Knew*
Galli-Rini, Anthony, *Method for Accordion*
Howard, John Tasker, *Our American Music*
Mason, Daniel G., *Tune In, America! A Study of Our Coming Musical Independence*
Mursell, J. and Glenn, M., *The Psychology of School Music Teaching*
Pratt, Carroll, *The Meaning of Music*
Stringfield, Lamar, *America and Her Music*

**N. Musical Compositions**

**Chamber Music**   George Antheil, *Six Little Pieces for String Quartet*; Ruth Crawford, *String Quartet*; Elliot Griffis, *Violin Sonata*; Daniel G. Mason, *Serenade for String Quartet*; Harl McDonald, *Piano Trio No. 1*; Quincy Porter, *String Quartet No. 4*; David S. Smith, *String Sextet*; Virgil Thomson, *String Quartet No. 1—Serenade for Flute and Violin*; Edgard Varèse, *Ionisation* (percussion); Mark Wessel, *String Quartet—Prelude and Fugue for String Quartet*; Clarence White, *String Quartet No. 1—String Quartet No. 2*.

**Choral/Vocal**   Samuel Barber, *Dover Beach, Opus 3*; John Alden Carpenter, *Song of Faith* (chorus and orchestra); Robert Delaney, *John Brown's Body* (Pulitzer Prize); Humphrey Stewart, *Missa pro defunctis*; Edwin John Stringham, *Pilgrim Fathers* (cantata); Virgil Thomson, *Stabat Mater* (soprano and strings)—*La Belle en Dormant* (soprano and piano); Hugo Weisgall, *Four Impressions* (Bearns Prize).

**Concertos**   Samuel Barlow, *Piano Concerto*; Marc Blitzstein, *Piano Concerto*; Radie Britain, *Rhapsodie Phantasie* (piano and orchestra); Arthur Farwell, *Symphonic Study No. 6: Mountain Vision* (piano concerto); Edward Burlingame Hill, *Piano Concertino*; Arne Oldberg, *Piano Concerto No. 2* (Hollywood Bowl Prize); Emerson Whithorne, *Violin Concerto*.

**Operas**   Paul Hastings Allen, *La piccola Figaro*; George Antheil, *Helen Retires*; Marc Blitzstein, *The Harpies*; Rossetter Gleason Cole, *The Maypole Lovers* (Bispham Medal); Harry L. Freeman, *Uzziah*; Eleanor Freer, *A Legend of Spain*; Richard Hageman, *Caponsacchi* (Bispham Medal); Mabel Wood Hill, *The Jolly Beggars* (operetta); Mary Carr Moore, *Los rubios*; Bernard Rogers, *The Marriage of Aude* (Bispham Medal).

**Orchestra/Band**    Arthur Cohn, *Suite for Orchestra*; Mabel Wheeler Daniels, *Deep Forest*; Isadore Freed, *Jeux de Timbres*; George Gershwin, *Orchestral Rhapsody No. 2*; Parks Grant, *Symphonic Fantasia*; Ferde Grofé, *Grand Canyon Suite*; Henry Hadley, *Silhouettes—San Francisco*; Richard Hammond, *Carnival*; Roy Harris, *Toccata for Orchestra*; Ethel G. Hier, *Choréographe* (ballet); Philip James, *Station WGZBX*; Boris Koutzen, *Valley Forge*; John Powell, *Natchez on the Hill*; Wallingford Riegger, *Fantasy and Fugue, Opus 10*; Carl Ruggles, *Sun-Treader*; Charles S. Skilton, *Overture in E Major*; John Philip Sousa, *Marches—The Aviator's March—A Century of Progress—The Circumnavigator's March—Kansas Wildcats—Northern Pines*; Leo Sowerby, *Passacaglia, Interlude and Fugue*; Lamar Stringfield, *A Negro Parade*.

**Piano/Organ**    Isadore Freed, *Sonorités Rhythmiques*; Gian Carlo Menotti, *Variations on a Theme of Schumann*; Arthur Shepherd, *Eclogue No. 1*; Gerald Strang, *Mirrororrim*; Hugo Weisgall, *Sonata No. 1 in F-Sharp Minor*.

**Symphonies**    Robert Russell Bennett, *Abraham Lincoln Symphony*; Nicolai Berezowsky, *Symphony No. 1, Opus 12*; Philip G. Clapp, *Symphony No. 9 in E-Flat Minor, "The Pioneers"*; Edwin Gerschefski, *Classic Symphony*; Richard Hammond, *Sinfonietta*; Hunter Johnson, *Symphony No. 1*; Dane Rudhyar, *Sinfonietta*; Frederick Search, *Symphony No. 2*; Tibor Serly, *Symphony No. 1*; Randall Thompson, *Symphony No. 2*; Virgil Thomson, *Symphony No. 2*; Joseph F. Wagner, *Sinfonietta Americana*.

# 1932

☀

## Historical Highlights

Franklin D. Roosevelt becomes the 32nd president; Charles Lindbergh's son is kidnapped and murdered; army troops are called in to disperse the "Veteran's Army" camping out in Washington, DC; the Reconstruction Finance Corporation is founded; the first modern Winter Olympics take place in Lake Placid, New York; Japanese troops invade China.

## World Cultural Highlights

**World Art**    Barbara Hepworth, *Reclining Figure*; Pablo Picasso, *Girl before a Mirror*; Diego Rivera, *Detroit Industry*; Georges Rouault, *Christ Mocked by Soldiers*; Walter Sickert, *Miss Earhart's Arrival*.

**World Literature**    W. H. Auden, *The Orators*; Aldous Huxley, *Brave New World*; Sean O'Faolain, *Midsummer Night Madness*; Salvatore Quasimodo, *Oboe sommerso*.

**World Music**    Frederick Delius, *Prelude to Irmelin*; Sergei Prokofiev, *Piano Concerto No. 5*; Sergei Rachmaninoff, *Variations on a Theme of Corelli*; Dmitri Shostakovich, *Lady Macbeth of Mtsensk*.

**Miscellaneous**    The Ballet Russe de Monte Carlo is founded, as are the Boyd Neel Orchestra and London Philharmonic Orchestra; births include Peter Blake, Fernando Botero, Glenn Gould, and Rodion Shchedrin; deaths include Eugène d'Albert, René Bazin, Johanna Gadski, and Emil Paur.

## American Art and Literature Highlights

**Births/Deaths**    Births include artists Robert Bechtle, Richard Estes, R. B. Kitaj, and literary figures John G. Dunne, Jack Gelber, Rona Jaffe, John Jakes, Sylvia Plath, Gay Talese, and John Updike; deaths include art figures Alfred and Louis Maurer, Julius Melchers, and literary figures Charles W. Chesnutt, Hart Crane, Harold MacGrath, James Oppenheim, and Henry Kitchell Webster.

**Art Works**    Peter Blume, *Light of the World*; Charles Burchfield, *Old Farm House (September Sunlight)*; Morris Graves, *Falcon and Chalice*; Marsden Hartley, *Lost Country—Petrified*

*Sandhills*; Reginald Marsh, *Bread Line—No One Has Starved*; Henry V. Poor, *Grey Day*; Ben Shahn, *Passion of Sacco and Vanzetti*; Grant Wood, *Daughters of the American Revolution*; William Zorach, *Torso*.

**Literature**    Pearl Buck, *The Good Earth* (Pulitzer Prize); Erskine Caldwell, *Tobacco Road*; John Dos Passos, *1919*; James T. Farrell, *Young Lonigan*; Edna Ferber, *Dinner at Eight*; J. Hall and C. Nordhoff, *Mutiny on the Bounty*; Ernest Hemingway, *Death in the Afternoon*; Archibald MacLeish, *Conquistador* (Pulitzer Prize); Max Miller, *I Cover the Waterfront*; Thomas Stribling, *The Store* (Pulitzer Prize).

## Music—The Vernacular/Commercial Scene

**A. Births**    Johnny Adams (singer) February 28; Juke Boy Bonner (singer/guitarist) March 22; Dorsey Burnette (singer/writer) December 28; Johnny Cash (singer) February 26; James L. Cleveland (singer) December 5; Patsy Cline (singer) September 8; Albert Collins (guitarist/singer) October 1; Charlie Feathers (singer) June 12; Eydie Gorme (singer) August 16; Roland Hanna (pianist) February 10; Stonewall Jackson (singer) November 6; Leroy Jenkins (jazz violinist) March 11; Little Richard (pianist/singer) December 5; Jaye P. Morgan (singer); Carl Perkins (singer) April 9; Della Reese (singer) July 6; Debbie Reynolds (singer/actress) April 1; Charlie Rich (singer/writer) December 14; Keely Smith (singer) March 9; Mel Tillis (singer) August 8; Melvin Van Peebles (composer/lyricist); Dottie West (singer) October 11; John Williams (composer/conductor) February 8; Faron Young (singer) February 25.

**B. Deaths**    William Jerome (lyricist) June 25; Robert A. King (composer/lyricist) April 13; Bubber Miley (trumpeter) May 24; Chauncey Olcott (singer/composer) March 18; Frank Teschemacher (clarinetist/saxophonist) March 1; Florenz Ziegfeld (impresario) July 22.

**C. Biographical**

**Performing Groups**    Andrews Sisters; Dixieliners; Louisiana Shakers; New Orleans Feetwarmers; Spirits of Rhythm.

**New Beginnings**    Dorsey House (Chicago); André Kostelanetz Presents (radio); Bluebird Records (subsidiary, RCA Victor); National Convention of Gospel Choirs and Choruses (Chicago).

**Miscellaneous**    Ella Logan (Scottish singer) comes to the United States.

**E. Representative Works**

**Musicals**    Irving Berlin, *Face the Music*; Eubie Blake, *Shuffle Along of 1933*; Vernon Duke, *Walk a Little Faster*; J. Gorney and E. Y. Harburg, *Americana*; J. Kern and O. Hammerstein, *Music in the Air*; Cole Porter, *The Gay Divorcée*; A. Schwartz and H. Dietz, *Flying Colors*; V. Youmans and E. Heyman, *Through the Years*; V. Youmans and B. DeSylva, *Take a Chance*.

**Songs**    H. Arlen and T. Koehler, *I Gotta Right to Sing the Blues*; Gus Arnheim, *After All Is Said and Done*; Gene Autry, *That Silver-Haired Daddy of Mine*; George Bassman, *I'm Getting Sentimental Over You*; Thomas A. Dorsey, *Precious Lord, Take My Hand*; V. Duke and E. Y. Harburg, *April in Paris*; Duke Ellington, *It Don't Mean a Thing (If It Ain't Got That Swing)*; Herman Hupfield, *Let's Put Out the Lights and Go to Sleep*; Jimmy McHugh, *Don't Blame Me*; Arthur Schwartz, *Louisiana Hayride*.

**Other**    James P. Johnson, *Harlem Symphony*.

## Music—The Cultivated/Art Music Scene

**F. Births**    Elaine Barkin (composer) December 15; John B. Chance (composer) November 20; Michael Colgrass (composer) April 22; Mary Costa (soprano) April 5; Reri Grist (soprano) February 29; Ivan Davis (pianist) February 4; William Dooley (baritone) September 9; Enrico di Giuseppe (tenor) October 14; M. William Karlins (composer) February 25; Karl Kroeger (composer/musicologist) April 13; Marvin David Levy (composer) August 2; Henry Lewis (conductor) October 16; Jerome Lowenthal (pianist) February 11; Martin Mailman (composer/conductor) June 30; Joel Mandelbaum (composer) October 12; Anna Moffo (soprano) June 27; Pauline Oliveros (composer) May 30; Frank Rutkowski (harpsichord maker) December 12; Regina Sarfaty (mezzo-soprano); Joseph Silverstein (violinist/conductor) March 21; Wayne Slawson (composer/theorist) December 29; Patrick J. Smith (critic) December 11; Alan B. Stout (composer) November 26; Andrea Velis (tenor) June 7; Richard Westenburg (conductor) April 26; Ramon Zupko (composer) November 14.

**G. Deaths**   Franz X. Arens (German-born composer) January 28; Andreas Dippel (German-born tenor/impresario) May 12; George Eastman (art patron) March 14; Arthur Friedheim (German-born pianist) October 10; Charles H. Gabriel (composer/educator) September 14; Clayton Johns (pianist/composer) March 5; John Orth (organist) May 3; John P. Sousa (bandmaster/composer) March 6; Albert A. Stanley (organist) May 19; Humphrey John Stewart (British-born organist) December 28; Henry B. Tremaine (piano maker) May 13; Clarence Whitehill (bass-baritone) December 18.

**H. Debuts**

**United States**   E. Power Biggs (British organist—New York), James Melton (tenor—New York), Carlo Morelli (Chilean baritone—Chicago), Egon Petri (German pianist—New York), Izler Solomon (conductor—Lansing, Michigan), Henri Temianka (Polish violinist—New York).

**Metropolitan Opera**   Rose Bampton (soprano), Richard Bonelli (baritone), Armando Borgioli (Italian bass), Göta Ljunberg (Swedish soprano), Francesco Merli (Italian tenor), Tito Schipa (Italian tenor).

**I. New Positions**

**Conductors**   Basil Cameron (Seattle Symphony Orchestra—to 1938); Wassili Leps (Providence Symphony Orchestra—to 1941).

**Educational**   Charles Warren Fox (Eastman—to 1970); Roy Harris (Juilliard); A. Tillman Merritt (Harvard—to 1972); Quincy Porter (Vassar—to 1938); Leo Sowerby (American Conservatory, Chicago—to 1962).

**Other**   Herbert Elwell (music critic, *Cleveland Plain Dealer*—to 1964); Irving Kolodin (music critic, *New York Sun*—to 1950); Edwin John Stringham (music editor, American Book Co.—to 1939).

**J. Honors and Awards**

**Honors**   Ernst Bacon (Pulitzer Travel Scholarship); Walter Damrosch (American Academy); Vittorio Giannini (Rome Prize).

**K. Biographical**   Jelly d'Arányi makes a second concert tour of the United States; Artur Balsam (Polish pianist) tours the United States with Yehudi Menuhin; Elliott Carter receives his M.A. from Harvard and goes to Paris for a three-year stay studying with Nadia Boulanger; Alexei Haieff (Russian composer) comes to the United States; Jan Peerce begins singing at Radio City Music Hall; Ralph Vaughan Williams visits the United States and lectures at Bryn Mawr; John Finley Williamson again moves his Westminster Choir School, this time from Ithaca, New York, to Princeton, New Jersey.

**L. Musical Beginnings**

**Performing Groups**   Baltimore Opera Co.; Barrère-Britt-Salzedo Trio; Buffalo Philharmonic Orchestra; Curtis String Quartet (Philadelphia); Haydn Festival Choir (Indianapolis); Maganini Chamber Symphony (New York); Milwaukee Opera Co.; North Carolina Symphony Orchestra (Raleigh); Providence Symphony Orchestra (Rhode Island).

**Festivals**   Baldwin-Wallace Bach Festival (Berea, Ohio); Central City Opera Festival (Colorado); Yaddo Music Festival (Saratoga Springs, New York).

**Educational**   American Library of Musicology; University of Louisville School of Music.

**Other**   Aeolian American Corporation (merger of American Piano Co. and Aeolian Co.); Chamber Music Society of America; *Chord and Discord*; Columbia Concerts Corporation (Artists Management, Inc.); Radio City Music Hall (New York); Schlicker Organ Co. (Buffalo).

## M.  Music Publications

Bauer, M. and Peyser, E., *Music through the Ages*
Bernstein, Martin, *Score Reading*
Borowski, Felix, *The Standard Concert Guide*
Chaliapin, Feodor, *Man and Mask*
Earhart, Will, *Music to the Listening Ear*
Idelsohn, Abraham, *Jewish Liturgy and Its Development*
Karpeles, Maud, *English Folk Songs from the Southern Appalachians*
Kwalwasser, Jacob, *Problems in Public School Music*
Moore, Douglas, *Listening to Music*
Saminsky, Lazare, *Music of Our Day*
Strunk, Oliver, *State and Resources of Musicology in the United States*
Yasser, Joseph, *A Theory of Evolving Tonality*

## N.  Musical Compositions

**Chamber Music**   Samuel Barber, *Cello Sonata*; John J. Becker, *Soundpiece No. 1* (piano and string quartet); Charles W. Cadman, *Violin Sonata in G*; Arthur Cohn, *String Quartet No. 3*; Ulric Cole, *String Quartet*; Frederick S. Converse, *Piano Trio In E Minor*; Richard Donovan, *Sextet for Piano and Winds*; Arcady Dubensky, *String Quartet No. 1 in C*; Harry L. Freeman, *The Slave*; Sidney Homer, *Piano Quintet*; Dorothy James, *String Quartet in One Movement*; Harl McDonald, *Fantasy for String Quartet—Piano Trio No. 2*; Paul Nordoff, *String Quartet No. 1—Violin Sonata No. 1*; Frederick Search, *String Quartet No. 3*; Virgil Thomson, *String Quartet No. 2*; David Van Vactor, *Quintet for Flute and String Quartet* (Society for Publication of American Music Prize); Bernard Wagenaar, *String Quartet No. 2*; Adolph Weiss, *String Quartet No. 4*; Emerson Whithorne, *Violin Sonata*.

**Choral/Vocal**   John Cage, *Three Songs on Gertrude Stein*; Henry Hadley, *Belshazzar, Opus 112* (cantata); Philip James, *General William Booth Enters into Heaven*; Arthur Shepherd, *The Song of the Pilgrims* (cantata); Elie Siegmeister, *The Strange Funeral in Braddock* (song); Charles S. Skilton, *Ticonderoga* (cantata); Randall Thompson, *Americana*; Wintter Watts, *Circles* (song cycle).

**Concertos**   Ernst Bacon, *Symphonic Fugue* (piano and strings); John Alden Carpenter, *Patterns* (piano and orchestra); Edwin Gerschefski, *Concertino for Piano and Orchestra*; Frederick Jacobi, *Cello Concerto*; Paul Nordoff, *Piano Concerto No. 1*; Leo Sowerby, *Piano Concerto No. 2*; David Van Vactor, *Flute Concerto*; Hermann H. Wetzler, *Symphonie concertante* (violin and orchestra).

**Operas**   Marc Blitzstein, *The Condemned*; Charles W. Cadman, *South in Sonora* (operetta); Eleanor Freer, *Massimilliano, the Court Jester*; Vittorio Giannini, *Lucedia*; Louis Gruenberg, *The Emperor Jones* (Bispham Medal); Dorothy James, *Paolo and Francesca*; Nikolai Lopatnikoff, *Danton*; Otto Luening, *Evangeline*; Hugo Weisgall, *Night*; Clarence White, *Ouanga* (Bispham Medal).

**Orchestra/Band**   Joseph Achron, *Golem Suite*; George Antheil, *Morceau (The Creole)*; John J. Becker, *Dance Figure: Stagework No. 1* (ballet); Charles W. Cadman, *Hollywood Suite*; Richard Donovan, *Smoke and Steel* (symphonic poem); Arthur Farwell, *Prelude to a Spiritual Drama*; George Gershwin, *Cuban Overture*; David Guion, *Shingandi*; Douglas Moore, *Overture on an American Tune*; Solomon Pimsleur, *The Miracle of Life and the Mystery of Death* (symphonic poem); Quincy Porter, *Poem and Dance*; John Powell, *Natchez-on-the-Hill, Opus 30*; Wallingford Riegger, *Dichotomy, Opus 12*; David S. Smith, *1929—A Satire*; Lamar Stringfield, *The Legend of John Henry*.

**Piano/Organ**   Hans Barth, *Sonata No. 2*; Marion Bauer, *Dance Sonata*; Amy Beach, *Three Pianoforte Pieces, Opus 128*; Paul Creston, *Five Dances, Opus 1*; Arthur Farwell, *Two Composition, Opus 93*; Vivian Fine, *Four Polyphonic Pieces*; Nikolai Lopatnikoff, *Variations for Piano*; Florence Price, *Sonata in E Minor*; Vittorio Rieti, *Six Short Pieces*; Wallingford Riegger, *Four Tone Pictures, Opus 14*; Elie Siegmeister, *Theme and Variations No. 1;* Adolph Weiss, *Sonata*.

**Symphonies**   Ernst Bacon, *Symphony No. 1*; Nicolai Berezowsky, *Sinfonietta, Opus 17*; Elliot Griffis, *Symphony No. 1*; Herbert Inch, *Symphony*; Werner Janssen, *Louisiana Symphony*; Quinto Maganini, *Symphony in G Minor*; Harl McDonald, *Symphony No. 1, "The Santa Fe Trail"*; Florence Price, *Symphony No. 1 in E Minor* (Wanamaker Prize); Vittorio Rieti, *Symphony No. 3*; Tibor Serly, *Symphony No. 2*; Arthur Shepherd, *Sinfonia Domestica di Famiglia Blossom*; Mark Wessel, *Symphony*; Paul White, *Symphony in E Minor*.

# 1933

❋

## Historical Highlights

The 20th Amendment provides earlier swearing in of the elected president; the 21st Amendment repeals prohibition; Congress forms the National Recovery Administration (NRA), the Tennessee Valley Authority and Civilian Conservation Corps (CCC); Adolf Hitler is appointed Chancellor of Germany and pulls Germany out of the League of Nations and begins rearmament.

## World Cultural Highlights

**World Art**   Max Beckmann, *Departure* (beginning); Alberto Giacometti, *The Palace at 4 A.M.*; Henri Matisse, *The Dance*; Diego Rivera, *Man at the Crossroads*; Maurice de Vlaminck, *Les Gerber*.

**World Literature**   Noel Coward, *Design for Living*; James Hilton, *Lost Horizon*; Stephen Spender, *Poems*; Hugh Walpole, *Vanessa*; William Butler Yeats, *The Winding Stair and Other Poems*.

**World Music**   Joseph Jongen, *Symphonie Concertante*; Zoltán Kodály, *Dances of Galanta*; Olivier Messiaen, *L'Ascension*; Franz Schmidt, *Symphony No. 4*; Dmitri Shostakovich, *Piano Concerto No. 1*.

**Miscellaneous**   The Banff Centre and School of Fine Arts and Palestine Conservatory of Music and Dramatic Art open; births include Claudio Abbado, Montserrat Caballé, Jerzy Kosinski, and Krzystof Penderecki; deaths include Olaf Bull, Paul Ernst, John Galsworthy, and Stefan George.

## American Art and Literature Highlights

**Births/Deaths**   Births include art figures Dan Flavin, Sam Gilliam, Joseph Raffaele, Mark di Suvero, and literary figures John C. Gardner, Jr., Cormac McCarthy, Rod McKuen, Philip Roth, and Susan Sontag; deaths include artists John Haberle, James Kelly, George Luks, Robert Vonnoh, and literary figures Earl Derr Biggers, Ring Lardner, Sara Teasdale, and Henry Van Dyke.

**Art Works**   Gifford Beal, *Equestrian*; Charles Burchfield, *Ice Glare;* Marsden Hartley, *Eight Bells Folly: Memorial to Hart Crane*; Seymour Lipton, *Straphanger*; John Marin, *From the Bridge, New York City*; Paul Manship, *Prometheus* (Rockefeller Center); Waldo Peirce, *County Fair*; Horace Pippin, *The Buffalo Hunt*; Hugo Robus, *Girl Washing Her Hair*.

**Literature**   Hervey Allen, *Anthony Adverse*; Maxwell Anderson, *Both Your Houses* (Pulitzer Prize); Erskine Caldwell, *God's Little Acre*; Edgar Guest, *Life's Highway*; J. Hall and C. Nordhoff, *Men Against the Sea*; Robert Hillyer, *Collected Verse* (Pulitzer Prize); Sidney Kingsley, *Men in White* (Pulitzer Prize); Eugene O'Neill, *Ah, Wilderness!*; Elmer Rice, *We, the People*; Sara Teasdale, *Strange Victory*.

## Music—The Vernacular/Commercial Scene

**A. Births**   Jesse Belvin (singer) December 15; James Brown (singer/bandleader) May 3; Roy Clark (singer/guitarist) April 15; Robert Goulet (singer) November 26; Earl Grant (piano) January 20; John Handy II (saxophonist/composer) February 3; Bobby Helms (singer) August 15; Jerry Herman (composer/lyricist) July 10; Cissy Houston (singer); Quincy Jones (arranger/bandleader) March 14; Buddy Knox (singer) July 20; Jerry Leiber (songwriter) April 25; Bobby Lewis (singer)

February 17; Clyde McPhatter (singer) November 15; Willie Nelson (singer) April 30; Lloyd Price (singer) March 9; Chita Rivera (singer/dancer) January 23; Mike Seeger (folk singer) August 15; Wayne Shorter (saxophonist/composer) August 25; Nina Simone (singer); Cecil Taylor (pianist/composer) March 15; Joe Tex (singer) August 8; Tommy Tucker (singer) March 5; Conway Twitty (singer) September 1.

**B. Deaths**   Marie Cahill (singer) August 23; Freddie Keppard (cornetist) July 15; William H. Krell (bandleader/composer) September 30; Eddie Lang (guitarist) March 26; Jimmie Rodgers (singer/writer) May 26.

**C. Biographical**

**Performing Groups**   Benny Carter Big Band; Gil Evans Big Band; Jeter-Pillars Orchestra (St. Louis); Roberta Martin Singers; Pioneer Trio (Sons of the Pioneers).

**New Beginnings**   National Folk Festival Association (National Council for the Traditional Arts); *Tempo* (to 1941).

**Miscellaneous**   Desi Arnaz (Cuban bandleader/singer) comes to the United States.

**D. Publications**   G. P. Jackson, *White Spirituals in the Southern Uplands.*

**E. Representative Works:**

**Musicals**   Irving Berlin, *As Thousands Cheer* (revue); George and Ira Gershwin, *Pardon My English—Let Them Eat Cake*; R. Henderson, L. Brown, and B. DeSylva, *Strike Me Pink*; J. Kern and O. Harbach, *Roberta*; Cole Porter, *Nymph Errant*; H. Warren and A. Dubin, *42nd Street* (film); V. Youmans and G. Kahn and E. Eliscu, *Flying Down to Rio* (film).

**Songs**   Harold Arlen, *Stormy Weather*; H. Arlen, E. Y. Harburg, and B. Rose, *It's Only a Paper Moon*; Irving Caesar, *If I Forget You*; Hoagy Carmichael, *Lazybones*; F. Churchill and A. Ronell, *Who's Afraid of the Big Bad Wolf*; Billy J. Hill, *The Last Round-Up*; J. Little and J. Young, *In a Shanty in Old Shanty Town*; J. Livingston and M. Symes, *It's the Talk of the Town*; Harry Revel, *Did You Ever See a Dream Walking*; H. Spina and J. Burke, *Annie Doesn't Live Here Anymore*; Harry Warren, *Shuffle Off to Buffalo*; H. Warren and A. Dubin, *We're in the Money*.

**Other**   Alfred Newman, *I Cover the Waterfront* (film music); Max Steiner, *King Kong* (film music).

## Music—The Cultivated/Art Music Scene

**F. Births**   Alden Ashforth (composer) May 13; Easley Blackwood (composer/ pianist) April 21; John Browning (pianist) May 22; Jan DeGaetani (mezzo-soprano) July 10; Richard Dufallo (conductor/clarinetist) January 30; Robert Kern (baritone); David Lewin (theorist/composer) July 2; Ronald Lo Presti (composer) October 28; Spiro Malas (bass-baritone) January 28; W. Francis McBeth (composer) March 9; John Obetz (organist) June 29; Mel Powell (composer) February 12; Eric Salzman (composer/author) September 8; Don Smithers (trumpeter/musicologist) February 17; Joel Warren Spiegelman (composer) January 23; Morton Subotnick (composer) April 14; Bertram Turetzky (contrabassist) February 14.

**G. Deaths**   Blair Fairchild (composer) April 23; Eugen Haile (German-born composer) August 14; Benjamin Ives Gilman (ethnomusicologist) March 18; Sissieretta Jones (soprano) June 24; Emil Oberhoffer (German-born conductor) May 22; Albert Ross Parsons (pianist/composer) June 14; Charles A. Tindley (hymnist) July 26; Richard Henry Warren (organist) December 3.

**H. Debuts**

**United States**   Isobel Baillie (Scottish soprano—New York), Margaret Bonds (first black soloist with the Chicago Symphony Orchestra), Norman Cordon (baritone—Chicago), Julius Huehn (baritone—New York), Ray Lev (pianist—New York), Rudolf Serkin (Austrian pianist—Washington, DC), Leonard Shure (pianist—Boston).

**Metropolitan Opera**   Richard Crooks (tenor), Virgilio Lazzari (bass), Frida Leider (German soprano), Emanuel List (Austrian bass), Nino Martini (Italian tenor), Eidé Norena (Norwegian soprano), Maria Olczewska (German mezzo-soprano).

**I. New Positions**

**Conductors**   Otto Klemperer (Los Angeles Philharmonic Orchestra—to 1939); Karl Krueger (Kansas City Philharmonic Orchestra—to 1943); Frédérique Petrides (Orchestrette of New York); Artur Rodzinski (Cleveland Orchestra—to 1943); Dorsey Whittington (Birmingham [Alabama] Symphony Orchestra—to 1948).

**Educational**   Mabel Garrison (Smith College—to 1939); Paul Henry Lang (musicology, Columbia—to 1969); Hugo Leichtentritt (Harvard—to 1940); Arnold Schoenberg (Malkin Conservatory); Isabelle Vengerova (piano, Mannes); John W. Work, Jr. (Fisk University—to 1967).

**Other**   Deems Taylor (director, ASCAP—to 1966).

**J. Honors and Awards**

**Honors**   John Alden Carpenter (PhD, Wisconsin University); Philip James (National Institute).

**K. Biographical**   George Antheil returns permanently to the United States; George Balanchine (Russian choreographer), Arthur Balsam (Polish pianist), Paul Bekker (German musicologist), Frederick Dorian (Austrian critic), Igor Gorin (Russian baritone), Viktor Hollaender (German conductor/composer), Otto Klemperer (German conductor), Nicolas Nabokov (Russian composer), and Ignace Strasfogel (Polish conductor/pianist) all come to the United States; Vladimir Horowitz marries Arturo Toscanini's daughter, Wanda; Werner Josten and Artur Rodzinski become American citizens; Hugo Leichtentritt returns to the United States.

**L. Musical Beginnings**

**Performing Groups**   Alabama Symphony Orchestra (Birmingham Symphony Orchestra); Chicago Grand Opera Co. II; Dayton Civic Concert Band; Dayton Philharmonic Orchestra; Kansas City Philharmonic Orchestra; Little Rock Symphony Orchestra (to 1939); Orchestrette of New York; St. Paul Opera Association; San Diego Polyphonia; Oakland Symphony Orchestra; Wallenstein Sinfonietta.

**Educational**   Malkin Conservatory (Boston).

**Other**   Hammond Organ; National Association for American Composers and Conductors (National Association of Composers, USA in 1975).

**M. Music Publications**

Bauer, Marion, *Twentieth Century Music*
Coleman, R. H., *The American Hymnal* (Baptist)
Cowell, Henry, *American Composers on American Music*
Fisher, William A., *One Hundred and Fifty Years of Music Publishing in the United States*
Forsyth, Cecil, *Clashpans*
Peyser, Ethel, *How to Enjoy Music*
Piston, Walter, *Principles of Harmonic Analysis*
Spaeth, Sigmund, *The Art of Enjoying Music*

**N. Musical Compositions**

**Chamber Music**   Samuel Barlow, *Ballad and Scherzo for String Quartet*; Nicolai Berezowsky, *String Quartet, Opus 16*; John Cage, *Clarinet Sonata*; Arcady Dubensky, *String Sextet in C*; Frederick Jacobi, *String Quartet No. 2*; Wesley La Violette, *String Quartet No. 2*; Harl McDonald, *String Quartet on Negro Themes*; Douglas Moore, *String Quartet*; Walter Piston, *String Quartet No. 1—String Quartet No. 2*; Leroy Robertson, *Piano Quintet* (Society for the Publication of American Music Award); Arthur Shepherd, *String Quartet No. 1 in E Minor*; Leon Stein, *String Quartet No. 1*; Gerald Strang, *Clarinet Quintet*; Lamar Stringfield, *A Mountain Episode* (string quartet); Burnet Tuthill, *Nocturne* (flute and string quartet)—*String Quartet*; David Van Vactor, *Twenty-Four Etudes for Flute*.

**Choral/Vocal**   John J. Becker, *Missa Symphonica*; Seth Bingham, *Wilderness Stone*; Ernest Bloch, *Sacred Service*; Franz C. Bornschein, *Enchanted Isle*; Richard Donovan, *Four Songs for Soprano and String Quartet*; William Schuman, *Four Canonic Choruses*.

**Concertos**    Joseph Achron, *Violin Concerto No. 2, Opus 68*; John J. Becker, *Horn Concerto*; Ross Lee Finney, *Violin Concerto No. 1* (revised 1952); Arne Oldberg, *Violin Concerto*; David Stanley Smith, *Violin Concerto*.

**Operas**    Avery Claflin, *Hester Prynne*; Howard Hanson, *Merry Mount, Opus 31*; Hall Johnson, *Run Little Chillun* (folk opera); Gail Kubik, *American Caprice*; Mary Carr Moore, *Flutes of Jade Happiness*; Charles Skilton, *Mary Rose*.

**Orchestra/Band**    Samuel Barber, *The School for Scandal Overture* (Bearns Prize)—*Music for a Scene from Shelley*; John J. Becker, *Abongo, a Primitive Dance: Stagework No. 2* (ballet); Marc Blitzstein, *Surf and Seaweed* (suite); Charles W. Cadman, *Dark Dancers of the Mardi Gras*; John Alden Carpenter, *Sea Drift* (symphonic poem); Arcady Dubensky, *Prelude and Fugue*; Henry Eichheim, *Bali*; Carl Eppert, *The Wanderer's Night Song* (symphonic poem); Rudolph Ganz, *Animal Pictures*; Quinto Maganini, *A Night in the Tropics*; Burrill Phillips, *Selections from McGuffey's Reader*; Quincy Porter, *Sweeney Agonistes* (incidental music); Gardner Read, *The Painted Desert—Sketches of the City, Opus 26* (Juilliard Publication Award); Bernard Rogers, *Three Japanese Dances—Japanese Landscapes*; Elie Siegmeister, *American Holiday*; David S. Smith, *Overture, Tomorrow*; William Grant Still, *Suite, A Deserted Plantation*; Adolph Weiss, *Theme and Variations*; Paul White, *Five Miniatures*.

**Piano/Organ**    George Antheil, *La femme 100 têtes (Forty-Four Preludes and Percussive Dance)*; Samuel Barlow, *Spanish Quarter*; Arthur Berger, *Two Episodes*; Marc Blitzstein, *Piano Suite*; Paul Bowles, *Sonatina*; Ulric Cole, *Fantasy Sonata*; Richard Donovan, *Suite No. 1*; Ross Lee Finney, *Sonata in D Minor*; Isadore Freed, *Five Pieces Sonata*; Edwin Gerschetski, *Sonatina*; Paul Nordoff, *Variations on a Bavarian Dance Theme*; Halsey Stevens, *Sonata No. 1*.

**Symphonies**    Felix Borowski, *Symphony No. 1*; Aaron Copland, *Short Symphony*; Morton Gould, *American Symphonette No. 1*; Roy Harris, *Symphony 1933 (No. 1)*; Frances McCollin, *Sinfonietta No. 3*; Walter Piston, *Concerto for Orchestra*; N. Clark Smith, *Negro Choral Symphony*.

# 1934

✺

## Historical Highlights

President Roosevelt presents his "Good Neighbor Policy" in relations with Latin American countries; the Federal Communications Commission (FCC) is formed as is the Federal Housing Administration (FHA); Everglades National Park is formed; Adolf Hitler makes himself "Führer" of a "New Germany"; the S.S. Queen Mary is launched in England; the Dionne Quintuplets in Canada become the first known surviving quintuplets.

## World Cultural Highlights

**World Art**    Salvador Dali, *The Metamorphosis of Narcissus*; José Orozco, *American Civilization*; Robert Spencer, *The Angel*; Maurice de Vlaminck, *Letter to Bertha*.

**World Literature**    René Char, *Le Marteau sans Maître*; Robert Graves, *I, Claudius—Claudius the God*; James Hilton, *Goodbye Mr. Chips*; Dylan Thomas, *18 Poems*; Mary Travers, *Mary Poppins*.

**World Music**    Paul Hindemith, *Mathis der Maler* (opera); Sergei Prokofiev, *Lt. Kijé—Cello Concerto*; Sergei Rachmaninoff, *Rhapsody on a Theme of Paganini*; Ralph Vaughan Williams, *Symphony No. 4*.

**Miscellaneous**    The Toronto Symphony Orchestra and National Orchestra of French Radio are founded; the Glyndebourne Opera Festivals begin; births include Aldo Ceccato, Peter Maxwell Davies, and Phillippe Entremont; deaths include Theodor Däubler, Frederick Delius, Edward Elgar, and Gustav Holst.

## American Art and Literature Highlights

**Births/Deaths**   Births include art figures Sheila Hicks, John H. McCracken, Faith Ringgold, and literary figures Joan Didion, LeRoi Jones, Kate Millett, N. Scott Momaday, Mark Strand, and Jack Valentine; deaths include artists William Hays, John Kane, Gunnar Widforss, and literary figures Mary Austin, Charles S. Brooks, Porter E. Browne, Alice French, Julian Hawthorne, and Wallace Thurman.

**Art Works**   Ilya Bolotowsky, *In the Barber Shop*; Charles Burchfield, *The Parade*; Paul Cadmus, *The Fleet's In*; John S. Curry, *The Line Storm*; Edwin Dickinson, *Stranded Brig*; William Gropper, *Sweatshop*; George Grosz, *The Couple*; Reginald Marsh, *Negroes on Rockaway Beach*; Man Ray, *Observatory Time—The Lovers*; Ben Shahn, *The W.T.C.U. Parade*; Raphael Soyer, *In the City Park*.

**Literature**   James M. Cain, *The Postman Always Rings Twice*; James T. Farrell, *The Young Manhood of Studs Lonigan*; J. Hall and C. Nordhoff, *Pitcairn Island*; Josephine Johnson, *Now in November* (Pulitzer Prize); Caroline Miller, *Lamb in His Bosom* (Pulitzer Prize); John O'Hara, *Appointment in Samarra*; Irving Stone, *Lust for Life*; Audrey Wurdemann, *Bright Ambush* (Pulitzer Prize).

## Music—The Vernacular/Commercial Scene

**A. Births**   Pat Boone (singer) June 1; Johnny Burnette (singer/writer) March 28; Junior Cook (saxophonist) July 22; King Curtis (saxophonist) February 7; Arthur Davis (string bassist) December 5; Bobby Davis (singer) May 14; Marie Dressler (singer/actress) July 28; Don Ellis (trumpeter/bandleader) July 25; Vern Gosdin (singer) August 5; Eddy Harris (saxophonist) October 20 (?); Shirley Jones (singer/actress) March 31; Freddie King (guitarist) September 3; Steve Lacy (saxophonist/composer) July 23; Little Milton (guitarist/singer) September 7; John Loudermilk (singer/composer); Peter Nero (pianist) May 22; Billy Paul (singer) December 1; Otis Rush (singer/guitarist) April 29; Del Shannon (singer) December 30; Huey "Piano" Smith (pianist/writer) January 1; Junior Wells (harmonica player/singer) December 9; Jackie Wilson (singer) June 9.

**B. Deaths**   Leroy Carr (singer); Russ Columbo (singer/composer) September 2; Charley Patton (singer/guitarist) April 28; Joseph W. Stern (composer) March 31; Roy Turk (lyricist) November 30.

**C. Biographical**

**Performing Groups**   Tiny Bradshaw Big Band; Dorsey Brothers Orchestra; Benny Goodman Band; Ink Spots; Melodears; Louis Prima and His New Orleans Gang; Rhythm Kings Sextet (Chicago); Fats Waller and His Rhythm.

**New Beginnings**   Academy Awards (film song and film score); Acousti-Lectric Co.; Decca Records, American branch; *Down Beat: the Contemporary Music Magazine*; National Folk Festival (Washington, D.C.); Billy Rose's Music Hall (New York City); Muzak Co.

**D. Publications**   A/J.A. Lomax, *American Ballads and Folksongs*; John Jacob Niles, *Songs of the Hillfolk*; Minnie E. Sears, *Song Index Supplement: An Index to More than 7,000 Songs . . .* ; Sigmund Spaeth, *The Facts of Life in Popular Song*.

**E. Representative Works**

**Musicals**   H. Arlen, E. Y. Harburg, G. Gershwin, *Life Begins at 8:40*; Irving Berlin, *Kid Millions* (film); Rudolf Friml, *Music Hath Charms*; Moss Hart (lyricist), *The Great Waltz* (on music of Johann Strauss); Cole Porter, *Anything Goes*; Arthur Schwartz and H. Dietz, *Revenge with Music*.

**Songs**   Harold Arlen, *Let's Fall in Love*; F. Bernard and D. Smith, *Winter Wonderland*; Brooks Bowman, *East of the Sun*; Con Conrad, *The Continental* (Oscar); John F. Coots, *Santa Claus Is Coming to Town*; S. Coslow and A. Johnston, *Cocktails for Two—My Old Flame*; Peter De Rose, *Deep Purple*; Maria Grever, *What a Diff'rence a Day Makes*; S. Harmati and E. Heyman, *The Bluebird of Happiness*; W. J. Hill and P. DeRose, *Wagon Wheels*; R. Rainger, *Love in Bloom*; C.

Robinson, *Carry Me Back to the Lone Prairie*; R. Rodgers and L. Hart, *Blue Moon*; H. Warren and A. Dubin, *I'll String Along with You—I Only Have Eyes for You*; M. Wayne and A. Hoffman, *Little Man, You've Had a Busy Day*.

**Other**   Alfred Newman, *The Count of Monte Cristo* (film music); Max Steiner, *The Lost Patrol* (film music).

## Music—The Cultivated/Art Music Scene

**F. Births**   Augustin Anievas (pianist) June 11; Benjamin Boretz (composer/theorist) October 3; John Chowning (composer) August 22; Van Cliburn (pianist) July 12; Alan Curtis (musicologist/conductor) November 17; Conrad De Jong (composer) January 13; Sydney Hodkinson (composer) January 17; Henry Holt (conductor) April 11; Marilyn Horne (mezzo-soprano) January 16; Yuri Krasnapolsky (conductor) November 24; Samuel Lipman (pianist/critic) June 7; Robert Moog (electronics expert) May 23; Thomas Paul (bass) February 22; Roger Reynolds (composer) July 18; Michael Sahl (composer) September 2; George Shirley (tenor) April 18; Paul Sperry (tenor) April 14; James Tenney (composer/conductor) August 10; Benita Valente (soprano) October 19; Richard Wernick (composer) January 19; Christian Wolff (composer).

**G. Deaths**   Theodore Baker (music historian) October 13; Eleonora de Cisneros (mezzo soprano) February 3; Gilbert Combs (organist) June 4; Hugo Felix (Austrian-born composer) August 24; Philip Hale (critic) November 30; Otto Kahn (German-born art patron) March 29; Paul Kochański (Ukranian-born violinist) January 12; Ernest R. Kroeger (organist) April 7; Edwin Lemare (British-born organist) September 24; Henry Taylor Parker (critic) March 30; Frank Rush Webb (organist/bandmaster) October 20.

**H. Debuts**

**United States**   Joseph Bertonnelli (tenor—Chicago), Dino Borgioli (Italian tenor—Chicago), Todd Duncan (baritone—New York), Emanuel Feuermann (Austrian cellist—Chicago), Werner Jansson (conductor—New York), Beveridge Webster (pianist—New York), Earl Wild (pianist—New York), Paul Wittgenstein (Austrian pianist—Boston)

**Metropolitan Opera**   Anny Konetzni (Austrian soprano), Lotte Lehmann (German soprano), Ettore Panizza (Argentine conductor), John Charles Thomas (baritone).

**I. New Positions**

**Conductors**   Antonia Brico (Women's Symphony Orchestra of New York).

**Educational**   Ferdinand Dunkley (Loyola University, New Orleans); Glen Haydon (University of North Carolina, Chapel Hill—to 1966); Otto Luening (music head, Bennington College—to 1944); Louis Victor Saar (St. Louis Institute—to 1937); Oliver Strunk (music head, Library of Congress—to 1937); Ernst Toch (New School for Social Research, New York); Carl Weinrich (organ, Westminster Choir College—to 1940).

**Other**   Ernst Bacon (supervisor, Federal Music Project, San Francisco); Samuel Chotzinoff (music critic, *New York Post*—to 1941); Arthur Cohn (director, Fleisher Music Collection, Philadelphia); Winthrop Sargeant (music critic, *Brooklyn Eagle)*; Moses Smith (music critic, *Boston Evening Transcript*—to 1939).

**J. Honors and Awards**

**Honors**   Carl Engel (PhD, Oberlin).

**K. Biographical**   Joseph Achron moves to Hollywood and begins film work as well as concertizing; Mary Louise Curtis Bok marries violinist Efrem Zimbalist; Lillian Evanti becomes the first black opera singer since Adelina Patti to sing at the White House; Herbert Graf (Austrian impresario) comes to the United States; Erich Wolfgang Korngold (Austrian composer) is brought to Hollywood where he stays after Hitler's Anschluss in his native land; Paul Henry Lang becomes a United States citizen; Colin McPhee begins a two-year stay in Bali; Eugene Ormandy makes his first recordings with the Minneapolis Symphony Orchestra for RCA Victor; Arnold Schoenberg, fleeing the Eastern winter, moves to California; Ernst Toch, invited to the United States, begins teaching in New York; Franz Waxman (Polish-born composer/conductor) comes to the United States.

**L. Musical Beginnings**

**Performing Groups** Bach Choir of Philadelphia; Branscombe Chorale; Cantata Singers of New York; Dayton Music Appreciation Choral Club; Hartford Symphony Orchestra; Pittsburgh Bach Choir; Phil Spitalny and His All-Girl Orchestra; Walden String Quartet (Cleveland).

**Festivals** Berkshire Music Festival.

**Educational** Hans Hoffman School of the Fine Arts (New York); School of American Ballet (New York—by Balanchine); University of Arizona School of Music.

**Other** American Musicological Society (Philadelphia); Chicago Grant Park Summer Concerts; Phoenix Theater (New York); Wadsworth Atheneum (Hartford); War Memorial Opera House (San Francisco).

**M. Music Publications**

Fisher, William A., *Music Festivals in the United States*
Goetschius, Percy, *The Structure of Music*
Jackson, Judge, *The Colored Sacred Harp*
Morris, Harold, *Contemporary American Music*
Mursell, James L., *Human Values in Music Education*
Peyser, Ethel, *The Book of Culture: The Basis of a Liberal Education*
Saminsky, Lazare, *Music of the Ghetto and the Bible*
Spaeth, Sigmund, *Music for Everybody*
Thompson, Oscar, *Practical Musical Criticism*
Whitmer, T. Carl, *The Art of Improvisation: A Handbook of Principles and Methods*

**N. Musical Compositions**

**Chamber Music** John Alden Carpenter, *Piano Quintet*; Henry Eichheim, *Violin Sonata*; Lehman Engel, *String Quartet*; Arthur Farwell, *Violin Sonata in G Minor, Opus 96*; Ross Lee Finney, *Violin Sonata No. 1*; Henry Hadley, *String Quartet No. 2, Opus 132*; Edward Burlingame Hill, *Sextet for Piano and Winds*; Werner Janssen, *String Quartet No. 1*; Werner Josten, *String Quartet in A Major*; David S. Smith, *String Quartet No. 6 in C Major*; Gerald Strang, *String Quartet*; Edgard Varèse, *Ecuatorial*.

**Choral/Vocal** Marian Bauer, *Faun Song*; Arthur M. Curry, *The Winning of Amarac*; Paul Nordoff, *Secular Mass*; John Powell, *The Babe of Bethlehem*; Gardner Read, *Four Nocturnes, Opus 23* (alto orchestra); Arthur Shepherd, *A Ballad of Trees and the Master*; Virgil Thomson, *Seven Choruses from Euripides' "Medea"*; Hugo Weisgall, *Four Songs*; Pietro Yon, *The Triumph of St. Patrick*.

**Concertos** George Gershwin, *Variations, "I Got Rhythm"*; Edward Burlingame Hill, *Violin Concerto*; Mary Howe, *Castellana* (two pianos and orchestra); Hugh F. MacColl, *Ballad* (piano and orchestra); Mary Carr Moore, *Piano Concerto*; Florence Price, *Piano Concerto in F Minor*; Leo Sowerby, *Cello Concerto No. 2*.

**Operas** Samuel Barlow, *Mon ami Pierrot*; Harry L. Freeman, *The Zulu King*; William Grant Still, *Blue Steel*; Hugo Weisgall, *Lillith*.

**Orchestra/Band** Samuel Barlow, *Biedermeier Waltzes* (strings); Marion Bauer, *Sun Splendor*; Marc Blitzstein, *Variations for Orchestra*; Charles W. Cadman, *Trail Pictures*; Aaron Copland, *Statements for Orchestra*; Henry Eichheim, *Korean Sketch*; Arthur Fickénscher, *Out of the Gay Nineties*; Henry Hadley, *Scherzo Diabolique, Opus 135*; Roy Harris, *When Johnny Comes Marching Home: An American Overture*; Mabel Wood Hill, *The Adventures of Pinocchio* (ballet); Mary Howe, *Stars*; Werner Josten, *Serenade*; Daniel G. Mason, *Suite after English Folk Songs, Opus 32*; Robert McBride, *Mexican Rhapsody*; Frances McCollin, *Suite in F Major*; Nicolas

Nabokov, *Union Pacific* (ballet); Arne Oldberg, *The Sea* (symphonic poem); Walter Piston, *Prelude and Fugue for Orchestra*; Quincy Porter, *Antony and Cleopatra* (incidental music); John Powell, *A Set of Three*; Bernard Rogers, *American Frescoes*; Virgil Thomson, *A Bride for the Unicorn* (incidental music); Ernst Toch, *Big Ben, Opus 62*; David Van Vactor, *Overture to a Comedy I.*

**Piano/Organ**   Isadore Freed, *Lyrical Sonorities*; Frances McCollin, *Variations on an Original Theme in F Major.*

**Symphonies**   Nicolai Berezowsky, *Symphony No. 2, Opus 18*; William Dawson, *Negro Folk Symphony;* Arthur Farwell, *Rudolf Gott Symphony, Opus 95*; Roy Harris, *Symphony No. 2*; Harl McDonald, *Symphony No. 2, "Rhumba"*; Leo Ornstein, *Symphony*; Quincy Porter, *Symphony No. 1*; Florence B. Price, *Mississippi River Symphony*; Timothy Spelman, *Symphony in G Minor*; Joseph F. Wagner, *Symphony No. 1.*

# 1935

❀

## Historical Highlights

The Works Progress Administration (WPA) provides jobs on public projects for jobless workers; Congress passes the Social Security Act; the American Institute of Public Opinion is founded by George Gallup; the Committee for Industrial Organization (CIO) is founded; Alcoholics Anonymous is founded; Mussolini orders the invasion of Ethiopia; Hitler introduces military training in Germany and deprives the Jews of all rights of citizenship.

## World Cultural Highlights

**World Art**   Salvador Dali, *Giraffe on Fire*; Vasili Kandinsky, *Movement I*; Louis Lozowick, *The Pneumatic Drill;* René Magritte, *Les Promenades d'Euclide*; Henri Matisse, *The Pink Nude*; Pablo Picasso, *Minotauromachy.*

**World Literature**   Enid Bagnold, *National Velvet*; C. S. Forrester, *The African Queen*; T. E. Lawrence, *The Seven Pillars of Wisdom*; Emlyn Williams, *Night Must Fall.*

**World Music**   Alban Berg, *Violin Concerto—Lulu* (unfinished); Olivier Messiaen, *La Nativité du Seigneur*; Sergei Prokofiev, *Romeo and Juliet*; William Walton, *Symphony No. 1.*

**Miscellaneous**   The Société des Concerts Symphoniques de Montreal is formed; births include Christo, Luciano Pavarotti, and Aulis Sallinen; deaths include Alban Berg, Paul Dukas, Mikhail Ippolitov-Ivanov, Max Liebermann, Kasemir Malevich, and Paul Signac.

## American Art and Literature Highlights

**Births/Deaths**   Births include art figures Carl André, Eleanor Antin, Jim Dine, Richard Hunt, Mel Ramos, and literary figures Ellen Gilchrist, Ken Kesey, Judith Rossner, Jerome Rothenberg, Robert Silverberg, and Calvin Trillin; deaths include art figures Charles Demuth, Childe Hassam, Gaston Lachaise, Charles Niehaus, and literary figures Edwin A. Robinson and Anna D. Sedgwick.

**Art Works**   Paul Cadmus, *To the Lynching*; Arthur Dove, *Mars, Orange and Green*; William Glackens, *The Soda Fountain*; Chaim Gross, *Handlebar Riders*; Edward Hopper, *The House by the Railroad*; Leon Kroll, *Morning on the Cape*; Reginald Marsh, *Coney Island Beach*; Moses Soyer, *Artists on WPA*; Joseph Stella, *Voice of the Nightingale*; Grant Wood, *Death on the Ridge Road.*

**Literature**   Zoë Akins, *The Old Maid* (Pulitzer Prize); Maxwell Anderson, *Winterset* (New York Drama Critics' Award); Pearl Buck, *A House Divided*; Tristan Coffin, *Strange Holiness* (Pulitzer Prize); Harold L. Davis, *Honey in the Horn* (Pulitzer Prize); James N. Hall, *The Hurricane*; Robert Sherwood, *The Petrified Forest*; John Steinbeck, *Tortilla Flat*; Thomas Wolfe, *Of Time and the River.*

## Music—The Vernacular/Commercial Scene

**A. Births**  Herb Alpert (trumpeter) March 31; Big Twist (Larry Nolan—singer/bandleader); Billy Boy Arnold (singer/guitarist) September 16; Bobby Bare (singer) April 7; Richard Berry (pianist/writer) April 11; Sonny Bono (singer) February 12; Hank Cochran (singer/writer) August 2; George Coleman (saxophonist) March 8; Sam Cooke (singer/writer) January 22; Eddie Floyd (singer) June 25; Ronnie Hawkins (singer) January 10; De Wolf Hopper (singer/actor) September 23; Steve Lawrence (singer) July 8; Jerry Lee Lewis (singer) September 29; Ramsay Lewis, Jr. (piano) May 27; Loretta Lynn (singer) April 14; Johnny Mandel (composer/arranger) November 23; Johnny Mathis (singer) September 30; Barry McGuire (singer/writer) October 15; Samuel Moore (Sam and Dave—singer) October 12; Jerry Orbach (singer/actor) October 20; Esther Phillips (singer) December; John Phillips (folk singer) August 30; Elvis Presley (singer) January 8; Lou Rawls (singer) December 1; Peggy Seeger (folk singer) June 17; Justin Tubb (guitarist/singer) August 20; Gene Vincent (singer/writer) February 11; Bobby Vinton (singer) April 16; Johnny "Guitar" Watson (guitarist) February 3; Link Wray (guitarist) May 2.

**B. Deaths**  Ballard MacDonald (lyricist) November 17; Bennie Moten (pianist/bandleader) April 2.

**C. Biographical**

**Performing Groups**  Barons of Rhythm (Count Basie Orchestra); Blue Sky Boys (William and Earl Bolick); Chuck Wagon Gang; Tommy Dorsey Orchestra and the Clambake Seven; Benny Goodman Trio; International Orchestra (by Noble Sissle); Red Norvo Band.

**New Beginnings**  Your Hit Parade (radio).

**Miscellaneous**  Lotte Lenya comes to New York with Kurt Weill; Ray Noble (British bandleader) comes to the United States; Victor Young moves to Hollywood and joins Paramount Studios.

**D. Publications**  John Jacob Niles, *Songs of the Hill-Folk II*; Elie Siegmeister, *Negro Songs of Protest*.

**E. Representative Works**

**Musicals**  Irving Berlin, *Top Hat* (film); N. H. Brown and A. Freed, *Broadway Melody of 1936* (film); Cole Porter, *Jubilee*; Rodgers and Hart, *Jumbo*; S. Romberg and O. Hammerstein, *May Wine*; A. Schwartz and H. Dietz, *At Home Abroad*.

**Songs**  Fred E. Ahlert, *I'm Gonna Sit Right Down and Write Myself a Letter*; Jimmie Davis, *Nobody's Darling but Mine*; Duke Ellington, *In a Sentimental Mood*; E. Farley and M. Riley, *The Music Goes 'Round and 'Round*; B. Hanighen and J. Mercer, *The Dixieland Band*; Jimmy McHugh and D. Fields, *I'm in the Mood for Love—I Feel a Song Coming On*; Cole Porter, *Begin the Beguine*; S. Romberg and O. Hammerstein, *When I Grow Too Old to Dream*; H. Warren and A. Dubin, *Lullaby of Broadway* (Oscar)—*Don't Give Up the Ship*.

**Other**  Harold Arlen, *Mood in Six Minutes*; Eubie Blake, *Black Keys on Parade*; Nacio Herb Brown, *American Bolero*; Duke Ellington, *Echoes of Harlem (Cootie's Concerto)—Reminiscing in Tempo*; James P. Johnson, *Symphony in Brown—Jasmine Concerto*; Matty Malneck, *Park Avenue Fantasy*; Alfred Newman, *Les Misérables—Call of the Wild* (film music); Herbert Stothart, *Mutiny on the Bounty—A Tale of Two Cities* (film music); Max Steiner, *The Informer* (Oscar)—*The Three Musketeers* (film music).

## Music—The Cultivated/Art Music Scene

**F. Births**  Malcolm Bilson (pianist) October 24; Dominic Cossa (baritone) May 13; Richard A. Crawford (musicologist) May 21; John Eaton (composer) March 30; Malcolm Frager (pianist) January 15; Robert Freeman (musicologist) August 26; David Hamilton (critic) January 18; Frederick Hemke (saxophonist) July 11; Gilbert Kalish (pianist) July 2; Erich Kunzel (conductor) March 21; William Lewis (tenor) November 23; Alan Mandel (pianist) July 17; Sherrill Milnes (baritone) January 10; Gordon Mumma (composer) March 30; William Murray (baritone) March 13; John MacIvor Perkins (composer) August 2; Leon Plantinga (musicologist) March 25; Terry

Riley (composer/performer) June 24; Loren Rush (composer) August 23; Arlene Saunders (soprano) October 5; Peter Schickele (composer/humorist) July 17; Charles Treger (violinist) May 13; La Monte Young (composer) October 14.

**G. Deaths**    Alfredo Barili (pianist/composer) November 17; Sophie Braslau (contralto) January 23; Clarence Grant Hamilton (organist) February 14; Lucius Hosmer (composer) May 9; Charles Martin Loeffler (German-born composer) May 19; Felice Lyne (soprano) September 1; Francis Maclennan (tenor) July 17; Alfred G. Robyn (pianist/organist) October 18; Gustave Saenger (editor/arranger) December 10; Frances Saville (soprano) November 8; Kurt Schindler (German-born composer/conductor) November 16; Marcella Sembrich (Polish-born soprano) January 11; Herbert Witherspoon (bass/administrator) May 10.

**H. Debuts**

**United States**    Webster Aitken (pianist—New York), Raya Garbousova (Russian cellist—New York), Bidú Sayão (Brazilian soprano—New York), Joseph Schuster (Russian cellist—New York), Roman Totenberg (Polish violinist—New York), Rosalyn Tureck (pianist—New York).

**Metropolitan Opera**    Kirsten M. Flagstad (Norwegian soprano), Eduard Habich (German baritone), Julius Huehn (baritone), Helen Jepson (soprano), Charles Kullman (tenor), Marjorie Lawrence (Australian soprano), Carlo Morelli (Chilean baritone), Thelma Votipka (soprano), Gertrud Wettergren (Swedish contralto).

**I. New Positions**

**Conductors**    Ernst Hoffmann (Houston Symphony Orchestra—to 1947); Bertha W. Clark (Knoxville Symphony Orchestra—to 1946).

**Educational**    Igor Buketoff (Juilliard—to 1945); William D. Revelli (band, University of Michigan—to 1971); Rosario Scalero (Curtis Institute—to 1946); William Schuman (Sarah Lawrence College—to 1945); Roger Sessions (Princeton to 1944); Burnet Tuthill (music head, Southwestern University, Memphis—to 1959).

**Other**    Alfred Frankenstein (critic, *San Francisco Chronicle*); Edward Johnson (general manager, Metropolitan Opera—till 1950); Charles Seeger (music advisor, Washington, DC programs); Howard Taubman (music editor, *New York Times*); Alfred Wallenstein (music director, WOR, New York—to 1945).

**J. Honors and Awards**

**Honors**    Samuel Barber (Rome Prize); Howard Hanson and Leo Sowerby (National Institute); Carl Engel and Walter Piston (Coolidge Medal); Deems Taylor (American Academy).

**K. Biographical**    Dario D'Attili (Italian violin maker) comes with his family to the United States; Bernhard Heiden (German composer) moves to the United States; Rudolf Kolisch (Austrian violinist) and his quartet tour the United States and decide to settle here; Gian Carlo Menotti (Italian composer) moves to the United States but keeps his Italian citizenship; Ruth Posselt becomes the first female American violinist to tour the USSR; Gustav Schützendorf leaves the Metropolitan Opera and returns to Germany; Igor Stravinsky makes a second tour of the United States; Alec Templeton (British blind pianist) comes to the United States with a British jazz band and decides to stay; Paul Ulanowsky (Austrian pianist) comes to the United States as an accompanist to Enid Szantho.

**L. Musical Beginnings**

**Performing Groups**    Buffalo Philharmonic Orchestra; Chattanooga Symphony Orchestra; Cleveland Women's Orchestra; Knoxville Symphony Orchestra; New York Women's Orchestra.

**Festivals**    Carmel Bach Festival (California); Winter Park Bach Festival (Florida).

**Educational**    Academy of Vocal Arts (Philadelphia).

**Other**    *The American Music Lover*; Chappell Music Publishers, American Branch; Composers' Forum-Laboratory (New York); Composer's Press; Federal Music Project of the Works Progress Administration; Carl Fischer, Los Angeles Branch; Metropolitan Opera Guild; National Association of Performing Artists; Southern Music Co. (San Antonio, Texas).

**M. Music Publications**

Downes, Olin, *Symphonic Masterpieces*
Earhart, Will, *The Meaning and Teaching of Music*
Erskine, John, *A Musical Companion*
Ferguson, Donald, *A History of Musical Thought*
Finney, Theodore M., *A History of Music*
Goldman, Edwin F., *The Goldman Band System*
Handy, William C., *Negro Authors and Composers of the United States*
Miller, Dayton, *Anecdotal History of the Science of Sound*
Samaroff, Olga, *The Layman's Music Book*
Thompson, Oscar, *How to Understand Music*
Thompson, Randall, *College Music*

**N. Musical Compositions**

**Chamber Music**   John Cage, *Percussion Quartet*; Arthur Cohn, *String Quartets 4, 5*; Frederick S. Converse, *String Quartet in E Minor*; David Diamond, *Partita* (oboe, bassoon, and piano); Carl Eppert, *String Quartet No. 1 in G Minor*; Ross Lee Finney, *String Quartet No. 1*; Edward Burlingame Hill, *String Quartet*; Werner Janssen, *String Quartet No. 2*; Homer Keller, *String Quartet in One Movement*; Harrison Kerr, *String Quartet No. 1*; Erich W. Korngold, *String Quartet No. 2 in E Major, Opus 26*; Wiktor Labunski, *String Quartet No. 1*; Nikolai Lopatnikoff, *Piano Trio*; Daniel G. Mason, *Sentimental Sketches, Opus 34*; Paul Nordoff, *String Quartet No. 2*; Quincy Porter, *String Quartet No. 5*; Frederick Search, *String Quartet No. 4*; Elie Siegmeister, *String Quartet No. 1*; Leo Sowerby, *String Quartet No. 2*; Edwin John Stringham, *String Quartet in F Minor*.

**Choral/Vocal**   Marion Bauer, *Ragpicker's Love* (song cycle); Albert Hay Malotte, *The Lord's Prayer*.

**Concertos**   John Barrows, *Variations for Horn and Strings*; Nicolai Berezowsky, *Concerto Lirico, Opus 19, for Cello and Orchestra*; Vittorio Giannini, *Piano Concerto*; Frederick Jacobi, *Piano Concerto*; Robert Sanders, *Violin Concerto*; Arnold Schoenberg, *Violin Concerto*; Roger Sessions, *Violin Concerto*; William Grant Still, *Kaintuck* (piano and orchestra); Bernard Wagenaar, *Triple Concerto* (flute, cello, and harp).

**Operas**   Robert Russell Bennett, *Maria Malibran*; George Gershwin, *Porgy and Bess* (folk opera); Wesley La Violette, *The Enlightened One*; Quinto Maganini, *The Argonauts* (Bispham Medal); Douglas Moore, *White Wings*; Mary Carr Moore, *Legende provençale*; Kurt Weill, *Der Weg der Verheissung* (biblical drama).

**Orchestra/Band**   George Antheil, *Dreams* (ballet); Milton Babbitt, *Generatrix* (withdrawn); John J. Becker, *A Marriage with Space: Stagework No. 3* (ballet); Arcady Dubensky, *Tom Sawyer Overture*; Victor Herbert, *Festival March*; Gail Kubik, *Orchestral Suite*; Otto Luening, *Two Symphonic Interludes*; Hugh F. MacColl, *Romantic Suite in the Form of Variations*; Arthur Nevin, *Arizona* (symphonic poem); Burrill Phillips, *Courthouse Square—Sinfonia Concertante*; John Powell, *A Set of Three*; Albert Stoessel, *Early American Suite*; Ernst Toch, *Pinocchio*.

**Piano/Organ**   Ernest Bloch, *Piano Sonata*; David Diamond, *Sonatina*; Miriam Gideon, *Piano Suite No. 1, "Three-Cornered Pieces"*; Edward Burlingame Hill, *Jazz Studies No. 2–4* (two pianos); Eastwood Lane, *The Fourth of July* (orchestrated by Grofé); Leo Ornstein, *Five Water Colors*; Gardner Read, *Three Satirical Sarcasms, Opus 29*; George Tremblay, *Prelude and Dance*.

**Symphonies**   Philip G. Clapp, *Symphony No. 10 in F Major, "Heroic"*; Vittorio Giannini, *Symphony: In Memoriam Theodore Roosevelt*; Morton Gould, *American Symphonette No. 2*; Henry Hadley, *Symphony No. 5, "Connecticut," Opus 140*; Werner Josten, *Symphony No. 1*; Harl McDonald, *Symphony No. 3, "Lamentations of Fu Hsuan"*; William Schuman, *Symphony No. 1* (withdrawn); Emerson Whithorne, *Symphony No. 2* (Juilliard Publication Award).

# 1936

❉

## Historical Highlights

Franklin D. Roosevelt is re-elected president; Boulder (Hoover) Dam is completed; a 40-hour week is enforced for companies doing business with the government; the Merchant Marine is formed; the Ford Foundation is founded; Hitler occupies the Rhineland; the Spanish Civil War begins; Edward VIII abdicates the British throne to marry an American divorcée; the Rome-Berlin Axis is formed.

## World Cultural Highlights

**World Art** Pierre Bonnard, *The Garden*; Salvador Dali, *Autumn Cannibalism*; Piet Mondrian, *Composition in White, Black and Red*; Maurice de Vlaminck, *The Pot of Coffee*.

**World Literature** Daphne du Maurier, *Jamaica Inn*; Aldous Huxley, *Eyeless in Gaza*; Rebecca West, *The Thinking Reed*.

**World Music** Béla Bartók, *Music for Strings, Percussion and Celesta*; Carlos Chávez, *Sinfonia India*; Aram Khachaturian, *Piano Concerto*; Carl Orff, *Carmina Burana*; Dmitri Shostakovich, *Symphony No. 4*.

**Miscellaneous** The Brazilian Conservatory of Music opens; the USSR State Symphony Orchestra is founded; births include Charles Dutoit, Hans Haacke, and Lucas Samaras; deaths include Auguste Delacroix, Federico García Lorca, Alexander Glazunov, Maxim Gorky, Rudyard Kipling, and Ottorino Respighi.

## American Art and Literature Highlights

**Births/Deaths** Births include art figures Frank Stella, Lorado Taft, and literary figures Jean Marie Auel, Judith Ann Guest, Clarence Major, Larry McMurtry, Tom Robbins, C. K. Williams, Bari Wood, and Paul Zindel; deaths include art figures George Ennis, Ralph Goddard, Lorado Taft, and literary figures Mary Andrews, Finley P. Dunne, and Mourning Dove.

**Art Works** Alexander Archipenko, *Torso in Space*; Stuart Davis, *Abstract Landscape* (?); Arthur Dove, *Windy Morning*; Marsden Hartley, *The Old Bars, Dogtown*; Doris Lee, *Thanksgiving*; Reginald Marsh, *Monday Night at the Metropolitan*; Charles Sheeler, *City Interior*; Raphael Soyer, *Office Girls*; Grant Wood, *Spring Turning*.

**Literature** James M. Cain, *Double Indemnity*; Walter D. Edmonds, *Drums Along the Mohawk*; William Faulkner, *Absalom, Absalom!*; Robert Frost, *A Further Range* (Pulitzer Prize); M. Hart and G. S. Kaufman, *You Can't Take It with You* (Pulitzer Prize); Edgar Lee Masters, *Across Spoon River*; Margaret Mitchell, *Gone with the Wind* (Pulitzer Prize); Robert Sherwood, *Idiot's Delight* (Pulitzer Prize).

## Music—The Vernacular/Commercial Scene

**A. Births** Albert Ayler (saxophonist/bandleader) July 13; Hank Ballard (singer/writer) November 18; Solomon Burke (singer); Clarence Carter (singer/guitarist) January 14; Don Cherry (trumpeter/bandleader) November 18; Bobby Darin (singer) May 14; Bill Gaither (composer/publisher) March 28; Buddy Guy (guitarist) July 30; Tom T. Hall (singer/writer) May 25; Billy Higgins (drums) October 11; Buddy Holly (singer/writer) September 7; Engelbert Humperdinck (singer) May 2; Ernie K-Doe (singer) February 22; Doug Kershaw (fiddler/singer) January 24; Roland Kirk (saxophonist) August 7; Kris Kristofferson (singer/writer) June 22; Roger Miller (singer/writer) January 2; Roy Orbison (singer/writer) April 23; Eddie Palmieri (piano/bandleader?); Mort Schuman (songwriter) November 12.

**B. Deaths**   Anne Caldwell (lyricist); Marilyn Miller (singer/actress) April 7; Harry B. Smith (lyricist) January 1.

**C. Biographical**

**Performing Groups**   Deep River Boys; Golden West Cowboys; Benny Goodman Quartet; Harlem Hamfats; Woody Herman's Thundering Herd; Milt Larkin Big Band (Houston); Russ Morgan Band; Pace Gospel Choral Union (Pittsburgh); "Hot Lips" Page Band; Artie Shaw Band I; Orrin Tucker Band.

**New Beginnings**   Old Ship of Zion Music Co.

**Miscellaneous**   Vernon Duke (Vladimir Dukelsky) becomes an American citizen.

**D. Publications**   *Axel Christensen's Instruction Book for Modern Swing Music*; Maud Cuney-Hare, *Negro Musicians and Their Music*; R. N. Dett, *The Dett Collection of Negro Spirituals*; G. Herzog, *Research in Primitive and Folk Music in the United States*; Alain Locke, *The Negro and His Music*; A. and J. A. Lomax, *Negro Folk Songs as Sung by Leadbelly*; John Jacob Niles, *More Songs of the Hill Folk*.

**E. Representative Works**

**Musicals**   Irving Berlin, *Follow the Fleet* (film); Jerome Kern and D. Fields, *Swing Time* (film); Cole Porter, *Born to Dance* (film)—*Red, Hot and Blue*; Rodgers and Hart, *On Your Toes* (contains *Slaughter on Tenth Avenue*); Various composers, *The Show Is On*; Kurt Weill, *Johnny Johnson*.

**Songs**   Irving Berlin, *Let's Face the Music and Dance*; S. Cahn and S. Chaplin, *Shoe Shine Boy*; Walter Donaldson, *Mr. Meadowlark*; J. Kern and D. Fields, *The Way You Look Tonight* (Oscar); Billy J. Hill, *Empty Saddles*; Ledbetter and Lomax, *Goodnight, Irene*; M. Malneck and J. Mercer, *Goody, Goody*; Johnny Mercer, *I'm an Old Cowhand*; A. Nichols, S. Cahn, and S. Chaplin, *Until the Real Thing Comes Along*; Bob Nolan, *Cool Water*; Cole Porter, *I've Got You Under My Skin*; J. Van Heusen and J. Burke, *Pennies from Heaven*; Ted Weems, *The Martins and the Coys*.

**Other**   Artie Shaw, *Interlude in B-Flat* (string quartet and jazz band).

## Music—The Cultivated/Art Music Scene

**F. Births**   Martina Arroyo (soprano) February 2; Elaine Bonazzi (mezzo-soprano); Thomas Bricetti (conductor) January 14; John Covelli (conductor/pianist) October 12; Peter G. Davis (critic) May 3; James DePreist (conductor) November 21; Paul Freeman (conductor) January 2; Anthony J. Gnazzo (composer) April 21; Richard Jackson (musicologist) February 15; Richard Kapp (conductor) October 9; Fredrick Kaufman (composer/trumpeter) March 24; Eve Queler (conductor) January 1; Michael Rabin (violinist) May 2; Steve Reich (composer) October 3; Elliott Schwartz (composer) January 19; Jeanette Scovotti (soprano) December 5; Norman Scribner (conductor/composer) February 25; Lawrence Leighton Smith (conductor) April 8; Robert Suderburg (composer/pianist) January 28; Edward Tarr (trumpeter/musicologist) June 15; Noel Tyl (baritone) December 31; David Ward-Steinman (composer/educator) November 6; Robert White (tenor) October 27; David Zinman (violinist/conductor) July 9.

**G. Deaths**   William C. Carl (organist) December 8; Ossip Gabrilowitsch (Russian-born pianist/conductor) September 14; Philip Goepp (organist) August 25; Rubin Goldmark (composer/educator) March 6; Sandor Harmati (Hungarian-born violinist/conductor) April 4; Fred Jewell (bandmaster/publisher) February 11; Henry Schoenefeld (composer/conductor) August 4; Ernestine Schumann-Heink (Austrian-born mezzo-soprano) November 17; Josef Stransky (Czech-born conductor/art dealer) March 6; Ellison Van Hoose (tenor) March 24; Arthur B. Whiting (pianist/composer) July 20.

**H. Debuts**

**United States**   Ludwig Altman (German organist—San Francisco), John Barbirolli (British conductor—New York), Ania Dorfmann (Russian pianist—New York), Herta Glaz (Austrian contralto—tour), Dimitri Mitropoulos (Greek conductor—Boston), Leonard Pennario (pianist—Dallas), Rudolf Serkin (Austrian pianist—New York), Isaac Stern (Russian violinist—San Francisco).

**Metropolitan Opera**   Joseph Bentonelli (tenor), Vina Bovy (Belgian soprano), Arthur Carron (British tenor), Bruna Castagna (Italian mezzo-soprano), Norman Cordon (baritone), Dusolina Giannini (soprano), René Maison (Belgian tenor), Kerstin Thorborg (Swedish mezzo-soprano), Alice Tully (soprano—New York).

**Other**   Risë Stevens (mezzo-soprano—Prague).

## I. New Positions

**Conductors**   Franco Autori (Buffalo Philharmonic Orchestra—to 1945); John Barbirolli (New York Philharmonic Orchestra—to 1943); José Iturbi (Rochester Philharmonic Orchestra—to 1944); Dimitri Mitropoulos (Minneapolis Symphony Orchestra—to 1949); Pierre Monteux (San Francisco Symphony Orchestra—to 1952); Eugene Ormandy (Philadelphia Orchestra—sharing with Stokowski to 1938); Ernest Schelling (Baltimore Symphony Orchestra—to 1938); Izler Solomon (Illinois Symphony Orchestra—to 1941); Arthur Zack (New Orleans Philharmonic—to 1940).

**Educational**   Frederick Dorian (Carnegie-Mellon—to 1954); Frederick Jacobi (composition, Juilliard); Paul Pisk (Combs Conservatory—to 1941); Arnold Schoenberg (UCLA); Ernst Toch (USC).

**Other**   Putnam Aldrich (Boston Society of Ancient Instruments); Ernst Bacon (supervisor, WPA Federal Music Project of San Francisco); Samuel Chotzinoff (music consultant, NBC radio); Herbert Graf (producer, Metropolitan Opera); Cecil Smith (music critic, *Chicago Tribune*—to 1942); Deems Taylor (commentator, New York Philharmonic Orchestra broadcasts—to 1943); Oscar Thompson (editor, *Musical America*—to 1943).

## J. Honors and Awards

**Honors**   Kent Kennan (Rome Prize).

**K. Biographical**   Maurice Abravanel (Greek conductor) comes to the United States and conducts at the Metropolitan Opera; Ludwig Altman (German organist), Willi Apel (Polish musicologist), Hans T. David (German musicologist), Alice Ehlers (Austrian harpsichordist), Marcel Grandjany (French harpist), László Halász (Hungarian conductor), Walter Hinrichson (German publisher), Felix Labunski (Polish composer), Fritz Mahler (Austrian conductor), Hans Nathan (German musicologist), Paul Pisk (Austrian musicologist/composer), Boris Schwarz (Russian musicologist), Edward Steuermann (Polish pianist), and Roman Totenberg (Polish violinist) all come to the United States; Lucrezia Bori retires from opera; Saul Caston becomes assistant conductor of the Philadelphia Orchestra; Henry Cowell is sent to San Quentin on a morals charge; Margarete Dessoff returns to Switzerland; Roy Harris marries Beula Duffey (Johana).

## L. Musical Beginnings

**Performing Groups**   Negro Chorus of Los Angeles; New Orleans Philharmonic Symphony Orchestra.

**Festivals**   North Iowa Band Festival; Ravinia Festival (Chicago); Three Choirs Festival (New York).

**Educational**   Archives of Folk and Primitive Music (Columbia); Brevard Music Center (North Carolina); University of Pittsburgh Music Department.

**Other**   American Guild of Musical Artists; Neil A. Kjos Music Co. (Illinois); W. F. Ludwig Drum Co. (Chicago); Metropolitan Opera Auditions; National Singing Convention (Birmingham, Alabama); New Friends of Music (New York); *Opera News* (Metropolitan Opera); Society of the Classic Guitar (New York); Whittall Foundation (Library of Congress).

## M. Music Publications

Bekker, Paul, *The Story of the Orchestra*
Einstein, Alfred, *A Short History of Music*
Kolodin, Irving, *The Metropolitan Opera, 1883–1936*
Rosenfeld, Paul, *Discoveries of a Music Critic*
Samaroff, Olga, *The Magic World of Music*

Spaeth, Sigmund, *Great Symphonies*
Thompson, Oscar, *Tabulated Biographical History of Music*

**N. Musical Compositions**

**Chamber Music**   John J. Becker, *Soundpiece No. 2: String Quartet No. 1, "Homage to Haydn" — Soundpiece No. 3: Violin Sonata*; Paul Creston, *String Quartet, Opus 8*; Isadore Freed, *String Quartet No. 3*; Charles Jones, *String Quartet No. 1*; Boris Koutzen, *String Quartet No. 2*; Wesley La Violette, *String Quartet No. 3*; Joaquin Nin-Culmell, *Piano Quintet*; Arnold Schoenberg, *String Quartet No. 4, Opus 37*; William Schuman, *String Quartet No. 1*; Roger Sessions, *String Quartet No. 1*; Arthur Shepherd, *String Quartet No. 2 in D Minor*; David S. Smith, *String Quartet No. 8 in A*; Gustav Strube, *String Quartet No. 2*; George Tremblay, *String Quartet No. 1*; Burnet Tuthill, *Clarinet Quintet*; Edgard Varèse, *Density 21.5* (solo flute); Bernard Wagenaar, *String Quartet No. 3*.

**Choral/Vocal**   Ernst Bacon, *On Ecclesiastes*; Marion Bauer, *Four Songs for Soprano and String Quartet*; Arthur Farwell, *Four Emily Dickinson Songs, Opus 101*; Vittorio Giannini, *Requiem*; Daniel G. Mason, *Love Songs for Soprano and Orchestra*; Arthur Shepherd, *Invitation to the Dance* (chorus); David S. Smith, *Songs of Three Ages* (song cycle); Randall Thompson, *The Peaceable Kingdom*.

**Concertos**   Ernest Bloch, *Voice in the Wilderness* (cello and orchestra); John Alden Carpenter, *Violin Concerto*; David Diamond, *Violin Concerto No. 1*; Hunter Johnson, *Piano Concerto*; Harl McDonald, *Concerto for Two Pianos and Orchestra*; Leo Sowerby, *Organ Concerto in C*.

**Operas**   Samuel Barlow, *Amanda*; Eugene M. Bonner, *The Gods of the Mountain*; Arcady Dubensky, *On the Highway*; Gian Carlo Menotti, *Amelia Goes to the Ball*; Douglas Moore, *The Headless Horseman*; Charles S. Skilton, *The Day of Gayomair*; Albert Stoessel, *Garrick*.

**Orchestra/Band**   Ernst Bacon, *Country Roads, Unpaved* (suite); Samuel Barber, *Adagio for Strings, Opus 11* (from *String Quartet*); Franz C. Bornschein, *Leif Ericson* (symphonic poem); Charles W. Cadman, *American Suite* (strings); Aaron Copland, *El Salón Mexico*; Arcady Dubensky, *Serenade*; Lou Harrison, *Changing World* (ballet); Alan Hovhaness, *Prelude and Quadruple Fugue* (orchestrated 1954); Henry H. Huss, *Elegy*; Kent Kennan, *Night Soliloquy* (flute and strings); Colin McPhee, *Tabuh-Tabuhan*; Leo Ornstein, *Nocturne and Dance of the Fates*; Gardner Read, *Prelude and Toccata* (Juilliard Publication Award); Bernard Rogers, *The Supper at Emmaus*; Lazare Saminsky, *Three Shadows—Pueblo: A Moon Epic*; William Grant Still, *Beyond Tomorrow—Dismal Swamp* (symphonic poems); Lamar Stringfield, *From the Blue Ridge Mountains*; Virgil Thomson, *Hamlet—Macbeth* (incidental music)—*The Plow that Broke the Plains* (film music); Burnet Tuthill, *Laurentia, Opus 16* (symphonic poem); Vladimir Ussachevsky, *Theme and Variations*.

**Piano/Organ**   Josef Alexander, *Sonata No. 1*; Seth Bingham, *Carillon de Château-Thierry* (organ); Ernest Bloch, *Visions and Prophecies*; Paul Creston, *Sonata, Opus 9*; Arthur Farwell, *Prelude and Fugue, Opus 94—Two Tone-Pictures, Opus 104*; Gardner Read, *Passacaglia and Fugue, Opus 34* (organ—orchestrated 1938); Stefan Wolpe, *Four Studies in Basic Rows*.

**Symphonies**   Samuel Barber, *Symphony No. 1, Opus 9*; Felix Borowski, *Symphony No. 2*; Avery Claflin, *Symphony No. 1*; Frederick Converse, *Symphony No. 3 in F Major*; Anis Fuleihan, *Symphony No. 1*; Edward B. Hill, *Symphony No. 3 in G Major*; Werner Josten, *Symphony in F Major*; Wesley La Violette, *Symphony No. 1*; Daniel G. Mason, *Symphony No. 3, Opus 35, "Lincoln"*; Gardner Read, *Symphony No. 1, Opus 30* (New York Philharmonic Orchestra Prize); Bernard Rogers, *Symphony No. 3, "On a Thanksgiving Song"*; Bernard Wagenaar, *Symphony No. 3*; Meredith Willson, *Symphony No. 1*.

# 1937

☀

## Historical Highlights

The Golden Gate Bridge opens in San Francisco; Amelia Earhart Putnam disappears on a flight across the Pacific; DuPont Labs synthesizes nylon; E. H. Land founds the Polaroid Co.; the

Japanese attack United States and British boats in China; Neville Chamberlain becomes Prime Minister of Great Britain; the dirigible *Hindenburg* blows up while moored in New Jersey.

## World Cultural Highlights

**World Art**    Georges Braque, *Woman with a Mandolin*; Salvador Dali, *Inventions on the Monsters*; Henri Matisse, *The Lady in Blue*; Pablo Picasso, *Guernica*; Georges Rouault, *The Old King*.

**World Literature**    Jean Anouilh, *Traveler without Luggage*; Archibald Cronin, *The Citadel*; Erich Remarque, *Three Comrades*; J. R. R. Tolkien, *The Hobbit*; Evelyn Waugh, *A Handful of Dust*.

**World Music**    Béla Bartók, *Sonata for Two Pianos and Percussion*; Paul Hindemith, *Nobilissima Visione*; Darius Milhaud, *Scaramouche Suite*; Dmitri Shostakovich, *Symphony No. 5*.

**Miscellaneous**    The Lisbon Philharmonic Orchestra, the Swedish Symphony Orchestra and the Tokyo Symphony Orchestra are founded; births include Vladimir Ashkenazy, David Hockney, and Neeme Järvi; deaths include James Barrie, Allen Jones, Maurice Ravel, Albert Roussel, and Charles Widor.

## American Art and Literature Highlights

**Births/Deaths**    Births include art figures Red Grooms, Larry Poons, Edward Ruscha, and literary figures Joseph Epstein, Gail Godwin, Susan Howe, Arthur Kopit, John Perreault, Thomas Pynchon, Erich Segal, and Lanford Wilson; deaths include art figures Hugh Breckenridge, Edwin Child, Bruce Crane, Charles Eaton, Frederic MacMonnies, Henry O. Tanner, and novelist Edith Wharton.

**Art Works**    Alexander Archipenko, *Walking Woman*; Peter Blume, *The Eternal City*; Edwin Dickinson, *Composition with Still Life*; Philip Evergood, *American Tragedy*; Edward Hopper, *Cape Cod Evening*; Walt Kuhn, *Trio*; Robert Laurent, *The Triumph of the Egg*; Jack Levine, *The Feast of Pure Reason*; Theodore Roszak, *Construction in White*; Millard Sheets, *Birth of Spring*.

**Literature**    Maxwell Anderson, *High Tor* (New York Drama Critics' Award); Ernest Hemingway, *To Have and Have Not*; J. P. Marquand, *The Late George Apley* (Pulitzer Prize); Clifford Odets, *Golden Boy*; John O'Hara, *Butterfield 8*; John Steinbeck, *Of Mice and Men* (New York Drama Critics' Award); Jerome Weidman, *I Can Get It for You Wholesale*; Marya Zaturenska, *Cold Morning Sky* (Pulitzer Prize).

## Music — The Vernacular/Commercial Scene

**A. Births**    Bill Andersen (guitarist/singer) November 1; Ron Carter (string bass) May 4; Gene Chandler (singer) July 6; Alice Coltrane (pianist/harp) August 27; Dick Dale (guitarist) May 4; Charlie Daniels (singer/bandleader) October 28; Peter Duchin (bandleader) July 28; Don Everly (Everly Brothers) February 1; Freddy Fender (singer) June 4; Mickey Gilley (singer) March 9; Charlie Haden (string bass) August 6; Merle Haggard (singer) April 6; John Hartford (singer/writer) December 30; Jon Hassel (composer) March 22; Joe Henderson (saxophonist) April 24; Clarence "Frogman" Henry (singer/pianist) March 19; Wanda Jackson (singer/writer) October 20; Waylon Jennings (singer) June 15; Little Willie John (singer) November 15; Trini Lopez (singer/bandleader) May 15; Tom Paxton (folk singer/writer) October 31; Sonny Osborne (singer/banjoist) October 29; David Prater (Sam and Dave — singer) May 9; Jerry Reed (singer) March 20; Tommy Sands (singer) August 27; Bobby Scott (pianist/composer) January 29; Billie Jo Spears (singer) January 14; Billy Stewart (singer) March 24; Paul Stookey (Peter, Paul, and Mary) November 30; Mary Travers (Peter, Paul, and Mary) November 7; Frankie Valli (singer) May 3; Nancy Wilson (singer) February 20.

**B. Deaths**    Bessie Smith (singer) September 26.

**C. Biographical**

**Performing Groups**    Bunny Berigan Big Band (New York); Larry Clinton Orchestra; International Sweethearts of Rhythm; John Kirby Sextet (New York); Little Chicks (from the Chick Webb band); Glenn Miller Band; Savoy Sultans; Artie Shaw Band II; Wings Over Jordan.

**New Beginnings**   Musicraft Records (New York); *Southern Folklore Quarterly*.

**Miscellaneous**   Billie Holiday joins Count Basie's Orchestra as singer; Cole Porter loses the use of his legs in a riding accident on Long Island.

**D. Publications**   Ray Bauduc, *Dixieland Drumming*; G. P. Jackson, *Spiritual Folksongs of Early America*; John Jacob Niles, *Ballads, Carols and Tragic Legends from the Southern Appalachian Mountains*.

**E. Representative Works**

**Musicals**   H. Arlen and E. Y. Harburg, *Hooray for What!*; Irving Berlin, *On the Avenue* (film); Eubie Blake, *Swing It*; George and Ira Gershwin, *Shall We Dance?* (film); Cole Porter, *Rosalie* (film); Rodgers and Hart, *Babes in Arms—I'd Rather Be Right*; Harold Rome, *Pins and Needles*; A. Schwartz and H. Dietz, *Between the Devil*.

**Songs**   Harold Arlen, *In the Shade of the Old Apple Tree*; Irving Berlin, *I've Got My Love to Keep Me Warm*; L. Brown and S. Fain, *That Old Feeling*; Larry Clinton, *The Dipsy Doodle*; Cliff Friend, *The Merry-go-round Broke Down*; R. Friml and H. Stothart, *The Donkey Serenade*; Wilhelm Grosz, *Harbor Lights*; Erskine Hawkins, *Tuxedo Junction*; Harry Owens, *Sweet Leilani* (Oscar); R. Rainger and L. Robin, *Blue Hawaii*; Richard Whiting, *Too Marvelous for Words*.

**Other**   Frank Churchill, *Snow White and the Seven Dwarfs* (film music); Larry Clinton, *Study in Brown*; Duke Ellington, *Diminuendo and Crescendo in Blue* (jazz suite); Raymond Scott, *The Toy Trumpet*; Herbert Stothart, *The Good Earth* (film music); Dimitri Tiomkin, *Lost Horizon* (film music).

## Music—The Cultivated/Art Music Scene

**F. Births**   Edward Applebaum (composer) September 28; Patricia Brooks (soprano) November 7; Donald Buchla (electronics expert) April 17; Grace Bumbry (mezzo-soprano) January 4; Claudine Carlson (mezzo-soprano) February 26; David Del Tredici (composer) March 16; Brian Fennelly (composer) August 14; Joseph Flummerfelt (conductor) February 24; Catherine Gayer (soprano) February 11; Philip Glass (composer) January 31; Frederick Hammond (musicologist) August 7; Katherine Hoover (composer/conductor); Ruth Laredo (pianist) November 20; Robert Moran (composer) January 8; Paul Palombo (composer) September 10; Michael Ponti (pianist) October 29; Samuel Sanders (pianist) June 27; Stephen Simon (conductor) May 3; Judith Somogi (conductor) May 13; Felicia Weathers (soprano) August 13; Donald M. Wilson (composer) June 30; Olly Wilson (composer) September 7.

**G. Deaths**   Richard Aldrich (critic) June 2; Maurice Arnold (violinist/composer) October 23; Dan Beddoe (Welsh-born tenor) December 26; Paul Bekker (German-born musicologist) March 7; Frank H. Damrosch (German-born conductor) October 22; Clarence Eddy (organist) January 10; Arthur Foote (composer) April 8; Sam Franko (violinist/conductor) May 6; George Gershwin (composer/pianist) July 11; Henry Hadley (composer/conductor) September 6; William James Henderson (critic) June 5; Eduard Herrmann (German-born violinist/conductor) April 24; Julie Rivé-King (pianist) July 24; Caro Roma (soprano/composer) September 23; Louis Victor Saar (Dutch-born pianist/composer) November 23; Wallace A. Sabin (British-born organist) December 8; Marie Selika (soprano) May 19; Marcia Van Dresser (soprano) July 11.

**H. Debuts**

**United States**   Jussi Bjoerling (Swedish tenor—Chicago), Jorge Bolet (Cuban pianist—Philadelphia), Hugues Cuénod (Swiss tenor—tour), Antal Dorati (Hungarian conductor—Washington, DC), Maurice Eisenberg (cellist—New York), Ivan Galamian (Peruvian violinist—New York), Paul Hindemith (German violist—Washington, DC), Julius Katchen (pianist, age 11—Philadelphia), Marta Krásová (Czech mezzo-soprano—tour), Luboshutz and Nemenoff (duo-pianists—New York), Ginette Neveu (French violinist—tour), Rosa Pauly (Hungarian soprano—New York), Erna Sack (German soprano—Chicago).

**Metropolitan Opera**   John Brownlee (Australian baritone), Gina Cigna (French soprano), Carl

Hartmann (German tenor), Zinka Milanov (Yugoslavian soprano), Nicola Moscona (Greek bass), Bidú Sayão (Brazilian soprano), Carlo Tagliabue (Italian baritone), Jennie Tourel (Russian soprano), Helen Traubel (soprano), Robert Weede (baritone), Adolf Vogel (German bass-baritone).

## I. New Positions

**Conductors**   Werner Janssen (Baltimore Symphony Orchestra—to 1939); Fabien Sevitzky (Indianapolis Symphony Orchestra—to 1955); Fritz Stiedry (Orchestra, New Friends of Music, New York); Arturo Toscanini (NBC Symphony Orchestra); Robert Whitney (Louisville Orchestra—to 1967).

**Educational**   Wayne Barlow (Eastman—to 1978); Ernest Hutcheson (president, Juilliard—to 1945); Wiktor Labunski (Kansas City Conservatory—director in 1941); Paul Pisk (University of Redlands, chairman, 1948–51); Curt Sachs (NYU—to 1953); Halsey Stevens (Dakota Wesleyan University—to 1944); Oliver Strunk (musicology, Princeton—to 1966); Burnet C. Tuthill (director, Memphis College of Music—to 1959); John Vincent (music head, Western Kentucky State—to 1945).

**Other**   Robert Russell Bennett (president, American Society of Musical Arrangers); Harold Spivacke (head, Music Division, Library of Congress—to 1972); Oscar Thompson (music critic, *New York Sun*—to 1945); Powell Weaver (organ, First Baptist Church, Kansas City—to 1945); Ernest White (organ, Church of St. Mary the Virgin, New York—to 1958).

## J. Honors and Awards

**Honors**   Ernest Bloch (National Institute); Frederick Converse, Albert Spalding (American Academy).

**Awards**   Jorge Bolet (Naumburg Prize); John Edmunds (Bearns Prize).

**K. Biographical**   Daniele Amfitheatrov (Russian conductor) comes to the United States as assistant conductor of the Minnesota Symphony Orchestra; Jacob Avshalomov (composer/conductor) comes to the United States; Victor Babin (Russian pianist) moves to the United States with his wife, Vitya Vronsky; Carl Bamberger (Austrian conductor), Artur Holde (German conductor), Curt Sachs (German musicologist), Leo Schrade (German musicologist), and Hans Weisshaar (German violin maker) emigrate to the United States; Georges Barrère and E. Power Biggs become American citizens; Maria Callas moves to Greece for voice study; Lukas Foss (German composer/conductor) moves to the United States with his family; Bronislav Gimpel (Russian violinist) comes to the United States; William Primrose (Scottish violist) comes to the United States to play in Toscanini's NBC Symphony Orchestra.

## L. Musical Beginnings

**Performing Groups**   Dayton Civic Ballet Co.; Dayton Civic Harmonica Band; Dayton Philharmonic Youth Orchestra; Drake–Des Moines Symphony Orchestra; Jackson Music Association (Mississippi); Louisville Orchestra (Kentucky); NBC Symphony Orchestra (formed exclusively for Arturo Toscanini).

**Festivals**   Saratoga Music Festival (New York); Tanglewood Festival (Massachusetts).

**Educational**   Phi Beta Mu (University of Texas); Raisa-Rimini Singing School (Chicago).

**Other**   Santa Fe Concert (Community Concerts) Association.

## M. Music Publications

Bernstein, Martin, *An Introduction to Music*
Gleason, Harold, *Method of Organ Playing*
Huss, Winthrop and de Bekker, L., *The Encyclopedia of Music and Musicians*
Jackson, George P., *Spiritual Folk-songs of Early America*
Mursell, James L., *The Psychology of Music*
Slonimsky, Nicolas, *Music Since 1900*
Spaeth, Sigmund, *Stories behind the World's Great Music*
Taylor, Deems, *Of Men and Music*

Thompson, Oscar, *The American Singer*
Verrall, John, *Elements of Harmony*
Williams, Ernest S., *The Ernest S. Williams Modern Method for Trumpet or Cornet*

**N. Musical Compositions**

**Chamber Music** John J. Becker, *Soundpiece No. 4: String Quartet No. 2*; Charles W. Cadman, *Piano Quintet in G Minor*; Avery Claflin, *String Quartet*; Herbert Elwell, *String Quartet in E Minor*; Arthur Farwell, *Piano Quintet in E Minor, Opus 103*; Ross Lee Finney, *String Quartet No. 2—Viola Sonata No. 1*; Edward B. Hill, *Piano Quartet*; Harrison Kerr, *String Quartet No. 2*; Nicolas Nabokov, *String Quartet*; Quincy Porter, *String Quartet No. 6*; William Schuman, *String Quartet No. 2*.

**Choral/Vocal** Theodore Chanler, *Epitaphs* (song cycle); R. Nathaniel Dett, *The Ordering of Moses* (oratorio); Arthur Farwell, *Four Indian Songs, Opus 102*; William Schuman, *Pioneers—Choral Etude*; Charles S. Skilton, *Communion Service in C Major*; Virgil Thomson, *My Shepherd Will Supply My Needs—Scenes from the Holy Infancy*; Robert Ward, *Fatal Interview*.

**Concertos** Isidor Achron, *Piano Concerto No. 1*; Joseph Achron, *Violin Concerto No. 3, Opus 72*; John J. Becker, *Viola Concerto*; Anis Fuleihan, *Piano Concertos 1, 2*; Frederick Jacobi, *Violin Concerto*; Wiktor Labunski, *Piano Concerto in C Major*; Wesley La Violette, *Piano Concerto*; Walter Piston, *Concertino for Piano and Chamber Orchestra*; Vittorio Rieti, *Piano Concerto No. 2*; William Russell, *Trumpet Concerto*; Leo Sowerby, *Organ Concerto No. 1*.

**Operas** Marc Blitzstein, *The Cradle Will Rock* (musical play); Aaron Copland, *The Second Hurricane* (high school opera); Walter Damrosch, *The Man without a Country*; Vittorio Giannini, *The Scarlet Letter*; Louis Gruenberg, *Green Mansions*; Paul Nordoff, *Mr. Fortune*.

**Orchestra/Band** Samuel Barber, *First Essay for Orchestra, Opus 12*; Samuel Barlow, *Amphitryon 38* (incidental music); Ernest Bloch, *Evocations*; Charles W. Cadman, *Suite on American Folktunes*; Aaron Copland, *Music for Radio (Saga of the Prairie)*; Herbert Elwell, *Orchestral Sketches*; Arthur Fickénscher, *Variations on a Theme in Medieval Style* (strings); Vivian Fine, *The Race of Life* (ballet)—*Elegiac Song* (strings); Leo Ornstein, *Nocturne and Dance of the Fates*; Burrill Phillips, *Play Ball* (ballet); Quincy Porter, *Dance in Three-Time*; Wallingford Riegger, *Candide, Opus 24* (ballet); William Schuman, *Prelude and Fugue for Orchestra*; Elie Siegmeister, *Abraham Lincoln Walks at Midnight*; William Grant Still, *Lenox Avenue* (ballet); Virgil Thomson, *Antony and Cleopatra* (incidental music)—*The River* (film music)—*Filling Station* (ballet); Richard Yardumian, *Armenian Suite*.

**Piano/Organ** John J. Becker, *Soundpiece No. 5: Piano Sonata*; Paul Creston, *Two-Part Inventions, Opus 14*; Werner Josten, *Sonata No. 1*; Leo Sowerby, *Organ Suite*; Halsey Stevens, *Sonata No. 2*; Emerson Whithorne, *El Camino Real*.

**Symphonies** Ernst Bacon, *Symphony No. 2*; Nicolai Berezowsky, *Symphony No. 3, Opus 21*; Alan Hovhaness, *Symphony No. 1, Opus 17, "Exile"*; Harrison Kerr, *Symphony No. 2*; Harl McDonald, *Symphony No. 4, "Festival of the Workers"*; Walter Piston, *Symphony No. 1*; William Schuman, *Symphony No. 2*; David S. Smith, *Symphony No. 4, Opus 78*; William Grant Still, *Symphony No. 2 in G Minor*; David Van Vactor, *Symphony No. 1* (New York Philharmonic Prize); Emerson Whithorne, *Symphony No. 3*.

# 1938

❖

## Historical Highlights

The United States and Germany recall their respective ambassadors, thus breaking relations; Congress creates the Federal National Mortgage Association (FNMA) and sets up the House Committee on Un-American Activities; Orson Welles scares the nation with his broadcast of H. G.

Wells's *War of the Worlds*; Germany takes over Austria and is given the Czech Sudetenland by means of the Munich Pact sponsored by British Prime Minister Neville Chamberlain.

## World Cultural Highlights

**World Art**     Jean Arp, *Growth*; Salvador Dali, *Apparition of Face and Fruit-Dish*; Charles Despiau, *Assis*; Raoul Dufy, *Regatta*; Paul Klee, *A Park Near Lucerne;* Paul Nash, *Landscape from a Dream.*

**World Literature**     Jean Anouilh, *La Sauvage*; Graham Greene, *Brighton Rock*; André Malraux, *L'Espoir*; Daphne du Maurier, *Rebecca*; Jean-Paul Sartre, *Nausea*; George Bernard Shaw, *Geneva*.

**World Music**     Dmitri Kabalevsky, *Colas Breugnon*; Francis Poulenc, *Concerto for Organ, Strings and Timpani*; Sergei Prokofiev, *Alexander Nevsky*; Igor Stravinsky, *Dumbarton Oaks Concerto.*

**Miscellaneous**     The Lucerne Festivals begin in Switzerland and the Ibero-American Music Festival in Bogotá; births include Elly Ameling, Rudolf Nureyev, and Maxim Shostakovich; deaths include Gabriele d'Annunzio, Ernest Barlach, Feodor Chaliapin, Ernst Kirchner, and Alexander Kuprin.

## American Art and Literature Highlights

**Births/Deaths**     Births include art figures Janet Fish, Robert Graham, Nancy Holt, Sylvia Mangold, Brice Marden, Jim Nutt, and literary figures John Guare and Joyce Carol Oates; deaths include art figures George Barnard, Thomas Dewing, William Glackens, Sargent Kendall, Edmund Tarbell, and literary figures Mary H. Foote, Zona Gale, Owen Wister, and Thomas Wolfe.

**Art Works**     Milton Avery, *Seagulls, Gaspé*; Paul Cadmus, *Sailors and Floosies*; Arthur Dove, *Abstract, the Flour Mill*; Marsden Hartley, *The Fisherman's Last Supper*; Robert Laurent, *Kneeling Figure*; Jacob Lawrence, *Street Scene—Restaurant*; Jacques Lipchitz, *Prometheus with a Vulture*; Man Ray, *La Fortune*; José de Rivera, *Red and Black (Double Element)*; Henry Moore, *Recumbent Figures.*

**Literature**     Maxwell Anderson, *Knickerbocker Holiday*; William Faulkner, *The Unvanquished*; John G. Fletcher, *Selected Poems* (Pulitzer Prize); Marjorie Kinnan Rawlings, *The Yearling* (Pulitzer Prize); Robert Sherwood, *Abe Lincoln in Illinois* (Pulitzer Prize); John Steinbeck, *The Long Valley*; Thornton Wilder, *Our Town* (Pulitzer Prize); Richard Wright, *Uncle Tom's Children*.

## Music—The Vernacular/Commercial Scene

**A. Births**     Hoyt Axton (singer/writer) March 25; Jeff Barry (singer/writer) April 3; Carla Bley (composer/bandleader) May 11; JoAnne Brackeen (piano) July 26; James Burton (guitarist) August 21; J. J. Cale (singer/writer) December 5; Glen Campbell (singer) April 22; Bobby Charles (singer/writer); Dee Clark (singer) November 7; Eddie Cochran (singer/writer) October 3; Dave "Baby" Cortez (singer) August 13; Don Covay (singer/writer) March; Tyrone Davis (singer) May 4; Duane Eddy (guitarist) April 26; Connie Francis (singer) December 12; Dale Hawkins (singer/guitarist) August 23; David Houston (singer) December 9; Freddie Hubbard (trumpeter) April 7; Etta James (singer); Norma Jean (singer) January 30; Jack Jones (singer) January 14; Ben E. King (singer/writer) September 23; Gordon Lightfoot (guitarist/singer) November 17; Darlene Love (singer) July 26; Charley Pride (singer) March 18; Louie Ramírez (arranger/bandleader) February 24; Kenny Rogers (singer) August 21; Connie Stevens (singer/actress) August 8; Johnnie Taylor (singer) May 5; Allen Toussaint (singer/pianist/writer) January 14; Tina Turner (singer) November 26; McCoy Tyner (pianist) December 11; Maurice Williams (singer/writer) April 26; Bill Withers (singer) July 4; Peter Yarrow (Peter, Paul, and Mary) May 31.

**B. Deaths**     Con Conrad (composer) September 28; Benjamin R. Harney (ragtime pianist/writer) March 11; May Irwin (singer/actress) October 22; Joseph "King" Oliver (cornetist/bandleader) April 8; James Sylvester Scott (ragtime pianist) August 30; Edgar Smith (lyricist) March 8; James Thornton (singer/writer) July 27; Richard A. Whiting (songwriter) February 10.

**C. Biographical**

**Performing Groups**     Van Alexander Big Band; Blue Grass Boys; Les Brown's "Band of Renown"; Bill Doggett Band I; Roy Eldridge Band; Four Harmony Kings; Harry James Big Band; King Cole Trio (?); Gene Krupa Big Band I; The Pied Pipers; Jack Teagarden Band; Young Tuxedo Brass Band (New Orleans).

**New Beginnings**     Society for the Preservation and Encouragement of Barber Shop Quartet Singing in America (Oklahoma); *Swing: The Guide to Modern Music*.

**Miscellaneous**     Ernest Gold (Austrian composer) comes to the United States; Billie Holiday joins Artie Shaw's band, becoming the first black singer in a white band; Mabel Mercer comes to the United States and New York.

**D. Publications**     W. C. Handy, *Book of Negro Spirituals*; Winthrop Sargeant, *Jazz, Hot and Hybrid*.

**E. Representative Works**

**Musicals**     Irving Berlin, *Alexander's Ragtime Band* (film); S. Fain and I. Kahal, *Right This Way—Hellzapoppin*; George and Ira Gershwin, *Goldwyn Follies* (film); Frederick Loewe, *Great Lady*; Cole Porter, *You Never Know—Leave It to Me*; R. Rodgers, L. Hart, and J. Logan, *The Boys from Syracuse—I Married an Angel*; K. Weill and M. Anderson, *Knickerbocker Holiday*.

**Songs**     Irving Berlin, *God Bless America* (complete song); Johnny Burke and J. Monaco, *An Apple for the Teacher*; Hoagy Carmichael, *Small Fry*; J. Fred Coots and Haven Gillespie, *You Go to My Head*; Tommy Dorsey, *Boogie Woogie* (based on Pine Top Smith's song); Sammy Fain, *I'll Be Seeing You*; S. Gaillard and S. Stewart, *The Flat Foot Floogie*; Ray Noble, *Cherokee*; Ralph Rainger, *Thanks for the Memories* (Oscar); Harold Rome, *Sing Out the News*; H. Warren and J. Mercer, *Jeepers Creepers—You Must Have Been a Beautiful Baby*; Bob Will, *San Antonio Rose*.

**Other**     Leroy Anderson, *Jazz Pizzicato—Jazz Legato*; Frankie Carle and J. Lawrence, *Sunrise Serenade*; Hugo Friedhofer, *The Adventures of Marco Polo* (film music); Erich Korngold, *Adventures of Robin Hood* (film music—Oscar).

## Music—The Cultivated/Art Music Scene

**F. Births**     Thomas Beveridge (composer); William Bolcom (pianist/composer) May 26; Paul Chihara (composer) July 9; Gloria Coates (composer/performer) October 10; John Corigliano, Jr. (composer) February 16; Lyle Davidson (composer) February 25; Simon Estes (bass-baritone) February 2; Calvin Hampton (organist) December 31; John Harbison (composer) December 20; Michael Jaffee (early music performer) April 21; Roberta Knie (soprano) May 13; Anton Kuerti (pianist/composer) July 21; Douglas Leedy (composer/conductor) March 3; William T. McKinley (composer); Barton McLean (composer) April 8; Johanna Meier (soprano) February 13; Ellsworth Milburn (composer) February 6; Larry Palmer (organist/harpsichordist) November 13; Neva Pilgrim (soprano) November 21; Kenneth Riegel (tenor) April 29; Jerome Rose (pianist) August 12; Frederic Rzewski (pianist/composer) April 13; Harvey Sollberger (flutist/composer) May 11; Joan Tower (composer) September 6; Tatiana Troyanos (mezzo-soprano) September 12; Phil Winsor (composer) May 10; Charles Wuorinen (composer) June 9.

**G. Deaths**     Aurelio Giorni (Italian-born pianist) September 23; Alma Gluck (Romanian-born soprano) October 27; Leopold Godowsky (Lithuanian-born pianist/composer) November 21; Mary Elizabeth Salter (soprano) September 12; Antoinette Szumowska (Polish-born pianist) August 18.

**H. Debuts**

**United States**     Simon Barere (Russian pianist—New York), Joel Berglund (Swedish bass-baritone—Chicago), Dean Dixon (conductor—New York), Rudolf Firkusny (Czech pianist—New York), Massimo Freccia (Italian conductor—New York), Felix Galimir (Austrian violinist—New York), Szymon Goldberg (Polish violinist—New York), Mack Harrell (baritone—New York), Hilde Konetzni (Austrian soprano—tour), James Melton (tenor—Cincinnati), Jan Peerce (tenor—Philadelphia), Gertrude Pitzinger (Bohemian contralto—New York), Maria Reining (Austrian soprano—Chicago), Risë Stevens (mezzo-soprano—Philadelphia), Ebe Stignani (Italian mezzo-soprano—San Francisco), James Sykes (pianist—New York).

**Metropolitan Opera**   Jussi Björling (Swedish tenor), Maria Caniglia (Italian soprano), Mafalda Favero (Italian soprano), January Kiepura (Polish tenor), Erich Leinsdorf (Austrian conductor), Hans Nissen (German bass-baritone), Rosa Pauly (Hungarian soprano), Risë Stevens (mezzo-soprano), Leonard Warren (baritone).

**Other**   Maria Callas (soprano—Athens).

**I. New Positions**

**Conductors**   Kurt Herbert Adler (Chicago Opera—to 1943); Victor Alessandro (Oklahoma City Symphony Orchestra—to 1951); Erich Leinsdorf (German opera, Metropolitan Opera); Fritz Reiner (Pittsburgh Symphony Orchestra—to 1948); Hans Schwieger (Southern Symphony Orchestra—to 1941); Nicolai Sokoloff (Seattle Symphony Orchestra—to 1940); Burnet Tuthill (Memphis Symphony Orchestra—to 1946).

**Educational**   Wilfred C. Bain (dean of music, North Texas State University); Lucien Cailliet (USC—to 1945); Catharine Crozier (Eastman—to 1953); Marcel Grandjany (Juilliard—to 1975); Joseph Machlis (Queens—to 1974); Paul Nordoff (Philadelphia Conservatory—to 1943); Moshe Paranov (director, Hartt School—president in 1957); Quincy Porter (dean, New England Conservatory—director in 1942); Carl Ruggles (University of Miami); Robert L. Sanders (music dean, Indiana University—to 1947); Edwin J. Stringham (music chair, Queens—to 1946).

**Other**   Abraham Veinus (music research, RCA).

**J. Honors and Awards**

**Honors**   Walter Damrosch (American Academy Gold Medal); Walter Piston, Roger Sessions, Arthur Shepherd, and Randall Thompson (National Institute).

**Awards**   Jorge Bolet (Josef Hoffman Award); Carroll Glenn (Naumburg Award).

**K. Biographical**   Those coming to the United States include Kurt Herbert Adler, Walter Aschaffenburg, Erwin Bodky, Ingolf Dahl, Emanuel Feuermann, Paul Fromm, Jakob Gimpel, Walter Herbert, Hugo Kauder, Ernst Krenek, Alexander Lászlo, Siegmund Levarie, Hans Moldenhauer, Joaquin Nin-Culmell, Egon Petri, Karol Rathaus, Rudolf Réti, Moriz Rosenthal, Julius Rudel, Franz Rupp, Alexander Schneider, Elisabeth Schumann, Hans Schwieger, Fritz Stiedry, Kurt Stone, Karl Weigl, and Stefan Wolpe. Maurice Abravanel, caught up in Metropolitan Opera politics, moves to Broadway; Antonia Brico becomes the first woman to direct the New York Philharmonic Orchestra; Lily Pons marries conductor André Kostelanetz; Hilda Somer (Austrian pianist) is brought to the United States at age eight; William Steinberg (German conductor) becomes assistant to Toscanini at the NBC Symphony Orchestra; Paul Wittgenstein settles in New York and teaches privately.

**L. Musical Beginnings**

**Performing Groups**   Blaisdell Wind Quartet (New York); Boston Society of Ancient Instruments; Galimir String Quartet II; Louisville Chamber Music Society; New York Chamber Orchestra; Southern Symphony Orchestra (Columbia, South Carolina); Fred Waring Glee Club (by Robert Shaw).

**Festivals**   Stern Grove Midsummer Music Festival (San Francisco).

**Educational**   Drinker Library of Choral Music (Philadelphia); National Association of Choir Directors; University of Texas College of Fine Arts.

**Other**   American Accordionists' Association; American Composers Alliance; Arrow Music Press (New York); Griffith Music Foundation (Newark, New Jersey); Henry Hadley Foundation for the Advancement of American Music (New York); Tanglewood Music Shed; Whittall Pavilion (Library of Congress).

**M. Music Publications**

Dennée, Charles, *Musical Journeys*

Dickinson, George, *Classification of Music Compositions: A Decimal System*
Earhart, Will, *Elements of Music Theory*
Gilman, Lawrence, *Toscanini and Great Music*
Goldman, Richard F., *The Band's Music*
La Violette, Wesley, *Music and Its Makers*
Leichtentritt, Hugo, *Music, History and Ideas*
Mason, Daniel G., *Music in My Time*
Seashore, Carl E., *Psychology of Music*
Taubman, Howard, *Opera: Front and Back*
Wier, Albert, ed., *The Macmillan Encyclopedia of Music and Musicians*

**N. Musical Compositions**

**Chamber Music**   Amy Beach, *Piano Trio*; Lionel Nowak, *String Quartet*; Charles S. Skilton, *String Quartet in B Minor*; Leo Sowerby, *Clarinet Sonata* (Society for Publication of American Music Prize); Ernst Toch, *Piano Quintet, Opus 64*; Joseph Wood, *String Quartet No. 1*.

**Choral/Vocal**   John Cage, *Five Songs on e. e. cummings*; Ross Lee Finney, *Three 17th Century Lyrics*; Earl Robinson, *Ballad for Americans*; Arnold Schoenberg, *Kol Nidre, Opus 39*; Louise Talma, *The Hound of Heaven* (Stovall Prize); Vladimir Ussachevsky, *Jubilee Cantata*.

**Concertos**   John J. Becker, *Piano Concerto No. 2, "Satirico"*; Ernest Bloch, *Violin Concerto*; Henry Brant, *Clarinet Concerto*; David Diamond, *Cello Concerto*; Arcady Dubensky, *Fantasy on a Negro Theme* (tuba and orchestra); John Woods Duke, *Piano Concerto*; Louis Gruenberg, *Piano Concerto No. 2*; Wesley La Violette, *Violin Concerto No. 2*; Harold C. Morris, *Violin Concerto*; Bernard Rogers, *Soliloquy No. 2* (bassoon and orchestra).

**Operas**   Vittorio Giannini, *Beauty and the Beast*; Douglas Moore, *The Devil and Daniel Webster*; Lazare Saminsky, *Julian, the Apostate Caesar*; Julia Smith, *Cynthia Parker*.

**Orchestra/Band**   Wayne Barlow, *The Winter's Passed* (oboe and strings); William Bergsma, *Paul Bunyan* (ballet); Henry Brant, *Fisherman's Overture*; Aaron Copland, *Billy the Kid* (ballet)—*An Outdoor Overture*; Walter Piston, *The Incredible Flutist* (ballet); Wallingford Riegger, *Machine Ballet, Opus 28*; Tibor Serly, *The Pagan City* (tone poem); Virgil Thomson, *Androcles and the Lion* (incidental music); Ernst Toch, *The Idle Stroller Suite*; Karl Weigl, *Festival Overture*; Hugo Weisgall, *Quest* (ballet); Adolph Weiss, *Suite for Orchestra*.

**Piano/Organ**   Hans Barth, *Suite No. 1, Opus 20*; Amy Beach, *Five Improvisations, Opus 148*; Leonard Bernstein, *Sonata*; John Cage, *Metamorphosis—Bacchanale* (prepared piano); R. Nathaniel Dett, *Tropic Winter Suite*; Ernst Krenek, *Twelve Short Pieces, Opus 83*; Robert Palmer, *Sonata No. 1*; Vittorio Rieti, *Sonata in A-Flat Major*; Arthur Shepherd, *Capriccio No. 1*; George Tremblay, *Sonatas Nos. 1, 2*.

**Symphonies**   George Antheil, *Symphony No. 2*; Henry Cowell, *Symphony No. 2, "Anthropos"*; Morton Gould, *American Symphonette No. 3*; Parks Grant, *Symphony in D Minor*; Howard Hanson, *Symphony No. 3, Opus 33*; Kent Kennan, *Symphony*; Frederick Search, *Symphony No. 3*; Arthur Shepherd, *Symphony No. 2*; George Tremblay, *Chaparral Symphony*.

# 1939

❀

## Historical Highlights

The first splitting of the atom occurs at Columbia University; the Neutrality Act of 1939 permits sale of arms to France and England; the first helicopter is introduced by Igor Sikorsky; the New York World's Fair in the East and the San Francisco International Exposition both open; World War II begins as the Germans invade Poland and occupy the rest of Czechoslovakia; the Russo-Finnish War begins; the Spanish Civil War ends.

## World Cultural Highlights

**World Art**   André Derain, *Young Girl Peeling Fruit*; Paul Klee, *The Conquest of the Mountains*; Jean-Paul Laurent, *The Hunt and the Forester*; Antoine Pevsner, *Projection in Space*.

**World Literature**   Jean Giraudoux, *Ondine*; Christopher Isherwood, *Goodbye to Berlin*; James Joyce, *Finnegans Wake*; Richard Llewellyn, *How Green Was My Valley*; William Butler Yeats, *Last Poems*.

**World Music**   Béla Bartók, *String Quartet No. 6—Mikrokosmos*; Benjamin Britten, *Les Illuminations*; Zoltán Kodály, *Peacock Variations—Concerto for Orchestra*; Dmitri Shostakovich, *Symphony No. 6*.

**Miscellaneous**   The Geneva International Competition for Music Performers begins; births include Alan Ayckbourn, James Galway, and Seamus Heaney; deaths include Olav Dunn, Ludwig Fulda, Franz Schmidt, Antonio Ruiz, and William Butler Yeats.

## American Art and Literature Highlights

**Births/Deaths**   Births include art figures Larry Bell, Judy Chicago, Gary Kuehn, Richard Serra, and literary figures Margaret Atwood, Clark Coolidge, Charles Fuller, Tina Howe, and Robert Siegel; deaths include artists Frederick Frieseke, Robert Hallowell, Ernest Lawson, and literary figures Ford Maddox Ford, Zane Grey, Sidney Coe Howard, Philander Johnson, and Joel Elias Spingarn.

**Art Works**   Isobel Bishop, *Lunch Hour*; Alexander Brook, *Georgia Jungle*; Alexander Calder, *Lobster Trap and Fish Tail*; Edward Hopper, *New York Movie*; Jacob Lawrence, *Series: Harriet Tubman*; Reginald Marsh, *Ten Shots, Ten Cents*; Georgia O'Keeffe, *Red and Orange Hills*; Charles Sheeler, *Rolling Power*; Grant Wood, *In the Spring*.

**Literature**   Philip Barry, *The Philadelphia Story*; M. Hart and G. S. Kaufman, *The Man Who Came to Dinner*; Lillian Hellman, *The Little Foxes*; Katherine Porter, *Pale Horse, Pale Rider*; William Saroyan, *The Time of Your Life* (Pulitzer Prize—New York Drama Critics' Award); John Steinbeck, *The Grapes of Wrath* (Pulitzer Prize); Mark Van Doren, *Collected Poems* (Pulitzer Prize).

## Music—The Vernacular/Commercial Scene

**A. Births**   Luther Allison (guitarist/singer) August 17; Frankie Avalon (singer) September 18; William Bell (singer) July 16; Gary (US) Bonds (singer) June 6; Roy Buchanan (guitarist) September 23; Jerry Butler (singer) December 8; Nick Ceroli (drummer) December 22; David A. Coe (singer) September 6; Judy Collins (singer) May 1; Dion (DiMucci) (singer) July 18; Phil Everly (singer) January 19; John Fahey (guitarist) February 28; Roberta Flack (singer) February 10; Dallas Frazier (singer/writer) October 27; Marvin Gaye (singer/writer) April 2; Gerry Goffin (songwriter) February 11; Eddie Kendricks (singer) December 17; Barry Mann (songwriter) February 9; Barbara McNair (singer) March 4; Sal Mineo (singer) January 10; Ray Peterson (singer) April 23; Neil Sedaka (singer/writer) March 13; Del Shannon (singer) December 30; Grace Slick (singer/writer) October 30; Ray Stevens (singer/writer) January 24; Johnny Tillotson (singer) April 20; Gary Usher (singer/writer) (?); Al Wilson (singer) June 19; Nancy Wilson (singer) February 20; Paul Winter (saxophonist/composer) August 31.

**B. Deaths**   Harry Alford (composer) March 4; Herschel Evans (saxophonist) February 9; Abe Holzmann (ragtime composer/arranger) January 16; Tommy Ladnier (trumpeter) June 4; Gertrude "Ma" Rainey (singer) December 22; Fay Templeton (singer/actress) October 3; William "Chick" Webb (drummer/bandleader) June 16; Joe Young (singer/lyricist) April 21.

**C. Biographical**

**Performing Groups**   Carmen Cavallaro Band; Cotton Blossom Singers (Jackson Harmoneers); Five Blind Boys of Mississippi; Happyland Jubilee Singers (Five Blind Boys of Alabama); Coleman Hawkins Band; Mugsy Spanier's Ragtime Band; Summa Cum Laude Orchestra;

Tennessee State Sacred Harp Singing Association; Three Suns; Alec Wilder Octet.

**New Beginnings**   Big 3 Music Corporation (M-G-M Studios); Blue Note Record Co. (New York); Diamond Horseshoe (New York—by Billy Rose); *Jazz Information* (to 1942); *Jazzmen*; Novachord (by Laurens Hammond).

**Miscellaneous**   Carmen Miranda, the "Brazilian Bombshell," debuts on Broadway.

**D. Publications**   Wilder Hobson, *American Jazz Music*; I. Kolodin and B. Goodman, *The Kingdom of Swing*; S. Spaeth and R. Bruce, *How to Write Popular Songs*.

**E. Representative Works**

**Musicals**   Harold Arlen, *The Wizard of Oz* (film); Irving Berlin, *Carefree* (film); Jerome Kern and O. Hammerstein, *Very Warm for May*; Cole Porter, *Du Barry Was a Lady—You Never Know*; Rodgers and Hart, *Too Many Girls*; A. Schwartz and D. Fields, *Stars in Your Eyes*; Sam H. Stept, C. Tobias, and L. Brown, *Yokel Boy*.

**Songs**   H. Arlen and E. Y. Harburg, *Over the Rainbow* (Oscar); R. Bloom and J. Mercer, *Day In—Day Out*; L. Brown and W. Timm, *The Beer Barrel Polka*; J. Burke and F. Masters, *Scatterbrain*; Robert M. Crawford, *The Army Air Corps Song*; A. Dubin and V. Herbert, *Indian Summer*; J. Kennedy and M. Carr, *South of the Border*; Jerome Kern, *All the Things You Are*; Jack Lawrence, *If I Didn't Care*; A. H. Malotte and L. Morey, *Ferdinand, the Bull*.

**Other**   Glenn Miller, *Moonlight Serenade*; Max Steiner, *Gone with the Wind* (film music—Oscar); Fats Waller, *London Suite*.

## Music—The Cultivated/Art Music Scene

**F. Births**   Jon Appleton (composer) January 4; Arleen Augér (soprano) September 13; Jerome Barry (baritone) November 16; Lawrence Bernstein (musicologist) March 25; Bonnie Blackburn (musicologist) July 15; Charles Boone (composer) June 21; Gabriel Chodos (pianist) February 7; Erick Friedman (violinist) August 16; Joann Grillo (mezzo-soprano) May 14; Jonathan Harvey (cellist/composer); William Hellermann (composer/guitarist) July 15; William Hibbard (composer/violist) August 8; Grayson Hirst (tenor) December 27; Gwendolyn Killebrew (mezzo-soprano) August 26; Kenneth Klein (conductor) September 5; Barbara Kolb (composer) February 10; Robert L. Marshall (musicologist) October 12; Janis Martin (mezzo-soprano) August 16; Eugene Narmour (musicologist) October 27; Judith Nelson (soprano) September 10; Max Neuhaus (composer/percussionist) August 9; Joel Sachs (musicologist/pianist) December 19; Ann Schein (pianist) November 10; David Stock (composer/conductor) June 3; Richard A. Trythall (composer/pianist) July 25; Ralph Votapek (pianist) March 20; Neal Zaslaw (musicologist) June 28; Ellen Taaffe Zwilich (composer/violinist) April 30.

**G. Deaths**   Artur Bodanzky (conductor) November 23; Charles Dalmores (French-born tenor) December 6; Leandro Campanari (Italian-born violinist/conductor) April 22; Harold Flammer (publisher) October 22; Weston S. Gales (organist/conductor) October 21; Lawrence Gilman (critic) September 8; William Sherman Haynes (flute maker) January 28; Emma Juch (Austrian-born soprano) March 6; Waldo Selden Pratt (music historian) July 29; Ernest Schelling (composer/conductor) December 8.

**H. Debuts**

**United States**   Lorenzo Alvary (Hungarian bass—San Francisco), Kurt Baum (Czech tenor—Chicago), Clifford Curzon (British pianist—New York), William Masselos (pianist—New York), Dorothy Maynor (soprano—Tanglewood), Jarmila Novotná (Czech soprano—San Francisco), Paul Paray (French conductor—New York), Sigurd Rascher (German saxophonist—Boston), György Sándor (Hungarian pianist—New York), Leo Smit (pianist—New York).

**Metropolitan Opera**   Mack Harrell (baritone), Herbert Janssen (German baritone), Walter Olitzki (German baritone).

**I. New Positions**

**Conductors**   Quinto Maganini (Norwalk Symphony Orchestra—to 1978); Max Reiter (San Antonio Symphony Orchestra—to 1950).

**Educational**  Samuel Barber (Curtis Institute—to 1942); Joseph W. Clokey (dean, Fine Arts, Miami University—to 1946); Felix Deyo (director, Long Island Conservatory); Frederick Fennell (Eastman—to 1965); Irving Fine (Harvard—to 1950); Ernst Krenek (Vassar—to 1942); Rudolf Serkin (Curtis Institute); Carleton Sprague Smith (NYU—to 1967); Randall Thompson (director, Curtis Institute—to 1941); Eric Werner (Hebrew Union College, Cincinnati—to 1967).

**Other**  Paul Callaway (organist, Washington National Cathedral); Leonard Ellinwood (catalogist, Library of Congress); Robert Lawrence (music critic, *New York Herald Tribune*—to 1943); Charles Mills (critic, *Modern Music*—to 1947); Harold Schonberg (music critic, *American Music Lover*—to 1942); Alexander Schreiner (senior organist, Mormon Tabernacle—to 1977).

**K. Biographical**  Among the many emigrations to the United States are Samuel Adler's family, Peter Herman Adler, Lorenzo Alvary, Manfred F. Bukofzer, Adolf Busch, Mario Castelnuovo-Tedesco, Anthony Collins, Paul Dessau, Alfred Einstein, Emile Enthoven, Andor Foldes, Ivan Galamian, Raya Garbousova, Robert Goldsand, Otto Johannes Gombosi, Alexander Gretchaninov, Julius Herford, Erich Hertzmann, Karl Kohn, Fritz Kreisler, Nikolai Lopatnikoff, Paul Nettl, Raoul Pleskow, André Previn's family, Sigurd Rascher, Gerhard Samuel, György Sándor, George Schick, Artur Schnabel, Luigi Silva, Henry Swoboda, Bruno Walter, Eric Werner, and Eugene Zador. Marian Anderson scores a triumph singing at the Lincoln Memorial; Igor Gorin, Alexei Haieff, Fritz Mahler, Nicolas Nabokov, and Rudolph Serkin become American citizens; William Schwann opens a record store in Cambridge; Igor Stravinsky (Russian composer) comes to New York and gives the Norton lectures at Harvard; George Szell, in the United States when war begins in Europe, decides to stay; Jaromir Weinberger again moves to the United States where he settles permanently in St. Petersburg, Florida.

**L. Musical Beginnings**

**Performing Groups**  American Ballad Singers; American Ballet Theater; American Recorder Society; Brooklyn Chamber Music Society; Dallas Grand Opera Association; Pittsburgh Opera Society; Primrose String Quartet; San Antonio Symphony Orchestra; Tucson Boys' Choir.

**Educational**  Tau Beta Sigma Sorority (wind-band society).

**Other**  Allen Organ Co. (Allentown, Pennsylvania); American Music Center (New York); Broadcast Music, Inc. (BMI); Getzen Brass Instrument Co. (Elkhorn, Wisconsin); Jewish Music Forum; Words and Music (Shawnee Press, 1947).

**M. Music Publications**

Copland, Aaron, *What to Listen for in Music*
Dickinson, George S., *The Pattern of Music*
Gunn, Glenn D., *Music: Its History and Enjoyment*
Helm, Everett B., *The Beginnings of the Italian Madrigal and the Works of Arcadelt*
Kinscella, H. and Tierney, E., *Music in the Small School*
Mitchell, William, *Elementary Harmony*
Pratt, Waldo S., *The Music of the French Psalter of 1562*
Spaeth, Sigmund, *Music for Fun*
Taubman, Howard, *Music as a Profession*
Thompson, Oscar, ed., *The International Cyclopedia of Music and Musicians*
Thomson, Virgil, *The State of Music*
Weinstock, H. and Brockway, W., *Men of Music*

**N. Musical Compositions**

**Chamber Music**  Paul Creston, *Saxophone Sonata, Opus 19*; Arthur Fickénscher, *Piano Quintet*; Alexander Gretchaninov, *Clarinet Sonata No. 1*; Kent Kennan, *Sea Sonata* (violin and piano); Daniel G. Mason, *Variations on a Quiet Theme, Opus 40* (string quartet); Charles Mills, *String Quartet No. 1*; Robert Palmer, *String Quartet No. 1*; Vincent Persichetti, *String Quartet No. 1, Opus 7*; Walter Piston, *Violin Sonata*; Wallingford Riegger, *String Quartet No. 1, Opus 30*; William Schuman, *String Quartet No. 3*; Karl Weigl, *String Quartet No. 6—Piano Trio*.

**Choral/Vocal**  Mabel Wheeler Daniels, *Song of Jael*; Eleanor Freer, *Sonnets from the Portuguese* (after E. Browning); Vittorio Rieti, *Ulysses' Wanderings*; William Schuman, *Prologue* (chorus and orchestra)—*Prelude for Voices*; Louise Talma, *In Principio Erat Verbum* (Stovall Prize); Kurt Weill, *The Ballad of Magna Carta*.

**Concertos**    Samuel Barber, *Violin Concerto, Opus 14*; Wesley La Violette, *Concerto for String Quartet and Orchestra*; Walter Piston, *Violin Concerto No. 1*; Julia Smith, *Piano Concerto*.

**Operas**    John J. Becker, *Privilege and Privation: Stagework No. 5c*; Vittorio Giannini, *Blennerhasset*; Erich W. Korngold, *Die Kathrin*; Gian Carlo Menotti, *The Old Maid and the Thief* (radio opera); Eugene Zador, *Christoph Columbus*.

**Orchestra/Band**    Esther Ballou, *Suite for Chamber Orchestra*; Samuel Barlow, *Sousa ad Parnassum*; John J. Becker, *Rain Down Death: Stagework No. 5a* (incidental music)—*Orchestra Suite I*; William Bergsma, *San Francisco*; Leonard Bernstein, *The Birds* (incidental music); Aaron Copland, *Quiet City* (incidental music); Lou Harrison, *Green Mansions* (ballet); Ernst Krenek, *Symphonic Piece*; Otto Luening, *Symphonic Fantasia II*; Harl McDonald, *The Legend of the Arkansas Traveler*; Daniel G. Mason, *Prelude and Fugue for Strings, Opus 37*; Bernard Rogers, *Colors of War—The Song of the Nightingale*; William Schuman, *American Festival Overture—The Orchestra Song*; Robert Ward, *Ode for Orchestra*; Karl Weigl, *Old Vienna*; Jaromir Weinberger, *Variations and Fugue, "Under the Spreading Chestnut Tree"*; Richard Yardumian, *Symphonic Suite*.

**Piano/Organ**    Ingolf Dahl, *Prelude and Fugue*; Ross Lee Finney, *Piano Fantasy (Sonata No. 2)*; Kent Kennan, *Three Preludes*; Douglas Moore, *Passacaglia* (organ); Vincent Persichetti, *Sonata No. 1—Sonata No. 2*; Roger Sessions, *Pages From My Diary*; Jaromir Weinberger, *Bible Poems* (organ); Hugo Weisgall, *Piano Variations*.

**Symphonies**    George Antheil, *Symphony No. 3, "American"*; Felix Borowski, *Symphony No. 3*; Vittorio Giannini, *IBM Symphony*; Don Gillis, *Symphony No. 1*; Roy Harris, *Symphony No. 3*; Charles Jones, *Symphony No. 1*; Homer Keller, *Symphony No. 1*; Wesley La Violette, *Symphony No. 2*; Nikolai Lopatnikoff, *Symphony No. 2, Opus 24*; H. Owen Reed, *Symphony*; John Verrall, *Symphony No. 1*; Joseph Wood, *Symphony No. 1*.

# 1940

❀

## Historical Highlights

The census indicates a population of 132,165,000 in the United States; Franklin D. Roosevelt is elected for a third term as president; Congress passes a Selective Training and Service Act and the Smith Alien Act limiting the American Communist Party; President Roosevelt calls for defense buildup; Norway, France, and the Netherlands fall to the German war machine; Winston Churchill becomes British Prime Minister as Neville Chamberlain resigns; Leon Trotsky is assassinated in Mexico.

## World Cultural Highlights

**World Art**    Max Beckmann, *Circus Caravan*; Ludwig von Hofmann, *Spring*; Vasili Kandinsky, *Sky Blue*; Carl Milles, *The Meeting of the Waters*; John Piper, *St. Mary le Port, Bristol*.

**World Literature**    W. H. Auden, *Another Time*; Graham Greene, *The Power and the Glory*; Mikhail Sholokhov, *The Quiet Don*; Dylan Thomas, *Portrait of the Artist as a Young Dog*.

**World Music**    Benjamin Britten, *Sinfonia da Requiem*; Dmitri Kabalevsky, *The Comedians*; Aram Khachaturian, *Violin Concerto*; Anton Webern, *Variations for Orchestra, Opus 30*.

**Miscellaneous**    The Brazilian Symphony Orchestra of Rio de Janeiro, the Lithuanian Philharmonic Orchestra, and the Tokyo Philharmonic Orchestra are founded; births include Joseph Brodsky, Bruce Chatwin, and Siegfried Jerusalem; deaths include Verner von Heidenstam, Paul Klee, Selma Lagerlöf, Karl Muck, Donald Tovey, and Édouard Vuillard.

## American Art and Literature Highlights

**Births/Deaths**    Births include art figures Chuck Close, Nancy Graves, and literary figures Peter Benchley, John P. Coyne, Harold Jaffe, Paul Mariani, David Rabe, and Edmund White; deaths include art figures Jonas Lie, Allen Newman, Henry R. Poor, Charles Woodbury, and literary figures Dane Coolidge, F. Scott Fitzgerald, DuBose Heyward, Charles Markham, and Nathanael West.

**Art Works**  Hyman Bloom, *The Synagogue*; Stuart Davis, *Report from Rockport*; Lyonel Feininger, *Blue Sails*; Chaim Gross, *Girl on a Wheel*; Louis Guglielmi, *Relief Blues*; Morris Hirshfield, *Girl before a Mirror*; Edward Hopper, *Office at Night*; Loren MacIver, *Hopscotch*; Charles Sheeler, *Incantation*; David Smith, *Medals of Dishonor*; Max Weber, *The Hasidic Dance*.

**Literature**  Leonard Bacon, *Sunderland Capture and Other Poems* (Pulitzer Prize); Walter Clark, *The Oxbow Incident*; William Faulkner, *The Hamlet*; Ernest Hemingway, *For Whom the Bell Tolls*; John O'Hara, *Pal Joey*; Eugene O'Neill, *Long Day's Journey into Night* (Pulitzer Prize); Robert Sherwood, *There Shall Be No Night* (Pulitzer Prize); Upton Sinclair, *World's End*.

## Music — The Vernacular/Commercial Scene

**A. Births**  Roy Abrams (saxophonist/bandleader) January 23; George Adams (saxophonist/flutist) April 29; Steve Alaimo (songwriter) December 6; Arthur Alexander (singer) May 10; Roy Ayers (vibraphonist) September 10; Gary Bartz (saxophonist/composer) September 26; James Black (drummer) February 1; Arthur Blythe (saxophonist) July 5; Charles Brackeen (saxophonist) March 13; Anita Bryant (singer) March 25; Jimmie Clanton (singer) September 2; George Clinton (singer) July 22; Dash Crofts (singer/guitarist) August 14; Joey Dee (singer) June 11; Ellie Greenwich (singer/writer) October 23; Herbie Hancock (pianist/writer) April 12; Al Jarreau (singer) March 12; Carole King (singer/writer) February 9; "Chuck" Mangione (trumpeter/bandleader) November 29; Delbert McClinton (singer) November 4; Johnny Nash (singer) August 9; Rick Nelson (singer) May 8; Phil Ochs (folk singer/writer) December 19; "Smokey" Robinson (singer/writer) February 19; Pharoah Sanders (saxophonist) October 13; David Shaw (singer/writer) December 11; Nancy Sinatra (singer) June 8; Percy Sledge (singer) November 25; Phil Spector (writer/producer) December 26; Ralph Towner (guitarist) March 1; Dionne Warwick (singer) December 12; Paul Williams (singer/writer); Frank Zappa (composer) December 21.

**B. Deaths**  Johnny Dodds (clarinetist/saxophonist) August 8; Billy Hill (composer) December 24; V. O. Stamps (publisher) August 19.

**C. Biographical**

**Performing Groups**  Eddie Durham Big Band; Gramercy Five (Artie Shaw); Lionel Hampton Big Band; Vaughn Monroe Band; Original Gospel Harmonettes; Tony Pastor Band; Raymond Scott Big Band; Claude Thornhill Band; Yerba Buena Jazz Band (San Francisco).

**New Beginnings**  Keynote Records (New York); Martin and Morris Music Co. (Chicago): Solovox (by L. Hammond).

**Miscellaneous**  Bronislaw Kaper (Polish songwriter) comes to the United States.

**D. Publications**  John W. Work, Jr., *American Negro Songs and Spirituals*.

**E. Representative Works**

**Musicals**  Berlin and Ryskind, *Louisiana Purchase*; Eubie Blake, *Tan Manhattan*; Vernon Duke, *Cabin in the Sky*; B. Lane and E. Y. Harburg, *Hold on to Your Hats*; Cole Porter, *Panama Hattie — Broadway Melody of 1940* (film); Rodgers and Hart, *Pal Joey* (New York Drama Critics Award) — *Higher and Higher*.

**Songs**  G. Autry and P. Whitley, *Back in the Saddle Again*; R. Bloom and J. Mercer, *Fools Rush in*; A. P. Carter, *Wabash Cannon Ball*; Jimmy Davis, *You Are My Sunshine*; L. Harline and N. Washington, *When You Wish upon a Star* (Oscar); J. Kern and O. Hammerstein, *The Last Time I Saw Paris*; Lane and Loesser, *I Hear Music*; M. Lewis and N. Hamilton, *How High the Moon*; A. Lewis and L. Stock, *Blueberry Hill*; Ruth Lowe, *I'll Never Smile Again*; D. Raye and H. Prince, *Beat Me, Daddy, Eight to the Bar*; Don Raye, *This Is My Country*; J. Van Heusen and J. Burke, *Imagination*.

**Other**  Bernard Hermann, *Citizen Kane* (film music); Alfred Newman, *The Grapes of Wrath* (film music); Miklós Rózsa, *The Thief of Bagdad* (film music); Dimitri Tiomkin, *The Westerner* (film music).

## Music—The Cultivated/Art Music Scene

**F. Births**   Stephen Bishop-Kovacevich (pianist) October 17; Judith Blegen (soprano) April 27; Mark DeVoto (composer) January 11; Justino Díaz (bass) January 29; Helen Donath (soprano) July 10; Jon Gibson (saxophonist/flutist) March 11; Kay Griffel (soprano) December 26; Richard Kostelanetz (composer/critic) May 14; Shirley Love (mezzo-soprano) January 6; Stephen Pruslin (pianist) April 16; Phillip Rhodes (composer) June 6; Murry Sidlin (conductor) May 6; Alvin Singleton (composer) December 2; Olivia Stapp (soprano) May 30; William Workman (baritone) February 4.

**G. Deaths**   Frederick S. Converse (composer) June 8; Albert von Doenhoff (pianist/composer) October 3; Arthur Elson (music author) February 24; Viktor Hollaender (German-born conductor) October 24; Walter Keller (organist) July 7; Clara Anna Korn (composer/educator) July 14; Emma Nevada (soprano) June 20; Lewis Richards (harpsichordist) February 15; Bertram Shapleigh (composer/pianist) July 2; Arnold Volpe (Lithuanian-born conductor) February 2.

**H. Debuts**

**United States**   Peter Herman Adler (Czech conductor—New York), Eugene Conley (tenor—New York), Andor Foldes (Hungarian pianist—New York), Edward Kilenyi, Jr. (pianist—New York), Dorothy Kirsten (soprano—Chicago), Gerhard Pechner (German baritone—San Francisco), Tossy Spivakovsky (Russian violinist—New York).

**Metropolitan Opera**   Licia Albanese (Italian soprano), Salvatore Baccaloni (Italian bass), Alexander Kipnis (Russian bass), Jarmila Novotná (Czech soprano), Eleanor Steber (soprano), Sándor (Alexander) Svéd (Hungarian baritone).

**I. New Positions**

**Conductors**   Howard Barlow (Baltimore Symphony Orchestra—to 1943); Hans Heniot (Utah State Symphony Orchestra—to 1946); William F. Santelmann (United States Marine Band—to 1955); Ole Windingstad (New Orleans Philharmonic Symphony Orchestra—to 1944).

**Educational**   Ernest Bloch (Berkeley—to 1952); Otto Johannes Gombosi (University of Washington—to 1946); Paul Hindemith (Yale—to 1953); Ralph Kirkpatrick (Yale—to 1976); Leopold Mannes (Mannes School—to 1964); Douglas Moore (director, Columbia Music Department); Joaquin Nin-Culmell (Williams College, Massachusetts—to 1950); Robert Palmer (University of Kansas—to 1943); Egon Petri (Cornell—to 1946); Artur Schnabel (piano, University of Michigan—to 1945); Beveridge Webster (New England Conservatory—to 1946).

**Other**   Ludwig Altmann (organ, San Francisco Symphony Orchestra); Glenn D. Gunn (music critic, *Washington Times Herald*—to 1954); Gustave Reese (publications head, G. Schirmer); Virgil Thomson (music critic, *New York Herald-Tribune*—to 1954).

**J. Honors and Awards**

**Honors**   Stephen Foster (Hall of Fame for Great Americans); Walter Piston (American Academy of Arts and Sciences).

**Awards**   Sidney Foster (Leventritt Award); Abbey Simon (Naumburg Award).

**K. Biographical**   Further emigrations to the United States include Gerhard Albersheim (musicologist), Béla Bartók (pianist/composer), Rudolf Firkusny (pianist), Jerzy Fitelberg (composer), Claude Frank (pianist), Karl Geiringer (musicologist), Paul Hindemith (composer), Jascha Horenstein (conductor), Mieczyslaw Horszowski (pianist), Betsy Jolas (composer), Siegfried Landau (conductor), Jacob Lateiner (pianist), Edwin Lowinsky (musicologist), Darius Milhaud (composer), Vittorio Rieti (composer), Miklós Rózsa (composer), Max Rudolf (conductor), Felix Salzer (musicologist), Tossy Spivakovsky (violinist), and Joseph Szigeti (violinist). Henry Cowell is paroled from San Quentin; Igor Stravinsky marries Vera de Bosset and settles in Hollywood; Ernst Toch becomes an American citizen; Arturo Toscanini takes the NBC Symphony on a tour of South America; Hugo Weisgall receives a PhD in German literature.

**L. Musical Beginnings**

**Performing Groups**   All-American Youth Orchestra (by Leopold Stokowski); Arkansas State Symphony Orchestra (Little Rock); Baltimore Civic Opera Co.; Choral Guild of Atlanta; Janssen

Symphony Orchestra of Los Angeles; National Youth Administration Sinfonietta (New York); Utah State Symphony Orchestra.

**Festivals**   June Music Festival (Albuquerque, New Mexico).

**Educational**   Alice M. Ditson Fund (Columbia); Ornstein School of Music (Philadelphia).

**Other**   American Society of Piano Technicians; Berkshire (Tanglewood) Music Center (Massachusetts); *The Harmonizer*; Kleinhans Music Hall (Buffalo); Edgar M. Leventritt Foundation International Competition; National Music Council.

## M. Music Publications

Davison, Archibald, *Choral Conducting*
Kinscella, Hazel, *History Sings*
Kolodin, Irving, ed., *The Critical Composer*
Krenek, Ernst, *Studies in Counterpoint, Based on the Twelvetone Technique*
Levant, Oscar, *A Smattering of Ignorance*
Reese, Gustave, *Music in the Middle Ages*
Sachs, Curt, *The History of Musical Instruments*
Schillinger, Joseph, *Kaleidophone: New Resources of Melody and Harmony*
Seeger, Charles, *Music as Recreation*
Siegmeister, E. and Downes, O., *A Treasury of American Song*
Spaeth, Sigmund, *Great Program Music*
Taylor, Deems, *The Well Tempered Listener*

## N. Musical Compositions

**Chamber Music**   Leonard Bernstein, *Violin Sonata*; Cecil Burleigh, *Hymn to the Ancients* (piano quintet); David Diamond, *String Quartet No. 1*; Ross Lee Finney, *String Quartet No. 3*; Ellis Kohs, *String Quartet No. 1*; Leo Ornstein, *String Quartet No. 2*; Burrill Phillips, *String Quartet No. 1*; Quincy Porter, *Quintet* (flute and strings); Leroy Robertson, *String Quartet* (New York Music Critics' Award); Arthur Shepherd, *Quintet for Piano and Strings*; Leo Smit, *Sextet* (clarinet, bassoon, and strings); George Tremblay, *Modes of Transportation* (string quartet)—*Wind Quintet*; David Van Vactor, *String Quartet No. 1*; Joseph F. Wagner, *String Quartet*; Ben Weber, *Lyric Piece, Opus 7* (string quartet).

**Choral/Vocal**   Samuel Barber, *A Stopwatch and an Ordnance Map*; Richard Hammond, *Six Women's Choruses*; Victor Herbert, *Three Songs, Opus 15*; Kenneth Morris, *Just a Closer Walk with Thee* (gospel song); William Schuman, *This is Our Time*; Charles S. Skilton, *Zoo Fantastique*; Stefan Wolpe, *Unnamed Lands* (cantata).

**Concertos**   Henry Brant, *Violin Concerto*; Cecil Effinger, *Concerto Grosso*; Anis Fuleihan, *Concerto for Two Pianos*; Paul Hindemith, *Cello Concerto*; George F. McKay, *Violin Concerto*; Paul Nordoff, *Violin Concerto*; Alan Shulman, *Theme and Variations* (viola and orchestra); David Van Vactor, *Viola Concerto*; Bernard Wagenaar, *Violin Concerto*; Karl Weigl, *Rhapsody for Piano and Orchestra*.

**Operas**   Marc Blitzstein, *No for an Answer*; Paul Nordoff, *The Masterpiece*.

**Orchestra/Band**   Ernst Bacon, *A Drumlin Legend*; Marion Bauer, *Symphonic Suite for Strings, Opus 34*; John J. Becker, *Dance for Shakespeare's Tempest—When the Willow Nods: Stagework No. 5b* (incidental music); Leonard Bernstein, *The Peace* (incidental music); Henry Brant, *City Portrait* (ballet)—*The Great American Goof* (ballet); Arcady Dubensky, *Stephen Foster: Theme, Variations and Finale*; Lukas Foss, *The Tempest* (incidental music); Alexander Gretchaninov, *Rhapsody on a Russian Theme, Opus 147*; Lou Harrison, *Johnny Appleseed* (ballet); Paul Hindemith, *The Four Temperaments* (ballet); Harrison Kerr, *Dance Suite*; Sergei Rachmaninoff, *Symphonic Dances*; Gardner Read, *Pan e Dafni, Opus 53*; Bernard Rogers, *Dance of Salome*; Harold Shapero, *Nine-Minute Overture*; William Grant Still, *Miss Sally's Party* (ballet); Gustav Strube, *Harz Mountains* (symphonic poem); Virgil Thomson, *The Trojan Women* (incidental music); Jaromir Weinberger, *Prelude and Fugue on a Southern Folktune—Mississippi Rhapsody* (band).

**Piano/Organ**    Radie Britain, *Western Suite*; John Cage, *Bacchanale for Prepared Piano*; Lehman Engel, *Gates of Paradise*; Vivian Fine, *Suite in E-Flat*; Miriam Gideon, *Suite No. 2, "Sketches";* Nicolas Nabokov, *Sonata No. 2*; Arthur Shepherd, *Nocturne in F Minor*; Charles S. Skilton, *Five Miniatures*; David Stanley Smith, *Sonata No. 2*; Virgil Thomson, *Sonata No. 4.*

**Symphonies**    Hans Barth, *Symphony, "Prince of Peace," Opus 25*; Charles W. Cadman, *Symphony in E Minor, "Pennsylvania"*; Roy Harris, *Folksong Symphony (No. 4)*; Paul Hindemith, *Symphony in E-Flat Major*; Nicolas Nabokov, *Symphony No. 2, "Biblica"*; Florence B. Price, *Symphony No. 3 in C Minor*; Bernard Rogers, *Symphony No. 4 in G Minor*; Leo Sowerby, *Symphony No. 3*; Leon Stein, *Symphony No. 1 in C Major*; Igor Stravinsky, *Symphony in C*; Burnet Tuthill, *Symphony in C Major, Opus 21*; Meredith Willson, *Symphony No. 2.*

# 1941

☀

## Historical Highlights

The Japanese attack Pearl Harbor on December 7—Congress declares war on Japan; Germany and Italy declare war on the United States; Douglas MacArthur is made Supreme Allied Commander in the Pacific; Hitler invades Russia in June and begins the extermination of Jews; Roosevelt and Churchill sign the Atlantic Charter; the first commercial television broadcast is made.

## World Cultural Highlights

**World Art**    Max Beckmann, *Perseus*; Constantin Brancusi, *Cock Greeting the Sun*; John Nash, *Bombers Over Britain;* Diego Rivera, *Self-Portrait.*

**World Literature**    Bertolt Brecht, *Mutter Courage und ihre Kinder*; Noel Coward, *Blithe Spirit*; Archibald Cronin, *Keys of the Kingdom*; James Hilton, *Random Harvest.*

**World Music**    Olivier Messiaen, *Quartet for the End of Time* (written while in a prisoner of war camp); Arthur Honegger, *Symphony No. 2*; Richard Strauss, *Capriccio*; Michael Tippett, *A Child of Our Time.*

**Miscellaneous**    The London Baroque Ensemble is founded; births include Christopher Hogwood, Jorma Hynninen, Riccardo Muti, and Edo de Waart; deaths include James Joyce, Ignace Jan Paderewski, Rabindranath Tagore, Hugh Walpole, and Virginia Woolf.

## American Art and Literature Highlights

**Births/Deaths**    Births include art figures Jennifer Bartlett, Linda Benglis, Barry Le Va, Bruce Nauman, Martin Puryear, and literary figures Nora Ephron, Carter Ratcliff, Anne Rice, Paul Theroux, and Larry Woiwode; deaths include art figures Gutzon Borglum, Louis Eilshemius, Roland Perry, and literary figures Sherwood Anderson, Edward O'Brien, Lola Ridge, Elizabeth Roberts, and Constance Rourke.

**Art Works**    Ivan Albright, *That Which I Should Have Done I Did Not Do*; Arthur G. Dove, *Brothers #1*; Adolph Gottlieb, *Oedipus*; Robert Graves, *Little-Known Bird of the Inner Eye*; Louis Guglielmi, *Terror in Brooklyn*; Edward Hopper, *Nighthawks*; Jacob Lawrence, *Series: Migration of the Negro*; John Marin, *Circus Elephants*; Mark Tobey, *San Francisco Street.*

**Literature**    James Agee, *Let Us Now Praise Famous Men*; William R. Benét, *The Dust Which Is God* (Pulitzer Prize); James M. Cain, *Mildred Pierce*; Edna Ferber, *Saratoga Trunk*; Ellen Glasgow, *In This Our Life* (Pulitzer Prize); Lillian Hellman, *Watch on the Rhine* (New York Drama Critics' Award); James Thurber and E. Nugent, *The Male Animal.*

## Music—The Vernacular/Commercial Scene

**A. Births**    Paul Anka (singer) July 30; Joan Baez (folk singer) January 9; Homer Banks

(singer/writer) August 2; Captain Beefheart (singer/writer) January 15; Jan Berry (singer) April 3:
David Blue (singer/writer) February 18; Lester Bowie (trumpeter) October 11; Sandy Bull (guitarist) February 25; Henry Burr (singer) April 6; Vikki Carr (singer) July 19; Chubby Checker (singer) October 3; Guy Clark (singer) November 6; Earl T. Conley (singer) October 17; Chick Corea (pianist/composer) June 12; David Crosby (singer/guitarist) August 14; Neil Diamond (singer/writer) January 24; Lamont Dozier (songwriter) June 16; Dr. John (singer/writer); Bob Dylan (singer) May 24; Cass Elliot (singer) September 19; Shirley Ellis (singer); Bobby Goldsboro (singer) January 18; Tim Hardin (singer/writer) December 23; Richie Havens (singer/guitarist) January 21; Lonnie Mack (guitarist) July 18; (Harry) Nilsson (composer/singer) June 15; Johnny Paycheck (singer) May 31; Wilson Pickett (singer/writer) March 18; Gene Pitney (singer/writer) February 17; Otis Redding (singer/writer) September 9; Martha Reeves (singer) July 18; Leon Russell (guitarist/singer) April 2; Buffy Sainte-Marie (singer) February 20; Jim Seals (singer/guitarist) October 17; Paul Simon (singer/guitarist) October 13; Barrett Strong (singer/writer) February 5; Richie Valens (guitarist/singer) May 13.

**B. Deaths** Blind Boy Fuller (singer) February 13; Howard E. Johnson (lyricist) May 1; Gus Kahn (lyricist) October 8; Eddie Leonard (minstrel performer) July 29; Helen Morgan (singer) October 8; Jelly Roll Morton (pianist/composer) July 10; Victor Schertzinger (composer) October 26; James D. Vaughan (publisher/composer) February 9; Peetie Wheatstraw (singer/pianist) December 21.

**C. Biographical**

**Performing Groups** Almanac Singers; Artistry in Rhythm Orchestra (Stan Kenton); Lionel Hampton Big Band; Eddie Heywood Sextet; Eddie Howard Band; Artie Shaw Band III; Cootie Williams Dance Band.

**D. Publications** H. Dichter and E. Shapiro, *Early American Sheet Music, Its Lure and Lore, 1768–1889* (also *Handbook to Early American Sheet Music*); A. and J. A. Lomax, *Our Singing Country*; Harold Spivacke, *The Archive of American Folk Song in the Library of Congress*.

**E. Representative Works**

**Musicals** Ralph Blane and Hugh Martin, *Best Foot Forward*; Vernon Duke, J. Latouche, and H. Adamson, *Banjo Eyes*; Duke Ellington and Ben Webster, *Jump for Joy*; Cole Porter, *Let's Face It— You'll Never Get Rich* (film); S. Romberg and O. Hammerstein, *Sunny River*; Kurt Weill and I. Gershwin, *Lady in the Dark*.

**Songs** Elmer Albrecht and Dick Jurgens, *Elmer's Tune*; Harold Arlen and J. Mercer, *Blues in the Night*; Gene de Paul, *I'll Remember April*; Duke Ellington, *I've Got It Bad (And That Ain't Good)*; Alan R. Jones, *Easy Street*; Paul Madeira and J. Dorsey, *I'm Glad There Is You*; Donald Reid and S. Kaye, *Remember Pearl Harbor*; Jule Styne and F. Loesser, *I Don't Want to Walk Without You*; Don Swander and June Hershey, *Deep in the Heart of Texas*; Ernest Tubb, *Walking the Floor Over You*; Harry Warren and M. Gordan, *Chattanooga Choo Choo*.

**Other** Frank Churchill, *Dumbo* (film music—Oscar); Bernard Herrmann, *The Devil and Daniel Webster* (film music—Oscar); Alfred Newman, *How Green Was My Valley* (film music); Artie Shaw, *Concerto for Clarinet*.

## Music—The Cultivated/Art Music Scene

**F. Births** Stephen Albert (composer) February 6; Karan Armstrong (soprano) December 14; Charles Castelman (violinist) May 22; Marc-Antonio Consoli (composer) May 19; Kenneth Cooper (harpsichordist/musicologist) May 31; David H. Cope (composer/author) May 17; Curtis Curtis-Smith (composer) September 9; Pablo Elvira (baritone) September 24; Lawrence Foster (conductor) October 23; Philip Gossett (musicologist) September 27; Doris Hays (composer/pianist) August 6; Jackson Hill (musicologist) May 23; Gary Karr (string-bass virtuoso) November 20; Joel Krosnick (cellist) April 3; Jaime Laredo (violinist) June 7; John Nelson (conductor) December 6; Anthony Newman (harpsichordist) May 12; Ronald Perera (composer/educator) December 25; Paul Plishka (bass) August 28; Paula Robison (flutist) June 8; Jeffrey Van (guitarist) November 13; Richard Wilson (pianist/composer) May 15.

**G. Deaths**  Pearl G. Curran (composer) April 16; Cecil Forsyth (British-born composer/author) December 7; Melanie Kurt (Austrian-born soprano) March 11; Mischa Levitzki (Russian-born pianist) January 2; Ignace Jan Paderewski (Polish-born pianist) June 29; Gennaro Papi (Italian-born conductor) November 29; Charles S. Skilton (composer) March 12; Thomas Whitney Surette (music educator) May 19.

**H. Debuts**

**United States**  Catharine Crozier (organist—Washington, DC), Sidney Foster (pianist—New York), Jerome Hines (bass—San Francisco), William Kapell (pianist—New York), George London (baritone—Los Angeles), Robert Mann (violinist—New York), Luigi Silva (Italian cellist—Rochester), Abbey Simon (pianist—New York), Blanche Thebom (mezzo-soprano—New York).

**Metropolitan Opera**  Kurt Baum (Czech tenor), Nadine Conner (soprano), Edwin McArthur (conductor), Gerhard Pechner (German baritone), Jan Peerce (tenor), Stella Roman (Romanian soprano), Astrid Varnay (Swedish soprano), Bruno Walter (German conductor).

**I. New Positions**

**Conductors**  Thomas Beecham (Seattle Symphony Orchestra—to 1944); Mishel Piastro (Longines Symphonette—to 1966); Izler Solomon (Columbus Philharmonic Orchestra—to 1949).

**Educational**  Manfred Bukofzer (Berkeley—to 1955); Arnold Elston (University of Oregon—to 1958); Karl Geiringer (Boston University); George F. McKay (University of Washington—to 1968); Vincent Persichetti (head, theory/composition, Philadelphia Conservatory—to 1947); John D. Robb (chair, music department, University of New Mexico); Reginald Stewart (director, Peabody—to 1958); Randall Thompson (music head, University of Virginia, Charlottesville—to 1946); Efrem Zimbalist (director, Curtis Institute—to 1968).

**Other**  Henry Fillmore (president, American Bandmasters Association—to 1946); William D. Revelli (president, College Band Directors National Association—to 1945); Charles Seeger (music division, Pan-American Union).

**J. Honors and Awards**

**Honors**  Samuel Barber and Arthur Shepherd (National Institute); Frederick Woltmann (American Academy).

**Awards**  Harold Shapero (Rome Prize); William Kapell and Robert Mann (Naumburg).

**K. Biographical**  Those coming to the United States include Claudio Arrau (Chilean pianist), Jean Berger (German composer), Hermann Berlinski (German organist), Alexander Borovsky (Russian pianist), George Jellinek (Hungarian music author), Erich Itor Kahn (German pianist), Peter Jona Korn (German composer), Wanda Landowska (Polish harpsichordist), Ernst Lévy (Swiss pianist), Ursula Mamlok (German composer), Bohuslav Martinů (Czech composer), and Christian Wolff (French composer). Hugh Aitken enters NYU to study chemistry; Paul Althouse retires from the stage and concentrates on voice teaching; Aaron Copland visits Latin America as an envoy for the Department of Inter-American Affairs; Dean Dixon becomes the first black to conduct the New York Philharmonic Orchestra; Serge Koussevitzky, Felix Labunski, Paul Pisk, and Arnold Schoenberg become American citizens; Marjorie Lawrence is stricken with polio; Edwin McArthur becomes the first native American to conduct at the Metropolitan Opera.

**L. Musical Beginnings**

**Performing Groups**  Collegiate Chorale (New York); Greater Miami Opera Association; Longines Symphonette (New York); National Negro Opera Co.; New Music Group of Chicago; Syracuse Philharmonic Orchestra.

**Educational**  College Band Directors National Association; Domaine School for Conductors and Orchestral Players (Hancock, Maine).

**Other**  American Ballet Caravan (by Balanchine); Baptist Church Music Department; Hargail

Music (New York); International Music Co. (New York); New York Music Critics' Circle Award (to 1965).

## M. Music Publications

Bessaraboff, Nicholas, *Ancient European Musical Instruments*
Copland, Aaron, *Our New Music*
Dowling, L. and Shaw, A. ed., *The Schillinger System of Musical Composition*
Finney, Theodore M., *Hearing Music*
Gatti-Casazza, Giulio, *Memories of the Opera*
Graf, Herbert, *The Opera and Its Future in America*
Haydon, Glen, *Introduction to Musicology*
Howard, John T., *Our Contemporary Composers: American Music in the Twentieth Century*
Lang, Paul Henry, *Music in Western Civilization*
Piston, Walter, *Harmony*
Spaeth, Sigmund, *Fun with Music*
Weinstock, H. and Brockway, W., *The Opera: A History of Its Creation and Performance*

## N. Musical Compositions

**Chamber Music**   Milton Babbitt, *String Trio*; Arthur Berger, *Woodwind Quartet*; John Woods Duke, *String Quartet No. 1*; Louis Gruenberg, *String Quartet No. 2*; Peter Mennin, *String Quartet No. 1*; Vittorio Rieti, *String Quartet No. 2*; Harold Shapero, *String Quartet*; Randall Thompson, *String Quartet No. 1*; John Verrall, *String Quartet No. 1*; Adolph A. Weiss, *Violin Sonata*; Joseph Wood, *String Quartet No. 2*.

**Choral/Vocal**   Milton Babbitt, *Music for the Mass* (Bearns Prize); John Alden Carpenter, *Song of Freedom*; Daniel G. Mason, *Three Nautical Songs, Opus 38*; Florence Price, *Songs to the Dark Virgin*; William Grant Still, *Plain-Chant for America*; Ben Weber, *Five Songs, Opus 15*; John Wesley Work, *The Singers* (cantata).

**Concertos**   Robert Russell Bennett, *Violin Concerto*; Nicolai Berezowsky, *Viola Concerto, Opus 28—Clarinet Concerto, Opus 29*; Rudolph Ganz, *Piano Concerto*; Gail Kubik, *Violin Concerto*; William Latham, *Fantasy Concerto* (flute and strings); Nikolai Lopatnikoff, *Violin Concerto, Opus 26*; Darius Milhaud, *Piano Concerto No. 2, Opus 225*; Vincent Persichetti, *Concertino for Piano and Orchestra, Opus 16*.

**Operas**   Mabel Wood Hill, *The Rose and the Ring*; Clarence Loomis, *Fall of the House of Usher*; William Grant Still, *Troubled Island—A Bayou Legend*.

**Orchestra/Band**   Isidor Achron, *Suite Grotesque*; William Bergsma, *Gold and the Señor Commandante* (ballet); Ross Lee Finney, *Overture for a Drama*; Morton Gould, *Spirituals*; Alexander Gretchaninov, *Vers la victoire* (symphonic poem); Frances McCollin, *Suite for Strings*; Quincy Porter, *Music for Strings*; Wallingford Riegger, *Canon and Fugue in D Minor, Opus 33—Pilgrim's Progress, Opus 29* (ballet); William Schuman, *Newsreel for Orchestra*; David S. Smith, *Credo* (symphonic poem); William Grant Still, *Old California* (symphonic poem); Edwin J. Stringham, *Fantasy on an American Folk Tune*; Virgil Thomson, *Oedipus Tyrannos* (incidental music); David Van Vactor, *Overture to a Comedy II* (Juilliard Publishing Prize); Joseph F. Wagner, *Hudson River Legend*; Jaromir Weinberger, *Czech Rhapsody*; Stefan Wolpe, *Toccata*.

**Piano/Organ**   Hans Barth, *Suite No. 2, Opus 23*; Aaron Copland, *Sonata*; Vivian Fine, *Five Preludes*; Charles Mills, *Sonata No. 1*; Robert Palmer, *Three Preludes*; Quincy Porter, *Canon and Fugue* (organ); Arnold Schoenberg, *Variations on a Recitative, Opus 48* (organ); Harold Shapero, *Sonata for Piano, Four Hands*; Arthur Shepherd, *Nocturne No. 2—Capriccio No. 2*; Ben Weber, *Suite No. 1, Opus 8*; Jaromir Weinberger, *Organ Sonata*.

**Symphonies**   Milton Babbitt, *Symphony, 1941* (withdrawn); Robert Russell Bennett, *Symphony in D, "For the Dodgers"*; Paul Creston, *Symphony No. 1* (New York Music Critics' Award); David Diamond, *Symphony No. 1*; Morton Gould, *Latin-American Symphonette*; Parks Grant, *Symphony No. 2*; Elliot Griffis, *Symphony for Strings, "Fantastic Pursuit"*; Louis Gruenberg, *Symphony No.*

*2, Opus 43*; Edmund Haines, *Symphony No. 1*; Ellis Kohs, *Concerto for Orchestra*; Normand Lockwood, *Symphony*; Peter Mennin, *Symphony No. 1*; Charles Mills, *Symphony No. 1*; Walter Piston, *Sinfonietta*; William Schuman, *Symphony No. 3* (New York Music Critics' Award)— *Symphony No. 4*; Frederick Search, *Symphony No. 4*; Joseph F. Wagner, *Sinfonietta No. 2*; Robert Ward, *Symphony No. 1* (Juilliard Publishing Prize); Jaromir Weinberger, *Lincoln Symphony*; Eugene Zador, *Symphony No. 4, "Children's Symphony."*

# 1942

✺

## Historical Highlights

First nuclear chain reaction by Enrico Fermi occurs in Chicago; Dwight David Eisenhower becomes Commander of the United States forces in Europe; the Merchant Marine Academy is founded; a women's auxiliary corps is formed in all services; the United States invades Guadalcanal; the allies invade North Africa; the battle of Stalingrad begins in Russia; the battles of the Coral Sea and Midway halt the Japanese advance; 26 nations sign the United Nations agreement.

## World Cultural Highlights

**World Art**   Max Beckmann, *The Actors*; Pierre Bonnard, *L'Oiseau Bleu*; Georges Braque, *Patience*; Max Ernst, *Europe after the Rain*; Jack B. Yeats, *Two Travellers*.

**World Literature**   Albert Camus, *The Stranger*; Daphne du Maurier, *Frenchmen's Creek*; C. S. Lewis, *The Screwtape Letters*.

**World Music**   Carlos Chávez, *Toccata for Percussion*; Aram Khachaturian, *Gayne*; Sergei Prokofiev, *War and Peace*; Dmitri Shostakovich, *Symphony No. 7*; Richard Strauss, *Horn Concerto No. 2*.

**Miscellaneous**   The Conservatoire de Musique et de l'Art Dramatique opens in Montreal; births include Daniel Barenboim, Julio González, Eduardo Mata, and Maurizio Pollini; deaths include Léon Daudet, Frederick Stock, Felix Weingartner, Alexander Zemlinsky, and Stefan Zweig.

## American Art and Literature Highlights

**Births/Deaths**   Births include art figures Jon Borofsky and literary figures Michael Crichton, John Irving, Erica Jong, Garrison Keillor, William Matthews, Sharon Olds, and Martin Cruz Smith; deaths include art figures Cecilia Beaux, William Couper, John Flannagan, Frederic Ruckstull, Gertrude Whitney, Grant Wood, and literary figures Eleanor Atkinson, Will James, and Alice Caldwell Rice.

**Art Works**   Alexander Calder, *Red Petals*; John Rogers Cox, *Gray and Gold*; Arshile Gorky, *Mojave*; Marsden Hartley, *Evening Storm, Schoodic, Maine*; Walt Kuhn, *Girl from Madrid*; Jacob Lawrence, *Tombstones*; Robert Motherwell, *Spanish Picture with Window*; Jackson Pollock, *Male and Female*; Richard Pousette-Dart, *Symphony No. 1, The Transcendental*; Florine Stettheimer, *Cathedrals of Art*.

**Literature**   Maxwell Anderson, *The Eve of St. Mark*; Sally Benson, *Meet Me in St. Louis*; Pearl Buck, *Dragon Seed*; William Faulkner, *Go Down, Moses*; Robert Frost, *A Witness Tree* (Pulitzer Prize); McKinlay Kantor, *Gentle Annie*; Upton Sinclair, *Dragon's Teeth* (Pulitzer Prize); Thornton Wilder, *The Skin of Our Teeth* (Pulitzer); Philip G. Wylie, *Generation of Vipers*.

## Music—The Vernacular/Commercial Scene

**A. Births**   Mike Abene (pianist/arranger) July 2; Nickolas Ashford (singer) May 4; Len Barry (singer) June 12; Elvin Bishop (guitarist) October 21; Paul Butterfield (singer/bandleader) December 17; James Carr (singer) June 13; Harry Chapin (singer/writer) December 7; Lee Clayton (songwriter) October 29; Andrae Crouch (singer) July 1; Vic Dana (singer) August 26; Mac Davis (singer/writer) January 21; Jack DeJohnette (drums) August 9; Daryl Dragon (The Captain) August 27; Aretha Franklin (singer) March 25; Jerry Garcia (guitarist/composer) August 1; Art Garfunkel (singer) October 13; Dobie Gray (singer) July 26; Norman Greenbaum (singer/writer) November 20; Isaac Hayes (singer/writer) August 20; Jimi Hendrix (guitarist/singer) November 27; Oliver Lake (saxophonist/composer) September 14; Frankie Lymon (singer) September 30; Curtis Mayfield (singer/writer) June 3; Country Joe McDonald (singer/writer); Wayne Newton (singer) April 3; Lou Reed (singer/writer) March 2; Paul Revere (keyboards) January 7; Johnny Rivers (singer/writer) November 7; Billy Joe Royal (singer) April 3; Bobby Rydell (singer) April 26; Edwin Starr (singer) January 21; Barbra Streisand (singer/actress) April 24; B. J. Thomas (singer/writer) August 7; Carla Thomas (singer); James Blood Ulmer (guitarist) February 2; Jerry Jeff Walker (singer/writer) March 16; Tammy Wynette (singer/writer) May 5.

**B. Deaths** Bunny Berigan (trumpeter/bandleader) June 2; Jimmy Blanton (stringbassist) October; Charlie Christian (guitarist) March 2; Frank Churchill (composer) May 14; George M. Cohan (composer/promoter) November 5; Fred Fisher (composer) January 14; Irving Kahal (lyricist) February 7; Sidney D. Mitchell (lyricist) February 25; Ralph Rainger (songwriter) October 23.

**C. Biographical**

**Performing Groups** Spike Jones and His City Slickers; Cecil Scott Band II; Freddie Slack Band; Mary Lou Williams' Combo.

**New Beginnings** Acuff-Rose Publications (Nashville); Capitol Record Co. (Los Angeles); *Cashbox: The International Music-Record Weekly*; *Hit Parader*; Savoy Records (Newark); *Song Hits*.

**D. Publications** Douglas Gilbert, *Lost Chords: The Diverting Story of American Popular Songs*; A. Lomax and S. Cowell, *American Folk Song and Folk Lore*; Lydia Parrish, *Slave Songs of the Georgia Slave Islands*.

**E. Representative Works**

**Musicals** Irving Berlin, *This Is the Army*; Frederick Loewe, *The Life of the Party*; Richard Rodgers and L. Hart, *By Jupiter*; Harold Rome, *Let Freedom Sing*; Various, *Star and Garter*.

**Songs** H. Arlen and J. Mercer, *That Old Black Magic*; Bennie Benjamin, *When the Lights Go On Again All Over the World*; Irving Berlin, *White Christmas* (Oscar); Hoagy Carmichael, *Lamplighter's Serenade*; Duke Ellington, *Don't Get Around Much Any More*; Frank Loesser, *Praise the Lord and Pass the Ammunition*; Joe McCoy, *Why Don't You Do Right*; Glenn Miller, *Moonlight Cocktail*; V. Schertzinger and J. Mercer, *Tangerine*; J. Styne and S. Cahn, *I've Heard That Song Before*; Harry Warren and M. Gordon, *I Had the Craziest Dream—There Will Never Be Another You*.

**Other** Bernard Herrmann, *The Magnificent Ambersons* (film music); Earl Hines, *Piano Man*; Stan Kenton, *Concerto for Doghouse*; Alfred Newman, *The Black Swan* (film music); Miklós Rózsa, *The Jungle Book* (film music); Max Steiner, *Now, Voyager* (film music—Oscar).

## Music—The Cultivated/Art Music Scene

**F. Births** Richard J. Bunger (pianist) June 1; June Card (soprano) April 10; Joel Cohen (conductor/lutenist) May 23; Michael Devlin (baritone) November 27; Charles Dodge (composer) June 5; Stephen Gunzenhauser (conductor) April 8; David Holloway (baritone) November 12; Jonathan D. Kramer (composer/theorist) December 7; Steven Lubin (pianist) February 22; Priscilla McLean (composer) May 27; Charlie Morrow (composer) February 9; Samuel Ramey (baritone) March 28; Gerald Shapiro (composer) May 14; Jeffrey Siegel (pianist) November 18; Richard Stilwell (baritone) May 6; Richard Stoltzman (clarinetist) July 12.

**G. Deaths** Pasquale Amato (Italian-born baritone) August 12; Henry Eichheim (violinist/conductor) August 22; Emanuel Feuermann (Austrian-born cellist) May 25; Eleanor Everest Freer (composer) December 13; Charles Hackett (tenor) January 1; Alfred Hertz (German-born conductor) April 17;

Gustav Hinrichs (German-born conductor) March 26; Frank Holton (brass instrument maker) April 17; Arthur Pryor (trombone/bandmaster) June 18; Paul Reimers (German-born tenor) April 14; Anna Schoen-René (German-born singer) November 13; Edmund Severn (music educator) May 14; Frederick Stock (German-born conductor) October 20; Frederick J. Work (composer/educator) January 17.

### H. Debuts

**United States**   Howard Boatwright (violinist—New York), Lawrence Davidson (bass—Chicago), Leon Fleisher (pianist—San Francisco), Witold Malcuzynski (Polish pianist—New York), Nan Merriman (mezzo-soprano—Cincinnati), Zara Nelsova (Canadian cellist—New York), Regina Resnik (soprano—New York).

**Metropolitan Opera**   Lorenzo Alvary (Hungarian bass), Thomas Beecham (British conductor), Walter Cassel (baritone), Herta Glaz (Austrian contralto), Margaret Harshaw (mezzo-soprano), James Melton (tenor), George Szell (Hungarian conductor).

### I. New Positions

**Conductors**   Richard Bales (music director, National Gallery of Art); Fausto Cleva (San Francisco Opera Co.—to 1944); Arthur Cohn (Symphony Club of Philadelphia—to 1965); Reginald Stewart (Baltimore Symphony Orchestra—to 1952); George Szell (Metropolitan Opera—to 1946).

**Educational**   Boris Goldowsky (opera, New England Conservatory); Mieczyslaw Horszowski (piano, Curtis Institute); Ernst Krenek (Hamline College, St. Paul, Minnesota); Gregor Piatigorsky (Curtis Institute—to 1951; Quincy Porter (director, New England Conservatory—to 1946); Carl Weinrich (organ, Columbia—to 1952).

**Other**   Claudia Cassidy (music critic, *Chicago Tribune*); Max de Schauensee (music critic, *Philadelphia Evening Bulletin*); Deems Taylor (president, ASCAP—to 1948).

### J. Honors and Awards

**Honors**   John Alden Carpenter (American Academy); Bernard Herrmann and Robert McBride (American Academy and Institute).

**Awards**   Igor Buketoff (first Alice M. Ditson Award); Roy Harris (Coolidge Medal).

**K. Biographical**   Amy Beach's 75th birthday is celebrated by a chamber music festival in Washington, DC; Leonard Bernstein begins arranging pop songs for Harms-Remick Co.; Henry Cowell is given a full pardon by the Governor of California; Peggy Glanville-Hicks (Australian composer) comes to the United States; Vladimir Horowitz, Erich Leinsdorf, Nathan Milstein, Pierre Monteux, and Gregor Piatigorsky become American citizens; Lorin Maazel, age 12, conducts a full program with the New York Philharmonic Orchestra; Claudio Spies (Chilean composer/educator) comes to the United States.

### L. Musical Beginnings

**Performing Groups**   Bach Society of St. Louis; Cambridge Collegium Musicum (Cambridge Society for Early Music); Cathedral Choral Society (Washington, DC); Dallas Chamber Music Society; Hartt Opera Theater (Hartford); San Antonio Chamber Music Society; Seattle Youth Orchestra.

**Festivals**   American Music Festival (Washington, DC).

**Educational**   National Catholic Music Educators' Association; New England Conservatory Opera Workshop; Spokane Conservatory of Music.

**Other**   American Symphony Orchestra League (Washington, DC); Connecticut Opera Association; (Natalie) Koussevitzky Music Foundation (New York); Rocky Ridge Music Center (Colorado).

### M. Music Publications

Apel, Willi, *The Notation of Polyphonic Music: 900–1600*
Dorian, Frederick, *The History of Music in Performance*

Ewen, David, *The Book of Modern Composers*
Gleason, Harold, *Examples of Music before 1400*
Helm, Everett, *The Chansons of Arcadelt*
Howard, John Tasker, *This Modern Music*
Moore, Douglas, *From Madrigal to Modern Music: A Guide to Musical Styles*
Schnabel, Artur, *Music and the Line of Most Resistance*
Schoenberg, Arnold, *Models for Beginners in Composition*

## N. Musical Compositions

**Chamber Music**   Amy Beach, *Pastorale for Woodwind Quintet, Opus 151*; John J. Becker, *Soundpiece No. 6: Sonata for Flute and Clarinet*; William Bergsma, *String Quartet No. 1*; Andrew Imbrie, *String Quartet No. 1*; Carl McKinley, *String Quartet in One Movement*; Charles Mills, *String Quartet No. 2*; Robert Palmer, *Violin Sonata*; Arnold Schoenberg, *Ode to Napoleon, Opus 41*; John Verrall, *String Quartet No. 2*; Ben Weber, *String Quartet, Opus 12*; Karl Weigl, *String Quartet No. 7 in F Minor*.

**Choral/Vocal**   Seth Bingham, *Canticle of the Sun*; Paul Creston, *Dance Variations*; Irving Fine, *Three Choruses from Alice in Wonderland*; Lukas Foss, *The Prairie* (cantata— New York Music Critics' Award); Everett Helm, *Requiem*; George F. McKay, *Pioneers*; Roger Nixon, *Chinese Seasons* (song cycle); Bernard Rogers, *The Passion* (oratorio); William Schuman, *Secular Cantata No. 2: A Free Song* (Pulitzer Prize)   *Holiday Song —Requiescat* (treble choruses); Leo Sowerby, *Song of America*; Burnet C. Tuthill, *Big River*; Kurt Weill, *Three Walt Whitman Songs*.

**Concertos**   Isidor Achron, *Piano Concerto No. 2*; Jean Berger, *Caribbean Concerto* (harmonica and orchestra); Ulric Cole, *Piano Concerto No. 2*; David Diamond, *Concerto for Two Pianos*; Vernon Duke, *Violin Concerto*; Arthur Kreutz, *Violin Concerto*; Frances McCollin, *Variations on an Original Theme* (piano and orchestra); George F. McKay, *Cello Concerto*; Burrill Phillips, *Piano Concerto*; Arnold Schoenberg, *Piano Concerto, Opus 42*; William Schuman, *Piano Concerto*; David S. Smith, *Violin Concerto No. 2*; Mark Wessel, *Piano Concerto*.

**Operas**   Gian Carlo Menotti, *The Island God*; Deems Taylor, *Ramuntcho, Opus 23*; Randall Thompson, *Solomon and Balkis*; Joseph Wood, *The Mother* (Juilliard Prize).

**Orchestra/Band**   Samuel Barber, *Second Essay for Orchestra, Opus 17*; Henry Brant, *Downtown Suite*; Aaron Copland, *Lincoln Portrait—Rodeo* (ballet); Cecil Effinger, *Western Overture*; Herbert Elwell, *Introduction and Allegro*; Jerome Kern, *Mark Twain Suite*; George Kleinsinger, *A Western Rhapsody*; Erich Korngold, *Tomorrow, Opus 33* (symphonic poem); Harold C. Morris, *American Epic*; Gardner Read, *Night Flight*; Wallingford Riegger, *Passacaglia and Fugue, Opus 34*; Arthur Shepherd, *Hilaritas* (band); Igor Stravinsky, *Circus Polka—Danses Concertantes—Four Norwegian Moods*; Lamar Stringfield, *Peace* (symphonic poem); John Verrall, *Three Jacks* (ballet); Elinor R. Warren, *The Fountain*; Clarence White, *Kutamba Rhapsody*; Stefan Wolpe, *The Man from Midian* (ballet).

**Piano/Organ**   Arthur Berger, *Piano Fantasy*; Seth Bingham, *Twelve Hymn-Preludes for Organ*; Aaron Copland, *Danzón cubano* (two pianos—orchestrated 1944); Ross Lee Finney, *Sonata No. 3*; Everett Helm, *Sonata Brevis*; John La Montaine, *Sonata*; Charles Mills, *Sonata No. 2*; Lionel Nowak, *Flickers*; Robert Palmer, *Sonata No. 2*; Burrill Phillips, *Sonata No. 1*.

**Symphonies**   George Antheil, *Symphony No. 4, "1942"*; John J. Becker, *Symphony No. 5, "Homage to Mozart"—Symphony No. 6, "Out of Bondage"*; Leonard Bernstein, *Symphony No. 1, "Jeremiah"* (New York Music Critics' Award); Henry Brant, *Symphony* (first two movements withdrawn); John Alden Carpenter, *Symphony No. 2*; Philip G. Clapp, *Symphony No. 11 in C Major*; Henry Cowell, *Symphony No. 3, "Gaelic"*; Robert Delaney, *Symphony No. 1*; David Diamond, *Symphony No. 2*; Ross Lee Finney, *Symphony No. 1, "Communiqué"*; Roger Goeb, *Symphony No. 1*; Louis Gruenberg, *Symphony No. 3, Opus 44;* Alexei Haieff, *Symphony No. 1*; Roy Harris, *Symphony No. 5*; Wesley La Violette, *Symphony No. 4* (band); Bohuslav Martinů, *Symphony No. 1*; Frances McCollin, *Sinfonietta No. 4*; Charles Mills, *Symphony No. 2*; Jerome Moross, *Symphony*; Vincent Persichetti, *Symphony No. 1, Opus 18—Symphony No. 2, Opus 19*; Gardner Read,

*Symphony No. 2* (Paderewski Prize); Vittorio Rieti, *Symphony No. 4, "Tripartita"*; Leon Stein, *Symphony No. 2 in E Major* (Charles Cohen Award); Gerald Strang, *Symphony No. 1.*

# 1943

❋

## Historical Highlights

Roosevelt and Churchill meet in Casablanca and with Stalin at Tehran; Congress passes the "pay-as-you-go" income tax bill; the Pentagon building is finished in Washington, DC; the "big inch" gas pipeline begins operation between Texas and Pennsylvania; the Jefferson Memorial is dedicated; the Allies invade Sicily and Italy; the Italians withdraw from the conflict; General Eisenhower becomes Supreme Allied Commander in Europe; the Germans surrender at Stalingrad and North Africa.

## World Cultural Highlights

**World Art**    Constantin Brancusi, *The Flying Turtle*; Lucien Freud, *The Painter's Room;* Barbara Hepworth, *Sculpture with Color, Pale Blue and Red;* Henri Matisse, *Tabac Royal.*

**World Literature**    Jean-Paul Sartre, *The Flies—Being and Nothingness*; Hermann Hesse, *Das Glasperlenspiel*; Antoine de Saint-Exupéry, *The Little Prince.*

**World Music**    Benjamin Britten, *Serenade for Tenor, Horn and Strings*; Aram Khachaturian, *Symphony No. 2*; Dmitri Shostakovich, *Symphony No. 8*; Ralph Vaughan Williams, *Symphony No. 5.*

**Miscellaneous**    The Liverpool Symphony Orchestra in England and the Valencia Municipal Orchestra in Spain are founded; births include Vitaly Komar and Udo Zimmermann; deaths include Konstantin Balmont, Maurice Denis, and Henrik Pontoppidan.

## American Art and Literature Highlights

**Births/Deaths**    Births include artists Patry Denton, James Turrell, and literary figures Frederick Barthelme, Tess Gallagher, Louise Glück, Susan Isaacs, Charles Ludlum, Sam Shepard, and James Vincent Tate; deaths include art figures George Brewster, Ralph Clarkson, Marsden Hartley, and literary figures Stephen Vincent Benét, Charles Dobie, Cale Young Rice, and Alexander Woolcott.

**Art Works**    Milton Avery, *Pink Sky*; Max Beckmann, *Carnaval*; George Grosz, *The Wanderer*; Robert Gwathmey, *End of Day*; Marsden Hartley, *Dead Plover*; Walt Kuhn, *Show Girl in Armor*; Loren MacIver, *Red Votive Lights*; Piet Mondrian, *Broadway Boogie-Woogie*; Robert Motherwell, *Pancho Villa, Dead or Alive*; Jackson Pollack, *She-Wolf*; Charles Sheeler, *The Artist Looks at Nature.*

**Literature**    Stephen V. Benét, *Western Star* (Pulitzer Prize); Louis Bromfield, *Mrs. Parkington*; T. S. Eliot, *Four Quartets*; Martin Flavin, *Journey in the Dark* (Pulitzer Prize); William Saroyan, *The Human Comedy*; Max Shulman, *Barefoot Boy with Cheek*; Betty Smith, *A Tree Grows in Brooklyn*; Robert Penn Warren, *At Heaven's Gate.*

## Music—The Vernacular/Commercial Scene

**A. Births**    Barbara Acklin (singer/writer) February 28; Willie Alexander (pianist/singer); Eric Andersen (songwriter) February 14; Kenny Barron (pianist) June 9; George Benson (guitarist) March 22; Gary Burton (vibes) January 23; Roy C (singer); Lou Christie (singer) February 19; John Cipollina (guitarist) August 24; Jessi Colter (pianist/singer) May 25; Larry Coryell (guitarist) April 2; Jim Croce (singer/writer) January 10; John Denver (singer) December 31; Henry E. Dixey (singer/actor) February 25; Ral Donner (singer) February 10; Fabian (singer) February 6; Dick Feller (singer) January 2; John Hammond (singer) November 13; Brian Hyland (singer/writer) November 12; Julio Iglesias (singer) September 23; Millie Jackson (singer) July 15; Janis Joplin (singer) January 19; Marilyn McCoo (singer) September 30; Steve Miller (guitarist/bandleader) October 5; Joni Mitchell (singer/writer) November 7; Jim Morrison (singer) December 8; Maria Muldaur (singer) September 12; Randy Newman (singer/writer) November 28; K. T. Oslin (singer/writer); Maceo Parker (saxophonist) February 14; Van Dyke Parks (songwriter/producer) January 3; Bobby Sherman (singer/writer) July 18; David Soul (singer) August 28; Billy Swan (singer) May 12; Toni Tennille (singer) May 8; Bobby Vee (singer) April 30; Jim Weatherly (songwriter) March 17; Mary Wells (singer) May 13; Grover Washington, Jr. (saxophonist) December 12; Tony Joe White (guitarist/singer) July 23.

**B. Deaths**  Charles Neil Daniels (songwriter/publisher) January 23; Joseph McCarthy (lyricist) December 18; Neil Moret (composer/lyricist) January 21; Thomas "Fats" Waller (pianist/bandleader) December 15.

**C. Biographical**

**Performing Groups**  Art Tatum Trio.

**Miscellaneous**  Richard Rodgers forms a partnership with Oscar Hammerstein II.

**D. Publications**  Rudi Blesh, *This Is Jazz: A Series of Lectures Given at the San Francisco Museum*; Duke Ellington, *Piano Method for Blues*; Glenn Miller's *Method for Orchestral Arranging*; Woody Guthrie, *Bound for Glory*; G. P. Jackson, *White and Negro Spirituals—Down-East Spirituals and Others*.

**E. Representative Works**

**Musicals**  Oscar Hammerstein (lyrics), *Carmen Jones* (music of Bizet); Lerner and Loewe, *What's Up?*; Frank Loesser and A. Schwartz, *Thank Your Lucky Stars* (film); Cole Porter, *Something for the Boys—Something to Shout About* (film); Rodgers and Hammerstein, *Oklahoma* (Special Pulitzer Prize); Kurt Weill, S. J. Perelman, and O. Nash, *One Touch of Venus*.

**Songs**  L. Brown and B. Homer, *Sentimental Journey*; Al Dexter, *Pistol Packing Mama*; Herman Hupfield, *As Time Goes By*; J. Livingston and M. Drake, *Mairzy Doats*; Frank Loesser, *Spring Will Be a Little Late This Year*; F. Loesser and A. Schwartz, *They're Either Too Young or Too Old*; Jimmy McHugh and H. Adamson, *I Couldn't Sleep a Wink Last Night*; Jimmy Van Heusen and J. Burke, *Sunday, Monday and Always*; Oliver Wallace, *Der Führer's Face*; H. Warren and M. Gordon, *You'll Never Know* (Oscar).

**Other**  Duke Ellington, *Black, Brown and Beige—Blue Belles of Harlem* (jazz suite); Alfred Newman, *The Song of Bernadette* (film music—Oscar); David Rose, *Holiday for Strings*; Max Steiner, *Casablanca* (film music); Herbert Stothart, *The Human Comedy* (film music).

## Music—The Cultivated/Art Music Scene

**F. Births**  Alice Artzt (guitarist) March 16; James Atherton (tenor) April 27; Allan W. Atlas (musicologist) February 19; Stephen D. Burton (composer) February 24; William Cochran (tenor) June 23; William Duckworth (composer/author) January 13; George Edwards (composer) May 11; Rolf Gehlhaar (composer) December 30; Richard Goode (pianist) June 1; Anthony Iannaccone (composer) October 14; Ronald Jeffers (composer/conductor) March 25; Stephen Kates (cellist) May 7; Fred Lerdahl (composer/theorist) March 10; James Levine (pianist/conductor) June 23; William McGlaughlin (conductor) October 3; Meredith Monk (composer) November 20; Joan Morris (mezzo-soprano) February 10; Robert Morris (composer/theorist) October 19; Michael Murray (organist) March 19; Thomas Murray (organist) October 6; William Parker (baritone) August 5; Harvey Pittle (saxophonist) June 22; Dennis Riley (composer) May 28; Faye Robinson (soprano) November 2; Joseph Schwantner (composer) March 22; James Sellars (composer) October 8; Allen Strange (composer) June 26; James Tocco (pianist) September 21; Paul Zukofsky (violinist) October 22.

**G. Deaths**  Joseph Achron (violinist/composer) April 29; Timothée Adamowski (Polish-born violinist) April 18; Jean-Baptiste Beck (French-born musicologist) June 23; Jules Bledsoe (baritone) July 14; Carl Busch (Danish-born conductor) December 19; R. Nathaniel Dett (composer/pianist)

October 2; Maria Gay (Spanish-born contralto) July 29; Percy Goetschius (theorist/educator) October 29; Victor Harris (conductor/pianist) February 15; Jean Paul Kürsteiner (pianist/pedagogue) March 19; Arthur Nevin (composer/conductor) July 10; Alice Nielsen (soprano) March 8; Jane Osborn-Hannah (soprano) August 13; Sergei Rachmaninoff (Russian-born pianist/composer) March 28; Joseph Schillinger (Russian-born theorist) March 23; Albert Stoessel (violinist/conductor) May 12; Hermann Wetzler (organist/conductor) May 29; Huntington Woodman (organist) December 25; Pietro Alessandro Yon (Italian-born organist/composer) November 22.

### H. Debuts

**United States**   Leonard Bernstein (conductor—New York), Joseph Fuchs (violinist—New York), Eugene Istomin (pianist—Philadelphia), Byron Janis (pianist—New York), Jean Madeira (mezzo-soprano—Chautauqua), Henryk Szeryng (Polish violinist—New York).

**Metropolitan Opera**   Patrice Munsel (soprano), Martial Singher (French baritone).

### I. New Positions

**Conductors**   Kurt Herbert Adler (chorus master, San Francisco Opera); Désiré Defauw (Chicago Symphony Orchestra—to 1947); Karl Krueger (Detroit Symphony Orchestra—to 1949); Efrem Kurtz (Kansas City Philharmonic Orchestra—to 1948); Erich Leinsdorf (Cleveland Orchestra, only one year before army draft); Artur Rodzinski (New York Philharmonic Orchestra—to 1947); Alfred Wallenstein (Los Angeles Philharmonic Orchestra—to 1956).

**Educational**   Josef Alexander (Brooklyn College—to 1977); John J. Becker (Barat College, Illinois—to 1957); Igor Buketoff (Columbia—to 1947); Robert Palmer (Cornell—to 1980); Gardner Read (Kansas City Conservatory—to 1945).

**Other**   Jack Beeson (music critic, *Boston Transcript* and *New York Sun*); Albert Goldberg (music critic, *Chicago Tribune*—to 1946); Walter Herbert (general director, New Orleans Opera).

### J. Honors and Awards

**Honors**   Ernest Bloch (American Academy); Paul Creston and William Schuman (American Academy and Institute); Quincy Porter (Coolidge Medal and National Institute); Burnet Tuthill (doctorate, Chicago Musical College).

**Awards**   Carol Brice (Naumburg Award—first black American to win); Eugene Istomin (Leventritt); Constance Keene (Naumburg).

### K. Biographical   Béla Bartók, now quite ill, makes his last public appearance as a performer; Jean Berger, Walter Ducloux, László Halász, Maria Jeritza, Erich Korngold, Fritz Kreisler, Siegmund Levarie, Erica Morini, André Previn, Boris Schwarz, Roman Totenberg, Paul Ulanowsky, and Karl Weigl all become naturalized American citizens; Leonard Bernstein becomes assistant conductor of the New York Philharmonic Orchestra; Helen (Strassburger) Boatwright marries violinist Howard Boatwright; John Cage moves permanently to New York; Roque Cordero (Panamanian composer/conductor) receives a scholarship to the University of Minnesota; John Corigliano, Sr., becomes the first American-born and American-trained concertmaster of the New York Philharmonic Orchestra; Carroll Glenn marries pianist Eugene List; Marjorie Lawrence, battling back from polio, resumes her singing career.

### L. Musical Beginnings

**Performing Groups**   City Center Opera Co. (New York City Opera); National Gallery Orchestra (Washington, DC); New Orleans Opera Association.

**Other**   New York City Center of Music and Drama; *Notes* (Music Library Association); Pulitzer Prize for Music (Columbia University).

### M. Music Publications

Erskine, John, *The Philharmonic-Symphony Society of New York: Its First Hundred Years*
Ferguson, Donald, *A Short History of Music*
Geiringer, Karl, *Musical Instruments: Their History in Western Culture . . .*
Goldman, Richard F., *Landmarks of Early American Music*

Hindemith, Paul, *A Concentrated Course in Traditional Harmony*
Johnson, H. Earle, *Musical Interludes in Boston, 1795–1830*
Liebling, Estelle, *The Estelle Liebling Coloratura Digest*
Loesser, Arthur, *Humor in American Song*
Mursell, James L., *Music in American Schools*
Rubsamen, Walter, *Literary Sources of Secular Music in Italy (ca. 1500)*
Sachs, Curt, *The Rise of Music in the Ancient World*
Siegmeister, Elie, *The Music Lover's Handbook*
Spaeth, Sigmund, *A Guide to Great Orchestral Music*
Stokowski, Leopold, *Music for All of Us*

**N. Musical Compositions:**

**Chamber Music**   Aaron Copland, *Violin Sonata*; Cecil Effinger, *String Quartet No. 1*; Alexander Gretchaninov, *Clarinet Sonata No. 2*; Wesley La Violette, *Quintet for Flute and String Quartet*; Charles Mills, *String Quartet No. 3* (Roth Prize); Robert Palmer, *String Quartet No. 2*; Quincy Porter, *String Quartet No. 7*; Arthur Shepherd, *Divertissement for Wind Quintet*; Virgil Thomson, *Sonata for Flute Alone*; Ben Weber, *String Trio No. 1*.

**Choral/Vocal**   Ned Rorem, *The Seventieth Psalm*; Randall Thompson, *The Testament of Freedom*.

**Concertos**   Marion Bauer, *Piano Concerto, "American Youth," Opus 36*; Vernon Duke, *Cello Concerto*; Harl McDonald, *Violin Concerto*; Walter Piston, *Prelude and Allegro* (organ and orchestra); Lazare Saminsky, *The Vow (Piano Concerto)*.

**Operas**   Paul Bowles, *The Wind Remains*; Timothy Spelman, *The Courtship of Miles Standish*; William Grant Still, *A Southern Interlude*.

**Orchestra/Band**   George Antheil, *Decatur at Algiers*; Jacob Avshalomov, *The Taking of T'ung Kuan*; Richard Bales, *National Gallery Suite I*; Samuel Barber, *Commando March*; William Bergsma, *Music on a Quiet Theme*; Marc Blitzstein, *Freedom Morning* (symphonic poem); Cecil Burleigh, *Leaders of Men*; John Alden Carpenter, *The Anxious Bugler* (symphonic poem); Ross Lee Finney, *Variations, Fuguing, and Holiday* (Ditson Award); Morton Gould, *American Salute*; Richard Hageman, *The Crucible*; Paul Hindemith, *Symphonic Metamorphoses on Themes of Carl Maria von Weber*; Harl McDonald, *Suite, My Country at War*; Bohuslav Martinů, *Memorial to Lidice*; Douglas Moore, *In Memoriam* (symphonic poem); Gardner Read, *Overture No. 1, Opus 58* (Composers' Press Publishing Award); Wallingford Riegger, *Processional (Funeral March), Opus 36*; Lazare Saminsky, *East and West Suite*; Arnold Schoenberg, *Theme and Variations, Opus 43a*; William Schuman, *William Billings Overture—Prayer in Time of War*; Elie Siegmeister, *Ozark Set*; Gerald Strang, *Overland Trail Overture*; Hugo Weisgall, *Overture in F (American Comedy)*; Eugene Zador, *Biblical Scenes*.

**Piano/Organ**   Josef Alexander, *Sonata No. 2*; Esther Ballou, *Sonata No. 1 for Two Pianos*; Seth Bingham, *Baroques* (organ); Norman Dello Joio, *Sonata No. 1*; R. Nathaniel Dett, *Eight Bible Vignettes*; Harrison Kerr, *Sonata No. 2—Four Preludes*; Ernst Krenek, *Sonata No. 3, Opus 92/4*; Wiktor Labunski, *Variations on a Theme of Paganini*; Nikolai Lopatnikoff, *Sonata in E Major*; Vincent Persichetti, *Sonata No. 3*; Quincy Porter, *Six Miniatures*; Carl Ruggles, *Evocations* (organ—also for orchestra); William Schuman, *Three Score Set*; Arthur Shepherd, *Fantasy Concertante on "The Garden Hymn"* (organ)— *Capriccio No. 3*; David S. Smith, *Triumph and Peace* (organ); Louise Talma, *Sonata No. 1*.

**Symphonies**   Béla Bartók, *Concerto for Orchestra*; Robert Russell Bennett, *Four Freedoms Symphony*; Nicolai Berezowsky, *Symphony No. 4, Opus 27*; Avery Claflin, *Symphony No. 2*; Morton Gould, *Symphony No. 1*; Howard Hanson, *Symphony No. 4, "Requiem"* (Pulitzer Prize); Philip James, *Symphony No. 1*; Bohuslav Martinů, *Symphony No. 2*; Harold C. Morris, *Symphony No. 2, "Victory"*; Robert Palmer, *Concerto for Orchestra*; Walter Piston, *Symphony No. 2* (New York Music Critics' Award); Robert Sanders, *Symphony for Band*; William Schuman, *Symphony No. 5 (for Strings)*; David Van Vactor, *Symphony No. 2, "Music for the Marines."*

# 1944

☼

## Historical Highlights

Franklin D. Roosevelt is elected to an unprecedented fourth term as president; Allied world leaders meet at Dumbarton Oaks and Bretton Woods; the new rank of General of the Armies is given to Generals Eisenhower, MacArthur, Marshall, and Arnold; Congress passes the GI bill of rights; the Invasion of Europe takes place on June 6; the Japanese fleet is destroyed in the Battle of Leyte Gulf; Hitler begins using the V-1 and V-2 rocket bombs against England.

## World Cultural Highlights

**World Art**   Georges Braque, *Pumpkin Slice*; Alexandre Colin, *Liberation*; Henri Matisse, *The White Dress*; Georges Rouault, *Homo Homini Lupus*; Maurice Utrillo, *Rue Saint Rustique, Montmartre*.

**World Literature**   Ivo Andric, *The Bridge on the Drina*; W. Somerset Maugham, *The Razor's Edge*; George Orwell, *Animal Farm*; Franz Werfel, *Jacobowsky and the Colonel*.

**World Music**   Gottfried von Einem, *Concerto for Orchestra*; Aram Khachaturian, *Masquerade*; Olivier Messiaen, *Vingt Regards sur l'Enfant Jésus*; Sergei Prokofiev, *Cinderella—Symphony No. 5*.

**Miscellaneous**   The Chelsea Symphony Orchestra and City of Birmingham Symphony Orchestra are founded in England; births include Andrew Davis, Vladimir Spivakov, and Kiri Te Kanawa; deaths include Cécile Chaminade, Jean Giraudoux, Vasili Kandinsky, Aristide Maillol, and Edvard Munch.

## American Art and Literature Highlights

**Births/Deaths**   Births include art figures Chuck Forsman, Michael Heizer, Duarte Santos, Alan Shields, Alan Saret, and literary figures Janet Ann Dailey, Robert Morgan, Alice Walker, and Joy Williams; deaths include artists Piet Mondriaan, Florine Stettheimer, and literary figures George Ade, Irvin S. Cobb, Katherine Gerould, Hutchins Hapgood, Ida Tarbell, William A. White, and Harold Bell Wright.

**Art Works**   Arthur Dove, *That Red One*; Philip Evergood, *Don't Cry, Mother*; Arshile Gorky, *The Liver Is the Cock's Comb*; Morris Graves, *Sea, Fish and Constellation*; Robert Gwathmey, *Singing and Mending*; Seymour Lipton, *Folk Song*; Reginald Marsh, *Eyes Tested*; Ben Shahn, *The Red Stairway*; Clyfford Still, *Jamais*; Max Weber, *Crouched Figure*; William Zorach, *Victory* (marble).

**Literature**   Saul Bellow, *The Dangling Man*; John R. Hersey, *A Bell for Adano* (Pulitzer Prize); Charles Jackson, *Lost Weekend*; Margaret Landon, *Anna and the King of Siam*; Karl Shapiro, *V-Letter and Other Poems* (Pulitzer Prize); Ben Ames Williams, *Leave Her to Heaven*; Tennessee Williams, *The Glass Menagerie* (New York Drama Critics' Award); Kathleen Winsor, *Forever Amber*.

## Music—The Vernacular/Commercial Scene

**A. Births**   John Abercrombie (guitarist) December 16; Barbara Acklin (singer) February 28; Moe Bandy (singer) February 12; Archie Bell (singer) September 1; Michael Bloomfield (guitarist) July 28; Pete Cetera (singer/guitar) September 13; Rita Coolidge (singer) May 1; Jackie DeShannon (singer/writer) August 21; Michael Franks (songwriter) September 18; Kinky Friedman (songwriter) October 31; Bobbie Gentry (singer) July 27; Marvin Hamlisch (composer) June 2; Luther Ingram (singer/writer) November 30; Booker T. Jones (organist) September 12; Gladys Knight (singer) May 28; Patti LaBelle (singer) May 24; Brenda Lee (singer) December 11; Van McCoy (singer/writer) January 6; George McCrae (singer) October 19; Ronnie Milsap (singer) January 16; Tracy Nelson (singer/writer) December 27; Tony Orlando (singer) April 3; Eddie Rabbitt (singer) November 27; Susan Raye (singer) October 8; Diana Ross (singer) March 26; Boz Scaggs (singer) June 8; John Sebastian (songwriter) March 17; Woody Shaw (trumpeter) December 24; Frank Sinatra, Jr. (singer) January 10; Henry Threadgill (composer) February 15; Townes Van Zandt (singer/writer) March 7; Barry White (singer/writer) September 12; Johnny Winter (singer) February 23; Bobby Womack (guitarist/writer) March 4.

**B. Deaths**  Felix Bernard (piano/composer) October 20; Cecil Mack (lyricist); Glenn Miller (trombonist/bandleader) December 15 (?); Jimmy Noone (clarinetist/bandleader) April 19.

**C. Biographical**

**Performing Groups**  Frankie Carle Big Band; Billy Eckstine Jazz Band; Buddy Johnson Big Band; Gene Krupa Big Band II; Luis Russell Big Band; Artie Shaw Band IV.

**New Beginnings**  Black and White Record Co.; Burke–Van Heusen (Burran) Publishing Co.; DeLuxe Records (New Jersey); Jazz at the Philharmonic (Los Angeles); King Records (Cincinnati); New England Folk Festival (Natick, Massachusetts).

**Miscellaneous**  Jimmie Davis (country singer) is elected governor of Louisiana for the first term (second term, 1960–1964).

**E. Representative Works**

**Musicals**  Harold Arlen and E. Harburg, *Bloomer Girl*; Leonard Bernstein, B. Comden, and A. Green, *On the Town*; Ralph Blane and H. Martin, *Meet Me in St. Louis* (film); Phil Charig, D. Shapiro, M. Pascal, *Follow the Girls*; Chet Forrest and R. C. Wright, *Song of Norway* (based on music of Grieg); Burton Lane, *Laffing Room Only*; Cole Porter, *Mexican Hayride—Seven Lively Arts*.

**Songs**  Johnny Burke and J. Van Heusen, *Swinging on a Star* (Oscar); Burton Lane, *Feudin' and Fightin'*; Johnny Mercer, *Dream*; Johnny Mercer and H. Arlen, *Ac-cent-tchu-ate the Positive*; Cole Porter, *Don't Fence Me In*; Andy Razaf, *That's What I Like about the South*; Jule Styne and Sammy Cahn, *I'll Walk Alone—Saturday Night Is the Loneliest Night of the Week—There Goes That Song Again*; Karl Suessdorf, *Moonlight in Vermont*; Jimmy Van Heusen, *It Could Happen to You*.

**Other**  Duke Ellington, *Blutopia* (jazz suite); Hugo Friedhofer, *A Wing and a Prayer* (film music); Alfred Newman, *The Keys of the Kingdom* (film music); Max Steiner, *Since You Went Away* (Oscar).

## Music—The Cultivated/Art Music Scene

**F. Births**  William Hugh Albright (pianist/composer) October 20; Frank Becker (composer) March 29; Gene R. Bedient (organ builder) August 23; Daniel Chorzempa (organist) December 7; William Christie (harpsichordist/composer) December 19; Dennis Russell Davies (conductor) April 16; Brent Ellis (baritone) June 20; Richard Friedman (composer) January 6; Lynn Harrell (cellist) January 30; Lorin Hollander (pianist) July 19; Linda Kelm (soprano) December 11; Paul Lansky (composer) June 18; Bennett Lerner (pianist) March 21; Dennis McIntire (music historian) June 25; Barbara Nissman (pianist) December 31; Ursula Oppens (pianist) February 2; Anthony Paratore (pianist) June 17; Florence Quivar (mezzo-soprano) March 3; John Rahn (composer/theorist) February 26; Joshua Rifkin (musicologist) April 22; Stephen Scott (composer) October 10; Ellen Shade (soprano) February 17; Lucy Shelton (soprano) February 25; Leonard Slatkin (conductor) September 1; Michael Tilson Thomas (conductor) December 21; Patricia Wise (soprano) July 31; Eugenia (Rich) Zukerman (flutist) September 25.

**G. Deaths**  Amy (Mrs. H. H. A.) Beach (composer/pianist) December 27; Johanna M. Beyer (German-born composer/musicologist) January 9; Charles Douglas (organist) January 19; Carl Engel (German-born musicologist) May 6; John Homer Grunn (pianist/composer) June 6; Katherine Heyman (pianist) September 28; Arthur E. Johnstone (composer/educator) January 23; Edgar Stillman Kelley (composer) November 12; Josef Lhévinne (Russian-born pianist) December 2; Henry B. Pasmore (singer/composer) February 23; Leo Schulz (composer) August 12.

**H. Debuts**

**United States**   Richard Dyer-Bennet (British singer—New York), Donald Gramm (bass-baritone—Chicago), Grant Johannesen (pianist—New York), Robert Merrill (baritone—Trenton, New Jersey), Leonard Rose (cellist—New York), Richard Tucker (tenor—New York).

**Metropolitan Opera**   Emil Cooper (Russian conductor), Ella Flesch (Hungarian soprano), Martha Lipton (mezzo-soprano), Regina Resnik (soprano), Blanche Thebom (mezzo-soprano).

**Other**   Mimi Benzell (soprano—Mexico City).

**I. New Positions**

**Conductors**   Saul Caston (Denver Symphony Orchestra—to 1964); Massimo Freccia (New Orleans Philharmonic Symphony Orchestra—to 1952); Hans Schwieger (Fort Wayne Philharmonic Orchestra—to 1948); Henry Sopkin (Atlanta Youth Orchestra [Atlanta Symphony Orchestra in 1945]—to 1966).

**Educational**   Isadore Freed (director, Hartt School of Music—to 1960); Rudolf Kolisch (University of Wisconsin—to 1967); Otto Luening (director of opera, Columbia); Roger Sessions (Berkeley—to 1953).

**Other**   Gustave Reese (director of publications, Carl Fischer—to 1955).

**J. Honors and Awards**

**Honors**   David Diamond and Burrill Phillips (American Academy and Institute); Roy Harris and Quincy Porter (National Institute).

**K. Biographical**   Among those receiving American citizenship are Daniele Amfitheatrov, Jacob Avshalomov, Victor Babin, Claude Frank, Felix Galimir, Walter Herbert, Hugo Kauder, Peter Jona Korn, Efrem Kurtz, Nikolai Lopatnikoff, Hans Nathan, Vittorio Rieti, Julius Rudel, Artur Schnabel, Elisabeth Schumann, Hans Schwieger, William Steinberg, and Henry Swoboda. Leonard Bernstein stuns the music world when at the last minute he is called upon to substitute for an ailing Bruno Walter in a difficult New York Philharmonic Orchestra program; Eugene Ormandy parts with RCA Victor and begins a 25-year association with Columbia Records; Heitor Villa-Lobos makes his first visit to the United States.

**L. Musical Beginnings**

**Performing Groups**   Albeneri Trio (Benar Heifetz, Erich Kahn, Alexander Schneider); American Youth Orchestra (New York); Atlanta Youth Symphony Orchestra; Charleston Choral Society; Fort Wayne Philharmonic Orchestra; Jackson (Mississippi) Symphony Orchestra; Kroll String Quartet (to 1969); Springfield (Massachusetts) Symphony Orchestra and Chorus; New York City Symphony Orchestra (by Leopold Stokowski); Wichita Symphony Orchestra (Kansas).

**Educational**   Meadowmount School for String Players (Westport, New York); National Association of Teachers of Singing (NATS).

**Other**   Ampex Co.; National Society of Arts and Letters (Washington, DC); *The Score*.

**M. Music Publications**

Apel, Willi, *Harvard Dictionary of Music*
Boyden, David, *A Manual of Counterpoint Based on Sixteenth-Century Practice*
Crist, Bainbridge, *The Art of Setting Words to Music*
Downes, Edward O., *Adventures in Symphonic Music*
Erskine, John, *What Is Music?*
Ferguson, Donald, *On the Elements of Expression in Music*
Jacob, Gordon, *How to Read a Score*
Jackson, George P., *The Story of the Sacred Harp*
McHose, A. and Tibbs, R., *Sight Singing Manual*
Sachs, Curt, *The Evolution of Piano Music*

Siegmeister, Elie, *Work and Sing*
Veinus, Abraham, *The Concerto*

## N. Musical Compositions

**Chamber Music**  George Barati, *String Quartet No. 1*; William Bergsma, *String Quartet No. 2*; David Diamond, *String Quartet No. 2*; Cecil Effinger, *String Quartet No. 3*; Samuel Gardner, *String Quartet No. 2*; Charles Jones, *String Quartet No. 2*; Werner Josten, *Horn Sonata*; Boris Koutzen, *String Quartet No. 3*; Ernst Krenek, *String Quartet No. 7*; Lionel Nowak, *Violin Sonatina*; Vincent Persichetti, *String Quartet No. 2, Opus 24*; Leroy Robertson, *American Serenade* (string quartet); Arthur Shepherd, *String Quartet No. 3 in D Minor*; David Stanley Smith, *String Quartet No. 10*.

**Choral/Vocal**  Wayne Barlow, *Psalm XXIII*; Marion Bauer, *China, Opus 38*; Robert Delaney, *Western Star*; Herbert Elwell, *Blue Symphony* (song cycle); Arthur Farwell, *Twelve Emily Dickinson Songs, Opus 107*; Irving Fine, *The Choral New Yorker*; William Schuman, *Te Deum*; Arthur Shepherd, *Psalm XLII*; Leo Sowerby, *Canticle of the Sun* (Pulitzer Prize); Igor Stravinsky, *Babel*.

**Concertos**  Samuel Barber, *Capricorn Concerto, Opus 21*; Hans Barth, *Ten Etudes for Quarter-Tone Piano and Orchestra*; Charles W. Cadman, *Aurora Borealis* (piano and orchestra)—*A Mad Empress Remembers* (cello and orchestra); Vivian Fine, *Concertante* (piano and orchestra); Anis Fuleihan, *Violin Concerto No. 1*; Vittorio Giannini, *Violin Concerto*; Louis Gruenberg, *Violin Concerto*; Roy Harris, *Piano Concerto No. 1*; Everett Helm, *Kentucky Sonata* (violin and orchestra); Bohuslav Martinů, *Cello Concerto No. 2*; Lionel Nowak, *Concertino for Piano and Orchestra*; Leroy Robertson, *Rhapsody for Piano and Orchestra*; Gunther Schuller, *Horn Concerto No. 1*; Alan Shulman, *Pastorale and Dance* (violin and orchestra); Leo Sowerby, *Classic Concerto* (organ and strings).

**Operas**  Robert Russell Bennett, *The Kiss*; Arcady Dubensky, *Two Yankees in Italy*; Harry L. Freeman, *Zululand*; Frederick Jacobi, *The Prodigal Son* (Bispham Medal); Bernard Rogers, *The Warrior* (Ditson Award); Bernard Wagenaar, *Pieces of Eight* (Ditson Award).

**Orchestra/Band**  Richard Bales, *National Gallery Suite II*; John J. Becker, *Antigone* (incidental music), *The Snow Goose: A Legend of the Second World War*; Leonard Bernstein, *Fancy Free* (ballet); Ernest Bloch, *Suite Symphonique*; Aaron Copland, *Appalachian Spring* (Pulitzer Prize—New York Music Critics' Award); David Diamond, *Rounds for String Orchestra* (New York Music Critics' Award); Arthur Farwell, *Indian Suite, Opus 110*; Lukas Foss, *Ballets: The Heart Remembers—Within These Walls*; Don Gillis, *The Alamo* (tone poem); Paul Hindemith, *Hérodiade* (ballet); Ulysses Kay, *Overture, Of New Horizons*; Colin McPhee, *Four Iroquois Dances for Orchestra*; Gian Carlo Menotti, *Sebastian* (ballet); Burrill Phillips, *Scherzo for Orchestra*; Quincy Porter, *The Moving Tide*; William Schuman, *Variations on a Theme of Eugene Goossens—Circus Overture—Steel Town* (film music); David S. Smith, *The Apostle* (tone poem); William Grant Still, *Poem for Orchestra—Festive Overture* (Cincinnati Symphony Orchestra Prize); Igor Stravinsky, *Scenes de Ballet—Scherzo a la Russe*; Louise Talma, *Toccata for Orchestra*; Bernard Wagenaar, *Song of Mourning*.

**Piano/Organ**  Samuel Barber, *Four Excursions*; Jean Berger, *Five Compositions for Piano*; Norman Dello Joio, *Sonata No. 2*; Vivian Fine, *Rhapsody on a Russian Folk Song*; Alexander Gretchaninov, *Sonata No. 2*; Eastwood Lane, *Here Are Ladies (Five Pieces)*; Normand Lockwood, *Sonata*; Robert Palmer, *Sonata for Two Pianos*; Wallingford Riegger, *New and Old: Twelve Pieces for Piano, Opus 38*; Harold Shapero, *Sonata No. 1—Sonata No. 2—Sonata No. 3*; Elie Siegmeister, *American Sonata (No. 1)*; Virgil Thomson, *Ten Etudes*.

**Symphonies**  Samuel Barber, *Symphony No. 2, Opus 19*; Philip G. Clapp, *Symphony No. 12 in B-Flat Major, "Rime of the Ancient Mariner"*; Lukas Foss, *Symphony in G*; Morton Gould, *Symphony No. 2—Concerto for Orchestra*; Roy Harris, *Symphony No. 6, "Gettysburg"*; Beatrice Laufer, *Symphony No. 1*; Bohuslav Martinů, *Symphony No. 3*; Peter Mennin, *Symphony No. 2* (Bearns Prize—Gershwin Award); Darius Milhaud, *Symphony No. 2, Opus 247*; Wallingford Riegger, *Symphony No. 1* (withdrawn).

# 1945

☀

## Historical Highlights

President Roosevelt dies and Harry S. Truman becomes the 33rd president; the United Nations convenes in San Francisco; the first controlled atomic bomb test takes place in New Mexico; Germany surrenders, then Japan when atomic bombs are dropped on Hiroshima and Nagasaki; Clement Attlee becomes British prime minister; the Latin-American countries sign the Act of Chapultepec.

## World Cultural Highlights

**World Art** Max Beckmann, *Blindman's Bluff*; Otto Dix, *Saul and David*; Max Ernst, *The Temptation of St. Anthony*; Francis Gruber, *Job*; Pablo Picasso, *The Charnel House*; William Zorach, *Victory*.

**World Literature** Jean Giraudoux, *The Madwoman of Chaillot*; Federico García Lorca, *La casa de Bernarda Alba*; Evelyn Waugh, *Brideshead Revisited*.

**World Music** Benjamin Britten, *Peter Grimes*; Zoltán Kodály, *Missa Brevis*; Dmitri Shostakovich, *Symphony No. 9*; Richard Strauss, *Metamorphosen*; Michael Tippett, *Symphony No. 1*.

**Miscellaneous** The Rheinische Philharmonic Orchestra (Koblenz), the Hungarian Radio and Television Symphony Orchestra, and the Smetana Quartet (Prague) are formed; births include Radu Lupu, Alexander Melamid, and Itzhak Perlman; deaths include Béla Bartók, Pietro Mascagni, Alexei Tolstoy, Anton Webern, and Franz Werfel.

## American Art and Literature Highlights

**Births/Deaths** Births include art figures John Alexander, Gordon Matta-Clark, Susan Rothenberg, Charles Simonds, and literary figures Michael Cristofer, Annie Dillard, August Wilson, and Tobias Wolff; deaths include art figures Herbert Adams, A. Sterling Calder, and literary figures Robert Benchley, Ernst Cassirer, Benjamin DeCasseres, Theodore Dreiser, Ellen Glasgow, and Amélie Rives.

**Art Works** Ilya Bolotowsky, *Upright in Gold and Violet*; Chaim Gross, *Acrobatic Dancers*; Philip Guston, *If This Be Not I*; Yasuo Kuniyoshi, *The Headless Horse Who Wants to Jump*; Jacob Lawrence, *Series: John Brown*; Barnett Newman, *The Song of Orpheus*; Mark Rothko, *Baptismal Scene*; David Smith, *Pillar of Sunday*; Yves Tanguy, *The Rapidity of Sleep*.

**Literature** Mary Chase, *Harvey* (Pulitzer Prize); Thomas B. Costain, *The Black Rose*; Robert Frost, *A Masque of Reason*; Sinclair Lewis, *Cass Timberlane*; Betty MacDonald, *The Egg and I*; J. P. Marquand, *Repent in Haste*; Samuel Shellabarger, *The Captain from Castile*; John Steinbeck, *Cannery Row*; Jessamyn West, *The Friendly Persuasion*; Richard Wright, *Black Boy*.

## Music—The Vernacular/Commercial Scene

**A. Births** R. C. Bannon (singer) May 2; Little Eva (Boyd) (singer) June 29; Anthony Braxton (saxophonist/clarinetist) June 4; David Bromberg (guitarist/violinist) September 19; Kim Carnes (singer/writer) July 20; Johnny Cymbal (songwriter) February 3; Doris Duke (singer); José Feliciano (singer/writer) September 10; Wild Man Fischer (singer); John Fogerty (singer/guitarist) May 28; Jimmie Dale Gilmore (singer/guitarist) May 6; David Grisman (mandolin player/composer) March 23; Deborah Harry (singer) July 1; Donnie Hathaway (singer) October 1; Nona Hendryx (singer/writer) August 18; Keith Jarrett (pianist) May 8; Leo Kottke (guitarist) September 11; Don McLean (singer/composer) October 2; Lee Michaels (organist/singer) November 24; Bette Midler (singer/actress) December 1; Melba Moore (singer); Michael M. Murphey (singer/writer) March 4; Freda Payne (singer) September 19; Jeannie C. Riley (singer) October 19; Mitch Ryder (singer); David Sanborn (saxophonist/writer) July 30; Carly Simon (singer/writer) June 25; Stephen Stills (singer/guitarist) January 3; Tony Williams (drummer) December 12.

**B. Deaths** Al Dubin (lyricist) February 11; Gus Edwards (singer/composer) November 7; Clyde Hart (pianist) March 19; Jerome Kern (composer) November 11; Jimmy Monaco (composer) October 6.

**C. Biographical**

**Performing Groups** Davis Sisters; Everly Brothers; The Erroll Garner Trio; Dizzy Gillespie Big Band I and Sextet; The Ravens; The Sensational Nightingales; Ted Weems Band II.

**New Beginnings** Mercury Records; Modern Music Co. (Los Angeles); Philo (Aladdin) Records; Stamps Quartet Music Co. (Dallas).

**Miscellaneous** Jerome Kern is taken into the National Institute.

**D. Publications** John Jacob Niles, *The Anglo American Ballad Book.*

**E. Representative Works**

**Musicals** Morton Gould, B. Comden, and A. Green, *Billion Dollar Baby*; Lerner and Loewe, *The Day before Spring*; Richard Rodgers, *State Fair* (film); Rodgers and Hammerstein, *Carousel* (New York Drama Critics Award); Sigmund Romberg and M. D. Fields, *Up in Central Park.*

**Songs** Elly Beadell and N. Tollerton, *Cruising Down the River*; Ray Freedman and D. Thomas, *Sioux City Sue*; Bud Green, L. Brown, and B. Homer, *Sentimental Journey*; Walter Gross, *Tenderly*; Duke Ellington and J. Hodges, *I'm Beginning to See the Light*; Lionel Hampton, *Hey-Baba Re-Bop*; David Raksin, *Laura*; Rodgers and Hammerstein, *It Might as Well Be Spring* (Oscar); Harry Ruby and B. Kalmar, *Give Me the Simple Life*; Jule Styne and S. Cahn, *It's Been a Long, Long Time—Let It Snow, Let It Snow, Let It Snow*; Allie Wrubel and R. Gilbert, *Zip-A-Dee-Doo-Dah* (Oscar).

**Other** Duke Ellington, *New World a-Comin'* (jazz suite); Hugo Friedhofer, *Brewster's Millions* (film music); Miklós Rózsa, *Spellbound* (film music—Oscar); Alfred Newman, *A Bell for Adano— A Tree Grows in Brooklyn* (film music); Herbert Stothart, *National Velvet* (film music).

## Music —The Cultivated/Art Music Scene

**F. Births** Theodore Albrecht (conductor) September 24; Charles Amirkhanian (composer) January 19; Victoria Bond (conductor) May 6; Phyllis Bryn-Julson (soprano) February 5; Lenus Carlson (baritone) February 11; Barbara Conrad (mezzo-soprano) August 11; Leila Alice Cuberli (soprano) September 29; Misha Dichter (pianist) September 27; D'Anna Fortunato (mezzo-soprano) February 21; Isaiah Jackson (conductor) January 22; Martin Katz (pianist) November 27; Jane Marsh (soprano) June 25; John Mauceri (conductor) September 12; Julia Migenes (soprano) March 13; Jessye Norman (soprano) September 15; Thomas Pasatieri (composer) October 20; Maggi Payne (composer/flutist) December 23; Arnold Rosner (composer) November 8; David Schiff (composer) August 30; Barry Schrader (composer) June 26; Alan Titus (baritone) October 28; Frederica Von Stade (mezzo-soprano) June 1; Reynold Weidemaar (music educator) September 25; Susan Davenny Wyner (soprano) October 17; Judith Lang Zaimont (composer) November 8.

**G. Deaths** Béla Bartók (Hungarian-born composer) September 26; Herbert L. Clarke (cornetist/bandmaster) January 30; Harvey B. Gaul (composer/organist) December 1; Albino Gorno (Italian-born pianist) October 29; Helen Hopekirk (Scottish-born pianist) November 19; John Adam Hugo (pianist/composer) December 29; Leonard Liebling (pianist/critic) October 28; Edward B. Marks (publisher) December 17; Frank Metcalf (hymnist) February 25; Erno Rapee (Hungarian-born conductor) June 26; George C. Stebbins (hymnist) October 6.

**H. Debuts**

**United States** Jacob Lateiner (Cuban pianist—Philadelphia), Jerome Lowenthal (pianist—Philadelphia), Malcolm Sargent (British conductor—New York), Russell Sherman (pianist—New York), Nell Tangeman (Cincinnati), Ramón Vinay (Chilean baritone—New York), George Walker (pianist).

**Metropolitan Opera** Pierrette Alarie (Canadian soprano), Mimi Benzell (soprano), Fritz Busch (German conductor), Dorothy Kirsten (soprano), Robert Merrill (baritone), Torsten Ralf (Swedish tenor), Richard Tucker (tenor).

### I. New Positions

**Conductors**   Leonard Bernstein (New York City Symphony Orchestra); Antal Dorati (Dallas Symphony Orchestra—to 1949); Francis Madeira (Rhode Island Philharmonic Orchestra—to 1979); Max Rudolf (Metropolitan Opera—to 1958); William Steinberg (Buffalo Philharmonic Orchestra—to 1952).

**Educational**   Ernst Bacon (director, Syracuse University School of Music—to 1963); Jack Beeson (Columbia); Henry Brant (Columbia—to 1952); Ingolf Dahl (USC—to 1970); Donald Jay Grout (Cornell—to 1970); Mack Harrell (Juilliard—to 1956); Felix Labunski (Cincinnati College of Music); Nikolai Lopatnikoff (composition, Carnegie-Mellon—to 1969); Gardner Read (head, Cleveland Institute—to 1948).

**Other**   Roy Harris (head, music department, Office of War Information); Paul Henry Lang (editor, *Musical Quarterly*—to 1973); Henry Pleasants (European music critic, *New York Times*—to 1955); William Schuman (director of publications, G. Schirmer—to 1952).

### J. Honors and Awards

**Honors**   William Bergsma and Gian Carlo Menotti (American Academy and Institute); Alexander Schneider (Coolidge Medal).

**Awards**   Howard Hanson and Frank Wigglesworth (Ditson Award).

### K. Biographical   Licia Albanese, Manfred Bukofzer, Alfred Einstein, Marcel Grandjany, Karl Kohn, Ernst Krenek, Lotte Lehmann, Ursula Mamlok, Paul Nettl, Raoul Pleskow, Luigi Silva, and Igor Stravinsky all become naturalized American citizens; Richard Bonelli retires from the opera stage and concentrates on teaching voice; Alberto Ginastera, fired by Perón from his Argentine music post, comes to the United States; Gunther Schuller becomes principal horn in the Metropolitan Opera orchestra; Leopold Stokowski marries heiress Gloria Vanderbilt.

### L. Musical Beginnings

**Performing Groups**   Civic Light Opera Association of Pittsburgh; Mississippi Opera Association (Jackson); Pittsburgh Youth Symphony; Rhode Island Philharmonic Orchestra; Rochester Oratorio Society; San Antonio Opera Co.

**Educational**   Berklee College of Music (Boston); Institute of Renaissance and Baroque Music (American Institute of Musicology, Rome/Cambridge); Ohio State University School of Music; Oregon Conservatory of Music II (Portland—to 1954).

**Other**   George Gershwin Award; *Music of the West*.

### M. Music Publications

Antheil, George, *Bad Boy of Music*
Koch, Caspar, *Organ Student's Gradus ad Parnassum*
Krenek, Ernst, ed., *Hamline Studies in Musicology*
Slonimsky, Nicolas, *Music of Latin America*
Spaeth, Sigmund, *At Home with Music*
Thomson, Virgil, *The Musical Scene*

### N. Musical Compositions

**Chamber Music**   Samuel Adler, *String Quartet No. 1*; Ernest Bloch, *String Quartet No. 2*; Cecil Burleigh, *Two Essays in String Quartet: Illusion, Transition*; Arthur Cohn, *String Quartet No. 6*; Alvin Etler, *Quartet for Strings*; Edward Burlingame Hill, *Clarinet Quintet*; Frederick Jacobi, *String Quartet No. 3*; Ernst Kanitz, *Quintettino*; Erich W. Korngold, *String Quartet No. 3 in D Major*; Hugh F. MacColl, *String Quartet No. 2*; Conlon Nancarrow, *String Quartet No. 1*; Joaquin Nin-Culmell, *Six Variations on a Theme by Luis de Milán* (guitar); Gardner Read, *Piano Quintet, Opus 47*; Halsey Stevens, *Quintet* (flute, strings, piano—Society for Publication of American Music Prize); Powell Weaver, *Violin Sonata*.

**Choral/Vocal**   Miriam Gideon, *Hound of Heaven*; Ulysses Kay, *Song of Jeremiah* (cantata); William Latham, *Prayer after World War*; Frances McCollin, *Lincoln Lyrics* (cantata); Harl

McDonald, *Song of the Nations*; Robert Palmer, *Lincoln Walks at Midnight*; Lazare Saminsky, *Requiem*; Robert Sanders, *An American Psalm*; David Stanley Smith, *The Ocean*; Louise Talma, *Terre de France* (song cycle); Stefan Wolpe, *Yigdal* (cantata).

**Concertos**  Esther Ballou, *Piano Concerto No. 1*; Samuel Barber, *Cello Concerto* (New York Critics' Circle Award); Béla Bartók, *Piano Concerto No. 3* (finished by T. Serly)—*Viola Concerto* (realized by Tibor Serly from sketches); Nicolai Berezowsky, *Harp Concerto, Opus 31*; Arthur Cohn, *Variations for Clarinet (Saxophone) and Orchestra*; Cecil Effinger, *Suite for Cello and Orchestra*; Lehman Engel, *Violin Concerto*; Vittorio Giannini, *Trumpet Concerto*; Ernest Gold, *Piano Concerto*; Parks Grant, *Clarinet Concerto*; Paul Hindemith, *Piano Concerto*; Erich Korngold, *Violin Concerto in D Major, Opus 35*; Wiktor Labunski, *Variations for Piano and Orchestra*; Gian Carlo Menotti, *Piano Concerto in F Major*; Gardner Read, *Violin Concerto, Opus 55—Cello Concerto*; Gunther Schuller, *Cello Concerto*; Alexander Steinert, *Rhapsody for Clarinet and Orchestra*; Igor Stravinsky, *Ebony Concerto* (for Woody Herman); Paul White, *Andante and Rondo* (cello and orchestra).

**Operas**  John J. Becker, *Deirdre: Stagework No. 6*; Marc Blitzstein, *Goloopchik*; Louis Gruenberg, *Volpone*; Normand Lockwood, *The Scarecrow*; Gian Carlo Menotti, *The Medium*.

**Orchestra/Band**  Samuel Adler, *Epitaph for the Young American Soldier*; George Antheil, *Over the Plains*; Nicolai Berezowsky, *Introduction and Allegro, Opus 8*; Arthur Berger, *Three Pieces for String Orchestra*; Charles W. Cadman, *Overture, Huckleberry Finn Goes Fishing*; John Alden Carpenter, *The Seven Ages*; Arcady Dubensky, *Orientale*; Lukas Foss, *The Gift of the Magi* (ballet); Morton Gould, *Interplay* (ballet); Louis Gruenberg, *Americana—Music to an Imaginary Ballet*; Leroy Robertson, *Punch and Judy Overture*; Arnold Schoenberg, *Prelude "Genesis," Opus 44*; William Schuman, *Undertow* (ballet); Harold Shapero, *Serenade in D for Strings* (Bearns Prize); Elie Siegmeister, *Western Suite*; David Stanley Smith, *Daybreak*; William Grant Still, *From the Delta* (band); Lamar Stringfield, *Mountain Dawn*; Gustav Strube, *Peace Overture*; Joseph F. Wagner, *American Jubilee Overture*.

**Piano/Organ**  Jack Beeson, *Sonata No. 4*; Paul Bowles, *Six Preludes*; Paul Creston, *Six Preludes, Opus 38*; Robert Evett, *Sonata No. 1*; Ross Lee Finney, *Sonata No. 4, "Christmastime"*; Nicolas Flagello, *Three Dances*; Anis Fuleihan, *Sonorities*; Miriam Gideon, *Dances for Two Pianos*; Alexei Haieff, *Sonata for Two Pianos*; Roy Harris, *American Ballads*; Frederick Jacobi, *Fantasy Sonata*; Charles Mills, *Thirty Penitential Preludes*; Robert Palmer, *Toccata ostinato*; Gardner Read, *Sonata da Chiesa, Opus 61*; Arthur Shepherd, *In Modo Ostinato*; Virgil Thomson, *Portraits (in Five Volumes, 1929–1945)*.

**Symphonies**  Henry Brant, *Symphony, The 1930's*; Mark Brunswick, *Symphony in B-Flat Major*; Paul Creston, *Symphony No. 2*; David Diamond, *Symphony No. 3, 4*; Cecil Effinger, *Little Symphony No. 1*; Lehman Engel, *Symphony No. 2*; Roger Goeb, *Symphony No. 2*; Ray Green, *Symphony No. 2*; Harrison Kerr, *Symphony No. 2*; Arthur Kreutz, *Symphony No. 1*; Bohuslav Martinů, *Symphony No. 4*; Douglas Moore, *Symphony No. 2 in A Major*; John Powell, *Symphony in A Major (Virginia Symphony, 1951)*; Wallingford Riegger, *Symphony No. 2* (withdrawn); Vittorio Rieti, *Symphony No. 5*; Halsey Stevens, *Symphony No. 1*; William Grant Still, *Symphony No. 5, "Western Hemisphere"*; Igor Stravinsky, *Symphony in Three Movements*; Howard Swanson, *Symphony No. 1*; Joseph F. Wagner, *Symphony No. 2*; Karl Weigl, *Symphony No. 5, "Apocalyptic."*

# 1946

❁

## Historical Highlights

Winston Churchill in his "Iron Curtain" speech (Fulton, Missouri) coins the phrase "cold war"; the Philippines are given their independence; Congress lifts most price and wage controls from the war years and forms the Atomic Energy Commission; Trygve Lie is the first Secretary-General of the

United Nations; Charles de Gaulle resigns as French President; war criminal trials are held in Nuremberg.

## World Cultural Highlights

**World Art**    Otto Dix, *The Crucifixion*; George Grosz, *Peace II*.

**World Literature**    Nikos Kazantzakis, *Zorba, the Greek*.

**World Music**    Benjamin Britten, *Young Person's Guide to the Orchestra*; Arthur Honegger, *Symphony No. 3, "Liturgique"*; Aram Khachaturian, *Cello Concerto*; Sergei Prokofiev, *Symphony No. 6*.

**Miscellaneous**    The Darmstadt Contemporary Festivals begin; foundings include the Bamberg Symphony Orchestra, the Royal Philharmonic Orchestra (London), and Sydney Symphony Orchestra (Australia); births include Trevor Pinnock and Giuseppe Sinopoli; deaths include Charles Despiau, Manuel de Falla, Gerhardt Hauptmann, and H. G. Wells.

## American Art and Literature Highlights

**Births/Deaths**    Births include sculptor Alice Aycock, artists Lita Albuquerque, Dennis Ashbaugh, Mary Anna Goetz, Catharine Murphy, Roger Welch, and author Ron Silliman; deaths include art figures John Curry, Arthur Dove, Jules Guerin, Laszló Moholy-Nagy, Elie Nadelman, Horace Pippin, Joseph Stella, and literary figures Countee Cullen, Damon Runyon, and Booth Tarkington.

**Art Works**    William Baziotes, *Cyclops*; Charles Burchfield, *The Sphinx and the Milky Way*; David Hare, *The Couple*; Walt Kuhn, *Clown with White Tie*; Mauricio Lasansky, *Dachau*; Jack Levine, *Welcome Home*; Isamu Noguchi, *Humpty Dumpty*; Jackson Pollock, *Sounds in the Grass: Shimmering Substance*; David Smith, *Cello Player*; Max Weber, *Crouched Figure*.

**Literature**    Elizabeth Bishop, *North and South* (Pulitzer Prize); R. Crouse and H. Lindsay, *State of the Union* (Pulitzer Prize); Thomas Heggen, *Mr. Roberts*; Robert Lowell, *Lord Weary's Castle* (Pulitzer Prize); Carson McCullers, *A Member of the Wedding* (New York Drama Critics' Award); Robert Penn Warren, *All the King's Men* (Pulitzer Prize); Frank G. Yerby, *The Foxes of Harrow*.

## Music — The Vernacular/Commercial Scene

**A. Births**    Howard Bellamy (singer) February 2; Cher (La Pierre) (singer) May 20; Jimmy Buffett (singer) December 25; Richard Carpenter (singer) October 15; John Conlee (singer) August 11; Arthur Conley (singer) April 1; Keith Copeland (drummer) April 18; George Duke (pianist/composer) January 12; Lesley Gore (singer) May 2; Al Green (singer/writer) April 13; Brenda Holloway (singer/writer) June 21; Naomi Judd (singer) January 11; Andy Kim (singer/writer) December 5; Bobby Lewis (lutist) May 9; Gary Lewis (drummer/bandleader) July 31; Barry Manilow (pianist/composer) June 17; Buddy Miles (drummer/singer) September 5; Liza Minnelli (singer) February 12; Gram Parsons (singer/writer) November 5; Dolly Parton (singer) January 19; Billy Preston (singer/writer) September 9; John Prine (folk singer/writer) October 10; Linda Ronstadt (singer) July 15; Valerie Simpson (singer) August 26; Patti Smith (singer/writer) December 30; Joel Sonnier (singer) October 2; Tammi Terrell (singer) January 24; Jimmie Webb (singer/writer) August 15.

**B. Deaths**    James Tim Brymn (composer/bandleader) October 3; Ernie Erdman (songwriter) November 1; Lew Pollack (composer/lyricist) January 18; Riley Puckett (singer/guitarist) July 13; Mamie Smith (singer) October 30; Harry Von Tilzer (songwriter/publisher) January 10; Vincent Youmans (composer) April 5; Joe Young (lyricist).

**C. Biographical**

**Performing Groups**    Ray Anthony Band; The Chordettes; Clinch Mountain Boys; The Clovers; Pete Dailey's Chicagoans; Dizzy Gillespie Band II; Maddox Brothers and Rose; Pee Wee Hunt Sextet; Jazz Workshop Ensemble (by Dave Brubeck); George Lewis Ragtime Band (?); The Orioles; Buddy Rich Big Band; Stanley Brothers; Charlie Ventura Band.

**New Beginnings** Circle Records; Clef Records (by Mercury Records—Los Angeles); Dial Records (New York); People's Songs, Inc. (New York); Fender Electric Instruments Co.; Imperial Records; MGM Records; *The Songwriter's Review: The Guiding Light to Tin Pan Alley*; Specialty Records.

**D. Publications** Rudi Blesh, *Shining Trumpets: A History of Jazz*; Hoagy Carmichael, *The Stardust Road*; D. Dexter, Jr., *Jazz Cavalcade: The Inside Story of Jazz*; Philip D. Jordan, *Singin' Yankees*; Mezz Mezzrow and B. Wolfe, *Really the Blues*.

**E. Representative Works**

**Musicals** Harold Arlen and J. Mercer, *St. Louis Woman*; Harold Rome and A. E. Horwitt, *Call Me Mister*; Irving Berlin, *Blue Skies* (film); I. Berlin and D. Fields, *Annie Get Your Gun*; Duke Ellington, *Beggar's Holiday*; Jerome Kern and Oscar Hammerstein, *Centennial Summer*; Cole Porter, *Around the World*; J. Van Heusen and J. Burke, *Nellie Bly*.

**Songs** Harold Arlen and J. Mercer, *Come Rain or Come Shine*; Hoagy Carmichael, *Ole Buttermilk Sky*; Donald Gardner, *All I Want for Christmas Is My Two Front Teeth*; Jay Livington and R. Evans, *To Each His Own*; Johnny Mercer, *On the Achison, Topeka and Santa Fe* (Oscar); Josef Myrow, *You Make Me Feel So Young*; Jule Styne and Sammy Cahn, *Five Minutes More*; Charles Tobias and Nat Simon, *The Old Lamp Lighter*; Mel Tormé, *The Christmas Song (Chestnuts Roasting on an Open Fire)*.

**Other** Leroy Anderson, *Chicken Reel*; Duke Ellington, *Deep South Suite*; Hugo Friedhofer, *The Best Years of Our Lives* (film music—Oscar); Alfred Newman, *The Razor's Edge* (film music); Miklós Rózsa, *Spellbound* (film music); Max Steiner, *Saratoga Trunk* (film music); Dimitri Tiomkin, *Duel in the Sun* (film music).

## Music—The Cultivated/Art Music Scene

**F. Births** Martin Bresnik (composer) November 13, Barry Busse (tenor) August 18; James Oliver Buswell IV (violinist) December 4; Barbara Daniels (soprano) May 7; Brent Ellis (baritone) June 20; Ruth Falcon (soprano) November 2; Carole Farley (soprano) November 29; Janice Giteck (pianist) June 27; Pamela Hebert (soprano) August 31; Christopher Keene (conductor) December 21; Ralph Kirshbaum (cellist) March 4; John Kozar (pianist) June 12; Peter Lieberson (composer) October 25; James McCalla (musicologist) August 25; Susan McClary (musicologist) October 2; Carol Neblett (soprano) February 1; Marc Neikrug (pianist/composer) September 24; Paul Barbero (composer) July 25; Robert X. Rodriguez (composer) June 28; Bruce Saylor (composer) April 24; André Watts (pianist) June 20; Larry Wendt (composer) April 5.

**G. Deaths** Clarence C. Birchard (publisher) February 27; Carrie Jacobs Bond (composer) December 28; Charles Wakefield Cadman (composer) December 30; Charles Dennée (pianist/pedagogue) April 29; Edward Dickinson (organist) January 25; Hallett Gilberté (composer) January 5; Henriot Lévy (Polish-born pianist) June 16; Georg Liebling (German-born pianist) February 7; Antonio Paoli (Puerto Rican tenor) August 24; Paul Rosenfeld (critic) July 21; Moriz Rosenthal (Austrian-born pianist) September 3; Roland F. Seitz (bandmaster/publisher) December 29; Sigismond Stojowski (Polish-born pianist/conductor) November 5; Jeannette Thurber (art patron) January 2.

**H. Debuts**

**United States** Lucine Amara (soprano—San Francisco), Gold and Fizdale (piano duo—New York), Bernard Greenhouse (cellist—New York), Ida Haendel (Polish violinist—tour), Maryla Jonas (Polish pianist—New York), Charles Munch (French conductor—Boston), Patricia Neway (soprano—Chautauqua), Italo Tajo (Italian bass—Chicago), Giuseppe Valdengo (Italian baritone—New York), Camilla Williams (soprano—New York)

**Metropolitan Opera** Joel Berglund (Swedish bass-baritone), Dezső Ernster (Hungarian bass), Louis Fourestier (French conductor), Jerome Hines (bass), Irene Jordan (soprano), Fritz Stiedry (Austrian conductor), Set Svanholm (Swedish tenor), Ramón Vinay (Chilean baritone).

## I. New Positions

**Conductors**   Werner Janssen (Utah Symphony Orchestra—to 1947); William Strickland (Nashville Symphony Orchestra—to 1951); Fritz Stiedry (Metropolitan Opera—to 1958); George Szell (Cleveland Orchestra—to 1970).

**Educational**   William Bergsma (Juilliard—to 1963); Elliott Carter (Peabody—to 1948); Mario Castelnuovo-Tedesco (Los Angeles Conservatory); Edward T. Cone (Princeton—to 1985); Josef Fuchs (Juilliard); Robert Kelly (Indiana University—to 1976); Marilyn Mason (University of Michigan); Hans Nathan (musicology, Michigan State University—to 1981); Paul Nettl (Indiana University—to 1963); Quincy Porter (Yale—to 1965); John Vincent (UCLA—to 1969); Beveridge Webster (piano, Juilliard).

**Other**   Virgil Fox (organ, Riverside Church, New York—to 1965); Paul Hume (music editor, *Washington Post*); Harold Schonberg (music critic, *New York Sun*—to 1950).

## J. Honors and Awards

**Honors**   Marc Blitzstein, Norman Dello Joio, Otto Luening, Peter Mennin, Robert Palmer, and Robert Ward (American Academy and Institute); Howard Hanson (George Peabody); Ellis Kohs (Ditson Award); Quincy Porter (PhD, Yale); William Schuman (National Institute).

**Awards**   Arnold Eidus (Long-Thibaud); Gary Graffman (Rachmaninoff); Leonid Hambro (Naumburg); Jerome Hines (Caruso).

**K. Biographical**   Those becoming American citizens include Mario Castelnuovo-Tedesco, Alexander Gretchaninov, Paul Hindemith, Christopher Isherwood, Herbert Janssen, Siegfried Landau, Nikolai Malko, Dmitri Mitropoulos, Karol Rathaus, Artur Rubinstein, Max Rudolf, George Szell, Jennie Tourel, and Paul Wittgenstein; Adele Addison receives a scholarship to Westminster Choir College; Samuel Adler enters Boston University; Hugh Aitken marries educator Laura Tapia and enters Juilliard; Chou Wen-Chung (Chinese composer) comes to the United States to study architecture but soon changes to music; Aldo Parisot (Brazilian cellist) comes to United States, studies at Yale; Max Rosen retires from public performance and teaches; Arnold Schoenberg experiences a heart attack; Yma Sumac (Peruvian contralto/soprano) arrives in New York; Francis Thorne spends eight years in business and banking.

## L. Musical Beginnings

**Performing Groups**   Anchorage Symphony Orchestra (Alaska); Bach Aria Group (New York); Detroit Concert Band; Fine Arts Quartet (Chicago); Fort Worth Civic Opera Association; Houston Youth Symphony Orchestra; Juilliard String Quartet; Mobile Opera Guild (Alabama); Nashville Symphony Orchestra III; New England Opera Theater (Goldovsky Opera Institute, 1963); Portland (Oregon) Symphonic Choir; Texas Boys Choir (Fort Worth); Utah Symphony Orchestra (renamed Utah State Symphony Orchestra); Roger Wagner Chorale (Los Angeles).

**Festivals**   Caramoor Festival (Katonah, New York).

**Educational**   American String Teachers Association (Athens, Georgia); Juilliard School of Music (merger, Institute of Musical Art and Juilliard Graduate School).

**Other**   *The Instrumentalist*; *Journal of Renaissance and Baroque Music (Musica disciplina)*; G. Leblanc Corporation (Kenosha, Wisconsin); Hal Leonard Music Inc. (Winona, Minnesota).

## M. Music Publications

Apel, W. and Davison, A., *Historical Anthology of Music*
Babbitt, Milton, *The Function of Set Structure in the Twelve Tone System*
Davison, Archibald, *The Technique of Choral Composition*
Goldman, Richard F., *The Concert Band*
Graf, Max, *Modern Music—Composer and Critic*
Hindemith, Paul, *Elementary Training for Musicians*
Leichtentritt, Hugo, *Serge Koussevitzky, the Boston Symphony Orchestra and New American Music*
Rosenfeld, Paul, *On Music and Musicians*
Sachs, Curt, *The Commonwealth of Art*

**N. Musical Compositions**

**Chamber Music**   George Antheil, *String Quartet No. 3*; David Diamond, *String Quartet No. 3*; Irving Fine, *Violin Sonata*; Miriam Gideon, *String Quartet*; Andrew Imbrie, *Piano Trio*; Burrill Phillips, *Cello Sonata*; Quincy Porter, *Sonata for Horn and Piano*; Arnold Schoenberg, *String Trio, Opus 45*; Ralph Shapey, *String Quartet No. 1*; Halsey Stevens, *Piano Quartet*; Ernst Toch, *String Quartet No. 12, Opus 70*; George Walker, *String Quartet*; Ben Weber, *String Trio No. 2*.

**Choral/Vocal**   Marc Blitzstein, *Symphony: The Airborne*; Herbert Elwell, *Lincoln: Requiem Aeternam* (Paderewski Prize); Arthur Farwell, *Two Indian Choruses, Opus 111*; Ross Lee Finney, *Poor Richard* (song cycle); Lukas Foss, *Song of Songs*; Lou Harrison, *Easter Cantata*; Paul Hindemith, *When Lilacs Last in the Dooryard Bloom'd*; Felix Labunski, *Songs without Words* (soprano and strings); George Rochberg, *Songs of Solomon*; Hugo Weisgall, *Soldier Songs* (song cycle).

**Concertos**   George Antheil, *Violin Concerto*; Seth Bingham, *Organ Concerto*; Cecil Effinger, *Piano Concerto*; Irving Fine, *Violin Concerto*; Roy Harris, *Concerto for Two Pianos*; Erich Korngold, *Cello Concerto in C Major, Opus 37*; Ernst Krenek, *Piano Concerto No. 3*; Joaquin Nin-Culmell, *Piano Concerto*; Arthur Shepherd, *Violin Concerto*; Ben Weber, *Sinfonia for Cello and Orchestra*.

**Operas**   Alexander Gretchaninov, *The Marriage*; Gian Carlo Menotti, *The Telephone*.

**Orchestra/Band**   Ernst Bacon, *Ford's Theater*; Samuel Barber, *Medea* (ballet); Robert Russell Bennett, *Overture to an Imaginary Drama*; Leonard Bernstein, *Facsimile* (ballet); Marc Blitzstein, *Show* (ballet); Arthur Farwell, *The Heroic Breed, Opus 115*; Alexander Gretchaninov, *Festival Overture, Opus 178*; Ulysses Kay, *A Short Overture*; Burrill Phillips, *Tom Paine Overture*; Gardner Read, *Bell Overture, Opus 72*; Bernard Rogers, *Amphitryon Overture*; Arthur Shepherd, *Fantasy Overture on Down East Spirituals*; Leo Smit, *Yerma* (ballet); William Grant Still, *Suite, Archaic Ritual*; Igor Stravinsky, *Concerto in D* (strings).

**Piano/Organ**   Jack Beeson, *Sonata No. 5*; Arthur Berger, *Three Bagatelles*; Elliott Carter, *Sonata*; Norman Dello Joio, *Two Nocturnes*; Lejaren Hiller, *Sonata No. 1*; Frederick Jacobi, *Introduction and Toccata*; Charles Jones, *Sonata No. 1*; Tibor Serly, *Sonata in Modus Lascivus*; Roger Sessions, *Sonata No. 2*; Ralph Shapey, *Sonata No. 1*; Ernst Toch, *Profiles*; Joseph F. Wagner, *Sonata*; Jaromir Weinberger, *Six Religious Preludes* (organ).

**Symphonies**   Jacob Avshalomov, *Sinfonietta* (Naumburg Recording Award); Robert Russell Bennett, *Symphony*; Thomas Beversdorf, *Symphony No. 1*; Philip Bezanson, *Symphony No. 1*; Aaron Copland, *Symphony No. 3*; Henry Cowell, *Symphony No. 4, "Short Symphony"*; Cecil Effinger, *Symphony No. 2*; Louis Gruenberg, *Symphony No. 4, Opus 50*; Paul Hindemith, *Symphonia Serena*; George Kleinsinger, *Symphony No. 1*; Peter Jona Korn, *Symphony No. 1*; Arthur Kreutz, *Symphony No. 2*; Bohuslav Martinů, *Symphony No. 5*; Peter Mennin, *Symphony No. 3*; Darius Milhaud, *Symphony No. 3, Opus 271 (Te Deum)*; Harold C. Morris, *Symphony No. 3, "Amaranth"*; Vincent Persichetti, *Symphony No. 3, Opus 30*; William Schuman, *Symphony No. 6*; Roger Sessions, *Symphony No. 2* (New York Music Critics' Award); Halsey Stevens, *Symphony No. 3*; Bernard Wagenaar, *Symphony No. 4*.

# 1947

❄

## Historical Highlights

The Truman Doctrine seeks to keep the Americas free of Communist influence; Congress passes the Taft-Hartley Law limiting union power and the Marshall Plan to help developing countries; the Central Intelligence Agency (CIA) is formed; the United States Air Force becomes a separate entity; the Dead Sea Scrolls are discovered; Thor Heyerdahl sails his raft, *Kon-Tiki*, from South America to Polynesia.

## World Cultural Highlights

**World Art**   Max Ackermann, *Cheerfulness on White;* Max Bill, *Continuity;* Alberto Giacometti, *The Pointing Man*; Frida Kahlo, *Self-Portrait, Loose Hair;* Walter Sickert, *Ennui*.

**World Literature**   Jean Anouilh, *Ring Round the Moon*; Anne Frank, *The Diary of Anne Frank*; Jean Genet, *The Maids*; Malcolm Lowry, *Under the Volcano*; Thomas Mann, *Dr. Faustus*.

**World Music**   Benjamin Britten, *Albert Herring*; Hans Werner Henze, *Symphony No. 1*; Arthur Honegger, *Symphony No. 4, "Deliciae Basilienses"*; Ralph Vaughan Williams, *Symphony No. 6*.

**Miscellaneous**   The Edinburgh Music Festivals begin; the Osaka Symphony Orchestra (Japan), Queensland Symphony Orchestra (Brisbane), and Winnipeg Symphony Orchestra are founded; deaths include Tristan Bernard, Pierre Bonnard, Alfredo Casella, George Kolbe, and Willem Pijper.

## American Art and Literature Highlights

**Births/Deaths**   Births include literary figures Ann Beattie, Tom Clancy, Mark Helprin, David Alan Mamet, Douglas Messerli, Gregory Orr, Sara Paretsky, and Bob Perelman; deaths include sculptors Henry Kitson, Hermon MacNeil, and literary figures Louis K. Anspacher, Henry W. Boynton, Willa Cather, Hugh Lofting, Charles B. Nordhoff, and Jim Tully.

**Art Works**   William Baziotes, *The Dwarf*; Philip Evergood, *Flight of Fancy*; Arshile Gorky, *Agony*; Stanley Hayter, *Falling Figure*; Frederick Kiesler, *Totem of Religions*; Jack Levine, *Apteka*; Jackson Pollock, *Full Fathom Five*; Theodore Roszak, *The Spectre of Kitty Hawk*; Theodore Stamos, *Impulse of Remembrance*; Andrew Wyeth, *Dodges Ridge*.

**Literature**   W. H. Auden, *The Age of Anxiety* (Pulitzer Prize); Saul Bellow, *The Victim*; Sinclair Lewis, *Kingsblood Royal*; James Michener, *Tales of the South Pacific* (Pulitzer Prize); Arthur Miller, *All My Sons* (New York Drama Critics' Award); Sterling North, *So Dear to My Heart*; Tennessee Williams, *A Streetcar Named Desire* (Pulitzer Prize — New York Drama Critics' Award).

## Music — The Vernacular/Commercial Scene

**A. Births**   John Anderson (singer) December 13; Lynn Anderson (singer) September 26; Jerry Bergonzi (saxophonist); Shirley Brown (singer) January 6; Tim Buckley (singer/guitarist) February 14; Buckwheat Zydeco (singer) November 14; Jessi Colter (singer) May 25; Ry Cooder (singer/guitarist) March 15; Marilyn Crispell (piano) March 30; Kiki Dee (singer) March 6; Ruth Derringer (singer/guitarist) August 5; Arlo Guthrie (singer/writer) July 10; Sammy Hagar (singer/writer) October 13; Emmylou Harris (singer) April 12; John Hartford (singer) December 30; Don Henley (singer/writer) July 22; Tommy James (singer/guitarist) April 29; Melanie (Salfa — singer/guitarist) February 3; Barry Miles (drummer/pianist) March 28; Anne Murray (singer) June 20; Laura Nyro (singer/writer) October 18; Iggy Pop (singer) April 21; Mike Reid (composer) May 24; Minnie Riperton (singer) November 8; Carole Sager (singer); Carlos Santana (composer/bandleader); Bob Seger (singer/writer); Loudon Wainwright III (singer/writer) September 5; Joe Walsh (guitarist/singer) November 20; Jennifer Warnes (singer/writer) March 3; Warren Zevon (singer/writer) January 24.

**B. Deaths**   Thurland Chattaway (composer/lyricist) November 12; Walter Donaldson (composer/lyricist) July 15; Bert Kalmar (lyricist) September 18; Jimmie Lunceford (bandleader) July 12; Fate Marable (pianist/bandleader) January 16; Eva Tanguay (singer/dancer).

**C. Biographical**

**Performing Groups**   Cat Anderson Jazz Band; Pee Wee Crayton Trio; Experiment in Jazz (by Bill Russo); Benny Goodman Sextet; Skitch Henderson Dance Band; Woody Herman's Second Herd; Piccadilly Boys (Tito Puente's orchestra).

**New Beginnings**   Aristocrat Records (Chess in 1950); Atlantic Records; Audiophile Record Co.; *Country Song Roundup*; Dave Dreyer, Publisher, *Esquire's Jazz Book*; Folkways Records; Imperial Records; Kramer-Whitney Co.; Mercury Records; Ozark Folk Festival (Eureka Springs, Arkansas).

**Miscellaneous**   Billie Holiday is jailed on drug charges; Edith Piaf (French singer) tours the

United States; George Shearing (British jazz pianist) emigrates to the United States.

**D. Publications**  Theodor Adorno, *Composing for the Films*; G. Beall, *Frontiers of Jazz*; E. Condon and T. Sugrue, *We Called It Music: A Generation of Jazz*; N. Lloyd, *The Fireside Book of Favorite American Songs*; A. and J. A. Lomax, *Folk Song: USA*.

**E. Representative Works**

**Musicals**  Burton Lane and E. Y. Harburg, *Finian's Rainbow*; Lerner and Loewe, *Brigadoon* (New York Drama Critics' Award); Rodgers and Hammerstein, *Allegro*; Jule Styne and Sammy Cahn, *High Button Shoes*; K. Weill and L. Hughes, *Street Scene*.

**Songs**  Mack David, Al Hoffman, and Jerry Livingston, *Chi-Baba, Chi-Baba*; E. Goulding and M. Gordon, *Mam'selle*; Joe Greene, *Across the Alley from the Alamo*; Louise Massey and Lee Penny, *My Adobe Hacienda*; Jack McVea and Dan Howell, *Open the Door, Richard*; Carl Sigman and Bob Hilliard, *Bongo, Bongo, Bongo (I Don't Want to Leave the Congo)*; Jule Styne, *Time after Time*; Merle Travis, *Sixteen Tons*; Merle Travis and Tex Williams, *Smoke! Smoke! Smoke! (That Cigarette)*.

**Other**  Leroy Anderson, *Fiddle Faddle—Irish Suite*; Duke Ellington, *Liberian Suite*; Hugo Friedhofer, *A Star Is Born* (film music); Jimmy Giuffre, *Four Brothers* (for Woody Herman); Alfred Newman, *The Captain from Castile* (film music).

## Music—The Cultivated/Art Music Scene

**F. Births**  John Adams (composer) February 15; Laurie Anderson (composer/performer) March 1; Margarita Castro-Alberty (Puerto Rican soprano) October; Dale Duesing (baritone) September 26; Peter Gena (pianist/composer) April 27; Donald Grantham (composer) November 9; Sheri Greenawald (soprano) November 12; Irene Gubrud (soprano) January 4; D. Kern Holoman (musicologist/conductor) September 8; Young-Uck Kim (violinist) September 1; David Kuebler (tenor) July 23; Joan La Barbara (composer/performer) June 8; James Morris (bass-baritone) January 10; David Ott (composer) July 5; Christopher Parkening (guitarist) December 14; Lucy Peacock (soprano) June 21; Murray Perahia (pianist) April 19; Janet Perry (soprano) December 27; Neil Burton Rolnick (composer) October 22; David Rosenboom (composer/performer) September 9; Neil Rosensheim (tenor) November 27; Gerard Schwarz (conductor) August 19; Peter Serkin (pianist) July 24; Craig Smith (conductor) January 31; Carl Topilow (conductor) March 14.

**G. Deaths**  Lilian E. Blauvelt (soprano) August 29; Fannie Dillon (pianist/composer) February 21; Charles Farnsworth (music educator) May 22; William Foden (guitarist/composer) April 9; Felix Fox (German-born pianist) March 24; William Wade Hinshaw (baritone) November 27; Louise Homer (contralto) May 6; Karl Jörn (Latvian-born tenor) December 19; Grace Moore (soprano) January 26; Carl Adolph Preyer (German-born pianist) November 16; Corinne Rider-Kelsey (soprano) July 10; Harry R. Shelley (organist) September 12.

**H. Debuts**

**United States**  Eileen Farrell (soprano—tour), Ellen Faull (soprano—New York), Samson François (French pianist—New York), Claude Frank (German pianist—New York), Orazio Frugoni (Italian pianist—New York), Gary Graffman (pianist—Philadelphia), Helen Kwalwasser (violinist—New York), Beverly Sills (soprano—Philadelphia), Norman Treigle (bass—New Orleans), Alexis Weissenberg (Bulgarian pianist—New York).

**Metropolitan Opera**  Cloe Elmo (Italian mezzo-soprano), Daniza Ilitsch (Serbian soprano), Mihály Székely (Hungarian bass), Ferruccio Tagliavini (Italian tenor), Pia Tassinari (Italian soprano), Giuseppe Valdengo (Italian baritone).

**I. New Positions**

**Conductors**  Maurice Abravanel (Utah Symphony Orchestra—to 1979); John Barnett (Phoenix Symphony Orchestra—to 1949); H. Arthur Brown (Tulsa Philharmonic Orchestra—to 1958); Werner Janssen (Portland [Oregon] Symphony Orchestra—to 1949); Thor Johnson (Cincinnati Symphony Orchestra—to 1967); Erich Leinsdorf (Rochester Symphony Orchestra—to 1955); Fritz

Mahler (Erie Symphony Orchestra—to 1953); Moshe Paranov (Hartford Symphony Orchestra—to 1953); Artur Rodzinski (Chicago Symphony Orchestra—to 1948); David Van Vactor (Knoxville Symphony Orchestra—to 1972); Bruno Walter (New York Philharmonic Orchestra—to 1949).

**Educational**  Wilfred Conwell Bain (dean, School of Music, Indiana University—to 1973); Henry Brant (Juilliard—to 1954); Anthony Donato (Northwestern University—to 1976); Elliot Forbes (Princeton—to 1958); Richard Franko Goldman (Juilliard—to 1960); Leo Kraft (Queens College—to 1989); Peter Mennin (composition, Juilliard—to 1958); Egon Petri (Mills College—to 1957); Leonard Rose (Juilliard); David Van Vactor (University of Tennessee).

**Other**  Abram Chasins (music director, WQXR, New York); Donal Henahan (critic, *Chicago Daily News*—to 1967); Irving Kolodin (music critic, *Saturday Review*—to 1982); Winthrop Sargeant (music critic, *New Yorker*).

**J. Honors and Awards**

**Honors**  Louis Gruenberg, Paul Hindemith, and Bernard Rogers (National Institute); Alexei Haieff, Ulysses Kay, and Normand Lockwood (American Academy and Institute); Serge Koussevitzky (LL.D, Princeton); Arnold Schoenberg (American Academy); Virgil Thomson (French Legion of Honor).

**Awards**  John Alden Carpenter (American Academy Gold Medal); Andrew Imbrie (Rome Prize); Berl Senofsky (Naumburg); Alexis Weissenberg (Leventritt).

**K. Biographical**  Laurindo Almeida (Brazilian guitarist), Aaron Avshalomov (Russian composer), Paul Doktor (Austrian pianist), Wolfgang Fraenkel (German composer), Richard Hoffmann (Austrian musicologist), and K. B. Jirák (Czech conductor) come to the United States; Hermann Berlinski, Antal Dorati, Vladimir Golschmann, Edward Lowinsky, and Lauritz Melchior become American citizens; Sarah Caldwell becomes assistant to Boris Goldovsky at the New England Conservatory Opera; Aaron Copland again visits Latin America for the State Department; Serge Koussevitzky marries his second wife, Olga Naumoff; Ernst Krenek decides to try his luck in Los Angeles; Louis Lane begins working with Szell in Cleveland; Robert Starer (Austrian composer) enters Juilliard.

**L. Musical Beginnings**

**Performing Groups**  Amateur Chamber Music Players of Indianapolis; Anchorage Community Chorus (Alaska); Detroit Women's Symphony; Hollywood String Quartet; Houston Symphony Chorale; Little Orchestra Society of New York; Memphis Symphony Orchestra II; New Music Quartet (New York); Phoenix Symphony Orchestra; Singing City (Philadelphia choral group); Springfield Young People's Symphony Orchestra (Massachusetts); Tulsa Philharmonic Orchestra.

**Festivals**  Los Angeles Music Festival; Ojai Music Festival (California).

**Educational**  Music Academy of the West (Santa Barbara, California); Stanford University Music Department; Waring Music Workshop.

**Other**  Midwest National Band and Orchestra Clinic (Chicago); Shawnee Press (formerly Words and Music); Hans Weisshaar, violin maker and restorer (Hollywood); Wurlitzer Electronic Organ.

**N. Music Publications**

Bukofzer, Manfred, *Music in the Baroque Era*
Dorian, Frederick, *The Musical Workshop*
Einstein, Alfred, *Music in the Romantic Era*
Ferguson, Donald, *Piano Music of Six Great Composers*
Graf, Max, *From Beethoven to Shostakovich*
McHose, Allen, *Contrapuntal Harmonic Technique of the 18th Century*
Nettl, Paul, *The Story of Dance Music*
Piston, Walter, *Counterpoint*
Seashore, Carl E., *In Search of Beauty in Music: A Scientific Approach to Musical Esthetics*
Slonimsky, Nicolas, *Thesaurus of Scales and Melodic Patterns*

**N. Musical Compositions**

**Chamber Music**  John W. Duke, *String Quartet No. 2*; Ross Lee Finney, *String Quartet No. 4*;

William Flanagan, *Divertimento for String Quartet*; Lukas Foss, *String Quartet No. 1 in G*; Bohuslav Martinů, *Concerto da Camera (String Quartet No. 7)*; Walter Piston, *String Quartet No. 3*; Quincy Porter, *String Sextet on Slavic Folk Songs*; Wallingford Riegger, *String Quartet No. 2*; Ned Rorem, *String Quartet No. 1* (withdrawn); Ralph Shapey, *Piano Quintet*; Robert Starer, *String Quartet*; Adolph A. Weiss, *Sextet for Piano and Winds*.

**Choral/Vocal**    Ernst Bacon, *From Emily's Diary (Dickinson)*; Samuel Barber, *Knoxville: Summer of 1915, Opus 24*; Nicolai Berezowsky, *Gilgamesh* (cantata); Nicolas Nabokov, *The Return of Pushkin*; Arnold Schoenberg, *A Survivor from Warsaw, Opus 46*; Edgard Varèse, *Etude pour Espace*.

**Concertos**    David Diamond, *Violin Concerto No. 2*; Paul Hindemith, *Clarinet Concerto*; Ellis Kohs, *Cello Concerto*; William Schuman, *Violin Concerto;* Robert Starer, *Piano Concerto No. 1*; John Verrall, *Violin Concerto*.

**Operas**    Harry L. Freeman, *Allah*; Burrill Phillips, *Don't We All*; Roger Sessions, *The Trial of Lucullus*; Virgil Thomson, *The Mother of Us All*.

**Orchestra/Band**    George Antheil, *Autumn Song*; William Bergsma, *The Fortunate Islands*; John Cage, *The Seasons Ballet*; David Diamond, *Romeo and Juliet* (incidental music); Alvin Etler, *Passacaglia and Fugue for Orchestra*; Irving Fine, *Toccata Concertante*; Morton Gould, *Fall River Legend* (ballet); Lou Harrison, *Suite No. 1 for Strings*; Felix Labunski, *Variations for Orchestra*; Douglas Moore, *Farm Journal*; Robert Palmer, *Variations, Chorale and Fugue*; Gardner Read, *Pennsylvaniana Suite, Opus 67*; Leroy Robertson, *Trilogy*; Carl Ruggles, *Organum*; William Schuman, *Night Journey* (ballet); Leo Smit, *Virginia Sampler* (ballet); William Grant Still, *Wood Notes*; Igor Stravinsky, *Orpheus* (ballet); Hugo Weisgall, *Outpost* (ballet).

**Piano/Organ**    Hugh Aitken, *Sonatina*; Milton Babbitt, *Three Compositions*; Paul Bowles, *Sonata for Two Pianos*; David Diamond, *Sonata No. 1*; Ross Lee Finney, *Nostalgic Waltzes*; Lejaren Hiller, *Sonata No. 2*; Andrew Imbrie, *Sonata*; Charles Jones, *Sonata for Two Pianos*; Leon Kirchner, *Variations on "L'homme armé";* Gail Kubik, *Sonata*; Robert Moevs, *Sonatina*; Harold Shapero, *Variations in C Minor*; Leo Smit, *Five Pieces for Young People*; Stefan Wolpe, *Battle Piece*.

**Symphonies**    Henry Brant, *Symphony, The Promised Land*; Vernon Duke, *Symphony No. 3*; Cecil Effinger, *Symphony No. 1*; Don Gillis, *Symphony No. 5¹/₂*; Morton Gould, *Symphony No. 3*; Ernst Krenek, *Symphony No. 4*; Solomon Pimsleur, *Symphony of Terror and Despair*; Walter Piston, *Symphony No. 3* (Pulitzer Prize); Wallingford Riegger, *Symphony No. 3* (Pulitzer Prize—New York Music Critics' Award); Harold Shapero, *Symphony for Classical Orchestra*; Elie Siegmeister, *Symphony No. 1*; Leo Sowerby, *Symphony No. 4*; Gerald Strang, *Symphony No. 2*; Max Wald, *Symphony in F Major*; Robert Ward, *Symphony No. 2*; Karl Weigl, *Symphony No. 6 in A Minor*.

# 1948

❀

## Historical Highlights

Harry S. Truman scores an unexpected defeat over Thomas Dewey for his first full term as president; the Organization of American States (OAS) is formed; the first 200-inch telescope is installed at Mount Palomar; the electric transistor is unveiled by Bell Laboratories; the Berlin Airlift begins when Russian troops blockade all ground routes into the city; Israel is proclaimed a Jewish state with David Ben-Gurion as first Prime Minister; Mahatma Gandhi is assassinated in India.

## World Cultural Highlights

**World Art**    Fernand Léger, *Hommage à David*; Giacomo Manzù, *Cardinal;* Henri Matisse, *Large Interior in Red*.

**World Literature**    Christopher Fry, *The Lady's not for Burning*; Alan Paton, *Cry, the Beloved Country*; Jean-Paul Sartre, *Les Mains Sales*; Evelyn Waugh, *The Loved One*.

**World Music**   Pierre Boulez, *Les Soleil des Eaux*; Luigi Dallapiccola, *Il Prigioniero*; Hans Werner Henze, *Symphony No. 2—Whispers from Heavenly Death*; Olivier Messiaen, *Turangalila Symphony*.

**Miscellaneous**   The Aldeburgh Festival, Ansbach Bach Festival, and Bath Festival begin in England; births include Mikhail Baryshnikov and Eva Marton; deaths include Georges Bernanos, Franz Lehár, and Karl Schwitters.

## American Art and Literature Highlights

**Births/Deaths**   Births include artists Eric Fischl, Lois Lane, and literary figures Kathy Acker, John Calvin Batchelor, T. Coraghessan Boyle, Albert Goldbarth, Charles R. Johnson, and Heather McHugh; deaths include art figures George Ault, Arshile Gorky, Florine Stettheimer, and literary figures Gertrude Atherton, Eusebio Chacón, Susan Glaspell, Will Irwin, Louis V. Ledoux, and Genevieve Taggard.

**Art Works**   Peter Blume, *The Rock*; Herbert Ferber, *Labors of Hercules*; Morris Graves, *Han Bronze with Moon No. 1*; George Grosz, *Waving the Flag*; Edward Hopper, *Seven O'Clock*; Karl Knaths, *Indian Blanket*; Jacob Lawrence, *Series: In the Heart of the Black Belt*; Jacques Lipchitz, *The Sacrifice*; Man Ray, *As You Like It*; Barnett Newman, *Onement I*; Andrew Wyeth, *Christina's World*.

**Literature**   Maxwell Anderson, *Anne of the Thousand Days*; Truman Capote, *Other Voices, Other Rooms*; James G. Cozzens, *Guard of Honor* (Pulitzer Prize); William Faulkner, *Intruder in the Dust*; Ruth Herschberger, *Adam's Rib*; Norman Mailer, *The Naked and the Dead*; Peter Viereck, *Terror and Decorum* (Tietjens Prize—Pulitzer Prize); Tennessee Williams, *Summer and Smoke*.

## Music—The Vernacular/Commercial Scene

**A. Births**   Patti Austin (singer) August 10; Rubén Blades (singer/writer) July 16; Jackson Browne (singer/writer) October 9; T-Bone Burnett (singer/writer) January 14 (?); Larry Carlton (guitarist) March 2; Richie Cole (saxophonist/composer) February 29; Lacy J. Dalton (singer) October 13; Paul Davis (singer) April 21; Joe Ely (guitarist) February 9; Leon Everette (singer) June 21; Jesse Frederick (composer) June 25; Vincent Furnier (Alice Cooper—rock performer) February 4; Larry Gatlin (singer/writer) May 2; Steve Goodman (singer/writer) July 25; Daryl Hohl (Hall and Oates) October 11; Michael Kamen (composer/arranger); Kenny Loggins (singer/writer) January 7; Elliot Lurie (singer/writer) August 19; Barbara Mandrell (singer) December 25; Meatloaf (Marvin Aday—singer) September 27; Hugh Moffatt (trumpeter) November 10; Gary Morris (singer) December 7; Willie Nile (singer/writer) June 7; Ted Nugent (guitarist) December 11; Jeffrey Osborne (drummer/singer) March 9; Todd Rundgren (singer/writer) June 22; Stephen Schwartz (composer/lyricist) March 6; Tom Scott (saxophonist) May 19; Dan Seals (singer) February 8; Donna Summer (singer) December 31; James Taylor (singer/writer) March 12.

**B. Deaths**   J. Keirn Brennan (lyricist) February 4; Vernon Dalhart (singer) September 14; John Avery Lomax (folk singer) January 26; Red McKenzie (bandleader) February 7; Kerry Mills (composer/publisher) December 5; Paul Pratt (pianist/composer) July 7; John "Sonny Boy" Williamson (singer) June 1.

**C. Biographical**

**Performing Groups**   The Crows; The Foggy Mountain Boys; The Four Freshmen; Jordanaires; Perez Prado Mambo Band; The Weavers.

**New Beginnings**   Discovery Records (New York); Dixieland Jubilee (Los Angeles—to 1960); Fender Broadcaster (Telecaster) Guitar; Folkways Records; New Orleans Jazz Club; Ed Sullivan TV Show (Toast of the Town).

**D. Publications**   S. W. Finkelstein, *Jazz: a People's Music*; Burl Ives, *Wayfaring Stranger*; J. J. Niles, *Anglo-American Carol Study Book*; Ruth Crawford Seeger, *American Folk Songs for Children*; Sigmund Spaeth, *A History of Popular Music in America*.

**E. Representative Works**

**Musicals**   Irving Berlin, *Easter Parade* (film); R. Blane and H. Warren, *Summer Holiday* (film);

Charles Gaynor, *Lend an Ear*; J. P. Johnson, *Sugar Hill*; R. Lewine and A. Horwitt, *Make Mine Manhattan*; Frank Loesser, *Where's Charley*; J. McHugh and H. Adamson, *As the Girls Go*; Cole Porter, *The Pirate* (film); C. Porter and B. and S. Spewack, *Kiss Me, Kate*; Arthur Schwartz and Howard Dietz, *Inside USA*; Kurt Weill, *Down In the Valley*.

**Songs**   Harold Arlen and Leo Robin, *Hooray for Love*; David Barbour and Peggy Lee, *Mañana*; Roy Brodsky, *Red Roses for a Blue Lady*; Alex Kramer and J. Whitney, *Far-Away Places (with the Strange-Sounding Names)*; Jay Livingston and R. Evans, *Buttons and Bows* (Oscar); Frank Loesser, *Baby, It's Cold Outside—I'd Love to Get You on a Slow Boat to China*; Jimmy McHugh and H. Adamson, *It's a Most Unusual Day*; Redd Stewart and Pee Wee King, *Tennessee Waltz*; George Tibbles and R. Idriss, *The Woody Woodpecker Song*.

**Other**   Duke Ellington, *The Tattooed Bride* (jazz suite); Hugo Friedhofer, *Joan of Arc* (film music); Thelonious Monk, *Misterioso*; Alfred Newman, *Yellow Sky* (film music); Miklós Rózsa, *A Double Life* (film music—Oscar); Max Steiner, *Key Largo* (film music).

## Music—The Cultivated/Art Music Scene

**F. Births**   Jeannine Altmeyer (soprano) May 2; Carmen Balthrop (soprano) May 14; Kathleen Battle (soprano) August 13; Chester Biscardi (composer) October 19; Brenda Boozer (mezzo-soprano) January 25; Frederick Burchinal (baritone) December 7; John Cheek (baritone) August 17; Deborah Cook (soprano) July 6; Conrad Cummings (composer) February 10; Clamma Dale (soprano) July 4; Paul Demarinis (composer) October 6; James Fields (pianist) November 1; C. William Harwood (conductor) March 14; Daniel Heifetz (violinist) November 20; Barbara Hendricks (soprano) November 20; Ani Kavafian (violinist) May 10; Gilbert Levine (conductor) January 22; Catherine Malfitano (soprano) April 18; Leona Mitchell (soprano) October 13; Garrick Ohlsson (pianist) April 3; Joseph Paratore (pianist) March 19; Nathaniel Rosen (cellist) June 9; Fred Sherry (cellist/conductor) October 27; Robert Vodnoy (conductor) April 16; Sandra Walker (mezzo-soprano) October 1; Dan Welcher (composer) March 2.

**G. Deaths**   Isidor Achron (Polish-born pianist/composer) May 12; John Turnell Austin (British-born organist) September 17; Franz Bornschein (composer) June 8; George Boyle (Australian-born pianist/composer) June 20; William Arms Fisher (editor/publisher) December 18; Ferruccio Giannini (Italian-born tenor) September 17; Jacques Gordon (Ukranian-born violinist) September 15; Clara Damrosch Mannes (pianist/educator) April 25; Olga Samaroff (pianist/educator) May 17; Henry Dike Sleeper (organist) January 28; Oley Speaks (composer/baritone) August 27; George Templeton Strong (composer/artist) June 27; Rudolph Henry Wurlitzer (violin maker) May 27.

**H. Debuts**

**United States**   Adele Addison (soprano—Boston), Frances Bible (mezzo-soprano—New York), Paul Doktor (Austrian violist—Washington, DC), Kathleen Ferrier (British contralto—New York), Tito Gobbi (Italian baritone—San Francisco), Nicole Henriot (French pianist—New York), Lilian Kallir (Czech pianist—New York), Anton Kuerti (Austrian pianist—Cleveland), Seymour Lipkin (as conductor, Cleveland), Moura Lympany (British pianist), Alan Mandel (pianist—New York), Frederick Marvin (pianist—New York), Marko Rothmüller (Yugoslavian baritone—New York), Aksel Schiotz (Swedish tenor/baritone), Giorgio Tozzi (bass—New York).

**Metropolitan Opera**   Frank Guarrera (baritone), Jean Madeira (mezzo-soprano), Giuseppe di Stefano (Italian tenor), Italo Tajo (Italian bass).

**I. New Positions**

**Conductors**   Antonia Brico (Antonia Brico Symphony Orchestra); Igor Buketoff (Fort Wayne Philharmonic Orchestra—to 1966); Efrem Kurtz (Houston Symphony Orchestra—to 1954); Bennett Lipkin (Birmingham Symphony Orchestra—to 1960); Fritz Reiner (Metropolitan Opera—to 1953); Hans Schwieger (Kansas City Philharmonic Orchestra—to 1971).

**Educational**   Milton Babbitt (Princeton, second time); Bohuslav Martinů (Princeton); Gardner Read (Boston University School for the Arts—to 1978); Leroy Robertson (music chair, University of Utah—to 1963); George Rochberg (Curtis—to 1954); Boris Schwarz (music chair, Queens—to 1955); Randall Thompson (Harvard—to 1965); Abraham Veinus (Syracuse University); John Verrall (University of Washington—to 1973).

**Other**  Peggy Glanville-Hicks (music critic, *New York Herald Tribune*); Harold Schonberg (music critic, *Musical Courier*—to 1952); Cecil Smith (editor, *Musical America*—to 1951).

**J. Honors and Awards**

**Honors**  Lou Harrison and Vincent Persichetti (American Academy and Institute); Dean Dixon (Alice M. Ditson); Erich Itor Kahn (Coolidge); Virgil Thomson (National Institute).

**Awards**  Sidney Harth and Theodore Lettvin (Naumburg); Seymour Lipkin (Rachmaninoff).

**K. Biographical**  Irwin Bazelon makes New York his headquarters; Paul Dessau decides to return to Germany; Andor Foldes and Peggy Glanville-Hicks become American citizens; Jaime Laredo's family leaves Bolivia for the United States; Janos Starker (Hungarian cellist) settles in the United States and becomes principal cellist of the Dallas Symphony Orchestra; Alexander Tcherepnin comes to the United States on concert tour and is invited to teach at DePaul University in Chicago; Werner Torkanowsky (German conductor/violinist) comes to the United States; Friedrich Von Huene (Polish recorder/flute maker) emigrates to the United States

**L. Musical Beginnings**

**Performing Groups**  Amato Opera Theater (New York); Denver Philharmonic Orchestra (Businessman's Symphony Orchestra); Desert Singing Guild (Masterworks Chorale—Tucson); National Opera Association (Grass Roots Opera—Raleigh, North Carolina); New Orchestra of Los Angeles; New York Brass Ensemble; Robert Shaw Chorale; Tulsa Opera Club (Tulsa Opera, Inc.).

**Educational**  *Journal of the American Musicological Society.*

**Other**  Boelke-BoMart (Music Publishers, New York); Columbia Long-playing Record; K. G. Gemeinhardt Co. (Elkhart, Indiana); Louisville Orchestra Commissioning Project; National Baptist Music Convention; C. F. Peters, Music Publisher (New York); Society for Forgotten Music; *Symphony Magazine.*

**M. Music Publications**

Barlow, Harold, *A Dictionary of Musical Terms*
Cazden, Norman, *Musical Consonance and Dissonance*
Drinker, Sophie, *Music and Women*
Hindemith, Paul, *A Concentrated Course in Traditional Harmony II*
Howard, John Tasker, *The World's Great Operas*
Kanitz, Ernest, *A Counterpoint Manual: Fundamental Techniques of Polyphonic Music Writing*
Sachs, Curt, *Our Musical Heritage*
Schoenberg, Arnold, *Structural Functions of Harmony—Fundamentals of Musical Composition*
Thomson, Virgil, *The Art of Judging Music*
Toch, Ernst, *The Shaping Forces in Music*

**N. Musical Compositions**

**Chamber Music**  Hugh Aitken, *Short Suite* (wind quintet); Samuel Adler, *Violin Sonata No. 1*; Milton Babbitt, *Composition for Four Instruments* (New York Music Critics' Award)—*String Quartet No. 1*; Philip Bezanson, *String Quartet No. 1*; Elliott Carter, *Cello Sonata—Woodwind Quintet*; Jacob Druckman, *String Quartet No. 1*; Cecil Effinger, *String Quartet No. 4*; Irving Fine, *Partita for Wind Quintet* (New York Music Critics' Award); Karel Husa, *String Quartet No. 1*; Ellis Kohs, *String Quartet No. 2, "A Short Concert"*; Nikolai Lopatnikoff, *Violin Sonata No. 2*; Robert Parris, *String Quartet No. 1*; Wallingford Riegger, *String Quartet No. 3*; John Verrall, *String Quartet No. 3.*

**Choral/Vocal**  George Antheil, *Songs of Experience* (after Blake); Jacob Avshalomov, *How Long, O Lord* (cantata); Herbert Elwell, *Pastorale (Song of Solomon)*; Andrew Imbrie, *On the Beach at Night*; Peter Mennin, *Four Chinese Poems*; Igor Stravinsky, *Mass*; Louise Talma, *The Divine Flame* (oratorio).

**Concertos**    John J. Becker, *Violin Concerto*; Robert Russell Bennett, *Piano Concerto*; Nicolai Berezowsky, *Theremin Concerto*; Ernest Bloch, *Concerto Symphonique for Piano and Orchestra—Scherzo Fantasque* (piano and orchestra); John Alden Carpenter, *Carmel Concerto* (piano); Aaron Copland, *Clarinet Concerto*; Alvin Etler, *Concerto for String Quartet and String Orchestra*; Ross Lee Finney, *Piano Concerto No. 1*; Lukas Foss, *Piano Concerto No. 2* (New York Music Critics' Award); Alexei Haieff, *Violin Concerto*; Howard Hanson, *Piano Concerto*; Meyer Kupferman, *Piano Concerto No. 1*; Bohuslav Martinů, *Piano Concerto No. 3*; Nicolas Nabokov, *Flute Concerto*; Quincy Porter, *Viola Concerto*; Ned Rorem, *Piano Concerto No. 1* (withdrawn); Alan Shulman, *Cello Concerto*; William Grant Still, *From a Lost Continent* (piano and orchestra).

**Orchestra/Band**    George Antheil, *American Dance Suite I*; Thomas Beversdorf, *Mexican Portrait*; Marc Blitzstein, *The Guests* (ballet); Norman Dello Joio, *Variations, Chaconne and Finale* (New York Music Critics' Award); William Flanagan, *A Concert Overture*; Morton Gould, *Philharmonic Waltzes*; Lou Harrison, *Suite No. 2 for Strings*; Darius Milhaud, *Kentuckiana, Opus 287*; Robert Parris, *Symphonic Movement No. 1*; Walter Piston, *Suite No. 2*; Gardner Read, *Temple of St. Anthony*; George Rochberg, *Night Music* (Gershwin Award); Ned Rorem, *Overture in C* (Gershwin Award); Gunther Schuller, *Symphonic Study*; Seymour Shifrin, *Music for Orchestra*; Halsey Stevens, *A Green Mountain Overture*; Virgil Thomson, *Louisiana Story* (film music—Pulitzer Prize); Halsey Stevens, *A Green Mountain Overture*; Robert Ward, *Concert Piece for Orchestra—Jubilation Overture*.

**Piano/Organ**    Claus Adam, *Sonata*; Paul Bowles, *Six Latin-American Pieces*; John Cage, *Dream—In a Landscape*; Norman Dello Joio, *Sonata No. 3*; Robert Erickson, *Sonata*; Frederick Jacobi, *Suite Fantasque*; Leon Kirchner, *Sonata*; Ernst Krenek, *Sonata No. 4, Opus 114*; Douglas Moore, *Piano Suite*; Harold Shapero, *Sonata in F Minor*; Arthur Shepherd, *Eclogue No. 2 for Piano—Processional Festivo*; Seymour Shifrin, *Four Cantos*; Leo Smit, *Rural Elegy*; Leo Sowerby, *Sonata in D Major*; Robert Swanson, *Sonata No. 1*; Ben Weber, *Suite No. 2, Opus 27*; Stefan Wolpe, *Studies for Piano*.

**Symphonies**    Josef Alexander, *Symphony No. 1*; George Antheil, *Symphony No. 5, "Joyous"—Symphony No. 6, "After Delacroix"*; Hans Barth, *Symphony No. 2*; Norman Cazden, *Symphony*; Henry Cowell, *Symphony No. 5*; Herbert Inch, *Sinfonietta I*; Frederick Jacobi, *Symphony No. 2*; Ulysses Kay, *Concerto for Orchestra*; Homer Keller, *Symphony No. 2*; Peter Mennin, *Symphony No. 4, "The Cycle"*; Gardner Read, *Symphony No. 3, Opus 75* (Shell Publishing Award); Harold Shapero, *Sinfonia in C Minor (Traveler's Overture)*; Julia Smith, *Folkways Symphony*; Howard Swanson, *Short Symphony* (New York Music Critics' Award); John Verrall, *Symphony No. 2*.

# 1949

❀

## Historical Highlights

Congress ratifies the North Atlantic Treaty Organization (NATO); New York becomes the permanent home of the United Nations; a WAC Corporal rocket becomes the first to reach outer space; the Berlin Airlift ends after 328 days and Germany is divided into East and West; the Communists take over in China as the Nationalists are driven from the mainland to the island of Formosa; Russia explodes its first atomic bomb.

## World Cultural Highlights

**World Art**    Marc Chagall, *Red Sun*; Jacob Epstein, *Lazarus;* Alberto Giacometti, *The City Square;* Marino Marini, *Horse and Rider;* Henri Matisse, *Murals, Chapel of the Rosary, Venice;* Maurice de Vlaminck, *Les Blés.*

**World Literature**    Simone de Beauvoir, *The Second Sex*; Nancy Mitford, *Love in a Cold Climate*; George Orwell, *1984*; Albert Schweitzer, *Hospital in the Jungle.*

**World Music**   Benjamin Britten, *Spring Symphony*; Hans Werner Henze, *Symphony No. 3*; Dmitri Kabalevsky, *Cello Concerto*; Dmitri Shostakovich, *The Song of the Forests*.

**Miscellaneous**   The Bavarian Radio Symphony Orchestra, Hungarian State Philharmonic Orchestra and Symphony Orchestra of Rio de Janeiro are founded; deaths include James Ensor, Hans Kindler, Maurice Maeterlinck, José Orozco, Henri Rabaud, Nikos Skalkottas, and Richard Strauss.

## American Art and Literature Highlights

**Births/Deaths**   Births include sculptor Deborah Butterfield, artist Robert Kushner, poets Olga Broumas, Michael Waters, authors Jamaica Kincaid, Mary Robison, and Scott Turow; deaths include art figures Robert Aitken, Walt Kuhn, Furio Piccirilli, August Tack, and literary figures Hervey Allen, Mary Antin, Rex Beach, Alice Henderson, and Margaret Mitchell.

**Art Works**   Louise Bourgeois, *The Blind Leading the Blind*; Philip Evergood, *Leda in High Places*; Ellsworth Kelly, *Face of Stone Window*; Robert Motherwell, *Five in the Afternoon*; Louise Nevelson, *Archaic Figure with Star*; Isamu Noguchi, *Cronos*; Clayton Price, *Bird by the Sea*; Ben Shahn, *Death of a Miner*; Niles Spencer, *The Silver Tanks*; Yves Tanguy, *Fear*.

**Literature**   Nelson Algren, *The Man with the Golden Arm* (National Book Award); Maxwell Anderson, *Lost in the Stars*; Gwendolyn Brooks, *Annie Allen* (Pulitzer Prize); William R. Burnett, *The Asphalt Jungle*; E. Carey and F. Gilbreth, *Cheaper by the Dozen*; Arthur Miller, *Death of a Salesman* (Pulitzer Prize—New York Drama Critics' Award); Clifford Odets, *The Big Knife*; Eudora Welty, *The Golden Apples*.

## Music—The Vernacular/Commercial Scene

**A. Births**   Danny Adler (guitarist); Adrian Belew (guitarist) December 23; Eric Carmen (singer) August 11; Marshall Chapman (singer/guitarist) January 7; Martin Delray (singer) September 26; Donna Fargo (singer) November 10; Gloria Gaynor (singer) September 7; Billy Joel (singer/writer) May 9; Patti Lupone (singer) April 21; Susannah McCorkle (singer) January 1; Maureen McGovern (singer) July 27; Eddie Money (singer) March 21; Elliott Murphy (singer/writer) March 16; Holly Near (singer/writer) June 6; Ira Newborn (composer) December 12; John Oates (Hall and Oates) April 7; Stella Parton (singer) May 4; Bonnie Raitt (singer) November 8; Lionel Richie (singer/writer) June 20; Bruce Springsteen (singer/guitarist) September 23; Tom Waits (songwriter) December 7; Joe Louis Walker (singer/guitarist) December 26; Hank Williams, Jr. (singer) May 26.

**B. Deaths**   Ivie Anderson (singer) December 28; George Botsford (composer) February 11; Euday Bowman (ragtime pianist); "Fiddlin' John" Carson (fiddler) December 11; Buddy Clark (singer) October 1; Eddie De Lange (composer/lyricist) July 13; Blind Willie Johnson (singer/guitarist); "Bunk" Johnson (trumpeter) July 7; Leadbelly (Huddie Ledbetter—singer/guitarist) December 6; Paul Mares (trumpeter/composer) August 18; Big Eye Louis Nelson (clarinetist) August 20; Chris Smith (composer) October 4; Herbert Stothart (songwriter) February 1.

**C. Biographical**

**Performing Groups**   Dave Brubeck Trio and Octet; Drifting Cowboys I (Hank Williams); Dukes of Dixieland (New Orleans); Firehouse Five Plus Two; Five Keys; Four Aces; Hollywood Flame; Innovations in Modern Music Orchestra (Stan Kenton); Kings of Dixieland (Chicago); Saddlemen (Comets); George Shearing Quintet; Lennie Tristano Sextet.

**New Beginnings**   Derby Records (New York); Fantasy Records (Berkeley); Prestige Records (New York).

**Miscellaneous**   Mimi Benzell gives up opera to concentrate on pop music; Skitch Henderson joins the music staff of NBC; Les Paul marries Mary Ford; Ezio Pinza begins a second career on Broadway (*South Pacific*).

**D. Publications**   Leonard Feather, *Inside Bebop*; H. Johnson, *Thirty Negro Spirituals*.

**E. Representative Works**

**Musicals**   Irving Berlin and Lew Sherwood, *Miss Liberty*; Jule Styne and Leo Robin, *Gentlemen*

*Prefer Blondes*; Cole Porter, *Adam's Rib* (film); Rodgers and Hammerstein, *South Pacific* (Pulitzer Prize—Tony—New York Drama Critics' Award); Kurt Weill and M. Anderson, *Lost in the Stars*.

**Songs**   Evelyn Danzig, *Scarlet Ribbon*; Terry Gilkyson, *Cry of the Wild Goose*; Haven Gillespie and B. Smith, *That Lucky Old Sun*; Walter Heath and J. Lange, *Clancy Lowered the Boom*; B. E. Holland and L. Dozier, *Where Did Our Love Go?*; Stan Jones, *Ghost Riders in the Sky*; Johnny Lange, W. Heath, F. Glickman, *Mule Train*; Frank Loesser, *Baby, It's Cold Outside*; Johnny Marks, *Rudolph, the Red-Nosed Reindeer*; Roy Orbison and W. Dees, *Oh, Pretty Woman*; Irving Taylor and Ken Lane, *Everybody Loves Somebody*; Donna Summer and E. Hokenson, *Bad Girl*.

**Other**   Leroy Anderson, *Trumpeter's Lullaby*; Leonard Bernstein, *Prelude, Fugue and Riffs*; Alfred Newman, *Twelve O'Clock High* (film music); Lucky Roberts, *Park Avenue Polka*.

## Music—The Cultivated/Art Music Scene

**F. Births**   John Aler (tenor) October 4; Roberta Alexander (soprano) March 3; Wilhelmina Fernandez (soprano) January 5; Lawrence Ferrara (pianist) May 16; Primous Fountain III (composer) August 1; Isola Jones (mezzo-soprano) December 27; Gita Karasik (pianist) December 14; Joseph Kubera (pianist) May 25; Dan Steven Locklair (composer/organist) August 7; Alan Marks (pianist) May 14; Janis Mattox (composer) March 18; Robin McCabe (pianist) November 7; Stephen Paulus (composer) August 24; Sharon Robinson (cellist) December 2; Christopher Rouse (composer) February 15; Stephen Ruppenthal (composer/performer) June 3; Neil Shicoff (tenor) June 2; Ruth Welting (soprano) May 11; Edgar Warren Williams (composer/theorist) June 6; Carol Wincenc (flutist) June 29; Maurice Wright (composer/educator) October 17.

**G. Deaths**   Albert Ammons (pianist/composer) December 5; Samuel Baldwin (organist) September 15; Harry T. Burleigh (composer) September 12; Reinhold Faelten (pianist) July 17; Emilio de Gogorza (baritone) May 10; Helen Hood (composer) January 22; Hans Kindler (Dutch-born conductor/cellist) August 30; Rosa Olitzka (German-born contralto) September 29; Walter Olitzki (German-born baritone) August 2; Elie Robert Schmitz (French-born pianist) September 5; Carl E. Seashore (Swedish-born psychologist) October 16; David Stanley Smith (conductor/composer) December 17.

### H. Debuts

**United States**   Bethany Beardslee (soprano—New York), Guido Cantelli (Italian conductor), Joan Hammond (New Zealand soprano—New York), Sidney Harth (violinist—New York), Lili Kraus (Hungarian pianist—New York), Rafael Kubelik (Czech conductor—Chicago), Seymour Lipkin (pianist—New York), Yvonne Loriod (French pianist—Boston), Julian Olevsky (German violinist—New York), Marko Rothmüller (Yugoslavian baritone—New York), Samuel Sanders (pianist—New York).

**Metropolitan Opera**   Erna Berger (German soprano), Ferdinand Frantz (German bass-baritone), Peter Klein (German tenor), Jonel Perlea (Romanian conductor), Fritz Reiner (Hungarian conductor), Ljuba Welitsch (Bulgarian soprano).

**Other**   Herbert Handt (tenor—Vienna), Mildred Miller (soprano—Stuttgart), Nell Rankin (mezzo-soprano—Zürich).

### I. New Positions

**Conductors**   Peter Herman Adler (music director, NBC Opera Co.); Fausto Cleva (San Francisco Opera, second term—to 1955); Walter Hendl (Dallas Symphony Orchestra—to 1958); Robert Lawrence (Phoenix Symphony Orchestra—to 1952); Howard Mitchell (National Symphony Orchestra—to 1970); Dimitri Mitropoulos (New York Philharmonic Orchestra—to 1957); Charles Munch (Boston Symphony Orchestra—to 1962); Manuel Rosenthal (Seattle Symphony Orchestra—to 1951); James Sample (Portland [Oregon] Symphony Orchestra—to 1953).

**Educational**   Gorden Binkerd (University of Illinois—to 1971); Henry Cowell (Columbia—to 1965); Kent Kennan (University of Texas); Harrison Kerr (University of Oklahoma—to 1968); John Kirkpatrick (music chair, Cornell—to 1957); George Perle (University of Louisville—to 1957); Burrill Phillips (University of Illinois—to 1964); Elie Siegmeister (Hofstra University—to

1976); Robert Starer (Juilliard—to 1974); Hugo Weisgall (director, Baltimore Institute of Musical Arts).

## J. Honors and Awards

**Honors**    John Cage, Louis Mennini, Stefan Wolpe (American Academy); Igor Stravinsky (National Institute).

**Awards**    Gary Graffman (Leventritt); Grant Johannesen (Ostend).

**K. Biographical**    Ernst von Dohnányi settles in Florida and becomes composer-in-residence at Florida State University; John Hsu (Chinese cellist) emigrates to the United States; Jerome Kacinskas (Lithuanian conductor/composer) comes to the United States; Leontyne Price wins a scholarship to Juilliard; Ned Rorem begins eight years of study and travel in France and Morocco; Charles Rosen receives an MA degree in Romance Languages from Princeton; Joseph Rosenstock becomes an American citizen; Nicolas Roussakis (Greek composer) arrives in the United States; William Grant Still becomes the first black to have an opera performed by a major opera company (New York City Opera).

## L. Musical Beginnings

**Performing Groups**    Heifetz-Piatigorsky-Rubinstein Trio; Huntington (Long Island) Philharmonic Orchestra; La Salle String Quartet (Juilliard); Mannes Trio; NBC Television Opera Co.; New York Woodwind Quintet; Phoenix Boys Choir; Rackham Symphony Choir (Detroit); Salt Lake Symphonic Choir; Stanley String Quartet (University of Michigan).

**Festivals**    Goethe Bicentennial Convocation and Music Festival (Aspen Music Festival).

**Other**    Frank Music Corporation; Greater Louisville Foundation for the Arts; Hubbard and Dowd, Harpsichord Makers (Boston); *The Hymn*; Serge Koussevitzky Music Foundation (Library of Congress); *Long Playing Record Catalog* (Schwann); *The Music Index*; Naumburg Recording Award; Vanguard Recording Society (New York); Westminster Recordings.

## M. Music Publications

Einstein, Alfred, *The Italian Madrigal* (3 volumes)
Feldman, Morton, *Illusions*
Gleason, Harold, *Music Literature Outlines*
Haggin, B. H., *Music in the Nation*
McHose, A. and White, D., *Keyboard and Dictation Manual*
Partch, Harry, *Genesis of a New Music*
Rowen, Ruth H., *Early Chamber Music*
Saminsky, Lazare, *Living Music of the Americas*
Sargeant, Winthrop, *Geniuses, Goddesses and People*
Taylor, Deems, *Music to My Ears*
Ulrich, Homer, *The Education of a Concertgoer*

## N. Musical Compositions

**Chamber Music**    Hugh Aitken, *Chamber Concerto*; Marion Bauer, *Five Pieces for String Quartet*; Ross Lee Finney, *String Quartet No. 5*; Lejaren Hiller, *String Quartet No. 1*; Ulysses Kay, *String Quartet No. 1*; Leon Kirchner, *String Quartet No. 1* (New York Music Critics' Award); Darius Milhaud, *String Quartet No. 15*; Walter Piston, *Piano Quintet*; Wallingford Riegger, *Music for Brass Choir, Opus 45*; Ned Rorem, *Violin Sonata*; Arnold Schoenberg, *Phantasy for Violin and Piano, Opus 47*; Ralph Shapey, *String Quartet No. 2*; Seymour Shifrin, *String Quartet No. 1*; Halsey Stevens, *String Quartet No. 3—Bassoon Sonata*; John Verrall, *String Quartet No. 4*; Karl Weigl, *String Quartet No. 8*; Stefan Wolpe, *Violin Sonata*.

**Choral/Vocal**    Arthur Farwell, *Ten Emily Dickinson Songs, Opus 112*; Daniel G. Mason, *Soldiers, Opus 42* (song cycle); Arnold Schoenberg, *Dreimal Tausend Jahre, Opus 50a*; Halsey Stevens, *Six Millay Songs*; Russell Smith, *Songs of Innocence*; William Grant Still, *Songs of Separation*; Randall Thompson, *The Last Words of David*.

**Concertos**   Robert Russell Bennett, *Variations* (violin and orchestra); Paul Creston, *Piano Concerto*; Louis Gruenberg, *Cello Concerto, Opus 58*; Roy Harris, *Violin Concerto*; Paul Hindemith, *Concerto for Four Woodwinds, Harp and Orchestra—Concerto for Trumpet, Bassoon and Strings—Horn Concerto*; H. Owen Reed, *Cello Concerto*; Leroy Robertson, *Violin Concerto*; Dane Rudhyar, *Tripthong* (piano and orchestra); Burnet Tuthill, *Clarinet Concerto*; Richard Yardumian, *Violin Concerto*.

**Operas**   Marc Blitzstein, *Regina*; Carlisle Floyd, *Slow Dusk*; Lukas Foss, *The Jumping Frog of Calaveras County*; Gian Carlo Menotti, *The Consul* (Pulitzer Prize); Douglas Moore, *Giants in the Earth* (Pulitzer Prize); Vittorio Rieti, *Don Perlimplin*.

**Orchestra/Band**   George Antheil, *Tom Sawyer*; Irwin Bazelon, *Ballet Suite*; Robert Russell Bennett, *Suite of Old American Dances* (band); Jean Berger, *Creole Overture*; Philip Bezanson, *Overture, Cyrano de Bergerac*; Norman Cazden, *Three Ballads*; Richard Donovan, *Passacaglia on Vermont Folk Tunes*; Cecil Effinger, *Lyric Overture*; Nicolas Flagello, *Beowulf*; Lou Harrison, *Solstice—The Marriage at the Eiffel Tower* (ballets); Arthur Kreutz, *Hamlet* (incidental music); Salvatore Martirano, *The Cherry Orchard* (incidental music); Burrill Phillips, *Concerto Grosso* (string quartet and orchestra); H. Owen Reed, *La Fiesta Mexicana* (band/orchestra); William Schuman, *Judith* (ballet—New York Music Critic's Award); Robert Starer, *Prelude and Dance*; Virgil Thomson, *At the Beach—A Solemn Music* (band).

**Piano/Organ**   Samuel Barber, *Sonata, Opus 26*; John J. Becker, *Soundpiece No. 7* (two pianos); Arthur Berger, *Four Two-Part Inventions*; Ernest Bloch, *Six Preludes for Organ*; Paul Cooper, *Sonata No. 1*; Lucia Dlugoszewski, *Sonata No. 1*; Arthur Farwell, *Sonata, Opus 113*; Leon Kirchner, *Little Suite*; Benjamin Lees, *Sonata No. 1*; Peter Mennin, *Five Pieces*; Darius Milhaud, *Sonata No. 2, Opus 293*; Vincent Persichetti, *Sonatas No. 4, 5*; Gardner Read, *Organ Suite, Opus 81*; Ned Rorem, *Sonata No. 1*; Leo Smit, *Seven Characteristic Pieces—Variations in G Major*; Arthur Shepherd, *Eclogue No. 3*; Julia Smith, *Characteristic Suite*; Robert Starer, *Sonata No. 1*.

**Symphonies**   William Bergsma, *Symphony No. 1*; Leonard Bernstein, *Symphony No. 2, "Age of Anxiety"*; Philip James, *Symphony No. 2*; Ernst Krenek, *Symphony No. 5*; Gail Kubik, *Symphony No. 1*; George Rochberg, *Symphony No. 1*; David Stanley Smith, *Symphony No. 5*; William Grant Still, *Symphony No. 4, "Autochthonous"*; Randall Thompson, *Symphony No. 3*; George Tremblay, *Symphony in One Movement*.

# 1950

☀

## Historical Highlights

The census reveals a population of 151,326,000; Senator Joseph McCarthy begins his communist witchhunt in Washington; the Alger Hiss spy case takes place; the McCarran Internal Security Act tightens controls on Communists; President Truman approves the building of the hydrogen bomb; the Korean War begins; the Chinese enter the conflict when the Allies drive the Communists back to the Yalu River; apartheid riots begin in South Africa.

## World Cultural Highlights

**World Art**   Marc Chagall, *King David*; Alberto Giacometti, *Chariot*; Ludwig von Hofmann, *Elegy*; Pablo Picasso, *The She-Goat*; Samuel Scott, *Haitian Market*.

**World Literature**   Jean Anouilh, *The Rehearsal*; Christopher Fry, *Venus Observed*; Eugène Ionesco, *The Bald Soprano*.

**World Music**   Karl-Birger Blomdahl, *Symphony No. 3, "Facetter"*; Pierre Boulez, *Le Visage Nuptial*; Artur Honegger, *Symphony No. 5, "Di tre re"*; Heitor Villa-Lobos, *Erosion of the Amazon*.

**Miscellaneous**   Il Solisti di Zagreb, the Belfast Symphony Orchestra, and the Hungarian State

Folk Ensemble are founded; deaths include Charles Koechlin, Nicolai Miaskovsky, Vaslav Nijinsky, Rafael Sabatini, and George Bernard Shaw.

## American Art and Literature Highlights

**Births/Deaths**   Births include literary figures Charles Bernstein, Carolyn Forché, Gloria Naylor, and Wendy Wasserstein; deaths include art figures Max Beckmann, Allen Clark, Edgar McKillop, Alexander Proctor, and literary figures Irving Bacheller, William R. Benét, Edgar Lee Masters, Edna St. Vincent Millay, Agnes Repplier, Ridgely Torrence, and Clement Wood.

**Art Works**   William Baziotes, *Dragon*; Alexander Calder, *Red Gongs*; José de Creeft, *The Poet*; Stuart Davis, *Little Giant Still Life*; Chaim Gross, *Adolescent*; Edward Hopper, *Cape Cod Morning*; Willem de Kooning, *Woman*; Ibram Lassaw, *Milky Way*; Rico Lebrun, *The Crucifixion Triptych*; Barnett Newman, *The Wild*; Jackson Pollock, *Autumn Rhythm*; George Tooker, *The Subway—Bathers*.

**Literature**   e. e. cummings, *XAIPE*; A. B. Guthrie, Jr., *The Way West* (Pulitzer Prize); John R. Hersey, *The Wall*; William Inge, *Come Back, Little Sheba*; Henry M. Robinson, *The Cardinal*; Anya Seton, *Foxfire*; Isaac Bashevis Singer, *The Family Moskat*; Peter Taylor, *A Woman of Means*; Robert Penn Warren, *World Enough and Time*; Tennessee Williams, *The Rose Tattoo*.

## Music—The Vernacular/Commercial Scene

**A. Births**   David Bellamy (singer) September 16; Dee Dee Bridgewater (singer) May 27; Karen Carpenter (singer) March 2; David Cassidy (singer) April 12; Alex Chilton (singer/guitarist) December 28; Natalie Cole (singer) February 6; Willie Colon (trombonist/bandleader) April 28; Rodney Crowell (singer) August 7; Barbara Fairchild (singer) November 12; Becky Hobbs (pianist/writer) January 24; David Lynn Jones (singer) January 15; Tonio K. (singer/writer) July 4; Ronnie Laws (saxophonist) October 3; Ronnie McDowell (singer) March 26; Bobby McFerrin (singer/conductor) March 11; Thelonious Monk, Jr. (drummer/bandleader); Teddy Pendergrass (singer/writer) March 26; Tom Petty (singer) October 20; Billy Squier (guitarist) May 12; Stevie Wonder (singer/writer) May 13.

**B. Deaths**   Joseph A. Burke (songwriter) June 9; Buddy de Sylva (lyricist) July 11; Bertha Hill (singer) May 7; Charles L. Johnson (pianist/composer) December 28; Al Jolson (singer/actor) October 23; "Fats" Navarro (trumpeter) July 7.

**C. Biographical**

**Performing Groups**   The Basin Street Six (New Orleans); Billy May Band; Billy Ward and His Dominoes.

**New Beginnings**   Elektra Records; *Sing Out: The Folk Song Magazine*; Vanguard Records.

**Miscellaneous**   Fletcher Henderson suffers a stroke, leaving him partially paralyzed.

**D. Publications**   R. Blesh and H. Janis, *They All Played Ragtime—The True Story of an American Music*; Richard B. Harwell, *Confederate Music*; John Jacob Niles, *Shape-Note Study Book*; R. Crawford Seeger, *Animal Folk Songs for Children*; Arnold Shaw, *Lingo of Tin-Pan Alley*; C. Smith, *Musical Comedy in America*.

**E. Representative Works**

**Musicals**   Irving Berlin, Russel Crouse, and Howard Lindsay, *Call Me Madam*; Frank Loesser, *Guys and Dolls* (New York Drama Critics' Award); Cole Porter, *Out of This World*; Harold Rome, *Bless You All*.

**Songs**   Deacon Anderson, *Rag Mop*; Leroy Anderson, *Sleigh Ride*; Cy Coben, *The Ole Piano Roll Blues*; Mack David, *I Don't Care if the Sun Don't Shine*; Sammy Fain, *Dear Hearts and Gentle People*; Anton Karas, *The Third Man Theme*; Jay Livingston and R. Evans, *Mona Lisa* (Oscar)—*Silver Bells*; Bob Merrill, *If I Knew You Were Comin' I'd've Baked a Cake—How Much Is That Doggie in the Window*; Lloyd Price, *Lawdy Miss Clawdy*; Henry Stone and Jack Stapp, *Chattanoogie Shoe Shine Boy*.

**Other**   Leroy Anderson, *The Typewriter*; Duke Ellington, *Harlem (A Tone Parallel to Harlem)*;

Alfred Newman, *All About Eve* (film music); Max Steiner, *The Flame and the Arrow* (film music); Leith Stevens, *Destination Moon* (film music); Franz Waxman, *Sunset Boulevard* (film music — Oscar).

## Music — The Cultivated/Art Music Scene

**F. Births**    Beth Anderson (composer) January 3; Robert Black (pianist) April 28; Stephen G. Chatman (composer) February 28; Katherine Ciesinski (mezzo-soprano) October 13; James Conlon (conductor) March 18; Philip Creech (tenor) June 1; James W. Dietsch (baritone) March 21; Faith Esham (soprano); Maria Ewing (mezzo-soprano) March 27; Eugene N. Fodor (violinist) March 5; Lia Frey-Rabine (soprano) August 12; Gregory Fulkerson (violinist) May 9; Gail Gilmore (mezzo-soprano) September 21; David Golub (pianist) March 22; Michael R. Habermann (pianist) February 23; Thomas Harper (baritone); Mary Jane Johnson (soprano) March 22; Kathleen Kuhlmann (mezzo-soprano) December 7; Gary Lakes (tenor) September 26; Libby Larsen (composer) December 24; Barry McCauley (tenor) June 2; Janice Meyerson (mezzo-soprano); Elmer Oliveira (violinist) June 28; Leslie Richards (mezzo-soprano) February 19; Kay George Roberts (conductor) September 16; Michael Schelle (composer) January 22; Calvin Simmons (conductor/pianist) April 27; Daniel Victor Starr (theorist) September 8; Richard Vernon (bass).

**G. Deaths**    Walter Damrosch (German-born conductor); Carl Deis (organist) July 24; Giuseppe De Luca (Italian-born baritone); Henry P. Eames (pianist) November 25; Emile Enthoven (Dutch-born composer) December 26; John Lawrence Erb (pedagogue/author) March 17; Gottfried Galston (Austrian-born pianist) April 2; H. Willard Gray (publisher) October 22; Bruno Huhn (British-born pianist) May 13; Richard Kountz (composer) October 14; Albert Riemenschneider (organist/conductor) July 20; Minnie Saltzmann-Stevens (soprano) January 25; Edward Schneider (pianist/composer) July 1; Martinus Sieveking (Dutch-born pianist) November 26; Edyth Walker (mezzo-soprano) February 19; Kurt Weill (German-born composer).

**H. Debuts**

**United States**    Victoria de los Angeles (Spanish soprano — New York), Gina Bachauer (Greek pianist — New York), Aldo Ciccolini (Italian pianist — New York), Suzanne Danco (Belgian soprano), Mario Del Monaco (Italian tenor — San Francisco), Friedrich Gulda (Austrian pianist — New York), David Lloyd (tenor — New York), Cornell MacNeil (baritone — Philadelphia), Michael Rabin (violinist — New York), Gérard Souzay (French baritone — New York), Renata Tebaldi (Italian soprano — San Francisco), William Warfield (baritone — New York).

**Metropolitan Opera**    Lucine Amara (soprano), Fedora Barbieri (Italian mezzo-soprano), Eugene Conley (tenor), Mario Del Monaco (Italian tenor), Alberto Erede (Italian conductor), Hans Hotter (German bass-baritone), Roberta Peters (soprano), Paul Schlöffler (German bass-baritone), Cesare Siepi (Italian bass).

**I. New Positions**

**Conductors**    George Barati (Honolulu Symphony Orchestra and Opera — to 1967); Emerson Buckley (Miami Opera — to 1985); Désiré Defauw (Gary Symphony Orchestra — to 1958); Rafael Kubelik (Chicago Symphony Orchestra — to 1953); Edwin McArthur (Harrisburg Symphony Orchestra [Pennsylvania] — to 1974); Hugo Winterhalter (music director, RCA Victor — to 1963).

**Educational**    Willi Apel (musicology, Indiana University — to 1970); Irving Fine (Brandeis — to 1962); Josef Gingold (Western Reserve University — to 1960); H. Wiley Hitchcock (University of Michigan — to 1961); Paul Hume (Georgetown University — to 1977); Ellis Kohs (USC — to 1985); Joaquin Nin-Culmell (Berkeley — to 1974); Vittorio Rieti (Chicago Musical College — to 1953); Gunther Schuller (Manhattan School — to 1963).

**Other**    Rudolph Bing (manager, Metropolitan Opera — to 1972); Gustave Reese (president, American Musicological Society); Harold Schonberg (music critic, *The New York Times* — to 1980).

**J. Honors and Awards**

**Honors**    Andrew Imbrie and Ben Weber (American Academy); Percy Grainger (National Institute); Gail Kubik (Rome Prize).

**K. Biographical**	Betty Allen receives a private scholarship to the Hartford School of Music; Cathy Berberian marries composer Luciano Berio; Halim El-Dabh (Egyptian composer) comes to the United States as a Fulbright Scholar; the Louisville Orchestra avoids financial failure when Martha Graham dances in William Schuman's *Judith* for their benefit; Lauritz Melchior, at odds with Rudolph Bing, leaves the Metropolitan Opera permanently; Gundaris Poné (Latvian composer/conductor) comes to the United States; Arthur Shepherd retires from teaching; Lester Trimble goes to Paris to study with Boulanger, Milhaud, and Honegger.

**L. Musical Beginnings**

**Performing Groups**	American Arts Orchestra (radio orchestra); Baltimore Chamber Music Society; Hilltop Opera Co. (Baltimore); Philadelphia Woodwind Quintet; Portland (Oregon) Opera Association; Syracuse Friends of Chamber Music; Utah Chorale (Salt Lake Symphony Chorus in 1984).

**Festivals**	Aspen Music Festival (Colorado); Marlboro Festival (Vermont); Opera in the Ozarks (Eureka Springs, Arkansas).

**Educational**	Catholic University Music Dept.; Idyllwild School of Music (California); Inspiration Point Fine Arts Colony (Eureka Springs, Arkansas).

**Other**	*The Church Musician*; Hammond Chord Organ; National Association for Music Therapy; Weintraub Music Co. (New York).

**M. Music Publications**

Barlow, Harold, *A Dictionary of Vocal Themes*
Barzun, Jacques, *Berlioz and the Romantic Century*
Bukofzer, Manfred, *Studies in Medieval and Renaissance Music*
Crawford, Ruth P., *Animal Folk Songs for Children*
McHose, Allen I., *Musical Style 1850–1920*
Rudolf, Max, *The Grammar of Conducting*
Salzedo, Carlos, *The Art of Modulating*
Schoenberg, Arnold, *Style and Idea—Preliminary Exercises in Counterpoint* (published 1963)
Sessions, Roger, *The Musical Experience of Composer, Performer, Listener*
Spaeth, Sigmund, *Opportunities in Music Careers*
Strunk, Oliver, *Source Readings in Music History*
Vega, Aurelio de la, *The Negative Emotion*

**N. Musical Compositions**

**Chamber Music**	Samuel Adler, *String Quartet No. 2*; Milton Babbitt, *Composition for Viola and Piano*; Ernst Bacon, *String Quintet*; Thomas Beversdorf, *Cathedral Music* (brass); John Cage, *String Quartet*; Robert Erickson, *String Quartet No. 1*; Ross Lee Finney, *String Quartet No. 6*; Louis Gruenberg, *Violin Sonata No. 3*; Gene Gutchë, *String Quartet No. 3* (Minnesota State Prize); Peter Jona Korn, *String Quartet No. 1*; Leo Kraft, *String Quartet No. 1*; Hall Overton, *String Quartet No. 1*; Robert Palmer, *Piano Quintet*; Quincy Porter, *String Quartet No. 8*; Ned Rorem, *String Quartet No. 2*; Miklós Rozsa, *String Quartet*; Dane Rudhyar, *Piano Quintet*; William Schuman, *String Quartet No. 4*; Lester Trimble, *String Quartet No. 1*; David Van Vactor, *String Quartet No. 2*; Stefan Wolpe, *Quartet* (trumpet, tenor sax, piano, percussion).

**Choral/Vocal**	Hugh Aitken, *Mass*; Jean Berger, *Four Songs after Hughes*; Aaron Copland, *Twelve Songs of Emily Dickinson*; Miriam Gideon, *Sonnets from Shakespeare* (song cycle); Nicolas Nabokov, *La vita nuova*; Roger Nixon, *Six Moods of Love* (song cycle); Quincy Porter, *The Desolate City*; Wallingford Riegger, *Cantata, In Certainty of Song, Opus 46*; Bernard Rogers, *The Prophet Isaiah* (cantata); Ned Rorem, *Six Irish Poems*; Arnold Schoenberg, *De Profundis, Opus 50b—Modern Psalm, Opus 50c*; Ben Weber, *Symphony on Poems of William Blake*.

**Concertos**	Ernest Bloch, *Concertino for Flute, Viola and Strings*; David Diamond, *Piano Concerto*; Nicolas Flagelo, *Piano Concerto No. 1*; Alexei Haieff, *Piano Concerto No. 1* (New York Music Critics' Award); Leo Kraft, *Concerto No. 1 for Flute, Clarinet, Trumpet and Strings*; Ernst

Krenek, *Piano Concerto No. 4*; Bohuslav Martinů, *Double Violin Concerto No. 2*; Virgil Thomson, *Cello Concerto*.

**Operas**   Jack Beeson, *Jonah*; Nicolas Flagello, *Mirra*; Bernard Rogers, *The Veil*; William Grant Still, *Costaso*; Hugo Weisgall, *The Tenor*.

**Orchestra/Band**   Hugh Aitken, *Toccata for Orchestra*; Leonard Bernstein, *Peter Pan* (incidental music); Marc Blitzstein, *King Lear* (incidental music I); Herbert Elwell, *Ode for Orchestra*; Kenneth Gaburo, *On a Quiet Theme* (Gershwin Memorial Award); Don Gillis, *Tulsa* (symphonic portrait); Lou Harrison, *Almanac of the Seasons* (ballet); Lawrence Moss, *Orchestral Suite*; Vincent Persichetti, *Fairy Tale, Opus 48*; William Schuman, *George Washington Bridge* (winds); Lamar Stringfield, *About Dixie*.

**Piano/Organ**   Irwin Bazelon, *Suite for Young People—Five Pieces*; Seth Bingham, *Variation Studies* (organ); Norman Cazden, *Three New Sonatas*; Lucia Dlugoszewski, *Melodic Sonata*; William Flanagan, *Sonata*; Lejaren Hiller, *Sonata No. 3—Sonata No. 4*; Charles Jones, *Sonata No. 2*; Ernst Krenek, *Sonata No. 5, Opus 121*; Benjamin Lees, *Sonata No. 2*; Robert Moevs, *Sonata*; George Perle, *Sonata, Opus 27*; Vincent Persichetti, *Sonatas No. 6–8—Sonatinas No. 1–3*; Gardner Read, *Eight Preludes on Old Southern Hymns* (organ); Harold Shapero, *American Variations*; Leo Sowerby, *Whimsical Variations* (organ); Ben Weber, *Episodes—Fantasia*; Stefan Wolpe, *Music for a Dancer*.

**Symphonies**   Marion Bauer, *Symphony*; Thomas Beversdorf, *Symphony No. 2*; Philip Bezanson, *Symphony No. 2*; Henry Brant, *Symphony, Origins*; Paul Creston, *Symphony No. 3*; Halim El Dabh, *Symphony No. 1*; Miriam Gideon, *Symphonia Brevis*; Gene Gutchë, *Symphonies 1, 2*; Alan Hovhaness, *Symphony No. 9, Opus 80, "St. Vartan"*; Herbert Inch, *Sinfonietta II*; Ulysses Kay, *Sinfonia in E Major*; Ellis Kohs, *Symphony No. 1*; Meyer Kupferman, *Chamber Symphony (No. 1)*; William Latham, *Symphony No. 1*; Peter Mennin, *Symphony No. 5*; George Perle, *Symphony No. 2*; Walter Piston, *Symphony No. 4*; Ned Rorem, *Symphony No. 1*; Gunther Schuller, *Symphony for Brass and Percussion*; Harold Shapero, *Concerto for Orchestra*; Elie Siegmeister, *Symphony No. 2*; Robert Starer, *Symphony No. 1*; Ernst Toch, *Symphony No. 1, Opus 72*; Robert Ward, *Symphony No. 3*; Richard Yardumian, *Symphony No. 1, "Noah."*

# 1951

✹

## Historical Highlights

The 22nd Amendment, limiting the president to only two terms, is ratified; the United States signs the ANZUS Pact with Australia and New Zealand; President Truman removes General MacArthur from his Far East command; Julius and Ethel Rosenberg are sentenced to death for spying; the Korean peace talks begin at Panmunjom; Winston Churchill again becomes British Prime Minister.

## World Cultural Highlights

**World Art**   Salvador Dali, *Christ on the Cross*; Mario Marini, *Cavaliere;* Pablo Picasso, *Baboon and Young*; Stanley Spencer, *Silent Prayer*.

**World Literature**   W. H. Auden, *Nones*; Samuel Beckett, *Molloy—Malone meurt*; Eugène Ionesco, *La Légion;* Jean-Paul Sartre, *The Devil and the Good Lord*.

**World Music**   Benjamin Britten, *Billy Budd*; Francis Poulenc, *Stabat Mater*; Dmitri Shostakovich, *24 Preludes and Fugues*; Ralph Vaughan Williams, *The Pilgrim's Progress*.

**Miscellaneous**   The Bilbao Festival in Spain, Wexford Festival in Ireland, and the Wiener Festwochen begin; births include Cyprien Katsaris and Pascal Rogé; deaths include Fritz Busch, André Gide, Willem Mengelberg, and Artur Schnabel.

## American Art and Literature Highlights

**Births/Deaths**   Births include artists John Ahearn, Julian Schnabel, and literary figures Jorie

Graham, Craig Lucas, Terry McMillan, Ted Mooney, and Anna Quindlan; deaths include art figures Frank Benson, Charles Keck, Albert Laessle, John Sloan, and literary figures Abraham Cahan, Lloyd C. Douglas, John Erskine, James N. Hall, Harry Hervey, and Sinclair Lewis.

**Art Works**   Ilya Bolotowsky, *Configurations within a Diamond*; James Brooks, *Tondo*; Adolph Gottlieb, *Frozen Sounds No. 1*; Philip Guston, *The Clock*; Edward Hopper, *Rooms by the Sea*; Willem de Kooning, *Nightsquare*; Ibram Lassaw, *Galaxy of Andromeda*; John Marin, *Sea Piece— Boat Fantasy*; Ben Shahn, *Silent Music*; David Smith, *Hudson River Landscape*; Yves Tanguy, *The Invisibles*.

**Literature**   William Faulkner, *Requiem for a Nun*; James Jones, *From Here to Eternity* (National Book Award); Robert Lowell, *The Mills of the Kavanaughs*; Marianne Moore, *Collected Poems* (Pulitzer Prize—National Book Award); Conrad Richter, *The Town* (Pulitzer Prize); Carl Sandburg, *Complete Poems* (Pulitzer Prize); Herman Wouk, *The Caine Mutiny* (Pulitzer Prize).

## Music—The Vernacular/Commercial Scene

**A. Births**   Kathy Baillie (singer) February 20; Tommy Bolin (guitarist) August 1; Peabo Bryson (singer/writer) April 13; Jim Carroll (singer); Bootsy Collins (songwriter) October 26; Christopher Cross (singer) May 3; Anthony Davis (pianist/composer) February 20; Brad Fiedel (composer) March 10; Dan Fogelberg (guitarist/writer) August 13; Robben Ford (guitarist) December 16; Bill Frisell (guitarist) March 18; Steve Gatlin (singer) April 4; Crystal Gayle (singer) January 9; Andrew Gold (guitarist) August 2; Janis Ian (singer/writer) April 7; Mark Isham (composer) September 7; Nils Lofgren (guitarist/writer) June 21; Melissa Manchester (singer/writer) February 15; John Mellencamp (singer) October 7; Jonathan Richman (singer) May 16; Maggie Roche (singer) October 26; Judy Rodman (singer) May 23; Johnny Rodriguez (singer/guitar) December 10; John Scofield (guitarist) December 26; Luther Vandross (singer) April 20; Jimmie Vaughan (guitarist) March 20; Wendy Waldman (singer/writer); Deniece Williams (singer/writer) June 3.

**B. Deaths**   Harry Armstrong (composer/singer) February 28; Mildred Bailey (singer) December 12; Fanny Brice (singer/comedian); Sidney "Big Sid" Catlett (drummer) March 25; Eddy Duchin (pianist/bandleader) February 9; Herman Hupfield (composer) June 8; "Whispering" Jack Smith (singer) May; Robert B. Smith (lyricist) November 6; Egbert Van Alstyne (composer) July 9; Jimmy Yancey (pianist) September 17.

**C. Biographical**

**Performing Groups**   Big Four Jazz Quartet; Bill Doggett Band II; The Flamingos; Jimmy Hodges Sextet; Milt Jackson Quartet; Ahmad Jamal's Three Strings; Modern Jazz Quartet; James Moody Sextet; Buddy Morrow Band; Shenandoah Valley Boys; Jack Teagarden All Stars.

**New Beginnings**   Contemporary Records (Los Angeles); Dot Records; Fortune Records; *High Fidelity*; Storyville Records (Boston); Sun Records (Memphis); Lennie Tristano School of Jazz (New York); United Records (Chicago).

**Miscellaneous**   Alan Freed, Cleveland disk jockey, first coins the term "rock-and-roll" in reference to music.

**D. Publications**   Larry Freeman, *The Melodies Linger On: 50 Years of Popular Song*; Charles Haywood, *A Bibliography of North American Folklore and Folksong*.

**E. Representative Works**

**Musicals**   Sammy Fain and E. Y. Harburg, *Flahooley*; George and Ira Gershwin, *An American in Paris* (film—Oscar); Walter Kent and K. Gannon, *Seventeen*; Lerner and Loewe, *Paint Your Wagon*; Johnny Mercer, *Top Banana*; Rodgers and Hammerstein, *The King and I*; Arthur Schwartz and D. Fields, *A Tree Grows in Brooklyn*; Jule Styne, B. Comden, and A. Green, *Two on the Aisle*.

**Songs**   Ross Bagdasarian, *Come on-a My House*; N. Brodszky and S. Cahn, *Be My Love*; H. Carmichael and J. Mercer, *In the Cool, Cool, Cool of the Evening*; Irving Gordon, *Unforgettable*; Vaughn Horton, *Mockingbird Hill*; P. M. Howard and P. Weston, *Shrimp Boats*; Bob Merrill, *My Truly, Truly Fair*; J. Newman and P. Campbell, *Kisses Sweeter Than Wine*; Bernie Wayne and Lee Morris, *Blue Velvet*; Hank Williams, *Cold Cold Heart*.

**Other**  Leroy Anderson, *Syncopated Clock—Waltzing Cat—Belle of the Ball*; Bernard Herrmann, *The Day the Earth Stood Still* (film music); Thelonious Monk, *Criss-Cross*; Alfred Newman, *David and Bathsheba* (film music); Alex North, *A Streetcar Named Desire—Death of a Salesman* (film music); Miklós Rózsa, *Quo Vadis?* (film music); Franz Waxman, *A Place in the Sun* (film music—Oscar).

## Music—The Cultivated/Art Music Scene

**F. Births**  Mark Beudert (tenor) June 4; Rockwell Blake (tenor) January 10; Karen Bureau (soprano) February 3; Donald Crockett (composer/conductor) February 18; Thomas DeLio (composer/theorist) January 7; Paul Joseph Dresher (composer) January 8; Rinde Eckert (vocalist/composer) September 20; Carroll B. Freeman (tenor) December 16; Peter Gordon (composer/saxophonist) June 20; Richard Hayman (composer) July 29; Robin Heifetz (composer) August 1; Melanie Holliday (soprano) August 12; Timothy Jenkins (tenor) November 21; Gerald Levinson (composer); David Macbride (composer); Jeremy Menuhin (pianist/conductor) November 2; Kent Nagano (conductor) November 22; Liz Phillips (composer/artist) June 13; J. Patrick Raftery (baritone) April 4; Lawrence Rapchak (composer) May 7; Douglas Riva (pianist) August 16; David Starobin (guitarist) September 27; Frank Stemper (pianist/composer) October 19; Sharon Sweet (soprano) August 16; George Tsontakis (composer) October 24; Lois Vierk (composer) August 4; Ransom Wilson (flutist) October 25; Delores Ziegler (mezzo-soprano) September 4.

**G. Deaths**  Howard Brockway (composer/pianist) February 20; Mme. Charles Cahier (contralto) April 15; John Alden Carpenter (composer) April 26; Peter Dykema (music educator) May 13; John Erskine (pianist/educator) June 1; Jerzy Fitelberg (Polish-born composer) April 25; Olive Fremstad (soprano) April 21; Robert Henried (Austrian-born musicologist) September 3; Ernest Hutcheson (Australian-born pianist/composer) February 9; Serge Koussevitzky (Russian-born conductor) June 4; Eastwood Lane (composer) January 22; Hugo Leichtentritt (Polish-born musicologist) November 13; Kathleen Lockhart Manning (composer) March 20; Queena Mario (soprano) May 28; Elizabeth Quaile (Irish-born pianist) June 30; Francis Rogers (baritone) May 15; Léon Rothier (French-born bass) December 6; Artur Schnabel (Austrian-born pianist) August 15; Arnold Schoenberg (Austrian-born composer) July 13; Powell Weaver (pianist/composer) December 22.

**H. Debuts**

**United States**  Stephen Bishop-Kovacevich (pianist—San Francisco), Toshiya Eto (Japanese violinist—New York), Grace Hoffman (mezzo-soprano—New York), Paul Jacobs (pianist—New York), Charles Rosen (pianist—New York), Nicola Rossi-Lemeni (Italian bass—tour), Frans Vroons (Dutch tenor—San Francisco), Zvi Zeitlin (Yugoslav violinist—New York).

**Metropolitan Opera**  Victoria de los Angeles (Spanish soprano), Renato Capecchi (Italian baritone), Hilde Gueden (Austrian soprano), Fritz Krenn (Austrian bass), George London (bass-baritone), Mildred Miller (soprano), Elena Nikolaidi (Greek contralto), Nell Rankin (mezzo-soprano), Günther Treptow (German tenor).

**Other**  Claire Watson (soprano—Graz).

**I. New Positions**

**Conductors**  Victor Alessandro (San Antonio Symphony Orchestra—to 1976); Fausto Cleva (Metropoliatn Opera—to 1971); Guy Fraser Harrison (Oklahoma City Symphony Orchestra—to 1972); Paul Paray (French conductor—Detroit Symphony Orchestra—to 1963); Thomas Schippers (New York City Opera).

**Educational**  Leonard Bernstein (Brandeis—to 1955); Henry Cowell (Peabody—to 1956); Ben Johnston (University of Illinois—to 1983); Joseph Kerman (Berkeley—to 1971); Meyer Kupferman (composition, Sarah Lawrence College); Paul Pisk (University of Texas—to 1963); Leonard Rose (cello, Curtis—to 1962); Martial Singher (voice, Mannes College—to 1962); Roman Totenberg (strings, Mannes College—to 1957); Roger Wagner (music head, Marymount College, Los Angeles—to 1966).

**Other**  George Rochberg (editor, Theodore Presser Co.).

**J. Honors and Awards**

**Honors**   Henry Cowell (National Institute); Alan Hovhaness, Leon Kirchner, and Frank Wigglesworth (American Academy); Igor Stravinsky (American Academy Gold Medal).

**Awards**   Philippe Entremont (Long-Thibaud); Laurel Hurley (Naumburg).

**K. Biographical**   Luciano Berio and Luigi Dallapiccola (Italian composers) both make their first visits to the United States; Leonard Bernstein marries Felicia Montealegre Cohn; Margaret Buechner (German composer) comes to the United States; cellist Leonard Rose leaves the New York Philharmonic Orchestra and begins his solo career; Carlos Surinach (Spanish composer/conductor) settles in the United States; Joseph Szigeti becomes a US citizen.

**L. Musical Beginnings**

**Performing Groups**   Northwest Grand Opera Association (Seattle); San Francisco Boy's Chorus.

**Festivals**   Birmingham Festival of the Arts (Alabama).

**Educational**   National Association of College Wind and Percussion Instructors.

**Other**   American Music Editions; American Opera Society (New York); *The American String Teacher*; BMI Awards to Student Composers; Concert Artists Guild (New York).

**M. Music Publications**

Barbour, Murray, *Tuning and Temperament: A Historical Survey*
Graf, Herbert, *Opera for the People*
McHose, Allen I., *Basic Principles of the Technique of 18th Century Counterpoint*
Mursell, James L., *Music and the Classroom Teacher*
Nettl, Paul, *Forgotten Musicians*
Parrish, C. and Ohl, J. F., *Masterpieces of Music before 1750*
Rogers, Bernard, *The Art of Orchestration*
Rudolf, Réti, *The Thematic Process in Music*
Sendrey, Alfred, *Bibliography of Jewish Music*
Sessions, Roger, *Harmonic Practice*
Thomson, Virgil, *Music Right and Left*
Vega, Aurelio de la, *The New Romanticism*
Vincent, John, *The Diatonic Modes in Modern Music*

**N. Musical Compositions**

**Chamber Music**   Hugh Aitken, *String Trio*; Thomas Beversdorf, *String Quartet No. 1*; Elliott Carter, *String Quartet No. 1*; David Diamond, *String Quartet No. 4*; Morton Feldman, *Structures for String Quartet—Projections I–IV*; Alexei Haieff, *String Quartet*; Robert Helps, *String Quartet*; Lejaren Hiller, *String Quartet No. 2*; Andrew Imbrie, *String Quartet No. 2*; Charles Jones, *String Quartet No. 3*; Peter Mennin, *String Quartet No. 2*; Robert Palmer, *Wind Quintet—Viola Sonata*; Walter Piston, *String Quartet No. 4*; Wallingford Riegger, *Piano Quintet, Opus 47*; Vittorio Rieti, *String Quartet No. 3*; Roger Sessions, *String Quartet No. 2*; Ralph Shapey, *String Quartet No. 3*; Ben Weber, *String Quartet No. 2, Opus 35*; Stefan Wolpe, *Quartet* (oboe, cello, piano, percussion).

**Choral/Vocal**   George Antheil, *Eight Fragments from Shelley*; Milton Babbitt, *Du* (song cycle); Wayne Barlow, *Mass in G Major*; Ross Lee Finney, *Chamber Music* (32 songs after Joyce); Vincent Persichetti, *Harmonium, Opus 51* (song cycle after Stevens); Ned Rorem, *Cycle of Holy Songs*; Leo Smit, *A Choir of Starlings*; Virgil Thomson, *Five Songs to Poems of William Blake—Four Songs to Poems of Thomas Campion*; Robert Ward, *Sacred Songs for Pantheists*.

**Concertos**   Esther Ballou, *Prelude and Allegro for Piano and Strings*; Thomas Beversdorf, *Concerto for Two Pianos*; Ernest Bloch, *Suite Hébraïque* (viola/violin and orchestra); John Cage, *Concerto for Prepared Piano*; Paul Creston, *Concerto for Two Pianos*; Lou Harrison, *Suite for Violin, Piano and Chamber Orchestra*; Everett Helm, *Piano Concerto No. 1*; Harrison Kerr, *Violin Concerto*; Karl Kohn, *Sinfonia Concertante* (piano and orchestra); Nikolai Lopatnikoff, *Concerto for Two Pianos, Opus 33*; Otto Luening, *Louisville (Kentucky) Concerto*; Vittorio Rieti, *Concerto* *for Two Pianos*; Ned Rorem, *Piano Concerto No. 2*; Gerald Strang, *Cello Concerto*; David Van Vactor, *Violin Concerto*.

**Operas**   John J. Becker, *Faust: A Television Opera*; Leonard Bernstein, *Trouble in Tahiti*; Salvatore Martirano, *The Magic Stone*; Louis Mennini, *The Well*; Gian Carlo Menotti, *Amahl and the Night Visitors*; William Grant Still, *Mota*; Igor Stravinsky, *The Rake's Progress*; T. Carl Whitmer, *Oh, Isabel*.

**Orchestra/Band**   George Antheil, *Nocturne in Skyrockets*; Ernst Bacon, *From These States*; Philip Bezanson, *Fantasy, Fugue and Finale* (strings); Irving Fine, *Notturno for Harp and Strings*; William Flanagan, *A Concert Ode*; Howard Hanson, *Fantasy-Variations on a Theme of Youth, Opus 40*; Roy Harris, *Cumberland Concerto for Orchestra*; Robert Hall Lewis, *Concert Overture*; Robert Parris, *Symphonic Movement No. 2*; Bernard Rogers, *Leaves from the Tale of Pinocchio*; Gunther Schuller, *Dramatic Overture*; Ralph Shapey, *Fantasy for Symphony Orchestra*; Alan Shulman, *A Laurentian Overture*; Frank Wigglesworth, *Telesis*.

**Piano/Organ**   Hugh Aitken, *Four Pieces for Piano, Four Hands—Three Short Pieces*; William Bergsma, *Tangents*; John Cage, *Music of Changes*; Miriam Gideon, *Piano Suite No. 3*; Kent Kennan, *Two Preludes for Piano*; Leo Kraft, *Piano Variations*; Ernst Krenek, *Sonata No. 6, Opus 128*; Benjamin Lees, *Sonata for Two Pianos*; John Verrall, *Sonata*; George Walker, *Sonata No. 1*; Stefan Wolpe, *Seven Pieces*.

**Symphonies**   David Diamond, *Symphony No. 5*; Halim El-Dabh, *Symphony No. 2*; Alvin Etler, *Symphony*; Isadore Freed, *Symphony No. 2*; Paul Hindemith, *Symphony in B-Flat Major* (band)— *Symphony "Die Harmonie der Welt"*; Leon Kirchner, *Sinfonia*; Peter Jona Korn, *Symphony No. 2, Opus 13*; George F. McKay, *Evocation Symphony*; Vincent Persichetti, *Symphony No. 4, Opus 51*; John Powell, *Symphony on Virginia Folk Themes and in the Folk Modes*; Robert Starer, *Symphony No. 2*; Leon Stein, *Symphony No. 3 in A Major*; Alexander Tcherepnin, *Symphony No. 2 in E-Flat Major, Opus 77*; Ernst Toch, *Symphony No. 2, Opus 73*; Lester Trimble, *Symphony in Two Movements*; Joseph F. Wagner, *Symphony No. 3*; Ben Weber, *Symphony in Four Movements*.

# 1952

❀

## Historical Highlights

General Dwight D. Eisenhower is elected the 34th president; the first hydrogen bomb is exploded in the South Pacific; the McCarran-Walter Act reforms the immigration laws; the GI Bill of Rights for Korean veterans is passed; Puerto Rico becomes a member of the United States Commonwealth; Elizabeth II becomes British monarch on the death of her father; Juan Batista seizes power in Cuba; a Korean Armistice is declared.

## World Cultural Highlights

**World Art**   Marc Chagall, *Green Night*; Roberto Crippa, *Aurora Borealis*; Barbara Hepworth, *Evocation*; Georges Rouault, *The End of Autumn*; Stanley Spencer, *The Sabbath Breakers*.

**World Literature**   Jean Anouilh, *Waltz of the Toreadors*; Samuel Becket, *Waiting for Godot*; Agatha Christie, *The Mousetrap*; Dylan Thomas, *Under Milk Wood*.

**World Music**   Sergei Prokofiev, *Symphony No. 7*; Karlheinz Stockhausen, *Spiel*; Michael Tippett, *The Midsummer Marriage*; Ralph Vaughan Williams, *Sinfonia Antartica*.

**Miscellaneous**   The Shakespeare Festival, the Canadian Broadcasting Co. Symphony, and the Edmonton Symphony are founded in Canada; deaths include Frances Alda, Alfred Einstein, Paul Éluard, Henry Expert, and Ferenc Molnar.

## American Art and Literature Highlights

**Births/Deaths**   Births include artists David Bates, David Salle, sculptor Timothy Woodman, and literary figures Rita Dove, Beth Henley, Alice Hoffman, Jane Anne Phillips, and Amy Tan; deaths include art figures Oscar Berninghaus, Arthur Carles, Howard Christy, Jo Davidson, Bernard Karfiol, C. Chandler Ross, Adolph Weinman, and literary figures Eugene Jolas, Charles F. Oursler, and George Santayana.

**Art Works**   Leonard Baskin, *Mantegna at Eremitani*; Helen Frankenthaler, *Mountains and Seas*; Willem de Kooning, *Woman, No. 1*; Yasuo Kuniyoshi, *The Amazing Juggler*; Jack Levine, *King Saul*; John Marin, *The Written Sea*; Walter Murch, *Governor II*; Jackson Pollack, *Convergence*; Hugo Robus, *Passing Years*; Theodore Roszak, *Whaler of Nantucket*; Theodoros Stamos, *Greek Orison*.

**Literature**   Ralph Ellison, *The Invisible Man* (National Book Award); Edna Ferber, *Giant*; Ernest K. Gann, *The High and the Mighty*; Ernest Hemingway, *The Old Man and the Sea* (Pulitzer Prize); Joseph Kramm, *The Shrike* (Pulitzer Prize); Archibald MacLeish, *Collected Poems* (Pulitzer Prize—National Book Award); John Steinbeck, *East of Eden*; E. B. White, *Charlotte's Web*.

## Music—The Vernacular/Commercial Scene

**A. Births**   Ray Anderson (trombone) October 16; Karla Bonoff (songwriter) December 27; Billy Branch (harmonica) October 3; David Byrne (singer/writer) May 14; John Campbell (guitarist/singer); John Clayton (bass) August 8; Randy Crawford (singer) February 18; Mark Dresser (doublebass) September 26; Rudy Gatlin (singer) August 20; John Hiatt (singer/writer) August 20; James Ingram (singer) February 17; Grace Jones (singer/writer) May 19; Henry Kaiser (guitarist) September 19; George Lewis (trombonist) July 14; John McCutcheon (folk musician) August 14; Michael McDonald (singer/writer); Juice Newton (singer) February 18; Mandy Patinkin (singer/actor) November 30; Lee Ritenour (guitarist) January 11; Hilton Ruiz (pianist) May 29; Jules Shear (singer/writer) March 7; Ricky Van Shelton (singer) January 12; Janis Siegel (singer) July 23; Phoebe Snow (singer) July 17; George Strait (singer) May 18.

**B. Deaths**   Fletcher Henderson (pianist) December 29; John Kirby (string bass/bandleader) June 14; Gertrude Lawrence (actress/singer) September 6; "Uncle Dave" Macon (singer) March 22; Edward Madden (lyricist) March 11; Percy Wenrich (songwriter/pianist) March 17.

**C. Biographical**

**Performing Groups**   The Four Coins; The Hilltoppers; Kentucky Travelers; Gladys Knight and the Pips; Moonglows: Moroccos; Gerry Mulligan Quartet (Los Angeles); Sauter-Finnegan Orchestra; Spaniels; The Tams (Four Dots); Billy Taylor Trio; Tennessee Cutups.

**New Beginnings**   Old Town Records; Charles H. Pace Music Publishers (Pittsburgh); Pacific Jazz Records (Los Angeles); Sun Records.

**D. Publications**   G. P. Jackson, *Another Sheaf of White Spirituals*; Barry Ulanov, *A History of Jazz in America*.

**E. Representative Works**

**Musicals**   Ralph Blane, *Three Wishes for Jamie*; Vernon Duke and O. Nash, *Two's Company*; Frank Loesser, *Hans Christian Andersen* (film); Harold Rome and J. Logan, *Wish You Were Here*.

**Songs**   Irving Berlin, *Count Your Blessings*; Tommie Connor, *I Saw Mommie Kissing Santa Claus*; Bill Haley, *Rock a-Beatin' Boogie*; J. Leiber and M. Stoller, *Kansas City—Hound Dog*; B. Kaper and H. Deutsch, *Hi Lili, Hi Lo*; Dick Manning and Al Hoffman, *Takes Two To Tango*; Dmitri Tiomkin and Ned Washington, *Do Not Forsake Me* (*High Noon*—Oscar); Hank Williams, *Jambalaya—Your Cheatin' Heart*.

**Other**   Leroy Anderson, *Blue Tango*; Bernard Herrmann, *The Snows of Kilimanjaro* (film music); Richard Rodgers, *Victory at Sea* (TV film music); Miklós Rózsa, *Ivanhoe* (film music); George Shearing, *Lullaby of Birdland*; Dimitri Tiomkin, *High Noon* (film music).

## Music—The Cultivated/Art Music Scene

**F. Births**   June Anderson (soprano) December 30; William David Black (pianist) February 23; Gwendolyn Bradley (soprano) December 12; Rhys Chatham (composer) September 19; Kristine Ciesinski (soprano) July 5; Maggie Cole (harpsichordist); Janice Gail Eckhart (mezzo-soprano) July 21; Jill Feldman (soprano) April 21; Peter Garland (composer/publisher) January 27; Jay Mitchell Gottlieb (pianist) October 23; Jerry Hadley (tenor) June 16; Vernon Hartman (baritone) July 12; Scott Johnson (composer) May 12; Lia Kahler (mezzo-soprano); Kim Kashkashian (violist) August 31; Ida Kavafian (violinist) October 29; Linda Kobler (harpsichordist); Chris Merritt (tenor) September 27; Kathryn Montgomery (soprano) September 23; Beverly Morgan (soprano) March 17; Pamela Myers (soprano); Ashley Putnam (soprano) August 10; Linda Roark-Strummer (soprano); Megan Roberts (composer) October 12; Santiago Rodriguez (pianist) February 16; Gianna Rolandi (soprano) August 16; André-Michel Schub (pianist) December 26; Diana Soviero (soprano); Carol Vaness (soprano) July 27.

**G. Deaths**   Frances Alda (New Zealand soprano) September 18; Paul Hastings Allen (composer) September 28; Richard Buhlig (pianist) January 30; Adolf Busch (German-born violinist/composer) June 9; Rossetter Gleason Cole (organist/composer) May 18; Ruth Crawford (composer) November 18; Giuseppe Creatore (Italian-born conductor/impresario) August 15; Emma Eames (soprano) June 13; Alfred Einstein (German-born musicologist) February 13; Arthur Farwell (composer/publisher) January 20; Wallace Goodrich (organist/conductor) June 6; Frederick Jacobi (composer/conductor) October 24; Harry B. Jepson (organist) August 23; Ralph Kinder (organist) November 14; Riccardo Martin (tenor) August 11; Beryl Rubinstein (pianist/composer) December 29; Felix Salmond (British-born cellist) February 19; Elisabeth Schumann (German-born soprano) February 19.

**H. Debuts**

**United States**   John Alexander (tenor—Cincinnati), Augustin Anievas (pianist—New York), Donald Grobe (tenor—Chicago), Laurel Hurley (soprano—New York), Jean Langlais (French organist—tour), Jaime Laredo (Bolivian pianist—San Francisco), John Macurdy (bass—New Orleans), Lois Marshall (Canadian mezzo-soprano—New York), James McCracken (tenor—Central City, Colorado), Leontyne Price (soprano—New York), Gerald Tarack (violinist—New York), Beverly Wolff (mezzo-soprano—Philadelphia).

**Metropolitan Opera**   Sigurd Björling (Swedish baritone), Josef Greindl (German bass), Richard Holm (German tenor), Elisabeth Höngen (German mezzo-soprano), Hans Hopf (German tenor), Erich Kunz (Austrian bass), Brenda Lewis (soprano).

**I. New Positions**

**Conductors**   Samuel Adler (Seventh Army Symphony Orchestra); Edvard Fendler (Mobile Symphony Orchestra—to 1957); Massimo Freccia (Baltimore Symphony Orchestra—to 1959); Alexander Hilsberg (New Orleans Philharmonic Symphony Orchestra—to 1960); Leslie Hodge (Phoenix Symphony Orchestra—to 1959); William Steinberg (Pittsburgh Symphony Orchestra—to 1976).

**Educational**   Walter Aschaffenburg (composition, Oberlin—to 1987); Leslie Bassett (University of Michigan); Sarah Caldwell (director, Boston University Opera Workshop); Sidney Foster (Indiana University—to 1977); Scott Huston (Cincinnati Conservatory—to 1988); Earl Kim (Princeton—to 1967); Egon Petri (San Francisco Conservatory—to 1962); Jerome Rosen (University of California, Davis); Seymour Shifrin (Berkeley—to 1966); Edward Steuermann (piano, Juilliard—to 1964).

**Other**   George Rochberg (editor, Theodore Presser); Lester Trimble (music critic, *New York Herald-Tribune*—to 1962).

**J. Honors and Awards**

**Honors**   Robert Kurka (American Academy); Robert Moevs (Rome Prize); Edward Steuermann (Schoenberg Medal).

**Awards**   Van Cliburn (Chopin Prize); Mario Di Bonaventura (Besançon Competition); Leon Fleisher (Queen Elisabeth—first American to win).

**K. Biographical**   Victor Aitay, Paul Doktor, and Werner Torkanowsky become American citizens; Dominick Argento receives a Fulbright grant to study in Florence, Italy; Christoph von Dohnányi (German conductor) comes to the United States to study with his grandfather, Ernst von Dohnányi; Charles Munch takes the Boston Symphony Orchestra on its first European tour; Leontyne Price marries baritone William Warfield (divorced in 1972); Albert Schweitzer receives the Nobel Peace Prize for his work in Africa; guitarist John Williams wins a guitar audition and begins studying with Segovia.

**L. Musical Beginnings**

**Performing Groups**   Eastman Wind Ensemble; Gilbert and Sullivan Society (Houston); Hilltop Musical (Opera) Co. (Baltimore); Kentucky Opera Association (Louisville); New York Pro Musica (Pro Musica Antiqua); San Francisco Chamber Orchestra; Queens College Faculty String Quartet; Scottish Rite Symphony Orchestra (Syracuse, New York).

**Festivals**   Pittsburgh International Festival.

**Other**   *Bulletin of the American Composers' Alliance*; Composer's Facsimile Edition (American Composers Edition in 1972); Fromm Music Foundation (Harvard); Modern Music Masters Society (Park Ridge, Illinois); Recording Industries Association of America (RIAA); Southeastern Composers' League (South Carolina); Young Audiences (New York).

**M. Music Publications**

Copland, Aaron, *Music and Imagination*
Davison, Archibald, *Church Music: Illusion and Reality*
Hindemith, Paul, *A Composer's World*
Kennan, Kent, *The Technique of Orchestration*
Luening, Otto, *Electronic Tape Music*
Pratt, Carroll, *Music as the Language of Emotion*
Salzer, Felix, *Structural Hearing: Tonal Coherence in Music*
Slonimsky, Nicolas, *Lexicon of Musical Invective*
Smith, Cecil, *Worlds of Music*
Stevenson, Robert M., *Music in Mexico: A Historical Survey*
Ulrich, Homer, *Symphonic Music*

**N. Musical Compositions**

**Chamber Music**   Ernest Bloch, *String Quartet No. 3* (New York Music Critics' Award); John Cage, *4'33"* (for any instrument tacet); David M. Epstein, *String Quartet No. 1*; Irving Fine, *String Quartet*; Vivian Fine, *Violin Sonata*; Andrew Imbrie, *Serenade for Flute, Violin and Piano*; Peter Jona Korn, *Horn Sonata*; Billy Jim Layton, *Five Studies for Violin and Piano*; Benjamin Lees, *String Quartet No. 1*; Paul Nordoff, *Violin Sonata No. 2*; Robert Palmer, *Clarinet Quintet*; Robert Parris, *String Quartet No. 2*; Wallingford Riegger, *Woodwind Quintet, Opus 51*; George Rochberg, *String Quartet No. 1* (Society for Publication of American Music Prize); Alan Stout, *String Quartet No. 1*; Igor Stravinsky, *Octet*; Clifford Taylor, *Violin Sonata* (Harvey Gaul Prize); John Verrall, *String Quartet No. 5*.

**Choral/Vocal**   Jack Beeson, *Two Songs on Betjeman—Six Lyrics on English and American Poets*; Wallace Berry, *Spoon River*; Lukas Foss, *A Parable of Death* (cantata); Miriam Gideon, *Epitaphs for Robert Burns—Sonnets from "Fatal Interview"* (song cycles); Ulysses Kay, *Three Pieces after Blake*; Robert Starer, *Kohelet (Ecclesiastes)*; Igor Stravinsky, *Cantata*.

**Concertos**   George Barati, *Chamber Concerto*; Philip Bezanson, *Piano Concerto*; Ernest Bloch, *Concerto Grosso No. 2*; Morton Gould, *Concerto for Tap Dancer and Orchestra*; Ray Green, *Violin Concerto*; Scott Huston, *Toccata* (piano and orchestra); Ernst Krenek, *Violin Concerto No. 1*; Peter Mennin, *Concertato "Moby Dick"*; Gian Carlo Menotti, *Violin Concerto in A Minor*; Robert Muczynski, *Divertimento, Opus 2, for Piano and Orchestra*; Burrill Phillips, *Triple Concerto* (clarinet, viola, piano); Florence Price, *Violin Concerto No. 2*; Adolph Weiss, *Trumpet Concerto*.

**Electronic**    Otto Luening, *Fantasy in Space* (tape); Vladimir Ussachevsky, *Sonic Contours* (tape recorder).

**Operas**    George Antheil, *Volpone*; Donald Lybbert, *Monica*; Ned Rorem, *A Childhood Miracle*; Alexander Tcherepnin, *The Farmer and the Fairy* (Bispham Medal); Hugo Weisgall, *The Stranger*.

**Orchestra/Band**    George Antheil, *Capital of the World* (ballet); Samuel Barber, *Souvenirs* (ballet); Irwin Bazelon, *Concert Overture*; Arthur Berger, *Ideas of Order*; Jean Berger, *Petit Suite* (strings); Robert McBride, *Pumpkin Eater's Little Fugue*; Gian Carlo Menotti, *Apocalypse*; Charles Mills, *Theme and Variations*; Robert Mocvs, *Fourteen Variations for Orchestra*; Miklós Rozsa, *Variations on The Vintner's Daughter*; Arthur Shepherd, *Variations on an Original Theme*; Howard Swanson, *Music for Strings*; Clifford Taylor, *Theme and Variations* (National Symphony Orchestra Prize); Virgil Thomson, *King Lear* (incidental music)—*The Harvest According* (ballet); David Van Vactor, *Masque of the Red Death*; Christian Wolff, *Suite No. 1*.

**Piano/Organ**    Esther Ballou, *Music for the Theater* (two pianos); Jean Berger, *Sonatina*; Seth Bingham, *Thirty-Six Hymn and Carol Canons* (organ); Norman Dello Joio, *Aria and Toccata* (two pianos); Robert Evett, *Sonata No. 2*; Arthur Farwell, *Polytonal Studies, Opus 109*; Vivian Fine, *Piano Variations*; Ross Lee Finney, *Variations on a Theme by Alban Berg*; Lee Hoiby, *Five Preludes, Opus 7*; Alan Hovhaness, *Fantasy for Piano*; Jean Eichelberger Ivey, *Theme and Variations*; Ezra Laderman, *Sonata No. 1*; Robert Muczynski, *Five Sketches, Opus 3*; Robert Palmer, *Sonata for Piano, Four Hands*; Vincent Persichetti, *Sonata No. 9, Opus 50*; George Rochberg, *Twelve Bagatelles*; Ned Rorem, *Sonata No. 2*; Ralph Shapey, *Piano Suite*; Robert Starer, *Five Preludes*.

**Symphonies**    Jean Berger, *Sinfonia Breve*; Raynor Brown, *Symphony No. 1*; Edward T. Cone, *Symphony*; Henry Cowell, *Symphonies No. 6, 7, 8*; Paul Creston, *Symphony No. 4*; Emma Lou Diemer, *Symphony No. 1*; Cecil Effinger, *Symphony No. 4*; Roger Goeb, *Symphony No. 3*; Gene Gutché, *Symphony No. 3*; Roy Harris, *Symphony No. 7* (Naumburg Award); Erich Korngold, *Symphony in F-Sharp Major, Opus 40*; Gail Kubik, *Symphony Concertante* (Pulitzer Prize); Meyer Kupferman, *Little Symphony*; Wesley La Violette, *Symphony No. 3*; Harold Morris, *Symphony No. 3, "Amaranth"—Symphony No. 4*; Robert Parris, *Symphony*; Ralph Shapey, *Symphony No. 1*; Alexander Tcherepnin, *Symphony No. 3, Opus 83*; George Tremblay, *Symphony No. 2*; Joseph Wood, *Symphony No. 2*.

# 1953

❈

## Historical Highlights

The experimental Bell X-1A reaches a speed in excess of 1,600 mph; the Communist Party is forced to register as an agent of the USSR; the Refugee Relief Act allows people fleeing Communism to enter the United States; the Department of Health, Education, and Welfare (HEW) is formed; Joseph Stalin dies and Georgi Malenkov becomes Russian Premier; Russian tanks crush an East Berlin uprising; Dag Hammarskjöld is elected Secretary-General of the United Nations.

## World Cultural Highlights

**World Art**    Willi Baumeister, *Mortaruru with Red Overhead;* Georges Braque, *Apples;* Marc Chagall, *The Eiffel Tower*; Jean Dubuffet, *The Busy Life.*

**World Literature**    Jean Anouilh, *L'Alouette*; Samuel Beckett, *The Unnamable;* Arthur C. Clarke, *Childhood's End;* Jacques Cousteau, *Silent World.*

**World Music**    Benjamin Britten, *Gloriana*; Aram Khachaturian, *Spartacus*; Olivier Messiaen, *Réveil des oiseaux*; Dmitri Shostakovich, *Symphony No. 10*; William Walton, *Orb and Scepter March.*

**Miscellaneous**    The Bergen International Music Festivals begin; births include Riccardo Chailly,

Andras Schiff, and Hugh Wolff; deaths include Hilaire Belloc, Ivan Bunin, Émile Cammaerts, Raoul Dufy, Joseph Jongen, Sergei Prokofiev, Jérôme Tharaud, and Dylan Thomas.

## American Art and Literature Highlights

**Births/Deaths**  Births include artists David Beck, Robert Longo, Charles Ray, and Tom Waldron and novelists Brad Leithauser and Alice MacDermott; deaths include art figures James Fraser, John Marin, Everett Shinn, Niles Spencer, Bradley W. Tomlin, and literary figures Gordon Gerould, Elaine and Dora Goodale, Eugene O'Neill, Marjorie Kinnan Rawlings, and Ben Ames Williams.

**Art Works**  William Baziotes, *Primeval Landscape*; Stuart Davis, *Semé*; Helen Frankenthaler, *Open Wall*; Ellsworth Kelly, *Spectral Colors Arranged By Chance*; Jack Levine, *The Gangster Funeral*; Seymour Lipton, *Sanctuary*; Jackson Pollock, *Portrait and a Dream*; Abraham Rattner, *Composition with Three Figures*; Larry Rivers, *Washington Crossing the Delaware*; Jack Tworkov, *The Wheel*.

**Literature**  Saul Bellow, *The Adventures of Augie March* (National Book Award); Charles B. Catton, *A Stillness at Appomatox* (National Book Award); William Inge, *Picnic* (Pulitzer Prize—New York Drama Critics' Award); Arthur Miller, *The Crucible*; John Patrick, *Teahouse of the August Moon* (Pulitzer Prize—New York Drama Critics' Award); Theodore Roethke, *The Waking* (Pulitzer Prize).

## Music—The Vernacular/Commercial Scene

**A. Births**  Fred Ahlert (songwriter) October 20; Deborah Allen (singer/writer) September 30; Pat Benatar (singer) January 10; David Benoit (pianist/composer); Michael Bolton (singer) February 26; Michael Bonagura (singer) March 26; Angela Brown (singer); Billy Burnette (singer/guitarist) May 8; Jonathan "Rocky" Burnette (singer/writer) June 12; James Chance (saxophonist) April 20; Marshall Crenshaw (singer/writer) November 11; Meg Davis (singer/writer) January 28; Alex De Grassi (guitarist/composer) February 13; Ronnie Dunn (singer) June 1; Jon Faddis (trumpeter) July 24; Nanci Griffith (singer/writer) July 6; Jeff Hamilton (drummer) August 4; Craig Harris (trombonist) September 10; James Horner (composer/arranger) August 14; Hal Ketchum (singer) April 9; Chaka Khan (singer) March 23; Cyndi Lauper (singer) June 20; James Newton (jazz flutist) May 1; Terre Roche (singer) April 10; Michele Rosewomen (pianist) March 19; "Mad Dog" Watkins (guitarist/singer) July 19; Bobby Watson (saxophonist) August 23; Lucinda Williams (singer/writer) January.

**B. Deaths**  Irene Bordoni (singer) March 19; Peter De Rose (composer) April 24; George Pullen Jackson (folk singer) January 19; Ruth Crawford Seeger (folk song expert) November 18; Hank Williams (singer) January 1.

**C. Biographical**

**Performing Groups**  Chet Baker Big Band; The Cadillacs; The Chords; The Dells; Dreams (Lee Andrews and the Hearts); Drifters I; Les Elgart Band; The Harptones; The Larks (Meadowlarks); Osborne Brothers; The Platters; The Rivingtons; Max Roach Jazz Quartet; The Staples; The Willows.

**New Beginnings**  Bethlehem Record Co.; Delmark Records; Fender Stratocaster Guitar; Florida Folk Festival (White Springs); Hickory Records (Nashville); Institute of Jazz Studies; *Music, Books on Music, and Sound Recordings* (by Library of Congress); National Oldtime Fiddler's Contest (Weiser, Idaho); Riverside Records (New York); VeeJay Records.

**Miscellaneous**  Ray Conniff becomes music director for Columbia Records; an accident in concert results in Dizzy Gillespie's unique "bell-up" trumpet.

**D. Publications**  R. P. Crawford, *American Folk Songs for Christmas*; Miles M. Fisher, *Negro Slave Songs in the United States*; *The Burl Ives Songbook*.

**E. Representative Works**

**Musicals**  L. Bernstein, B. Comden, and A. Green, *Wonderful Town* (New York Drama Critics' Award); S. Fain and P. F. Webster, *Calamity Jane* (film—adapted for stage); C. Porter and A. Burrows, *Can-Can*; Rodgers and Hammerstein, *Me and Juliet*; J. Styne and B. Hilliard, *Hazel Flagg*; R. Wright and G. Forrest, *Kismet* (based on music of Borodin).

**Songs**  S. Fine and H. B. Gilbert, *The Moon Is Blue*; Arthur Hamilton, *Cry Me a River*; Fred Karger and Bob Wells, *From Here to Eternity*; Bob Merrill, *How Much Is That Doggie in the Window*; Marty Robbins, *Singin' the Blues*; L. Russell and B. Pepper, *Vaya Con Dios*; Al Stillman, E. Drake, and J. Shirt, *I Believe*; Harry Warren, *That's Amore*.

**Other**  Hugo Friedhofer, *Island in the Sky* (film music); Bernard Herrmann, *Beneath the Twelve-Mile Reef* (film music); Alfred Newman, *The Robe—Love Is a Many-Splendored Thing* (film music—Oscar); Miklós Rózsa, *Julius Caesar* (film music); Victor Young, *Shane* (film music).

## Music—The Cultivated/Art Music Scene

**F. Births**  Daniel Asia (composer); Richard Buckley (conductor) September 1; David Burgess (guitarist) August 22; Kaaren Erickson (soprano) February 9; Juliana Kathleen Gondale (soprano) May 20; Eric Halfvarson (bass); Janice Hall (soprano) September 28; Kevin Hanlon (composer) January 1; David Hykes (composer/performer) March 2; Mark Kaplan (violinist) December 30; Kenneth Kiesler (conductor) August 18; David Leisner (guitarist/composer) December 22; Lynne Lewandowski (harp maker) May 14; Peter Scott Lewis (composer); David Lively (pianist) June 27; Tod Machover (cellist/composer) November 24; Erie Mills (soprano) June 22; Claudette Peterson (soprano) July 15; Stephen Robinson (guitarist) August 16; Neil Rutman (pianist) July 12; Brian Schexnayder (baritone) September 18; Roberto Sierra (composer) October 9; Carl Stone (composer/performer) February 10; William Winant (percussionist) February 11; Hugh Wolff (conductor) October 21; John Zorn (composer) September 2.

**G. Deaths**  Suzanne Adams (soprano) February 5; John Parsons Beach (composer/pianist) November 6; Nicolai Berezowsky (Russian-born composer) August 27; Melville Antone Clark (harpsichord maker) December 11; Elizabeth Sprague Coolidge (art patron) November 4; Arthur M. Curry (composer/pedagogue) December 30; Eric De Lamarter (organist/conductor) May 17; Sidney Homer (composer) July 10; Henry Holden Huss (pianist/composer) September 17; William Kapell (pianist) October 29; Frank La Forge (pianist/composer) May 5; Henry C. Lahee (British-born musicologist) April 11; Virgilio Lazzari (Italian-born bass) October 4; Hugh F. MacColl (composer/organist) October 17; Daniel Gregory Mason (composer/educator) December 4; Gaetano Merola (Italian-born conductor/manager) August 30; T. Tertius Noble (British-born organist/composer) May 4; Florence Bea Price (composer/educator) June 3; Friedrich Schorr (Hungarian-born baritone) August 14; Albert Spaulding (violinist) May 26; Frank Edwin Ward (organist) September 15; Reinald Werrenrath (baritone) September 12.

**H. Debuts**

**United States**  Paul Badura-Skoda (Austrian pianist—New York), Inge Borkh (German soprano—San Francisco), Phillippe Entremont (French pianist—New York), Ferenc Fricsay (Hungarian conductor—Boston), Josef Krips (Austrian conductor—Buffalo), James Levine (age 10, as pianist), Karl Münchinger (German conductor—San Francisco), Elizabeth Schwarzkopf (German soprano—Carnegie Hall), Georg Solti (Hungarian conductor—San Francisco), Ludwig Suthaus (German tenor—San Francisco), Dubravka Tomsic (Yugoslav pianist—Chicago), Cesare Valletti (Italian tenor—San Francisco), Paul Zukofsky (violinist—New Haven, Connecticut).

**Metropolitan Opera**  Ettore Bastianini (Italian baritone), Lisa Della Casa (Swiss soprano), Jean Fenn (soprano), James McCracken (tenor), Josef Metternich (German baritone), Nicola Rossi-Lemeni (Italian bass), Irmgard Seefried (German soprano), Theodor Uppman (baritone), Cesare Valletti (Italian tenor), Sandra Warfield (mezzo-soprano).

**Other**  Irene Dalis (mezzo-soprano—Oldenburg).

**I. New Positions**

**Conductors**  Kurt Herbert Adler (artistic director, San Francisco Opera—to 1981); Fritz Mahler (Hartford Symphony Orchestra—to 1964); Fritz Reiner (Chicago Symphony Orchestra—to 1962).

**Educational**  Warren Benson (Ithaca College, New York—to 1967); Arthur Berger (Brandeis—to 1979); Paul Doktor (Mannes); Ernst C. Krohn (music director, St. Louis University—to 1963); Bruno Nettl (Wayne State University—to 1964); Claude Palisca (University of Illinois—to 1959);

Carl Parrish (Vassar—to 1965); Albert Seay (Colorado College); Roger Sessions (Conant Professor, Princeton—to 1965); Homer Ulrich (music chair, University of Maryland—to 1972).

**Other**  Samuel Adler (music director, Temple Emmanu-El, Dallas); John Brownlee (president, American Guild of Musical Artists—to 1967); James Lyons (music critic, *New York Herald Tribune*—to 1962).

## J. Honors and Awards

**Honors**  Peggy Glanville-Hicks, Roger Goeb, Nikolai Lopatnikoff, and Roger Sessions (American Academy); Karl L. King (PhD, Phillips University).

**Awards**  Elliott Carter (Rome Prize); Ellen Goldstein (Busoni); Betsy Jolas (Besançon).

**K. Biographical**  Leonard Bernstein becomes first American to conduct at La Scala; Victor Borge begins a three-year run on Broadway with his Comedy in Music show; Mattiwilda Dobbs becomes the first black person to sing at La Scala; Pozzi Escot (Peruvian composer) and Rolf Gehlhaar (German composer) emigrate to the United States; Szymon Goldberg becomes a US citizen; Margaret Harshaw makes her Covent Garden debut; Vladimir Horowitz begins a long semi-retirement, giving only occasional performances or recordings; Ticho Parly (Danish tenor) comes to the United States and studies at Indiana University; Helen Traubel leaves the Metropolitan Opera after quarrels with Rudolf Bing and concentrates on Broadway and films.

## L. Musical Beginnings

**Performing Groups**  American Ballet Center (New York); Merce Cunningham Dance Co.; Lyric Art Quartet-Quintet (Houston); Miami Beach Symphony Orchestra; Portland Lyric Theater (Maine); Santa Fe (Rio Grande) Symphony Orchestra.

**Festivals**  New Hampshire Music Festival (Center Harbor); Peninsula Music Festival (Fish Creek, Wisconsin).

**Educational**  American School Band Directors Association (Michigan); Columbia University Tape Studio; National Catholic Bandmasters' Association (Notre Dame).

**Other**  *Ethnomusicology*; Louisville Records; Ronald A. Wilford and Associates, Artist Management.

## M. Music Publications

Barlow, Wayne, *Foundations of Music*
Dickinson, George, *The Study of Music as a Liberal Art*
Ellinwood, Leonard, *The History of American Church Music*
Nettl, Bruno, *North American Indian Musical Styles*
Read, Gardner, *Thesaurus of Orchestral Devices*
Russell, George, *The Lydian Chromatic Concept of Tonal Organization*
Sachs, Curt, *Rhythm and Tempo: A Study in Music History*
Seeger, Charles, *Music and Society: Some New World Evidence of Their Relationship*
Stevenson, Robert M., *Patterns of Protestant Church Music*
Weinstock, Herbert, *Music as an Art*

## N. Musical Compositions

**Chamber Music**  Samuel Adler, *String Quartet No. 3*; Milton Babbitt, *Woodwind Quartet*; Leslie Bassett, *Trio for Viola, Clarinet and Piano*; Jack Beeson, *Viola Sonata*; William Bergsma, *String Quartet No. 3*; Easley Blackwood, *Viola Sonata*; Ernest Bloch, *String Quartet No. 4*; Earl Brown, *Folio* (unspecified instrumentation); Ross Lee Finney, *Piano Quintet No. 1*; Lejaren Hiller, *String Quartet No. 3;* Karel Husa, *String Quartet No. 2*; Andrew Imbrie, *String Quartet No. 2*; Clarence Loomis, *String Quartet No. 1*; Wallingford Riegger, *Concerto for Piano and Woodwind Quintet, Opus 53*; George Rochberg, *Chamber Symphony* (Naumburg Recording Award); Ralph Shapey, *String Quartet No. 4*; Leo Sowerby, *Festival Musick*; Halsey Stevens, *Horn Sonata*; Alan Stout, *String Quartets No. 1, 2*; Ernst Toch, *String Quartet No. 13*; Burnet Tuthill, *String Quartet*.

**Choral/Vocal**  Jacob Avshalomov, *Tom o'Bedlam* (New York Music Critics' Award); Richard

Bales, *The Confederacy*; Samuel Barber, *Hermit Songs*; Wallace Berry, *Canticle on a Judaic Text*; Cecil Effinger, *The St. Luke Christmas Story*; Herbert Elwell, *The Forever Young*; Roy Harris, *Abraham Lincoln Walks at Midnight*; Normand Lockwood, *The Prairie*; Louis Mennini, *Mass*; Leroy Robertson, *Book of Mormon* (oratorio); Ned Rorem, *Five Songs for High Voice and Orchestra—Poèmes pour la Paix* (song cycle); Halsey Stevens, *Four Songs of Love and Death*; Virgil Thomson, *Kyrie*.

**Concertos**  Hugh Aitken, *Piano Concerto*; Esther Ballou, *Concertino for Oboe and Strings*; Arcady Dubensky, *Trombone Concerto*; Robert Erickson, *Fantasy for Cello and Orchestra*; Roger Goeb, *Violin Concerto*; Leon Kirchner, *Piano Concerto No. 1* (Naumburg Award); Nicolas Nabokov, *Cello Concerto, "Les hommages"*; Quincy Porter, *Concerto Concertante for Two Pianos and Orchestra* (Pulitzer Prize); Wallingford Riegger, *Variations for Piano and Orchestra*; Vittorio Rieti, *Cello Concerto No. 2*; Robert Starer, *Piano Concerto No. 2*; Paul Turok, *Violin Concerto*.

**Operas**  Samuel Barber, *A Hand of Bridge*; Peggy Glanville-Hicks, *The Transposed Heads*; Clarence Loomis, *The Captive Woman*; Gian Carlo Menotti, *The Saint of Bleecker Street* (Pulitzer Prize); William Schuman, *The Mighty Casey*; Julia Smith, *Cockcrow*; Peter Westergaard, *Charivari*.

**Orchestra/Band**  Warren Benson, *A Delphic Serenade*; Thomas Beversdorf, *New Frontiers*; Henry Brant, *Antiphony I* (five orchestral groups); Lee Hoiby, *Suite No. 2, Opus 8*; Billy Jim Layton, *An American Portrait*; Jerome Moross, *The Last Judgment*; Ron Nelson, *Savannah River Holiday*; Gardner Read, *Toccata Giocosa, Opus 94*; William Schuman, *Voyage for a Theater* (ballet); Leo Smit, *Concert Overture, The Parcae*; Leo Sowerby, *Fantasy Portrait*; Halsey Stevens, *Triskelion*; Igor Stravinsky, *Tango*; Virgil Thomson, *The Grass Harp* (incidental music); Richard Wernick, *The Trojan Women* (incidental music).

**Piano/Organ**  Earle Brown, *25 Pages for 1 to 25 Pianos*; John Cage, *Music for Piano*; Ingolf Dahl, *Sonata Seria*; Robert Evett, *Sonata No. 3*; Miriam Gideon, *Six Cuckoos in Quest of a Composer*; Mel Powell, *Sonatina*; William Schuman, *Voyages*; Leo Smit, *Fantasy: The Farewell*; Alexander Tcherepnin, *Twelve Preludes, Opus 85*; George Walker, *Sonata No. 1*; Stefan Wolpe, *Enchantments*.

**Symphonies**  Samuel Adler, *Symphony No. 1*; Henry Cowell, *Symphony No. 9—Symphony No. 10*; Miriam Gideon, *Symphonia Brevis*; Alan Hovhaness, *Symphony No. 5, Opus 170*; Ernst Krenek, *Symphony, "Pallas Athene"*; William Latham, *Symphony No. 2*; Benjamin Lees, *Symphony No. 1*; Bohuslav Martinů, *Fantaisies Symphoniques (Symphony No. 6—New York Critics' Circle Award)*; Peter Mennin, *Symphony No. 6*; Robert Muczynski, *Symphony, Opus 5*; Robert Palmer, *Symphony No. 1*; Vincent Persichetti, *Symphony No. 5, "For Strings," Opus 61*; Seymour Shifrin, *Chamber Symphony*; Frank Wigglesworth, *Symphony No. 1*.

# 1954

☼

## Historical Highlights

The first atomic powered submarine, the *Nautilus*, is launched; the Communist party loses its legal status in the United States; racial segregation in public schools is outlawed by the Supreme Court; the Air Force Academy opens in Colorado Springs; the United States signs a mutual defense treaty with Japan; the French are driven out of Vietnam, which is now divided into North and South; the Southeast Asia Treaty Organization (SEATO) is created; Russia blocks all efforts to unify Germany.

## World Cultural Highlights

**World Art**  Marc Chagall, *The Red Roofs*; Salvador Dali, *The Crucifixion*; Fernand Léger, *Acrobat on a Horse*; Pablo Picasso, *Sylvette*.

**World Literature**   Kingsley Amis, *Lucky Jim*; Cecil Day-Lewis, *Collected Poems*; William Golding, *Lord of the Flies*; J. R. R. Tolkien, *The Lord of the Rings*.

**World Music**   Benjamin Britten, *The Turn of the Screw*; Witold Lutoslawski, *Concerto for Orchestra*; Edgard Varèse, *Deserts*; Ralph Vaughan Williams, *Tuba Concerto*; Iannis Xenakis, *Metastasis*.

**Miscellaneous**   The Gothenburg School of Music opens; the Cork International Choral Festival and Swedish Contemporary Music Festival begin; deaths include Franz Bengtsson, André Derain, Wilhelm Furtwängler, James Hilton, Clemens Krauss, and Henri Matisse.

## American Art and Literature Highlights

**Births/Deaths**   Births include artists Gerald Berg, Holly Lane, and literary figures Lorna Dee Cervantes, Louise Erdrich, Harvey Fierstein, and Elizabeth Tallent; deaths include artists Mary Longman, Reginald Marsh, and literary figures Walter Arensberg, Leonard Bacon, Maxwell Bodenheim, Joseph Hergesheimer, William March (Campbell), Samuel Shellabarger, and Rita Weiman.

**Art Works**   Isobel Bishop, *Snack Bar*; Hans Burkhardt, *Bikini (Hydrogen Bomb)*; Stuart Davis, *Colonial Cubism*; Philip Evergood, *American Shrimp Girl*; Balcomb Greene, *Composition: The Storm*; Jasper Johns, *Construction with a Piano*; Jack Levine, *Election Night*; Rudy Pozzatti, *The Grasshopper*; Robert Rauschenburg, *Yoicks*; Charles Sheeler, *Architectural Cadences*.

**Literature**   e. e. cummings, *Poems 1923–1954*; William Faulkner, *A Fable* (Pulitzer Prize—National Book Award); Evan Hunter, *The Blackboard Jungle*; Robinson Jeffers, *Hungerfield and Other Poems* (Pulitzer Prize); Marianne Moore, *The Fables of La Fontaine*; Wallace Stevens, *Collected Poems* (Pulitzer—National Book Award); William C. Williams, *Desert Music and Other Poems*.

## Music—The Vernacular/Commercial Scene

**A. Births**   Danielle Alexander (singer/writer) December 2; John Anderson (singer) December 13; Tim Berne (saxophonist) October 16; Angela Bofill (singer); T. Graham Brown (singer) October 30; Jann Browne (singer) March 14; Peter Case (singer/writer) April 5; Eugene Chadbourne (guitarist) January 4; Robert Cray (singer/guitarist); Rob Crosby (singer) April 25; Al DiMeola (guitarist) July 22; Ricky Ford (saxophonist) March 4: Dennis Gonzalez (trumpeter/producer) August 15; Nanci Griffith (singer) July 6; Tim Hagans (trumpeter/composer) August 19; Bruce Hornsby (pianist/singer) November 23; Jermaine Jackson (singer) December 11; Rickie Lee Jones (singer) November 8; Louise Mandrell (singer) July 13; Alexander O'Neal (singer) November 14; Ray Parker, Jr. (guitarist/writer) May 1; John Schneider (actor/singer) April 8; Ricky Skaggs (singer) July 18; Stevie Ray Vaughan (guitarist) October 3; Steve Wariner (singer) December 25.

**B. Deaths**   Johnny Ace (singer/writer) December 25; Alger "Texas" Alexander (singer) April 16; Oscar "Papa" Celestin (trumpeter/bandleader) December 15; Rosamond Johnson (singer/composer) November 11; Arthur J. Johnston (lyricist/composer) May 1; "Hot Lips" Page (trumpeter) November 5; Fred Rose (singer/writer); Louis Silver (pianist/composer) March 26.

**C. Biographical**

**Performing Groups**   The Blossoms; The Blue Notes; Brown-Roach Jazz Quintet; The Cadets; Ray Charles Dance Band; The Crew Cuts; The (Jazz) Crusaders; The Four Tops; Jazz Messengers (by Art Blakey); McGuire Sisters; The Olympics (Challengers); The Pastels; The Penguins; The Sensations; The Tarriers; Otis Williams and the Charms.

**New Beginnings**   City Center Light Opera Co. (New York); Kool Newport Jazz Festivals.

**D. Publications**   Louis Armstrong, *Satchmo: My Life in New Orleans*; Norman Lloyd, *The Fireside Book of Love Songs*; A. P. Merriam and R. J. Benford, *A Bibliography of Jazz*; R. G. Reisner, *The Literature of Jazz*.

**E. Representative Works**

**Musicals**   Richard Adler and J. Ross, *Pajama Game*; Harold Arlen and T. Capote, *House of Flowers*;

Irving Berlin, *There's No Business Like Show Business* (film); Leonard Bernstein, *On the Waterfront* (film); J. Moross and J. Latouche, *The Golden Apple* (New York Drama Critics' Award); H. Rome, S. N. Behrman, and J. Logan, *Fanny*; A. Schwartz and D. Fields, *By the Beautiful Sea*; J. Styne, B. Comden, and A. Green, *Peter Pan*; Sandy Wilson, *The Boy Friend*.

**Songs**  Robert Allen and Al Stillman, *Home for the Holidays*; T. Blackburn and G. Burns, *The Ballad of Davy Crockett*; Charles Calhoun, *Shake, Rattle and Roll*; G. Cory and D. Cross, *I Left My Heart in San Francisco*; Melvin Endsley, *Singing the Blues*; Fain and Webster, *Secret Love*; Stuart Hamblen, *This Ole House*; J. McHugh and M. Parish, *Dream, Dream, Dream*; Jule Styne and Sammy Cahn, *Three Coins in the Fountain* (Oscar); Sid Tepper and Roy Bennett, *The Naughty Lady of Shady Lane*.

**Other**  Leroy Anderson, *Sandpaper Ballet*; Gene V. De Paul, *Seven Brides for Seven Brothers* (film music —Oscar); Miklós Rózsa, *Knights of the Round Table* (film music); Max Steiner, *The Caine Mutiny* (film music); Dimitri Tiomkin, *The High and the Mighty* (film music—Oscar).

## Music—The Cultivated/Art Music Scene

**F. Births**  Gary Arvin (pianist) May 24; Endre Balogh (violinist); Robert Beaser (composer); Gerald Berg (composer); Rebecca Blankenship (soprano) March 24; Thomas G. Dickinson (pianist) January 5; Susan Dunn (soprano) July 23; Warren Ellsworth (tenor) October 28; Susan Pearl Finger (pianist/musicologist) March 15; Michael Jon Fink (composer/performer) December 7; Eliot Fisk (guitarist) August 10; Stephen Jaffe (composer) December 30; Nancy Johnson (soprano); Tedd Joselson (pianist) October 4 (in Belgium); Pamela Hamblin (soprano) June 14; Aleck Karis (pianist) January 21; Gregory Kunde (tenor); Jennifer Lane (mezzo-soprano) November 25; Michael Lipman (cellist) March 15; Cheryl Ann Parrish (soprano) November 6; Tobias Picker (composer/ pianist) July 18; Larry Polansky (composer/theorist) October 16; Evelyn de la Rosa (soprano) March 8; Patricia Schuman (soprano) February 4; Clare Shore (composer); Gregory Lee Stapp (bass) May 19; Neal Stulberg (conductor) April 12; Stephanie Sundine (soprano).

**G. Deaths**  Paul Althouse (tenor) February 6; Philipp Greeley Clapp (composer) April 9; Arthur Fickénscher (composer/pianist) March 15; Harry L. Freeman (composer) March 24; Edwin Grasse (violinist/composer) April 8; Heinrich Hammer (German-born violinist/conductor) October 28; Mabel Wood Hill (composer) March 1; Allen C. Hinckley (bass) January 28; Charles E. Ives (composer) May 19; Leon Rains (bass) June 11; Karol Rathaus (Polish-born composer) November 21; Will Rossiter (British-born composer/publisher) June 10; Rosario Scalero (Italian-born composer) December 25; Fritzi Scheff (Austrian-born soprano) April 8; Yvonne de Tréville (soprano) January 25; Max Wald (composer) August 14.

## H. Debuts

**United States**  Betty Allen (mezzo-soprano—New York), David Bar-Illan (Israeli pianist—New York), Maria Callas (soprano—Chicago), Rosanna Carteri (Italian soprano—San Francisco), Mary Curtis-Verna (soprano—San Franciso), Gloria Davy (soprano—New York), Natalie Hinderas (pianist—New York), Marilyn Horne (mezzo-soprano—Los Angeles), John Reardon (baritone—New York), Regina Sarfaty (mezzo-soprano—Boston), Giulietta Simionato (Italian mezzo-soprano—Chicago), Thomas Stewart (baritone—New York), Edward Van Beinum (Dutch conductor—Philadelphia).

**Metropolitan Opera**  Charles Anthony (tenor), Kurt Böhme (German bass), Fernando Corena (Swiss bass), Otto Edelmann (Austrian bass-baritone), Rosalind Elias (mezzo-soprano), Christel Goltz (German soprano), Calvin Marsh (baritone), Louis Sgarro (bass).

**Other**  Jean Cox (Kiel); Charles Holland (tenor—Paris).

## I. New Positions

**Conductors**  Joel Cohen (Boston Camerata); Enrique Jordá (San Francisco Symphony Orchestra—to 1963); Milton Katims (Seattle Symphony Orchestra—to 1975); Josef Krips (Buffalo Philharmonic Orchestra—to 1963).

**Educational**    Julius Baker (Juilliard—to 1980); Karel Husa (composition, Cornell University); Leon Kirchner (professor, Mills College—to 1960); Edward Lippman (Columbia University); William O. Smith (University of Southern California—to 1960).

**Other**    Carol Fox (general manager, Lyric Theater of Chicago); Paul Henry Lang (music critic, *New York Herald Tribune*—to 1963).

## J. Honors and Awards

**Honors**    Ingolf Dahl, Colin McPhee, and Hugo Weisgall (American Academy); Carl Ruggles (National Institute).

**Awards**    John Browning (Steinway Centennial Award); Van Cliburn (Leventritt Award); Billy Jim Layton (Rome Prize); Aldo Mancinelli (Busoni).

**K. Biographical**    Grace Bumbry wins on Arthur Godfrey's Talent Scouts program; William Dawson retires as director of the Tuskegee Choir; Karel Husa leaves Paris and comes to the United States; Jerome Kacinskas and János Starker become American citizens; Abraham Kaplan (Israeli conductor) moves to New York to attend Juilliard; Gladys Swarthout retires to Florence, Italy; Arturo Toscanini gives his last concert with NBC Symphony Orchestra and retires to Italy; Ralph Vaughan Williams makes a second lecture tour of the United States.

## L. Musical Beginnings

**Performing Groups**    Boston Camerata; Chamber Music Society of Little Rock (Arkansas); Contemporary Chamber Players (University of Chicago); Dedham Chorus (Massachusetts); Festival Quartet (Aspen, Colorado); Lyric Theater (Opera) of Chicago; "Music in Our Time" Series, 92nd Street YM–YWHA, New York.

**Educational**    Louisville Academy of Music (Kentucky).

**Other**    American Choral Foundation; American Prix de Rome; Alexander Broude, Inc., Music Publisher; Central Opera Service (Metropolitan Opera); Composers Recordings, Inc.; Eric Herz Harpsichords, Inc. (Harvard, Massachusetts); R. A. Moog Co. (Trumansburg, New York); Musicwriter (patented by Cecil Effinger); San Francisco Opera Auditions.

## M. Music Publications

Balanchine, George, *Balanchine's Complete Stories of Great Ballets*
Fennell, Frederick, *Time and the Winds*
Ferguson, Donald N., *Masterworks of the Orchestra Repertoire*
Friskin, J. and Freundlich, I., *Music for the Piano*
Levarie, Siegmund, *Fundamentals of Harmony*
Loesser, Arthur, *Men, Women and Pianos: A Social History*
Reed, H. Owen, *Basic Music*
Robb, John D., *Hispanic Folk Songs of New Mexico*

## N. Musical Compositions

**Chamber Music**    Milton Babbitt, *String Quartet No. 2*; Leslie Bassett, *String Quintet*; Earl Brown, *Four Systems* (unspecified instrumentation); Mario Davidovsky, *String Quartet No. 1*; Arcady Dubensky, *String Quartet No. 2 in B-Flat*; Robert Evett, *Piano Quintet*; Harold Farberman, *Evolution*; Vivian Fine, *Composition for String Quartet*; Jack Gottlieb, *String Quartet*; Charles Jones, *String Quartet No. 4*; Hall Overton, *String Quartet No. 2*; Robert Palmer, *String Quartet No. 3*; Halsey Stevens, *Piano Trio No. 3*; Alan Stout, *String Quartet No. 3*; Louise Talma, *String Quartet*.

**Choral/Vocal**    Dominick Argento, *Five Songs about Spring*; Samuel Barber, *Prayers of Kierkegaard, Opus 30*; Margaret Bonds, *The Ballad of the Brown King*; Henry Brant, *Millennium II*; Irving Fine, *Childhood Fables for Grownups*; George Rochberg, *David, the Psalmist*; Ned Rorem, *Eight Poems by Whitman*; Eric Salzman, *Cummings Set* (song cycle); Roger Sessions, *The Idyll of Theocritus*; Harold Shapero, *Hebrew Cantata*; William Grant Still, *A Psalm for Living*; Igor Stravinsky, *In Memoriam Dylan Thomas*.

**Concertos**    Ernest Bloch, *Symphony for Trombone and Orchestra*; Benjamin Boretz, *Concerto*

*Grosso for Strings*; Cecil Effinger, *Symphonie Concertante* (harp, piano, and orchestra); Robert Evett, *Cello Concerto*; Andrew Imbrie, *Violin Concerto*; Robert Muczynski, *Piano Concerto, Opus 7*; Robert Parris, *Piano Concerto*; Miklós Rózsa, *Violin Concerto*; Virgil Thomson, *Concerto for Flute, Strings, Harp, and Percussion*; Lester Trimble, *Concerto for Winds and Strings*; Ben Weber, *Violin Concerto*.

**Electronic**   Vladimir Ussachevsky and Otto Luening, *A Poem in Cycles and Bells* (orchestra and tape); Edgard Varèse, *Déserts* (instruments and tape).

**Operas**   George Antheil, *The Brothers—Venus in Africa*; Wallace Berry, *The Admirable Bashville*; Aaron Copland, *The Tender Land*; Carlisle Floyd, *Susannah* (New York Music Critics' Award); Arthur Kreutz, *The University Greys*; Bernard Rogers, *The Nightingale.*

**Orchestra/Band**   Samuel Adler, *Toccata for Orchestra*; Hugh Aitken, *Short Suite for Strings*; Leonard Bernstein, *Serenade*; Felix Borowski, *The Mirror* (symphonic poem); Morton Gould, *Showpiece for Orchestra*; Ulysses Kay, *Serenade*; Martin Mailman, *Autumn Landscape* (Edward Benjamin Award); Colin McPhee, *Transitions*; George Perle, *Rhapsody for Orchestra*; Quincy Porter, *The Merry Wives of Windsor* (incidental music); Leo Sowerby, *All on a Summer's Day* (tone poem); Halsey Stevens, *Four Short Pieces*; Igor Stravinsky, *Agon* (ballet), Randall Thompson, *A Trip to Nahant* (symphonic fantasy); Virgil Thomson, *Ondine* (incidental music); Ben Weber, *Prelude and Passacaglia*; Clarence White, *Elegy* (Benjamin Award).

**Piano/Organ**   John Cage, *34' 46.776"* (prepared piano); Benjamin Lees, *Ten Pieces*; Robert Muczynski, *Six Preludes, Opus 6*; Vincent Persichetti, *Sonatinas 4–6*; Ralph Shapey, *Sonata Variations*; Louise Talma, *Six Etudes*; Jaromir Weinberger, *Dedications—Five Preludes* (organ).

**Symphonies**   Josef Alexander, *Symphony No. 2*; John J. Becker, *Symphony No. 7, "Sermon on the Mount"*; Thomas Beversdorf, *Symphony No. 3*; Easley Blackwood, *Chamber Symphony, Opus 2*; Barney Childs, *Symphony No. 1*; Paul Cooper, *Symphony No. 1*; Henry Cowell, *Symphony No. 11*; David Diamond, *Symphony No. 6*; Cecil Effinger, *Symphony No. 3*; Roger Goeb, *Symphony No. 4*; Howard Hanson, *Symphony No. 5, "Sinfonia sacra"*; Lejaren Hiller, *Symphony No. 1*; Alan Hovhaness, *Symphony No. 2, "Mysterious Mountain"*; Homer Keller, *Symphony No. 3*; Harrison Kerr, *Symphony No. 3*; Felix Labunski, *Symphony No. 2 in D Major*; Nikolai Lopatnikoff, *Symphony No. 3, Opus 35*; Paul Nordoff, *Symphony No. 1, "Winter"*; Walter Piston, *Symphony No. 5*; Dane Rudhyar, *Syntony No. 5*; Carlos Surinach, *Sinfonietta flamenca*; Howard Swanson, *Concerto for Orchestra*.

# 1955

❉

## Historical Highlights

The AF of L and the CIO merge into one organization; the United States and Canada approve the Distant Early Warning Line (DEW) against surprise Communist attack; public school desegregation is ordered by the Supreme Court; the first United States "advisors" enter South Vietnam; the oral contraceptive, the "pill," goes on the market; Anthony Eden replaces Churchill as British prime minister; Malenkov resigns and Nikolai Bulganin becomes Russian leader.

## World Cultural Highlights

**World Art**   Salvador Dali, *The Lord's Supper*; Barbara Hepworth, *Two Figures (Menhirs);* Hans Hofmann, *Exuberance*; Oscar Kokoschka, *Thermopylae Triptych*; Pablo Picasso, *Jacqueline in a Turkish Vest—Women of Algiers.*

**World Literature**   Kingsley Amis, *That Uncertain Feeling*; Enid Bagnold, *The Chalk Garden*; Jean Genet, *The Balcony*; Philip Larkin, *The Less Deceived.*

**World Music**   Pierre Boulez, *Le Marteau sans Maître*; Hans Werner Henze, *Symphony No. 4*; Rodion Shchedrin, *The Humpback Horse*; Ralph Vaughan Williams, *Symphony No. 8.*

**Miscellaneous**    The Municipal Philharmonic of Chile is founded; the Athens Festival of the Arts begins; births include Simon Rattle; deaths include Georges Enescu, Fernand Léger, Thomas Mann, and Maurice Utrillo.

## American Art and Literature Highlights

**Births/Deaths**    Births include novelists John Grisham, Jay McInerney, and poet Cathy Song; deaths include art figures Mabel Dwight, William Leigh, Carl Milles, Yves Tanguy, Bessie P. Vonnoh, and literary figures James Agee, Robert Coffin, Weldon Kees, Robert Sherwood, Leonora Speyer, Wallace Stevens, and Walter White.

**Art Works**    Philip Evergood, *Woman at the Piano*; Leon Golub, *Damaged Man*; David Hare, *Head of an Animal*; Grace Hartigan, *Shinnecock Canal*; Jasper Johns, *Target with Four Faces*; Franz Kline, *Accent Grave*; Lee Krasner, *Blue Level*; Robert Rauschenberg, *Satellite*; Kay Sage, *Tomorrow Is Never*; Charles Sheeler, *Golden Gate*.

**Literature**    Maxwell Anderson, *The Bad Seed*; W. H. Auden, *Shield of Achilles* (National Book Club Award); Elizabeth Bishop, *Cold Spring* (Pulitzer Prize); William Inge, *Bus Stop*; MacKinlay Kantor, *Andersonville* (Pulitzer Prize); Norman Mailer, *Deer Park*; Tennessee Williams, *Cat on a Hot Tin Roof* (Pulitzer Prize—New York Drama Critics' Award); Herman Wouk, *Marjorie Morningstar*.

## Music—The Vernacular/Commercial Scene

**A. Births**    Dan Barrett (trombonist) December 14; Kix Brooks (singer) May 12; Carlene Carter (singer) September 26; Rosanne Cash (singer) May 24; Jeff Clayton (saxophonist) February 16; Dean Dillon (singer) March 26; Steve Earle (singer/guitarist) January 17; Bill Lloyd (singer) December 6; Reba McEntire (singer) March 28; Pat Metheny (guitarist) August 12; David Murray (saxophonist) February 19; Adam Nussbaum (drummer) November 29; Paul Overstreet (singer) March 17; Dee Snider (singer) March 15; Keith Whitley (singer) July 1; Lil' Ed Williams (guitarist); Cassandra Wilson (singer) December 4.

**B. Deaths**    Gus Arnheim (composer/bandleader) September 11; Axel W. Christensen (pianist) August 17; James P. Johnson (pianist/composer) November 17; Lillian Lorraine (singer/actress) April 17; Carmen Miranda (singer) August 5; Charlie "Bird" Parker (saxophonist) March 12; Al Piantadosi (songwriter) April 8; Jerry Ross (singer/writer) November 11; Andrew B. Sterling (lyricist) August 11.

**C. Biographical**

**Performing Groups**    The BoDeans; Jimmy Bowen and the Rhythm Orchids; The Cleftones; The Coasters; The Danderliers; Danny and the Juniors (Juvenairs); Miles Davis Quintet; The Falcons; The Five Satins; Pete Fountain and His Three Coins; Frankie Lymon and the Teenagers; Harold Melvin and the Blue Notes; The Miracles; The Monotones; Parliament; The Rays; The Rivieras; The Silhouettes; The Tokens; The Vibrations (Jayhawks).

**New Beginnings**    Argo (Cadet) Records (Chicago); Atco Records (subsidiary of Atlantic Records); Liberty Records.

**Honors and Awards**    Richard Rodgers (National Institute of Arts and Letters).

**Miscellaneous**    "Cannonball" Adderley gives up teaching and moves to New York; Francis Thorne leaves the business world and begins six years of jazz piano playing.

**D. Publications**    Leonard Feather, *The Encyclopedia of Jazz*; Langston Hughes, *Famous Negro Music Makers—First Book of Jazz*; Marion S. Revett, *A Minstrel Town*; Jean Ritchie, *Singing Family of the Cumberlands*; Ruth Crawford Seeger, *American Folk Songs for Christmas*; Nat Shapiro and Nat Hentoff, eds., *Hear Me Talkin' to Ya: The Story of Jazz as Told by the Men Who Made It*.

**E. Representative Works**

**Musicals**    Richard Adler and J. Ross, *Damn Yankees*; Albert Hague and A. B. Horwitt, *Plain and Fancy*; Carolyn Leigh, *Heidi* (television—on music of R. Schumann); C. Porter, G. S. Kaufman, and L. MacGrath, *Silk Stockings*; Rodgers and Hammerstein, *Pipe Dream*.

**Songs** Ray Heindorf and Sammy Cahn, *Pete Kelly's Blues*; Pearl King and Dave Bartholomew, *I Hear You Knockin' (But You Can't Come in)*; Little Richard, *Tutti Frutti*; Alex North, *Unchained Melody*; S. Tepper and R. C. Bennett, *I'm Gettin' Nuttin' for Christmas*; James Van Heusen and Sammy Cahn, *Love and Marriage* (Oscar)—*The Tender Trap*.

**Number One Hits** *Autumn Leaves* (Roger Williams); *Love Is a Many Splendored Thing* (Four Aces); *Rock Around the Clock* (Bill Haley and the Comets); *Sixteen Tons* (Tennessee Ernie Ford); *The Yellow Rose of Texas* (Mitch Miller).

**Other** Elmer Bernstein, *The Man with the Golden Arm* (film music); Morton Gould, *Derivations for Clarinet and Jazz Band*; Bernard Herrmann, *The Kentuckian* (film music); Morgan Lewis, *The Unconquered* (film music—Oscar); Alex North, *Unchained—The Rose Tattoo* (film music); Gunther Schuller, *Symphonic Tribute to Duke Ellington*.

## Music—The Cultivated/Art Music Scene

**F. Births** Gregg Baker (baritone) December 7; Lawrence Bakst (tenor); Pamela Coburn (soprano) March 29; Stephen Drury (pianist) April 13; Diamanda Galas (composer) August 29; Kathryn Gamberoni (soprano) January 11; Robert Gambill (tenor); Kyle Gann (composer/critic) November 21; Susan Greene (musicologist/educator) January 1; Thomas Hampson (baritone) June 28; Allen Benedict Ho (musicologist) March 30; John Edward Holmquist (guitarist) February 7; Julie Kaufmann (soprano) May 25; Ron Kuivila (composer) December 19; Kevin J. Langan (bass) April 1; Yo-Yo Ma (cellist) October 7, Mark McGurty (composer) April 28; Michael Myers (tenor), Gerard Joseph Pape (composer) April 22; Eugene Perry (baritone); JoAnn Pickens (soprano); Gino Quilico (baritone) April 29; Susan Quittmeyer (mezzo-soprano); Marilyn Schmiege (mezzo-soprano); Cheryl Studer (soprano) October 24; Robert Taub (pianist) December 25; Benjamin Verdery (guitarist) October 1; Peter Zazofsky (violinist).

**G. Deaths** Marion Bauer (composer/author) August 9; Manfred Bukofzer (German-born musicologist) December 7; F. Melius Christiansen (Norwegian-born conductor) June 1; Olin Downes (musicologist/critic) August 22; Florence Easton (British-born soprano) August 13; Otto Gombosi (Hungarian-born musicologist) February 17; Mayhew Lake (composer/conductor) March 16; Harl McDonald (composer) March 30; Homer Rodeheaver (singer/publisher) December 18; Vincent F. Safranek (Bohemian-born bandmaster) September 7.

### II. Debuts

**United States** Géza Anda (Hungarian pianist—Philadelphia), Carlo Bergonzi (Italian tenor—Chicago), Richard Cassilly (tenor—New York), Jörg Demus (Austrian pianist—New York), Mattiwilda Dobbs (soprano—San Francisco), Mignon Dunn (mezzo-soprano—New Orleans), Dietrich Fischer-Dieskau (German baritone—Cincinnati), Ezio Flagello (bass—Ellenville, New York), Emil Gilels (Russian pianist—Philadelphia), Ivry Gitlis (Israeli violinist), Carlo Maria Giulini (Italian conductor—Chicago), Glenn Gould (Canadian pianist—Washington, DC), Lorin Hollander (pianist, age 11—New York), Alicia de Larrocha (Spanish pianist—Los Angeles), Evelyn Lear (soprano—New York), Richard Lewis (British tenor—San Francisco), Pilar Lorengar (Spanish soprano—New York), Barry Morell (tenor—New York), David Oistrakh (Russian violinist—New York), Fernando Previtali (Italian conductor—Cleveland), Louis Quilico (Canadian baritone—New York), Joseph Rouleau (Canadian bass—New Orleans), Teresa Stich-Randall (soprano—Chicago).

**Metropolitan Opera** Marian Anderson (contralto), Giuseppe Campora (Italian tenor), Ralph Herbert (baritone), Laurel Hurley (soprano), Robert McFerrin (baritone), Thomas Schippers (conductor), Renata Tebaldi (Italian soprano), Giorgio Tozzi (bass), Hermann Uhde (German baritone).

**Other** Anna Moffo (soprano—Spoleto).

### I. New Positions

**Conductors** Theodore Bloomfield (Portland [Oregon] Symphony Orchestra—to 1959); Margaret Hillis (New York City Opera); Siegfried Landau (Brooklyn Philharmonia—to 1971);

Jonel Perlea (Connecticut Symphony Orchestra—to 1978); Albert F. Schoepper (United States Marine Band—to 1972); Leopold Stokowski (Houston Symphony Orchestra—to 1961).

**Educational**   Claus Adam (Juilliard); Gilbert Chase (director, School of Music, University of Oklahoma); Richard Crocker (Yale—to 1963); Catharine Crozier (Rollings College—to 1969); John Hsu (Cornell University); Menahem Pressler (piano, Indiana University); Vittorio Rieti (composition, Queens College—to 1960); John M. Ward (musicology, Harvard).

**Other**   Paul Henry Lang (president, International Musicological Society—to 1958); Howard Taubman (music critic, *The New York Times*—to 1960).

## J. Honors and Awards

**Honors**   Henry Brant, Irving Fine, Walter Piston, and Adolph Weiss (American Academy); Richard Rodgers and Edgard Varèse (National Institute).

**Awards**   Henry Brant (Prix Italia); John Browning (Leventritt); Berl Senofsky (Queen Elizabeth); Shirley Verrett (Marion Anderson).

**K. Biographical**   Marion Anderson becomes the first black singer at the Metropolitan Opera; Evelyn Lear marries baritone Thomas Stewart; Robert McFerrin becomes the first black male to join the Metropolitan Opera; Ilhan Mimaroglu (Turkish composer) comes to the United States and settles in New York; Zara Nelsova and Yma Sumac become American citizens; Vladimir Pleshakov (Russian pianist) comes to the United States and begins the study of medicine; Joan Tower returns to the United States after many years in South America; Shirley Verrett wins on Arthur Godfrey's Talent Scouts.

## L. Musical Beginnings

**Performing Groups**   Anchorage Civic Opera; Beaux Arts String (Trio) Quartet; Brooklyn Philharmonia (Philharmonic Orchestra) (Academy); Cleveland Orchestra Chorus; Greater Denver Opera Co.; Festival Piano Quartet (Aspen); Houston Ballet; Houston Grand Opera Co.; Masterwork Chorus and Orchestra (New York); Gregg Smith Singers (Los Angeles); St. Olaf Lutheran Choir; West Bay Opera of Palo Alto.

**Festivals**   Empire State Music Festival.

**Educational**   Institute of Puerto Rican Culture; Society for Ethnomusicology (Philadelphia).

**Other**   Composers Recordings, Inc. (CRI); C. B. Fisk, Inc., Organ Builders; Institute of Puerto Rican Culture; National Opera Association (NOA—National Music Council).

## M. Music Publications

Chase, Gilbert, *America's Music: From the Pilgrims to the Present*
Chotzinoff, Samuel, *A Lost Paradise: Early Reminiscences*
Cowell, Henry, *Charles Ives and His Music*
Erickson, Robert, *The Structure of Music*
Finney, Theodore, *We Have Made Music*
Forte, Allen, *Contemporary Tone-Structures*
Kolodin, Irving, *Orchestral Music*
Kwalwasser, Jacob, *Exploring the Musical Mind*
Machlis, Joseph, *The Enjoyment of Music*
Piston, Walter, *Orchestration*
Pleasants, Henry, *The Agony of Modern Music*
Rochberg, George, *The Hexachord and its Relation to the Twelve-tone Row*
Schonberg, Harold, *Chamber and Solo Instrument Music*

## N. Musical Compositions

**Chamber Music**   Thomas Beversdorf, *String Quartet No. 2*; Henry Brant, *Encephalograms II* (soprano and seven instruments)—*Labyrinth I*—*Labyrinth II*; Allen Brings, *Clarinet Sonata*; George Crumb, *Cello Sonata*; Ross Lee Finney, *String Quartet No. 7*; Benjamin Lees, *String Quartet No. 2*; David Martin Levy, *String Quartet*; Nikolai Lopatnikoff, *String Quartet No. 3, Opus*

*36*; Eric Salzman, *String Quartet*; Arthur Shepherd, *String Quartet No. 4 in C Major*; Alan Stout, *String Quartet No. 4*; William Sydeman, *String Quartet—Woodwind Quintet*; Lester Trimble, *String Quartet No. 2, "Pastorale"*; Paul Turok, *String Quartet No. 1*; Burnet Tuthill, *String Quartet No. 2*; Richard Wernick, *Four Pieces for String Quartet*.

**Choral/Vocal**   Josef Alexander, *Canticle of Night*; Richard Bales, *The Republic* (cantata); Avery Claflin, *Lament for April 15*; Aaron Copland, *Canticle of Freedom*; David M. Epstein, *The Seasons* (song cycle); Ellis Kohs, *Lord of the Ascendant*; Ned Rorem, *The Poet's Requiem*; Halsey Stevens, *Ballad of William Sycamore*; William Grant Still, *Rhapsody*; Igor Stravinsky, *Canticum sacrum ad honorem Sancti Marci nominis*; Alexander Tcherepnin, *The Lost Flute* (song cycle).

**Concertos**   Nicolas Flagello, *Piano Concerto No. 2—Violin Concerto*; Gene Gutchë, *Piano Concerto* (Gottschalk Gold Medal); Benjamin Lees, *Piano Concerto No. 1*; Mana Zucca, *Violin Concerto*; Robert Parris, *Concerto for Five Kettledrums*; Vittorio Rieti, *Piano Concerto No. 3*.

**Electronic**   Vladimir Ussachevsky, *A Piece for Tape Recorder*.

**Operas**   George Antheil, *The Wish*; Marc Blitzstein, *Reuben, Reuben*; Jack Gottlieb, *Tea Party*; Louis Gruenberg, *Antony and Cleopatra*; Ulysses Kay, *The Boor*; Louis Mennini, *The Rope*; Robert Ward, *He Who Gets Slapped (Pantaloon)*.

**Orchestra/Band**   Samuel Adler, *A Feast of Light—Summer Stock Overture*; Leonard Bernstein, *Salome* (incidental music); Marc Blitzstein, *King Lear* (incidental music II); Ernest Bloch, *Proclamation*; Irving Fine, *Serious Song: A Lament for Strings*; Morton Gould, *Jekyll and Hyde Variations*; Alexei Haieff, *Ballet in E*; Peter Jona Korn, *Variations on a Tune from The Beggar's Opera*; Robert Moevs, *Three Symphonic Pieces*; Gardner Read, *Vernal Equinox, Opus 96*; Harold Shapero, *Credo*; Ralph Shapey, *Challenge—The Family of Man*; Igor Stravinsky, *Greetings Prelude*; Clarence White, *Dance Rhapsody*.

**Piano/Organ**   Esther Ballou, *Sonata*; Gordon Binkerd, *Sonata No. 1*; Jacob Druckman, *The Seven Deadly Sins*; Halim El-Dabh, *Mekta in the Art of Kita*; Alexei Haieff, *Sonata*; Ezra Laderman, *Sonata No. 2*; Darius Milhaud, *Petite Suite, Opus 348* (organ); Douglas Moore, *Four Pieces*; Vincent Persichetti, *Sonata No. 10, Opus 67*; Leo Smit, *Sonata in One Movement*; Louise Talma, *Sonata No. 2*; Alexander Tcherepnin, *Eight Pieces*.

**Symphonies**   Gordon Binkerd, *Symphony No. 1*; Ernest Bloch, *Symphony in E-Flat Major*; Jean Eichelberger Ivey, *Festive Symphony*; Gail Kubik, *Symphony No. 2*; W. Francis McBeth, *Symphony No. 1*; Darius Milhaud, *Symphony No. 6, Opus 343—Symphony No. 7, Opus 344*; Paul Nordoff, *Symphony No. 2, "Tranquil"*; Hall Overton, *Symphony No. 1 for Strings*; Walter Piston, *Symphony No. 6*; Robert Sanders, *Symphony in A Major*; Leo Smit, *Symphony No. 1 in E-Flat* (New York Music Critics' Award); Ernst Toch, *Symphony No. 3, Opus 75* (Pulitzer Prize); Paul Turok, *Symphony*.

# 1956

❁

## Historical Highlights

Dwight D. Eisenhower is elected to a second term as president; work begins on the interstate highway system; the Agricultural (Soil Bank) Act pays farmers to remove cropland from production; Albert B. Sabin perfects his oral polio vaccine; Egypt nationalizes the Suez Canal; warfare with France and England ends; Russian tanks crush Hungarian uprising; "de-Stalinization" begins in Russia.

## World Cultural Highlights

**World Art**   Alberto Giacometti, *Femme Assise;* Richard Hamilton, *Just What Is It That Makes Today's Home So Different, So Appealing?*; Barbara Hepworth, *Orpheus*; Joern Utzon, *Sydney Opera House* (Australia).

**World Literature**   Jean Anouilh, *Poor Bits;* Winston Churchill, *History of the English Speaking Peoples*; John Osborne, *Look Back in Anger*.

**World Music**   Luciano Berio, *Nones*; Benjamin Britten, *Prince of the Pagodas*; Dmitri Kabalevsky, *Symphony No. 5*; Karlheinz Stockhausen, *Gesang der Jünglinge*; William Walton, *Cello Concerto*.

**Miscellaneous**   The Australian Opera Co. and Brisbane Conservatory of Music open; the Japan State Philharmonic is founded; deaths include Max Beerbohm, Bertolt Brecht, Reinhold Glière, Alan Milne, and Emil Nolde.

## American Art and Literature Highlights

**Births/Deaths**   Deaths include art figures Gifford Beal, Lyonel Feininger, Louis Guglielmi, Jackson Pollock, John Storrs, and literary figures Louis Bromfield, Christopher La Farge, Robert M. Lovett, Charles MacArthur, John McClure, Percy MacKaye, Henry L. Mencken, and Leonora Speyer.

**Art Works**   Paul Cadmus, *Bar Italia*; Philip Guston, *The Street*; Ibram Lassaw, *Procession*; Rico Lebrun, *Buchenwald Pit*; Richard Lippold, *Variations in a Sphere, No. 10: The Sun*; Loren MacIver, *The Street*; Louise Nevelson, *The Royal Voyage*; Robert Rauschenberg, *Gloria*; Hugo Robus, *Water Carrier*; Theodore J. Roszak, *Sea Sentinel*; H. C. Westermann, *A Soldier's Dream*.

**Literature**   Nelson Algren, *A Walk on the Wild Side*; Elizabeth Bishop, *Poems, North and South* (Pulitzer Prize); F. Goodrich and A. Hackett, *Diary of Anne Frank* (Pulitzer Prize — New York Drama Critics' Award); Grace Metalious, *Peyton Place*; Wright Morris, *Field of Vision* (National Book Award); John O'Hara, *Ten North Frederick* (National Book Award); Dore Schary, *Sunrise at Campobello* (five Tonys); Richard Wilbur, *Things of This World* (Pulitzer Prize — National Book Award).

## Music — The Vernacular/Commercial Scene

**A. Births**   Suzy Bogguss (singer) December 30; Debby Boone (singer) September 22; Mark Collie (singer) January 18; Steve Coleman (saxophonist) September 20; John Debney (composer) August 18; Michael Feinstein (pianist/singer) September 7; Gregg Field (drummer) February 21; Kenny G. (saxophonist) June 5; Dan Hartman (saxophonist) November 4; Chris Isaak (singer/writer) June 26; Freddie Jackson (singer) October 2; Robert Earl Keen, Jr. (singer) January 11; Tina Marie (singer) March 5; Charly McClain (singer) March 25; Lee Roy Parnell (singer) December 21; Billy Smith (singer) November 11; Rex Smith (singer) September 19; Doug Stone (singer) June 19; Sylvia (Allen) (singer) December 9; Diane Warren (songwriter) September 7; Michael Wycoff (singer); Dwight Yoakam (singer/writer) October 23.

**B. Deaths**   Clifford Brown (trumpeter) June 26; Mort Dixon (lyricist) March 23; Tommy Dorsey (trombonist/bandleader) November 26; Elsie Janis (singer/actress) February 26; Tommy Johnson (singer/guitarist) November 1; Isham Jones (songwriter/bandleader) October 19; John LaTouche (lyricist) August 7; Adrian Rollini (saxophonist) May 15; Jean Schwartz (composer) September 30; Art Tatum (pianist) November 4; Frankie Trumbauer (saxophonist) June 11; Albert Von Tilzer (songwriter/publisher) October 1; Victor Young (conductor/arranger) November 11.

**C. Biographical**

**Performing Groups**   "Cannonball" Adderley Jazz Quintet; The Bobbettes; The Chantels; The Crests; Del-Vikings; Dreamlovers; The Four Seasons; John Fred and His Playboy Band; Jimmy Giuffre Trio; Ramsay Lewis Trio; Little Joe and the Thrillers; Shelly Manne Quintet; The Mello-Kings; The Ramrods; Royal Teens; Horace Silver Jazz Quintet; The Tymes.

**New Beginnings**   *Down Beat Yearbook*.

**D. Publications**   E. Condon and R. Gehman, *Eddie Condon's Treasury of Jazz*; W. L. Grossman and J. W. Farrell, *The Heart of Jazz*; Stephen Longstreet, *The Real Jazz, Old and New*; Marshall W. Stearns, *The Story of Jazz*.

**E. Representative Works**

**Musicals**   Leonard Bernstein, *Candide*; J. Bock and G. O. Weiss, *Mr. Wonderful*; H. Karr and M. Dubey, *Happy Hunting*; Lerner and Loewe, *My Fair Lady* (New York Drama Critics' Award); Frank

Loesser, *Most Happy Fella* (New York Drama Critics' Award); F. Luther, *Tom Sawyer* (television); G. de Paul and J. Mercer, *Li'l Abner*; Cole Porter, *High Society* (film); F. Spielman and J. Torre, *The Stingiest Man in Town*; J. Styne, B. Comden, and A. Green, *Bells Are Ringing*.

**Number One Hits** *Don't Be Cruel/Hound Dog—Heartbreak Hotel—I Want You, I Need You, I Love You—Love Me Tender* (Elvis Presley); *Lisbon Antigua* (Nelson Riddle); *Memories Are Made of This* (Dean Martin); *My Prayer* (The Platters); *Poor People of Paris* (Les Baxter); *Rock and Roll Waltz* (Kay Starr); *Singing the Blues* (Guy Mitchell); *The Wayward Wind* (Gogi Grant).

**Other** Elmer Bernstein, *The Ten Commandments* (film music); Duke Ellington, *Night Creature* (jazz band and orchestra); Miklós Rózsa, *Lust for Life* (film score); Dimitri Tiomkin, *Giant* (film music); Victor Young, *Around the World in Eighty Days* (film score).

## Music—The Cultivated Art/Music Scene

**F. Births** Barbara Bonney (soprano) April; Michael Gandolfi (composer); Nancy Gustafson (soprano) June 27; Mark Bowman Hester (tenor) June 27; Sharon Isbin (guitarist) August 7; Jeffrey Kahane (pianist) September 12; Richard Leech (tenor); Stephen Mackey (composer); Dorothy Madison (soprano) January 12; Andrea Matthews (soprano) November 6, Rhonda Jackson McAfee (mezzo-soprano) May 1; Sylvia McNair (soprano) June 23; Steven Mercurio (conductor); Timothy Noble (baritone), Christopher O'Riley (pianist) April 17; Michael Pugliese (percussionist/composer) September 26; Ned Rothenberg (composer) September 15; Neal Wilson (tenor) June 4.

**G. Deaths** Hans Barth (German-born composer/pianist) December 8; Felix Borowski (British-born composer/critic) September 6; Lorenzo Camilieri (Greek-born conductor) April 20; Robert Delaney (composer) September 21; Ferdinand Dunkley (British-born organist) January 5; Henry Fillmore (bandmaster/composer) December 7; George Foote (composer) March 25; Edwin Franko Goldman (bandmaster/composer) February 21; Alexander Gretchaninov (Russian-born composer) January 4; Arthur M. Hartmann (violinist) March 30; Rupert Hughes (music author) September 9; Erich Itor Kahn (German-born pianist/composer) March 5; Guy Maier (pianist/educator) September 24; Max Rosen (violinist) December 16; Cecil Smith (critic) May 28; Isabelle Vengerova (Russian-born pianist) February 7; Henry W. Wehrmann, Jr. (violinist/composer) October 21; Jacob Weinberg (Russian-born pianist/composer) November 2.

**H. Debuts**

**United States** McHenry Boatwright (baritone—Boston), John Browning (pianist—New York), Boris Christoff (Bulgarian bass—San Francisco), Maureen Forrester (Canadian contralto—New York), Louis Kentner (Hungarian pianist—New York), Kurt Leimer (Austrian pianist—New York), Chester Ludgin (baritone—New Orleans), Birgit Nilsson (Swedish soprano—Hollywood), Judith Raskin (soprano—Central City, Colorado), Mstislav Rostropovich (Russian cellist—New York), Leonie Rysanek (Austrian soprano—San Francisco), Ravi Shankar (Indian sitar player—tour).

**Metropolitan Opera** Carlo Bergonzi (Italian tenor), Maria Callas (soprano), Mattiwilda Dobbs (soprano), Tito Gobbi (Italian baritone), Jean Morel (French conductor), Enzo Sordello (Italian baritone), Antonietta Stella (Italian soprano).

**I. New Positions**

**Conductors** Eduard van Beinum (Los Angeles Philharmonic Orchestra—to 1959); Louis Lane (associate, Cleveland Orchestra—to 1973); Erich Leinsdorf (New York City Opera); Izler Solomon (Indianapolis Symphony Orchestra—to 1976).

**Educational** John Brownlee (director, Manhattan School—to 1969); Norman Dello Joio (Mannes—to 1972); Jacob Druckman (Juilliard—to 1972); Vittorio Giannini (Curtis); Hans Heinz (voice, Juilliard); Charles Kullman (Indiana University—to 1971); Ron Nelson (Brown University—music chair 1963–1973); György Sándor (piano, SMU—to 1961); Robert Whitney (dean, University of Louisville Music School—to 1972).

**Other** Kurt Herbert Adler (general director, San Francisco Opera); Paul Creston (president, National Association of American Composers and Conductors); Robert Ward (managing editor, Galaxy Music—to 1966).

## J. Honors and Awards

**Honors**   Elliott Carter and Ernst Toch (National Institute); Aaron Copland (American Academy Gold Medal); Ross Lee Finney, Robert Moevs, and Igor Stravinsky (American Academy).

**Awards**   Victor Alessandro (Alice M. Ditson Award); John Browning (Queen Elisabeth Second); Abraham Kaplan (Frank Damrosch Prize).

**K. Biographical**   Leonardo Balada (Spanish composer) wins a scholarship to the New York College of Music; Marc-Antonio Consoli (Italian composer) comes to the United States for music study; William Dawson is sent by the State Department to train choruses in Spain; Ani and Ida Kavafian (Turkish-born violinists) come with their families to the United States and settle in Detroit; Janos Kiss (Hungarian composer) emigrates to the United States; Bohuslav Martinů accepts a professorship in the American Academy in Rome; Gundaris Poné and Nicolas Roussakis become American citizens; Zoltán Rozsnyai (Hungarian conductor) flees Hungary after the attempted freedom revolution and comes to the United States; José Serebrier (Uruguayan conductor) moves to the United States and enters Curtis Institute.

## L. Musical Beginnings

**Performing Groups**   Chicago Children's Choir; Clarion Concerts (New York); Cleveland Modern Dance Association; Joffrey Ballet Co.; Memphis Opera Theater; Newark Chamber Orchestra; Opera Association of New Mexico (Santa Fe); Opera Society of Washington (DC); Rhode Island Civic Chorale; West Bay Opera (San Francisco).

**Festivals**   Alaska Festival of Music (Anchorage).

**Educational**   Indiana University Folklore Archives.

**Other**   Ford Auditorium (Detroit); Moravian Music Foundation (Winston-Salem, North Carolina); Musicians Guild of America; Organ Historical Society (Richmond, Virginia); Schilke Music Products (Chicago); Violoncello Society.

## M. Music Publications

Barzun, Jacques, *Music in American Life*
Boatwright, Howard, *Introduction to the Theory of Music*
Boyden, David D., *An Introduction to Music*
Haggin, B. H., *The Listener's Musical Companion*
Kerman, Joseph, *Opera as Drama*
Meyer, Leonard, *Emotion and Meaning in Music*
Mursell, James L., *Music Education: Principles and Programs*
Peyser, Ethel, *How Opera Grew*
Sessions, Roger, *Reflections on the Music Life in the United States*
Shanet, Howard, *Learn to Read Music*
Sowerby, Leo, *Ideals in Church Music*

## N. Musical Compositions

**Chamber Music**   Samuel Adler, *Violin Sonata No. 2*; Dominick Argento, *String Quartet*; Arthur Berger, *Chamber Music for Thirteen Instruments*; Ernest Bloch, *String Quartet No. 5*; Robert Erickson, *String Quartet No. 2*; Irving Fine, *Fantasia for String Trio*; Ulysses Kay, *String Quartet No. 2*; Billy Jim Layton, *String Quartet in Two Movements*; Henri Lazarof, *String Quartet No. 1*; Robert Hall Lewis, *String Quartet No. 1*; Vincent Persichetti, *Piano Quintet, Opus 66*; Walter Piston, *Wind Quintet*; Eric Salzman, *Flute Sonata*; Halsey Stevens, *Trumpet Sonata*; John Verrall, *String Quartet No. 6*.

**Choral/Vocal**   George Antheil, *Cabeza de Vaca* (cantata); Dominick Argento, *Ode to the West Wind*; Richard Bales, *The Union*; Philip Bezanson, *The Word of Love* (song cycle); Carlisle Floyd, *Pilgrimage* (cantata); Felix Labunski, *Images of Youth* (cantata); Billy Jim Layton, *Three Dylan Thomas Poems*; Robert Palmer, *Of Night and the Sea* (cantata); Burrill Phillips, *The Return of Odysseus* (secular cantata); Wallingford Riegger, *A Shakespeare Sonnet, Opus 63*; Arthur Shepherd, *A Psalm of the Mountains*; Leo Sowerby, *The Throne of God*; Halsey Stevens, *Sonetto del Petrarca*; Peter Westergaard, *The Plot against the Giant (Cantata No. 1)*.

**Concertos**   Benjamin Boretz, *Violin Concerto*; Paul Creston, *Violin Concerto*; Harold Farberman, *Bassoon Concerto*; Andrew Imbrie, *Little Concerto for Piano, Four Hands, and Orchestra*; Peter Jona Korn, *Saxophone Concerto*; Peter Mennin, *Violin Concerto*; Robert Parris, *Viola Concerto*; Daniel Pinkham, *Violin Concerto*; Roger Sessions, *Piano Concerto*; Elie Siegmeister, *Clarinet Concerto*; Howard Swanson, *Piano Concerto*; Joseph F. Wagner, *Violin Concerto No. 2*.

**Electronic**   L. Hiller and L. Isaacson, *Illiac Suite* (string quartet); Otto Luening, *Theater Piece No. 2*.

**Operas**   John J. Becker, *The Queen of Cornwall*; Jack Beeson, *The Sweet Bye and Bye*; William Bergsma, *The Wife of Martin Guerre*; Leonard Bernstein, *Candide*; Norman Dello Joio, *The Trial at Rouen (Triumph of St. Joan II*—New York Music Critics' Award); Ulysses Kay, *The Juggler of Our Lady*; Douglas Moore, *The Ballad of Baby Doe* (New York Music Critics' Award); Ron Nelson, *The Birthday of the Infanta*; Ned Rorem, *The Robbers*; Robert Starer, *The Intruder*; William Grant Still, *The Pillar*; Lazar Weiner, *The Golem*; Hugo Weisgall, *Six Characters in Search of an Author*.

**Orchestra/Band**   Dominick Argento, *The Resurrection of Don Juan* (ballet); Arthur Berger, *Polyphony*; Philip Bezanson, *Anniversary Overture* (band); Marc Blitzstein, *Volpone* (incidental music); Ernest Bloch, *Suite Modale* (flute and strings); Henry Cowell, *Variations for Orchestra*; Alvin Etler, *Dramatic Overture*; Howard Hanson, *Elegy in Memory of Serge Koussevitzky*; Karel Husa, *Fantasies*; Robert Kurka, *Suite, The Good Soldier Schweik*; Donald Martino, *Contemplations*; Gian Carlo Menotti, *The Unicorn, the Gorgon and the Manticore* (ballet); Joaquín Nin-Culmell, *Yerma* (incidental music); William Schuman, *New England Triptych—Chester Overture* (band); Virgil Thomson, *King John* (incidental music); Charles Wuorinen, *Music for Orchestra*.

**Piano/Organ**   Robert Evett, *Sonata No. 4*; Ross Lee Finney, *Inventions*; Robert Helps, *Three Etudes*; Leo Kraft, *Sonata*; Ezra Laderman, *Three Pieces*; Benjamin Lees, *Sonata No. 3 (Sonata Breve)*; Robert Palmer, *Evening Music*; George Rochberg, *Sonata-fantasia*; Ralph Shapey, *Mutations*; Seymour Shifrin, *Trauermusik*; Halsey Stevens, *Six Preludes—Three Short Preludes for Organ*.

**Symphonies**   Barney Childs, *Symphony No. 2*; Avery Claflin, *Four Pieces for Orchestra (Symphony No. 3)*; Paul Cooper, *Symphony No. 2*; Henry Cowell, *Symphony No. 12*; Paul Creston, *Symphony No. 5*; Halim El-Dabh, *Symphony No. 3*; Peter Jona Korn, *Symphony No. 3*; Gail Kubik, *Symphony No. 3*; Meyer Kupferman, *Symphony No. 4—Lyric Symphony*; Vincent Persichetti, *Symphony for Band (No. 6)*; Wallingford Riegger, *Symphony No. 4*; George Rochberg, *Symphony No. 2* (Naumburg Recording Prize); Ned Rorem, *Symphony No. 2*; Stefan Wolpe, *Symphony*.

# 1957

❋

## Historical Highlights

The Eisenhower Doctrine provides aid for Middle Eastern countries to fight against Communism; the Civil Rights Commission is founded; the Straits of Mackinac bridge opens in Michigan; "under God" is added to the pledge of allegiance; the European Economic Community (common market) is founded; *Sputnik I*, the first orbiting spacecraft, is sent up by the Russians.

## World Cultural Highlights

**World Art**   Henri-Georges Adam. *Beacon of the Dead* (Auschwitz); Marc Chagall, *Self-Portrait*; Norbert Kricke, *Water Forest* (Gelsenkirchen); Pablo Picasso, *Las Meninas*.

**World Literature**   Samuel Beckett, *Endgame;* Jean Genet, *The Balcony;* Ted Hughes, *The Hawk in the Rain*; John Osborne, *The Entertainer*; Boris Pasternak, *Doctor Zhivago*.

**World Music**   Francis Poulenc, *The Dialogues of the Carmelites*; Dmitri Shostakovich, *Piano Concerto No. 2—Symphony No. 11, "1905"*; Ralph Vaughan Williams, *Symphony No. 9*.

**Miscellaneous**   The Institute for Contemporary Music opens in Tokyo; Colin Carr and Shlomo Mintz are born; deaths include Constantin Brancusi, Joyce Cary, Percy W. Lewis, Diego Rivera, Jean Sibelius, and Arturo Toscanini.

## American Art and Literature Highlights

**Births/Deaths**  Births include literary figures David H. Hwang, Tama Janowitz, and Mona Simpson; deaths include art figures Maurice Sterne, Pavel Tchelitchew, Mahonri Young, and literary figures Sholem Asch, Badger Clark, Peter B. Kyne, Gabriela Mistral, Christopher Morley, Anne Parrish, Kenneth Roberts, and Laura Wilder.

**Art Works**  Josef Albers, *Homage to the Square: "Ascending"*; William Baziotes, *Mammoth*; Richard Diebenkorn, *Man and Woman in a Large Room*; Robert Goodnough, *The Struggle*; Seymour Lipton, *Pioneer*; Isamu Noguchi, *The Family*; Richard Pousette-Dart, *Spanish Presence*; Mark Rothko, *Light Cloud, Dark Cloud*; Raphael Soyer, *Farewell to Lincoln Square*; Andrew Wyeth, *Brown Swiss*.

**Literature**  James Agee, *A Death in the Family* (Pulitzer Prize); John Cheever, *The Wapshot Chronicle* (National Book Award); William Faulkner, *The Town*; Ketti Frings, *Look Homeward, Angel* (Pulitzer Prize—New York Drama Critics' Award); William Inge, *The Dark at the Top of the Stairs*; Chin Yang Lee, *Flower Drum Song*; Wright Morris, *The Field of Vision* (National Book Award); Robert P. Warren, *Promises: Poems 1954–1956* (Pulitzer Prize—National Book Award).

## Music—The Vernacular/Commercial Scene

**A. Births**  Geri Allen (pianist) June 12; Anita Baker (singer) December 20; Laura Branigan (singer) July 3; Holly Dunn (singer) August 22; Gloria Estefan (singer) September 1; Vince Gill (singer) April 5; Patty Loveless (singer) January 4; Lyle Lovett (singer/writer) November 1; Cheryl Lynn (singer) March 11; Donny Osmond (singer) December 9; Emily Remler (guitarist/singer) September 18; Joe Satriani (guitarist) July 15; Liz Story (pianist); Pam Tillis (singer) July 24; Tony Vega (singer) July 13.

**B. Deaths**  Belle Baker (singer) April 28; Gene Buck (singer/writer) February 25; Jimmy Dorsey (clarinetist/bandleader) June 12; Abe Lyman (drummer/bandleader) October 23; Walter Page (string bass/bandleader) December 20.

**C. Biographical**

**Performing Groups**  Aquatones; The Capris; The Champs; Ray Conniff Singers; Country Gentlemen; The Crescendos; Danny and the Juniors; The Elegants; The Esquires; The Fireballs; The Fireflies; The Five Duotones; Buddy Holly and the Crickets; The Impressions; Isley Brothers; Johnny and the Jammers; Kingston Trio; Lambert, Hendricks and Ross; Little Anthony and the Imperials; The Mar-Keys; Mastersounds Jazz Quartet; The Miracles; Oak Ridge Boys; The Osmonds; The Quin-Tones; The Royaltones (Paragons); The Satintones; The Shells; The Three Sounds.

**New Beginnings**  American Bandstand (national network); Cameo-Parkway Records; Hi Records; National Academy of the Recording Arts and Sciences; School of Jazz (Lenox, Massachusetts); Stax (Satellite) Records; Verve Records.

**Miscellaneous**  Count Basie's band plays a command performance for Queen Elizabeth of England.

**D. Publications**  Jack Burton, *The Index of American Popular Music*; David Ewen, *Panorama of American Popular Music*; Leonard Feather, *The Book of Jazz from Then till Now: A Guide to the Entire Field*; Nat Shapiro and Nat Hentoff, *The Jazz Makers*; Studs Terkel, *Giants of Jazz*.

**E. Representative Works**

**Musicals**  H. Arlen and E. Y. Harburg, *Jamaica*; L. Bernstein and J. Robbins, *West Side Story*; George Kleinsinger and Joe Darion, *Shinbone Alley*; R. Merrill and G. Abbott, *New Girl in Town*; Cole Porter, *Les Girls* (film); Rodgers and Hammerstein, *Cinderella* (television); Meredith Willson, *The Music Man* (New York Drama Critics' Award).

**Number One Hits**  *All Shook Up—Jailhouse Rock/Treat Me Nice—Teddy Bear—Too Much* (Elvis Presley); *April Love—Love Letters In the Sand* (Pat Boone); *Diana* (Paul Anka); *Honeycomb*

(Jimmie Rodgers); *Party Doll* (Buddy Knox); *Round and Round* (Perry Como); *Tammy* (Debbie Reynolds); *That'll Be the Day* (The Crickets); *You Send Me* (Sam Cooke); *Young Love* (Tab Hunter).

**Other**　Duke Ellington and Billy Strayhorn, *Such Sweet Thunder* (jazz suite)—*A Drum Is a Woman*; G. Evans and M. Davis, *Miles Ahead*; Thelonious Monk, *'Round Midnight*; Harry Ruby, *The Real McCoys* (television theme); George Russell, *Concerto for Billy the Kid*; James Van Heusen and Sammy Cahn, *All the Way* (Oscar).

## Music—The Cultivated/Art Music Scene

**F. Births**　Louis Gentile (tenor) September 2; Craig S. Goodman (flutist/conductor) July 6; Marcus Haddock (tenor) June 19; Derek Han (pianist); David Lang (composer) January 8; Mark Laycock (conductor) August 30; Susanne Mentzer (mezzo-soprano) January 21; Paul Moravec (composer) November 2; Michael Morgan (conductor) September 17; Kurt Ollmann (baritone) January 19; Keith Olson (tenor); Peter Sellars (opera director) September 27.

**G. Deaths**　Frances Densmore (ethnomusicologist) June 5; Weldon Hart (composer/violinist) November 20; Josef Hofmann (Polish-born pianist) February 16; Erich Wolfgang Korngold (Czech-born composer) November 29; Robert Kurka (composer) December 12; Gustave Langenus (Belgian-born clarinetist) January 30; Mary Carr Moore (composer/educator) January 9; Ezio Pinza (Italian-born bass) May 9; Rudolph Réti (Serbian born theorist) February 7; Rose Laura Sutro (pianist) January 11.

**H. Debuts**

**United States**　Daniel Barenboim (Argentine pianist—New York), Herbert Beattie (bass—New York), Lili Chookasian (contralto—Chicago), Justino Díaz (bass—Puerto Rico), Albert Fuller (harpsichordist—New York), Aase Loveberg (Norwegian soprano—Philadelphia), Johanna Martzy (Hungarian violinist), Robert Miller (pianist—New York), Anna Moffo (soprano—Chicago), Gianni Raimondi (Italian tenor—San Francisco), Rita Streich (German soprano—San Francisco), Jess Thomas (tenor—San Francisco).

**Metropolitan Opera**　Karl Böhm (Austrian conductor), Mary Curtis-Verna (soprano), Irene Dalis (mezzo-soprano), Ezio Flagello (bass), Nicolai Gedda (Swedish tenor), Flaviano Labo (Italian tenor), Martha Mödl (German mezzo-soprano), Robert Nagy (tenor), Marianne Schech (German soprano), Mario Sereni (Italian baritone), Wolfgang Windgassen (German tenor).

**Other**　Cathy Berberian (soprano—Naples), Gloria Davy (soprano—Nice), William Dooley (baritone—Heidelberg).

**I. New Positions**

**Conductors**　Richard P. Condie (Mormon Tabernacle Choir—to 1974); Edvard Fendler (Beaumont Symphony Orchestra—to 1971); Margaret Hillis (Chicago Symphony Chorus); Julius Rudel (New York City Opera—to 1979); Kenneth Schermerhorn (American Ballet Theater—to 1967).

**Educational**　Samuel Adler (North Texas State University—to 1966); John Barrows (horn, Yale—to 1961); Henry Brant (Bennington College—to 1980); Walter Kaufmann (Indiana University—to 1977); Robert McBride (University of Arizona); George Perle (University of California, Davis—to 1961); Mel Powell (Yale—to 1969); Leo Smit (UCLA—to 1963); Hugo Weisgall (Juilliard—to 1970).

**Other**　Lucien Cailliet (music director, G. Leblanc Corporation); John Crosby (general director, Santa Fe Opera Co.); David Hall (music editor, *Stereo Review*); James Lyons (editor, *American Record Guide*); Lester Trimble (music critic, *The Nation*—to 1962).

**J. Honors and Awards**

**Honors**　Theodore Ward Chanler (Waite Award); Lukas Foss, Lee Hoiby, and Seymour Shifrin (American Academy); William Schuman (Brandeis); Ernst Toch (National Institute).

**Awards**  Sidney Harth (Wieniawski Second); Anton Kuerti (Leventritt); Jerome Lowenthal (Busoni and Darmstadt); Leslie Parnas (Casals Prize); Regina Sarfaty (Naumburg); William O. Smith (Rome Prize).

**K. Biographical**  Walter Kaufmann (German musicologist) comes to the United States; Varujan Kojian (Lebanese-born conductor) comes to the United States and studies at Curtis Institute; Henri Lazarof (Bulgarian composer) comes to the United States and enters Brandeis University; Vaclav Nelhybel (Czech composer/conductor) comes to the United States; Steve Reich receives a degree in philosophy (with honors) from Cornell; Roger Reynolds receives a degree in engineering physics; Elliott Schwartz receives a BA degree from Columbia; Robert Starer becomes an American citizen; Robert Suderburg graduates *summa cum laude* from the University of Minnesota; Mihály Virizlay (Hungarian cellist) comes to the United States.

## L. Musical Beginnings

**Performing Groups**  American Wind Symphony (Pittsburgh); Chicago Symphony Chorus; Dallas Civic Opera; Improvisation Chamber Ensemble (UCLA—by Lukas Foss); New York Chamber Soloists; Omaha Opera Co.; Philharmonica Hungarica (New York); Richmond Symphony Orchestra (Virginia); Santa Fe Opera Co.; Montana String Quartet.

**Festivals**  Festival Casals (Puerto Rico); Santa Fe Opera Festival (New Mexico).

**Educational**  College Music Society (Boulder, Colorado); Institute of Medieval Music (New York).

**Other**  Bell Telephone Laboratories Computer Music Studio (Murray Hill, New Jersey); Bohemian Composers Group (Louisiana); Harpsichord Music Society (New York); *Journal of Music Theory*; Rutkowski and Robinette, Harpsichord Makers (New York); Sewanee Summer Music Center (Tennessee); Southern Music Publishing Co. (San Antonio); Summy-Birchard Co. (Evanston—by merger); World Music Bank for International Exchange and Promotion of Contemporary Music.

## M. Music Publications

Bukofzer, Manfred, *The Place of Musicology in American Institutions of Higher Learning*
Chasins, Abram, *Speaking of Pianists*
Dallin, Leon, *Techniques of Twentieth Century Composition*
Diller, Angela, *The Splendor of Music*
Howard, J. T. and Bellows, G.K., *A Short History of Music in America*
Hume, Paul, *Our Music, Our Schools and Our Culture*
Lyons, J. and Howard, J., *Modern Music*
McCutchan, Robert, *Hymn Tune Names: Their Sources and Significance*
Ratner, Leonard, *Music: The Listener's Art*
Reese, Gustave, *Fourscore Classics of Music Literature*
Saminsky, Lazare, *Physics and Metaphysics of Music . . .*
Ulrich, Homer, *Music: A Design for Listening*
Wittgenstein, Paul, *School for the Left Hand*

## N. Musical Compositions

**Chamber Music**  Hugh Aitken, *Quintet for Oboe and String Quartet*; Leslie Bassett, *Five Pieces for String Quartet*; Ernest Bloch, *Piano Quintet No. 2*; Henry Brant, *Hieroglyphics I—Millennium III*; Ingolf Dahl, *Piano Quintet*; Vivian Fine, *String Quartet*; Andrew Imbrie, *String Quartet No. 3*; John La Montaine, *String Quartet, Opus 16*; Robert Moevs, *String Quartet*; Mel Powell, *Piano Quintet—Piano Trio*; Gardner Read, *String Quartet, Opus 100*; Halsey Stevens, *Septet* (winds and strings); William Grant Still, *Four Indigenous Portraits*; Alan Stout, *String Quartet No. 5*; Aurelio de la Vega, *String Quartet, "In Memoriam Alban Berg"*; Peter Westergaard, *String Quartet*.

**Choral/Vocal**  Josef Alexander, *Songs for Eve*; Jacob Avshalomov, *Inscriptions at the City of Brass*; Leonard Bernstein, *Harvard Choruses*; Richard Donovan, *Five Elizabethan Lyrics*; Cecil Effinger, *The Invisible Fire* (oratorio); Howard Hanson, *Song of Democracy*; Daniel Pinkham, *Christmas Cantata—Easter Cantata*; Randall Thompson, *Ode to the Virginian Voyage*.

**Concertos**  Ernst Bacon, *Elegy* (oboe and strings); George Barati, *Cello Concerto*; Avery Claflin, *Piano Concerto*; Herbert Elwell, *Concert Suite for Violin and Orchestra*; Robert Evett, *Piano Concerto*; Walter Piston, *Viola Concerto* (New York Music Critics' Award); Russell Smith, *Piano Concerto No. 2*; Richard Yardumian, *Passacaglia, Recitatives and Fugue (Piano Concerto)*; Ben Weber, *Rapsodie concertante* (viola and orchestra).

**Electronic**  Bülent Arel, *Music for String Quartet and Tape*.

**Operas**  Dominick Argento, *The Boor*; Samuel Barber, *Vanessa* (Pulitzer Prize); John Eaton, *Ma Barker*; William Flanagan, *Bartleby*; Paul Hindemith, *Die Harmonie der Welt*; David Marvin Levy, *The Tower*; Jerome Moross, *Gentlemen, Be Seated*; Vittorio Rieti, *The Pet Shop*.

**Orchestra/Band**  Hugh Aitken, *Seven Pieces for Chamber Orchestra—Partita No. 1*; Richard Bales, *National Gallery Suite III, "American Design"*; Elaine Barkin, *Essay for Orchestra*; Wayne Barlow, *Night Song*; Aaron Copland, *Orchestral Variations*; Norman Dello Joio, *Meditations on Ecclesiastes* (Pulitzer Prize); David Diamond, *The World of Paul Klee*; Robert Erickson, *Variations for Orchestra*; Ross Lee Finney, *Variations for Orchestra*; Ferde Grofé, *Death Valley Suite*; Howard Hanson, *Mosaics*; Darius Milhaud, *Aspen Serenade, Opus 361*; Burrill Phillips (incidental music); Quincy Porter, *The Mad Woman of Chaillot* (incidental music); Mel Powell, *Stanzas*; Wallingford Riegger, *Festival Overture*; Halsey Stevens, *Music for String Orchestra*; William Grant Still, *Little Red Schoolhouse*; Lester Trimble, *Sonic Landscape*.

**Piano/Organ**  Hugh Aitken, *Seven Bagatelles*; Milton Babbitt, *Partitions*; Gordan Binkerd, *Organ Service*; John Cage, *Winter Music* (1–20 pianos); Chou Wen-Chung, *The Willows Are New*; Edward T. Cone, *Prelude, Passacaglia and Fugue*; Aaron Copland, *Piano Fantasy*; John Eaton, *Piano Variations*; Carlisle Floyd, *Sonata*; Ray Green, *Dance Sonata No. 2*; Jean Eichelberger Ivey, *Sonata*; Benjamin Lees, *Six Ornamental Etudes*; Robert Muczynski, *Sonata No. 1, Opus 9*; George Tremblay, *Sonata No. 3*; David Ward-Steinman, *Sonata*; George Walker, *Sonata No. 2*; Christian Wolff, *Duo for Pianists*.

**Symphonies**  Samuel Adler, *Symphony No. 2*; Gordon Binkerd, *Symphony No. 2*; William Bolcom, *Symphony*; Raynor Brown, *Symphony No. 2*; Alvin Etler, *Concerto for Orchestra*; Harold Farberman, *Symphony*; Alexei Haieff, *Symphony No. 2* (based on *Sonata for Two Pianos, 1945*); Robert Helps, *Symphony No. 1* (Naumburg Foundation Prize); Charles Jones, *Symphony No. 2*; Ellis Kohs, *Symphony No. 2*; John La Montaine, *Symphony No. 1, Opus 28*; W. Francis McBeth, *Symphony No. 2*; Colin McPhee, *Symphony No. 2, "Pastorale"*; Roger Sessions, *Symphony No. 3*; Elie Siegmeister, *Symphony No. 3*; Halsey Stevens, *Sinfonia Breve*; Alexander Tcherepnin, *Symphony No. 4 in E Major, Opus 91*; Ernst Toch, *Symphony No. 4, Opus 80*.

# 1958

☀

## Historical Highlights

Alaska is taken into the Union as the 49th state; the National Aeronautics and Space Administration (NASA) is formed; *Pioneer I* and *Explorer I* are launched; the atomic submarine *Nautilus* crosses the North Pole under the ice; transatlantic jet service begins; Egypt and Syria unite to form the United Arab Republic; Charles de Gaulle becomes president under a new French constitution.

## World Cultural Highlights

**World Art**  Karel Appel, *Flowering Heads;* Corneille, *Spanish Town;* Alberto Giacometti, *Annette Assise;* Johann Hofmann, *Golden Blaze*; Norbert Kricke, *Raumplastik;* Anton Tàpies, *Grey Ochre*.

**World Literature**  Bertolt Brecht, *Der Aufhaltsame Aufstieg des Arturo Ui*; Harold Pinter, *The Birthday Party*; E. B. White, *The Once and Future King* (tetralogy completed).

**World Music**    Witold Lutoslawski, *Funeral Music*; Toshiro Mayuzumi, *Nirvana Symphony*; Olivier Messiaen, *Catalogue d'Oiseaux*; Francis Poulenc, *La Voix Humaine*; Michael Tippett, *Symphony No. 2*.

**Miscellaneous**    The George Enescu Festival begins in Romania and the Festival of Two Worlds in Spoleto; births include Yefim Bronfman, Ivo Pogorelich, and Esa-Pekka Salonen; deaths include Alfred Noyes, Georges Rouault, Florent Schmitt, Ralph Vaughan Williams, and Maurice de Vlaminck.

## American Art and Literature

**Births/Deaths**    Deaths include art figures Guy Pène Du Bois, John Gregory, Jan Müller, and literary figures Zoë Akins, James B. Cabell, Grace Walcott Conkling, Rachel Crothers, Dorothy Canfield Fisher, George J. Nathan, Mary Roberts Rinehart, Antoinette Scudder, and Mary S. Watts.

**Art Works**    Isabel Bishop, *Subway Scene*; Sam Francis, *Shining Black*; Jasper Johns, *Light Bulb II*; Ellsworth Kelly, *Ralph Vaughan Williams*; Edward Kienholz, *The Beanery*; Ibram Lassaw, *Galactic Cluster I*; Jacques Lipchitz, *Between Heaven and Earth*; Henry Moore, *Reclining Figure (UNESCO)*; Jan Müller, *Jacob's Ladder*; Louise Nevelson, *Sky Cathedral*; Hugo Robus, *Meditating Girl*.

**Literature**    E. Burdick and W. Lederer, *The Ugly American*; Truman Capote, *Breakfast at Tiffany's*; Stanley Kunitz, *Selected Poems, 1928–1958* (Pulitzer Prize); Bernard Malamud, *The Magic Barrel* (National Book Award); Archibald MacLeish, *J. B.* (Pulitzer Prize); Theodore Roethke, *Words for the Wind* (National Book Award); Leon Uris, *Exodus*; Tennessee Williams, *Suddenly Last Summer*.

## Music—The Vernacular/Commercial Scene

**A. Births**    Howard Alden (guitarist) October 17; Joe Bowie (trombonist); Belinda Carlisle (singer) August 17; Mary Chapin Carpenter (singer) February 21; Shawn Colvin (singer/writer) January 10; Joe Diffie (singer) December 28; Paul Evans (singer/writer) March 5; Béla Fleck (banjo) July 10; Alan Jackson (singer) October 17; Michael Jackson (singer) August 29; Sammy Kershaw (singer) February 24; Madonna (singer) August 16; Prince (singer) June 7; Shannon (Greene—singer); Marty Stuart (singer) September 30; Aaron Tippin (singer) July 3; Tanya Tucker (singer) October 10; Shelley West (singer) May 23; Brooks Williams (guitar) November 10.

**B. Deaths**    Tiny Bradshaw (piano/bandleader) November 26; Big Bill Broonzy (singer) August 14; Lew Brown (lyricist) February 5; Alfred Bryan (lyricist) April 1; Rex Griffin (singer) October 7; William C. Handy (trumpeter/composer) March 28; Artie Matthews (composer) October 25; Harry Revel (songwriter) November 3.

**C. Biographical**

**Performing Groups**    The Belmonts; Brothers Four; The Caravans; The Casinos; The Castells; The Classics (originally Perennials); The Contours; Joey Dee and the Starliters; Dion and the Belmonts; The Fleetwoods; Greenbriar Boys; The Kingsmen; Chad Mitchell Trio; The O'Jays; New Lost City Ramblers; Olympia Brass Band (New Orleans); The Primes; Bill Russo Orchestra; The Shirelles; Stars of Faith; The Teddy Bears; The Tokens; The Wallers.

**New Beginnings**    *Allen's Poop Sheet* (to 1974); *Coda: The Jazz Magazine*; Country Music Association; Gold Record Awards; Grammy Awards; Hifijazz Records (Hollywood); *The Jazz Review*; William Ransom Hogan Jazz Archive (Tulane University); Monterey Jazz Festivals (California); United Artists Records (New York); United Nations Jazz Society; Warner Brothers Records.

**Miscellaneous**    Lalo Schifrin (Argentine pianist/conductor) comes to the United States as arranger for Xavier Cugat's band.

**D. Publications**    Samuel Charters, *Jazz: New Orleans, 1885–1957*; David Ewen, *Complete Book of American Musical Theater*; Stephen Longstreet, *Encyclopédie du Jazz*; Hazel Meyer, *The Gold in Tin Pan Alley*; Elizabeth R. Montgomery, *The Story behind Popular Songs*.

### E. Representative Works

**Musicals** Richard Adler, *The Gift of the Magi* (television); Leroy Anderson and W. and J. Kerr, *Goldilocks*; Jerry Bock and S. Harnick, *The Body Beautiful*; Lerner and Loewe, *Gigi* (film—Oscar for title song); Jay Livingston and Ray Evans, *Oh, Captain*; Cole Porter, *Aladdin* (television); Rodgers and Hammerstein, *Flower Drum Song*; J. Styne, B. Comden, A. Green, *Say, Darling*.

**Number One Hits** *All I Have to Do Is Dream* (Everly Brothers); *At the Hop* (Danny and the Juniors); *The Chipmunk Song* (Chipmunks with David Seville); *Don't/I Beg of You—Hard Headed Woman* (Elvis Presley); *It's All in the Game* (Tommy Edwards); *It's Only Make Believe* (Conway Twitty); *Little Star* (The Elegants); *Poor Little Fool* (Ricky Nelson); *The Purple People Eater* (Sheb Wooley); *Tequila* (The Champs); *To Know Him Is to Love Him* (Teddy Bears); *Tom Dooley* (Kingston Trio); *Twilight Time* (The Platters); *Volare* (Domenico Modugno); *Witch Doctor* (David Seville).

**Other** David Butolph, *Maverick* (television theme); Hugo Friedhofer, *The Young Lions* (film music); Henry Mancini, *Peter Gunn* (television theme); David Rose, *The Stripper*; Francis Thorne, *Broadway and 52nd Street*; Dimitri Tiomkin, *The Old Man and the Sea* (film music—Oscar)—*Rawhide* (television theme).

## Music—The Cultivated/Art Music Scene

**F. Births** Eve Beglarian (composer) July 22; Heidi Bergman (violinist) July 19; Barbara Carter (soprano); Kathleen Cassello (soprano); Cynthia Haymon (soprano); Claire Fox Hillard (conductor) August 30; Frank Lopardo (tenor); Catherine Mardiello (pianist) February 21; Aprile Millo (soprano) April 14; Derek Lee Ragin (counter-tenor) June 17; Thomas Randle (tenor) December 21; Teresa Ringholz (soprano) December 30; Marta Senn (mezzo-soprano); Franul Tichel (composer); Diana Walker (soprano); Deborah Voight (soprano).

**G. Deaths** Bentley Ackley (hymnist/editor) September 3; Louis d'Angelo (baritone) August 9; Edward S. Barnes (organist) February 14; Erwin Bodky (pianist/musicologist) December 6; Frances M. Clark (music educator) June 14; Gaston-Marie Déthier (Belgian-born organist) May 26; Eva Gauthier (Canadian mezzo-soprano) December 26; A. A. Harding (bandmaster) December 3; Judge Jackson (composer/compiler) April 7; Artur Rodzinski (Polish-born conductor) November 27; Ernest C. Schirmer (publisher) February 15; Arthur Shepherd (composer) January 12; Lily Strickland (composer/pianist) June 6; Marie Sundelius (soprano) June 26; Thomas Tapper (music educator) February 24; Emerson Whithorne (pianist/composer) March 25.

### H. Debuts

**United States** Martina Arroyo (soprano—New York), Vladimir Ashkenazy (Russian pianist—tour), Teresa Berganza (Spanish mezzo-soprano—Dallas), Mary Costa (soprano—Los Angeles), Jan DeGaetani (mezzo-soprano—New York), Sylvia Fisher (Australian soprano—Chicago), Bernard Haitink (Dutch conductor—Los Angeles), Gita Karasik (pianist—San Francisco), Leonid Kogan (Russian violinist—Boston), Robert Muczynski (pianist—New York), Ticho Parly (Danish tenor—New Orleans), Itzhak Perlman (Israeli violinist—Ed Sullivan TV show), Arlene Saunders (soprano—New York), Peter Serkin (pianist—Marlboro), Jeffrey Siegel (pianist—Chicago), Stanislaw Skrowaczewski (Polish conductor—Cleveland).

**Metropolitan Opera** Inge Borkh (German soprano), Gloria Davy (soprano), Mignon Dunn (mezzo-soprano), Grace Hoffman (mezzo-soprano), William Lewis (tenor), Barry Morell (tenor), Mario Zanasi (Italian baritone).

**Other** Ann Schein (pianist—London).

### I. New Positions

**Conductors** John Barnett (music director, National Orchestral Association); Leonard Bernstein (New York Philharmonic Orchestra—to 1969); Vladimir Golschmann (Tulsa Philharmonic Orchestra—to 1961); Robert Irving (New York City Ballet); Paul Kletzki (Dallas Symphony Orchestra—to 1961); Leopold Ludwig (San Francisco Opera—to 1968); Max Rudolf (Cincinnati

Symphony Orchestra—to 1970); Edouard Van Remoortel (St. Louis Symphony Orchestra—to 1962); George Schick (Metropolitan Opera—to 1969).

**Educational**    Dominick Argento (University of Minnesota); Easley Blackwood (University of Chicago); Henry L. Clarke (University of Washington—to 1977); Arnold Elston (Berkeley—to 1971); Elliot Forbes (Harvard); Lejaren Hiller (University of Illinois—to 1968); Thor Johnson (Northwestern University—to 1964); Peter Mennin (director, Peabody—to 1962); Claudio Spies (Swarthmore College—to 1970); Janos Starker (Indiana University); Peter Westergaard (Columbia—to 1966).

**Other**    Eric Salzman (music critic, *The New York Times*—to 1962).

## J. Honors and Awards

**Honors**    Samuel Barber (American Academy); Leonard Bernstein (Ditson); Julius Rudel (National Arts Club Medal); Roger Sessions (Brandeis); Paul Wittgenstein (PhD, Philadelphia Musical Academy).

**Awards**    Van Cliburn (Tchaikovsky, piano); Ivan Davis (Busoni and Casella); Shirley Verrett (Naumburg).

## K. Biographical

Leonard Bernstein becomes the first American-born conductor of the New York Philharmonic Orchestra; Carlos Chávez (Mexican composer/conductor) becomes the Charles Eliot Norton lecturer at Harvard; Chou Wen-chung, Rolf Gehlhaar, and Alexander Tcherepnin become US citizens; Mario Davidovsky (Argentine composer) studies at Berkshire and stays in the United States; President Eisenhower signs the National Cultural Center Act, establishing the Kennedy Center for the Performing Arts; Herbert Graf returns to Europe; Kyrill Kondrashin becomes the first Soviet conductor to visit the United States; the Romero family of guitarists (Celedonio, Celin, Pepe, Angel) emigrates to the United States; János Starker begins a solo career as cellist; Karlheinz Stockhausen (German composer) begins a lecture tour of the United States

## L. Musical Beginnings

**Performing Groups**    Atlanta Community Orchestra; Boston Opera Group (Opera Co. of Boston); Clarion Music Society; Denver Lyric Theater; Lenox String Quartet (Berkshire Center); Lyric Opera of Kansas City; Milwaukee Symphony Orchestra; Phoenix Bach and Madrigal Society; Puerto Rico Symphony Orchestra.

**Festivals**    Fort Wayne Fine Arts Festival; Inter-American Music Festival (Washington, DC).

**Educational**    Cooperative Studio for Electronic Music (Ann Arbor, Michigan); Experimental Music Studio, University of Illinois; University of California at Davis Music Department.

**Other**    *American Choral Review*; Clarion Music Society (New York); Music at the Vineyards (Saratoga, California); Music Critics Association (MCA); Piano Technicians Guild (by merger); Rodgers Organ Co.; Society for the Preservation of the American Musical Heritage; *Stereo Review*; Takoma Records.

## M. Music Publications

Kolodin, Irving, (ed.) *The Composer as Listener: A Guide to Music—The Musical Life*
Krenek, Ernst, *Tonal Counterpoint in the Style of the 18th Century*
Krueger, Karl, *The Way of the Conductor: His Origins, Purpose and Procedures*
Parrish, Carl, *A Treasury of Early Music*
Rudolf Réti, *Tonality—Atonality—Pantonality*
Saminsky, Lazare, *Essentials of Conducting*
Sargeant, Winthrop, *Listening to Music*
Veinus, Abraham, *Understanding Music: Style, Structure and History*
Wagner, Joseph, *Orchestration*

## N. Musical Compositions

**Chamber Music**    Hugh Aitken, *Serenade for Ten Instruments*; T. J. Anderson, *String Quartet No.*

*1*; Leslie Bassett, *Woodwind Quintet*; Arthur Berger, *String Quartet*; Gordon Binkerd, *String Quartet No. 1*; Easley Blackwood, *String Quartet No. 1*; Howard Boatwright, *Quartet for Clarinet and Strings*; Benjamin Boretz, *String Quartet*; Ingolf Dahl, *String Quartet No. 2*; Mario Davidovsky, *String Quartet No. 2*; John Eaton, *String Quartet No. 1*; Ross Lee Finney, *String Quintet*; Leon Kirchner, *String Quartet No. 2* (New York Music Critics' Award); Meyer Kupferman, *String Quartet No. 4*; George Perle, *String Quintet, Opus 35*; Burrill Phillips, *String Quartet No. 2*; Quincy Porter, *String Quartet No. 9*; Roger Sessions, *String Quintet*; Ralph Shapey, *String Quartet No. 5*; Alan Stout, *Clarinet Quintet*; William Sydeman, *Concerto da Camera No. 1* (Pacifica Foundation Award).

**Choral/Vocal**    Hugh Aitken, *Cantata No. 1*; Dominick Argento, *Six Elizabethan Songs*; Ernst Bacon, *By Blue Ontario* (cantata); Thomas Beversdorf, *The Rock* (oratorio); Philip Bezanson, *Song of the Cedar* (cantata); Howard Boatwright, *Mass in C Major*; Henry Brant, *In Praise of Learning*; Salvatore Martirano, *O, O, O, O, that Shakespeherian Rag*; William Schuman, *Carols of Death*; Seymour Shifrin, *Cantata to Sophoclean Choruses*; Igor Stravinsky, *Threni: id est Lamentationes Jeremiae prophetae*; Randall Thompson, *Requiem*.

**Concertos**    William Bergsma, *Concerto for Wind Quintet*; John Cage, *Concerto for Piano and Orchestra*; Edward T. Cone, *Violin Concerto*; Donald Erb, *Chamber Concerto for Piano and Strings*; Alvin Etler, *Concerto for Violin and Wind Quintet*; Harold Farberman, *Timpani Concerto*; Lee Hoiby, *Piano Concerto No. 1*; Benjamin Lees, *Violin Concerto*, *Peter Menuin*, *Piano Concerto*; Tibor Serly, *Concerto for Two Pianos*; Robert Starer, *Concerto for Viola, Strings and Percussion*.

**Electronic**    Kenneth Gaburo, *Antiphony I*; Otto Luening, *Dynamophonic Suite*; Vladimir Ussachevsky, *Studies in Sound Plus*; Edgard Varèse, *Poème électronique* (tape).

**Operas**    Paul Bowles, *Yerma*; Nicolas Flagello, *The Sisters*; Carlisle Floyd, *Wuthering Heights*; Lee Hoiby, *The Scarf*; David Martin Levy, *Escorial*; Gian Carlo Menotti, *Maria Golovin*; Nicolas Nabokov, *The Holy Devil*; Ned Rorem, *Eagles*; William Grant Still, *Minette Fontaine*; Louise Talma, *The Alcestiad* (Marjorie Peabody Award); Hugo Weisgall, *Purgatory*.

**Orchestra/Band**    Samuel Adler, *Jubilee*; T. J. Anderson, *Pyknon Overture*; Jacob Avshalomov, *Phases of the Great Land*; John J. Becker, *Madeleine and Judas* (incidental music); Jean Berger, *Short Overture*; Marc Blitzstein, *A Midsummer's Night Dream* (incidental music)—*A Winter's Tale* (incidental music)—*Lear: A Study for Orchestra*; Ernest Bloch, *Two Last Poems* (flute and orchestra); John Eaton, *Tertullian Overtures*; Halim El-Dabh, *Bacchanalia—Clytemnestra* (dance drama); Howard Hanson, *Summer Seascape*; Leo Kraft, *Variations for Orchestra*; Nikolai Lopatnikoff, *Music for Orchestra, Opus 39*; Ray Luke, *Orchestra Suite No. 1*; William Mayer, *Overture for an American*; George Rochberg, *Cheltenham Concerto*; Gunther Schuller, *Spectra*; Ralph Shapey, *Ontogeny*; Seymour Shifrin, *Three Pieces for Orchestra*; Halsey Stevens, *Five Pieces for Orchestra—Symphonic Dances*; William Sydeman, *Orchestral Abstractions*; Elinor Warren, *The Crystal Lake*; Richard Wernick, *The Emperor's Nightingale* (ballet).

**Piano/Organ**    Esther Ballou, *Sonata No. 2 for Two Pianos*; Leslie Bassett, *Voluntaries for Organ*; Jean Berger, *Caribbean Cruise* (two pianos); Lucia Dlugoszewski, *Music for the Left Ear*; Robert Helps, *Starscape*; Norman Lloyd, *Sonata*; Donald Martino, *Piano Fantasy*; W. Francis McBeth, *Three Pieces*; William Schuman, *Three Piano Moods*; William Sydeman, *Piano Variations*.

**Symphonies**    Easley Blackwood, *Symphony No. 1*; Raynor Brown, *Symphony No. 3*; Henry Cowell, *Symphony No. 13, "Madras"*; Cecil Effinger, *Little Symphony No. 2—Symphony No. 5*; David M. Epstein, *Symphony No. 1*; Ross Lee Finney, *Symphony No. 2*; Lukas Foss, *Symphony of Chorales*; Paul Hindemith, *Pittsburgh Symphony*; Benjamin Lees, *Symphony No. 2*; Charles Mills, *Crazy Horse Symphony*; Vincent Persichetti, *Symphony No. 7*; Ned Rorem, *Symphony No. 3*; Roger Sessions, *Symphony No. 4*; William Grant Still, *Symphony No. 3, "Sunday Symphony"*; Clifford Taylor, *Symphony No. 1*; Gil Trythall, *Symphony No. 1*; Robert Ward, *Symphony No. 4*; Frank Wigglesworth, *Symphony No. 2*; Joseph Wood, *Symphony No. 3*; Charles Wuorinen, *Symphony No. 1*.

# 1959

❋

## Historical Highlights

Hawaii becomes the 50th state; Russia's Nikita Khrushchev and Cuba's Fidel Castro make tours of the United States; the St. Lawrence Seaway officially opens; NASA begins its astronaut program; the *Savannah*, the first atom-powered cargo ship, is launched; a Russian rocket sends back close up photos before hitting the moon; an Antarctica Treaty is signed; the Chinese crush a Tibetan freedom uprising.

## World Cultural Highlights

**World Art**    André Beaudin, *La Lune de Mai*; Fernando Botero, *Mona Lisa, Age 12*; Marc Chagall, *La Champ de Mars*; Meret Oppenheim, *Spring Banquet;* Victor Vasarely, *Supernovae*.

**World Literature**    Jean Anouilh, *Becket*; Bertolt Brecht, *St. Joan of the Stockyards;* Jean Genet, *Les Nègres*; Günther Grass, *The Tin Drum*; Eugène Ionesco, *The Killer*.

**World Music**    Henri Dutilleux, *Symphony No. 2*; Krzysztoff Penderecki, *Psalms of David*; Francis Poulenc, *Gloria*; Dmitri Shostakovich, *Cello Concerto No. 1*; Karlheinz Stockhausen, *Zyklus*.

**Miscellaneous**    The Academy of St. Martin-in-the-Fields is founded in England and the Vancouver Opera Co. in Canada; deaths include Eduard van Beinum, Curt Sachs, and Heitor Villa-Lobos.

## American Art and Literature Highlights

**Births/Deaths**    Births include author Susan Faludi; deaths include art figures John Carroll, Jacob Epstein, George Grosz, and literary figures Maxwell Anderson, Raymond Chandler, Sarah N. Claghorn, Octavus Roy Cohen, Edgar A. Guest, Wallace Irwin, Reginald Wright Kauffman, and architect Frank Lloyd Wright.

**Art Works**    Milton Avery, *Tangerine Moon and Wine Dark Sea*; Leonard Baskin, *Man with Owl*; José de Creeft, *Alice in Wonderland*; Jasper Johns, *False Start*; Seymour Lipton, *Prophet*; Morris Louis, *Faces*; Robert Motherwell, *Monster (for Charles Ives)*; Robert Rauschenberg, *Canyon*; Frank Stella, *Marriage of Reason and Squalor*; George Tooker, *Waiting Room*; Peter Voulkos, *Feather Rock*.

**Literature**    Saul Bellow, *Henderson the Rain King*; Allen S. Drury, *Advise and Consent* (Pulitzer Prize); Lorraine Hansberry, *A Raisin in the Sun* (New York Drama Critics' Award); Philip Roth, *Goodbye Columbus* (National Book Award); Delmore Schwartz, *Summer Knowledge* (Bollingen Prize); William Snodgrass, *Heart's Needle* (Pulitzer Prize); Robert L. Taylor, *Travels of Jamie McPheeters* (Pulitzer Prize); Tennessee Williams, *Sweet Bird of Youth*.

## Music—The Vernacular/Commercial Scene

**A. Births**    Cindy Blackman (percussionist) November 18; Shaun Cassidy (singer) September 27; Marc Cohn (singer/pianist) July 5; Radney Foster (singer) July 20; Stanley Jordan (pianist/guitarist) July 31; Kathy Mattea (singer) June 21; Stephanie Mills (singer); Lorrie Morgan (singer) June 27; Marie Osmond (singer) October 13; Marc Shaiman (composer) October 22; Randy Travis (singer) May 4; Suzanne Vega (singer/writer) August 12; Jody Watley (singer) January 30; "Weird Al" Yankovic (singer).

**B. Deaths**    Sidney Bechet (clarinetist) May 14; Warren "Baby" Dodds (drummer) February 14; Mack Gordon (composer/lyricist) March 1; Guitar Slim (guitarist) February 7; Billie Holiday (singer) July 17; Buddy Holly (singer/writer) February 3; Charlie Johnson (pianist/bandleader) December 13; Sam M. Lewis (lyricist) November 22; George W. Meyer (songwriter) August 28; Jack Norworth (composer/lyricist) September 1; Richie Valens (singer/composer) February 3; Lester Young (saxophonist) March 15.

## C. Biographical

**Performing Groups**   "Cannonball" Adderley Jazz Quintet II; AfroJazz Sextet (Herbie Mann); Bill Black Combo; The Dovells; Drifters II; Bill Evans Trio; The Fendermen; Gospel Chimes; Jazztet (by Art Farmer); Jive Five; Quincy Jones Big Band; The Lettermen; The Limeliters; The Majors; The Marvelows; Thelonious Monk Big Band; Wes Montgomery Trio; Ohio Players; The Orlons; Randy and the Rainbows; The Ronettes; The Sheppards; Soulful Inspirations; Sunny and the Sunglows; The Supremes; Tavares; The Versatones (Ventures).

**New Beginnings**   Motown Records; Newport Folk Festival; Tamla Records.

**Miscellaneous**   Louis Armstrong suffers a heart attack.

**D. Publications**   Whitney Balliett, *The Sound of Surprise*; Oscar Brand, *Bawdy Songs and Backroom Ballads*; Samuel Charters, *The Country Blues*; Nat Hentoff, *Jazz*; D. D. Lawrence, *Folklore Songs of the United States*; Alan Lomax, *Leadbelly: A Collection of World Famous Songs*; Francis Newton, *The Jazz Scene*; Martin Williams (ed.), *The Art of Jazz: Essays on the Nature and Development of Jazz*.

## E. Representative Works

**Musicals**   H. Arlen and J. Mercer, *Saratoga*; Rick Besoyan, *Little Mary Sunshine*; J. Bock and S. Harnick, *Fiorello* (Pulitzer Prize—New York Drama Critics' Award); A. Hague and D. Fields, *Redhead*; Bob Merrill, J. Stein, and R. Russell, *Take Me Along*; M. Rodgers and M. Barer, *Once Upon a Mattress*; Rodgers and Hammerstein, *The Sound of Music*; Harold Rome, *Destry Rides Again*; J. Styne and S. Sondheim, *Gypsy*.

**Number One Hits**   *The Battle of New Orleans* (Johnny Horton); *A Big Hunk O'Love* (Elvis Presley); *Come Softly to Me—Mr. Blue* (The Fleetwoods); *The Happy Organ* (Dave "Baby" Cortez); *Heartaches by the Number* (Guy Mitchell); *Kansas City* (Wilbert Harrison); *Lonely Boy* (Paul Anka); *Mack the Knife* (Bobby Darin); *Sleep Walk* (Santo and Johnny); *Smoke Gets in Your Eyes* (The Platters); *Stagger Lee* (Lloyd Price); *The Three Bells* (The Browns); *Venus—Why* (Frankie Avalon).

**Other**   David Amram, *J. R.* (film music—Pulitzer Prize); J. Livingston and R. Evans, *Bonanza* (television theme); Miklós Rózsa, *Ben Hur* (film music—Oscar); B. Russell, *Jazz in the Space Age*; H. Simeone and N. Onorati, *The Little Drummer Boy*; Max Steiner, *A Summer Place* (film music); James Van Heusen and Sammy Cahn, *High Hopes* (Oscar).

## Music—The Cultivated/Art Music Scene

**F. Births**   John F. Bertles (composer) January 28; Karen Huffstodt (soprano) December 31; Barbara Jane Kilduff (soprano) May 31; Andrew Litton (conductor) May 16.

**G. Deaths**   George Antheil (composer/pianist) February 12; Gustave L. Becker (pianist/educator) February 25; Felix Deyo (composer/pianist) June 21; Edwin A. Fleisher (art patron) January 9; Walter Helfer (composer) April 16; Edward Johnson (tenor/impresario) April 20; Maryla Jonas (Polish-born pianist) July 3; Wanda Landowska (Polish-born harpsichordist) August 16; Mario Lanza (tenor) October 7; David Mannes (violinist/conductor) April 25; Walter Naumburg (art patron) October 17; Ethel Newcomb (pianist) July 3; Curt Sachs (German-born musicologist) February 5; Lazare Saminsky (Russian-born composer/conductor) June 30; Frederick P. Search (cellist/conductor) November 9; Lamar E. Stringfield (composer/flutist) January 21; T. Carl Whitmer (organist) May 30; Ole Windingstad (Norwegian-born conductor/composer) June 3.

## H. Debuts

**United States**   Michel Block (Belgian pianist—New York), Gré Brouwenstijn (Dutch soprano—Chicago), Ivan Davis (pianist—New York), Zara Dolukhanova (Russian mezzo-soprano—tour), Geraint Evans (British baritone—San Francisco), Enrico di Giuseppe (tenor—New Orleans), Reri Grist (soprano—Santa Fe), Sena Jurinac (Yugoslavian soprano—San Franciso), Igor Kipnis (harpsichordist—New York), Ralph Kirshbaum (cellist—Dallas), Peter Maag (Swiss conductor—Cincinnati), Spiro Malas (bass-baritone—Baltimore), João Carlos Martins (Brazilian pianist—Washington, DC), Christopher Parkening (guitarist—Los Angeles), Georges Prêtre (French conductor—Chicago), George Shirley (tenor—Woodstock, New York), Gabriella Tucci (Italian soprano—San Francisco), Silvio Varviso (Swiss conductor—San Francisco), Ralph Votapek (pianist—New York).

**Metropolitan Opera**   Martina Arroyo (soprano), Kim Borg (Finnish bass), Oskar Czerwenka (Austrian bass), Christa Ludwig (German-soprano), Cornell MacNeil (baritone), Anna Moffo (soprano), Birgit Nilsson (Swedish soprano), Marko Rothmüller (Yugoslavian baritone), Leonie Rysanek (Austrian soprano), Giulietta Simionato (Italian mezzo-soprano), Elisabeth Söderström (Swedish soprano), Teresa Stratas (Canadian soprano).

**Other**   Grace Bumbry (mezzo-soprano—London), Barry McDaniel (baritone—Stuttgart).

## I. New Positions

**Conductors**   Peter Herman Adler (Baltimore Symphony Orchestra—to 1968); Piero Bellugi (Portland [Oregon] Symphony Orchestra—to 1961); Theodore Bloomfield (Rochester Philharmonic Orchestra—to 1963); Louis Lane (Akron, Ohio, Symphony Orchestra—to 1983); Gerhard Samuel (Oakland Symphony Orchestra—to 1971); Fabien Sevitzky (University of Miami Symphony Orchestra—to 1965); Guy Taylor (Phoenix Symphony Orchestra—to 1969).

**Educational**   Milton Babbitt (director, Columbia-Princeton Electronic Music Center); Richard Burgin (Boston University—to 1962); George Crumb (University of Colorado—to 1964); Leon Fleisher (Peabody); Allen Forte (Yale); Claude Palisca (Yale); Daniel Pinkham (New England Conservatory); Jesús Maria Sanromá (Puerto Rico Conservatory—to 1980); Morton Subotnick (Mills College—to 1966); William Sydeman (Mannes College—to 1970).

**Other**   Stanley Adams (president, ASCAP—to 1980).

## J. Honors and Awards

**Honors**   Agustin Anievas (Concert Artists Guild Award); Milton Babbitt, Noel Lee, and Virgil Thomson (American Academy); Leonard Bernstein (Gold Baton); Marc Blitzstein (National Institute); Ernest Bloch (Brandeis); Karl Geiringer (American Academy of Arts and Sciences).

**Awards**   Stuart Canin (Paganini); Malcolm Frager (Leventritt Award); Jaime Laredo (Queen Elisabeth); Joseph Silverstein (Queen Elisabeth Third); Ralph Votapek (Naumburg).

**K. Biographical**   Bülent Arel (Turkish composr) comes to the United States and works as a technician at the Columbia-Princeton Electronic Music Center; Anshel Brusilow is appointed concertmaster of the Philadelphia Orchestra; Sergei Conus (Russian pianist/composer) comes to the United States; Karel Husa, Henri Lazarof, and Carlos Surinach become American citizens; Mehli Mehta (Indian violinist) comes to the United States and joins the Curtis String Quartet; Thea Musgrave (Scottish composer) comes to the United States on a scholarship to Berkshire; Fritz Noack (German organ builder) emigrates to the United States, going to work for the Estey Organ Co.; Thomas Schippers takes the New York Philharmonic Orchestra on a concert tour of Russia; Aurelio de la Vega (Cuban composer/author) moves permanently to the United States and settles in California.

## L. Musical Beginnings

**Performing Groups**   Chicago Little Symphony; Philadelphia String Quartet; St. Paul Chamber Orchestra (Minnesota).

**Educational**   Columbia-Princeton Electronic Music Center; Merce Cunningham School of Dance; Houston Ballet Academy.

**Other**   American Choral Director's Association; *The Choral Journal*; Houston Friends of Music; International Congress of Strings (Oklahoma).

## M. Music Publications

Avshalomov, Jacob, *Music Is Where You Make It I*
Bernstein, Leonard, *The Joy of Music*

Bronson, Bertrand, *The Festival Tunes of the Child Ballads I*
Burk, John N., *Mozart and His Music*
Chase, Gilbert, *The Music of Spain*
Chasins, Abram, *The Van Cliburn Legend*
Hiller, L. and Isaacson, L., *Experimental Music*
Kennan, Kent, *Counterpoint Based on 18th-Century Practice*
Krenek, Ernst, *Modal Counterpoint in the Style of the 16th Century*
Leonard, Charles, *Foundations and Principles of Music Education*
Spaeth, Sigmund, *Fifty Years with Music*
Werner, Eric, *The Sacred Bridge: Literary Parallels in Synagogue and Early Church*

**N. Musical Compositions**

**Chamber Music**   Hugh Aitken, *Quartet for Clarinet and Strings*; John J. Becker, *Soundpiece No. 8: String Quartet No. 3*; Elliott Carter, *String Quartet No. 2* (Pulitzer Prize—New York Music Critics' Award); Paul Cooper, *String Quartet No. 3*; Leo Kraft, *String Quartet No. 2*; Ezra Laderman, *String Quartet No. 1*; George Perle, *Wind Quintet No. 1*; Vincent Persichetti, *String Quartet No. 3, Opus 81*; Mel Powell, *Filigree Setting* (string quartet); Terry Riley, *Spectra*; Ezra Sims, *String Quartet No. 1*; Alan Stout, *String Quartet No. 6*; Aurelio de la Vega, *Quintet for Winds*.

**Choral/Vocal**   Hugh Aitken, *Cantata No. 2*; Wayne Barlow, *Missa Sancti Thomae*; Leslie Bassett, *For City, Nation, World* (cantata); Philip Bezanson, *Songs of Innocence*; Margaret Bonds, *Mass in D Minor*; William Flanagan, *The Lady of Tearful Regret*; Nicolas Nabokov, *Four Poems by Pasternak*; Robert Starer, *Ariel: Visions of Isaiah*; Halsey Stevens, *A Testament of Life—Two Shakespeare Songs*; Randall Thompson, *Frostiana*.

**Concertos**   Josef Alexander, *Concertino for Trumpet and Strings*; David Amram, *Shakespearean Concerto*; Thomas Beversdorf, *Violin Concerto*; John La Montaine, *Piano Concerto, Opus 9* (Pulitzer Prize); Paul Nordoff, *Piano Concerto No. 2, "Gothic"*; Robert Parris, *Violin Concerto*; Walter Piston, *Concerto for Two Pianos*; Gundaris Poné, *Violin Concerto*; Quincy Porter, *Harpsichord Concerto*; Wallingford Riegger, *Variations for Violin and Orchestra*; Igor Stravinsky, *Movements for Piano and Orchestra*; John Verrall, *Piano Concerto*.

**Operas**   Samuel Adler, *The Outcasts of Poker Flat*; Philip Bezanson, *Western Child*; Marc Blitzstein, *Juno*; Jonathan Elkus, *The Outcasts of Poker Flat*; Nicolas Flagello, *The Judgment of St. Francis*; Martin Mailman, *The Hunted*; Hugo Weisgall, *The Gardens of Adonis*; Richard Wernick, *Maggie*; Frank Wigglesworth, *Between the Atoms and the Stars*.

**Orchestra/Band**   Hugh Aitken, *Partita No. 2 for Orchestra*; David Amram, *Autobiography*; T. J. Anderson, *Introduction and Allegro for Orchestra*; Wayne Barlow, *Rota*; Irwin Bazelon, *Overture, "The Taming of the Shrew"*; Jack Beeson, *Transformations*; Morton Feldman, *Atlantis*; Irving Fine, *Blue Towers*; Peggy Glanville-Hicks, *Saul and the Witch of Endor* (ballet); Andrew Imbrie, *Legend*; Meyer Kupferman, *Variations for Orchestra*; Richard Maxfield, *Five Movements for Orchestra* (Gershwin Memorial Award); Joaquin Nin-Culmell, *Don Juan* (ballet); Gunther Schuller, *Seven Studies on Themes of Paul Klee*; Ralph Shapey, *Rituals*; William Sydeman, *Study for Orchestra I*; Alexander Tcherepnin, *Symphonic Prayer, Opus 93*; Robert Washburn, *Three Pieces for Orchestra*.

**Piano/Organ**   Stephen Albert, *Two Toccatas*; Robert Ashley, *Sonata*; Esther Ballou, *Variations, Scherzo and Fugue*; Samuel Barber, *Nocturne (Homage to John Field)*; William Bolcom, *Romantic Pieces*; John Corigliano, *Kaleidoscope* (two pianos); Ingolf Dahl, *Sonata Pastorale*; Morton Feldman, *Last Pieces*; Robert Helps, *Recollections*; Benjamin Lees, *Kaleidoscopes*; Gordon Mumma, *Piano Suite*; Hall Overton, *Polarities No. 1*; Burrill Phillips, *Sinfonia Brevis* (organ); George Rochberg, *Bartókiana*; Seymour Shifrin, *The Modern Temper* (four hands); Elie Siegmeister, *Three Moods*; Robert Starer, *Fantasia concertante*.

**Symphonies**   Jack Beeson, *Symphony No. 1 in A Major*; Robert Russell Bennett, *Commemoration Symphony*; Gordon Binkerd, *Symphony No. 3*; David Diamond, *Symphony No. 7*; Emma Lou Diemer, *Symphony No. 2*; Gene Gutchë, *Symphony No. 4* (Albuquerque Prize); Alan Hovhaness, *Symphony No. 6, "Celestial Gate"—Symphony No. 7* (winds); Benjamin Lees, *Concerto for*

*Orchestra*; Ray Luke, *Symphony No. 1*; Kirke Mechem, *Symphony No. 1*; George Perle, *Symphony for Band*; Gardner Read, *Symphony No. 4*; Bernard Rogers, *Symphony No. 5, "Africa"*; Alan Stout, *Symphony No. 1*; David Van Vactor, *Symphony No. 3*; David Ward-Steinman, *Symphony No. 1* (BMI Award—Bearns Prize); Robert Washburn, *Symphony No. 1*; Charles Wuorinen, *Symphonies No. 2, 3*.

# 1960

❁

## Historical Highlights

The census indicates a population of 179,323,000; John F. Kennedy becomes the 35th president; the U-2 spy plane is shot down by the Russians over their territory; Congress passes a Civil Rights Act; the Peace Corps is founded; the nuclear submarine *Triton* circles the world underwater; the European Free Trade Association is formed; France explodes its first atomic bomb.

## World Cultural Highlights

**World Art**   Karel Appel, *Red Nude; Woman with Ostrich*; John Bratby, *Gloria with Sunflower*; Marc Chagall, *Sirene au pin;* Norbert Kricke, *Space Sculpture*; Giorgio Morandi, *Still Life*.

**World Literature**   Joy Adamson, *Born Free*; Eugène Ionesco, *Rhinocéros*; Harold Pinter, *The Caretaker*.

**World Music**   Pierre Boulez, *Pli Selon Pli*; Benjamin Britten, *The Midsummer Night's Dream*; Krzysztof Penderecki, *Threnody for the Victims of Hiroshima*; William Walton, *Symphony No. 2*.

**Miscellaneous**   The National Symphony of Havana is founded; the Adelaide (Australia) Festival of the Arts begins; Barry Douglas and Sergei Edelmann are born; deaths include Hugo Alfvén, Massimo Bontempelli, Albert Camus, and Boris Pasternak.

## American Art and Literature Highlights

**Births/Deaths**   Deaths include art figures Ernest Blumenschein, Leon Dabo, Rudolph Evans, David Park, and literary figures Franklin P. Adams, Harold L. Davis, Zora Neale Hurston, Harry H. Kemp, J. P. Marquand, Ruth Suckow, Richard N. Wright, and Audrey May Wurdemann.

**Art Works**   Richard Anuszkiewicz, *Plus Reversed*; Alexander Calder, *The Cock's Comb*; Gene Davis, *Homage to Matisse*; Philip Evergood, *Virginia in the Grotto*; Leon Golub, *The Burnt Man*; Adolph Gottlieb, *Green Expanding*; Ellsworth Kelly, *Blue, Green, Yellow, Orange, Red*; Gabriel Kohn, *Azimuth*; Seymour Lipton, *Crusader*; Louise Nevelson, *Great Night Column*.

**Literature**   Edward F. Albee, *The Zoo Story and Other Plays*; John Barth, *The Sotweed Factor*; Harper Lee, *To Kill a Mockingbird* (Pulitzer Prize); Robert J. Lowell, *Life Studies* (National Book Award); Phyllis McGinley, *Times Three: Selected Verse* (Pulitzer Prize); Flannery O'Connor, *The Violent Bear It Away*; Anne Sexton, *To Bedlam and Part Way Back*; John Updike, *Rabbit, Run*.

## Music—The Vernacular/Commercial Scene

**A. Births**   Afrika Bambaataa (disc jockey) October 4; Lionel Cartwright (singer/writer) February 10; Donald "Duck" Harrison (saxophonist) June 23; Evelyn "Champagne" King (singer) July 1; Joan Jett (guitarist/singer) September 22; Brandon Marsalis (saxophonist/bandleader) August 26; Robbie Nevil (singer/writer) October 2; Wallace Roney (trumpeter) May 25; Terry Smith (singer) June 15; Steve Vai (guitarist) June 6.

**B. Deaths**   Jusse Belvin (singer) February 6; Phil Charig (composer) August 31; Bobby Clark (composer/singer) February 12; Eddie Cochran (singer) April 17; Oscar Hammerstein II (librettist/lyricist) August 23; Al Hoffman (songwriter) July 21; Jennifer Holliday (singer) October 19; Johnny Horton (singer) November 5; Joseph F. Lamb (composer) September 3; Oscar Pettiford (bass/bandleader) September 8.

**C. Biographical**

**Performing Groups**  The Chiffons; The Chi-Lites; John Coltrane Jazz Band; The Dimensions; The Devotions; The Fascinations; The Intruders; Tommy James and the Shondells; The Kingsmen; The Marvelettes; Mighty Clouds of Joy; The Radiants; Paul Revere and the Raiders; Saints and Sinners; The Spinners; The Velvets; The Vogues (Val-Aires).

**New Beginnings**  Arhoolie Records; Impulse! Record Co. (New York); Jazz Artists Guild; Minit Records; Motown Records and Publishing Co. (Detroit).

**D. Publications**  Oscar Brand, *Folk Songs for Fun*; Dom Cerulli et al., *The Jazz Word*; Stanley Green, *The World of Musical Comedy*; Nat Hentoff, *Jazz Street;* Alan Lomax, *Folk Songs of North America . . . ;* Bruno Nettl, *An Introduction to Folk Music in the United States*; Leroy Ostransky, *The Anatomy of Jazz*; Hugues Panassié, *The Real Jazz*; R. G. Reisner, *The Jazz Titans; Including "The Parlance of Hip."*

**E. Representative Works**

**Musicals**  J. Bock and S. Harnick, *Tenderloin*; C. Coleman and C. Leigh, *Wildcat*; Lerner and Loewe, *Camelot*; Frank Loesser, *Greenwillow*; Harvey Schmidt and Tom Jones, *The Fantasticks*; C. Strouse and L. Adams, *Bye Bye Birdie*; J. Styne, B. Comden, and A. Green, *Do Re Mi*; Meredith Willson, *The Unsinkable Molly Brown*.

**Number One Hits**  *Alley-Oop* (Hollywood Argyles); *Are You Lonesome Tonight?—It's Now or Never—Stuck On You* (Elvis Presley); *Cathy's Clown* (Everly Brothers); *El Paso* (Marty Robbins); *Everybody's Somebody's Fool—My Heart Has a Mind of Its Own* (Connie Francis); *Georgia on My Mind* (Ray Charles); *I Want to Be Wanted—I'm Sorry* (Brenda Lee); *Itsy Bitsy Teeny Weeny Yellow Polka Dot Bikini* (Brian Hyland); *Mr. Custer* (Larry Verne); *Running Bear* (Johnny Preston); *Save the Last Dance for Me* (The Drifters); *Stay* (Maurice Williams and the Zodiacs); *Teen Angel* (Mark Dinning); *Theme, "A Summer Place"* (Percy Faith); *The Twist* (Chubby Checker).

**Other**  Duke Ellington and Billy Strayhorn, *Suite Thursday—Turacet* (incidental music); Ernest Gold, *Exodus* (film music—Oscar); Manos Hadjidakis and Billy Towne, *Never on Sunday* (Oscar); Max Roach, *Freedom Now Suite*; Miklós Rózsa, *El Cid* (film music).

## Music—The Cultivated/Art Music Scene

**F. Births**  Harolyn Blackwell (soprano); Christine Brewer (soprano); Andrew Cooperstock (pianist) July 9; Sidney Corbett (composer) April 26; Robert Dennison (pianist) June 10; Damon Evans (tenor); JoAnn Falletta (conductor); Renée Fleming (soprano); Bonita Glenn (soprano); Susan Graham (mezzo-soprano); Jane Henschel (contralto); Kamran Ince (composer) May 6; Camelia Johnson (soprano); Daniel S. Katz (musicologist) November 12; Daniel Kleinknecht (conductor) May 5; Pamela Kuhn (soprano); Jennifer Larmore (mezzo-soprano); Susan Roberts (soprano); Anna Steiger (soprano) February 13; Dawn Upshaw (soprano) July 17.

**G. Deaths**  Alfred Ackley (hymnist/singer) July 3; Alberto Bimboni (Italian-born pianist/composer) June 18; Mario Castelnuovo-Tedesco (Italian-born composer) March 16; Joseph W. Clokey (organist) September 14; James F. Cooke (author/composer) March 3; Ellabelle Davis (soprano) November 15; Désiré Defauw (Belgian-born conductor) July 25; Ruth Lynda Deyo (pianist) March 4; Fay Foster (pianist) April 17; Isadore Freed (Russian-born composer) November 10; Povla Frijsh (Danish-born soprano) July 10; Mack Harrell (baritone) January 29; Edward Burlingame Hill (composer) July 9; Frances McCollin (composer/conductor) February 26; Giorgio Polacco (Italian-born conductor) April 30; Hugh Porter (organist/educator) September 22; John Charles Thomas (baritone) December 13; Lawrence Tibbett (baritone) July 15; Armand Tokatyan (Bulgarian-born tenor) June 12; Leonard Warren (baritone) March 4; Clarence C. White (violinist/composer) June 30.

**H. Debuts**

**United States**  Antonio de Almeida (Brazilian conductor—New York), Cathy Berberian (mezzo-soprano—Berkshire), Patricia Brooks (soprano—New York), Eugene Fodor (violinist—Denver), Lawrence Foster (conductor—Los Angeles), Kay Griffel (soprano—Chicago), Lynn Harrell (cellist—New York), Marilyn Horne (mezzo-soprano—San Francisco), Jean Kraft (mezzo-soprano—New York), Sviatoslav Richter (Russian pianist—tour), Renata Scotto (Italian soprano—Chicago), Jeanette Scovotti (soprano—Boston), Joan Sutherland (Australian soprano—Dallas), Herta Töpper (Austrian mezzo-soprano—San Francisco), Benita Valente (soprano—New York).

**Metropolitan Opera**   Piero Cappuccilli (Italian baritone), Eileen Farrell (soprano), Kerstin Meyer (Swedish mezzo-soprano), Hermann Prey (German baritone), Anneliese Rothenberger (German soprano), Georg Solti (Hungarian conductor), Gabriella Tucci (Italian soprano), Jon Vickers (Canadian tenor).

**Other**   Helen Donath (soprano—Cologne), Olivia Stapp (mezzo-soprano—Spoleto).

## I. New Positions

**Conductors**   Erich Kunzel (Rhode Island Philharmonic Orchestra—to 1965); Siegfried Landau (Chattanooga Opera—to 1973); Stanislaw Skrowaczewski (Minneapolis Symphony Orchestra—to 1979); Arthur Winograd (Birmingham, Alabama, Symphony Orchestra—to 1964); James Yestadt (New Orleans Philharmonic Symphony Orchestra—to 1963).

**Educational**   Elliott Carter (Yale—to 1962); Philip Farkas (Indiana University—to 1982); Josef Gingold (Indiana University); Martha Lipton (Indiana University); Roger Nixon (San Francisco State); Vittorio Rieti (New York College of Music); George Rochberg (chair, music, University of Pennsylvania—to 1968); Elliott Schwartz (University of Massachusetts, Amherst—to 1964); Charles Seeger (UCLA—to 1970); Abbey Simon (Indiana University—to 1974); Gil Trythall (Knox College—to 1975).

**Other**   Paul Creston (director, ASCAP—to 1968); Allen Forte (music editor, *Journal of Music Theory*); Harold Schonberg (music editor, *The New York Times*—to 1980).

## J. Honors and Awards

**Honors**   Richard Bales (Ditson); Arthur Berger, Easley Blackwood, Salvatore Martirano, and Gunther Schuller (American Academy); Leonard Bernstein (*Musical America's* Musician of the Year); Aaron Copland (Brandeis); Ernst Krenek (National Institute); Edward MacDowell (Hall of Fame); Carl Ruggles (PhD, University of Vermont); Thomas Scherman (National Arts Club Medal); Louise Talma (Waite Award).

**Awards**   Ivan Davis (Liszt Award); Malcolm Frager (Queen Elizabeth First); Joseph Silverstein (Naumburg).

**K. Biographical**   Samuel Adler marries poet Carol Ellen Stalker and tours Europe for the State Department; Stephen Albert studies with Blomdahl in Stockholm and enters Philadelphia Musical Academy; Grace Bumbry makes her stage debut in Paris; Herbert Handt makes his conducting debut in Rome; Ruth (Meckler) Laredo marries violinist Jaime Laredo (divorced 1976); George London becomes the first American to sing the role of Moussorgsky's "Boris" at the Bolshoi; Lorin Maazel becomes the first American to conduct at Bayreuth; Juan Orrega-Salas (Chilean composer) moves to the United States; Seiji Ozawa (Japanese conductor) studies at Berkshire by arrangement of Charles Munch and wins the Koussevitzky Prize; Joseph Szigeti retires to Switzerland; Ivan Tcherepnin becomes an American citizen.

## L. Musical Beginnings

**Performing Groups**   American Brass Quintet (New York); American Wind Symphony Orchestra (Pittsburgh); Camerata Singers; Contemporary Chamber Ensemble (New York); Dallas Civic Chorus; Dayton Opera Association; Hawaii Opera Theater; New York Camerata Singers; Oakland Symphony Chorus (California); Pittsburgh Oratorio Society; San Francisco Chamber Music Society; Tucson Youth Symphony.

**Educational**   Gaylord Music Library (Washington University); Puerto Rican Conservatory of Music; Yale Electronic Music Studio.

**Other**   *The American Recorder*; Henri Elkan Music Publishers, Inc.; Edward MacDowell Medal; Metropolitan Opera Studio; National Band Association (NBA); Fritz Noack Organ Co. (Lawrence, Massachusetts); Society for Asian Music (New York); Friedrich Von Huene, Recorder/Flute Maker (Waltham, Massachusetts).

## M. Music Publications

Bacon, Ernst, *Words on Music*
Chávez, Carlos, *Musical Thought*
Copland, Aaron, *Copland on Music*
Grout, Donald Jay, *A History of Western Music*
Hanson, Howard, *Harmonic Materials of Modern Music*
Kauder, Hugo, *Counterpoint: An Introduction to Polyphonic Composition*
Lang, Paul H., *Problems of Modern Music*
Meyer, L. and Cooper, G., *The Rhythmic Structure of Music*
Tureck, Rosalyn, *An Introduction to the Performance of Bach*
Wagner, Joseph, *Scoring for Band*

## N. Musical Compositions

**Chamber Music**   Leonardo Balada, *Violin Sonata*; Wallace Berry, *String Quartet No. 1*; Easley Blackwood, *String Quartet No. 2, Opus 6—Violin Sonata, Opus 7*; Aaron Copland, *Nonet*; David Diamond, *String Quartet No. 5*; Donald Erb, *String Quartet No. 1*; Harold Farberman, *String Quartet*; Ross Lee Finney, *String Quartet No. 8*; Jean Eichelberger Ivey, *String Quartet*; Pauline Oliveros, *Variations for Piano Sextet* (Pacifica Foundation Prize); Robert Palmer, *String Quartet No. 4*; George Perle, *Wind Quintet No. 2—String Quartet No. 5*; Vittorio Rieti, *String Quartet No. 4*; Terry Riley, *String Quartet*; Elie Siegmeister, *String Quartet No. 2*; William Grant Still, *Lyric String Quartet*; Alan Stout, *String Quartet No. 7*; Clifford Taylor, *String Quartet No. 1*; Francis Thorne, *String Quartet No. 1*; Bernard Wagenaar, *String Quartet No. 4*.

**Choral/Vocal**   Samuel Adler, *Shir Chadash* (synagogue service); Hugh Aitken, *Cantata No. 3*; David Amram, *Friday Evening Service*; Milton Babbitt, *Composition for Tenor and Six Instruments*; Roberta Bitgood, *Joseph* (cantata); Halim El-Dabh, *The Egyptian Series—The Islamic Series*; Carlisle Floyd, *The Mystery* (song cycle); Lukas Foss, *Time Cycle* (New York Music Critics' Award); Roy Harris, *Canticle of the Sun*; Andrew Imbrie, *Drumtaps* (cantata); Vincent Persichetti, *Mass, Opus 84*; Gardner Read, *The Prophet* (oratorio); Robert Suderburg, *Concert Mass*; Virgil Thomson, *Missa pro defunctis*; Burnet Tuthill, *Requiem, Opus 38*.

**Concertos**   Samuel Barber, *Toccata Festiva, Opus 36* (organ and orchestra); Robert Russell Bennett, *Harp and Cello Concerto*; Paul Creston, *Violin Concerto No. 2*; Alvin Etler, *Concerto for Wind Quintet and Orchestra*; Leon Kirchner, *Concerto for Violin, Cello, Ten Winds and Percussion*; Henri Lazarof, *Viola Concerto*; Walter Piston, *Violin Concerto No. 2*; Gunther Schuller, *Contrasts for Wind Quintet and Orchestra*; Elie Siegmeister, *Flute Concerto*.

**Electronic**   Bülent Arel, *Electronic Music I* (tape); Otto Luening, *Gargoyles*; Gordon Mumma, *Sinfonia* (instruments and tape); Mel Powell, *Electronic Setting*.

**Operas**   Radie Britain, *Kuthara*; Anis Fuleihan, *Vasco*; Paul Hindemith, *The Long Christmas Dinner*; Harrison Kerr, *The Tower of Kel*; Lawrence Moss, *The Brute*; Vittorio Rieti, *The Clock*.

**Orchestra/Band**   T. J. Anderson, *New Dances*; George Barati, *The Dragon and the Phoenix*; Samuel Barber, *Die Natali—Choral Prelude for Christmas, Opus 37*; Irwin Bazelon, *Ballet Centauri 17*; Arthur Berger, *Chamber Concerto*; William Bergsma, *Chameleon Variations*; Marc Blitzstein, *Toys in the Attic* (incidental music); Henry Brant, *Atlantis*; Morton Feldman, *The Swallows of Sanangan*; Irving Fine, *Diversions for Orchestra*; Vivian Fine, *Alcestis* (ballet); William Flanagan, *Notations*; Karel Husa, *Mosaïques*; Ezra Laderman, *Song of Songs* (Biblical ballet); John La Montaine, *Overture, From Sea to Shining Sea, Opus 30*; Nikolai Lopatnikoff, *Festival Overture, Opus 40*; Robert Palmer, *Memorial Music*; George Perle, *Three Movements for Orchestra*; George Rochberg, *Time Span I*; Robert Starer, *The Dybbuk—The Story of Esther* (ballets); William Grant Still, *The Peaceful Land* (National Music Clubs Prize); Morton Subotnick, *The Balcony* (incidental music); Carlos Surinach, *Acrobats of God—David and Bathsheba* (ballets); Hugo Weisgall, *Appearances and Entrances*.

**Piano/Organ**   Samuel Adler, *Toccata, Recitation and Postlude* (organ); David Amram, *Sonata*; John J. Becker, *Improvisation for Organ*; Gordon Binkerd, *Entertainments*; William Bolcom, *Twelve Etudes*; Mario Castelnuovo-Tedesco, *Sonatina zoologica, Opus 187*; David Cope, *Sonata*

*No. 1*; Emma Lou Diemer, *Ten Hymn Preludes* (organ); Nicolas Flagello, *Prelude, Ostinato and Fugue, Opus 30*; Jack Gottlieb, *Sonata*; George F. McKay, *Suite on 16th Century Hymns* (organ); Vincent Persichetti, *Organ Sonata, Opus 86*; Burrill Phillips, *Sonata No. 4*; Gardner Read, *Six Preludes on Old Southern Hymns* (organ); Halsey Stevens, *Ritratti—Portraits for Piano*.

**Symphonies**   Samuel Adler, *Symphony No. 3, "Diptych"*; Thomas Beversdorf, *Symphony No. 4*; Henry Cowell, *Symphony No. 14, 15, "Thesis"*; David Diamond, *Symphony No. 8*; Robert Evett, *Symphony No. 1*; Ross Lee Finney, *Symphony No. 3*; Arthur Frackenpohl, *Symphony for Strings*; Vittorio Giannini, *Symphony No. 4*; Lejaren Hiller, *Symphony No. 2*; Alan Hovhaness, *Symphony No. 11, "All Men Are Brothers"—Symphony No. 12, Opus 188*; David Martin Levy, *Symphony*; Louis Mennini, *Symphony No. 1, "Da Chiesa"*; Walter Piston, *Symphony No. 7* (Pulitzer Prize); William Schuman, *Symphony No. 7*; Francis Thorne, *Symphony No. 1*; Aurelio de la Vega, *Symphony in Four Parts*; Frank Wigglesworth, *Symphony No. 3*.

# 1961

✺

## Historical Highlights

The attempted invasion of Cuba at the Bay of Pigs fails; Alan Shepard and Gus Grissom make the first American suborbital flights while Russian Yuri Gagarin becomes the first man in space; the 23rd Amendment gives the vote to residents of the District of Columbia; the Communists begin building the Berlin Wall; the Union of South Africa leaves the British Commonwealth.

## World Cultural Highlights

**World Art**   Marc Chagall, *The Twelve Tribes of Israel* (stained glass); Jean Dubuffet, *Exode;* Hans Hofmann, *The Golden Wall*; Yves Klein, *Monochrome Blue*; Remedios Varo, *Toward the Tower*.

**World Literature**   Samuel Beckett, *Oh! Les Beaux Jours*; V. S. Naipaul, *A House for Mr. Biswas*; Muriel Spark, *The Prime of Miss Jean Brodie*; Yevgeny Yevtushenko, *Babi Yar*.

**World Music**   Hans Werner Henze, *Elegie für Junge Liebende*; Zoltán Kodály, *Symphony*; Krzysztof Penderecki, *Fluorescences*; Dmitri Shostakovich, *Symphony No. 12*; Michael Tippett, *King Priam*.

**Miscellaneous**   The Zagreb Festival of Contemporary Music begins; births include Stephen Hough, Cecile Licad and Nadja Salerno-Sonnenberg; deaths include Sir Thomas Beecham, Blaise Cendrars, Paul Landowski, Antoine Pevsner, and Václav Talich.

## American Art and Literature Highlights

**Births/Deaths**   Deaths include art figures Arthur Lee, Leo Lentelli, "Grandma" Moses, Max Weber, and literary figures Josephine Dodge Bacon, Thomas Bell, Hilda Doolittle, Jessie R. Fauset, Kenneth Fearing, Dashiell Hammett, Moss Hart, Ernest Hemingway, Robert S. Hillyer, George S. Kaufman, Julia Peterkin, Henry M. Robinson, and James Thurber.

**Art Works**   Leon Golub, *Colossal Man*; Robert Indiana, *American Dream I*; Jasper Johns, *Zero Through Nine*; Ellsworth Kelly, *Red, White and Blue*; Alfred Leslie, *The Red Side*; Henry Moore, *Reclining Mother and Child*; Louise Nevelson, *Dawn Light*; Kenneth Noland, *Reverberation*; Larry Rivers, *The Last Civil War Veteran*; James Rosenquist, *I Love You with My Ford*; Wayne Thiebaud, *Pie Rows*.

**Literature**   Abe Burrows, *How To Succeed in Business without Really Trying* (Pulitzer Prize); Alan Dugan, *Poems 1* (Pulitzer Prize—National Book Award); Joseph Heller, *Catch-22*; Tad Mosel, *All the Way Home* (Pulitzer Prize—New York Drama Critics' Award); Edwin G. O'Connor, *The Edge of Sadness* (Pulitzer Prize); Walker Percy, *Poems* (National Book Award); J. D. Salinger, *Franny and Zooey*; John Steinbeck, *The Winter of Our Discontent*; Irving Stone, *The Agony and the Ecstasy*.

## Music—The Vernacular/Commercial Scene

**A. Births**   Oleta Adams (singer); Matt Catingub (saxophonist/arranger) March 25; Billy Ray Cyrus (singer) August 25; Davis Daniel (singer) March 1; Iris DeMent (singer); Melissa Etheridge (guitarist/singer) May 29; Leif Garrett (singer) November 8; k. d. lang (singer) November 2; Wynton Marsalis (trumpeter) October 18; Eddie Santiago (singer) (?); Keith Sweat (singer) July 22.

**B. Deaths**   Joseph E. Howard (composer/lyricist) May 19; Nick La Rocca (cornetist/bandleader) February 22; Alphonse Picou (clarinetist) February 4; Blanche Ring (singer/actress) January 13.

**C. Biographical**

**Performing Groups**   The Angels; The Beach Boys; The Bel-Airs; The Chambers Brothers; Chicago's Experimental Band; Clarke-Boland Big Band; Crystals; Cyrkle; Dick and DeeDee; The Gems (Lovettes); The Honeys (Rovell Sisters); Jay and the Americans; The Journeymen; The Kentucky Colonels; The Manhattans; New Christy Minstrels; La Perfecta (Eddie Palmieri band); Peter, Paul, and Mary; Red Onion Jazz Band; Shep and the Limelites; Jr. Walker and the All Stars; Paul Winter Sextet; Young Men from New Orleans (Disneyland).

**New Beginnings**   Gaither Music Co. (Alexandria, Indiana); Charlie Parker Records (New York); Preservation Hall (New Orleans); Reprise Records (by Frank Sinatra); Southside Records, Wand Records.

**Honors**   Hank Williams, Jimmie Rodgers, Fred Rose (Country Music Hall of Fame).

**D. Publications**   Linnell Gentry, *A History and Encyclopedia of Country, Western, and Gospel Music*; Isaac Goldberg, *Tin Pan Alley: A Chronicle of American Popular Music*; N. Hentoff, *The Jazz Life*; John Jacob Niles, *Ballad Book of John Jacob Niles*; Paul Oliver, *The Meaning of the Blues*; Bill Russo, *Composing for the Jazz Orchestra*.

**E. Representative Works**

**Musicals**   Richard Adler, *Kwamina*; Johnny Burke, *Donnybrook!*; E. Y. Harburg, *Happiest Girl in the World* (music of Offenbach); Jerry Herman, *Milk and Honey* (Tony); Loesser, Burrows, and Weinstock, *How to Succeed in Business without Really Trying* (Pulitzer Prize—New York Drama Critics' Award—Tony); Bob Merrill and M. Stewart, *Carnival* (New York Drama Critics' Award); A. Schwartz and H. Dietz, *The Gay Life*; J. Styne, B. Comden, and A. Green, *Do Re Mi—Subways Are for Sleeping*.

**Number One Hits**   *Big Bad John* (Jimmy Dean); *Blue Moon* (The Marcels); *Calcutta* (Lawrence Welk); *Hit the Road Jack* (Ray Charles); *The Lion Sleeps Tonight* (The Tokens); *Michael* (The Highwaymen); *Moody River* (Pat Boone); *Mother-in-Law* (Ernie K-Doe); *Please Mr. Postman* (The Marvelettes); *Pony Time* (Chubby Checker); *Quarter to Three* (Gary U.S. Bonds); *Runaround Sue* (Dion); *Runaway* (Del Shannon); *Running Scared* (Roy Orbison); *Surrender* (Elvis Presley); *Take Good Care of My Baby* (Bobby Vee); *Tossin' and Turnin'* (Bobby Lewis); *Travelin' Man* (Ricky Nelson); *Will You Love Me Tomorrow* (The Shirelles); *Wonderland by Night* (Bert Kaempfert).

**Other**   Elmer Bernstein, *Summer and Smoke* (film music—Oscar); Gil Evans and Miles Davis, *Sketches from Spain*; Henry Mancini, *Breakfast at Tiffany's* (film score—Oscar); Henry Mancini and Johnny Mercer, *Moon River* (Oscar); David Raksin, *Ben Casey* (theme); Miklós Rózsa, *King of Kings* (film music).

## Music—The Cultivated/Art Music Scene

**F. Births**   Kallen Esperian (soprano) June 8; Rafael Figueroa (Puerto Rican cellist) March 27; Dylana Jenson (violinist) May 14; Mark Edward Laubach (organist) January 18; Cecile Licad (pianist) May 11; Lowell Liebermann (composer/pianist) February 22; Najda Salerno-Sonnenberg (violinist) January 10; Vincenzo Scuderi (tenor); Patricia Spence (mezzo-soprano) January 12; Michael Torke (composer/pianist) September 22.

**G. Deaths** John J. Becker (composer) January 21; Theodore W. Chanler (critic/composer) July 27; Archibald Davison (conductor/educator) February 6; Percy Grainger (Australian-born pianist) February 20; Alexander Hilsberg (Polish-born violinist/conductor) August 10; James Melton (tenor) April 21; Wallingford Riegger (composer) April 2; Luigi Silva (Italian-born cellist) November 29; Ernest M. Skinner (organ builder) October 27; William T. Upton (musicologist) January 19; Paul Wittgenstein (Austrian-born pianist) March 3.

## H. Debuts

**United States**   Sesto Bruscantini (Italian baritone—Chicago), Dominic Cossa (baritone—New York), Dennis Russell Davies (pianist—Toledo), Plácido Domingo (Spanish tenor—Dallas), Sixten Ehrling (Swedish conductor—Detroit), Henry Holt (Austrian conductor—Los Angeles), James King (tenor—San Francisco), Seiji Ozawa (Japanese conductor—New York), Thomas Paul (bass—New York), Paul Plishka (bass—Paterson, New Jersey), Paula Robison (flutist—New York), Santiago Rodriguez (pianist, age 9—New Orleans), Graziella Sciutti (Italian soprano—San Francisco).

**Metropolitan Opera**   John Alexander (tenor), Ingrid Bjoner (Norwegian soprano), Franco Corelli (Italian tenor), Phyllis Curtin (soprano), Gottlob Frick (German bass), Sándor Konya (Hungarian tenor), Leontyne Price (soprano), George Shirley (tenor), Teresa Stich-Randall (soprano), Joan Sutherland (Australian soprano), Silvio Varviso (Swiss conductor), Galina Vishnevskaya (Russian soprano), Eberhard Wächter (Austrian baritone).

**Other**   Stephen Bishop-Kovacevich (pianist—London), Catherine Gayer (soprano—Venice), Felicia Weathers (soprano—Zürich).

## I. New Positions

**Conductors**   Franco Autori (Tulsa Philharmonic Orchestra—to 1971); John Barbirolli (Houston Symphony Orchestra—to 1967); Frederik Prausnitz (New England Conservatory Symphony Orchestra—to 1969); Paul Wolfe (Florida West Coast Symphony Orchestra).

**Educational**   Victor Babin (director, Cleveland Institute—to 1972); Robert Baker (dean of music, Union Seminary—to 1973); H. Wiley Hitchcock (Hunter College—to 1971); Abraham Kaplan (Juilliard—to 1977); Leon Kirchner (Harvard); George Perle (Queens—to 1984); György Sándor (University of Michigan—to 1981); David Ward-Steinman (San Diego State); Roman Totenberg (chair, string department, Boston University—to 1978).

## J. Honors and Awards

**Honors**   Maurice Abravanel (Ditson); Aaron Copland (MacDowell Medal); Norman Dello Joio (National Institute); Arthur Judson (Gold Baton); Leontyne Price (*Musical America* Musician of the Year); Wallingford Riegger (Brandeis—Creative Arts Award); Roger Sessions (American Academy Gold Medal); Halsey Stevens, Lester Trimble, and Yehudi Wyner (American Academy).

**Awards**   Agustin Anievas (Mitropoulos Prize); Leslie Bassett (Rome Prize); Jerome Rose (Busoni); Elaine Skorodin (Paganini Second); Werner Torkanowsky (Naumburg).

**K. Biographical**   Grace Bumbry becomes the first black artist to sing at Bayreuth; Kyung-Wha Chung (Korean violinist) and Myung-Wha Chung (cellist) come to New York and enter Juilliard; Halim El-Dabh becomes an American citizen; Hans-Heinz Dräger (German musicologist) comes to the United States and teaches at the University of Texas; Horacio Gutiérrez leaves Castro's Cuba for the United States; James Levine enters Juilliard; Sergiu Luca (Romanian violinist) comes to the United States; Seiji Ozawa is invited by Bernstein to be his assistant in New York; Margaret Leng Tan (Malaysian pianist) comes to the United States; Pinchas Zuckerman (Israeli violinist) enters Juilliard on a scholarship provided by Isaac Stern.

## L. Musical Beginnings

**Performing Groups**   Accademia Monteverdiana (New York); Aeolian Chamber Players (New York); Amor Artis Chorale and Orchestra (Yale); California Chamber Symphony Orchestra; Dorian Wind Quintet (Berkshire); Japanese Philharmonic Orchestra of Los Angeles; Musica Aeterna Orchestra and Chorus (New York); Philadelphia Chamber Orchestra; Piccolo Opera Co. (Detroit); Spring Opera Theater (San Francisco).

**Educational**   California Institute of the Arts; California State University, Northridge, Electronic Music Studio; Duke University Music Department; San Francisco Tape Music Center (Conservatory).

**Other** Friends of French Opera; Heifetz-Piatigorsky Concerts (Los Angeles); Knoxville Civic Auditorium (Tennessee); Latin American Music Center (Indiana University); Young Concert Artists (New York).

## M. Music Publications

Cage, John, *Silence*
Cohn, Arthur, *The Collector's Twentieth-century Music in the Western Hemisphere*
Ewen, David, *New Book of Modern Composers*
Forte, Allen, *The Compositional Matrix*
Graf, Herbert, *Producing Opera for America*
Goldman, Richard F., *The Wind Band: Its Literature and Technique*
Kohs, Ellis, *Music Theory*
Machlis, Joseph, *Introduction to Contemporary Music*
Ottman, Robert, *Elementary Harmony, Theory and Practice—Advanced Harmony, Theory and Practice*
Persichetti, Vincent, *Twentieth Century Harmony: Creative Aspects and Practice*
Pleasants, Henry, *Death of a Music?*
Siegmeister, Elie, *Invitation to Music*
Slenczynska, Ruth, *Music at Your Fingertips*
Walter, Bruno, *Of Music and Music-Making*

## N. Musical Compositions

**Chamber Music** David Amram, *String Quartet*; Philip Bezanson, *String Quartet No. 2*; Gordon Binkerd, *String Quartet No. 2*; Easley Blackwood, *Pastorale and Variations, Opus 11* (wind quintet); Earl Brown, *Available Forms I*; John Cage, *Variations I* (any number of performers); David Cope, *String Quartet No. 1*; Robert Evett, *Piano Quartet*; Morton Feldman, *Two Pieces for Clarinet and String Quartet—Durations III, IV, V*; Ross Lee Finney, *Piano Quintet No. 2*; Nicolas Flagello, *Harp Sonata*; Charles Jones, *String Quartet No. 5*; Ulysses Kay, *String Quartet No. 3*; Louis Mennini, *String Quartet*; Robert Muczynski, *Flute Sonata*; Terry Riley, *String Trio*; George Rochberg, *String Quartet No. 2*; Loren Rush, *String Quartet in C-Sharp Minor*; Ezra Sims, *String Quartet No. 2*; Alan Stout, *String Quartet No. 8*; William Sydeman, *Woodwind Quintet No. 2*; John Verrall, *String Quartet No. 7*; Robert A. Wykes, *Piano Quintet*.

**Choral/Vocal** Hugh Aitken, *Cantatas No. 4, 5*; Henry Brant, *Fire in Cities*; Miriam Gideon, *Songs of Voyage* (song cycle); Pauline Oliveros, *Sound Patterns* (Gaudeamus Foundation Prize); Quincy Porter, *Symptoms of Love* (song cycle); Ned Rorem, *King Midas* (song cycle); William Grant Still, *From the Hearts of Women* (song cycle); Halsey Stevens, *Cuatro canciones*; Igor Stravinsky, *A Sermon, a Narrative and a Prayer*; Randall Thompson, *The Nativity according to St. Luke*; Peter Westergaard, *Leda and the Swan (Cantata No. III)*.

**Concertos** Samuel Adler, *Rhapsody for Violin and Orchestra*; Wayne Barlow, *Images for Harp and Orchestra*; William Bolcom, *Concertante* (violin, flute, oboe and orchestra); Henry Brant, *Violin Concerto with Lights*; Elliott Carter, *Double Concerto for Harpsichord and Piano* (New York Music Critics' Award); Henri Lazarof, *Concerto for Piano and Chamber Group*; Mel Powell, *Setting* (cello and orchestra); Ben Weber, *Piano Concerto, Opus 52*.

**Electronic** Bülent Arel, *Stereo Electronic Music I* (tape); Robert Ashley, *# + Heat* (electronic theater)—*Public Opinion Descends upon the Demonstrators* (electronic theater); Milton Babbitt, *Composition for Synthesizer*; Mario Davidovsky, *Electronic Study I*; Lejaren Hiller, *Nightmare Music*; Mel Powell, *Electronic Setting No. 1*; Vladimir Ussachevsky, *Creation Prologue* (four choruses and tape).

**Operas** Dominick Argento, *Colonel Jonathan the Saint*; Norman Dello Joio, *Blood Moon*; Cecil Effinger, *Pandora's Box* (children's opera); Harold Farberman, *Medea* (chamber opera); Kenneth Gaburo, *The Widow*; Vittorio Giannini, *The Harvest*; Douglas Moore, *The Wings of the Dove*; Francis Thorne, *Fortuna*; Robert Ward, *The Crucible* (Pulitzer Prize—New York Music Critics' Award).

**Orchestra/Band**   Samuel Adler, *Southwestern Sketches* (band); Hugh Aitken, *The Moirai* (ballet); Ernst Bacon, *Erie Waters*; Leslie Bassett, *Five Movements for Orchestra*; Alvin Etler, *Triptych for Orchestra*; Felix Labunski, *Symphonic Dialogues*; Martin Mailman, *Suite in Three Movements*; Gardner Read, *Night Flight, Opus 44*; William Schuman, *A Song of Orpheus*; Robert Starer, *Samson Agonistes* (ballet)—*Prelude and Rondo Giocoso*; Edgard Varèse, *Nocturnal* (completed by Chou Wen-Chung).

**Piano/Organ**   William Bolcom, *Fantasy Sonata No. 1*; Robert Evett, *Six Etudes*; Ross Lee Finney, *Sonata Quasi una Fantasia*; Lejaren Hiller, *Sonata No. 5*; Halsey Stevens, *Piano Fantasia*; William Sydeman, *Sonata*; Alexander Tcherepnin, *Sonata No. 2, Opus 94*.

**Symphonies**   Josef Alexander, *Symphony No. 3*; T. J. Anderson, *Classical Symphony*; Easley Blackwood, *Symphony No. 2, Opus 9*; Emma Lou Diemer, *Symphony No. 3*; Alexei Haieff, *Symphony No. 3*; Lou Harrison, *Symphony on G*; Alan Hovhaness, *Symphony No. 14, Opus 194, "Ararat"* (winds); Juan Orrego-Salas, *Symphony No. 3, Opus 50*; Daniel Pinkham, *Symphony No. 1*; Francis Thorne, *Symphony in One Movement*; Ernst Toch, *Symphony No. 5, "Jephtha"*; Richard Trythall, *Symphony*; George Walker, *Symphony*.

# 1962

☀

## Historical Highlights

John Glenn becomes the first American in space; *Mariner II* is sent to the planet Venus; the first *Telstar* satellite is launched; the Cuban Missile Crisis causes a confrontation between the United States and Russia; Cuba is expelled from the Organization of American States; the Century 21 Exposition opens in Seattle; U Thant is elected Secretary-General of the United Nations.

## World Cultural Highlights

**World Art**   Hans Arp, *Femme-Amphore;* Anthony Caro, *Early One Morning*; Arne Jones, *Dodeka;* Yves Klein, *Fire Painting*; Ernst Wilhelm Noy, *Forboggen;* Graham Sutherland, *Owl in Tree Form*.

**World Literature**   Anthony Burgess, *A Clockwork Orange*; Len Deighton, *The Ipcress File*; Doris Lessing, *The Golden Notebook*; Alexander Solzhenitsyn, *One Day in the Life of Ivan Denisovich*.

**World Music**   Benjamin Britten, *War Requiem*; Hans Werner Henze, *Symphony No. 5*; Krzysztof Penderecki, *Stabat Mater*; Dmitri Shostakovich, *Symphony No. 13, "Babi Yar,"* Iannis Xenakis, *ST/10*.

**Miscellaneous**   The German avant-garde art group Fluxus is formed; deaths include Richard Aldington, Kirsten Flagstad, Eugene Goossens, Jacques Ibert, and Yves Klein.

## American Art and Literature Highlights

**Births/Deaths**   Deaths include art figures Franz Kline, Morris Louis, Ivan Mestrovic, Boardman Robinson, August Savage, Kurt Seligmann, Eugene Speicher, and literary figures William S. B. Braithwaite, Frederick H. Brennan, e. e. cummings, William Faulkner, Robinson Jeffers, Nina Putnam, and George Sylvester Viereck.

**Art Works**   Thomas Hart Benton, *Opening of the West*; Jasper Johns, *Fool's House*; Alex Katz, *Washington Crossing the Delaware*; R. B. Kitaj, *Welcome Every Dread*; Lee Krasner, *Cobalt Night*; Roy Lichtenstein, *Forget It! Forget Me!*; Claes Oldenburg, *Dual Hamburger*; Edward Ruscha, *Large Trademark with Eight Spotlights*; George Segal, *Bus Riders*; Wayne Thiebaud, *Pie Table*.

**Literature**   Edward Albee, *Who's Afraid of Virginia Woolf?* (New York Drama Critics' Award); James Baldwin, *Another Country*; James Clavell, *King Rat*; William Faulkner, *The Reivers*

(Pulitzer Prize); James Jones, *The Thin Red Line*; Tennessee Williams, *Night of the Iguana* (New York Drama Critics' Award); William C. Williams, *Pictures from Brueghel and Other Poems* (Pulitzer Prize).

## Music—The Vernacular/Commercial Scene

**A. Births**   Paula Abdul (singer) June 19; Clint Black (singer) February 4; Terence Blanchard (trumpeter) March 13; Rob Brown (saxophonist) February 27; Jon Bon Jovi (singer) March 2; Garth Brooks (singer) February 2; Sheryl Crow (singer/writer) February 11; James McMurtry (singer/writer) March 18; Terence Trent D'Arby (singer) March 15; Billy Dean (singer) April 2; Bill Morissey (singer/writer) August 11; Mark O'Connor (fiddler) August 4.

**B. Deaths**   Harry Carroll (songwriter) December 26; Jesse Crawford (organist) May 28; Victor Moore (singer/actor) July 23.

**C. Biographical**

**Performing Groups**   Bloodstone; Bob B. Soxx and the Blue Jeans; Booker T. and the MGs; The Castaways; The Chantays; The Creators (Ad Libs); The Dartells; The Dillards; El Gran Combo; Labelle; Manhattan; Martha and the Vandellas; The McCoys; Moe and the Mavericks; Orchestra USA; Orquesta Broadway, The Persuasions; ? and the Mysterians; The Righteous Brothers; The Sentinals; The Standells; Surfaris; The Temptations; The Trashmen; The Whispers

**New Beginnings**   A and M Records; *BMI: The Many Worlds of Music*; *Jazz and Pop: The Magazine about Music*; Limelight Records (subsidiary of Mercury); Philadelphia Folk Festival.

**D. Publications**   *Esquire's World of Jazz*; Whitney Balliett, *Dinosaurs in the Morning*; Jack Burton, *The Blue Book of Tin Pan Alley I*; S. Charters and L. Kunstadt, *Jazz: A History of the New York Scene*; David Ewen, *Popular American Composers from Revolutionary Times to the Present*; Hans Nathan, *Dan Emmett and the Rise of Early Negro Minstrelsy*; Martin Williams, ed., *Jazz Panorama*.

**E. Representative Works**

**Musicals**   I. Berlin, H. Lindsay, and R. Crouse, *Mr. President*; Leslie Bricusse and Anthony Newley, *Stop the World—I Want to Get Off*; C. Coleman and C. Leigh, *Little Me*; J. Kander and J. and W. Goldman, *A Family Affair*; R. Rodgers and S. Taylor, *No Strings*; Harold Rome, *I Can Get It for You Wholesale*; Stephen Sondheim, *A Funny Thing Happened on the Way to the Forum*; C. Strouse and L. Adams, *All American*.

**Number One Hits**   *Big Girls Don't Cry—Sherry* (The Four Seasons); *Breaking Up Is Hard to Do* (Neil Sedaka); *Don't Break the Heart That Loves You* (Connie Francis); *Duke of Earl* (Gene Chandler); *Good Luck Charm* (Elvis Presley); *He's a Rebel* (The Crystals); *Hey! Baby* (Bruce Channel); *I Can't Stop Loving You* (Ray Charles); *Johnny Angel* (Shelley Fabares); *The Loco-Motion* (Little Eva); *Monster Mash* (Bobby "Boris" Pickett); *Peppermint Twist* (Joey Dee and the Starliters); *Roses Are Red (My Love)* (Bobby Vinton); *Sheila* (Tommy Roe); *Soldier Boy* (The Shirelles); *Stranger on the Shore* (Mr. Acker Bilk); *The Stripper* (David Rose); *Telstar* (The Tornadoes).

**Other**   Leroy Anderson, *Home Stretch*; Jerry Goldsmith, *Lonely Are the Brave* (film music); Henry Mancini, *Days of Wine and Roses* (film score—Oscar for song); Bronislaw Kaper, *Mutiny on the Bounty* (film music); Thelonious Monk, *Five Spot Blues—Bolivar Blues*; Morty Norman, *James Bond Theme*.

## Music—The Cultivated/Art Music Scene

**F. Births**   Richard William Dowling (pianist) September 6; Ken Noda (pianist/composer) October 5; Emily White (pianist) December 15.

**G. Deaths**   Louis Bernstein (publisher) February 15; G. Clara Clemens (contralto) November 19; Edouard Déthier (Belgian-born violinist) February 19; Irving Fine (composer) August 23; Fraser

Gange (Scottish-born baritone) July 1; Artur Holde (German-born conductor/critic) June 23; Edwin Arthur Kraft (organist) July 15; Fritz Kreisler (violinist) January 29; Charles O'Connell (conductor) September 1; Egon Petri (German-born pianist) May 27; Solomon Pimsleur (pianist) April 22; Toscha Seidel (Russian-born violinist) November 15; Bruno Walter (German-born conductor) February 17; Harriet Ware (pianist/composer) February 9; Wintter Watts (composer) November 1; Florence Wickham (contralto) October 20.

## H. Debuts

**United States**   Grace Bumbry (mezzo-soprano—the White House), Jeanne-Marie Darré (French pianist—New York), Richard Goode (pianist—New York), Joan Grillo (mezzo-soprano—New York), Heinz Holliger (oboist—tour), Gilbert Kalish (pianist—New York), Gary Karr (string bass—New York), Alfredo Kraus (Spanish tenor—Chicago), Albert Lance (Australian tenor—tour), Ruth Laredo (pianist—New York), Wilma Lipp (Austrian soprano—San Francisco), Shirley Love (mezzo-soprano—Baltimore), Edith Peineman (German violinist—tour), André Previn (conductor—St. Louis), Helge Rosvaenge (Danish tenor—tour), Ann Schein (pianist—New York), Tamás Vásáry (Hungarian pianist—New York).

**Metropolitan Opera**   Lili Chookasian (contralto), Régine Crespin (French soprano), Murray Dickie (Scottish tenor), Rita Gorr (Belgian mezzo-soprano), Raina Kabaivanska (Bulgarian soprano), Gerda Lammers (German soprano, John Macurdy (bass), Janis Martin (mezzo-soprano), Judith Raskin (soprano), Jeanette Scovotti (soprano), Jess Thomas (tenor), Hertha Töpper (Austrian mezzo-soprano), Otto Weiner (Austrian baritone).

**Other**   Nancy Tatum (soprano—Saarbrücken), Shirley Verrett (mezzo-soprano—Spoleto).

## I. New Positions

**Conductors**   Arthur Bennett Lipkin (Portland [Maine] Symphony Orchestra—to 1967); Donald Johanos (Dallas Symphony Orchestra—to 1970); Erich Leinsdorf (Boston Symphony Orchestra—to 1969); Zubin Mehta (Los Angeles Philharmonic Orchestra—to 1978); Maurice Peress (Corpus Christi Symphony Orchestra—to 1975); Jacques Singer (Portland [Oregon] Symphony Orchestra—to 1972).

**Educational**   Luciano Berio (Mills College—to 1963); Edith Borroff (University of Wisconsin—to 1966); David Burge (University of Colorado); Karl Geiringer (University of California, Santa Barbara—to 1972); Margaret Harshaw (Indiana University); Henri Lazarof (UCLA); Peter Mennin (president, Juilliard—to 1983); Gregor Piatigorsky (University of Southern California—to 1976); Leo Treitler (University of Chicago—to 1966); Nicholas Van Slyck (director, Longy School of Music—to 1976).

**Other**   Elliott W. Galkin (music critic, *Baltimore Sun*); William Schuman (president, Lincoln Center).

## J. Honors and Awards

**Honors**   Ernst Bacon, John La Montaine, George Rochberg, and William Sydeman (American Academy); Howard Hanson (National Arts Club Medal); Leon Kirchner (National Institute—American Academy of Arts and Sciences); Igor Stravinsky (*Musical America* Musician of the Year); Edgard Varèse (Brandeis).

**Awards**   Marvin David Levy (Rome Prize); Charles Treger (Wieniawski); Ralph Votapek (Cliburn).

**K. Biographical**   Esther Ballou becomes the first woman composer to have a work premiered at the White House; James DePreist becomes paralyzed in both legs from poliomyelitis; Jerome Hines sings the role of Boris Godunov in Moscow with Premier Khrushchev present; Joseph Kalichstein (Israeli pianist) emigrates to the United States to study at Juilliard; Vaclav Nelhybel and Mihály Virizlay become American citizens; Shulamit Ran (Israeli composer) comes to the United States to study; Fritz Reiner resigns his Chicago Symphony Orchestra post owing to ill health; Igor Stravinsky is allowed to visit Russia after a 50-year absence.

## L. Musical Beginnings

**Performing Groups**   American Symphony Orchestra (founded by Leopold Stokowski); Group for Contemporary Music (Columbia University); Kenneth Jewell Chorale (Detroit); Minnesota Opera Co.; Opera Theater of Rochester; Texas Girls' Choir (Fort Worth).

**Festivals**  Eastern Music Festival (North Carolina); Grand Teton Music Festival (Jackson, Wyoming); International Carillon Festival (Springfield, Illinois); Lake George Opera Festival (Glens Falls, New York).

**Educational**  Interlochen Arts Academy (Michigan).

**Other**  American Harp Society (New York); A-R Editions (New Haven); Arkansas Arts Center (Little Rock); *Clavier*; Cliburn International Piano Competition; College of Church Musicians (Washington, DC); Delius Association of Florida (Jacksonville); Jewish Liturgical Music Society of America; Judson, O'Neill, Beall and Steinway (Arthur Judson Management, 1969); International Conference of Symphony and Opera Musicians (ICSOM); Kraushaar Auditorium (Baltimore); *Perspectives of New Music*; Philharmonic Hall (Avery Fisher Hall—New York); Martha Baird Rockefeller Fund for Music; Seattle Center Opera House (old Civic Auditorium); Kurt Weill Foundation for Music.

## M. Music Publications

Farkas, Philip, *The Art of Brass Playing*
Forte, Allen, *Tonal Harmony*
Frackenpohl, Arthur R., *Harmonization at the Piano*
Galamian, I. and Green, E. A., *Principles of Violin Playing and Teaching*
Galamian, I. and Newmann, F., *Contemporary Violin Technique*
Mates, Julian, *The American Musical State before 1800*
Perle, George, *Serial Composition and Atonality*
Ratner, Leonard, *Harmony: Structure and Style*
Rudolf Réti, *Tonality in Modern Music*
Schuller, Gunther, *Horn Technique*
Stein, Leon, *Structure and Style*

## N. Musical Compositions

**Chamber Music**  Stephen Albert, *Illuminations*; David Amram, *Dirge and Variations* (violin, cello and piano)—*Three Songs for Marlboro* (horn and cello); Robert Ashley, *Fives*; Leonardo Balada, *Concerto for Cello and Nine Instruments*; George Barati, *String Quartet No. 2*; Leslie Bassett, *String Quartet No. 3—Piano Quintet*; William Bolcom, *Octet*; David Diamond, *String Quartet No. 6*; Lejaren Hiller, *String Quartet No. 5*; Ezra Laderman, *String Quartet No. 2*; Henri Lazarof, *String Quartet No. 2*; Robert Hall Lewis, *String Quartet No. 2*; Martin Mailman, *String Quartet*; Walter Piston, *String Quartet No. 5* (New York Music Critics' Award); Bernard Rogers, *Violin Sonata*; Seymour Shifrin, *String Quartet No. 2*; Ezra Sims, *String Quartet No. 3*; Alan Stout, *String Quartet No. 9—String Quartet No. 10*; Igor Stravinsky, *Eight Instrumental Miniatures*; Louise Talma, *Violin Sonata*; George Tremblay, *String Quartet No. 2*; Christian Wolff, *For Five or Ten People*.

**Choral/Vocal**  Samuel Adler, *The Vision of Isaiah* (cantata); Leonardo Balada, *Cuatro Canciones de la Provincia de Madrid*; Esther Ballou, *Early American Portrait*; Samuel Barber, *Andromache's Farewell*; Jean Berger, *Fiery Furnace* (cantata); Howard Boatwright, *Passion According to St. Matthew*; Morton Feldman, *The O'Hara Songs*; Ross Lee Finney, *Earthrise: A Trilogy Concerned with the Human Dilemma, Pt. I*; William Flanagan, *Chapter from Ecclesiastes*; Jean Eichelberger Ivey, *Woman's Love* (song cycle); Ulysses Kay, *Choral Triptych*; Meyer Kupferman, *Infinities 4— Infinities 6*; Gundaris Poné, *Daniel propheta* (oratorio); Halsey Stevens, *Magnificat*.

**Concertos**  T. J. Anderson, *Six Pieces for Clarinet and Chamber Orchestra*; Samuel Barber, *Piano Concerto* (Pulitzer Prize); Robert Russell Bennett, *Concerto for Violin, Piano and Orchestra*; Alvin Etler, *Clarinet Concerto*; Gene Gutché, *Violin Concerto* (City of Trieste Prize); Paul Hindemith, *Organ Concerto*; Vincent Persichetti, *Piano Concerto, Opus 90*; Gunther Schuller, *Piano Concerto No. 1*; Lester Trimble, *Five Episodes for Piano and Orchestra*; Ramon Zupko, *Violin Concerto* (City of Trieste Prize).

**Electronic**  Mario Davidovsky, *Electronic Study II*; Kenneth Gaburo, *Antiphony II* (voice and tape)—*Antiphony III*; Gordon Mumma, *Epoxy*; Mel Powell, *Electronic Setting No. 2*.

**Operas**   Carlisle Floyd, *The Passion of Jonathan Wade*; William Grant Still, *Highway 1, USA*; Igor Stravinsky, *The Flood* (television opera); Ernst Toch, *The Last Tale*.

**Orchestra/Band**   Samuel Adler, *Elegy for String Orchestra*; Hugh Aitken, *I Odysseus*; Earl Brown, *Available Forms II* (two conductors); Aaron Copland, *Connotations for Orchestra*; William Kraft, *American Carnival Overture*; W. Francis McBeth, *Band Suite No. 2*; Joaquin Nin-Culmell, *Diferencias for Orchestra*; George Perle, *Serenade No. 1*; George Rochberg, *Time-Span II*; Robert Starer, *Phaedra* (ballet); Carlos Surinach, *Feast of Ashes* (ballet); Robert Washburn, *St. Lawrence Overture*.

**Piano/Organ**   Esther Ballou, *Passacaglia and Toccata* (organ); Paul Creston, *Three Narratives, Opus 79*; George Crumb, *Five Pieces*; Nicolas Flagello, *Sonata, Opus 38*; Benjamin Lees, *Three Preludes*; W. Francis McBeth, *Five Projections*; Gordon Mumma, *Gestures II*; Leo Sowerby, *Bright, Blithe and Brisk* (organ); Halsey Stevens, *Three Pieces for Organ*; Robert Suderburg, *Six Moments*; Louise Talma, *Passacaglia and Fugue*; Clifford Taylor, *Nine Studies*; Ernst Toch, *Sonata, Four Hands*; Richard Trythall, *Three Pieces*; David Van Vactor, *Five Pieces*.

**Symphonies**   Jacob Avshalomov, *Symphony, "The Oregon"*; Wayne Barlow, *Sinfonia da camera*; Irwin Bazelon, *Symphony No. 1—Symphony No. 2, "Testament to a Big City"—Symphony No. 3*; Warren Benson, *Symphony for Drums and Wind Orchestra*; Henry Cowell, *Symphony No. 16, "Icelandic"*; Irving Fine, *Symphony*; Gene Gutchë, *Symphony No. 5 for Strings* (Espla Award); Roy Harris, *Symphony No. 8, "San Francisco"—Symphony No. 9*; Alan Hovhaness, *Symphonies No. 15, "Silver Pilgrimage"—Symphony No. 16, Opus 202*; Charles Jones, *Symphony No. 3*; Beatrice Laufer, *Symphony No. 2*; Colin McPhee, *Symphony No. 3*; Hall Overton, *Symphony No. 2*; Julia Perry, *Symphony No. 2*; Quincy Porter, *Symphony No. 2*; William Schuman, *Symphony No. 8*.

# 1963

❊

## Historical Highlights

President Kennedy is assassinated and Lyndon B. Johnson becomes the 36th president—Lee Harvey Oswald, the accused assassin, is killed by Jack Ruby; a "hot line" telephone between Moscow and Washington, DC, becomes a reality; a ban on atmospheric nuclear tests is signed; scientists discover quasars in outer space; France vetoes Great Britain's entry into the European Common Market.

## World Cultural Highlights

**World Art**   Philip King, *Genghis Khan;* Richard Lippold, *Orpheus and Apollo*; Marino Marini, *Portrait, Hans Arp;* Arnoldo Pomodoro, *Sphere I;* Miroslav Sutej, *Bombardment of the Optic Nerve II*.

**World Literature**   Daphne du Maurier, *The Birds*; John le Carré, *The Spy Who Came in from the Cold*; Yukio Mishima, *The Sailor Who Fell from Grace with the Sea*.

**World Music**   Havergal Brian, *Symphony No. 21*; Dmitri Kabalevsky, *Requiem*; Karlheinz Stockhausen, *Plus-Minus*; William Walton, *Variations on a Theme of Hindemith*.

**Miscellaneous**   Alexander Solzhenitsyn is censured by the Soviet government; Yehudi Menuhin School of Music opens in England; Anne Sophie Mutter is born; deaths include Georges Braque, Jean Cocteau, Aldous Huxley, Francis Poulenc, Fritz Reiner, and Jacques Villon.

## American Art and Literature Highlights

**Births/Deaths**   Births include artist Bruno Surdo and author Naomi Wolf; deaths include art figures William Baziotes, Joe Jones, Jacob Lawrence, Lee Lawrie, Kay Sage, and literary figures Van

Wyck Brooks, W. E. B. DuBois, Robert Frost, Oliver H. P. La Farge, Clifford Odets, Sylvia Plath, Theodore Roethke, Evelyn Scott, and William Carlos Williams.

**Art Works**   Richard Anuszkiewicz, *Injured by Green*; Alexander Calder, *Under the White Sickle Moon*; Red Grooms, *Coney Island*; Robert Indiana, *Demuth American Dream No. 5*; Ellsworth Kelly, *Blue, Red, Green*; Roy Lichtenstein, *Wham!*; Larry Rivers, *Dutch Masters and Cigars I*; Edward Ruscha, *Standard Station*; George Segal, *Gas Station*; Jack Tworkov, *West 23rd*; Tom Wesselmann, *T.V. Set*.

**Literature**   Shirley Hazzard, *Cliffs of Fall and Other Stories*; Sylvia Plath, *Ariel*; John Crowe Ransom, *Selected Poems* (National Book Award); Maurice Sendak, *Where the Wild Things Are*; Neil Simon, *Barefoot in the Park*; Louis Simpson, *At the End of the Open Road* (Pulitzer Prize); John Updike, *The Centaur* (National Book Award); Kurt Vonnegut, Jr., *Cat's Cradle*; William C. Williams, *Paterson*.

## Music—The Vernacular/Commercial Scene

**A. Births**   Tori Amos (pianist/writer) August 22; Regina Belle (singer) July 15; Mark Chesnutt (singer) September 6; Taylor Dayne (singer); M. C. Hammer (rap); Whitney Houston (singer) August 9; Marcus Roberts (piano) August 7; Tim Ryan (singer) February 4; Rachel Sweet (singer); Travis Tritt (singer) February 9; Vanessa Williams (singer) March 18.

**B. Deaths**   Harry Akst (songwriter) March 31; Irving Aronson (composer/bandleader) May 10; Sonny Clark (piano) January 13; Patsy Cline (singer) March 5; Skinnay Ennis (singer/bandleader) June 3; Otto Harbach (lyricist) January 24; Max Hoffmann (composer/arranger) May 21; Eddie Howard (singer/bandleader) May 23; Elmore James (guitar) May 24; Lizzie Miles (singer) March 17; Charles Henry Pace (composer/publisher) December 16; Dick Powell (singer/actor) January 3; J. Russel Robinson (pianist/writer) September 30; Dave Stamper (songwriter) September 18; Dinah Washington (singer) December 14; Ted Weems (bandleader) May 6.

**C. Biographical**

**Performing Groups**   Paul Butterfield Blues Band; The Buckaroos; The Crossfires; The Dynamic Superiors; Even Dozen Jug Band; Exile; Bobby Fuller Four; The Gentrys; Goldie and the Gingerbreads; Holy Modal Rounders; Jim Kweskin Jug Band; Garnet Mimms and the Enchanters; New Jazz Orchestra; New York Contemporary Five; The Shilohs; Sonny and Cher; Styx; The Turtles.

**New Beginnings**   Arkansas Folk Festival; Britt Festivals (Jacksonville, Oregon); Colorado Jazz Party (private); *The Jazzologist* (to 1983); *Music City News*; New Orleans Jazz Club of California; Red Bird Records.

**D. Publications**   Amiri Baraka, *Blues People*; Samuel Charter, *The Poetry of the Blues*; Harold Courlander, *Negro Folk Music, USA*; Benny Green, *The Reluctant Art: The Growth of Jazz*; LeRoi Jones, *Blues People: Negro Music in White America*.

**E. Representative Works**

**Musicals**   Lionel Bart, *Oliver!* (United States premiere); Rick Besoyan, *The Student Gypsy, or The Prince of Liederkranz*; Bock and Harnick, *She Loves Me*; B. A. Grael, *The Streets of New York*; H. Schmidt and T. Jones, *110 in the Shade*; A. Schwartz and H. Dietz, *Jennie*; Meredith Willson, *Here's Love*.

**Number One Hits**   *Blue Velvet* (Bobby Vinton); *Deep Purple* (Nino Tempo and April Stevens); *Dominique* (The Singing Nun); *Easier Said Than Done* (The Essex); *Fingertips* (Stevie Wonder); *Go Away Little Girl* (Steve Lawrence); *He's So Fine* (The Chiffons); *Hey Paula* (Paul and Paula); *I Will Follow Him* (Little Peggy March); *I'm Leaving It Up to You* (Dale and Grace); *If You Wanna Be Happy* (Jimmy Soul); *It's My Party* (Lesley Gore); *My Boyfriend's Back* (The Angels); *Our Day Will Come* (Ruby and the Romantics); *So Much in Love* (The Tymes); *Sugar Shack* (Jimmy Gilmer and the Fireballs); *Sukiyaki* (Kyu Sakamoto); *Surf City* (Jan and Dean); *Walk Like a Man* (The Four Seasons); *Walk Right in* (The Rooftop Singers).

**Other** Duke Ellington, *My People—Perfume Suite—Timon of Athens* (incidental music); Ernest Gold, *It's a Mad, Mad, Mad, Mad World* (film music); Henry Mancini, *The Pink Panther* (film music); Lalo Schifrin, *Jazz Faust*; Dimitri Tiomkin, *55 Days at Peking* (film music); James Van Heusen and Sammy Cahn, *Call Me Irresponsible* (Oscar).

## Music—The Cultivated Art/Music Scene

**F. Births** Leonard Mark Anderson (pianist) October 8; Tzimon Barto (pianist/conductor) January 2; Linda Ruth Holzer (pianist) August 9; Kevin Kenner (pianist) May 19; Caroline J. Shoemaker (composer/performer) April 9.

**G. Deaths** Fredric Fradkin (violinist) October 3; Amelita Galli-Curci (Italian-born soprano) November 26; Mabel Garrison (soprano) August 20; Heinrich Gebhard (pianist/composer) May 5; Erich Hertzmann (German-born musicologist) March 3; Werner Josten (German-born conductor/composer) February 6; Thurlow Lieurance (composer) October 9; Margarete Matzenauer (Hungarian-born soprano) May 19; John Powell (pianist/musicologist) August 15; Rosa Raisa (Polish-born soprano) September 28; Vladimir Rosing (Russian-born tenor) November 24; Felix Slatkin (violinist/conductor) February 8; Alec Templeton (British-born pianist) March 28; John S. Thompson (pianist/pedagogue) March 1; Carl H. Tollefsen (violinist/educator) December 10.

**H. Debuts**

**United States** Peter van der Bilt (Dutch bass-baritone—San Francisco), Alfred Brendel (Austrian pianist—New York), James Oliver Buswell IV (violinist—St. Louis), Sergiu Comissiona (Romanian conductor—tour), Michael Devlin (bass-baritone—New Orleans), Stephen Kates (cellist—New York), Young-Uck Kim (violinist—Philadelphia), Jerome Lowenthal (pianist—New York), Adriana Maliponte (Italian soprano—Philadelphia), Danica Mastilović (Yugoslav soprano—Chicago), John Ogdon (British pianist—New York), John Pritchard (British conductor—Pittsburgh), Tatiana Troyanos (mezzo-soprano—New York), André Watts (pianist—New York), John Williams (Australian guitarist—tour).

**Metropolitan Opera** Franz Allers (Czech conductor), Justino Díaz (bass), Joann Grillo (mezzo-soprano), Shirley Love (mezzo-soprano), Léopold Simoneau (Canadian tenor).

**I. New Positions**

**Conductors** Emerson Buckley (Fort Lauderdale Symphony Orchestra); Eleazar Carvalho (St. Louis Symphony Orchestra—to 1968); Sixten Ehrling (Detroit Symphony Orchestra—to 1973); Lukas Foss (Buffalo Philharmonic Orchestra—to 1970); Josef Krips (San Francisco Symphony Orchestra—to 1970); Jean Martinon (Chicago Symphony Orchestra—to 1968); Kenneth Schermerhorn (New Jersey Symphony Orchestra—to 1968); Werner Torkanowsky (New Orleans Philharmonic Symphony Orchestra—to 1977).

**Educational** William Bergsma (director of music, University of Washington—to 1971); Salvatore Martirano (University of Illinois); Vincent Persichetti (chair of composition, Juilliard); Paul Pisk (Washington University, St. Louis—to 1972); Ray Robinson (dean, Peabody—assistant director, 1966–1969); Eleanor Steber (head, voice department, Cleveland Institute—to 1972); Lester Trimble (University of Maryland—to 1968); Gideon W. Waldrop (dean, Juilliard—to 1985); Yehudi Wyner (Yale School of Music—to 1973).

**Other** Hermann Berlinski (music, DC Hebrew Congregation); Calvin Hampton (organ, Calvary Episcopal Church, New York—to 1983); Alan Rich (music critic, *New York Herald Tribune*—to 1967); Eric Salzman (music critic, *New York Herald Tribune*—to 1966); Lester Trimble (music critic, *Washington Evening Star*—to 1968); Hugo Weisgall (president, American Music Center—to 1973).

**J. Honors and Awards**

**Honors** Victor Alessandro and Emerson Buckley (Alice M. Ditson Award); Marian Anderson and Rudolf Serkin (Medal of Freedom); Elliott Carter (American Academy of Arts and Sciences); Chou

Wen-Chung, Mel Powell, and Vladimir Ussachevsky (American Academy); Paul Creston and Olga Koussevitzky (National Arts Club Medal); Erich Leinsdorf (*Musical America* Musician of the Year); Nikolai Lopatnikoff (National Institute); Walter Piston (Brandeis).

**Awards**  Ezra Laderman (Rome Prize); Arnold Steinhardt (Queen Elisabeth Third).

**K. Biographical**  Hans Werner Henze (German composer) visits the United States for the premiere of his *Fifth Symphony*; Christopher Keene enters Berkeley to study history; cellist Zara Nelsova marries pianist Grant Johannesen; William Primrose, after suffering a heart attack, begins concentrating on teaching; Richard Stolzman enters Indiana University as a voice major.

**L. Musical Beginnings**

**Performing Groups**  Composers String Quartet (New England Conservatory); Greater Des Moines Youth Symphony; High Tor Opera Co. (New York); Norman Luboff Choir; Lyric Opera Theater of Phoenix; Pittsburgh Madrigal Singers; St. Petersburg (Florida) Symphony Orchestra; Seattle Opera Association; Tulsa Youth Symphony.

**Festivals**  Cabrillo Music Festival (Aptos, California); Taos School of Music Chamber Music Festival (New Mexico).

**Educational**  Harlem School of the Arts; National Association of Organ Teachers; University of New Orleans Music Department.

**Other**  Center for Creative and Performing Arts (SUNY, Buffalo); Clowes Memorial Hall (Indianapolis); Seesaw Music Corporation (New York); Zondervan Publishing (Grand Rapids, Michigan—purchase of Singspiration Co.).

**M. Music Publications**

Bacon, Ernst, *Notes on the Piano*
Donato, Anthony, *Preparing Music Manuscript*
Gebhard, Heinrich, *The Art of Pedaling*
Hubbard, Frank, *Harpsichord Regulating and Repairing*
Machlis, Joseph, *American Composers of Our Time*
Nettl, Paul, *The Dance in Classical Music*
Pisk, P. and Ulrich, H., *A History of Music and Musical Style*
Primrose, William, *Technique Is Memory*
Ritchie, Jean, *The Dulcimer Book*
Schonberg, Harold, *The Great Pianists*
Smith, Leland, *Handbook of Harmonic Analysis*
Spaeth, Sigmund, *The Importance of Music*

**N. Musical Compositions**

**Chamber Music**  Samuel Adler, *String Quartet No. 4*; Charles Amirkhanian, *Canticle No. 1—Canticle No. 2*; David Amram, *The Wind and the Rain* (violin and piano); T. J. Anderson, *Five Bagatelles* (oboe, violin, and harpsichord); Robert Ashley, *In Memoriam . . . Crazy Horse*; Irwin Bazelon, *Brass Quintet*; Luciano Berio, *Sequenza II* (harp); David Cope, *String Quartet No. 2*; John Corigliano, *Violin Sonata*; Cecil Effinger, *String Quartet No. 5*; Alvin Etler, *String Quartet No. 1—Brass Quintet*; Morton Feldman, *Vertical Thoughts I, II, III, IV, V*; Nicolas Flagello, *Violin Sonata, Opus 41*; Lukas Foss, *Echoi*; Alexei Haieff, *Cello Sonata*; Peter Jona Korn, *String Quartet No. 2*; Clarence Loomis, *String Quartet No. 2*; George Rochberg, *Piano Trio*; Ralph Shapey, *String Quartet No. 6*; George Tremblay, *String Quartet No. 4*; Robert Washburn, *String Quartet*; Richard Wernick, *String Quartet No. 1*; Peter Westergaard, *Variations for Six Players*.

**Choral/Vocal**  Stephen Albert, *Supernatural Songs*; Jacob Avshalomov, *City upon a Hill*; Howard Boatwright, *Canticle of the Sun*; Earl Brown, *From Here*; Donald Erb, *Cummings Cycle*; Morton Feldman, *Chorus and Instruments I*; Miriam Gideon, *The Condemned Playground* (song cycle); Paul Hindemith, *Mass*; Anthony Iannaccone, *Magnificat*; William Kraft, *Silent Boughs* (song cycle); Daniel Pinkham, *Requiem*; H. Owen Reed, *A Tabernacle for the Sun*; Ned Rorem, *Poems of Love and the Rain*; Igor Stravinsky, *Abraham and Isaac*; Randall Thompson, *A Feast of Praise* (cantata).

**Concertos**   Ernst Bacon, *Piano Concerto No. 1, "Riolama"*; Paul Chihara, *Viola Concerto*; Nicolas Flagello, *Piano Concerto No. 3*; Benjamin Lees, *Oboe Concerto*; Joaquín Nin-Culmell, *Cello Concerto*; Shulamit Ran, *Capriccio for Piano and Orchestra*; Eric Stokes, *A Center Harbor Holiday* (tuba and orchestra); Alexander Tcherepnin, *Piano Concerto No. 5, Opus 96*; Joseph F. Wagner, *Organ Concerto*.

**Electronic**   Mario Davidovsky, *Synchronism No. 1*; Tod Dockstader, *Water Music*; L. Hiller and R. Baker, *Computer Cantata*; Lejaren Hiller, *Seven Electronic Studies*; Salvatore Martirano, *Three Electronic Dances*; Gordon Mumma, *Megaton for Wm. Burroughs*; Mel Powell, *Events*; Terry Riley, *Mescalin Mix* (tape); Aurelio de la Vega, *Coordinates for Magnetic Tape*.

**Operas**   Dominick Argento, *Christopher Sly—The Masque of Angels*; Philip Bezanson, *Stranger in Eden*; Marc Blitzstein, *The Magic Barrel—Idiots First* (unfinished); Jonathan Elkus, *Medea*; Carlisle Floyd, *The Sojourner and Mollie Sinclair*; Peggy Glanville-Hicks, *Sappho*; Andrew Imbrie, *Three against Christmas*; Gian Carlo Menotti, *Le dernier sauvage—Labyrinth* (television opera); Roger Sessions, *Montezuma*; Hugo Weisgall, *Athaliah*.

**Orchestra/Band**   Leslie Bassett, *Variations for Orchestra* (Pulitzer Prize); Warren Benson, *Theme and Excursions*; William Bergsma, *In Celebration*; Thomas Beversdorf, *Variations (Threnody) for Orchestra*; Henry Brant, *Voyage Four*; Gene Gutchë, *Ghenghis Khan*; Ulysses Kay, *Fantasy Variations*; Leo Kraft, *Three Pieces for Orchestra*; William Mayer, *Snow Queen* (ballet); W. Francis McBeth, *Chant and Jubilo* (band); Ned Rorem, *Lions*; William Schuman, *The Orchestra Song*; William Grant Still, *Folk Suite* (band)—*Miniature Overture*; Carlos Surinach, *Symphonic Variations*; William Sydeman, *Study for Orchestra II*; Francis Thorne, *Elegy for Orchestra*; Robert Ward, *Invocation and Toccata*; Elinor Warren, *Along the Western Shore*.

**Piano/Organ**   Samuel Adler, *Sonata Breve for Piano*; Leonardo Balada, *The Seven Last Words* (organ); Paul Cooper, *Sonata No. 2*; Karl Kohn, *Partita*; Benjamin Lees, *Sonata No. 4*; Peter Mennin, *Sonata*; Hall Overton, *Sonata*; Loren Rush, *Hexahedron*; Robert Starer, *Sketches in Color I*; Charles Wuorinen, *Piano Variations*.

**Symphonies**   Irwin Bazelon, *Symphony Concertante*; Leonard Bernstein, *Symphony No. 3, "Kaddish"*; Henry Cowell, *Symphony No. 17*; Alan Hovhaness, *Symphony No. 17, Opus 203— Symphony No. 18, "Circe"*; Ernst Kanitz, *Symphony No. 1, "Sinfonia Breve"*; Karl Korte, *Symphony No. 2*; Ray Luke, *Symphony No. 2*; W. Francis McBeth, *Symphony No. 3* (Hanson Prize); Peter Mennin, *Symphony No. 7, "Variation-Symphony"*; Louis Mennini, *Symphony No. 2, "Da Festa"*; Daniel Pinkham, *Symphony No. 2*; Ernst Toch, *Symphony No. 5, "Rhapsodic Poem"— Symphony No. 6*.

# 1964

☀

## Historical Highlights

Lyndon Johnson elected to his first full term as president; the Civil Rights Act of 1964 is passed; the 24th Amendment abolishes the Southern Poll Tax; the New York World's Fair and the Verrazano Narrows Bridge opens; *Mariner IV* is launched toward Mars; the surgeon general reports a definite link between smoking and cancer; Kosygin and Brezhnev oust Khrushchev from power in Russia.

## World Cultural Highlights

**World Art**   Barbara Hepworth, *Four Squares with Two Circles;* Johann Hofmann, *The Man with the Yellow Pants*; Pablo Picasso, *Girl in Sling Chair*; Michelangelo Pistoletto, *Pax Vobiscum*.

**World Literature**   Chinua Achebe, *Arrow of God;* Anthony Burgess, *The Long Day Wanes;* Joe Orton, *Entertaining Mr. Sloane*; Harold Pinter, *The Homecoming*.

**World Music**   Pierre Boulez, *Figures*; Dmitri Kabalevsky, *Cello Concerto No. 2*; Akira Miyoshi, *Concerto for Orchestra*; Dmitri Shostakovich, *Execution of Stepan Razin*; Iannis Xenakis, *Eonta*.

**Miscellaneous**   Jean-Paul Sartre refuses the Nobel Prize for literature; deaths include Brendan Behan, Pierre Monteux, Sean O'Casey, Edwin Pratt, Edith Sitwell, and Ernst Toch.

## American Art and Literature Highlights

**Births/Deaths**   Deaths include art figures Alexander Archipenko, Jon Corbino, Stuart Davis, Rico Lebrun, Gerald Murphy, Hugo Robus, and literary figures Nathan Asch, Rachel Carson, Bret Ellis, Hermann Hagedorn, Amory Hare, Ben Hecht, Grace Metalious, (Mary) Flannery O'Connor, Robert H. Schauffler, and Carl Van Vechten.

**Art Works**   Stuart Davis, *Blips and Ifs*; Helen Frankenthaler, *Interior Landscape*; Adolph Gottlieb, *Orb*; Robert Indiana, *Eat*; Jasper Johns, *Painted Bronze*; R. B. Kitaj, *The Ohio Gang*; Sol LeWitt, *Muybridge I*; Kenneth Noland, *Bend Sinister*; Larry Poons, *Nixe's Mate*; Robert Rauschenberg, *Retroactive*; Moses Soyer, *Three Brothers*; Wayne Thiebaud, *Bikini*; Ernest Trova, *Falling Man Series*.

**Literature**   Edward Albee, *Tiny Alice*; Saul Bellow, *Herzog* (National Book Award); John Berryman, *Seventy-Seven Dream Songs* (Pulitzer Prize); John Cheever, *The Wapshot Scandal*; Richard Condon, *An Infinity of Mirrors*; Shirley Ann Grau, *Keepers of the House* (Pulitzer Prize); Theodore Roethke, *The Far Field* (National Book Award); Hubert Selby, Jr., *Last Exit to Brooklyn*.

## Music — The Vernacular/Commercial Scene

**A. Births**   Tracy Chapman (singer/writer) March 30; Cliff Eidelman (composer/arranger) December 5; Skip Ewing (singer/writer) February 6; Vincent Herring (saxophonist) November 19; Lenny Kravitz (songwriter) May 26; Richard Marx (singer/writer) September 16; Rockwell (Kenneth Gordy — singer) March 15; Trisha Yearwood (singer) September 19.

**B. Deaths**   Nacio Herb Brown (songwriter) September 28; Johnny Burke (lyricist/publisher) February 25; Johnny Burnette (singer/writer) August 1; Eddie Cantor (singer/actor) October 10; Bo Carter (singer) September 21; Samuel Cooke (singer) December 10; Eric Allan Dolphy (saxophonist/clarinetist) June 29; Meade "Lux" Lewis (pianist) June 7; Cole Porter (composer) October 15; Don Redman (composer/arranger) November 30; Jim Reeves (singer/writer) July 31; Sam Stept (songwriter) December 2; Jack Teagarden (trombonist/singer) January 15.

**C. Biographical**

**Performing Groups**   Albert Ayler Jazz Quartet (New York); Beau Brummels; Captain Beefheart and His Magic Band; The Blues Magoos; The Byrds; The Charlatans; Chocolate Watch Band; Count Five; The Critters; The Delfonics; Dramatics (originally Sensations); The Dixie Cups; Fifth Estate; Hearts and Flowers; The Ides of March; Illusion; The Jackson Five; Jazz Composer's (Guild) Orchestra; The Knickerbockers; Kool and the Gang; The Leaves; Gary Lewis and the Playboys; The Mothers of Invention; New York Art Quartet; New York Big Band; The Shangri-Las; Sir Douglas Quintet; The T-Bones; The Van Dykes.

**New Beginnings**   Autumn Records; Country Music Foundation (Nashville); Galaxy Records (Berkeley); International Association of Jazz Record Collectors (Pittsburgh); Kansas City Jazz, Inc.

**Miscellaneous**   The Beatles and the Rolling Stones make their US debuts; Tex Ritter is inducted into the Country Music Hall of Fame.

**D. Publications**   Jerry Coker, *Improvising Jazz*; David Dachs, *Anything Goes: The World of Popular Music*; Dave Dexter, Jr., *The Jazz Story: From the 90's to the 60's*; David Ewen, *The Life and Death of Tin Pan Alley*; Robert Gold, *The Jazz Lexicon*; *The Folk Songs of Peggy Seeger*.

**E. Representative Works**

**Musicals**   Walter Marks, *Bajour*; Jerry Bock and S. Harnick, *Fiddler on the Roof* (New York Drama Critics Award — nine Tonys); Erwin Drake, *What Makes Sammy Run?;* Jerry Herman, *Hello, Dolly!* (New York Drama Critics' Award — Tony); H. Martin and T. Gray, *High Spirits*; Stephen Sondheim, *Anyone Can Whistle*; C. Strouse and L. Adams, *Golden Boy*; J. Styne, B. Comden, and A. Green, *Fade Out — Fade In*; J. Styne and B. Merrill, *Funny Girl*.

**Number One Hits**   *Baby Love—Come See About Me—Where Did Our Love Go* (The Supremes); *Can't Buy Me Love—A Hard Day's Night—I Feel Fine—I Want to Hold Your Hand—Love Me Do—She Loves You* (The Beatles); *Chapel of Love* (The Dixie Cups); *Do Wah Diddy Diddy* (Manfred Mann); *Everybody Loves Somebody* (Dean Martin); *Hello, Dolly!* (Louis Armstrong); *The House of the Rising Sun* (The Animals); *I Get Around* (Beach Boys); *Leader of the Pack* (The Shangri-Las); *Mr. Lonely—There! I've Said It Again* (Bobby Vinton); *My Guy* (Mary Wells); *Oh, Pretty Woman* (Roy Orbison); *Rag Doll* (The Four Seasons); *Ringo* (Lorne Greene); *A World Without Love* (Peter and Gordon).

**Other**   Duke Ellington, *Far East Suite*; Jerry Goldsmith, *Seven Days in May* (film music); Henry Mancini, *A Shot in the Dark* (film score); Charlie Mingus, *Meditations on Integration*; R. M. and R. B. Sherman, *Mary Poppins* (film music—Oscar for song *Chim Chim Cheree*).

## Music—The Cultivated/Art Music Scene

**F. Births**   Frederic Chiu (pianist); Mia Chung (pianist) October 9; John Keyes (tenor); Augusta Read Thomas (composer) April 24.

**G. Deaths**   Marc Blitzstein (composer) January 22; Samuel Chotzinoff (pianist/critic) February 9; Norman Cordon (baritone) March 1; Maud Fay (soprano) October 7; Nicolai Graudan (Russian-born cellist) August 9; Louis Gruenberg (Russian-born composer) June 10; John Tasker Howard (musicologist) November 20; Mary Howe (composer/pianist) September 14; Donald MacArdle (musicologist) December 23; Albert Hay Malotte (composer) November 16; Leopold Mannes (pianist/composer) August 11; Colin McPhee (composer/ethnomusicologist) January 7; Harold C. Morris (composer/pianist) May 6; Moses Smith (critic) July 27; Edward Steuermann (Polish-born pianist) November 11; Ernst Toch (Austrian-born composer) October 1; George Wedge (music educator/organist) October 31; William C. White (bandmaster/composer) September 30; John Finley Williamson (conductor/educator) May 28.

**H. Debuts**

**United States**   Pierre Boulez (French conductor—New York), Charles Castleman (violinist—New York), Fiorenza Cossotto (Italian contralto—Chicago), Nicolai Ghiaurov (Bulgarian bass—Chicago), David Golub (pianist—Dallas), Wilhelm Kempff (German pianist—New York), Ivan Moravec (Czech pianist—New York), Elmar Oliveira (violinist—Hartford), John Owings (pianist), Wolfgang Sawallisch (German conductor—tour), Hermann Scherchen (German conductor—Philadelphia), Josef Suk (Czech violinist—Cleveland).

**Metropolitan Opera**   Luigi Alva (Peruvian tenor), Gabriel Bacquier (French baritone), Mary Costa (soprano), William Dooley (baritone), Geraint Evans (British baritone), Igor Gorin (bass), Donald Gramm (bass-baritone), Michael Langdon (British bass), Georges Prêtre (French conductor), Elisabeth Schwarzkopf (German soprano), David Ward (Scottish bass).

**Other**   Roberta Knie (soprano—Hagen).

**I. New Positions**

**Conductors**   Emerson Buckley (music director, Seattle Opera); Vladimir Golschmann (Denver Symphony Orchestra—to 1970); Amerigo Marino (Birmingham Symphony Orchestra (Alabama)—to 1985); László Somogyi (Rochester Philharmonic Orchestra—to 1969); Arthur Winograd (Hartford Symphony Orchestra—to 1985).

**Educational**   Philip Bezanson (music head, University of Massachusetts); Howard Boatwright (dean of music, Syracuse University); Walter Hendl (director, Eastman—to 1972); Thor Johnson (director, Interlochen—to 1967); Eugene List (Eastman—to 1975); Mehli Mehta (UCLA—to 1976); Robert Moevs (Rutgers); Bruno Nettl (University of Illinois); Gunther Schuller (Yale—to 1967); Ralph Shapey (University of Chicago); Henri Temianka (CSU, Long Beach—to 1976); Charles Wuorinen (Columbia University—to 1971).

**Other**   Elaine Barkin (coeditor, *Perspectives of New Music*); Robert Commanday (music critic, *San Francisco Chronicle*); Shirley Fleming (editor, *Musical America*—to 1991); Glynn Ross, general manager, Seattle Opera—to 1983); Paul Turok (reviewer, *Music Journal*—to 1980); Richard Westenburg (organ, choir, Central Presbyterian Church, New York—to 1974).

## J. Honors and Awards

**Honors**   Samuel Adler (Ives Award); Leslie Bassett, Gordon Binkerd, and Hall Overton (American Academy); Aaron Copland (Presidential Medal of Freedom); Ingolf Dahl (Alice M. Ditson Award); James DePreist (Mitropoulos); Milton Katims (Ditson Award); Carl Ruggles (Brandeis); William Schuman (National Arts Club Medal); Lawrence Leighton Smith (Mitropoulos Award); Richard Trythall (Rome Prize).

**Awards**   Itzhak Perlman (Leventritt); Michael Ponti (Busoni); Paula Robison (Munich—shared).

**K. Biographical**   James DePreist begins a conducting career in Europe; Akiro Endo and Walter Kaufmann become American citizens; Leon Fleisher begins to notice finger problems in his right hand; Christopher Keene neglects his history studies and organizes an opera group on the Berkeley campus; James Levine becomes assistant conductor of the Cleveland Orchestra; Nicolas Slonimsky retires from teaching; Tomás Svoboda (Czech composer) settles in the United States, continuing music study in California; Chinary Ung (Cambodian-born composer) comes to the United States.

## L. Musical Beginnings

**Performing Groups**   American Youth Symphony Orchestra (Los Angeles); Boston Symphony Chamber Players; Fort Worth Schola Cantorum (Texas); Louisville Bach Society; Oakland Youth Symphony (California); Rochester Chamber Orchestra; San Diego Opera Co.; Seattle Opera Association; Waverly Consort (New York).

**Festivals**   Bar Harbor Music Festival (Maine), Berkshire Festival of Contemporary Music; Meadow Brook Festival (Rochester, Minnesota).

**Educational**   Bowdoin College Music Press; Institute of American Music (Eastman); Jewish Music Research Center (Hebrew University); University of Chicago Press.

**Other**   Blaisdell Memorial Center (Honolulu); Dorothy Chandler Pavilion (Louisiana); Composers Theatre (New York); *Journal of Band Research*; Lincoln Center Music Theater; New York State Theater; William P. Ross Harpsichord Shop (Boston); Something Else Press; *Schwann-2: Record and Tape Guide*.

## M. Music Publications

Chotzinoff, Samuel, *A Little Nightmusic*
Creston, Paul, *Principles of Rhythm*
Duckles, Vincent, *Music Reference and Research Materials*
Ferguson, Donald, *Image and Structure in Chamber Music*
Gleason, H. and Marrocco, W., *Music in America*
Johnson, H. Earle, *Operas on American Subjects*
Lowens, Irving, *Music and Musicians in Early America*
Read, Gardner, *Music Notation: A Manual of Modern Practice*
Reed, H. O. and Harder, P., *Basic Contrapuntal Techniques*

## N. Musical Compositions

**Chamber Music**   Samuel Adler, *Piano Trio No. 1—Introduction and Capriccio* (harp); Stephen Albert, *Imitations for String Quartet—Canons for String Quartet*; David Amram, *Violin Sonata*; Wallace Berry, *String Quartet No. 2*; Paul Cooper, *String Quartet No. 4*; George Crumb, *Four Nocturnes* (violin and piano); David Diamond, *String Quartets 7, 8*; Donald Martino, *Concerto for Wind Quintet*; Walter Piston, *Piano Quartet—String Sextet*; Terry Riley, *In C*; Leon Stein, *String Quartet No. 3*; Stefan Wolpe, *Chamber Piece No. 1*; Christian Wolff, *For One, Two or Three People*.

**Choral/Vocal**   Hugh Aitken, *Mass II*; David Amram, *A Year in Our Land* (cantata); Margaret Bonds, *Fields of Wonder (after Hughes)*; Richard Felciano, *Four Poems from the Japanese*; Miriam Gideon, *Questions on Nature* (song cycle); Nicolas Nabokov, *Five Poems by Anna Akhmatova*;

Bernard Rogers, *The Light of Man* (oratorio); Eric Salzman, *In Praise of the Owl and the Cuckoo*; Seymour Shifrin, *Satires of Circumstance*; Halsey Stevens, *Siete canciones*; Virgil Thomson, *The Feast of Love*; David Ward-Steinman, *Song of Moses* (oratorio); Ben Weber, *The Ways* (song cycle).

**Concertos**   Hugh Aitken, *Partita for String Quartet and Orchestra*; Leonardo Balada, *Piano Concerto*; Esther Ballou, *Guitar Concerto—Piano Concerto No. 2*; Wallace Berry, *Piano Concerto*; William Bolcom, *Concerto Serenade* (violin and strings); Benjamin Lees, *Concerto for String Quartet and Orchestra*; Robert Parris, *Flute Concerto—Trombone Concerto*; Halsey Stevens, *Cello Concerto*; Louise Talma, *Dialogues for Piano and Orchestra*.

**Electronic**   Robert Ashley, *Combination Wedding and Funeral—Kitty Hawk (An Antigravity Piece)—The Wolfman Tape*; Milton Babbitt, *Philomel*; Tod Dockstader, *Quartermass—Two Moons of Quartermass*; Kenneth Gaburo, *Fat Millie's Lament—The Wasting of Lucrecetzia*.

**Operas**   Marc Blitzstein, *Sacco and Vanzetti* (unfinished); Avery Claflin, *Uncle Tom's Cabin*; John Eaton, *Heracles*; Richard Felciano, *Sir Gawain and the Green Knight*; Arthur Frackenpohl, *Domestic Relations*; Lee Hoiby, *Natalia Petrovna*; Gian Carlo Menotti, *Martin's Lie*; Thomas Pasatieri, *The Trysting Place*; Robert Ward, *The Lady from Colorado*.

**Orchestra/Band**   Hugh Aitken, *Partitas No. 3, 4*; Dominick Argento, *Royal Invitation, or Homage to the Queen of Tonga—St. Joan* (incidental music)—*Volpone* (incidental music); Louis Ballard, *Fantasy Aborigine I*; Margaret Bonds, *The Migration*; George Edwards, *Two Pieces for Orchestra*; Jonathan Elkus, *Will of Stratford* (incidental music); William Flanagan, *Narrative*; Alan Hovhaness, *Floating World, "Ukiyo"*; John La Montaine, *Birds of Paradise*; Hall Overton, *Sonorities*; Eric Stokes, *Three Sides of a Town*; Igor Stravinsky, *Variations for Orchestra*; Morton Subotnick, *Galileo* (incidental music); David Ward-Steinman, *Western Orpheus*; Eugene Zador, *Festival Overture*.

**Piano/Organ**   Leslie Bassett, *Four Statements for Organ*; Leonard Bernstein, *Five Anniversaries*; Earle Brown, *Corroborree* (three pianos); David Burge, *Eclipse II*; Paul Creston, *Metamorphoses, Opus 84*; Emma Lou Diemer, *Toccata* (organ); Morton Feldman, *Piano Piece*; Robert Muczynski, *A Summer Journal, Opus 19*; George Perle, *Short Sonata*; Burrill Phillips, *Organ Sonata*; Gardner Read, *Five Polytonal Etudes, Opus 116*; Elie Siegmeister, *Sonata No. 2*.

**Symphonies**   T. J. Anderson, *Symphony in Three Movements*; Henry Cowell, *Symphony No. 18*; Donald Erb, *Symphony of Overtures*; Ezra Laderman, *Symphony No. 1*; Robert Hall Lewis, *Symphony No. 1*; Nikolai Lopatnikoff, *Concerto for Orchestra*; Ray Luke, *Symphony No. 3*; Martin Mailman, *Sinfonietta*; Julia Perry, *Symphony No. 4*; Roger Sessions, *Symphony No. 5*; Leo Sowerby, *Symphony No. 5*; Francis Thorne, *Symphony No. 2*; Ernst Toch, *Symphony No. 7*; David Van Vactor, *Sinfonia Breve*; Richard Yardumian, *Symphony No. 2, "Psalms."*

# 1965

❁

## Historical Highlights

The first American "space walks" take place on the third and fourth *Gemini* flights following Russia's premiere; the Watts riots take place in Los Angeles causing great damage; the Department of Housing and Urban Development (HUD) is created; Congress passes the Medicare and Medicaid programs for the aged; United States planes bomb North Vietnam in retaliation for Communist attacks.

## World Cultural Highlights

**World Art**   Hans Arp, *Fruit Agressif;* Corneille, *Fascination of the Island;* Salvador Dali, *Bust of Dante;* Lucia Fontana, *Spatial Concept;* Alberto Giacometti, *Caroline;* Pablo Picasso, *Self-Portrait.*

**World Literature**   Italo Calvino, *Cosmicomics*; John Fowles, *The Magus*; Gunter Grass, *Dog Years.*

**World Music**   Pierre Boulez, *Éclat*; Giselher Klebe, *Jacobowsky and the Colonel*; Witold Lutoslawski, *Paroles Tissées*; Rodion Shchedrin, *Symphony No. 2, "24 Preludes."*

**Miscellaneous**   Russian author Mikhail Sholokhov receives the Nobel Prize for literature; deaths include Julián Carrillo, Winston Churchill, Myra Hess, Zoltán Kemémy, Hans Knappertsbusch, W. Somerset Maugham, and Albert Schweitzer.

## American Art and Literature Highlights

**Births/Deaths**   Deaths include art figures Milton Avery, Joseph Badger, Frederick Kiesler, Charles Sheeler, David Smith, Abraham Walkowitz, literary figures Joseph Auslander, Thomas B. Costain, T. S. Eliot, Lorraine Hansberry, Willard Motley, and Thomas S. Stribling.

**Art Works**   Frank Gallo, *Male Image*; John Hultberg, *The Great Glass Roof*; Jasper Johns, *Edingsville*; Joseph Kosuth, *One and Three Chairs*; Roy Lichtenstein, *Moonscape*; John McCracken, *Rainmaker*; Larry Poons, *Away Out on the Mountains*; Larry Rivers, *Jim Dine Storm Window*; George Segal, *Girl in Doorway*; Raphael Soyer, *Homage to Thomas Eakins*; Andrew Wyeth, *Weather Side*.

**Literature**   Abe Burrows, *Cactus Flower*; James Dickey, *Buckdancer's Choice* (National Book Award); Frank Gilroy, *The Subject Was Roses* (Pulitzer Prize—New York Drama Critics' Award); Arthur Hailey, *Hotel*; Robin Moore, *The Green Berets*; Katherine Anne Porter, *Collected Stories* (Pulitzer Prize—National Book Award); Neil Simon, *The Odd Couple*; Lanford Wilson, *Balm in Gilead*.

## Music—The Vernacular/Commercial Scene

**A. Births**   Marty Brown (singer) July 25; Karyn White (singer) October 14.

**B. Deaths**   Dave Barbour (guitarist/writer) December 11; Earl Bostic (saxophonist/bandleader) October 28; Nat "King" Cole (singer) February 15; Tadd Dameron (pianist/composer) March 8; Alan Freed (disk jockey) January 20; Spike Jones (musical satirist) May 1; "Red" Nichols (cornetist/bandleader) June 28; Frank Proffitt (banjo maker); Ted Snyder (songwriter) July 16; Frank Stamps (publisher) February 12, Claude Thornhill (composer/pianist) July 1; Harry Tierney (songwriter/pianist) March 22; Clarence Williams (pianist) November 6; Spencer Williams (composer) July 14; R. Miller "Sonny Boy" Williamson (singer) May 25.

**C. Biographical**

**Performing Groups**   The Amboy Dukes; A.M.M.; The Arbors; The Association; The Barbarians; Big Brother and the Holding Co.; Blues Project; The Buckinghams; Cannibal and the Headhunters; Choir; Country Joe and the Fish; The Cowsills; Daily Flash; The Disciples; The Doors; Electric Prunes; The Fantastic Four; The Flamin' Groovies; The Fugs; The Grateful Dead; The Good Rats; Great Society; International Submarine Band; The Jaggerz; Jazzmobile; Jefferson Airplane (Jefferson Starship—1974); Thad Jones–Mel Lewis Big Band; The Left Banke; Lost and Found; Love; The Lovin' Spoonful; Mad River; The Mamas and the Papas; MC5; The Monkees; Music Machine (Ragamuffins); Notes From the Underground; Peaches and Herb; Pearls Before Swine; Quicksilver Messenger Service; The Remains; The Seeds; Sopwith Camel; The Strangeloves; The 13th Floor Elevators; The Trammps; Untraditional Jazz Improvisational Team (New York); The Velvet Underground; We Five; The Youngbloods; The (Young) Rascals.

**New Beginnings**   Association for the Advancement of Creative Musicians (AACM); Dunhill Records; National Ragtime Festival (St. Louis); Rodgers and Hammerstein Archives of Recorded Sound (New York); Revelation Records (Los Angeles).

**Honors**   Ernest Tubb (Country Music Hall of Fame).

**D. Publications**   Jack Burton, *The Blue Book of Tin Pan Alley II*; Josh Dunson, *Freedom in the Air: Song Movements of the '60's*; R. M. Lawless, *Folksingers and Folksongs in America*; Wilfrid Mellers, *Music in a New Found Land: Themes and Developments in the History of American Music*; B. Nettl, *Folk and Traditional Music of the Western Continents*; Irwin Stambler, *Encyclopedia of Popular Music*.

### E. Representative Works

**Musicals**    L. Bricusse and A. Newley, *The Roar of the Greasepaint—The Smell of the Crowd* (United States premiere); M. Grudeff and R. Jessel, *Baker Street*; J. Kander and F. Ebb, *Flora, the Red Menace*; M. Leigh and J. Darion, *Man of La Mancha* (New York Drama Critics' Award—Tony); A. J. Lerner and B. Lane, *On a Clear Day You Can See Forever*; R. Rodgers and S. Sondheim, *Do I Hear a Waltz?*; Harold Rome, *The Zulu and the Zayda*; J. Van Heusen and S. Cahn, *Skyscraper*.

**Number One Hits**    *Back in My Arms Again—I Hear a Symphony—Stop! In the Name of Love* (The Supremes); *Downtown* (Petula Clark); *Eight Days a Week—Help!—Ticket to Ride—Yesterday* (The Beatles); *Eve of Destruction* (Barry McGuire); *Game of Love* (Wayne Fontana and the Mindbenders); *Get Off My Cloud—(I Can't Get No) Satisfaction* (Rolling Stones); *Hang on Sloopy* (The McCoys); *Help Me Rhonda* (Beach Boys); *I Can't Help Myself* (The Four Tops); *I Got You Babe* (Sonny and Cher); *I'm Henry VIII, I Am—Mrs. Brown, You've Got a Lovely Daughter* (Herman's Hermits); *I'm Telling You Now* (Freddie and the Dreamers); *Mr. Tambourine Man—Turn! Turn! Turn!* (The Byrds); *My Girl* (The Temptations); *Over and Over* (Dave Clark Five); *This Diamond Ring* (Gary Lewis and the Playboys); *You've Lost That Lovin' Feelin'* (The Righteous Brothers).

**Other**    Duke Ellington, *The Golden Broom and the Green Apple—Virgin Islands Suite—In the Beginning God*; J. Mandel and P. F. Webster, *The Shadow of Your Smile* (Oscar); Alex North, *The Agony and the Ecstasy* (film music); Lalo Schifrin, *Jazz Suite on the Mass Texts*.

## Music—The Cultivated/Art Music Scene

**F. Births**    Peter Kelly (composer); John Moran (composer); Kurt Nikkanen (violinist) December; Paula Rasmussen (mezzo-soprano).

**G. Deaths**    Henry Cowell (composer) December 10; Henry S. Drinker, Jr. (dilettante) March 9; John Hays Hammond, Jr. (organ builder) February 12; Edwin Hughes (pianist) July 17; Herbert Janssen (German-born baritone) June 3; Nina Koshetz (Russian-born soprano) May 14; Clarence Loomis (pianist/composer) July 3; Léa Luboshutz (Russian-born violinist) March 18; Jeanette MacDonald (soprano) January 14; Carl Parrish (musicologist) November 27; Tito Schipa (Italian-born tenor) December 16; Gustave Schirmer III (publisher) May 28; Nicolai Sokoloff (Russian-born violinist) September 25; Sigmund Spaeth (musicologist) November 11; Nell Tangeman (mezzo-soprano) February 15; Edgard Varèse (French-born composer) November 6.

### H. Debuts

**United States**    Jacqueline du Pré (British cellist—New York), Brent Ellis (baritone—Santa Fe), Peter Frankl (Hungarian pianist—Dallas), Sergiu Luca (Romanian violinist—Philadelphia), Julia Migenes (soprano—New York), Luciano Pavarotti (Italian tenor—Miami), Neva Pilgrim (New York), Kenneth Riegel (tenor—Santa Fe), Yakov Zak (Russian pianist—tour).

**Metropolitan Opera**    Grace Bumbry (mezzo-soprano), Montserrat Caballé (Spanish soprano), Mirella Freni (Italian soprano), Nicolai Ghiaurov (Bulgarian bass), Zubin Mehta (Indian conductor), Sherrill Milnes (baritone), Kostas Paskalis (Greek baritone), Helga Pilarczyk (German soprano), Gianni Raimondi (Italian tenor), John Reardon (baritone), Renata Scotto (Italian soprano), Gérard Souzay (French baritone), Felicia Weathers (soprano).

**Other**    Kenneth Cooper (harpsichordist—London), Simon Estes (bass-baritone—Berlin), Jane Marsh (soprano—Spoleto), William Workman (baritone—Hamburg).

### I. New Positions

**Conductors**    David Burge (Boulder Philharmonic Orchestra—to 1972); László Halász (Eastman—to 1967).

**Educational**    Lucian Berio (Juilliard—to 1972); George Crumb (University of Pennsylvania); Emma Lou Diemer (University of Maryland—to 1970); David Ewen (University of Miami); Frederick Fennell (University of Miami); Vittorio Giannini (director, North Carolina School of the

Arts); Robert Muczynski (head, composition, University of Arizona—to 1988); William Primrose (Indiana University—to 1972); Walter Rubsamen (music chair, UCLA—to 1973); Harvey Sollberger (Columbia Universtiy—to 1983).

**Other**    Martin Bernheimer (music editor, *Los Angeles Times*); David Hamilton (music division, W. W. Norton Co.); Thomas Murray (organ, Immanuel Presbyterian Church, Los Angeles—to 1973).

### J. Honors and Awards

**Honors**    Stephen Albert (Rome Prize); Jacob Avshalomov (Alice M. Ditson Award); Milton Babbitt and Vincent Persichetti (National Institute); Elliott Carter (Brandeis); Mario Davidovsky, Earl Kim, and Harvey Sollberger (American Academy); Vladimir Horowitz (*Musical America* Musician of the Year); Richard Kostelanetz (Pulitzer for Music Criticism); David Martin Levy (Rome Prize); Leontyne Price (Medal of Freedom); William Schuman (Brandeis Medal); Edgard Varèse (MacDowell Medal); Charles Whittenberg (Rome Prize).

**K. Biographical**    Marian Anderson gives her farewell tour; Erich Kunzel becomes assistant to Max Rudolf at the Cincinnati Symphony Orchestra; Bruno Maderna (Italian composer) is invited by Sarah Caldwell to come to Boston and conduct his opera; Randall Thompson decides to retire from teaching; Michael Tippett (British composer) makes his first visit to the United States.

### L. Musical Beginnings

**Performing Groups**    Choral Arts Society of Washington; Concerto Soloists (Philadelphia); Greater Miami Symphony Orchestra (Florida Philharmonic Orchestra); Los Angeles Master Chorale and Sinfonia; Omaha Regional Ballet Co.; Phoenix Opera Co.

**Festivals**    Bowdoin Summer Music Festival; New College Music Festival (Saratosa, California); New York Philharmonic in the Parks.

**Educational**    North Carolina School of the Arts (Winston Salem).

**Other**    Marc Blitzstein Award for Musical Theater; *Current Musicology*; National Foundation on the Arts and the Humanities (National Endowment for the Arts and National Endowment for the Humanities); Naumburg Chamber Music Award; Rochester Music Publishers; Thorne Music Fund.

### M. Music Publications

Boyden, David D., *History of Violin Playing from Its Origins to 1761*
Cohn, Arthur, *Twentieth-century Music in Western Europe*
Dickinson, George, *A Handbook of Style in Music*
El-Dabh, Halim, *The Derabucca: Hand Techniques in the Art of Drumming*
Goldman, Richard F., *Harmony in Western Music*
Hubbard, Frank, *Three Centuries of Harpsichord Making*
Johnson, H. Earle, *Hallelujah, Amen! The Story of the Handel and Haydn Society of Boston*
Levant, Oscar, *The Memoirs of an Amnesiac*
Seay, Albert, *Music in the Medieval World*
Serly, Tibor, *A Second Look at Harmony*
Siegmeister, Elie, *Harmony and Melody*

### N. Musical Compositions

**Chamber Music**    Samuel Adler, *Violin Sonata No. 3*; William Bolcom, *String Quartet No. 8*; Earl Brown, *String Quartet 1965*; Donald Erb, *Antipodes for String Quartet and Percussion*; Alvin Etler, *String Quartet No. 2*; Richard Felciano, *Contractions* (woodwind quintet); Anthony Iannaccone, *String Quartet*; Clarence Loomis, *String Quartet No. 3*; Gunther Schuller, *String Quartet No. 2*; Joseph Schwantner, *Diaphonia Intervallum* (Bearns Prize); Leon Stein, *String Quartet No. 4*; Halsey Stevens, *Cello Sonata*.

**Choral/Vocal**    Stephen Albert, *Winter Songs—Wedding Songs*; Leonard Bernstein, *Chichester Psalms*; Roberta Bitgood, *Let There Be Light* (cantata); Richard Felciano, *Captives*; Ross Lee Finney, *Nun's Priest's Tale*; Daniel Pinkham, *St. Mark Passion*; Leo Sowerby, *Solomon's Garden*; Randall Thompson, *Passion According to St. Luke*; Robert Ward, *Sweet Freedom Songs*.

**Concertos**   David Amram, *Horn Concerto*; Leonardo Balada, *Guitar Concerto*; Easley Blackwood, *Oboe Concerto*; Henry Cowell, *Harp Concerto*; Harold Farberman, *Concerto for Alto Sax and Strings*; Ross Lee Finney, *Concerto for Percussion and Orchestra*; Anis Fuleihan, *Violin Concerto No. 2*; Karel Husa, *Concerto for Brass Quintet and Orchestra*; Donald Martino, *Piano Concerto*; Tibor Serly, *Concertino 3 Times 3* (piano and orchestra); Alexander Tcherepnin, *Piano Concerto No. 6, Opus 99*; Charles Wuorinen, *Piano Concerto No. 1*.

**Electronic**   Robert Ashley, *Night Train* (electronic theater)—*Orange Dessert* (electronic theater); Larry Austin, *The Maze*; Kenneth Gaburo, *Lemon Drops*; Salvatore Martirano, *Underworld* (mixed media); Gordon Mumma, *Le Corbusier*; Morton Subotnick, *Serenade No. 3*; Vladimir Ussachevsky, *Of Wood and Brass* (tape); Charles Wuorinen, *Orchestral and Electronic Exchanges*.

**Operas**   David Amram, *The Final Ingredient* (television opera); Jack Beeson, *Lizzie Borden*; Cecil Effinger, *Cyrano de Bergerac*; Ezra Laderman, *Air Raid*; Thomas Pasatieri, *The Women—The Flowers of Ice*; Ned Rorem, *Miss Julie*.

**Orchestra/Band**   Samuel Adler, *Festive Prelude* (band); David Amram, *King Lear Variations* (wind band); Dominick Argento, *Variations for Orchestra: The Mask of Night*; Milton Babbitt, *Relata I*; Richard Bales, *National Gallery Suite IV, "American Chronicle"*; George Barati, *Polarization*; Irwin Bazelon, *Excursions*; Easley Blackwood, *Symphonic Fantasy, Opus 17*; Margaret Bonds, *Montgomery Variations*; Michael Colgrass, *Sea Shadow*; Edward T. Cone, *Music for Strings*; Vivian Fine, *My Son, My Enemy* (ballet); Robert Hall Lewis, *Three Pieces for Orchestra*; Robert McBride, *Country Music Fantasy*; Robert Muczynski, *Symphonic Dialogues, Opus 20*; Nicolas Nabokov, *Don Quixote* (ballet); Robert Palmer, *A Centennial Overture*; Burrill Phillips, *Soleriana Concertante*; George Rochberg, *The Alchemist* (incidental music); William Schuman, *The Witch of Endor* (ballet)— *Philharmonic Fanfare*; Elliott Schwartz, *Music for Orchestra*; Robert Starer, *Mutabili (Variants for Orchestra)*; William Sydeman, *Study for Orchestra III*; Aurelio de la Vega, *Analigus*.

**Piano/Organ**   William Bolcom, *Dream Music I*; John Eaton, *Microtonal Fantasy for Two Pianos*; Richard Felciano, *Gravities* (piano, four hands); Ben Johnston, *Sonata for Microtonal Piano*; Leo Kraft, *Statements and Commentaries*; Vincent Persichetti, *Sonata No. 11, Opus 101*; Raoul Pleskow, *Music for Two Pianos*; Roger Sessions, *Sonata No. 3*; Leo Sowerby, *Sinfonia Brevis for Organ*; Robert Starer, *Sonata No. 2*.

**Symphonies**   Irwin Bazelon, *Symphony No. 4*; Easley Blackwood, *Symphony No. 3, Opus 14*; William Bolcom, *Symphony (Oracles)*; Henry Cowell, *Symphony No. 19—Symphonies 20, 21* (unfinished); Robert Evett, *Symphony No. 2—Symphony No. 3*; Roy Harris, *Symphony No. 10, "Abraham Lincoln"*; Anthony Iannaccone, *Symphony No. 1*; Andrew Imbrie, *Symphony No. 1*; Charles Jones, *Symphony No. 4*; Ernst Kanitz, *Symphony No. 2, "Sinfonia Seria"*; Walter Piston, *Symphony No. 8*; Gunther Schuller, *Symphony*; Leo Smit, *Symphony No. 2*; Clifford Taylor, *Symphony No. 2*.

# 1966

☀

## Historical Highlights

President Lyndon Johnson tours the Far East; Robert C. Weaver becomes the first black to be appointed to a cabinet post; the Soviet *Luna 9* and the American *Surveyor I* land on the moon; the first space docking is achieved; President de Gaulle orders NATO forces out of France; the so-called "cultural revolution" begins in China.

## World Cultural Highlights

**World Art**   Georg Baselitz, *Ein neuer Typ;* Marc Chagall, *Le Triomphe de la musique*; Salvador Dali, *Tuna Fishing*.

**World Literature**  Jean Genet, *Les Paravents*; Graham Greene, *The Comedians*; Seamus Heaney, *Death of a Naturalist;* Yevgeny Yevtushenko, *Bratskaya Station.*

**World Music**  Benjamin Britten, *The Burning Fiery Furnace*; Hans Werner Henze, *Muses of Sicily*; Krzysztof Penderecki, *Passion According to St. Luke*; Dmitri Shostakovich, *Cello Concerto No. 2.*

**Miscellaneous**  L'Orchestre de Paris and the Ulster Symphony of Ireland are founded; deaths include Jan (Hans) Arp, André Breton, C. S. Forester, Alberto Giacometti, and Tristan Klingsor.

## American Art and Literature Highlights

**Births/Deaths**  Deaths include art figures Alfeo Faggi, Leo Freedlander, Malvina Hoffman, Hans Hofmann, Paul Manship, Maxfield Parrish, Frederick Sievers, William Zorach, and literary figures George A. Chamberlain, Cyril Hume, William McFee, Anne Nichols, Kathleen Norris, Delmore Schwartz, Lillian Smith, and Mary Heaton Vorse.

**Art Works**  Alexander Calder, *The Sail*; Helen Frankenthaler, *Mauve District*; Red Grooms, *Loft on 26th Street*; Robert Grosvenor, *Tenerife*; Paul Jenkins, *Sun Over the Hourglass*; Edward Kienholz, *The State Hospital*; Nicholas Krushenick, *King Kong*; Sol LeWitt, *Open Modular Cube*; Richard Lindner, *Rock—Rock*; Jules Olitski, *C + J and B*; Lucas Samaras, *Mirrored Room*; George Segal, *Diner*.

**Literature**  Edward Albee, *A Delicate Balance* (Pulitzer Prize); John Barth, *Giles Goat Boy*; Truman Capote, *In Cold Blood*; Allen S. Drury, *Capable of Honor*; Richard Eberhart, *Selected Poems* (Pulitzer Prize), Bernard Malamud, *The Fixer* (Pulitzer Prize—National Book Award); Walker Percy, *The Last Gentleman*; Anne Sexton, *Live or Die* (Pulitzer Prize); Neil Simon, *Sweet Charity*.

## Music—The Vernacular/Commercial Scene

**A. Births**  Janet Jackson (singer) May 16; Wynonna Judd (singer); Stacy Lattislaw (singer) November 25.

**B. Deaths**  Mississippi John Hurt (guitarist) July 3; Papa Jack Laine (drummer/bandleader) June 1; "Bud" Powell (pianist) August 1; Billy Rose (lyricist) February 10; Abner Silver (composer/lyricist) November 24; Sophie Tucker (singer) February 9.

**C. Biographical**

**Performing Groups**  The American Breed; Blue Image; Buffalo Springfield; Canned Heat; Chicago Loop; The Clique; Creedence Clearwater Revival; Earth Quake; Fifth Dimension; The Flock; Grass Roots; Grease Band; Harpers Bizarre; Jimi Hendrix Experience; The Hombres; Iron Butterfly; Kaleidoscope; Leather Coated Minds; Lynyrd Skynyrd; Merry-Go-Round; Steve Miller Band; Moby Grape; Mother Earth; Nitty Gritty Dirt Band; The Originals; Peanut Butter Conspiracy (Ashes); Red Crayola; Buddy Rich Band II; The Royal Guardsmen; Santana; Savoy Brown (Blues Band); Soul Survivors; Spanky and Our Gang; Vanilla Fudge; West Coast Pop Art Experimental Band.

**New Beginnings**  AACM Festival; *Bluegrass Unlimited*; Boston Globe Jazz Festival; Jazz Composer's Orchestral Association; Memphis Blues Festival; Milestone Records; Sire Records.

**Miscellaneous**  David Baker becomes chair of jazz studies at Indiana University; Helen Reddy (Australian singer) comes to the United States; The Who make their US debut tour.

**D. Publications**  Whitney Balliett, *Such Sweet Thunder*; Leonard Feather, *The Encyclopedia of Jazz in the Sixties*; Charles Keil, *Urban Blues*; Henry A. Kmen, *Music in New Orleans: The Formative Years, 1791–1841*; Robert Shelton, *The Country Music Story: A Picture History of Country and Western Music*; Martin Williams, *Where's the Melody? A Listener's Introduction to Jazz.*

**E. Representative Works**

**Musicals**  J. Bock and S. Harnick, *The Apple Tree*; C. Coleman and D. Fields, *Sweet Charity*;

Jerry Herman, *Mame* (Tony); J. Kander and F. Ebb, *Cabaret* (New York Drama Critics' Award—Tony); H. Schmidt and T. Jones, *I Do! I Do!*; C. Strouse and L. Adams, *It's a Bird, It's a Plane, It's Superman*; J. Van Heusen and S. Cahn, *Walking Happy*.

**Number One Hits**　*The Ballad of the Green Berets* (Sgt. Barry Sadler); *Cherish* (The Association); *Good Lovin'* (The Young Rascals); *Good Vibrations* (Beach Boys); *Hanky Panky* (Tommy James and the Shondells); *I'm a Believer—Last Train to Clarksville* (The Monkees); *Lightnin' Strikes* (Lou Christie); *Monday, Monday* (The Mamas and the Papas); *My Love* (Petula Clark); *96 Tears* (? and the Mysterians); *Paint It Black* (Rolling Stones); *Paperback Writer—We Can Work It Out* (The Beatles); *Poor Side of Town* (Johnny Rivers); *Reach Out, I'll Be There* (The Four Tops); *(You're My) Soul and Inspiration* (Righteous Brothers); *The Sounds of Silence* (Simon and Garfunkel); *Strangers in the Night* (Frank Sinatra); *Summer in the City* (Lovin' Spoonful); *Sunshine Superman* (Donovan); *These Boots Are Made For Walking* (Nancy Sinatra); *When a Man Loves a Woman* (Percy Sledge); *Wild Thing* (The Troggs); *Winchester Cathedral* (New Vaudeville Band); *You Can't Hurry Love—You Keep Me Hangin' On* (The Supremes).

**Other**　Jerry Goldsmith, *The Blue Max* (film music); Johnny Mandel, *The Russians Are Coming, The Russians Are Coming* (film music); Alex North, *Who's Afraid of Virginia Woolf* (film music); Nino Rota, *Romeo and Juliet* (film music).

## Music—The Cultivated/Art Music Scene

**F. Births**　Dolora Zajick (mezzo-soprano).

**G. Deaths**　Mario Chamlee (tenor) November 13; Vittorio Giannini (composer) November 28; Noah Greenberg (conductor/musicologist) January 9; Richard Hageman (Dutch-born composer/conductor) March 6; Glen Haydon (musicologist) May 8; Jan Kiepura (Polish-born tenor) August 15; Otto Kinkeldey (musicologist) September 19; Boris Koutzen (Russian-born composer) December 10; Victor Küzdö (Hungarian-born violinist) February 24 (age 106); Florence Macbeth (soprano) May 5; Joseph Maddy (music educator) April 18; Carl McKinley (composer/organist) July 24; Lee Pattison (pianist) December 22; Louis Persinger (violinist) December 31; Quincy Porter (composer) November 12; Deems Taylor (composer/author) July 3.

**H. Debuts**

**United States**　Janet Baker (British mezzo-soprano—San Francisco), Phyllis Bryn-Julson (soprano—Boston), Mischa Dichter (pianist—Boston), Christiane Eda-Pierre (French soprano—Chicago), Oscar Ghiglia (Italian guitar—New York), Elisabeth Grümmer (German soprano—New York), Robert Hale (baritone—New York), Ralph Holmes (British violinist—New York), Gwyneth Jones (British soprano—New York), Alan Marks (pianist—St. Louis), Eve Queler (conductor—Fair Lawn, New Jersey), Margarita Rinaldi (Italian soprano—Dallas), Helen Watts (British contralto—New York), Patricia Wise (soprano—Kansas City).

**Metropolitan Opera**　Walter Berry (Austrian bass-baritone), Plácido Domingo (Spanish tenor), Loren Driscoll (tenor), Lamberto Gardelli (Italian conductor), Reri Grist (soprano), James King (tenor), Alfredo Kraus (Spanish tenor), Pilar Lorengar (Spanish soprano), Ticho Parly (Danish tenor), Thomas Stewart (baritone), Virginia Zeani (Romanian soprano).

**Other**　Edward Sooter (tenor—Bremerhaven).

**I. New Positions**

**Conductors**　John Nelson (Greenwich Philharmonia, Connecticut—to 1974).

**Educational**　Paul Chihara (UCLA—to 1974); Roque Cordero (Indiana University—to 1969); Edward O. D. Downes (Queens College—to 1983); Maureen Forrester (Philadelphia Academy of Music—to 1971); Jacob Lateiner (Juilliard); Aldo Parisot (cello, New England Conservatory—to 1970); Roger Reynolds (UC, San Diego); William O. Smith (University of Washington); Morton Subotnick (NYU—to 1969); Italo Tajo (voice, Cincinnati Conservatory); Henry Weinberg (Queens College); Richard Wilson (Vassar—to 1985).

**Other**　David Amram (composer-in-residence, New York Philharmonic Orchestra); Larry Austin (editor, *Source*—to 1971); Edward T. Cone (editor, *Perspectives of New Music*—to 1972); Frederick Swann (organ, Riverside Church, New York—to 1982).

## J. Honors and Awards

**Honors** Walter Aschaffenburg and Ralph Shapey (American Academy); David Diamond (American Academy and National Institute); Yehudi Menuhin (*Musical America* Musician of the Year); Harry Partch (Waite Award); Carlos Surinach (Arnold Bax Medal); Virgil Thomson (American Academy Gold Medal); Stefan Wolpe (National Institute and Brandeis).

**Awards** Mischa Dichter, Simon Estes, and Stephen Kates (Tchaikovsky Silver Medals); Lawrence Foster (Koussevitzky); Jane Marsh (Tchaikovsky, Voice); Robert Menga (Paganini Second); Garrick Ohlsson (Busoni); Paula Robison (Geneva); Barry Snyder (Cliburn Second).

**K. Biographical** Licia Albanese sings the final role of her opera career in the old Metropolitan Opera house; Theodore Antoniou (Greek composer) tours the United States through the courtesy of the United States State department; Niccolò Castiglioni (Italian pianist/composer) and Dinu Ghezzo (Romanian conductor/composer) come to the United States; Erich Kunzel takes the Cincinnati Symphony Orchestra on a tour of the Far East; Sergiu Luca, Stanislaw Skrowaczewski, Claudio Spies, and Aurelio de la Vega all become naturalized American citizens; Beverly Sills sings with the Metropolitan Opera company in a park concert in New York; Oliver Strunk retires from teaching at Princeton and moves to Italy.

## L. Musical Beginnings

**Performing Groups** Arkansas Symphony Orchestra; Chamber Symphony of Philadelphia; Newark Boys Chorus and School; Newark Little Symphony; San Francisco Conservatory Artists Ensemble (New Music Ensemble); Sonic Arts Union; Washington (DC) Performing Arts Society; Western Opera Theater (San Francisco).

**Festivals** Florida International Festival (Daytona Beach); Flagstaff Festival of the Arts (Arizona); Mostly Mozart Festival (Lincoln Center summer festival); Saratoga Festival of the Performing Arts.

**Educational** International Bach Institute; Kreeger Music Building, American University.

**Other** Affiliate Artists, Inc.; American Society of University Composers (Society of Composers, Inc.); Association for Recorded Sound Collections (Virginia); Philipp R. Belt Piano Workshop (New Hampshire); Buchla Associates (Berkeley); CBS Musical Instruments; Jesse H. Jones Hall (Houston); Metropolitan Opera House (Lincoln Center—New York); Répertoire International de Littérature Musicale (RILM); Saratoga Performing Arts Center (New York).

## M. Music Publications

Aldrich, Putnam, *Rhythm in Seventeenth-Century Italian Monody*
Austin, William, *Music in the 20th Century*
Berry, Wallace, *Form in Music*
Chasins, Abram, *The Appreciation of Music*
Elston, Arnold, *A Modern Guide to Symphonic Music*
Hamm, Charles E., *Opera*
Krenek, Ernst, *Exploring Music*
Lowens, Irving, *Source Readings in American Music History*
Pleasants, Henry, *The Great Singers*
Stevenson, Robert M., *Protestant Church Music in America: A Short Survey of Men and Movements from 1564 to the Present*
Talma, Louise, *Harmony for the College Student*
Verrall, John, *Fugue and Invention in Theory and Practice*

## N. Musical Compositions

**Chamber Music** Samuel Adler, *Seven Epigrams for Woodwind Sextet—Cello Sonata*; Charles Amirkhanian, *Canticle No. 3—Canticle No. 4* (percussion); David Amram, *Fanfare and*

*Processional* (brass quintet); T. J. Anderson, *Connections* (string quintet); Bülent Arel, *For Violin and Piano*; Milton Babbitt, *Sextets*; Leonardo Balada, *Geometria No. 1*; Arthur Berger, *Septet*; Wallace Berry, *String Quartet No. 3*; Henry Brant, *Hieroglyphics II*; David Diamond, *String Quartet No. 9*; Jacob Druckman, *String Quartet No. 2*; Morton Feldman, *First Principles I*; Andrew Imbrie, *Cello Sonata*; Ben Johnston, *String Quartet No. 3*; Leon Kirchner, *String Quartet No. 3* (Pulitzer Prize); Leo Kraft, *Concerto No. 2 for Thirteen Instruments—String Quartet No. 3*; Ezra Laderman, *String Quartet No. 3*; Lawrence Moss, *Windows*; George Rochberg, *Black Sounds* (Prix Italia); Seymour Shifrin, *String Quartet No. 3*; Robert Ward, *String Quartet*.

**Choral/Vocal**    Samuel Adler, *Behold Your God* (cantata); Dominick Argento, *The Revelation of St. John the Divine*; Luciano Berio, *Sequenze III*; William Bolcom, *Morning and Evening Songs (after Blake)*; David Del Tredici, *Syzygy*; David Epstein, *Fancies* (song cycle); Miriam Gideon, *Rhymes from the Hill*; Daniel Pinkham, *Jonah* (oratorio); Ned Rorem, *Hearing—Sun* (song cycles); Robert Starer, *Joseph and His Brothers* (cantata); Igor Stravinsky, *Requiem Canticles*.

**Concertos**    William Bergsma, *Violin Concerto*; John Eaton, *Concert Piece for Syn-ket and Orchestra*; Donald Erb, *Concerto for Percussion and Orchestra*; Lukas Foss, *Concert for Cello, Orchestra and Tape*; Marc Neikrug, *Piano Concerto*; George Perle, *Cello Concerto*; Walter Piston, *Variations for Cello and Orchestra*; Miklós Rózsa, *Piano Concerto*; Francis Thorne, *Piano Concerto No. 1*; David Ward-Steinman, *Cello Concerto*.

**Electronic**    Jacob Druckman, *Animus I* (trombone and tape); John Eaton, *Concert Piece No. 2* (syn-ket); Ilhan Mimaroglu, *Agony*; Gordon Mumma, *Mesa*; Pauline Oliveros, *Big Mother Is Watching You*.

**Operas**    Samuel Barber, *Antony and Cleopatra*; William Flanagan, *The Ice Age* (unfinished); Carlisle Floyd, *Markheim*; Douglas Moore, *Carry Nation*; Thomas Pasatieri, *La Divina—Padrevia*; Gunther Schuller, *The Visitation*; Peter Westergaard, *Mr. and Mrs. Discobolos* (after Lear).

**Orchestra/Band**    Dominick Argento, *S. S. Glencairn* (incidental music); Leonardo Balada, *Guernica*; Earl Brown, *Modules I—Modules II*; Michael Colgrass, *As Quiet As*; Cecil Effinger, *Landscape*; Herbert Elwell, *Symphonic Sketches*; Richard Felciano, *Mutations*; Morton Gould, *Venice* (two orchestras and brass); Lee Hoiby, *After Eden* (ballet); Henri Lazarof, *Structures sonores* (La Scala Award); Jerome Moross, *Variations on a Waltz*; Miklós Rózsa, *Sinfonia Concertante*; Morton Subotnick, *Danton's Death* (incidental music).

**Piano/Organ**    Hugh Aitken, *Piano Fantasy*; Luciano Berio, *Sequenza IV (piano)*; Easley Blackwood, *Symphonic Episode for Organ, Opus 18*; Morton Feldman, *Two Pieces for Three Pianos*; Vivian Fine, *Four Piano Pieces*; Lawrence Moss, *Omaggio I*; Robert Muczynski, *Sonata No. 2, Opus 22*; Ralph Shapey, *Mutations II*.

**Symphonies**    Alan Hovhaness, *Symphony No. 19, Opus 217, "Vishnu"*; Anthony Iannaccone, *Symphony No. 2*; Juan Orrego-Salas, *Symphony No. 4, Opus 59, "Of the Distant Answer"*; Robert Palmer, *Symphony No. 2*; Julia Perry, *Symphony No. 6*; Gunther Schuller, *Concerto for Orchestra I, "Gala Music"*; Roger Sessions, *Symphony No. 6*; Alan Stout, *Symphony No. 2*.

# 1967

❀

## Historical Highlights

President Johnson meets with Russian Premier Kosygin in New Jersey; Thurgood Marshall becomes the first black Supreme Court Justice; the 25th Amendment on vice-presidential appointment is ratified; notable race riots take place in Detroit; Puerto Rico votes to remain a part of the United States Commonwealth.

## World Cultural Highlights

**World Art**    Karel Appel, *Personnage—Angry Landscape;* Anthony Caro, *Deep Body Blue*; Marc

Chagall, *The Blue Village*; Gottfried Honegga, *Volume II;* Joan Miró, *Alicia.*

**World Literature**　Alan Ayckbourn, *Relatively Speaking*; Christopher Isherwood, *Meeting by the River*; Robert K. Massie, *Nicholas and Alexandra*; Gabriel Márquez, *One Hundred Years of Solitude*.

**World Music**　Alberto Ginastera, *Bomarzo*; Hans Werner Henze, *Moralities—Doublebass Concerto*; Krzysztof Penderecki, *Dies Irae (Auschwitz Oratorio)*; Dmitri Shostakovich, *Violin Concerto No. 2*.

**Miscellaneous**　The Fires of London and the London Early Music Consort are founded; the Brighton Music Festivals begin; deaths include Zoltán Kodály, René Magritte, John E. Masefield, André Maurois, and Malcolm Sargent.

## American Art and Literature Highlights

**Births/Deaths**　Deaths include artists Charles Burchfield, Edward Hopper, Ad Reinhardt, and literary figures William R. Burlingame, Elizabeth Daly, Martin Flavin, Langston Hughes, Carson McCullers, Dorothy Parker, Elmer L. Rice, Carl Sandburg, and Nathan Eugene Toomer.

**Art Works**　Leonard Baskin, *Icarus*, Robert Bechtle, *'61 Pontiac*; Roy Lichtenstein, *Modern Painting of Sun's Rays*; Bruce Nauman, *From Hand to Mouth*; Barnett Newman, *Broken Obelisk*; Gene Pelham, *Noi*; Robert Rauschenberg, *Booster*; José de Rivera, *Infinity*; George Segal, *The Restaurant Window*; Tony Smith, *Smoke*, Paul Thek, *The Tomb– Death of a Hippie*; Peter Voulkos, *Pirelli*.

**Literature**　Edward F Albee, *A Delicate Balance* (Pulitzer Prize); Anthony Hecht, *The Hard Hours* (Pulitzer Prize); James Merrill, *Nights and Days* (National Book Award); Marianne Moore, *Complete Poems* (Poetry Society Gold Medal); Harold Pinter, *The Homecoming* (New York Drama Critics' Award); William Styron, *The Confessions of Nat Turner* (Pulitzer Prize); Thornton Wilder, *The Eighth Day* (National Book Award).

## Music—The Vernacular/Commercial Scene

**A. Births**　Harry Connick, Jr. (pianist/composer) September 11; Juliana Hatfield (singer/writer/guitarist) July 27; Timmy T(orres—singer) September 21.

**B. Deaths**　Henry "Red" Allen (trumpeter) April 17; LaVerne Andrews (Andrews Sisters); Jimmy Archey (trombone) November 16; Buster Bailey (clarinetist) April 12; Billy Banks (singer) October 9; John Coltrane (saxophonist) July 17; Ida Cox (singer) November 10; Woody Guthrie (folk singer) October 3; Edmond Hall (clarinetist) February 11; Otis Redding (singer); Stuff Smith (jazz violinist) September 25; "Muggsy" Spanier (cornetist) February 12; Billy Strayhorn (pianist/composer) May 31; Franz Waxman (composer) February 24; Paul Whiteman (bandleader) December 29.

**C. Biographical**

**Performing Groups**　The Band; Blood, Sweat and Tears; Blue Cheer; The Box Tops; Chicago; Clover; Commander Cody and His Lost Planet Airmen; The Commodores; Earth Opera; The Electric Flag; Elephant's Memory; Every Mother's Son; Firesign Theater; Fraternity of Man; Friends of Distinction; Gap Band; J. Geils Band; Golden Dawn; Edwin Hawkins Singers; Here and Now; Hour Glass; Iggy Pop and the Stooges; The James Gang; Joy of Cooking; (H. P.) Lovecraft; Mandrake Memorial; The Meters; Muscle Shoals; Nazz; New York Jazz Sextet (?); NRBQ; Osmosis; Gary Puckett and the Union Gap; REO Speedwagon; The Rockets; Kenny Rogers and the First Edition; Rotary Connection; Sagittarius; Santana; Sly and the Family Stone; Sound Rhythm Section; Spirit; Steppenwolf; Strawberry Alarm Clock; Billy Taylor Jazzmobile; Tower of Power; Paul Winter Consort; Tyrannosaurus Rex; West.

**Miscellaneous**　Tony Bennett performs at the White House for Prime Minister Sato of Japan.

**New Beginnings**　*ASCAP Today*; Association for the Advancement of Creative Musicians (Chicago); Berkeley Jazz Festival; Buddah Records; Country Music Foundation Library and Media Center (Nashville); Festival of American Folklife (Smithsonian Museum); *Guitar Player*

*Magazine*; Master Jazz Recording Co.; Monterey International Pop Festival (California); Presleys' Mountain Music Jubilee Theater (Branson, Missouri); *Rolling Stone*.

**D. Publications**   S. Charters, *The Bluesman: The Story and the Music of the Men Who Made the Blues*; Lucy M. Garrison et al., *Slave Songs of the United States*; L. Jones, *Black Music*; B. Kessel, *The Guitar: A Tutor*; L. Levy, *Grace Notes in American History: Popular Sheet Music from 1820 to 1900*; G. Simon, *The Big Bands*; M. Williams, *Jazz Masters of New Orleans*.

**E. Representative Works**

**Musicals**   E. Bernstein and C. Leigh, *How Now, Dow Jones*; N. Ford and G. Cryer, *Now Is the Time for All Good Men*; Clark Gesner, *You're a Good Man, Charlie Brown*; M. Hadjidakis and J. Darion, *Illya Darling*; G. H. MacDermot, J. Rado, and G. Ragni, *Hair*; Bob Merrill, *Henry, Sweet Henry*; J. Styne, B. Comden, A. Green, *Hallelujah, Baby!* (Tony).

**Number One Hits**   *All You Need Is Love—Hello Goodbye—Penny Lane* (The Beatles); *Daydream Believer* (The Monkees); *Groovin'* (The Young Rascals); *The Happening—Love Is Here and Now You're Gone* (The Supremes); *Happy Together* (The Turtles); *Incense and Peppermints* (Strawberry Alarm Clock); *Kind of a Drag* (The Buckinghams); *The Letter* (The Box Tops); *Light My Fire* (The Doors); *Ode to Billie Joe* (Bobbie Gentry); *Respect* (Aretha Franklin); *Ruby Tuesday* (Rolling Stones); *Something Stupid* (Nancy and Frank Sinatra); *To Sir with Love* (Lulu); *Windy* (The Association).

**Other**   Elmer Bernstein, *Thoroughly Modern Millie* (film score—Oscar); Leslie Bricusse, *Doctor Dolittle* (Oscar for song *Talk to the Animals*); Duke Ellington, *Murder in the Cathedral* (jazz suite); Lalo Schifrin, *Mission Impossible* (theme music).

## Music—The Cultivated/Art Music Scene

**F. Births**   Joshua Bell (violinist) December 9; James Bobrick (baritone) February 6.

**G. Deaths**   Nathan Broder (musicologist) December 16; Hans T. David (German-born musicologist) October 30; Sophie Drinker (musicologist) September 6; Nelson Eddy (baritone) March 6; Mischa Elman (Russian-born violinist) April 5; Geraldine Farrar (soprano) March 11; Elliot Griffes (pianist/composer) June 8; William Kincaid (flutist) March 27; Dorothée Manski (German-born soprano) February 24; Geoffery O'Hara (composer) January 31; James Pease (bass-baritone) April 26; David Poleri (tenor) December 13; Fabien Sevitzky (Russian-born conductor) February 2; Franz Waxman (Polish-born conductor/composer) February 24; Jaromir Weinberger (Czech-born composer) August 8; John W. Work, Jr. (composer/conductor) May 17.

**H. Debuts**

**United States**   Carlos Barbosa-Lima (Brazilian guitarist—tour), Stuart Burrows (British tenor—San Francisco), Guy Chauvet (French tenor—San Francisco), Myung-Wha Chung (Korean cellist—San Francisco), Joseph Kalichstein (Israeli pianist—New York), James Morris (bass-baritone—Baltimore), John Nelson (conductor—New York), Anthony Newman (harpsichordist—New York), Magda Olivero (Italian soprano—Dallas), Erna Spoorenberg (Dutch soprano—New York), Uto Ughi (Italian violinist—New York), Ragnar Ulfung (Norwegian tenor—San Francisco), José Van Dam (Belgian bass-baritone—Santa Fe), Ingvar Wixell (Swedish baritone—Chicago).

**Metropolitan Opera**   Teresa Berganza (Spanish mezzo-soprano), Marie Collier (Australian soprano), Cristina Deutekom (Dutch soprano), Peter Glossop (British conductor), Elisabeth Grümmer (German soprano), Gundula Janowitz (German soprano), Gwendolyn Killebrew (mezzo-soprano), Tom Krause (Finnish baritone), Evelyn Lear (soprano), Jeannette Pilou (Italian soprano), Paul Plishka (bass), Lucia Popp (Czech soprano), Karl Ridderbusch (German bass), Peter Schreier (German tenor).

**Other**   Arleen Augér (soprano—Vienna).

**I. New Positions**

**Conductors**   Thor Johnson (Nashville Symphony Orchestra—to 1975); Edwin McArthur (opera, Eastman—to 1972); Jorge Mester (Louisville Orchestra—to 1980); André Previn (Houston

Symphony Orchestra—to 1969); Zoltán Rozsnyai (San Diego Symphony Orchestra—to 1971); Robert Shaw (Atlanta Symphony Orchestra—to 1988); Paul Vermel (Portland [Maine] Symphony Orchestra—to 1975).

**Educational**   Robert Erickson (UC, San Diego); Richard Felciano (Berkeley); Earl Kim (Harvard); Pauline Oliveros (UC, San Diego—to 1981); Gunther Schuller (president, New England Conservatory—to 1977); Gerald Shapiro (Brown University); Russell Sherman (piano chair, New England Conservatory); Robert Ward (chancellor, North Carolina School of the Arts—to 1972).

**Other**   John S. Edwards (general manager, Chicago Symphony Orchestra—to 1984); Donal Henahan (music critic, *The New York Times*); Lester Trimble (composer-in-residence, New York Philharmonic Orchestra); Arthur Woodbury (editor, *Source*—to 1972).

## J. Honors and Awards

**Honors**   William Bergsma, Gunther Schuller, Robert Ward (National Institute); George Crumb, Donald Martino, and Charles Wuorinen (American Academy); Ross Lee Finney (Brandeis); Douglas Moore (National Arts Club Medal).

**Awards**   Edward Auer (Long-Thibaud); Kyung-Wha Chung (Leventritt Award).

**K. Biographical**   Arleen Augér wins a contest enabling her to go to Vienna where she is accepted by the Opera; Horacio Gutiérrez and Varujan Kojian become American citizens; Byron Janis discovers Chopin's lost *Waltz in G-Flat Major*; Tania León (Cuban pianist/composer) comes to the United States; Alexander Tcherepnin is invited back to the Soviet Union.

## L. Musical Beginnings

**Performing Groups**   Albuquerque Civic Light Opera; Arizona Chamber Orchestra (Tucson); Augusta Opera (Georgia); Bronx Opera Co. (New York); Cincinnati Orchestra Association; Continuum (contemporary music group); New Jersey Symphony Chorus; Edward Tarr Brass Ensemble.

**Festivals**   Indiana State University Contemporary Music Festival; Lincoln Center Summer Festival; Rhode Island Verdi Festival.

**Educational**   Ali Akbar College of Music (San Francisco); Electronic Music Studio, San Francisco State University; Institute for Studies in American Music (Kansas City); International Institute for the String Bass.

**Other**   *American Harp Journal*; American Liszt Society (Baltimore); *American Organist*; Mark Educational Recordings, Inc.; *Music Forum*; Merriweather Post Pavilion of Music (Maryland); Deems Taylor Award (ASCAP).

## M. Music Publications

Apel, Willi, *Geschichte der Orgel- und Klaviermusik*
Benson, Warren, *Creative Projects in Musicianship*
Cross, Lowell, *A Bibliography of Electronic Music*
Fischer, Irwin, *A Handbook of Modal Counterpoint*
Kraft, Leo, *A New Approach to Ear Training*
Rorem, Ned, *Music from Inside Out*
Salzman, Eric, *Twentieth-century Music: An Introduction*
Schonberg, Harold, *The Great Conductors*
Schwartz, E. and Childs, B., *Contemporary Composers on Contemporary Music*
Thomson, Virgil, *Music Reviewed, 1940–1954*
Watanabe, Ruth, *Introduction to Music Research*
Winternitz, Emanuel, *Musical Instruments and Their Symbolism in Western Art*
Yates, Peter B., *Twentieth Century Music*

## N. Musical Compositions

**Chamber Music**   Claus Adam, *String Trio*; Leonardo Balada, *Geometria II*; Leslie Bassett, *Nonet* (woodwinds, brass, and piano); Luciano Berio, *Sequenze VI* (viola); Easley Blackwood, *Piano Trio*,

*Opus 22*; William Bolcom, *Session III—Session IV*; John Eaton, *Vibrations* (flute, 2 oboes tuned a quarter-tone apart); George Edwards, *String Quartet No. 1*; Alvin Etler, *Sonic Sequence for Brass Quintet*; Morton Feldman, *First Principles II*; Vivian Fine, *Quintet* (string quartet, trumpet and piano); Hall Overton, *String Quartet No. 3*; George Perle, *Wind Quintet No. 3*; Seymour Shifrin, *String Quartet No. 4*; Leon Stein, *String Quartet No. 5*; Robert Suderburg, *Chamber Music II*; Randall Thompson, *String Quartet No. 2 in G Major*; Francis Thorne, *String Quartet No. 2*; Stefan Wolpe, *Chamber Piece No. 2*.

**Choral/Vocal**   Samuel Adler, *The Binding* (oratorio); Leonardo Balada, *Three Cervantinas* (song cycle); Vivian Fine, *Epitaph*; William Mayer, *Eve of St. Agnes*; Gian Carlo Menotti, *Canti della lon-tananza* (song cycle); Halsey Stevens, *Campion Suite—Te Deum*; Louise Talma, *A Time to Remember*; Randall Thompson, *A Psalm of Thanksgiving* (cantata).

**Concertos**   Easley Blackwood, *Violin Concerto, Opus 21*; Alvin Etler, *Concerto for Brass Quintet, Strings and Percussion*; Philip Glass, *Violin Concerto*; Marc Neikrug, *Clarinet Concerto*; Robert Parris, *Concerto for Percussion, Violin, Cello and Piano*; Walter Piston, *Clarinet Concerto*; Shulamit Ran, *Symphonic Poem for Piano and Orchestra*; Robert Starer, *Concerto for Violin, Cello and Orchestra*; Burnet Tuthill, *Trombone Concerto*.

**Electronic**   Mario Davidovsky, *Synchronism No. 4*; Richard Felciano, *Glossolalia*; Kenneth Gaburo, *Antiphony IV*; Alvin Lucier, *Whistlers*; Gordon Mumma, *Hornpipe*; Pauline Oliveros, *Beautiful Soop*; Frederic Rzewski, *Impersonation*; Elliott Schwartz, *Elevator Music* (any instrument); Morton Subotnick, *Silver Apples of the Moon* (tape); David Ward-Steinman, *Now Music*.

**Operas**   Dominick Argento, *The Shoemaker's Holiday* (ballad opera); Robert Ashley, *That Morning Thing*; Jonathan Elkus, *The Mandarin*; Ezra Laderman, *Shadows among Us*; Marvin David Levy, *Mourning Becomes Electra*; Roger Nixon, *A Bride Comes to Yellow Sky*; Thomas Pasatieri, *The Penitentes*; Gardner Read, *Villon*; Robert Starer, *Pantagleize*; Eugene Zador, *The Scarlet Mill*.

**Orchestra/Band**   Hugh Aitken, *Partita for Band*; Dominick Argento, *Oresteia* (incidental music); Louis Ballard, *The Four Moons* (ballet); Philip Bezanson, *Capriccio Concertante*; Aaron Copland, *Inscape*; George Crumb, *Echoes of Time and the River* (Pulitzer Prize); David Epstein, *Sonority Variations*; Morton Feldman, *In Search of an Orchestration*; Ross Lee Finney, *Symphonie Concertante*; Carlisle Floyd, *Introductions, Aria and Dance*; Lukas Foss, *Baroque Variations*; Morton Gould, *Vivaldi Gallery*; Lee Hoiby, *Landscape* (ballet); Henri Lazarof, *Mutazione*; Ray Luke, *Orchestra Suite No. 2*; Donald Martino, *Mosaic for Grand Orchestra*; Nicolas Nabokov, *Symphonic Variations*; Gunther Schuller, *Triplum I*; Elie Siegmeister, *Theme and Variations No. 2*; Robert Starer, *Six Variations with Twelve Tones*; Carlos Surinach, *Agathe's Tale* (ballet).

**Piano/Organ**   William Albright, *Organbook I*; Josef Alexander, *Ten Bagatelles*; Mario Castelnuovo-Tedesco, *Introduction, Aria and Fugue* (organ); David Cope, *Sonata No. 4*; Norman Dello Joio, *Five Images* (piano, four hands); Ilhan Mimaroglu, *Twelve Preludes*; Juan Orrego-Salas, *Sonata, Opus 60*; Leo Sowerby, *Passacaglia for Organ*; Robert Stewart, *Variations*.

**Symphonies**   Samuel Adler, *Symphony No. 4, "Geometrics"*; Irwin Bazelon, *Symphony No. 5*; Nicolas Flagello, *Symphony No. 1*; Anis Fuleihan, *Symphony No. 2*; Don Gillis, *Symphony No. 10*; Howard Hanson, *Symphony No. 6*; Roy Harris, *Symphony No. 11*; Ulysses Kay, *Symphony*; Kirke Mechem, *Symphony No. 2*; Nicolas Nabokov, *Symphony No. 3*; Vincent Persichetti, *Symphony No. 8, Opus 106*; Roger Sessions, *Symphony No. 7*.

# 1968

✸

## Historical Highlights

Richard M. Nixon is elected the 37th president; candidate Robert Kennedy is assassinated in Los Angeles and Martin Luther King in Memphis; *Apollo 8* puts the first men in orbit around the moon;

direct airline service begins between the United States and Russia; Korean Peace talks resume in Paris; the Communists crush democratic uprisings in Czechoslovakia.

## World Cultural Highlights

**World Art** Giovanni Anselmo, *Torsione;* Karel Appel, *Donna Cubista;* Mario Mertz, *Lingotto—Unreal City;* Pierre Soulages, *Painting, May 9, 1968.*

**World Literature** Václav Havel, *The Increased Difficulty of Concentration;* Alexander Solzhenitsyn, *The First Circle—Cancer Ward.*

**World Music** Havergal Brian (age 92), *Symphonies No. 31, 32;* Peter Maxwell Davies, *Taverner;* Hans Werner Henze, *The Raft of the Medusa;* Karlheinz Stockhausen, *Aus den Sieben Tagen.*

**Miscellaneous** The Scottish Baroque Ensemble and Saar Radio Chamber Orchestra are founded; the Helsinki Music Festivals begin; deaths include Karl-Birger Blomdahl, Max Brod, Marcel Duchamp, Salvatore Quasimodo, and Alexander Yashin.

## American Art and Literature Highlights

**Births/Deaths** Deaths include artists Douglas Crockwell, Adolf Dehn, and literary figures Witter Bynner, Neal Cassady, Olive Dargan (Fielding Burke), George Dillon, Glenn Dresbach, Edna Ferber, Fannie Hurst, Howard Lindsay, Edwin Greene O'Connor, Conrad Richter, Upton Sinclair, and John Steinbeck.

**Art Works** Herbert Bayer, *Aging Star*, Hans Burkhardt, *Mai Lai;* Walter De Maria, *Earthroom;* Gregory Gillespie, *Doll Child;* Alex Katz, *Ada with a Superb Lily;* Edward Kienholz, *Portable War Memorial;* Lee Krasner, *The Green Fuse;* Seymour Lipton, *Laureate;* Isamu Noguchi, *Red Cube;* George Rickey, *Unstable Cube;* Sheldon C. Schoneberg, *Tambourine;* Andrew Wyeth, *Barn Loft.*

**Literature** Saul Bellow, *Mosby's Memoirs and Other Stories;* Jerzy Kosinski, *Steps* (National Book Award); Norman Mailer, *Armies of the Night* (Pulitzer Prize); N. Scott Momaday, *House Made of Dawn* (Pulitzer Prize); Howard Sackler, *The Great White Hope* (Pulitzer Prize—New York Drama Critics' Award); Neil Simon, *Plaza Suite;* John Updike, *Couples;* Gore Vidal, *Myra Breckenridge.*

## Music—The Vernacular/Commercial Scene

**A. Births** Big Daddy Kane (singer) September 10; Tracy Lawrence (singer) January 27; Shelby Lynne (singer) October 22; Charlie Sexton (guitarist/singer) August 11.

**B. Deaths** James "Kokomo" Arnold (singer/guitarist); Ziggy Elman (trumpeter/bandleader) June 26; Red Foley (singer) September 19; Little Willie John (singer) May 27; George Lewis (clarinetist) December 31; Little Walter (harmonica player) February 15; Frankie Lymon (singer) February 28; Wes Montgomery (guitarist) June 15; Liz Phair (singer); Charles "Lucky" Roberts (pianist/composer) February 5; Willard Robison (singer/writer) June 24.

**C. Biographical**

**Performing Groups** Allman Brothers Band; The Archies; Art Ensemble of Chicago; Brass Construction; Brooklyn Bridge; Cold Blood; The Corvettes; Crosby, Stills, and Nash; The Emotions; Grand Funk (Railroad); Dan Hicks and His Hot Licks; Dr. Hook and the Medicine Show; The Flaming Embers; The Flying Burrito Brothers; The Fourth Way; Herbie Hancock Sextet; It's a Beautiful Day; Mandrill; Chuck Mangione Quartet; Ohio Express; Pacific Gas and Electric; The People; Poco; Project Soul (Con Funk Shun); Redbone; Rhinoceros; Sha Na Na; The Stylistics; Three Dog Night; 360 Degree Music Experience; World's Greatest Jazz Band; Zephyr.

**New Beginnings** Baldknobber's Theater (Branson, Missouri); Black Artists Group (St. Louis); Gospel Music Workshop of America; Hot Wax Records; National Association of Jazz Educators (NAJE); Milwaukee Summerfest; *Rag Times.*

**Honors** Bob Wills (Country Music Hall of Fame).

**D. Publications** Amiri Baraka, *Black Music;* Avril Dankworth, *Jazz: An Introduction to Its Musical Basis;* David Ewen, *Composers for the American Theater;* Alan Lomax, *Folk Song Syle* *and Culture*; Bill C. Malone, *Country Music,USA*; Bill Russo, *Jazz Composition and Orchestration*; Gunther Schuller, *Early Jazz: Its Roots and Musical Development*.

### E. Representative Works

**Musicals**   B. Bacharach and H. David, *Promises, Promises*; George M. Cohan, *George M.* (tribute revue); W. H. Hester and D. Apolinar, *Your Own Thing*; J. Kander and F. Ebb, *Zorba—The Happy Time*; Walter Marks, *Golden Rainbow*; Paul Nassau and Oscar Brand, *Education of H\*Y\*M\*A\*N K\*A\*P\*L\*A\*N*; H. Peretti, L. Creatore, and G. D. Weiss, *Maggie Flynn*; J. Wise and R. Miller, *Dames at Sea*.

**Number One Hits**   *The Dock of the Bay* (Otis Redding); *Grazing in the Grass* (Hugh Masekela); *Green Tambourine* (Lemon Pipers); *Harper Valley P.T.A.* (Jeannie C. Riley); *Hello I Love You* (The Doors); *Hey Jude* (The Beatles); *Honey* (Bobby Goldsboro); *I Heard It Through the Grapevine* (Marvin Gaye); *Judy in Disguise* (John Fred and His Playboy Band); *Love Child* (Diana Ross and the Supremes); *Love Is Blue* (Paul Mauriat); *Mrs. Robinson* (Simon and Garfunkel); *People Got to Be Free* (The Rascals); *This Guy's in Love with You* (Herb Alpert); *Tighten Up* (Archie Bell and the Drells).

**Other**   David Baker, *Black America: To the Memory of Martin Luther King* (jazz cantata); Alan and Marilyn Bergman and Michel Legrand, *The Windmills of Your Mind* (Oscar); Carla Bley, *A Genuine Tong Funeral*; Duke Ellington, *Second Sacred Concert—Latin American Suite*; Jerry Goldsmith, *Planet of the Apes* (film music); Miklós Rózsa, *The Green Berets* (film music); R. M. and R. B. Sherman, *Chitty Chitty Bang Bang* (film music).

## Music—The Cultivated/Art Music Scene

**G. Deaths**   Frank Black (conductor) January 29; Angela Diller (pianist/pedagogue) April 30; Granville English (composer) September 1; Sylvia Kenney (musicologist) October 31; Edward Kilenyi, Sr. (Hungarian-born composer/violinist) August 15; Ray Lev (Russian-born pianist) May 20; Charles Munch (French-born conductor) November 6; Verne Q. Powell (woodwind maker) February 3; Bernard Rogers (composer) May 24; Leo Sowerby (organist) July 7; Fritz Stiedry (Austrian-born conductor) August 9.

### H. Debuts

**United States**   Elly Ameling (Dutch soprano—New York), Kyung-Wha Chung (Korean violinist—New York), Marisa Galvany (soprano—Seattle), Franco Gulli (Italian violinist—Dallas), David Holloway (baritone—Kansas City), Werner Hollweg (German tenor), Aram Khachaturian (Washington, DC, as conductor), David Lively (pianist—St. Louis), Evelyn Mandac (Filipino soprano—Mobile, Alabama), Murray Perahia (pianist—New York), Maurizio Pollini (Italian pianist), Jerzy Semkow (Polish conductor—Boston), Anja Silja (German soprano—Chicago); John Stewart (tenor—Santa Fe).

**Metropolitan Opera**   Giacomo Aragall (Spanish tenor), Fiorenza Cossotto (Italian contralto), Barbra Ericson (Swedish mezzo-soprano), Hildegard Hillebrecht (German soprano), Zoltán Kelemen (Hungarian bass), Edda Moser (German soprano), Luciano Pavarotti (Italian tenor), Anna Reynolds (British mezzo-soprano), Gerhard Stolze (German tenor), Martti Talvela (Finnish bass), Josephine Veasey (British mezzo-soprano), Shirley Verrett (mezzo-soprano), Teresa Zylis-Gara (Polish soprano).

### I. New Positions

**Conductors**   Theo Alcantara (Orchestra, University of Michigan—to 1973); Igor Buketoff (St. Paul Opera—to 1974); Henry Lewis (New Jersey Symphony Orchestra—to 1976); Eve Queler (Opera Orchestra of New York); Kenneth Schermerhorn (Milwaukee Symphony Orchestra—to 1980); José Serebrier (Cleveland Philharmonic Orchestra—to 1971); Walter Susskind (St. Louis Symphony Orchestra—to 1975).

**Educational**   Wayne Barlow (director, Eastman Electronic Studio—to 1974); Jack Beeson (music chair, Columbia University—to 1972); Jorge Bolet (Indiana University—to 1977); Earle Brown (Peabody—to 1973); Richard Franko Goldman (director, Peabody); Ulysses Kay (Lehman College, CUNY); Lili Kraus (Texas Christian University—to 1983); Anthony Newman (Juilliard—to 1973); Rudolf Serkin (director, Curtis Institute—to 1976); Ralph Votapek (Michigan State University); Richard Wernick (University of Pennsylvania); Peter Westergaard (Princeton).

**Other**   John Kirkpatrick (curator, Ives Collection, Yale); Alan Rich (music critic, *New York*—to 1981); José Serebrier (composer-in-residence, Cleveland Symphony Orchestra—to 1970); Lester Trimble (music critic, *Stereo Review*—to 1974).

## J. Honors and Awards

**Honors**   Leonard Bernstein (National Arts Club Medal); John Cage (American Academy and Institute); David Del Tredici, William Flanagan, Ned Rorem, and Francis Thorne (American Academy); Roger Sessions (MacDowell Medal); Leopold Stokowski (Gold Baton); Virgil Thomson (Brandeis); Henry Weinberg (Rome Prize).

**Awards**   Mario Di Bonaventura (Arnold Bax); François Huybrechts (Mitropoulos); Jorge Mester (Naumburg); Jessye Norman (Munich); Garrick Ohlsson (Montreal); John Owings (Liszt); Paula Page (Geneva); Jeffrey Siegel (Queen Elisabeth Third); Michael Tilson Thomas (Koussevitzky).

**K. Biographical**   William Albright enters the Paris Conservatory; Myung-Whun Chung arrives in New York and enters Mannes; Arpad Joó (Hungarian conductor) emigrates to the United States; Jorge Mester becomes an American citizen; Brian Priestman becomes resident conductor of the Baltimore Symphony Orchestra; Samuel Ramey graduates from Wichita State and tours with the Grass Roots Opera Co.; William Schuman suffers a heart attack and resigns from his Lincoln Center post; Roger Sessions gives the Norton lectures at Harvard; Leonard Slatkin becomes assistant to Susskind in St. Louis Symphony Orchestra; Pinchas Zukerman marries flutist Eugenia Rich.

## L. Musical Beginnings

**Performing Groups**   Camerata Symphony Orchestra; Chamber Music Society of Lincoln Center; Cleveland String Quartet; Connecticut String Orchestra; Dayton Contemporary Dance Co.; Philip Glass Ensemble; Houston Civic Symphony Orchestra; Opera Orchestra of New York; Pocket Opera (San Francisco).

**Festivals**   Blossom Music Festival (Ohio); Romantic Music Festival (Indianapolis); Sevenars Summer Music Festival (Worthington, Massachusetts); Waterloo Music Festival (Stanhope, New Jersey).

**Educational**   Ives Oral History Project (Yale).

**Other**   *Asian Music*; Ernest Bloch Society; Blossom Music Center (Cuyahoga Falls, Ohio); John Brombaugh, Organ Builder (Middletown, Ohio); Garden State Arts Center (New Jersey); International Record Critics Awards (IRCA); *The Opera Journal*; Pacific World Artists; People-to-People Music Committee (for international relations); Powell Symphony Hall (St. Louis); San Antonio Theater for the Performing Arts; Santa Fe Opera House; Society of Black Composers.

## M. Music Publications

Ashbrook, William, *The Operas of Puccini*
Balanchine, George, *Balanchine's New Complete Stories of Great Ballets*
Bookspan, Martin, *Masterpieces of Music and Their Composers*
Cone, Edward T., *Musical Form and Musical Performance*
Feldman, Morton, *False Relationships and the Extended Ending*
Foster, William P., *Band Pageantry*
Gaston, E. Thayer, *Music in Therapy*
Hines, Jerome, *This Is My Story, This Is My Song*
Kaufmann, Walter, *The Ragas of North India*
Kerman, Joseph, *History of Art and Music*
Levarie, S. and Lévy, E., *Tone: A Study in Musical Acoustics*
Palisca, Claude, *Baroque Music*
Rorem, Ned, *Music and People*
Taubman, Howard, ed., *The New York Times Guide to Listening Pleasure*

## N. Musical Compositions

**Chamber Music**   David Amram, *Wind Quintet*; Earle Brown, *Event: Synergy II*; Paul Cooper, *Concert for Winds, Percussion and Piano*; David Diamond, *String Quartet No. 10*; Donald Erb, *Three Pieces for Brass Quintet and Piano*; Philip Glass, *Pieces in the Shape of a Square* (two flutes); Karel Husa, *String Quartet No. 3* (Pulitzer Prize); Karl Kohn, *Impromptus* (wind octet);

Ezra Laderman, *Double Helix* (flute, oboe, string quartet); Lawrence Moss, *Exchanges*; Richard Wilson, *String Quartet No. 1*.

**Choral/Vocal**    Samuel Adler, *From Out of Bondage* (cantata); Stephen Albert, *Bacchae—Wolf Time*; Dominick Argento, *A Nation of Cowslips—Letters from Composers* (tenor and guitar); Wayne Barlow, *Wait for the Promise of the Father* (cantata); Luciano Berio, *Sinfonia*; Philip Bezanson, *That Time May Cease and Midnight Never Come*; David Burge, *A Song of Sixpence*; Michael Colgrass, *The Earth's a Baked Apple*; Cecil Effinger, *Paul of Tarsus* (oratorio); Nicolas Flagello, *Te Deum for Mankind*; Ned Rorem, *Some Trees* (song cycle).

**Concertos**    Samuel Adler, *Concerto for Winds, Brass and Percussion*; Easley Blackwood, *Flute Concerto*; John Corigliano, *Piano Concerto*; David Diamond, *Violin Concerto No. 3*; Alvin Etler, *Concerto for String Quartet and Orchestra*; Ross Lee Finney, *Piano Concerto No. 2*; Ezra Laderman, *Flute Concerto, "Celestial Bodies"*; Henri Lazarof, *Cello Concerto*; Robert Moevs, *Concerto grosso* (Stockhausen Prize); Gunther Schuller, *Doublebass Concerto*; Elliott Schwartz, *Magic Music* (piano and orchestra); Leo Smit, *Piano Concerto*; John Verrall, *Viola Concerto*; Robert Ward, *Piano Concerto*.

**Electronic**    Jacob Druckman, *Animus II* (soprano, two percussion, tape); John Eaton, *Duet for Syn-ket and Synthesizer*; Kenneth Gaburo, *Antiphony V* (piano and tape); Steve Reich, *Pendulum Music*; Terry Riley, *A Rainbow in the Curved Air*; Eric Salzman, *Feedback*; Ezra Sims, *McDowell's Fault, or the Tenth Sunday after Trinity*; Morton Subotnick, *Lamination* (orchestra and tape); William Sydeman, *Projections No. 1*; Vladimir Ussachevsky, *Computer Piece No. 1*.

**Operas**    David Amram, *Twelfth Night*; Jean Berger, *Pied Piper* (musical play); Halim El-Dabh, *Black Epic*; Robert Erickson, *Cardenitas 68* (monodrama); Gian Carlo Menotti, *Help, Help, the Globolinks!*; Ned Rorem, *Bertha*; Eric Stokes, *Horspfal*; Virgil Thomson, *Lord Byron*; Hugo Weisgall, *Nine Rivers from Jordan*.

**Orchestra/Band**    Samuel Adler, *City by the Lakes*; Milton Babbitt, *Relata II*; Paul Chihara, *Forest Music*; Karel Husa, *Music for Prague 1968* (band); Beatrice Laufer, *Dialogues*; Robert McBride, *Symphonic Melody*; Thomas Pasatieri, *Invocations*; George Perle, *Serenade No. 2*; H. Owen Reed, *The Turning Mind*; William Schuman, *To Thee, Old Cause*; Robert Starer, *The Lady of the House of Sleep* (ballet); Halsey Stevens, *Threnos: In Memoriam Quincy Porter*.

**Piano/Organ**    William Bolcom, *Garden of Eden Suite*; Richard Felciano, *On the Divine Presence* (organ); Ross Lee Finney, *Thirty-Two Piano Games*; Scott Huston, *Diorama* (organ); Karl Kohn, *Recreations*.

**Symphonies**    Josef Alexander, *Symphony No. 4*; T. J. Anderson, *Chamber Symphony*; Leonardo Balada, *Sinfonia en Negro: Homage to Martin Luther King*; Alan Hovhaness, *Symphony No. 20, Opus 223, "Three Journeys to a Holy Mountain"*; Karl Korte, *Symphony No. 3*; Benjamin Lees, *Symphony No. 3*; Alex North, *Symphony No. 2*; Julia Perry, *Symphony USA*; William Schuman, *Symphony No. 9, "Le Fosse Ardeatine"*; Roger Sessions, *Symphony No. 8*; Lester Trimble, *Symphony No. 2*; John Verrall, *Symphony No. 3*.

# 1969

☀

## Historical Highlights

Neil Armstrong and Edwin Aldrin become the first men on the moon; the My Lai Massacre by American troops comes to light as the United States begins a troop pullout in Vietnam; Strategic Arms Limitations Talks (SALT) begin; Charles de Gaulle resigns and Georges Pompidou becomes French president; the supersonic transport, *Concorde*, makes its first trial flight.

## World Cultural Highlights

**World Art**    Karel Appel, *La Hollandaise;* Fernandez Arman, *Glove Torso;* Georg Baselitz, *Der Wald auf den Kopf;* Anthony Caro, *Piece LXXXII;* Barbara Hepworth, *Maquette for Divided Circle*.

**World Literature**  John Fowles, *The French Lieutenant's Woman*; Seamus Heaney, *Door Into the Dark;* Vladimir Nabokov, *Ada*; Joe Orton, *What the Butler Saw.*

**World Music**  Peter Maxwell Davies' *Eight Songs for a Mad King*; Hans Werner Henze, *Symphony No. 6*; Krzysztof Penderecki, *The Devils of Louduon*; Dmitri Shostakovich, *Symphony No. 14.*

**Miscellaneous**  The Opéra de Lyon is founded in France; deaths include Ernest Ansermet, Salvatore Baccaloni, Wilhelm Backhaus, Otto Dix, Walter Gropius, and Osbert Sitwell.

## American Art and Literature Highlights

**Births/Deaths**  Deaths include art figures Louis Bouché, Thomas Jones, Ben Shahn, and literary figures Cornelia Cannon, Frederick M. Clapp, Grace Crowell, Floyd Dell, Max Eastman, Josephine Herbst, Jack Kerouac, Theodore Pratt, and John Kennedy Toole.

**Art Works**  Ilya Bolotowsky, *Scarlet Diamond*; Louise Bourgeois, *Cumul I*; Alexander Calder, *La Grande Vitesse*; Ron Davis, *Red L*; Jim Dine, *Name Painting*; Helen Frankenthaler, *Commune*; Ellsworth Kelly, *Thirteen Panels: Spectrum V*; Leon Kroll, *Majestic Elms*; Richard Pousette-Dart, *Presence, Red*; George Rickey, *Two Rectangles Gyratory*; Frank Stella, *River of Ponds II.*

**Literature**  John Berryman, *The Dream Songs* (National Book Award—Bollingen Prize); Robin Moore, *The French Connection*; Joyce C. Oates, *Them* (National Book Award); Mario Puzo, *The Godfather*; Philip Roth, *Portnoy's Complaint*; Neil Simon, *Last of the Red Hot Lovers*; Jean Stafford, *Collected Stories* (Pulitzer Prize); Kurt Vonnegut, Jr., *Slaughterhouse Five.*

## Music—The Vernacular/Commercial Scene

**A. Births**  Bobby Brown (singer/writer) February 5; Martika (singer) May 18.

**B. Deaths**  Spade Cooley (fiddler) November 5; Vernon Duke (Vladimir Dukelsky—composer) January 17; Pops Foster (string bass) October 30; Judy Garland (singer/actress) June 22; Leigh Harline (composer) December 18; Coleman Hawkins (saxophonist) May 19; Frank Loesser (librettist/composer) July 26; Ella Logan (singer) May 1; Jimmy McHugh (composer) May 23; William McKinney (drummer/bandleader) October 14; Russ Morgan (trombonist/arranger) August 7; Tony Pastor (bandleader) October 31; "Pee Wee" Russell (clarinetist) February 15; Josh White (singer/guitarist) September 5.

**C. Biographical**

**Performing Groups**  Alabama; Area Code 615; Black Oak Arkansas; Blue Oyster Cult; Bread; Brownsville Station; Cactus; Chairmen of the Board; Crazy Horse; Earth, Wind and Fire; Flash Cadillac and the Continental Kids; Funkadelic; Grand Funk Railroad; Hall and Oates, Rock Duo; The Honey Cone; The Hues Corporation; Lakeside; Lifetime; Little Feat; Love Unlimited; Manhattan Transfer; Mason Profitt; Mountain; New Riders of the Purple Sage; Jimmy Owen Quartet Plus One; Seals and Crofts; The Shaggs; White Trash; Tony Williams Lifetime; ZZ Top.

**New Beginnings**  Altamont Festival; Amos Records; *Creem*; Collective Black Artists; Concord Summer Jazz Festival (California); Hee Haw (television); Jazz Institute of Chicago; Mississippi River Festival (Edwardsville, Illinois); National Academy of Popular Music; New Orleans Jazz and Heritage Festival; Shelter Records.

**Honors**  Gene Autry (Country Music Hall of Fame); Duke Ellington (Medal of Honor).

**Miscellaneous**  Jethro Tull makes its first United States tour; The Woodstock Rock Music Festival takes place in New York.

**D. Publications**  David Baker, *Jazz Improvisation: A Comprehensive Method of Study*; Jimmy Giuffre, *Jazz Phrasing and Interpretation: Aspects of Jazz Performance*; Henry Pleasants, *Serious Music, and All That Jazz*; Lillian Roxon, *Rock Encyclopedia*; Arnold Shaw, *The Rock Revolution*; I. Stambler and G. Landon, *Encyclopedia of Folk, Country and Western Music.*

**E. Representative Works**

**Musicals**  Al Carmines and M. I. Fornes, *Promenade*; S. Edwards and P. Stone, *1776* (New York Drama Critics' Award); J. Herman, J. Lawrence, and R. E. Lee, *Dear World*; A. Previn and A. J. Lerner, *Coco*; H. Schmidt and T. Jones, *Celebration*; Peter Townshend, *Tommy* (rock opera).

**Number One Hits**    *Aquarius/Let the Sunshine In—Wedding Bell Blues* (Fifth Dimension); *Come Together—Something* (The Beatles); *Crimson and Clover* (Tommy James and the Shondells); *Dizzy* (Tommy Roe); *Everyday People* (Sly and the Family Stone); *Get Back* (Beatles with Billy Preston); *Honky Tonk Women* (Rolling Stones); *I Can't Get Next to You* (The Temptations); *In the Year 2525* (Zager and Evans); *Leaving on a Jet Plane* (Peter, Paul, and Mary); *Love Theme, "Romeo and Juliet"* (Henry Mancini); *Na Na Hey Hey Kiss Him Goodbye* (Steam); *Someday We'll Be Together* (Diana Ross and the Supremes); *Sugar, Sugar* (The Archies); *Suspicious Minds* (Elvis Presley).

**Other**    Dave Brubeck, *The Gates of Justice* (oratorio); Mort Stevens, *Hawaii Five-O* (theme music).

## Music—The Cultivated Art/Music Scene

**F. Births**    Tara Noval (violinist) February 6.

**G. Deaths**    Clarence Adler (pianist) December 24; John Brownlee (Australian-born baritone) January 10; Bainbridge Crist (composer) February 7; William Flanagan (composer) August 31; Hazel Harrison (pianist) April 28; Walter Hinrichsen (publisher) July 21; Julius Katchen (pianist) April 29; A. Walter Kramer (critic/publisher) April 8; Arthur Loesser (pianist/author) January 4; Giovanni Martinelli (Italian-born tenor) February 2; Douglas Moore (composer) July 25; Gladys Swarthout (contralto) July 7.

**H. Debuts**

**United States**    Arleen Augér (soprano—New York), Endre Balogh (violinist—Los Angeles), Aldo Ceccato (Italian conductor—Chicago), Christoph von Dohnányi (German conductor—Chicago), Christoph Eschenbach (German pianist—Cleveland), Carole Farley (soprano—New York), Nelson Freire (Brazilian pianist—New York), Miriam Fried (Romanian violinist—New York), Karine Georgian (Russian cellist—New York), Grayson Hirst (tenor—Washington, DC), Ani Kavafian (violinist—New York), Patricia Kern (British soprano—Washington, DC), Raymond Leppard (British conductor/harpsichordist—New York), Johanna Meier (soprano—New York), Carol Neblett (soprano—New York), Margaret Price (British soprano—San Francisco), Nathaniel Rosen (cellist—Los Angeles), Fred Sherry (cellist—New York), Paul Sperry (tenor—New York), Pauline Tinsley (British soprano—Santa Fe), Claire Watson (soprano—New York), Pinchas Zukerman (Israeli violinist—New York).

**Metropolitan Opera**    Theo Adam (German bass-baritone), Karan Armstrong (soprano), Renata Bruson (Italian baritone), Carlo Franci (Italian conductor), Rita Orlandi-Malaspina (Italian soprano).

**Other**    Alice Artzt (guitarist—London), Jessye Norman (soprano—Berlin), Janet Perry (soprano—Linz).

**I. New Positions**

**Conductors**    Sergiu Comissiona (Baltimore Symphony Orchestra—to 1984); Phillip Spurgeon (Phoenix Symphony Orchestra—to 1971); Georg Solti (Chicago Symphony Orchestra—to 1991); William Steinberg (Boston Symphony Orchestra—to 1972); Yuri Krasnapolsky (Omaha Symphony Orchestra—to 1975).

**Educational**    John Harbison (MIT—to 1982); Paul Palombo (Cincinnati Conservatory—to 1978); Mel Powell (California Institute of the Arts); Alfred Reed (University of Miami); Roger Reynolds (UC, San Diego); Phillip Rhodes (University of Louisville); Ray Robinson (president, Westminster Choir College—to 1987); George Schick (president, Manhattan School—to 1976); Morton Subotnick (California Institute of the Arts); Paul Zukofsky (SUNY, Stony Brook).

**Other**    Peter Herman Adler (music/art director, National Educational Television); Louis Ballard (music supervisor, United States Bureau of Indian Affairs); Alice Tully (chairperson, Chamber Music Society of Lincoln Center).

**J. Honors and Awards**

**Honors**    Samuel Adler (doctorate, SMU); Elliott Carter, Jacob Druckman, Nicolas Roussakis, and

Claudio Spies (American Academy); Andrew Imbrie (National Institute); Christopher Keene (Julius Rudel Award); Ernst Krenek (Brandeis); Barbara Kolb (Rome Prize, first American woman to win); Loren Rush (Rome Prize).

**Awards**   William Cochran (Melchior Award); Daniel Heifetz (Merriweather Post Competition); Joseph Kalichstein (Leventritt); Ralph Kirshbaum (Cassadó Competition); Karl Korte (Queen Elisabeth Second); Kathleen Lenski (Paganini Second); Ursula Oppens (Busoni).

**K. Biographical**   Putnam Aldrich retires from teaching; David Amram tours Brazil for the US State Department; T. J. Anderson becomes the first black composer-in-residence for the Atlanta Symphony Orchestra; Theodore Antoniou (Greek composer) emigrates to the United States; Leonard Bernstein is named Conductor Laureate to the New York Philharmonic Orchestra; Carlo Maria Giulini becomes Principal Guest Conductor of the Chicago Symphony Orchestra; George Szell becomes senior guest conductor of the New York Philharmonic Orchestra; Michael Tilson Thomas is recommended by William Steinberg to be assistant conductor of the Boston Symphony Orchestra.

**L. Musical Beginnings**

**Performing Groups**   Berkeley Symphony Orchestra (California); Da Capo Chamber Players (Columbia University); Janus Chorale of New York; Kent Opera Co. (Ohio); Light Opera of Manhattan; Los Angeles Chamber Orchestra; Portland String Quartet (Maine); Rascher Saxophone Quartet; Tokyo String Quartet (New York); Vermeer String Quartet; Western Wind (vocal ensemble).

**Festivals**   New England Bach Festival; Newport Music Festival (Rhode Island); Riemenschneider Bach Institute.

**Other**   Association of Independent Composers and Performers; Gene R. Bedient Organ Co. (Lincoln, Nebraska); Belwin Mills Publishing Co. (by merger); Century II Concert Hall (Wichita, Kansas); Carl Fischer, San Francisco Branch; Judd Concert Artist Bureau (New York); Mother Mallard's Portable Masterpiece Co. (electronic ensemble); Milwaukee Performing Arts Center; National Opera Institute (National Institute for Music Theater); Pearson Electronic Sound Studio (Colorado Springs); Shaw Concerts, Inc.; Alice Tully Hall (Lincoln Center).

**M. Music Publications**

Baron, Samuel, *Chamber Music for Winds*
Berry, W. and Chudacoff, E., *Eighteenth-Century Imitative Counterpoint*
Cage, John, *Notations*
Ewen, David, *Composers Since 1900*
Hitchcock, H. Wiley, *Music in the United States: A Historical Introduction*
Hoover, Cynthia A., *Harpsichords and Clavichords*
Kolodin, Irving, *The Continuity of Music: A History of Influence*
Reed, H.O. and Leach, J., *Scoring for Percussion*
Rich, Alan, *Music: Mirror of the Arts*
Salzer, F. and Schachter, C., *Counterpoint in Composition: The Study of Voice Leading*
Starer, Robert, *Rhythmic Training*
Verrall, John, *Basic Theory of Scales, Modes and Intervals*
Zuckermann, Wolfgang, *The Modern Harpsichord*

**N. Musical Compositions**

**Chamber Music**   Elaine Barkin, *String Quartet*; Warren Benson, *String Quartet*; Luciano Berio, *Sequenze VII* (oboe); Norman Cazden, *Piano Trio*; Alvin Etler, *Clarinet Sonata No. 2*; Philip Glass, *Music in Eight Parts—Music in Fifths—Music in Similar Motion*; John Harbison, *Piano Trio*; Andrew Imbrie, *String Quartet No. 4*; Karl Kohn, *Interlude I* (flute, strings)—*II* (piano, strings); Marc Neikrug, *String Quartet No. 1*; George Perle, *String Quartet No. 6*; Steve Reich, *Four Log Drums*; Paul Turok, *String Quartet No. 2*; Stefan Wolpe, *String Quartet No. 2*; Victor Young, *String Quartet No. 5*.

**Choral/Vocal**    Samuel Adler, *A Whole Bunch of Fun* (secular cantata); David Amram, *Three Songs for America*; T. J. Anderson, *Variations on a Theme by M. B. Tolson*; Leonardo Balada, *Maria Sabina*; Leslie Bassett, *Moon Canticle*; David Del Tredici, *An Alice Symphony*; Ross Lee Finney, *The Remorseless Rush of Time*; Scott Huston, *The Oratorio of Understanding*; Peter Mennin, *Cantata de Virtute: Pied Piper of Hamlin*; Lawrence Moss, *Ariel*; Vincent Persichetti, *The Creation* (oratorio); Phillip Rhodes, *Autumn Setting*; Ned Rorem, *War Scenes* (song cycle); Louise Talma, *The Tolling Bell*; Richard Wernick, *Moonsongs from the Japanese*.

**Concertos**    Esther Ballou, *Konzertstück for Viola and Orchestra*; George Barati, *Baroque Quartet Concerto*; Robert Helps, *Piano Concerto No. 1*; Leo Kraft, *Concerto No. 3 for Cello, Winds and Percussion—Wind Quintet and Percussion*; Ray Luke, *Piano Concerto* (Queen Elisabeth Prize); Vittorio Rieti, *Violin Concerto No. 2*; Ned Rorem, *Piano Concerto in Six Movements*; Halsey Stevens, *Concerto for Clarinet and Strings*.

**Electronic**    Theodore Antoniou, *Events III* (orchestra, tape, slides); Bülent Arel, *Capriccio for TV* (tape); Robert Ashley, *The Wolfman Motorcity Revue* (electronic theater); Leslie Bassett, *Collect*; Jacob Druckman, *Animus III* (clarinet and tape); Robert Erickson, *Pacific Sirens*; Anthony Gnazzo, *Ten Pieces for Pauline Oliveros*; Gordon Mumma, *Beam*; Ezra Sims, *A Frank Overture—Four Dented Interludes and Coda*; Allen Strange, *The Hairbreath Ring Screamers*; Gil Trythall, *The Electric Womb*; Charles Wuorinen, *Time's Encomium* (tape—Pulitzer Prize).

**Operas**    Jack Beeson, *My Heart's in the Highlands*; Thomas Beversdorf, *The Hooligan*; Carlisle Floyd, *Of Mice and Men*; John La Montaine, *Erode, the Greate*; Ned Rorem, *Three Sisters Who Are Not Sisters*; Leo Smit, *The Alchemy of Love*; Frank Wigglesworth, *The Willowdale Handcar*.

**Orchestra/Band**    Leslie Bassett, *Colloquy for Orchestra*; Edward T. Cone, *Variations for Orchestra*; Donald Erb, *The Seventh Trumpet*; Morton Feldman, *On Time and the Instrumental Factor*; Morton Gould, *Soundings*; Leon Kirchner, *Music for Orchestra*; Beatrice Laufer, *Eight Orchestral Vignettes*; Bernard Rands, *Wildtrack 1*; Gunther Schuller, *Shapes and Designs*; William Schuman, *In Praise of Shahn*; Robert Suderburg, *Orchestra Music I*; Robert Washburn, *North Country Sketch*; Peter Westergaard, *Tuckets and Sennets* (band).

**Piano/Organ**    Elaine Barkin, *Six Pieces for Piano*; Arthur Berger, *Five Pieces for Piano*; Gordon Binkerd, *Concert Set for Piano—Piano Miscellany*; Paul Cooper, *Cycles*; Emma Lou Diemer, *Toccata and Fugue* (organ); Philip Glass, *Music in Contrary Motion* (organ); Raoul Pleskow, *Three Bagatelles*; Charles Wuorinen, *Sonata No. 1, Broken Sequences*.

**Symphonies**    Irwin Bazelon, *Symphony No. 6*; Roy Harris, *Symphony No. 12, "Pere Marquette"* (tenor and orchestra); Charles Jones, *Symphony No. 5*; Ezra Laderman, *Symphony No. 2, "Luther"*; Martin Mailman, *Symphony No. 3*; Julia Perry, *Symphony No. 8*; George Rochberg, *Symphony No. 3* (with chorus); Robert Starer, *Symphony No. 3*; Francis Thorne, *Symphony No. 3*.

# 1970

☀

## Historical Highlights

The Census indicates a US population of 203,810,000; Congress passes the Omnibus Crime Control Act; AMTRAK, national rail passenger service, is formed by Congressional action; student riots on Kent State campus bring retaliation by Federal forces; Newark elects the first black mayor of a major United States city; a Soviet spacecraft sends data back from the surface of Venus.

## World Cultural Highlights

**World Art**    Olle Baertling, *Yoyan*; Fernando Botero, *The Coffee Break;* Jorge Castillo, *Jardin de Boissano;* Salvador Dali, *The Hallucinogenic Toreador;* Mario Marini, *Cavallo con Cavaliere*.

**World Literature**    *New English Bible: Old Testament*; Simone de Beauvoir, *The Coming of Age;* Ted Hughes, *Crow;* Tom Stoppard, *After Magritte*.

**World Music**   Benjamin Britten, *Owen Wingrave*; Henri Dutilleux, *Cello Concerto*; Olivier Messiaen, *La Transfiguration*; Krzysztof Penderecki, *Kosmogonia*; Michael Tippett, *The Knot Garden*.

**Miscellaneous**   The Bangkok Opera is founded in Thailand and Opera Rara in London; the Nottingham Music Festival in England and the Kuhmo Festival in Finland begin; deaths include Sir John Barbirolli, E. M. Forster, François Mauriac, and Nelly Sachs.

## American Art and Literature Highlights

**Births/Deaths**   Deaths include art figures Romaine Brooks, Beniamino Bufano, William Johnson, Robert Laurent, Barnett Newman, Waldo Peirce, Henry V. Poor, Mark Rothko, and literary figures Louise Bogan, John Dos Passos, Lorine Niedecker, John H. O'Hara, Erich Maria Remarque, Wilbur D. Steele, Jean S. Untermeyer, and Anzia Yezierska.

**Art Works**   Richard Estes, *Cafeteria*; Nancy Graves, *Bones, Skins, Feathers*; Red Grooms, *Discount Store*; Duane Hanson, *Tourists*; Edward Hicks, *Fugue Rothschild*; Edward Kienholz, *Roxy's*; Henry Moore, *Square Form with Cut*; Isamu Noguchi, *In Stillness Moving*; Larry Rivers, *Black Olympia*; Herbert Shuptrine, *Sea of Snow*; Mark di Suvero, *X Delta*; Andrew Wyeth, *Indian Summer*.

**Literature**   Saul Bellow, *Mr. Sammler's Planet* (National Book Award); Charles Gordone, *No Place to Be Somebody* (Pulitzer Prize); W. S. Merwin, *The Carrier of Ladders* (Pulitzer Prize—rejected); Mona Van Duyn, *To See, To Take* (National Book Award); Paul Zindel, *The Effect of Gamma Rays on Man-in-the-Moon Marigolds* (Pulitzer Prize—New York Drama Critics' Award).

## Music—The Vernacular/Commercial Scene

**A. Births**   Beck (Hansen—songwriter) July 8; Mariah Carey (singer/writer) March 22; Debbie Gibson (singer/writer) August 31; Queen Latifah (Dana Owens—singer/actress) March 18.

**B. Deaths**   Albert Ayler (saxophonist/bandleader) November; Perry "Mule" Bradford (composer/pianist) April 20; Gene Gifford (guitarist/arranger) November 12; L. Wolfe Gilbert (songwriter) July 12; Earl Grant (pianist) June 10; Ray Henderson (composer) December 31; Jimi Hendrix (guitarist/singer) September 18; Johnny Hodges (saxophonist) May 11; Lonnie Johnson (singer/guitarist) June 16; Janis Joplin (singer) October 4; John Jacob Loeb (composer) March 2; Alfred Newman (composer/conductor) February 17; Billy Stewart (singer) January 17; Tammi Terrell (singer) March 16; Charles Tobias (lyricist) July 6; Harry M. Woods (songwriter) January 13.

**C. Biographical**

**Performing Groups**   Aerosmith; Asleep at the Wheel; Chase; Circle; Copperhead; Crabby Appleton; Doobie Brothers; Fanny; Free Movement; Grootna; Heart; Hoo Doo Rhythm Devils; Kansas; M'Boom; Oregon; Rare Earth; The Raspberries; Redeye; The Residents; Boz Scaggs Band; Stoneground; Terry and the Pirates; Undisputed Truth; Wackers; Weather Report; Wiregrass Sacred Harp Singers (Alabama).

**New Beginnings**   Chiaroscuro Record Co. (New York); Creative World Records; *Journal of Country Music*; *Living Blues: The Journal of the American Blues Tradition*.

**Honors**   Duke Ellington (American Academy and Institute); Bill Monroe (Country Music Hall of Fame).

**Miscellaneous**   Elton John tours the United States; Elvis Presley joins Johnny Cash, Peggy Lee, and Pearl Bailey for a concert at the White House.

**D. Publications**   Laurindo Almeida, *Contemporary Moods for Classical Guitar*; David Baker, *Black Music in Our Culture*; David Ewen, *Great Men of American Popular Song*; Paul Oliver, *Aspects of the Blues Tradition*; P. Rivelli and R. Levin, *Giants of Black Music*; Arnold Shaw, *The World of Soul: Black America's Contribution to the Pop Music Scene*; Martin Williams, *The Jazz Tradition*.

**E. Representative Works**

**Musicals**   J. Bock and S. Harnick, *The Rothschilds*; S. Freeman and F. Underwood, *Lovely Ladies, Kind Gentlemen*; L. Grossman and H. Hackady, *Minnie's Boys*; R. Rodgers and M. Charnin, *Two*

*By Two*; S. Sondheim and H. Prince, *Company* (Tony—New York Drama Critics' Award); C. Strouse and L. Adams, *Applause*; G. Geld, P. Udell, and P. Rose, *Purlie*; Various composers, *Oh, Calcutta!*

**Number One Hits**   *ABC—I Want You Back—I'll Be There—The Love You Save* (The Jackson Five); *Ain't No Mountain High Enough* (Diana Ross); *American Woman/No Sugar Tonight* (Guess Who); *Bridge Over Troubled Waters* (Simon and Garfunkel); *(They Long to Be) Close to You* (Carpenters); *Cracklin' Rosie* (Neil Diamond); *Everything Is Beautiful* (Ray Stevens); *I Think I Love You* (Partridge Family); *The Long and Winding Road/For You Blue—Let It Be* (The Beatles); *Make It with You* (Bread); *Mama Told Me (Not to Come)* (Three Dog Night); *My Sweet Lord/Isn't It a Pity* (George Harrison); *Raindrops Keep Fallin' on My Head* (Oscar—B. J. Thomas); *The Tears of a Clown* (Smokey Robinson and the Miracles); *Thank You/Everybody Is a Star* (Sly and the Family Stone); *Venus* (Shocking Blue); *War* (Diana Ross).

**Other**   William Bolcom, *Fourteen Piano Rags*; Ray Copeland, *Classical Jazz Suite in Six Movements*; Duke Ellington, *The River*; Jerry Goldsmith, *Tora! Tora! Tora!* (film music); John Handy II, *Concerto for Jazz Soloist and Orchestra*; Arthur James and Fred Karlin, *For All We Know* (Oscar); Johnny Mandel, *M\*A\*S\*H* (film music); Oliver Nelson, *A Black Suite*.

## Music—The Cultivated Music Scene

**F. Births**   Wendy Fang Cheng (pianist/composer) July 22; Anne Akiko Meyers (violinist).

**G. Deaths**   Mimi Benzell (soprano) December 23; Mary Louise Curtis Bok (art patron) January 4; Saul Caston (conductor/trumpeter) July 28; Ingolf Dahl (Swedish-born composer) August 6; Richard F. Donovan (organist/conductor) August 22; Anis Fuleihan (Cypriot composer/conductor) October 11; Fortune Gallo (impresario) March 28; Hall Johnson (conductor) April 30; Ethel Leginska (British-born pianist) February 26; Estelle Liebling (Swiss-born soprano) September 25; George Frederick McKay (composer) October 4; Jonel Perlea (Romanian-born conductor) July 29; Mishel Piastro (Russian-born violinist) April 10; David Saperton (pianist) July 5; Timothy M. Spelman (composer) August 21; Phil Spitalny (conductor) October 11; Ottilie Sutro (pianist) September 12; George Szell (Hungarian-born conductor) July 29.

**H. Debuts**

**United States**   Joyce Castle (mezzo-soprano—San Francisco), Gabriel Chodos (pianist—New York), Ryland Davies (British tenor—San Francisco), Brigitte Fassbänder (German mezzo-soprano—San Francisco), Daniel Heifetz (violinist—Washington, D.C.), Marie Krebs (German pianist—tour), Joel Krosnick (cellist—New York), Teresa Kubiak (Polish soprano—New York), Yvonne Minton (Australian mezzo-soprano—Chicago), Pandit Pran Nath (Indian composer/performer—New York), Garrick Ohlsson (pianist—New York), Richard Stilwell (baritone—New York), Ruth Welting (soprano—New York).

**Metropolitan Opera**   Judith Blegen (soprano), Helge Brilioth (Swedish tenor), Dominic Cossa (baritone), Gilda Cruz-Romo (Mexican soprano), Enrico di Giuseppe (tenor), Jean Kraft (mezzo-soprano), Giangiacomo Guelfi (Italian baritone), Marilyn Horne (mezzo-soprano), Leopold Ludwig (Austrian conductor), Edith Mathis (Swiss soprano), Ruggero Raimondi (Italian bass), Ursula Schröder-Feinen (German soprano), Frederica Von Stade (mezzo-soprano).

**I. New Positions**

**Conductors**   Anshel Brusilow (Dallas Symphony Orchestra—to 1973); Antal Dorati (National Symphony Orchestra—to 1977); Eduardo Mata (Phoenix Symphony Orchestra); Seiji Ozawa (San Francisco Symphony Orchestra—to 1976); Maurice Peress (Austin Symphony Orchestra—to 1973); Brian Priestman (Denver Symphony Orchestra—to 1978); Thomas Schippers (Cincinnati Symphony Orchestra—to 1977).

**Educational**   Hugh Aitken (music chair, William Paterson College); Leonardo Balada (Carnegie-Mellon); John M. Perkins (music chair, Washington University—to 1975); Max Rudolf (opera, Curtis—to 1973); Joseph Schwantner (Eastman); Russell Smith (University of New Orleans—to 1975); Claudio Spies (Princeton); Frank Wigglesworth (CUNY—to 1976); Olly Wilson (Berkeley); Christian Wolff (Columbia—to 1976); Christoph Wolff (Columbia University).

**Other**   Craig Smith (music director, Emmanuel Church, Boston); Patrick J. Smith (editor, *Musical Newsletter*—to 1977).

## J. Honors and Awards

**Honors**   William Albright and Morton Feldman (American Academy); Milton Babbitt (Brandeis); Lewis Lockwood (Alfred Einstein Award); Peter Mennin (National Arts Club Medal); Nicolas Nabokov (National Institute); Eugene Ormandy (Medal of Freedom); Gunther Schuller (Ditson Award); William Schuman (MacDowell Medal).

**Awards**   Ralph Kirshbaum (Tchaikovsky); Garrick Ohlsson (Chopin); David Perlonga (Rome Prize); Nathaniel Rosen (Piatigorsky).

**K. Biographical**   Emanuel Ax becomes an American citizen and graduates from Columbia with a degree in French; István Kertész is chosen by members of the Cleveland Orchestra as their conductor but the board hires Lorin Maazel; Otto Luening retires from active teaching; Thea Musgrave returns to the United States as a visiting professor in California; Garrick Ohlsson becomes the first American to win the Chopin competition in Warsaw; André Previn marries his third wife, actress Mia Farrow; Steve Reich spends the summer studying drumming at the University of Ghana in Africa; Terry Riley goes to India to study Indian music; Tibor Szász (Romanian pianist) comes to the United States.

## L. Musical Beginnings

**Performing Groups**   Cincinnati Ballet Co.; Cleveland Philharmonia Chorale; Des Moines Ballet Co.; Detroit Youth Orchestra; Manhattan String Quartet; New England Contemporary Music Ensemble; New York Electronic Ensemble; St. Louis Youth Symphony Orchestra; Tanglewood Festival Chorus.

**Other**   ARP Instruments (Newton Highlands, Massachusetts); Council of Creative Artists, Libraries, and Museums; Feedback Studio Verlag, New Cologne; *Music Cataloging Bulletin*; Opera America; Puget Music Publications (Seattle); Quog Music Theater (New York).

## M. Music Publications

Borroff, Edith, *Music of the Baroque*
Cope, David II., *Notes in Discontinuum*
Creston, Paul, *Creative Harmony*
Frankenstein, Alfred, *A Modern Guide to Symphonic Music*
Helm, Everett, *Composer, Performer, Public*
Klaus, Kenneth, *The Romantic Period in Music*
Reimer, Bennett, *A Philosophy of Music Education*
Rorem, Ned, *Critical Affairs* (Deems Taylor Award)
Sessions, Roger, *Questions about Music*
Smith, Julia, ed., *Directory of American Women Composers*
Smith, Patrick J., *The Tenth Muse*
Stevenson, Robert M., *Philosophies of American Music History—Renaissance and Baroque Musical Sources in the Americas*
Talma, L. et al., *Functional Harmony*

## N. Musical Compositions

**Chamber Music**   John Adams, *Piano Quintet*; Hugh Aitken, *Trios for Eleven Instruments*; Milton Babbitt, *String Quartet No. 3—String Quartet No. 4*; Leonardo Balada, *Mosaico* (brass quintet); William Bergsma, *String Quartet No. 4*; Alvin Etler, *Violin Concerto for Seven Instruments*; Morton Feldman, *The Viola in My Life I, II, III—Madame Press Died Last Week at Ninety*; Philip Glass, *Music with Changing Parts*; Barbara Kolb, *Trobar Clus*; John Lessard, *Wind Quintet II*; Joseph Schwantner, *Consortium I*; Lester Trimble, *Panels I*; Charles Wuorinen, *Ringing Changes* (percussion).

**Choral/Vocal**   Leslie Bassett, *Celebration: in Praise of Earth*; John Eaton, *Mass*; George Edwards, *The Captive*; Cecil Effinger, *The Long Dimension*; Howard Hanson, *The Mystic Trumpeter*; Ezra

Laderman, *And David Wept*; Vincent Persichetti, *A Net of Fireflies, Opus 115* (song cycle); Daniel Pinkham, *Ascension Cantata*; Roger Sessions, *When Lilacs Last in the Dooryard Bloom'd* (cantata); Seymour Shifrin, *Chronicles*; Alan Stout, *Nocturne*; William Sydeman, *Maledictions*; Hugo Weisgall, *Fancies and Inventions* (song cycle).

**Concertos**   Samuel Adler, *Organ Concerto*; David Amram, *Triple Concerto* (woodwind quartet, brass quartet, jazz quartet, and orchestra)—*Elegy for Violin and Orchestra*; Wayne Barlow, *Saxophone Concerto* (band); Robert Russell Bennett, *Guitar Concerto*; Easley Blackwood, *Piano Concerto, Opus 24*; Barney Childs, *Clarinet Concerto*; Marvin David Levy, *Piano Concerto*; Witold Lutoslawski, *Cello Concerto*; Gian Carlo Menotti, *Triplo Concerto a tre* (three trios and orchestra); Robert Palmer, *Piano Concerto*; Daniel Pinkham, *Organ Concerto*; Walter Piston, *Fantasia for Violin and Orchestra*.

**Electronic**   Bülent Arel, *Stereo Electronic Music II* (tape); Robert Ashley, *Fancy Free* (electronic theater)—*It's There* (electronic theater); Milton Babbitt, *Phonemena*; Mario Davidovsky, *Synchronisms No. 6* (Pulitzer Prize); Robert Erickson, *Oceans* (trumpet and tape); Richard Felciano, *Soundings for Mozart—Frames and Gestures*; Brian Fennelly, *SUNYATA*; Gordon Mumma, *Conspiracy 8*; Mel Powell, *Cantilena*; Ezra Sims, *Elina's Piece*.

**Operas**   Luciano Berio, *Opera*; Lucia Dlugoszewski, *The Heidi Songs*; Jonathan Elkus, *Helen in Egypt*; Lee Hoiby, *Summer and Smoke*; Ben Johnston, *Carmilla*; Ulysses Kay, *The Capitoline Venus*; Ned Rorem, *Fables* (six short operas).

**Orchestra/Band**   William Albright, *Alliance*; Jean Berger, *Divertissement for Strings*; Alan Hovhaness, *And God Created Great Whales*; Elliott Schwartz, *Island*; Roger Sessions, *Rhapsody for Orchestra*; Frank Wigglesworth, *Three Portraits for Strings*.

**Piano/Organ**   William Bolcom, *Chorale and Prelude on Abide with Me* (organ); Emma Lou Diemer, *Celebration* (organ); Henri Lazarof, *Cadence IV*; Robert Hall Lewis, *Serenade I*; Donald Martino, *Pianississimo*; George Perle, *Suite in C*; Steve Reich, *Four Organs*; Loren Rush, *Soft Music, Hard Music* (three amplified pianos); Howard Swanson, *Sonata No. 2*; Paul Turok, *Three Transcendental Etudes*.

**Symphonies**   Samuel Adler, *Sinfonietta*; Nicolas Flagello, *Symphony No. 2, "Symphony of the Winds"*; Alan Hovhaness, *Symphony No. 21, Opus 234, "Etchmiadzin"*; Andrew Imbrie, *Symphony No. 2—Symphony No. 3* (Hinrichson Award); Ray Luke, *Symphony No. 4*; W. Francis McBeth, *Symphony No. 4*; Julia Perry, *Symphony No. 9*; Vincent Persichetti, *Symphony No. 9, "Sinfonia Janiculum," Opus 113*; Elie Siegmeister, *Symphony No. 4*; Alan Stout, *Symphony No. 4*; Howard Swanson, *Symphony No. 3*; George Tremblay, *Symphony No. 3*.

# 1971

❀

## Historical Highlights

The voting age in the United States is lowered to 18 via the 26th Amendment; *Mariner 9* goes into orbit around Mars; the United States blockade of North Vietnam begins; the United States table tennis team are the first Americans to enter China in almost 20 years; cigarette advertisements are banned from television; the Soviets land two space probes on Mars.

## World Cultural Highlights

**World Art**   Fernando Botero, *The Military Junta*; Jean Dubuffet, *Le Compersé;* Vuillard Vicente, *Afternoon*.

**World Literature**   E. M. Forster, *Maurice* (posthumous publication); Alexander Solzhenitsyn, *August, 1914*; Yevgeny Yevtushenko, *Stolen Apples*.

**World Music**   Alberto Ginastera, *Beatrix Cenci*; Vagn Holmboe, *Symphony No. 10*; Krzysztof Penderecki, *Utrenja*; Edmund Rubbra, *Symphony No. 8*; Dmitri Shostakovich, *Symphony No. 15*.

**Miscellaneous**   The Banff Festival of the Arts is founded; the Mexican State Symphony Orchestra is founded; Chilean poet Pablo Neruda receives the Nobel Prize for literature; deaths include Margarethe Arndt-Ober, Thurston Dart, Marcel Dupré, and George Seferis.

## American Art and Literature Highlights

**Deaths**   Deaths include art figures Rockwell Kent, Karl Knaths, Henry Mattson, Irene Pereira, George Picken, and literary figures Archie Binns, Harvey Fergusson, Helen Hull, Manfred Lee (Ellery Queen), Ogden Nash, James R. Ullman, and Philip G. Wylie.

**Art Works**   Ilya Bolotowsky, *Vibrant Red*; Robert Cottingham, *ART*; Duane Hanson, *Lady at Table*; Al Held, *The Albany Mural*; Robert Indiana, *LOVE*; Luis Jimenez, *Barfly*; Roy Lichtenstein, *Mirror No. 3*; Malcolm Morley, *Los Angeles Yellow Pages*; Ed Moses, *Indian Blanket Series*; Jack Tworkov, *Partitions*; Tom Wesselman, *Big Brown Nude*; Dalhart Windberg, *Sand Dunes*.

**Literature**   John Guare, *The House of Blue Leaves* (New York Drama Critics' Award); Jerzy Kosinski, *Being There*; Howard Moss, *Selected Poems* (National Book Award); Flannery O'Connor, *The Complete Stories* (National Book Award); Irving Stone, *Passions of the Mind*; John Updike, *Rabbit Redux*; Joseph Wambaugh, *The New Centurions*; Herman Wouk, *The Winds of War*.

## Music — The Vernacular/Commercial Scene

**A. Births**   Mary J. Blige (singer) January 11; Tiffany (Darwish—singer) October 2; Alison Krauss (fiddler) July 23.

**B. Deaths**   Lil Armstrong (pianist/singer) August 27; Louis Armstrong (trumpeter/bandleader) July 6; Edward "Zez" Confrey (pianist) November 22; King Curtis (saxophonist) August 13; Ted Fiorito (bandleader) July 22; Lennie Hayton (pianist) April 24; Bob Hilliard (lyricist) February 1; Joe Jordan (pianist/arranger) September 11; Wynton Kelly (pianist) April 12; Ted Lewis (clarinetist/bandleader) August 25; Jim Morrison (singer) July 3; Junior Parker (harmonica player/singer) November 18; Ben Pollack (drummer/bandleader) June 7; Charlie Shavers (trumpeter) July 8; Arthur Smith (violinist) February 28; Max Steiner (composer) December 28; Joe Sullivan (pianist/writer) October 13; Gene Vincent (singer/writer) October 12.

**C. Biographical**

**Performing Groups**   Air; Ambrosia; Atlanta Rhythm Section; Big Star; Climax; Charlie Daniel's Band; Country Gazette; The Eagles; Jo Jo Gunne; Herbie Hancock Sextet; Mahavishnu Orchestra; Manassas; New Black Eagle Jazz Band; New York Dolls; The Ozark Mountain Daredevils; Pure Prairie League; Return to Forever; Revolutionary Ensemble; Seldom Scene; Sparks; A Taste of Honey; Marshall Tucker Country/Rock Band.

**New Beginnings**   Alligator Records (Chicago); Black Jazz Record Co. (Glenview, Illinois); Philo International Records; *Popular Music and Society*.

**D. Publications**   D. Baker, *Techniques of Improvisation*; W. Balliett, *Ecstasy at the Onion*; Rudi Blesh, *Combo: USA: Eight Lives in Jazz*; Tony Heilbut, *The Gospel Sound: Good News and Bad Times*; Lester Levy, *Flashes of Merriment: a Century of Humorous Songs in America*; R. J. Martinez, *Portraits of New Orleans Jazz: Its People and Places*; John Rublowsky, *Black Music in America*; Arnold Shaw, *The Street That Never Slept: New York's Fabled 52nd Street*.

**E. Representative Works**

**Musicals**   Andrew Lloyd Webber, *Jesus Christ, Superstar* (United States premiere); G. H. MacDermot and J. Guare, *Two Gentlemen of Verona*; J. Kander and F. Ebb, *70, Girls, 70*; Skip Redwine and Larry Franks, *Frank Merriwell (or Honor Challenged)*; Claiborne F. Richardson, *The Grass Harp*; Stephen L. Schwartz, *Godspell*; Stephen Sondheim, *Follies* (New York Drama Critics' Award).

**Number One Hits**   *Brand New Key* (Melanie); *Brown Sugar* (Rolling Stones); *Family Affair* (Sly and the Family Stone); *Go Away Little Girl* (Donny Osmond); *Gypsys, Tramps and Thieves* (Cher); *How Do You Mend a Broken Heart?* (Bee Gees); *Indian Reservation* (The Raiders); *It's Too Late/I Feel the Earth Move* (Carole King); *Joy to the World* (Three Dog Night); *Just My Imagination* (The

Temptations); *Knock Three Times* (Dawn); *Maggie May/Reason to Believe* (Rod Stewart); *Me and Bobby McGee* (Janis Joplin); *One Bad Apple* (The Osmonds); *Theme from "Shaft"* (Oscar—Isaac Hayes); *Uncle Albert/Admiral Halsey* (Paul and Linda McCartney); *Want Ads* (The Honey Cone); *You've Got a Friend* (James Taylor).

**Other**   Dave Brubeck, *Truth Is Fallen*; Neil Diamond, *African Trilogy*; Duke Ellington, *Afro-Eurasian Eclipse* (jazz suite)—*New Orleans Suite*; Jerry Goldsmith, *The Mephisto Waltz* (film music); John LaMontaine, *Invocation for Jazz Band*.

## Music—The Cultivated Art/Music Scene

**F. Births**   Gil Shaham (violinist).

**G. Deaths**   Edward Ballantine (composer) July 2; Mark Brunswick (composer) May 26; Fausto Cleva (Italian-born conductor) August 6; Mabel Wheeler Daniels (composer) March 10; Arnold Elston (composer) June 6; Ethel G. Hier (pianist/composer) January 14; Julius Huehn (baritone) June 8; Alton Jones (pianist) January 2; Karl L. King (bandmaster/composer) March 31; Pierre Luboshutz (Russian-born pianist) April 17; William Mitchell (musicologist) August 17; Leroy Robertson (composer) July 25; Carl Ruggles (composer) October 24; Igor Stravinsky (Russian-born composer) April 6; Bernard Wagenaar (Dutch-born composer/conductor) May 19; Herbert Weinstock (musicologist) October 21; Adolph Weiss (composer) February 21.

**H. Debuts**

**United States**   Douglas Ahlstedt (tenor—San Francisco), Endre Balogh (pianist—New York), Agnes Baltsa (Greek mezzo-soprano—Houston), Viorica Cortez (Romanian mezzo-soprano—Seattle), Claudia Cummings (soprano—San Francisco), Robert Dennison (pianist—Philadelphia), Helga Dernesch (Austrian soprano—Chicago), Helen Donath (soprano—San Francisco), Zoltán Kocsis (Hungarian pianist—tour), Barbara Nissman (pianist—Philadelphia), Cristina Ortiz (Brazilian pianist—New York), Kun-Woo Paik (Korean pianist—New York), Harvey Pittel (saxophonist—Boston), Kiri Te Kanawa (New Zealand soprano—Santa Fe), Eugenia Zukerman (flutist—New York).

**Metropolitan Opera**   Jeannine Altmeyer (soprano), Stuart Burrows (British tenor), Gerd Feldhoff (German baritone), Leo Goeke (tenor), Benno Kusche (German bass-baritone), James Levine (conductor), Catarina Ligendza (Swedish soprano), Adriana Maliponte (Italian soprano), James Morris (bass-baritone), John Pritchard (British conductor), Arlene Saunders (soprano).

**I. New Positions**

**Conductors**   Pierre Boulez (New York Philharmonic Orchestra—to 1977); Harold Farberman (Oakland Symphony Orchestra—to 1979); Lawrence Foster (Houston Symphony Orchestra—to 1978); Skitch Henderson (Tulsa Philharmonic Orchestra—to 1974); Jorge Mester (Kansas City Philharmonic Orchestra—to 1974); Frederik Prausnitz (Syracuse Symphony Orchestra—to 1974); Michael Tilson Thomas (Buffalo Philharmonic Orchestra—to 1979).

**Educational**   Bülent Arel (SUNY, Stony Brook); Emma Lou Diemer (UC, Santa Barbara); Paul Doktor (Juilliard); John Eaton (Indiana University); H. Wiley Hitchcock (Brooklyn College); Anthony Iannaccone (Eastman); Karl Korte (University of Texas); Louis Krasner (New England Conservatory); Ezra Laderman (SUNY, Binghamton—to 1982); Harvey Phillips (Indiana University); Terry Riley (Mills College—to 1980); Charles Rosen (SUNY, Stony Brook); Eleanor Steber (voice, Juilliard); Lester Trimble (Juilliard).

**Other**   Rhys Chatham (music director, New York Kitchen); Charles Dodge (president, American Composers Alliance—to 1975).

**J. Honors and Awards**

**Honors**   Maurice Abravanel (Ditson); Elliott Carter (American Academy Gold Medal); Barbara Hendricks (soprano—Geneva); Sydney Hodkinson, Fred Lerdahl, and Roger Reynolds (American Academy); Earl Kim (Brandeis); Louis Lane (Mahler Medal); Eugene O'Brien (Rome Prize);

Harold C. Schonberg (Pulitzer for Music Criticism); William Schuman (MacDowell Medal); William Grant Still (doctorate, University of Arkansas); Michael Tilson Thomas (*Musical America* Musician of the Year); Ben Weber (National Institute).

**Awards**  Myung-Wha Chung (Geneva); Ani Kavafian (Naumburg); Diane Walsh (Kapell Second); Mark Westcott (Kapell First).

**K. Biographical**  Kathleen Battle, graduating from Cincinnati Conservatory, begins teaching in grade school; Myung-Wha Chung becomes an American citizen; Lynn Harrell leaves the Cleveland Symphony Orchestra and begins a solo career; Margaret Harris becomes the first black woman to conduct a major orchestra (Chicago Symphony Orchestra); Wiktor Labunski retires from teaching; Darius Milhaud resigns his teaching at Mills College because of the increasing severity of his arthritis; Thea Musgrave marries American violinist Peter Mark; William D. Revelli retires from teaching; Klaus Tennstedt has his passport wrongly stamped by a Russian official and chooses to stay in the West.

**L. Musical Beginnings**

**Performing Groups**  Annapolis Brass Quintet; Arizona Opera Co. (Phoenix); Concord String Orchestra (New Hampshire); Empire Brass Quintet (Berkshire); Houston Pops Orchestra; Michigan Opera Theater; Opera/South (Jackson, Mississippi); Philadelphia Singers; Norman Scribner Choir (Washington, DC); Speculum Musicae (New York).

**Festivals**  Chamber Music Northwest Festival (Portland, Oregon); Festival-Institute at Round Top (Texas).

**Educational**  Center for Music Experiment, University of California, San Diego; Institute for Studies in American Music (Brooklyn College, New York).

**Other**  American Musical Instrument Society (New York); *American Musical Instrument*; Greater Hartford Arts Council; John F. Kennedy Center for the Performing Arts (DC); Kirana Center for Indian Classical Music (New York); The Kitchen (New York); Music Hall of the Tucson Community Center; Music of the Baroque (Chicago); Power Center for the Performing Arts (University of Michigan); Répertoire International d'Iconographie Musicale; The Leo Sowerby Society; Wolftrap Farm Park for the Performing Arts (Vienna, Virginia).

**M. Music Publications**

Adler, Samuel, *Anthology for the Teaching of Choral Conducting*
Ballou, Esther, *Creative Explorations of Musical Elements*
Borroff, Edith, *Music in Europe and the United States: A History*
Cope, David, *New Directions in Music*
Harrison, Lou, *Music Primer*
Hood, Mantle, *The Ethnomusicologist*
Hoover, Cynthia A., *Music Machines: American Style*
Krohn, Ernst C., *Missouri Music*
Lawrence, Robert, *A Rage for Opera*
Peyser, Joan, *The New Music: The Sense behind the Sound*
Southern, Eileen, *The Music of Black Americans*
Thomson, Virgil, *American Music Since 1910*

**N. Musical Compositions**

**Chamber Music**  Samuel Adler, *Histrionics*; Stephen Albert, *Cathedral Music*; Theodore Antoniou, *Cheironomiai*; Leslie Bassett, *Sextet for Piano, Viola and String Quartet*; Elliott Carter, *String Quartet No. 3* (Pulitzer Prize); Paul Chihara, *Ceremony I*; Aaron Copland, *Threnody I (Igor Stravinsky: In Memoriam)*; John Eaton, *Sonority Movement* (flute and nine harps)—*Piano Trio: in Memoriam Mario Cristini*; George Edwards, *Kreuz und Quer*; David Epstein, *String Quartet No. 2*; Donald Erb, *Fanfare for Brass and Percussion*; Arthur Frackenpohl, *String Quartet*; Steve Reich, *Drumming*; Joseph Schwantner, *Consortium II*; Charles Wuorinen, *String Quartet No. 1*.

**Choral/Vocal**  Ernst Bacon, *Requiem, "The Last Invocation"*; Samuel Barber, *The Lovers, Opus*

*43*; Leonard Bernstein, *Mass* (theater piece); David Del Tredici, *Adventures Underground*; Morton Feldman, *Chorus and Orchestra I*; Vivian Fine, *Sounds of the Nightingale*; Alexei Haieff, *Caligula* (baritone and orchestra); John Harbison, *Five Songs of Experience* (after Blake); Jean Eichelberger Ivey, *Three Songs of the Night*; Thomas Pasatieri, *Heloise and Abelard* (song cycle); Ned Rorem, *Ariel* (song cycle); William Schuman, *Declaration Chorale—Mail Order Madrigals*; Richard Wernick, *A Prayer for Jerusalem* (Naumburg Recording Prize).

**Concertos**   David Amram, *Bassoon Concerto*; Warren Benson, *Horn Concerto*; Morton Feldman, *The Viola in My Life IV*; William Mayer, *Octagon* (piano and orchestra); Walter Piston, *Flute Concerto*; André Previn, *Guitar Concerto*; Shulamit Ran, *Concertpiece for Piano and Orchestra*; Miklós Rózsa, *Cello Concerto*; Roger Sessions, *Concerto for Cello, Violin and Orchestra*.

**Electronic**   Luciano Berio, *Memory for Electric Piano and Electric Harpsichord*; Kenneth Gaburo, *Antiphony VI*; Priscilla McLean, *Spectra I*; Allen Strange, *Switchcraft*; Morton Subotnick, *Sidewinder* (tape); Vladimir Ussachevsky, *Conflict*; David Ward-Steinman, *Kaleidoscope—Vega*.

**Operas**   Samuel Adler, *The Wrestler* (biblical opera); Dominick Argento, *Postcard from Morocco*; Thomas Beversdorf, *Vision of Christ* (mystery play); John Eaton, *Myshkin* (Peabody and Ohio State Awards); Halim El-Dabh, *Opera Flies*; Harold Farberman, *The Losers*; Gian Carlo Menotti, *The Most Important Man*; Thomas Pasatieri, *Calvary*.

**Orchestra/Band**   Stephen Albert, *Leaves from the Golden Notebook*; T. J. Anderson, *Intervals*; Wayne Barlow, *Hampton Beach Overture*; William Bergsma, *Changes*; Philip Bezanson, *Sinfonia Concertante*; Gordon Binkerd, *A Part of Heaven*; William Bolcom, *Commedia for Chamber Orchestra*; Ross Lee Finney, *Spaces*; Carlisle Floyd, *Overture, In Celebration*; Alexander Tcherepnin, *Russian Sketches, Opus 106*; Charles Wuorinen, *Grand Bamboula* (strings); Ramon Zupko, *Radiants*.

**Piano/Organ**   William Albright, *Organbook II*; T. J. Anderson, *Watermelon*; William Bolcom, *Hydraulis* (organ); Norman Dello Joio, *Lyric Pieces*; Jacob Druckman, *Synapse*; Hall Overton, *Polarities No. 2*; Leo Ornstein, *Some New York Scenes—A Morning in the Woods*; George Perle, *Six Etudes*; Vincent Persichetti, *Parable VI, Opus 117* (organ); George Rochberg, *Carnival Music*.

**Symphonies**   Samuel Adler, *Concerto for Orchestra*; Paul Cooper, *Symphony No. 3 for Strings*; Alan Hovhaness, *Symphony No. 22, Opus 236, "City of Light"*; Robert Hall Lewis, *Symphony No. 2*; Nikolai Lopatnikoff, *Symphony No. 4, Opus 46*; Alex North, *Symphony No. 3*; David Van Vactor, *Symphony No. 4, "Walden"* (with chorus); Elinor Warren, *Symphony in One Movement*.

# 1972

✿

## Historical Highlights

Richard M. Nixon is re-elected president and makes a successful visit to Red China; the Watergate Affair begins when five men are arrested for breaking into the Democratic headquarters in Washington, DC; the Selective Service comes to an end; Georgia governor George Wallace is shot while campaigning for president.

## World Cultural Highlights

**World Art**   Fernando Botero, *Fruit Basket*; Sergio de Camargo, *Carrara Marble Piece;* Willem de Kooning, *The Clam Digger*; Paul De Vree, *Lady Chatterley;* Meret Oppenheim, *Le Secret de la Végétation*.

**World Literature**   Chinua Achebe, *Girls at War;* Margaret Drabble, *The Needle's Eye*; James Herriot, *All Creatures Great and Small*; Ted Hughes, *Selected Poems: 1957–1967*.

**World Music**   Luigi Nono, *Piano Concerto No. 1*; Andrzej Panufnik, *Violin Concerto*; Krzysztof Penderecki, *Cello Concerto*; Rodion Shchedrin, *Anna Karenina*; Michael Tippett, *Symphony No. 3*.

**Miscellaneous**   The National Conservatory of Music opens in Venezuela; the Wiener Urtext Editions are founded in Austria; German author Heinrich Böll receives the Nobel Prize for literature; deaths include Havergal Brian, Dino Buzzati, Robert Casadesus, Jules Romain, and Stefan Wolpe.

## American Art and Literature Highlights

**Births/Deaths**   Deaths include art figures Joseph Cornell, Fritz Glarner, Hobson Pittman, Karl Zerbe, and literary figures Sally Benson, John Berryman, Padraic Colum, Jean Garrigue, Paul Goodman, Ruth McKenney, Marianne Moore, Kenneth Patchen, Ezra Pound, Betty Smith, Mark Van Doren, and Edmund Wilson.

**Art Works**   Jack Beal, *Danae*; Ilya Bolotowsky, *Diamond with Yellow and Orange*; Jean Dubuffet, *Group of Four Trees*; David Hockney, *Panama Hat*; Alex Katz, *Face of a Poet*; Lee Krasner, *Rising Green*; Mauricio Lasansky, *Quetzalcoatl*; Roy Lichtenstein, *Still Life with Goldfish*; Georgia O'Keeffe, *Black Rock, Blue Sky*; Charles Simonds, *People Who Live in a Circle*.

**Literature**   A. R. Ammons, *Collected Poems* (National Book Award); John Barth, *Chimera* (National Book Award); Maxine Kumin, *Up Country* (Pulitzer Prize); Ira Levin, *The Stepford Wives*; Jason Miller, *That Championship Season* (Pulitzer Prize—New York Drama Critics' Award); Wallace Stegner, *Angle of Repose* (Pulitzer Prize); Eudora Welty, *The Optimist's Daughter* (Pulitzer Prize).

## Music — The Vernacular/Commercial Scene

**B. Deaths**   May Aufderheide (composer) September 1; Gene Austin (singer) January 24; Lovie Austin (pianist) July 10; Phil Baxter (composer/bandleader) November 2; Big Maybelle (singer) January 23; Don Byas (saxophonist) August 24; Gary Davis (guitarist/singer) May 5; Robert E. Dolan (composer/arranger) September 26; Mississippi Fred Dowell (singer) July 3; Rudolf Friml (composer) November 12; Mahalia Jackson (singer) January 27; Bill Johnson (string bassist) December 3; Clyde McPhatter (singer) June 13; Tony Parenti (clarinetist/saxophonist) April 17; Harry Richman (composer/singer) November 3; Jimmy Rushing (singer) June 8; T. Texas Tyler (singer) January 28.

**C. Biographical**

**Performing Groups**   B. T. Express; John Cafferty and the Beaver Brown Band; Captain Beyond; Devo; The Droogs; Graham Central Station; Harlem Blues and Jazz Band; Hot Tuna; Kansas; Kiss; The Motels; New England Conservatory Ragtime Ensemble; Orleans; Paraphernalia; Petra; Shadowfax; Starcastle; Steely Dan; Suicide; Stories; Supersax; Tierra; Tipica 73; The Tubes; Wizzard.

**New Beginnings**   Ann Arbor Jazz and Blues Festival; *Bim, Bam, Boom: The Magazine Devoted to the History of Rhythm and Blues*; Bix Beiderbecke Memorial Jazz Festival; Eubie Blake Music, Publishing and Recording Co.; *Country Music*; *Music Yearbook*; New York Jazz Musician's Festival; Northwest Regional Folklife Festival (Seattle); Anita O'Day (Emily) Records; Texas Folklife Festival (San Antonio).

**Honors**   Jimmie Davis (Country Music Hall of Fame).

**Miscellaneous**   Cleo Laine comes to the United States.

**D. Publications**   Alan Dawson, *Blues and Old Time Signatures*; Don Ellis, *The New Rhythm Book*; Edward Lee, *Jazz: An Introduction*; Charles Nanry, ed., *American Music from Storyville to Woodstock*; J. M. Schwartz, *The Incompleat Folksinger*; Ian Whitcomb, *After the Ball: Pop Music from Rag to Rock*; A. Wilder and J. T. Maher, *American Popular Song: The Great Innovators*.

**E. Representative Works**

**Musicals**   Micki Grant, *Don't Bother Me I Can't Cope*; J. H. Jacobs and W. Casey, *Grease*; G. MacDermot and Gore, *Via Galactica*; S. Schwartz and R. O. Hirson, *Pippin*; C. Strouse and L. Adams, *I and Albert*; J. Styne and B. Merrill, *Sugar*.

**Number One Hits**   *Alone Again* (Gilbert O'Sullivan); *American Pie* (Don McLean); *Baby Don't Get Hooked On Me* (Mac Davis); *Ben* (Michael Jackson); *Black and White* (Three Dog Night); *Brandy* (Looking Glass); *Candy Man* (Sammy Davis, Jr.); *The First Time Ever I Saw Your Face* (Roberta Flack); *Heart of Gold* (Neil Young); *A Horse with No Name* (America); *I Am Woman* (Helen Reddy); *I Can See Clearly Now* (Johnny Nash); *I'll Take You There* (The Staple Singers); *Lean On Me* (Bill Withers); *Let's Stay Together* (Al Green); *Me and Mrs. Jones* (Billy Paul); *My Ding-a-Ling* (Chuck Berry); *Oh Girl* (The Chi-Lites); *Papa Was a Rollin' Stone* (The Temptations); *Song Sung Blue* (Neil Diamond); *Without You* (Nilsson).

**Other**   T. J. Anderson, *Swing Set*; Al Kasha and Joel Hirschorn, *The Poseidon Adventure* (film music—Oscar for song *The Morning After*).

## Music—The Cultivated Art/Music Scene

**G. Deaths**   Howard Barlow (conductor) January 31; Seth Bingham (organist/composer) June 21; John Chance (composer) August 16; Lucile Crews (composer) November 3; Richard Crooks (tenor) September 29; Cliff Edwards (singer) July 18; Maurice Eisenberg (cellist) December 13; Richard Ellsasser (organist) August 9; Rudolf Granz (Swiss-born pianist) August 2; Vladimir Golschmann (Russian-born conductor) March 1; Ferde Grofé (arranger/composer) April 3; Hugo Kauder (Austrian-born composer) July 22; Margaret Ruthven Lang (composer) May 29 (age 104); Oscar Levant (pianist/author) August 14; Jean Madeira (mezzo-soprano) July 10; Paul Nettl (Czech-born musicologist) January 8; Hall Overton (composer) November 24; Michael Rabin (violinist) January 19; Alexander Smallens (Russian-born conductor) November 24; Helen Traubel (soprano) July 28; Robert Weede (baritone) July 9; Stefan Wolpe (German-born composer) April 4.

**H. Debuts**

**United States**   Irina Arkhipova (Russian mezzo-soprano—San Francisco), Teresa Mary Cahill (British soprano—Santa Fe), José Carreras (Spanish tenor—New York), Robert Davidovici (Romanian violinist—New York), Miklós Erdély (Hungarian conductor—San Antonio), Julie Hamari (Hungarian mezzo-soprano—Chicago), Pamela Hebert (soprano—New York), Anne Howells (British mezzo-soprano—Chicago), David Kuebler (tenor—Santa Fe), Berit Lindholm (Swedish soprano—San Francisco), Jesús López-Cobos (Spanish conductor—San Francisco), Radu Lupu (Romanian pianist—Cleveland), Catherine Malfitano (soprano—Colorado), Leona Mitchell (soprano—San Francisco), Kathryn Montgomery (soprano—Bloomington, Indianapolis), Riccardo Muti (Italian conductor—Philadelphia), Wieslaw Ochman (Polish tenor—Chicago), Katia Ricciarelli (Italian soprano—Chicago), Faye Robinson (soprano—New York), Neil Rosensheim (tenor—Florida), Steffan Scheja (Swedish pianist—New York), Ellen Shade (soprano—Pittsburgh), Peter Strummer (Austrian bass-baritone—Atlanta), Richard Vernon (bass—Memphis), Sandra Walker (mezzo-soprano—San Francisco), Carol Wincenc (flutist—New York), Susan Davenny Wyner (soprano—New York).

**Metropolitan Opera**   Peter Herman Adler (conductor), Christoph von Dohnányi (German conductor), Rita Hunter (British soprano), Gwyneth Jones (British soprano), Peter Maag (Swiss conductor), Barry McDaniel (baritone), Gustav Neidlinger (German bass-baritone), Louis Quilico (Canadian baritone), Anja Silja (German soprano), Hans Sotin (German bass), Roger Soyer (French bass), Ragnar Ulfung (Norwegian tenor), Christine Weidinger (soprano).

**Other**   Kathleen Battle (soprano—Spoleto).

**I. New Positions**

**Conductors**   Dennis Russell Davies (St. Paul Chamber Orchestra); Peter Erös (San Diego Symphony Orchestra—to 1980); Dale Harpham (United States Marine Band—to 1974); François Huybrechts (Wichita Symphony Orchestra—to 1977); Daniel Lewis (Pasadena Symphony Orchestra—to 1983); Lorin Maazel (Cleveland Orchestra—to 1982).

**Educational**   John Adams (San Francisco Conservatory—to 1982); T. J. Anderson (music chair, Tufts); Chou Wen-chung (Columbia); Roque Cordero (Illinois State); Norman Dello Joio (dean,

Boston University School of Fine Arts—to 1979); Martin Feldman (SUNY, Buffalo); Franco Gulli (Indiana University); Howard Shanet (music head, Columbia University—to 1978).

**Other** Schuyler Chapin (general manager, Metropolitan Opera—to 1975); Martin Feinstein (director, Kennedy Center, Washington, DC); Claude Palisca (director, International Musicological Society—to 1977); Andrew Porter (music critic, *New Yorker*); Edward Waters (Music, Library of Congress).

## J. Honors and Awards

**Honors** Earle Brown, John Eaton and John Harbison (American Academy); Elliott Galkin (Deems Taylor Award); Margaret Hillis (doctorate, Indiana University); Louis Lane (Ditson); Irving Lowens (Deems Taylor Award); Vittorio Rieti (Waite Award); Robert Ward (PhD, Duke—National Institute).

**Awards** Curtis O. Curtis-Smith (Koussevitzky Prize); Mario Davidovsky (Naumburg); Eugene Fodor (Paganini); Marian Hahn (Kapell Second); Murray Perahia (Leeds); Jeffrey Swann (Queen Elisabeth Second); Ellen Wasserman (Kapell).

**K. Biographical** Colin Davis becomes Principal Guest Conductor of the Boston Symphony Orchestra; Goeran Gentele is appointed manager at the Metropolitan Opera but dies before the year is up; Jascha Heifetz retires from active concert life; Milton Katims takes the Seattle Symphony Orchestra on a concert tour of Alaska; Henry Lewis becomes the first black to conduct at the Metropolitan Opera; Gerard Schwarz joins the New York Philharmonic Orchestra as trumpeter; Yasunao Tone (Japanese composer) comes to the United States and settles in New York; Ellen Taaffe Zwilich enters Juilliard.

## L. Musical Beginnings

**Performing Groups** American Chamber Trio; Arizona Opera Co. (Tucson); Brandenburg Players (New York); Hartford Chorale; New York Lyric Opera Co.; Orpheus (Chamber Orchestra—New York); Portland Choral Arts Society (Maine); Sequoia String Quartet (California Institute of Arts); Syracuse Society for New Music; Tashi; West Virginia Opera Theater (Charleston); Whitewater Opera Co. (Richmond, Indiana).

**Festivals** Aston Magna Baroque Festival; Castle Hill Baroque and Classical Music Festival (Ipswich, Massachusetts); Garth Newel Chamber Music Festival (Hot Springs, Virginia); Sitka Summer Music Festival (Sitka, Virginia); Western Arts Music Festival (Laramie, Wyoming).

**Other** Affiliate Artists' Exxon/Art Endowment Conductors Program (New York); Marian Anderson Fellowship (New York); Aston Magna Foundation for Music (New York); Black Artist Group (St. Louis); Patricia Corbett Pavilion (University of Cincinnati); Maurice Gusman Philharmonic Hall (Miami); Indiana University Musical Arts Center; *Soundings*; Symphony Hall (Phoenix, Arizona); Tubists Universal Brotherhood Association; Unpublished Editions (Printed Editions).

## M. Music Publications

Adler, Samuel, *Choral Singing: An Anthology*
Bing, Rudolf, *5,000 Nights at the Opera*
Boulton, Laura, *Musical Instruments of World Cultures*
Chasins, Abram, *Music at the Crossroads*
Downes, Edward O., *Perspectives in Musicology*
Duerkson, George, *Teaching Instrumental Music*
Hutcheson, Jere, *Musical Form and Analysis*
Kerman, Joseph, *Listen*
Krohn, Ernst C., *Music Publishing in the Middle Western States before the Civil War*
Schwarz, Boris, *Music and Musical Life in Soviet Russia: 1917–70*
Southern, Eileen, *Readings in Black American Music*
Strange, Allen, *Electronic Music: Systems, Techniques and Controls*

### N. Musical Compositions

**Chamber Music**   Arthur Berger, *Trio for Guitar, Violin and Piano*; William Bolcom, *String Quartet No. 9 (Novella)*; Paul Chihara, *Ceremony II* (flute, two cellos, piano); Lejaren Hiller, *String Quartet No. 6*; Marc Neikrug, *String Quartet No. 2*; Robert Parris, *The Book of Imaginary Beings*; George Perle, *Sonata quasi una fantasia* (clarinet and piano); Vincent Persichetti, *String Quartet No. 4*; George Rochberg, *String Quartet No. 3*; Ralph Shapey, *String Quartet No. 7*; Seymour Shifrin, *String Quartet No. 5*; Harvey Sollberger, *The Two and the One* (amplified cello and percussion); Lester Trimble, *Panels II* (13 instruments); Charles Wuorinen, *Violin Variations*.

**Choral/Vocal**   Dominick Argento, *To Be Sung upon the Water* (song cycle); Louis Ballard, *Portrait of Will Rogers* (cantata); Samuel Barber, *Three Songs, Opus 45*; Gloria Coates, *Five Poems of Emily Dickinson*; David Del Tredici, *Vintage Alice*; John Eaton, *Ajax*; Morton Feldman, *Voice and Instruments I—Voice and Instruments II*; John La Montaine, *Wilderness Journal*; Ronald Perera, *Five Summer Songs*; Ned Rorem, *Last Poems of Wallace Stevens* (song cycle); Leo Smit, *Caedmon*; Vladimir Ussachevsky, *Missa Brevis*; Hugo Weisgall, *Translations* (song cycle).

**Concertos**   David Amram, *Violin Concerto*; Leonardo Balada, *Sinfonia Concertante* (guitar and orchestra); Leslie Bassett, *Forces* (violin, cello, piano, orchestra); Cecil Effinger, *Violin Concerto*; Morton Feldman, *Cello and Orchestra*; Andrew Imbrie, *Cello Concerto*; Donald Martino, *Cello Concerto*; Bernard Rands, *Mésalliance* (piano and orchestra); Robert Starer, *Piano Concerto No. 3*; Charles Wuorinen, *Violin (Amplified) Concerto No. 2*.

**Electronic**   Charles Amirkhanian, *Just* (tape)—*Sound Nutrition* (tape); Wayne Barlow, *Soundscapes* (orchestra and tape); David Cope, *Spirals* (tuba and tape); Barbara Kolb, *Soundings*; Donald Martino, *Augenmusik*; Priscilla McLean, *Spectra II*; Ezra Sims, *Thirty Years Later—Wall to Wall*; David Ward-Steinman, *Nova, Arcturus*.

**Operas**   Jean Berger, *Yiphth and His Daughter*; John Eaton, *The Three Graces* (theater piece); Carlisle Floyd, *Flower and Hawk* (monodrama); Thomas Pasatieri, *The Black Widow—The Trial of Mary Lincoln*.

**Orchestra/Band**   Dominick Argento, *A Ring of Time*; Elaine Barkin, *Plus ça change*; Earle Brown, *Time Spans*; Aaron Copland, *Three Latin Sketches* (chamber orchestra); Jacob Druckman, *Windows* (Pulitzer Prize); George Edwards, *Monopoly* (band and piano); Richard Felciano, *Galactic Rounds*; Jean Eichelberger Ivey, *Forms in Motion*; William Schuman, *Voyage for Orchestra*; Elliott Schwartz, *Dream Overture*; Aurelio de la Vega, *Intrada*.

**Piano/Organ**   Josef Alexander, *Twelve Pieces in the Attic* (piano); Gloria Coates, *Structures*; George Crumb, *Makrokosmos I* (amplified piano); David Diamond, *Sonata No. 2*; Lejaren Hiller, *Sonata No. 6*; Anthony Iannaccone, *Keyboard Essays*; Homer Keller, *Sonata*; John Lessard, *Twelve Sketches* (piano, four hands); Francis Thorne, *Sonata*; David Ward-Steinman, *Sonata for Fortified Piano*.

**Symphonies**   Leonardo Balada, *Steel Symphony*; Ross Lee Finney, *Symphony No. 4*; Alan Hovhaness, *Symphony No. 23, Opus 249, "Ani"* (band); Scott Huston, *Symphony No. 4 for Strings*; Meyer Kupferman, *Symphony No. 6, "Ying Yang"*; Virgil Thomson, *Symphony No. 3*.

# 1973

☀

## Historical Highlights

Vice President Spiro Agnew resigns after being convicted of income tax evasion; Gerald R. Ford becomes vice president; seven of the Watergate participants are given jail sentences; the House studies possible impeachment of President Nixon; an Arab oil embargo causes an energy crisis in the West; another Arab attack on Israel fails.

## World Cultural Highlights

**World Art**   Balthus, *The Card Players*; Claudio Bravo, *Before the Game;* Lucien Freud, *Large Interior, W. 9;* Marcus Lüpertz, *Death and the Artist;* Malcolm Morley, *Piccadilly Circus.*

**World Literature**   Alan Ayckbourn, *The Norman Conquests*; Bernard Malamud, *Rembrandt's Hat*; Peter Shaffer, *Equus*; Alexander Solzhenitsyn, *The Gulag Archipelago.*

**World Music**   Malcolm Arnold, *Symphony No. 7*; Luciano Berio, *Concerto for Two Pianos*; Benjamin Britten, *Death in Venice*; Hans Werner Henze, *Tristan*; Krzysztof Penderecki, *Symphony No. 1.*

**Miscellaneous**   The Sydney Opera House opens and the London Academy of Ancient Music is founded; deaths include W. H. Auden, Pablo Casals, Noel Coward, Jascha Horenstein, Pablo Neruda, Pablo Picasso, and J. R. R. Tolkien.

## American Art and Literature

**Births/Deaths**   Deaths include art figures Philip Evergood, Carl Holty, Anna Huntington, Jacques Lipchitz, Louis Lozowick, Stanton Macdonald-Wright, and literary figures Pearl Buck, Mary Ellen Chase, Willliam M. Inge, John G. Neihardt, William Lindsay White, and Margaret Wilson.

**Art Works**   Linda Benglis, *Omega*; Thomas Hart Benton, *County Politics*; Ilya Bolotowsky, *Deep Blue Diamond*; Robert Graham, *Eight Heads*; Al Held, *South Southwest*; David Hockney, *Still Life with Book*; Lee Krasner, *Peacock*; Brice Marden, *Grove Group*; Richard Pousette-Dart, *Merging Presences*; George Segal, *Abraham's Sacrifice of Isaac*; William T. Wiley, *With Few Exceptions.*

**Literature**   Erica Jong, *Fear of Flying*; Robert T. Lowell, *The Dolphin* (Pulitzer Prize); Joyce C. Oates, *Do with Me What You Will*; Thomas Pynchon, *Gravity's Rainbow* (National Book Award); Irwin Shaw, *Evening in Byzantium*; Isaac Bashevis Singer, *A Crown of Feathers and Other Stories* (National Book Award); Lanford Wilson, *The Hot l Baltimore* (New York Drama Critics' Award).

## Music—The Vernacular/Commercial Scene

**B. Deaths**   David Akeman (Stringbean—comedian/banjoist) November 10; Eddie Condon (guitarist/writer) August 4; Jim Croce (folk singer) September 29; Bobby Darin (singer) December 20; Arthur Freed (lyricist) April 12; Ralph Freed (songwriter) February 13; Betty Grable (singer/actress) July 3; J. C. Higginbotham (trombonist) May 26; Ted Koehler (lyricist) January 17; Gene Krupa (bandleader/drums) October 16; Vaughn Monroe (singer/bandleader) May 21; Edward "Kid" Ory (trombonist/bandleader) January 23; Gram Parsons (singer) September 19; Speckled Red (singer/pianist) January 2; Andy Razaf (lyricist) February 3; Tito Rodriguez (singer/bandleader) February 28; Willie "the Lion" Smith (pianist) April 18; Clara Ward (singer) January 16; Hugo Winterhalter (conductor) September 17.

**C. Biographical**

**Performing Groups**   Blackbyrd; The Dixie Dregs; Ethnic Heritage Ensemble; The Family of Mann (Herbie Mann band); Journey; KC and the Sunshine Band; The Legends of Jazz; Los Lobos; The Miami Latin Boys (Sound Machine); Pablo Cruise; Pavlov's Dog; Stray Dog; Sweet Honey in the Rock; Television; George Thorogood and the Destroyers; Twisted Sister.

**New Beginnings**   Berkeley Records; *The Black Perspective in Music*; Concord Records; Crossover Records; *Journal of Jazz Studies*; Laurel Records; Pablo Recording Co. (Los Angeles); *Popular Periodical Index*; *Rock Scene*; Survival Records.

**Honors**   Chet Atkins and Patsy Cline (Country Music Hall of Fame).

**Miscellaneous**   Merle Haggard, Frank Sinatra, and Billy Taylor perform at the White House.

**D. Publications**   David Baker, *Jazz Styles and Analysis: Trombone*; William E. Bolcom, *Reminiscing with Sissle and Blake*; J. Buerkle and D. Barker, *Bourbon Street Black: The New Orleans Black Jazzman*; Charlie Byrd, *Charlie Byrd's Melodic Method for Guitar*; R. P. Christeson, *The Old-time Fiddler's Repertory I*; J. L. Collier, *Inside Jazz*; E. Condon and H. O'Neal, *The Eddie Condon Scrapbook of Jazz*; B. Cook, *Listen to the Blues.*

### E. Representative Works

**Musicals**   L. Bernstein and R. Wilbur, *Candide* (based on 1956 opera—New York Drama Critics' Award); C. Coleman and D. Fields, *Seesaw*; M. Dubey and D. Fuller, *Smith*; N. Ford and G. Cryer, *Shelter*; Cary Hoffman and Ira Gasman, *What's a Nice Country Like You Doing in a State Like This?*; Stephen Sondheim, *A Little Night Music* (New York Drama Critics' Award); J. Woldin and R. Brittan, *Raisin*.

**Number One Hits**   *Angie* (Rolling Stones); *Bad, Bad Leroy Brown—Time in a Bottle* (Jim Croce); *Brother Louie* (Stories); *Crocodile Rock* (Elton John); *Delta Dawn* (Helen Reddy); *Frankenstein* (Edgar Winter Group); *Give Me Love* (George Harrison); *Half-Breed* (Cher); *Keep On Truckin'* (Eddie Kendricks); *Killing Me Softly with His Song* (Roberta Flack); *Let's Get It On* (Marvin Gaye); *Love Train* (The O'Jays); *Midnight Train to Georgia* (Gladys Knight and the Pips); *The Most Beautiful Girl* (Charlie Rich); *My Love* (Paul McCartney and Wings); *The Night the Lights Went Out in Georgia* (Vicki Lawrence); *Photograph* (Ringo Starr); *Superstitious—You Are the Sunshine of My Life* (Stevie Wonder); *Tie a Yellow Ribbon Round the Ole Oak Tree* (Dawn); *Top of the World* (Carpenters); *Touch Me in the Morning* (Diana Ross); *We're an American Band* (Grand Funk); *Will It Go Round in Circles* (Billy Preston); *You're So Vain* (Carly Simon).

**Other**   Duke Ellington, *Third Sacred Concert*; Arthur Smith, *Dueling Banjos*; Billy Taylor, *Suite for Jazz Piano and Orchestra*.

## Music—The Cultivated Art/Music Scene

**F. Deaths**   Esther Ballou (composer) March 12; Nicholas Bessaraboff (instrument maker) November 10; Alvin D. Etler (composer) June 13; Laurens Hammond (electronic instrument maker) July 1; William F. Ludwig (German-born percussionist) June 14; James Lyons (critic) November 13; Edith Mason (soprano) November 26; Francis Macmillen (violinist) July 14; Lauritz Melchior (Danish-born tenor) March 18; Walter Rubsamen (musicologist) June 19; Fernando Sacconi (Italian-born violin maker) June 26; Joseph Szigeti (Hungarian-born violinist) February 19; Jennie Tourel (mezzo-soprano) November 23; Mark E. Wessel (composer) May 2; Paul White (composer) May 31; Jacques Wolfe (Romanian-born composer) June 22.

### H. Debuts

**United States**   Emanuel Ax (pianist—New York), Carmen Balthrop (soprano—Washington, DC), Jean-Philippe Collard (French pianist—San Francisco), Ileana Cotrubas (Romanian soprano—Chicago), Barbara Daniels (soprano—Florida), Maria L. Ewing (mezzo-soprano—Chicago), Sylvia Geszty (Hungarian soprano—Los Angeles), Dylana Jenson (violinist—New York), Aung-Sook Lee (Korean soprano—Chicago), Shlomo Mintz (Israeli violinist—New York), Joan Morris (soprano—New York), Jessye Norman (soprano—New York), Elmar Oliveira (violinist—New York), Felicity Palmer (British soprano—Houston), Samuel Ramey (bass—New York), Alberto Remedios (British tenor—San Francisco), Linda Zoghby (soprano—Chicago).

**Metropolitan Opera**   Betty Allen (mezzo-soprano), Richard Cassilly (tenor), Carlo Cossuta (Italian tenor), Rafael Kubelik (Czech conductor), Teresa Kubiak (Polish soprano), Mady Mesplé (French soprano), Yvonne Minton (Australian mezzo-soprano), Kenneth Riegel (tenor), Rita Shane (soprano), Huguette Tourangeau (Canadian mezzo-soprano), Benita Valente (soprano), Ingvar Wixell (Swedish baritone).

**Other**   Lia Frey-Rabine (soprano—Bern), Melanie Holliday (soprano—Hamburg), Gilbert Levine (conductor—Paris), Emily Rawlins (Basel).

### I. New Positions

**Conductors**   Peter Herman Adler (American Opera Center, Juilliard); Kazuyoshi Akiyama (American Symphony Orchestra—to 1978); Theo Alcantara (Grand Rapids Symphony Orchestra—to 1978); Aldo Ceccato (Detroit Symphony Orchestra—to 1977); Arpad Joo (Knoxville Symphony Orchestra—to 1978); Louis Lane (Dallas Symphony Orchestra—to 1978); James Levine (principal conductor, Metropolitan Opera—director, Ravinia Festival, Chicago); Seiji Ozawa (Boston

Symphony Orchestra); Lawrence Leighton Smith (Portland Symphony Orchestra [Oregon]—to 1980).

**Educational**   Milton Babbitt (Juilliard); Wayne Barlow (Dean of Graduate Studies, Eastman); William Bolcom (University of Michigan); Anthony di Bonaventura (piano, Boston University); Anshel Brusilow (North Texas State University—to 1982); Jan De Gaetani (Eastman School); Grant Johansen (Cleveland Institute—to 1985); Harold S. Powers (Princeton, musicology); Shulamit Ran (University of Chicago).

**Other**   Richard Dyer (music critic, *Boston Globe*); Ezra Laderman (president, American Music Center—to 1976); Thomas Murray (organ/choir, St. Paul's Episcopal Cathedral, Boston—to 1980); Eileen Southern (editor, *The Black Perspective in Music*).

## J. Honors and Awards

**Honors**   Rudolf Bing (National Arts Club Medal); Roy Harris (Brandeis); Lou Harrison and Vladimir Ussachevsky (National Institute); Betsy Jolas, Barbara Kolb, and William Schuman (American Academy); Joseph Kerman and Edward E. Lowinsky (American Academy of Arts and Sciences); John Philip Sousa (Hall of Fame for Great Americans).

**Awards**   Richard Goode (Clara Haskil); Margie Huffman (Kapell Third); Ida Kavafian (Vianna da Motta); Alan Marks (Kapell Second); Murray Perahia (Queen Elizabeth); James Tocco (Munich).

## K. Biographical   Myung-Whun Chung and Janos Kiss become American citizens; Ervin Nyiregyházi, at age 70, makes a comeback recital in San Francisco; Eugene Ormandy takes the Philadelphia Orchestra to China on a cultural exchange visit; Mark Peskanov (Russian violinist) comes to the United States and studies with Dorothy DeLay at Juilliard; Steve Reich begins studying Far East music cultures; Gerard Schwarz, at Aspen, is called on to substitute at the last minute as conductor for an ailing Eleazar de Carvalho and makes a grand debut; Peter Serkin returns to an active musical life.

## L. Musical Beginnings

**Performing Groups**   Albuquerque Opera Theater; Arkansas Opera Theater; Cleveland Opera Theater (Lyric Opera Cleveland); Composers Inside Electronics (performance ensemble); Des Moines Metro Opera; Hartford Chamber Orchestra; Korean Classical Music and Dance Co. (Los Angeles); Kronos String Quartet; New Wilderness Preservation Band; Northwest Chamber Orchestra (Seattle).

**Festivals**   Des Moines Metro Opera Summer Festival; Santa Fe Chamber Music Festival (New Mexico).

**Educational**   Experimental Music Studio (MIT).

**Other**   Des Moines Hall of the Performing Arts in the Harmon Fine Arts Center; Roy Harris Archives (CSU); Minnesota Composers Forum; *Modern Liturgy*; New Orleans Theater of the Performing Arts.

## M. Music Publications

Ballard, Louis, *My Music Reaches to the Sky*
Cooper, Paul, *Perspectives in Music Theory*
Cuyler, Louise, *The Symphony*
Forte, Allen, *The Structure of Atonal Music*
Haggin, B. H., *A Decade of Music*
Krueger, Karl, *The Musical Heritage of the United States: The Unknown Portion*
Sargeant, Winthrop, *Divas: Impressions of Today's Sopranos*
Schwartz, Elliott, *Electronic Music: A Listener's Guide*
Stevenson, Robert M., *Foundations of New World Opera*
Temianka, Henri, *Facing the Music*
Trythall, Gilbert, *Principles and Practice of Electronic Music*
Ulrich, Homer, *A Survey of Choral Music*

### N. Musical Compositions

**Chamber Music**  John Adams, *American Standard*; Beth Anderson, *Music for Charlemagne Palestine*; T. J. Anderson, *Beyond Silence*; Philip Bezanson, *Petite Suite* (woodwinds); Easley Blackwood, *Violin Sonata*; Aaron Copland, *Threnody II (Beatrice Cunningham: In Memoriam)*; Curtis Curtis-Smith, *Five Sonorous Inventions*; Lukas Foss, *MAP*; Lou Harrison, *Suite for Violin and American Gamelan*; Ben Johnston, *String Quartet No. 4*; Donald Martino, *Notturno* (Pulitzer Prize); George Perle, *String Quartet No. 7*; Gundaris Poné, *Diletti dialettici*; Joseph Schwantner, *In Aeternum*; Elie Siegmeister, *String Quartet No. 3*; Lester Trimble, *Panels III*; Richard Wernick, *String Quartet No. 2*.

**Choral/Vocal**  William Albright, *An Alleluia Super-round*; Dominick Argento, *Jonah and the Whale* (oratorio); Philip Bezanson, *St. Judas* (oratorio); Henry Brant, *An American Requiem*; Ezra Laderman, *The Questions of Abraham* (opera-cantata); Marvin D. Levy, *Masada* (oratorio—revised 1987); Robert Parris, *Walking Around*; Stephen Paulus, *Three Elizabethan Songs*; Daniel Pinkham, *Daniel in the Lion's Den*; William Schuman, *Concerto on Old English Rounds* (viola and women's chorus); Robert Starer, *Images of Man*; Louise Talma, *Voices of Spring*; Virgil Thomson, *Cantata on Poems of Edward Lear*.

**Concertos**  Claus Adam, *Cello Concerto*; George Barati, *Piano Concerto*; Morton Feldman, *String Quartet and Orchestra*; Ross Lee Finney, *Violin Concerto No. 2*; Lou Harrison, *Concerto for Organ, Percussion and Orchestra*; Andrew Imbrie, *Piano Concerto No. 1*; William Kraft, *Piano Concerto*; Henri Lazarof, *Flute Concerto*; Halsey Stevens, *Double Concerto for Violin, Cello and Strings*; Charles Wuorinen, *Concerto No. 2 for Piano (Amplified) and Orchestra*.

**Electronic**  Charles Amirkhanian, *Seatbelt Seatbelt* (tape); Gloria Coates, *Natural Voice and Electronic Sound*; Mario Davidovsky, *Synchronism No. 7*; Barton McLean, *Genesis*; Priscilla McLean, *Night Images*; Gordon Mumma, *Cybersonic Cantilevers*; Loren Rush, *A Little Traveling Music*; Elliott Schwartz, *Scales and Arpeggios*; David Tudor, *Rainforest IV*.

**Operas**  Samuel Adler, *The Lodge of Shadows* (music drama); Beth Anderson, *Queen Christina*; William Bergsma, *The Murder of Comrade Sharik*; John Eaton, *The Lion and Androcles* (children's opera); Halim El-Dabh, *Ptahmose and the Magic Spell* (operatic trilogy); Gian Carlo Menotti, *Tamu-Tamu*; Nicolas Nabokov, *Love's Labour's Lost*; Eric Salzman, *Lazarus*; Robert Ward, *Claudia Legare*.

**Orchestra/Band**  David Amram, *Brazilian Memories*; Leonardo Balada, *Auroris*; William Bolcom, *Summer Divertimento*; Paul Chihara, *Ceremony III*; Karl Kohn, *Prophet Bird—Innocent Psaltery*; Robert Moevs, *Main-travelled Roads (Symphonic Piece No. 4)*; Bernard Rands, *Wildtrack 2*; George Rochberg, *Imago mundi*; Ellen Taaffe Zwilich, *Symposium for Orchestra*.

**Piano/Organ**  Aaron Copland, *Proclamation*; George Crumb, *Makrokosmos II* (amplified piano); Curtis Curtis-Smith, *Rhapsodies*; Robert Helps, *Three Hommages*; Steve Reich, *Six Pianos*; Ralph Shapey, *Thirty-One Variations (Fromm Variations)*; Robert Starer, *Sketches in Color II—Stone Ridge Set*; Clifford Taylor, *Thirty Ideas for Piano*; Charles Wuorinen, *Twelve Short Pieces*.

**Symphonies**  Easley Blackwood, *Symphony No. 4*; Alan Hovhaness, *Symphony No. 24, "Majnun"—Symphony No. 25, "Odysseus"*; Ezra Laderman, *Symphony No. 3, "Jerusalem"*; Peter Mennin, *Symphony No. 8*; Vittorio Rieti, *Symphony No. 6*; Ben Weber, *Sinfonia Clarion*.

# 1974

☀

## Historical Highlights

Richard Nixon, under threat of impeachment, becomes the first president to resign his office; Gerald Ford becomes the first president who was never elected as vice president; President Ford gives a full pardon to Nixon; price and wage controls are ended; the OPEC countries end the oil embargo; Helmut Schmidt becomes chancellor of West Germany; Yitzhak Rabin becomes prime minister of Israel.

## World Cultural Highlights

**World Art**   Pierre Alechinsky, *Monsieur Hume;* Jean-Pierre Bertrand, *The Fifty-Four Days of Robinson Crusoe;* Rufino Tamayo, *The Juggler;* Victor Vasarely, *Pai-Ket.*

**World Literature**   Donald Bartholme, *Guilty Pleasures;* Philip Larkin, *High Windows;* John LeCarré, *Tinker, Tailor, Soldier, Spy;* Tom Stoppard, *Travesties.*

**World Music**   Peter Maxwell Davies, *Miss Donnithorne's Maggot;* Olivier Messiaen's *Des Canyons aux Étoile;* Krzysztof Penderecki, *Magnificat;* William Walton, *Magnificat.*

**Miscellaneous**   The Artur Rubinstein International Piano Competition is founded in Israel; the Scottish Chamber Orchestra is founded in Edinburgh; deaths include Kurt Atterberg, H. E. Bates, Knud Jeppesen, André Jolivet, Pär Lagerkvist, and Frank Martin.

## American Art and Literature Highlights

**Deaths**   Deaths include art figures Adolph Gottlieb, Morris Kantor, Leon Kroll, Gabriel Kohn, Moses Soyer, and literary figures Margaret Clapp, Margaret Leech, Walter Lippman, Sterling North, John C. Ransom, Anne Sexton, Jacqueline Susann, and Parker Tyler.

**Art Works**   Robert Arneson, *The Palace at 9 A.M.;* Ronald Davis, *Bent Beam;* Don Eddy, *New Shoes for Four;* Helen Frankenthaler, *Rapunzel;* R. B. Kitaj, *Autumn of Central Paris;* Roy Lichtenstein, *Still Life with "Dance";* Brice Marden, *Star;* Robert Morris, *Labyrinth;* Nam June Paik, *TV Buddha;* George Rickey, *Two Open Rectangles Eccentric;* Sylvia Stone, *Manhattan Express.*

**Literature**   Peter Benchley, *Jaws;* Annie Dillard, *Pilgrim at Tinker Creek* (Pulitzer Prize); E. L. Doctorow, *Ragtime* (National Book Critics' Award); Marilyn Hacker, *Presentation Piece* (National Book Award); David Mamet, *Sexual Perversity in Chicago;* John Nichols, *The Milagro Beanfield War;* Robert Stone, *Dog Soldiers* (National Book Award); Lanford Wilson, *The Mound Builders.*

## Music — The Vernacular/Commercial Scene

**B. Deaths**   Gene Ammons (saxophonist/bandleader) August 6; Roy Bargy (ragtime pianist/composer) January 16; Arthur "Big Boy" Crudup (singer) March 28; Sam Donahue (saxophonist/bandleader) March 22; Duke Ellington (composer/bandleader) May 24; Dorothy Fields (lyricist/librettist) March 28; Cliff Friend (songwriter) June 27; Paul Gonsalves (saxophonist) May 17; Ivory Joe Hunter (pianist/singer/writer) November 8; Tex Ritter (singer) January 2; Harry Ruby (songwriter/lyricist) February 23; Blossom Seeley (singer/dancer) April 17; Peter Wendling (pianist/composer) April 7.

**C. Biographical**

**Performing Groups**   The Amazing Rhythm Aces; Braxton Quartet; Cameo; Cheap Trick; The Dictators; Dr. Buzzard's Original Savannah Band; The Fabulous Thunderbirds; Fireball (?); The L. A. Four; Mink Deville; Montrose; Mother's Finest; New Grass Revival; New York Jazz Repertory Co.; The Outlaws; The Ramones; Starland Vocal Band; Utopia; Van Halen.

**New Beginnings**   Arista Records (New York); Scott Joplin Ragtime Festival (Sedalia, Missouri); *Mississippi Rag: The Voice of Traditional Jazz and Ragtime;* New England Fiddling Contest; *Pickin': the Magazine of Bluegrass and Old-Time Country Music;* Sacramento Dixieland Jubilee.

**Miscellaneous**   Olivia Newton-John makes her first United States tour.

**D. Publications**   Stanley Dance, *The World of Swing;* Roger Kinkle, *Complete Encyclopedia of Popular Music and Jazz* (4 volumes); Albert McCarthy, *Big Band Jazz;* Henry Pleasants, *The Great American Popular Singers;* Irwin Stambler, *Encyclopedia of Pop, Rock, and Soul;* Robert C. Toll, *Blacking Up: The Minstrel Show in Nineteeth-Century America.*

**E. Representative Works**

**Musicals**   Jerry Herman, *Mack and Mabel;* Frank Loesser, *Hans Christian Andersen* (based on 1952 film); Cole Porter, *Cole* (tribute revue); Robert B. and Richard M. Sherman, *Over Here;* C. Strouse and R. Rogers, *The Truth About Cinderella;* Jule Styne and Leo Robin, *Lorelei.*

**Number One Hits**   *Angie Baby* (Helen Reddy); *Annie's Song—Sunshine on My Shoulders* (John Denver); *Band on the Run* (Paul McCartney and Wings); *Bennie and the Jets* (Elton John); *Billy, Don't Be a Hero* (Do Donaldson and the Heywoods); *Can't Get Enough of Your Love, Babe* (Barry White); *Cat's in the Cradle* (Harry Chapin); *Dark Lady* (Cher); *Feel Like Makin' Love* (Roberta Flack); *(You're) Having My Baby* (Paul Anka and Odia Coates); *I Can Help* (Billy Swan); *I Honestly Love You* (Olivia Newton-John); *I Shot the Sheriff* (Eric Clapton); *The Joker* (Steve Miller Band); *The Loco-Motion* (Grand Funk); *The Night Chicago Died* (Paper Lace); *Rock Me Gently* (Andy Kim); *Rock the Boat* (Hues Corporation); *Rock Your Baby* (George McCrae); *Seasons in the Sun* (Terry Jacks); *Show and Tell* (Al Wilson); *Sundown* (Gordon Lightfoot); *Then Came You* (Dionne Warwick); *TSOP* (MFSB and the Three Degrees); *The Way We Were* (Oscar—Barbra Streisand); *Whatever Gets You Thru the Night* (John Lennon); *You Ain't Seen Nothing Yet* (Bachman-Turner Overdrive); *You Haven't Done Nothin'* (Stevie Wonder); *You're Sixteen* (Ringo Starr).

**Other**   Mark Bucci, *Joining! Departure! Arrival!*; Marvin Hamlisch, *The Way We Were* (film music—Oscar); Al Kasha/Joel Hirschorn, *We May Never Love Like This Again* (Oscar); Nelson Riddle, *The Great Gatsby* (film music—Oscar).

## Music—The Cultivated/Art Music Scene

**G. Deaths**   John Barrows (horn player) January 11; Karin Branzell (Swedish-born contralto) December 14; Eddy Brown (violinist) June 14; John Challis (harpsichord maker) September 6; Clara Edwards (singer/composer) January 17; Herbert Elwell (composer/critic) April 17; Edmund Haines (composer) July 5; Sol Hurok (impresario) March 5; Wiktor Labunski (Russian-born pianist/composer) January 26; Quinto Maganini (conductor/arranger) March 10; Harry Partch (composer/performer) September 3; Marie Powers (soprano) December 27; Robert Sanders (composer) December 26; Herman Schlicker (organ builder) December 4; Edwin John Stringham (composer/educator) July 1; Alexander Tcherepnin (composer) September 29; Joseph F. Wagner (composer/conductor) October 12; John M. Williams (pianist/pedagogue) December 6.

### H. Debuts

**United States**   Maurice André (French trumpeter—tour), Katharine Ciesinski (mezzo-soprano—Philadelphia), Pablo Elvira (Puerto Rican baritone—tour), Eric Ericson (Swedish conductor—Washington, DC), Ruth Falcon (soprano—New York), Sheri Greenawald (soprano—New York), Barbara Hendricks (soprano—San Francisco), Timothy Jenkins (tenor—Fort Worth), Tedd Joselson (pianist—Philadelphia), Ava June (soprano—San Francisco), Kurt Masur (German conductor—Cleveland), Kurt Moll (German bass—San Francisco), Gaetane Prouvost (French violinist—New York), Sharon Robinson (cellist—New York), André-Michel Schub (pianist—New York), Diana Soviero (soprano—St. Paul), Klaus Tennstedt (German conductor—Boston), Anna Tomowa-Sintow (Bulgarian soprano—San Francisco), Hans Vonk (Dutch conductor—San Francisco).

**Metropolitan Opera**   Steuart Bedford (British conductor), José Carreras (Spanish tenor), Brigitte Fassbänder (German mezzo-soprano), Jon Garrison (tenor), Manfred Jungwirth (Austrian bass), Paolo Montarsolo (Italian bass), Peter Pears (British tenor), John Shirley-Quirk (British baritone), John Stewart (tenor), Kiri Te Kanawa (New Zealand soprano), Lucia Valentini-Terrani (Italian mezzo-soprano).

### I. New Positions

**Conductors**   Akira Endo (Austin Symphony Orchestra—to 1983); Jack T. Kline (United States Marine Band—to 1979); Yuri Krasnapolsky (Des Moines Symphony Orchestra—to 1987); Erich Kunzel (New Haven Symphony Orchestra—to 1977); Thomas Lewis (Tulsa Philharmonic Orchestra—to 1977); Maurice Peress (Kansas City Philharmonic Orchestra—to 1980); David Zinman (Rochester Philharmonic Orchestra—to 1985).

**Educational**   John Alexander (voice, Cincinnati Conservatory); Agustin Anievas (Brooklyn College); Gerard Béhague (University of Texas); Lawrence F. Bernstein (music chair, University of Pennsylvania—to 1977); James Oliver Buswell IV (Indiana University—to 1986); Phyllis Curtin (Yale—to 1983); Phillip Rhodes (Carleton College, Minnesota); Tossy Spivakovsky (Juilliard); Robert Suderburg (chancellor, North Carolina School of the Arts); William Warfield (University of Illinois).

**Other**  Gerard Béhague (editor, *Ethnomusicology*); Richard Westenburg (music director, Cathedral Church of St. John the Divine—to 1986).

**J. Honors and Awards**

**Honors**  Lawrence F. Bernstein (Alfred Einstein Award); Sarah Caldwell (*Musical America* Musician of the Year); Van Cliburn (National Arts Club Medal); Richard Felciano, Raoul Pleskow, and Olly Wilson (American Academy); Nancy Hanks (Gold Baton); Walter Piston and Martha Graham (MacDowell Medal); Frederik Prausnitz (Mahler Medal); Roger Sessions (Special Pulitzer); Louise Talma (American Academy and National Institute); Alexander Tcherepnin (National Institute).

**Awards**  Dickran Atamian (Kapell Second); Emanuel Ax (Rubinstein); Lynn Chang (Paganini Second—no First); Eugene Fodor (Tchaikovsky Second, Violin—no First); Eugene Indjic (Rubinstein Second); Paratore Brothers (Munich); André-Michel Schub (Naumburg); Maurice Wright (Bearns); Ellen Taaffe Zwilich (Coolidge).

**K. Biographical**  Mikhail Baryshnikov defects to the West while touring with the Bolshoi Ballet; Kurt Masur brings the Leipzig Gewandhaus Orchestra on a United States tour, the first East German orchestra in the United States; Jessye Norman moves to Europe and takes up residency in London, Mstislav Rostropovich (Russian cellist/conductor) and his wife, Galina Vishnevskaya (Russian soprano), leave Russia after losing their Russian citizenship and settle in the United States; Gunther Schuller and the New England Conservatory Ragtime Ensemble perform for Italian President Giovanni Leone at the White House; Louise Talma becomes the first woman to be taken into the American Academy of Arts and Letters.

**L. Musical Beginnings**

**Performing Groups**  Amadé Trio; American String Quartet; Ars Nova Orchestra; Atlanta Symphony Youth Orchestra; Audubon String Quartet; Cincinnati Chamber Orchestra; Dayton Bach Society; Denver Children's Chorale; Duo Geminiani (early music duo); Electronic Weasel Ensemble; Ensemble for Early Music (New York); Feld Ballet Co.; Group for New Music (Pro Musica Moderna (University of Massachusetts); Opera Theatre of Syracuse (Opera Co., 1984); Oregon Repertory Singers; San Francisco Contemporary Music Players; Tarack Chamber Players.

**Festivals**  Artpark Festival (Lewiston, New York).

**Educational**  Arnold Schoenberg Institute (USC); Ernst Toch Archive (UCLA).

**Other**  Ambassador Auditorium (Los Angeles); American Society for Jewish Music; Birmingham Concert Hall (Alabama); Centre for American Music (Staffordshire, England); Contemporary Music Forum (Washington, DC); Meet the Composer Program; Minneapolis Orchestral Hall; New Music for Young Ensembles (New York); Norlin Foundation; Serge Modular Music Systems (California); David Sutherland Harpsichord Shop (Ann Arbor).

**M. Music Publications**

Benson, Warren, *Compositional Process and Writing Skills*
Cone, Edward T., *The Composer's Voice*
Craft, Robert, *Prejudices in Disguise*
Etler, Alvin, *Making Music: An Introduction to Theory*
Krenek, Ernst, *Horizons Circled: Reflection on My Music*
Reich, Steve, *Writings about Music*
Rorem, Ned, *The Final Diary, 1961–1972* (Deems Taylor Award)
Strunk, Oliver, *Essays on Music in the Western World*
Tremblay, George, *The Definitive Cycle of the 12-tone Row and Its Application in All Fields of Composition, including the Computer*
Turetzky, Bertram, *The Contemporary Contrabass*
Vinton, John, *Dictionary of Contemporary Music*
Westergaard, Peter, *An Introduction to Tonal Theory*
Willis, Thomas, *The Chicago Symphony Orchestra*

**N. Musical Compositions**

**Chamber Music**  William Albright, *Seven Deadly Sins*; David Amram, *Fanfare for Brass and*

*Percussion*; Chester Biscardi, *Orpha*; Howard Boatwright, *String Quartet No. 2*; Norman Dello Joio, *String Quartet*; Morton Feldman, *Instruments I—Instruments II*; Brian Fennelly, *String Quartet*; Philip Glass, *Music in Twelve Parts*; Ezra Laderman, *String Quartet No. 4*; Robert Palmer, *Piano Quartet No. 2*; Joseph Schwantner, *Autumn Canticles* (piano trio); Seymour Shifrin, *Piano Trio*; Carlos Surinach, *String Quartet*; Lester Trimble, *Panels IV*; Ellen Taaffe Zwilich, *Sonata in Three Movements* (violin and piano—Viotti Prize)—*String Quartet*.

**Choral/Vocal**    William Albright, *Mass in D—Chichester Mass*; Josef Alexander, *Aspects of Love*; Beth Anderson, *Joan* (oratorio); Dominick Argento, *From the Diary of Virginia Woolf* (Pulitzer Prize); Leonardo Balada, *No-Res*; Wayne Barlow, *Voices of Darkness*; John Biggs, *Songs of Love, Laughter and Tears* (song cycle); Chester Biscardi, *Heabakes—Five Sapphic Lyrics*; Jacob Druckman, *Lamia*; George Edwards, *Exchange-Misère*; David Epstein, *Night Voices*; Donald Erb, *New England's Prospect* (oratorio); Richard Felciano, *Te Deum*; John Harbison, *Elegiac Songs*; John La Montaine, *Mass of Nature*; Thomas Pasatieri, *Rites of Passage*; George Perle, *Songs of Praise and Lamentation*; Elie Siegmeister, *A Cycle of Cities*; Richard Wernick, *Songs of Remembrance* (song cycle); Olly Wilson, *SpiritSong*.

**Concertos**    Leonardo Balada, *Concerto for Piano, Winds and Percussion*; Harold Farberman, *Violin Concerto*; Ross Lee Finney, *Alto Sax Concerto*; Andrew Imbrie, *Piano Concerto No. 2*; Peter Lieberson, *Cello Concerto*; Marc Neikrug, *Viola Concerto*; George Rochberg, *Violin Concerto*; Elliott Schwartz, *The Harmony of Maine* (synthesizer and orchestra); Elie Siegmeister, *Piano Concerto*; Robert Suderburg, *Piano Concerto, "within the mirror of time"*; Carlos Surinach, *Piano Concerto*; Clifford Taylor, *Piano Concerto*.

**Electronic**    Charles Amirkhanian, *She she and she* (tape); Milton Babbitt, *Reflections for Piano and Tape*; David Cope, *Arena* (cello and tape)—*Paradigm* (violin, piano and tape); Conrad Cummings, *Subway Songs*; Mario Davidovsky, *Synchronism No. 8*; Kenneth Gaburo, *Antiphony VII*; Salvatore Martirano, *Shop Talk*; Priscilla McLean, *Dance of Dawn*; Elliott Schwartz, *Spaces*.

**Operas**    Samuel Adler, *The Disappointment* (ballad opera); Hugh Aitken, *Fables*; Dominick Argento, *A Water Bird Talk* (monodrama); John Harbison, *Winter's Tale*; John La Montaine, *Be Glad Then America*; Thomas Pasatieri, *The Seagull*; Eric Salzman, *The Conjurer*; Robert Starer, *The Last Lover*.

**Orchestra/Band**    Jean Berger, *Short Symphony*; William Bergsma, *A Carol on Twelfth Night*; Leonard Bernstein, *Dybbuk* (ballet); Paul Chihara, *Ceremony IV*; Gloria Coates, *The Planets*; Robert Erickson, *Rainbow Rising*; John Lessard, *Pastimes and Alleluia*; Robert Parris, *Angels*; Raoul Pleshkow, *Three Pieces for Orchestra*; Ned Rorem, *Air Music* (Pulitzer Prize); Gunther Schuller, *Four Soundscapes (Hudson Valley Reminiscences)*; William Schuman, *Prelude for a Great Occasion*; Robert Starer, *Holy Jungle* (ballet); Carlos Surinach, *Chronique* (ballet).

**Piano/Organ**    Josef Alexander, *Twelve Signs of the Zodiac*; Norman Cazden, *Six Preludes and Fugues*; George Crumb, *Makrokosmos III (Music for a Summer Evening)* (two amplified pianos and two percussionists); Ezra Laderman, *Momenti*; Robert Muczynski, *Sonata No. 3, Opus 35*; Leo Ornstein, *Biography in Sonata Form*; Leo Smit, *Martha Through the Looking Glass*; Joseph F. Wagner, *Twelve Concert Preludes* (organ); Richard Wilson, *Eclogue*; Richard Yardumian, *Fantasy No. 2*.

**Symphonies**    Leon Stein, *Symphony No. 4*.

# 1975

☀

## Historical Highlights

Two attempts are made on President Ford's life in California; union official Jimmy Hoffa mysteriously disappears and is believed to be murdered; all United States troops and civilians are hurriedly evacuated from Vietnam as the Communists take over the whole country; Russian cosmonauts and United States astronauts perform a joint linkup in space; the European Space Agency is founded.

## World Cultural Highlights

**World Art**    Elizabeth Frink, *Horse Lying Down;* David Hockney, *The Rake's Progress* (stage settings); Anselm Kiefer, *Sea Lion;* F. E. McWilliam, *Peace C.;* Victor Pasmore, *Brown Symphony.*

**World Literature**    Alan Ayckbourn, *Absurd Person Singular*; Harold Pinter, *No Man's Land.*

**World Music**    Jacques Charpentier, *Saxophone Concerto*; Joonas Kokkonen, *The Last Temptation*; Witold Lutoslawski, *Les Espaces du Sommeil*; Andrzej Panufnik, *Symphony for Spheres.*

**Miscellaneous**    The Robert Casadesus International Piano Competition begins in Paris; the Takács String Quartet is founded in Hungary; deaths include Michael Ayrton, Boris Blacher, Arthur Bliss, Barbara Hepworth, Alexis Léger, and Dmitri Shostakovich.

## American Art and Literature Highlights

**Births/Deaths**    Deaths include art figures Thomas Hart Benton, James Chapin, George Morris, Fairfield Porter, and Louis Slobodkin, and literary figures Hannah Arendt, Walker Evans, Arthur Kober, Vincent Sheean, Rex Stout, and Thornton Wilder.

**Art Works**    Ron Davis, *Diamond in a Box*; Richard Estes, *Central Savings*; Philip Guston, *Head and Bottle*; Jasper Johns, *Weeping Woman*; Alex Katz, *Six Women*; Ellen Lanyon, *Cobra*; Sol LeWitt, *Four-Part Modular Cube*; Larry Poons, *Bear Mary's Painting*; Fairfield Porter, *Back Yards*; Theodore Roszak, *Vigil*; Frank Stella, *Jardin Botanico I*; Ernest Trova, *Three Walking Poets.*

**Literature**    Edward F. Albee, *Seascape* (Pulitzer Prize); John Ashbery, *Self-Portrait in a Convex Mirror* (National Book Award—National Book Critics' Award); Saul Bellow, *Humboldt's Gift* (Pulitzer Prize); William Gaddis, *J. R.* (National Book Award); David Mamet, *American Buffalo* (New York Drama Critics' Award); Michael Shaara, *The Killer Angels* (Pulitzer Prize).

## Music—The Vernacular/Commercial Scene

**A. Births**    Lalo Rodríguez (singer) May 16; Tony Thompson (singer) September 2.

**B. Deaths**    "Cannonball" Adderley (saxophonist) August 8; Leroy Anderson (composer/conductor) May 18; Shelton Brooks (songwriter/pianist) September 6; Tim Buckley (singer/guitarist) June 29; Lefty Frizzell (singer) July 19; Louis Jordan (saxophonist/singer) February 4; Vincent Lopez (pianist/bandleader) September 20; George Morgan (guitarist/writer) July 7; Oliver Nelson (composer) October 28; Noble Sissle (singer/lyricist) December 17; T-Bone Walker (guitarist/singer) March 17; Bob Wills (fiddler/bandleader) March 13.

**C. Biographical**

**Performing Groups**    Angel; Boston; Capp-Pierce Juggernaut (Orchestra); Desmond Child and Rouge; Coral Reefer Band; The Cramps; Dave and Sugar; Molly Hatchet; The Heartbreakers and Johnny Thunder; Heath Brothers Band; Greg Kihn Band; Lone Star; Miami Sound Machine; Pere Ubu; Tom Petty and the Heartbreakers; Quiet Riot; Real Kids; The Runaways; Silver Convention; Southside Johnny and the Asbury Jukes; Spyro Gyra; Starland Vocal Band; The Talking Heads; .38 Special; The Tubes; United Jazz and Rock Ensemble; Zapp; Zebra.

**New Beginnings**    Catalyst Record Co. (Los Angeles); Horizon Records (Los Angeles); Malaco Records; *Songwriters Magazine*; Xanadu Records (New York).

**Miscellaneous**    Billy Taylor receives a DME from the University of Massachusetts.

**D. Publications**    Bob Artis, *Bluegrass: . . . The Story of an American Musical Tradition*; Jerry Coker, *The Jazz Idiom*; Arthur Davis, *The Arthur Davis Method of Double Bass*; Peter Gammond, *Scott Joplin and the Ragtime Era*; André Hodeir, *Jazz: Its Evolution and Essence*; Jack Hurst, *Nashville's Grand Ole Opry*; Lester Levy, *Give Me Yesterday: America in Song, 1890–1920*; Steven D. Price, *Old as the Hills: The Story of Bluegrass Music.*

**E. Representative Works**

**Musicals**   Gary Geld and Peter Udell, *Shenandoah*; L. Grossman and H. Hackady, *Goodtime Charley*; Marvin Hamlisch and Edward Kleban, *A Chorus Line* (Pulitzer Prize—Tony—New York Drama Critics' Award); J. Kander and F. Ebb, *Chicago*; *Rodgers and Hart* (tribute revue); Charlie Smalls, *The Wiz*; R. H. Waldman and A. Uhry, *The Robber Bridegroom*.

**Number One Hits**   *Bad Blood—Laughter in the Rain* (Neil Sedaka); *Before the Next Teardrop Falls* (Freddy Fender); *Best of My Love* (Eagles); *Black Water* (Doobie Brothers); *Fame* (David Bowie); *Fire* (Ohio Players); *Get Down Tonight—That's the Way* (KC and the Sunshine Band); *He Don't Love You (Like I Love You)* (Tony Orlando and Dawn); *The Hustle* (Soul City Symphony); *I'm Sorry/Calypso—Thank God I'm a Country Boy* (John Denver); *Jive Talkin'* (Bee Gees); *Lady Marmalade* (Labelle); *Let's Do It Again* (Staple Singers); *Love Will Keep Us Together* (Captain and Tennille); *Lovin' You* (Minnie Riperton); *Lucy in the Sky with Diamonds—Island Girl* (Elton John); *Mandy* (Barry Manilow); *My Eyes Adored You* (Frankie Valli); *Pick Up the Pieces* (Average White Band); *Please, Mr. Postman* (Carpenters); *Rhinestone Cowboy* (Glen Campbell); *Shining Star* (Earth, Wind and Fire); *Sister Golden Hair* (America); *You're No Good* (Linda Ronstadt).

**Other**   Dave Brubeck, *La Fiesta de la Posada*; Keith Carradine, *I'm Easy* (Oscar); Henry Mancini, *Return of the Pink Panther* (film music); John Williams, *Jaws* (film music—Oscar); Judith Lang Zaimont, *Judy's Rag*.

## Music—The Cultivated/Art Music Scene

**G. Deaths**   Carl Becker (violin maker) August 6; Joseph Bentonelli (tenor) April 4; Philip Bezanson (composer) March 11; John Corigliano, Sr. (violinist) September 1; Milton Cross (music historian) January 3; Robert Evett (composer) February 3; Karl Gehrkens (music educator) February 28; Marcel Grandjany (French-born harpist) February 24; Walter Herbert (German-born conductor) September 14; Bernard Herrmann (composer/conductor) December 24; Philip James (composer) November 1; Thor Johnson (conductor) January 16; Arthur Judson (concert manager) January 29; Ernst C. Krohn (musicologist) March 21; Nicola Moscona (German-born bass) September 17; Benno Rabinof (violinist) July 2; Oscar Rasbach (composer) March 24; Robert Stolz (Austrian-born composer/conductor); Norman Treigle (bass-baritone) February 16; Richard Tucker (tenor) January 8.

**H. Debuts**

**United States**   Norman Bailey (British baritone—New York), John Cheek (bass-baritone—Chicago?), Clamma Dale (soprano—New York), Justus Frantz (German pianist—New York), Pavel Kogan (Russian violinist—Philadelphia), Robert Lloyd (British bass-baritone—San Francisco), Eva Marton (Hungarian soprano—New York), Ermanno Mauro (Italian-born tenor—New York), Robin McCabe (pianist—New York), Yevgeni Nesterenko (Russian bass—New York), Elena Obraztsova (Russian mezzo-soprano—tour), Maria Pellegrini (Italian soprano—Pittsburgh), Claudette Peterson (soprano—San Francisco), Gianna Rolandi (soprano—New York), Mstislav Rostropovich (as conductor—San Francisco), Neil Shicoff (tenor—Cincinnati), Vladimir Spivakov (Russian violinist—New York).

**Metropolitan Opera**   Wolfgang Brendel (German baritone), Ryland Davies (British tenor), Andrew Foldi (Hungarian bass), Maureen Forrester (Canadian contralto), Elizabeth Harwood (British soprano), Anne Howells (British mezzo-soprano), Roberta Knie (soprano), Berit Lindholm (Swedish soprano), Evelyn Mandac (Filipino soprano), Danica Mastilović (Yugoslav soprano), Donald McIntyre (New Zealand bass-baritone), Leona Mitchell (soprano), Wieslaw Ochman (Polish tenor), Magda Olivero (Italian soprano), Katia Ricciarelli (Italian soprano), Beverly Sills (soprano), José Van Dam (Belgian bass-baritone).

**Other**   Lella Cuberli (soprano—Budapest), Gail Gilmore (mezzo-soprano—Krefeld), Lynne Strow-Piccolo (soprano—Siena).

### I. New Positions

**Conductors**   Christopher Keene (Syracuse Symphony Orchestra—to 1984); James Levine (music director, Metropolitan Opera).

**Educational**   David Burge (Eastman); Louise Cuyler (Smith College); Ian Hobson (University of Illinois); Eugene List (piano, NYU); Itzhak Perlman (violin, Brooklyn College); Bernard Rands (UC, San Diego); Robert X. Rodriguez (University of Texas); Elliott Schwartz (music chair, Bowdoin College—to 1985); Leonard Stein (USC); Risë Stevens (president, Mannes—to 1978); Leo Treitler (musicology, SUNY, Stony Brook); Gil Trythall (Virginia University).

**Other**   Roberta Bitgood (president, American Guild of Organists -to 1981); Anthony Bliss (director, Metropolitan Opera); George London (director, Opera Society of Washington).

### J. Honors and Awards

**Honors**   Martin Bresnick (Rome Prize); Marc Antonio Consoli, Charles Dodge and Christian Wolff (American Academy); George Crumb and Hugo Weisgall (National Institute); John S. Edwards (Gold Baton); Elliott Galkin (Deems Taylor – second award), Miriam Gideon (American Academy and Institute); Eugene Ormandy (*Musical America* Musician of the Year); Leo Ornstein (Marjorie Peabody Award); Vincent Persichetti (Brandeis); Alice Tully (National Arts Club Medal).

**Awards**   Lynn Harrell and Murray Perahia (Avery Fisher); Sharon Isbin (Toronto); Julian Martin (Kapell Third); Elmar Oliveira and Joy Simpson (Naumburg); Santiago Rodriguez (Kapell).

**K. Biographical**   Joshua Bell, age 7, solos with the Bloomington Symphony Orchestra in Indiana; William Bolcom marries mezzo-soprano Joan Morris; Semyon Bychkov and his wife leave Russia for the United States; Paul Creston retires from teaching; Edo De Waart is appointed Principal Guest Conductor of the San Francisco Symphony Orchestra; Cho-Liang Lin (Chinese violinist) comes to the United States to study at Juilliard; Riccardo Muti becomes Principal Guest Conductor of the Philadelphia Orchestra; Bernard Rands (British composer) comes to the United States and settles in California; Elizabeth Schwarzkopf makes her farewell concert tour of the United States; Calvin Simmons becomes assistant to Zubin Mehta in Los Angeles; Ellen Taaffe Zwilich becomes the first woman to receive a DMA in composition at Juilliard.

### L. Musical Beginnings

**Performing Groups**   Classic Opera of Miami; Glimmerglass Opera Co. (Cooperstown, New York); Harmonic Choir (New York); Indianapolis Opera; Minot Opera Association (North Dakota); New York New Music Ensemble; Pennsylvania Opera Theatre; Primavera String Quartet (New York); Syracuse University Oratorio Society; Twentieth Century Consort (Washington, DC); Virginia Opera Association (Norfolk); Youngstown Opera Co.

**Festivals**   Cullowhee Music Festival (North Carolina); Pacific Northwest Wagner Festival (Seattle).

**Educational**   Stanford Center for Computer Research in Music and Acoustics; String Revival (Columbia); Teacher's Institute of Lincoln Center; Kenneth Warren and Son (Chicago) School of Violinmaking.

**Other**   American Council of Learned Societies; Conductor's Guild (sponsor, ASOL); *Ear Magazine*; Avery Fisher Prize; Hartford Civic Center; International Brass Society; International League of Women Composers (Knoxville); Margun Music (for American Music); *Musica judaica*; New World Records (Milwaukee); *Northwest Arts* (magazine); Real Art Ways (Hartford); Sonneck Society; Eleanor Steber Music Foundation; Richard Tucker Music Foundation.

### M. Music Publications

Appleton, J. and Perera, R., *Development and Practice of Electronic Music*
Ballard, Louis, *Music of North American Indians*
Bazelon, Irwin, *Knowing the Score: Notes on Film Music*
Bennett, Robert R., *Instrumentally Speaking*

Erickson, Robert, *Sound Structures in Music*
Fink, Roberts, and Ricci, *The Language of Twentieth Century Music*
Hixon, Don and Don H., *Women in Music*
Lawrence, Vera B., *Music for Patriots, Politicians, and Presidents* (Deems Taylor Award)
Reynolds, Roger, *Mind Models: New Forms of Musical Experience*
Shanet, Howard, *Philharmonic: A History of New York's Orchestra*
Vercoe, Barry, *Man–Computer Interaction in Creative Applications*

## N. Musical Compositions

**Chamber Music**   Claus Adam, *String Quartet*; Samuel Adler, *String Quartet No. 6*; Theodore Antoniou, *Circle of Accusation*; Daniel Asia, *String Quartet No. 1*; Elaine Barkin, *Inward and Outward Bound*; Leslie Bassett, *Wind Music* (sextet); Irwin Bazelon, *Woodwind Quintet*; Paul Cooper, *String Quartet No. 5*; Ben Johnston, *String Quartet No. 5*; George Rochberg, *Piano Quintet*; Joseph Schwantner, *Canticle of the Evening Bells*; Lester Trimble, *Panels V (String Quartet No. 3)—Panels VI (Quadraphonics)* (percussion); Frank Wigglesworth, *Woodwind Quintet*.

**Choral/Vocal**   John Adams, *Grounding*; T. J. Anderson, *Horizons '76*; Wayne Barlow, *Voices of Faith*; Elliott Carter, *A Mirror on Which to Dwell*; Lee Hoiby, *Galileo Galilei* (oratorio); William Mayer, *Spring Came on Forever*; Daniel Pinkham, *Four Elegies*; Raoul Pleshkow, *Cantata No. 1*; Bernard Rands, *Wildtrack 3*; Ned Rorem, *Serenade on Five English Poems* (song cycle); William Schuman, *The Young Dead Soldiers*; Tibor Serly, *The Pleiades*; Robert Starer, *Journals of a Songmaker*; Alan Stout, *Passion*; Randall Thompson, *A Concord Cantata*; Hugo Weisgall, *Song of Celebration*.

**Concertos**   John Corigliano, *Oboe Concerto*; Morton Feldman, *Piano and Orchestra*; Halsey Stevens, *Viola Concerto*; Burnet Tuthill, *Tuba Concerto*; George Walker, *Piano Concerto*.

**Electronic**   Charles Amirkhanian, *Beemsterboer* (tape); Ruth Anderson, *Sound Environment* (sound sculpture); Kenneth Gaburo, *My, My, My, What a Wonderful Fall*; Anthony Gnazzo, *Compound Skill Fracture*; Barton McLean, *The Sorcerer Revisited*; Roger Reynolds, *Voicespace I, "Still"*; Morton Subotnick, *Two Butterflies* (amplified orchestra).

**Operas**   Jack Beeson, *Captain Jinks of the Horse Marines*; Jean Berger, *The Cherry Tree Carol* (liturgical drama); Philip Glass, *Einstein on the Beach*; Paul Turok, *Richard III*; Charles Wuorinen, *The W. of Babylon* ("Baroque burlesque").

**Orchestra/Band**   Jacob Avshalomov, *Raptures for Orchestra on Madrigals of Gesualdo*; Leonardo Balada, *Homage to Casals—Homage to Sarasate*; Leslie Bassett, *Echoes from an Invisible World*; Irwin Bazelon, *A Quiet Piece for a Violent Time*; Earle Brown, *Cross Sections and Color Fields*; Cecil Effinger, *Capriccio*; Donald Erb, *Music for a Festive Occasion*; Brian Fennelly, *In Wildness Is the Preservation of the World*; Lee Hoiby, *Music for Celebration, Opus 30*; Robert Hall Lewis, *Nuances II*; Otto Luening, *Symphonic Interlude III*; Michael McNabb, *Solstice*; Gundaris Poné, *Avanti!* (Friedheim Award); Ned Rorem, *Assembly and Fall*; Nicolas Roussakis, *Ode and Cataclysm*; Eric Stokes, *The Continental Harp and Band Report*; Virgil Thomson, *Parson Weems and the Cherry Tree* (ballet); Charles Wuorinen, *A Reliquary for Igor Stravinsky*.

**Piano/Organ**   William Albright, *Sweet Sixteenths*; Karel Husa, *Sonata No. 2*; Ezra Laderman, *Preludes for Organ in Different Forms*; Peter Lieberson, *Piano Fantasy*; Jerome Moross, *Sonata for Piano, Four Hands*; Gardner Read, *Sonoric Fantasia No. 4* (organ and percussion); Ned Rorem, *Eight Etudes*; Roger Sessions, *Five Pieces*; Alan Stout, *Sonata for Two Pianos*; George Walker, *Sonata No. 3*.

**Symphonies**   Samuel Adler, *Symphony No. 5, "We Are the Echoes"*; William Bergsma, *Symphony No. 2: Voyages*; Paul Chihara, *Ceremony V: Symphony in Celebration (No. 1)*; Paul Cooper, *Symphony No. 4, "Landscape"*; Roy Harris, *Bicentennial Symphony (No. 13)*; Alan Hovhaness, *Symphony No. 26, Opus 280, "Consolation"*; Scott Huston, *Symphony No. 5*; Otto Luening, *Wisconsin Symphony*; William Schuman, *Symphony No. 10, "American Muse"*; Elie Siegmeister, *Symphony No. 5, "Visions of Time"*; David Van Vactor, *Symphony No. 5*.

# 1976

✸

## Historical Highlights

Jimmy Carter is elected the 39th president during nationwide bicentennial celebrations; *Viking One* and *Viking Two* make soft landings on Mars; *Pioneer Ten* passes through Saturn's rings on its way to outer space; Conrail is formed to control the bankrupt northeastern railroads; civil war between Christians and Moslems breaks out in Lebanon.

## World Cultural Highlights

**World Art**  Augustin Cardena, *Femme au Repos;* Eduardo Chillida, *Peine del Viante;* Chryssa, *Rhythms;* Anthony Green, *The Red Bathroom;* Malcolm Morley, *The Age of Catastrophe.*

**World Literature**  Colleen McCullough, *The Thorn Birds*; Oscar Villegas, *Atlantida.*

**World Music**  Peter Maxwell Davies, *Symphony No. 1*; Henryk Górecki, *Symphony of Sorrowful Songs (No. 3)*; Hans Werner Henze, *We Come to the River*; Witold Lutoslawski, *Mi-Parti.*

**Miscellaneous**  The Tallis Scholars are founded in London, the Bohuslav Martinů Trio in Holland, and the Instituto Superior de Arte in Cuba; deaths include Benjamin Britten, Agatha Christie, Deryck Cooke, Max Ernst, Rudolf Kempe, and Jean Martinon.

## American Art and Literature Highlights

**Births/Deaths**  Deaths include art figures Josef Albers, Alexander Calder, Man Ray, Mark Tobey, and literary figures Paul Gallico, Louis Ginsberg, Alfred Kreymborg, Alexander Laing, Walter Lowenfels, Charles Reznikoff, H. Allen Smith, Wilbert Snow, and Edward Tanner (Patrick Dennis).

**Art Works**  Will Barnet, *Atlantis*; Paul Cadmus, *Subway Symphony*; Jim Dine, *So Many Different Colors*; Audrey Flack, *Queen*; Jasper Johns, *End Papers*; Anselm Kiefer, *Sea Lion*; R. B. Kitaj, *If Not, Not*; Elizabeth Murray, *Beginner*; Lowell Nesbitt, *Amber Beads and Mask*; Beverly Pepper, *Phaedra*; Mark di Suvero, *For Handel*; Ernest Trova, *Abstract Variations*; Andrew Wyeth, *Sea Boots.*

**Literature**  Don DeLillo, *Ratner's Star*; John Gardner, *October Light* (National Book Critics' Award); Alex Haley, *Roots* (Special Pulitzer); Ira Levin, *The Boys from Brazil*; Neil Simon, *California Suite*; Wallace Stegner, *The Spectator Bird* (National Book Award); Leon Uris, *Trinity*; Gore Vidal, *1876*; Kurt Vonnegut, Jr., *Slapstick*; Paul Zindel, *Pardon Me, You're Stepping on My Eyeball.*

## Music—The Vernacular/Commercial Scene

**B. Deaths**  Tommy Bolin (guitar) December 4; Connee Boswell (singer) October 11; Percy Faith (conductor/arranger) February 9; Jesse "Lone Cat" Fuller (guitarist/singer) January 29; Jerry Gray (bandleader/arranger) August 10; Bobby Hackett (cornetist/guitarist) June 7; Howlin' Wolf (singer) January 10; Buell Kazee (folk singer) August 31; Chris Kenner (singer/writer) January 25; Freddie King (guitarist) December 28; Edgar Leslie (lyricist); Mance Lipscomb (guitarist/fiddler) January 30; Johnny Mercer (bandleader/writer) June 25; Sal Minco (singer) February 12; Phil Ochs (singer/writer) April 8; Victoria Spivey (pianist/singer) October 3; Ned Washington (lyricist) December 20.

**C. Biographical**

**Performing Groups**  Willie Alexander and the Boom Boom Band; American Flyer; Atlantic Starr; Beausoleil; The B-52s; The Cars; Chic; Crime; The Dead Boys; The Feelies; The Fleshtones; David Grisman Quintet; Richard Hell and the Voidoids; High Inergy; Old and New Dreams; Pez Band; Siouxsie and the Banshees; Stuff; The Weirdos; Wild Cherry; World Saxophone Quartet.

**New Beginnings**   *Cadence Magazine: The American Review of Jazz and Blues*; Central Illinois Jazz Festival (Decatur); *Jazz Magazine*; Chicago Jazz Archive (University of Chicago); *Journal of Popular Culture*; *Songsmith's Journal*.

**Honors**   Scott Joplin (Special Pulitzer); Kitty Wells (Country Music Hall of Fame).

**D. Publications**   Christa Dixon, *Negro Spirituals: From Bible to Folk Song*; Stanley Green, *Encyclopedia of the Musical Theater*; Richard Jackson, *Popular Songs in Nineteenth-Century America*; Dan Morgenstern, *Jazz People*; Tony Palmer, *All You Need Is Love: The Story of Popular Music*; Larry Sandberg and Dick Weissman, *The Folk Music Sourcebook*; Valerie Wilmer, *The Face of Black Music*.

**E. Representative Works**

**Musicals**   L. Bernstein and A. J. Lerner, *1600 Pennsylvania Avenue*; J. Kander and F. Ebb, *2 X 5* (tribute revue); A. L. Webber and T. Rice, *Joseph and the Amazing Technicolor Dream Coat* (United States premiere); Bill Solly and Dick Vosburgh, *The Great American Backstage Musical*; Stephen Sondheim, *Pacific Overtures* (New York Drama Critics' Award); Various composers, *Bubbling Brown Sugar* (revue)—*Your Arms Too Short to Box with God*.

**Number One Hits**   *Afternoon Delight* (Starland Vocal Band); *Boogie Fever* (The Sylvers); *Convoy* (C. W. McCall); *December, 1963* (The Four Seasons); *Disco Duck* (Rick Dees and His Cast of Idiots); *Disco Lady* (Johnnie Taylor); *Don't Go Breaking My Heart* (Elton John and Kiki Dee); *A Fifth of Beethoven* (Big Apple Band); *50 Ways to Leave Your Lover* (Paul Simon); *I Write the Songs* (Barry Manilow); *If You Leave Me Now* (Chicago); *Kiss and Say Goodbye* (Manhattans); *Let Your Love Flow* (Bellamy Brothers); *Love Hangover—"Mahogany" Theme* (Diana Ross); *Love Machine* (The Miracles); *Love Rollercoaster* (Ohio Players); *Play That Funky Music* (Wild Cherry); *Rock 'n Me* (Steve Miller Band); *Saturday Night* (Bay City Rollers); *Shake Your Booty* (KC and the Sunshine Band); *Silly Love Songs* (Wings); *"S.W.A.T." Theme* (Rhythm Heritage); *Tonight's the Night* (Rod Stewart); *Welcome Back* (John Sebastian); *You Should Be Dancing* (Bee Gees).

**Other**   Anthony Braxton, *Creative Orchestra Music*; Jerry Goldsmith, *The Omen* (film music—Oscar); Henry Mancini, *Silver Streak* (film music).

## Music—The Cultivated/Art Music Scene

**G. Deaths**   Victor Alessandro (conductor) November 27; Alexander Brailowsky (Russian-born pianist) April 25; Dean Dixon (conductor) November 3; Samuel Dushkin (Polish-born violinist) June 24; Frank Hubbard (harpsichord maker) February 25; Rosina Lhevinne (Russian-born pianist) November 9; Nikolai Lopatnikoff (Estonian-born composer/pianist) October 7; Mieczyslaw Munz (Polish-born pianist) August 25; Gregor Piatigorsky (Russian-born cellist) August 6; Walter Piston (composer/educator) November 12; Elisabeth Rethberg (German-born soprano) June 6; Paul Robeson (baritone) January 23; Clifton Williams (bandmaster/composer) February 12.

**H. Debuts**

**United States**   John Aler (tenor—New York), Dmitri Alexeev (Russian pianist—Chicago), Lazar Berman (Russian pianist—tour), Robert Black (pianist—New York), Gwendolyn Bradley (soprano—Lake George, New York), Yefim Bronfman (Israeli pianist—Marlboro, Vermont), Mark Butler (Canadian violinist—New York), Philip DeGroote (South African cellist—New York), Eliot Fisk (guitarist—New York), Giuseppe Giacomini (Italian tenor—Cincinnati), Nigel Kennedy (British violinist—New York), Andreas Klein (German pianist—New York), Bennett Lerner (pianist—New York), Luis Lima (Argentine tenor—New York), Cho-Liang Lin (Chinese violinist—Philadelphia), Ashley Putnam (soprano—Norfolk), Simon Rattle (British conductor—tour); Julien Robbins (bass—Philadelphia), Louise Williams (British violinist—New York).

**Metropolitan Opera**   Norman Bailey (British baritone), Hildegard Behrens (German soprano), Sarah Caldwell (conductor), James Conlon (conductor), Jean Cox (tenor), Stafford Dean (British bass), Simon Estes (bass-baritone), Maria Ewing (soprano), Gianandrea Gavazzeni (Italian conductor), René Kollo (German tenor), Eva Marton (Hungarian soprano), Johanna Meier (soprano),

Elena Obraztsova (Russian mezzo-soprano), Alberto Remedios (British tenor), Ellen Shade (soprano), Neil Shicoff (tenor), Richard Stilwell (baritone), Alan Titus (baritone), Tatiana Troyanos (mezzo-soprano), Ruth Welting (soprano).

**Others**  Frederick Burchinal (baritone — Amsterdam).

## I. New Positions

**Conductors**  Michael Charry (Nashville Symphony Orchestra — to 1982); Bruce Hangen (Portland [Maine] Symphony Orchestra); Walter Hendl (Erie Symphony Orchestra, Pennsylvania); Rainer Miedél (Seattle Symphony Orchestra); John Nelson (Indianapolis Symphony Orchestra — to 1987); Frederik Prausnitz (Peabody Symphony Orchestra and Opera); André Previn (Pittsburgh Symphony Orchestra — to 1984); Gerard Schwarz (Eliot Feld Dance Co.); Robert Vodnoy (Northwest Indiana Symphony Orchestra).

**Educational**  Schuyler Chapin (dean, Columbia School of the Arts); John Crosby (president, Manhattan School — to 1985); Irene Dalis (San Jose State University); Charles Hamm (Dartmouth); Gary Karr (Hartt School of Music); Louis Krasner (New England Conservatory); Milton Katims (University of Houston — to 1984); Joseph Machlis (Juilliard); William Masselos (Juilliard); Frederik Prausnitz (Peabody); Eileen Southern (Harvard); Christoph Wolff (Harvard).

**Other**  James Levine (music director, Metropolitan Opera).

## J. Honors and Awards

**Honors**  Dominick Argento, Robert Helps, Robert Hall Lewis, and Richard Wernick (American Academy); Samuel Barber (American Academy Gold Medal); Leslie Bassett and Jack Beeson (American Academy and Institute); Jack Beeson (National Arts Club Medal); William Dawson (Alabama Hall of Fame); Arthur Fiedler (Gold Baton); Ashley Putnam (Weyerhauser Award); Artur Rubinstein (*Musical America* Musician of the Year and Medal of Freedom); José Serebrier (Ditson).

**Awards**  Dickran Atamian and Clamma Dale (Naumburg); Karen Eley (Paganini Second); Douglas Humphreys (Bachauer); Christopher Giles (Bachauer Second); Ani Kavafian (Avery Fisher); Ursula Oppens (Avery Fisher); Peter Orth (Kapell Second).

**K. Biographical**  Maurice Abravanel undergoes open-heart surgery; Yefim Bronfman (Israeli pianist) emigrates to the United States; Sarah Caldwell becomes the first woman to conduct at the Metropolitan Opera; Sergice Comissiona and Horacio Gutiérrez become American citizens; Raymond Leppard (British conductor/harpsichordist) settles in the United States; Steve Reich studies Hebrew ritual for a year; Artur Rubinstein retires from public recital life owing to increasing blindness.

## L. Musical Beginnings

**Performing Groups**  American Composers Orchestra (New York); Atlanta Lyric Opera Co.; Austin Civic Wind Ensemble; (New) Cleveland Opera; Denver Early Music Consort; Des Moines Community Orchestra; Emerson String Quartet (Juilliard); Folger Music Consort (Washington, DC); Opera Ebony (Philadelphia); Philadelphia Opera Theater; Russian Orchestra of the Americas; St. Louis Symphony Chorus; St. Louis Opera Theatre; Salt Lake Pro Musica; San Francisco Early Music Society; Utah Opera Co.

**Festivals**  Festival of Contemporary Music (New York); June in Buffalo (New York); SMU Conservatory Summer Music Festival (Dallas, Texas).

**Educational**  American Institute for Verdi Studies (New York); *Journal of the Arnold Schoenberg Institute*; New School of Music (Cambridge, Massachusetts).

**Other**  Gina Bachauer International Piano Competition; Crouse-Hinds Concert Theater (Syracuse Civic Center); Female Composers of America (American Women Composers); ICM Artists; Kazuko Hillyer International Concert Arts Society; Sacred Music Society of America (New York); Scottsdale Center for the Arts (Phoenix, Arizona); Society of Advertising Music Producers, Arrangers, and Composers (SAMPAC).

## M. Music Publications

Berry, Wallace, *Structural Functions in Music*
Borroff, Edith, *Music in Perspective*
Cope, David H., *New Music Composition—New Music Notation*
Downes, Edward, *New York Philharmonic Guide to the Symphony*
Eaton, John C., *Involvement with Music: New Music since 1950*
Kohs, Ellis, *Musical Form: Studies in Analysis and Synthesis*
Kolodin, Irving, *The Opera Omnibus: Four Centuries of Critical Give and Take*
Kraft, Leo, *Gradus: An Integrated Approach to Harmony, Counterpoint and Analysis*
Lowens, Irving, *Bibliography of Songsters Printed in America before 1821*
Read, Gardner, *Contemporary Instrumental Techniques*
Serly, Tibor, *Modus Lascivus: The Road to Enharmonicism*

## N. Musical Compositions

**Chamber Music**   Hugh Aitken, *Tromba*; Elaine Barkin, *String Trio*; Chester Biscardi, *Piano Trio*; Gloria Coates, *String Quartet No. 3*; Curtis Curtis-Smith, *Unisonics* (saxophone and piano); Mario Davidovsky, *String Quartet No. 3*; Ezra Laderman, *String Quartet No. 5*; Leo Ornstein, *String Quartet No. 3*; Steve Reich, *Music for Eighteen Musicians*; William Schuman, *Amaryllis*.

**Choral/Vocal**   David Amram, *The Trail of Beauty*; Louis Ballard, *Thus Spake Abraham* (cantata); Jack Beeson, *From a Watchtower* (five songs); Henry Brant, *Spatial Concerto (Questions from Genesis)*; Paul Chihara, *Missa Carminum*; John Corigliano, *Dylan Thomas Trilogy*; Norman Dello Joio, *Mass*; David Del Tredici, *Final Alice*; Harold Farberman, *War Cry on a Prayer Feather*; Morton Feldman, *Voice, Violin, and Piano*; Vivian Fine, *Three Sonnets from Keats*; John Harbison, *The Flower-fed Buffaloes*; Daniel Pinkham, *The Passion of Judas*; Ned Rorem, *Women's Voices* (song cycle); William Schuman, *Casey at the Bat*; Leo Smit, *At the Corner of the Sky*; Robert Starer, *The People, Yes*; Robert A. Wykes, *Adequate Earth* (oratorio).

**Concertos**   Claus Adam, *Concerto Variations for Cello and Orchestra*; Leonardo Balada, *Concerto for Four Guitars and Orchestra*; George Barati, *Guitar Concerto*; Leslie Bassett, *Concerto for 2 Pianos*; William Bolcom, *Piano Concerto*; Michael Colgrass, *Concertmasters*; Donald Erb, *Trombone Concerto—Cello Concerto;* Robert Helps, *Piano Concerto No. 2*; Robert Kelly, *Viola Concerto*; Benjamin Lees, *Concerto for Woodwind Quintet and Orchestra—Variations for Piano and Orchestra*; Walter Piston, *Concerto for String Quartet, Winds and Percussion*; Gundaris Poné, *Horn Concerto*; Gunther Schuller, *Violin Concerto—Horn Concerto No. 2*; Elliott Schwartz, *Janus* (piano and orchestra); Elie Siegmeister, *Double Concerto* (violin, piano); Francis Thorne, *Violin Concerto*.

**Electronic**   John Adams, *Onyx* (tape); Charles Amirkhanian, *Mahogany Ballpark* (tape); Beth Anderson, *Soap Tuning—Zen Piece* (theater pieces); Anthony Gnazzo, *The Art of Canning Music*; Lejaren Hiller, *Electronic Sonata—Midnight Carnival*; Gordon Mumma, *Passenger Pigeon 1776–1976*; Roger Reynolds, *Voicespace II, "A Merciful Coincidence"*; David Tudor, *Forest Speech*; Olly Wilson, *Sometimes* (tenor and tape).

**Operas**   Dominick Argento, *The Voyage of Edgar Allan Poe*; Robert Ashley, *Music with Roots in the Aether*; Ernst Bacon, *Dr. Franklin* (musical play); Carlisle Floyd, *Bilby's Doll*; Andrew Imbrie, *Angle of Repose*; Jean Eichelberger Ivey, *Testament of Eve* (monodrama); Ulysses Kay, *Jubilee*; Leon Kirchner, *Lily*; Gian Carlo Menotti, *The Hero*; Thomas Pasatieri, *Inez de Castro—Washington Square*; Eric Salzman, *Stauf*; Hugo Weisgall, *Jennie, or the Hundred Nights*.

**Orchestra/Band**   Samuel Adler, *Concertino No. 2 for String Orchestra*; Louis Ballard, *Fantasy Aborigine II*; Irwin Bazelon, *Detonations*; Norman Dello Joio, *Colonial Variations*; Morton Feldman, *Orchestra*; Sydney Hodkinson, *Edge of the Olde One*; Nikolai Lopatnikoff, *Melting Pot* (ballet); Robert Mills, *Symphonic Ode*; Ron Nelson, *Five Pieces after Paintings by Andrew Wyeth*; Lester Trimble, *Panels for Orchestra*; Richard Wernick, *Visions of Wonder and Terror* (Pulitzer Prize).

**Piano/Organ**   William Albright, *Five Chromatic Dances*; Arthur Berger, *Composition for Piano, Four Hands*; William Bolcom, *Mysteries* (organ); George Edwards, *Draconian Measures*; Richard Felciano, *On the Heart of the Earth* (organ); Barbara Kolb, *Appello*; Leo Kraft, *Ten Short Pieces*; Robert Muczynski, *Maverick Pieces*; George Perle, *Six Etudes*; George Rochberg, *Partita Variations*; Ned Rorem, *A Quaker Reader* (organ); Dane Rudhyar, *Theurgy—Transmutation*; Clifford Taylor, *Thirty-Six More Ideas*; George Walker, *Sonata No. 2*; Charles Wuorinen, *Sonata No. 2*.

**Symphonies**   William Bergsma, *Symphony No. 2, "Voyages"*; Howard Boatwright, *Symphony*; Morton Gould, *Symphony of Spirituals*; Alan Hovhaness, *Symphonies No. 27–31*; Henri Lazarof, *Chamber Symphony*; Gian Carlo Menotti, *Symphony No. 1, "The Halcyon"*; George Rochberg, *Symphony No. 4*; Gunther Schuller, *Concerto for Orchestra II*; Joseph F. Wagner, *Symphony No. 4*; Robert Ward, *Symphony No. 5, "Canticles of America."*

# 1977

✿

## Historical Highlights

All Vietnam draft evaders are pardoned by President Carter; the Department of Energy is formed; a severe energy crisis marks the winter months; the Panama Canal Treaty is signed, providing for the eventual ownership of the Canal by Panama; territorial waters are extended to 200 miles off the coast; Egypt and Israel begin peace talks.

## World Cultural Highlights

**World Art**   Balthus, *Nude in Profile;* Marc Chagall, *American Windows (Chicago)*; David Hockney, *Looking at Pictures on a Screen*; Heinz Mack, *Light Column, Munich;* Bridget Riley, *Green Dominance.*

**World Literature**   Alan Ayckbourn, *Bedroom Farce;* Kingsley Amis, *Jake's Thing;* James Herriot, *All Things Wise and Wonderful*; Barbara Pym, *Quartet in Autumn.*

**World Music**   Andrzej Panufnik, *Sinfonia Mistica*; Krzysztof Penderecki, *Violin Concerto—De Profundis*; Michael Tippett, *Symphony No. 4—Ice Break*; Malcolm Williamson, *Symphony No. 4.*

**Miscellaneous**   The Institut de Recherche et de Coordination Acoustique/Musique (IRCAM) opens in Paris; deaths include Richard Addinsell, Thomas Blackburn, Witold Malcuzynski, and John Nash.

## American Art and Literature Highlights

**Births/Deaths**   Deaths include artists Naum Gabo, Henry P. Gray, William Gropper, and literary figures James M. Cain, John Dickson Carr, Edward Dahlberg, James Jones, MacKinlay Kantor, Robert Traill Lowell, Jr., Vladimir Nabokov, Anaïs Nin, and Louis Untermeyer.

**Art Works**   Jack Beal, *Murals, Department of Labor Building, D.C.*; Robert Bechtle, *Watsonville Patio*; Edward Kienholz, *The Art Show*; R. B. Kitaj, *The Orientalist*; Willem de Kooning, *North Atlantic Light*; Robert Kushner, *Empty Pagoda*; Robert Longo, *The American Soldier*; Claes Oldenburg, *Batcolumn*; Miriam Schapiro, *Anonymous Was a Woman.*

**Literature**   Michael Cristofer, *The Shadow Box* (Pulitzer Prize); Robert Lowell, *Day by Day* (National Book Critics' Award); James A. McPherson, *Elbow Room* (Pulitzer Prize); Toni Morrison, *Song of Solomon* (National Book Critics' Award—National Book Award); Howard Nemerov, *Collected Poems* (Pulitzer Prize); Wendy Wasserstein, *Uncommon Women and Others.*

## Music—The Vernacular/Commercial Scene

**B. Deaths**   Puddinghead Battle (trumpeter/arranger) February 6; Stoney Cooper (folk singer)

March 22; Bing Crosby (singer) October 14; Paul Desmond (saxophonist) May 30; "Sleepy" John Estes (singer) June 5; Joe Garland (composer/arranger) April 21; Erroll Garner (pianist) January 2; Buddy Johnson (pianist/bandleader) February 9; Roland Kirk (saxophonist) December 5; Sam Lanin (clarinetist/bandleader) May 5; Guy Lombardo (bandleader); Elvis Presley (singer) August 16; Ethel Waters (singer/actress) September 1.

## C. Biographical

**Performing Groups**   The Avengers; Black Flag; The Buggles; Centaurus; Creed; The Dickies; Dils; DNA; Drifting Cowboys II (by Hank Williams); Grand Master Flash and the Furious Five; The Germs; Godz; Legs Diamond; Lipps, Inc.; Love of Life Orchestra; Mandingo Griot Society; Menudo (Puerto Rican group); The Misfits; Neville Brothers; 1994; Ozone; The Romantics; ROVA Saxophone Quartet; Shalamar; S.O.S. Band; String Trio of New York; The Sugar Hill Gang; The Village People; X; The Zantees.

**New Beginnings**   Artists House Records (New York); Bee Hive Record Co. (Chicago); Big Bands International; Jazz World Society; Russian River Jazz Festival (California); Songwriters Hall of Fame; Women's Jazz Festival (Kansas City).

**Honors**   Merle Travis (Country Music Hall of Fame).

**D. Publications**   J. L. Collier, *The Great Jazz Artists*; Richard Crawford, *The Civil War Song*; Joan Dew, *Singers and Sweethearts: The Women of Country Music*; Dena Epstein, *Sinful Tunes and Spirituals: Black Folk Music to the Civil War*; David Ewen, *All the Years of American Popular Music*; Arthur Jackson, *The World of Big Bands: The Sweet and Swinging Years*; Frederick Tillis, *Jazz Theory and Improvisation*.

## E. Representative Works

**Musicals**   C. Coleman and M. Stewart, *I Love My Wife*; J. Kander and F. Ebb, *The Act*; Cole Porter, *Unsung Cole* (tribute revue); Shire and Maltby, *Starting Here, Starting Now*; Stephen Sondheim, *Side by Side by Sondheim* (tribute review); C. Strouse and M. Charnin, *Annie* (New York Drama Critics' Award).

**Number One Hits**   *Best of My Love* (The Emotions); *Blinded by the Light* (Manfred Mann's Earth Band); *Car Wash* (Rose Royce); *Da Doo Ron Ron* (Shaun Cassidy); *Dancing Queen* (Abba); *Don't Give Up On Us* (David Soul); *Don't Leave Me This Way* (Thelma Houston); *Dreams* (Fleetwood Mac); *Evergreen* (Oscar—Barbra Streisand); *Gonna Fly Now* (Bill Conti); *Got to Give It Up* (Marvin Gaye); *Hotel California—New Kid in Town* (Eagles); *How Deep Is Your Love* (Bee Gees); *I Just Want to Be Your Everything* (Andy Gibb); *I Wish—Sir Duke* (Stevie Wonder); *I'm Your Boogie Man* (KC and the Sunshine Band); *Looks Like We Made It* (Barry Manilow); *Rich Girl* (Hall and Oates); *Southern Nights* (Glen Campbell); *Torn Between Two Lovers* (Mary MacGregor); *Undercover Angel* (Alan O'Day); *When I Need You—You Make Me Feel Like Dancing* (Leo Sayer); *You Don't Have to Be a Star* (Marilyn McCoo and Billy Davis); *You Light Up My Life* (Oscar—Debby Boone).

**Other**   Stephen Sondheim, *The Seven Percent Solution* (film music); John Williams, *Close Encounters of the Third Kind—Star Wars* (film music—Oscar).

# Music—The Cultivated/Art Music Scene

**G. Deaths**   Kurt Adler (pianist/conductor) September 21; E. Power Biggs (organist) March 10; Gena Branscombe (composer) July 26; Maria Callas (soprano) September 16; Irwin Fischer (composer) May 7; Sidney Foster (pianist) February 7; Roland Hayes (tenor) January 1; Helen Hewitt (musicologist) March 19; Jacob Kwalwasser (educator) August 7; Paul Nordoff (composer/therapist) January 18; Carmela Ponselle (mezzo-soprano) June 13; Gustave Reese (musicologist) September 7; Thomas Schippers (conductor) December 16; Harold Spivacke (musicologist) May 9; Leopold Stokowski (conductor) September 13; Grete Stückgold (British-born soprano) September 13; John Vincent (composer) January 21.

## H. Debuts

**United States**   Elizabeth Bainbridge (British mezzo-soprano—Chicago), William D. Black (pianist—New York), Barry Busse (tenor—Houston), Kristine Ciesinski (soprano—New York), David Duesing (baritone—San Francisco?), Faith Esham (soprano—New York), Wilhelmenia Fernandez (soprano—Houston), Michael Habermann (pianist—New York), Eric Halfvarson (bass—Houston), Janice Hall (soprano—Wolf Trap), Vernon Hartman (baritone—Philadelphia), Sylvia Ho (Chinese pianist—New York), Peter Hofmann (German tenor—San Francisco), Gwynne Howell (British bass—Chicago), Linda Kelm (soprano—Seattle), Gidon Kremer (Latvian violinist), Steven Lubin (pianist—New York), Silvia Marcovici (Romanian violinist—New York), Yuri Masurok (Polish baritone—San Francisco), Barry McCauley (tenor—San Francisco), Michael Myers (tenor—Central City), Pamela Myers (soprano—San Francisco), Ken Noda (pianist—Minneapolis), Patricia Payne (New Zealand soprano—San Francisco), Linda Roark-Strummer (soprano—St. Louis), Hanna Schwarz (German mezzo-soprano—San Francisco), Tibor Szász (Romanian pianist—New York), Alexander Toradze (Russian pianist—New York), Carol Vaness (soprano—San Francisco), Sarah Walker (British mezzo-soprano—Chicago).

**Metropolitan Opera**   James Atherton (tenor), Carmen Balthrop (soprano), Josephine Barstow (British soprano), John Brecknock (British tenor), Claudine Carlson (mezzo-soprano), John Cheek (bass-baritone), Maria Chiara (Italian soprano), Ileana Cotrubas (Romanian soprano), Carole Ann Farley (soprano), Edita Gruberová (Czech soprano), Isola Jones (mezzo-soprano), Florence Quivar (mezzo-soprano), Sylvia Sass (Hungarian soprano), Bernard Weikl (Austrian baritone).

**Other**   Sharon Isbin (guitarist—London), James Tocco (pianist—Vienna).

**I. New Positions**

**Conductors**   Sergiu Comissiona (American Symphony Orchestra, New York—to 1982); Dennis Russell Davies (American Composers Orchestra); Edo de Waart (San Francisco Symphony Orchestra—to 1985); Antal Dorati (Detroit Symphony Orchestra—to 1981); François Huybrechts (San Antonio Symphony Orchestra); Erich Kunzel (Cincinnati Pops); Eduardo Mata (Dallas Symphony Orchestra); Thomas Michalak (New Jersey Symphony Orchestra—to 1983); Mstislav Rostropovich (National Symphony Orchestra); Jerzy Semkow (St. Louis Symphony Orchestra—to 1979); Leonard Slatkin (New Orleans Philharmonic Symphony Orchestra—to 1979); Judith Somogi (Utica Symphony Orchestra); Walter Susskind (Cincinnati Symphony Orchestra—to 1980).

**Educational**   Jorge Bolet (Curtis); Elliott Galkin (director, Peabody—to 1982); Boris Goldovsky (Curtis); Grant Johannesen (president, Cleveland Institute—to 1984); Abraham Kaplan (University of Washington); Theodore Lettvin (University of Michigan—to 1987); Zinka Milanov (Curtis); Nicolas Roussakis (Rutgers); Abbey Simon (University of Houston); James Tocco (Indiana University); Earl Wild (Juilliard); Richard Westenburg (choral head, Juilliard—to 1989).

**Other**   Allen Forte (president, Society for Music Theory); Joan Peyser (editor, *Musical Quarterly*—to 1984); Patrick J. Smith (president, Music Critics Association—to 1981).

**J. Honors and Awards**

**Honors**   Bethany Beardslee (doctorate, Princeton); Paul Cooper and Paul Lansky (American Academy); Arthur Fiedler (Medal of Freedom—National Arts Club Medal); Plácido Domingo (*Musical America* Musician of the Year); Avery Fisher (Gold Baton); Leon Kirchner (Brandeis); Samuel Lipman (Deems Taylor, music criticism); Irving Lowens (Deems Taylor II); Virgil Thomson (MacDowell Medal).

**Awards**   Christopher Giles (Bachauer First); Aprile Millo (Farrar); Edward Newman (Kapell Second); Tobias Picker (Bearns); Nathaniel Rosen (Naumburg); André-Michel Schub (Fisher); Jeffrey Shumway (Bachauer Second); Richard Stoltzman (Fisher); Jeffrey Swann (Cliburn Third).

**K. Biographical**   Victoria Bond becomes the first woman to receive a doctorate in conducting from Juilliard; Gunther Herbig (Czech conductor) becomes Principal Guest Conductor of the Dallas Symphony Orchestra; Thomas Schippers, made Conductor Emeritus of the Cincinnati Symphony Orchestra, learns of his lung cancer; Dmitri Stikovetsky (Russian violinist) comes to the United States.

**L. Musical Beginnings**

**Performing Groups**   Austin Civic Orchestra; Chamber Music America (New York); Cincinnati

Pops Orchestra; Dallas Symphony Chorus; Los Angeles Piano Quartet; Ninety Second Street "Y" Chamber Orchestra (New York); John Oliver Chorale (Massachusetts); Opera for Youth (Sarasota, Florida); Pittsburgh New Music Ensemble; Relache (new music ensemble); Schoenberg (Columbia) String Quartet; Tremont String Quartet (New York); Young People's Philharmonia (Springfield, Massachusetts); Zeitgeist.

**Festivals**  Chamber Music West (San Francisco Conservatory); Colorado Music Festival (Boulder); Festival of Two Worlds (Spoleto, USA—Charleston, South Carolina); West Coast Festival of Sound Poetry (San Francisco).

**Educational**  International Index of Dissertations (AMS).

**Other**  American Artists International Foundation; American Music/Theater Group (Illinois); Association of Concert Bands (Allentown, Pennsylvania); Association of Professional Vocal Ensembles (Chicago); *Computer Music Journal*; Cumberland County Civic Center (Maine); *Fanfare*; Jackson Arts Center (Mississippi); Music Library Association Publication Prizes; Pianists Foundation of America; Tulsa Performing Arts Center.

## M. Music Publications

Behague, Gerard, *Music in Latin America: An Introduction*
Carter, Elliott, *The Writings of Elliott Carter: An American Composer Looks at Modern Music*
Chapin, Schuyler, *Musical Chairs: A Life in the Arts*
Hemke, Frederick, *The Teacher's Guide to the Saxophone*
Lippman, Edward, *A Humanistic Philosophy of Music*
Perle, George, *Twelve-tone Tonality*
Salzman, E. and Sahl, M., *Making Changes: A Practical Guide to Vernacular Harmony*
Seeger, Charles, *Studies in Musicology, 1935–75—Essays for a Humanist* (editor)
Tarr, Edward, *Die Trompete*
Vinton, John, *Essays after a Dictionary*

## N. Musical Compositions

**Chamber Music**  David Amram, *Native American Portraits*; Larry Austin, *Phantasmagoria*; Seymour Barab, *String Quartet*; Gloria Coates, *String Quartet No. 4*; Paul Cooper, *String Quartet No. 6*; Homer Keller, *Cello Sonata*; Harvey Sollberger, *Flute and Drums*; Robert Starer, *Piano Quartet*; Joan Tower, *Amazon I*.

**Choral/Vocal**  Stephen Albert, *To Wake the Dead*; Milton Babbitt, *A Solo Requiem*; Warren Benson, *Five Lyrics of Louise Bogan*; Leonard Bernstein, *Songfest*; George Crumb, *Star Child*; Mario Davidovsky, *Scenes from Shir-ha-shirim (Song of Solomon)*; Miriam Gideon, *Songs of Youth and Madness*; Robert Helps, *Gossamer Noons*; Stephen Paulus, *Canticles: Songs and Rituals for Easter and the May*; Hale Smith, *Toussaint L'Ouverture 1803*.

**Concertos**  Samuel Adler, *Flute Concerto*; Theodore Antoniou, *Double Concerto for Percussion and Orchestra*; William Bergsma, *Sweet Was the Song the Virgin Sung: Tristan Revisited* (viola and orchestra); John Corigliano, *Clarinet Concerto*; Andrew Imbrie, *Flute Concerto*; Karl Korte, *Piano Concerto*; Ezra Laderman, *Viola Concerto*; Donald Martino, *Triple Concerto* (clarinet, bass, and contrabass clarinets); Vincent Persichetti, *English Horn Concerto, Opus 137*; Shulamit Ran, *Piano Concerto*; Gardner Read, *Piano Concerto, Opus 130*; Robert Suderburg, *Percussion Concerto*.

**Electronic**  Conrad Cummings, *Endangered Species*; Jacob Druckman, *Animus IV*; Anthony Gnazzo, *Begin Again*; Alvin Lucier, *Music on a Long Thin Wire*; Salvatore Martirano, *Fast Forward*; Priscilla McLean, *Invisible Chariots*; Allen Strange, *Soundbeams*.

**Operas**  T. J. Anderson, *The Shell Fairy* (operetta); Seymour Barab, *Little Stories in Tomorrow's Paper*; Morton Feldman, *Neither* (monodrama); Vivian Fine, *The Women in the Garden*; John Harbison, *Full Moon in March*; Jerome Moross, *Sorry, Wrong Number*; Thea Musgrave, *Mary, Queen of Scots*; Eric Stokes, *The Jealous Cellist*.

**Orchestra/Band**  Samuel Adler, *Aeolus, King of the Winds*; David Amram, *Overture for Brass and Percussion;* Dominick Argento, *In Praise of Music*; Ernst Bacon, *Over the Waters Overture*;

Louis Ballard, *Fantasy Aborigine III*; Leslie Bassett, *Sounds, Shapes and Symbols* (band); Jean Berger, *Diversion for Strings*; Leonard Bernstein, *Overture, Slava!*; Chester Biscardi, *At the Still Point*; William Bolcom, *Seattle Slew Suite*; Jacob Druckman, *Chiaroscuro*; Anne LeBaron, *Metamorphosis* (Bearns Prize); Ned Rorem, *Sunday Morning*; Dane Rudhyar, *Cosmic Cycle*; Joseph Schwantner, *And the Mountains Rising Nowhere* (winds); Francis Thorne, *Spoon River Overture*; Aurelio de la Vega, *Adiós* (Friedheim Award).

**Piano/Organ**  John Adams, *China Gates—Phrygian Gates*; John Corigliano, *Etude Fantasy*; Morton Feldman, *Piano*; Miriam Gideon, *Sonata*; Alan Hovhaness, *Sonata Ananda—Sonata Fred the Cat—Sonata Mt. Ossipee*; Leo Kraft, *Ten Short Pieces for Piano*; Daniel Pinkham, *Blessings* (organ); Shulamit Ran, *Hyperbolae*; Frederic Rzewski, *The People United Will Never Be Defeated—Four Pieces*; Roger Sessions, *Five Pieces*; Louise Talma, *Textures*.

**Symphonies**  Elliott Carter, *A Symphony of Three Orchestras*; Ross Lee Finney, *Concerto for Strings*; Howard Hanson, *Symphony No. 7, "A Sea Symphony"*; Alan Hovhaness, *Symphony No. 32—Symphony No. 33—Symphony No. 34*; Henri Lazarof, *Concerto for Orchestra*; Vittorio Rieti, *Symphony No. 7*; Francis Thorne, *Symphony No. 4*.

# 1978

✸

## Historical Highlights

Diplomatic relations are officially established between the United States and Communist China; Menachem Begin of Israel and Anwar Sadat of Egypt meet at Camp David in Maryland to discuss peace between the two countries; Congress ratifies the Panama Canal Treaty; the first successful transatlantic balloon crossing is made; riots against the Shah break out in Iran.

## World Cultural Highlights

**World Art**  Malcolm Morley, *Ultimate Anxiety—M.A.S.H.*; Meret Oppenheim, *The Green Spectator;* Jeffrey Shaw, *Moonlight Goose*.

**World Literature**  Graham Greene, *The Human Factor*; Czeslaw Milosz, *Bells in Winter*; Harold Pinter, *Betrayal.*

**World Music**  Henri Dutilleux, *Timbres, espace, mouvement*; György Ligeti, *The Grand Macabre*; Krzysztof Penderecki, *Paradise Lost*; Aulis Sallinen, *The Red Line*.

**Miscellaneous**  Grieg Hall is dedicated in Bergen, Norway; the Dresden Opera Festivals begin; the Opera North Co. is founded in Leeds, England; deaths include Carlos Chávez, Giorgio de Chirico, Aram Khachaturian, Alexander Kipnis, and Willem von Otterloo.

## American Art and Literature Highlights

**Deaths**  Deaths include art figures Harry Bertoia, Edwin Dickinson, Lorser Feitelson, Paul Jennewein, John Koch, Gabriel Kohn, Gordon Matta-Clark, Abraham Rattner, Norman Rockwell, and literary figures Faith Baldwin, Katherine G. Biddle, James G. Cozzens, Phyllis McGinley, John Hall Wheelock, Margaret Widdemer, and Louis Zukofsky.

**Art Works**  Robert Arneson, *Splat*; Jack Beal, *Prudence, Avarice, Lust, Justice, Anger*; Ron Davis, *Wedge Wave*; Jim Dine, *Self-Portrait with Cigar*; Richard Estes, *Downtown*; Roy Lichtenstein, *Self-Portrait*; Elizabeth Murray, *Parting and Together*; Susan Rothenberg, *The Smoker*; Frank Stella, *Harewa*; Cy Twombly, *Series: Fifty Days at Iliam*; H. C. Westermann, *Big Leaguer*.

**Literature**  Donald Coburn, *The Gin Game* (Pulitzer Prize); John Irving, *The World According to Garp* (National Book Award); Arthur Kopit, *Wings*; Tim O'Brien, *Going After Cacciato* (National Book Award); Sam Shepard, *Buried Child* (Pulitzer Prize); Isaac Bashevis Singer, *Shosha*; Robert P. Warren, *Now and Then: Poems 1976–1978* (Pulitzer Prize); Herman Wouk, *War and Remembrance*.

## Music—The Vernacular/Commercial Scene

**B. Deaths**   Milton Ager (pianist/composer) July 5; Johnny Bond (songwriter) June 29; Juke Boy Bonner (singer/guitarist) June 29; Alex Bradford (singer/writer) February 15; Maybelle Carter (singer) October 23; Don Ellis (trumpeter/bandleader) December 17; Ruth Etting (singer/actress) September 24; Enoch Light (bandleader) July 31; Ray Noble (bandleader) April 2; Louis Prima (trumpeter/singer) August 24; Lennie Tristano (pianist) November 18; Joe Venuti (violinist) August 14; Peggy Wood (singer/actress) March 18.

**C. Biographical**

**Performing Groups**   Avatar; Blind Illusion; Breathless; The dBs; The Dead Kennedys; DeBarge; Larry Gatlin and the Gatlin Brothers; Girlschool; The Go-Gos; Holly and the Italians; The Hooters; The Knack; Lovely Music, Ltd.; The Plasmatics; The Pretenders; The Radiators; Redd Kross; Spider; Stone City Band; Storm; Survivor; Toto; 20/20; The Waitresses.

**New Beginnings**   Atlanta Free Jazz Festival; DAAGNIM (Dallas Association for Avant Garde and Neo Impressionistic Music); Delta Blues Museum (Clarksdale, Mississippi); *Imagine Magazine*; Newport Jazz Saratoga (Saratoga Springs); *New Wave Rock*; Paradise Valley Jazz Party; Rhino Records; Solar Records.

**Honors**   Grandpa Jones (Country Music Hall of Fame); Richard Rodgers (Kennedy Center).

**Miscellaneous**   Eubie Blake, at the ripe old age of 95, performs at the White House; Jimmy Giuffre begins teaching at the New England Conservatory.

**D. Publications**   Gerald Bordman, *The American Musical Theatre: A Chronicle*; Douglas Green, *Country Roots: The Origins of Country Music*; D. A. Jasen and T. J. Tichenor, *Rags and Ragtime: A Musical History*; Kenny Rogers and Len Epand, L., *Making It with Music*; Arnold Shaw, *Honkers and Shouters: The Golden Years of Rhythm and Blues*.

**E. Representative Works**

**Musicals**   Eubie Blake, *Eubie* (tribute revue); C. Coleman, B. Comden, A. Green, *On the Twentieth Century*; Fremont and Willens, *Piano Bar*; Carol Hall, *The Best Little Whorehouse in Texas*; C. Lederer and L. Davis, *Timbuktu* (black casting of *Kismet*); M. W. Marvin and C. Durang, *A History of the American Film*; Charles Strouse, *By Strouse* (revue); Fats Waller, *Ain't Misbehavin'* (New York Drama Critics Award).

**Number One Hits**   *Baby Come Back* (Player); *Boogie Oogie Oogie* (A Taste of Honey); *Le Freak* (Chic); *Grease* (Frankie Valli); *Hot Child in the City* (Nick Gilder); *If I Can't Have You* (Yvonne Elliman); *Kiss You All Over* (Exile); *MacArthur Park* (Donna Summer); *Miss You* (Rolling Stones); *Saturday Night Fever—Stayin' Alive* (Bee Gees); *Shadow Dancing—(Love Is) Thicker than Water* (Andy Gibb); *Three Times a Lady* (Commodores); *Too Much, Too Little, Too Late* (Johnny Mathis and Deniece Williams); *With a Little Luck* (Wings); *You Don't Bring Me Flowers* (Barbra Streisand and Neil Diamond); *You Needed Me* (Anne Murray); *You're the One That I Want* (John Travolta and Olivia Newton-John).

**Other**   Anthony Braxton, *For Four Orchestras*; Dave Brubeck, *Beloved Son*; Paul Jabara, *Last Dance* (Oscar); Henry Mancini, *House Calls—Who Is Killing the Great Chefs of Europe?* (film music); John Williams, *Superman* (film music).

## Music—The Cultivated/Art Music Scene

**G. Deaths**   Claire Coci (organist) September 30; Theodore M. Finney (musicologist) May 19; Don Gillis (composer) January 10; Carl Hugo Grimm (organist) October 25; Michel Gusikoff (violinist/composer) July 10; Charles Haubiel (composer) August 26; Oswald Jonas (Austrian-born musicologist) March 19; Ernest Kanitz (Austrian-born composer) April 7; Harrison Kerr (composer/educator) August 15; Alexander Kipnis (Russian-born bass) May 14; Rudolf Kolisch (Austrian-born violinist) August 1; Wesley La Violette (composer) July 29; Raymond Michalski (bass) December 24; Nicolas Nabokov (Russian-born composer) April 6; Tibor Serly (Hungarian-born composer/theorist) October 8; William Steinberg (German-born conductor) May 16; William Grant Still (composer) December 3; Howard Swanson (composer) November 12; David M. Williams (organist) March 13.

## H. Debuts

**United States**    June Anderson (soprano—New York), David Atherton (British conductor—San Francisco), Frederick Burchinal (baritone—New York), Robert Cohen (British cellist—Tanglewood), Sandro De Palma (Italian pianist—New York), Yuri Egorov (Russian pianist—New York), Jerry Hadley (tenor—Sarasota), Lee Hoiby (as pianist—New York), Jeffrey Kahane (pianist—San Francisco), Ida Kavafian (violinist—New York), Emma Kirkby (British soprano—tour), John Kozar (pianist—New York), Katia and Marielle Labèque (French pianists—Los Angeles), André Laplante (Canadian pianist—New York), Lowell Lieberman (pianist—New York), Erie Mills (soprano—St. Louis), Kurt Nikkanen (violinist—New York), Peter Rösel (German violinist—tour), András Schiff (Hungarian pianist—New York), Gregory Lee Stapp (bass—Philadelphia), David Starobin (guitarist—New York), Nunzio Todisco (Italian tenor), Delores Ziegler (mezzo-soprano—Knoxville), Krystian Zimerman (Polish pianist), Marilyn Zschau (soprano—New York).

**Metropolitan Opera**    John Aler (tenor), Arleen Augér (soprano), Kathleen Battle (soprano), Michael Devlin (bass-baritone), Pablo Elvira (baritone), Håkan Hagegård (Swedish baritone), Luis Lima (Argentine tenor), Jesus López-Cobos (Spanish conductor), Ermanno Mauro (Canadian tenor), Kurt Moll (German bass), Marianna Nicolescu (soprano), Siegmund Nimsgern (German bass-baritone), Ana Tomowa-Sintow (Bulgarian soprano), Iulia Varady (Romanian soprano).

**Other**    Marilyn Schmiege (mezzo-soprano—Wuppertal).

## I. New Positions

**Conductors**    Theo Alcantara (Phoenix Symphony Orchestra—to 1989); Carlo Maria Giulini (Los Angeles Philharmonic Orchestra—to 1983); Stephen Gunzenhauser (Delaware Symphony Orchestra); Luis Herrera de la Fuente (Oklahoma Symphony Orchestra—to 1988); Zubin Mehta (New York Philharmonic Orchestra—to 1991); Kent Nagano (Berkeley Symphony Orchestra); Brian Priestman (Florida Philharmonic Orchestra); Zoltán Rozsnyai (Knoxville Symphony Orchestra—to 1985); Gerard Schwarz (Los Angeles Chamber Orchestra—to 1986); Murry Sidlin (Tulsa Philharmic Orchestra—to 1980).

**Educational**    Eugene Conley (North Texas State); Andrew Foldi (Cleveland Institute); Szymon Goldberg (Juilliard and Yale—to 1982); Robert Helps (University of Southern Florida); Jonathan D. Kramer (Cincinnati Conservatory—to 1990); Paul Palombo (music director—University of Washington); Christopher Rouse (University of Michigan—to 1981); Roman Totenberg (director, Longy School, Massachusetts—to 1985); Yehudi Wyner (dean of music, SUNY, Purchase—to 1982).

**Other**    Ezra Laderman (music director, National Endowment for the Arts).

## J. Honors and Awards

**Honors**    Marian Anderson (Congressional Gold Medal—Kennedy Center); Wallace Berry, Curtis Curtis-Smith and Elie Siegmeister (American Academy); John Cage (American Academy of Arts and Sciences); Elliott Carter (Handel Medallion); Aaron Copland (Gold Baton); Jacob Druckman and George Perle (American Academy and Institute); Avery Fisher (National Arts Club Medal); Artur Rubinstein (Kennedy Center); Dane Rudhyar (Marjorie Peabody Waite Award).

**Awards**    Gregory Allen (Queen Elisabeth Second); James Barbagallo (Kapell Second); Rockwell Blake (Tucker); Boris Bloch (Busoni); Arthur Greene (Bachauer); Kevin Hanlon (Bearns); Dylana Jensen (Tchaikovsky Second, Violin); Yo-Yo Ma (Fisher); Aprile Millo (Caballé); Edward Newman (Bachauer Second); Elmar Oliveira (Tchaikovsky, shared First—first American violinist to win); Murray Perahia (Edison Prize); Nathaniel Rosen (Tchaikovsky, Cello); Carol Wincenc (Naumburg).

**K. Biographical**   Myung-Whun Chung becomes associate conductor of the Los Angeles Philharmonic Orchestra; Bella Davidovich (Russian pianist) emigrates to the United States; Simon Estes, as Wagner's Dutchman, becomes the first black to sing a lead role at Bayreuth; Yoel Levi (Romanian-born conductor) comes to the United States as assistant to Maazel in Cleveland; the Metropolitan Opera presents *La Bohème*, the first live telecast from New York; the White House begins a PBS series on Sunday afternoons beginning with Vladimir Horowitz.

**L. Musical Beginnings**

**Performing Groups**   Chanticleer (San Francisco); Four Corners Opera Association (Farmington, New Mexico); Honolulu Symphony Chorus; Knoxville (Tennessee) Opera Co.; Meredith Monk Vocal Ensemble; Mozartean Players (New York); (New) Pittsburgh Chamber Orchestra; Pittsburgh Chamber Opera Theater; Providence Opera Theater (Rhode Island); San Francisco Chamber Soloists; Wachovia Little Symphony (senior citizens).

**Festivals**   Basically Bach Festival (New York); Puerto Rico Biennials of Twentieth-Century Music; Festival of a Thousand Oaks (Peru, Nebraska); North Country Chamber Players Summer Festival (New Hampshire).

**Other**   ASCAP Foundation Grants to Young Composers; Cincinnati Composer's Guild; Community Artist Residency Training (CART); Denver Center for the Performing Arts; Noah Greenberg Award; Houston Cultural Arts Council; *Inter-American Review*; Kennedy Center Friedheim Awards; Shaw Attractions, Inc.

**M. Music Publications**

Artzt, Alice, *The Art of Practicing*
Cage, John, *Writings through Finnegans Wake*
Duckworth, William, *Theoretical Foundations of Music*
Forte, Allen, *The Harmonic Organization of the Rite of Spring*
Gutchë, Gene, *Music of the People*
Harris, Ernest, *Music Educations: A Guide to Information Sources*
Hoppin, Richard, *Medieval Music*
Kraft, Leo et al., *A New Approach to Keyboard Harmony*
Mordden, Ethan, *Opera in the Twentieth Century*
Read, Gardner, *Modern Rhythmic Notation*

**N. Musical Compositions**

**Chamber Music**   John Adams, *Shaker Loops*; Samuel Adler, *Piano Trio No. 2*; Leslie Bassett, *String Quartet No. 4*; John Harbison, *Quintet for Winds*; Charles Jones, *String Quartet No. 7*; Fred Lerdahl, *String Quartet No. 1*; Robert Palmer, *Cello Sonata No. 1*; Steve Reich, *Music for a Large Ensemble*; George Rochberg, *String Quartet No. 4* (Friedheim Award)—*String Quartets No. 5, 6 (Concord Quartets)*; Gerhard Samuel, *String Quartet No. 1*; Joseph Schwantner, *Sparrows*; Clifford Taylor, *String Quartet No. 2*.

**Choral/Vocal**   Theodore Antoniou, *Circle of Thanatos and Genesis*; Daniel Asia, *Sand II*; Elliott Carter, *Syringa*; George Edwards, *Veined Variety*; Ross Lee Finney, *Earthrise: A Trilogy Concerned with the Human Dilemma, Part III*; Kenneth Gaburo, *Subito*; Charles Jones, *The Fond Observer* (song cycle); Raoul Pleshka, *Cantata No. 2*; Robert Starer, *Transformation* (song cycle); George Walker, *Mass*.

**Concertos**   Jacob Druckman, *Viola Concerto*; Donald Erb, *Concerto for Keyboards and Orchestra*; Morton Feldman, *Flute and Orchestra*; John Harbison, *Piano Concerto* (Friedheim Award); Leon Kirchner, *Music for Flute and Orchestra*; William Kraft, *Tuba Concerto*; Meyer Kupferman, *Piano Concerto No. 2*; Ezra Laderman, *Violin Concerto—Piano Concerto No. 1*; Jerome Moross, *Concerto for Flute and Strings*; Gunther Schuller, *Contrabassoon Concerto*; Carlos Surinach, *Concerto for Harp and Orchestra*; Lester Trimble, *Harpsichord Concerto*.

**Electronic**   Charles Amirkhanian, *Audience* (tape); Beth Anderson, *Morning View and Maiden Spring* (mixed media); Alvin Lucier, *Ghosts*; Salvatore Martirano, *Fifty One*; Michael McNabb, *Dream-song*; Frederic Rzewski, *Squares*; Elliott Schwartz, *California Games*; Gil Trythall, *Luxikon I*.

**Operas**   William Albright, *The Magic City*; Dominick Argento, *Miss Havisham's Fire*; Jack Beeson, *Dr. Heidegger's Fountain of Youth*; John Eaton, *Danton and Robespierre*; Ezra Laderman, *Galileo Galilei*; Libby Larsen, *The Words upon the Windowpane*; Marvin David Levy, *The Balcony*; Eric Salzman, *Noah*; Robert Starer, *Apollonia*.

**Orchestra/Band**   Richard Adler, *Memory of a Childhood*; Samuel Adler, *A Little Night and Day Music* (band); Samuel Barber, *Third Essay for Orchestra, Opus 47*; Henry Brant, *Trinity of Spheres*; Michael Colgrass, *Déjà Vu* (Pulitzer Prize); Joaquin Nin-Culmell, *Le rêve de Cyrano* (ballet); Roger Reynolds, *Fiery Winds*; William Schuman, *In Sweet Music*; Joseph Schwantner, *Aftertones of Infinity* (Pulitzer Prize); Carlos Surinach, *The Owl and the Pussycat* (ballet).

**Piano/Organ**   William Albright, *The King of Instruments—Organbook III*; Leonardo Balada, *Persistencies*; George Crumb, *Makrokosmos IV (Celestial Mechanics)* (amplified piano, four hands); Richard Felciano, *In Celebration of Golden Rain* (gamelan and organ); Vivian Fine, *Momenti*; Marc Neikrug, *Cycle of Seven*; Stephen Paulus, *Five Translucent Landscapes*; Ralph Shapey, *Twenty-One Variations*; Howard Swanson, *Sonata No. 3*; Nancy Van de Vate, *Sonata No. 1—Nine Preludes*.

**Symphonies**   Alan Hovhaness, *Symphonies No. 35–39*; Henri Lazarof, *Symphony*; Gerhard Samuel, *Symphony: Out of Time*; Roger Sessions, *Symphony No. 9*; Clifford Taylor, *Symphony No. 3*; Charles Wuorinen, *Two-Part Symphony—Percussion Symphony*.

# 1979

❀

## Historical Highlights

Inflation in the United States reaches a record 13%; a near-disaster at Three Mile Island in Pennsylvania almost causes a panic; the American Embassy in Teheran is stormed and 50 Americans taken hostage by the Iranians the Shah flees the country and the Ayatollah Khomeini takes over and proclaims an Islamic Republic; Margaret Thatcher becomes Britain's first woman Prime Minister.

## World Cultural Highlights

**World Art**   Fernando Botero, *Still Life in Front of a Window*; Joseph Beuys, *Aus Berlin*; Paul Delvaux, *La Pose;* John Hoyland, *North Sound;* Roland Piché, *White Space Frame*.

**World Literature**   John Le Carré, *Smiley's People*; Caryl Churchill, *Cloud Nine;* Nadine Gordimer, *The Burger's Daughter*; V. S. Naipaul, *A Bend in the River;* Peter Shaffer, *Amadeus*.

**World Music**   Arne Nordheim, *The Tempest*; Aulis Sallinen, *Symphony No. 4*; Alfred Schnittke, *Symphony No. 2, "St. Florian"*; Karlheinz Stockhausen, *Michaels Jugend—Michaels Heimkehr*.

**Miscellaneous**   Berwald Hall opens in Stockholm; the Singapore Symphony Orchestra is founded; the Buxton Festivals begin in Derbyshire, England; deaths include Nadia Boulanger, Sonya Delauney, Pietro Lazzari, Paul Paray, Jean Rhys, and Konstantin Simonov.

## American Art and Literature Highlights

**Births/Deaths**   Deaths include artist Fletcher Martin and literary figures Elizabeth Bishop, James T. Farrell, S. J. Perelman, Cornelia Otis Skinner, Jean Stafford, and Alan Tate.

**Art Works**   Isobel Bishop, *Variations on a Theme of Walking*; Louise Bourgeois, *Partial Recall*; Sandro Chia, *In Strange and Gloomy Waters*; Judy Chicago, *Dinner Party*; Jim Dine, *Our Dreams Still Point North*; Eric Fischl, *Women in Water*; Robert Graham, *Dance Figure I*; Philip Guston, *Entrance*; Henry Moore, *Upright Motive No. 9*; Lowell Nesbitt, *Dark Brown Iris on White*.

**Literature**   John Cheever, *Stories of John Cheever* (Pulitzer Prize); Donald Justice, *Selected Poems* (Pulitzer Prize); Philip Levine, *Ashes* (National Book Award—National Book Critics' Award); Norman Mailer, *The Executioner's Song* (Pulitzer Prize); Neil Simon, *They're Playing Our*

*Song*; William Styron, *Sophie's Choice* (National Book Award); Lanford Wilson, *Talley's Folly* (Pulitzer Prize—New York Drama Critics' Award); Tom Wolfe, *The Right Stuff*.

## Music—The Vernacular/Commercial Scene

**B. Deaths**    Milton Ager (songwriter) May 6; Josephine Baker (singer) April 12; Dorsey Burnette (singer/writer) August 19; Louis Busch (pianist) September 19; Gus Cannon (singer/banjoist) October 15; Donny Hathaway (singer/writer) January 13; Pee Wee Hunt (trombonist/bandleader) June 22; Stan Kenton (bandleader) August 25; Van McCoy (singer/writer) July 6; Charlie Mingus (string bass/writer) January 5; Minnie Riperton (singer) July 12; Richard Rodgers (composer) December 30; Nat Simon (composer) September 5; Al Stillman (lyricist) February 17; Jimmie Tarlton (singer) November 29; Dimitri Tiomkin (composer) November 11.

### C. Biographical

**Performing Groups**    Bad Brains; Beat; Berlin; The Blasters; Brave Combo; The Bush Tetras; Joe "King" Carrasco and the Crowns; Christian Death; Dakota; The Durocs; Flipper; Force M.D.s; Georgia Satellites; G-Force; Hüsker Dü; The Knack; Huey Lewis and the News; Lounge Lizards; Material; The Minutemen; Mission of Burma; Modern Lovers; Oingo Boingo; Pearl Harbor and the Explosions; Pylon; Romeo Void; Rossington-Collins Band; 707; Social Distortion; Spy; Steps Ahead; The Stray Cats.

**New Beginnings**    Chicago Jazz Festival; Geffen Records; Houston Jazz Festival; Real Art Ways August Jazz Festival; *Songwriter's Market*.

**Honors**    Hank Snow (Country Music Hall of Fame); Ella Fitzgerald (Kennedy Center).

**D. Publications**    Whitney Balliett, *American Singers*; Dizzy Gillespie, *To Be or Not to Bop*; W. P. Gottlieb, *The Golden Age of Jazz*; Charles Hamm, *Yesterdays: Popular Song in America*; F. Kaufman and J. P. Guckin, *The African Roots of Jazz*; John S. Roberts, *The Latin Tinge: The Impact of Latin American Music on the United States*; George Simon et al., *The Best of the Music Makers*.

### E. Representative Works

**Musicals**    S. Downs and R. Martin, *Festival*; M. Hamlisch and C. B. Sager, *They're Playing Our Song*; Jerry Herman, *The Grand Tour*; B. Lane and A. J. Lerner, *Carmelina*; A. L. Webber and T. Rice, *Evita* (United States premiere); R. Rodgers, M. Charnin, and G. Jessel, *I Remember Mama*; G. Sherman and P. Udell, *Comin' Uptown*; Stephen Sondheim, *Sweeney Todd*; Various composers, *Sugar Babies*.

**Number One Hits**    *Babe* (Styx); *Bad Girls—Hot Stuff* (Donna Summer); *Do Ya Think I'm Sexy* (Rod Stewart); *Don't Stop 'Til You Get Enough* (Michael Jackson); *Escape (Piña Colada Song)* (Rupert Holmes); *Good Times* (Chic); *Heartache Tonight* (Eagles); *Heart of Glass* (Blondie); *I Will Survive* (Gloria Gaynor); *Knock On Wood* (Amii Stewart); *Love You Inside Out—Too Much Heaven—Tragedy* (Bee Gees); *My Sharona* (The Knack); *No More Tears* (Barbra Streisand and Donna Summers); *Pop Muzik* (M); *Reunited* (Peaches and Herb); *Ring My Bell* (Anita Ward); *Rise* (Herb Alpert); *Sad Eyes* (Robert John); *Still* (Commodores); *What a Fool Believes* (Doobie Brothers).

**Other**    Norman Gimbel, *It Goes Like It Goes* (Oscar); Henry Mancini, *10—Nightwing* (film scores); Johnny Mandel, *Being There* (film music); Cecil Taylor, *Tetra Stomp: Eatin' Rain in Space*.

## Music—The Cultivated/Art Music Scene

**G. Deaths**    Alan Crofoot (tenor) March 5; Arthur Fiedler (conductor) July 10; Bronislav Gimpel (Austrian-born violinist) May 1; Roy Harris (composer) October 1; Karl Krueger (conductor) July 21; Dorothea Dix Lawrence (soprano/folklore scholar) May 23; Marjorie Lawrence (Australian-born soprano) January 13; Arthur Mendel (musicologist) October 14; Julia Perry (composer) April 29; Thomas Scherman (conductor) May 14; Seymour Shifrin (composer/educator) September 26; Chester Watson (bass) January 8; Ben Weber (composer) May 9.

### H. Debuts

**United States**    Gabriela Benacková (Czech soprano—New York), Isobel Buchanan (Scottish soprano—Santa Fe), Livia Budai (Hungarian mezzo-soprano—San Francisco), Robert Cohen (British cellist—tour), Bella Davidovich (Russian pianist—New York), Warren Ellsworth (tenor—Houston), Aage Haugland (Danish bass-baritone—St. Louis), Sharon Isbin (guitarist—New York), Kathleen Kuhlmann (mezzo-soprano—Chicago), Gregory Kunde (tenor—Chicago), Kevin J. Langan (bass—New Jersey Opera), David Leisner (guitarist—New York), Mimi Lerner (Polish mezzo-soprano—New York), Cecile Licad (Filipino pianist—Tanglewood), Elizabeth Mead (Australian pianist—New York), Anne Murray (Irish mezzo-soprano—New York), Mikhail Pletnev (Russian pianist—New York), Leslie Richards (mezzo-soprano—San Diego), Evelyn de la Rosa (soprano—San Francisco), Stefania Toczyska (Polish mezzo-soprano—San Francisco), Christian Zacharias (German pianist—Boston).

**Metropolitan Opera**    Agnes Baltsa (Greek mezzo-soprano), Christian Boesch (Austrian baritone), Norma Burrowes (British soprano), Philip Creech (tenor), Mariella Devia (Italian soprano), Dale Duesing (baritone), Brent Ellis (baritone), Marisa Galvany (soprano), Aage Haugland (Danish bass-baritone), Timothy Jenkins (tenor), William Johns (tenor), Dimitri Kavrakos (bass), David Kuebler (tenor), Catherine Malfitano (soprano), Seth McCoy (tenor), Julia Migenes (soprano), Carol Neblett (soprano), Julien Robbins (bass), Gianna Rolandi (soprano), Haralm Stamm (German bass), Jocelyn Taillon (French contralto).

**Other**    Barbara Bonney (soprano—Darmstadt); John E. Holmquist (guitarist—London); Ken Noda (pianist—London); Deborah Sasson (soprano—Hamburg).

## I. New Positions

**Conductors**    John R. Bourgeois (United States Marine Band); Gaetano Delogu (Denver Symphony Orchestra—to 1986); John De Main (Houston Grand Opera); Philippe Entremont (New Orleans Philharmonic Symphony Orchestra—to 1986); Donald Johanos (Honolulu Symphony Orchestra and Opera); Christopher Keene (Long Island Philharmonic Orchestra—to 1990); Neville Marriner (Minnesota Symphony Orchestra); Julius Rudel (Buffalo Philharmonic Orchestra—to 1985); Calvin Simmons (Oakland Symphony Orchestra—to 1982); Leonard Slatkin (St. Louis Symphony Orchestra).

**Educational**    Betty Allen (director, Harlem School of the Arts); Theodore Antoniou (composition, Boston University); Arthur Berger (New England Conservatory); Sharon Isbin (Manhattan School—to 1984); Leon Plantinga (music chair, Yale—to 1986); William Primrose (Brigham Young University—to 1982); Robert Ward (Duke); Richard Wilson (music chair, Vassar—to 1982).

**Other**    Charles Dodge (president, American Music Center); Donal Henahan (music critic, *The New York Times*); Robert Shaw (National Council on the Arts); Beverly Sills (general manager, New York City Opera).

## J. Honors and Awards

**Honors**    Henry Brant, Paul Chihara, Vivian Fine, Robert Starer, and Morton Subotnick (American Academy); Aaron Copland and Martha Graham (Kennedy Center Honors); Howard Hanson, Ulysses Kay, and Ned Rorem (American Academy and Institute); Eugene Ormandy (Gold Baton).

**Awards**    Gregory Allen (Bachauer Third); Emanuel Ax (Avery Fisher); Michael Blum (Kapell Third); Panayis Lyras (Bachauer); Peter Orth (Naumburg); Cynthia Raim (Haskil); Dmitri Stikovetsky (Kreisler); Marc Silverman (Bachauer Second); Calvin Simmons (Stokowski); Diana Soviero (Tucker); Marioara Trifan (Kapell).

**K. Biographical**    Maurice Abravanel, on his doctor's orders, retires as Conductor Emeritus of the Utah Symphony Orchestra; Claudio Arrau and Philip Brett become American citizens; Antal Dorati takes the Detroit Symphony Orchestra on its first international tour; Sergei Edelmann (Russian pianist) emigrates to the United States; Leon Fleisher undergoes surgery for his hand problems; Gary Graffman retires from performance with right hand problems; Birgit Nilsson settles her tax dispute with the IRS and gives her first United States performance in five years; Seiji Ozawa takes the Boston Symphony Orchestra to China; Isaac Stern is invited to China to advise in their music programs.

## L. Musical Beginnings

**Performing Groups**    Atlanta Civic Opera; Boston Philharmonic Orchestra; Berkeley Opera

(Commedia dell'Opera); Brass Chamber Music Society of Annapolis; Jupiter Symphony Orchestra (New York); Lehigh Valley Chamber Orchestra; Opera Midwest (Evanston, Illinois); Orchestra of the Twentieth Century (New York); Soviet Emigré Orchestra (Tchaikovsky Chamber Orchestra); Texas Chamber Orchestra (Houston); Tulsa Little Symphony Orchestra (Oklahoma Sinphonia).

**Festivals**  InterArts Summer Festival (Honolulu); New Music America Festival (New York); Skaneateles Festival (New York); Soviet Emigré Music Festival (New York); University of Hawaii Summer Music Festival.

**Other**  American Opera Project (San Francisco); Atlantic Center for the Arts (Florida); Ralph Bailey Concert Hall (Fort Lauderdale); Bowling Green Arts Center (Ohio); GunMar Music; Roy Harris Society; Eleanor Steber Music Foundation Vocal Competition; Leopold Stokowski Conducting Prize; Symphony Hall (Salt Lake City); Terrace Theater (Washington, DC).

## M. Music Publications

Adler, Samuel, *Singing and Hearing*
Block and Neuls-Bates, *Women in American Music*
Cage, John, *Empty Words*
Creston, Paul, *Rational Metric Notation*
Dempster, Stuart, *The Modern Trombone: A Definition of Its Idioms*
Epstein, David M., *Beyond Orpheus: Studies in Musical Structures*
Johnson, H. Earle, *First Performances in America to 1900: Works with Orchestra*
Lipman, Samuel, *Music after Modernism* (Deems Taylor Award)
Ratner, Leonard, *Classic Music: Expression, Form and Style*
Read, Gardner, *Style and Orchestration*
Rowen, Ruth H., *Music through Sources and Documents*
Sessions, Roger, *Roger Sessions on Music: The Collected Essays*
Wuorinen, Charles, *Simple Composition*

## N. Musical Compositions

**Chamber Music**  Leslie Bassett, *Sextet*; Paul Creston, *Suite for Saxophone Quartet*; Norman Dello Joio, *Trumpet Sonata*; Morton Feldman, *String Quartet No. 1*; John Harbison, *Woodwind Quintet*; Lou Harrison, *String Quartet Set*; Lejaren Hiller, *String Quartet No. 7*; Karl Korte, *Piano Trio*; Raoul Pleshkow, *String Quartet*; Steve Reich, *Variations for Winds, Strings and Keyboards*; George Rochberg, *String Quartet No. 7* (with baritone); Francis Thorne, *String Quartet No. 3*; Charles Wuorinen, *String Quartet No. 2*.

**Choral/Vocal**  Gloria Coates, *Leonardo da Vinci* (oratorio); George Crumb, *Apparition: Elegiac Songs and Vocalises for Soprano and Amplified Piano*; George Edwards, *The Leaden Echo and the Golden Echo*; Miriam Gideon, *The Resounding Lyre—Voices from Elysium* (song cycles); William Kraft, *The Sublime and the Beautiful* (song cycle); Meyer Kupferman, *A Nietzsche Cycle*; Robert Parris, *Three Lyrics by Ben Jonson*; George Perle, *Thirteen Dickinson (Emily) Songs*; Daniel Pinkham, *When God Arose—Hezekiah* (oratorios); Ned Rorem, *The Nantucket Songs*; Frederic Rzewski, *Four North American Ballads*; William Schuman, *Time to the Old* (song cycle); Joseph Schwantner, *Sparrows*; Seymour Shifrin, *Five Last Songs*; John Verrall, *Songs of Nature* (song cycle).

**Concertos**  David Epstein, *Violin Concerto*; Morton Feldman, *Violin and Orchestra*; Earl Kim, *Violin Concerto*; Peter Jona Korn, *Trumpet Concerto*; Leo Kraft, *Concerto No. 4 for Piano and Fourteen Instruments*; George Perle, *Concertino for Piano, Winds and Timpani*; Ned Rorem, *Concerto for Cello, Piano and Orchestra*; Miklós Rózsa, *Viola Concerto*; Frederic Rzewski, *A Long Time Man* (piano and orchestra); Gunther Schuller, *Trumpet Concerto*; William Schuman, *Three Colloquies for Horn and Orchestra*; Ramon Zupko, *Windsongs* (piano and orchestra).

**Electronic**  Charles Amirkhanian, *Dreams Freud Dreamed* (tape); Laurie Anderson, *Americans on the Move*; Ruth Anderson, *Centering*; David Cope, *Glassworks* (two pianos and tape); Jean

Eichelberger Ivey, *Sea-change* (orchestra, tape); Joan La Barbara, *The Executioner's Bracelet*; Alvin Lucier, *Solar Sounder 1;* Ray Luke, *Medea*; Salvatore Martirano, *She Spoke*; Allen Strange, *Second Book of Angels*.

**Operas** Theodore Antoniou, *Periander;* Lee Hoiby, *Something New for the Zoo*; Gian Carlo Menotti, *La Loca*; Thea Musgrave, *A Christmas Carol*; Richard Owen, *May Dyer*; Thomas Pasatieri, *Three Sisters*; Stephen Paulus, *The Village Singer;* Paul Turok, *A Secular Masque*.

**Orchestra/Band** John Adams, *Common Tones in Simple Time*; William Bolcom, *Humoresk*; Jacob Druckman, *Aureole*; Morton Gould, *Burchfield Gallery*; Barbara Kolb, *Grisaille*; Benjamin Lees, *Mobiles for Orchestra*; Joan Tower, *Amazon II*.

**Piano/Organ** Samuel Adler, *Sonatina*; Josef Alexander, *Nine Etudes*; Chester Biscardi, *Mestiere*; William Bolcom, *Three Gospel Preludes* (organ); Donald Erb, *Nightmusic II*; Otto Luening, *Short Sonatas No. 5–7*; Robert Palmer, *Sonata No. 3*; Vittorio Rieti, *Twelve Preludes*; Frederic Rzewski, *Down by the River Side*; Elie Siegmeister, *Sonata No. 3*.

**Symphonies** William Bolcom, *Symphony for Chamber Orchestra (No. 3)*; Alan Hovhaness, *Symphonies 40–43, 45*; Martin Mailman, *Symphony No. 2*; Eric Stokes, *Symphony, Book I*; Ellen Taaffe Zwilich, *Chamber Symphony.*

# 1980

❀

## Historical Highlights

The United States Olympic Committee votes to boycott the Summer Olympics in Moscow; Ronald Reagan is elected the 40th president; an attempt to free the Iranian hostages by force fails; Mount St. Helens in Washington state erupts with a gigantic explosion; workers in Poland form an independent union, Solidarity; Iraq goes to war with Iran.

## World Cultural Highlights

**World Art** Enzo Cucchi, *Fish on the Back of the Adriatic Sea*; Claudio Parmiggiani, *Atena Ermetica;* Vettor Pisani, *Oedipus and the Sphinx*; Peter Stämpfli, *Zeus*.

**World Literature** Italo Calvino, *Italian Folktales;* J. M. Coetzee, *Waiting for the Barbarians;* Umberto Eco, *The Name of the Rose*; William Golding, *Rites of Passage*.

**World Music** Oliver Knussen, *Where the Wild Things Are*; Krzysztof Penderecki, *Symphony No. 2, "Christmas"*; Karlheinz Stockhausen, *Donnerstag*; John Tavener, *Akhmatova: Requiem*.

**Miscellaneous** The first Lyons Berlioz Festival takes place in France; the Opéra de Montreal is founded; deaths include Oskar Kokoschka, Marino Marini, Allan Pettersson, Jean-Paul Sartre, and Graham Sutherland.

## American Art and Literature Highlights

**Births/Deaths** Deaths include art figures Robert Brackman, Alexander Brook, Philip Guston, Clyfford Still, and literary figures Herbert S. Agar, Marc Connelly, George P. Elliot, Robert E. Hayden, Sam Levinson, Henry Miller, Mary O'Hara, Katherine Anne Porter, Muriel Rukeyser, and James A. Wright.

**Art Works** Jim Dine, *The Yellow Robe*; Jack Beal, *Harvest*; Nancy Graves, *Trace*; David Hockney, *Mulholland Drive*; Alex Katz, *Ada and Alex*; Lee Krasner, *Series: Solstice*; Jacob Lawrence, *Exploration*; Roy Lichtenstein, *Head*; Jim Nutt, *Ah Ha (It Is!)*; Martin Puryear, *Bower*; David Salle, *Hundreds of Tons*; Sandy Skoglund, *Radioactive Cats*; Andrew Wyeth, *Day Dream (Helga)*.

**Literature** Edward Albee, *The Lady from Dubuque*; Shirley Hazzard, *The Transit of Venus* (National Book Critics' Award); Wright Morris, *Plains Song* (National Book Award); Lisel Mueller,

*The Need to Hold Still* (National Book Award); James Schuyler, *The Morning of the Poem* (Pulitzer Prize); Jessamyn West, *Double Discovery*.

## Music—The Vernacular/Commercial Scene

**B. Deaths**  Harold Adamson (songwriter) August 17; Louis Alter (composer) November 3; Herman Autrey (trumpeter/singer) June 14; Barney Bigard (clarinetist) June 27; Henry Byrd (Professor Longhair) January 30; Gower Champion (choreographer) August 25; Bill Evans (pianist) September 15; Jimmy Forrest (saxophonist/bandleader) August 26; Jane Froman (singer) April 22; Tim Hardin (singer/writer) December 29; Dick Haymes (singer) March 30; John Jacob Niles (folk singer/collector) March 1; Alec Wilder (composer) December 24.

**C. Biographical**

**Performing Groups**  Bad Religion; Balkan Rhythm Band (Chicago); The Bongos; The Circle Jerks; The Contortions; Culprit; Forester Sisters (?); Franke and the Knockouts; Free Flight; Gun Club; The Indigo Girls; Kid Creole and the Coconuts; King's X; Kix; Legendary Blues Band; The Meat Puppets; Missing Persons; New York Saxophone Quartet; Poison Idea; Quarterflash; R.E.M.; The Replacements; Rodney-Sullivan Quintet; The Rods; The Smithereens; Steeplechase; Take 6; Throwing Muses.

**New Beginnings**  Clearwater Jazz Holiday (Florida); Four AD Records; Montreux-Detroit International Jazz Festival; Teresa Records (California); Was Trax Records (Chicago).

**Honors**  Eubie Blake (Peabody Medal); Johnny Cash and the Sons of the Pioneers (Country Music Hall of Fame); Dexter Gordon (Jazz Hall of Fame).

**Miscellaneous**  Ex-Beatle John Lennon is shot and killed in New York.

**D. Publications**  Edward A. Berlin, *Ragtime: A Musical and Cultural History*; Michael B. Druxman, *The Musical: From Broadway to Hollywood*; Leonard Feather, *The Passion for Jazz*; Fred Hill, *Grass Roots*; Richard Kislan, *The Musical: A Look at the American Musical Theater*; Henry Sampson, *Blacks in Blackface*; Nicholas E. Tawa, *Sweet Songs for Gentle Americans: The Parlor Song in America*.

**E. Representative Works**

**Musicals**  C. Coleman and M. Stewart, *Barnum*; F. Lazarus, J. Herman, Vosburgh, *A Day in Hollywood—A Night in the Ukraine*; Frank Loesser, *Perfectly Frank* (tribute revue); M. Mandel and N. Sachs, *My Old Friend*; Strouse and Rogers, *Charlie and Algernon*.

**Number One Hits**  *Another Brick in the Wall* (Pink Floyd); *Another One Bites the Dust—Crazy Little Thing Called Love* (Queen); *Call Me* (Blondie); *Coming Up* (Paul McCartney); *Do That To Me One More Time* (Captain and Tennille); *Funkytown* (Lipps, Inc.); *It's Still Rock and Roll To Me* (Billy Joel); *Lady* (Kenny Rogers); *Magic* (Olivia Newton-John); *Please Don't Go* (KC and the Sunshine Band); *Rock with You* (Michael Jackson); *Sailing* (Christopher Cross); *(Just Like) Starting Over* (John Lennon); *Upside Down* (Diana Ross); *Woman in Love* (Barbra Streisand).

## Music—The Cultivated/Art Music Scene

**G. Deaths**  Richard Bonelli (baritone) June 7; Cecil Burleigh (composer/violinist) July 28; Norman Cazden (composer/musicologist) August 18; Wilbur Chenoweth (pianist/composer) March 23; William D. Denny (composer/violist) September 2; Jessica Dragonette (soprano) March 18; Henri Elkan (Belgian-born publisher) June 12; Virgil Fox (organist) October 25; Harold Gleason (organist/musicologist) June 28; Richard Franko Goldman (bandmaster) January 19; José Iturbi (Spanish-born pianist/conductor) June 28; Hilde Konetzni (soprano) April 20; William Kroll (violinist) March 10; Richard Lert (Austrian-born conductor) April 25; Norman Lloyd (composer/theorist) July 31; Paolo Martucci (Italian-born pianist) October 18; Lina Pagliughi (soprano) October 1; Oliver Strunk (musicologist) February 24; Walter Susskind (Czech-born conductor) March 25; Ernest White (organist) September 21.

**H. Debuts**

**United States**  Pascal Devoyon (French pianist), Richard Estes (tenor—New York), Theodora

Geraets (Dutch violinist—St. Louis), Jorma Hynninen (Finnish baritone—New York), Marek Janowski (Polish conductor—Chicago), Young-Mi Kim (Korean soprano—New York), Margaret Marshall (Scottish soprano—Boston), Valerie Masterson (British soprano—San Francisco), Sylvia McNair (soprano—Indianapolis), Aprile Millo (soprano—Salt Lake City), Anne-Sophie Mutter (German violinist—New York), Inga Nielsen (Danish soprano—New York), Bent Norup (Danish baritone—Portland, Oregon), Dano Raffanti (Italian tenor—Dallas), J. Patrick Raftery (baritone—Chicago), Julian Rodescu (Romanian bass—New York), Annerose Schmidt (German pianist—New York), Raili Viljakainen (Finnish soprano—New York); Neal Wilson (tenor—Wolf Trap).

**Metropolitan Opera**   Christiane Eda-Pierre (Martinique soprano), Dalmacio Gonzalez (Spanish tenor), Peter Hofmann (German tenor), Siegfried Jerusalem (German tenor), Benjamin Luxon (British baritone), Franz Mazura (Austrian bass-baritone), Leo Nucci (Italian baritone), Patricia Payne (New Zealand soprano), Emily Rawlins (soprano), David Rendall (British tenor), Brian Schexnayder (baritone), Edward Sooter (tenor), Jeffrey Tate (British conductor), Domenico Trimarchi (Italian bass-baritone).

**Other**   D'Anna Fortunato (mezzo-soprano—Paris), Jeffrey Gall (counter-tenor—Spoleto), Pamela Hamblin (soprano—Karlsruhe); Nancy Johnson (soprano—Detmold).

## I. New Positions

**Conductors**   Igor Buketoff (Texas Chamber Orchestra); James DePreist (Oregon Symphony Orchestra), Akira Endo (Louisville Orchestra—to 1983); Michael Gielen (Cincinnati Symphony Orchestra to 1986), Varujan Kojian (Utah Symphony Orchestra—to 1983); Joel Lazar (Tulsa Philharmonic Orchestra—to 1983); Riccardo Muti (Philadelphia Orchestra—to 1992); Lawrence Leighton Smith (San Antonio Symphony Orchestra to 1983), John Williams (Boston Pops); Pinchas Zukerman (St. Paul Chamber Orchestra—to 1986).

**Educational**   Julius Baker (Curtis); David Bar-Illan (Mannes); Thomas DeLio (University of Maryland); Szymon Goldberg (Curtis); Gary Graffman (Curtis); Stephen Kates (Brooklyn College, CUNY); Robert Morris (Eastman); Marni Nixon (Music Academy of the West); Ned Rorem (Curtis), Ann Schein (Peabody); Carol Wincenc (Manhattan School); Judith Lang Zaimont (Peabody).

**Other**   Gerard Béhague (editor, *Latin American Music Review*); Héctor Campos-Parsi (music advisor, Administration for the Development of Arts and Culture, Puerto Rico); Marta Casals Istomin (artistic director, Kennedy Center—to 1990); Paul Turok (reviewer, *Ovation* and *Fanfare*).

## J. Honors and Awards

**Honors**   Dominick Argento and Gunther Schuller (American Academy and Institute); Claudio Arrau (Bülow Medal); Samuel Barber (MacDowell Medal); Leonard Bernstein (Peabody Medal); Andrew Imbrie (American Academy of Arts and Sciences); Zubin Mehta (*Musical America* Musician of the Year); Leontyne Price, Leonard Bernstein, and Agnes DeMille (Kennedy Center); Eric Salzman (Prix Italia for *Civilization and its Discontents*); Beverly Sills (Medal of Freedom—Gold Baton).

**Awards**   Claus Adam (Friedheim); Gregory Allen (Rubinstein First); James Barbagallo (Bachauer Second); Martin Bresnick (Ancona); Faith Esham, Irene Gubrud, Jan Opalach and Lucy Shelton (Naumburg); Richard Goode (Fisher); Duane Hulbert (Bachauer); Barry McCauley (Tucker); Robert McDonald (Kapell, shared Second, no First); John Anthony Lennon (Rome Prize); Peter Zazofsky (Queen Elisabeth Second).

**K. Biographical**   Ilona Brown brings the Academy of St. Martin-in-the-Fields on its first tour of the United States; Thomas Hampson wins first prize in the Metropolitan Opera auditions but chooses to go to Europe for experience; Neeme Järvi (Estonian-born conductor) leaves Russia and emigrates to the United States; Kazimierz Kord becomes Principal Guest Conductor of the Cincinnati Symphony Orchestra; Eugene Ormandy officially resigns as conductor of the Philadelphia Orchestra; Tibor Szász becomes an American citizen.

## L. Musical Beginnings

**Performing Groups**   Ax-Ma-Kim Trio; Chamber Music Plus (Hartford); Chamber Opera Theater of New York; Cleveland Chamber Symphony; Da Vinci String Quartet; Las Vegas Symphony

Orchestra; Los Angeles Opera Repertory Theater; Res Musica (Maryland); Opera San Jose; Solisti New York.

**Festivals**   Cape and Islands Chamber Music Festival (New York); Connecticut Harp Festival; International Brass Quintet Festival (Baltimore); National Sacred Harp Singing Convention (Birmingham, Alabama); New and Unusual Music Festival (San Francisco); Summer Opera Festival (San Francisco).

**Other**   *Alaska New Music Forum*; Black Music Colloquium; *Black Music Research Journal*; Louise M. Davies Symphony Hall (San Francisco); De Vos Hall for the Performing Arts (Grand Rapids, Michigan); Charles Ives Center for American Music; Andrew Jackson Hall (Nashville); *Journal of the Conductors' Guild*; *Ovation: The Magazine for Classical Music Listeners*; Oscar Mayer Auditorium and Madison Civic Center (Wisconsin); Music Associates of America; Pavarotti International Voice Competition (Philadelphia); Washington Opera (DC); Weigel Hall (Ohio State University); *Winds Quarterly*.

## M. Music Publications

De Gaetani, Jan, *The Complete Sightsinger*
Felciano, Richard, *Orchestration*
Kohs, Ellis, *Musical Composition: Projects in Ways and Means*
Kolodin, Irving, *In Quest of Music*
LePage, Jane, *Women Composers, Conductors, and Musicians of the Twentieth Century*
Rahn, John, *Basic Atonal Theory*
Reed, H. O. and Sidnell, R., *The Materials of Music Composition*
Robb, John D., *Hispanic Folk Music of New Mexico and the Southwest*
Stone, Kurt, *Music Notation in the Twentieth Century: A Practical Guide*
Tyler, James, *The Early Guitar*
Wolfe, Richard J., *Early American Music Engraving and Printing*
Zaimont, Judith L., *Twentieth Century Music: An Analysis and Appreciation*

## N. Musical Compositions

**Chamber Music**   Stephen Albert, *Music from the Stone Harp*; John Alexander, *Hexagon* (piano and wind quintet); David Amram, *Landscapes* (percussion); Leonardo Balada, *Sonata for 10 Wind Instruments*; Leslie Bassett, *Trio for Violin, Clarinet and Piano*; Arthur Berger, *Piano Trio*; William Bolcom, *Brass Quintet*; Mario Davidovsky, *String Quartet No. 4*; Earl Kim, *Twelve Caprices for Solo Violin*; Ezra Laderman, *String Quartet No. 6*; Henri Lazarof, *String Quartet No. 3*; Stephen Paulus, *Music for Contrasts* (string quartet); George Rochberg, *Octet: a Grand Fantasia*; Joan Tower, *Petroushskates*; Paul Turok, *String Quartet No. 3*.

**Choral/Vocal**   John Adams, *Harmonium*; Warren Benson, *Songs for the End of the World—Moon Rain and Memory Jane*; Earle Brown, *Windsor Jambs*; David Del Tredici, *In Memory of a Summer Day* (Pulitzer Prize); Miriam Gideon, *Morning Star—Spirit above the Dust* (song cycles); Lee Hoiby, *The Italian Lesson*; Robert Kelly, *Rural Songs*; William Mayer, *Enter Ariel* (song cycle); Stephen Paulus, *Letters for the Times*; Bernard Rands, *Canti lunatici* (song cycle); Ned Rorem, *The Santa Fe Songs*; Francis Thorne, *The Eternal Light*; Richard Wernick, *A Poison Tree*; Charles Wuorinen, *The Celestial Sphere*.

**Concertos**   Donald Erb, *Trumpet Concerto*; John Harbison, *Violin Concerto*; Lee Hoiby, *Piano Concerto No. 2*; Tobias Picker, *Piano Concerto*; Robert Starer, *Violin Concerto*; Carlos Surinach, *Violin Concerto*; Richard Wernick, *Cello Concerto*.

**Electronic**   Ruth Anderson, *Communications* (text piece); Joan La Barbara, *October Music: Star Showers and Extraterrestrials*; Alvin Lucier, *Music for Pure Waves*; Roger Reynolds, *Voicespace III, "Eclipse"*; Terry Riley, *Embroidery—Chorale of the Blessed Day*.

**Operas**   Dominick Argento, *Miss Havisham's Wedding Night* (monodrama); John Eaton, *The Cry of Clytaemnestra*; Carlisle Floyd, *Willie Stark*; Philip Glass, *Satyagraha*; Kirke Mechem, *Tartuffe*; Thea Musgrave, *The Last Twilight* (theater piece); Thomas Pasatieri, *Before Breakfast*; Eric

Salzman, *Civilization and Its Discontents* (Prix Italia); David Schiff, *Gimpel the Fool*.

**Orchestra/Band**   Richard Adler, *Yellowstone Overture*; Leonard Bernstein, *Divertimento for Orchestra*; Jacob Druckman, *Prism*; Robert Erickson, *East of the Beach*; Richard Felciano, *Orchestra*; Morton Feldman, *The Turfan Fragments*; Sydney Hodkinson, *Sinfonia concertante*; Karel Husa, *The Trojan Women* (ballet); Ezra Laderman, *Summer Solstice*; Henri Lazarof, *Mirrors, Mirrors . . .* (ballet); Robert Hall Lewis, *Moto*; Robert Moevs, *Prometheus: Music for Small Orchestra I*; Joaquín Nin-Culmell, *Cymbeline* (incidental music); Raoul Pleshkow, *Music for Orchestra*; Joseph Schwantner, *First Morning of the World* (wind ensemble); Eric Stokes, *The Phonic Paradigm*; Vladimir Ussachevsky, *Dances and Fanfares for a Festive Occasion*.

**Piano/Organ**   Leslie Bassett, *Liturgies for Organ*; Leonard Bernstein, *Touches*; William Bolcom, *Monsterpieces (and Others)*; David Burge, *Three Variations on "Simple Gifts"*; Elliott Carter, *Night Fantasies*; Michael Colgrass, *Tales of Power*; George Crumb, *A Little Suite for Christmas*; Norman Dello Joio, *Concert Variations*; Morton Feldman, *Principal Sound* (organ); Ross Lee Finney, *Youth's Companion*; Dick Higgins, *Piano Album*; Robert Muczynski, *Masks, Opus 40*; Vincent Persichetti, *Sonata No. 12, Opus 145, Song of David* (organ); Elie Siegmeister, *Prelude, Blues and Toccata (Sonata No. 4)*; William Sydeman, *Short Piano Pieces*; Richard Trythall, *Twelve Pieces*; Robert Ward, *Three Celebrations of God in Nature* (organ).

**Symphonies**   Irwin Bazelon, *Symphony No. 7, "Ballet for Orchestra"*; Alan Hovhaness, *Symphony No. 44, Opus 339*; Ezra Laderman, *Symphony No. 4*; Charles Mills, *Symphony No. 5*; George Perle, *A Short Symphony*; David Van Vactor, *Symphony No. 6*; Robert A. Wykes, *A Lyric Symphony*.

# 1981

☼

## Historical Highlights

The Iranian-held hostages are released on President Reagan's inauguration day; John Hinckley, Jr., trying to assassinate the president, wounds him and others; the space shuttle *Columbia* orbits the earth for two days before making a safe return; federal air controllers on strike are dismissed by President Reagan; Sandra Day O'Connor becomes the first woman supreme court justice.

## World Cultural Highlights

**World Art**   Balthus, *Painter and His Model;* Corneille, *Le Grand Oiseau de l'Été;* Barry Flanagan, *Boxing Ones;* Anselm Kiefer, *Landscape with Wing;* Malcolm Morley, *Underneath the Lemon Tree*.

**World Literature**   Jorge Luis Borges, *Borges: A Reader;* Taylor Caldwell, *Answer as a Man*; Colleen McCullough, *An Indecent Obsession*; D. M. Thomas, *The White Hotel*.

**World Music**   Pierre Boulez, *Repons*; Peter Maxwell Davies, *Symphony No. 2*; Joonas Kokkonen, *Requiem*; Per Norgard, *Symphony No. 4*; Andrzej Panufnik, *Sinfonia Votiva*.

**Miscellaneous**   The Luciano Pavarotti Voice Competitions begin; the USSR International Music Festivals begin; deaths include Enid Bagnold, Karl Böhm, Ilya Bolotowsky, A. J. Cronin, Pamela Johnson, Kyrill Kondrashin, and Lotte Lenya.

## American Art and Literature Highlights

**Deaths**   Deaths include art figures Ilya Bolotowsky, Theodore Roszak, Isaac Soyer, and literary figures Nelson Algren, Mary C. Chase, Paddy Chayefsky, Elizabeth F. Corbett, Ketti Frings, Isabella Gardner, Meyer Levin, Anita Loos, and William Saroyan.

**Art Works**   Carl André, *Hellgate*; Jack Beal, *The Painting Lesson*; Greg Constantine, *Artists' Licenses*; John De Andrea, *Seated Man and Woman*; Richard Diebenkorn, *Ocean Park*; Robert

Kushner, *Song of the Sphinx*; James McGarrell, *Travestimento*; Joan Miró, *Miró's Chicago*; Judy Pfaff, *Dragons*; Mel Ramos, *Artist's Studio, No. 1*; James Rosenquist, *Star Thief*; David Salle, *Rational Censor*.

**Literature**    Alice Adams, *Rich Rewards*; A. R. Ammons, *A Coast of Trees* (National Book Critics' Award); Thomas Berger, *Reinhardt's Women*; Harvey Fierstein, *Torch Song Trilogy*; Charles Fuller, *A Soldier's Play* (Pulitzer Prize—New York Drama Critics' Award); Arthur Miller, *The American Clock*; Thomas Robbins, *Still Life with Woodpecker*; Irwin Shaw, *Bread upon the Waters*.

## Music—The Vernacular/Commercial Scene

**B. Deaths**    Cat Anderson (trumpeter) April 29; Michael Bloomfield (guitarist) February 15; Henry Brown (pianist) June 28; Roy James Brown (singer) May 25; Hoagy Carmichael (composer/pianist) December 27; Harry Chapin (singer/writer) July 16; Bob Eberly (singer) November 17; Hugo Friedhofer (composer) May 17; Bill Haley, Jr. (guitarist/singer) February 9; Edgar Y. Harburg (lyricist/librettist) March 5; Lee Hays (folk singer) August 26; George "Pee Wee" Herman (trumpeter/clarinetist) June 20; Helen Humes (singer) September 13; Walter "Furry" Lewis (guitarist) September 14; Russell Procope (clarinetist/saxophonist) January 21; Eddie Sauter (composer/arranger) April 21; Hazel Scott (pianist/singer) October 2; Billy Sherwood (trumpeter/bandleader) January 23; Harry Warren (songwriter) September 22; Mary Lou Williams (pianist) May 28.

**C. Biographical**

**Performing Groups**    Anthrax; Asia; The Bangles; The Beastie Boys; Blackheart; Concrete Blonde; Giuffria; The Golden Palominos; Great White; Green on Red (originally, Surfers); Grupo Niche; Icon; Jason and the Scorchers; Joshua; Jump Up; Die Kreuzen; Let's Active; Manowar; Metallica; Ministry; Mötley Crüe; Naked Prey; New Edition; Pandemonium; Pantera; Prime Time; Queensrÿche; Quest; Rank and File; Ratt; Savage Grace; Shanghai; Sonic Youth; Soul Asylum; Stetsasonic; Sugarcreek; 10,000 Maniacs; The Time; Was (Was Not); Xebron.

**New Beginnings**    *Black Music Newsletter*; Bridge Records; Chicago Blues Archive; Epitaph Records; *Jazz Line*; Herbie Mann Music; MTV.

**Honors**    Count Basie (Kennedy Center); Eubie Blake (Medal of Freedom).

**Miscellaneous**    Eliane Elias (Brazilian pianist) moves to the United States.

**D. Publications**    Jack DeJohnette, *The Art of Modern Jazz Drumming*; David Evans, *Big Road Blues: Tradition and Creativity in the Folk Blues*; Vincent Lynch and Bill Henkin, *Jukebox: The Golden Age*; Harvey Rachlin, *The Encyclopedia of the Music Business*.

**E. Representative Works**

**Musicals**    Harry Chapin, *Cotton Patch Gospel*; J. Kander and F. Ebb, *Woman of the Year*; Henry Krieger and Tom Eyer, *Dreamgirls*; Stephen Sondheim, *Merrily We Roll Along*; Charles Strouse and Lee Adams, *Bring Back Birdie*; Thomas Tierney and Ted Drachman, *Susan B!*; M. Valenti and D. Driver, *Oh! Brother!*; James C. Wann, *Pump Boys and Dinettes*.

**Number One Hits**    *Arthur's Theme (Best That You Can Do)* (Oscar—Christopher Cross); *Bette Davis Eyes* (Kim Carnes); *Celebration* (Kool and the Gang); *Endless Love* (Diana Ross and Lionel Richie); *I Love a Rainy Night* (Eddie Rabbitt); *Jessie's Girl* (Rick Springfield); *Keep on Loving You* (REO Speedwagon); *Kiss on My List—Private Eyes* (Hall and Oates); *Morning Train* (Sheena Easton); *9 to 5* (Oscar—Dolly Parton); *The One That You Love* (Air Supply); *Physical* (Olivia Newton-John); *Rapture—The Tide Is High* (Blondie); *Stars on 45 Medley*.

**Other**    Duke Ellington, *Sophisticated Ladies*.

## Music—The Cultivated/Art Music Scene

**G. Deaths**    Webster Aitken (pianist) May 11; Samuel Barber (composer) January 23; Robert Russell Bennett (composer/arranger) August 18; Thomas Beversdorf (trombonist/composer) February 15; Richard Burgin (Polish-born violinist/conductor) April 29; Louis Cheslock (composer/violinist) July 19; Eugene Conley (tenor) December 18; Alice Ehlers (Austrian-born harpsichordist) March 1; Alfred Frankenstein (critic) June 21; Ivan Galamian (Peruvian-born violinist) April 14; David Guion (composer) October 17; Howard Hanson (composer/educator) February 26; Hershy Kay (composer/arranger) December 2; Robert Lawrence (conductor/critic) August 9; Mana-Zucca (piano/composer) March 8; Sylvia Marlowe (harpsichordist) December 11; John McCormack (tenor) July 3; Hephzibah Menuhin (pianist) January 1; Mischa Mischakoff (Russian-born violinist) February 1; Rosa Ponselle (soprano) May 25.

## H. Debuts

**United States**  Gerd Albrecht (German conductor—San Francisco), Joshua Bell (violinist—Philadelphia), Margarita Castro-Alberty (Puerto Rican soprano—New York), Ghena Dimitrova (Bulgarian soprano—Dallas), Janis Gail Eckhart (mezzo-soprano—New York), Kathryn Gamberoni (soprano—St. Louis), Gail Gilmore (mezzo-soprano—New York), Linda Gray (Scottish soprano—Dallas), Sylvia Greenberg (Romanian soprano—Chicago), Irene Gubrud (soprano—St. Paul), Dénes Gulyás (Hungarian tenor—Philadelphia), Gottfried Hornik (Austrian baritone—San Francisco), Mary Jane Johnson (soprano—New York), Hans Kann (Austrian pianist—tour), Veronica Jochum (German pianist—New York), Veronica Kincses (Hungarian soprano—Chicago), Gary Lakes (tenor—Seattle), Susanne Mentzer (mezzo-soprano—Houston), Chris Merritt (tenor—New York), Christopher O'Riley (pianist New York), Ivo Pogorelich (Yugoslavian pianist—New York), Mikhail Rudy (Russian pianist—Cleveland), Heinrich Schiff (Austrian cellist Cleveland), Kathryn Selby (Australian pianist—New York), Stephanie Sundine (soprano New York), Robert Taub (pianist—New York), Hiroshi Wakasugi (Japanese conductor—Boston).

**Metropolitan Opera**  Thomas Allen (British baritone), Rockwell Blake (tenor), Gwendolyn Bradley (soprano), Sesto Bruscantini (Italian baritone), Zdislava Donat (Polish soprano), Birgit Finnilä (Swedish contralto), Manfred Jung (German tenor), Gary Lakes (tenor), Dano Raffanti (Italian tenor), Eva Randová (Czech mezzo-soprano), Martti Salminen (Finnish bass), Richard Vernon (bass), Spas Wenkoff (Bulgarian tenor), Susan Davenny Wyner (soprano), Heinz Zednik (Austrian tenor).

**Other**  D'Anna Fortunato (Paris—with Boston Opera Co.), Robert Gambill (tenor—Milan); Thomas Hampson (baritone—Düsseldorf).

## I. New Positions

**Conductors**  David Atherton (San Diego Symphony Orchestra—to 1987); Alvaro Cassuto (National Orchestra Association, New York—to 1987); Lukas Foss (Milwaukee Symphony Orchestra—to 1986); Kenneth Klein (Santa Cruz [California] Symphony Orchestra—to 1985); Hugh Wolff (Northeastern Pennsylvania Philharmonic Orchestra—to 1986).

**Educational**  Mario Davidovsky (Columbia); Mark DeVoto (Tufts); Donald Erb (Southern Methodist University); Eileen Farrell (voice, Hartt); Joan Morris (University of Michigan); Thomas Murray (Yale); Jan Peerce (voice, Mannes); Christopher Rouse (Eastman); Carl Topilow (Cleveland Institute); Donald H. White (music chair, Central Washington University—to 1990).

**Other**  Anthony Bliss (general manager, Metropolitan Opera); William Kraft (composer-in-residence, Los Angeles Philharmonic Orchestra—to 1985); Ardis Krainik (general manager, Chicago Lyric Theater).

## J. Honors and Awards

**Honors**  Maurice Abravanel (Gold Baton); Peter Herman Adler, Marian Anderson, and Carleton Sprague Smith (Peabody); Martin Bernheimer (Pulitzer for Music Criticism); Leonard Bernstein, Robert Erickson, Meyer Kupferman, and Ursula Mamlok (American Academy); Kevin Hanlon (Koussevitzky); Otto Luening (Brandeis); Donald Martino (American Academy and Institute); Gunther Schuller (National Arts Club Medal); William Schuman (Schuman); Rudolf Serkin (Kennedy Center).

**Awards**  Nina Bodnar-Horton (Long-Thibaud); Colin Carr and Nadja Salerno-Sonnenberg (Naumburg); C. William Harwood (Stokowski); Gary Lakes (Melchior); Cecile Licad (Leventritt);

Panayis Lyras (Cilburn Second); Gundaris Poné (Trieste); J. Patrick Raftery (Tucker); Santiago Rodriguez (Cliburn Third); André-Michel Schub (Cliburn); Nina Tichman (Kapell Second).

**K. Biographical**   Kurt Herbert Adler retires as director of the San Francisco Opera and is appointed conductor emeritus; Peter Herman Adler retires from the active music scene; Christian Badea becomes an American citizen; Sarah Caldwell takes the Boston Opera Company on a tour of China; Antal Dorati resigns his post with the Detroit Symphony Orchestra becoming Conductor Emeritus; János Kárpáti (Hungarian musicologist) lectures at Harvard; Johanna Meier becomes the first native-born American to sing Isolde at Bayreuth; Conlon Nancarrow visits the United States after 40 years in Mexico; Simon Rattle is appointed Principal Guest Conductor of the Los Angeles Philharmonic Orchestra; Maxim Shostakovich and his son defect to the West and settle in the United States; Michael Tilson Thomas becomes Principal Guest Conductor of the Los Angeles Philharmonic Orchestra.

**L. Musical Beginnings**

**Performing Groups**   Alexander String Quartet (New York); Austin Symphonic Band; Baroque Virtuosi (California); E.A.R. (new music ensemble, California); Greensboro Opera Co. (North Carolina); Kalichstein-Laredo-Robinson Trio; Opera Colorado; Opera St. Paul; Philharmonia Baroque (Berkeley); San Francisco Youth Orchestra; Tallahassee Symphony Orchestra.

**Festivals**   Bach Aria Festival and Institute (Stony Brook, New York); Boston Early Music Festival and Exhibition; Chamber Music in Historic Sites (Louisiana); International Festival of the Art Song (Milwaukee); Maryland Handel Festival (College Park, Maryland).

**Educational**   Conductor's Institute (West Virginia); San Diego Opera Institute; Tureck Bach Institute.

**Other**   Baird Music Hall (Buffalo); Broude Trust for the Publication of Musicological Editions; Composers in Red Sneakers (Boston); Friends of the Gamelan, Inc.; *Keyboard Classics*; National Foundation for Advancement in the Arts; *Psychomusicology*; William Schuman Award (Columbia).

**M. Music Publications**

Ceely, Robert, *Electronic Music Resource Book*
Cohen, Aaron, *International Encyclopedia of Women Composers*
Duckworth, William, *The Language of Experimental Music*
Escot, P. and Cogan, R., *Sonic Design: Practice and Problems*
Farrell, S. C., *Dictionary of Contemporary American Musical Instrument Makers*
Hamilton, David, *Metropolitan Opera Encyclopedia*
Helm, Everett, *Music and Tomorrow's Public*
Jablonski, Edward, *Encyclopedia of American Music*
Krummel, D. W. et al., *Resources of American Music History*
Sándor, György, *On Piano Playing: Motion, Sound and Expression*

**N. Musical Compositions**

**Chamber Music**   Samuel Adler, *String Quartet No. 7*; Ernst Bacon, *Piano Trio*; Elaine Barkin, *Impromtu* (piano trio); Earle Brown, *Folio II*; Jacob Druckman, *String Quartet No. 3*; Donald Erb, *Hair of the Wolf-full Moon* (string quartet); Richard Felciano, *Crystals* (string quartet); John Harbison, *Piano Quintet*; Benjamin Lees, *String Quartet No. 3*; Robert Hall Lewis, *String Quartet No. 3*; Tod Machover, *String Quartet No. 1*; Ned Rorem, *Quintet* (clarinet, bassoon, violin, cello, piano); Gerhard Samuel, *String Quartet No. 2*; Joseph Schwantner, *Music of Amber* (Friedheim Award); Charles Wuorinen, *Horn Trio*.

**Choral/Vocal**   Samuel Adler, *Snow Tracks*; Hugh Aitken, *Cantata No. 6*; Stephen Albert, *Into Eclipse* (song cycle); Dominick Argento, *I Hate and I Love* (song cycle); Leonard Bernstein, *Olympic Hymn*; Howard Boatwright, *A Song for St. Cecilia's Day*; Elliott Carter, *In Sleep, In Thunder* (song cycle); David Del Tredici, *Happy Voices* (Friedheim Award)—*All in the Golden Afternoon—Quaint Events*; Miriam Gideon, *A Woman of Valor* (song cycle); Gerald Levinson, *Black Magic/White Magic* (song cycle); William Mayer, *Passage* (song cycle); Paul Moravec,

*Missa Miserere*; Ronald Perera, *The White Whale*; Daniel Pinkham, *The Conversion of Saul* (oratorio); Steve Reich, *Tehillim*; Terry Riley, *G-Song*.

**Concertos**    William Albright, *Bacchanal* (organ and orchestra); George Barati, *Branches of Time* (two pianos and orchestra); Paul Chihara, *Saxophone Concerto*; Brian Fennelly, *Tropes and Echos*; Ellis Kohs, *Violin Concerto*; Ezra Laderman, *Concerto for String Quartet and Orchestra*; Robert Muczynski, *Saxophone Concerto, Opus 41*; Tobias Picker, *Violin Concerto*; Gunther Schuller, *Piano Concerto No. 2*; Stanislaw Skrowaczewski, *Clarinet Concerto*; Robert Suderburg, *Harp Concerto*; Lester Trimble, *Violin Concerto*.

**Electronic**    Conrad Cummings, *Dinosaur Music*; Michael McNabb, *Love in the Asylum*; Mel Powell, *Three Synthesizer Settings*; Terry Riley, *Sunrise of the Planetary Dream Collector*; Gil Trythall, *Luxikon II*; David Tudor, *Phonemes*.

**Operas**    Hugh Aitken, *Felipe*; Halim El-Dabh, *Drink of Eternity* (opera pageant); Carlisle Floyd, *Willie Stark*; Thea Musgrave, *An Occurrence at Owl Creek Bridge*; Ron Nelson, *Hamaguchi*; Burrill Phillips, *The Unforgiven*; George Rochberg, *The Confidence Man*; Robert Ward, *Abelard and Heloise*.

**Orchestra/Band**    Beth Anderson, *Overture for Band, Revelation*; Dominick Argento, *Fire Variations—Eight Variations and Finale*; Milton Babbitt, *Ars Combinatoria*; John Cage, *Dance Four Orchestras*; Donald Erb, *Sonneries*; Karel Husa, *The Trojan Women* (ballet); William Kraft, *Settler's Suite*; John La Montaine, *Concerto for String Orchestra*; Marc Neikrug, *Mobile for Orchestra*; Stephen Paulus, *Spectra*; Raoul Pleshkow, *Four Bagatelles for Orchestra*; Gundaris Poné, *La serenissima* (City of Trieste Prize—Whitney Prize); Christopher Rouse, *The Infernal Machine*; Elie Siegmeister, *Fantasies in Line and Color: Five American Paintings*; Virgil Thomson, *Thoughts for Strings*; Joan Tower, *Sequoia*; Paul Turok, *Ultima Thule*; Nancy Van der Vate, *Dark Nebulae*; Olly Wilson, *Lumina*; Ramon Zupko, *Rituals and Dances*.

**Piano/Organ**    Gordon Binkerd, *Sonata No. 2*; Michael Colgrass, *Metamusic*; George Crumb, *Gnomic Variations*; Morton Feldman, *Triadic Memories*; Lukas Foss, *Solo for Piano*; Dick Higgins, *Sonata for Prepared Piano*; Donald Martino, *Fantasies and Impromtus*; Leo Ornstein, *Sonata No. 6* (?).

**Symphonies**    Richard Brooks, *Symphony in One Movement*; John Eaton, *Symphony No. 2*; John Harbison, *Symphony No. 1*; Alan Hovhaness, *Symphonies No. 46, 47, 49*; Scott Huston, *Symphony No. 6, "The Human Condition"*; Meyer Kupferman, *Symphony No. 10, "FDR"*; Peter Mennin, *Symphony No. 9, "Sinfonia capricciosa"*; Vittorio Rieti, *Symphony No. 8*; Roger Sessions, *Concerto for Orchestra* (Pulitzer Prize); Leo Smit, *Symphony No. 3*; Richard Yardumian, *Symphony No. 3*.

# 1982

❀

## Historical Highlights

The Equal Rights Amendment fails to get ratification; the recession deepens, especially in the northern states; John Hinckley, the President's would-be assassin, is found insane; deliberately tainted Tylenol kills several in Chicago; martial law is declared in Poland and the Solidarity union is outlawed; Deng Xiaoping becomes top man in Communist China.

## World Cultural Highlights

**World Art**    Ilya Borofsky, *Running Man*; Fernando Botero, *Man on Horseback;* Enzo Cucchi, *Under the Wind;* Rainer Fetting, *Tänzer II;* Markus Lüpertz, *Orpheus in Hell*.

**World Literature**    Athol Fugard, *Master Harold . . . and the Boys*; William Golding, *A Moving Target*; Graham Greene, *Monsignor Quixote*; Thomas Keneally, *Schindler's Ark*.

**World Music**    Leonardo Balada, *Zapata!*; Witold Lutoslawski, *Symphony No. 3*; Krzysztof Penderecki, *Cello Concerto No. 2*; Aulis Sallinen, *Shadows*; Alfred Schnittke, *Violin Concerto No. 4*.

**Miscellaneous**   The Barbican Centre for Arts and Conferences opens in London; the Icelandic Opera Co. is founded; deaths include Louis Aragon, Clifford Curzon, Glenn Gould, Ngaio Marsh, and Ben Nicholson.

## American Art and Literature Highlights

**Deaths**   Deaths include art figures Raymond Jonson, Umberto Romano, Jack Tworkov, and literary figures Djuna Barnes, John Cheever, Babette Deutsch, John Gardner, Granville Hicks, Richard Jessup, Archibald MacLeish, Ayn Rand, Kenneth Rexroth, Howard Sackler, and Marya Zaturenska.

**Art Works**   David Beck, *Bandshell of Myopic Orchestra*; Helen Frankenthaler, *Fireworks*; Jasper Johns, *Perilous Night*; Robert Moskowitz, *Red Mill*; Elizabeth Murray, *Yikes*; Michael Ott, *Carpenter's Level*; Nam June Paik, *V-yramid*; Martin Puryear, *Sanctuary*; David Salle, *Normal Sentences*; Julian Schnabel, *Hope*; Kenneth Snelson, *Mozart*; Jacqueline Winsor, *Exploded Piece*.

**Literature**   Saul Bellow, *The Dean's December*; Richard Condon, *Prizzi's Honor*; Mark Helprin, *Ellis Island and Other Stories*; John Irving, *Hotel New Hampshire*; Helen H. Santmyer, *And Ladies of the Club*; Martin Cruz Smith, *Gorky Park*; John Updike, *Rabbit Is Rich* (National Book Award—National Book Critics' Award); Alice Walker, *The Color Purple* (Pulitzer Prize—National Book Award).

## Music—The Vernacular/Commercial Scene

**B. Deaths**   Ray Bloch (conductor/arranger) March 29; Sam Coslow (composer/lyricist); Sonny Greer (drummer) March 23; Al Haig (pianist) November 16; Sam "Lightnin'" Hopkins (singer/guitarist) January 30; Thelonious Monk (pianist/composer) February 17; Art Pepper (saxophonist) June 15; Eleanor Powell (singer/dancer) February 11; Marty Robbins (singer/writer) December 8; Nat Shilkret (composer/arranger); Charlie Spivak (trumpet/bandleader) March 1; Sonny Stitt (saxophonist) June 15; Joe Tex (singer) August 12; Tommy Tucker (singer) January 22; Jimmie Wakely (singer) September 23; Roy Webb (composer) December 10; Big Joe Williams (singer/guitarist) December 17.

**C. Biographical**

**Performing Groups**   Big Black; Bitch (Betsy in 1988); Cobra; Crimson Glory; The Cutting Crew; Death Angel; Dio; DRI; Faith No More; Fates Warning; The Forester Sisters; Gang Green; Girls Next Door; Go West; Helstar; Hot Streak; Levert; The Long Ryders; Mr. Mister; Public Enemy; Rock City Angels; Scandal; Scratch Acid; Slayer; Special EFX; Steeler; The Streets; The Weather Girls; Yard Trauma.

**New Beginnings**   *Annual Review of Jazz Studies*; Blues Heaven Foundation (Chicago); Greenwich Village Jazz Festival; GRP Records; Mid-America Jazz Festival (St. Louis); *New Music*; Sunnyside Records.

**Honors**   Benny Goodman (Kennedy Center); Kate Smith (Medal of Freedom).

**D. Publications**   James McCalla, *Jazz: A Listener's Guide*; Robert Palmer, *Deep Blues*; Billy Taylor, *Jazz Piano: History and Development*.

**E. Representative Works**

**Musicals**   L. Grossman, B. Comden, and A. Green, *A Doll's Life*; Larry Grossman and Hal Hackady, *Snoopy*; Gerald J. Markoe and M. E. Colby, *Charlotte Sweet*; A. Menken and H. Ashman, *Little Shop of Horrors*; James Quinn and Alaric Jans, *Do Black Patent Leather Shoes Really Reflect Up?*; Andrew Lloyd Webber, *Cats*; Maury Yeston, *Nine*.

**Number One Hits**   *Abracadabra* (Steve Miller Band); *Centerfold* (J. Geils Band); *Chariots of Fire* (Vangelis); *Don't You Want Me* (The Human League); *Ebony and Ivory* (Paul McCartney and Stevie Wonder); *Eye of the Tiger* (Survivor); *Hard to Say I'm Sorry* (Chicago); *I Can't Go for That—Maneater* (Hall and Oates); *I Love Rock and Roll* (Joan Jett and the Blackhearts); *Jack and Diane* (John Cougar); *Mickey* (Toni Basil); *Truly* (Lionel Richie); *Up Where We Belong* (Oscar—Joe Cocker and Jennifer Warnes); *Who Can It Be Now?* (Men at Work).

**Other**  William Bolcom, *Ragomania* (orchestra); Anthony Braxton, *For Two Pianos*; Henry Mancini, *Victor-Victoria* (film music—Oscar); John Williams, *E. T.* (film music—Oscar).

## Music—The Cultivated/Art Music Scene

**G. Deaths**  Samuel Barlow (composer) September 19; Mildred Dilling (harpist/educator) December 30; Lehman Engel (composer/conductor) August 29; Igor Gorin (Russian-born baritone) March 24; Frederick Jagel (tenor) July 5; Maria Jeritza (Czech-born soprano) July 10; William Primrose (Scottish-born violist) May 1; Artur Rubinstein (Polish-born pianist) December 20; Max de Schauensee (Italian-born tenor/critic) July 24; Renold Schilke (trumpet maker) September 5; Calvin Simmons (conductor) August 21; George Tremblay (pianist/composer) July 14; Burnet Tuthill (composer/conductor) January 18; Lazar Weiner (Russian-born pianist/composer) January 10; Albert Weisser (musicologist) March 13.

**H. Debuts**

**United States**  Francisco Araiza (Mexican tenor—San Francisco), Enzo Dara (Italian bass—New York), Barry Douglas (Irish pianist—New York), Susan Dunn (soprano—Peoria, Illinois), Jeffrey Gall (counter-tenor—San Francisco), Thomas Hampson (baritone—St. Louis), Horst Hiestermann (German tenor—Dallas), Charles Holland (tenor—New York), Yuzuko Horigome (Japanese violinist—Tanglewood), Jacek Kasprzyk (Polish conductor—Detroit), Midori (Japanese violinist—New York), Noriko Ogawa (Japanese pianist—New York), Keith Olson (tenor—New York), Michala Petri (Danish recorder virtuoso—New York), Rosalind Plowright (British mezzo-soprano—Philadelphia), Laszlo Polgar (Hungarian bass—Philadelphia), Vladimir Popov (Russian tenor—Portland), Teresa Ringholz (soprano—San Francisco), Douglas Riva (pianist—New York), Nadja Salerno-Sonnenberg (violinist—New York), Marta Senn (mezzo-soprano—Washington, DC), Dimitri Sgouros (Greek pianist—New York), Giuseppe Sinopoli (Italian conductor—Los Angeles), David Thomas (British bass—Hollywood).

**Metropolitan Opera**  Ara Berberian (bass), Carlo Bini (Italian tenor), Karen Bureau (soprano), Margarita Castro-Alberty (Puerto Rican soprano), Riccardo Chailly (Italian conductor), Barbara Conrad (mezzo-soprano), Kay Griffel (soprano), Anton Guadagno (Italian conductor), Angeles Gulin (Spanish soprano), Bernard Haitink (Dutch conductor), Julia Hamari (Hungarian mezzo-soprano), Anthony Laciura (tenor), J. Patrick Raftery (baritone), Olivia Stapp (soprano), Linda Zoghby (soprano).

**Other**  Pamela Coburn (soprano—Munich), Thomas Harper (baritone—Coburg), Lia Kahler (mezzo-soprano—Holland), Michael Morgan (conductor—Vienna), Gil Shaham (violinist—Jerusalem).

**I. New Positions**

**Conductors**  Isaiah Jackson (Flint Symphony Orchestra, Michigan); Christopher Keene (New York City Opera); Kenneth Klein (New York Virtuosi); David Zinman (Baltimore Symphony Orchestra).

**Educational**  Anshel Brusilow (Southern Methodist University); Bella Davidovich (Juilliard); Peter Erös (Peabody); Sidney Harth (Yale); Ani Kavafian (Mannes); Seth McCoy (voice, Eastman); Leslie Parnas (St. Louis Conservatory); György Sándor (Juilliard); Werner Torkanowsky (Carnegie-Mellon); Robert Washburn (dean, Crane School of Music—to 1985).

**Other**  John Adams (composer-in-residence, San Francisco Symphony Orchestra); Jacob Druckman (composer-in-residence, New York Philharmonic Orchestra); Donald Erb (president, American Music Center—to 1986); John Harbison (composer-in-residence, Pittsburgh Symphony Orchestra—to 1984); Terence A. McEwen (general manager, San Francisco Opera); Joseph Schwantner (composer-in-residence, St. Louis Symphony Orchestra—to 1985).

**J. Honors and Awards**

**Honors**  Milton Babbitt (Special Pulitzer); Chou Wen-Chung, Mario Davidovsky, and George Walker (American Academy and Institute); Elliott Galkin and Gunther Schuller (George Peabody);

Vladimir Horowitz (Wolf Foundation); Jessye Norman (*Musical America* Musician of the Year); Eugene Ormandy (Kennedy Center Honors); William Schuman (American Academy Gold Medal); Ralph Shapey (MacArthur Fellow); James Tenney and Ramon Zupko (American Academy).

**Awards**   Michael Gurt (Bachauer); Horacio Gutiérrez (Fisher); Michael Lewin (Kapell, shared Second—no First Prize); Alexander Markov (Paganini Second); Russell Patterson (Ditson); Gundaris Poné (Friedheim); Thomas Riehl (Naumburg).

**K. Biographical**   Claudio Abbado becomes Principal Guest Conductor of the Chicago Symphony Orchestra; William Christie becomes the first American to be appointed professor at the Paris Conservatory; Leon Fleisher, after 17 years, redebuts with a two-handed repertoire; Midori moves permanently to New York; Vladimir Popov (Russian tenor) emigrates to the United States; Bright Sheng (Chinese composer) emigrates to the United States.

**L. Musical Beginnings**

**Performing Groups**   Back Bay Brass Quintet (Boston); Baton Rouge Opera Co.; Cathedral Symphony Orchestra of New Jersey; Choral Arts Society of Philadelphia; Newberry Consort (Chicago); New York Virtuosi; Philharmonia Baroque Orchestra of the West; Portland Chamber Music Society (Maine).

**Festivals**   Music Festival of Arkansas (Fayetteville); New World Festival of the Arts (Miami); Redwoods Summer Music Festival (Santa Rosa, California); Rockport Chamber Music Festival (Massachusetts); Sandpoint Music Festival (Idaho); Seattle Chamber Music Festival; Sun Valley Music Festival (Idaho).

**Educational**   Alaska Conservatory of Music (Anchorage).

**Other**   Artistic Ambassador Program (United States Information Agency); Association for Classical Music (New York); Austin Performing Arts Center; Gina Bachauer International Piano Competition (Salt Lake City); *Chamber Music Quarterly*; Compact Disc; Contemporary Trends (Houston); George Eastman Prize; Great Plains Chamber Music Institute (Kansas); Hult Center for the Performing Arts (Eugene, Oregon); Indianapolis International Violin Competition; *The Journal of Musicology*; Joseph Meyerhoff Symphony Hall (Baltimore); Rudolf Nissim Composer Competition; Nonesuch Commission Award; George M. Sullivan Arena (Anchorage); Wharton Center for the Performing Arts (Michigan State University); Xerox Pianists Program.

**M. Music Publications**

Barzun, Jacques, *Critical Questions on Music and Letters, Culture and Biography*
Cage, John, *Themes and Variations*
Ewen, David, *American Composers: A Biographical Dictionary*
Futrell, Jon, ed., *The Illustrated Encyclopedia of Black Music*
Hamilton, David, *The Listener's Guide to Great Instrumentalists*
Leinsdorf, Erich, *The Composer's Advocate: A Radical Orthodoxy for Musicians*
Lipman, Samuel, *The House of Music: Art in an Era of Institutions*
Merriman, Margaret, *A New Look at 16th Century Counterpoint*
Schrader, Barry, *Introduction to Electro-acoustic Music*
Southern, Eileen, *Biographical Dictionary of Afro-American and African Musicians*
Valenti, Fernando, *The Harpsichord: A Dialogue for Beginners*

**N. Musical Compositions**

**Chamber Music**   John Adams, *Grand Pianola Music*; William Albright, *The Enigma Syncopations*; Milton Babbitt, *String Quartet No. 5*; Ernst Bacon, *Cello Sonata—Violin Sonata*; William Bergsma, *String Quartet No. 5*; Wallace Berry, *String Quartet No. 4*; James Cohn, *Concerto da Camera*; George Edwards, *String Quartet No. 2*; Morton Feldman, *For John Cage* (violin and piano); Fred Lerdahl, *String Quartet No. 2*; Mel Powell, *String Quartet 1982 (No. 2)*; George Rochberg, *String Quintet—Between Two Worlds* (flute and piano); Christopher Rouse, *String Quartet*; Frederic Rzewski, *Antigone-Legend* (violin and piano); Richard Wilson, *String Quartet No. 3*.

**Choral/Vocal**   Josef Alexander, *Rossettiana*; Dominick Argento, *The André Expedition* (song cycle); Milton Babbitt, *The Head of the Bed*; Morton Feldman, *Three Voices for Joan La Barbara*; John Harbison, *Mirabal Songs*; Andrew Imbrie, *A Song for St. Cecilia's Day*; Bernard Rands, *Canti del sole* (song cycle—Pulitzer Prize); Ned Rorem, *After Long Silence* (song cycle); Frederic Rzewski, *Antigone-Legend*; Joseph Schwantner, *Magabunda: Four Poems of Agueda Pizarro*; Charles Wuorinen, *Mass*; Yehudi Wyner, *On This Most Voluptuous Night* (song cycle).

**Concertos**   Ernst Bacon, *Piano Concerto No. 2*; Leonardo Balada, *Violin Concerto*; Leslie Bassett, *Concerto Grosso* (brass quintet and band); Irwin Bazelon, *Tides*; Michael Colgrass, *Piano Concerto*; Rolf Gehlhaar, *Tokamak* (piano and orchestra); William Kraft, *Interplay for Cello and Orchestra*; Ernst Krenek, *Organ Concerto—Cello Concerto—Violin Concerto No. 2*; Ezra Laderman, *Concerto for Flute, Bassoon and Orchestra*; John La Montaine, *Symphonic Variations, Opus 50*; Benjamin Lees, *Double Concerto for Cello, Piano and Orchestra*; Martin Mailman, *Violin Concerto* (Queen Marie-José Prize); William Mayer, *Inner and Outer Strings*; Gian Carlo Menotti, *Piano Concerto No. 2*; Marc Neikrug, *Violin Concerto*; George Walker, *Cello Concerto*.

**Electronic**   Charles Amirkhanian, *Dog of Stravinsky* (tape); Easley Blackwood, *Twelve Microtonal Etudes for Synthesizer*; Paul Dresher, *Industrial Strength Music*; David A. Jaffe, *Silicon Valley Breakdown*; Karl Korte, *Hill Country Birds*; Joan La Barbara, *Autumn Signal*; Barton McLean, *The Electric Sinfonia—The Last Ten Minutes*; Steve Reich, *Vermont Counterpoint*; Roger Reynolds, *Archipelago*; Morton Subotnick, *Liquid Strata*; David Ward-Steinman, *Intersections*.

**Operas**   T. J. Anderson, *Soldier Boy, Soldier*; Robert Ashley, *Atalanta (Acts of God)*; Leonardo Balada, *Hangman, Hangman!*; Philip Glass, *The Photographer*; Jack Gottlieb, *The Movie Opera*; Scott Huston, *Blind Girl*; Jean Eichelberger Ivey, *Birthmark*; Gian Carlo Menotti, *A Bride from Pluto*; Stephen Paulus, *The Postman Always Rings Twice*; Daniel Pinkham, *The Dreadful Dining Car*; William Sydeman, *Aria da capo*; George Tremblay, *The Phoenix: A Dance Symphony*; Gil Trythall, *The Terminal Opera*; Robert Ward, *Minutes till Midnight*.

**Orchestra/Band**   Richard Adler, *Wilderness Suite*; Theodore Antoniou, *The GBYSO Music*; George Barati, *Confluence*; Earle Brown, *Sounder Rounds*; Marc-Antonio Consoli, *Afterimages*; John Corigliano, *Echoes of Forgotten Rites*; Paul Dresher, *Channels Passing/Study for Variations*; Robert Erickson, *Aurora*; Vivian Fine, *Drama for Orchestra*; Lukas Foss, *Exeunt*; Morton Gould, *Housewarming*; Janos Kiss, *Quo Vadis* (symphonic poem); Joan Tower, *Amazon III*; Ramon Zupko, *Canti terrae*.

**Piano/Organ**   William Albright, *That Sinking Feeling* (organ); Theodore Antoniou, *Prelude and Toccata*; Milton Babbitt, *About Time*; Elaine Barkin, *At the Piano*; Irwin Bazelon, *Repercussions* (two pianos); Arthur Berger, *Perspectives III* (four hands); Gordon Binkerd, *Sonata No. 3*; William Bolcom, *Gospel Preludes II—Gospel Preludes III* (organ); George Crumb, *Pastoral Drone* (organ); Vivian Fine, *Double Variations for Piano*; Alan Hovhaness, *Sonata Mt. Chocorua*; David Noon, *Three Etudes*; Elie Siegmeister, *Three Studies*; Hugo Weisgall, *Sonata No. 2*.

**Symphonies**   Warren Benson, *Symphony No. 2, "Lost Songs"* (band); Paul Chihara, *Symphony No. 2*; Paul Creston, *Symphony No. 6 for Organ and Orchestra*; Curtis Curtis-Smith, *GAS! (The Great American Symphony)*; Alan Hovhaness, *Symphony No. 48—Symphonies 50–58*; Ezra Laderman, *Symphony No. 5, "Isaiah"*; Tobias Picker, *Symphony No. 1*; Ellen Taaffe Zwilich, *Symphony No. 1: Three Movements for Orchestra* (Pulitzer Prize).

# 1983

❖

## Historical Highlights

The United States sponsors an invasion of Grenada to overthrow the Marxist regime there; Sally Ride becomes the first American woman in space; American Telephone and Telegraph is forced to divide into smaller companies; Barney Clark becomes the first man to receive an artificial heart; Acquired

Immune Deficiency Syndrome (AIDS) becomes the newest scare disease; the Russians break off arms talks with the West.

## World Cultural Highlights

**World Art**  Ilya Borofsky, *Molecule Man with Briefcase*; Anselm Kiefer, *To the Unknown Painter;* Malcolm Morley, *Day Fishing at Heraklion*; Hak Chul Shin, *History of a Modern Korea*.

**World Literature**  Maeve Binchy, *Light a Penny Candle;* John Le Carré, *The Little Drummer Girl*; Gabriel Garcia Márquez, *Chronicle of a Death Foretold*; Fay Weldon, *Life and Loves of a She-Devil*.

**World Music**  Iain Hamilton, *Lancelot*; Hans Werner Henze, *The English Cat*; Witold Lutoslawski, *Chaim I*; Olivier Messiaen, *St. Francis of Assisi*; Michael Tippitt, *The Mask of Time*.

**Miscellaneous**  The New Opera Co. of Israel is founded; the Lahti Performing Arts Center opens in Finland; deaths include Sir Adrian Boult, Kenneth Clark, José Gutierrez, Richard Llewellyn, Igor Markevitch, Joan Miró, William Walton, and Rebecca West.

## American Art and Literature Highlights

**Births/Deaths**  Deaths include art figures Ivan Albright, Allyn Cox, Julian Levi, Richard Stankiewicz, and literary figures Henry Chapin, William Goyen, Ross MacDonald, Vincent McHugh, Josephina Niggli, and Tennessee Williams.

**Art Works**  Sandro Chia, *Young Man with Red Arm*; Greg Constantine, *Van Gogh Visits New York*; Eric Fischl, *A Visit to/a Visit from/the Island*; Al Held, *Mantegna's Edge*; Jasper Johns, *Racing Thoughts*; Robert Longo, *Ornamental Love*; Malcolm Morley, *Day Fishing in Heraklion*; Sandy Skoglund, *Maybe Babies*; Wayne Thiebaud, *Dark Lipstick*; Andrew Wyeth, *United States Navy*.

**Literature**  Nora Ephron, *Heartburn*; William Kennedy, *Ironweed* (National Book Critics'); Galway Kinnell, *Selected Poems* (National Book Award); Neil Simon, *Brighton Beach Memoirs* (New York Drama Critics' Award); Tom Stoppard, *The Real Thing* (New York Drama Critics' Award); Paul Theroux, *Mosquito Coast*; John Updike, *Hugging the Shore* (National Book Award—Pulitzer Prize).

## Music — The Vernacular/Commercial Scene

**B. Deaths**  Sweet Emma Barrett (pianist/singer) January 28; Eubie Blake (pianist/writer) February 12; Karen Carpenter (singer) February 4; Cliff Carlisle (singer/writer) April 5; Sam Chatmon (guitarist) February 2; Rafael Cortijo (Puerto Rican percussionist/bandleader); Howard Dietz (lyricist) July 30; Al Donahue (bandleader) February 20; Ira Gershwin (lyricist) August 17; Earl "Fatha" Hines (pianist) April 22; Harry James (bandleader/trumpeter) July 6; Bronislaw Kaper (composer) April 26; Carolyn Leigh (lyricist) November 19; Freddy Martin (bandleader) September 30; Muddy Waters (singer) April 30; Roosevelt Sykes (bandleader/composer) July 11; Merle Travis (singer/guitarist) October 20.

**C. Biographical**

**Performing Groups**  Alcatrazz; The Allies; American Music Club; Autograph; Black Sheep; Bon Jovi; Carnivore; Cinderella; The Crumbsuckers; Dark Angel; Death; Eleventh Dream Day; Exile; Grupo Fascinación; Hurricane; Living Color; Lizzie Borden; Lone Justice; Megadeth; Mobo Band (by K. Watanabe); Nasty Savage; Obsession; Poison; Possessed; Q5; Red Hot Chili Peppers; Run DMC; Savatage; Sawyer Brown; Shire; Sojourn; Stryper; Surface; 'Til Tuesday; 29th Street Saxophone Quartet; White Lion; The Young Fresh Fellows.

**New Beginnings**  Roy Clark's Celebrity Theater (Branson, Missouri); International Association for the Study of Popular Music, American Chapter; Jacksonville Jazz Festival; Mosaic Records; *RPM (Reviews of Popular Music)*.

**Honors**  "Little Jimmy" Dickens (Country Music Hall of Fame); Ella Fitzgerald (Peabody Award); Mabel Mercer (Medal of Freedom); Frank Sinatra (Kennedy Center); Stephen Sondheim (American Academy and Institute).

**D. Publications**  Mark Booth, *American Popular Music: A Reference Guide*; Lehman Engel, *Getting the Show On*; C. Friedman and G. Giddins, *A Moment's Notice: Portraits of American Jazz Musicians*; Ethan Mordden, *The Hollywood Musical*; Mary Unterbrink, *Jazz Women at the Keyboard*.

**E. Representative Works**

**Musicals**  Jerry Herman, *La Cage aux Folles* (Tony); David Shire and R. Malty, *Baby*; Various composers, *Amen Corner—5-6-7-8 . . . Dance!*

**Number One Hits**  *Africa* (Toto); *All Night Long* (Lionel Richie); *Baby, Come To Me* (Patti Austin and James Ingram); *Beat It—Billie Jean* (Michael Jackson); *Come On Eileen* (Dexys Midnight Runners); *Down Under* (Men at Work); *Every Breath You Take* (The Police); *Flashdance* (Oscar—Irene Cara); *Islands in the Stream* (Kenny Rogers and Dolly Parton); *Let's Dance* (David Bowie); *Maniac* (Michael Sembello); *Say, Say, Say* (Paul McCartney and Michael Jackson); *Sweet Dreams (Are Made of This)* (Eurythmics); *Tell Her About It* (Billy Joel); *Total Eclipse of the Heart* (Bonnie Tyler).

**Other**  Anthony Braxton, *On Four Compositions (Quartet) 1983*; Irene Cara/Giorgio Moroder, *Flashdance* (film music—Oscar)

## Music—The Cultivated/Art Music Scene

**G. Deaths**  Claus Adam (Austrian-born cellist/composer) July 4; George Balanchine (Russian-born ballet impresario) April 30; Cathy Berberian (soprano) March 6; Charles Benton Fisk (organ maker) December 16; Charles Warren Fox (musicologist) October 15; Carroll Glenn (bass bariTone) June 2; Donald Gramm (bass-baritone) June 2; Carroll Hollister (pianist) October 1; Paul Jacobs (harpsichordist/pianist) September 25; Charles Kullman (tenor) February 8; Irving Lowens (musicologist/critic) November 14; Peter Mennin (composer/administrator) June 17; Jerome Moross (composer); Boris Schwarz (Russian-born violinist/musicologist) December 31; Gerald Strang (composer) November 2; Marion Talley (soprano) January 3; Alfred Wallenstein (cellist/conductor) February 8; Emanuel Winternitz (Austrian-born musicologist) August 22.

**H. Debuts**

**United States**  Evelyn Brunner (Swiss soprano—Baltimore), Li-Ly Chang (Chinese—New York), Mia Chung (pianist—Washington, DC), Paul Coletti (Scottish violist—New York), Elizabeth Connell (South African soprano—New York), Lella Cuberli (soprano—New York), Alberto Cupido (Italian tenor—San Francisco), Mark Elder (British conductor—Chicago), Mechthild Gessendorf (German soprano—Tulsa), Reiner Goldberg (German tenor—New York), Roland Hermann (German baritone—New York), Ian Hobson (British pianist—New York), Melanie Holliday (soprano—Houston), Patrizia Kwella (British soprano—San Diego), Jean-Philippe Lafont (French bass-baritone—New York), Karita Mattila (Finnish soprano—Washington, DC), Mikael Melbye (Danish baritone—Santa Fe), Corneliu Murgu (Romanian tenor—Philadelphia), Cheryl Ann Parrish (soprano—San Francisco), Janet Perry (soprano—Washington, DC), Stephen Robinson (guitarist—New York), Gabriele Schnaut (mezzo-soprano—Chicago), Dmitri Sitkovetsky (Ukrainian violinist—Chicago), John Tomlinson (British bass—San Francisco), Dawn Upshaw (soprano—New York), Diana Walker (soprano—New York), Ortrun Wenkel (German contralto—San Francisco).

**Metropolitan Opera**  Roberta Alexander (soprano), Silvano Carroli (Italian baritone), Barbara Daniels (soprano), Stefka Evstatieva (Bulgarian soprano), Vernon Hartman (baritone), Sergei Koptchak (Czech bass), Spiro Malas (bass-baritone), Jessye Norman (soprano), Benedetta Pecchioli (Italian mezzo-soprano), Juan Pons (Spanish baritone), Klaus Tennstedt (German conductor), Gösta Winbergh (Swedish tenor).

**Other**  Derek Lee Ragin (counter-tenor—Innsbruck), Anna Steiger (soprano—Glyndebourne).

**I. New Positions**

**Conductors**  Christian Badea (Columbus Symphony Orchestra); Emerson Buckley (Oakland Symphony Orchestra); Sergiu Comissiona (Houston Symphony Orchestra); Kenneth Klein (South Dakota Symphony Orchestra); Kenneth Schermerhorn (Nashville Symphony Orchestra—to 1988); Gerard Schwarz (Seattle Symphony Orchestra); Jerzy Semkow (Rochester Philharmonic

Orchestra); Joseph Silverstein (Utah Symphony Orchestra); Lawrence Leighton Smith (Louisville Orchestra).

**Educational** Bethany Beardslee (Brooklyn College); Colin Carr (New England Conservatory); Phyllis Curtin (dean, Boston University School of the Arts); Kenneth Gaburo (University of Iowa); Henry Holt (USC Opera); Aleck Karis (Columbia); Jaime Laredo (violin, St. Louis Conservatory); Harvey Sollberger (Indiana University); Gabriella Tucci (Indiana University).

**Other** Margaret Bent (president, American Musicological Society); Speight Jenkins (general manager, Seattle Opera); Libby Larsen (composer-in-residence, Minnesota Symphony Orchestra—to 1987); Stephen Paulus (composer-in-residence, Minnesota Symphony Orchestra—to 1987); John Rahn (editor, *Perspectives of New Music*).

## J. Honors and Awards

**Honors** Milton Babbitt, Paul Fromm (Peabody); Elliott Carter (MacDowell Medal); Schuyler Chapin (National Arts Club Medal); Lukas Foss (American Academy and Institute, Brandeis); Morton Gould (Gold Baton); Betsy Jolas (American Academy and Institute); Nathan Milstein (*Musical America* Musician of the Year); Bernard Rands, Bruce Saylor and Joan Tower (American Academy); Peter Sellars (MacArthur Fellow); Virgil Thomson (Kennedy Center).

**Awards** Susan Dunn (Tucker); Stephen Hough (Naumburg); Jeffrey Kahane (Rubinstein); Elmar Oliveira (Avery Fisher); Peter Serkin (Siena).

**K. Biographical** Charles Dutoit becomes Principal Guest Conductor of the Minnesota Symphony Orchestra; Raymond Leppard becomes an American citizen and Principal Guest Conductor of the St. Louis Symphony Orchestra; Bernard Rands becomes an American citizen; George Rochberg retires from teaching to devote full time to composing; Alexander Toradze (Russian pianist) settles in the United States; David Zinman becomes Principal Guest Conductor of the Baltimore Symphony Orchestra; Ellen Taaffe Zwilich becomes the first woman to win a Pulitzer Prize for composition.

## L. Musical Beginnings

**Performing Groups** Harmonia Opera (New York); Indiana Opera Theater; Music Camerit (Hebrew Art School, New York); San Francisco Chamber Symphony; Santa Fe Desert Chorale.

**Festivals** American Music Theater Festival (Philadelphia); Bridgehampton Chamber Music Festival (New York); Connecticut Early Music Festival; Lake Tahoe Summer Music Festival; Next Wave Festival (Brooklyn, New York); San Antonio Festival; Southeastern Music Center Summer Festival (Georgia).

**Educational** Virginia School of the Arts (Lynchburg).

**Other** *American Music*; Finger Lakes Performing Arts Center (Rochester); Huang Harmonicas (Farmingdale, New York); Kentucky Center for the Arts (Louisville); New Albion Records; *The Opera Quarterly*; Alexander Tcherepnin Society (New York).

## M. Music Publications

Apel, Willi, *Die italienische Violinmusik im 17. Jahrhundert*
Deutsch, Diana, ed., *Music Perception*
Hamm, Charles E., *Music in the New World*
Harder, Paul, *Music Manuscript Technique*
Lerdahl, F. and Jackendoff, R., *A Generative Theory of Tonal Music*
Levarie, S. and Lévy, E., *Musical Morphology: A Discourse and a Dictionary*
Levy, Kenneth, *Music: A Listener's Introduction*
Pellegrino, Ron, *The Electronic Arts of Sound and Light*
Prausnitz, Frederik, *Score and Podium: A Complete Guide to Conducting*
Rockwell, John, *All American Music: Composition in the Late Twentieth Century*
Schwarz, Boris, *Great Masters of the Violin*

## N. Musical Compositions

**Chamber Music** John Cage, *Thirty Pieces for String Quartet*; Morton Feldman, *String Quartet No. 2*; Lukas Foss, *Percussion Quartet*; Arthur Frackenpohl, *Tuba Sonata*; Philip Glass, *String*

*Quartet No. 2: Company*; Alexei Haieff, *Wind Quintet*; William Kraft, *Gallery '83*; Ezra Laderman, *String Quartet No. 7—Double String Quartet*; John Anthony Lennon, *Ghostfires* (guitar); Donald Martino, *String Quartet* (Friedheim Award); Robert Palmer, *Cello Sonata No. 2*; George Rochberg, *Piano Quartet*; Gunther Schuller, *Duologue*; Harvey Sollberger, *The Humble Heart* (woodwind quintet); Francis Thorne, *String Quartet No. 4*.

**Choral/Vocal**   Theodore Antoniou, *Prometheus* (cantata); Mario Davidowsky, *Romancero*; Cecil Effinger, *Cantata, Opus 111: From Ancient Prophets*; Carlisle Floyd, *Citizen of Paradise* (song cycle); Miriam Gideon, *Wing'd Hour* (song cycle); Aaron Jay Kernis, *Morningsongs* (song cycle); Thomas Pasatieri, *Mass*; Ronald Perera, *Earthsongs*; Mel Powell, *Strand Settings: Darker* (song cycle); Terry Riley, *The Medicine Wheel—Song of the Emerald Runner*; Ned Rorem, *An American Oratorio*.

**Concertos**   David Amram, *Honor Song* (cello and orchestra); Leslie Bassett, *Concerto Lyrico* (trombone and orchestra); Irwin Bazelon, *Piano Concerto*; Chester Biscardi, *Piano Concerto*; William Bolcom, *Violin Concerto*; Emma Lou Diemer, *Trumpet Concerto*; Meyer Kupferman, *Tuba Concerto*; Benjamin Lees, *Concerto for Brass Choir and Orchestra*; Peter Lieberson, *Piano Concerto*; Peter Mennin, *Flute Concerto*; Gian Carlo Menotti, *Doublebass Concerto*; Tobias Picker, *Piano Concerto No. 2, "Keys to the City"*; Gunther Schuller, *Saxophone Concerto*; Joseph Schwantner, *Distant Runes and Incantations* (piano and orchestra); Ralph Shapey, *Double Concerto for Violin and Cello*; Elie Siegmeister, *Violin Concerto*; Richard Wilson, *Bassoon Concerto*.

**Electronic**   Laurie Anderson, *United States (two evening musical happening)*; Paul Dresher, *Dark Blue Circumstance*; Alvin Lucier, *Seesaw*; Tod Machover, *Electronic Etudes*; Terry Riley, *The Ethereal Time Shadow—Offering to Chief Crazy Horse*; Loren Rush, *The Digital Domain*.

**Operas**   Robert Ashley, *Perfect Lives (Private Parts)*; Elaine Barkin, *Women's Voices* (theater piece); Leonard Bernstein, *A Quiet Place*; Paul Dresher, *Are Are*; Ulysses Kay, *Frederick Douglass*; William Mayer, *A Death in the Family—One Christmas Long Ago*; Richard Owen, *The Death of the Virgin*; Thomas Pasatieri, *Maria Elena*.

**Orchestra/Band**   Curtis Curtis-Smith, *Variations on "Amazing Grace"* (with organ); George Edwards, *Moneta's Mourn*; Donald Erb, *Prismatic Variations*; Harold Farberman, *Shapings*; John Harbison, *Ulysses Bow—Ulysses Raft* (ballets); William Kraft, *Gallery 83*; Ezra Laderman, *Sonore*; Witold Lutoslawski, *Chaim I*; Robert Moevs, *Pandora: Music for Small Orchestra II*; Stephen Paulus, *Seven Short Pieces for Orchestra*; George Perle, *Serenade No. 3*; Gardner Read, *Astral Nebulae*; Steve Reich, *The Desert Music*; Nicolas Roussakis, *Fire and Earth and Water and Air*; Gerhard Samuel, *AGAM* (ballet); Hugo Weisgall, *Prospect*; Frank Wigglesworth, *Aurora*; Ellen Taaffe Zwilich, *Prologue and Variations*.

**Piano/Organ**   Theodore Antoniou, *Entrata*; Milton Babbitt, *Playing for Time—Canonical Form*; Leslie Bassett, *Repercussions* (two pianos); Gordon Binkerd, *Sonata No. 4*; Joel Chadabe, *Variations*; George Crumb, *Processional*; David Diamond, *Prelude, Fantasy and Fugue*; Emma Lou Diemer, *Romantic Suite* (organ); Rolf Gehlhaar, *Cusps, Swallowtails and Butterflies*; Anthony Iannaccone, *Variations for Organ*; Benjamin Lees, *Fantasy Variations*; Otto Luening, *Sonority Forms I*; Robert Muczynski, *Dream Cycle, Opus 44*; Burrill Phillips, *Commentaries*; Nancy Van de Vate, *Sonata No. 2*.

**Symphonies**   Karel Husa, *Symphony No. 2, "Reflections"—Concerto for Wind Ensemble* (Sudler International Prize); Meyer Kupferman, *Symphony No. 11*; Ezra Laderman, *Symphony No. 6*; Martin Mailman, *Symphony No. 3*; Stephen Paulus, *Concerto for Orchestra*; Elie Siegmeister, *Symphony No. 6*; David Van Vactor, *Symphony No. 7*.

# 1984

❀

## Historical Highlights

Ronald Reagan, re-elected president, visits China; the space shuttle *Challenger* succeeds in retrieving a satellite for repairs in space; the Louisiana Exposition opens in New Orleans; the Communist countries boycott the Summer Olympics in Los Angeles; Indira Gandhi of India dies at the hands of her own guard; Margaret Thatcher escapes an attempt on her life.

## World Cultural Highlights

**World Art**    Georg Baselitz, *Das Liebespaar;* Tony Cragg, *Spectrum;* Leon Golub, *Mercenaries V*; Malcolm Morley, *Farewell to Crete*; Rufino Tamayo, *Cabeza en Azul*.

**World Literature**    Julian Barnes, *Flaubert's Parrot*; Athol Fugard, *The Road to Mecca;* Milan Kundera, *The Unbearable Lightness of Being*; Yevgeny Yevtushenko, *Wild Berries*.

**World Music**    Hans Werner Henze, *Symphony No. 7*; Alun Hoddinott, *Symphony No. 6*; Aulis Sallinen, *The King Goes Forth to France*; Alfred Schnittke, *Symphony No. 4*; Andrew Lloyd Webber, *Requiem*.

**Miscellaneous**    The Castello Svevo International Festival in Sicily and the Havana International Festival of Contemporary Music begin; deaths include Vicente Alexandre, Ania Dorfman, Elizabeth Goudge, Jorge Guillen, Liam O'Flaherty, J. B. Priestley, and Mikhail Sholokhov.

## American Art and Literature Highlights

**Births/Deaths**    Deaths include artists Peter Hurd, Lee Krasner, Alice Neel, Emanuel Romano, and literary figures Richard Brautigan, Truman Capote, Michel Foucault, Albert Halper, Lillian Hellman, George Oppen, Irwin Shaw, Jesse Stuart, and Jessamyn West.

**Art Works**    Robert Arneson, *Ground Zero*; Larry Bell, *Triangles on Grid*; Louise Bourgeois, *Velvet Eyes*; Jean Dubuffet, *Monument with Standing Beast*; Red Grooms, *Picasso in the South of France*; Martin Puryear, *Night and Day*; John Register, *Pink Cadillac*; Susan Rothenberg, *Mondrian*; Julian Schnabel, *King of the Wood*; Frank Stella, *Abercrombie's Curtain*; Jamie Wyeth, *Breakfast at Sea*.

**Literature**    Alison Lurie, *Foreign Affairs* (Pulitzer Prize); Helen MacInnes, *Ride a Pale Horse*; Jay McInerney, *Bright Lights, Big City*; Sharon Olds, *The Dead and the Living* (National Book Critics' Award); Richard Price, *The Breaks*; Sam Shepard, *Fool for Love*; Arthur Wilson, *Ma Rainey's Black Bottom* (New York Drama Critics' Award).

## Music — The Vernacular/Commercial Scene

**B. Deaths**    Count Basie (pianist/bandleader) April 26; Lenny Breau (guitarist) August 8; Ray Copeland (trumpeter/arranger) May 19; Ral Donner (singer) April 6; Carmen Dragon (conductor) March 28; William "Red" Garland (pianist) April 23; Marvin Gaye (singer) April 1; Steve Goodman (singer/writer) September 20; Claude Hopkins (pianist/bandleader) February 19; Alberta Hunter (singer) October 17; Ina Ray Hutton (bandleader) February 19; Gordon Jenkins (arranger) April 24; Bessie Jones (folk singer) September 4; Shelly Manne (drummer/bandleader) September 26; Percy Mayfield (singer/writer) August 11; Mabel Mercer (singer) April 20; Ethel Merman (singer) February 15; Abe Olman (songwriter) January 4; Esther Phillips (singer) August 7; Leo Robin (lyricist) December 29; Arthur Schwartz (composer) September 3; Ada "Bricktop" Smith (singer) January 31; Larry Stock (pianist/composer) May 4; Big Mama Thornton (singer) July 25; Ernest Tubb (singer) September 6; Paul Francis Webster (lyricist) March 18; Meredith Willson (composer) June 15; Jackie Wilson (singer) January 21.

**C. Biographical**

**Performing Groups**    The A-Bones; A.D.; Aftermath; Aviator; Blessed Death; Camper Van Beethoven; Cult Jam; Detente; Dinosaur, Jr.; Flotsam and Jetsam; Heavy D. and the Boyz; Heir Apparent; Heretic; Hirax; The Honeydrippers; HSAS; The Jets; Leaders Jazz Sextet; Metal Church; Morbid Angel; Neon Cross; Omen; Overkill; Primus; The Range; Screaming Trees; Sentinel Beast; Soundgarden; Tangler; Tesla; They Might Be Giants; Timbuk 3; Warrant; W.A.S.P.

**New Beginnings**    JVC Jazz Festival Newport; Los Angeles Classic Jazz Festival; National Jazz Service Organization; Pittsburgh Jazz Festival; Leon Russell Enterprises (Nashville).

**Honors**    Floyd Tillman (Country Music Hall of Fame); Lena Horne and Arthur Miller (Kennedy Center).

**D. Publications**   R. P. Christeson, *The Old-time Fiddler's Repertory II*; Nicholas Tawa, *A Music for Millions: Antebellum Democratic Attitudes and the Birth of American Popular Music*.

**E. Representative Works**

**Musicals**   J. Kander and F. Ebb, *The Rink*; Galt MacDermot and William Dumaresq, *The Human Comedy*; Stephen Sondheim, *Sunday in the Park with George*.

**Number One Hits**   *Against All Odds* (Phil Collins); *Caribbean Queen (No More Love on the Run(* (Billy Ocean); *Footloose* (Kenny Loggins); *Hello* (Lionel Richie); *I Just Called to Say I Love You* (Oscar—Stevie Wonder); *Jump* (Van Halen); *Karma Chameleon* (Culture Club); *Let's Go Crazy* (Prince and the Revolution); *Let's Hear It for the Boy* (Deniece Williams); *Like a Virgin* (Madonna); *Missing You* (John Waite); *Out of Touch* (Hall and Oates); *Owner of a Lonely Heart* (Yes); *The Reflex* (Duran Duran); *Time After Time* (Cyndi Lauper); *Wake Me Up Before You Go-Go* (Wham); *What's Love Got To Do With It?* (Tina Turner); *When Doves Cry* (Prince).

**Other**   Jan Hammer, *Miami Vice Theme*; Randy Newman, *The Natural* (film music); Ray Parker, Jr., *Theme from Ghostbusters*; Prince, *Purple Rain* (Oscar).

## Music—The Cultivated/Art Music Scene

**G. Deaths**   Otto Edwin Albrecht (musicologist) July 5; Lucien Cailliet (French-born composer/arranger) December 27; Olaf Christiansen (conductor) April 12; Samuel Gardner (Russian-born violinist/composer) January 23; Calvin Hampton (organist) August 5; Walter Kaufmann (Czech-born musicologist) September 9; Ralph Kirkpatrick (harpsichordist) April 13; Alfred Knopf (publisher) August 11; Gail Kubik (composer) July 20; Jan Peerce (tenor) December 15; Judith Raskin (soprano) December 21; Leonard Rose (cellist) November 16; Jesús María Sanromá (Puerto Rican pianist) October 12; Albert Seay (musicologist) January 7; Reginald Stewart (Scottish-born pianist/conductor) July 8; Randall Thompson (composer) July 9; Barbara Troxell (soprano) September 23; Fred Waring (conductor/publisher) July 29.

**H. Debuts**

**United States**   Sergiu Celibadache (Romanian conductor—New York), Michael Collins (British clarinetist—New York), Imogen Cooper (British pianist), Sergei Edelmann (Russian pianist—Chicago), Anne Gjevang (Norwegian mezzo-soprano—Chicago), Christopher Hogwood (British conductor—Chicago), Stephen Hough (British pianist—New York), Linda Kobler (harpsichordist—New York), Mischa Lefkowitz (Latvian violinist—New York), Frank Lopardo (tenor—St. Louis), Andrea Matthews (soprano—Virginia City), Rhonda Jackson McAfee (mezzo-soprano—St. Louis), Marie McLaughlin (Scottish soprano—Washington, DC), Hermann Michael (German conductor—Seattle), Diana Montague (British mezzo-soprano—Chicago), Jon Kimura Parker (Canadian pianist—New York), Esa-Pekka Salonen (Finnish conductor—Los Angeles), Galina Stamenova (Bulgarian violinist—Dallas), Cheryl Studer (soprano—Chicago), Marcel Vanaud (Belgian baritone—Pittsburgh), Frank Peter Zimmermann (German violinist—Pittsburgh).

**Metropolitan Opera**   Francisco Araiza (Mexican tenor), Julie Hamari (Hungarian mezzo-soprano), Jorma Hynninen (Finnish baritone), Marek Janowski (Polish conductor), Artur Korn (German bass), Aprile Millo (soprano), Franz Nentwig (German bass-baritone), Vladimir Popov (Russian tenor), Samuel Ramey (bass), Dawn Upshaw (soprano), Carol Vaness (soprano), Ute Vinzing (German soprano).

**I. New Positions**

**Conductors**   Christoph von Dohnányi (Cleveland Orchestra); Günther Herbig (Detroit Symphony Orchestra—to 1990); Lorin Maazel (program consultant, Pittsburgh Symphony Orchestra); John Mauceri (American Symphnoy Orchestra—to 1987); Jorge Mester (Pasadena Symphony Orchestra); Bernard Rubenstein (Tulsa Philharmonic Orchestra); Gunther Schuller (Spokane Symphony Orchestra).

**Educational**   Donald Erb (Indiana University); Sharon Isbin (Mannes); Anna Moffo (voice, NYU); Joseph W. Polisi (president, Juilliard); Charles Treger (president, Meadowmount School, Connecticut).

**Other**   Bruce Crawford (general manager, Metropolitan Opera); Eric Salzman (editor, *Musical Quarterly*); Elliott Schwartz (chairman, American Society of University Composers—to 1987).

**J. Honors and Awards**

**Honors**   Martin Bookspan (National Arts Club Medal); Elliott Carter (George Peabody Medal); David Del Tredici (American Academy and Institute); Richard D. Freed (Deems Taylor); William Kraft and Ellen Taaffe Zwilich (American Academy); James Levine (*Musical America* Musician of the Year); Gian Carlo Menotti and Isaac Stern (Kennedy Center); Paul Moravec (Rome Prize).

**Awards**   David Buechner (Bachauer); Kenneth Jean (Stokowski); Jon Klibonoff (Bachauer Second); Tod Machover (Koussevitzky); Gundaris Poné (Louisville); Roger Roloff (Tucker).

**K. Biographical**   Phyllis Curtin retires from all public performance; Bella Davidovich becomes a naturalized American citizen; Plácido Domingo conducts at the Metropolitan Opera; Eugene Ormandy, after suffering a January heart attack, cancels all conducting engagements for the future; Gunther Schuller hands in his resignation as artistic director at the Berkshire Music Center; Judith Somogi becomes the first woman to conduct at Milan's La Scala.

**L. Musical Beginnings**

**Performing Groups**   Abel-Steinberg-Winant Trio; Cavani String Quartet (Cleveland); Concert Opera Association of San Francisco; Concordia (New York Chamber Orchestra); Paul Dresher Ensemble; Manhattan Chamber Orchestra; New Orchestra of Boston; North Beach Grand Opera (Opera Nova); Renaissance City Chamber Players (Detroit); Santa Fe Symphony Orchestra.

**Festivals**   Grand Canyon Chamber Music Festival; International Festival of the Americas (Miami).

**Educational**   La Guardia High School of Music and the Arts (New York); Fritz Reiner Center for Contemporary Music (Columbia).

**Other**   Braun Music Center (Stanford); Center for Black Music Research (Chicago); *Chamber Music Magazine*; Circle Theater (restoration—Indianapolis); *Essays on Modern Music*; Filene Center (Wolf Trap Farm); Grawemeyer Awards (University of Louisville); Miami Center for the Fine Arts; *Opus*; Riverbend Music Center (Cincinnati); Arlene Schnitzer Concert Hall (Portland, Oregon); Society for Electro-Acoustic Music in the United States.

**M. Music Publications**

Craft, Robert, *Present Perspectives*
Goldovsky, Boris, *Good Afternoon, Ladies and Gentlemen*
Hines, Jerome, *Great Singers on Great Singing*
Kirkpatrick, Ralph, *Interpreting Bach's Well-tempered Clavier: A Performer's Discourse of Method*
Machover, Tod, *Some Thoughts on Computer Music*
Oliveros, Pauline, *Software for People: Collected Writings 1963–80*
Rochberg, George, *The Aesthetics of Survival: A Composer's View of Twentieth-century Music*
Rorem, Ned, *Setting the Tone: Essays and a Diary*
Werner, Eric, *The Sacred Bridge II: Literary Parallels in Synagogue and Early Churches*

**N. Musical Compositions**

**Chamber Music**   William Albright, *Saxophone Sonata*; Milton Babbitt, *Sheer Pluck* (guitar)—*Composition for Guitar*; Arthur Berger, *Wind Quintet*; Morton Feldman, *For Philip Guston*; Lukas Foss, *Trio for Violin, Horn and Piano*; John Harbison, *String Quartet No. 1—Twilight Music*; Charles Jones, *String Quartet No. 8*; Ellis Kohs, *String Quartet No. 3*; William Kraft, *Weavings* (string quartet and percussion); George Perle, *Wind Quintet No. 4* (Pulitzer Prize); Wayne Peterson, *String Quartet*; Shulamit Ran, *String Quartet*; Terry Riley, *Cadenza on the Night Plain* (string quartet); Bright Sheng, *String Quartet No. 1—String Quartet No. 2*; Ellen Taaffe Zwilich, *Double Quartet for Strings*.

**Choral/Vocal**   Stephen Albert, *Into Eclipse*; Henry Brant, *Western Springs: A Spatial Assembly for Two Orchestras, Two Choruses and Two Jazz Combos*; Andrew Imbrie, *Requiem: In Memoriam John H. Imbrie*; John La Montaine, *The Marshes of Glynn*; Roger Nixon, *A Narrative of Tides* (song cycle).

**Concertos** Byron Adams, *Violin Concerto*; Hugh Aitken, *Violin Concerto No. 1*; Michael Colgrass, *Chaconne for Viola and Orchestra*; Donald Erb, *Clarinet Concerto—Contrabassoon Concerto*; Brian Fennelly, *Concerto for Sax and Strings*; Morton Gould, *Flute Concerto*; William Kraft, *Concerto for Timpani and Orchestra*; Meyer Kupferman, *Clarinet Concerto*; Ezra Laderman, *Cello Concerto*; Juan Orrego-Salas, *Violin Concerto, Opus 86*; Robert Palmer, *Concerto for Two Pianos, Two Percussionists, Strings and Brass*; George Rochberg, *Oboe Concerto*; Ned Rorem, *Violin Concerto—Organ Concerto*; Joan Tower, *Cello Concerto*: George Walker, *Violin Concerto*; Robert Ward, *Saxophone Concerto*; Richard Wernick, *Violin Concerto* (Friedheim Award); Charles Wuorinen, *Piano Concerto No. 3—Rhapsody for Violin and Orchestra*.

**Electronic** Charles Amirkhanian, *Martinique and the Course of Abstraction* (tape); Ruth Anderson, *Time and Tempo* (sound sculpture); Paul Dresher, *Other Fire*; Richard Felciano, *Kindertotenlieder*; Kenneth Gaburo, *Antiphony VIII, "Revolution"* (percussion and tape); Joan La Barbara, *Time(d) Trials and Unscheduled Events*; Alvin Lucier, *Spinner*; Tod Machover, *Spectres Parisiens*; Roger Reynolds, *Transfigured Wind II*.

**Operas** Dominick Argento, *Casanova's Homecoming*, Robert Ashley, *Atalanta Strategy*; Leonardo Balada, *Zapata!*, Paul Dresher, *See Hear*; Ross Lee Finney, *Weep Torn Land*; Philip Glass, *Akhnaton*; Thea Musgrave, *Harriet, the Woman Called Moses*.

**Orchestra/Band** Theodore Antoniou, *The Magic World* (ballet); David Amram, *Across the Wide Missouri, a Musical Tribute to Harry S. Truman—Andante and Variations on a Theme for Macbeth* (band); Leslie Bassett, *Colors and Contours* (band); William Bolcom, *Orphée-Sérénade*; John Cage, *A Collection of Rocks*; George Crumb, *A Haunted Landscape*; Paul Dresher, *Re:act:ion*; Vivian Fine, *Poetic Fires*; Karel Husa, *Symphonic Suite*; Libby Larsen, *Overture: Parachute Dancing*; Robert Moevs, *Symphonic Piece No. 5*; Ron Nelson, *Aspen Jubilee*; Stephen Paulus, *Ordway Overture*; Gundaris Poné, *American Portraits*; Bernard Rands, *Le Tambourin, Suite No. 1—Suite No. 2*; Christopher Rouse, *Gorgon*; Gunther Schuller, *Jubilee Music*; Joseph Schwantner, *A Sudden Rainbow*; Ralph Shapey, *Groton: Three Movements for Young Orchestra*; Robert Starer, *Hudson Valley Suite—Symphonic Prelude*; David Ward-Steinman, *Olympics Overture*; Frank Wigglesworth, *Sea Winds*; Charles Wuorinen, *Movers and Shakers;* Ellen Taaffe Zwilich, *Celebration for Orchestra*.

**Piano/Organ** George Barati, *B.U.D. Piano Sonata*; Leslie Bassett, *Seven Preludes*; William Bergsma, *Variations for Piano*; Ross Lee Finney, *Narrative in Retrospect*; Charles Jones, *Sonata for Piano, Four Hands*; Leon Kirchner, *Five Pieces*; Benjamin Lees, *Fantasy Variations*; George Perle, *Six New Etudes*; Tobias Picker, *Pian-o-rama* (two pianos); Terry Riley, *The Harp of New Albion*; George Rochberg, *Four Short Sonatas*; Frederic Rzewski, *A Machine* (two pianos).

**Symphonies** Stephen Albert, *Symphony: RiverRun* (Pulitzer Prize); Ezra Laderman, *Symphony No. 7*; Libby Larsen, *Symphony No. 1: Water Music*; Henri Lazarof, *Icarus (Concerto for Orchestra No. 2)*; Vittorio Rieti, *Symphony No. 9*; George Rochberg, *Symphony No. 5*; Francis Thorne, *Symphony No. 5*; David Van Vactor, *Symphony No. 8*; George Walker, *Sinfonia No. 1*; Olly Wilson, *Sinfonia*; Richard Wilson, *Symphony No. 1*.

# 1985

❊

## Historical Highlights

President Reagan undergoes cancer surgery and meets with Russian Premier Gorbachev in Geneva; RCA sells out to General Electric Corporation; the Gramm-Rudman bill that is supposed to end the federal deficit is passed; E. F. Hutton, one of the largest brokerage houses, pleads guilty to fraud and manipulation of accounts; 25,000 die in a volcano eruption in Colombia.

## World Cultural Highlights

**World Art** Christo wraps the Pont Neuf in Paris; Anna Esposito, *Woman's Belongings;* Hans Haacke, *MetroMobilitan*; Anselm Kiefer, *Midgard*; Leon Kossoff, *A Street in Willesden*.

**World Literature**   Isabel Allende, *The House of the Spirits*; Maeve Binchy, *Echoes;* Italo Calvino, *Mr. Palomar*; John Fowles, *A Maggot*; Carlos Fuentes, *The Old Gringo*.

**World Music**   Henri Dutilleux, *Concerto for Violin and Orchestra*; Aulis Sallinen, *Symphony No. 5*; Rodion Shchedrin, *The Seagull*; Udo Zimmermann, *Die Weisse Rose*.

**Miscellaneous**   The Queensland Performing Arts Complex opens in Australia; the Festa Musicale Stiana begins in Italy; the Glenn Gould Memorial Foundation is founded; deaths include Italo Calvino, Marc Chagall, Jean Dubuffet, Robert Graves, Philip Larkin, and José Rivera.

## American Art and Literature Highlights

**Births/Deaths**   Deaths include artists Gene B. Davis, Eric Sloane, and literary figures Abe Burrows, Taylor Caldwell, Robert S. Fitzgerald, Alfred Hayes, Helen MacInnes, Robert Nathan, Theodore Sturgeon, E. B. White, and Bernard Wolfe.

**Art Works**   Rex Brandt, *Pirate's Cove*; Richard Estes, *Times Square at 3:53 P.M., Winter*; Eric Fischl, *Manhattoes*; Jane Freilicher, *Outside World*; Nancy Graves, *Looping*; Alex Katz, *Green Cap*; Jeff Koons, *Series, Equilibrium*; Loren MacIver, *Plateau du fromage de chèvre*; Elizabeth Murray, *Kitchen Painting*; Martin Puryear, *The Spell*; George Sugarman, *Waltz*; Andrew Wyeth, *Refuge (Helga)*.

**Literature**   E. L. Doctorow, *World's Fair* (National Book Award); Rita Dove, *Thomas and Beulah* (Pulitzer Prize); Ellen Gilchrist, *Victory Over Japan* (National Book Award); Louise Glück, *The Triumph of Achilles* (National Book Critics' Award); Neil Simon, *Biloxi Blues*; Anne Tyler, *The Accidental Tourist* (National Book Critics' Award); August Wilson, *Fences* (Pulitzer Prize—Tony).

## Music—The Vernacular/Commercial Scene

**B. Deaths**   Kenny Baker (singer); Nick Ceroli (drummer) August 11; Kenny Clarke (drummer) January 25; Larry Clinton (bandleader/arranger) May 2; J. Fred Coots (composer) April 8; "Blind John" Davis (pianist) October 12; Johnny Desmond (singer) September 6; Morton Downey (singer) October 25; Johnny Guanieri (pianist) January 7; Tommy Jarrell (violinist/banjoist) January 28; Jo Jones (drummer) September 3; Philly Joe Jones (drummer) August 30; Wayne King (bandleader) July 16; Kay Kyser (bandleader) July 23; Johnny Marks (songwriter) September 3; Irving Mills (impresario/publisher) April 21; Little Brother Montgomery (pianist/singer) September 6; Rick Nelson (singer) December 31; Nelson Riddle (bandleader/arranger) October 6; John "Zoot" Sims (saxophonist) March 23; "Big Joe" Turner (singer) November 24; Dickie Wells (trombonist) November 12; Charles "Cootie" Williams (trumpeter/bandleader) September 15.

**C. Biographical**

**Performing Groups**   Bloodgood; Edie Brickell and the New Bohemians; Cryptic Slaughter; Damien Thorne; Death Mask; De La Soul; Desert Rose Band; Al DiMeola Project; Elektric Band (by Chick Corea); Extreme; The Faith Brothers; Forbidden (Evil); Guns n' Roses; Guy; GWAR; Juggernaut; King Diamond; L 7; Meanstreak; Zodiac Mindwarp and the Love Reaction; Mordred; New Kids on the Block; Nuclear Assault; Realm; Restless Heart; Sanctuary; School of Violence; The Silos; Southern Pacific; SWA; Sweethearts of the Rodeo; 2 Live Crew; White Zombies.

**New Beginnings**   Federation of Jazz Studies; Jazz in July (New York); Landmark Records; Live Aid Concerts; Manassas Jazz Festival; Popular Music Research Center (University of Nevada).

**Honors**   Alan J. Lerner (Kennedy Center).

**D. Publications**   J. E. Hasse, editor, *Ragtime: Its History, Composers and Music*; Neil Rosenberg, *Bluegrass: A History*; Arnold Shaw, *Dictionary of American Pop/Rock*; Ryan J. Thomson, *The Fiddler's Almanac*; Don Waller, *The Motown Story*.

**E. Representative Works**

**Musicals**   Dan Goggin, *Nunsense*; Jerry Herman, *Jerry's Girls* (revue); Rupert Holmes, *The Mystery of Edwin Drood*; Andrew Lloyd Webber, *Song and Dance*; Roger Miller, *Big River: The Adventures of Huckleberry Finn* (Tony).

**Number One Hits**   *Broken Wings* (Mr. Mister); *Can't Fight This Feeling* (REO Speedwagon); *Careless Whisper*—*Everything She Wants* (Wham); *Crazy for You* (Madonna); *Don't You (Forget about Me)* (Simple Minds); *Everybody Wants to Rule the World*—*Shout* (Tears for Fears); *Everytime You Go Away* (Paul Young); *Heaven* (Bryan Adams); *I Want to Know What Love Is* (Foreigner); *Miami Vice Theme* (Jan Hammer); *Money for Nothing* (Dire Straits); *Oh Sheila* (Ready for the World); *One More Night*—*Sussudio* (Phil Collins); *Part-Time Lover* (Stevie Wonder); *The Power of Love* (Huey Lewis and the News); *St. Elmo's Fire* (John Parr); *Saving All My Love for You* (Whitney Houston); *Say You, Say Me* (Oscar—Lionel Richie); *Separate Lives* (Phil Collins and Marilyn Martin); *Take on Me* (a-ha); *A View to a Kill* (Duran Duran); *We Are the World* (USA for Africa); *We Built This City* (Starship).

**Other**   Anthony Braxton, *Quartet (London) 1985*—*Quartet (Birmingham) 1985*; Quincy Jones, *The Color Purple* (film score).

## Music—The Cultivated/Art Music Scene

**G. Deaths**   Carol Brice (contralto) February 15; Winifred Cecil (soprano) September 13; Richard P. Condie (conductor) December 22; Paul Creston (composer) August 24; Vincent H. Duckles (musicologist) July 1; David Ewen (critic) December 28; Eugene List (pianist) March 1; George London (baritone) March 24; Julian Olevsky (German-born violinist) May 23; Eugene Ormandy (Hungarian-born conductor) March 12; Joseph Rosenstock (Polish-born conductor) October 17; Roger Sessions (composer) March 16; Richard Yardumian (composer) August 15; Efrem Zimbalist (Russian-born violinist) February 22.

**H. Debuts**

**United States**   Pierre Amoyal (French violinist—New York), Bernard d'Ascoli (French pianist—Houston), Christine Cairns (Scottish soprano—Los Angeles), Damon Evans (tenor—New York), Claus Peter Flor (German conductor—Los Angeles), Cecilia Gasdia (Italian soprano—Philadelphia), Andrei Gavrilov (Russian pianist—New York), Matt Haimovitz (Israeli cellist—New York), Cynthia Haymon (soprano—Santa Fe), Fiamma Izzo d'Amico (Italian soprano—Houston), Nigel Kennedy (British violinist—tour), Michael Lipman (cellist—Pittsburgh), Waltraud Meier (German mezzo-soprano—Dallas), António Meneses (Brazilian cellist—tour), Suzanne Murphy (Irish soprano—New York), Anne Sophie Mutter (German violinist—Washington, DC), János Nágy (Hungarian tenor), Catherine Nardiello (pianist—Bethesda, Maryland), Wolfgang Neumann (Austrian tenor—Dallas), Neil Rutman (pianist—New York), Anne Sofie von Otter (German mezzo-soprano—Chicago), Yan Pascal Tortelier (French conductor—Seattle); Yoko Watanabe (Japanese soprano—Los Angeles).

**Metropolitan Opera**   Gregg Baker (baritone), Elizabeth Connell (South African soprano), Yun Deng (Chinese mezzo-soprano), Helga Dernesch (Austrian mezzo-soprano), Kaaren Erickson (soprano), George Fortune (baritone), Dénes Gulyás (Hungarian tenor), Mari Anne Häggander (Swedish soprano), Gwynne Howell (British bass), Camelia Johnson (soprano), Philip Langridge (British tenor), Barry McCauley (tenor), Kathryn Montgomery (soprano), Ann Murray (Irish mezzo-soprano), Václav Neumann (Czech conductor), García Navarro (Spanish conductor), Christof Perick (German conductor), Margaret Price (British soprano), Giuseppe Sinopoli (Italian conductor), Eric Strummer (Austrian bass-baritone), Giuseppe Taddei (Italian baritone), Marilyn Zschau (soprano).

**Other**   Kathleen Cassello (soprano—Hamburg), Deborah Cook (soprano—Glyndebourne), Sharon Sweet (soprano—Munich).

**I. New Positions**

**Conductors**   Kazuyoshi Akiyama (Syracuse Symphony Orchestra); Herbert Blomstedt (San Francisco Symphony Orchestra); Semyon Bychkov (Buffalo Philharmonic Orchestra); Paul Polivnick (Alabama Symphony Orchestra); André Previn (Los Angeles Philharmonic Orchestra); Jerzy Semkow (Rochester Philharmonic Orchestra); Neal Stulbert (New Mexico Symphony Orchestra—to 1993); Kirk Trevor (Knoxville Symphony Orchestra); Hugh Wolff (New Jersey Symphony Orchestra); David Zinman (Baltimore Symphony Orchestra).

**Educational**   Martina Arroyo (voice, Louisiana State University); David Cerone (president, Cleveland Institute); Lewis Lockwood (president, American Musicological Society); Robert Suderburg (Williams College, Massachusetts); Richard Wilson (music chair, Vassar, second term— to 1988).

**Other**   Stephen Albert (composer-in-residence, Seattle Symphony Orchestra); Leon Fleisher (artistic director, Tanglewood); John Harbison (composer-in-residence, Los Angeles Philharmonic Orchestra—to 1989); Tobias Picker (composer-in-residence, Houston Symphony Orchestra); Christopher Rouse (composer-in-residence, Indianapolis Symphony Orchestra); Alvin Singleton (composer-in-residence, Atlanta Symphony Orchestra—to 1988); Joan Tower (composer-in-residence, St. Louis Symphony Orchestra); Charles Wuorinen (composer-in-residence, San Francisco Symphony Orchestra—to 1987).

## J. Honors and Awards

**Honors**   Leonard Bernstein (American Academy Gold Medal); Elliott Carter, Martha Graham, Leontyne Price and Alice Tully (National Medal of Arts); David Diamond (Schuman); Donald Erb, John McLennan, and Ezra Sims (American Academy); Morton Gould (National Arts Club Medal); Yehudi Menuhin (Legion of Honor, France); Joseph Meyerhoff, Julius Rudel, and William Schuman (Peabody Medal); George Perle (National Academy of Arts and Sciences); George Rochberg and Charles Wuorinen (American Academy and Institute); William Schuman (Special Pulitzer—Gold Baton); Beverly Sills (Kennedy Center).

**Awards**   Mark Beudert (Pavarotti); Robert Erickson (Friedheim Award); Jo Ann Falletta (Stokowski); James McCalla (Bowdoin); Aprile Millo (Tucker); Mark Peskanov (Isaac Stern); Jeffrey Siegel (Kapell); Christopher Trakas and Dawn Upshaw (Naumburg); Hugh Wolff (Seaver).

**K. Biographical**   Richard Bales retires as Music Director of the National Gallery of Art; Christopher Hogwood takes the Academy of Ancient Music on its first American tour; Milton Katims is invited to China to give master viola classes at the Shanghai Conservatory; Evelyn Lear and Leontyne Price give their farewell Metropolitan Opera performances; Rudolph Serkin celebrates his 50th year as a performer with a Carnegie Hall recital; Leonard Slatkin takes the St. Louis Symphony Orchestra on a tour of Europe.

## L. Musical Beginnings

**Performing Groups**   Atlantic Brass Quintet (Boston); Boston Early Music Festival Orchestra; Detroit Symphony Chorus; Lark String Quartet (St. Paul); Lyric Opera Theater of Baton Rouge; Merrimack Lyric Opera (Lowell, Massachusetts); Pacific Chamber Orchestra; Virtuosi della Rosa (Portland, Oregon).

**Festivals**   Deer Valley International Chamber Music Festival (Utah); OK Mozart Festival (Oklahoma); Pensacola Chamber Music Festival (Florida); Sedona Chamber Music Festival (Arkansas).

**Educational**   Foundation for the Advancement of Education in Music; Darius Milhaud Archive (Mills College).

**Other**   Affiliate Artists Seaver Conducting Award; American Music Week; Composer's Guild, Inc. (New York); Murray Dranoff International Two Piano Competition (Miami); Houston Lyric Theater Center; Newport Classic Recordings (Providence); Ordway Music Theater (St. Paul); Symphony Hall (renovated Fox Theater—San Diego); Texas Composers Forum.

## M. Music Publications

Basquin, Peter et al., *Explorations in the Arts*
Blackwood, Easley, *The Structure of Recognizable Diatonic Tunings*
Butterworth, Neil, *Dictionary of American Composers*
Crawford, Richard A., *Studying American Music*
Dodge, C. and Jerse, T., *Computer Music: Synthesis, Composition and Performance*
Feldman, Morton, *Essays*
Gauldin, Robert L., *A Practical Approach to Sixteenth-Century Counterpoint*

Jacobson, Robert, *Magnificence—Onstage at the Metropolitan Opera*
Machover, Tod, *The Extended Orchestra*
Mordden, Ethan, *Demented: The World of the Opera Diva*
Nettl, Bruno, *The Western Impact on World Music: Change, Adaptation and Survival*
Plantinga, Leon, *Romantic Music: A History of Musical Style in Nineteenth-Century Europe*
Roads, Curtis, *Composers and the Computer*
Schonberg, Harold, *The Glorious Ones: Classical Music's Legendary Performers*
Stowall, Robin, *Violin Technique and Performance Practice*

### N. Musical Compositions

**Chamber Music**  Samuel Adler, *Double Portrait*; Elliott Carter, *Penthode* (five instrumental quartets); Cecil Effinger, *String Quartet No. 6*; Morton Feldman, *Piano and String Quartet*; Philip Glass, *String Quartet No. 3: Mishima*; John Harbison, *String Quartet*; Stephen Jaffe, *The Rhythm of the Running Plough*; William Kraft, *Melange*; Tod Machover, *Nature's Breath*; Robert Muczynski, *Woodwind Quintet, Opus 45*; Steve Reich, *New York Counterpoint*; George Rochberg, *To the Dark Wood*; Ned Rorem, *Septet: Scenes from Childhood*; William Schuman, *Dances; Divertimento for Woodwind Quintet and Percussion*; Ralph Shapey, *Kroslish Sonate*; Jan Swafford, *Midsummer Variations* (piano quintet); Kevin Volans, *White Man Sleeps*; Charles Wuorinen, *Horn Trio Continued*; Yehudi Wyner, *String Quartet*; Jay Alan Yim, *Autumn Rhythm* (string quartet).

**Choral/Vocal**  Stephen Albert, *Flower of the Mountain*; Thomas Beveridge, *Radha Sings: Songs and Dances of Celestial Love*; Miriam Gideon, *Creature to Creature* (song cycle); Lee Hoiby, *Psalm Ninety-three*; Donald Martino, *The White Island*; William Schuman, *On Freedom's Ground: An American Cantata*; Hugo Weisgall, *Lyrical Interval* (song cycle); Michael White, *Songs from Another Time*.

**Concertos**  David Amram, *Travels* (trumpet and orchestra); Milton Babbitt, *Piano Concerto*; Lukas Foss, *Renaissance Concerto* (flute and orchestra); John Harbison, *Concerto for Oboe, Clarinet and Strings*; Lou Harrison, *Piano Concerto*; Jean Eichelberger Ivey, *Violin Concerto—Cello Concerto*; Henri Lazarof, *Violin Concerto*; Anthony Newman, *Viola Concerto*; Juan Orrego-Salas, *Piano Concerto No. 2, Opus 93*; Christopher Rouse, *Doublebass Concerto*; Gunther Schuller, *Bassoon Concerto, "Eine kleine Fagottmusik"—Viola Concerto*; Stanislaw Skrowaczewski, *Violin Concerto*; Joan Tower, *Piano Concerto, "Homage to Beethoven"*; Nancy Van der Vate, *Distant Worlds* (violin and orchestra).

**Electronic**  William Albright, *Sphaera*; Larry Austin, *Montage: Themes and Variations* (violin and tape); Joan La Barbara, *Loose Tongues*; Paul Lansky, *Idle Chatter*; Alvin Lucier, *Serenade*; Morton Subotnick, *The Key to Songs*.

**Operas**  Chester Biscardi, *Tight Rope*; John Eaton, *The Tempest*; Philip Glass, *The Juniper Tree*; Stephen Paulus, *The Woodlanders*; Elie Siegmeister, *Lady of the Lake*.

**Orchestra/Band**  John Adams, *Harmonielehre*; Henry Brant, *Desert Music*; Chou Wen-Chung, *Beijing in the Mist*; Curtis Curtis-Smith, *Celebration*; David Del Tredici, *March to Tonality*; Paul Dresher, *Slow Fire*; Halim El-Dabh, *Rhapsodia Egyptia-Brasileira*; Brian Fennelly, *Fantasy Variations;* Morton Gould, *Classical Variations on Colonial Themes*; Libby Larsen, *Coriolis*; Otto Luening, *Symphonic Fantasias 5, 6—Symphonic Interlude No. 4*; Witold Lutoslawski, *Chaim II*; Gerard Pape, *Cosmos*; Raoul Pleshkow, *Six Epigrams for Orchestra*; Mel Powell, *Modules*; Bernard Rands, *Ceremonial I*; Christopher Rouse, *Phantasmata*; Elliott Schwartz, *Celebrations/Reflections: A Time Warp*; Joan Tower, *Island Rhythms Overture*; Hugo Weisgall, *Tekiator*; Charles Wuorinen, *Prelude to Kullervo*; Ellen Taaffe Zwilich, *Concerto Grosso 1985*.

**Piano/Organ**  Milton Babbitt, *Lagniappe*; Mario Davidovsky, *Capriccio* (two pianos); Emma Lou Diemer, *Little Suite* (organ); John Harbison, *Sonata No. 1, "Roger Sessions: In Memoriam"*; Anthony Iannaccone, *Two-Piano Inventions*; Peter Liebeson, *Bagatelles*; Dan Locklair, *The Breakers Pound* (harpsichord); Ralph Shapey, *Variations* (organ); Robert Starer, *Four Seasonal Pieces*; Virgil Thomson, *Three Voluntaries for Organ*; George Walker, *Sonata No. 4*; Richard Wilson, *Fixations—Intercalation*.

**Symphonies**    Samuel Adler, *Symphony No. 6*; David Diamond, *Symphony No. 9*; Donald Erb, *Concerto for Orchestra*; Leo Kraft, *Symphony in One Movement*; Benjamin Lees, *Symphony No. 4, "Memorial Candles"*; Robert Hall Lewis, *Symphony No. 3*; Stephen Paulus, *Symphony in 3 Movements, "Soliloquy"*; Daniel Pinkham, *Symphony No. 3*; Ned Rorem, *String Symphony*; Gunther Schuller, *Farbenspiel (Concerto for Orchestra III)*; Ralph Shapey, *Symphonie Concertante*; Lester Trimble, *Symphony No. 3, "The Tricentennial"*; Ellen Taaffe Zwilich, *Symphony No. 2*.

# 1986

❀

## Historical Highlights

The space shuttle *Challenger* blows up after liftoff, killing the entire crew; the White House scandal over Iranian aid surfaces; the United States bombs Libya in retaliation for the bombing of a West Berlin disco; Reagan and Gorbachev meet in a shortened meeting in Iceland and fail to agree on arms limitation; Russia suffers a major nuclear accident at Chernobyl.

## World Cultural Highlights

**World Art**    Kenneth Armitage, *Blasted Oak;* Carlos Battaglia, *Imbrie;* Max Bill, *Continuity;* Romare Bearden, *The Evening of the Blue Snake*; Tony Cragg, *The Worm Returns;* Anselm Kiefer, *Iron Path.*

**World Literature**    Margaret Atwood, *The Handmaid's Tale*; Ruth Jhabvala, *Out of India*; Iris Murdoch, *The Good Apprentice*; Henri Troyat, *Sylvie*; Alec Waugh, *Brideshead Benighted.*

**World Music**    Hans Werner Henze, *Guitar Concerto*; Andrzej Panufnik, *Symphony No. 10, "Symphony of Hope"*; Krzysztof Penderecki, *The Black Mask*; Aulis Sallinen, *Symphony No. 5.*

**Miscellaneous**    The Hong Kong Academy for the Performing Arts opens; the Beijing Concert Hall opens in China; deaths include Simone de Beauvoir, Joseph Beuys, Jean Genet, Christopher Isherwood, Lili Kraus, Henry Moore, Peter Pears, and Edmund Rubbra.

## American Art and Literature Highlights

**Births/Deaths**    Deaths include art figures Dorothea Greenbaum, Seymour Lipton, Reuben Nakian, Georgia O'Keeffe, Marguerite T. Zorach, and literary figures William Barrett, John Ciardi, Laura Hobson, John D. MacDonald, and Bernard Malamud.

**Art Works**    Chuck Close, *Leslie*; Greg Constantine, *Picasso Visits Chicago*; Leon Golub, *Three Seated Black Men*; Alex Katz, *Joan*; Jeff Koons, *Rabbitt*; Randall Lake, *Rococo Punk*; Ellen Lanyon, *Camel Rock Meets the Dartmour Granite at Parmidgian Lake*; Robert Longo, *All You Zombies*; Tom Marioni, *Birds of a Feather*; Louise Nevelson, *Nocturnal Symphony*; Jules Olitski, *Lakshmi Stream.*

**Literature**    Pat Conroy, *The Prince of Tides*; Louise Erdrich, *The Beet Queen*; Jim Harrison, *The Theory and Practice of Rivers and Other Poems*; Edward Hirsch, *Wild Gratitude* (National Book Critics' Award); James A. Michener, *Texas*; Gloria Naylor, *Linden Hills*; Lawrence Sanders, *The Fourth Deadly Sin*; Neil Simon, *Broadway Bound*; Peter H. Taylor, *A Summons to Memphis.*

## Music — The Vernacular/Commercial Scene

**B. Deaths**    Pepper Adams (saxophonist/composer) September 10; Harold Arlen (composer) April 23; Desi Arnaz (Cuban bandleader) November 2; Clyde Bernhardt (trombonist/bandleader) May 20; W. Herbert Brewster (singer/writer) October 14; Eddie "Lockjaw" Davis (saxophonist) November 3; Lee Dorsey (singer/writer) December 1; Esquerita (singer/pianist); Benny Goodman (bandleader/clarinetist) June 13; Horace Heidt (bandleader) December 1; Thad Jones (trumpeter/bandleader) August 20; Alan Jay Lerner (lyricist/librettist) June 14; Gordon MacRae (singer/actor) January 24; Kate Smith (singer) June 17; Sonny Terry (harmonica player/writer) March 11; Rudy Vallee (singer/bandleader) July 3; Teddy Wilson (pianist) July 31; Estelle "Mama" Yancey (singer).

**C. Biographical**

**Performing Groups**   American Jazz Orchestra (New York); Blake Babies; Blanchard-Harrison Band; Bricklin; Cacophony; City; Danzig; Deee-Lite; Dr. Mastermind; Drive, She Said; EPMD; Exposé; Firehose; Highway 101; Jazzy Jeff and the Fresh Prince; Jungle Brothers; The Kentucky Headhunters; The Lemonheads; Material Issue; Naughty by Nature; Princess Pang; The Pixies; Salt-N-Pepa; Shark Island; Silent Rage; Skid Row; Sweet Sensation; Third Kind of Blue; Urge Overkill; Vixen; Wendy and Lisa; Winger.

**New Beginnings**   Boxcar Willie's Branson Theater (Missouri); Thelonious Monk Institute of Jazz.

**Honors**   Ray Charles (Kennedy Center); Alan Lomax (Medal of Arts).

**D. Publications**   Whitney Balliett, *American Musicians: 56 Portraits in Jazz*; Francis Davis, *In the Moment: Jazz in the 1980's*; Roman Iwaschkin, *Popular Music: A Reference Guide*; Henry Martin, *Enjoying Jazz*; Wilfrid Mellers, *Angels of the Night*; Paul Oliver and Max Harrison, *The New Grove Gospel, Blues and Jazz*.

**E. Representative Works**

**Musicals**   Anthony Davis, *X: The Life and Times of Malcolm X*; Duke Ellington, *Queenie Pie* (unfinished); Marvin Hamlisch, *Smile*; Jerome Kern, *Ladies and Gentlemen, Jerome Kern* (tribute review); Neil Simon, *Into the Light*; C. Strouse and S. Schwartz, *Rags*.

**Number One Hits**   *Addicted to Love* (Robert Palmer); *Amanda* (Boston); *Glory of Love* (Peter Cetera); *Greatest Love of All—How Will I Know* (Whitney Houston); *Higher Love* (Steve Winwood); *Holding Back the Years* (Simply Red); *Invisible Touch* (Genesis); *Kiss* (Prince); *Kyrie* (Mr. Mister); *Live to Tell—Papa Don't Preach* (Madonna); *The Next Time I Fall* (Peter Cetera and Amy Grant); *On My Own* (Patti Labelle and Michael McDonald); *Sara* (Starship); *Sledgehammer* (Peter Gabriel); *Stuck With You* (Huey Lewis and the News); *Take My Breath Away* (Oscar—Berlin); *That's What Friends Are For* (Dionne and Friends); *There'll Be Sad Songs* (Billy Ocean); *These Dreams* (Heart); *True Colors* (Cyndi Lauper); *Venus* (Bananarama); *Walk Like an Egyptian* (Bangles); *The Way It Is* (Bruce Hornsby and the Range); *When I Think of You* (Janet Jackson); *You Give Love a Bad Name* (Bon Jovi).

**Other**   Herbie Hancock, *Round Midnight* (film music—Oscar); James Horner, *Aliens* (film music).

## Music—The Cultivated/Art Music Scene

**G. Deaths**   Wheeler Beckett (conductor) January 25; David D. Boyden (musicologist) September 18; George Cehanovsky (Russian-born baritone) March 25; Celius Dougherty (pianist) December 22; Dusolina Giannini (soprano) June 26; Sascha Gorodnitzki (Russian-born pianist) April 4; Donald Grobe (tenor) April 1; Lili Kraus (Hungarian-born pianist) November 6; Allen Irvine McHose (theorist) September 14; Thomas Michalak (Polish-born conductor) July 10; Louise Parker (contralto) September 15; Felix Salzer (Austrian theorist/pedagogue) August 12; Winthrop Sargent (critic) August 15; Lester Trimble (composer) December 31; Claire Watson (soprano) July 16; Robert Whitney (conductor) November 22.

**H. Debuts**

**United States**   Tzimon Barto (pianist—New York), Gabriela Benacková (Russian soprano—San Francisco), Paata Burchuladze (Russian bass—Philadelphia), Helena Doese (Swedish soprano—Houston), Linda Finnie (Czech mezzo-soprano—Chicago), Elizabeth Gale (British soprano—San Diego), Della Jones (British mezzo-soprano), Cyprien Katsaris (French pianist—New York), Leonidas Kavakos (Greek violinist—Santa Barbara), Felicity Lott (British soprano—New York),

Olli Mustonen (Finnish pianist—Newport), Anton Nel (South African pianist—New York), Alan Oke (British bass—Boston), Eugene Perry (baritone—New York), Vyacheslav Polozov (Ukrainian tenor—Pittsburgh), Gino Quilico (baritone—San Francisco), Thomas Sanderling (Russian conductor), Marilyn Schmiege (mezzo-soprano—New York), Ilona Tokody (Hungarian soprano—San Diego), Eduard Tumagian (Romanian baritone—Pittsburgh), Dolora Zajick (mezzo-soprano—San Francisco).

**Metropolitan Opera**   Christian Badea (conductor), Lando Bartolini (Italian tenor), Sylvain Cambreling (French conductor), Myung-Whun Chung (Korean conductor), Hugues Cuénod (Swiss tenor), Faith Esham (soprano), Cecilia Gasdia (Italian soprano), Mechthild Gessendorf (German soprano), Gail Gilmore (mezzo-soprano), Thomas Hampson (baritone), Kathryn Harries (British soprano), Barbara Hendricks (soprano), Gottfried Hornik (Austrian baritone), Taro Ichihara (Japanese tenor), Gary Lakes (tenor), Marie McLaughlin (Scottish soprano), Marita Napier (South African soprano), Stanford Olsen (tenor), Juan Pons (Spanish baritone), Leslie Richards (mezzo-soprano), Diana Soviero (soprano), Sarah Walker (British mezzo-soprano), Yoko Watanabe (Japanese soprano).

**Other**   Dorothy Madison (soprano—London).

## I. New Positions

**Conductors**   Victoria Bond (Roanoke Symphony Orchestra); Christopher Hogwood (Boston Handel and Haydn Society); James Levine (artistic director, Metropolitan Opera); Jésus López-Cobos (Cincinnati Symphony Orchestra); Zdenek Mácal (Milwaukee Symphony Orchestra); Andrew John Massey (Rhode Island Philharmonic Orchestra); William McGlaughlin (Kansas City Symphony Orchestra); Maxim Shostakovich (New Orleans Philharmonic Symphony Orchestra); Edo de Waart (Minnesota Symphony Orchestra).

**Educational**   James O. Buswell IV (New England Conservatory); Robert Fitzpatrick (dean, Curtis); Leon Fleisher (piano, Curtis Institute); Lynn Harrell (USC, Los Angeles); Gideon W. Waldrop (president, Manhattan School—to 1988).

**Other**   Earle Brown (president, American Music Center); Kyle Gann (music reviewer, *Village Voice*, New York); Morton Gould (president, ASCAP); John Pritchard (music director, San Francisco Opera); Christopher Rouse (composer-in-residence, Baltimore Symphony Orchestra—to 1989).

## J. Honors and Awards

**Honors**   Marian Anderson and Aaron Copland (Medal of Arts); Milton Babbitt and Morton Gould (American Academy); Paul Fromm (Gold Baton); Boris Goldovsky (Peabody Medal); Philip Gossett (Deems Taylor); Vladimir Horowitz (Medal of Freedom); Milton Katims (Toscanini Award); Yehudi Menuhin (Kennedy Center); Claude V. Palisca and George Rochberg (American Academy of Arts and Sciences); George Perle and Charles Wuorinen (MacArthur Fellow); Itzhak Perlman (Medal of Freedom); Isaac Stern (*Musical America* Musician of the Year—Wolf Foundation); Frederica Von Stade (National Arts Club Medal).

**Awards**   Andres Diaz (Naumburg); Barry Douglas (Tchaikovsky); Arthur Greene (Kapell); Stanford Olson (Steber); Richard Stolzman (Fisher); Dolora Zajic (Tucker); Richard Wilson (Hinrichsen).

**K. Biographical**   Leonard Bernstein sues G. Schirmer for breach of contract; Catharine Comet becomes the first woman to be conductor of a fully professional orchestra in Grand Rapids, Michigan; Barry Doubles is the first Westerner to win the Tchaikovsky competition since 1958; Vladimir Horowitz returns with a triumphant recital tour to his native Russia after 61 years of exile; Joseph Silverstein takes the Utah Symphony Orchestra on a concert tour of both Berlins, the first American orchestra to do so; Leonard Slatkin takes the St. Louis Symphony Orchestra on a Far East concert tour.

## L. Musical Beginnings

**Performing Groups**   Austin Lyric Opera; Boston Composers Orchestra; Cleveland Youth

Orchestra; Illinois Chamber Orchestra; Los Angeles Music Center Opera; Miami City Ballet; Washington Guitar Quintet.

**Festivals** Mackinac Island Music Festival (Michigan); Nakamichi Baroque Music Festival (UCLA); New Hampshire Music Festival; Omaha Festival of Contemporary Music.

**Other** American Berlin Opera Foundation; Czech Music Society of St. Louis; Richard Gaddes Fund for Young Singers (St. Louis Opera); Great Woods Center for the Performing Arts (Massachusetts); Orange County Performing Arts Center (Segerstrom Hall—California).

## M. Music Publications

Craven, Robert R., *Symphony Orchestras of the United States*
Dox, Thurston J., *American Oratorios and Cantatas*
Hitchcock and Sadie, *New Grove Dictionary of American Music*
Lippman, Edward A., *Musical Aesthetics: A Historical Reader*
Peyser, Joan, ed., *The Orchestra: Origins and Transformations*
Polansky, Larry, *New Instrumentation and Orchestration*
Schuller, Gunther, *Musings: The Musical Worlds of Gunther Schuller*
Slonimsky, Nicolas, *Supplement to Music Since 1900*

## N. Musical Compositions

**Chamber Music** Milton Babbitt, *Joy of More Sextets*; Easley Blackwood, *Cello Sonata*; Elliott Carter, *String Quartet No. 4*; Morton Feldman, *Coptic Light*; Meyer Kupferman, *The Fires of Prometheus* (trumpet and two pianos); Andrew Imbrie, *Dream Sequence*; Ezra Laderman, *String Quartet No. 8*; Roger Reynolds, *The Behavior of Mirrors* (solo guitar).

**Choral/Vocal** David Del Tredici, *Child Alice*; Emma Lou Diemer, *Peace Cantata*; John Harbison, *The Flight into Egypt* (Pulitzer Prize); Jonathan Harvey, *Forms of Emptiness*; Joan La Barbara, *Helga's Lied*; Libby Larsen, *Coming Forth into Day*; Bernard Rands, *Requiescant*; Ellen Taaffe Zwilich, *Seven Motets for the Liturgical Year*.

**Concertos** Stephen Albert, *Violin Concerto in One Movement*; George Barati, *Violin Concerto*; Donald Erb, *Concerto for Brass and Orchestra*; Richard Felciano, *Organ Concerto*; Leo Kraft, *Concerto No. 5 for Oboe and Strings—Concerto No. 6 for Clarinet and Orchestra*; William Kraft, *Veils and Variations* (horn and orchestra—Friedheim Award); Roger Reynolds, *The Dream of the Infinite Room* (cello and orchestra); Ralph Shapey, *Concerto for Piano, Cello and String Orchestra* (Friedheim Award); Rand Steiger, *Double Concerto*; Joan Tower, *Piano Concerto, "Homage to Beethoven"*; Nancy Van de Vate, *Violin Concerto*; Richard Wernick, *Viola Concerto*; Ellen Taaffe Zwilich, *Piano Concerto*.

**Electronic** Paul Dresher, *Water Dreams*; John Rahn, *Kali*; Roger Reynolds, *Vertigo—The Vanity of Words: Voicespace V*.

**Operas** John Adams, *The Chairman Dances*; John Corigliano, *A Figaro for Antonia*; Sorrel Hays, *Love in Space*; Lee Hoiby, *The Tempest*; Gian Carlo Menotti, *Goya*; William Neill, *The Guilt of Lillian Sloan*.

**Orchestra/Band** Leonard Bernstein, *Jubilee Games*; Elliott Carter, *A Celebration of Some 100 X 150 Notes*; John Corigliano, *Fantasia on an Ostinato*; Jacob Druckman, *Athanor*; Philip Glass, *A Descent into the Maelstrom* (dance piece); William Kraft, *Of Ceremonies, Pageants and Celebrations*; Ezra Laderman, *Pentimento*; Otto Luening, *Symphonic Fantasias 7, 8—Symphonic Interlude No. 5*; William T. McKinley, *Boston Overture*; Gundaris Poné, *Titzarin*; Steve Reich, *Three Movements for Orchestra*; Joan Tower, *Silver Ladders* (Grawemeyer Prize); Chinary Ung, *Inner Voices*.

**Piano/Organ** Chester Biscardi, *Sonata*; Richard Felciano, *Five Short Pieces*; Morton Feldman, *Palais de mari*; Alan Hovhaness, *Blue Job Mountain Sonata*; Andrew Imbrie, *Daedalus*; George Perle, *Sonatina*; Paul Reale, *Sonata Brahmsiana*; Nancy Van der Vate, *Twelve Pieces on One to Twelve Notes*.

**Symphonies** Irwin Bazelon, *Symphony No. 8 for Strings*; Karel Husa, *Concerto for Orchestra*;

Benjamin Lees, *Symphony No. 5*; Peter Lieberson, *Symphony*; Stephen Paulus, *Symphony in Three Movements (Soliloquy)*; Tobias Picker, *Symphony No. 2*; Christopher Rouse, *Symphony No. 1*; Elie Siegmeister, *Symphony No. 7*; Stanislaw Skrowaczewski, *Concerto for Orchestra*; Richard Wilson, *Symphony No. 2*.

# 1987

☀

## Historical Highlights

President Reagan proposes the first trillion-dollar budget; the Wall Street crash in October ruins many; Texaco, Inc. goes into bankruptcy; sex scandals end the presidential quest of Senator Hart and cause the fall of televangelists Jim and Tammy Bakker; Chrysler buys out American Motors; Premier Gorbachev of Russia announces his new policy of "glasnost" (openness).

## World Cultural Highlights

**World Art**   George Andreas, *Conflict;* Augustine Cardenas, *Acueducto;* Anselm Kiefer, *Osiris and Isis*; Baltasar Lobo, *Grande Jeune Fille à Genoux;* Rufine Tamayo, *Dos Hermanos*.

**World Literature**   Brian Moore, *The Colour of Blood*; Henri Troyat, *Third Happiness*; Amos Tutuola, *Pauper, Brawler and Slanderer*.

**World Music**   Malcolm Arnold, *Symphony No. 9*; Michael Schelle, *Concerto for Two Pianos and Orchestra*; Robert Simpson, *Symphony No. 9*; John Tavener, *The Protecting Veil*.

**Miscellaneous**   The Glenn Gould Performing Prize is set up in Canada; the National Theater opens in Taipei, Taiwan; deaths include Jean Anouilh, Leon Berkowitz, Peter Fingesten, Eugen Jochum, Dmitri Kabalevsky, André Masson, and Maria von Trapp.

## American Art and Literature Highlights

**Births/Deaths**   Deaths include artists Raphael Soyer, Myron Stout, Andy Warhol, and literary figures James Baldwin, Erskine Caldwell, John Logan, Charles Ludlum, Robert Ludlum, Howard Moss, and Marguerite Yourcenar.

**Art Works**   Jack Beal, *The Sense of Smell*; Robert Bourdon, *Blue Velvet*; Anthony Caro, *Chicago Fugue*; Eric Fischl, *The Evacuation of Saigon*; Helen Frankenthaler, *Tout à Coup*; Grace Hartigan, *L. A. Boudoir*; Edward Kienholz, *Shine on Shine*; Lucio Pozzi, *Orpheus Re-Membered*; Susan Rothenberg, *Vertical Spin*; David Salle, *Coming and Going*; Andy Warhol, *Beethoven*.

**Literature**   Toni Morrison, *Beloved* (Pulitzer Prize—Kennedy Book Award); Walker Percy, *The Thanatos Syndrome*; Reynolds Price, *Kate Vaiden* (National Book Critics' Award); Philip Roth, *The Counter-Life* (National Book Critics' Award); Sam Shepard, *A Lie of the Mind* (New York Drama Critics' Award); August Wilson, *The Piano Lesson* (Pulitzer Prize—New York Drama Critics' Award).

## Music—The Vernacular/Commercial Scene

**B. Deaths**   Fred Astaire (singer/dancer) June 22; Boudleaux Bryant (songwriter) June 30; Paul Butterfield (singer/bandleader) May 3 (?); Clifton Chenier (singer/accordionist); Elizabeth "Libba" Cotten (singer/guitarist) June 29; Eddie Durham (trombonist/arranger) March 6; Woody Herman (bandleader/clarinetist) October 29; Sammy Kaye (bandleader) June 2; Liberace (pianist) February 4; Jerry Livingston (composer) July 1; Howard McGhee (trumpeter) July 17; Joseph Meyer (songwriter) June 22; Turk Murphy (trombonist/composer) May 30; Joseph Myrow (songwriter) December 24; Buddy Rich (drummer/bandleader) April 2; Maxine Sullivan (singer) April 7; Kid Thomas (Valentine) (trumpeter/bandleader) June 16.

**C. Biographical**

**Performing Groups**   Alice in Chains; Anatasia Screamed; Atheist; Atrophy; Babes in Toyland;

B.A.L.L.; Bang Tango; Bongwater; Britny Fox; The Bulletboys; China Sky; Color Me Badd; Dangerous Toys; The Dharma Bums; Femme Fatale; Firehose; Fugazi; L. A. Guns; The Lemon Pipers; Nine Inch Nails; Nirvana; The O'Kanes; Pariah; Saraya; Souled America; Stone Temple Pilots; Uncle Sam; Uncle Tupelo; Wreckx-N-Effect.

**New Beginnings**　International Foundation for Jazz; SOS Productions (Pennsylvania).

**Honors**　Perry Como and Sammy Davis, Jr. (Kennedy Center); Ella Fitzgerald (National Medal of Arts); Benny Goodman (posthumous National Arts Club Medal).

**D. Publications**　Amiri and Amina Baraka, *The Music: Reflections on Jazz and Blues*; Jason Berry et al., *Up from the Cradle of Jazz: New Orleans Music since World War II*; Roy Carr et al., *The Hip: Hipsters, Jazz and the Beat Generation*; Leonard Feather, *The Jazz Years: Earwitness to an Era*; Ira Gitler, *Swing to Bop: An Oral History of the Transition in Jazz in the 1940's*; Neil Leonard, *Jazz: Myth and Religion*; R. Pattison, *The Triumph of Vulgarity: Rock Music in the Mirror of Romanticism*; David Szatmary, *Rockin' in Time: A Social History of Rock and Roll*.

**E. Representative Works**

**Musicals**　Andrew Lloyd Webber, *Starlight Express*; C. M. Schönberg and H. Kretzmer, *Les Misérables* (United States debut); Stephen Sondheim, *Into the Woods* (New York Drama Critics' Prize)

**Number One Hits**　*Alone* (Heart); *Always* (Atlantic Starr); *Bad* (Michael Jackson); *La Bamba* (Los Lobos); *Didn't We Almost Have It All—I Wanna Dance with Somebody (Who Loves Me)* (Whitney Houston); *(I Just) Died In Your Arms* (Cutting Crew); *Faith* (George Michael); *Head to Toe—Lost in Emotion* (Lisa Lisa and Cult Jam); *Heaven Is a Place on Earth* (Belinda Carlisle); *Here I Go Again* (Whitesnake); *I Just Can't Stop Loving You* (Michael Jackson and Siedah Garrett); *I Knew You Were Waiting* (Aretha Franklin and George Michael); *I Still Haven't Found What I'm Looking For* (U2); *I Think We're Alone Now* (Tiffany); *Jacob's Ladder* (Huey Lewis and the News); *Lean On Me* (Club Nouveau); *Livin' on a Prayer* (Bon Jovi); *Nothing's Gonna Stop Us Now* (Starship); *Open Your Heart—Who's That Girl* (Madonna); *Shake You Down* (Gregory Abbott); *Shakedown* (Bob Seger); *(I've Had) The Time of My Life* (Oscar—Bill Medley and Jennifer Warnes); *You Keep Me Hangin' On* (Kim Wilde).

**Other**　Dave Brubeck, *I See, Satie*.

## Music—The Cultivated/Art Music Scene

**G. Deaths**　James Atherton (tenor) November 20; Carl Bamberger (Austrian-born conductor) July 18; John Ness Beck (composer) June 25; Walter R. Boelke (publisher) January 25; Abram Chasins (pianist/author) June 21; Morton Feldman (composer) September 3; Paul Fromm (patron) July 4; Donald Jay Grout (musicologist) March 9; Jascha Heifetz (Russian-born violinist) December 10; Natalie Hinderas (pianist) June 22; Charles Holland (tenor) November 7; Egon Kenton (Hungarian-born violinist/musicologist) December 3; Norman Luboff (conductor) September 22; Edwin McArthur (conductor/pianist) February 24; Hans Moldenhauer (German-born musicologist) October 19; Erwin Nyiregyházi (Hungarian-born pianist) April 13; Vincent Persichetti (composer) August 14; Joy Simpson (soprano) March 25; Izler Solomon (conductor) December 6.

**H. Debuts**

**United States**　Andreas Bach (German pianist—New York), Olaf Bär (German baritone—Chicago), Giovanni Battel (Italian pianist—San Francisco), Michel Dalberto (French pianist), Vladimir Feltsman (Russian pianist—Washington, DC), Nuccia Focile (Italian soprano—Philadelphia), Natalia Gutman (Russian cellist—tour), Judith Kellock (soprano—New York), Sergei Leiferkus (Russian baritone—Boston), Jan Vogler (German cellist—Chicago), Mitsuko Uchida (Japanese pianist—New York), Maria Zampieri (Italian soprano—San Francisco).

**Metropolitan Opera**　Bruno Beccaria (Italian tenor), Livia Budai (Hungarian mezzo-soprano), Paata Burchuladze (Russian bass), Peter Dvorsky (Czech tenor), Jean Fournet (French conductor),

Sonya Ghazarian (Lebanese soprano), Gail Gilmore (mezzo-soprano), Anne Gjevang (Norwegian mezzo-soprano), Jerry Hadley (tenor), Horst Hiestermann (German tenor), Gregory Kunde (tenor), Johanna Meier (German mezzo-soprano), Waltraud Meier (German mezzo-soprano), Erie Mills (soprano), Diana Montague (British mezzo-soprano), Vyacheslav Polokov (Ukrainian tenor), Gino Quilico (baritone), Susan Quittmeyer (mezzo-soprano), Jan Hendrik Rootering (German bass), Neil Rosenshein (tenor), Ralf Weikert (Austrian conductor).

### I. New Positions

**Conductors**  Theo Alcantara (Pittsburgh Opera); Sergiu Comissiona (New York City Opera); Isaiah Jackson (Dayton Philharmonic Orchestra); Raymond Leppard (Indianapolis Symphony Orchestra); Andrew John Massey (Fresno Philharmonic Orchestra); Geoffrey Simon (Albany Symphony Orchestra).

**Educational**  Simon Estes (voice, Juilliard); Theodore Lettvin (Rutgers University).

**Other**  Spiros Argiris (music director, Spoleto, United States); John Corigliano (composer-in-residence, Chicago Symphony Orchestra); Lee Goldstein (composer-in-residence, Chicago Lyric Opera); James W. Pruett (chief, Music Division, Library of Congress).

### J. Honors and Awards

**Honors**  Hugh Aitken, Joel Hoffman and Dennis Riley (American Academy); Leonard Bernstein (MacDowell Medal); Dennis Russell Davies (Ditson Award); Betty Freeman and Isaac Stern (Gold Baton); Kamran Ince (Rome Prize); Barbara Kolb and Tod Machover (Friedheim); Donald Martino (American Academy of Arts and Sciences); Nathan Milstein (Kennedy Center); Jessye Norman (Ph.D., Harvard); Mstislav Rostropovich (*Musical America* Musician of the Year); William Schuman (National Medal of Arts); Gerard Schwarz (National Arts Club Medal).

**Awards**  Harry Dworchak (Tucker); Anton Nel (Naumburg); Mark Peskanov (Frederick Mann Award); William Wolfram (Kapell Second—no First).

### K. Biographical  
Phyllis Curtin is invited to Beijing, where she gives master classes in voice at the Conservatory; Maria Ewing leaves the Metropolitan Opera after performance differences with James Levine; Vladimir Feltsman, released from eight years of virtual house arrest in the Soviet Union, comes to the United States; Yoel Levi becomes an American citizen; Gilbert Levine becomes the first American conductor to be appointed to an Eastern European orchestra (Crakow); Lorin Maazel takes the Pittsburgh Symphony Orchestra on a concert tour of China; John Nelson takes the Indianapolis Symphony Orchestra on its first international tour; the Toscanini Legacy (notes, scores, letters, etc.) is donated to the music library at Lincoln Center.

### L. Musical Beginnings

**Performing Groups**  New World Symphony (Miami); Orion String Quartet; St. Cecilia Orchestra (New York).

**Festivals**  Bang on a Can Festival (New York); International Festival of Music at Purgatory (Colorado); Mendocino Music Festival (California); Mozart in Monterey; Sound Celebration (Louisville, Kentucky).

**Educational**  Opera/Music Theater Institute (New Jersey).

**Other**  Foundation for Musical Performance (New York); Glimmerglass Opera House (Cooperstown, New York); International New Music Composer's Group (New York); Pacific Contemporary Music Center; Tampa Performing Arts Complex; Gus S. Wortham Theater Center (Houston).

### M. Music Publications

Babbitt, Milton, *Words about Music*  
Devenney, David P., *Nineteenth-Century American Choral Music*  
Dunsby, J. and Whittall, A., *Music Analysis in Theory and Practice*  
Friedberg, Ruth, *American Art Song and American Poetry III: The Century Advances*  
Gauldin, Robert, *A Practical Approach to Eighteenth-Century Counterpoint*

Green, Elizabeth, *The Dynamic Orchestra* . . .
Hazen, Margaret and Robert, *The Music Men: . . . Brass Bands in America, 1800–1920*
Heussenstamm, George, *The Norton Manual of Music Notation*
LePage, Jane, *Women Composers, Conductors . . . of the Twentieth Century III*
Lewin, David, *Generalized Musical Intervals and Transformations*
Morris, Robert, *Composition with Pitch-Classes: A Theory of Compositional Design*
Read, Gardner, *Source Book of Proposed Music Notation Reforms*
Winsor, Phil, *Computer-Assisted Music Composition*

## N. Musical Compositions

**Chamber Music**   William Albright, *Clarinet Quintet*; Curtis Curtis-Smith, *Fantasy Pieces* (violin and piano); John Davison, *Sonata Pastorale*; David Diamond, *Cello Sonata No. 2*; Emma Lou Diemer, *String Quartet No. 1*; Donald Erb, *Views of Space and Time*; Richard Felciano, *Shadows*; Glenn Gass, *Piano Quartet*; John Harbison, *String Quartet No. 2*; Andrew Imbrie, *String Quartet No. 5*; William Kraft, *Quartet for the Love of Time*; Meyer Kupferman, *Summer Music*; Lowell Liebermann, *Flute Sonata*; David Macbride, *Three Dances* (string quartet); Stephen Paulus, *String Quartet No. 2*; Ned Rorem, *Bright Music*; Gunther Schuller, *String Quartet No. 3*; Ezra Sims, *Clarinet Quintet*; Robert Starer, *Kaaterskill Quartet*; Louise Talma, *Conversations* (flute and piano); Chinary Ung, *Spiral I*; Charles Wuorinen, *String Quartet No. 3*.

**Choral/Vocal**   Beth Anderson, *Dreaming Fields* (song cycle); Dominick Argento, *Te Deum*; Milton Babbitt, *Three Cultivated Choruses*; Irwin Bazelon, *Legends and Love Letters*; Barbara Feldman, *Variations for String Quartet and Chorus*; John Harbison, *The Natural World*; Aaron Jay Kernis, *Love Scenes* (song cycle); Gunther Schuller, *Thou Art the Son of God* (cantata); Ralph Shapey, *Songs of Joy*; Ellen Taaffe Zwilich, *What Is Pink?*

**Concertos**   Philip Glass, *Violin Concerto*; Donald Erb, *Brass Concerto*; Karel Husa, *Organ Concerto, "The Sunlights"*; Ezra Laderman, *Concerto for Violin, Cello and Orchestra*; György Ligeti, *Piano Concerto*; Donald Martino, *Saxophone Concerto*; Marc Neikrug, *Concerto for String Quartet and Orchestra*; Stephen Paulus, *Violin Concerto*; André Previn, *Piano Concerto*; Bernard Rands, *Hiraeth* (cello and orchestra); Charles Wuorinen, *Five* (cello concerto).

**Electronic**   Paul Lansky, *Just More Idle Chatter*; Gordon Mumma, *Aleutian Displacement—Begault Meandown Sketches*; Diane Thome, *Ringing, Stillness, Pearl Light* (piano and tape).

**Operas**   John Adams, *Nixon in China*; Richard Brooks, *Moby Dick*; John Cage, *Europera 1—Europera 2*; Ross Lee Finney, *Computer Marriage*; Tod Machover, *Valis*; Richard Owen, *Abigail Adams*.

**Orchestra/Band**   Margaret Buechner, *The Old Swedes Church*; George Edwards, *Heraclitean Fire*; Philip Glass, *The Light*; Meyer Kupferman, *Wings of the Highest Tower*; Libby Larsen, *What the Monster Saw*; Anne LeBaron, *Strange Attractors*; Dan Locklair, *Creation's Seeing Order*; David Macbride, *Three Dances*; George Perle, *Dance Overture*; Wayne Peterson, *Trilogy*; Gundaris Poné, *Overture, La Bella Veneziana*; Steve Reich, *The Four Sections*; Joseph Schwantner, *Toward Light*; Bright Sheng, *H'UN (Lacerations): In Memoriam 1966–1976*; Nancy Van de Vate, *Chernobyl*; Charles Wuorinen, *Overture: Bamboula Beach*; Ellen Taaffe Zwilich, *Tanzspiel* (ballet).

**Piano/Organ**   William Albright, *Symphony for Organ*; Daniel Asia, *Scherzo Sonata*; Leslie Bassett, *Five Configurations*; William Bolcom, *Twelve New Etudes* (Pulitzer Prize); Curtis Curtis-Smith, *Fantasy Pieces*; Emma Lou Diemer, *Variations* (piano, four hands); Ross Lee Finney, *Narrative in Retrospect*; Karel Husa, *Frammenti* (organ); Andrew Imbrie, *Organ Prelude—Three Piece Suite* (piano); Aaron Jay Kernis, *Poisoned Nocturnes*; Andrew Stiller, *The Water Is Wide, Daisy Bell*.

**Symphonies**   Daniel Asia, *Symphony No. 1*; William Bolcom, *Symphony No. 4*; John Harbison, *Symphony No. 2*; Roger Reynolds, *Symphony: Vertigo*; George Rochberg, *Symphony No. 6*; Richard Wernick, *Symphony No. 1*.

# 1988

✹

## Historical Highlights

George Bush is elected the 41st president; the space shuttle *Discovery* puts the United States back in the space program after more than two years of delay; President Reagan visits Moscow and Premier Gorbachev visits the United States; several ethics charges against Reagan aides shake the White House; a ceasefire is called in the Iraq-Iran war; Russia decides to pull out of Afghanistan.

## World Cultural Highlights

**World Art**    Fernando Botero, *Woman with Cigarette;* Anna Esposito, *Neapolitan Mosaic;* Charles Greeley, *Nude Descending Spiral*; Howard Hodgkin, *Bed in Venice*; Gerhard Richter, *Betty.*

**World Literature**    Maeve Binchy, *Silver Wedding;* Peter Carey, *Oscar and Lucinda*; Gabriel García Marquez, *Love in the Time of Cholera*; Fay Weldon, *The Hearts and Lives of Man.*

**World Music**    George Lloyd, *Symphony No. 7;* Jay Reise, *Rasputin*; Alfred Schnittke, *Violin Concerto No. 4*; Robert Simpson, *Symphony No. 10*; Karlheinz Stockhausen, *Montag aus Licht.*

**Miscellaneous**    The D'Oyly Carte Opera Co. is reborn in England; the Paris Philharmonic Orchestra is founded; deaths include René Char, Antal Dorati, Alan Paton, Miguel Piñero, Eugene Mravinsky, and Sacheverell Sitwell.

## American Art and Literature Highlights

**Births/Deaths**    Deaths include art figures Romare Bearden, Isabel Bishop, Robert Gwathmey, Stanley W. Hayter, Louise Nevelson, Isamu Noguchi, Charles Pollack, and literary figures Raymond Carver, Robert Duncan, Rose Franken, Nancy Hale, and Max Shulman.

**Art Works**    Brad Faegre, *Alchemy*; Audrey Flack, *Islandia*; Nancy Graves, *Peripeteia '88*; Robert Longo, *Dumb Running*; Linda S. Moore, *Maple Road*; Catherine Murphy, *Summer, Hyde Park*; Jules Olitski, *Gold Blaze*; Martin Puryear, *Maroon*; Larry Rivers, *Dancer in an Abstract Field*; Bruno Surdo, *The Artist's Studio*; Mark di Suvero, *Symbiosis*; Ross Wetzel, *National C. R.*

**Literature**    Thomas Berger, *The House Guest*; Pete Dexter, *Paris Trout* (National Book Award); Donald Hall, *The One Day* (National Book Critics' Award); Neil Sheehan, *A Bright Shining Lie* (National Book Award); Neil Simon, *Rumors*; C. K. Williams, *Flesh and Blood* (National Book Critics' Award); August Wilson, *Joe Turner's Come and Gone* (New York Drama Critics' Award).

## Music—The Vernacular/Commercial Scene

**B. Deaths**    Joe Albany (pianist) January 11; Chet Baker (trumpeter) May 13; Ray Bauduc (percussionist) January 8; Brook Benton (singer) April 9; James Black (drummer) August 30; Lawrence Brown (trombonist) September 5; Beulah Bryant (singer) January 31; Roy Buchanan (guitarist) August 14; Billy Butterfield (trumpeter/bandleader) March 18; Warren Casey (composer/lyricist); Al Cohn (saxophonist/composer) February 15; Billy Daniels (singer) October 7; Dennis Day (singer) May 22; Gene De Paul (composer/pianist) February 27; Gil Evans (bandleader/arranger) March 20; Son House (guitarist/singer) October 19; Frederick Loewe (librettist/lyricist) February 14; Joshua Logan (librettist/director) July 12; Sallie Martin (singer) June 18; Leon McAuliffe (guitarist) August 20; Memphis Slim (pianist/singer) February 24; Sy Oliver (arranger/trumpeter) May 27; Roy Orbison (singer/writer) December 6; Charlie Palmieri (pianist/bandleader) September; David Prater (Sam and Dave); Charlie Rouse (saxophonist) November 30; Sylvester (singer) December 16; Eddie "Cleanhead" Vinson (saxophonist) July 2.

**C. Biographical**

**Performing Groups**    Apocrypha; Arrested Development; Bad English; Bell Biv Devoe; The Black Crowes; Boyz II Men; Danger, Danger; The Digital Underground; D'Molls; Dream Theatre;

En Vogue; Gang Starr; Jesus Jones; Jodeci; Junkyard; Mason Dixon; Mr. Big; Mudhoney; Ned's Atomic Dustbin; Nelson; New Frontier; Dan Reed Network; Shout; The Spin Drs.; Third Base; Toad the Wet Sprocket; The Traveling Wilburys; A Tribe Called Quest.

**Honors**   Loretta Lynn and Roy Rogers (Country Music Hall of Fame); Max Roach (MacArthur Fellow).

**Miscellaneous**   James Brown is sentenced to six and a half years on drug charges but serves only two.

**D. Publications**   James Collier, *The Reception of Jazz in America*; Daphne D. Harrison, *Black Pearls: Blues Queens of the 1920's*; Val Hicks, *Heritage of Harmony*; Richard Jackson, *Democratic Souvenirs: An Historical Anthology of Nineteenth-Century American Music*; Barry Kernfeld, *The New Grove Dictionary of Jazz*; T. Krasker and R. Kimball, *Catalog of the American Musical*; Paul Oliver, *Blues Off the Record: Thirty Years of Blues Commentary*; Russell Sanjek, *American Popular Music and Its Business: The First Four Hundred Years*.

**E. Representative Works**

**Musicals**   Andrew Lloyd Webber, *Phantom of the Opera* (United States premiere); Various composers, *The Gospel at Colonus*.

**Number One Hits**   *Anything For You* (Gloria Estefan and the Miami Sound Machine); *Baby, I Love Your Way* (Will to Power); *Bad Medicine* (Bon Jovi); *Could've Been* (Tiffany); *Dirty Diana— Man in the Mirror—The Way You Make Me Feel* (Michael Jackson); *Don't Worry, Be Happy* (Bobby McFerrin), *Every Rose Has Its Thorn* (Poison); *Father Figure—Monkey—One More Try* (George Michael); *The Flame* (Cheap Trick); *Foolish Beat* (Debbie Gibson); *Get Out of My Dreams, Get Into My Car* (Billy Ocean); *Got My Mind Set on You* (George Harrison); *Groovy Kind of Love* (Phil Collins); *Hold on to the Nights* (Richard Marx); *Kokomo* (Beach Boys); *Look Away* (Chicago); *Love Bites* (Def Leppard); *Need You Tonight* (INXS); *Never Gonna Give You Up—Together Forever* (Rick Astley); *Red Red Wine* (UB40); *Roll With It* (Steve Winwood); *Seasons Change* (Exposé); *So Emotional—Where Do Broken Hearts Go* (Whitney Houston); *Sweet Child o' Mine* (Guns 'n Roses); *Wild, Wild West* (The Escape Club); *Wishing Well* (Terence Trent D'Arby);

**Other**   Dave Brubeck, *Four New England Pieces*; Alan Silvestri, *Who Framed Roger Rabbit?* (film music); Carly Simon, *Let the River Run* (Oscar—from *The Working Girl*).

## Music—The Cultivated/Art Music Scene

**G. Deaths**   Kurt Herbert Adler (Austrian-born conductor/administrator) February 9; Jeanne Behrend (pianist/educator) March 20; Irving Kolodin (critic) April 29; Boris Kremenliev (Bulgarian-born musicologist) April 25; Raymond Lewenthal (pianist) November 21; Amerigo Marino (conductor) April 26; James McCracken (tenor) April 30; Howard Mitchell (cellist/conductor) June 22; Burrill Phillips (composer) June 22; John Reardon (baritone) April 16; Judith Somogi (conductor) March 23; Henry Sopkin (conductor) March 1; Eric Werner (Austrian-born musicologist) July 28.

**H. Debuts**

**United States**   Leonard Mark Anderson (pianist—New York), Vladimir Chernov (Russian baritone—Boston), Barry Douglas (Irish pianist—New York), Valeria Esposito (Italian soprano—Houston), Robert Hayward (British bass-baritone—Houston), Ben Heppner (Canadian tenor—Chicago), Nancy Johnson (soprano—San Francisco), Klaus König (German tenor—Houston), Jennifer Ruth Lane (mezzo-soprano—Santa Fe), Sophie Larson (Austrian soprano—New York), Mario Luperi (Italian bass—Pittsburgh), Neil Mackie (British tenor—Ojai), Mary Mills (soprano—Houston), Anne-Sofie Mutter (German violinist—New York), Maria-João Pires (Portugese pianist—New York), Donato Renzetti (Italian conductor—Chicago), Petteri Salomaa (Finnish baritone—San Francisco), Nadine Secunde (soprano—Chicago), Peter Seiffert (German tenor—Philadelphia), Raphael Wallfisch (British cellist—Indianapolis), David Wehr (conductor—New York).

**Metropolitan Opera**  Barbara Bonney (soprano), Frederick Burchinal (baritone), Katherine Ciesinski (soprano), Martine Dupuy (French mezzo-soprano), Mark Elder (British conductor), Carlos Feller (Polish bass), Alain Fondary (French baritone), Jeffrey Gall (counter-tenor), Cynthia Haymon (soprano—Santa Fe), Sumi Jo (Korean soprano), Philip Joll (British baritone), Carlos Kleiber (Austrian conductor), Toni Kramer (German tenor), Jean-Philippe Lafont (French bass), Veriano Luchetti (Italian tenor), Nicola Martinucci (Italian tenor), Silvia Mosca (Italian soprano), Wolfgang Neumann (Austrian tenor), Claudio Nicolai (German baritone), Timothy Noble (baritone), Anne Sofie von Otter (Swedish mezzo-soprano), Marcello Panni (Italian conductor), Derek Lee Ragin (countertenor), Donald Runnicles (British conductor), Hanna Schwarz (German mezzo-soprano), Cheryl Studer (soprano), Birgitta Svendsón (Swedish mezzo-soprano), Stefania Toczyska (Polish mezzo-soprano), Jeffrey Wells (bass), Ekkehard Wlaschiha (German baritone), Dolora Zajick (mezzo-soprano).

## I. New Positions

**Conductors**  Christoph Eschenbach (Houston Symphony Orchestra); Yoel Levi (Atlanta Symphony Orchestra); Zdenek Mácal (San Antonio Symphony Orchestra—to 1992); Michael Palmer (New Haven Symphony Orchestra); Hugh Wolff (St. Paul Chamber Orchestra).

**Educational**  Richard E. Adams (dean, Manhattan School of Music); Daniel Asia (composition head, University of Arizona, Tucson); Jeffrey Kahane (piano, Eastman).

**Other**  David Del Tredici (composer-in-residence, New York Philharmonic Orchestra); Donald Erb (composer-in-residence, St. Louis Symphony Orchestra); Jonathan Kramer (composer-in-residence, Cincinnati Symphony Orchestra); Lofti Mansouri (general manager, San Francisco Opera); Stephen Paulus (composer-in-residence, Atlanta Symphony Orchestra).

## J. Honors and Awards

**Honors**  Alexander Schneider (Kennedy Center); Rudolf Serkin and Virgil Thomson (Medal of Arts); Robert Shaw (Golden Baton); Isaac Stern (National Arts Club Medal); Francis Thorne (American Academy and Institute).

**Awards**  Alan Chow (Bachauer Second); Leonidas Kavakos (Naumburg); David Korevaar (Kapell Second—no First); Richard Leech (Tucker); Gundaris Poné (Enescu); André Watts (Fisher).

**K. Biographical**  Béla Bartók's remains are returned to Hungary for reburial; Stuart Challender takes the Sydney, Australia, Symphony Orchestra on a concert tour of the United States; Peter Maxwell Davies brings the Scottish Chamber Orchestra on a tour of the United States; Vladimir Horowitz donates his collection of papers and recordings to Yale University; Cho-Liang Lin becomes an American citizen; Eduardo Mata is appointed Principal Guest Conductor of the Pittsburgh Symphony Orchestra; Christopher Parkening performs at the White House; Simon Rattle takes the City of Birmingham Symphony Orchestra on a concert tour of the United States; Robert Shaw takes his Atlanta Symphony Orchestra and Chorus on a European concert tour; Jeffrey Tate brings the English Chamber Orchestra on a tour of the United States.

## L. Musical Beginnings

**Festivals**  Bravo! Colorado Music Festival (Vail); Colorado Mahlerfest (Boulder); New York International Festival of the Arts.

**Educational**  New World School of the Arts (Miami).

**Other**  Marian Anderson Award for American Singers; Benedum Center (Pittsburgh); Hildegard Publishing Co. (New York); James McCracken Memorial Fund for Young Tenors (New York); World Cello Congress (Maryland).

## M. Music Publications

Austin, L. and Clark, T., *Learning to Compose: Modes, Materials and Models of Musical Invention*
Clark, J. Bunker, *The Dawning of American Keyboard Music*
DeVenney, David P., *Early American Choral Music*

Forbes, Elliot, *A History of Music at Harvard to 1972*
Galkin, Elliott, *A History of Orchestral Conducting*
Kivy, Peter, *Osmin's Rage: Philosophical Reflections on Opera, Drama and Text*
Kramer, Jonathan, *The Time of Music—Listen to the Music*
Lester, Joel, *Analytic Approaches to Twentieth-Century Music*
Reynolds, Roger, *A Searcher's Path: A Composer's Ways*
Rorem, Ned, *Settling the Score: Essays on Music*
Tenney, James, *A History of Consonance and Dissonance*
Turek, Ralph, *Elements of Music: Vol. 1, Concepts and Applications*
Watkins, Glenn, *Soundings: Music in the Twentieth Century*

## N. Musical Compositions

**Chamber Music**   William Albright, *Abiding Passions* (woodwind quintet); Leslie Bassett, *Brass Quintet*; William Bolcom, *String Quartet No. 10*; John Corigliano, *Voyage* (flute and string quintet); George Edwards, *Parallel Convergences*; Richard Felciano, *Furies*; Aaron Jay Kernis, *Invisible Mosaic II*; William Kraft, *Quartet for Percussion*; Henri Lazarof, *Piano Trio*; Donald Martino, *From the Other Side*; Conlon Nancarrow, *String Quartet No. 3*; Marc Neikrug, *Stars the Mirror* (string quartet); Gerard J. Pape, *String Quartet No. 2*; Tobias Picker, *Piano Quintet*; Bernard Rands, *. . . in the Receding Mist . . .* ; Steve Reich, *Different Trains*; George Rochberg, *Violin Sonata*; Christopher Rouse, *String Quartet No. 2*; William Schuman, *String Quartet No. 5*; Richard Wernick, *String Quartet No. 3*; Charles Wuorinen, *Violin Sonata*.

**Choral/Vocal**   Samuel Adler, *Stars in the Dust* (oratorio); Leslie Bassett, *Pierrot Songs*; Emma Lou Diemer, *Christmas Cantata*; Lukas Foss, *With Music Strong*; John Harbison, *Simple Daylight*; Stephen Jaffe, *Four Songs with Ensemble*; Libby Larsen, *Three Summer Scenes*; Marc Neikrug, *Nachtlieder*; Stephen Paulus, *Voices*; Roger Reynolds, *Whispers Out of Time* (Pulitzer Prize)—*Not Only Night*; Ned Rorem, *Goodbye, My Fancy*; Ralph Shapey, *Songs of Life*; Yehudi Wyner, *Leonardo Vincitore*.

**Concertos**   Hugh Aitken, *Violin Concerto No. 2*; Elliott Carter, *Oboe Concerto*; Marc-Antonio Consoli, *Cello Concerto*; Morton Gould, *Concerto Grosso*; John Harbison, *Concerto for Double Brass Choir and Orchestra*; Karel Husa, *Trumpet Concerto—Cello Concerto*; Libby Larsen, *Trumpet Concerto*; Henri Lazarof, *Concertante for Horns and Strings*; Robert Hall Lewis, *Invenzione*; Witold Lutoslawski, *Piano Concerto No. 1*; Gerard J. Pape, *Piano Concerto*; Gunther Schuller, *Flute Concerto*; Joseph Schwantner, *Piano Concerto*; Robert Starer, *Clarinet Concerto—Cello Concerto*; Michael Torke, *Copper* (brass quintet and orchestra); Joan Tower, *Clarinet Concerto*; Nancy Van de Vate, *Krakow Concerto* (percussion and orchestra); Ellen Taaffe Zwilich, *Trombone Concerto*.

**Electronic**   Larry Austin, *Sonata Concertante* (piano and tape); Joan La Barbara, *Urban Tropics*; Paul Lansky, *Notjustmoreidlechatter*; Mel Powell, *Computer Prelude*; Roger Reynolds, *Versions/Stages I–IV*; Michael Torke, *Black and White*.

**Operas**   Dominick Argento, *The Aspern Papers*; Philip Glass, *1000 Airplanes on the Roof* (theater piece)—*The Making of the Representative for Planet 8*; Jack Gottlieb, *Death of a Ghost*; Marc Neikrug, *Los Alamos*; Lawrence Rapchak, *The Lifework of Juan Diaz*.

**Orchestra/Band**   John Adams, *Fearful Symmetries*; William Albright, *Chasm: Symphonic Fragment*; Elliott Carter, *Remembrance*; Emma Lou Diemer, *Serenade for String Orchestra*; Donald Erb, *Solstice*; Philip Glass, *The Canyon*; Meyer Kupferman, *Savage Landscape*; Joan La Barbara, *Urban Tropics*; Marvin D. Levy, *Arrows of Time*; Robert Hall Lewis, *Invenzione*; Dan S. Locklair, *Rubrica*; Alvin Lucier, *Silver Streetcar for the Orchestra*; William Mayer, *Of Rivers and Trains*; Gerard Pape, *Three Faces of Death*; Bernard Rands, *. . . Body and Shadow . . .* ; Ned Rorem, *A Quaker Reader*; Lalo Shifrin, *Songs of the Aztecs*; Andrew Stiller, *A Periodic Table of Elements* (chamber orchestra); Morton Subotnick, *A Desert Flowers*; Dana Wilson, *Piece of Mind*; Richard Wilson, *Suite for Small Orchestra*; Ellen Taaffe Zwilich, *Symbolon*.

**Piano/Organ** Larry Austin, *Violet's Invention*; Emma Lou Diemer, *Space Suite*; Lou Harrison, *A Summerfield Set*; Roger Reynolds, *Variation*.

**Symphonies** Irwin Bazelon, *Symphony No. 8 1/2*; Anthony Iannaccone, *Sinfonia concertante*; Meyer Kupferman, *Jazz Symphony*; George Perle, *Sinfonietta I*.

# 1989

❀

## Historical Highlights

The savings and loan bailout begins at taxpayers' expense; Colin Powell becomes the first black Chairman of the Joint Chiefs of Staff; the *Exxon Valdez* oil spill in Alaska occurs; Oliver North convicted in Iran-Gate affair; troops invade Panama seeking General Noriega; the Berlin Wall comes down as Communism begins crumbling; the Chinese crush student demonstrators in Tiananmen Square; Deng Xiaoping resigns.

## World Cultural Highlights

**World Art** George Andreas, *Physis;* John Chamberlain, *Scotch Vapor;* Pierre Fakhoury, *Basilica of Our Lady of Peace* (Ivory Coast—tallest church in Christendom); Rufino Tamayo, *Ancestor*.

**World Literature** John Banville, *The Book of Evidence;* Salman Rushdie, *The Satanic Verses* (the Iranian government sentences Rushdie to death); Claude Simon, *L'Acacia*.

**World Music** Peter Maxwell Davies, *Symphony No. 4*; Arvo Pärt, *Miserere*; Robert Simpson, *Flute Concerto*; Roger Steptoe, *Clarinet Concerto*.

**Miscellaneous** Compact discs replace records in the music stores; deaths include Samuel Beckett, Salvador Dali, Herbert von Karajan, Daphne du Maurier, Giuseppe Patané, and Martti Talvela.

## American Art and Literature Highlights

**Births/Deaths** Deaths include sculptor Richmond Barthé and literary figures Donald Barthelme, Sterling A. Brown, Bruce Chatwin, Malcolm Cowley, Emily Kimbrough, Mary McCarthy, Frederic Prokosch, Irving Stone, May Swenson, Robert Penn Warren, and Glenway Wescott.

**Art Works** Jack Beal, *Sense of Hearing*; Robert Bechtle, *Vicente Avenue Intersection*; Robert Cottingham, *Blues*; Brad Faegre, *Roaring Santa Fe #3751*; Eric Fischl, *By the River*; Helen Frankenthaler, *Gateway*; Joan Griswold, *Ice*; Garland Robinette, *Peter Fountain: Portrait of a Jazz Great*; Susan Rothenberg, *Blue U-Turn*; Wayne Thiebaud, *Steep Street*; George Wexler, *View from Miller's Farm*.

**Literature** E. L. Doctorow, *Billy Bathgate* (National Book Critics' Award); Allan Gurganus, *Oldest Confederate Widow Tells All*; Donald Hall, *The One Day* (National Book Critics' Award); Bharati Mukherjee, *The Middleman and Other Stories* (National Book Critics' Award); Amy Tan, *The Joy Luck Club*.

## Music—The Vernacular/Commercial Scene

**B. Deaths** Bob Allen (singer) April 24; Irving Berlin (composer) September 22; Archie Bleyer (bandleader/arranger) March 20; Will Bradley (trombonist) July; Archie Campbell (humorist/guitarist) August 29; John Cipollina (guitarist) May 29; Arnett Cobb (saxophonist) March 24; Cousin Joe (ukelele player/pianist) October 2; William "Wild Bill" Davison (cornetist) November 14; Roy Eldridge (trumpeter) February 26; Sammy Fain (composer) December 6; Johnny Green (pianist/arranger) May 15; Stuart Hamblen (singer/writer) March 8; Eddie Heywood (pianist/arranger) January 2; Bradley Kincaid (folk singer/guitarist) September 23; Rose Murphy (singer/pianist) November 16; Woody Shaw (trumpeter) May 11; Tommy Tucker (bandleader) July 11; Keith Whitley (singer) May 8.

## C. Biographical

**Performing Groups**   C + C Music Factory; Damn Yankees; Every Mother's Nightmare; Green Day; Helmet; Pavement; P M Dawn; Smashing Pumpkins; Snap!; The Texas Tornadoes; Walter Trout Band; Two Nice Girls; Wilson Phillips.

**New Beginnings**   Criterion Center Stage Right (off-Broadway house); Jazzpar Prize; SBK Records.

**Honors**   Dizzy Gillespie (National Medal of Arts); Mary Martin and Harry Belafonte (Kennedy Center).

**D. Publications**   Linda Dahl, *Stormy Weather: The Music and Lives of a Century of Jazzwomen*; Leonard Lyons, *The Great Jazz Pianists, Speaking of Their Lives and Music*; Peter van der Merwe, *Origins of the Popular Style*; Thomas L. Riis, *Just Before Jazz: Black Music Theater in New York, 1890–1915*; Gunther Schuller, *The Swing Era: The Development of Jazz 1930–1945*; Allen Woll, *Black Musical Theatre: From Coontown to Dreamgirls*.

## E. Representative Works

**Musicals**   C. Coleman and A. E. Hotchner, *Welcome to the Club*; C. Coleman and D. Zippel, *City of Angels* (New York Drama Critics' Award—Tony); Carman Moore, *Franklin and Eleanore*; Various composers, *Jerome Robbins' Broadway* (revue); M. Weston, R. Wright, and G. Forrest, *Grand Hotel*.

**Number One Hits**   *Another Day in Paradise—Two Hearts* (Phil Collins); *Baby Don't Forget My Number—Blame It on the Rain—Girl I'm Gonna Miss You* (Milli Vanilli); *Batdance* (Prince); *Cold Hearted—Forever Your Girl—Straight Up* (Paula Abdul); *Don't Wanna Lose You* (Gloria Estefan); *Eternal Flame* (Bangles); *Good Thing- She Drives Me Crazy* (Fine Young Cannibals); *Hangin' Tough—I'll Be Loving You (Forever)* (New Kids on the Block); *I'll Be There For You* (Bon Jovi); *If You Don't Know Me By Now* (Simply Red); *Like a Prayer* (Madonna); *Listen To Your Heart— The Look* (Roxette); *The Living Years* (Mike and the Mechanics); *Lost In Your Eyes* (Debbie Gibson); *Miss You Much* (Janet Jackson); *Right Here Waiting—Satisfied* (Richard Marx); *Rock On* (Michael Damian); *Toy Soldiers* (Martika); *We Didn't Start the Fire* (Billy Joel); *When I See You Smile* (Bad English); *When I'm With You* (Sheriff); *Wind Beneath My Wings* (Bette Midler).

**Other**   Elmer Bernstein, *My Left Foot* (film music); Henry Connick, Jr., *When Harry Met Sally* (film music); George Fenton, *We're No Angels* (film music); James Horner, *Field of Dreams* (film music); Michael Kamen, *License to Kill* (film music); Wynton Marsalis, *Majesty of the Blues*.

# Music—The Cultivated/Art Music Scene

**G. Deaths**   Josef Alexander (composer) December 23; Kurt Baum (Czech-born tenor) December 27; Antonia Brico (conductor) August 3; Emerson Buckley (conductor) November 17; Paul Doktor (Austrian-born violist) June 21; Jan De Gaetani (mezzo-soprano) September 15; Karl Geiringer (Austrian-born musicologist) January 10; Jakob Gimpel (Austrian-born pianist) March 12; Vladimir Horowitz (Russian-born pianist) November 5; Hans Nathan (German-born musicologist) August 4; Genia Nemenoff (French-born pianist) September 19; Halsey Stevens (composer) January 20; Kurt Stone (German-born musicologist) June 15; Virgil Thomson (composer/critic) September 30; Donald Voorhees (conductor) January 10.

## H. Debuts

**United States**   Gary Arvin (pianist—New York), Valerie Grace Ashworth (British pianist—New York), James Bobrick (tenor—Denver), Barbara Bonney (soprano—Chicago), Andrea Cappelletti (Italian violinist), Andrew Cooperstock (pianist—New York), Helen Field (British soprano— Houston), Judith Howard (British soprano—Seattle), Paolo Kudriavchenko (Russian tenor— Miami), Anthony Michaels-Moore (British baritone—Philadelphia), Sharon Sweet (soprano—San Francisco), Barseg Tumanyan (Armenian bass-baritone—Boston), Günther Wand (German conductor—Chicago), Franz Welser-Moest (Austrian conductor—St. Louis), Philip Zawisza (baritone—Chicago).

**Metropolitan Opera**   June Anderson (soprano), Ghena Dimitrova (Bulgarian soprano), Kallen Esperian (soprano), Ruth Falcon (soprano), Robert Gambill (tenor), Nancy Gustafson (soprano), Alan Held (baritone), Sumi Jo (Korean soprano), Donald Kaasch (tenor), Kathleen Kuhlmann (mezzo-soprano), Richard Leech (tenor), Andrew Litton (conductor), Frank Lopardo (tenor), Susanne Mentzer (mezzo-soprano), Heidi Grant Murphy (soprano), Neil Rosensheim (tenor), Nunzio Todisco (Italian tenor), Wendy White (mezzo-soprano), Delores Ziegler (mezzo-soprano).

## I. New Positions

**Conductors**   Dennis Russell Davies (Brooklyn Philharmonic Orchestra); Mark Philip Elder (Rochester Philharmonic Orchestra); James Sedares (music director, Phoenix Symphony Orchestra).

**Educational**   Edward Applebaum (composition, Florida State University); Dennis Russell Davies (music director, Brooklyn Academy of Music); Sidney Harth (Carnegie-Mellon); Ezra Laderman (dean, Yale School of Music).

**Other**   Christopher Keene (general director, New York City Opera); George Perle (composer-in-residence, San Francisco Symphony Orchestra—to 1991); Bernard Rands (composer-in-residence, Philadelphia Orchestra).

## J. Honors and Awards

**Honors**   John Cage (American Academy); Vladimir Horowitz (Medal of Arts); Ursula Mamlok (Hinrichsen Award); Gunther Schuller (Schuman Award); Willliam Schuman (Kennedy Center); Gerard Schwarz (Ditson Award); Ralph Shapey (American Academy and Institute).

**Awards**   Chinary Ung (Grawemeyer).

## K. Biographical   Mikhail Baryshnikov, at odds with the board of trustees, resigns as artistic director of the American Ballet Theater; Yefim Bronfman (Israeli pianist) becomes an American citizen; Congress prohibits the National Endowment for the Arts from funding works deemed obscene; Timothy Jenkins suffers a spinal injury in a fall during performance.

## L. Musical Beginnings

**Performing Groups**   Barati Ensemble (California); Borromeo String Quartet; St. Lawrence String Quartet.

**Festivals**   "Mainly Mozart," A Viennese Summerfest (Atlanta, Georgia).

**Other**   Maria Callas International Club; Morton Meyerson Symphony Center (Dallas).

## M. Music Publications

Adler, Samuel, *The Study of Orchestration*
Berry, Wallace, *Musical Structure and Performance*
Cone, E. and Morgan, P., *Music: A View from Delft: Selected Essays*
Dufallo, Richard, *Trackings: Composers Speak with Richard Dufallo*
Fink, Michael J., *Inside the Music Business: Music in Contemporary Life*
Galkin, Elliott, *A History of Orchestral Conducting*
Kivy, Peter, *Sound Sentiment: An Essay on the Musical Emotions*
Kostelanetz, Richard, *On Innovative Musicians*
Lester, Joel, *Analytic Approaches to Twentieth-Century Music*
Levy, Kenneth, *Music: A Listener's Introduction*
McClary, S. and Leppert, R., *Music and Society: The Politics of Composition, Performance and Reception*
Meyer, Leonard, B., *Style and Music: Theory, History and Ideology*
Pleasants, Henry, *Opera in Crisis: Tradition, Present, Future*
Thomson, Virgil, *Music with Words: A Composer's View*
Ward-Steinman, David, *Toward a Comparative Structural Theory of the Arts*

## N. Musical Compositions

**Chamber Music**   Daniel Asia, *Piano Quartet*; Milton Babbitt, *Consortini for Chamber Ensemble*; John Cage, *Four* (string quartet); Donald Erb, *String Quartet No. 2*; Philip Glass, *String Quartet No. 4: Boczak*; Katherine Hoover, *Quintet (Da Pacem)*; Andrew Imbrie, *Piano Trio No. 2*; Ben

Johnston, *Ponder Nothing* (solo clarinet); Barbara Kolb, *Extremes* (flute and cello); Gerard Pape, *Five Pieces for Saxophone and Piano*; George Perle, *String Quartet No. 8, "Windows of Order"*; Jan Swafford, *They Who Hunger* (piano quartet); Robert Ward, *Appalachian Ditties and Dances* (violin and piano); Richard Wernick, *String Sextet*; Olly Wilson, *A City Called Heaven*; Charles Wuorinen, *String Sextet*.

**Choral/Vocal**   John Adams, *The Wound-Dresser* (baritone and orchestra); Neely Bruce, *Eight Ghosts*; John Harbison, *Words from Paterson*; Stephen Jaffe, *Fort Juniper Songs;* Mark Louis Lehman, *Pilgrim Songs*; Steve Mackay, *Among the Vanishing*; Ned Rorem, *The Auden Poems*; Ralph Shapey, *Songs of Love*; Charles Wuorinen, *Genesis* (oratorio).

**Concertos**   John Adams, *Eros Piano* (piano and orchestra); Barney Childs, *Timpani Concerto*; David Diamond, *Kaddish* (cello and orchestra); John Harbison, *Viola Concerto*; Barbara Kolb, *Voyants* (piano and orchestra); Libby Larsen, *Concerto: Cold, Silent Snow* (flute and orchestra); Henri Lazarof, *Clarinet Concerto*; Marc Neikrug, *Flute Concerto*; Anthony Newman, *Adagio and Rondo* (piano and orchestra); Gunther Schuller, *Concerto for Piano Three Hands*; Francis Thorne, *Piano Concerto No. 3*; Michael Torke, *Rust* (piano and winds) — *Slate* (chamber group and orchestra); Joan Tower, *Flute Concerto*; Richard Wernick, *Piano Concerto*.

**Electronic**   Elaine Barkin, *To Whom It May Concern*; Joan La Barbara, *L'albero Della Foglie Azzure*; Paul Lansky, *Not so Heavy Metal*; Gerard Pape, *The Burning Thing* (flute and tape); Ezra Sims, *Flight*; Morton Subotnick, *And the Butterflies Began to Sing.*

**Operas**   Stephen Burton, *An American Triptych*; Chou Wen-Chung, *Echoes from the Gorge*; David Cope, *Cradle Falling*; Paul Dresher, *Power Failure*; David Lang, *Judith and Holofernes*; Libby Larsen, *Beauty and the Beast*; Anne LeBaron, *The E and O Line*; Richard Owen, *Tom Sawyer*; Ronald Perera, *The Yellow Wallpaper*, William Schuman, *A Question of Taste*.

**Orchestra/Band**   William Bolcom, *Etudes for Orchestra*; John Cage, *Twenty-Three* (strings); Elliott Carter, *Three Occasions for Orchestra*; Jacob Druckman, *Brangle*; Philip Glass, *Itaipú*, Morton Gould, *Notes of Remembrance*; Anthony Iannaccone, *Whispers of Heavenly Death*; Barbara Kolb, *The Enchanted Loom — Voyants*; Leo Kraft, *Pacific Bridges* (strings and clarinet); William Kraft, *Vintage Renaissance — Contextures II: The Final Beast*; Otto Luening, *Symphonic Fantasia No. 9*; Tod Machover, *Desires*; Salvatore Martirano, *LON/dons*; Joseph Schwantner, *Freeflight*; Joan Tower, *Island Prelude*; Richard Wilson, *Articulations*.

**Piano/Organ**   William Albright, *Whistler Nocturnes* (organ); Gerald Berg, *Variation Set*; John Cage, *2squared* (two pianos, four hands) — *Swinging*; Michael Colgrass, *The Schubert Birds*; George Crumb, *Zeitgeist* (two amplified pianos); Emma Lou Diemer, *Preludes to the Past* (organ); Stephen Jaffe, *Double Sonata* (two pianos); Leon Kirchner, *Interlude for Piano*; Gerald Levinson, *Morning Star* (two pianos); Dan Locklair, *Fantasy Brings the Day* (harpsichord); David Macbride, *Chartres*; Ned Rorem, *Organbooks I, II, III.*

**Symphonies**   John Corigliano, *Symphony No. 1*; Richard Danielpour, *Symphony No. 3, "Journey without Distance"*; David Diamond, *Sinfonietta*; Donald Erb, *Symphony for Winds*; Aaron Jay Kernis, *Symphony in Waves*; Andrzej Panufnik, *Symphony No. 10*; Daniel Pinkham, *Symphony No. 4*; Lawrence Rapchak, *Sinfonia antiqua*; George Rochberg, *Symphony No. 6*; Elie Siegmeister, *Symphony No. 8*; Robert Ward, *Symphony No. 6*; Ellen Taaffe Zwilich, *Symphony for Winds*.

# 1990

❁

## Historical Highlights

General Noriega surrenders to United States troops, who are then pulled out of Panama; John Poindexter convicted in the Iran-Contra affair; troops are sent to Saudi Arabia following the Iraqi invasion of Kuwait; East and West Germany are united; the USSR comes to an official end; Lech Walesa is elected Polish president; John Major becomes the new British prime minister.

## World Cultural Highlights

**World Art**    Leon Kossoff, *Christchurch Spitalfields, Morning;* A. R. Penck, *Castle;* Leonid Sokov, *Meeting of Two Sculptures—Lenin and Giacometti;* Susana Solano, *End of the 90's.*

**World Literature**    A. S. Byatt, *Possession;* J. M. Coetzee, *Age of Iron;* John Le Carré, *The Russian House;* Edna O'Brien, *Lantern Slides;* Henri Troyat, *David's Wife.*

**World Music**    Aulis Sallinen, *Symphony No. 6;* Peter Schat, *The Heavens;* Leif Segerstam, *Symphony No. 15, "Ecliptic Thoughts"—Symphony No. 16;* Robert Simpson, *Symphony No. 11.*

**Miscellaneous**    Restoration of Michelangelo's Sistine Chapel paintings is completed; Meeting of the Worlds Festivals begin in Finland and Pacific Music Festivals in Japan; deaths include Damasos Alonso, Roald Dahl, Lawrence Durrell, Alberto Moravia, Malcolm Muggeridge, and Patrick White.

## American Art and Literature Highlights

**Births/Deaths**    Deaths include artists Balcomb Greene, Ralph Humphrey, and literary figures Norman Cousins, Walker Percy, Anya Seton and Irving Wallace.

**Art Works**    David Beck, *Movie Palace;* Andrew S. Conklin, *Fulton Street Station;* Bryan Keeler, *Hallelujah Bass;* Roy Lichtenstein, *Airplane* (bronze); Robert Morris, *In World, In Body, In Mind;* Auseklis Ozols, *Louisiana Palette;* Ann Marie Rousseau, *The Poet's Room;* Frank Stella, *Knights and Squires;* Wayne Thiebaud, *Dark Candles;* Robert Vickrey, *After the Swim;* Jane Wilson, *Snowy Light.*

**Literature**    John Casey, *Spartina* (National Book Award); John Guare, *Six Degrees of Separation* (New York Drama Critics' Award); Charles Johnson, *The Middle Passage* (National Book Award); John Updike, *Rabbit at Rest* (National Book Critics' Award); Geoffrey Ward, *Transparent Gestures* (National Book Critics' Award); Mona Van Duyn, *Near Changes* (Pulitzer Prize).

## Music—The Vernacular/Commercial Scene

**B. Deaths**    Pearl Bailey (singer) August 17; Carl Belew (songwriter) November; Big Twist (Larry Nolan—singer/bandleader) March 14; Art Blakey (drummer) October 16; Lee Castle (trumpeter/bandleader) November 16; Carmen Cavallaro (pianist/bandleader); June Christy (singer) June 21; Dee Clark (singer) December 7; Xavier Cugat (bandleader) October 27; Sammy Davis, Jr. (singer) May 16; Bobby Day (singer) July; Tom Fogerty (guitarist) September 6; Sergio Franchi (tenor) May 1; Dexter Gordon (saxophonist) April 25; Jay Gorney (composer) June 14; Mel Lewis (drummer/bandleader) February 2; Mary Martin (singer/actress) November 3; Clyde McCoy (trumpeter/bandleader) June 1; Johnnie Ray (singer) February 24; Emily Remler (guitarist/singer) May 4; David Rose (composer) August 23; Del Shannon (singer/writer) February 8; Joe Turner (pianist) July 21; Gary Usher (singer/writer) May 25; Jimmy Van Heusen (songwriter) February 7; Sarah Vaughan (singer) April 3; Stevie Ray Vaughan (guitarist) August 27.

**C. Biographical**

**Performing Groups**    Basehead; Big F; Bikini Kill; The Breeders; The Disposable Heroes of HipHoprisy; The Flecktones; Galactic Cowboys; Hi-Five; Hole; The House of Pain; Kik Tracee; Kill for Thrills; Liquid Jesus; Mindfunk; Pearl Jam; Shai; Slaughter; Tuff; Ugly Kid Joe.

**New Beginnings**    Mel Tillis Showroom (Branson, Missouri).

**Honors**    Tennessee Ernie Ford (Country Music Hall of Fame); Dizzy Gillespie and Jule Styne (Kennedy Center).

**Miscellaneous**    Harry Connick, Jr., and Peter Nero perform at the White House; Gloria Estefan undergoes back surgery following a serious bus/car collision.

**D. Publications**    Samuel A. Floyd, Jr., ed., *Black Music in the Harlem Renaissance: A Collection of Essays;* Philip Furia, *Poets of Tin Pan Alley;* Mickey Hart, *Drumming at the Edge of Magic: A Journey into the Spirit of Percussion;* Nicholas E. Tawa, *The Way to Tin Pan Alley: American Popular songs, 1866–1910.*

**E. Representative Works**

**Musicals**   Andrew Lloyd Webber, *Aspects of Love*; Stephen Sondheim, *Assassins*.

**Number One Hits**   *Because i Love You (The Postman Song)* (Stevie B); *Black Cat—Escapade* (Janet Jackson); *Black Velvet* (Alannah Myles); *Blaze of Glory* (Bon Jovi); *Close to You* (Maxi Priest); *Hold On—Release Me* (Wilson Phillips); *How Am I Supposed to Live Without You* (Michael Bolton); *I Don't Have the Heart* (James ingram); *I'll Be Your Everything* (Tommy Page); *I'm Your Baby Tonight* (Whitney Houston); *Ice Ice Baby* (Vanilla Ice); *If Wishes Came True* (Sweet Sensation); *It Must Have Been Love* (Roxette); *Love and Affection* (Nelson); *Love Takes Time— Vision of Love* (Mariah Carey); *Love Will Lead You Back* (Taylor Dayne); *Nothing Compares 2 U* (Sinead O'Connor); *Opposites Attract* (Paula Abdul and the Wild Pair); *Praying for Time* (George Michael); *She Ain't Worth It* (Glenn Medeiros); *Step by Step* (New Kids on the Block); *Vogue* (Madonna).

**Other**   Elmer Bernstein, *The Field* (film music); Alan Menken, *The Little Mermaid* (film music— Oscar for song *Under the Sea*); Stephen Sondheim, *Sooner or Later* (Oscar—from film *Dick Tracy*).

## Music—The Cultivated/Art Music Scene

**G. Deaths**   Peter Herman Adler (Czech-born conductor) October 2; John Alexander (tenor) December 8; Ludwig Altman (German-born organist/composer) November 27; Ernst Bacon (composer) March 16; Leonard Bernstein (conductor/composer) October 14; Jorge Bolet (Cuban-born pianist) October 16; Aaron Copland (composer) December 2; William Levi Dawson (composer) May 2; Cecil Effinger (composer) December 22; Peter Racine Fricker (British-born composer) February 1; Elliott Galkin (conductor/critic) May 24; Albert Goldberg (critic) February 4; Werner Janssen (conductor) September 19; Paul Pisk (Austrian-born composer/musicologist) January 12; Hugh Ross (British-born conductor) January 20; Zoltán Rozsnyai (Hungarian-born conductor) September 10; Martial Singher (French born baritone) March 10; Eleanor Steber (soprano) October 3; Fernando Valente (harpsichord) September 6.

**H. Debuts**

**United States**   Kelly Anderson (bass-baritone—Indianapolis), Leif Ove Andsnes (Norwegian pianist—Cleveland), Ainhoa Arteta (Spanish soprano—Palm Beach), Stephen Barlow (British conductor—San Francisco), Ales Barta (Czech organist—New York), Rebecca Blankenship (soprano—San Francisco), Bettina Boller (Swiss violinist—New York), Pamela Coburn (soprano—Los Angeles), Vladimir Grishko (Ukrainian tenor—Baton Rouge), Dmitri Hvorostovsky (Russian baritone—New York), Irina/Maxim Jeleznov (Russian duo-pianists—Hartford), Ljubov Kazarnovskaya (Russian soprano—Boston), Dimitri Kharitonov (Russian baritone—Chicago), Evgeny Kissin (Russian pianist—New York), Köhler (German countertenor—Washington, DC), Joanna Kozlowska (Polish soprano—New York), Valeria Popova (Bulgarian soprano— Milwaukee), Claire Powell (British mezzo-soprano—San Francisco), Patricia Racette (soprano— San Francisco), Heidi Skok (mezzo-soprano—Pittsburgh), Maxim Vengerov (Russian violinist— New York), Yoko Watanabe (Japanese soprano—Boston), Janice Watson (British soprano—New York).

**Metropolitan Opera**   Kathleen Cassello (soprano), Richard Cowan (baritone), Dwayne Croft (baritone), Susan Dunn (soprano), Franco Farina (tenor), Haijing Fu (Chinese baritone), Maria Guleghina (Ukranian soprano), Jerry Hadley (tenor), Robert Hale (baritone), Uwe Heilmann (German tenor), Peter Kazaras (tenor), Felicity Lott (British soprano), Lars Magnussen (Swedish tenor), Karita Mattila (Finnish soprano), John Horton Murray (German tenor), Rico Saccini (conductor), Ludmila Schemtchuk (Russian mezzo-soprano), Patricia Schuman (soprano), Stephanie Sundine (soprano), Sharon Sweet (soprano), Deon Van der Walt (South African tenor).

**I. New Positions**

**Conductors**   Neeme Järvi (Detroit Symphony Orchestra); Carl St. Clair (Pacific Symphony Orchestra); Christopher Wilkins (San Antonio Symphony Orchestra).

**Educational**   Dennis Russell Davies (director, Brooklyn Academy of Music); Joseph Flummerfelt (chorus, New England Conservatory); Kyle Gann (Bucknell University); Elmar Oliveira (Manhattan School of Music).

**Other**   Hugo Weisgall (president, American Academy and Institute of Arts and Letters); Richard Westenburg (music director, Fifth Avenue Presbyterian Church, New York).

## J. Honors and Awards

**Honors**   David Lang (Rome Prize); Mstislav Rostropovich (Ditson); Elie Siegmeister (American Academy and Institute); George Tsontakis and Chinary Ung (Friedheim).

**Awards**   Sergei Babayan (Casadesus); Grace Bumbry (Tibbett); Renee Fleming (Richard Tucker); Sylvia McNair (Marion Anderson); Christopher Taylor (Tchaikovsky); Joan Tower (Grawemeyer); Deborah Voight (Ponselle).

**K. Biographical**   Régine Crespin and Joan Sutherland announce their retirement from the opera stage; Mstislav Rostropovich has his Russian citizenship restored and makes a triumphant tour of the USSR with the National Symphony Orchestra.

## L. Musical Beginnings

**Performing Groups**   Ars Poetica Chamber Orchestra (Detroit); Boston Opera Theater; Dayton Philharmonic Gospel Choir; Hollywood Bowl Orchestra.

**Festivals**   Bard Music Festival (New York); Laurel Festival of the Arts at Jim Thorpe, Pennsylvania; Festival in the Sun (Tucson); Music at the Gainey Center.

**Other**   Carlos Moseley Music Pavilion (New York).

## M. Music Publications

Cohn, Arthur, *Encyclopedia of Chamber Music*
Finney, Ross Lee, *Thinking About Music: Collected Writings*
Kerman, Joseph, *Contemplating Music: Challenges to Musicology*
Kivy, Peter, *Music Alone: Philosophical Reflections on the Purely Musical Experience*
Narmour, Eugene, *The Analysis and Cognition of Basic Melodic Structures*
Nicholls, David, *American Experimental Music, 1890–1940*
Perle, George, *The Listening Composer*
Read, Gardner, *Twentieth-Century Microtonal Notation*
Slonimsky, Nicolas, *Lectionary of Music*
Treitler, Leo, *Music and the Historical Imagination*

## N. Musical Compositions

**Chamber Music**   James Cohn, *Piano Trio*; Donald Crockett, *Celestial Mechanics* (oboe and string quartet); Barbara Feldman, *The Immutable Silence*; Philip Glass, *Hydrogen Jukebox*; Karel Husa, *String Quartet No. 4, "Poems"*; Aaron Jay Kernis, *String Quartet, "Musica Celestis"*; Gerald Levinson, *Dreamlight*; Steven MacKay, *On All Fours* (string quartet); William Thomas McKinley, *Six Romances, "Secrets of the Heart"* (flute and piano); Daniel Pinkham, *String Quartet*; Roger Reynolds, *Dionysus* (octet); Ezra Sims, *Concert Piece for Viola*; Robert Vodnoy, *Percussion Concussion*; Robert Ward, *Violin Sonata No. 2*; Ellen Taaffe Zwilich, *Clarinet Quintet*.

**Choral/Vocal**   Ben Johnston, *Calamity Jane to Her Daughter*; Stephen Jaffe, *Fort Juniper Songs*; Aaron Jay Kernis, *Brilliant Sky, Infinite Sky* (song cycle); Ernst Krenek, *Opus Sine Nomine* (oratorio); Robert Hall Lewis, *Kantaten*; Gian Carlo Menotti, *For the Death of Orpheus*; Christopher Rouse, *Karolju*.

**Concertos**   Stephen Albert, *Cello Concerto*; Elliott Carter, *Violin Concerto*; Curtis Curtis-Smith, *Violin Concerto—Concerto for Piano, Left Hand*; Emma Lou Diemer, *Marimba Concerto*; Morton Gould, *Diversions* (tenor saxophone and orchestra); John Anthony Lennon, *Zingari* (guitar and orchestra); George Perle, *Piano Concerto No. 1*; Mel Powell, *Duplicates* (piano and orchestra—Pulitzer Prize); Nancy Van de Vate, *Viola Concerto*; Ellen Taaffe Zwilich, *Flute Concerto—Oboe Concerto*.

**Electronic**  Charles Amirkhanian, *Vers Les Anges*; Larry Austin, *Transmission Two: The Great Excursion*; Joan La Barbara, *In the Dreamtime*; Paul Lansky, *QuakerBridge*; Alvin Lucier, *Amplifiers and Reflectors—Music for Piano and Amplified Sonorous Vessels*; John Rahn, *Miranda*; Diane Thome, *The Ruins of the Heart*.

**Operas**  Peggy Glanville-Hicks, *Beckett*; Joan La Barbara, *Events in the Elsewhere*; John Moran, *The Manson Family*; Hugo Weisgall, *Esther*; Peter Westergaard, *The Tempest*.

**Orchestra/Band**  Daniel Asia, *Black Light*; Henry Brant, *Prisons of the Mind*; Margaret Buechner, *Elizabeth* (ballet); Michael Colgrass, *Snow Walker*; Jacob Druckman, *Overture, Summer Lightning*; Tan Dun, *Death and Fire—Orchestral Theatre I*; Lukas Foss, *Celebration*; William Kraft, *Vintage 1990–91*; David Lang, *International Business Machine*; Otto Luening, *Symphonic Fantasia No. 10*; David Ott, *Music of the Canvas;* Stephen Paulus, *Street Music*; Wayne Peterson, *The Widening Gyre*; Christopher Rouse, *Concerto for Strings—Karolju*; Joseph Schwantner, *A Play of Shadows* (flute and orchestra); Elie Siegmeister, *Figures in the Wind*; Michael Tilson Thomas, *From the Diary of Anne Frank* (with narrator); Robert Ward, *The Scarlet Letter* (ballet); Charles Wuorinen, *Astra*.

**Piano/Organ**  Aaron Jay Kernis, *Before Sleep and Dreams*; Libby Larsen, *Aspects of Glory* (organ); Raoul Pleskow, *Sonata*.

**Symphonies**  Daniel Asia, *Symphony No. 2*; Easley Blackwood, *Symphony No. 5*; Henry Brant, *Spatial Symphony*; John Harbison, *Symphony No. 3*; Robert Hall Lewis, *Symphony No. 4*; David Ott, *Symphony No. 1*; Daniel Pinkham, *Symphony No. 4*; Shulamit Ran, *Symphony* (Pulitzer Prize—Friedheim Award); Roger Reynolds, *Symphony: Myths*; George Walker, *Sinfonia No. 2*; Marilyn Ziffrin, *Symphony for Voice and Orchestra*.

# 1991

☀

## Historical Highlights

Operation Desert Storm drives the Iraqis out of Kuwait in less than two weeks but leaves all Kuwaiti oil wells burning; Saddam Hussein remains in power in Iraq; Boris Yeltsin is elected president of a new Russia; an attempted coup against Gorbachev is thwarted by the people and the military together; civil war begins in Yugoslavia.

## World Cultural Highlights

**World Art**  Susana Amunderain, *Red Stripe: Bar*; Eduardo Arroyo, *Granada*; Fernando Botero, *Madre e Hijo*; Francesca Clemente, *Tree of Life*; Baltasar Lobo, *L'ile du Levant*.

**World Literature**  Douglas Coupland, *Generation X: Tales for an Accelerated Culture*; Nadine Gordimer, *Jump and Other Stories*; Graham Greene, *The Last Word and Other Stories*.

**World Music**  Olivier Messiaen, *Eclairs sur l'Au-delà*; Andrzej Panufnik, *Cello Concerto*; Krzysztof Penderecki, *King Ubu*; Aulis Sallinen, *Kullervo*; Michael Tippitt, *Byzantium*.

**Miscellaneous**  South African author Nadine Gordimer receives the Nobel Prize for literature. Deaths include Claudio Arrau, Margot Fonteyn, Zino Francescatti, Natalia Ginzburg, Graham Greene, Wilhelm Kempff, Giacomo Manzù, Sean O'Faolain, Andrzej Panufnik, Rufino Tamayo, and Jean Tinguely.

## American Art and Literature Highlights

**Births/Deaths**  Deaths include art figures Herbert Ferber, Chaim Gross, Robert Motherwell, Jane Piper, Joyce Treiman, and literary figures John C. Crosby, Ernest K. Gann, Theodor (Dr. Seuss) Geisel, A. B. Guthrie, Jr., Jerzy Kosinski, Howard Nemerov, James Schuyler, Isaac Bashevis Singer, Thomas Tryon, and Frank Yerby.

**Art Works**   Dennis Ashbaugh, *Designer Gene*; Grace Hartigan, *Broadway Corrida*; Roy Lichtenstein, *Interior with Mirrored Wall*; Hansen Mulford, *Low Tide*; Larry Rivers, *Matisse in Nice: Large Leaves*; Gary Stephan, *Oceans and Ovens*; Wayne Thiebaud, *Tied Ties*; Kent Ullberg, *Sailfish in Three States of Ascending*; Curt Walters, *Lydian Variegations (Grand Canyon)*.

**Literature**   Susan Faludi, *Backlash* (National Book Critics' Award); Philip Levine, *What Work Is* (National Book Award); Alexandra Ripley, *Scarlett*; Norman Rush, *Mating* (National Book Award); Neil Simon, *Lost in Yonkers* (Pulitzer Prize—Tony); Jane Smiley, *A Thousand Acres* (National Book Critics' Award—Pulitzer Prize); James Tate, *Selected Poems* (Pulitzer Prize).

## Music — The Vernacular/Commercial Scene

**B. Deaths**   Charlie Barnet (saxophone/bandleader) September 4; Gene Clark (singer/writer) May 24; Wilbur "Buck" Clayton (trumpeter/arranger) December 8; James Cleveland (singer/composer) February 9; Miles Davis (trumpeter) September 28; Richard Dyer-Bennett (folk singer) December 14; Tom Fogerty (singer) September; Tennessee Ernie Ford (singer) October 17; Lawrence "Bud" Freeman (tenor saxophonist) March 15; Slim Gaillard (singer/writer) February 26; Stan Getz (saxophonist) June 6; Jimmy McPartland (trumpeter/bandleader) March 13; Alex North (composer) September 8; Webb Pierce (singer) February 24; "Doc" Pomus (songwriter) March 14; Earl Robinson (composer) July 20; David Ruffin (singer) June 1; Mort Shuman (songwriter) November 2; Jabbo Smith (trumpeter/ singer) January 16; Dottie West (singer) September 4; Jack Yellen (lyricist/composer) April 17.

**C. Biographical**

**Performing Groups**   Counting Crows; The Four Horsemen; Kris Kross; The Persistence of Memory Orchestra.

**New Beginnings**   Lollapalooza Travelling Music Festival.

**Honors**   Roy Acuff, Betty Comden, Adolph Green (Kennedy Center); John O. Crosby, Roy Acuff (Medal of Arts); Merle Haggard, George Jones, Ray Price (Country Music Hall of Fame).

**D. Publications**   Garvin Bushell and Mark Tucker, *Jazz from the Beginning*; Samuel Charters, *Roots of the Blues: An African Search*; Mickey Hart, *Planet Drum: A Celebration of Percussion and Rhythm*.

**E. Representative Works**

**Musicals**   C. Coleman, B. Comden, and A. Green, *Will Rogers Follies* (Tony); J. Kander and F. Ebb, *The World Goes 'Round*; C. Strouse and R. Maltby, Jr., *Nick and Nora*.

**Number One Hits**   *All the Man that I Need* (Whitney Houston); *Baby Baby* (Amy Grant); *Black or White* (Michael Jackson); *Coming Out of the Dark* (Gloria Estefan); *Cream* (Prince and the New Power Generation); *Emotions—I Don't Wanna Cry—Someday* (Mariah Carey); *The First Time* (Surface); *Gonna Make You Sweat* (C + C Music Factory); *Good Vibrations* (Marky Mark and the Funky Bunch); *I Adore Mi Amor* (Color Me Badd); *(Everything I Do) I Do for You* (Bryan Adams); *I Like the Way* (Hi-Five); *Joyride* (Roxette); *Justify My Love* (Madonna); *Love Will Never Do (Without You)* (Janet Jackson); *More Than Words* (Extreme); *One More Try* (Timmy T); *The Promise of a New Day—Rush Rush* (Paula Abdul); *Romantic* (Karyn White); *Set Adrift on Memory Bliss* (P. M. Dawn); *Unbelievable* (EMF); *When a Man Loves a Woman* (Michael Bolton); *You're in Love* (Wilson Phillips).

**Other**   John Barry, *Dances with Wolves* (film music—Oscar); Anthony Braxton, *Quartet (Willisau) 1991*; Dave Brubeck, *Joy in the Morning*; Michael Kamen, *Robin Hood: Prince of Thieves* (film music); Alan Menken and Howard Ashman, *Beauty and the Beast* (film score—Oscar).

## Music — The Cultivated/Art Music Scene

**G. Deaths**   Claudio Arrau (Chilean-born pianist) June 8; Anthony Bliss (administrator) August 10; Frederick Dorian (Austrian-born author) January 24; Malcolm Frager (pianist) June 20; Martha Graham (choreographer) April 1; Scott Huston (composer) March 1; Robert Irving (conductor)

September 16; Gunnar Johansen (Danish-born pianist/composer) May 25; John Kirkpatrick (pianist) November 8; Ernst Krenek (Austrian-born composer) December 23; Paul Henry Lang (musicologist/critic) September 21; Nicola Rossi-Lemeni (Italian-born bass) March 12; Rudolf Serkin (Austrian-born pianist) May 8; Elie Siegmeister (composer) March 10; Frank Valentino (baritone) June 14; Elinor Remick Warren (pianist) April 27.

### H. Debuts

**United States** Alexander Barantschik (Russian violinist—tour), Thomas Booth (tenor—New York), Sarah Briggs (British pianist—San Francisco), Sarah Chang (violinist—Philadelphia), Maggie Cold (harpsichordist—New York), Daniele Gatti (Italian conductor—Chicago), Graciola von Glydenfeldt (Argentine soprano—Cincinnati), Thomas Harper (baritone—Seattle), Laurence Jackson (British violinist—tour), Ewa Malas-Godlewska (Polish soprano—Houston), Juri Maruzin (Russian tenor San Francisco), Elena Mirtova (Russian soprano—Omaha), Yoshiko Okada (Japanese pianist—New York), Alexander Paley (Russian pianist—Denver), Peter Rose (British bass—San Francisco), Lars Vogt (German pianist—Los Angeles), Peter Weber (Austrian baritone—Dallas).

**Metropolitan Opera** Gabriela Benacková (Czech soprano), Kenn Chester (tenor), Tracy Dahl (Canadian soprano), Helen Donath (soprano), John Fiore (Italian conductor), Lauren Flanigen (soprano), Lucio Gallo (Italian baritone), Manfred Hemm (Austrian baritone), Ben Heppner (Canadian tenor), Brian Hilt (tenor), Elizabeth Holleque (soprano), Lucina d'Intino (Italian mezzo-soprano), Anthony Rolfe Johnson (British tenor), François Loup (Swiss baritone), Mark Oswald (baritone), Herbert Perry (bass-baritone), Jane Shaulis (mezzo-soprano), Heidi Skok (mezzo-soprano), Peter Straka (Czech tenor), Ruth Ann Swenson (soprano), Michael Sylvester (tenor), Deborah Voight (soprano).

### I. New Positions

**Conductors** JoAnn Falletta (Virginia Symphony Orchestra); Kurt Masur (New York Philharmonic Orchestra); John Mauceri (Hollywood Bowl Orchestra); Steven Mercurio (Opera Co. of Philadelphia); Christof Perick (Los Angeles Chamber Orchestra); Paul Salamunovich (Los Angeles Master Chorale); Wolfgang Sawallisch (Philadelphia Orchestra); Christopher Wilkins (San Antonio Symphony Orchestra).

**Educational** Lawrence Foster (director, Aspen Festival and School); Christopher Rouse (Eastman); Alexander Toradze (Indiana University, South Bend).

**Other** Deborah Broda (director, New York Philharmonic Orchestra); Ardis Krainik (president, Opera America); Shulamit Ran (composer-in-residence, Chicago Symphony Orchestra).

### J. Honors and Awards

**Honors** Maurice Abravanel (National Medal of Arts); John Corigliano and Ezra Laderman (American Academy); Gian Carlo Menotti (*Musical America's* Musician of the Year); Majorie Merryman (Hinrichsen); Gunther Schuller (MacArthur Fellow); Ralph Shapey and William Kraft (Friedheim); Robert Shaw (Kennedy Center Honors); Nicolas Slonimsky (American Academy and Institute).

**Awards** Pavel Berman (Indianapolis); Yefim Bronfman (Avery Fisher); Hans Choi and Deborah Voigt (Tchaikovsky); Renee Fleming (Tucker); Denyce Graves (Marian Anderson); Tim Tobin (Melchior); Wendy Warner (Rostropovich).

**K. Biographical** The New Orleans Symphony Orchestra is discontinued due to financial problems.

### L. Musical Beginnings

**Educational** Leonard Bernstein Center for Education Through the Arts (Nashville).

**Other** Broward Center for the Performing Arts (Fort Lauderdale); Gilmore Artist Award (Kalamazoo); Singers Development Foundation.

### M. Music Publications

Booth, John E., *The Critic, Power, and the Performing Arts*

Cope, David, *Computer Analysis of Musical Style*
Kivy, Peter, *Sound and Semblance: Reflections on Musical Representation*
McClary, Susan, *Power and Desire in Seventeenth-Century Music—Feminine Endings: Music, Gender and Sexuality*
Narmour, Eugene, *The Analysis and Cognition of Melodic Complexity*
Tawa, Nicholas E., *The Coming of Age of American Art Music*

### N. Musical Compositions

**Chamber Music**  Milton Babbitt, *None but the Lonely Flute*; Gerald Berg, *Odd Trio* (violin, marimba, guitar); Elliott Carter, *Scrivo in vento* (solo flute); Donald Erb, *Drawing Down the Moon* (piccolo and percussion); Barbara Feldman, *Pure Difference*; Maurice Gardner, *Piano Quintet*; Richard Hervig, *Off Center*; Stephen Jaffe, *String Quartet No. 1*; Joan La Barbara, *Awakenings*; Libby Larsen, *Quartet Schoenberg, Schenker, Schillinger*; Nicholas Maw, *Piano Trio*; Tobias Picker, *Invisible Lilacs*; Ned Rorem, *String Quartet No. 3*; Harold Schiffman, *Rhapsody for Guitar*; Chinary Ung, *String Quartet No. 1*; Robert Vodnoy, *Suite for Unaccompanied Violin*.

**Choral/Vocal**  David Diamond, *Psalm 98*; Pauline Oliveros, *In Memoriam Mr. Whitney*; Daniel Pinkham, *Advent Cantata*; Ralph Shapey, *Centennial Celebration*; Charles Wuorinen, *A Winter's Tale* (soprano and six instruments).

**Concertos**  Emma Lou Diemer, *Piano Concerto*; John Harbison, *Oboe Concerto*; Jean Eichelberger Ivey, *Voyager* (cello and orchestra); Ezra Laderman, *Piano Concerto No. 2*; Libby Larsen, *Piano Concerto: Since Armstrong*; Lowell Liebermann, *Piano Concerto No. 2*; Andrzej Panufnik, *Cello Concerto*; Stephen Paulus, *Trumpet Concerto—Organ Concerto*; Tobias Picker, *Viola Concerto*; Ned Rorem, *Piano Concerto for the Left Hand*; Christopher Rouse, *Violin Concerto*; Joseph Schwantner, *Concerto for Percussionist and Orchestra*; Ralph Shapey, *Concerto Fantastique*; Michael Torke, *Piano Concerto*; Richard Wilson, *Piano Concerto*; Ellen Taaffe Zwilich, *Oboe Concerto*.

**Electronic**  Larry Austin, *La Barbara: The Name, the Sounds, the Music*; Roger Reynolds, *The Ivanov Suite—Versions/Stages*; Neil Rolnick, *ElectriCity* (sextet and electronics); Morton Subotnick, *All My Hummingbirds Have Alibis*.

**Operas**  John Adams, *The Death of Klinghoffer*; John Corigliano, *The Ghosts of Versailles*; Ulysses Kay, *Frederick Douglass*; Robert Moran, *From the Towers of the Moon*; Gerard J. Pape, *Weaveworld*; Roger Reynolds, *The Bacchae*.

**Orchestra/Band**  John Adams, *El Dorado* (orchestra); Elliott Carter, *Anniversary*; Michael Colgrass, *Arctic Dreams* (band); Donald Erb, *Ritual Observances*; Edward Knight, *Big Shoulders* (Rudolf Nissim Award); Libby Larsen, *Ghosts of an Old Ceremony*; Peter Lieberson, *World's Turning*; Otto Luening, *Symphonic Fantasia*; Wayne Peterson, *The Face of the Night, The Heart of the Dark* (Pulitzer Prize); Bernard Rands, *Ceremonial 3*; Roberto Sierra, *Tropicalia*; Robert Ward, *Byways of Memories*.

**Piano/Organ**  Milton Babbitt, *Preludes, Interludes and Postlude*; William Bolcom, *Recuerdos* (two pianos); Emma Lou Diemer, *Three Pieces*; Ross Lee Finney, *Narrative in Argument*; Dan Steven Locklair, *Voyage* (organ); Donald Martino, *Twelve Preludes;* Frederic Rzewski, *Ludes—Sonata*.

**Symphonies**  Leslie Bassett, *Concerto for Orchestra*; Henri Lazarof, *Symphony No. 2*; Marc Neikrug, *Symphony No. 1*; David Ott, *Symphony No. 2*; George Perle, *Sinfonietta II*; Joan Tower, *Concerto for Orchestra*; Dan Welcher, *Symphony No. 1*.

# 1992

✸

## Historical Highlights

Bill Clinton is elected the 42nd president; R. H. Macy and Co. and TWA. file for bankruptcy; a House bank scandal involving over 300 in Congress arouses the ire of the nation; a break in the tunnel system under the river floods the basements of downtown Chicago; fighting intensifies between Serbs and the Bosnians; Czechoslovakia splits into its two component parts.

## World Cultural Highlights

**World Art**   Georg Baselitz, *More Blondes*; Luigi Carboni, *Shaded Black*; Sandro Chia, *Donna Enigmatica*; Tony Cragg, *Eroded Landscape*.

**World Literature**   Peter Ackroyd, *English Music*; Ian McEwan, *Black Dogs*; Maeve Binchy, *The Copper Beech*; Ben Okri, *The Famished Road*.

**World Music**   Ingvar Lidholm, *Dream Play*; Wolfgang Rihm, *Gesungene Zeit*; Rodion Shchedrin, *Piano Concerto No. 4;* Alfred Schnittke, *Life with an Idiot*; John Tavener, *We Shall See Him as He Is*.

**Miscellaneous**   Krzysztof Penderecki wins the Grawemeyer Award; deaths include Francis Bacon, Günther Bialas, Geraint Evans, José Guerrero, Charles Groves, William Mathias, Olivier Messiaen, John Piper, Jean Poiret, and Eberhard Wächter.

## American Art and Literature Highlights

**Births/Deaths**   Deaths include art figures Robert Arneson, Peter Blume, Aaron Bohrod, James Brooks, David Hare, Richard Pousette-Dart, David Von Schlegell, and literary figures Isaac Asimov, Kay Boyle, Laurie Colwin, Louise Field Cooper, Pietro Di Donato, Alex Haley, Walt Morey, and Joseph Yates.

**Art Works**   Richard Artschwager, *Door/Door*; Patry Denton, *Playin' Marbles*; Eric Fischl, *Dog, Boy and Woman*; Janet Fish, *Bait*; Jasper Johns, *Mirror's Edge*; Jack Levine, *On the Block*; Roy Lichtenstein, *Interior with Skyline*; Jules Olitski, *Dark Delilah*; Philip Pearlstein, *Entrance to Lincoln Tunnel*; James Rosenquist, *Gift Wrapped Doll*; Esteban Vicente, *Song*; Jamie Wyeth, *Bi-Coastal*.

**Literature**   Robert Butler, *A Good Scent from a Strange Mountain* (Pulitzer Prize); Clarissa Estes, *Women Who Run with Wolves*; Louise Gluck, *The Wild Iris* (Pulitzer Prize); Tony Kushner, *Angels in America: Millennium Approaches* (Pulitzer Prize—Tony—New York Drama Critics' Award); Toni Morrison, *Jazz*; Susan Sontag, *The Volcano Lover*; Wendy Wasserstein, *The Sisters Rosensweig*.

## Music—The Vernacular/Commercial Scene

**B. Deaths**   Roy Acuff (singer) November 23; Ed Blackwell (drummer) October 7; Red Callender (string bass/tuba player) March 8; Junior Cook (saxophonist) February 3; James "Thunderbird" Davis (singer/guitarist) January 24; Willie Dixon (singer/string bassist) January 29; Alfred Drake (singer) July 25; Jack Dupree (pianist) January 21; Allan Jones (singer) June 27; Albert King (guitarist/singer); Andy Kirk (bandleader) December 11; Roger Miller (singer/writer) October 25; Mary Osborne (guitarist) March 3; Sammy Price (pianist) April 14; Andy Russell (singer) April 16; Sylvia Syms (singer) May 10; Charlie Ventura (saxophonist/bandleader) January 17; Lawrence Welk (bandleader) May 17; Mary Wells (singer) July 26.

**C. Biographical**

**Performing Groups**   Belly; Porno for Pyros.

**Honors**   Garth Brooks (ASCAP Voice of Music Award); Lionel Hampton (Kennedy Center); Minnie Pearl, Earl Scruggs, and Billy Taylor (National Medal of Arts); Max Roach (American Eagle); Stephen Sondheim (National Medal of Arts—refused).

**D. Publications**   Prince Dorough, *Popular-Music Culture in America*; Ted Gioia, *West Coast Jazz: Modern Jazz in California, 1945–1960*; Colin Larkin, ed., *Guinness Encyclopedia of Popular Music*; Burton W. Peretti, *The Creation of Jazz: Music, Race and Culture in Urban America*; Susan Porter, *With an Air Debonair*.

**E. Representative Works**

**Musicals**   Susan Birkenhead (lyrics), *Jelly's Last Jam*; William Finn and James Lapine, *Falsettos*; J.

Kander and F. Ebb, *Kiss of the Spider Woman* (Tony—New York Drama Critics' Award); D. Levine and P. Kellogg, *Anna Karenina*; J. Lunden and A. Perlman, *Wings*; Stephen Sondheim, *Putting It Together*.

**Number One Hits**    *All 4 Love* (Color Me Badd); *Alone With You* (Tevin Campbell); *Baby-Baby-Baby* (TLC); *Baby Got Back* (Sir Mix-a-Lot); *The Best Things in Life Are Free* (Luther Vandross and Janet Jackson); *Black or White* (Michael Jackson); *Boot Scootin' Boogie* (Brooks and Dunn); *Do It to Me* (Lionel Ritchie); *Don't Let the Sun Go Down on Me* (George Michael and Elton John); *End of the Road* (from "Boomerang"—Boyz II Men); *How Do You Talk to an Angel* (The Heights); *If I Didn't Have You* (Randy Travis); *I Will Always Love You* (Whitney Houston); *I'll Be There* (Mariah Carey); *I'm Too Sexy* (Right Said Fred); *I Still Believe in You* (Vince Gill); *Jump* (Kris Kross); *Love's Got a Hold on You* (Alan Jackson); *Real Love* (Mary J. Blige); *The River* (Garth Brooks); *Save the Best for Last* (Vanessa Williams); *This Used to Be My Playground* (Madonna); *To Be With You* (Mr. Big).

**Other**    Dave Brubeck, *Earth Is Our Mother*; Michael Kamen, *Shining Through* (film music); Alan Menken and Tim Rice, *Whole New World* (Oscar); Alan Silvestri, *Ferngully* (film music).

## Music—The Cultivated/Art Music Scene

**G. Deaths**    Stephen Albert (composer) December; Vitya Vronsky Babin (pianist) June 28; John Cage (composer) August 12; Gilbert Chase (critic/musicologist) February 22; Philip Farkas (horn virtuoso) December 21; Andor Foldes (Hungarian-born pianist) February 9; Dorothy Kirsten (soprano) November 18; William Masselos (pianist) October 23; Nathan Milstein (Russian-born violinist) December 21; Stella Roman (Romanian-born soprano) February 12; William Russell (composer); Andrew Schenk (conductor) February 19; William Schuman (composer/administrator) February 15; Henri Temianka (Scottish-born violinist/conductor) November 7; Werner Torkanowsky (conductor) October 20; Roger Wagner (conductor) September 17.

**H. Debuts**

**United States**    Ildebrando D'Arcangelo (Italian bass-baritone), José Azocar (Chilean tenor—Miami), Alexander Baillie (British cellist—Washington, DC), Renate Behle (Austrian soprano—Austin), Heather Dials (mezzo-soprano—Charleston), Elizabeth Futral (soprano—New York), Gegam Grigorian (Armenian tenor—New York), Ilya Kaler (Russian violinist—Newport), Sergei Larin (Lithuanian tenor—San Francisco), François Le Roux (French baritone—San Francisco), Stefan Margita (Czech tenor—Chicago), Michele Pertusi (Italian bass—Chicago), Michel Poulet (French cellist—tour), Shira Rabin (Israeli violinist—Philadelphia), Giuseppe Sabbatini (Italian tenor—Chicago), Mark Wigglesworth (British conductor—Philadelphia).

**Metropolitan Opera**    Raymond Aceto (bass), Vladimir Chernov (Russian baritone), Anne Evans (British soprano), Roberto Frontali (Italian baritone), Kim Josephson (baritone), Ljubov Kazarnovskaya (Russian soprano), Sergei Leiferkus (Russian baritone), Ion Marin (Romanian conductor), Sylvia McNair (soprano), Marie Plette (soprano), Christopher Robertson (baritone), Hao Jiang Tian (Chinese baritone), Veronica Villarroel (Chilean soprano).

**I. New Positions**

**Conductors**    Zuohuang Chen (Rhode Island Philharmonic Orchestra); David Alan Miller (Albany Symphony Orchestra); Donald Runnicles (music director, San Francisco Opera); Esa-Pekka Salonen (Los Angeles Philharmonic Orchestra); Wolfgang Sawallisch (Philadelphia Orchestra).

**Educational**    Marta Casals Istomin (president, Manhattan School of Music); Peter Serkin (piano, Curtis Institute).

**J. Honors and Awards**

**Honors**    Elliott Carter (American Eagle); Leon Fleisher (American Academy of Arts and Sciences); John Harbison and Ellen Taafe Zwilich (American Academy and Institute); Steven Mayer (Liszt Award); Shulamit Ran (Friedheim); Charles Rosen (Peabody Medal); Mstislav Rostropovich (Kennedy Center); Gunther Schuller (MacArthur Fellow); Robert Shaw (National

Medal of Arts—*Musical America's* Musician of the Year); David Tudor (John Cage Award).

**Awards**   Judy Berry (Caruso); Awadagin Pratt (Naumburg); Ruth Ann Swenson (Tucker); Philip Zawisza (Anderson).

**K. Biographical**   Ignace Jan Paderewski's body is returned to his native Warsaw; Awadagin Pratt becomes the first black to win first prize in a major competition; Esa-Pekka Salonen takes the Los Angeles Philharmonic Orchestra to the Salzburg Festival, the first American orchestra to be invited; Jennie Tourel's private papers are donated to the Archives at Boston University.

**L. Musical Beginnings**

**Performing Groups**   Louisiana Philharmonic Orchestra (replaces defunct New Orleans Symphony Orchestra); Overlook Lyric Theatre (Woodstock, New York); Brentanoo String Quartet.

**Other**   Asian American Arts Alliance; Aaron Copland Fund for Music (AMC); Kravis Center for the Performing Arts (West Palm Beach, Florida); Midori Foundation; Music for All Seasons (New Jersey); New England Conservatory/Piatigorsky Artist Award.

**M. Music Publications**

Koohgarian, Richard, *American Orchestral Music: A Performance Catalogue*
Littlejohn, David, *The Ultimate Art: Essays Around and About Opera*
Owen, Harold, *Modal and Tonal Counterpoint: From Josquin to Stravinsky*
Page, Tim, *Music from the Road: Views and Reviews 1978–1992*
Paynter, John, *Sound and Structure*
Sadie, Stanley, ed., *The New Grove Dictionary of Opera*
Steane, John B., *Voices: Singers and Critics*
Tawa, Nicholas E., *Mainstream Music of Early Twentieth Century America*

**N. Musical Compositions**

**Chamber Music**   Robert Ashley, *Outcome Inevitable*; Earl Brown, *Tracking Pierrot* (violin and piano); Elliott Carter, *Trilogy—Quintet for Piano and Winds*; John Cage, *13*; James Cohn, *Wind Quintet No. 2*; Emma Lou Diemer, *Sextet*; Stephen Jaffe, *Pedal Point*; Wayne Peterson, *String Quartet No. 2*; Ralph Shapey, *Trio Concertante* (violin, piano, percussion)—*Trio 1992* (violin, cello, piano); Robert Wernick, *Saxophonist Quartet*; Charles Wuorinen, *Saxophonist Quartet*.

**Choral/Vocal**   Leonardo Balada, *Thunderous Scenes*; Mario Castelnuovo-Tedesco, *Coplas* (song cycle); Richard Danielpour, *Sonnets to Orpheus*; Barbara Feldman, *Infinite Other* (chorus and chamber group); John Harbison, *The Rewaking* (soprano and string quartet); Meyer Kupferman, *Ice Cream Concerto*; Lowell Lieberman, *A Poet to His Beloved*; Steven MacKay, *Physical Property* (soprano and electric guitar); André Previn, *Honey and Rue* (song cycle); Robert Starer, *Nishmat Adam* (song cycle).

**Concertos**   Paul Chihara, *Violin Concerto*; Donald Erb, *Violin Concerto*; John Harbison, *Oboe Concerto*; Andrew Imbrie, *Piano Concerto No. 3*; Leon Kirchner, *Cello Concerto*; Lowell Liebermann, *Piano Concerto No. 2—Flute Concerto*; George Perle, *Piano Concerto No. 2*; Christopher Rouse, *Trombone Concerto* (Pulitzer Prize)—*Cello Concerto*; Lalo Schifrin, *Concerto of the Americas* (piano and orchestra); Roberto Sierra, *Of Discoveries* (two guitars and orchestra); David Soldier, *Ultraviolet Railroad* (violin, cello, and orchestra); Augusta Read Thomas, *Triple Concerto . . . night's midsummer blaze* (flute, viola, harp—Nissim Prize); Joan Tower, *Violin Concerto*; Chinary Ung, *Triple Concerto*; Ellen Taaffe Zwilich, *Flute Concerto*.

**Electronic**   Mario Davidovsky, *Synchronisms No. 10*; John Eaton, *Genesis*; Richard Karpen, *Denouement*; Tod Machover, *Bounce*; Gerard Pape, *Varesia Variations—Prélude Electronique*; David Tudor, *Neural Syntheses 6–9*.

**Operas**   Leonardo Balada, *The Death of Columbus;* William Bolcom, *McTeague*; Anthony Davis, *Tania*; Philip Glass, *The Voyage*; Robert Greenleaf, *Under the Arbor*; Meyer Kupferman, *The Proscenium*; Libby Larsen, *A Wrinkle in Time*; Meredith Monk, *Atlas*; Robert Moran, *Desert of Roses*; Robert X. Rodriguez, *Frida: The Story of Frida Kahlo*; Bright Sheng, *The Song of Majnun*; Gil Trythall, *The Pastimes of Lord Caitanya*.

**Orchestra/Band**    Henry Brant, *500: Hidden Hemisphere* (four bands and steel band); Margaret Buechner, *The American Civil War*; Curtis Curtis-Smith, *Piano Trio No. 2*; John Eaton, *Peer Gynt Music*; Donald Harris, *Mermaid Variations*; Anthony Ianaccone, *Night Rivers*; Libby Larsen, *The Atmosphere as a Fluid System*; Stephen MacKay, *TILT*; Gary Powell Nash, *In Memoriam: Sojourner Truth*; Daniel Pinkham, *Overture Concertante*; Mel Powell, *Settings for Small Orchestra*; Terry Riley, *The Sands*.

**Piano/Organ**    William Albright, *Flights of Fancy* (organ); Richard Danielpour, *Enchanted Garden*; Emme Lou Diemer, *Four Biblical Settings* (organ); Tod Machover, *Bounce*.

**Symphonies**    Daniel Asia, *Symphony No. 3, "Celebration"*; Leonardo Balada, *Symphony No. 4, "Lausanne"*; Irwin Bazelon, *Symphony No. 9, "Sunday Silence";* David Diamond, *Symphony No. 11*; Philip Glass, *Low Symphony*; Anthony Ianaccone, *Symphony No. 3, "Night Rivers"*; Witold Lutoslawski, *Symphony No. 4*; David Ott, *Symphony No. 3*; Daniel Pinkham, *Christmas Symphony*; Augusta Read Thomas, *Symphony No. 1, "Air and Angels"*; Ellen Taaffe Zwilich, *Symphony No. 3*.

# 1993

☀

## Historical Highlights

Some of the worst flooding in US history takes place in the midwest during the summer months—estimated damages over 12 billion dollars; the Branch Davidian cult in Waco, Texas, comes to a fiery end following an FBI standoff; the World Trade building in New York City is bombed by Arab terrorists; Republicans win big in several state elections; the Brady Gun Bill is signed into law.

## World Cultural Highlights

**World Art**    Sandro Chia, *Prisonnier Jaune, Vert, Bleu*; Antony Gormley, *Testing a World View*; Marcus Lüpertz, *The Warrior*; Arturo Rivera, *Stabat Mater II*; Hervé Télémaque, *L'ile aux nègres*.

**World Literature**    Roddy Doyle, *Paddy Clarke Ha Ha Ha*; Vikram Seth, *A Suitable Boy*; Tom Stoppard, *Arcadia*; Banana Yoshimoto, *Kitchen*.

**World Music**    Harrison Birtwistle, *Antiphonies*; Sofia Gubaidulina, *String Quartet No. 4*; Hans Werner Henze, *Symphony No. 8*; Nicholas Maw, *Violin Concerto*; Alfred Schnittke, *Symphony No. 7*.

**Miscellaneous**    Deaths include William Pène du Bois, Anthony Burgess, Boris Cristoff, William Golding, Erich Leinsdorf, Rudolf Nureyev, and Robert Westall.

## American Art and Literature Highlights

**Births/Deaths**    Deaths include art figures Peter Agostini, Richard Diebenkorn, Carl Morris, Lowell Nesbitt, Leo Smith, and literary figures John Ashworth, Nina Berberova, Robert Crichton, Peter DeVries, James Leo Herlihy, John Hersey, Irving Howe, Margaret Landon, and Wallace E. Stegner.

**Art Works**    Alice Aycock, *Some Night Action*; Will Barnet, *Three Chairs*; Marc Solomon Dennis, *Playing a Trick on the Elk (Religion)*; Jim Dine, *Gold*; Glenna Goodacre, *Vietnam Women's Memorial*; Nancy Grimes, *Allegory of Touch*; John MacCracken, *Universe Treasure*; Malcolm Morley, *Icarus*; Robert Rauschenberg, *Bicycloid VI*; Frank Stella, *The Town-Ho's Story*.

**Literature**    Mark Doty, *My Alexandria* (National Book Critics' Award); Thomas King, *Green Grass, Running Water*; Tony Kushner, *Angels in America: Perestroika* (Tony); Mary Oliver, *New and Selected Poems* (National Book Award); E. Annie Proulx, *The Shipping News* (National Book Award—Pulitzer Prize); May Sarton, *Collected Poems*; Neil Simon, *Laughter on the 23rd Floor*.

## Music—The Vernacular/Commercial Scene

**B. Deaths**    Arthur Alexander (singer) June 9; Sammy Cahn (lyricist) January 15; John Campbell (singer/guitarist) June 13; Albert Collins (guitarist/singer) November 24; Bob Crosby (bandleader)

March 9; Johnny Cymbal (songwriter) March 15; Thomas A. Dorsey ("father" of gospel music) January 23; Billy Eckstine (singer/bandleader) March 8; "Dizzy" Gillespie (trumpeter/bandleader) January 6; Erskine Hawkins (trumpeter/bandleader) November 11; David Houston (singer) November 30; Marv Johnson (singer) May 15; Helen O'Connell (singer) September 9; Mitchell Parish (lyricist) March 31; Sun Ra (Herman Blount—pianist/bandleader) May 30; Harold Rome (songwriter) October 26; Ann Ronell (songwriter) December 25; Johnny Sayles (singer) August 17; James "Son" Thomas (guitarist/singer) June 26; Al Trace (bandleader/writer) August 31; Luther Tucker (guitarist) June 17; Conway Twitty (singer) June 5; June Valli (singer) March 12; Bernie Wayne (composer); Frank Zappa (bandleader/composer) December 4.

### C. Biographical

**Performing Groups**   Smoking Popes; Xscape.

**New Beginnings**   Marshall Vente Jazz Festival (Chicago).

**Honors**   Dizzy Gillespie (American Academy); Lena Horne (American Eagle); Willy Nelson (Country Music Hall of Fame), Stephen Sondheim (Kennedy Center); Marion Williams (MacArthur Fellow—Kennedy Center).

**Miscellaneous**   Ella Fitzgerald loses both legs to complications of diabetes; Michael Jackson is charged with child molestation, but settles out of court.

**D. Publications**   M. A. Bufwach and R. K. Oermann, *Finding Her Voice: The Saga of Women in Country Music*; Lawrence Cohn, *Nothing But the Blues*; Ross Firestone, *Swing, Swing, Swing: The Life and Times of Benny Goodman;* David Lee Joyner, *American Popular Music*; William H. Kenney, *Chicago Jazz: A Cultural History, 1904–1930*; M. McKee and F. Chisenhall, *Beale Street Black and Blue: Life and Music on Black America's Main Street*; M. Roberts, *Romance, Swing and the Blues*; M. Tucker, *The Duke Ellington Reader*; Robert Walser, *Running with the Devil: Power, Gender and Madness in Heavy Metal Music*.

### E. Representative Works

**Musicals**   Flaherty and Ahrens, *My Favorite Year*; Hamlisch and Zippel, *The Goodbye Girl*; Jule Styne, *The Red Shoes*; Andrew Lloyd Webber, *Sunset Boulevard*; Monk Rowe, *Cheeks* (Dizzy Gillespie tribute); Willy Russell, *Blood Brothers* (United States premiere); Carly Simon, *Romulus Hunt* (pop "opera"); C. Strouse and T. Meehan, *Annie Warbucks*.

**Number One Hits**   *Again—That's the Way Love Goes* (Janet Jackson); *Ain't Going Down (Til the Sun Comes Up)—That Summer* (Garth Brooks); *Alibis* (Tracy Lawrence); *Can I Trust You with My Heart?* (Travis Tritt); *Can't Help Falling In Love* (from "Sliver"—UB40); *Chattahoochee* (Alan Jackson); *Dreamlover—Hero* (Mariah Carey); *Easy Come, Easy Go* (George Strait); *Freak Me* (Silk); *Gangsta Lean* (DRS); *Hip Hop Hooray* (Naughty by Nature); *I Will Always Love You* (from "Bodyguard"—Whitney Houston); *Informer* (Snow); *I'd Do Anything for Love (But I Won't Do That)* (Meat Loaf); *Just Kickin' It* (Xscape); *Knockin' Da Boots* (H Town); *Lately* (Jodeci); *Right Here (Human Nature)—Weak* (SWV); *Should've Been a Cowboy* (Toby Keith); *What Part of Me* (Lorrie Morgan); *When My Ship Comes In* (Clint Black).

**Other**   Bruce Broughton, *Tombstone* (film music); Ry Cooder, *Geronimo* (film music); Marcus Roberts, *Romance, Swing and the Blues*; John Williams, *Jurassic Park* (film music).

## Music—The Cultivated/Art Music Scene

**G. Deaths**   Maurice Abravanel (conductor) September 22; Marian Anderson (contralto) April 8; Arleen Augér (soprano) June 10; Patricia Brooks (soprano) January 22; Agnes de Mille (ballet choreographer) October 7; Kenneth Gaburo (composer/writer) January 26; Szymon Goldberg (violinist/conductor) July 20; Brian Hilt (tenor) April 6; Mieczyslaw Horszowski (Polish-born pianist—age 100) May 22; Carlos Montoya (guitarist) March 3; Rudolf Nureyev (Russian-born ballet star) January 6; Kevin Oldham (composer) March 12; William Parker (baritone) March 29; Marko Rothmüller (Yugoslavian-born baritone) January 20; Alexander Schneider (violinist/conductor) February 2; Italo Tajo (Italian-born bass) March 29; Jess Thomas (tenor) October 11; Tatiana Troyanos (mezzo-soprano) August 21; Alice Tully (soprano/art patron).

## H. Debuts

**United States**   Roberto Aronica (Italian tenor—San Francisco), Cecilia Bartoli (Italian mezzo-soprano—Houston), Jeffrey Black (Australian baritone—Los Angeles), Anne Bolstad (Norwegian soprano—Omaha), Olga Borodina (Russian mezzo-soprano—New York), Sally Burgess (South African mezzo-soprano—Portland, Oregon), Joseph Cornwell (British tenor—Boston), Cristina Gallardo-Domas (Chilean soprano—Philadelphia), Sonia Ganassi (Italian mezzo-soprano—Washington, DC), Wolfgang Holzmair (Austrian baritone—New York), Michiyoshi Inoue (Japanese conductor—Chicago), Mari Krikorian (Bulgarian soprano—Los Angeles), Solveig Kringelborn (Norwegian soprano—Los Angeles), Marjana Lipovsek (Slovenian contralto—Chicago), Vardan Mamikonian (Armenian pianist—New York), Alastair Miles (British bass—San Francisco), Elisabeth Norberg-Schulz (Norwegian soprano—Chicago), Simone Pedroni (Italian pianist—Pasadena), Alfredo Perl (Chilean pianist—Florida), Awagadin Pratt (pianist—Chicago), Carlo Rizzi (Italian conductor—Chicago), Christian Tetzlaff (German violinist—New York), Isabelle Vernet (French mezzo-soprano—Chicago).

**Metropolitan Opera**   Simone Alaimo (Italian bass), Fabio Armilliato (Italian tenor), Vladimir Atlantov (Russian tenor), Elizabeth Carter (soprano), Tiziana Fabbricini (Italian soprano), Angela Gheorghiu (Romanian soprano), Eric Halfvarson (bass), Matthias Hölle (German bass), Kristján Jóhannson (Icelandic soprano), Vincenzo La Scola (Italian tenor), Thomas Moser (tenor), Helmut Pampuch (German tenor), Françoise Pollet (French soprano), Carlo Rizzi (Italian conductor), Michael Schade (Canadian tenor), Wolfgang Schmidt (German tenor), Peter Seiffert (German tenor), Nina Warren (soprano), Carol Yahr (soprano).

## I. New Positions

**Conductors**   Sixten Ehrling (orchestras, Manhattan School of Music); Vjekoslav Sutej (Houston Grand Opera).

**Educational**   Bruce MacCombie (dean, Boston University School of the Arts); David Starobin (guitar, Manhattan School of Music).

**Other**   Graeme Jenkins (music director, Dallas Opera); Regina Resnik (president, American Guild of Musical Artists).

## J. Honors and Awards

**Honors**   Dominick Argento (OPERA America Award); William Bolcom (American Academy); Karel Husa (Grawemeyer); Marilyn Horne and Robert Shaw (Medal of Arts); Kurt Masur (*Musical America's* Musician of the Year); Roberta Peters (American Eagle); George Solti (Kennedy Center).

**Awards**   Jerry Hadley (Callas); Steven Isserlis (Piatigorsky); Nancy Maultsby (Marian Anderson); Leon McCawley (Beethoven); Ruth Ann Swenson (Tucker); Christopher Taylor (Cliburn Third); Deborah Voigt (Tucker).

**K. Biographical**   Maurice Abravanel has the Salt Lake City Music Hall renamed in his honor; Hobart Earle brings the Odessa Symphony Orchestra of the Ukraine on its first American tour; Gilbert Levine brings the Cracow Philharmonic Orchestra on its first US tour; Christa Ludwig makes her final appearances at the Metropolitan Opera and Carnegie Hall; while at the Salzburg Festival, Anne Manson becomes the first woman to conduct the Vienna Philharmonic; the Swedish Folksopers makes its US debut in Brooklyn; composer Jerry Williams and lyricists Dave Vest and Glenn Warren receive the one million dollar contest prize for a new national anthem (*America, My America*).

## L. Musical Beginnings

**Performing Groups**   Pocket Opera Co. (Chicago).

**Other**   American Friends of the Kirov Maryinsky Theater (New York); John and Irving Harris Concert Hall (Aspen); Stanley C. Harrison Opera House (renovation of USO center for Virginia Opera); Ivo Pogorelich International Piano Competition (Pasadena, California).

## M. Music Publications

Aiello, Rita and Sloboda, J., *Musical Perceptions*
Brooks, Iris, ed., *New Music Across America*

Dizikes, John, *Opera in America: A Cultural History* (National Book Critics' Award)
Hiley, David, *Western Plainchant, A Handbook*
James, Jamie, *The Music of the Spheres: Music, Science and the Natural Order of Things*
Schwartz, E. and Godfrey, D., *Music Since 1945: Issues, Materials and Literature*

**N. Musical Compositions**

**Chamber Music**    Gavin Bryar, *Three Elegies for Nine Clarinets*; Stephen Jaffe, *Triptych* (piano and woodwind quintet); Victoria Jordanova, *Four Preludes for Harp—Variations for Harp*; Meyer Kupferman, *Chaconne Sonata* (flute and piano); Tod Machover, *Forever and Ever* (hyperviolin and chamber group); Frederic Rzewski, *Crusoe* (percussion, keyboard, and woodwinds); Ralph Shapey, *Dinosaur Annex*; Leon Stein, *Quintet for Clarinet and String Quartet*.

**Choral/Vocal**    Paul Dresher, *Awed Behavior*; Bernard Rands, *Songs of the Eclipse*; Roger Reynolds, *Odyssey*; David Soldier, *War Prayer*; Robert Ward, *Songs for Ravenscroft*; Howard Whitaker, *Prayers of Habakkuk*; Olly Wilson, *I Shall Not Be Moved*.

**Concertos**    John Adams, *Violin Concerto*; William Bolcom, *Lyric Concerto for Flute and Orchestra*; John Corigliano, *Troubadours* (guitar and orchestra); Richard Danielpour, *Piano Concerto No. 2—Metamorphosis for Piano and Orchestra*; Karel Husa, *Violin Concerto*; William Thomas McKinley, *Concert Variations for Violin, Viola and Orchestra—Viola Concerto No. 3*; Ned Rorem, *English Horn Concerto*; Christopher Rouse, *Cello Concerto—Flute Concerto*; Charles Wuorinen, *Concerto for Saxophonist Quartet*; Ellen Taaffe Zwillich, *Bassoon Concerto  Horn Concerto*.

**Electronic**    Gerard Pape, *Two Electro-Acoustic Songs*; Diane Thome, *The Palaces of Memory* (tape and chamber ensemble).

**Operas**    Dominick Argento, *The Dream of Valentine*; David Carlson, *The Midnight Angel*; Conrad Cummings, *Tonkin*; Philip Glass, *Orphée*; Daron Aric Hagen, *Shining Brow* (opera); William Harper, *El Greco*; Bern Herbolsheimer, *Mark Me Twain*; Ezra Laderman, *Marilyn*; Libby Larsen, *Mrs. Dalloway*; Frank Lewin, *Burning Bright*; Gian Carlo Menotti, *Singing Child*; Steve Reich, *The Cave*; James Sellars, *The World Is Round*; Morton Subotnick, *Jacob's Room*; Robert Ward, *Roman Fever*; Lawrence Widdoes, *How to Make Love*; Frank Zappa, *Civilization, Phaze III* (opera-pantomime).

**Orchestra/Band**    Leonardo Balada, *Music for Oboe and Orchestra*; Elliott Carter, *Partita*; John Harbison, *Gli accordi piu usati* (chamber orchestra); Shulamit Ran, *Legends*; Bernard Rands, *. . . where the Murmurs die . . .*; Carlos Surinach, *Symphonic Melismas*; Frank Tichel, *Radiant Voices*.

**Piano/Organ**    Jonathan Kramer, *Notta Sonata* (with percussion); Gunther Schuller, *Sonata/Fantasia*; Joan Tower, *Stepping Stones* (two pianos).

**Symphonies**    Leslie Bassett, *Concerto for Symphony Orchestra*; Brian Fennelly, *A Thoreau Symphony*; Henri Lazarof, *Symphony No. 2*; Bernard Rands, *Symphony*; Roger Reynolds, *Symphony, "The Stages of Life."*

# 1994

❁

## Historical Highlights

A major earthquake strikes Los Angeles; CIA official Aldrich Ames is arrested for spying; four defendants are found guilty and sentenced in the World Trade Center bombing; former president Richard Nixon dies; thousands die in Rwandan bloodbath; Israel and the Palestinians sign accord; the English Channel Tunnel is inaugurated; Haitian leaders agree to leave and allow President Aristide to return to power.

## World Cultural Highlights

**World Art**    Luigi Carboni, *Gold Oxidation*; Stefano Di Stasio, *The Coordinates of Solitaire*; Joan Giordano, *Guardian*; George Pusenkoff, *Strong Feelings*; David Schluss, *Trio*.

**World Literature**   Thomas Flanagan, *The End of the Hunt*; V. S. Naipaul, *A Way in the World*; Salman Rushdie, *East, West*.

**World Music**   Peter Maxwell Davies, *Symphony No. 5*; Jost Meier, *The Dreyfus Affair;* Alfred Schnittke, *Symphony No. 8*; Judith Weir, *Blond Eckbert*; John Tavener, *The Apocalypse*.

**Miscellaneous**   The Tel Aviv Opera House and the Gothenburg Opera House open; deaths include Pierre Boulle, James Clavell, Norman Del Mar, Paul Delvaux, Gottlob Frick, and Eugene Ionesco.

## American Art and Literature Highlights

**Births/Deaths**   Deaths include art figures Dorothy Dehner, Sam Francis, Alexander Hogue, Donald C. Judd, John Rewald, Sylvia R. Weis, Carolyn Wyeth, and literary figures Robert Bloch, Cleanth Brooks, Amy Clampitt, Ralph Waldo Ellison, and Peter Taylor.

**Art Works**   John Alexander, *The Conversation*; Anthony Caro, *Halifax Steps-Spirals*; Laurie Fendrich, *Screaming Mimi's*; William King, *Harmonia*; Roy Lichtenstein, *Nude with Blue Hair*; Melissa Meyer, *Blame It on My Youth*; Malcolm Morley, *Salvonia*; James Rosenquist, *Military Intelligence*; Kiki Smith, *Mary Magdalene*; Frank Stella, *Ohonoo*; Mark Tansey, *Landscape*.

**Literature**   Edward Albee, *Three Tall Women* (Pulitzer Prize—New York Drama Critics' Award); Richard Condon, *Prizzi's Money*; E. L. Doctorow, *The Waterworks*; David Mamet, *The Village*; Mark Rudman, *Rider* (National Book Critics' Award); Robert Shenkkan, *The Kentucky Cycle* (Pulitzer Prize); Alexander Theroux, *Primary Colors*; John Updike, *The Afterlife and Other Stories*.

## Music—The Vernacular/Commercial Scene

**B. Deaths**   Stanley Adams (lyricist) January 27; Lee Allen (saxophonist) October 26; Danny Barker (guitarist) March 13; Cab Calloway (singer/bandleader) November 18; Kurt Cobain (guitarist/singer) April 8; Dorothy Collins (singer) July 21; Leonard Feather (critic/author) September 22; Walter Kent (songwriter) March 1; Henry Mancini (composer/pianist) June 14; Richard Allen Markowitz (composer) December 6; Carmen McRae (singer) November 10; Dennis Morgan (tenor/actor) September 7; Harry Nilsson (singer/writer) January 15; Dinah Shore (singer) February 24; Ginny Simms (singer) April 4; Willie Mae Ford Smith (gospel singer) February 2; Jule Styne (composer) September 20; Harry Tobias (lyricist) December 15; Earle Warren (saxophonist/singer) June 4; Marion Williams (singer) July 2.

**C. Biographical**

**Performing Groups**   Mighty Blue Kings; Polara.

**New Beginnings**   Skyline Stage, Navy Pier (Chicago).

**Prizes and Honors**   Ornette Coleman and Anthony Braxton (MacArthur Fellows); Aretha Franklin and Pete Seeger (Kennedy Center).

**Miscellaneous**   Marilyn Bergman is unanimously elected president of ASCAP; Barbra Streisand returns to the concert stage after a ten-year absence.

**D. Publications**   Martha Bayles, *The Loss of Beauty and Meaning in American Popular Music*; Paul Berliner, *Thinking in Jazz: The Infinite Art of Improvisation*; Betty Comden, *Off Stage*; David L. Lewis, *The Portable Harlem Renaissance Reader*; Cecelia Tichi, *High Lonesome: The American Culture of Country Music*.

**E. Representative Works**

**Musicals**   Alan Menken, *Beauty and the Beast* (based on the Disney movie); Stephen Sondheim, *Passion* (Tony); Mike Stoller and Jerry Leiber, *Baby, That's Rock 'n Roll*.

**Number One Hits**   *All For Love* (Bryan Adams, Rod Stewart, and Sting); *Any Time, Any Place/And On and On* (Janet Jackson); *Be My Baby Tonight* (John Michael Montgomery); *Bump n' Grind* (B. Kelly); *Can We Talk?* (Tevin Campbell); *Creep* (TLC); *Cry for You* (Jodeci); *Here Comes the Hotstepper* (Ini Kamoze); *Hero* (Mariah Carey); *If the Good Die Young* (Tracy Lawrence); *I Swear* (All-4-One); *I'll Make Love to You—On Bended Knee* (Boyz II Men); *I Wanna Be Down* (Brandy); *Livin' on Love—Summertime Blues* (Alan Jackson); *My Love* (Little Texas); *No Doubt*

*About It—Wink* (Neal McCoy); *The Power of Love* (Celine Dion); *Practice What You Preach* (Barry White); *The Sign* (Ace of Base); *Stay (I Missed You)* (from "Reality Bites"—Lisa Loeb and Nine Stories); *Third Rock from the Sun* (Joe Diffie); *Understanding* (Xscape); *XXX's and OOO's* (Trisha Yearwood).

**Other**  Eliot Goldenthal, *Interview with the Vampire* (film music); Jerry Goldsmith, *The Shadow* (film music); Wynton Marsalis, *In This House, On This Morning*; Ennio Morricone, *Wolf* (film music); Howard Shore, *Philadelphia* (film music); John Williams, *Schindler's List* (film music).

## Music—The Cultivated/Art Music Scene

**G.  Deaths**  Artur Balsam (Polish-born pianist) September 1; William Bergsma (composer) March 18; McHenry Boatwright (baritone) November 8; Gene Boucher (baritone) January 31; Rudolf Firkusny (Czech-born pianist) July 19; Avery Fisher (art patron) February 26; Nicolas Flagello (composer/conductor) March 16; Thomas Fulton (conductor) August 4; Giulio Gari (Romanian-born tenor) April 15; Lejaren Hiller (composer) January 26; Joseph Levine (conductor/pianist) March 23; Samuel Lipman (pianist/critic) December 17; Herva Nelli (Italian-born soprano) May 31; Jarmila Novotna (Czech-born soprano) February 9; Thomas Palmer (baritone) June 11; William Revelli (bandmaster) July 16; Vittorio Rieti (Italian-born composer) February 19; Nicolas Roussakis (composer) October 23; Carlton Sprague Smith (musicologist/librarian) September 19; Ignace Strasfogel (Polish-born conductor/pianist) February 6; David Van Vactor (composer) March 24; Andrea Velis (tenor) October 4.

**H.  Debuts**

**United States**  Mark Anderson (pianist—New York), Barry Banks (British tenor—Chicago), Frederic Chiu (pianist—New York), Jane Eaglen (British soprano—Seattle), David Hobson (Australian tenor—San Francisco), Vladimir Matorin (Russian bass—Chicago), Eldar Nebolsin (pianist—New York), Christiane Oelze (German soprano—Atlanta), Deborah Riedel (Australian soprano—San Diego), Roberto Servile (baritone—San Francisco), Heikki Siukkola (Finnish tenor—Philadelphia).

**Metropolitan Opera**  Alexander Anisimov (Russian bass), Ainhoa Arteta (Spanish soprano), Natalie Dessay (French soprano), Barbara Devers (mezzo-soprano), Vladimir Galouzine (Russian tenor), Galina Gorchakova (Russian soprano), Ann Howard (British mezzo-soprano), Pierre Lefèbvre (Canadian tenor), Mary Mills (soprano), Kent Nagano (conductor), Stefano Palatchi (Spanish bass), Bruno Praticò (Italian bass), Peter Riberi (tenor), Bryn Terfel (Welsh bass), Ramon Vargas (Mexican tenor).

**I.  New Positions**

**Conductors**  Andrew Litton (Dallas Symphony Orchestra); Duain Wolfe (Chicago Symphony Chorus).

**Other**  Luciano Berio (composer-in-residence, Harvard); Shulamit Ran (composer-in-residence, Chicago Lyric Opera); Beverly Sills (chairperson, Lincoln Center).

**J.  Honors and Awards**

**Honors**  Morton Gould (Kennedy Center); Karel Husa, Steve Reich and Robert Starer (American Academy); Christa Ludwig (*Musical America's* Musician of the Year); Gerhard Samuel (Ditson Award); Hugo Weisgall (Academy Gold Medal).

**Awards**  Mark Anderson (Kapell); Nicholas Angelich (Bachauer); Russell Braun (George London); Patrick Denniston (James McCracken); Juliette Kang (Indianapolis); Kevin Kenner (Chopin); Jennifer Larmore and Marie Plette (Tucker); Emily Magee (MacAllister); Garrick Ohlsson (Avery Fisher); Earle Patriarco (Nilsson); Patricia Racette (Marian Anderson); Theresa Santiago (Naumburg); Karen Slack (Ponselle).

**K.  Biographical**  Kathleen Battle is fired by the Metropolitan Opera because of her temperamental actions; Carlo Bergonzi gives his farewell concert in Carnegie Hall in April; James Levine announces his resignation as head of Chicago's Ravinia Festival and Christoph Eschenbach is named as his replacement; Andrew Litton takes his Bournemouth Symphony Orchestra on its first-ever tour of the United States; the Swedish Folk Opera (founded 1976) makes its US debut in New York; Andrius Zlabys (Lithuanian pianist) comes to Interlochen for further music study.

**L. Musical Beginnings**

**Performing Groups**   Ensemble Kalinda Chicago.

**Other**   Broward Center for the Performing Arts (Fort Lauderdale); Electronic Music Foundation (Albany); Morton Gould Award (ASCAP); Gerda Lissner Foundation; Seiji Ozawa Hall (Tanglewood).

**M. Music Publications**

Jellinek, George, *History Through the Opera Glass*
La Rue, C. Steven, *International Dictionary of Opera*
Plotkin, Fred, *Opera 101: A Complete Guide to Learning and Loving Opera*
Rorem, Ned, *Knowing When to Stop: A Memoir*
Rosen, Charles, *The Frontiers of Meaning: Three Informal Lectures on Music*

**N. Musical Compositions**

**Chamber Music**   Easley Blackwood, *Clarinet Sonata in A Minor, Opus 37—Sonatina for Piccolo Clarinet, Opus 38*; Maurice Gardner, *String Quartet No. 2*; James MacMillan, *Kiss on Wood* (violin and piano); Joan Tower, *Night Fields* (string quartet)—*Très lent, "In Memoriam Olivier Messiaen"* (cello and piano); Charles Wuorinen, *Piano Quintet*.

**Choral/Vocal**   William Bolcom, *Let Evening Come* (cantata); Richard Danielpour, *Songs to Orpheus*; John Harbison, *Chorale Cantata*; Dorothy Lang, *Life Cycle*; Dan Locklair, *Brief Mass*; Roger Reynolds, *Last things, I think, to think about . . .* ; Ned Rorem, *Songs of Sadness*.

**Concertos**   John Adams, *Violin Concerto* (Grawemeyer Prize); Chen Yi, *Piano Concerto*; Richard Danielpour, *Cello Concerto*; Lukas Foss, *Piano Concerto for the Left Hand*; John Harbison, *Cello Concerto*; Leon Kirchner, *Music for Cello and Orchestra* (Friedheim Award); Thomas Ludwig, *Violin Concerto*; David Ott, *Piano Concerto*; Stephen Paulus, *Double Concerto, "The Veil of Illusion"*; Gunther Schuller, *Organ Concerto*; Joseph Schwantner, *Concerto for Percussion*; Steven Stucky, *Double Flute Concerto*; Michael Torke, *Guitar Concerto*; Dan Welcher, *Piano Concerto, "Shiva's Drums"*; Ellen Taaffe Zwilich, *American Concerto* (trumpet and orchestra)—*Double Concerto* (violin and cello).

**Electronic**   Diane Thome, *Masks of Eternity*.

**Operas**   Jack Beeson, *Cyrano*; Philip Glass, *La Belle et la Bête* (to accompany the Jean Cocteau film); Tania León, *Scourge of Hyacinths*; Robert Moran, *The Dracula Diary*; Thea Musgrave, *Simón Bolívar*; Bruce Saylor, *Orpheus Descending*; Eric Stokes, *Apollonia's Circus*; Conrad Susa, *Dangerous Liaisons*; Augusta Read Thomas, *Ligeia*; Stewart Wallace, *Harvey Milk*.

**Orchestra/Band**   Morton Gould, *Stringmusic* (Pulitzer Prize); Barbara Kolb, *All in Good Time*; Dan Locklair, *Hues for Orchestra*; Fred Lerdahl, *Quiet Music*; Stephen Mackay, *Eating Greens*; Nicholas Maw, *Odyssey*; Michael Torke, *Javelin*; Joan Tower, *Duets*.

**Symphonies**   Peter Alexander, *Symphony No. 1* (Rudolf Nissim Prize); Philip Glass, *Symphony No. 2*; Gerald Levinson, *Symphony No. 2*; Christopher Rouse, *Symphony No. 2*; Richard Wernick, *Symphony No. 2*.

# 1995

☀

## Historical Highlights

A car bomb blows up a federal building in downtown Oklahoma City, killing 167 people; Timothy McVeigh and Terry Nichols are indicted for the blast; Bosnians, Croats, and Serbs begin peace talks—United States troops enter Bosnia; Russian troops enter the breakaway state of Chechnya;

leaders of Egypt, Israel, Jordan, and the PLO begin peace talks in Cairo; Israeli Prime Minister Yitzhak Rabin is assassinated.

## World Cultural Highlights

**World Art**   Richard Deacon, *Beauty and the Beast*; Markus Lüpertz, *Odalisque*; Annette Messger, *Penetration*.

**World Literature**   Maeve Binchy, *The Glass Lake*; Nicholas Evans, *The Horse Whisperers*; Salman Rushdie, *The Moor's Last Sigh*.

**World Music**   Harrison Birtwistle, *Panic*; Pierre Boulez, *Notations V–VIII*; York Höller, *Aura*; Giya Kancheli, *Lament (in Memory of Luigi Nono)*.

**Miscellaneous**   The Cite de la Musique opens in Paris; deaths include Kingsley Amis, Anatole Fistoulari, Alexander Gibson, James Herriot, Vladimir Maximov, Arturo Benedetti Michelangeli, Vaclav Neumann, Shura Cherkassky, and Ferruccio Tagliavini.

## American Art and Literature Highlights

**Births/Deaths**   Deaths include Ian Ballantine, Stanley Elkin, Charles Gordone, Nancy Graves, Albert Hackett, Paul Horgan, Ray Johnson, Sidney Kingsley, George McNeil, James Ingram Merrill, John Patrick, May Sarton, Irving Shulman, Peter Taylor, Calder Willingham, and Robert Zelazny.

**Art Works**   Jonathan Borofsky, *Man with a Heart*; Louise Bourgeois, *Januarye Addams Tribute* (Chicago); Chuck Close, *Dorothea*; Jim Dine, *Very Picante*; Gregory Green, *Nuclear Device #1*; Richard Hunt, *Steelaway*; Brice Marden, *Daoist Portrait*; Owen Morrel, *Lighthouse*; Catherine Murphy, *Translucent Curtain*; Robert Rauschenberg, *Glacier*; Frank Stella, *Imaginary Places*.

**Literature**   Pat Conroy, *Beach Music*; Horton Foote, *The Young Man from Atlanta* (Pulitzer Prize); John Grisham, *The Rainmaker*; Philip Levine, *Simple Truth*; Terence McNally, *Master Class*; Harold Pinter, *Moonlight*; Carol Shields, *The Stone Diaries* (National Book Critics' Award — Pulitzer Prize); Neil Simon, *London Suite*; Amy Tan, *The Hundred Secret Senses*; Anne Tyler, *Ladder of Years*.

## Music — The Vernacular/Commercial Scene

**B. Deaths**   Laurindo Almeida (guitarist/composer) July 26; Maxine Andrews (singer) October 21; Ralph Blane (songwriter/arranger) November 13; Don Cherry (trumpeter) September 19; Earl Coleman (singer) July 12; Jerry Garcia (singer/guitarist) August 8; Phil Harris (singer/bandleader) August 11; Julius Hemphill (saxophonist/writer) April 2; Burl Ives (folk singer) April 14; Dean Martin (singer/actor) December 25; Ray McKinley (drummer/bandleader) May 7; Charlie Rich (singer) July 25; Ron Richardson (singer) April 5; Art Taylor (drummer) February 6; Junior Walker (saxophonist) November 23; Ronnie White (songwriter) August 26.

**C. Biographical**

**Performing Groups**   Nuttin' Nyce.

**New Beginnings**   Rock 'n Roll Hall of Fame (Cleveland); Express Yourself Festival (Chicago).

**Prizes and Honors**   B. B. King (Kennedy Center); Bill Monroe (Medal of Arts); Diane Warren (ASCAP Voice of Music Award).

**Miscellaneous**   Latin American singer Selena is murdered by her manager.

**D. Publications**   Donald Clarke, *The Rise and Fall of Popular Music*; Samuel A. Floyd, Jr., *The Power of Black Music: Interpreting Its History from Africa to the United States*; William Hyland, *The Song Is Ended: Songwriters and American Music*; Robert Palmer, *Rock and Roll: An Unruly History*.

**E. Representative Works**

**Musicals**   Jonathan Larson, *Rent*; Jeffery Lunden and Arthur Perlman, *Another Midsummer Night*; Melissa Manchester and Jeffrey Sweet, *I Sent a Letter to My Love*; Henry Mancini and

Leslie Bricusse, *Victor/Victoria*; Randy Newman, *Faust*; Thomas Tierney and John Forster, *Eleanor*; Frank Wildhorn and Leslie Bricusse, *Jekyll and Hyde*.

**Number One Hits**    *Creep—Waterfalls* (TLC); *Exhale* (Whitney Houston); *Fantasy* (Mariah Carey); *Gangsta's Paradise* (Coolio); *Have You Ever Really Loved a Woman?* (Bryan Adams); *I Like It, I Love It* (Tim McGraw); *Kiss From a Rose* (Seal); *No More "I Love You's"* (Annie Lennox); *Not on Your Love* (Jeff Carson); *One Sweet Day* (Mariah Carey and Boyz II Men); *She's Every Woman* (Garth Brooks); *Someone Else's Star* (Bryan White); *Take a Bow* (Madonna); *That's as Close as I Get to Loving You* (Aaron Tippin); *This Is How We Do It* (Montell Jordon); *Who Can I Run To?* (Xscape); *You Are Not Alone* (Michael Jackson).

**Other**    James Horner, *Braveheart—Jumanji* (film music); James Newton Howard, *Waterworld* (film music).

## Music—The Cultivated/Art Music Scene

**G. Deaths**    Christine Dethier (violinist) December 1; Robert Fizdale (pianist) December 6; Joseph Gingold (violinist) January 11; Alexander Goudonov (ballet) May 18; Ulysses Kay (composer) May 20; Christopher Keene (conductor) October 8; Louis Krasner (violinist/educator) May 4; Eduardo Mata (Mexican-born conductor) January 4; Erica Morini (Austrian-born violinist) November 1; Miklós Rózsa (composer) July 27; Max Rudolf (conductor) February 28; Leonard Shure (pianist) February 28; Nicholas Slonimsky (Russian-born pianist/composer/lexicographer) December 25; Frederic Waldman (conductor) December 1.

**H. Debuts**

**United States**    Nicholas Angelich (French pianist—New York), Patricia Bardon (San Francisco), Arnaldo Cohen (Brazilian pianist—Lexington, Kentucky), Monica Groop (Finnish mezzo-soprano—Los Angeles), Angelika Kirchschlager (Austrian mezzo-soprano—New York), Frances Lucey (Irish soprano—New York), Michail Milanov (Bulgarian bass—Portland, Oregon), Anna Netrebko (Russian soprano—San Francisco), Luba Orgonasova (Czech soprano—Chicago), Falk Struckmann (German bass-baritone—Chicago), Christian Thielemann (German conductor—New York).

**Metropolitan Opera**    Daniel Beckwith (conductor), Barbara Frittoli (Italian soprano), Marcello Giordani (Italian tenor), Galina Gorchakova (Russian soprano), Sheri Greenawald (soprano), Gregam Grigorian (Russian tenor), Dimitri Hvorostovsky (Russian baritone), John Keyes (tenor), Richard Margison (Canadian tenor), Elizabeth Norberg-Schulz (Norwegian soprano), Daniel Oren (Israeli conductor), Patricia Racette (soprano), Nina Rautio (Russian soprano), Joan Rodgers (British soprano), Larissa Rudakova (Russian soprano), Bryn Terfel (Welsh bass-baritone), Jean-Luc Viala (French tenor), Stephen West (bass-baritone), Janet Williams (soprano).

**I. New Positions**

**Conductors**    Christoph Eschenbach (Ravinia Festival); Keith Lockhart (Boston Pops); Robert Spano (Brooklyn Philharmonic Orchestra).

**Educational**    Marilyn Horne (voice director, Music Academy of the West).

**J. Honors and Awards**

**Honors**    Licia Albanese, David Diamond (Medal of Arts); Marilyn Horne (*Musical America's* Musician of the Year—Kennedy Center); Meredith Monk (MacArthur Fellow); Hugo Weisgall (Schuman Award); Olly Wilson (American Academy).

**Awards**    Michelle De Young (Marian Anderson); Paul Groves (Tucker); Lisa Kim (Yehudi Menuhin); Samantha Yvonne McElhaney (Ponselle); Jon Nakamatsu (Chopin); Patricia Racette (Anderson).

**K. Biographical**    Dutch soprano Elly Ameling makes her farewell tour of the United States; the Chicago Symphony Orchestra begins a major renovation of Orchestra Hall; Kent Nagano takes the Opera de Lyons to San Francisco on its first visit to the United States; Joseph Silverstein announces his retirement from the Utah Symphony Orchestra in 1998; Hans Vonk (Dutch conductor) is named to succeed Leonard Slatkin in St. Louis in 1996.

## L. Musical Beginnings

**Performing Groups**   Anonymous Four; Chicago String Quartet.

**Festivals**   Amadeus Festival (New Jersey).

**Other**   Leonard Bernstein Jerusalem International Conducting Competition; Elysium Recordings, Inc.; Kurt Weill Prize.

## M. Music Publications

Borroff, Edith, *Music Melting Round: A History of Music in the United States*
Duckworth, William, *Talking Music: Conversations with . . . Experimental Composers*
Peyser, Joan, *Music of My Time*
Rosen, Charles, *The Romantic Generation*
Sadie, Julie and Samuel, Rhian, *Norton/Grove Dictionary of Women Composers*
Smith, Geoff and Nicola W., *New Voices: American Composers Talk about Their Music*
Steinberg, Michael, *The Symphony: A Listener's Guide*

## N. Musical Compositions

**Chamber Music**   Elliott Carter, *String Quartet No. 5*; John Corigliano, *String Quartet;* Richard Danielpour, *String Quartet No. 3, "Psalms of Sorrow"*; Stephen Mackey, *No Two Breaths*; George Rochberg, *Clarinet Concerto*; Ned Rorem, *String Quartet No. 4*; Richard Warnick, *String Quartet No. 5.*

**Choral/Vocal**   William Bolcom, *A Walt Whitman Triptych*; Elliot Goldenthal, *Fire Water Paper: A Vietnam Oratorio*; Lee Hoiby, *I Was There*; Marta Ptasznska, *Holocaust Memorial Cantata*; Ned Rorem, *More Than a Day* (cycle); Joseph Schwantner, *Evening Land* (soprano and orchestra).

**Concertos**   William Bolcom, *Concerto for Two Pianos, Left Hand* (or two concertos for one piano, left hand); James Grant, *Piano Concerto*; Lowell Liebermann, *Concerto for Flute and Harp*; Stephen Mackey, *Banana/Dump Truck* (cello and orchestra)—*Deal* (electric guitar and orchestra); George Rochberg, *Clarinet Concerto*; John Williams, *Bassoon Concerto*; Ellen Taaffe Zwilich, *Triple Concerto.*

**Electronic**   Robert Gibson, *Ex Machina for Computer Generated Tape;* Roger Reynolds, *Watershed III.*

**Operas**   Victoria Bond, *Travels*; David Carlson, *Dreamkeepers*; David Lang, *Modern Painters*; Stephen Paulus, *The Woman at Otowi Crossing*; Michael Reid, *Different Fields*; Nancy Van de Vate, *Der Herrscher und Das Mädchen.*

**Orchestra/Band**   John Adams, *Lollapalooza*; Henry Brant, *Plowshares and Swords*; Elliott Carter, *Adagio Tenebroso*; Richard Danielpour, *Toward the Splendid City*; Stephen Hartke, *Ascent of the Equestrian in a Balloon*; Bernard Rands, *Canzoni per orchestra*; Carlos Rodriquez, *Fábulas*; Michael Torke, *The Telephone Book—New York December* (string orchestra).

**Piano/Organ**   Ned Rorem, *Six Variations for Two Pianos.*

**Symphonies**   Lou Harrison, *Symphony No. 3*; Judith Lang Zaimont, *Symphony No. 1.*

# Selected Bibliography

Anderson, E. Ruth, *Contemporary American Composers, Second Edition*. Boston: G. H. Hall & Co., 1982.

Bierley, Paul E., *John Philip Sousa, American Phenomenon*. Englewood Cliffs, NJ: Prentice-Hall, Inc., 1973.

Biracree, Tom, *The Country Music Almanac*. New York: Prentice Hall, 1993.

Booth, Mark W., *American Popular Music: A Reference Guide*. Westport, CT: Greenwood Press, 1983.

Bronson, Fred, *Billboard Book of Number One Hits, Third Edition*. New York: Billboard Books, 1992.

Butterworth, Neil, *A Dictionary of American Composers*. New York: Garland Publishing Co., 1984.

Clarke, Donald, ed., *The Penguin Encyclopedia of Popular Music*. London: Viking Penguin, Inc., 1989.

Cummings, David M., ed., *International Who's Who in Music and Musician's Directory, Eleventh Edition*. Cambridge, England: International Who's Who in Music, 1994.

Dox, Thurston J., *American Oratorios and Cantatas*. New York: Scarecrow Press, 1986.

Ewen, David, *All the Years of American Popular Music*. Englewood Cliffs, NJ: Prentice-Hall, Inc., 1977.

Ewen, David, *American Composer: A Biographical Dictionary*. New York: G. P. Putnam's Sons, 1982.

Ewen, David, *American Songwriters*. New York: The H. W. Wilson Co., 1987.

Ewen, David, *Great Men of American Popular Song*. Englewood Cliffs, NJ: Prentice-Hall, Inc., 1970.

Fitzgerald, Gerald et al., eds. *Annals of the Metropolitan Opera*. New York: Metropolitan Opera Guild, Inc., 1989.

Gammond, Peter, *The Oxford Companion to Popular Music*. New York, Oxford University Press, 1993.

Gänzl, Kurt and Lamb, Andrew, *Gänzl's Book of the Musical Theatre*. New York: Schirmer Books, 1989.

Grout, Donald J. and Palisca, Claude V., *A History of Western Music, Fourth Edition*. New York, W. W. Norton & Co., 1988.

Hall, Charles J., *An Eighteenth-Century Musical Chronicle*. Westport, CT: Greenwood Press, 1990.

Hall, Charles J., *A Nineteenth-Century Musical Chronicle*. Westport, CT: Greenwood Press, 1989.

Hall, Charles J., *A Twentieth-Century Musical Chronicle*. Westport, CT: Greenwood Press, 1989.

Hoover, Kathleen and Cage, John, *Virgil Thomson*. New York: Thomas Yoseloff, 1959.

Howard, John Tasker, *Ethelbert Nevin*. New York: Thomas Crowell Co., 1935.

Howe, M. A. DeWolfe, *The Boston Symphony Orchestra*. Boston: Houghton Mifflin Co., 1914.

Jacobs, Dick and Harriet, *Who Wrote That Song?* Cincinnati: Writer's Digest Books, 1994.

Johnson, H. Earle, *Musical Interludes in Boston*. New York: Columbia University Press, 1943.

Jones, F. O., *A Handbook of American Music and Musicians*. New York: Da Capo Press (reprint of 1886 original), 1971.

Kernfeld, Barry, ed., *The New Grove Dictionary of Jazz*. New York: Groves Dictionaries of Music, 1988.

Kimball, Robert, ed., *Cole*. New York: Holt, Rinehart & Winston, 1971.

Lane, Hana Umlauf, ed., *The World Almanac Book of Who*. New York: World Almanac Publications, 1980.

Larkin, Colin, ed., *The Guiness Encyclopedia of Popular Music*. Chester, CT: Guinness Publishers, 1992.

Lax, Roger and Smith, Frederick, *The Great Song Thesaurus, Second Edition*. New York: Oxford University Press, 1989.

Loggins, Vernon, *Where the Word Ends*. Baton Rouge: Louisiana State University Press, 1958.

Loucks, Richard, *Arthur Shepherd, American Composer*. Provo, UT: Brigham Young University Press, 1980.

Machlis, Joseph, *Introduction to Contemporary Music, Second Edition*. New York: W. W. Norton & Co., 1961.

Morgan, Robert P., *Twentieth-Century Music*. New York: W. W. Norton & Co., 1991.

Morton, Brian and Collins, Pamela, ed., *Contemporary Composers*. Chicago: St. James Press, 1992.

*Music in Colonial Massachusetts*. Boston: Colonial Society of Massachusetts, 1980.

Ochoa, George and Corey, Melinda, *The Timeline Book of the Arts*. New York, Ballantine Books, 1995.

Paine, J. K. et al., *Famous Composers and Their Works*. Boston: J. B. Millet Co.,      1909.

Reis, Claire R., *Composers in America*. New York: Da Capo Press, 1977.

Rich, Maria F., ed., *Who's Who in Opera*. New York, Arno Press, 1976.

Richards, Tad and Shestack, M. B., *The New Country Music Encyclopedia*. New York: Simon & Schuster, 1993.

Romanowski, Patricia and George-Warren, Holly, ed., *The New Rolling Stone Encyclopedia of Rock & Roll*. New York: Rolling Stone Press, 1995

Sadie, Stanley, ed., *The New Grove Dictionary of Opera*. London: Macmillan Press, Ltd., 1992.

Seltsam, William H., *Metropolitan Opera Annals*. New York: The H. W. Wilson Co., 1947.

Semler, Isobel P. and Underwood, P., *Horatio Parker*. New York: G. P. Putnam's Sons, 1942.

Shanet, Howard, *Philharmonic: A History of New York's Orchestra*. New York: Doubleday and Co., 1975.

Slonimsky, Nicolas, ed., *Baker's Biographical Dictionary of Musicians, Eighth Edition*. New York: Schirmer Books, 1992.

Slonimsky, Nicolas, *Music Since 1900, Fifth Edition*. New York: Schirmer Books, 1994.

Upton, William T., *William Henry Fry*. New York: Thomas Crowell, 1954.

Waten, Edward N., *Victor Herbert*. New York: Macmillan, 1955.

Watkins, Glenn, *Soundings: Music in the Twentieth Century*. New York: Schirmer Books, 1988.

Wilder, Alec, *American Popular Song*. New York: Oxford University Press, 1972.

Wold, Milo et al., *An Outline History of Western Music, Seventh Edition*. Dubuque, IA: Wm. C. Brown, 1990.

Numerous magazines and periodicals including the following:
    *American Music*
    *American Record Guide*
    *Current Biography*
    *Facts on File*
    *Fanfare*
    *Musical America*
    *Newsweek*
    *Opera News*
    *Stereo Review*
    *Time*

# Music Index

## A

A & M Records – 1962C
AACM Festival – 1966C
A-R Editions – 1962L
Abarbanell, Lina – 1905H
Abba – 1977E
Abbado, Claudio – 1982K
Abbey, Henry – 1883I
Abbott, Emma – 1850F, 1872K, 1877H, 1891G
Abbott, Emma, Opera Co. – 1878L
Abbott, Gregory – 1987E
Abdul, Paula – 1962A, 1989E, 1990E, 1991E
Abel-Steinberg-Winant Trio – 1984L
Abene, Mike – 1942A
Abercrombie, John – 1944A
A-Bones – 1984C
Abott, Bessie – 1906H
Abrahams, Maurice
   *Get Out & Get Under* – 1913E
   *Hitchy-Koo* – 1912E
   *Ragtime Cowboy Joe* – 1912E
   *Twentieth Century Rag* – 1914E
Abrahams, Maurice, Publishing Co. – 1923C
Abrams, Muhal Richard – 1930A
Abrams, Roy – 1940A
Abravanel, Maurice – 1936K, 1938K, 1947I, 1961J, 1971J, 1976I, 1979K, 1981J, 1991J, 1993K
Academy Awards, Film Music – 1934C
Academy of Vocal Arts – 1935L
Accademia dei Dilettanti di Musica – 1928L
Accademia Monteverdiana – 1961L
Accone, Frank d' – 1931C
Ace, Johnny – 1929A, 1954B
Ace of Base – 1994E
Aceto, Raymond – 1992H
Achron, Isidor – 1928K, 1948G
   *Piano Concerto No. 1* – 1937N
   *Suite Grotesque* – 1941N
Achron, Joseph – 1925K, 1934K, 1943G
   *Golem Suite* – 1932N
   *Konzertanten-Kapelle* – 1928N
   *Violin Concerto No. 1* – 1925N
   *Violin Concerto No. 2* – 1933N
   *Violin Concerto No. 3* – 1937N
Ackley, Alfred H. – 1887F, 1960G
Ackley, Bentley D. – 1872F, 1908K
Acklin, Barbara – 1943A

Ackté, Aïno – 1904H
Acousti-Lectric Co. – 1934C
Acuff, Roy – 1903A, 1966C, 1991C, 1992B
Acuff-Rose Publications – 1942C
A.D. – 1984C
Adam, Claus – 1929K, 1955I, 1980J, 1983G
   *Cello Concerto* – 1973N
   *Concerto Variations* – 1976N
   *Piano Sonata* – 1948N
   *String Quartet* – 1975N
   *String Trio* – 1967N
Adam, Stanley – 1994B
Adam, Theo – 1969H
Adamowski, Joseph – 1889K, 1903I, 1930G
Adamowski, Timothée – 1879HK, 1908I, 1943G
Adamowski String Quartet – 1888L
Adamowski Trio – 1896L
Adams, A. Emmett
   *Bells of St. Mary's, The* – 1917E
Adams, Bryan – 1985E, 1991E, 1994E
Adams, Byron – 1955F
   *Violin Concerto* – 1984N
Adams, Charles R. – 1834F, 1856H, 1877K, 1879K, 1900G
Adams, F. W. – 1787F, 1859G
Adams, George – 1940A
Adams, John – 1947F, 1972I, 1982I
   *American Standard* – 1973N
   *Chairman Dances, The* – 1986N
   *China Gates* – 1977N
   *Common Tones in Simple Time* – 1979N
   *Death of Klinghoffer, The* – 1991N
   *El Dorado* – 1991N
   *Eros Piano* – 1989N
   *Fearful Symmetries* – 1988N
   *Grand Pianola Music* – 1982N
   *Grounding* – 1975N
   *Harmonielehre* – 1985N
   *Harmonium* – 1980N
   *Lollapalooza* – 1995N
   *Nixon in China* – 1987N
   *Onyx* – 1976N
   *Phrygian Gates* – 1977N
   *Piano Quintet* – 1970N
   *Shaker Loops* – 1980N
   *Violin Concerto* – 1993N
   *Wound-Dresser, The* – 1989N

---

❖

---

Vernacular/Commercial Music Scene
A *Births*   B *Deaths*   C *Biographical*   D *Publications*
E *Representative Pieces*

Cultivated/Art Music Scene
F *Births*   G *Deaths*   H *Debuts*   I *New Positions*   J *Honors and Awards*
K *Biographical*   L *Musical Beginnings*   M *Publications*   N *Compositions*

Adams, Johnny – 1932A
Adams, Lee – 1924A
Adams, Marie "TV Mama" – 1925A
Adams, Nathan – 1783F, 1864G
Adams, Pepper – 1930A, 1986B
Adams, Richard E. – 1988I
Adams, Stanley – 1907A, 1959I, 1994B
Adams, Stephen
  Holy City, The – 1905N
Adams, Suzanne – 1872F, 1895H, 1898K, 1899H,
  1953G
Adamson, Harold – 1906A, 1980B
Adderley, J. "Cannonball" – 1928A, 1955C,
  1975B
Adderley Jazz Quintet – 1956C
Adderley Jazz Quintet II – 1959C
Adderley, Nat – 1931A
Addison, Adele – 1925F, 1946K, 1948H
Adesdi Chorus (New York) – 1924L
Adgate, Andrew – 1762F, 1790K, 1793G
  Lessons for the Uranian Society – 1785M
  Philadelphia Harmony – 1789N
  Rudiments of Music, The – 1788N
  Select Psalms & Hymns for Use of Mr. Adgate's
    Pupils – 1787N
Adkins, Morton – 1877F
Adler, Clarence – 1914H, 1969G
Adler, Danny – 1949A
Adler, Kurt – 1977G
Adler, Kurt Herbert – 1938IK, 1943I, 1953I, 1956I,
  1988GK
Adler, Larry – 1914F
Adler, Peter Herman – 1939K, 1940H, 1949I, 1959I,
  1972H, 1973I, 1969I, 1981JK, 1990G
Adler, Richard
  Damn Yankees – 1955E
  Gift of the Magi – 1958E
  Kwamina – 1961E
  Memory of a Childhood – 1978N
  Pajama Game – 1954E
  Wilderness Suite, The – 1982N
  Yellowstone Overture – 1980N
Adler, Samuel – 1939K, 1946K, 1952I, 1953I,
  1957I, 1960K, 1969J
  Aeolus, King of the Winds – 1977N
  Anthology for the Teaching of Choral Conducting
    – 1971M
  Behold Your God – 1966N
  Binding, The – 1967N
  Cello Sonata – 1966N
  Choral Singing: An Anthology – 1972M
  City by the Lakes – 1968N
  Concerto for Orchestra – 1971N
  Disappointment, The – 1974N
  Double Portrait – 1985N
  Elegy for String Orchestra – 1962N
  Epitaph for . . . American Soldiers – 1945N
  Feast of Light, A – 1955N
  Flute Concerto – 1977N

From Out of Bondage – 1968N
Jubilee – 1958N
Little Night & Day Music, A – 1978N
Lodge of Shadows, The – 1973N
Organ Concerto – 1970N
Outcasts of Poker Flat – 1959N
Piano Sonatina – 1979N
Piano Trio No. 1 – 1964N
Piano Trio No. 2 – 1978N
Rhapsody for Violin & Orchestra – 1961N
Shir Chadash – 1960N
Sinfonietta – 1970N
Singing & Hearing – 1979M
Snow Tracks – 1981N
Sonata Breve for Piano – 1963N
Southwestern Sketches – 1961N
Stars in the Dust – 1988N
String Quartet No. 1 – 1945N
String Quartet No. 2 – 1950N
String Quartet No. 3 – 1953N
String Quartet No. 4 – 1963N
String Quartet No. 6 – 1975N
Study of Orchestration, The – 1989M
Summer Stock Overture – 1955N
Symphony No. 1 – 1953N
Symphony No. 2 – 1957N
Symphony No. 3 – 1960N
Symphony No. 4 – 1967N
Symphony No. 5 – 1975N
Symphony No. 6 – 1985N
Toccata, Recitation & Postlude – 1960N
Toccata for Orchestra – 1954N
Violin Sonata No. 1 – 1948N
Violin Sonata No. 2 – 1956N
Violin Sonata No. 3 – 1965N
Vision of Isaiah – 1962N
Whole Bunch of Fun, A – 1969N
Wrestler, The – 1971N
Ad Libs – 1962C
Adorno, Theodor
  Composing for the Films – 1947D
Aeolian American Corporation – 1932L
Aeolian Chamber Players (New York) – 1961L
Aeolian Organ & Music Co. – 1888L
Aeolian Vocalists – 1842L
Aeolian-Skinner Organ Co. – 1931L
Aeolian Weber Piano & Pianola Co. – 1903L
Aerosmith – 1970C
Affiliate Artists, Inc. – 1966L
Afrika Bambaataa – 1960A
AfroJazz Sextet – 1959C
Aftermath – 1984C
Ager, Milton – 1893A, 1979B
  Ain't She Sweet – 1927E
  Bagdad – 1924E
  Happy Days Are Here Again – 1929E
  I'm Nobody's Baby – 1921E
  I Wonder What's Become of Sally? – 1924E
  Louisville Lou – 1923E

---

❖

---

## Vernacular/Commercial Music Scene

A *Births*    B *Deaths*    C *Biographical*    D *Publications*
E *Representative Pieces*

---

**Cultivated/Art Music Scene**

F *Births*     G *Deaths*     H *Debuts*     I *New Positions*     J *Honors and Awards*
K *Biographical*     L *Musical Beginnings*     M *Publications*     N *Compositions*

❀

**Vernacular/Commercial Music Scene**
A *Births*    B *Deaths*    C *Biographical*    D *Publications*
E *Representative Pieces*

*Last of the Mohicans* – 1916N
*Milda* – 1913N
*O Munasterio* – 1911N
*Piccola Figaro, La* – 1931N
*Serenade* -1928N
*Symphony No. 6* – 1910N
Allen, Richard  – 1760F, 1831G
  *Collection of Spiritual Songs & Hymns* – 1801M
Allen, Robert
  *Home for the Holidays* – 1954E
Allen, Thomas – 1981H
Allen, Thomas S.
  *By the Watermelon Vine* – 1904E
  *Lindy Lou* – 1904E
Allen, W. F. et al., *Slave Songs of the United States*
  1867M
Allen's Poop Sheet – 1958C
Allers, Frank – 1963H
All-4-One – 1994E
Allies – 1983C
Alligator Records – 1971C
Allison, Luther – 1939A
Allison, Mose – 1927A
Allman Brothers Band – 1968C
Allyn & Bacon, Music Publishers  1816L
Almanac Singers – 1941C
Almeida, Antonio de – 1960H
Almeida, Laurindo – 1947K, 1995B
  *Contemporary Moods for Classical Guitar* –
  1970D
Almquist, Carl Jonas – 1851K
Alpert, Herb – 1935A, 1968E, 1979E
Altamont Festival – 1969C
Alten, Bella – 1904H
Alter, Louis – 1902A, 1980B
  *Manhattan Serenade* – 1928E
Altglass, Max – 1913K, 1924H
Althouse, Monroe  1853F, 1924G
Althouse, Paul – 1899F, 1913H, 1941J, 1954G
Altman, Ludwig – 1936HK, 1940I, 1990G
Altmeyer, Jeannine – 1948F, 1971H
Alva, Luigi – 1964H
Alvarez, Albert – 1899H
Alvarez, Chico – 1920A
Alvary, Lorenzo – 1939HK, 1942H
Alvary, Max – 1805H
Amadé Trio – 1974L
Amara, Lucine – 1927F, 1946H, 1950H
Amato Opera Theater – 1948L
Amato, Pasquale – 1908H, 1942G
Amazing Rhythm Aces – 1974C
Amboy Dukes – 1965C
Ambrosia – 1971C
Ameling, Elly – 1968H, 1995K
America – 1972E, 1975E
American Academy & Institute of Fine Arts – 1886L
American Academy in Rome – 1921L
American Academy of Teachers of Singing – 1922L
American Academy of Arts & Letters – 1904L

American Accordionists' Association – 1938L
American Artists International Foundation – 1977L
American Arts Orchestra – 1950L
American Association of Composers – 1928L
American Association of University Women
  Education Fund – 1882L
American Ballad Singers – 1939L
American Ballet Caravan – 1941L
American Ballet Center – 1953L
American Ballet Theater – 1939L
American Bandmasters' Association – 1929L
American Bandstand – 1957C
American Berlin Opera Foundation – 1986L
American Brass Quintet (New York) – 1960L
*American Deed, The* – 1983C
American Cabinet Organ – 1861L
American Chamber Trio – 1972L
American Choral Directors' Association – 1959L
American Choral Foundation – 1954L
*American Choral Review* – 1958L
American College of Musicians – 1884L
American Composers Alliance – 1938L
American Composers Orchestra – 1976L
American Composers' Project – 1925L
American Conservatory at Fontainebleau – 1921L
American Council of Learned Societies – 1975L
American Federation of Jazz Studies – 1985C
American Federation of Musicians – 1896L
American Flyer – 1976C
American Folksong Festival – 1930C
American Friends of the Kirov Maryinsky Theater –
  1993L
American Gramophone Co. – 1887L
American Guild of Musical Artists – 1936L
American Guild of Organists – 1896L
*American Harp Journal* – 1967L
American Harp Society – 1962L
American Institute for Verdi Studies – 1976L
American Institute of Applied Music – 1886L
American Institute of Musicology – 1945L
American Jazz Orchestra – 1986C
American Library of Musicology – 1932L
American Liszt Society – 1967L
*American Music* – 1983L
American Music Association – 1856L
American Music Center – 1939L
American Music Club – 1983C
American Music Editions – 1951L
American Music Festival (D.C.) – 1942L
American Music Guild – 1921L
*American Music Journal* – 1854L, 1900L
*American Music Lover, The* – 1935L
American Music/Theater Group – 1977L
American Music Theater Festival – 1983L
American Music Week – 1985L
*American Musical Instrument* – 1971L
American Musical Instrument Society – 1971L
*American Musical Magazine* – 1786L
*American Musical Miscellany, The* – 1798L

---

## Cultivated/Art Music Scene

F *Births*    G *Deaths*    H *Debuts*    I *New Positions*    J *Honors and Awards*
K *Biographical*    L *Musical Beginnings*    M *Publications*    N *Compositions*

*American Musical Times, The* – 1847L
American Musicological Society (Philadelphia) –
    1934L
American National Orchestra – 1923L
American Opera Co. – 1885L
American Opera Project (San Francisco) – 1979L
American Opera Society – 1951L
American Orchestral Society – 1920L
*American Organist, The* – 1918L, 1967L
American Piano Co. – 1908L
American Prix de Rome – 1954L
American Publisher's Copyright League – 1886L
American Record Co. – 1929C
*American Record Guide* – 1926L
*American Recorder, The* – 1960L
American Recorder Society – 1939L
American Rome Prize – 1905L
American School Band Director's Association –
    1953L
American School of Classical Studies – 1895L
American Symphony Orchestra – 1894L
American Symphony Orchestra (Stokowski) –
    1962L
American Society for Jewish Music – 1974L
American Society of Ancient Instruments –
    1925L
American Society of Composers, Authors &
    Publishers – 1914L
American Society of Piano Technicians – 1940L
American Society of University Composers – 1966L
American Steam Music Co. – 1855L
American String Quartet – 1974L
*American String Teacher, The* – 1951L
American String Teachers' Association – 1946L
American Symphony Orchestra League – 1942L
American Wind Symphony – 1957L
American Women Composers – 1976L
American Youth Orchestra – 1944L
Americans, The – 1961C
Amfitheatrov, Daniele – 1937K, 1944K
Amirkhanian, Charles – 1945F
    *Audience* – 1978N
    *Beemsterboer* – 1975N
    *Canticles 1 & 2* – 1963N
    *Canticles 3 & 4* – 1966N
    *Dog of Stravinsky* – 1982N
    *Dreams Freud Dreamed* – 1979N
    *Mahogany Ballpark* – 1976N
    *Martinique & Course of Abstraction* – 1984N
    *Seatbelt Seatbelt* – 1973N
    *She she & she* – 1974N
    *Sound Nutrition* – 1972N
    *Vers Les Anges* – 1990N
AMM – 1965C
Ammons, Albert – 1907F, 1949G
Ammons, Gene – 1925A, 1974B
Amor Artis Chorale & Orchestra – 1961L
Amos Records – 1969C
Amos, Tori – 1963A

Amoyal, Pierre – 1985H
Ampex Co. – 1944L
Amram, David – 1930F, 1966I, 1969K
    *Across the Wide Missouri* – 1984N
    *Andante & Variations (band)* – 1984N
    *Autobiography for Strings* – 1959N
    *Bassoon Concerto* – 1971N
    *Brazilian Memories* – 1973N
    *Dirge & Variations* – 1962N
    *Final Ingredient, The* – 1965N
    *Friday Evening Service* – 1960N
    *Horn Concerto* – 1965N
    *Landscapes* – 1980N
    *Native American Portraits* – 1977N
    *Overture, Brass & Percussion* – 1977N
    *Piano Sonata* – 1960N
    *Shakespearean Concerto* – 1959N
    *String Quartet* – 1961N
    *Three Songs for America* – 1969N
    *Trail of Beauty, The* – 1976N
    *Travels* – 1985N
    *Triple Concerto* – 1970N
    *Twelfth Night* – 1968N
    *Violin Concerto* – 1972N
    *Violin Sonata* – 1964N
    *Wind & the Rain, The* – 1963N
    *Year in Our Land, A* – 1964N
Amsterdam Musical Association – 1906C
Anastasia Screamed – 1987C
Anchorage Civic Opera – 1955L
Anchorage Community Chorus – 1947L
Anchorage Symphony Orchestra – 1946L
Ancona, Mario – 1893H
Anda, Géza – 1955H
Andersen, Eric – 1943A
Anderson, Beth – 1950F
    *Dreaming Fields* – 1987N
    *Joan* – 1974N
    *Morning View & Maiden Spring* – 1978N
    *Music for Charlemagne Palestine* – 1973N
    *Overture for Band* – 1981N
    *Queen Christina* – 1973N
    *Revelation* – 1981N
    *Soap Tuning* – 1976N
    *Zen Piece* – 1976N
Anderson, Bill – 1937A
Anderson, Cat – 1916A, 1981B
Anderson, Cat, Jazz Band – 1947C
Anderson, Deacon
    *Rag Mop* – 1950E
Anderson, Ivie – 1905A, 1949B
Anderson, John – 1954A
Anderson, June – 1952F, 1989H, 1978H
Anderson, Kelly – 1990H
Anderson, Laurie – 1947F
    *America on the Move* – 1979N
    *United States* – 1983N
Anderson, Leonard Mark – 1963F, 1988H
Anderson, Leroy – 1908A, 1931I, 1975b

---

※

---

## Vernacular/Commercial Music Scene
A *Births*    B *Deaths*    C *Biographical*    D *Publications*
E *Representative Pieces*

❁

## Cultivated/Art Music Scene

---

### Vernacular/Commercial Music Scene

A *Births*    B *Deaths*    C *Biographical*    D *Publications*
E *Representative Pieces*

*Jonah & the Whale* – 1973N
*Letters from Composers* – 1968N
*Masque of Angels, The* – 1963N
*Miss Havisham's Fire* – 1978N
*Miss Havisham's Wedding Night* – 1980N
*Nation of Cowslips, A* – 1968N
*Ode to the West Wind* – 1956N
*Oresteia* – 1967N
*Postcard from Morocco* – 1971N
*Resurrection of Don Juan* – 1956N
*Revelation of St. John the Divine* – 1966N
*Ring of Time, A* – 1972N
*S. S. Glencairn* – 1966N
*St. Joan* – 1964N
*Shoemaker's Holiday, The* – 1967N
*Six Elizabethan Songs* – 1958N
*String Quartet* – 1956N
*Te Deum* – 1987N
*To Be Sung upon the Water* – 1972N
*Variations: Mask of Night* – 1965N
*Volpone* – 1964N
*Voyage of Edgar Allan Poe* – 1976N
*Water Bird Talk, A* – 1974N
Argiris, Spiros – 1987I
Argo Records – 1955C
Arhoolie Records – 1960C
Arimondi, Vittorio – 1895H
Arista Records – 1974C
Aristocrat Records – 1947C
Arkansas Arts Center – 1962L
Arkansas Folk Festival – 1963C
Arkansas Opera Theater – 1973L
Arkansas Symphony Orchestra – 1966L
Arkansas State Symphony Orchestra – 1940L
Arizona State U. School of Music – 1885L
Arkhipova, Irina – 1972H
Arkin, Alan
Arlen, Harold – 1905A, 1986B
*Bloomer Girl* – 1944E
*Blues in the Night* – 1941E
*Come Rain or Come Shine* – 1946E
*Hooray for Love* – 1948E
*Hooray for What!* – 1937E
*House of Flowers* – 1954E
*I Gotta Right to Sing the Blues* – 1932E
*I Love a Parade* – 1931E
*In the Shade of the Old Apple Tree*
  – 1937E
*It's Only a Paper Moon* – 1933E
*Let's Fall in Love* – 1934E
*Life Begins at 8:40* – 1934E
*Mood in Six Minutes* – 1935E
*Over the Rainbow* – 1939E
*St. Louis Woman* – 1946E
*Saratoga* – 1959E
*Stormy Weather* – 1933E
*That Old Black Magic* – 1942E
*Wizard of Oz, The* – 1939E
*You Said It* – 1930E
Armilliato, Fabio – 1993H

Armstrong, Harry – 1951B
*Goodbye, Eyes of Blue* – 1898E
Armstrong, Henry W.
*Sweet Adeline* – 1903E
Armstrong, Karan – 1941F, 1969H
Armstrong, Lil – 1898A, 1971B
Armstrong, Louis – 1898A, 1924C, 1959C, 1964E, 1971B
*Satchmo: My Life In New Orleans* – 1954D
Arnaz, Desi – 1933C, 1986B
Arndt, Felix
*Nola* – 1915E
Arnheim, Gus – 1897A, 1955B
*After All Is Said & Done* – 1932E
*I Cried for You* – 1923E
*Sweet & Lovely* – 1931E
Arnheim, Gus, Big Band – 1928C
Arnold, Billy Boy – 1935A
Arnold, Eddie – 1918A
Arnold, James "Kokomo" – 1901A, 1968B
Arnold, Maurice – 1865F, 1937G
Arnold, Richard – 1853K, 1918G
Arnoldson, Sigrid – 1893H
Aronica, Roberto – 1993H
Aronson, Irving – 1963B
ARP Instruments – 1970L
Arrau, Claudio – 1923H, 1941K, 1979K, 1980J, 1991G
Arrested Development – 1988C
Arrow Music Press – 1938L
Arroyo, Martina – 1936F, 1958H, 1959H, 1985I
Ars Poetica Chamber Orchestra – 1990L
Ars Nova Orchestra – 1974L
Art Ensemble of Chicago – 1968V
Art Publication Society – 1912L
Arteta, Ainhoa – 1990H, 1994H
Arthur, Alfred – 1844F
Arthur Pryor Band – 1903L
Artis, Bob
*Bluegrass:...an American Musical Tradition* – 1975D
Artistic Ambassador Program – 1982L
Artistry in Rhythm Orchestra – 1941C
Artists House Records – 1977C
Arto Records – 1920C
Artôt, Alexandre-Joseph – 1843H
Artpark (Lewiston) – 1974L
Artpark Festival (N.Y.) – 1974L
Artzt, Alice – 1943G, 1969H
Arvin, Gary – 1954F, 1989H
*Art of Practicing, The* – 1978M
Arvin, Gary – 1954F, 1989H
Asaf, George
*Pack Up Your Troubles in Your Old Kit Bag* – 1915E
*ASCAP Biographical Dictionary of Composers, Authors & Publishers* – 1948M
*ASCAP Today* – 1967C

---

## Cultivated/Art Music Scene
F *Births*    G *Deaths*    H *Debuts*    I *New Positions*    J *Honors and Awards*
K *Biographical*    L *Musical Beginnings*    M *Publications*    N *Compositions*

ASCAP Foundation Grants to Young Composers –
  1978L
Aschaffenburg, Walter – 1938K, 1952I, 1966J
Ascoli, Bernard d' – 1985H
Ashbrook, William – 1922F
  *Operas of Puccini, The* – 1968M
Asheville Mountain Dance and Folk Festival –
  1928C
Ashford, Nickolas – 1943A
Ashforth, Alden – 1933F
Ashkenazy, Vladimir – 1958H
Ashley, Robert – 1930F
  *# + Heat* – *1961N*
  *Atalanta (Acts of God)* – *1982N*
  *Atalanta Strategy* – *1984N*
  *Combination Wedding & Funeral* – *1964N*
  *Fancy Free* – *1970N*
  *Fives* – *1962N*
  *In Memoriam...Crazy Horse* – *1963N*
  *It's There* – *1970N*
  *Kitty Hawk* – *1964N*
  *Music with Roots in the Aether* – *1976N*
  *Night Train* – *1965N*
  *Orange Dessert* – *1965N*
  *Outcome Inevitable* – *1992N*
  *Perfect Lives (Private Parts)* – *1983N*
  *Piano Sonata* – *1959N*
  *That Morning Thing* – *1967N*
  *Wolfman Motorcity Revue* – *1969N*
  *Wolfman Tape, The* – *1964N*
Ashley Slave Band – 1836L
Ashworth, Charles S. – 1804I
Ashworth, Valerie Grace – 1989H
Asia – 1981C
Asia, Daniel – 1953F, 1988I
  *At the Far Edge* – *1991N*
  *Black Light* – *1990N*
  *Piano Quartet* – *1989N*
  *Sand II* – *1978N*
  *Scherzo Sonata* – *1987N*
  *String Quartet No. 1* – *1975N*
  *Symphony No. 1* – *1987N*
  *Symphony No. 2* – *1990N*
  *Symphony No. 3* – *1992N*
Asian American Arts Alliance – 1992L
Asleep at the Wheel – 1970C
Aspen Festival Piano Quartet – 1955L
Aspen Festival Quartet – 1954L
Aspen Music Festival – 1950L
Associated Glee Clubs of America – 1924L
Associated Music Publishers – 1927L
Association, The – 1965C, 1966E, 1967E
Association for Advancement of Creative Musicians
  – 1965L
Association for Classical Music – 1982L
Association for Recorded Sound Collections –
  1966L
Association of American Women Composers –
  1926L

Association of Concert Bands – 1977L
Association of Independent Composers &
  Performers – 1969L
Association of Professional Vocal Ensembles –
  1977L
Astaire, Fred – 1987B
Astley, Rick – 1988E
Aston Magna Baroque Festival – 1972L
Aston Magna Foundation – 1972L
Astor, John Jacob – 1783K, 1786K
Asylum Records – 1971C
Atamian, Dickran – 1974J, 1976J
Atcher, Bob – 1914A
Atco Records – 1955C
Atherton, David – 1978H, 1981I
Atherton, James – 1943F, 1977H, 1987G
Atheist – 1987C
Atkins, Boyd – 1900A
Atkins, Chet – 1924A, 1971C, 1973C, 1975C,
  1976C
Atlanta, Georgia
  *Century Music Club* – *1901L*
  *Choral Guild* – *1940L*
  *Civic Opera* – *1979L*
  *Community Orchestra* – *1958L*
  *Free Jazz Festival* – *1978C*
  *Lyric Opera Co.* – *1976L*
  *Music Club* – *1915L*
  *Music Festival Association* – *1909L*
  *Symphony Youth Orchestra* – *1974L*
  *Viennese Summerfest* – *1989L*
  *Youth Symphony* – *1944L*
Atlanta Rhythm Section – 1971C
Atlantic Brass Quintet – 1985L
Atlantic Center for the Arts (FL) – 1979L
Atlantic Records – 1947C
Atlantic Starr – 1976C, 1987E
Atlantov, Vladimir – 1993H
Atlas, Allan W. – 1943F
Atrophy – 1987C
Atteridge, Harold
  *By the Beautiful Sea* – *1914E*
Attili, Dario d' – 1935K
Atwill & Co., San Francisco – 1849L
Atwill, Joseph – 1811F, 1891G
Atwill, Joseph, & Co., Publishers – 1852L
Aubigne, Lloyd d' – 1895H
Audiophile Record Co. – 1947C
Audsley, George A. – 1892K
  *Temple of Tone, The* – *1925M*
  *Art of Organ Building, The* – *1905M*
Audubon String Quartet – 1974L
Auer, Edward – 1967J
Auer, Leopold – 1918K, 1919H, 1928I
  *Violin Playing as I Teach It* – *1921M*
  *Masterworks & Their Interpretation* – *1925M*
Aufderheide, May – 1888A, 1972B
  *Blue Ribbon Rag* – *1910E*
  *Dusty Rag* – *1908E*

*Novelty Rag* – 1911E
*Richmond Rag* – 1909E
*Thriller, The* – 1909E
*Totally Different Rag* – 1910E
Augér, Arleen – 1939F, 1967HK, 1969H, 1970H, 1993G
Augusta (GA) Opera – 1967L
Aus der Ohe, Adele – 1886H
Austin, Texas
　　Civic Orchestra – 1977L
　　Civic Wind Ensemble – 1976L
　　Lyric Opera – 1986L
　　Musical Union – 1886L
　　Performing Arts Center – 1982L
　　Symphonic Band – 1981L
　　Symphony Orchestra – 1911L
Austin Lyceum – 1841L
Austin, Elizabeth – 1827H
Austin, Florence – 1884F, 1901H, 1927G
Austin, Gene – 1900A, 1972B
　　*How Come You Do Me Like You Do* – 1924E
Austin, John Turnell – 1869F, 1889K, 1948G
Austin, Larry – 1930F, 1966I
　　*La Barbara:...* – 1991N
　　*Learning to Compose* – 1988M
　　*Maze, The* – 1965N
　　*Montage: Themes & Variations* – 1985N
　　*Phantasmagoria* – 1977N
　　*Sonata Concertante* – 1988N
　　*Transmission Two* – 1990N
　　*Violet's Invention* – 1988N
Austin, Lovie – 1887A, 1972B
Austin, Patti – 1948A, 1983E
Austin, William – 1920F
　　*Music in the 20th Century* – 1966M
Austral, Florence – 1925H
Autograph – 1983C
Autoharp – 1885L
Autori, Franco – 1928F, 1936G
Autrey, Herman – 1904A, 1980B
Autry, Gene – 1907A, 1969C
　　*Back in the Saddle Again* – 1940E
　　*That Silver-Haired Daddy of Mine* – 1932E
Autumn Records – 1964C
Avalon, Frankie – 1939A, 1959E
Avatar – 1978C
Avengers – 1977C
Average White Band – 1975E
Averill, Perry – 1862F, 1895H
Aviator – 1984C
Avshalomov, Aaron – 1947K
Avshalomov, Jacob – 1937K, 1944K, 1965J
　　*City Upon a Hill* – 1963N
　　*How Long, O Lord* – 1948N
　　*Inscriptions, City of Brass* – 1956N
　　*Music is Where You Make It I* – 1959M
　　*Phases of the Great Land* – 1958N
　　*Raptures for Orchestra* – 1975N
　　*Sinfonietta* – 1946N

*Symphony, "The Oregon"* – 1962N
*Taking of T'ung Kuan* – 1943N
*Tom o'Bedlam* – 1953N
Ax-Ma-Kim Trio – 1980L
Ax, Emanuel – 1970K, 1973H, 1974J, 1979J
Axton, Hoyt – 1938A
Ayer, Nat D.
　　*If You Were the Only Girl in the World* – 1916E
Ayers, Roy – 1940A
Ayler, Albert – 1936A, 1970B
Ayler, Albert, Jazz Quartet – 1964C
Ayres, Frederick – 1876F, 1926G
　　*Cello Sonata* – 1926N
　　*Overture, From the Plains* – 1914N
　　*Piano Trio, Op. 13* – 1914N
　　*String Quartet* – 1916N
　　*Two Fugues, Op. 9* – 1910N
　　*Violin Sonata No. 1* – 1914N
　　*Violin Sonata No. 2* – 1926N
Azocar, José – 1992H

## B

Babayan, Sergei – 1990J
Babbitt, Harry – 1913A
Babbitt, Milton – 1916F, 1931K, 1948I, 1959IJ, 1965J, 1970J, 1973I, 1982J, 1983J, 1986J
　　*About Time* – 1982N
　　*Ars combinatoria* – 1981N
　　*Composition for 4 Instruments* – 1948N
　　*Composition for Guitar* – 1984N
　　*Composition for Synthesizer* – 1961N
　　*Composition for Viola & Piano* – 1950N
　　*Composition, Tenor & 6 Instruments* – 1960N
　　*Consortini for Chamber Ensemble* – 1989N
　　*Du* – 1951N
　　*Function of Set Structure in the 12-Tone System* – 1946M
　　*Generatrix* – 1935N
　　*Head of the Bed, The* – 1982N
　　*Joy of More Sextets* – 1986N
　　*Lagniappe* – 1985N
　　*Music for the Mass* – 1941N
　　*None But the Lonely Flute* – 1992N
　　*Partitions* – 1957N
　　*Philomel* – 1964N
　　*Phonemena* – 1970N
　　*Piano Concerto* – 1985N
　　*Playing for Time* – 1983N
　　*Preludes, Interludes & Postlude* – 1991N
　　*Reflections, Piano & Tape* – 1974N
　　*Relata I* – 1965N
　　*Relata II* – 1968N
　　*Sextets* – 1966N
　　*Sheer Pluck* – 1984N
　　*Solo Requiem, A* – 1977N
　　*String Quartet No. 1* – 1948N
　　*String Quartet No. 2* – 1954N
　　*String Quartets 3 & 4* – 1970N
　　*String Quartet No. 5* – 1982N

---

❊

## Cultivated/Art Music Scene

F *Births*　　G *Deaths*　　H *Debuts*　　I *New Positions*　　J *Honors and Awards*
K *Biographical*　　L *Musical Beginnings*　　M *Publications*　　N *Compositions*

Babbitt, Milton (continued)
   *String Trio* – 1941N
   *Symphony, 1941* – 1941N
   *Three Compositions for Piano* – 1947N
   *Three Cultivated Choruses* – 1987N
   *Woodwind Quartet* – 1953N
   *Words about Music* – 1987M
Babcock Brothers Piano Co. – 1809L
Babcock, Alpheus – 1785F, 1842G
Babes in Toyland – 1987C
Babin, Victor – 1937K, 1944K, 1961I
Babin, Vitya Vronsky – 1992G
Baccaloni, Salvatore – 1930H, 1940H
Bach Aria Festival – 1981L
Bach, Andreas – 1987H
Bach, Christopher, Orchestra – 1855L
Bach, Vincent – 1914K, 1923K
Bach, Vincent, Co. – 1919L
Bacharach, Burt – 1928A
Bachauer, Gina – 1950H
Bachauer International Piano Competition – 1976L,
   1982L
Bachman-Turner Overdrive – 1974E
Back Bay Brass Quintet – 1982L
Back Stage Club – 1924C
Backhaus, Wilhelm – 1912H
Bacon Piano Co. (NY) – 1789L
Bacon, Ernst – 1898F, 1925I, 1928I, 1932J, 1934I,
   1936I, 1945I, 1962J, 1990G
   *Cello Sonata* – 1982N
   *Country Roads, Unpaved* – 1936N
   *Dr. Franklin* – 1976N
   *Drumlin Legend, A* – 1940N
   *Eire Waters* – 1961N
   *Elegy, Oboe & Strings* – 1957N
   *Fantasy & Fugue for Orchestra* – 1926N
   *Ford's Theater* – 1946N
   *From Emily's Diary* – 1947N
   *From These States* – 1951N
   *Notes of the Piano* – 1963M
   *On Ecclesiastes* – 1936N
   *Our Musical Idiom* – 1917M
   *Over the Waters Overture* – 1977N
   *Piano Concerto No. 1* – 1963N
   *Piano Concerto No. 2* – 1982N
   *Piano Trio* – 1981N
   *Requiem* – 1971N
   *String Quintet* – 1950N
   *Symphonic Fugue* – 1932N
   *Symphony No. 1* – 1932N
   *Symphony No. 2* – 1937N
   *Violin Sonata* – 1982N
   *Words on Music* – 1960M
Bacon, Leonard
   *Hymns & Sacred Songs* – 1823M
Bacon, Thomas – 1758K, 1762K, 1768G
Bacquier, Gabriel – 1964H
Bada, Angelo – 1908H
Bad Brains – 1979C

Badea, Christian - 1981K, 1983I, 1986H
Bad English – 1988C, 1989E
Badger, Alfred – 1815F, 1834K, 1892G
Badger, Alfred, Flute Shop – 1846L
Bad Religion – 1980C
Badura-Skoda, Paul – 1953H
Baermann, Carl – 1881HK
Baez, Joan – 1941A
Bagdasarian, Ross
   *Come-on-a My House* – 1951E
Bagley, Edwin E. – 1922G
   *National Emblem March* – 1906N
Bailey Concert Hall (Fort Lauderdale) –
   1979L
Bailey, Buster – 1902A, 1967B
Bailey, Lillian – 1881K
Bailey, Mildred – 1907A, 1951B
Bailey, Norman – 1975H, 1976H
Bailey, Pearl – 1918A, 1978C, 1990B
Baillie, Alexander – 1992H
Baillie, Isobel – 1933H
Baillie, Kathy – 1951A
Bain, Wilfred C. –1938I, 1947I
Bainbridge, Elizabeth – 1977H
Baker & Scribner – 1846L
Baker Family Singers – 1881L
Baker, Belle – 1957B
Baker, Benjamin Franklin – 1811F, 1841I, 1850I,
   1889G
   *Baker's Church Music* – 1855M
   *Storm King, The* – 1856N
   *Thorough-Bass & Harmony* – 1870M
Baker, Bonnie – 1918A
Baker, Chet – 1929A, 1988B
Baker, Chet, Big Band – 1953C
Baker, David – 1931A, 1966C
   *Black America* – 1968E
   *Black Music in Our Culture* – 1970D
   *Jazz Improvisation* – 1969D
   *Jazz Styles & Analysis: Trombone* – 1973D
   *Techniques of Improvisation* – 1971D
Baker, Gary
   *I Swear* – 1994E
Baker, Gregg – 1955F, 1985H
Baker, Israel – 1921F
Baker, Janet – 1966H
Baker, Josephine – 1906A, 1925C, 1979B
Baker, Julius –1915F, 1954I, 1980I
Baker, Kenny – 1912A, 1985B
Baker, LaVern – 1929A
Baker, Robert S. – 1916F, 1961I
Baker, Theodore – 1851F, 1874K, 1882K, 1891K,
   1892I, 1926K, 1934G
   *Biographical Dictionary of Music, A* – 1900M
   *Dictionary of Musical Terms, A* – 1895M
   *Pronouncing Pocket Manual of Musical Terms* –
   1905M
Baklanov, George – 1911H
Bakst, Lawrence – 1955F

---

❖

**Vernacular/Commercial Music Scene**
A *Births*   B *Deaths*   C *Biographical*   D *Publications*
E *Representative Pieces*

Balada, Leonardo – 1956K, 1970I
  Auroris – 1973N
  Concerto, Cello & 9 Instruments – 1962N
  Concerto, 4 Guitars – 1976N
  Concerto, Piano, Winds & Percussion – 1974N
  Cuatro Canciones de la Provincia de Madrid,
    1962N
  Death of Columbus – 1992N
  Geometria No. 1 – 1966N
  Geometria II- 1967N
  Guernica – 1966N
  Guitar Concerto – 1965N
  Hangman, Hangman! – 1982N
  Homage to Casals – 1975N
  Homage to Sarasate – 1975N
  Maria Sabina – 1969N
  Mosaico – 1970N
  Persistencies – 1978N
  Piano Concerto – 1964N
  Seven Last Words, The – 1963N
  Sinfonia concertante – 1972N
  Sinfonia en Negro – 1968N
  Sonata for 10 Winds – 1980N
  Steel Symphony – 1972N
  Symphony No. 4 – 1992N
  Three Cervantinas – 1967N
  Thunderous Scenes – 1992N
  Violin Concerto – 1982N
  Violin Sonata – 1960N
  Zapata! – 1984N
Balanchine, George – 1933K, 1983G
  Balanchine's Complete Stories of Great Ballets –
    1954M
  Balanchine's New...Stories of Great Ballets –
    1968N
Balatka String Quartet – 1850L
Balatka Academy of Musical Art – 1879L
Balatka, Hans – 1849K, 1850I, 1860I, 1899G
Baldknobber's Theater – 1968C
Baldwin Piano Co. – 1862L
Baldwin, Dalton – 1931F
Baldwin, Samuel – 1862F, 1907I, 1949G
Baldwin-Wallace Bach Festival – 1932L
Baldwin-Wallace Conservatory of Music – 1913L
Bales, Richard – 1915F, 1942I, 1960J, 1985K
  Confederacy, The – 1953N
  National Gallery Suite I – 1943N
  National Gallery Suite II – 1944N
  National Gallery Suite III – 1957N
  National Gallery Suite IV – 1965N
  Republic, The – 1955N
  Union, The – 1956N
Balkan Rhythm Band – 1980C
B.A.L.L. – 1987C
Ball, Ernest R. – 1927B
  Heart of Paddy Whack, The – 1914E
  Let the Rest of the World Go By – 1919E
  Little Bit of Heaven, A – 1914E
  Love Me & the World is Mine – 1906E

  Manual of the Sacred Choir – 1849M
  Mother Machree – 1910E
  When Irish Eyes Are Smiling – 1912E
Ballantine, Edward – 1886G, 1912I
  By a Lake in Russia – 1922N
  Eve of St. Agnes, The – 1917N
  From the Garden of Hellas – 1923N
  Prelude, the Delectable Forest – 1914N
Ballard, Hank – 1936A
Ballard, Louis – 1931F, 1969I
  Fantasy Aborigine I – 1964N
  Fantasy Aborigine II – 1976N
  Fantasy Aborigine III – 1977N
  Four Moon, The – 1967N
  My Music Reaches to the Sky – 1973M
  Music of North American Indians – 1975M
  Portrait of Will Rogers – 1972N
  Thus Spake Abraham – 1976N
Balliett, Whitney
  American Musicians, 56 Portraits in Jazz –
    1986D
  American Singers – 1979D
  Dinosaurs in the Morning – 1962D
  Ectasy at the Onion – 1971D
  Sound of Surprise, The – 1959D
  Such Sweet Thunder – 1966D
Ballou, Esther – 1915F, 1962K, 1973G
  Concertino, Oboe & Strings – 1953N
  Creative Explorations of Musical Elements –
    1971M
  Early American Portrait – 1962N
  Guitar Concerto – 1964N
  Konzertstück, Viola & Orchestra – 1969N
  Music for the Theater – 1952N
  Passacaglia & Toccata – 1962N
  Piano Concerto No. 1 – 1945N
  Piano Concerto No. 2 – 1964N
  Piano Sonata – 1955N
  Prelude & Allegro – 1951N
  Sonata No. 1 for 2 Pianos – 1943N
  Sonata No. 2 for 2 Pianos – 1958N
  Suite for Chamber Orchestra – 1939N
  Variations, Scherzo & Fugue – 1959N
Ballou, Silas
  New Hymns for Various Subjects – 1785M
Balmer, Charles – 1836K
  St. Louis Fireman's Parade March – 1847N
Balmer & Weber Music House – 1848L
Balogh, Endre – 1954F, 1969H, 1971H
Balogh, Ernö – 1924K
Balsam, Artur – 1932K, 1933K, 1994G
Balthrop, Carmen – 1948F, 1973H, 1978H
Baltimore, Maryland
  Academy of Music (Peabody) – 1857L
  Chamber Music Society – 1950L
  Civic Opera Co. – 1940L
  Kraushaar Auditorium – 1962L
  Lyric Theater – 1894L
  Meyerhoff Symphony Hall – 1982L

---

### Cultivated/Art Music Scene

F *Births*    G *Deaths*    H *Debuts*    I *New Positions*    J *Honors and Awards*
K *Biographical*    L *Musical Beginnings*    M *Publications*    N *Compositions*

Baltimore, Maryland (continued)
   *Opera Co. – 1932L*
   *Oratorio Society – 1882L*
   *Philpot's Hill Theater – 1786L*
   *Symphony Orchestra – 1914L*
Baltsa, Agnes – 1971H, 1979H
Bamberger, Carl – 1937K, 1987G
Bamboschek, Giuseppe – 1913K, 1919H
Bampton, Rose – 1909F, 1929H, 1932H
Bananarama – 1986E
Band, The – 1967C
Bandrowski, Alexander von – 1902H
Bandwagon – 1967C
Bandy, Moe – 1944A
Bang on a Can Festival – 1987L
Bangles, The – 1981C, 1986E, 1989E
Bang Tango – 1987C
Banks, Barry – 1994H
Banks, Billy – 1908A, 1967B
Banks, Homer – 1941A
Banner Record Co. – 1922C
Bannon, R. C. – 1945A
Baptist Church Music Dept. – 1941L
Bar Harbor Music Festival – 1964L
Bar-Illan, David – 1954H, 1980I
Barab, Seymour – 1921F
   *Little Stories... – 1977N*
   *String Quartet – 1977N*
Baraka, Amiri
   *Black Music – 1968D*
   *Blues People – 1963D*
   *Music: Reflections on Jazz & Blues, The – 1987D*
Barantschik, Alexander – 1991H
Barati Ensemble – 1989L
Barati, George –1950I
   *Baroque Quartet Concerto – 1969N*
   *Branches of Time – 1981N*
   *B.U.D. Piano Sonata – 1984N*
   *Cello Concerto – 1957N*
   *Chamber Concerto – 1952N*
   *Confluence – 1982N*
   *Dragon & the Phoenix, The – 1960N*
   *Guitar Concerto – 1976N*
   *Piano Concerto – 1973N*
   *Polarization – 1965N*
   *String Quartet No. 1 – 1944N*
   *String Quartet No. 2 – 1962N*
   *Violin Concerto – 1986N*
Barbagallo, James – 1978J, 1980J
Barbarians, The – 1965C
Barber, Samuel – 1910F, 1928K, 1935J, 1939I,
   1941J, 1958J, 1976J, 1980J, 1981G
   *Adagio for Strings – 1936N*
   *Andromache's Farewell – 1962N*
   *Antony & Cleopatra – 1966N*
   *Capricorn Concerto – 1944N*
   *Cello Concerto – 1945N*
   *Cello Sonata – 1932N*
   *Commando March – 1943N*
   *Dover Beach – 1931N*

*Essay No. 1 – 1937N*
*Essay No. 2 – 1942N*
*Essay No. 2 – 1978N*
*Essay No. 3 – 1978N*
*Four Excursions – 1944N*
*Hand of Bridge, A – 1953N*
*Hermit Songs – 1953N*
*Knoxville: Summer of 1915 – 1947N*
*Lovers, The – 1971N*
*Natali, Die – 1960N*
*Piano Concerto – 1962N*
*Piano Sonata – 1949N*
*Prayers of Kierkegaard – 1954N*
*School for Scandal Overture – 1933N*
*Serenade – 1928N*
*Seven Nursery Songs – 1923N*
*Souvenirs – 1952N*
*Stopwatch & an Ordnance Map – 1940N*
*Symphony No. 1 – 1936N*
*Symphony No. 2 – 1944N*
*Toccata Festiva – 1960N*
*Vanessa – 1957N*
*Violin Concerto – 1939N*
*Violin Sonata – 1928N*
Barbieri, Fedora – 1950H
Barbirolli, John – 1936HI, 1961I
Barbosa-Lima, Carlos – 1967H
Barbour, Dave – 1912A, 1965B
Barbour, J. Murray – 1897F
   *Tuning & Temperament: a Historical Survey –*
   1951M
Bard Music Festival – 1990L
Bare, Bobby – 1935A
Barenboim, Daniel – 1957H
Barere, Simon – 1938H
Bargy, Roy – 1894A, 1974B
Barili, Alfredo – 1854F, 1865H, 1935G
Barker/Bray
   *Indian Princess, The – 1808N*
   *Tears & Smiles – 1807N*
Barker, Danny – 1909A, 1994B
Barkin, Elaine – 1932F, 1964I
   *At the Piano – 1982N*
   *Essay for Orchestra – 1957N*
   *Impromtu – 1981N*
   *Inward & Outward Bound – 1975N*
   *Plus ça Change – 1972N*
   *String Trio – 1976N*
   *To Whom It May Concern – 1989N*
   *Women's Voices – 1983N*
Barlow, Harold – 1915A
Barlow, Howard – 1892F, 1923I, 1927I, 1940I,
   1972G
   *Dictionary of Vocal Themes, A – 1950M*
   *Dictionary of Musical Terms, A – 1948M*
Barlow, Samuel – 1892F, 1982G
   *Alba – 1927N*
   *Amanda – 1936N*
   *Amphyitryon – 1937N*
   *Ballo Sardo – 1928N*

---

❄

## Vernacular/Commercial Music Scene
A *Births*   B *Deaths*   C  *Biographical*   D *Publications*
E *Representative Pieces*

---

### Cultivated/Art Music Scene

F *Births*    G *Deaths*    H *Debuts*    I *New Positions*    J *Honors and Awards*
K *Biographical*    L *Musical Beginnings*    M *Publications*    N *Compositions*

---

**Vernacular/Commercial Music Scene**
A *Births*    B *Deaths*    C *Biographical*    D *Publications*
E *Representative Pieces*

---

## Cultivated/Art Music Scene

F *Births*    G *Deaths*    H *Debuts*    I *New Positions*    J *Honors and Awards*
K *Biographical*    L *Musical Beginnings*    M *Publications*    N *Compositions*

Bekker, Paul – 1933K, 1937G
  *Story of the Orchestra, The* – 1936M
Belafonte, Harry – 1927A, 1989C
Bel-Airs – 1961C
Belew, Adrian – 1948A
Belew, Carl – 1931A, 1990B
Belgian School of Violin – 1908L
Bell Telephone Computer Studio – 1957L
Bell, Archie – 1944A, 1968E
Bell, Joshua – 1967F, 1975K, 1981H
Bell, William – 1939A
Bellamann, Henry
  *Music Teacher's Notebook, A* – 1920M
Bellamy Brothers – 1976E
Bellamy, David – 1950A
Bellamy, Howard – 1946A
Bell Biv DeVoe – 1988C
Belle, Regina – 1963A
Bellezza, Vincenza – 1926H
Bellson, Louie – 1924A
Bellstedt, Herman – 1913I
Bellugi, Piero – 1959I
Belmonts, The – 1957C
Belt, P. R., Piano Workshop – 1966L
Belvin, Jusse – 1933A, 1960B
Belwin Mills Publishing Co. – 1969L
Belwin, Inc. – 1918L
Benacková, Gabriela – 1979H, 1991H
Benatar, Pat – 1953A
Bender, Paul – 1922H
Bendix, Max – 1910H
Beneke, Tex – 1914A
Benjamin, Bennie
  *When the Lights Go On Again* – 1942E
Bennett, Robert Russell – 1937I, 1981G
  *Abraham Lincoln Symphony* – 1931N
  *Commemoration Symphony* – 1959N
  *Concerto for Harp & Cello* – 1960N
  *Concerto for Violin & Piano* – 1962N
  *Endymion* – 1927N
  *Four Freedoms Symphony* – 1943N
  *Guitar Concerto* – 1970N
  *Instrumentally Speaking* – 1975M
  *Kiss, The* – 1944N
  *Maria Malibran* – 1935N
  *Organ Sonata* – 1929N
  *Overture to an Imaginary Drama* – 1946N
  *Piano Concerto* – 1948N
  *Suite, Old American Dances* – 1949N
  *Symphony* – 1946N
  *Symphony in D, "For the Dodgers"* – 1941N
  *Variations for Violin & Orchestra* – 1949N
  *Violin Concerto* – 1941N
Bennett, Tony – 1926A, 1967C
Benoit, David – 1953A
Benson, George – 1943A
Benson, Joan – 1929F
Benson, Warren – 1924F, 1953I
  *Compositional Process & Writing Skills* – 1974M

*Creative Projects in Musicianship* – 1967M
*Delphic Serenade, A* – 1953N
*5 Lyrics of Louise Bogan* – 1977N
*Horn Concerto* – 1971N
*Moon Rain & Memory Jane* – 1982N
*Songs for the End of the World* – 1980N
*String Quartet* – 1969N
*Symphony for Drums & Winds* – 1962N
*Symphony No. 2* – 1982N
*Theme & Excursions* – 1963N
Bent, Margaret – 1983I
Benton, Brook – 1931A, 1988B
Bentonelli, Joseph – 1925H, 1934H, 1936H, 1975G
Benzell, Mimi – 1922F, 1944H, 1945H, 1949C,
  1970G
Beranek, Leo L. – 1914F
Berberian, Cathy – 1925F, 1950K, 1957H, 1960H,
  1983G
Berezowsky, Nicolai – 1922K, 1928K, 1953G
  *Clarinet Concerto* – 1941N
  *Concerto Lirico, Op. 19* – 1935N
  *Gilgamesh* – 1947N
  *Harp Concerto* – 1945N
  *Sinfonietta* – 1932N
  *String Quartet* – 1933N
  *Symphony No. 1* – 1931N
  *Symphony No. 2* – 1934N
  *Symphony No. 3* – 1937N
  *Symphony No. 4* – 1943N
  *Theremin Concerto* – 1948N
  *Viola Concerto* – 1941N
  *Violin Concerto* – 1930N
Berg, Gerald – 1954F
  *Odd Trio* – 1991N
  *Variation Set* – 1989N
Berganza, Teresa – 1958H, 1967H
Berger, Arthur – 1912F, 1953I, 1979I, 1960J
  *Chamber Concerto* – 1960N
  *Chamber Music for 13 Instruments* – 1956N
  *Composition, Piano, 4 Hands* – 1976N
  *Ideas of Order* – 1952N
  *Perspectives III* – 1982N
  *Piano Fantasy* – 1942N
  *Piano Trio* – 1980N
  *Polyphony* – 1956N
  *Septet* – 1966N
  *String Quartet* – 1958N
  *Three Pieces, String Orchestra* – 1945N
  *Trio for Guitar, Violin & Piano* – 1972N
  *Two-Part Inventions, Four* – 1949N
  *Wind Quintet* – 1984N
  *Woodwind Quartet* – 1941N
Berger, Erna – 1949H
Berger, Jean – 1941K, 1943K
  *Caribbean Cruise* – 1958N
  *Cherry Tree Carol, The* – 1975N
  *Creole Overture* – 1949N
  *Diversion for Strings* – 1977N
  *Divertissement for Strings* – 1970N

---

Vernacular/Commercial Music Scene
A *Births*    B *Deaths*    C *Biographical*    D *Publications*
E *Representative Pieces*

Fiery Furnace – 1962N
5 Compositions for Piano – 1944N
Trio, Guitar, Violin & Piano – 1972N
Petit Suite – 1952N
Piano Sonatina – 1952N
Pied Piper – 1968N
Short Overture – 1958N
Short Symphony – 1974N
Sinfonia Breve – 1952N
Yiphth & His Daughter – 1972N
Berger, Rudolf – 1914H
Berglund, Joel – 1938H, 1946H
Bergman, Heidi – 1958F
Bergman, Marilyn – 1994C
Bergonzi, Carlo – 1955H, 1994K
Bergonzi, Jerry   1947A
Bergsma, William – 1921F, 1945J, 1946I, 1963I,
    1967J, 1994G
    Carol on Twelfth Night, A – 1974N
    Chameleon Variations – 1960N
    Changes – 1971N
    Concerto for Wind Quintet – 1958N
    Fortunate Islands, The – 1947N
    Gold & the Senor Commandante – 1941N
    In Celebration – 1963N
    Murder of Comrade Sharik, The – 1973N
    Music on a Quiet Theme   1943N
    Paul Bunyan – 1938N
    San Francisco – 1939N
    String Quartet No. 1 – 1942N
    String Quartet No. 2 – 1944N
    String Quartet No. 3 – 1953N
    String Quartet No. 4   1970N
    String Quartet No. 5 – 1982N
    Sweet Was the Song the Virgin Sung – 1977N
    Symphony No. 1 – 1949N
    Symphony No. 2 – 1976N
    Tangents – 1951N
    Variations for Piano – 1984N
    Violin Concerto – 1966N
    Wife of Martin Guerre, The   1956N
Berigan, Bunny – 1908A, 1942B
Berigan, Bunny, Big Band – 1937C
Berio, Luciano – 1950K, 1951K, 1962I, 1965I,
    1994I
    Opera – 1970N
    Sequenze II – 1963N
    Sequenze III – 1966N
    Sequenze IV – 1966N
    Sequenze VI – 1967N
    Sequenze VII – 1969N
    Sinfonia – 1968N
Berkeley Jazz Festival – 1967C
Berkeley Opera – 1979L
Berkeley Symphony Orchestra – 1969L
Berklee College of Music – 1945L
Berkshire Festival, Contemporary Music – 1964L
Berkshire Music Center – 1940L
Berkshire Music Festival – 1934L

Berkshire String Quartet – 1913L
Berlin – 1979C, 1986E
Berlin, E. A.
    Ragtime: a Musical & Cultural History – 1980D
Berlin, Irving – 1989B
    Alexander's Ragtime Band – 1911E
    Alexander's Ragtime Band (film) – 1938E
    All By Myself – 1921E
    Always – 1925E
    Annie, Get Your Gun – 1946E
    As Thousands Cheer – 1933E
    Blue Skies – 1927E
    Blue Skies (film) – 1946E
    Call Me Madam – 1950E
    Carefree – 1939E
    Century Girl, The – 1916E
    Cocoanuts, The – 1925E
    Count Your Blessings – 1952E
    Easter Parade (film) – 1948E
    Face the Music – 1932E
    Follow the Fleet – 1936E
    God Bless America – 1918E
    Hallelujah – 1929E
    I've Got My Love to Keep Me Warm – 1937E
    Kid Millions – 1934E
    Let's Face the Music & Dance -1936E
    Louisiana Purchase – 1940E
    Mr. President – 1962E
    Miss Liberty – 1949E
    Music Box Revue 1921-22 – 1921E
    Music Box Revue 1922-23 – 1922E
    On the Avenue   1937E
    Pretty Girl is Like a Melody, A – 1919E
    Putting On the Ritz – 1930E
    Ragtime Violin – 1911E
    Reaching for the Moon – 1931E
    School-House Blues – 1921E
    Stop! Look! Listen! – 1915E
    That International Rag – 1913E
    There's No Business Like Show Business (film) –
        1954E
    This Is the Army – 1942E
    Top Hat – 1935E
    Watch Your Step – 1914E
    White Christmas – 1942E
    Yip, Yip, Yaphank   1918E
    Ziegfeld Follies of 1919 – 1919E
    Ziegfeld Follies of 1920 – 1920E
    Ziegfeld Follies of 1927 – 1927E
Berlin, Irving, Music, Inc. – 1919C
Berliner, Paul
    Thinking in Jazz:...Art of Improvisation – 1994D
Berlinski, Hermann – 1941K, 1947K, 1963I
Berman, Jerry – 1933A
Berman, Lazar – 1976H
Berman, Pavel – 1991J
Bernard, Felix – 1944B
    Dardanella – 1919E
    Winter Wonderland – 1934E

Bernard, George
  *Old Rugged Cross, The* – 1913N
Bernard, Gus W.
  *Colored Aristocracy Cakewalk* – 1899E
Berne, Tim – 1954A
Bernhardt, Clyde – 1905A, 1986B
Bernheimer, Martin – 1965I, 1981J
Bernie, Ben
  *Sweet Georgia Brown* – 1925E
Bernstein Center, Education Thru the Arts – 1991L
Bernstein, Elmer – 1922A
  *Field, The* – 1990E
  *How Now, Dow Jones* – 1967E
  *Magnificent Seven, The* – 1960E
  *Man with the Golden Arm, The* – 1955E
  *My Left Foot* – 1989E
  *Summer & Smoke* – 1961E
  *Ten Commandments, The* – 1956E
  *Thoroughly Modern Millie* – 1967E
Bernstein, Lawrence – 1939F, 1974IJ
Bernstein, Leonard – 1918F, 1942K, 1943HK,
  1944K, 1945I, 1951IK,1953K, 1958IJK, 1959J,
  1960J, 1968J, 1969K, 1980J, 1981J, 1985J, 1986K,
  1987J, 1990G
  *Birds, The* – 1939N
  *Candide* – 1956N
  *Candide (musical)* – 1973E
  *Chichester Psalms* – 1965N
  *Divertimento for Orchestra* – 1980N
  *Dybbuk* – 1974N
  *Facsimile* – 1946N
  *Fancy Free* – 1944N
  *Five Anniversaries* – 1964N
  *Harvard Choruses* – 1956N
  *Joy of Music, The* – 1959M
  *Jubilee Games* – 1986N
  *Mass* – 1971N
  *Olympic Hymn* – 1981N
  *On the Town* – 1944E
  *On the Waterfront* – 1954E
  *Overture, Slava* – 1977N
  *Peace, The* – 1940N
  *Peter Pan* – 1950N
  *Piano Sonata* – 1938N
  *Prelude, Fugue & Riffs* – 1949E
  *Quiet Place, A* – 1983N
  *Salome* – 1955N
  *Serenade* – 1954N
  *1600 Pennsylvania Avenue* – 1976E
  *Songfest* – 1977N
  *Symphony No. 1* – 1942N
  *Symphony No. 2* – 1949N
  *Symphony No. 3* – 1963N
  *Touches* – 1981N
  *Trouble in Tahiti* – 1951N
  *Violin Sonata* – 1940N
  *West Side Story* – 1957E
  *Wonderful Town* – 1953E
Bernstein, Leonard, Conducting Comp. – 1995L

Bernstein, Louis – 1962G
Bernstein, Martin – 1904F, 1926I
  *Introduction to Music, An* – 1937M
  *Score Reading* – 1932M
Berry, Bill – 1930A
Berry, "Chu" – 1908A
Berry, Chuck – 1926A, 1972E
Berry, Jan – 1941A
  *Up from the Cradle of Jazz* – 1987D
Berry, Judy – 1992J
Berry, Richard – 1935A
Berry, Wallace – 1928F, 1966H, 1978J
  *Admirable Bashville, The* – 1954N
  *Canticle on a Judaic Text* – 1953N
  *Eighteenth-century Imitative Counterpoint* –
    1969M
  *Form in Music* – 1966M
  *Musical Structure & Performance* – 1989M
  *Piano Concerto* – 1964N
  *Spoon River* – 1952N
  *String Quartet No. 1* – 1960N
  *String Quartet No. 2* – 1964N
  *String Quartet No. 3* – 1966N
  *String Quartet No. 4* – 1982N
  *Structural Functions in Music* – 1976M
Beserkley Records – 1973C
Bertles, John F. – 1959F
Berwald, William – 1921I
Besanzoni, Gabriella – 1919H
Besoyan, Rick
  *Little Mary Sunshine* – 1959E
  *Student Gypsy, The* – 1963E
Bessaraboff, Nicholas – 1915K, 1973G
  *Ancient European Musical Instruments* – 1941M
Bethlehem Record Co. – 1953C
Bethune, Blind Tom – 1908G
  *Battle of Manassas, The* – 1861N
Beudert, Mark – 1951F, 1985J
Beversdorf, Thomas – 1924F, 1981G
  *Cathedral Music* – 1950N
  *Concerto for 2 Pianos* – 1951N
  *Hooligan, The* – 1969N
  *Mexican Portrait* – 1948N
  *New Frontiers* – 1953N
  *Rock, The* – 1958N
  *String Quartet No. 1* – 1951N
  *String Quartet No. 2* – 1955N
  *Symphony No. 1* – 1946N
  *Symphony No. 2* – 1950N
  *Symphony No. 3* – 1954N
  *Symphony No. 4* – 1960N
  *Variations for Orchestra* – 1963N
  *Violin Concerto* – 1959N
  *Vision of Christ* – 1971N
Beveridge, Thomas
  *Radha Sings* – 1985N
Beyer, Johanna M. – 1924K, 1944G
Bezanson, Philip – 1916G, 1964I, 1975G
  *Fantasy, Fugue & Finale* – 1951N

---

❀

**Vernacular/Commercial Music Scene**
A *Births*   B *Deaths*   C *Biographical*   D *Publications*
E *Representative Pieces*

Overture, Cyrano de Bergerac – 1949N
Piano Concerto – 1952N
St. Judas – 1973N
Sinfonia Concertante – 1971N
Songs of Innocence – 1959N
Stranger in Eden – 1963N
String Quartet No. 1 – 1947N
String Quartet No. 2 – 1961N
Symphony No. 1 – 1946N
Symphony No. 2 – 1950N
Western Child – 1959N
Word of Love, The – 1956N
B-52's, The – 1976C
Bible, Frances – 1927F, 1948H
Bigard, Barney – 1906A, 1988B
Big Apple Band – 1976E
Big Bands International – 1977C
Big Black – 1982C
Big Brother and the Holding Company – 1965C
Big Daddy Kane – 1968A
Bigelow, F. E.
    Our Director – 1926N
Big T – 1990C
Big Four Jazz Quartet – 1951C
Biggs, E. Power – 1932H, 1937K, 1977G
Biggs, John
    Songs of Love, Laughter & Tears – 1974N
Big Maybelle – 1920A, 1972B
Big Star – 1971C
Big Three Corporation – 1939C
Big Twist – 1937A, 1990B
Bikini Kill – 1990C
Bilk, Mr. Acker – 1962E
Bilson, Malcolm – 1935F
Bilt, Peter van der – 1963H
Bim, Bam, Boom:...History of Rhythm and Blues –
    1972C
Bimboni, Alberto – 1912K
    Winona – 1926N
Binder, Abraham
    Holy Land Impressions – 1927N
    Overture, The Pioneers – 1927N
Bing, Rudolph - 1950I, 1973J
    5,000 Nights at the Opera – 1972M
    Knight at the Opera, A – 1981M
Bingham, Seth – 1908I, 1912I, 1919I, 1972G
    Baroques – 1943N
    Canticle of the Sun – 1942N
    Carillon de Château-Thierry – 1936N
    Harmonies of Florence – 1928N
    Memories of France – 1920N
    Organ Concerto – 1946N
    Passacaglia for Orchestra – 1918N
    Pioneer America – 1925N
    String Quartet – 1916N
    Suite for 9 Winds – 1915N
    Suite for Organ – 1923N
    36 Hymn & Carol Canons for Organ – 1952N
    Twelve Hymn-Preludes for Organ – 1942N

Variation Studies for Organ – 1950N
Wall Street Fantasy – 1916N
Wilderness Stone – 1933N
Binkerd, Gordon – 1916F, 1949I, 1964J
    Concert Set for Piano – 1969N
    Entertainments – 1960N
    Organ Service – 1957N
    Part of Heaven, A – 1971N
    Piano Miscellany – 1969N
    Piano Sonata No. 1 – 1955N
    Piano Sonata No. 2 – 1981N
    Piano Sonata No. 3 – 1982N
    Piano Sonata No. 4 – 1983N
    String Quartet No. 1 – 1958N
    String Quartet No. 2 – 1961N
    Symphony No. 1 – 1955N
    Symphony No. 2 – 1957N
    Symphony No. 3 – 1959N
Bini, Carlo – 1982H
Birchard, Clarence C. – 1946G
Birchard, C. C., Co. – 1901L
Bird, Arthur H. – 1923G
    Concert Fantasia – 1904N
    Four Pieces for Piano – 1910N
    Three Miniature Poems – 1912N
    Two Decimettes – 1901N
Birge, Edward B.
    History of Public School Music in the United
    States – 1928M
Birmingham Concert Hall – 1974L
Birmingham Festival of the Arts – 1951L
Biscardi, Chester – 1948F
    At the Still Point – 1977N
    Five Sapphic Lyrics – 1974N
    Heabakes – 1975N
    Mestiere – 1979N
    Orpha – 1974N
    Piano Concerto – 1983N
    Piano Sonata – 1986N
    Piano Trio – 1976N
    Tight Rope – 1985N
Bishop, Elvin – 1942A
Bishop-Kovacevich, Stephen – 1940F, 1951H
Bispham, David – 1921G
Bispham Medal – 1921L
Bitch – 1982C
Bitgood, Roberta – 1908F, 1975I
    Joseph – 1960N
    Let There Be Light – 1965N
Bjoner, Ingrid – 1961H
Björling, Jussi – 1937H, 1938H
Björling, Sigurd – 1952H
Black and White Records – 1944C
Black Artist Group – 1968C
Black Bottom Stompers – 1927C
Black Crowes – 1988C
Black Eagle Jazz Band, New – 1971C
Black Flag – 1977C
Black Jazz Record Co. – 1971C

---

## Cultivated/Art Music Scene

F *Births*    G *Deaths*    H *Debuts*    I *New Positions*    J *Honors and Awards*
K *Biographical*    L *Musical Beginnings*    M *Publications*    N *Compositions*

Black Music Colloquium – 1980L
*Black Music Newsletter* – 1981C
*Black Music Research Journal* – 1980L
Black Oak Arkansas – 1969C
*Black Perspective in Music, The* – 1973C
Black Sheep – 1983C
Black Swan Record Co. – 1921C
Black, Bill, Combo – 1959C
Black, Clint – 1962A
Black, Frank – 1928I, 1968G
Black, James – 1940A, 1988B
Black, Jeffrey – 1993H
Black, Johnny S.
   *Paper Doll* – 1915E
Black, Robert – 1950F, 1976H
Black, William David – 1952F, 1977H
Blackburn, Bonnie – 1939F
Blackburn, Tom
   *Ballad of Davy Crockett* – 1954E
Blackbyrd – 1973C
Blackhearts, The – 1981C, 1982E
Blackman, Cindy – 1959A
Blackwell, Ed – 1992B
Blackwell, Harolyn – 1960F
Blackwell, Otis – 1931A
   *Breathless* – 1958E
Blackwood, Easley – 1933F, 1958I, 1960J
   *Cello Sonata* – 1986N
   *Chamber Symphony, Op. 2* – 1954N
   *Clarinet Sonata, Op. 37* – 1994N
   *Flute Concerto* – 1968N
   *Oboe Concerto* – 1965N
   *Pastorale & Variations* – 1961N
   *Piano Concerto* – 1970N
   *Piano Trio, Op. 22* – 1967N
   *Sonata for Violin & Piano* – 1973N
   *Sonatina for Piccolo Carinet* – 1994N
   *String Quartet No. 1* – 1958N
   *String Quartet No. 2* – 1960N
   *Structure of Recognizable Diatonic Tunings* –
    1985M
   *Symphonic Episode (organ)* – 1966N
   *Symphonic Fantasy* – 1965N
   *Symphony No. 1* – 1958N
   *Symphony No. 2* – 1961N
   *Symphony No. 3* – 1965N
   *Symphony No. 4* – 1973N
   *Symphony No. 5* – 1990N
   *12 Microtonal Etudes* – 1982N
   *Violin Concerto* – 1967N
   *Viola Sonata* – 1953N
   *Violin Sonata, Op. 7* – 1960N
Blades, Rubén – 1948S
Blaisdell Memorial Center (Hawaii) – 1964L
Blaisdell Wind Quartet – 1938L
Blake Babies – 1986C
Blake, Charles Dupee – 1903B
Blake, Charlotte
   *That Tired Rag* – 1911E

Blake, Eubie – 1978C, 1980C, 1981C, 1983B
   *Black Keys on Parade* – 1935E
   *Bugle Call Rag* – 1916E
   *Chevy Chase Rag* – 1914E
   *Classical Rag* – 1912E
   *Elsie* – 1923E
   *Eubie* – 1978E
   *Fizz Water Rag* – 1914E
   *Lew Leslie's Blackbirds of 1930* – 1930E
   *Love Will Find a Way* – 1921E
   *Shuffle Along of 1933* – 1932E
   *Swing It* – 1937E
   *Tan Manhattan* – 1940E
Blake, Eubie, Music Co. – 1972C
Blake, Rockwell – 1951F, 1978J, 1981H
Blakey, Art – 1919A, 1990B
Blanchard, Terence – 1962A
Blanchard-Harrison Band – 1986C
Blanchart, Ramón – 1907H
Bland, Bobby – 1930A
Bland, James – 1911B
Blane, Ralph – 1914A
   *Best Foot Forward* – 1941E
   *Meet Me in St. Louis* – 1944E
   *Summer Holiday* (film) – 1948E
   *Three Wishes for Jamie* – 1951E
Blankenship, Rebecca – 1954F, 1990H
Blanton, Jimmy – 1918A, 1942B
Blass, Robert – 1930G
Blasters – 1979C
Blauvelt, Lilian – 1947G
Bledsoe, Jules – 1924H, 1943G
Blegen, Judith – 1940F, 1970H
Blesh, Rudi
   *Combo: USA: Eight Lives in Jazz* – 1971D
   *Shining Trumpets: a History of Jazz* – 1946D
   *They All Played Ragtime* – 1950D
   *This Is Jazz:..Lectures Given at the San Francisco*
    *Museum* – 1943D
Blessed Death – 1984C
Bley, Carla – 1938A
   *Genuine Tong Funeral, A* – 1968E
Bleyer, Archie – 1909A, 1989B
Blige, Mary J. – 1971A
Blind Illusion – 1978C
Bliss, Anthony – 1975I, 1981I, 1991G
Blitz, Julian Paul – 1913I
Blitzstein, Marc – 1905F, 1946J, 1959J, 1964G
   *Cain* – 1930N
   *Condemned, The* – 1932N
   *Cradle Will Rock, The* – 1937N
   *Four Whitman Songs* – 1928N
   *Freedome Morning* – 1943N
   *Goloopchik* – 1945N
   *Guest, The* – 1948N
   *Harpies, The* – 1931N
   *King Lear I* – 1950N
   *King Lear II* – 1955N
   *Juno* – 1959N

---

**Vernacular/Commercial Music Scene**
A  *Births*    B  *Deaths*    C  *Biographical*    D  *Publications*
E  *Representative Pieces*

*Lear: A Study for Orchestra* – 1958N
*Magic Barrel, The* – 1963N
*Midsummer Night's Dream* – 1958N
*No for an Answer* – 1940N
*Parabola & Circula* – 1929N
*Piano Concerto* – 1931N
*Piano Percussion Music* – 1929N
*Piano Sonata* – 1927N
*Piano Suite* – 1933N
*Regina* – 1949N
*Reuben, Reuben* – 1955N
*Sacco & Vanzetti* – 1964N
*Sarabande for Orchestra* – 1926N
*String Quartet* – 1930N
*Surf & Seaweed* – 1933N
*Symphony: The Airborne* – 1946N
*Toys in the Attic* – 1960N
*Triple Sec* – 1928N
*Variations for Orchestra* – 1934N
*Volpone* – 1956N
Blitzstein, Marc, Award – 1965L
Bloch, Boris – 1978J
Bloch, Ernest – 1916K, 1920I, 1924K, 1925I, 1936J, 1940I, 1943J, 1959J
*America: an Epic Rhapsody* – 1926N
*Baal Shem* – 1923N
*Concertino, Flute, Viola, Strings* – 1950N
*Concerto Grosso No. 1* – 1925N
*Concerto Grosso No. 2* – 1952N
*Concerto Symphonique* – 1948N
*Evocations* – 1937N
*From Jewish Life* – 1924N
*Helvetia* – 1929N
*Hiver* – 1904N
*In the Mountains, Night* – 1925N
*Israel* – 1916N
*Piano Quintet* – 1923N
*Piano Sonata* – 1935N
*Poems of the Sea* – 1922N
*Printemps* – 1905N
*Proclamation* – 1955N
*Sacred Service* – 1933N
*Schelomo* – 1916N
*Scherzo Fantasque* – 1948N
*String Quartet No. 1* – 1916N
*String Quartet No. 2* – 1945N
*String Quartet No. 3* – 1952N
*String Quartet No. 4* – 1953N
*String Quartet No. 5* – 1956N
*Suite Hébraïque* – 1951N
*Suite Symphonique* – 1944N
*Suite, Viola & Orchestra* – 1919N
*Symphony in c#* – 1902N
*Symphony in E-flat* – 1955N
*Symphony, Trombone & Orchestra* – 1954N
*Three Jewish Poems* – 1913N
*Two Last Poems* – 1958N
*Violin Concerto* – 1938N
*Violin Sonata No. 1* – 1920N

*Violin Sonata No. 2* – 1924N
*Visions & Prophecies* – 1936N
*Voice in the Wilderness* – 1936N
Bloch, Ernest, Society – 1968L
Bloch, Ray – 1982B
Block, Michel – 1959H
*Women in American Music* – 1979M
Blomstedt, Herbert – 1927F, 1985H
Blondie – 1975C, 1979E, 1980E, 1981E
Bloodgood – 1985C
Blood, Sweat and Tears – 1967C
Bloodstone – 1962C
Bloom, Rube
*Fools Rush In* – 1940E
*Give Me the Simple Life* – 1945E
Bloomfield, Michael – 1944A, 1981B
Bloomfield, Theodore – 1923F, 1955I, 1959I
Blossom Music Center – 1968L
Blossom Music Festival (Ohio) – 1968L
Blossom, Henry – 1919B
Blossoms – 1954C
Blue Cheer – 1967C
Blue Devils – 1925C
Blue Grass Boys – 1938C
Blue Jay Singers – 1926C
Blue Note Record Co. – 1939C
Blue Notes – 1954C
Blue Oyster Cult – 1969C
Blue Ribbon Band – 1929C
Blue Sky Boys – 1935C
Blue, David – 1941A
Bluebird Records – 1932C
*Bluegrass Unlimited* – 1966C
Blues Heaven Foundation – 1982C
Blues Image – 1966C
Blues Magoos – 1964C
Blues Project – 1965C
Blumenfeld, Harold – 1923F
Blum, Michael – 1979J
Blythe, Arthur – 1940A
BMI Awards to Student Composers – 1951L
*BMI: The Many Worlds of Music* – 1962C
Boatwright, Helen – 1916F, 1943K
Boatwright, Howard – 1918F, 1942H, 1943K, 1964I
*Canticle of the Sun* – 1963N
*Introduction to the Theory of Music* – 1956M
*Mass in C* – 1958N
*Passion According to St. Matthew* – 1962N
*Quartet, Clarinet & Strings* – 1958N
*Song for St. Cecilia's Day, A* – 1981N
*String Quartet No. 2* – 1974N
*Symphony* – 1976N
Boatwright, McHenry – 1928F, 1956H, 1994G
Bobbettes, The – 1956C
Bobick, James – 1967F, 1989H
Bock, Jerry – 1928A
*Apple Tree, The* – 1966E
*Body Beautiful, The* – 1958E
*Fiddler on the Roof* – 1964E

---

### Cultivated/Art Music Scene
F *Births*    G *Deaths*    H *Debuts*    I *New Positions*    J *Honors and Awards*
K *Biographical*    L *Musical Beginnings*    M *Publications*    N *Compositions*

Bock, Jerry (continued)
  *Fiorello* – 1959E
  *Mr. Wonderful* – 1956E
  *Rothschilds, The* – 1970E
  *She Loves Me* – 1962E
Bockelmann, Rudolph – 1930H
Bodanzky, Arthur – 1915HI, 1939G
BoDeans, The – 1985C
Bodky, Erwin – 1938K, 1958G
Bodnar-Horton, Nina – 1981J
Boelke-Bomart, Inc., Publishers – 1948L
Boelke, Walter R. – 1987G
Boesch, Christian – 1979H
Bofill, Angela – 1954A
Bogguss, Suzy – 1956A
Böhme, Kurt – 1954H
Böhm, Karl – 1957H
Bohnen, Michael – 1923H
Boise, Otis Bardwell – 1912G
  *Music & Its Masters* – 1902M
Bok, Mary Louise Curtis – 1934K, 1970G
Bolcom, William – 1938F, 1973I, 1975K, 1993J
  *Brass Quintet* – 1980N
  *Commedia for Chamber Orchestra* – 1971N
  *Concerto Serenade* – 1964N
  *Concerto, Two Pianos, Left Hand* – 1995N
  *Dream Music I* – 1965N
  *Etudes for Orchestra* – 1989N
  *Fantasy Sonata No. 1* – 1961tN
  *Fourteen Piano Rags* – 1970E
  *Garden of Eden Suite* – 1968N
  *Gospel Preludes II, III* – 1982N
  *Humoresk* – 1979N
  *Hydraulis* – 1971N
  *Let Evening Come* – 1994N
  *Lyric Concerto for Flute* – 1993N
  *McTeague* – 1992N
  *Monsterpieces* – 1980N
  *Morning & Evening Songs* – 1966N
  *Mysteries* – 1976N
  *Octet* – 1962N
  *Orphée-Sérénade* – 1984N
  *Piano Concerto* – 1976N
  *Ragomania* – 1982E
  *Recuerdos for Two Pianos* – 1995N
  *Reminiscing with Sissle & Blake* – 1973D
  *Romantic Pieces for Piano* – 1959N
  *Seattle Slew Suite* – 1977N
  *Session III, IV* – 1967N
  *String Quartet No. 8* – 1965N
  *String Quartet No. 9* – 1972N
  *String Quartet No. 10* – 1988N
  *Summer Divertimento* – 1973N
  *Symphony* – 1957N
  *Symphony (Oracles)* – 1965N
  *Symphony for Chamber Orchestra* – 1979N
  *Symphony No. 4* – 1987N
  *Three Gospel Preludes* – 1979N
  *12 Etudes for Piano* – 1960N

  *12 New Etudes for Piano* – 1987N
  *Violin Concerto* – 1983N
  *Walt Whitman Triptych, A* – 1995N
Bolet, Jorge – 1937HJ, 1938J, 1969I, 1977I,
  1990G
Bolin, Tommy – 1951A, 1976B
Boller, Bettina – 1990H
Bolstad, Anne – 1993H
Bolton, Michael – 1953A, 1990E, 1991E
Bonagura, Michael – 1953A
Bonaventura, Anthony di – 1930F, 1973I
Bonaventura, Mario di – 1924F, 1952J, 1968J
Bonazzi, Elaine – 1936F
Bonci, Alessandro – 1906H, 1907H
Bond, Carrie Jacobs – 1946G
  *Half Minute Songs* – 1911N
  *I Love You Truly* – 1901E
  *Just A-Wearyin' for You* – 1901E
  *Perfect Day, A* – 1909E
  *Sandman, The* – 1912N
Bond, Johnny – 1915A, 1978B
Bond, Victoria – 1945F, 1977K, 1986I, 1988I
Bonds, Gary U. S. – 1939A, 1961E
Bonds, Margaret – 1913F, 1933H
  *Ballad of the Brown King* – 1954N
  *Mass in D* – 1959N
  *Migration, The* – 1964N
  *Montgomery Variations* – 1965N
Bonelli, Richard – 1915H, 1932H, 1945K,
  1980G
Bongos, The – 1980C
Bongwater – 1987C
Bon Jovi, Jon – 1962A, 1983C, 1986E, 1988E,
  1989E, 1990E
Bonner, Eugene M.
  *Barbara Fritchie* – 1917N
  *Celui Qui Espousa une Femme Muette* – 1923N
  *Fields of Wonder* – 1964N
  *Gods of the Mountains* – 1936N
  *Piano Quintet* – 1925N
  *Venetian Glass Nephew, The* – 1927N
  *Whispers of Heavenly Death* – 1925N
Bonner, Juke Boy – 1932A, 1978B
Bonnet, Joseph – 1917H
Bonney, Barbara – 1956F, 1988H
Bono, Cher – 1946A
Bono, Sonny – 1935A
Bonoff, Karla – 1932A
Booker T. and the MG's – 1961C
Bookspan, Martin – 1984J
  *Masterpieces of Music & Their Composers* –
  1968M
Boone, "Blind" – 1927A
Boone, Charles – 1939F
Boone, Debby – 1956A, 1977E
Boone, Pat – 1934A, 1957E, 1961E
Booth, John E.
  *The Critic, Power, & the Performing Arts* –
  1991M

---

❖

Vernacular/Commercial Music Scene
  A *Births*    B *Deaths*    C *Biographical*    D *Publications*
E *Representative Pieces*

Booth, Mark
  *American Popular Music: A Reference Guide* –
    1983D
Booth, Thomas – 1991H
Boozer, Brenda – 1948F
Borchard, Adolphe – 1910H
Bordman, Gerald
  *American Musical Theatre: A Chronicle, The* – 1978D
Bordoni, Irene – 1953B
Boretz, Benjamin – 1934F
  *Concerto Grosso for Strings* – 1954N
  *String Quartet* – 1958N
  *Violin Concerto* – 1956N
Borg, Kim – 1959H
Borge, Victor – 1953K
Borgioli, Armando – 1932H
Borgioli, Dino – 1934H
Bori, Lucrezia – 1912H, 1936K
Borkh, Inge – 1953H, 1958H
Bornschein, Franz – 1919I, 1940G
  *Enchanted Isle, The* – 1933N
  *Leif Ericson*   1936N
  *Old Louisiana* – 1930N
  *Onawa* – 1916N
  *Phantom Canoe, The* – 1916N
  *Sea God's Daughter, The* – 1924N
  *Vision of Sir Launfal* – 1928N
Borodina, Olga – 1993H
Borovsky, Alexander – 1941K
Borowski, Felix – 1916I, 1925I, 1956G
  *Allegro de Concert* – 1915N
  *Ecce Homo* – 1923N
  *Elegie Symphonique* – 1919N
  *Mirror, The* – 1954N
  *Piano Concerto* – 1913N
  *Semiramis* – 1925N
  *Standard Concert Guide, The* – 1932M
  *Standard Operas, The* – 1928M
  *Symphony No. 1* – 1933N
  *Symphony No. 2* – 1936N
  *Symphony No. 3* – 1939N
Borroff, Edith – 1925F, 1962I
  *Music in Perspective* – 1976M
  *Music in Europe and the United States* – 1971M
  *Music Melting Round: A History...* – 1995M
  *Music of the Baroque* – 1970M
Borromeo String Quartet – 1989L
Borwick, Leonard – 1911H
Boskerck, F. S. von
  *Semper Paratus* – 1928N
Bosse Music Book Publishers – 1912L
Bostic, Earl – 1913A, 1965B
Boston – 1975C, 1986E
Boston, Massachusetts
  *Berklee College of Music* – 1945C
  *Camerata* – 1954L
  *Chamber Orchestra* – 1927L
  *Choral Arts Society* – 1901L
  *Civic Orchestra* – 1925L

*Composers Orchestra* – 1986L
*Early Music Festival* – 1981L
*Early Music Festival Orch.* – 1985L
*Esplanade Concerts* – 1929L
*Flute Players Club* – 1920L
*Globe Jazz Festival* – 1966C
*Longy School of Music* – 1916L
*Malkin Conservatory* – 1933L
*Mallet & Graupner Music Academy* – 1801L
*New Orchestra* – 1984L
*Opera Co.* – 1909L
*Opera Group* – 1958L
*Opera House* – 1909L
*Opera Theater* – 1990L
*People's Symphony Orchestra* – 1920L
*Philharmonic Orchestra* – 1979L
*School of Music* – 1910L
*Sinfonietta* – 1924L
*Society of Ancient Instruments* – 1938L
*Symphony Chamber Players* – 1964L
Boswell Sisters – 1925C
Boswell, Connie – 1907A, 1976B
Botsford, George – 1949B
  *Boomerang Rag* – 1916E
  *Buckeye Rag* – 1913E
  *Chatterbox Rag* – 1910E
  *Eskimo Rag* – 1912E
  *Grizzly Bear Rag* – 1910E
  *Incandescent Rag* – 1913E
  *Universal Rag* – 1913E
Botta, Luca – 1913H
Bottesini, Giovanni – 1947H
Bottje, Will Gay – 1925F
Boucher, Gene – 1994G
Boudleaux, Felice – 1925A
Boughton, Bruce
  *Tombstone* – 1993E
Bouhy, Jacques – 1985I
Boulez, Pierre – 1964H, 1971I
Boulton, Laura
  *Musical Instruments of World Cultures* – 1972M
Bourgeois, John R. – 1979I
Bournemouth Symphony Orchestra – 1994K
Bovy, Vina – 1936H
Bowdoin College Music Press – 1964L
Bowdoin Summer Music Festival – 1965L
Bowen, Jimmy – 1955C
Bower, R. H.
  *Lonely Romeo, A* – 1919E
Bowie, David – 1971C, 1975E, 1983E
Bowie, Joe – 1958A
Bowie, Lester – 1941A
Bowles, Paul F. – 1910F
  *Six Latin-American Pieces* – 1948N
  *Six Preludes* – 1945N
  *Sonata for 2 Pianos* – 1947N
  *Sonatina* – 1933N
  *Wind Remains, The* – 1943N
  *Yerma* – 1958N

---

❊

## Cultivated/Art Music Scene

F *Births*      G *Deaths*      H *Debuts*      I *New Positions*      J *Honors and Awards*
K *Biographical*      L *Musical Beginnings*      M *Publications*      N *Compositions*

---

❖

---

Vernacular/Commercial Music Scene

A  *Births*     B  *Deaths*     C  *Biographical*     D  *Publications*
E  *Representative Pieces*

Brevard Music Center – 1936L
Brewer, Christine – 1960F
Brewer, John H. – 1931G
Brewer, Teresa – 1931A
Brewster, W. Herbert – 1986B
Brice, Carol – 1918F, 1943J, 1985G
Brice, Fanny – 1951B
Bricetti, Thomas – 1936F
Brickell, Edie – 1985C
Bricklin – 1986C
Brico, Antonia – 1902F, 1934I, 1938K, 1948I, 1989G
Bricusse, Leslie
   *Roar of the Greasepaint—The Smell of the |*
   *Crowd* – 1965E
   *Stop the World—I Want to Get Off* – 1962E
Bridge Records – 1981C
Bridgehampton Chamber Music Festival –
   1983L
Bridgewater, Dee Dee – 1950A
Briggs, Sarah – 1991H
Brilioth, Helge – 1970H
Brings, Allen
   *Clarinet Sonata* – 1955N
Britain, Radie – 1908F
   *Heroic Poem* – 1929N
   *Kuthara* – 1960N
   *Rhapsodie Phantasie* – 1931N
   *Western Suite* – 1940N
Britny Fox – 1987C
Britt Festival – 1963C
Broadcast Music, Inc. – 1939L
Brockway, Howard – 1903I, 1910J, 1951G
   *Sylvan Suite* – 1903
Borda, Deborah – 1991I
Broder, Nathan – 1905F, 1967G
Brodsky, Roy
   *Red Roses for a Blue Lady* – 1948E
Brodszky, Nicholas
   *Be My Love* – 1951E
Bromberg, David – 1945A
Brombough, John, Organ Builder – 1968L
Bronfman, Yefim – 1976HK, 1989K, 1991J
Bronskaja, Eugenia – 1909H
Bronson, Bertrand
   *Festival Tunes of the Child Ballads I, The* –
   1959M
Bronx Opera Co. – 1967L
Brook Mays Music Co. – 1901L
Brook, Barry S. – 1918F
Brooklyn Bridge – 1968C
Brooks, Garth – 1962A, 1991C
Brooks, Iris
   *New Music Across America* – 1993M
Brooks, Joseph
   *You Light Up My Life* – 1977E
Brooks, Kix – 1955A
Brooks, Patricia – 1937F, 1960H, 1993G
Brooks, Richard J. G.
   *Moby Dick* – 1987N
   *Symphony in One Movement* – 1981N

Brooks, Shelton – 1975B
   *Darktown Strutters Ball* – 1917E
   *Some of These Days* – 1910E
Broonzy, Big Bill – 1958B
Brothers Four – 1958C
Brothers, Leighton
   *Steamboat Bill* – 1910E
Broude, Alexander – 1909F
Broude, Alexander, Inc. – 1954L
Broude Brothers Publishers – 1929L
Broude Trust for...Musicological Editions –
   1981L
Brouwenstijn, Gré – 1959H
Broward Center for the Performing Arts – 1991L
Brown-Roach Quintet – 1954C
Brown, A. Seymour
   *Oh You Beautiful Doll* – 1911E
Brown, Angela – 1953A
Brown, Bobby – 1969A
Brown, Clarence "Gatemouth" – 1924A
Brown, Cleo – 1909A
Brown, Clifford – 1930A, 1956B
Brown, Earle – 1926F, 1968I, 1972J, 1986I
   *Available Forms I* – 1961N
   *Available Forms II* – 1962N
   *Corrobboree* – 1964N
   *Cross Sections & Color Fields* – 1975N
   *Event: Synergy II* – 1968N
   *Folio I* – 1953N
   *Folio II* – 1981N
   *Four Systems* – 1954N
   *From Here* – 1963N
   *Modules I & II* – 1966N
   *Sounder Rounds* – 1982N
   *String Quartet 1965* – 1965N
   *Time Spans* – 1972N
   *Tracking Pierrot* – 1992N
   *Twenty-Five Pages* – 1953N
   *Windsor Jambs* – 1980N
Brown, Eddy – 1915H
Brown, Eddy, String Quartet – 1922L
Brown, H. Arthur – 1947I
Brown, Henry – 1981B
Brown, Howard M.
   *Instrumental Music Printed before 1600* – 1965M
Brown, Iona – 1980K
Brown, James – 1933A, 1988C
Brown, Lawrence – 1907A, 1988B
Brown, Les – 1912A, 1947C
Brown's, Les, Band of Renown – 1938C
Brown, Lester R.
   *Sentimental Journey* – 1943E
Brown, Lew – 1958B
   *Beer Barrel Polka, The* – 1939E
Brown, Marty – 1965A
Brown, Milton – 1903A
Brown, Nacio Herb – 1964B
   *American Bolero* – 1935E
   *Broadway Melody* – 1929E
   *Broadway Melody of 1936* – 1935E
Brown, Nellie E. – 1924G

---

❈

### Cultivated/Art Music Scene

F *Births*   G *Deaths*   H *Debuts*   I *New Positions*   J *Honors and Awards*
K *Biographical*   L *Musical Beginnings*   M *Publications*   N *Compositions*

Brown, Ray – 1926A
Brown, Raynor – 1912F
   *Symphony No. 1* – 1952N
   *Symphony No. 2* – 1957N
   *Symphony No. 3* – 1958N
Brown, Rob – 1962S
Brown, Roy James – 1925A, 1981B
Brown, Ruth – 1928A
Brown, Shirley – 1947A
Brown, T. Graham – 1954A
Brown, William – 1787KN
Browne, Jackson – 1948A
Browne, Jann – 1954A
Browning, John – 1933F, 1954J, 1955J, 1956HJ
Brownlee, John – 1926H, 1937H, 1953I, 1956I,
   1966I, 1969G
Browns, The – 1959E
Brownsville Station – 1969C
Brubeck, Dave – 1920A
   *Beloved Son* -1978E
   *Earth is Our Mother* – 1992E
   *Fiesta de la Posada, La* – 1975E
   *Four New England Pieces* – 1988E
   *Gates of Justice, The* – 1969E
   *I See, Satie* – 1987E
   *Joy in the Morning* – 1991E
   *Truth is Fallen* – 1971E
Brubeck, Dave, Trio & Octet – 1949C
Bruce, Neely
   *Eight Ghosts* – 1989N
Bruckner Society of America – 1931L
Brune, Alfred
   *Fairy Tale, A* – 1920N
   *Overture, A Twilight Picture* – 1917N
Bruner, Cliff – 1915A
Brunner, Evelyn – 1983H
Brunswick, Mark – 1902F, 1971G
   *Symphony in B-Flat* – 1945N
Brunswick Record Co. – 1921C
Bruscantini, Sesto – 1961H, 1981H
Brusilow, Anshel – 1928F, 1959K, 1970I, 1973I,
   1981I
Bruson, Renata – 1969H
Bryan, Alfred – 1948B
Bryant, Anita – 1940A
Bryant, Beulah – 1918A, 1988B
Bryant, Boudleaux – 1920A, 1987B
Bryant, Felice – 1991C
   *All I Have To Do Is Dream* – 1958E
   *Bye, Bye, Love* – 1957E
Bryar, Gavin
   *3 Elegies for 9 Clarinets* – 1994N
Brymn, James Tim – 1946A
Bryn-Julson, Phyllis – 1945F, 1966H
Bryson, Peabo – 1951A
B. T. Express – 1972C
Bucci, Mark
   *Joining! Departure! Arrival!* – 1971E
Buchanan, Isobel – 1979H

Buchanan, Roy – 1939A, 1988B
Bucharoff, Simon
   *Modern Pianist's Textbook, The* – 1931M
Buchla, Donald – 1937F
Buchla Associates – 1966L
Buck, Dudley – 1909G
Buck, Gene – 1929I, 1957B
Buckaroos, The – 1963C
Buckinghams, The – 1965C, 1967E
Buckley, Emerson – 1916F, 1950I, 1963IJ, 1963J,
   1964I, 1983I, 1989G
Buckley, Richard – 1953F
Buckley, Tim – 1947A, 1975B
Buckwheat Zydeco – 1947A
Budai, Livia – 1979H, 1987H
Budapest String Quartet – 1917L
Buddah Records – 1967C
Buechner, David – 1984J
Buechner, Margaret – 1951K
   *American Civil War, The* – 1992N
   *Elizabeth* – 1990N
   *Old Swedes Church, The* – 1987N
Buelow, George J. – 1929F
Buerkle, Jack V.
   *Bourbon Street Black* – 1973D
Buffalo Springfield – 1966C
Buffalo, New York
   *Baird Music Hall* – 1981L
   *Center for Creative & Performing Arts* –
     *1963L*
   *Guido Chorus* – 1904L
   *June in Buffalo* – 1976L
   *Kleinhans Music Hall* – 1940L
   *Musica Sacra Society* – 1920L
   *Philharmonic Orchestra* – 1935L
   *Philharmonic Society* – 1908L
   *Shea's Buffalo Theater* – 1926L
   *Symphony Society* – 1921L
   *Temple of Music* – 1901L
Buffett, Jimmy – 1946A
Bufwach, M. A.
   *Finding Her Voice:...Women in Country Music* –
     1993D
Buggles – 1977C
Buhlig, Richard – 1901H, 1907H, 1917I,
   1952G
Buketoff, Igor – 1915F, 1935I, 1942J, 1943I, 1948I,
   1968I, 1980I
Bukofzer, Manfred – 1939K, 1941I, 1945K,
   1955G
   *Music in the Baroque Era* – 1947M
   *Place of Musicology in American Institutions...* –
     1957M
   *Studies in Medieval & Renaissance Music* –
     1950M
Bull, Sandy – 1941A
Bulletboys – 1987C
*Bulletin of the American Composers' Alliance* –
   1952L

---

❀

Vernacular/Commercial Music Scene
A *Births*    B *Deaths*    C *Biographical*    D *Publications*
E *Representative Pieces*

---

Cultivated/Art Music Scene

F *Births*   G *Deaths*   H *Debuts*   I *New Positions*   J *Honors and Awards*
K *Biographical*   L *Musical Beginnings*   M *Publications*   N *Compositions*

Bychkov, Semyon – 1975K, 1985I
Byrd, Charlie – 1925A
  *Melodic Method for Guitar* – 1973D
Byrds, The – 1964C, 1965E
Byrne, David – 1952A

# C

C + C Music Factory – 1989C, 1991E
C.S.U., Northridge, Electronic Music Studio –
  1961L
C., Roy – 1943A
Caballé, Montserrat – 1965H
Cabrillo Music Festival – 1963L
Cacophony – 1986C
Cactus – 1969C
Cadek School of Music – 1904L
*Cadence Magazine: American Review of Jazz and
  Blues, The* – 1976C
*Cadenza, The* – 1894L
Cadets, The – 1954C
Cadillacs, The – 1953C
Cadman, Charles Wakefield – 1881F, 1903K, 1908I,
  1909K, 1917K, 1926J, 1946G
  *American Suite* – 1936N
  *At Dawning* – 1906N
  *Aurora Borealis* – 1944N
  *Belle of Havana, The* – 1928N
  *Dark Dancers of the Mardi Gras* – 1933N
  *Father of Waters, The* – 1928N
  *Four American Songs* – 1907N
  *From Wigwam & Teepee* – 1914N
  *Garden of Mystery, The* – 1925N
  *Ghost of Lollypop By* – 1926N
  *Hollywood Suite* – 1932N
  *Jeanne d'Arc* – 1906N
  *Land of the Misty Water* – 1912N
  *Mad Empress Remembers, A* – 1944N
  *Oriental Suite* – 1921N
  *Overture, Huckleberry Finn* – 1945N
  *Piano Quintet in g* – 1937N
  *Piano Sonata in A* – 1915N
  *Piano Trio in D* – 1913N
  *Prairie Sketches* – 1906N
  *Rappaccini's Daughter* – 1925N
  *Rubaiyat of Omar Khayyám* – 1921N
  *Sayonara* – 1910N
  *Shanewis* – 1918N
  *South in Sonora* – 1932N
  *Suite on American Folktunes* – 1937N
  *Sunset Trail, The* – 1922N
  *Symphony in e, "Pennsylvania"* – 1940N
  *Trail Pictures* – 1934N
  *Thunderbird Suite* – 1914N
  *Violin Sonata in G* – 1932N
  *Vision of Sir Launfal* – 1909N
  *Willow Wind, The* – 1922N
  *Witch of Salem, A* – 1926N
Cady, C. M. – 1857I
Cady, Calvin B. – 1880I

*Caecilia* – 1877L
Caesar, Irving – 1895A
  *If I Forget You* – 1933E
  *I've Heard That Song Before* – 1942E
Cafferty, John, & the Beaver Brown Band – 1972C
Cage, John – 1912F, 1930K, 1943K, 1949J, 1968J,
  1978J, 1989J, 1992G
  *Bacchanale for Prepared Piano* – 1940N
  *Clarinet Sonata* – 1933N
  *Concerto for Piano and Orchestra, 1958N*
  *Concerto for Prepared Piano* – 1951N
  *Dance Four Orchestras* – 1981N
  *Empty Words* – 1979M
  *Europeras 1 & 2* – 1987N
  *Five Songs on e.e. cummings* – 1938N
  *Four* – 1989N
  *In a Landscape* – 1948N
  *Metamorphosis* – 1938N
  *Music for Piano* – 1953N
  *Music of Changes* – 1951N
  *Notations* – 1969M
  *Piano Concerto* – 1958N
  *Percussion Quartet* – 1935N
  *Seasons Ballet, The* – 1947N
  *Silence* – 1961M
  *String Quartet* – 1950N
  *Themes & Variations* – 1982M
  *Three Songs on Gertrude Stein* – 1932N
  *13* – 1992N
  *Thirty Pieces for 5 Orchestras* – 1981N
  *34' 46.776"* – 1954N
  *Twenty-Three* – 1989N
  *Variations I* – 1961N
  *Winter Music* – 1957N
  *Writings through Finnegan's Wake* – 1978M
  *Year from Monday, A* – 1967M
  *2squared* – 1989N
  *4', 33"* – 1952N
Cahier, Mrs. Charles – 1870F, 1904H, 1951G
Cahill, Marie – 1870A, 1933B
Cahill, Teresa Mary – 1972H
Cahn, Sammy – 1913A, 1993B
  *Saturday Night Is the Loneliest Night* – 1944E
  *Shoe Shine Boy* – 1936E
Cailliet, Lucien – 1923K, 1938I, 1957I, 1984G
Cairns, Christine – 1985H
Caldwell, Anne – 1867A, 1936B
Caldwell, Sarah – 1924F, 1947K, 1952I, 1974J,
  1976HK, 1981K
Caldwell, William
  *Union Harmony, The* – 1837M
Cale, J. J. – 1938A
Calhoun, Charles
  *Shake, Rattle & Roll* – 1954E
California Chamber Symphony Orchestra – 1961L
California Institute of the Arts – 1961L
California Ramblers – 1921C
Callahan, J. Will
  *Smiles* – 1917E

---

Vernacular/Commercial Music Scene
A *Births*    B *Deaths*    C *Biographical*    D *Publications*
E *Representative Pieces*

Callas, Maria – 1923F, 1937K, 1938H, 1954H, 1955H, 1977G
Callas, Maria, International Club – 1990L
Callaway, Paul – 1939I
Callender, Red – 1916A, 1992B
Calliet, Lucien – 1915K
Calliope – 1845L
Calloway, Cab – 1907A, 1994B
  *Minnie the Moocher – 1931E*
Calvé, Emma – 1893H
Cambreling, Sylvain – 1986H
Cambridge Collegium Musicum – 1942L
Cameo – 1974C
Cameo-Parkway Records – 1957C
Camerata Singers – 1960L
Camerata Symphony Orchestra – 1968L
Cameron, Basil – 1932I
Camilieri, Lorenzo – 1914K, 1921K
Campanari, Giuseppe – 1884K, 1893H, 1894H
Campanari, Leandro – 1881HK, 1939G
Campanini, Cleofonte – 1883H, 1906K, 1913I, 1906I, 1910I, 1919G
Campanini, Italo – 1873H, 1883H
Campbell, Archie – 1914A, 1987B
Campbell, Glen – 1936A, 1967C, 1968C, 1975E, 1977E
Campbell, John – 1952A, 1993B
Campbell, Lucie E. – 1885F
Campbell-Tipton, Louis
  *Legends, Two – 1908N*
  *Sonata Heroic – 1904N*
Campbell-Watson, Frank
  *Modern Elementary Harmony – 1930M*
  *University Course of Music Study – 1923M*
Camper Van Beethoven – 1984C
Campora, Giuseppe – 1955H
Campos-Parsi, Héctor – 1980I
Candidus, William – 1840F, 1867H
Caniglia, Maria – 1938H
Canin, Stuart – 1959J
Canned Heat – 1966C
Cannibal & the Headhunters – 1965C
Cannon, Gus – 1883A, 1979B
Cannon, Hughie
  *Bill Bailey, Won't You...- 1902E*
Cannon's Jug Stompers – 1928C
Cantelli, Guido – 1949G
Cantor, Eddie – 1892A, 1964B
Cape & Islands Chamber Music Festival – 1980L
Capecchi, Renato – 1951H
Capitol Record Co. – 1942C
Capoul, Joseph – 1883H, 1888H
Cappa, Carlo Alberto – 1858K
Cappelletti, Andrea – 1989H
Capp-Pierce Juggernaut – 1975C
Cappuccilli, Piero – 1960H
Capris, The – 1957C
Capron, Henri – 1785H, 1794K
Captain and Tennille – 1975E, 1980E

Captain Beefheart and his Magic Band – 1964C
Captain Beyond – 1972C
Cara, Irene
  *Flashdance – 1983E*
Caradori-Allen, Madame – 1837H
Caramoor Festival (N.Y.) – 1946L
Carapetyan, Armen – 1908F
Caravans, The – 1958C
Card, June – 1942F
Carden, Allen Dickenson – 1792F, 1859G
  *Missouri Harmony, The – 1820M*
  *United States Harmony – 1829M*
  *Western Harmony – 1824M*
Cardinal Record Co. – 1920C
Cardwell School of Music – 1927L
Carey, Mariah – 1970A, 1990E, 1991E, 1992E, 1993E, 1994E
Carhart & Needham, Reed Organs – 1846L
Carl, William C. – 1865F, 1882I, 1892I, 1936G
  *Master Studies for the Organ – 1907M*
  *Historical Organ Collection – 1919M*
Carle, Frankie – 1903A
  *Sunrise Serenade – 1938C*
Carle, Frankie, Big Band – 1944C
Carle, Richard – 1871A
Carlisle, Belinda – 1958A, 1987E
Carlisle, Bill – 1908A
Carlisle, Cliff – 1904A, 1983B
Carlisle, Kitty – 1914A
Carlson, Claudine – 1937F, 1977H
Carlson, David
  *Midnight Angel, The – 1993N*
Carlson, Lenus – 1945F
Carlton, Larry – 1948A
Carmel Bach Festival – 1935L
Carmen, Eric – 1949A
Carmichael, Hoagy – 1899A, 1981B
  *Georgia On My Mind – 1930E*
  *In the Cool, Cool, Cool of the Evening – 1951E*
  *Lamplighter's Serenade – 1942E*
  *Lazy River – 1931E*
  *Lazybones – 1933E*
  *Ole Buttermilk Sky – 1946E*
  *Small Fry – 1938E*
  *Stardust – 1927E*
  *Stardust Road, The – 1946E*
  *Rockin' Chair – 1929E*
  *Washboard Blues – 1926E*
Carmines, Al
  *Promenade – 1969E*
Carnegie, Andrew – 1835F, 1919G
Carnegie Corporation of New York – 1911L
Carnes, Kim – 1945A, 1981E
Carnivore – 1983C
Carpenter, John Alden – 1876F, 1897K, 1906K, 1909K, 1918J, 1933J, 1942J, 1947J, 1951G
  *Adventures in a Perambulator – 1914N*
  *Anxious Bugler, The – 1943N*
  *Birthday of the Infanta – 1917N*

---

### Cultivated/Art Music Scene

F *Births*     G *Deaths*     H *Debuts*     I *New Positions*     J *Honors and Awards*
K *Biographical*     L *Musical Beginnings*     M *Publications*     N *Compositions*

Carpenter, John Alden (continued)
  *Brangelbrink – 1896N*
  *Carmel Concerto – 1948N*
  *Concertino for Piano & Orchestra – 1917N*
  *Gitanjali – 1913N*
  *Impromptu, 1913N*
  *Krazy Kat – 1921N*
  *Little Dutch Girl, The – 1900N*
  *Nocturne for Piano – 1898N*
  *Patterns – 1932N*
  *Piano Concertino – 1915N*
  *Piano Quintet – 1934N*
  *Piano Sonata No. 1 – 1897N*
  *Pilgrim Vision, A – 1920N*
  *Polonaise Américaine – 1912N*
  *Sea Drift – 1933N*
  *Seven Ages, The – 1945N*
  *Skyscrapers – 1924N*
  *Song of Faith – 1931N*
  *Song of Freedom – 1941N*
  *Strawberry Night Festival Music – 1896N*
  *String Quartet – 1927N*
  *Suite for Orchestra – 1909N*
  *Symphony No. 1 – 1917N*
  *Symphony No. 2 – 1942N*
  *Violin Concerto – 1936N*
  *Violin Sonata – 1911N*
  *Water-Colors – 1916N*
Carpenter, Karen – 1950A, 1983B
Carpenter, Mary Chapin – 1958A, 1991C
Carpenter, Richard – 1946A
Carpenters, The – 1970E, 1973E, 1975E
Carr, Benjamin – 1793K, 1794H, 1797K, 1801I,
  1804K, 1807I, 1810K, 1816I, 1822K, 1831G
  *Analytical Instructor, The – 1826M*
  *Applicazione adolcita, Opus 6 – 1809N*
  *Archers, The, or, Mountaineers of Switzerland –*
    *1796N*
  *Caledonian Frolic, The – 1793N*
  *Dead March & Monody for General Washington –*
    *1800N*
  *Federal Overture – 1794N*
  *Four Ballads – 1794N*
  *Four Ballads from Rodeby, Opus 10 – 1813N*
  *History of England, The, Opus 11 – 1814N*
  *Lessons & Exercises in Vocal Music, Opus 8 –*
    *1811N*
  *Macbeth – 1795N*
  *Musical Bagatelles, Opus 13 – 1820N*
  *Philander & Silvia – 1792N*
  *Poor Jack – 1795N*
  *Sacred Airs, Opus 16 – 1830N*
  *Siege of Tripoli, Opus 4 – 1804N*
  *Six Ballads from "Lady of the Lake," Opus 7 –*
    *1810N*
  *Six Canzonets, Opus 14 – 1824N*
  *Six Piano Sonatas – 1796N*
  *Six Progressive Sonatinas – 1812N*
  *Three Ballads, Opus 2 – 1799N*

Carr, Colin – 1981J, 1983I
Carr, James – 1942A
Carr, Joseph – 1819G
Carr, Joseph, Publishing House – 1794L
Carr, Leroy – 1899A
Carr, Roy
  *The Hip: Hipsters, Jazz & the Beat Generation –*
    *1987D*
Carr, Vikki – 1941A
Carrasco, Joe "King," and the Crowns – 1979C
Carr's Musical Repository, Phil. – 1793L
Carr's Musical Repository, N.Y. – 1794L
*Carr's Musical Miscellany – 1812L*
Carrell, James P. – 1787F, 1854G
  *Songs of Zion – 1821M*
  *Virginia Harmony, The – 1831M*
Carreño, Teresa – 1862H, 1872K, 1875K, 1892K,
  1902K, 1917G
Carreras, José – 1972H, 1974H
Caroli, Silvano – 1983H
Carroll, Earl
  *So Long, Letty – 1916E*
Carroll, Earl
  *Vanities – 1923C*
Carroll, Harry – 1892A, 1962B
  *Little Blue Devil, The – 1919E*
Carroll, Jim – 1951A
Carron, Arthur – 1936H
Carruth, Hayden
  *Sitting In:...Jazz, Blues & Related Topics –*
    *1993D*
Cars, The – 1976C
Carson, "Fiddlin' John" – 1868A, 1949B
Carter Family – 1927C, 1970C
Carter, A. P. – 1891A
  *Wabash Cannon Ball – 1940E*
Carter, Benny – 1907A
Carter, Benny, Band – 1933C
Carter, Betty – 1930A
Carter, Bo – 1893A, 1964B
Carter, Carlene – 1955A
Carter, Clarence – 1936A
Carter, Elizabeth – 1993H
Carter, Elliott – 1908F, 1932K, 1946I, 1950J,
  1953J, 1956J, 1960I, 1963J, 1965J, 1969J,
  1971J
  *Adagio Tenebroso – 1995N*
  *Celebration of Some 100 X 150 Notes – 1986N*
  *Cello Sonata – 1948N*
  *Double Concerto – 1961N*
  *In Sleep, In Thunder – 1981N*
  *Mirror on Which to Dwell, A – 1975N*
  *Night Fantasies – 1980N*
  *Oboe Concerto – 1988N*
  *Partita – 1993N*
  *Penthode – 1985N*
  *Piano Sonata – 1946N*
  *Remembrance – 1988N*
  *Scrivo in vento – 1991N*

---

❖

**Vernacular/Commercial Music Scene**
A *Births*    B *Deaths*    C *Biographical*    D *Publications*
E *Representative Pieces*

---

❀

## Cultivated/Art Music Scene

F *Births*   G *Deaths*   H *Debuts*   I *New Positions*   J *Honors and Awards*
K *Biographical*   L *Musical Beginnings*   M *Publications*   N *Compositions*

Ceroli, Nick – 1939A, 1985B
Cerone, David – 1985I
Ceruli, Dom
*Jazz Word, The – 1960D*
Cetera, Peter – 1944A, 1986E
Chadabe, Joel
*Variations for Piano – 1983N*
Chadbourne, Eugene – 1954A
Chadwick, George W. – 1854F, 1876IK, 1877K,
1878K, 1880IK, 1882I, 1890I, 1897I, 1898J, 1905J,
1909J, 1928J, 1931G
*Adonais Overture – 1900N*
*Angel of Death – 1919N*
*Anniversary Overture – 1922N*
*Aphrodite – 1913N*
*Cleopatra – 1904N*
*Dedication Ode – 1886N*
*Euterpe Overture – 1906N*
*Everywoman – 1911N*
*Five Pieces for Piano – 1905N*
*Four Irish Songs – 1909N*
*Harmony: a Course of Study – 1897M*
*Joshua – 1909N*
*Judith – 1900N*
*Lily Nymph, The – 1893N*
*Lochinvar – 1897N*
*Love's Sacrifice – 1916N*
*Melpomene Overture – 1887N*
*Miller's Daughter Overture – 1886N*
*Noel – 1908N*
*Ode, Opening Chicago World's Fair –*
*1892N*
*Padrone, The – 1915N*
*Pastoral Prelude, A – 1894N*
*Phoenix Expirans – 1891N*
*Piano Quintet in E-Flat – 1888N*
*Pilgrims, The – 1891N*
*Quiet Lodging, The – 1892N*
*Rip Van Winkle Overture – 1879N*
*Sinfonietta in D – 1904N*
*String Quartet No. 1 – 1878N*
*String Quartet No. 2 – 1878N*
*String Quartet No. 3 in D – 1885N*
*String Quartet No. 4 in E Minor – 1896N*
*String Quartet No. 5 in D Minor – 1898N*
*Suite in Variation Form – 1923N*
*Suite Symphonique in E-flat – 1909N*
*Symphonic Sketches – 1904N*
*Symphony No. 1 – 1882N*
*Symphony No. 2 in B-Flat – 1886N*
*Symphony No. 3 in F – 1894N*
*Tabasco – 1894E*
*Tam O'Shanter – 1915N*
*Ten Canonic Studies for Organ – 1885N*
*Thalia Overture – 1883N*
*Theme, Variations & Fugue – 1908N*
*Viking's Last Voyage, The – 1881N*
Chailly, Riccardo – 1982H
Chairmen of the Board – 1969C

Chaliapin, Feodor – 1907H
*Man & Mask – 1932M*
*Pages from My Life – 1927M*
Challender, Stuart – 1988K
Challis, Bill – 1904A
Challis, John – 1907F
Challis Harpsichord Co. – 1930L
Chamber Music America – 1977L
*Chamber Music Magazine – 1984L*
Chamber Music Northwest Festival – 1971L
Chamber Music Plus – 1980L
*Chamber Music Quarterly – 1982L*
Chamber Music Society of America – 1932L
Chamber Music West – 1977L
Chambers Brothers, The – 1961C
Chamlee, Mario – 1892F, 1916H, 1920H, 1966G
Champaign – 1981C
Champion, Gower – 1921A, 1980B
Champion Records – 1925C
Champs, The – 1957C, 1958E
Chance, James – 1953A
Chance, John B. – 1932F
Chandler, David Hiram – 1843I
Chandler, Gene – 1937A, 1962E
Chang, Sarah – 1991H
Chang, Li-Ly – 1983H
Chang, Lynn – 1974J
Chanler, Theodore W. – 1902F, 1957J, 1961G
*Epitaphs – 1937N*
Channel, Bruce – 1962E
Channing, Carol – 1921A
Chantays – 1962C
Chantels – 1956C
Chanticleer – 1978L
Chapin, Anzi – 1768F, 1835G
Chapin, Harry – 1942A, 1974E, 1981B
*Cat's in the Cradle – 1974E*
*Cotton Patch Gospel – 1981E*
Chapin, Lucius – 1760F, 1842G
Chapin, Schuyler – 1923F, 1972I, 1976I, 1983J
*Musical Chairs: a Life in the Arts – 1977M*
Chapman, Maria W.
*Songs of the Free & Hymns of Christian Freedom*
*– 1836M*
Chapman, Marshall – 1949A
Chapman, Tracy – 1964A
Chappell Music, U.S. Branch – 1935L
Charig, Phil – 1902A, 1960B
*Follow the Girls – 1944E*
Charlatans, The – 1964C
Charles, Bobby – 1938A
Charles, Ernest – 1895F
Charles, Ray – 1930A, 1960E, 1961E, 1962E,
1986C
Charles, Ray, Dance Band – 1954C
Charleston, South Carolina
*Broad Street Theater – 1793L*
*Charleston Theater – 1773L*
*Choral Society – 1944L*

---

❖

---

Vernacular/Commercial Music Scene
A *Births*    B *Deaths*    C *Biographical*    D *Publications*
E *Representative Pieces*

---

### Cultivated/Art Music Scene

F *Births*    G *Deaths*    H *Debuts*    I *New Positions*    J *Honors and Awards*
K *Biographical*    L *Musical Beginnings*    M *Publications*    N *Compositions*

Chicago, Illinois (continued)
*Symphony Chorus* – *1957L*
*Symphony Orchestra* – *1891L*
*Tremont Music Hall* – *1850L*
*Vocal Normal School* – *1912L*
*Weber Hall* – *1883L*
*Women's String Quartet* – *1926L*
*Women's Symphony Orchestra* – *1925L*
Chicago Loop – 1966C
Chicago String Quartet
Chickasaw Syncopators – 1927C
Chickering, Jonas – 1797F, 1818K, 1853G
Chickering, Thomas E. – 1824F, 1871G
Chiffons, The – 1960C, 1963E
Chihara, Paul – 1938F, 1966I, 1979J
*Ceremony I* – *1971N*
*Ceremony II* – *1972N*
*Ceremony III* – *1973N*
*Ceremony IV* – *1974N*
*Forest Music* – *1968N*
*Missa Carminum* – *1976N*
*Saxophone Concerto* – *1981N*
*Symphony No. 1* – *1975N*
*Symphony No. 2* – *1982N*
*Viola Concerto* – *1963N*
*Violin Concerto* – *1992N*
Child, Desmond, & Rouge – 1975C
Child, Ebenezer – 1770F, 1866G
*Sacred Musician, The* – *1804M*
Child's Grand Opera House – 1884L
Childs, Barney – 1926F
*Clarinet Concerto* – *1970N*
*Symphony No. 1* – *1954N*
*Symphony No. 2* – *1956N*
*Timpani Concerto* – *1989N*
Chi-Lites, The – 1960C
Chilton, Alex – 1950A
China Sky – 1987C
Chiu, Frederic – 1964F, 1994H
Chocolate Watch Band – 1964C
Chodos, Gabriel – 1939F, 1970H
Choi, Hans – 1991J
*Choir: a Monthly Journal of Church Music* –
1899L
Chookasian, Lili – 1921F, 1957H, 1962H
*Choral Advocate & Singing-Class Journal* – 1850L
*Choral Journal, The* – *1959L*
*Chord & Discord* – *1932L*
Chordettes – 1946C
Chords, The – 1953C
Chorzempa, Daniel – 1944F
Chotzinoff, Samuel – 1889F, 1925I, 1934I, 1936I,
1964G
*Day's at the Morn* – *1964M*
*Little Nightmusic, A* – *1964M*
*Lost Paradise: Early Reminiscences, A* – *1955M*
Chou Wen-Chung - 1946K, 1958K, 1963J, 1972I,
1982J
*Beijing in the Mist* – *1985N*

*Echoes from the Gorge* – *1989N*
*Willows Are New, The* – *1957N*
Chow, Alan – 1988J
Chowning, John – 1934F
Christensen, Axel – 1881A, 1955B
*Cauldron Rag, The* – *1909E*
*Christensen's Rag-time Instruction Book for Piano*
– *1904D*
*Instruction Book for Jazz & Novelty Piano*
*Playing* – *1927D*
*Instruction Book for Modern Swing Music* –
*1936D*
Christeson, R. P.
*Old-time Fiddler's Repertory I* – *1973D*
*Old-time Fiddler's Repertory II* – *1984D*
Christian, Charlie – 1916A, 1942B
Christian Death – 1979C
Christian's, Frank, Ragtime Band – 1910C
Christiani, Adolf
*Principles of Musical Expression in Piano*
*Playing* - *1886M*
Christiansen, F. Melius – 1888K, 1903I, 1955G
Christiansen, Fredrik
*Practical Modulation* – *1916M*
Christiansen, Olaf – 1901F, 1984G
Christie, Lou – 1943A, 1966E
Christie, William – 1944F, 1982K
Christie, Winifred – 1919H
Christoff, Boris – 1956H
Christy's Minstrels – 1843L
Christy, Edwin P. – 1815A, 1862B
*Farewell (Good Night) Ladies* – *1842M*
Christy, George
*Essence of Kentucky, The* – *1862E*
Christy, June – 1925A, 1990B
Christy Minstrels, New – 1961C
Chuck Wagon Gang – 1935C
Chung, Kyung-Wha – 1961K, 1967J, 1968H, 1971J
Chung, Mia – 1964F, 1983H
Chung, Myung-Wha – 1961K, 1967H, 1971K
Chung, Myung-Whun – 1968K, 1973K, 1978K,
1986H
*Church Musician, The* – *1950L*
*Church Music Review* – *1901L*
Church, John, & Co. – 1869L
*Church's Musical Visitor* – *1871L*
Churchill, Frank E. – 1901A, 1942B
*Dumbo* – *1941E*
*Snow White & the Seven Dwarfs* – *1937E*
*Who's Afraid of the Big, Bad Wolf?* – *1933E*
Chusid, Martin – 1925F
Ciccolini, Aldo – 1950H
Ciesinski, Katharine – 1950F, 1974H, 1988H
Ciesinski, Kristine – 1952F, 1977H
Cigna, Gina – 1937H
Cincinnati, Ohio
*Ballet Co.* – *1970L*
*Beethoven Society* – *1873L*
*Cecilia Society* – *1856L*

---

※

---

**Vernacular/Commercial Music Scene**
A *Births*    B *Deaths*    C *Biographical*    D *Publications*
E *Representative Pieces*

---

❖

---

### Cultivated/Art Music Scene
F *Births*    G *Deaths*    H *Debuts*    I *New Positions*    J *Honors and Awards*
K *Biographical*    L *Musical Beginnings*    M *Publications*    N *Compositions*

Clayton, Buck – 1911A, 1991B
Clayton, Jeff – 1955A
Clayton, John – 1952A
Clayton, Lee – 1942A
Clearwater Jazz Holiday – 1980C
Clef Club – 1910L
*Clef, The* – 1913L
Clef Records – 1946C
Cleftones, The – 1955C
Clemens, Clara – 1874F, 1904H, 1909K, 1962G
  *Development of Song, The* – 1924M
Clemens, Hans – 1930H
Clement, Ada, Music School – 1917L
Clément, Edmond – 1909H
Clemm, John Gottlob – 1762G
Cleva, Fausto – 1920HK, 1931K, 1942I, 1949I,
  1951I, 1971G
Cleveland, Ohio
  *Chamber Music Society – 1918L*
  *Chamber Symphony – 1980L*
  *Conservatory of Music – 1871L*
  *Gesangverein – 1854L*
  *Grand Orchestra – 1902L*
  *Gray's Armory – 1893L*
  *Harmonic Society – 1837L*
  *Hruby Conservatory of Music – 1918L*
  *Institute of Music – 1920L*
  *Lyric Opera – 1973L*
  *Mendelssohn Society – 1850L*
  *Messiah Civic Chorus – 1921L*
  *Modern Dance Association – 1956L*
  *Mozart Society – 1837L*
  *Music School Settlement – 1912L*
  *Musical Arts Association – 1915L*
  *Opera Theater – 1973L*
  *Opera (New) – 1976L*
  *Orchestra – 1918L*
  *Orchestra Chorus – 1955L*
  *Philharmonia Chorale – 1970L*
  *Philharmonic Society – 1881L*
  *Sacred Music Society – 1842L*
  *St. Cecilia Society – 1852L*
  *School of Music – 1885L*
  *Severance Hall – 1931L*
  *Singer's Club – 1891L*
  *Symphony Orchestra – 1910L*
  *String Quartet – 1968L*
  *Vocal Society – 1873L*
  *West Side Musical College – 1900L*
  *Women's Orchestra – 1935L*
  *Youth Orchestra – 1986L*
Cleveland, James L. – 1932A, 1991B
Cleveland, Jimmy – 1926A
Cliburn International Piano Competition – 1962L
Cliburn, Van – 1934F, 1952J, 1954J, 1958J, 1974J
Clifton, Arthur – 1832G
Climax – 1971C
Clinch Mountain Boys – 1946C
Cline, Patsy – 1932A, 1963B, 1973C

Clinton, George – 1940A
Clinton, Larry – 1909A, 1985B
  *Dipsy Doodle, The* – 1937E
  *Study in Brown* – 1937E
Clinton, Larry, Orchestra – 1937C
Clique – 1966C
Clokey, Joseph W. – 1890F, 1939I
Clooney, Rosemary – 1928A
Clouds of Joy – 1929C
Clough & Warren Organ Co. – 1850L
Clover – 1967C
Clovers – 1946C
Club Nouveau – 1987E
Coasters, The – 1955C
Coates, Albert – 1920H
Coates, Eric
  *Sleepy Lagoon* – 1930E
Coates, Gloria – 1938F
  *Five Poems of Dickinson* – 1972N
  *Leonardo da Vinci* – 1979N
  *Natural Voice & Electronic Sound* – 1973N
  *Planets, The* – 1974N
  *String Quartet No. 3* – 1976N
  *String Quartet No. 4* – 1977N
  *Structures* – 1972N
Coates, Odia – 1974E
Cobain, Kurt – 1994BC
Cobb, Arnett – 1918A, 1989B
Cobb, George L.
  *Russian Rag* – 1918E
Cobb, Will D. – 1876A, 1930B
  *I Can't Tell Why I Love You, But I Do* – 1900E
  *Waltz Me Around Again, Willie* – 1906E
Coben, Cy
  *Ole Piano Roll Blues, The* – 1950E
Cobra – 1982C
Coburn, Pamela – 1955F, 1982H, 1990H
Cochran, Eddie – 1938A, 1960B
Cochran, Hank – 1935A
Cochran, William – 1943F, 1969J
Coci, Claire – 1912F, 1978G
Cocker, Joe – 1982E
Cocoanut Grove Orchestra – 1930C
*Coda: The Jazz Magazine* – 1958C
Cody, Commander, and his Lost Planet Airmen –
  1968C
Coe, David A. – 1939A
Coerne, Louis A. – 1870F, 1890K, 1905K, 1910I,
  1915I, 1922G
  *Evolution of Modern Orchestration* –
    1908M
  *Excalibur* – 1921N
  *Hiawatha* – 1893N
  *Organ Concerto in E* – 1892N
  *String Quartet in c, Op. 19* – 1893N
  *Suite for Strings in D Minor* – 1892N
  *Trojan Women* – 1917N
  *Woman of Marblehead, A* – 1897N
  *Zenobia* – 1902N

---

※

---

Vernacular/Commercial Music Scene
A *Births*    B *Deaths*    C *Biographical*    D *Publications*
E *Representative Pieces*

---

❈

## Cultivated/Art Music Scene

F *Births*　　G *Deaths*　　H *Debuts*　　I *New Positions*　　J *Honors and Awards*
K *Biographical*　　L *Musical Beginnings*　　M *Publications*　　N *Compositions*

Collard, Jean-Philippe – 1973H
*Collection of Psalms & Hymns for Public Worship*
    (Unitarian) – 1799M
Collective Black Artists – 1969C
College Band Directors Nat'l Association – 1941L
College Music Society (CO) – 1957L
College of Church Musicians – 1962L
Collegium Musicum der Germaine (NC) – 1786L
Collie, Mark – 1956A
Collier, James L.
    *Great Jazz Artists, The* – 1977D
    *Inside Jazz* – 1973D
    *Reception of Jazz in America: A New View* –
        1988D
Collier, Marie – 1967H
Collings, Judy – 1939A
Collins, Anthony – 1939K
Collins, Dorothy – 1994B
Collins, Michael – 1984H
Collins, Phil – 1984E, 1985E, 1988E, 1989E
Colon, Willie – 1950A
Color Me Badd – 1987C, 1991E, 1992E
Colorado Jazz Party – 1963C
Colorado Mahlerfest – 1988L
Colorado Music Festival – 1977L
Colson, Pauline – 1860H
Colter, Jessi – 1947A
Coltrane, Alice – 1937A
Coltrane, John – 1926A, 1967B
Coltrane Quartet – 1910C
Coltrane, John, Jazz Band – 1960C
Columbia Broadcasting Symphony – 1927L
Columbia Concerts Corporation – 1932L
Columbia Phonograph Co. – 1889L
Columbia Record Co. – 1903L
Columbia University Tape Studio – 1953L
Columbia-Princeton Electronic Center – 1959L
Columbo, Russ – 1908A, 1934B
Columbo, Russ, Big Band – 1931C
Colvin, Shawn – 1958A
Combs, Gilbert R. – 1863F, 1934G
Comden, Betty – 1915A, 1991C
    *Off Stage* – 1994D
Comet, Catharine – 1986K
Comets (Saddlemen) – 1949C
Comissiona, Sergiu – 1963H, 1969I, 1976K 1977I,
    1983I, 1987I
Commanday, Robert – 1922F, 1964I
Commander Cody and His Lost Planet Airmen –
    1967C
Commodores, The – 1967C, 1978E, 1979E
Community Artist Residency Training – 1978L
Como, Perry – 1912A, 1957E 1987C
Compact Disc – 1982L
Composers' Facsimile Edition – 1952L
Composers' Guild, Inc. – 1985L
Composers' Press – 1935L
Composers' String Quartet – 1963L
Composers in Red Sneakers – 1981L

Composers Inside Electronics – 1973L
Composers Recordings, Inc. – 1954L, 1955L   ???
*Composium* – 1971L
*Computer Music Journal* – 1977L
Concert Artists Guild – 1951L
Concord Records – 1973C
Concord String Orchestra – 1971L
Concord Summer Jazz Festival – 1969C
Concord Summer School of Music – 1915L
Concordia – 1984L
Concordia Publishing House – 1869L
Concrete Blonde – 1981C
Condie, Richard P. – 1957I, 1985G
Condon, Eddie – 1905A, 1973B
    *Eddie Condon Scrapbook of Jazz* – 1973D
    *Eddie Condon's Treasury of Jazz* – 1956D
    *We Called It Music: a Generation of Jazz* –
        1947D
Conductor's Guild – 1975L
Conductors' Institute (WV) – 1981L
Cone, Edward T. – 1917F, 1946I, 1966I
    *Composer's Voice, The* – 1974M
    *Music: A View from Delft: Selected Essays* –
        1989M
    *Music for Strings* – 1965N
    *Musical Form & Musical Performance* – 1968M
    *Prelude, Passacaglia & Fugue* – 1957N
    *Symphony* – 1952N
    *Variations for Orchestra* – 1967N
    *Violin Concerto* – 1958N
Confrey, Edward "Zez" – 1895A, 1971B
    *Dizzy Fingers* – 1923E
    *Kitten on the Keys* – 1921E
    *Modern Novelty Piano Solos* – 1923D
Con Funk Shun – 1968C
Conlee, John – 1946A
Conley, Earl Thomas – 1941A
Conley, Eugene – 1940H, 1950H, 1978I, 1981G
Conlon, James – 1950F, 1976H
Conn-Dupont Co. – 1875L
Connecticut Early Music Festival – 1983L
Connecticut Harp Festival – 1980L
Connecticut Opera Association – 1942L
Connecticut String Orchestra – 1968L
Connecticut Yankees – 1928C
Connell, Elizabeth – 1983H, 1985H
Connell, Horatio – 1876F
Conner, Chris – 1927A
Conner, Nadine – 1941H
Conner, Raymond
    *Carpet Rags* – 1903E
Connick, Harry, Jr. – 1967A, 1980C
    *When Harry Met Sally* – 1989E
Conniff, Ray – 1916A, 1953C
Conniff, Ray, Singers – 1957C
Connor, Tommie
    *I Saw Mommie Kissing Santa Claus* – 1952E
Conover Brother Music Store – 1871L
Conrad, Barbara – 1945F, 1982H

---

⚙

## Vernacular/Commercial Music Scene
A *Births*     B *Deaths*     C *Biographical*     D *Publications*
E *Representative Pieces*

Conrad, Con – 1891A, 1938B
  *Barney Google* – 1923E
  *Continental, The* – 1934E
  *Ma! He's Making Eyes at Me* – 1921E
  *Margie* – 1920E
  *Moonlight* – 1921E
Conried, Heinrich – 1878I, 1892I, 1903I
Consoli, Marc-Antonio – 1941F, 1956K, 1975J
  *Afterimages* – 1982N
  *Cello Concerto* – 1988N
Constantino, Florencio – 1906H
Contemporary Music Forum (D.C.) – 1974L
*Contemporary Music Magazine* – 1934C
Contemporary Records – 1951C
Conti, Bill – 1977E
Continental Vocalists – 1853C
*Continuum* – 1967L
Contortions – 1980C
Contours, The – 1958C
Conus, Sergei – 1959K
Converse, Charles – 1832F, 1918G
  *American Overture on Hail, Columbia* – 1869N
  *God With Us* – 1887N
Converse, Frederick S. – 1871F, 1889K, 1893K,
  1896K, 1898K, 1899I, 1903I, 1908J, 1920I, 1940G
  *Answer of the Stars, The* – 1920N
  *Belle Dame sans Merci, La* – 1902N
  *Endymion's Narrative* – 1901N
  *Euphrosyne Overture* – 1903N
  *Festival of Pan, The* – 1900N
  *Job* – 1906N
  *Mystic Trumpeter, The* – 1904N
  *Night & Day* – 1901N
  *Peace Pipe, The* – 1914N
  *Piano Trio in E Minor* – 1932N
  *Pipe of Desire, The* – 1905N
  *Sacrifice* – 1910N
  *String Quartet in E Minor* – 1935N
  *Symphony No. 1 in d* – 1898N
  *Symphony No. 3* – 1936N
  *Violin Concerto* – 1902N
Conway's Military Band School – 1922L
Conway, Patrick – 1867F, 1929G
Cooder, Ry – 1947A
  *Geronimo* – 1993E
Cook, Barbara – 1927A, 1973D
  *Listen to the Blues* – 1973D
Cook, Benjamin
  *Three Songs from Shakespeare* – 1793N
Cook, Deborah – 1948F, 1985H
Cook, Junior – 1934A, 1992B
Cook, Will Marion – 1865F
  *Bon Bon Buddy* – 1907E
  *Clorindy* – 1898E
  *Collection of Negro Songs* – 1912D
  *In Dahomey* – 1903E
  *Sons of Ham* – 1900E
Cooke, James F. – 1875F, 1908I, 1960G
  *Great Pianists on Piano Playing* – 1914M

  *Great Singers on the Art of Singing* – 1921M
  *Standard History of Music* – 1910M
Cooke, Sam – 1935A, 1957E, 1964B
Cooley, Spade – 1910A, 1969B
Coolidge, Elizabeth Sprague – 1864F, 1953G
Coolidge, Elizabeth S., Foundation – 1925L
Coolidge, Peggy Stuart – 1913F
Coolidge, Rita – 1944A
Coolidge Auditorium, Library of Congress – 1925L
Coolidge Chamber Music Festival – 1918L
Coon-Sanders Nighthawks – 1918C
Cooper, Alice – 1948A
Cooper, Emil – 1944H
Cooper, Imogen – 1984H
Cooper, Kenneth – 1941F, 1965H
Cooper, Paul – 1926F, 1977J
  *Concert for Winds, Perc. & Piano* – 1968N
  *Cycles* – 1969N
  *Perspectives in Music Theory* – 1973M
  *Piano Sonata I* – 1949N
  *Piano Sonata II* – 1963N
  *String Quartet No. 2* – 1954N
  *String Quartet No. 3* – 1959N
  *String Quartet No. 4* – 1966N
  *String Quartet No. 5* – 1975N
  *String Quartet No. 6* – 1977N
  *Symphony No. 1* – 1954N
  *Symphony No. 2* – 1956N
  *Symphony No. 3* – 1971N
  *Symphony No. 4* – 1975N
Cooper, Stoney T. – 1918A, 1977B
Cooper, Wilma Lee – 1921A
Cooperative Studio for Electronic Music – 1958L
Coopersmith, J. M. – 1903F
Cooperstock, Andrew – 1960F, 1989H
Coots, J. Fred – 1897A, 1985B
  *Love Letters in the Sand* – 1931E
  *Sally, Irene & Mary* – 1922E
  *Santa Claus Is Coming to Town* – 1934E
  *Sons O' Guns* – 1929E
  *You Go To My Head* – 1938E
Cope, David H. – 1941F
  *Arena* – 1974N
  *Computer Analysis of Musical Style* – 1991M
  *Cradle Falling* – 1989N
  *Glassworks* – 1979N
  *New Directions in Music* – 1971M
  *New Music Composition* – 1976M
  *New Music Notation* – 1976M
  *Notes in Discontinuum* – 1970M
  *Paradigm* – 1974N
  *Piano Sonata No. 1* – 1960N
  *Piano Sonata No. 4* – 1967N
  *Spirals* – 1972N
  *String Quartet No. 1* – 1961N
  *String Quartet No. 2* – 1963N
Copeland, Keith – 1946A
Copeland, Ray – 1926A, 1984B
  *Classic Jazz Suite* – 1970E

---

❄

## Cultivated/Art Music Scene
  F *Births*    G *Deaths*    H *Debuts*    I *New Positions*    J *Honors and Awards*
  K *Biographical*    L *Musical Beginnings*    M *Publications*    N *Compositions*

---

**Vernacular/Commercial Music Scene**
A *Births*     B *Deaths*     C *Biographical*     D *Publications*
E *Representative Pieces*

Cowell, Henry – 1897F, 1912K, 1929K, 1936K, 1940K, 1942K, 1948J, 1949I, 1951IJ, 1965G
*American Composers on American Music* – 1933M
*Banshee, The* – 1925N
*Harp Concerto* – 1965N
*Ives, Charles, & His Music* – 1955M
*New Musical Resources* (pub. 1930) – 1919M
*Piano Concerto* – 1928N
*Quartet Euphometric* – 1919N
*Symphony No. 1* – 1918N
*Symphony No. 2* – 1938N
*Symphony No. 3* – 1942N
*Symphony No. 4* – 1946N
*Symphony No. 5* – 1948N
*Symphonies 6-8* – 1952N
*Symphonies 9, 10* – 1953N
*Symphony No. 11* – 1954N
*Symphony No. 12* – 1956N
*Symphony No. 13* – 1958N
*Symphonies 14, 15* – 1960N
*Symphony No. 16* – 1962N
*Symphony No. 17* – 1963N
*Symphony No. 18* – 1964N
*Symphonies 19-21* – 1965N
*Tides of Manaunaun, The* – 1917N
*Variations for Orchestra* – 1956N
Cowsills, The – 1965C
Cox, Ida – 1896A, 1967B
Cox, Jean – 1922F, 1954H, 1976H
Cozad, Irene
*Eatin' Time Rag* – 1913E
Crabbé, Armand – 1907H
Crabby Appleton – 1970C
Craft, Robert – 1923F
*Prejudices in Disguise* – 1974M
*Present Perspectives* – 1984M
Craighead, David – 1924F
Cramps, The – 1975C
Craven, Robert R.
*Symphony Orchestras of the U.S.* – 1986M
Crawford, Bruce – 1984I
Crawford, Jesse – 1895A, 1926C, 1962B
Crawford, Randy – 1952A
Crawford, Richard A. – 1935F
*Civil War Song, The* – 1977M
*Studying American Music* – 1985M
Crawford, Robert M.
*Army Air Corps Song, The* – 1939E
Crawford, R. P.
*American Folk Songs for Christmas* – 1953D
Crawford, Ruth – 1901F, 1921K, 1931K, 1952G
*Animal Folk Songs for Children* – 1950M
*Five Preludes for Piano* – 1925N
*Four Preludes for Piano* – 1928N
*String Quartet* – 1931N
*Violin Sonata* – 1926N
Cray, Robert – 1954A
Crayton, Pee Wee – 1914A, 1985B

Crayton, Pee Wee, Trio – 1947C
Crazy Horse – 1969C
Creamer, Henry – 1930B
*If I Could Be With You One Hour Tonight* – 1926E
*'Way Down Yonder in New Orleans* – 1922E
Creative World Records – 1970C
Creatore, Giuseppe – 1952G
Creech, Philip – 1950F, 1979H
Creed – 1977C
Creedence Clearwater Revival – 1967C
*Creem* – 1969C
Crehore, Benjamin – 1831G
Crehore, George – 1765F
Cremonini, Giuseppe – 1895H
Crenshaw, Marshall – 1954A
Creole Band, Original – 1908C
Creole Jazz Band, King Oliver's – 1920C
Creole Jazz Band – 1915C
Creole Orchestra, Original (L.A.) – 1912C
Crescendos – 1957C
Crespin, Régine – 1962H, 1990K
Creston, Paul – 1906F, 1943J, 1956I, 1963J, 1968I, 1975K, 1985G
*Concerto for 2 Pianos* – 1951N
*Creative Harmony* – 1970M
*Dance Variations* – 1942N
*Five Dances, Opus 1* – 1932N
*Metamorphoses* – 1964N
*Piano Concerto* – 1949N
*Piano Sonata, Op. 9* – 1936N
*Principles of Rhythm* – 1964M
*Rational Metric Notation* – 1979M
*Saxophone Sonata* – 1939N
*Six Piano Preludes* – 1945N
*String Quartet, Op. 8* – 1936N
*Suite for Sax Quartet* – 1979N
*Symphony No. 1* – 1941N
*Symphony No. 2* – 1945N
*Symphony No. 3* – 1950N
*Symphony No. 4* – 1952N
*Symphony No. 5* – 1956N
*Symphony No. 6* – 1982N
*Three Narratives for Piano* – 1962N
*Two-Part Inventions* – 1937N
*Violin Concerto No. 1* – 1956N
*Violin Concerto No. 2* – 1960N
Crests, The – 1956C
Crew Cuts, The – 1954C
Crews, Lucile – 1888F
Crickets, The – 1957CE
Crime – 1976C
Crimi, Giulio – 1916H, 1918H
Crimson Glory – 1982C
Crispell, Marilyn – 1947A
Crist, Bainbridge – 1883F, 1969G
*Abisharika* – 1921N
*Art of Setting Words to Music, The* – 1944M
*Colored Stars* – 1921N
*Drolleries from an Oriental Doll's House* – 1920N

---

## Cultivated/Art Music Scene

F *Births*    G *Deaths*    H *Debuts*    I *New Positions*    J *Honors and Awards*
K *Biographical*    L *Musical Beginnings*    M *Publications*    N *Compositions*

Crist, Bainbridge (continued)
  *Egyptian Impressions* – 1914N
  *Pied de la Momie, Le* – 1915N
Critters – 1964C
Croce, Jim – 1943A, 1973BE
Crocker, Richard – 1927F, 1955I
  *Listening to Music* – 1971M
Crockett, Donald – 1951F
  *Celestial Mechanics* – 1990N
Crockett, E. I.
  *Rock-a-Bye, Baby* – 1887E
Crofoot, Alan – 1979G
Croft, Dwayne – 1990H
Crofts, Dash – 1940A
Crooks, Richard – 1900F, 1930H, 1933H, 1972G
Crosby, Bing – 1904A, 1977B
Crosby, Bob – 1913A, 1993B
Crosby, David – 1941A
Crosby, Fanny J. – 1828F, 1864K, 1915G
Crosby, John – 1926F, 1957I, 1976I, 1991C
Crosby, Rob – 1954A
Crosby, Stills and Nash – 1968C
Cross, Christopher – 1951A, 1980E, 1981E
Cross, Lowell,
  *Bibliography of Electronic Music, A* – 1967M
Cross, Milton – 1975G
Crossfires – 1963C
Crossley, Ada – 1903H
Crossover Records – 1973C
Crouch, Andrae – 1942A
Crouse-Hinds Concert Theater (Syracuse) – 1976L
Crow, Sheryl – 1962A
Crowell, Rodney – 1950A
Crows, The – 1948C
Crozier, Catharine – 1914F, 1938I, 1941H, 1955I
Crudup, Arthur "Big Boy" – 1905A, 1974B
Crumb, George – 1929F, 1959I, 1965I, 1967J, 1975J
  *Apparition* – 1979N
  *Cello Sonata* – 1955N
  *Echoes of Time & the River* – 1967N
  *Five Pieces for Piano* – 1962N
  *Four Nocturnes, Violin & Piano* – 1964N
  *Gnomic Variations* – 1981N
  *Haunted Landscape, A* – 1984N
  *Little Suite for Christmas* – 1980N
  *Makrokosmos I* – 1972N
  *Makrokosmos II* – 1973N
  *Makrokosmos III* – 1974N
  *Makrokosmos IV* – 1978N
  *Pastoral Drone* – 1982N
  *Star Child* – 1977N
  *Zeitgeist* – 1989N
Crumbsuckers – 1983C
Crusaders, The (Jazz) – 1954C
Cruz-Romo, Gilda – 1970H
Cryptic Slaughter – 1985C
Crystals, The – 1961C, 1962E
Cuberli, Lella – 1945F, 1975H, 1983H
Cuénod, Hugues – 1937H, 1986H

Cugat, Xavier – 1900A, 1958C, 1990B
Cullowhee Music Festival (NC) – 1975L
Culp, Julia – 1913H
Culprit – 1980C
Cult Jam – 1984E
Culture Club – 1984E
Cumberland County Civic Center – 1977L
Cummings, Claudia – 1971H
Cummings, Conrad
  *Dinosaur Music* – 1981N
  *Endangered Species* – 1977N
  *Subway Songs* – 1974N
  *Tonkin* – 1993N
Cuney-Hare, Maud
  *Negro Musicians & Their Music* – 1936D
Cunningham, Merce – 1919F
Cunningham, Merce, Dance Co. – 1953L
Cunningham, Merce, School of Dance – 1959L
Cupido, Alberto – 1983H
Curran, Pearl G. – 1875F, 1941G
  *Current Musicology* – 1965L
Curry, Arthur M. – 1866F, 1915I
  *Atala* – 1911N
  *Winning of Amarac, The* – 1934N
Curtin, Phyllis – 1922F, 1961H, 1974I, 1983I,
  1984K, 1987K
Curtis Institute of Music – 1924L
Curtis String Quartet – 1932L
Curtis, Alan – 1934F
Curtis, King – 1934A, 1971B
Curtis, Natalie – 1875A, 1921G
  *Hampton Series of Negro Folk Songs* – 1918D
  *Indians' Book, The* – 1907M
  *Songs and Tales from the Dark Continent* –
  1920D
  *Songs of Ancient America* – 1905M
Curtis-Smith, Curtis – 1941F, 1972J, 1978J
  *Celebration* – 1985N
  *Fantasy Pieces* – 1987N
  *5 Sonorous Inventions* – 1973N
  *GAS! (Great American Symphony)* – 1982N
  *Piano Concerto, Left Hand* – 1990N
  *Piano Trio No. 2* – 1992N
  *Rhapsodies* – 1973N
  *Unisonics* – 1976N
  *Variations on "Amazing Grace"* – 1983N
  *Violin Concerto* – 1990N
Curtis-Verna, Mary – 1954H. 1957H
Curzon, Clifford – 1939H
Cushman, Charlotte – 1816FF 1835H, 1886G
Cutler, Henry Stephen – 1825F, 1902G
Cutter, Benjamin – 1857F
Cutting Crew – 1982C, 1987E
Cuvillier, John B. – 1827I
Cuvillier, Joseph – 1829I
Cuyler, Louise E. – 1908F, 1929I, 1975I
  *Symphony, The* – 1973M
Cymbal, Johnny – 1945A, 1993B
Cyrkle – 1961C

---

❁

---

## Vernacular/Commercial Music Scene
A *Births*     B *Deaths*     C *Biographical*     D *Publications*
E *Representative Pieces*

Cyrus, Billy Ray – 1961A
Czerwenka, Oskar – 1959H

# D

DAAGNIM – 1978C
Da Capo Chamber Players (Columbia) – 1969L
Dachs, David
  *Anything Goes: The World of Popular Music* –
    1964D
Dacre, Harry
  *Bicycle Built for Two, A* – 1892E
  *Playmates* – 1889E
Dadmun, John W. – 1819F, 1890G
  *Revival Melodies* – 1858M
Daffan, Ted – 1912A
Dahl, Ingolf – 1938K, 1945I, 1954J, 1964J, 1970G
  *Piano Quintet* – 1956N
  *Prelude & Fugue for Piano* – 1939N
  *Sonata Pastorale* – 1959N
  *Sonata Seria* – 1953N
  *String Quartet No. 2* – 1958N
Dahl, Linda
  *Stormy Weather: . . . a Century of Jazzwomen* –
    1989D
Dahl, Tracy – 1991H
Dailey's, Pete, Chicagoans – 1946C
Daily Flash – 1965C
Dakota – 1979C
Dalberto, Michel – 1987H
Dale and Grace – 1963E
Dale, Clamma – 1948F, 1975H, 1976J
Dale, Dick – 1937A
Dalhart, Vernon – 1883A, 1948B
Dalis, Irene – 1925F, 1953H, 1957H, 1976I
Dallapiccola, Luigi – 1951K
Dallas, Texas
  *Chamber Music Society* – 1942L
  *Civic Chorus* – 1960L
  *Civic Opera* – 1957L
  *Fair Park Music Hall* – 1925L
  *Grand Opera Association* – 1939L
  *Meyerson Symphony Center* – 1989L
  *(New) Opera House* – 1904L
  *Opera House* – 1883L
  *Philharmonic Society* – 1887L
  *Symphony Chorus* – 1977L
  *Symphony Club* – 1900L
Dallin, Leon
  *Techniques of Twentieth Century Composition* –
    1957M
Dal Monte, Toti – 1924H
Dalmorès, Charles – 1906H, 1939G
Dalton, Lacy J. – 1948A
Daly, Joseph
  *Chicken Reel, The* – 1910E
Dambois, Maurice – 1917AH
Dameron, Tadd – 1917A, 1965B
Damian, Michael – 1989E
Damien Thorne – 1985C

Damn Yankees – 1989C
Damone, Vic – 1928A
Damrosch, Frank – 1871K, 1897I, 1904J, 1937G
Damrosch, Leopold – 1871HIK, 1880K, 1884H,
    1885G
  *Ruth & Naomi* – 1875N
Damrosch, Walter – 1871K, 1883J, 1885HI, 1902I,
    1927I, 1932J, 1937J, 1950G
  *Cyrano de Bergerac* – 1913N
  *Man Without a Country* – 1937N
Damrosch Opera Co. – 1894L
Dana, Vic – 1942A
Dana, William Henry – 1846F, 1916G
  *Instrumentation for Military Bands* – 1876M
  *Orchestration* – 1875M
  *Practical Harmony* – 1884M
  *Practical Thorough-Bass* – 1873M
Dance, Stanley
  *World of Swing, The* – 1974D
Danco, Suzanne – 1950H
Danderliers – 1955C
Danger, Danger – 1988C
Dangerous Toys – 1987C
Daniel, Davis – 1961A
Daniel, Oliver – 1911F
Danielpour, Richard
  *Cello Concerto* – 1994N
  *Enchanted Garden* – 1992N
  *Piano Concerto No. 2* – 1993N
  *Songs to Orpheus* – 1994N
  *Sonnets to Orpheus* – 1992N
  *String Quartet No. 3* – 1995N
  *Symphony No. 3* – 1989N
Daniels & Russell, Publishers – 1901L
Daniels, Barbara – 1946F, 1973H, 1983H
Daniels, Billy – 1915A, 1988B
Daniels, Charles Neil – 1943B
  *You Tell Me Your Dream* – 1908E
Daniels, Charlie – 1937A
Daniels, Charlie, Band – 1971C
Daniels, Mabel Wheeler – 1878F, 1971G
  *American Girl in Munich, An* – 1905M
  *Deep Forest* – 1931N
  *Desolate City, The* – 1913N
  *Exsultate Deo* – 1929N
  *Holy Star, The* – 1928N
  *Peace with a Sword* – 1917N
  *Song of Jael* – 1939N
  *Songs of Elfland* – 1924N
Danks, Hart P. – 1834F, 1903B
  *Anna Lee* – 1856E
  *Don't Be Angry with Me, Darling* – 1870E
  *Pauline* – 1872E
  *Silver Threads Among the Gold* –
    1872E
Dankworth, A.
  *Jazz: an Introduction to Its Musical Basis* –
    1968D
Dannreuther, Gustav – 1877K, 1907I

---

## Cultivated/Art Music Scene

F *Births*    G *Deaths*    H *Debuts*    I *New Positions*    J *Honors and Awards*
K *Biographical*    L *Musical Beginnings*    M *Publications*    N *Compositions*

Dannreuther String Quartet – 1884L
Danny and the Juniors – 1957C, 1958E
Danzig – 1986C
Danzig, Evelyn
 *Scarlet Ribbon* – 1949E
Dara, Enzo – 1982H
D'Arby, Terence Trent – 1962A, 1988E
Dare, Elkanah K. – 1782F, 1826G
 *Periodical Harmony, The* – 1810M
Darin, Bobby – 1936A, 1959E, 1973B
Dark Angels – 1983C
Dark Clouds of Joy – 1926C
Darley, F. T. S.
 *Cities of the Plain, The* – 1855N
Darling, Edward
 *Big Pony* – 1887E
Darracott, William, Jr. – 1799F, 1868G
Darré, Jeanne-Marie – 1962H
Dartells – 1962C
Dartmouth Handel Society – 1807L
D'Ascoli, Bernard – 1988H
Dave and Sugar – 1975C
Davenport, Cow Cow
 *Mama Don't Allow* – 1929E
David, Hal – 1921A
David, Hans T. – 1936K, 1967G
David, Mack – 1912A
 *Chi-Baba, Chi-Baba* – 1947E
 *I Don't Care If the Sun Don't Shine* – 1950E
Davidovich, Bella – 1978K, 1979H, 1982I,
 1984K
Davidovici, Robert – 1972H
Davidovsky, Mario – 1958K, 1965J, 1972J, 1981I,
 1982J
 *Electronic Study I* – 1961N
 *Electronic Study II* – 1962N
 *Romancero* – 1983N
 *Scenes from Shir-ha-shirim* – 1977N
 *String Quartet No. 1* – 1954N
 *String Quartet No. 2* – 1958N
 *String Quartet No. 3* – 1976N
 *String Quartet No. 4* – 1980N
 *Synchronism No. 1* – 1963N
 *Synchronism No. 4* – 1967N
 *Synchronism No. 6* – 1970N
 *Synchronism No. 7* – 1973N
 *Synchronism No. 8* – 1974N
 *Synchronism No. 10* – 1992N
Davidson, Lawrence – 1942H
Davidson, Lyle – 1938F
Davies, Benjamin – 1893H
Davies, Dennis Russell – 1944F, 1961H, 1972I,
 1977I, 1987J, 1989I, 1990I
Davies, Peter Maxwell – 1980K
Davies, Ryland – 1970H, 1975H
Da Vinci Quartet – 1980L
Davis, Anthony
 *Tania* – 1992N
 *X: Life & Times of Malcolm X* – 1986E

Davis, Arthur – 1934A
 *Method of Double Bass* – 1975D
Davis, Benny – 1895A
Davis, Billy – 1977E
Davis, Blind John – 1913A, 1985B
Davis, Bobby – 1934A
Davis, Colin – 1972K
Davis, Eddie "Lockjaw" – 1922A, 1986B
Davis, Ellabelle – 1907F, 1960G
Davis, Francis
 *In the Moment: Jazz in the 1980's* – 1986D
Davis, Gary – 1896A, 1972B
Davis, Gussie L. – 1863A, 1899B
 *Lighthouse by the Sea, The* – 1886E
Davis, Ivan – 1932F, 1958J, 1959H, 1960J
Davis, James "Thunderbird" – 1992B
Davis, Jessie Bartlett – 1860F, 1905G
Davis, Jimmie – 1902A, 1944C, 1972C
 *Nobody's Darling But Mine* – 1935E
 *You Are My Sunshine* – 1940E
Davis, John – 1815I
Davis, Mac – 1942A, 1972E
Davis, Meg – 1953A
Davis, Miles – 1926A, 1991B
Davis, Miles, Quintet – 1955C
Davis, Paul – 1948A
Davis, Peter G. – 1936F
Davis, Pierre – 1837I
Davis, Sammy, Jr. – 1925A, 1972E, 1987C,
 1990B
Davis, Skeeter – 1931A
Davis, Tyrone – 1938A
Davis Sisters – 1945C
Davison, Archibald – 1883F, 1961G
 *Choral Conducting* – 1940M
 *Church Music: Illusion & Reality* – 1952M
 *Hero & Leander* – 1908N
 *Music Education in America* – 1926M
 *Protestant Church Music in America* – 1920M
 *Technique of Choral Composition, The* –
 1946M
 *Tragic Overture* – 1918N
Davison, John
 *Sonata Pastorale* – 1987N
Davison, Wild Bill – 1906A, 1989B
Davisson, Ananias – 1780F, 1857G
 *Introduction to Sacred Music, An* – 1821M
 *Kentucky Harmony* – 1816M
 *Small Collection of Sacred Music, A* – 1826M
 *Supplement to the Kentucky Harmony* – 1820M
Davy, Gloria – 1931F, 1957H, 1958H
Dawn – 1971E, 1973E, 1975E
Dawn, P. M. – 1991E
Dawson, Alan
 *Blues & Old Time Signatures* – 1972D
 *Manual for the Modern Drummer, A* – 1964M
Dawson, William – 1898F, 1925K, 1927K, 1930I,
 1954K, 1956K, 1976J, 1990G
 *Negro Folk Symphony* – 1934N

❀

**Vernacular/Commercial Music Scene**
A *Births*   B *Deaths*   C *Biographical*   D *Publications*
E *Representative Pieces*

---

❖

---

### Cultivated/Art Music Scene

F *Births*     G *Deaths*     H *Debuts*     I *New Positions*     J *Honors and Awards*
K *Biographical*     L *Musical Beginnings*     M *Publications*     N *Compositions*

Dello Joio, Norman (continued)
  *Meditations on Ecclesiastes* – 1957N
  *Piano Sonata No. 1* – 1943N
  *Piano Sonata No. 2* – 1944N
  *Piano Sonata No. 3* – 1948N
  *String Quartet* – 1974N
  *Trial at Rouen, The* – 1956N
  *Trumpet Sonata* – 1979N
  *Variations, Chaconne & Finale* – 1948N
Dells, The – 1953C
Delmark Records – 1953C
Del Monaco, Mario – 1950H
Delmore, Alton – 1908A
Delmore, Rabon – 1910A
Delna, Marie – 1910H
Delogu, Gaetano – 1979I
Del Puente, Giuseppe – 1878H, 1883H
Delray, Martin – 1949A
Delta Blues Museum – 1978C
Delta Omicron Music Fraternity – 1909L
Del Tredici, David – 1937F, 1968J, 1984J, 1988I
  *Adventures Underground* – 1971N
  *Alice Symphony, An* – 1969N
  *All in the Golden Afternoon* – 1981N
  *Child Alice* – 1986N
  *Final Alice* – 1976N
  *Happy Voices* – 1981N
  *In Memory of a Summer Day* – 1980N
  *March to Tonality* – 1985N
  *Quaint Events* – 1981N
  *Syzygy* – 1966N
  *Vintage Alice* – 1972N
De Luca, Giuseppe – 1915H, 1950G
De Lucia, Fernando – 1894H
De Lulli, Arthur
  *Celebrated Chop Waltz (Chopsticks)* – 1877E
DeLuxe Records – 1944C
Del-Vikings – 1956C
DeMacchi, Maria – 1904H
De Main, John – 1979I
De Marchi, Emilio – 1901H
DeMent, Iris – 1961A
Demensions – 1960A
DeMille, Agnes – 1909F, 1980J, 1993G
Dempster, Stuart
  *Modern Trombone, The* – 1979M
Demus, Jörg – 1955H
Dencke, Jeremiah – 1761K, 1795G
  *Liebesmahl* – 1765N
Deng, Yun – 1985H
Denishawn School of Dancing – 1915L
Dennée, Charles – 1863F, 1883I, 1946G
  *Musical Journeys* – 1938M
Dennison, Robert 1960F, 1971H
Denniston, Patrick – 1994J
Denny, William D. – 1910F, 1980G
Densmore, Frances – 1867F, 1957G
  *American Indians & Their Music, The* – 1926M
  *Chippewa Music* – 1913M

Denton, Carl - 1918I
Denver, Colorado
  *Amateur Symphony Orchestra* – 1900L
  *Arion Singing Society* – 1904L
  *Center for the Performing Arts* – 1978L
  *Children's Chorale* – 1974L
  *Choral Society* – 1890L
  *Chorus Club* – 1882L
  *City Band* – 1861L
  *College of Music* – 1925L
  *of Music* – 1887L
  *Early Music Consort* – 1976L
  *German Männerchor* – 1870L
  *Grand Opera Co.* – 1915L
  *Greater Denver Opera Co.* – 1955L
  *Innes School of Music* – 1916L
  *Lyric Theater* – 1958L
  *Municipal Band* – 1887L
  *Musical Union* – 1867L
  *Opera Co.* – 1955L
  *Phil. Orchestra (Businessman's Symphony
    Orchestra)* – 1948L
  *Sax Horn Band* – 1860L
  *String Quartet* – 1921L
  *Tabor Opera House* – 1881L
  *Wolcott Conservatory* – 1920L
Denver U. School of Music – 1879L
Denver, John – 1943A, 1974E, 1975E
De Palma, Sandro – 1978H
De Paul, Gene – 1919A, 1988B
  *I'll Remember April* – 1941E
  *Li'l Abner* – 1956C
  *Seven Brides for Seven Brothers* – 1954E
DePreist, James – 1936F, 1962K, 1964JK, 1980I
Derby Records – 1949C
Dernesch, Helga – 1971H, 1985H
De Reske, Edouard – 1891H
De Reske, Jean – 1891H
De Rose, Peter – 1900A, 1953B
  *Deep Purple* – 1934E
  *Wagon Wheels* – 1931E
  *When Your Hair Has Turned to Silver* –
    1931E
Derringer, Rick – 1947A
De Sabata, Victor – 1927H
Des Marais, Paul – 1920F
Des Moines, Iowa
  *Ballet Co.* – 1970L
  *Civic Music Association* – 1925L
  *Community Orchestra* – 1976L
  *Eisteddfod Association* – 1914L
  *Hall of the Performing Arts (Harmon Fine Arts
    Center)* – 1973L
  *Metro Opera* – 1973L
  *Metro Opera Festival* – 1973L
  *Music College* – 1888L
  *Youth Symphony Orchestra* – 1963L
Desert Rose Band – 1985c
Desert Singing Guild – 1948L

---

### Vernacular/Commercial Music Scene
A *Births*    B *Deaths*    C *Biographical*    D *Publications*
E *Representative Pieces*

---

## Cultivated/Art Music Scene

F *Births*     G *Deaths*     H *Debuts*     I *New Positions*     J *Honors and Awards*
K *Biographical*     L *Musical Beginnings*     M *Publications*     N *Compositions*

Diamond, David (continued)
  *Violin Concerto No. 2* – 1947N
  *Violin Concerto No. 3* – 1968N
  *World of Paul Klee, The* – 1957N
Diamond, Neil – 1941A, 1970E, 1972E
  *African Trilogy* – 1971E
Diaz, Andres – 1986J
Díaz, Justino – 1940F, 1957H, 1963H
Diaz, Rafaelo – 1884F, 1911H, 1918H
Dichter, H.
  *Early American Sheet Music, Its Lure & Lore,*
    *1768-1889* – 1941D
Dichter, Mischa – 1945F, 1966HJ
Dick and Deedee – 1961C
Dickens, "Little Jimmy" – 1920A, 1983C
Dickie, Murray – 1962H
Dickies, The – 1977C
Dickinson, Clarence – 1873F, 1912I
  *Excursions in Musical History* – 1917M
  *Technique & Art of Organ Playing* – 1921M
Dickinson, Edward – 1893F, 1946G
  *Education of the Music Lover, The* – 1911M
  *Music & Higher Education* – 1915M
  *Spirit of Music, The* – 1925M
Dickinson, George – 1888F
  *Classification of Music Compositions* – 1938M
  *Foretokens of the Tonal Principle* – 1923M
  *Growth & Use of Harmony, The* – 1927M
  *Handbook of Style in Music, A* – 1965M
  *Pattern of Music, The* – 1939M
  *Study of Music as a Liberal Art, The* –
    1953M
Dickinson, John
  *Liberty Song, The* – 1768N
Dickinson, Thomas G. – 1954F
Dictators – 1974C
Diddley, Bo – 1928A
Didur, Adamo – 1907H, 1908H
Die Kreuzen – 1981C
Diemer, Emma Lou – 1927F, 1965I, 1971I
  *Celebration* – 1970N
  *Christmas Cantata* – 1988N
  *Four Biblical Settings* – 1992N
  *Little Suite for Organ* – 1985N
  *Marimba Concerto* – 1990N
  *Peace Cantata* – 1986N
  *Piano Concerto* -1991N
  *Preludes to the Past* – 1989N
  *Romantic Suite for Organ* – 1983N
  *Serenade for Strings* – 1988N
  *Sextet* – 1992N
  *Space Suite* – 1988N
  *String Quartet No. 1* – 1987N
  *Symphony No. 1* – 1952N
  *Symphony No. 2* – 1959N
  *Symphony No. 3* – 1961N
  *Ten Hymn Preludes* – 1960N
  *Three Preludes for Piano* – 1991N
  *Toccata & Fugue for Piano* – 1969N

  *Toccata for Organ* – 1964N
  *Trumpet Concerto* – 1983N
Dietsch, James W. – 1950A
Dietz, Howard – 1896A, 1983B
Diffie, Joe – 1958A
Digital Underground – 1988C
Dillards, The – 1962C
Diller-Quaile School of Music – 1921L
Diller, Angela – 1877F, 1968G
  *Splendor of Music, The* – 1957M
Dilling, Mildred – 1894F, 1982G
Dillon, Dean – 1955A
Dillon, Fannie – 1881F, 1947G
Dillon, Harry/John
  *Do, Do. My Huckleberry Do* – 1893E
Dillon, William A.
  *I Want a Girl Just Like the Girl* – 1911E
Dils – 1977C
DiMeola, Al – 1954A
DiMeola, Al, Project – 1985C
Dimitrova, Ghena – 1981H, 1989H
Dinning, Mark – 1960E
Dinosaur, Jr. – 1984C
Dio – 1982C
Dion, Celine – 1994E
Dion (DiMucci) – 1939A, 1961E
Dion and the Belmonts – 1958C
Dionne and Friends – 1986E
Dippel, Andreas – 1890H, 1910I, 1932G
Dire Straits – 1985E
Disciples, The – 1965C
Discovery Records – 1948C
Disposable Heroes of HipHoprisy – 1990C
Distin, Henry – 1903G
Distin, Henry, Instruments – 1884L
Ditson, Alice M., Fund – 1940L
Ditson, Oliver – 1811F, 1875K, 1888G
Ditson, Oliver, & Co. – 1835L
Dixey, Henry E. – 1943A
Dixie Cups, The – 1964CE
Dixie Dregs – 1973C
Dixie Duo (Blake & Sissle) – 1915C
Dixie Hummingbirds – 1928C
Dixieland Jazz Band, Original – 1916C
Dixieland Jubilee – 1948C
Dixieliners – 1932C
Dixon, Bill – 1925A
Dixon, Christa
  *Negro Spirituals: From Bible to Folk Song* –
    1976D
Dixon, Dean – 1915F, 1938H, 1941K, 1948J, 1976G
Dixon, G. W.
  *Long Tail Blue* – 1827N
Dixon, James – 1928F
Dixon, Mort – 1892A, 1956B
Dixon, Willie – 1915A, 1992B
Dizikes, John
  *Opera In America: a Cultural History* – 1991M
DKG Institute of Musical Art – 1913L

---

❄

Vernacular/Commercial Music Scene
A *Births*     B *Deaths*     C *Biographical*     D *Publications*
E *Representative Pieces*

Dlugoszewski, Lucia – 1931A
*Heidi Songs, The* – 1970N
*Melodic Sonata* – 1950N
*Music for the Left Ear* – 1958N
*Piano Sonata No. 1* – 1949N
D'Molls – 1988C
DNA – 1977C
Doane, George Washington – 1799F
Doane, William H. – 1832F, 1915G
Dobbins, B.
*Contemporary Jazz Pianist, The* – 1978D
Dobbs, Mattiwilda – 1925F, 1953K, 1955H
Dobyns, Geraldine
*Possum Rag* – 1906E
Dockstader, Lew – 1924B
Dockstader's Minstrels – 1901C
Dockstader, Tod
*Quartermass* – 1964N
*Two Moons of Quartermass* – 1964N
*Water Music* – 1963N
Dr. Buzzard's Original Savannah Band – 1974C
Dr. Hook and the Medicine Show – 1968C
Dr. John – 1942A
Dr. Mastermind – 1986C
Dodds & Claus Piano Co. (NY) 1791L
Dodds, Warren "Baby" – 1898A, 1959B
Dodds, Johnny – 1892A, 1940B
Dodge, Charles – 1942F, 1971I, 1975J, 1979I
*Computer Music: Synthesis, Composition &
Performance* – 1985M
Dodsworth, Allen – 1817F, 1896G
*Dodsworth Brass Band School* – 1853M
Dodsworth, Harvey B. – 1822F, 1891G
Dodsworth, Thomas – 1825K
Dodsworth's Band – 1860L
Doenhoff, Albert von – 1880F, 1905H, 1940G
Doese, Helena – 1986H
Doggett, Bill – 1916A
Doggett, Bill, Band I – 1938C
Doggett, Bill, Band II – 1951C
Dohnányi, Christoph von – 1952K, 1969H, 1972H,
1984G
Dohnányi, Ernst von – 1899H, 1949K
Doktor, Paul – 1947K, 1948H, 1952K, 1953I, 1971I,
1989G
Dolci, Alexandro – 1918H
Dolan, Robert E. – 1972B
Dolge, Alfred
*Pianos & Their Makers* – 1911M
*Pianos & Their Makers II* – 1913M
Dolphy, Eric Allan – 1928A, 1964B
Dolukhonova, Zara – 1959H
Domaine School for Conductors &...Players – 1941L
Domingo, Plácido – 1961H, 1966H, 1977J, 1984K
Domino, "Fats" – 1928A
Domino Records – 1924C
Donahue, Al – 1983B
Donahue, Jack – 1930B
Donahue, Sam – 1918A, 1974B

Donalda, Pauline – 1906H
Donaldson, Bo – 1974E
Donaldson, Walter – 1893A, 1947B
*Carolina in the Morning* – 1922E
*Daughter of Rosie O'Grady, The* – 1918E
*How You Gonna Keep 'Em Down on the Farm* –
1919E
*Makin' Whoopee* – 1928E
*Mr. Meadowlark* – 1936E
*My Blue Heaven* – 1924E
*My Buddy* – 1922E
*Silks & Satins* – 1920E
*Whoopee* – 1928E
*Yes, Sir, That's My Baby* – 1925E
Donaldson, Douglas and Gumble – 1928C
Donath, Helen – 1940F, 1960H, 1971H, 1991H
Donato, Anthony – 1909F, 1947I
*Preparing Music Manuscript* – 1963M
Donat, Zdislava – 1981H
Donnelly, Dorothy 1880A, 1928B
Donner, Ral – 1943A, 1984B
Donovan – 1966E
Donovan, Richard F. – 1891F, 1970G
*Five Elizabethan Lyrics* – 1957N
*Four Songs, Soprano & SQ* – 1933N
*Passacaglia on Vermont Folk Tunes* – 1949N
*Piano Suite I* – 1933N
*Sextet, Piano & Winds* – 1932N
*Smoke & Steel* – 1932N
*Wood-Notes* – 1925N
Doobie Brothers – 1970C, 1975E, 1979E
Dooley, William – 1932F, 1957H, 1964H
Doolittle, Eliakim – 1772F, 1850G
*Hornet Stinging the Peacock* – 1812E
Doors, The – 1965C, 1967E, 1968E
Doppler, Arpád – 1880H
Dorati, Antal – 1937H, 1945I, 1947K, 1970I, 1977I,
1979K, 1981K
Dorfmann, Ania – 1936H
Dorian Wind Quintet – 1961L
Dorian, Frederick – 1933K, 1936I, 1991G
*History of Music in Performance, The* – 1942M
*Musical Workshop, The* – 1947M
Doring, Ernest M. – 1877F
Dorough, Prince
*Popular-Music Culture in America* – 1992D
Dorsey Brothers Orchestra – 1934C
Dorsey, Jimmy – 1904A, 1957B
Dorsey, Lee – 1926A, 1986B
Dorsey, Thomas A. – 1899A, 1993B
*Precious Lord, Take My Hand* – 1932E
Dorsey, Thomas A., Gospel Songs Pub. Co. – 1931C
Dorsey, Tommy – 1905A, 1956B
*Boogie Woogie* – 1938E
Dorsey, Tommy, Orchestra – 1935C
Dossenbach-Klingenberg School of Music – 1913L
Dot Records – 1951C
Dougherty, Celius – 1902F, 1986G
Douglas Casino (Cotton Club) – 1918C

---

## Cultivated/Art Music Scene
F *Births*    G *Deaths*    H *Debuts*    I *New Positions*    J *Honors and Awards*
K *Biographical*    L *Musical Beginnings*    M *Publications*    N *Compositions*

Douglas, Barry – 1982F, 1986JK, 1988H
Douglas, Charles W. – 1867F, 1944G
Dovells, The – 1959C
Dow, Peggy
   *Collection of Camp-meeting Hymns* – 1816M
Dowd, William R. – 1922F
Dowling, L./Shaw, A. ed.
   *Schillinger System of Musical Composition* –
   1941M
Dowling, Richard W. – 1962F
*Down Beat* – 1934C
*Down Beat Yearbook* – 1956C
Downer, Joseph – 1787K
Downes, Edward O. – 1911F, 1966I
   *Adventures in Symphonic Music* – 1944M
   *New York Philharmonic Guide to the Symphony* –
   1976M
   *Perspectives in Musicology* – 1972M
Downes, Olin – 1886G, 1906I, 1924I, 1955G
   *Lure of Music, The* – 1918M
   *Symphonic Broadcasts* – 1931M
   *Symphonic Masterpieces* – 1935M
Downey, Morton – 1985M
Downs, Stephen
   *Festival* – 1979E
Dox, Thurston J.
   *American Oratorios & Cantatas* – 1986M
Dozier, Lamont – 1941A
Dräger, Hans-Heinz – 1961K
Dragon, Carmen – 1914A, 1984B
Dragon, Daryl (The Captain) – 1942A
Dragonette, Jessica – 1980G
Drake, Alfred – 1914A, 1992B
Drake, Earl Ross – 1865F, 1916G
Drake, Ervin
   *What Makes Sammy Run?* – 1964E
Drake University Auditorium – 1905L
Drake-Des Moines Symphony Orchestra –
   1937L
Dramatics – 1964C
Dranoff Two Piano Competition – 1985L
Draper, G. H.
   *St. Louis Grand March, The* – 1839N
Dreamlovers – 1956C
Dream Theatre – 1988C
Dream Syndicate, The – 1981C
Dreams – 1953C
Drells, The – 1968E
Dresel, Otto – 1848H, 1852K, 1890G
Dresher, Paul – 1951F
   *Are Are* – 1983N
   *Awed Behavior* – 1993N
   *Channels Passing* – 1982N
   *Dark Blue Circumstance* – 1983N
   *Industrial Strength Music* – 1982N
   *Other Fire* – 1984N
   *Power Failure* – 1989N
   *Re:act:ion* – 1984N
   *See Hear* – 1984N

   *Slow Fire* – 1985N
   *Water Dreams* – 1986N
Dresher, Paul, Ensemble – 1984L
Dresser, Mark – 1952A
Dresser, Paul – 1858A
   *Blue & the Gray, The* – 1900E
   *Come Tell Me What's Your Answer, Yes or No?* –
   1898E
   *Convict & the Bird, The* – 1888E
   *In Good Old New York Town* – 1899E
   *Just Tell Them That You Saw Me* – 1895E
   *Letter That Never Came, The* – 1886E
   *On the Banks of the Wabash Far Away* – 1897E
   *Outcast Unknown, The* – 1887E
   *Pardon That Came Too Late, The* – 1891E
Dressler, Marie – 1934A
Dreyer, Dave
   *Me & My Shadow* – 1927E
DRI – 1982C
Drifters, The – 1953C, 1960E
Drinker Library of Choral Music – 1938L
Drinker, Henry S., Jr. – 1880F, 1965G
Drinker, Sophie – 1888F, 1967G
   *Music & Women* – 1948M
Driscoll, Loren – 1928F, 1966H
Drive, She Said – 1986C
Droogs – 1972C
Drouet, Louis François – 1854H
Drucker, Stanley – 1929F
Druckman, Jacob – 1928F, 1956I, 1969J, 1982I
   *Animus I* – 1966N
   *Animus II* – 1968N
   *Animus III* – 1969N
   *Animus IV* – 1977N
   *Athanor* – 1986N
   *Aureole* – 1979N
   *Brangle* – 1989N
   *Chiaroscuro* – 1977N
   *Lamia* – 1974N
   *Overture, Summer Lightning* – 1990N
   *Prism* – 1980N
   *Seven Deadly Sins, The* – 1955N
   *String Quartet No. 1* – 1948N
   *String Quartet No. 2* – 1966N
   *String Quartet No. 3* – 1981N
   *Synapse* – 1971N
   *Viola Concerto* – 1978N
   *Windows* – 1972N
Drury, Stephen – 1955F
Dubensky, Arcady
   *Downtown* – 1930N
   *Fantasy on a Negro Theme* – 1938N
   *From Old Russia* – 1927N
   *On the Highway* – 1936N
   *Orientale* – 1945N
   *Prelude & Fugue* – 1933N
   *Russian Bells* – 1928N
   *Stephen Foster* – 1940N
   *String Quartet No. 1* – 1932N

---

❖

### Vernacular/Commercial Music Scene
A *Births*   B *Deaths*   C *Biographical*   D *Publications*
E *Representative Pieces*

## Cultivated/Art Music Scene

F *Births*   G *Deaths*   H *Debuts*   I *New Positions*   J *Honors and Awards*
K *Biographical*   L *Musical Beginnings*   M *Publications*   N *Compositions*

Eastman Wind Ensemble – 1952L
Easton, Florence – 1904K, 1915H, 1917H, 1955G
Easton, Sheena – 1981E
Eaton, E. K.
  *Eaton's Series of National & Popular Songs I –*
  1852D
  *Eaton's Series of National & Popular Songs II –*
  1853D
  *Twelve Pieces of Harmony for Military Brass*
  *Bands –* 1846N
Eaton, John – 1935F, 1971I, 1972J
  *Ajax –* 1972N
  *Concert Piece, Syn-ket & Orchestra –* 1966N
  *Concert Piece No. 2 (Syn-ket) –* 1966N
  *Cry of Clytaemnestra, The –* 19980N
  *Danton & Robespierre –* 1978N
  *Duet for Syn-ket & Synthesizer –* 1968N
  *Genesis –* 1992N
  *Heracles –* 1964N
  *Involvement with Music: New Music since 1950 –*
  1976M
  *Lion & Androcles, The –* 1973N
  *Ma Barker –* 1957N
  *Mass –* 1970N
  *Microtonal Fantasy, 2 Pianos –* 1965N
  *Myshkin –* 1971N
  *Peer Gynt Music –* 1992N
  *Piano Trio –* 1971N
  *Piano Variations –* 1957N
  *Sonority Movement –* 1971N
  *String Quartet No. 1 –* 1958N
  *Symphony No. 2 –* 1981N
  *Tempest, The –* 1985N
  *Tertullian Overture –* 1958N
  *Three Graces, The –* 1972N
  *Vibrations –* 1967N
Eberly, Bob – 1981B
*Echo: a Music Journal –* 1883L
Eckert, Rinde – 1951F
Eckhard, Jacob – 1776K, 1786I, 1809I
  *Choral-book –* 1816M
  *Naval Song (Pillar of Glory) –* 1813N
Eckhart, Janis – 1952F, 1981H
Eckstine, Billy – 1914A, 1993B
Eckstine, Billy, Jazz Band – 1944C
Eda-Pierre, Christiane – 1966H, 1980H
Eddy, Clarence – 1851F, 1937G
  *Church & Concert Organist I, The –* 1882M
  *Church & Concert Organist II, The –* 1885M
  *Method for Pipe Organ, A –* 1917M
  *Organ in Church, The –* 1887M
Eddy, Duane – 1938A
Eddy, Nelson – 1901F, 1922H, 1924H, 1967AG
Edelmann, Otto – 1954H
Edelmann, Sergei – 1979K, 1984H
*Edison Phonograph Monthly –* 1903C
Edison, Harry "Sweets" – 1915A
Edmunds, John – 1913F, 1937J
Edson, Lewis – 1748F, 1820G

Edson, Lewis, Jr. – 1771F, 1845G
Edvina, Marie-Louise – 1915H
Edwards, Clara – 1887F, 1974G
Edwards, Cliff – 1972G
Edwards, George – 1943F
  *Captive, The –* 1970N
  *Draconian Measures –* 1976N
  *Exchange-Misère –* 1974N
  *Heraclitean Fire –* 1987N
  *Kreuz und Quer –* 1971N
  *Leaden Echo & the Golden Echo –* 1979N
  *Moneta's Mourn –* 1983N
  *Monopoly –* 1972N
  *Parallel Convergences –* 1988N
  *String Quartet No. 1 –* 1967N
  *String Quartet No. 2 –* 1982N
  *2 Pieces for Orchestra –* 1964N
  *Veined Variety –* 1978N
Edwards, Gus – 1879A, 1945B
  *By the Light of the Silvery Moon –* 1909E
  *Goodbye, Little Girl, Goodbye –* 1904E
  *I'll Be With You When Roses Bloom.. –* 1901E
  *In My Merry Oldsmobile –* 1905E
  *School Days –* 1907E
Edwards, Gus, Publishing Co. – 1906C
Edwards, John S. – 1967I, 1975J
Edwards, Julian – 1888K, 1900C, 1910G
  *Brian Boru –* 1896N
  *Dolly Varden –* 1901N
  *Goddess of Truth, The –* 1896N
  *I Couldn't Stand to See My Baby Lose –* 1899E
  *Jupiter –* 1892N
  *King Rene's Daughter –* 1893E
  *Lazarus –* 1907N
  *Madeleine, or, the Magic Kiss –* 1894E
  *Patriot, The –* 1907N
  *Wedding Day, The –* 1897N
  *When Johnny Comes Marching Home –* 1902E
Edwards, Sherman
  *1776 –* 1969E
Edwards, Tommy – 1922A, 1958E
Effinger, Cecil – 1914F, 1990G
  *Cantata: From Ancient Prophets –* 1983N
  *Concerto Grosso –* 1940N
  *Cyrano de Bergerac –* 1965N
  *Invisible Fire, The –* 1957N
  *Landscape –* 1966N
  *Little Symphony No. 1 –* 1945N
  *Little Symphony No. 2 –* 1958N
  *Long Dimension, The –* 1970N
  *Lyric Overture –* 1949N
  *Pandora's Box –* 1961N
  *Paul of Tarsus –* 1968N
  *Piano Concerto –* 1946N
  *St. Luke Christmas Story –* 1953N
  *String Quartet No. 1 –* 1943N
  *String Quartet No. 3 –* 1944N
  *String Quartet No. 4 –* 1948N
  *String Quartet No. 5 –* 1963N

---

❄

## Vernacular/Commercial Music Scene
A *Births*    B *Deaths*    C *Biographical*    D *Publications*
E *Representative Pieces*

---

## Cultivated/Art Music Scene

F *Births*   G *Deaths*   H *Debuts*   I *New Positions*   J *Honors and Awards*
K *Biographical*   L *Musical Beginnings*   M *Publications*   N *Compositions*

Ellington, Duke (continued)
*Piano Method for Blues* – 1943D
*Reminiscing in Tempo* – 1935E
*River, The* – 1970E
*Sacred Concert II* – 1968E
*Sacred Concert III* – 1973E
*Satin Doll* – 1958E
*Soda Fountain Rag* – 1914E
*Sophisticated Ladies* – 1981E
*Such Sweet Thunder* – 1957E
*Suite Thursday* – 1960E
*Tattooed Bride, The* – 1948E
*Timon of Athens* – 1963E
*Turacet* – 1960E
*Virgin Islands Suite* – 1965E
Ellinwood, Leonard – 1905F, 1939I
*History of American Church Music, The-* 1953M
Elliot, Cass – 1941A
Elliott, Alonzo
*There's a Long, Long Trail* – 1913E
Elliott, Mildred – 1903H
Elliott, Ramblin' Jack – 1931A
Ellis, Brent – 1946F, 1965H, 1979H
Ellis, Don – 1934A, 1978B
*New Rhythm Book, The* – 1972D
Ellis, Shirley – 1941A
Ellison-White Conservatory – 1918L
Ellsasser, Richard – 1972G
Ellsworth, Warren – 1954F, 1979H
Elman String Quartet – 1926L
Elman, Mischa – 1908H, 1911K, 1967G
Elman, Ziggy – 1914A, 1968B
Elmblad, Johannes – 1887H
Elmo, Cloe – 1947H
Elson, Arthur – 1873F, 1920I, 1940G
*Book of Musical Knowledge* – 1915M
*Critical History of the Opera, A* – 1901M
*Music Club Programs from All Nations* – 1907M
*Musician's Guide, The* – 1913M
*Orchestra Instruments & Their Use* – 1902M
*Pioneer School Music Course* – 1917M
*Women's Work in Music* – 1903M
Elson, Louis Charles – 1848F, 1877K, 1880I, 1886I, 1888I, 1920G
*Children in Music* – 1918M
*Curiosities of Music* – 1880M
*Elson's Music Dictionary* – 1905M
*Elson's Pocket Music Dictionary* – 1907M
*European Reminiscences, Musical & Otherwise* – 1891M
*Great Composers & Their Works* – 1898M
*History of American Music, The* – 1904M
*History of German Song, A* – 1888M
*Mistakes & Disputed Points in Music* – 1910M
*Modern Music & Musicians* – 1912M
*National Music of America & Its Sources, The* – 1899M
*Realm of Music, The* – 1892M
*Shakespeare in Music* – 1901M

*Theory of Music, The* – 1890M
*Women in Music* – 1918M
Elston, Arnold - 1907F, 1941I, 1958I, 1971G
*Modern Guide to Symphonic Music, A* – 1966M
Elvira, Pablo – 1941F, 1974H
Elwell, Herbert – 1898F, 1923J, 1928I, 1932I, 1974G
*Blue Symphony* – 1944N
*Concert Suite, Violin & Orchestra* – 1957N
*Divertimento for String Quartet* – 1929N
*Forever Young, The* – 1953N
*Happy Hypocrite, The* – 1925N
*Introduction & Allegro* – 1942N
*Lincoln: Requiem Aeternam* – 1946N
*Ode for Orchestra* – 1950N
*Orchestral Sketches* – 1937N
*Piano Quintet* – 1923N
*Piano Sonata* – 1926N
*Pieces for Piano* – 1928N
*String Quartet in e* – 1937N
*Symphonic Sketches* – 1966N
*Three Piano Preludes* – 1930N
*Violin Sonata* – 1927N
Elwes, Gervase – 1909H
Ely, Joe – 1947A
Elysium Recordings, Inc. – 1995L
Emerson, Allen & Manning's Minstrels – 1868C
Emerson Record Co. – 1916C
Emerson String Quartet – 1976L
Emerson, Luther O. – 1820F, 1895K, 1915G
*Golden Harp, The* – 1860M
*Golden Wreath, The* – 1857M
*Harp of Judah, The* – 1863M
*Jubilate* – 1866M
*Merry Chimes* – 1865M
*Romberg Collection, The* – 1853M
*Sabbath Harmony, The* – 1860M
Emerson, William
*Collection...Suitable for Private Devotion...* – 1808M
Emery, Stephen A. – 1841F, 1867I, 1891G
*Elements of Harmony* – 1880M
*Foundation Studies in Pianoforte Playing* – 1882M
EMF – 1991E
Emmett, Daniel – 1815F, 1854I, 1858C, 1904B
*Blue Tail Fly, De* – 1846N
*Boatman's Dance, De* – 1843N
*Dan Roach* – 1859E
*Dixie* – 1859E
*Jordan Is a Hard Road to Travel* – 1853E
*My Old Aunt Sally* – 1843N
*Old Dan Tucker* – 1843N
*Turkey in the Straw* – 1859E
Emmett, Joseph K.
*Emmett's Lullaby* – 1878E
*Fritz Among the Gypsies* – 1882E
*Fritz in a Madhouse* – 1890E
*Fritz in Ireland* – 1879E

---

❖

Vernacular/Commercial Music Scene
A *Births*    B *Deaths*    C *Biographical*    D *Publications*
E *Representative Pieces*

❀

## Cultivated/Art Music Scene

F *Births*   G *Deaths*   H *Debuts*   I *New Positions*   J *Honors and Awards*
K *Biographical*   L *Musical Beginnings*   M *Publications*   N *Compositions*

❖

Vernacular/Commercial Music Scene
A *Births*    B *Deaths*    C *Biographical*    D *Publications*
E *Representative Pieces*

---

## Cultivated/Art Music Scene

F *Births*    G *Deaths*    H *Debuts*    I *New Positions*    J *Honors and Awards*
K *Biographical*    L *Musical Beginnings*    M *Publications*    N *Compositions*

Farrar, Geraldine – 1882F, 1899K, 1901H, 1906H, 1922K, 1967G
Farrell, Eileen – 1920F, 1947H, 1960H, 1981I
Farrell, S.C.
  *Dictionary of Contemporary American...Instrument Makers* – 1981M
Farwell, Arthur – 1872F, 1893K, 1897K, 1899K, 1909I, 1910K, 1927I, 1952G
  *Academic Overture, "Cornell"* – 1900N
  *American Indian Melodies, Opus 11* – 1900N
  *Americana, Op. 78* – 1927N
  *Ballade, Opus 1* – 1898N
  *Caliban, Op. 47* – 1915N
  *Dawn, Op. 12* – 1901N
  *Death of Virginia, The* – 1894N
  *Domain of Hurakan* – 1902N
  *Evergreen Tree, The* – 1917N
  *Folksongs of the West & South* – 1905N
  *From Mesa & Plain* – 1905N
  *Fugue Fantasy, Op. 44* – 1914N
  *Gods of the Mountains, The* – 1927N
  *Heroic Breed, The* – 1946N
  *Hymn to Liberty* – 1910N
  *Impressions of the Wa-Wan Ceremony* – 1905N
  *Indian Songs, Three, Op. 32* – 1908N
  *Indian Suite* – 1944N
  *In the Tetons* – 1930N
  *Joseph & His Brethren* – 1912N
  *Letter to American Composers, A* – 1903M
  *Owasco Memories, Opus 8* – 1899N
  *Piano Quintet in e* – 1937N
  *Piano Sonata, Op. 113* – 1949N
  *Polytonal Studies for Piano* – 1952N
  *Prelude to a Spiritual Drama* – 1932N
  *Rudolf Gott Symphony* – 1934N
  *String Quartet, Op. 65* – 1922N
  *Symbolist Study No. 1* – 1901N
  *Symbolist Study No. 2* – 1904N
  *Symbolist Study No. 3* – 1905N
  *Symbolist Studies 4 & 5* – 1906N
  *Symbolist Study No. 6* – 1912N
  *Symphonic Poem on March, March* – 1921N
  *Symphonic Study: Mountain Vision* – 1931N
  *Ten Emily Dickinson Songs* – 1949N
  *Three Poems by Shelley* – 1914N
  *To Morfydd* – 1903N
  *Twelve Emily Dickinson Songs* – 1944N
  *Two Compositions for Piano* – 1932N
  *Vale of Enitharmon* – 1930N
  *Violin Sonata, Op. 80* – 1927N
  *Violin Sonata in g, Op. 96* – 1934N
Fascinations – 1960C
Fassbänder, Brigitte – 1970H, 1974H
Fate's Warning – 1982C
*Father Kemp's Old Folk's Concert Tunes* – 1860D
Faulds, Stone & Morse, Publishers – 1854L
Faull, Ellen – 1918F, 1947H
Favero, Mafalda – 1938H

Fay, Amy – 1844F, 1876H, 1903H , 1928G
  *Music Study in Germany* – 1880M
Fay, Maude – 1879F, 1906H, 1916H, 1964G
Fearis, John S.
  *Beautiful Isle of Somewhere* – 1897E
Feather, Leonard – 1935K, 1994B
  *Book of Jazz from Then Till Now, The* – 1957D
  *Encyclopedia of Jazz* – 1955D
  *Encyclopedia of Jazz in the Sixties* – 1966D
  *Inside Bebop* – 1949D
  *Jazz Years, The: Earwitness to an Era* – 1987D
  *Passion for Jazz, The* – 1980D
Feathers, Charlie – 1932A
Federal Music Project – 1935L
Feedback Studio Verlag (New Cologne) – 1970L
Feelies, The – 1976C
Feinhals, Fritz – 1908H
Feinstein, Martin – 1972I
Feinstein, Michael – 1956A
Feist, Leo, Publisher – 1895C
Felciano, Richard J. – 1930F, 1967I, 1974J
  *Captives* – 1965N
  *Contractions* – 1965N
  *Crystals* – 1981N
  *Four Poems from the Japanese* – 1964N
  *Frames & Gestures* – 1970N
  *Furies* – 1988N
  *Galactic Rounds* – 1972N
  *Glossolalia* – 1967N
  *Gravities* – 1965N
  *In Celebration of Golden Rain* – 1978N
  *Kindertotenlieder* – 1984N
  *Mutations* – 1966N
  *On the Divine Presence* – 1968N
  *On the Heart of the Earth* – 1976N
  *Orchestra* – 1980N
  *Orchestration* – 1980M
  *Organ Concerto* – 1986N
  *Shadows* – 1987N
  *Sir Gawain & the Green Knight* – 1964N
  *Soundings for Mozart* – 1970N
  *Te Deum* – 1974N
  *5 Short Piano Pieces* – 1986N
Feld Ballet Co. – 1974L
Feldhoff, Gerd – 1971H
Feldman, Barbara
  *Immutable Silence, The* – 1990N
  *Infinite Other* – 1992N
  *Pure Difference* – 1991N
  *Variations for String Quartet & Chorus* – 1987N
Feldman, Jill – 1952F
Feldman, Morton – 1926F, 1972I, 1978J, 1987G
  *Atlantis* – 1959N
  *Cello & Orchestra* – 1972N
  *Chorus & Instruments I* – 1963N
  *Chorus & Orchestra I* – 1971N
  *Coptic Light* – 1986N
  *Durations III, IV & V* – 1961N

❄

Vernacular/Commercial Music Scene
A *Births*     B *Deaths*     C *Biographical*     D *Publications*
E *Representative Pieces*

---

## Cultivated/Art Music Scene

F *Births*    G *Deaths*    H *Debuts*    I *New Positions*    J *Honors and Awards*
K *Biographical*    L *Musical Beginnings*    M *Publications*    N *Compositions*

Finck, Henry T. (continued)
  *Musical Progress:...Problems in the Tone World* –
    1923M
  *My Adventures in the Golden Age...* – 1926M
  *Songs & Song Writers* – 1900M
  *Success in Music & How it is Won* – 1909M
Fine Arts Quartet – 1946L
Fine Young Cannibals – 1989E
Fine, Irving – 1914F, 1939I, 1950I, 1955J, 1962G
  *Alice in Wonderland Choruses* – 1942N
  *Blue Towers* – 1959N
  *Childhood Fables for Grownups* – 1954N
  *Choral New Yorker* – 1944N
  *Diversions for Orchestra* – 1960N
  *Fantasia for String Trio* – 1956N
  *Notturno for Harp & Strings* – 1951N
  *Partita for Wind Quintet* – 1948N
  *Serious Song:...for Strings* – 1955N
  *String Quartet* – 1952N
  *Symphony* – 1962N
  *Toccata Concertante* – 1947N
  *Violin Concerto* – 1946N
  *Violin Sonata* – 1946N
Fine, Sylvia
  *Moon Is Blue, The* – 1953E
Fine, Vivian – 1913F, 1979J
  *Alcestis* – 1960N
  *Composition for String Quartet* – 1954N
  *Concertante* – 1944N
  *Drama for Orchestra* – 1982N
  *Double Variations for Piano* – 1982N
  *Elegiac Song* – 1937N
  *Epitaph* – 1967N
  *Four Piano Pieces* – 1966N
  *Four Polyphonic Piano Pieces* – 1932N
  *Five Piano Preludes* – 1941N
  *Momenti* – 1978N
  *My Son, My Enemy* – 1965N
  *Piano Suite in E-Flat* – 1940N
  *Piano Variations* – 1952N
  *Poetic Fires* – 1984N
  *Race of Life, The* – 1937N
  *Rhapsody, Russian Folk Song* – 1944N
  *Quintet* (with trumpet) – 1967N
  *Sounds of the Nightingale* – 1971N
  *String Quartet* – 1956N
  *Three Sonnets from Keats* – 1976N
  *Violin Sonata* – 1952N
  *Women in the Garden, The* – 1977N
Fink/Roberts/Ricci
  *Language of Twentieth Century Music* – 1975M
Fink, M. J.
  *Inside the Music Business: Music in
    Contemporary Life* – 1989M
Finger Lakes Performing Arts Center – 1983L
Finger, Susan Pearl – 1954F
Fink, Michael Jon – 1954F
Finkelstein, S. W.
  *Jazz: a People's Music* – 1948D

Finn, William
  *Falsettos* – 1992E
Finnegan, Bill – 1917A
Finney, Ross Lee – 1906F, 1956J, 1967J
  *Chamber Music* – 1951N
  *Computer Marriage* – 1987N
  *Concerto for Strings* – 1977N
  *Earthrise* – 1962N
  *Earthrise III* – 1978N
  *Narrative in Argument* – 1991N
  *Narrative in Retrospect* – 1987N
  *Overture for a Drama* – 1941N
  *Percussion Concerto* – 1965N
  *Piano Concerto No. 1* – 1948N
  *Piano Concerto No. 2* – 1968N
  *Piano Fantasy (Sonata 1)* – 1939N
  *Piano Quintet No. 1* – 1953N
  *Piano Quintet No. 2* – 1961N
  *Piano Sonata in D Minor* – 1933N
  *Piano Sonata No. 3* – 1942N
  *Piano Sonata No. 4* – 1945N
  *Poor Richard* – 1946N
  *Remorseless Rush of Time, The* – 1969N
  *Saxophone Concerto* – 1974N
  *Sonata Quasi una Fantasia* – 1961N
  *Spaces* – 1971N
  *String Quartet No. 1* – 1935N
  *String Quartet No. 2* – 1937N
  *String Quartet No. 3* – 1940N
  *String Quartet No. 4* – 1947N
  *String Quartet No. 5* – 1949N
  *String Quartet No. 6* – 1950N
  *String Quartet No. 7* – 1955N
  *String Quartet No. 8* – 1960N
  *String Quintet* – 1958N
  *Symphony No. 1* – 1942N
  *Symphony No. 2* – 1958N
  *Symphony No. 3* – 1960N
  *Symphony No. 4* – 1972N
  *Thinking About Music: Writings* – 1990M
  *Three 17th C. Lyrics* – 1938N
  *Thirty-Two Piano Games* – 1968N
  *Variations for Orchestra* – 1943N
  *Variations, Fuguing & Holiday* – 1943N
  *Variations on a Theme by Berg* – 1952N
  *Viola Sonata No. 1* – 1937N
  *Violin Concerto No. 1* – 1933N
  *Violin Concerto No. 2* – 1973N
  *Violin Sonata No. 1* – 1934N
  *Weep Torn Land* – 1984N
Finney, Theodore M. – 1902F, 1978G
  *Hearing Music* – 1941M
  *History of Music, A* – 1935M
  *We Have Made Music* – 1955M
Finnie, Linda – 1986H
Finnilä, Birgit – 1981H
Fiore, John – 1991H
Fiorito, Ted – 1900A, 1971B
  *Charley, My Boy* – 1924E

---

❄

Vernacular/Commercial Music Scene
A *Births*      B *Deaths*      C *Biographical*      D *Publications*
E *Representative Pieces*

Fiot & Meignen, Publishers – 1835L
Fiqué, Karl – 1887K, 1930G
Fireballs, The – 1957C, 1963E
Firefall – 1974C
Fireflies – 1957C
Firehose – 1987C
Firehouse Five Plus Two – 1949C
Firesign Theater – 1967C
Firestone, Ross
   *Swing, Swing, Swing: Life & Times of Benny*
   *Goodman* – 1993D
Firkusny, Rudolf – 1938H, 1940K, 1994G
First Edition – 1967C
Firth & Hall – 1827L
Firth, John – 1789F, 1864G
Firth, John, Piano & Publishing Co. – 1815L
Fischer, Carl – 1923G
Fischer, Carl, Publishing Co. – 1872L
Fischer, Carl, Boston Branch – 1909L
Fischer, Carl, Los Angeles Branch – 1935L
Fischer, Carl, San Francisco Branch – 1969L
Fischer, Clare – 1928A
Fischer, Emil F. – 1885H
Fischer, Fred – 1900C, 1942B
   *Chicago* – 1922E
   *Come, Josephine, in My Flying Machine* – 1910E
   *Peg O' My Heart* – 1913E
Fischer, Irwin – 1903F, 1928I
   *Handbook of Modal Counterpoint, A* – 1967M
Fischer, J. & C., Pianos – 1840L
Fischer, Wild Man – 1945A
Fischer, William G. – 1835F, 1912B
Fischer-Dieskau, Dietrich – 1955H
Fisher, Avery – 1906F, 1977J, 1978J, 1994G
Fisher, Avery, Prize – 1975L
Fisher, Eddie – 1928A
Fisher, Fred, Publisher – 1905C
Fisher, Joseph – 1901G
Fisher, J., & Brother, Publisher – 1864L
Fisher, Mark
   *When You're Smiling* – 1928E
Fisher, Miles M.
   *Negro Slave Songs in the United States* – 1953D
Fisher, Sylvia – 1958H
Fisher, William Arms – 1861F, 1948G
   *Music Festivals in the United States* – 1934M
   *Music That Washington Knew, The* – 1931M
   *Notes on Music in Old Boston* – 1918M
   *Ye Olde New England Psalm Tunes (1620-1820)...*
   – 1930M
   *150 Years of Music Publishing in the United*
   *States* – 1933M
Fisk U. Music Dept. – 1885L
Fisk Jubilee Singers – 1871L
Fisk, C. B., Organ Builder – 1955L
Fisk, Charles Benton – 1925F, 1983G
Fisk, Eliot – 1954F, 1976H
Fiske, Isaac – 1820F, 1894G
Fitelberg, Jerzy – 1940K, 1951G

Fitzgerald, Ella – 1918A, 1979C, 1983C, 1987C
Fitzpatrick, Robert – 1986I
Five Blind Boys of Alabama – 1939C
Five Blind Boys of Mississippi – 1939C
Five Dutones – 1957C
Five Keys – 1949C
Five Satins – 1955C
Fizdale, Robert – 1920F, 1995G
Flack, Roberta – 1939A, 1972E, 1973E, 1974E
Flagello, Ezio – 1931F, 1955H, 1957H, 1994G
Flagello, Nicolas – 1928F, 1994G
   *Beowulf* – 1949N
   *Harp Sonata* – 1961N
   *Judgment of St. Francis* – 1959N
   *Mirra* – 1950N
   *Piano Concerto No. 1* – 1950N
   *Piano Concerto No. 2* – 1955N
   *Piano Concerto No. 3* – 1963N
   *Piano Sonata* – 1962N
   *Prelude, Ostinato & Fugue* – 1960N
   *Sisters, The* – 1958N
   *Symphony No. 1* – 1967N
   *Symphony No. 2* – 1970N
   *Te Deum for Mankind* – 1968N
   *Three Dances* – 1945N
   *Violin Concerto* – 1955N
   *Violin Sonata* – 1963N
Flagg, Josiah – 1737F, 1771K, 1795G
   *Collection of the Best Psalm Tunes, A* – 1764M
   *Sixteen Anthems...to Which is Added a Few Psalm*
   *Tunes* – 1766M
Flagstad, Kirsten – 1935H
Flagstaff Festival of the Arts – 1966L
Flaherty, Stephen
   *My Favorite Year* – 1993E
Flaming Ember – 1968C
Flamingos – 1951C
Flamin' Groovies – 1965C
Flammer, Harold – 1889F, 1939G
Flammer, Harold, Inc. – 1917L
Flanagan, Tommy – 1930A
Flanagan, William – 1923F, 1968J, 1969G
   *Bartleby* – 1957N
   *Chapter from Ecclesiastes* – 1962N
   *Concert Ode, A* – 1951N
   *Concert Overture, A* – 1948N
   *Divertimento for String Quartet* – 1947N
   *Ice Age, The* – 1966N
   *Lady of Tearful Regret, The* – 1959N
   *Narrative* – 1964N
   *Notations* – 1960N
   *Piano Sonata* – 1950N
Flanigen, Lauren – 1991H
Flash Cadillac & the Continental Kids – 1969C
Flatt, Lester – 1914A, 1979B, 1985C
Fleck, Béla – 1958A
Flecktones – 1990C
Fleetwood Mac – 1977E
Fleetwoods, The – 1958C, 1959E

---

## Cultivated/Art Music Scene

F *Births*   G *Deaths*   H *Debuts*   I *New Positions*   J *Honors and Awards*
K *Biographical*   L *Musical Beginnings*   M *Publications*   N *Compositions*

Fleischer, Edytha – 1926H
Fleisher, Edwin A. – 1877F, 1959G
Fleisher, Leon – 1928F, 1942H, 1952J, 1959I,
  1964K, 1979K, 1982K, 1985I, 1986I, 1992J
Fleming, Renée – 1960F, 1990J, 1991J
Fleming, Shirley – 1964I
Flesch, Carl – 1913H
Flesch, Ella – 1944H
Fleshtones – 1976C
Fleta, Miguel – 1923H
Fletcher, Alice C. – 1838F, 1923G
  *Indian Games & Dances* – 1915M
  *Indian Story & Song from North America* –
    1900M
Fletcher, Grant – 1913F
Flipper – 1979C
Flock – 1966C
Floersheim, Otto – 1880I
Flonzaley String Quartet – 1902L
Flor, Claus Peter – 1985H
Florida Folk Festival – 1953C
Florida International Festival – 1966L
Florida State School of Music – 1902L
Floridia, Pietro – 1904K
Florio, Caryl – 1857K, 1920G
  *Allegro de Concert* – 1879N
  *Clairvoyance* – 1866N
  *Crown of the Year, The* – 1887N
  *Gulda* – 1879N
  *Ice Witch, The* – 1866N
  *Introduction, Theme & Variations* – 1879N
  *Marche des Fées* – 1870N
  *Marche Triomphale* – 1878N
  *Night at Bethlehem, The* – 1891N
  *Piano Concerto* – 1875N
  *Piano Quartet* – 1870N
  *Piano Trio in D* – 1866N
  *Reverie & Scherzo* – 1872N
  *Song of the Elements* – 1872N
  *String Quartet No. 1* – 1877N
  *String Quartet No. 2* – 1878N
  *String Quartet No. 3* – 1896N
  *Symphonies 1 & 2* – 1887N
  *Textbook of Practical Harmony, A* – 1892M
  *Tours de Mercure, Les* – 1869N
  *Uncle Tom's Cabin* – 1882N
Flotsam & Jetsam – 1984C
Floyd, Carlisle – 1926F
  *Bilby's Doll* – 1976N
  *Citizen of Paradise* – 1983N
  *Flower & Hawk* – 1972N
  *Introductions, Aria & Dance* – 1967N
  *Markheim* – 1966N
  *Mystery, The* – 1960N
  *Of Mice & Men* – 1969N
  *Overture, In Celebration* – 1971N
  *Passion of Jonathan Wade, The* – 1962N
  *Piano Sonata* – 1957N
  *Pilgrimage* – 1956N

*Slow Dusk* – 1949N
*Sojourner & Molly Sinclair, The* – 1963N
*Susannah* – 1954N
*Willie Stark* – 1981N
*Wuthering Heights* – 1958N
Floyd, Eddie – 1935A
Floyd, Samuel, Jr.
  *Black Music in the Harlem Renaissance* – 1990D
  *Power of Black Music, The* – 1995B
Flummerfelt, Joseph – 1937F, 1990I
Flying Burrito Brothers – 1968C
Flynn, Joseph
  *Down Went McGinty* – 1889E
Focile, Nuccia – 1987H
Foden, William – 1860F, 1947G
  *Foden's Grand Method for Guitar* – 1921M
Fodor, Eugene – 1950F, 1960H, 1972J, 1974J
Foerster, Adolph – 1854F, 1927G
Fogelberg, Dan – 1951A
Fogerty, John – 1945A
Fogerty, Tom – 1990B
Foggy Mountain Boys – 1948C
Fohstrom, Alma – 1885H, 1888H
Foldes, Andor – 1939K, 1940H, 1948K, 1992G
Foldi, Andrew – 1975H, 1978I
Foley, Red – 1910A, 1967C, 1968B
Foli, A. J. (Signor) – 1878H, 1899G
*Folio: Journal of Music, Art & Literature, The* –
  1869L
*Folk Song Magazine, The* – 1950C
Folkways Records – 1947C
Fondary, Alain – 1988H
Fontana, Wayne – 1965E
Foote, Arthur – 1853F, 1870K, 1875K, 1876I, 1878I,
  1898J, 1909I , 1921I, 1937G
  *Cello Concerto, Opus 33* – 1893N
  *Farewell of Hiawatha, The, Opus 11* – 1885N
  *Four Character Pieces after Omar Khayyam* –
    1900N
  *Four Pieces after Omar Khayyám* – 1912N
  *Francesca da Rimini* – 1890N
  *In the Gateway of Ispahan* – 1914N
  *In the Mountains, Opus 14* – 1886N
  *Modern Harmony in Its Theory & Practice* –
    1905M
  *Modulation & Related Harmonic Questions* –
    1919M
  *Nocturne & Scherzo* – 1918N
  *Piano Quartet in C, Opus 23* – 1890N
  *Piano Quintet, Opus 38* – 1897N
  *Piano Trio No. 1, Opus 5* – 1883N
  *Piano Trio No. 2* – 1908N
  *Serenade, Opus 25, for Strings* – 1891N
  *Skeleton in Armor, The, Opus 28* – 1891N
  *Some Practical Things in Piano-Playing* – 1909M
  *String Quartet No. 1, Opus 4* – 1883N
  *String Quartet No. 2, Opus 32* – 1893N
  *String Quartet No. 3* – 1911N
  *Suite for Strings, Op. 63* – 1907N

---

❀

**Vernacular/Commercial Music Scene**
A *Births*   B *Deaths*   C *Biographical*   D *Publications*
E *Representative Pieces*

---

## Cultivated/Art Music Scene

F *Births*    G *Deaths*    H *Debuts*    I *New Positions*    J *Honors and Awards*
K *Biographical*    L *Musical Beginnings*    M *Publications*    N *Compositions*

Foster, Stephe (continued)
  *What Must a Fairy's Dream Be* – 1847N
  *White House Chairs, The* – 1847N
Foster, William P. – 1919F
  *Band Pageantry* – 1968M
Foundation for...Advancement of Education in
  Music – 1985L
Foundation for Music Performance (N.Y.) –
  1987L
Fountain, Clarence – 1929A
Fountain, Pete – 1930A
Fountain, Pete, and his Three Coins – 1955C
Fountain, Primous, III – 1949F
Four Aces, The – 1949C
Four AD Records – 1980C
Four Aims (Tops) – 1953C, 1965E, 1966E
Four Coins – 1952C
Four Corners Opera Association (NM) – 1978L
Four Freshmen – 1948C
Four Harmony Kings – 1938C
Four Horsemen – 1991C
Four Seasons – 1956C, 1962E, 1963E, 1964E,
  1976E
Fourestier, Louis – 1946H
Fournet, Jean – 1987H
Fourth Way – 1968C
Fox-Buonameci School of Pianoforte Playing –
  1898L
Fox, Carol – 1954I
Fox, Charles Warren – 1904F, 1932I, 1983G
Fox, Felix – 1897K, 1947G
Fox, Harry, Agency, Inc. – 1927L
Fox, Hattie A.
  *Now I Lay Me Down to Sleep* – 1866E
Fox, Sam, Publisher – 1906L
Fox, Virgil – 1912F, 1946I, 1980G
Fox, Will
  *Twelve Months Ago Tonight* – 1887E
Foy, Eddie – 1854A, 1928B
Frackenpohl, Arthur B. – 1924F
  *Domestic Relations* – 196Nt
  *Harmonization at the Piano* – 1962M
  *String Quartet* – 1971N
  *Symphony for Strings* – 1960N
  *Tuba Sonata* – 1973N
Fradkin, Fredric – 1892F, 1911H, 1963G
Fraenkel, Wolfgang – 1947K
Frager, Malcolm – 1935F, 1959J, 1960J, 1991G
Franchi, Sergio – 1990B
Franci, Carlo – 1969H
Francis, Connie – 1938A, 1960E, 1962E
Franco-American Musical Society – 1920L
François, Samson – 1947H
Frank Music Corporation – 1949L
Frank, Claude – 1940K, 1944K, 1947H
Frankenstein, Alfred – 1906F, 1935I, 1981G
  *Modern Guide to Symphonic Music, A* –
    1970M
  *Syncopating Saxophones* – 1925M

Franke, Paul – 1920F
Franke, Tony – 1905H
Franke & the Knockouts – 1980C
Frankl, Peter – 1965H
Franklin, Aretha – 1942A, 1967E, 1987E, 1994C
Franklyn Music Warehouse – 1817L
Franko, Nahan – 1861F, 1869H, 1930G
Franko, Nahan, Orchestra – 1889L
Franko, Sam – 1857F, 1869H, 1937G
Franks, Michael – 1944A
Frantz, Ferdinand – 1949H
Frantz, Justus – 1975H
Fraternity of Man – 1967C
Frazier, Dallas – 1939A
Freccia, Massimo – 1938H, 1944I, 1952I
Fred, John/Playboy Band – 1956C, 1968E
Freddie/Dreamers – 1965E
Frederick, Jesse – 1948A
Free Flight – 1980C
Freed, Alan – 1922A, 1951C, 1965B
Freed, Arthur – 1894A, 1973B
Freed, Isadore – 1900F, 1944I, 1960G
  *Five Pieces for Piano* – 1933N
  *Homo Sum* – 1930N
  *Jeux de Timbres* – 1930N
  *Lyrical Sonorities* – 1934N
  *Piano Sonata* – 1933N
  *Sonorités Rhythmiques* – 1931N
  *String Quartet No. 1* – 1925N
  *String Quartet No. 2* – 1930N
  *String Quartet No. 3* – 1936N
  *Symphony No. 1* – 1942N
  *Symphony No. 2* – 1951N
Freed, Ralph – 1973B
Freed, Richard D. – 1984J
Freedman, Max C.
  *Rock Around the Clock* – 1953E
  *Sioux City Sue* – 1945E
Freeman School of Music – 1911L
Freeman, Betty – 1921F, 1987J
Freeman, Bud – 1906A, 1991B
Freeman, Carroll B. – 1951F
Freeman, Harry L. – 1869F, 1911I
  *African Kraal* – 1903N
  *Allah* – 1947N
  *Athalia* – 1916N
  *Leah Kleschna* – 1930N
  *Martyr, The* – 1893N
  *Octoroon, The* – 1904N
  *Prophecy, The* – 1912N
  *Slave, The* – 1932N
  *Tryst, The* – 1909N
  *Uzziah* – 1931N
  *Valdo* – 1906N
  *Vendetta* – 1923N
  *Voodoo* – 1914N
  *Zulu King, The* – 1934N
  *Zuluki* – 1898N
  *Zululand* – 1944N

---

Vernacular/Commercial Music Scene
A *Births*    B *Deaths*    C *Biographical*    D *Publications*
E *Representative Pieces*

---

### Cultivated/Art Music Scene

F  *Births*    G  *Deaths*    H  *Debuts*    I  *New Positions*    J  *Honors and Awards*
K  *Biographical*    L  *Musical Beginnings*    M  *Publications*    N  *Compositions*

Fry, William Henry (continued)
  *Notre Dame de Paris* – 1864N
  *Overture, Aurelia the Vestal* – 1838N
  *Overture, Evangeline* – 1860N
  *Overture, Macbeth* – 1862N
  *Overture, The World's Own* – 1857N
  *Sacred Symphony, Hagar in the Wilderness* –
    1854N
  *Santa Claus Symphony* – 1853N
  *Stabat Mater* – 1856N
Fryer, George H. – 1914H
Fu, Haijing – 1990H
Fuchs, Joseph – 1900F, 1943H, 1946I
Fuchs, Lillian – 1903F, 1926H
Fucik, Julius
  *Entry of the Gladiators* – 1900N
Fugazi – 1987C
Fugs, The – 1965C
Fuleihan, Anis – 1915K, 1919H, 1925K,
  1970G
  *Concerto for 2 Pianos* – 1940N
  *Piano Concertos No. 1 & 2* – 1937N
  *Sonorities* – 1945N
  *Symphony No. 1* – 1939N
  *Symphony No. 2* – 1967N
  *Vasco* – 1960N
  *Violin Concerto No. 1* – 1944N
  *Violin Concerto No. 2* – 1965N
Fulkerson, Gregory – 1950F
Fuller, Albert – 1957H
Fuller, Blind Boy – 1941B
Fuller, Bobby, Four – 1963C
Fuller, David – 1927F
Fuller, Jesse "Lone Cat" – 1896A, 1976B
Fuller, Margaret – 1844I, 1850G
Fulson, Lowell – 1921A
Fulton, Thomas – 1994G
Funk, Joseph – 1778F, 1862G
  *Allgemein Nützliche Choral-Music, Die* –
    1816M
  *Compilation of Genuine Church Music* –
    1832M
  *Harmonia Sacra* – 1851M
Funkadelic – 1969C
Funky Bunch – 1991E
Furber, Douglas
  *Limehouse Blues* – 1922E
Furia, Philip
  *Poets of Tin Pan Alley* – 1990D
Fürsch-Madi, Emmy – 1874H, 1883H, 1894G
Furst, W. W.
  *Bohemia* – 1896E
  *Fleur-De-Lis* – 1895E
  *Isle of Champagne, The* – 1892E
  *Princess Nicotine* – 1893E
Furtwängler, Wilhelm – 1925H
Futral, Elizabeth – 1992H
Futrell, Jon
  *Illustrated Encyclopedia of Black Music* – 1982M

# G

G., Kenny – 1956A
Gabriel, Charles H. – 1856F, 1932G
  *Glory Song, The* – 1900N
  *Gospel Songs & Their Writers* – 1915M
  *His Eye Is On the Sparrow* – 1905N
Gabriel, Peter – 1986E
Gabrilowitsch, Ossip - 1900HK, 1918I, 1919K,
  1936G
Gaburo, Kenneth – 1926F, 1983I
  *Antiphony I* – 1958N
  *Antiphony II, III* – 1962N
  *Antiphony IV* – 1967N
  *Antiphony V* – 1968N
  *Antiphony VI* – 1971N
  *Antiphony VII* – 1974N
  *Antiphony VIII* – 1984N
  *Fat Millie's Lament* – 1964N
  *Lemon Drops* – 1965N
  *On a Quiet Theme* – 1950N
  *Wasting of Lucretia, The* – 1964N
  *Widow, The* – 1961N
Gaddes, Richard, Fund for Young Singers – 1986L
Gadski, Johanna – 1900H
Gaillard, Slim – 1916A, 1991B
  *Flat Foot Floogie, The* – 1938E
Gaither, Bill – 1936A
Gaither Music Co. – 1961C
Galajikian, Florence G. – 1900F
Galamian, Ivan – 1937H, 1939K, 1981G
  *Contemporary Violin Technique* – 1962M
  *Principles of Violin Playing & Teaching* – 1962M
Galas, Diamanda – 1955F
Galactic Cowboys – 1990C
Galaxy Music Corporation – 1931L
Galaxy Records – 1964C
Gale, Elizabeth – 1986H
Gales, Weston S. – 1877F, 1914I, 1939G
Galimir, Felix – 1938H, 1944K
Galimir String Quartet II – 1938L
Galkin, Elliott W. – 1921F, 1962I, 1972J, 1975J,
  1977I, 1982J, 1990G
  *History of Orchestral Conducting* – 1989M
Gall, Jeffrey – 1982H, 1980H, 1988H
Gallardo-Domas, Cristina – 1993H
Galla-Rini, Anthony – 1904F
  *Galla-Rini Accordion Primer* – 1958M
  *Method for Accordion* – 1931M
Gallico, Paolo – 1892K
  *Apocalypse, The* – 1922N
  *Euphorion* – 1923N
  *Septet* – 1924N
Galli-Curci, Amelita – 1916H, 1921H, 1963G
Gallo, Fortune – 1895K, 1970G
Gallo, Lucio – 1991H
Gall, Yvonne – 1918H
Galouzine, Vladimir – 1994H
Galston, Gottfried – 1912H, 1927K, 1950G
Galvany, Marisa – 1968H, 1979H

---

❖

**Cultivated/Art Music Scene**
F  *Births*     G  *Deaths*     H  *Debuts*     I  *New Positions*     J  *Honors and Awards*
K  *Biographical*     L  *Musical Beginnings*     M  *Publications*     N  *Compositions*

Gems (Lovettes) – 1961C
Gemünder, August – 1846K, 1852K, 1895G
Gemunder, Austin M. – 1862F, 1928G
Gemünder, George – 1847K, 1899G
Gena, Peter – 1947F
Genesis – 1986E
Gennett Record Co. – 1917C
Gensler, Lewis E.
    *Queen High* – 1926E
Gentele, Göran – 1972K
Gentile, Louis – 1957F, 1983H
Gentle, Alice – 1888F, 1918H
Gentry, Bobbie – 1944A, 1967CE, 1970C
Gentry, Linnell
    *History & Encyclopedia of Country...and Gospel*
    *Music* – 1961D
Gentrys – 1963C
George, D.
    *Wreck of the Old '97* – 1903E
George, Earl – 1924F
Georgia Satellite – 1979C
Georgian, Karine – 1969H
Geraets, Theodora – 1980H
Gerhardt, Elena – 1912H
Gericke, Wilhelm – 1884I, 1898I
German Saengerbund of North America – 1849L
Germania Band (Reading, PA) – 1887L
Germantown Conservatory of Music – 1906L
Germs – 1977C
Gerschefski, Edwin – 1909F, 1926K
    *Classic Symphony* – 1931N
    *Concertino, Piano & Orchestra* – 1932N
    *Piano Sonatina* – 1933N
Gershwin, George – 1898F, 1910K, 1912K, 1937G
    *American in Paris, An* – 1928N
    *American in Paris, An* (film) – 1951E
    *Cuban Overture* – 1932n
    *Dangerous Maid, A* – 1921E
    *Delicious* – 1931E
    *Drifting Along with the Tide* – 1921E
    *Funny Face* – 1927E
    *George White Scandals* – 1920E
    *Girl Crazy* – 1930E
    *Goldwyn Follies* – 1938E
    *Of Thee I Sing* – 1931E
    *La, La, Lucille* – 1919E
    *Lady, Be Good* – 1924E
    *Let Them Eat Cake* – 1933E
    *Oh, Kay!* – 1926E
    *Our Nell* – 1922E
    *Pardon My English* – 1933E
    *Piano Concerto in F* – 1925N
    *Porgy & Bess* – 1935N
    *Rhapsody in Blue* – 1924N
    *Rhapsody No. 2* – 1931N
    *Rosalie* – 1928E
    *Shall We Dance?* – 1937E
    *Show Girl* – 1929E
    *Somebody Loves Me* – 1924E

    *Song of the Flame* – 1925E
    *Strike Up the Band* – 1930E
    *Swanee* – 1919E
    *Sweet Little Devil* – 1924E
    *Three Piano Preludes* – 1926N
    *Tiptoes* – 1925E
    *Treasure Girl* – 1928E
    *Variations, I Got Rhythm* – 1934N
Gershwin, George, Award – 1945L
Gershwin, Ira – 1983B
Gerster, Etelka – 1878H
Gerville-Réache, Jeanne – 1907H
Gesner, Clark
    *You're a Good Man, Charlie Brown* – 1967E
Gessendorf, Mechthild – 1983H, 1986H
Geszty, Sylvia – 1973H
Getz, Stan – 1927A, 1991B
Getzen Brass Instrument Co. – 1939L
G-Force – 1979C
Ghazarian, Sonya – 1987H
Gheorghiu, Angela – 1993H
Ghezzo, Dinu – 1966K
Ghiaurov, Nicolai – 1964H, 1965H
Ghiglia, Oscar – 1966H
Ghitalla, Armando – 1925F
Giacomini, Giuseppe – 1976H
Giannini, Dusolina – 1902F, 1923H, 1936H, 1986G
Giannini, Ferruccio – 1885K, 1891H, 1948G
Giannini, Vittorio – 1903F, 1932J, 1956I, 1965I,
    1966G
    *Beauty & the Beast* – 1938N
    *Blennerhasset* – 1939N
    *Harvest, The* – 1961N
    *IBM Symphony* – 1939N
    *Lucedia* – 1932N
    *Piano Concerto* – 1935N
    *Requiem* – 1936N
    *Scarlet Letter, The* – 1937N
    *Symphony: In Memoriam T.R.* – 1935N
    *Symphony No. 4* – 1960N
    *Trumpet Concerto* – 1945N
    *Violin Concerto* – 1944N
Gibb, Andy – 1977E, 1978E
Gibbs, Arthur H.
    *Runnin' Wild* – 1922E
Gibbs, Georgia – 1920A
Giblin, Irene
    *Chicken Chowder Rag* – 1905E
    *Sleepy Lou Rag* – 1906E
Gibson Mandolin-Guitar Co. – 1902C
Gibson, Bob – 1931A
Gibson, Debbie – 1970A, 1988E, 1989E
Gibson, Don
    *I Can't Stop Loving You* – 1958E
    *Oh, Lonesome Me* – 1958E
Gibson, Jon – 1940F
Gibson, Orville – 1856A, 1918B
Gibson, Robert
    *Ex Machina* – 1995N

---

❋

---

Vernacular/Commercial Music Scene

A *Births*    B *Deaths*    C *Biographical*    D *Publications*
E *Representative Pieces*

Giddings, T. P.
  *Instrumental Technique for Orchestra & Band* –
    1926M
Gideon, Miriam – 1906F, 1975J
  *Condemned Playground* – 1963N
  *Creature to Creature* – 1985N
  *Dances for Two Pianos* – 1945N
  *Epitaphs for Robert Burns* – 1952N
  *Hound of Heaven* – 1945N
  *Morning Star* – 1980N
  *Piano Sonata* – 1977N
  *Piano Suite No. 1* – 1935N
  *Piano Suite No. 2* – 1940N
  *Piano Suite No. 3* – 1951N
  *Questions on Nature* – 1964N
  *Resounding Lyre, The* – 1979N
  *Rhymes from the Hill* – 1966N
  *6 Cuckoos in Quest of a Composer* – 1953N
  *Songs of Voyage* – 1961N
  *Songs of Youth & Madness* – 1977N
  *Sonnets from Shakespeare* – 1950N
  *Spirit above the Dust* – 1980N
  *String Quartet* – 1946N
  *Symphonia Brevis* – 1950N
  *Voices from Elysium* – 1979N
  *Wind's Hour* – 1983N
  *Woman of Valor, A* – 1981N
Gielen, Michael – 1980I
Gieseking, Walter – 1926H
Gifford, Gene – 1970B
Gigli, Beniamino – 1920H
Gilbert & Sullivan – 1879K
Gilbert, Douglas
  *Lost Chords: the Story of American Popular
    Songs* – 1942D
Gilbert, Fred
  *Man That Broke the Bank at Monte Carlo, The* –
    1892E
Gilbert, Henry F. – 1868F, 1886K, 1889K, 1928G
  *Americanesque* – 1903N
  *Celtic Songs* – 1905N
  *Dance in the Place Congo* – 1908N
  *Fantasy in Delft* – 1920N
  *Fish Wharf Rhapsody* – 1909N
  *Hymn to America* – 1915N
  *Indian Scenes* – 1912N
  *Indian Sketches* – 1914N
  *Intimate Story of Tribal Life* – 1911N
  *Island of the Fay* – 1904N
  *Negro Dances* – 1914N
  *Negro Rhapsody* – 1912N
  *Riders to the Sea* – 1904N
  *Six Indian Sketches* – 1921N
  *Six Pieces, Op. 19* – 1927N
  *Strife* – 1910N
  *Symphonic Piece* – 1925N
  *Three American Dances* – 1911N
  *Three Tone Pictures, Op. 5* – 1914N
  *To Thee, America* – 1914N

  *Uncle Remus* – 1906N
  *Verlaine Moods, Two* – 1903N
Gilbert, L. Wolfe – 1886A, 1970B
  *Down Yonder* – 1922E
Gilberté, Hallett – 1872F, 1946G
Gilchrist, Frederick
  *Psalm 46* – 1882N
Gilchrist, William Wallace – 1846F, 1874I, 1878J,
    1882I, 1898J, 1916G
  *Easter Idyll, An* – 1907N
  *Eight Songs* – 1885N
  *Lamb of God, The* – 1909N
  *Legend of the Bended Spear* – 1888N
  *Prayer & Praise* – 1888N
  *Symphonic Poem in g* – 1910N
  *Symphony in C* – 1891N
Gilder, Nick – 1978E
Gilels, Emil – 1955H
Giles, Christopher – 1976J, 1977J
Giles, Imogene
  *Red Peppers* – 1907E
Gilfert's Music Repository (SC) – 1813L
Gilfert, Charles H. – 1800H, 1817I, 1829G
Gilfert, Charles, Music Publisher – 1815L
Gilham, W. B.
  *Aeolian Lyrist* – 1834M
Gilibert, Charles – 1900H
Gilibert, Gilibert – 1910G
Gilkyson, Terry
  *Cry of the Wild Goose* – 1949E
Gill, Vince – 1957A, 1990C
Gillespie, Dizzy – 1917A, 1953C, 1989C, 1990C,
    1993BC
  *To Be or Not to Bop* – 1979D
Gillespie, Dizzy, Big Band I – 1945C
Gillespie, Dizzy, Big Band II – 1946C
Gillespie, Dizzy, Sextet – 1945C
Gillespie, Haven
  *That Lucky Old Sun* – 1949E
  *You Go to My Head* – 1938E
Gillet, Wheeler
  *Virginia Sacred Minstrel, The* – 1817M
Gilley, Mickey – 1937A
Gillingham, George – 1793HK, 1826G
Gillis, Don – 1912F, 1970G
  *Alamo, The* – 1944N
  *Symphony No. 1* – 1939N
  *Symphony No. 51/2* – 1947N
  *Symphony No. 10* – 1967N
  *Tulsa* – 1950N
Gilly, Dinh – 1909H
Gilman, Benjamin Ives – 1852F, 1933G
Gilman, Lawrence – 1878F, 1901I, 1915I, 1923I,
    1939G
  *Aspects of Modern Opera* – 1909M
  *Music of Tomorrow & Other Studies* – 1907M
  *Nature in Music & Other Studies* – 1914M
  *Phases of Modern Music* – 1904M
  *Stories of Symphonic Music* – 1907M

---

### Cultivated/Art Music Scene

F *Births*    G *Deaths*    H *Debuts*    I *New Positions*    J *Honors and Awards*
K *Biographical*    L *Musical Beginnings*    M *Publications*    N *Compositions*

Gilman, Lawrence (continued)
   *Toscanini & Great Music* – 1938M
Gilmer, Jimmy – 1963E
Gilmore Artist Award – 1991L
Gilmore, Graves & Co., Brass Instr. – 1864L
Gilmore, Gail – 1950F, 1975H, 1981H, 1986H
Gilmore, Jimmie Dale – 1945A
Gilmore, Patrick S. – 1829F, 1849K, 1852I, 1853I,
   1855I, 1858I, 1869K, 1873I, 1892G
   *Famous 22nd Regiment March* – 1882N
   *When Johnny Comes Marching Home Again* –
   1863E
Gilmore's Band – 1858L
Gimpel, Bronislav – 1937K, 1979G
Gimpel, Jacob – 1938K, 1989G
Ginastera, Alberto – 1945K
Gingold, Josef – 1909F, 1926H 1950I, 1960I, 1995G
Gioia, Ted
   *West Coast Jazz, 1945-1960* – 1992D
Giordani, Marcello – 1995H
Giorni, Aurelio – 1914K, 1938G
Giraldoni, Eugenio – 1904H
Girlschool – 1978C
Girls Next Door – 1982C
Giteck, Janice – 1946F
Gitler, Ira
   *Swing to Bop* – 1987D
Gitlis, Ivry – 1955H
Giuffre, Jimmy – 1921A, 1978C
   *Four Brothers* – 1947E
   *Jazz Phrasing & Interpretation* – 1969D
Giuffre, Jimmy, Trio – 1956C
Giuffria – 1981C
Giulini, Carlo Maria – 1955H, 1969K, 1978I
Giuseppe, Enrico di – 1932F, 1959H, 1970H
Gjevang, Anne – 1984H, 1987H
Glanville, Roberta – 1904H
Glanville-Hicks, Peggy – 1942K, 1948IK, 1953J
   *Beckett* – 1990N
   *Sappho* – 1963N
   *Saul & the Witch of Endor* – 1959N
   *Transposed Heads, The* – 1953N
Glass, Philip – 1937F
   *Akhnaton* – 1984N
   *Belle et la Bête, La* – 1994N
   *Canyon, The* – 1988N
   *Descent into the Maelstrom* – 1986N
   *Einstein on the Beach* – 1975N
   *Itaipú* – 1989N
   *Juniper Tree, The* – 1985N
   *Light, The* – 1987N
   *Low Symphony* – 1992N
   *Making of the Representative for Planet 8* –
   1988N
   *Music in Contrary Motion* – 1969N
   *Music in Eight Parts* – 1969N
   *Music in Fifths* – 1969N
   *Music in Similar Motion* – 1969N
   *Music in Twelve Parts* – 1974N

   *Music with Changing Parts* – 1970N
   *Orphée* – 1993N
   *Photographer, The* – 1982N
   *Pieces in the Shape of a Square* – 1968N
   *Satyagraha* – 1980N
   *String Quartet No. 2: Company* – 1983N
   *String Quartet No. 3: Mishima* – 1985N
   *String Quartet No. 4: Boczak* – 1989N
   *Symphony No. 2* – 1994N
   *Violin Concerto* – 1987N
   *Voyage, The* – 1992N
   *1000 Airplanes on the Roof* – 1988N
Glass, Philip, Ensemble – 1968L
Glassychord (Glass Harmonica) – 1761L
Glaz, Herta – 1936H, 1942H
Gleason, Frederick – 1848F, 1884I, 1900I,
   1903G
   *Auditorium Festival Ode* – 1889N
   *Edris* – 1896N
   *Montezuma* – 1885N
   *Otho Visconti* – 1877N
   *Song of Life, The* – 1899N
Gleason, Harold – 1892F, 1921I, 1980G
   *Examples of Music before 1400* – 1942M
   *Method of Organ Playing* – 1937M
   *Music in America* – 1964M
   *Music Literature Outlines* – 1949M
Gleck, Henry T. – 1890I
Glenn, Bonita – 1960F
Glenn, Carroll – 1918F, 1938J, 1943K, 1983G
Glimmerglass Opera Co. – 1975L
Glimmerglass Opera House – 1987L
Glossop, Peter – 1967H
Glover, Charles
   *Rose of Tralee, The* – 1912E
Gluck, Alma – 1884F, 1890K, 1909H, 1938G
Glydenfeldt, Graciela von – 1991H
Gnazzo, Anthony J. – 1936F
   *Art of Canning Music, The* – 1976N
   *Begin Again* – 1977N
   *Compound Skill Fracture* – 1975N
   *Ten Pieces for Pauline Oliveros* – 1969N
Gobbi, Tito – 1948H, 1955H
Gockel, August – 1853H
Goddard, Arabella – 1873H
Goddard, Josiah
   *New & Beautiful Collection, A* – 1798M
Godowsky, Leopold – 1884H, 1890I, 1891K, 1895I,
   1938G
Godz – 1977C
Goeb, Roger – 1914F, 1953J
   *Symphony No. 1* – 1942N
   *Symphony No. 2* – 1945N
   *Symphony No. 3* – 1952N
   *Symphony No. 4* – 1954N
   *Violin Concerto* – 1953N
Goeke, Leo – 1971H
Goepp, Philip – 1864F, 1891K, 1936G
   *Annals of Music in Philadelphia...* – 1896M

---

❀

**Vernacular/Commercial Music Scene**
A  *Births*    B  *Deaths*    C  *Biographical*    D  *Publications*
E  *Representative Pieces*

Goetschius, Percy – 1853F, 1876K, 1890IK, 1892I,
  1896K, 1905I, 1943G
  *Counterpoint* – 1902M
  *Essentials of Music History* – 1913M
  *Homophonic Forms of Musical Composition* –
    1889M
  *Larger Forms of Musical Composition* – 1915M
  *Lessons in Music Form* – 1904M
  *Masters of the Symphony* – 1929M
  *Material Used in Musical Composition* – 1882M
  *Structure of Music, The* – 1934M
  *Theory & Practice of Tone Relations* – 1882M
Goetz, E. Ray
  *Orchid, The* – 1907E
Goetze, Marie – 1890H
Goffin, Gerry – 1939A
Gogorza, Emilio de – 1874F, 1897H, 1912K, 1949G
Go-Go's, The – 1978C
Gold & Fizdale – 1946H
Gold, Andrew – 1951A
Gold, Arthur – 1919F
Gold, Ernest – 1938C
  *It's a Mad, Mad, Mad, Mad World* – 1963E
  *Piano Concerto* – 1945N
  *Exodus* – 1960E
Gold, Robert
  *Jazz Lexicon: The Folk Songs of Peggy Seeger* –
    1964D
Goldbeck, Robert    1857K, 1908G
  *Encyclopedia of Music Education* – 1903M
Goldberg, Albert – 1898F, 1925I, 1943I, 1990G
Goldberg, Isaac
  *Tin Pan Alley:...the American Popular Music
    Racket* – 1930D
  *Tin Pan Alley: A Chronicle of American Popular
    Music* – 1961D
Goldberg, Reiner – 1983H
Goldberg, Szymon – 1938H, 1953K, 1978H, 1980I,
  1993G
Golde, Walter – 1887F
Golden Dawn – 1967C
Golden Palominos, The – 1981C
Golden, John L.
  *Sunshine Girl, The* – 1912E
Golden West Cowboys – 1936C
Goldenthal, Bobby – 1968E
Goldenthal, Elliot
  *Fire Water Paper: A Vietnam Oratorio* – 1995N
Goldie & the Gingerbreads – 1963C
Goldman Band – 1911L
Goldman, Edwin Franko – 1878F, 1956G
  *Band Guide & Aid to Teachers* -1916M
  *Goldman Band System, The* – 1935M
  *On the Mall* – 1923N
  *Pride of America March* – 1911N
Goldman, Richard Franko – 1910F, 1947I, 1968I,
  1980G
  *Band's Music, The* – 1938M
  *Concert Band, The* – 1946M

*Harmony in Western Music* – 1965M
*Landmarks of Early American Music* – 1943M
*Wind Band: its Literature & Technique, The* –
  1961M
Goldman, Robert
  *First Impressions* – 1959E
Goldmark, Rubin – 1872F, 1894K, 1924I, 1936G
  *Call of the Plains* – 1915N
  *Hiawatha* – 1900N
  *Negro Rhapsody, A* – 1922N
  *Piano Quartet* – 1909N
  *Requiem* – 1919N
  *Samson* – 1914N
Goldovsky Opera Institute    1946L
Goldovsky, Boris – 1930K, 1942I, 1977I, 1986J
  *Good Afternoon, Ladies & Gentlemen* – 1984M
Goldsand, Robert – 1927H, 1939K
Goldsboro, Bobby – 1941A, 1968E
Goldsmith, Jerry – 1929A
  *Blue Max, The* – 1966E
  *Lonely Are the Brave* – 1962E
  *Mephisto Waltz, The* – 1971E
  *Omen, The* – 1976E
  *Planet of the Apes* – 1968E
  *Seven Days in May* – 1964E
  *Shadow, The* – 1994E
  *Tora! Tora! Tora!* – 1970E
Goldstein, Ellen – 1953J
Goldstein, Lee – 1987I
Golschmann, Vladimir – 1931I, 1947K, 1958I,
  1964I, 1972G
Golson, Benny – 1929S
Goltz, Christel – 1954H
Golub, David – 1950G, 1964H
Gombosi, Otto J. – 1939K, 1940I, 1955G
Gondale, Juliana Kathleen – 1953F
Gonsalves, Paul – 1920A, 1974B
Gonzalez, Dennis – 1954C
Gonzalez, Dalmacio – 1980H
Gooch, William
  *Reuben & Rachel* – 1871E
Good, Dolly – 1915A
Goodale, Ezekiel
  *Instrumental Director* – 1819L
Goode, Richard – 1943F, 1962H, 1973J, 1980J
Goodman, Alfred
  *Lady in Ermine, The* – 1922R
Goodman, Benny – 1909A, 1982C, 1986B, 1987C
Goodman, Benny, Band – 1934C
Goodman, Benny, Quartet – 1936C
Goodman, Benny, Sextet – 1947C
Goodman, Benny, Trio – 1935C
Goodman, Craig S. – 1957F
Goodman, Steve – 1948A, 1984B
Good Rats, The – 1965C
Goodrich, Alfred
  *Art of Song, The* – 1888M
  *Complete Musical Analysis* – 1889M
Goodrich, John Wallace – 1871F, 1897I, 1931I

---

### Cultivated/Art Music Scene

F *Births*    G *Deaths*    H *Debuts*    I *New Positions*    J *Honors and Awards*
K *Biographical*    L *Musical Beginnings*    M *Publications*    N *Compositions*

Goodrich, Walter – 1902I
Goodrich, William M. – 1777F, 1833G
Goodrich, William, Organ Builder – 1804L
Goodwin, J. C.
  *Love Will Find a Way* – 1890E
Goodson, Katharine – 1907H
Goossens, Eugene – 1923I, 1931I
Gorchakova, Galina – 1994H, 1995H
Gordon String Quartet – 1930L
Gordon, Dexter – 1923A, 1980C, 1990B
Gordon, Jacques – 1913K, 1948G
Gordon, Mack – 1904A, 1959B
Gordon, Peter – 1951F
Gordon, Stephen T. – 1890G
Gordon, Stephen T., Publishing Co. – 1846L
Gore, Lesley – 1946A, 1963E
Gorin, Igor – 1933K, 1939K, 1964H, 1982G
Goritz, Otto – 1903H
Gorme, Eydie – 1932A
Gorney, Jay – 1896A, 1990B
  *Americana* – 1932E
  *Brother, Can You Spare a Dime?* –
    1930E
Gorno, Albino – 1881K, 1945C
Gorodnitzki, Sascha – 1904F, 1930J, 1986G
Gorr, Rita – 1962H
Gosdin, Vern – 1934A
Gospel Chimes – 1959C
Gospel Harmonettes, Original – 1940C
Gospel Music Workshop of America – 1968C
Gossett, Philip – 1941F, 1986J
Gotham-Attucks Music Pub. – 1986C
Gottlieb, Jack S. – 1930F
  *Death of a Ghost* – 1978N
  *Movie Opera, The* – 1982N
  *Piano Sonata* – 1960N
  *String Quartet* – 1954N
  *Tea Party* – 1955N
Gottlieb, Jay Mitchell – 1952F
Gottlieb, W. P.
  *Golden Age of Jazz, The* – 1979D
Gottschalk, Louis M. – 1829F 1835K, 1836K,
  1842K, 1844H, 1846K, 1851K, 1853H, 1854K,
  1856K, 1857K, 1861K, 1862K, 1865K, 1869G
  *La Bamboula* – 1845N
  *Bananier, Le* – 1850N
  *Banjo, The* – 1854N
  *Chanson des Negres* – 1850N
  *Charles IX* – 1869N
  *Cocoyé* – 1854N
  *Danse des Ombres* – 1851N
  *Danza* – 1857N
  *Dying Poet, The* – 1864N
  *Dying Swan, The* – 1869N
  *Escenas Campestres* – 1860N
  *Fantasy on "God Save the Queen"* – 1851N
  *Gallina, La* – 1863N
  *Grand Tarantelle* – 1868N
  *Isaura de Salerno* – 1869N

*Last Hope, The* – 1854N
*Maiden's Blush, The* – 1864N
*Mancenillier, Le* – 1849N
*Manchega* – 1856N
*Marche Funèbre, Opus 61* – 1854N
*Marche Solennelle* – 1868N
*Mélancholie, La* – 1847N
*Moissonneuse, Le* – 1847N
*Morte?, Opus 50* – 1868N
*National Glory* – 1853N
*Night in the Tropics, A* – 1859N
*Notes of a Pianist* – 1881M
*Ojos Criollos* – 1859N
*Printemps d'amour* – 1855N
*Savane, La* – 1846N
*Souvenir de la Havane* – 1859N
*Souvenir de Puerto Rico* – 1857N
*Souvenirs d'Andalousie* – 1851N
*Stringmusic* – 1994N
*Symphony No. 2, "A Montevideo"* – 1868N
*Union, The* – 1862N
Goudoever, Henri van – 1921H
Goudonov, Alexander – 1995G
Gould, Glenn – 1955H
Gould, Morton – 1913F, 1983J, 1985J, 1986IJ,
  1994J
  *American Salute* – 1943N
  *American Symphonette No. 1* – 1933N
  *American Symphonette No. 2* – 1935N
  *American Symphonette No. 3* – 1938N
  *Billion Dollar Baby* – 1945E
  *Burchfield Gallery* – 1979N
  *Classical Variations, Colonial Themes* – 1985N
  *Concerto for Orchestra* – 1944N
  *Concerto for Tap Dancer* – 1952N
  *Derivations, Clarinet & Jazz Band* – 1955E
  *Diversions* – 1990N
  *Fall River Legend* – 1947N
  *Flute Concerto* – 1984N
  *Housewarming* – 1982N
  *Interplay* – 1945N
  *Jekyll & Hyde Variations* – 1955N
  *Latin-American Symphonette* – 1941N
  *Notes of Remembrance* – 1989N
  *Philharmonic Waltzes* – 1948N
  *Showpiece for Orchestra* – 1954N
  *Soundings* – 1969N
  *Spirituals* – 1941N
  *Symphony of Spirituals* – 1976N
  *Symphony No. 1* – 1943N
  *Symphony No. 2* – 1944N
  *Symphony No. 3* – 1947N
  *Venice* – 1966N
  *Vivaldi Gallery* – 1967N
Gould, Morton, Award (ASCAP) – 1994L
Gould, Nathaniel D. – 1781F, 1798K, 1805I, 1864G
  *History of Church Music in America* – 1853M
  *National Church Harmony* – 1832M
  *Social Harmony* – 1823M

---

Vernacular/Commercial Music Scene

A *Births*    B *Deaths*    C *Biographical*    D *Publications*
E *Representative Pieces*

Goulding, Edmund
  *Mam'selle* – 1947E
Goulet, Robert – 1933A
Gow, George
  *Structure of Music, The* – 1895M
Go West – 1982C
Grable, Betty – 1918A, 1973B
Grael, B. A.
  *Streets of New York* – 1963E
Graf, Herbert – 1934K, 1936I, 1958K
  *Opera and Its Future in America, The* – 1941M
  *Opera for the People* – 1951M
  *Producing Opera for America* – 1961M
Graf, Max
  *Composer and Critic* – 1946M
  *From Beethoven to Shostakovich* – 1947M
  *Modern Music* – 1946M
Graffman, Gary – 1928F, 1936I, 1946J, 1947H, 1949J, 1979K, 1980I
Grafulla, Claudio S. – 1838K, 1880G
Graham, Charles
  *If the Waters Could Speak As They Flow* – 1887E
  *Picture That's Turned to the Wall, The* – 1891E
  *Two Little Girls in Blue* – 1893E
Graham, Martha – 1893F, 1926K, 1950K, 1974J, 1979J, 1985J, 1991G
Graham, Susan – 1960F
Graham Central Station – 1972C
Grainger, Percy – 1914K, 1915H, 1918K, 1950J, 1961G
  *Handel in the Strand* – 1912N
  *Suite, In a Nutshell* – 1916N
Gram, Hans – 1785K, 1804G
  *America* – 1791N
  *Death Song of an Indian Chief* – 1791N
Gramercy Five (Artie Shaw) – 1940C
Gramm, Donald – 1927F, 1944H, 1964H, 1983G
Grammy Awards – 1958C
Gran Combo, El – 1962C
Grand Army of the Republic Band – 1869L
Grand Canyon Chamber Music Festival – 1984L
Grand Funk (Railroad) – 1968C, 1973E, 1974E
Grand Master Flash and the Furious Five – 1977C
Grand Ole Opry – 1925C
Grand Teton Music Festival – 1962L
Grandjany, Marcel – 1924H, 1936K, 1938I, 1945K, 1975G
Grange, Anna Caroline de la – 1855H
Grannis, S. M.
  *Do They Miss Me at Home?* – 1852E
Grant, Amy – 1986E, 1991E
Grant, Earl – 1933A, 1970B
Grant, Gogi – 1924f, 1956E
Grant, James
  *Piano Concerto* – 1995N
Grant, Micki
  *Don't Bother Me, I Can't Cope* – 1972E
Grant, Parks – 1910F
  *Clarinet Concerto* – 1945N

  *Overture, Macbeth* – 1930N
  *Symphonic Fantasia* – 1931N
  *Symphony in d* – 1938N
  *Symphony No. 2* – 1941N
Grantham, Donald – 1947F
Grass Roots, The – 1966C
Grass Roots Opera – 1948L
Grasse, Edwin – 1884F, 1954G
Grassi, Alex de – 1953A
Grateful Dead, The – 1965C
Grau, Maurice – 1849F, 1891I, 1907G
Grau, Maurice, Opera Co. – 1898L
Graudan, Nicolai – 1964G
Graupner, Catherine C. – 1821G
Graupner, Gottlieb – 1795HK, 1796IK, 1808K, 1809I, 1836G
  *Rudiments of the Art of Playing the Piano Forte* – 1806M, 1819M
Graupner Music Store & Publisher – 1800L
Graves, Denyce – 1991J
Graves, Samuel – 1794I, 1878G
Graves, Samuel, & Co. – 1830L
Graveure, Louis – 1914H
Grawemeyer Prize – 1984I
Gray, Delores – 1924A
Gray, Dobie – 1942A
Gray, H. Willard – 1894K, 1950G
Gray, H. W., Co., Inc. – 1906L
Gray, Jerry – 1915A, 1976B
Gray, Linda – 1981H
Gray, Matthias, Music Store – 1859L
Gray, Matthias, Co., Publishers – 1858L
Gray, William B.
  *She Is More To Be Pitied Than Censured* – 1894E
Graziani, Francesco – 1854H
Grazzi, Amadeo – 1883H
Grease Band – 1966C
Great Society – 1965C
Great White – 1981C
Great Woods Center, Performing Arts – 1986L
Great Plains Chamber Music Institute – 1982L
Greatorex, Henry W. – 1836K, 1858G
  *Collection of Sacred Music* – 1851M
Greco, Buddy – 1926A
Green, Adolph – 1915A, 1991C
Green, Al – 1946A, 1972E
Green, Benny
  *Reluctant Art: The Growth of Jazz, The* – 1963D
Green, Bud
  *Sentimental Journey* – 1945E
Green, Douglas
  *Country Roots: The Origins of Country Music* – 1978D
Green, Eddie
  *Good Man is Hard to Find, A* – 1918E
Green, Elizabeth A. – 1906F
  *Dynamic Orchestra..., The* – 1987M
Green, John – 1908F
  *Body & Soul* – 1930E

---

## Cultivated/Art Music Scene

F *Births*   G *Deaths*   H *Debuts*   I *New Positions*   J *Honors and Awards*
K *Biographical*   L *Musical Beginnings*   M *Publications*   N *Compositions*

Green, Johnny – 1908A, 1989B
Green, Ray
  *Dance Sonata No. 2* – 1952N
  *Symphony No. 2* – 1945N
  *Violin Concerto* – 1952N
Green, Stanley
  *Encyclopedia of the Musical Theater* – 1976D
  *World of Musical Comedy, The* – 1960D
Greenawald, Sheri – 1947F, 1974H
Greenbaum, Norman – 1942C
Greenberg, Noah – 1919F, 1966G
Greenberg, Noah, Award – 1978L
Greenberg, Sylvia – 1981H
Greenbriar Boys – 1958C
Green Day – 1989C
Greene, Arthur – 1978J, 1986J
Greene, Harry P. – 1893H
Greene, Joseph P.
  *Across the Alley from the Alamo* – 1947E
Greene, Lorne – 1964E
Greene, Susan – 1955F
Greenfield, Elizabeth Taylor – 1819F, 1851H,
  1854K, 1876G
Greenhouse, Bernard – 1916F, 1946H
Greenleaf, Robert
  *Under the Arbor* – 1992N
Green On Red – 1981C
Greensboro Opera Co. (NC) – 1981L
Greenwich, Ellie – 1948A
Greenwich House Music School – 1906L
Greenwood, Francis
  *Collection of Psalms & Hymns for Sacred
  Worship* – 1830M
Greenwood, Lee – 1983C
Greer, Sonny – 1895A, 1982B
Greindl, Josef – 1952H
Grenville, Lillian – 1888F, 1906H, 1910H
Gretchaninov, Alexander – 1929K, 1939K, 1946K,
  1956G
  *Clarinet Sonata No. 1* – 1940N
  *Clarinet Sonata No. 2* – 1943N
  *Festival Overture* – 1946N
  *Marriage, The* – 1946N
  *Piano Sonata No. 2* – 1944N
  *Rhapsody on a Russian Theme* – 1940N
  *Vers la victoire* – 1941N
Gretsch Guitar Manufacturing Co. – 1883C
Grever, Maria
  *What a Diff'rence a Day Makes* – 1934E
Grider, Rufus – 1817F
  *Historical Notes on Music in Bethlehem, PA* –
  1873M
Grienauer, Alois – 1888H
Griffel, Kay – 1940F, 1960H, 1982H
Griffes, Charles Tomlinson – 1884F, 1903K, 1907I,
  1920G
  *Bacchanale* – 1919N
  *Fantasy Pieces, Op. 6* – 1915N
  *Five Poems, Op. 10* – 1917N

*Kairn of Koridwen, The* – 1916N
*Notturno for Orchestra* – 1918N
*Overture* – 1905N
*Piano Sonata* – 1918N
*Pleasure Dome of Kubla Khan* – 1912N
*Roman Sketches* – 1915N
*Symphonische Phantasie* – 1907N
*Three Poems, Op. 9* – 1916N
*Three Preludes for Piano* – 1919N
*Three Tone Images, Op. 3* – 1914N
*Three Tone Pictures, Op. 5* – 1914N
Griffin, Rex – 1912A, 1958B
Griffis, Elliot – 1893F, 1967G
  *Piano Sonata* – 1919N
  *String Quartet No. 2* – 1930N
  *Symphony for Strings* – 1941N
  *Symphony No. 1* – 1932N
  *Violin Sonata* – 1931N
Griffith Music Foundation – 1938L
Griffith, Nanci – 1954A
Griffith, Yeatman – 1898H
Griggs, S. S., & Co. – 1848L
Grigorian, Gegam – 1992H, 1995H
Grillo, Joann – 1939F, 1962H, 1963H
Grimes, Tiny – 1916A
Grimm, Carl Hugo – 1890F
Grishko, Vladimir – 1990H
Grisi, Giulia – 1854H
Grisman, David – 1945A
Grisman, David, Quintet – 1976C
Grist, Reri – 1932F, 1959H, 1966H
Griswold, Gertrude – 1861F
Griswold, Putnam – 1875F, 1911H, 1914G
Grobe, Charles – 1839K, 1879G
  *Battle of Buena Vista, Opus 101* – 1847N
  *Beauties of Beethoven* – 1860N
  *Buds & Blossoms* – 1867N
  *Centennial Memorial March* – 1875N
  *Grobe's Parlour Music* – 1856N
  *Ladies' Pets;..Waltzes, Marches, Polkas* –
  1853N
  *Melodies of the Day* – 1857N
  *Mnemosyne, Opus 14* – 1842N
  *Music of the Union, Opus 1348* – 1861N
  *New Method for the Pianoforte* – 1859M
  *United States Grand Waltz, Opus 43* – 1845N
  *Variations on "Come Home, Father"* – 1866N
  *Variations on "Dixie's Land"* – 1860N
  *Variations on "My Old Kentucky Home"* – 1853N
Grobe, Charles, Musical Agency – 1862L
Grobe, Donald – 1929F, 1952H, 1986G
Grofé, Ferde – 1892F, 1972G
  *Death Valley Suite* – 1957N
  *Grand Canyon Suite* – 1931N
  *Mississippi Suite* – 1925N
Groop, Monica – 1995H
Grootna – 1970C
Gross, Walter
  *Tenderly* – 1945E

---

❖

---

Vernacular/Commercial Music Scene
A *Births*    B *Deaths*    C *Biographical*    D *Publications*
E *Representative Pieces*

Grossman, B.
  *Doll's Life, A* – 1982E
Grossman, Larry
  *Goodtime Charley* – 1975E
  *Minnie's Boys* – 1970E
  *Snoopy* – 1982E
Grossman, W. L.
  *Heart of Jazz, The* – 1956D
Grosz, Wilhelm
  *Harbor Lights* – 1937E
Groton Academy (NH) – 1793L
Group for Contemporary Music – 1962L
Group for New Music (U. of MA) – 1974L
Grout, Donald Jay – 1902F, 1945I, 1987G
  *History of Western Music, A* – 1960M
Groves, Paul – 1995I
GRP Records – 1982C
Gruber, Edmund L.
  *Caissons Go Rolling Along, The* – 1908E
Gruberová, Edita – 1977H
Grudeff, Marion
  *Baker Street* – 1965E
Gruenberg, Eugene – 1928G
  *Violinist's Manual, The* – 1897M
Gruenberg, Louis – 1884F, 1912II, 1947J, 1964G
  *Americana* – 1945N
  *Antony & Cleopatra* – 1955N
  *Bride of the Gods, The* – 1913N
  *Cello Concerto* – 1949N
  *Creation, Op. 23* – 1926N
  *Daniel Jazz* – 1923E
  *Dumb Wife, The* – 1921N
  *Emperor Jones, The* – 1932N
  *Enchanted Isle, The* – 1927N
  *Four Diversions, Op. 32* – 1930N
  *Green Mansions* – 1937N
  *Hill of Dreams, The* – 1919N
  *Jack & the Beanstalk* – 1930N
  *Music to an Imaginary Ballet* – 1945N
  *Piano Concerto No. 1* – 1914N
  *Piano Concerto No. 2* – 1938N
  *Piano Quintet* – 1929N
  *String Quartet No. 2* – 1941N
  *Symphony No. 1* – 1919N
  *Symphony No. 2* – 1941N
  *Symphony No. 3* – 1942N
  *Symphony No. 4* – 1946N
  *Violin Sonata No. 1* – 1912N
  *Violin Sonata No. 2* – 1924N
  *Violin Sonata No. 3* – 1950N
  *Volpone* – 1945N
  *Witch of Brocken* – 1912N
Grümmer, Elisabeth – 1966H, 1967H
Grundman, Clare – 1913F
Grunewald, Louis – 1852K, 1915G
Grunewald, Louis, Dealer/Publisher – 1858L
Grunn, John Homer – 1888F, 1944G
Grupo Fascinación – 1983C
Grupo Niche – 1981C

Guadagnini, Luigi – 1883H
Guadagno, Anton – 1982H
Guanieri, Johnny – 1917A, 1985B
Guarrera, Frank – 1923F, 1948H
Gubrud, Irene – 1947F, 1980J, 1981H
Gudehus, Heinrich – 1890H
Gueden, Hilde – 1951H
Guelfi, Giangiacomo – 1970H
Guess Who – 1970E
Guggenheim, Daniel – 1856F, 1930G
Guggenheim Fellowship Program – 1925L
Guggenheim Foundation – 1924L
  *Guiding Light to Tin Pan Alley, The* – 1946C
Guilbert, Yvette – 1895H
Guilmant, Alexander – 1903K
Guion, David – 1892F, 1981G
  *Mother Goose Suite* – 1930N
  *Southern Nights Suite* – 1922N
  *Shigandi* – 1932N
Guiraud, Ernest – 1837F, 1892G
  *Gretna Green* – 1873N
*Guitar Player Magazine* – 1967C
Guitar Slim – 1926A, 1959B
Gulda, Friedrich – 1950H
Guleghina, Maria – 1990H
Gulin, Angeles – 1982H
Gulli, Franco – 1968H, 1972I
Gulyás, Dénes – 1981H, 1985H
Gumble, Albert
  *Chanticleer Rag* – 1910E
Gun Club – 1980C
GunMar Music – 1979L
Gunn School of Music & Dramatic Art –
  1922L
Gunn, Glenn D. – 1874F, 1910I, 1922I, 1940I
  *Course on the History and Aesthetics of Music* –
    1912M
  *Music: Its History & Enjoyment* – 1939M
Guns n' Roses – 1985C, 1988E
Gunzenhauser, Stephen – 1942F, 1978I
Gurt, Michael – 1982J
Gusikoff, Michel – 1893F, 1920H
Gusman, Maurice, Philharmonic Hall – 1972L
Gustafson, Nancy – 1956F, 1989H
Gustafson, William – 1887F, 1920H, 1931G
Gutché, Gene – 1925K
  *Ghenghis Khan* –1963N
  *Music of the People* – 1978M
  *Symphonies No. 1 & 2* – 1950N
  *Symphony No. 3* – 1952N
  *Symphony No. 4* – 1960N
  *Symphony No. 5 for Strings* – 1962N
Guthrie, Arlo – 1947A
Guthrie, Woody – 1912A, 1967B
  *Bound for Glory* – 1943D
Gutiérrez, Horacio – 1961K, 1967K, 1976K, 1982J
Gutiérrez y Espinosa, Felipe – 1825F, 1858I, 1899G
Gutman, Natalia – 1987H
Guy – 1985C

---

❁

## Cultivated/Art Music Scene

  F *Births*    G *Deaths*    H *Debuts*    I *New Positions*    J *Honors and Awards*
  K *Biographical*    L *Musical Beginnings*    M *Publications*    N *Compositions*

Guy, Buddy – 1936A
GWAR – 1986C

# H

Haar, James – 1929F
Habermann, Michael R. – 1950F, 1977H
Habich, Edward – 1930H, 1935H
Hackett, Bobby – 1915A, 1976B
Hackett, Charles – 1889F, 1915H, 1916K, 1918H, 1942G
Hackley, E. Azalia – 1867F, 1901H, 1922G
Haddock, Marcus – 1957F
Haden, Charlie – 1937A
Hadjidakis, Manos
    *Ilya Darling* – 1967E
    *Never On Sunday* – 1960E
Hadley, Henry K. – 1871F, 1894K, 1895I, 1904K, 1909I, 1911I, 1920HK, 1924J, 1925J, 1929I, 1937G
    *Azora* – 1915N
    *Belshazzar* – 1932N
    *Bianca* – 1916N
    *Christmas Cantata* – 1922N
    *Cleopatra's Night* – 1918N
    *Culprit Fay, The* – 1909N
    *Golden Prince, The* – 1914N
    *Happy Jack* – 1889N
    *Herod Overture* – 1901N
    *In Music's Praise* – 1899N
    *In Bohemia, Opus 28* – 1900N
    *Lucifer* – 1913N
    *Merlin & Vivian* – 1906N
    *Nancy Brown* – 1903E
    *New Earth, The* – 1919N
    *Nightingale & the Rose* – 1911N
    *Ocean, The* – 1921N
    *Oriental Suite* 1903N
    *Othello Overture* – 1919N
    *Piano Quintet, Op. 50* – 1919N
    *Princess of Ys, The* – 1903N
    *Resurgam, Op. 98* – 1922N
    *Safié, Op. 63* – 1909N
    *Salome, Op. 55* – 1905N
    *San Francisco* – 1931N
    *Scherzo Diabolique* – 1934N
    *Silhouettes* – 1931N
    *Streets of Pekin, The* – 1930N
    *String Quartet No. 2* – 1934N
    *Symphony No. 1, "Youth & Life"* – 1897N
    *Symphony No. 2* – 1901N
    *Symphony No. 3* – 1906N
    *Symphony No. 4* – 1911N
    *Symphony No. 5* – 1935N
Hadley, Henry, Foundation...for American Music – 1938L
Hadley, Jerry – 1952F, 1978H, 1987H, 1993J
Haendel, Ida – 1946H
Hagans, Tim – 1954A
Hagen, Elizabeth C. von – 1809G

Hagen, Francis F. – 1815F
Hagen, Theodore – 1854K, 1871G
Hagar, Sammy – 1947A
Hagegård, Håkan – 1978H
Hageman, Richard – 1906K, 1966G
    *Caponsacchi* – 1931N
    *Crucible, The* – 1943N
Hagen, Daron Aric
    *Shining Brow* – 1993tN
Hagen, Francis F. – 1907G
Häggander, Mari Anne – 1985H
Haggard, Merle – 1937A, 1973E, 1984C, 1991C
Haggin, B. H.
    *Decade of Music, A* – 1973M
    *Listener's Musical Companion, The* – 1956M
    *Music in the Nation* – 1949M
    *Music Observed* – 1964M
Hague, Albert
    *Plain & Fancy* – 1955E
    *Redhead* – 1959E
Hahn, Marian – 1972J
Haieff, Alexei – 1932K, 1939K, 1947J
    *Ballet in E* – 1955N
    *Caligula* – 1971N
    *Cello Sonata* – 1963N
    *Piano Concerto No. 1* – 1950N
    *Piano Sonata* – 1955N
    *Sonata for Two Pianos* – 1945N
    *String Quartet* – 1951N
    *Symphony No. 1* – 1942N
    *Symphony No. 2* – 1957N
    *Symphony No. 3* – 1961N
    *Violin Concerto* – 1948N
    *Wind Quintet* – 1983N
Haig, Al – 1924A, 1982B
Haile, Eugen – 1903K, 1933G
Haimovitz, Matt – 1985H
Haines Brothers Piano Co. – 1851L
Haines, Edmund – 1914F, 1974G
    *Symphony No. 1* – 1941N
Haitink, Bernard – 1958H, 1982H
Halasz, László – 1936K, 1943K, 1965I
Hale, Philip – 1854F, 1880K, 1890I, 1891I, 1897I, 1904I, 1934G
Hale, Robert – 1966H, 1990H
Haley, Bill – 1925A, 1981B
    *Rock-a-Beatin' Boogie* – 1952E
Halfvarson, Eric – 1953F, 1977H, 1993H
Halir, Carl – 1896H
Hall and Oates – 1969C, 1977E, 1981E, 1982E, 1984E
Hall Johnson Choir – 1930L
Hall, Mack Co. – 1895L
Hall of Fame for Great Americans – 1900L
Hall, Labagh & Co., Organ Builders – 1846L
Hall & Quinby Brass Instruments – 1862L
Hall & Erben, Organ Builders – 1824L
Hall, Carol
    *Best Little Whorehouse in Texas* – 1978E

---

✦

## Vernacular/Commercial Music Scene
A *Births*    B *Deaths*    C *Biographical*    D *Publications*
E *Representative Pieces*

Hall, David – 1916F, 1957I
Hall, David C. – 1822F, 1853I, 1900G
Hall, Edmond – 1901A, 1967B
Hall, Frederick D. – 1898F
Hall, Janice – 1953F, 1977H
Hall, Jim – 1930A
Hall, Marie – 1905H
Hall, Robert Browne – 1858F, 1907G
Hall, Thomas – 1791F, 1874G
Hall, Thomas, Organ Builder – 1811L
Hall, Tom T. – 1936A
Hall, Walter Henry – 1896I
Hall, Wendell W.
    *It Ain't Gonna Rain No Mo'* – 1923E
Hall, William – 1796F, 1874G
Hall, William, Piano Co. – 1820L
Hall, William, & Son – 1847L
Hamari, Julia – 1972H, 1982H
Hamblen, Stuart – 1908A, 1989B
    *This Ole House* – 1954E
Hamblin, Pamela – 1954F, 1980H
Hambourg, Mark – 1899H
Hambro, Leonid – 1946J
Hamerik, Asger – 1871I, 1900K
    *Requiem, Opus 34* – 1887N
    *Symphonie Lyrique, Opus 33* – 1885N
    *Symphonie Majesteuse, Opus 35* –
    1889N
    *Symphonie Poétique, Opus 26* – 1880N
    *Symphonie Sérieuse, Opus 36* – 1891N
    *Symphonie Tragique, Opus 32* – 1883N
Hamilton Organ Co. – 1889L
Hamilton, Arthur
    *Cry Me a River* – 1953E
Hamilton, Chico – 1921A
Hamilton, Clarence Grant – 1865F, 1935G
    *Epochs in Musical Progress* – 1926M
    *Outlines of Music History* – 1908M
    *Piano Music, Its Composers & Characteristics* –
    1925M
    *Piano Teaching* – 1910M
    *Sound & Its Relation to Music* – 1911M
    *What Every Piano Pupil Should Know* –
    1928M
Hamilton, David – 1935F, 1965I
    *Listener's Guide to Great Instrumentalists* –
    1982M
    *Metropolitan Opera Encyclopedia* – 1981M
Hamilton, Harley – 1898I
Hamilton, Jeff – 1953A
Hamilton, Jimmy – 1917A
Hamlisch, Marvin – 1944A
    *Chorus Line, A* – 1975E
    *Goodbye Girl, The* – 1993E
    *Smile* – 1986E
    *They're Playing Our Song* – 1979E
    *Way We Were, The* – 1974E
Hamm, Charles – 1925F, 1976I
    *Music in the New World* – 1983M

    *Opera* – 1966M
    *Yesterdays: Popular Song in America* – 1979D
Hammer, Heinrich – 1908K, 1954G
Hammer, Jan
    *Miami Vice Theme* – 1984E
Hammer, M. C. – 1963A
Hammerstein Opera House – 1908L
Hammerstein, Oscar, I – 1919G
    *Santa Maria* – 1896E
Hammerstein, Oscar, II – 1895A, 1943C, 1960B
Hammond Chord Organ – 1950L
Hammond Clock (Organ) Co. – 1928L
Hammond Instrument Co. – 1929L
Hammond Organ – 1933L
Hammond, Frederick – 1937F
Hammond, Joan – 1949H
Hammond, John – 1943A
Hammond, John Hays, Jr. – 1888F, 1965G
Hammond, Laurens – 1895F, 1973G
Hammond, Richard – 1896F
    *Carnival* – 1931N
    *Fiesta* – 1929N
    *Five Chinese Fairy Tales* – 1921N
    *Oboe Sonata* – 1924N
    *Sea of Heaven, The* – 1929N
    *Sinfonietta* – 1931N
    *Six Women's Choruses* – 1940N
Hampden County Musical Association (MA) –
    1889L
Hampson, Thomas – 1955F, 1980K, 1981H, 1982H,
    1986H
Hampton, Calvin – 1938F, 1963I, 1984G
Hampton, Lionel – 1909A, 1992C
    *Hey-Baba-Re-Bop* – 1945E
Hampton, Lionel, Big Band – 1940C
Hanby, Benjamin Russel – 1833A, 1867B
    *Darling Nellie Gray* – 1856E
Hanchett, Henry G. – 1853F, 1879H, 1918G
    *Art of the Musician, The* – 1905M
    *Introduction to the Theory of Music, An* – 1918M
    *Teaching as a Science* – 1882M
Hancock, Herbie – 1940A
    *Round Midnight* – 1986E
Hancock, Herbie, Sextet – 1968C
Handel Society of Dartmouth – 1780L
Handley, J. J.
    *Sleep, Baby, Sleep* – 1885E
Handt, Herbert – 1926F, 1949H, 1960K
Handy, John, II – 1933A
    *Concerto for Jazz Soloist* – 1970E
Handy, William C. – 1873A, 1958B
    *Aunt Hagar's Blues* – 1920E
    *Beale Street Blues* – 1916E
    *Book of Negro Spirituals* – 1938D
    *Joe Turner Blues* – 1915E
    *John Henry Blues* – 1922E
    *Memphis Blues* – 1909E
    *Negro Authors & Composers of the U.S.* – 1935D
    *St. Louis Blues* – 1914E

---

### Cultivated/Art Music Scene

F *Births*    G *Deaths*    H *Debuts*    I *New Positions*    J *Honors and Awards*
K *Biographical*    L *Musical Beginnings*    M *Publications*    N *Compositions*

---

---

### Cultivated/Art Music Scene

F *Births*    G *Deaths*    H *Debuts*    I *New Positions*    J *Honors and Awards*
K *Biographical*    L *Musical Beginnings*    M *Publications*    N *Compositions*

---

❀

---

### Vernacular/Commercial Music Scene

A  *Births*     B  *Deaths*     C  *Biographical*     D  *Publications*
E  *Representative Pieces*

We Parted by the River – 1866E
Write Me a Letter from Home – 1866E
Hayter, A. U. – 1873G
Hayton, Lennie – 1908A, 1971B
Hayward, Robert – 1988H
Haywood, Charles – 1904F
  Bibliography of North American Folklore &
    Folksong – 1951D
Haywood, Eddie, Sextet – 1941C
Hazen, M.R.
  Music Men, The – 1987M
Hazlewood, Lee – 1929A
Heart – 1970C, 1986E, 1987E
Heartbreakers and Johnny Thunder – 1975C
Hearts & Flowers – 1964C
Heath Brothers Band – 1975C
Heath, Walter H.
  Clancy Lowered the Boom – 1949E
Heavy D. and the Boyz – 1984C
Hebert, Pamela – 1946F, 1972H
Heckscher, Céleste de Longpré – 1860F, 1928G
Hedmont, Charles – 1857F
Hee Haw (TV) – 1969C
Hefti, Neal – 1922A
Heiden, Bernhard – 1935K
Heidt, Horace – 1901A, 1986B
Heifetz-Piatigorsky-Rubinstein Trio – 1949L
Heifetz-Piatigorsky Concerts (LA) – 1961L
Heifetz, Daniel – 1948F, 1969J, 1970H
Heifetz, Jascha – 1917H, 1925K, 1972K, 1987G
Heifetz, Robin – 1951F
Heights, The – 1992E
Heilbut, Tony
  Gospel Sound: Good News & Bad Times, The –
    1971D
Heilmann, Uwe – 1990H
Hein, Silvio – 1879A
Heindorf, Ray John
  Pete Kelly's Blues – 1955E
Heink, Ernestine Schumann – 1898H
Heinrich, Anthony Philip – 1805K, 1810K, 1817K,
  1826K, 1832K, 1837K, 1856K
  Boadicèa Overture – 1845N
  Chromatic Ramble of the Peregrine Harmonist –
    1820N
  Complaint of Longan the Mingo Chief – 1834N
  Concerto for the Kent Bugle – 1834N
  Dawning of Music in Kentucky, Opus 1 – 1820N
  Elegia Impromtu – 1837N
  Gran Sinfonia Eroica – 1835N
  Grand American National Chivalrous Symphony
    – 1837N
  Hunters of Kentucky, The – 1837N
  Indian War Council, The – 1834N
  Jäger's Adieu, The – 1835N
  Jubilee, The – 1841N
  Mocking Bird to the Nightingale, The – 1834N
  Oratorio of the Pilgrim Fathers – 1842N
  Ornithological Combat of Kings, The – 1847N

Pocahontas – 1837N
Pushmataha – 1831N
Schiller – 1834N
Sinfonia Romantico (Bohemia) – 1837N
Sylviad – 1823N
To the Spirit of Beethoven – 1846N
Tower of Babel, The – 1834N
Treaty of William Penn with the Indians – 1834N
Warrior's March, The – 1845N
Western Minstrel, The, Opus 2 – 1820N
Wildwood Troubadour, The – 1853N
Heinrich, Max – 1886H
Heinz Hall for the Performing Arts – 1927L
Heinz, Hans – 1956I
Heir Apparent – 1984C
Held, Alan – 1989H
Held, Anna – 1869C, 1918B
Helfer, Walter – 1896F
Hell, Richard, and the Voidoids – 1976C
Hellermann, William – 1939F
Helm, Everett Burton – 1913F
  Beginnings of the Italian Madrigal... – 1939M
  Chansons of Arcadelt, The – 1942M
  Composer, Performer, Public – 1970M
  Kentucky Sonata – 1944N
  Music & Tomorrow's Public – 1981M
  Piano Concerto – 1951N
  Requiem – 1942N
  Sonata Brevis – 1942N
Helmet – 1989C
Helms, Bobby – 1033A
Helps, Robert – 1928F, 1976J, 1978I
  Gossamer Noons – 1977N
  Piano Concerto No. 1 – 1969N
  Piano Concerto No. 2 – 1976N
  Recollections 1959N
  Starscape – 1958N
  String Quartet – 1951N
  Three Etudes for Piano – 1956N
  Three Homages – 1973N
  Symphony No. 1 – 1957N
Helstar – 1982C
Hemke, Frederick – 1935F
  Teacher's Guide to the Saxophone, The – 1977M
Hemm, Manfred – 1991H
Hemmenway, James – 1800F, 1849G
  Cupid's Frolic – 1819N
  Generall Lafayette's Trumpet March & Quick Step
    – 1824N
  Miss Billing's Waltz – 1819N
  New Year & Courtsy Cotillions, The – 1827N
  Philadelphia Grand Entre Waltz, The – 1819N
  Philadelphia Grand March – 1823N
  Philadelphia Hop Waltz, The – 1826N
  Philadelphia Serenading Grand March – 1826N
  Washington Grays' Bugle Quick Step – 1821N
  Washington Grays' Grand March – 1825N
Hempel, Frieda – 1912H
Hemphill, Julius – 1995B

---

Cultivated/Art Music Scene
  F Births      G Deaths      H Debuts      I New Positions      J Honors and Awards
  K Biographical      L Musical Beginnings      M Publications      N Compositions

Hempsted Music Store – 1851L
Henahan, Donal – 1947I, 1967I, 1980I
Henderson, Fletcher – 1897A, 1950C, 1952B
Henderson, Fletcher, Jazz Band – 1923C
Henderson, Joe – 1937A
Henderson, Ray – 1896A, 1970B
   *Alabamy Bound* – 1925E
   *Big Boy* – 1925E
   *Birth of the Blues* – 1926E
   *Bye, Bye, Blackbird* – 1926E
   *Five Foot Two, Eyes of Blue* – 1925E
   *Flying High* – 1930E
   *Follow Through* – 1929E
   *Georgette* – 1922E
   *Good News* – 1927E
   *Hold Everything* – 1928E
   *Singing Fool, The* – 1929E
   *Strike Me Pink* – 1933E
   *That Old Gang of Mine* – 1923E
Henderson, Skitch – 1918A, 1949C, 1971I
Henderson, Skitch, Dance Band – 1947C
Henderson, William J. – 1855F, 1887I, 1902I, 1920I, 1924I, 1937G
   *Art of the Singer, The* – 1906M
   *Early History of Singing* – 1921M
   *How Music Developed* – 1898M
   *Modern Musical Drift* – 1904M
   *Orchestra & Orchestral Music, The* – 1899M
   *Preludes & Studies* – 1891M
   *Story of Music, The* – 1889M
   *What is Good Music?* – 1898M
Hendl, Walter – 1917F, 1949I, 1964I, 1976I
Hendricks and Ross – 1957C
Hendricks, Barbara – 1948F, 1971H, 1974H, 1986H
Hendrickson, George
   *Union Harmony, The* – 1848M
Hendrickson, William D.
   *Spanish Cavalier, The* – 1881E
Hendrix, Jimi – 1942A, 1970B
Hendrix, Jimi, Experience – 1966C
Hendryx, Nona – 1945A
Heniot, Hans – 1940I
Henley, Don – 1947A
Henninges, Dona – 1860F
Henriot, Nicole – 1948H
Henry, Clarence "Frogman" – 1945A
Henschel, George – 1880H, 1881I
Henschel, Jane – 1960F
Henschel, Lillian – 1868F, 1876H, 1901G
Hensel, Heinrich – 1911H
Hensler, Elise – 1836F
Hentoff, Nat
   *Jazz* – 1959D
   *Jazz Life, The* – 1961D
   *Jazz Street* – 1960D
Henze, Hans Werner – 1963K
Heppner, Ben – 1988H, 1991H

Herbert, Victor – 1876K, 1886K, 1887HK, 1893I, 1898I, 1924K, 1908J, 1924G
   *Ameer, The* – 1899E
   *American Fantasia for Orchestra* – 1898N
   *Angel Face* – 1919E
   *Anthem of Lambs* – 1897N
   *Aschenbrödel March* – 1910N
   *Auditorium Festival March* – 1901N
   *Babes in Toyland* – 1903E
   *Babette* – 1903E
   *Badinage for Orchestra* – 1895N
   *Belle of Pittsburgh, The* – 1895N
   *Blümlein an Herzen, Opus 4* – 1884N
   *Captive, The* – 1891N
   *Cello Concerto No. 1* – 1894N
   *Cello Concerto No. 2* – 1898N
   *Christ is Risen* – 1904N
   *Cosmopolitan* – 1923N
   *Cyrano de Bergerac* – 1899E
   *Debutante, The* – 1914E
   *Dolly Dollars, Miss* – 1905E
   *Dream City* – 1906E
   *Dream Girl, The* – 1924E
   *Duchess, The* – 1911E
   *Easter Dawn, An* – 1905N
   *Eight Songs, Opus 10, 13, 14* – 1889N
   *Eileen* – 1917E
   *Eldorado* – 1894N
   *Enchantress, The* – 1911E
   *Encore, L'* – 1910N
   *Fall of a Nation, The* – 1916E
   *Fantasia for Violin & Orchestra* – 1893N
   *Fantasy on a Schubert Theme* – 1891N
   *Festival March* – 1935N
   *Fight is Made & Won, The* – 1897N
   *Fortune Teller, The* – 1898E
   *Girl in the Spotlight, The* – 1920E
   *Gold Bug, The* – 1896E
   *Honeymoon* – 1887N
   *Humoresque for Woodwinds* – 1898N
   *Ice-Water Galop* – 1894N
   *Idol's Eye, The* – 1897E
   *Indian Summer* – 1919E
   *Irish Rhapsody* – 1892N
   *It Happened in Nordland* – 1904E
   *Jester's Serenade, The* – 1908N
   *Lady of the Slipper, The* – 1912D
   *Little Nemo* – 1908E
   *Madcap Duchess, The* – 1913E
   *Madeleine* – 1913N
   *Magic Knight, The* – 1906E
   *Mlle. Fifi* – 1905E
   *Mlle. Modiste* – 1905E
   *March of the 22nd Regiment* – 1898N
   *McKinley Inauguration* – 1897N
   *Mélodie for Cello & Piano* – 1893N
   *Natouma* – 1911N
   *Naughty Marietta* – 1910E
   *Old Dutch* – 1909E

---

❖

**Vernacular/Commercial Music Scene**
A *Births*    B *Deaths*    C *Biographical*    D *Publications*
E *Representative Pieces*

---

## Cultivated/Art Music Scene

F *Births*    G *Deaths*    H *Debuts*    I *New Positions*    J *Honors and Awards*
K *Biographical*    L *Musical Beginnings*    M *Publications*    N *Compositions*

Hewitt, James (continued)
  *Theme with 30 Variations in D* – 1806N
  *Three Sonatas for Pianoforte, Op. 5* – 1796N
  *Wild Goose Chase, The* – 1800N
  *Wounded Hussar, The* – 1800N
  *Yankee Doodle with Variations* – 1810N
Hewitt, John Hill – 1801F, 1825K, 1838K, 1841I,
  1890G
  *All Quiet Along the Potomac Tonight* – 1863E
  *Fairy Bridal, The* – 1845N
  *Flora's Festival* – 1838N
  *Jephtha* – 1845N
  *King Linkum the First* – 1863N
  *Knight of the Raven Black Plume* –
  1835N
  *Musical Enthusiast, The* – 1872N
  *Revellers, The* – 1848N
  *Shadows on the Wall* – 1877M
  *Vivandiere, The* – 1863N
Hewitt, Sophia Henrietta – 1799F
Heyman, Edward – 1907A
Heyman, Henry C. – 1855F, 1870K, 1877K, 1924G
Heyman, Katherine – 1944G
  *Relation of Ultra-Modern to Archaic Music* –
  1921M
Heywood, Eddie – 1915A, 1989B
Heywoods, The – 1974E
Hiatt, John – 1952A
Hi-Five – 1990C, 1991E
Hibbard, William – 1939F
Hickory Records – 1953C
Hicks, Dan, and His Hot Licks – 1968C
Hicks, Stanley – 1911A
*Heritage of Harmony* – 1988D
Hier, Ethel G. – 1889F, 1971G
  *Choréographe* – 1931N
Hiestermann, Horst – 1982H, 1987H
Hifijazz Records – 1958C
Higginbotham, J. C. – 1973B
Higgins Brothers, Publishers – 1855L
Higgins, Billy – 1936A
Higgins, Dick
  *Piano Album* – 1980N
  *Sonata for Prepared Piano* – 1981N
Higgins, Hiram Murray – 1820F, 1897G
Higginson, Henry Lee – 1834F, 1919G
*High Fidelity* – 1951L
High Inergy – 1976C
Highway 101 – 1986C
Highwaymen, The – 1961E
Hildegard Publishing Co. – 1988L
Hildegarde – 1906A
Hill, Bertha – 1905A, 1958B
Hill, Billy – 1899A, 1940B
Hill, Edward Burlingame – 1872F, 1894K, 1908I,
  1916J, 1960G
  *Clarinet Quintet* – 1945N
  *Clarinet Sonata* -1927N

*Lilacs* – 1927N
*Modern French Music* – 1924M
*Nun of the Perpetual Adoration* – 1907N
*Pan the Star* – 1914N
*Parting of Lancelot & Guinevere* – 1915N
*Piano Concertino* – 1931N
*Piano Quartet* – 1937N
*Prelude to the Trojan Women* – 1920N
*Sextet, Piano & Winds* – 1934N
*Stevensonia Suite I* – 1917N
*Stevensonia Suite II* – 1922N
*String Quartet* – 1935N
*Symphony No. 1* – 1927N
*Symphony No. 2* – 1929N
*Symphony No. 3* – 1936N
*Violin Concerto* – 1934N
Hill, Fred
  *Grass Roots* – 1980D
Hill, Jackson – 1941F
Hill, Mabel Wood – 1870F, 1954G
  *Adventures of Pinocchio* – 1934N
  *Jolly Beggars, The* – 1931N
  *Rose & the Ring, The* – 1941N
Hill, Patty/Mildred
  *Good Morning to All* – 1893E
Hill, Ureli Corelli – 1802F, 1831K, 1875G
  *Kentucky Characteristic Grand March, The* –
  1855N
Hill, Uri Keeler – 1780F, 1805I, 1810K, 1836K,
  1844G
  *Handelian Repository, The* – 1814M
  *Number of Original Airs, Duettos & Trios* –
  1803M
  *Sacred Minstrel, The* – 1806s
  *Solfeggio Americano* – 1820M
  *Vermont Harmony, The* – 1801M
Hill, William J.
  *Empty Saddles* – 1936E
  *Last Round-Up, The* – 1933E
  *Wagon Wheels* – 1934E
Hillard, Claire Fox – 1958F
Hillebrecht, Hildegard – 1968H
Hillegas Music Shop – 1759L
Hiller, Lejaren – 1924F, 1958I, 1994G
  *Computer Cantata* – 1963N
  *Electronic Sonata* – 1976N
  *Experimental Music* – 1959M
  *Iliac Suite* – 1956N
  *Midnight Carnival* – 1976N
  *Nightmare Music* – 1961N
  *Piano Sonata No. 1* – 1946N
  *Piano Sonata No. 2* – 1947N
  *Piano Sonatas 3 & 4* – 1950N
  *Piano Sonata No. 5* – 1961N
  *Piano Sonata No. 6* – 1972N
  *Seven Electronic Studies* – 1963N
  *String Quartet No. 1* – 1949N
  *String Quartet No. 2* – 1951N

❖

Vernacular/Commercial Music Scene
A *Births*    B *Deaths*    C *Biographical*    D *Publications*
E *Representative Pieces*

---

## Cultivated/Art Music Scene

F *Births*  G *Deaths*  H *Debuts*  I *New Positions*  J *Honors and Awards*
K *Biographical*  L *Musical Beginnings*  M *Publications*  N *Compositions*

Hoffmann, Max – 1873A, 1963B
*Parisian Model, A* – 1906E
*Young Turk, The* – 1910E
Hoffmann, Richard – 1847HK, 1947K
*In Memoriam L. M. G.* – 1870N
Hoffmann, Ernst – 1935I
Hofmann, Josef – 1887H, 1894I, 1926IK, 1957IG
*Piano Playing* – 1908M
*Piano Questions Answered* – 1909M
Hofmann, Peter – 1977H, 1980H
Hogan, Ernest – 1909B
*All Coons Look Alike To Me* – 1896E
Hogan, William Ransom, Jazz Archive – 1958C
Hogwood, Christopher – 1984H, 1985K, 1986I
Hohl, Daryl (Hall & Oates) – 1948A
Hohnstock, Edele
*Diamant, Le: Polka Brillante* – 1894N
Hoiby, Lee – 1926F, 1957J, 1978H
*After Eden* – 1966N
*Five Preludes for Piano* – 1952N
*Galileo Galilei* – 1975N
*Italian Lesson, The* – 1980N
*I Was There* – 1995N
*Landscape* – 1967N
*Music for Celebration* – 1975N
*Natalia Petrovna* – 1964N
*Orchestral Suite No. 2* – 1953N
*Piano Concerto No. 1* – 1958N
*Piano Concerto No. 2* – 1980N
*Scarf, The* – 1958N
*Something New for the Zoo* – 1979N
*Summer & Smoke* – 1970N
*Tempest, The* – 1986N
Holcomb, Roscoe – 1913A
Holde, Artur – 1937K, 1962G
Holden, Oliver – 1765F, 1783K, 1878K, 1818K, 1844G
*American Harmony* – 1792M
*Charlestown Collection of Sacred Songs* – 1803M
*Coronation* – 1792N
*Dirge* – 1899N
*Federal Harmony, The* – 1788M
*From Vernon's Mount Behold the Hero Rise* – 1899N
*Massachusetts Compiler of Theoretical Principles* – 1795M
*Modern Collection of Sacred Music* – 1800M
*Plain Harmony* – 1800M
*Union Harmony, The* – 1793M
*Vocal Companion* – 1807M
*Worcester Collection, The* – 1797M
Holden, Oliver, Music Store (SC) – 1790L
Hole – 1990C
Holiday, Billie – 1915A, 1937C, 1938C, 1947C, 1959B
Hollaender, Viktor – 1933K, 1940G
Holland, Brian
*Baby Love* – 1964E

*I Hear a Symphony* – 1965E
*Stop! In the Name of Love* – 1965E
*Where Did Our Love Go?* – 1949E
Holland, Charles – 1909F, 1954H, 1982H, 1987G
Holland, Justin – 1819F, 1848K, 1887G
*Holland's Comprehensive Method for the Guitar* – 1874M
*Holland's Modern Method for the Guitar* – 1876M
Hollander, Lorin – 1944F, 1955H
Hölle, Matthias – 1993H
Holliday, Jennifer – 1960A
Holliday, Melanie –1951F, 1973H, 1983H
Holliger, Heinz – 1962H
Hollingsworth, Stanley – 1924F
Hollister, Carroll – 1901F, 1983G
Holloway, Brenda – 1946A
Holloway, David – 1942F, 1968H, 1973H
Hollweg, Werner – 1968H
Holly, Buddy – 1936A, 1959B
Holly, Buddy, and the Crickets – 1957C
Holly & the Italians – 1978C
Hollywood Argyles, The – 1959E
Hollywood Bowl Concerts – 1922L
Hollywood Bowl Orchestra – 1990L
Hollywood Flame – 1949C
Hollywood String Quartet – 1947L
Holm, Richard – 1952H
Holmes, Ralph – 1966H
Holmes, Rupert – 1979E
*Mystery of Edwin Drood, The* – 1985E
Holmes, William H.
*Hand That Rocks the Cradle, The* – 1895E
Holmquist, John Edward – 1955F, 1979H
Holoman, D. Kern – 1947F
Holst, Edvard – 1899G
*1999* – 1897E
Holst, Gustav – 1923K
Holt, Henry – 1934F, 1961H, 1983I
Holtkamp Organ Co. – 1855L
Holton, Frank – 1858F, 1918K, 1942G
Holy Modal Rounders – 1963C
Holyoke, Samuel – 1762F, 1789K, 1792K, 1800K, 1820G
*Christian Harmonist, The* – 1804M
*Columbian Repository of Sacred Harmony* – 1802M
*Hark from the Tombs* – 1800N
*Harmonia Americana* – 1791M
*Instrumental Assistant, The* – 1800M
*Instrumental Assistant II* – 1807M
*Washington* – 1790N
Holzer, Linda Ruth – 1963F
Holzmair, Wolfgang – 1993H
Holzmann, Abe – 1874A, 1939B
Hombres – 1966C
Homer, Louise – 1871F, 1895K, 1898H, 1899K, 1900H, 1947G
Homer, Sidney – 1864F, 1895K, 1953G
*Fall of the House of Usher* – 1920N

---

✦

## Vernacular/Commercial Music Scene
A *Births*　　B *Deaths*　　C *Biographical*　　D *Publications*
E *Representative Pieces*

---

## Cultivated/Art Music Scene

F *Births*   G *Deaths*   H *Debuts*   I *New Positions*   J *Honors and Awards*
K *Biographical*   L *Musical Beginnings*   M *Publications*   N *Compositions*

Houston, Texas (continued)
  *Ballet Academy – 1959L*
  *Civic Symphony Orchestra – 1968L*
  *Contemporary Trends – 1982L*
  *Cultural Arts Council – 1978L*
  *Friends of Music – 1959L*
  *Gilbert & Sullivan Society – 1952L*
  *Grand Opera Co. – 1955L*
  *Jazz Festival – 1979C*
  *Jones, Jesse H., Hall – 1966L*
  *Lyric Theater Center – 1985L*
  *Pops Orchestra – 1971L*
  *Symphony Chorale – 1947L*
  *Symphony Orchestra – 1913L*
  *Wortham, Gus S., Theater Center – 1987L*
  *Youth Symphony Orchestra – 1946L*
Houston, Cisco – 1918A
Houston, Cissy – 1933A
Houston, David – 1938A, 1966C, 1993B
Houston, Thelma – 1977E
Houston, Whitney – 1963A, 1985E, 1986E, 1987E, 1988E, 1990E, 1991E, 1992E, 1993E
Hovhaness, Alan – 1911F, 1951J
  *Fantasy for Piano – 1952N*
  *Floating World, "Ukiyo" – 1964N*
  *God Created Great Whales, And – 1970N*
  *Prelude & Quadruple Fugue – 1936N*
  *Symphony No. 1 – 1937N*
  *Symphony No. 9 – 1950N*
  *Symphony No. 5 – 1953N*
  *Symphony No. 6 & 7 – 1959N*
  *Symphony No. 2, "Mysterious Mountain" –*
    *1954N*
  *Symphonies 11 & 12 – 1960N*
  *Symphony No. 13 – 1954N*
  *Symphony No. 14 – 1961N*
  *Symphonies 15 & 16 – 1962N*
  *Symphonies 17 & 18 – 1963N*
  *Symphony No. 19 – 1966N*
  *Symphony No. 20 – 1968N*
  *Symphony No. 21 – 1970N*
  *Symphony No. 22 – 1971N*
  *Symphony No. 23 – 1972N*
  *Symphonies 24 & 25 – 1973N*
  *Symphony No. 26 – 1975N*
  *Symphonies 27-31 – 1976N*
  *Symphonies 32-34 – 1977N*
  *Symphonies 35-39 – 1978N*
  *Symphonies 40-43, 45 – 1979N*
  *Symphony No. 44 – 1980N*
  *Symphonies 46, 47 & 49 – 1981N*
  *Symphonies 48, 50-58 – 1982N*
Howard, Ann – 1994H
Howard, Eddie – 1914A, 1963B
Howard, Eddie, Band – 1941C
Howard, Emmons – 1845F, 1931G
Howard, Emmons, Organ Builder – 1883L
Howard, Frank
  *When the Robins Nest Again – 1883E*

Howard, Joe
  *The Sweetest Girl in Paris – 1918E*
Howard, John E. – 1867A
  *Hello, My Baby – 1899E*
  *Mary Blane – 1847N*
Howard, John Tasker – 1890F, 1964G
  *Our American Music – 1931M*
  *Our Contemporary Composers – 1941M*
  *Short History of Music in America, A – 1957M*
  *This Modern Music – 1942M*
  *World's Great Operas, The – 1948M*
Howard, Joseph E. – 1941B
  *I Wonder Who's Kissing Her Now? – 1909E*
  *Stubborn Cinderella, A – 1908E*
  *Time, the Place & the Girl, The – 1907E*
  *Umpire, The – 1905E*
Howard, Judith – 1989H
Howard, Kathleen – 1914H, 1916H
Howard, Paul M.
  *Shrimp Boats – 1951E*
Howard, Rollin
  *You Never Miss the Water Till the Well Runs Dry –*
    *1874E*
Howe, Elias – 1820F, 1895G
  *Complete Ball-Room Hand Book – 1858C*
  *Musician's Companion, First Part – 1844M*
Howe, Elias, Music Publishing – 1860L
Howe, Elias, Music Shop – 1842L
Howe, Julia Ward – 1908J
Howe, Mary – 1882F, 1964G
  *Castellana – 1934N*
  *Piano Quintet – 1923N*
  *Poème for Orchestra – 1924N*
  *Stars – 1934N*
  *Violin Sonata – 1922N*
Howell, Gwynne – 977H, 1985H
Howells, Anne – 1972H, 1975H
Howland, William L.
  *Sarrona – 1903N*
Howley, Haviland & Co. – 1894C
Howlin' Wolf – 1910A, 1976B
Hoyt, Charles H. – 1900B
Hruby Conservatory of Music – 1918L
HSAS – 1984C
Hsu, John – 1949K, 1955I
Huang Harmonicas (Farmingdale, N.Y.) – 1983L
Hubard, W. L., ed.
  *American History & Encyclopedia of Music I –*
    *1908M*
Hubbard & Dowd, Harpsichord Makers – 1949L
Hubbard, Frank – 1920F, 1976G
  *Harpsichord Regulating & Repairing – 1963M*
  *Three Centuries of Harpsichord Making – 1964M*
Hubbard, Freddie – 1938A
Hubbard, James M.
  *My Last Cigar – 1848N*
Hubbard, John – 1759F, 1810G
  *Essay on Music – 1807N*
  *Harmonia Selecta – 1789N*

---

❖

---

## Vernacular/Commercial Music Scene
A *Births*    B *Deaths*    C *Biographical*    D *Publications*
E *Representative Pieces*

Hubbell, Raymond – 1879A
  *Bachelor Belles, The* – 1910E
  *Fantana* – 1905E
  *Girl From Cook's, The* – 1927E
  *Jolly Bachelors, The* – 1910E
  *Kiss Burglar, The* – 1918E
  *Man from Cook's, The* – 1912E
  *Poor Butterfly* – 1916E
  *Winsome Widow, A* – 1911E
Hubbard, William, ed.
  *American History & Encyclopedia of Music* –
  1910M
Huberdeau, Gustave – 1908H
Huberman, Bronislaw – 1896H
Hubert, Albert – 1909H
Huehn, Julius – 1904F, 1933H, 1935H, 1971G
Hues Corporation – 1969C, 1974E
Huffman, Margie – 1973J
Huffstodt, Karen – 1954F
Hughes, Edwin – 1884F, 1917H, 1965G
Hughes, Langston
  *Famous Negro Music Makers* – 1955D
  *First Book of Jazz, The* – 1955D
Hughes, Miss – 1831H
Hughes, Rupert – 1872F, 1956G
  *American Music* – 1914M
  *Contemporary American Composers* – 1900M
  *Love Affairs of the Great Musicians* – 1903M
  *Musical Guide, The* – 1903M
  *Music Lovers' Encyclopedia* – 1912M
Hugo, John Adam – 1945G
  *Temple Dancer, The* – 1919N
Huhn, Bruno – 1891K, 1896H, 1950G
Hulbert, Duane – 1980J
Hult Center for the Performing Arts – 1982L
Human League – 1982E
Hume, Paul – 1915F, 1946I, 1950I
  *Our Music, Our Schools & Our Culture* – 1957M
Humes, Helen – 1913A, 1981B
Humiston, William H.
  *Southern Fantasie* – 1913N
  *Suite in f#* – 1911N
Humperdinck, Engelbert – 1936A
Humphraville, Angus
  *Missouri Lays & Other Western Ditties* – 1821M
Humphreys, Douglas – 1976J
Huneker, James G. – 1857F, 1888I, 1891I, 1900I,
  1919I, 1921G
  *Book of Temperaments, A* – 1904M
  *Development of the Piano, The* – 1915M
  *Melomaniacs* – 1902M
  *Mezzotints in Modern Music* – 1899M
  *Philharmonic Society of New York, The* – 1917M
  *Visionaries* – 1905M
Hunt, Pee Wee – 1907A, 1979B
Hunt, Pee Wee, Sextet – 1946C
Hunter, Alberta – 1895A, 1984B
Hunter, Charles – 1876A, 1906B
  *Cotton Bolls Rag* – 1901E

  *Queen of Love* – 1901E
  *Tennessee Tantalizer, A* – 1900E
  *Tickled to Death* – 1899E
Hunter, Ivory Joe – 1914A, 1974B
Hunter, Janie – 1918A
Hunter, Rita – 1972H
Hunter, Tab – 1931A, 1957E
Huntington (Long Island) PO – 1949L
Huntington Symphony Orch. – 1963L
Huntington, Daniel
  *Classical Church Music* – 1812M
Huntington, Jonathan – 1771F, 1806K, 1812K,
  1838G
  *Albany Collection, The* – 1800M
  *Apollo Harmony, The* – 1806M
  *English Extracts, The* – 1809M
Hupfield, Charles F. – 1799K, 1812K, 1864G
  *Musical Preceptor* – 1808M
Hupfield, Herman – 1894A, 1951B
  *As Time Goes By* – 1943E
  *Let's Put Out the Lights* – 1932E
Hurley, Laurel – 1927F, 1951J, 1952H, 1955H
Hurok, Sol – 1888F, 1906K, 1914K, 1974G
Hurricane – 1983C
Hurst, Jack
  *Nashville's Grand Ole Opry* – 1975D
Hurt, Mississippi John – 1893A, 1966B
Husa, Karel – 1954IK, 1959K, 1993J, 1994J
  *Cello Concerto* – 1988N
  *Concerto for Brass Quintet* – 1965
  *Concerto for Orchestra* – 1986N
  *Concerto for Wind Ensemble* – 1983N
  *Fantasies for Orchestra* – 1956N
  *Frammenti* – 1987N
  *Mosaïques* – 1960N
  *Organ Concerto, "Sunlights"* – 1987N
  *Piano Sonatas 2 – 5* – 1975N
  *Prague 1968* – 1968N
  *String Quartet No. 1* – 1948N
  *String Quartet No. 2* – 1953N
  *String Quartet No. 3* – 1968N
  *String Quartet No. 4* – 1990N
  *Symphonic Suite* – 1984N
  *Trumpet Concerto* – 1988N
  *Trojan Women, The* – 1980N
  *Violin Concerto* – 1993N
Hüsker Dü – 1979C
Husky, Ferlin – 1927A
Huss, George John – 1848K, 1858I, 1904G
  *Capriccietto alla Militaire* – 1869N
  *Impromtu* – 1860N
  *Papillon, Le* – 1860N
  *Six Études Speciales* – 1877N
  *Studies of Seconds* – 1877N
Huss, Henry Holden – 1862F, 1953G
  *Ave Maria, Opus 4* – 1890N
  *Ballade in F Major* – 1885N
  *Cleopatra's Death* – 1898N
  *Elegy* – 1936N

---

### Cultivated/Art Music Scene

F *Births*   G *Deaths*   H *Debuts*   I *New Positions*   J *Honors and Awards*
K *Biographical*   L *Musical Beginnings*   M *Publications*   N *Compositions*

✧

Vernacular/Commercial Music Scene
A *Births*     B *Deaths*     C *Biographical*     D *Publications*
E *Representative Pieces*

## Cultivated/Art Music Scene

F *Births*  G *Deaths*  H *Debuts*  I *New Positions*  J *Honors and Awards*
K *Biographical*  L *Musical Beginnings*  M *Publications*  N *Compositions*

Ives, Burl – 1909A, 1995B
  *Burl Ives Songbook, The* – 1953D
  *Wayfaring Stranger* – 1948D
Ives, Charles E. – 1874F, 1893I, 1898K, 1900I,
  1908K, 1911K, 1918K, 1922K, 1954G
  *Anti-Abolitionist Riots* – 1908N
  *Celestial Country, The* – 1899N
  *Central Park in the Dark* – 1906N
  *Charlie Rutledge* – 1921N
  *Children's Hour, The* – 1901N
  *Chromâtimemelôdtune* – 1919N
  *Circus Band March* – 1894N
  *Country Band March* – 1903N
  *Decoration Day* – 1912N
  *Emerson Overture* – 1907N
  *Fourth of July, The* – 1913N
  *From the Steeples & Mountains* – 1902N
  *Fugue in Four Keys on The Shining Shore* –
    1897N
  *General William Booth* – 1914N
  *Gong on the Hook & Ladder* – 1911N
  *Halloween* – 1906N
  *Harvest Home Chorales* – 1901N
  *Lincoln, the Great Commoner* – 1912N
  *Matthew Arnold Overture* – 1912N
  *Overture & March "1776"* – 1903N
  *Piano Sonata No. 1* – 1909N
  *Piano Sonata No. 2, "Concord"* – 1915N
  *Piano Trio* – 1911N
  *Psalm 14* – 1899N
  *Psalm 25* – 1901N
  *Psalm 40* – 1894N
  *Psalm 42* – 1888N
  *Psalm 54* – 1894N
  *Psalm 67* – 1894N
  *Psalm 100* – 1899N
  *Psalm 135* – 1900N
  *Psalm 150* – 1894N
  *Quarter-tone Chorale* – 1914N
  *Robert Browning Overture* – 1912N
  *Set for Theater Orchestra* – 1906N
  *Set No. 1 for Small Orchestra* – 1911N
  *Set No. 2 for Orchestra* – 1915N
  *Set No. 3 for Orchestra* – 1918N
  *Some Southpaw Pitching* – 1909N
  *String Quartet No. 1* – 1896N
  *String Quartet No. 2* – 1913N
  *Symphony No. 1* – 1898N
  *Symphony No. 2* – 1902N
  *Symphony No. 3* – 1904N
  *Symphony No. 4* – 1916N
  *Thanksgiving* – 1904N
  *Three Marches for Band* – 1892N
  *Three-Page Sonata* – 1905N
  *Three Places in New England* – 1912N
  *Three Quarter-tone Pieces* – 1924N
  *Tone Roads* – 1915N
  *Unanswered Question, The* – 1906N
  *Variations on America* – 1891N

  *Violin Sonata (KW 4)* – 1902N
  *Violin Sonata No. 1* – 1908N
  *Violin Sonata No. 2* – 1910N
  *Violin Sonata No. 3* – 1914N
  *Violin Sonata No. 4* – 1916N
  *Washington's Birthday* – 1909N
Ives, Charles, Center for American Music – 1980L
Ives Oral History Project (Yale) – 1968L
Ivey, Jean Eichelberger – 1923F
  *Birthmark* – 1982N
  *Cello Concerto* – 1985N
  *Festive Symphony* – 1955N
  *Forms in Motion* – 1972N
  *Piano Sonata* – 1957N
  *Sea-change* – 1979N
  *String Quartet* – 1960N
  *Testament of Eve* – 1976N
  *Theme & Variations* – 1952N
  *Three Songs of the Night* – 1971N
  *Violin Concerto* – 1985N
  *Voyager* – 1991N
  *Woman's Love* – 1962N
Ivogün, Maria – 1923H, 1926H
Iwaschkin, Roman
  *Popular Music: A Reference Guide* – 1986D
Izzo d'Amico, Fiamma – 1985H

# J
"J. K."
  *Yellow Rose of Texas, The* – 1858E
Jabara, Paul
  *No More Tears* – 1979E
Jablonski, Edward
  *Encyclopedia of American Music* – 1981M
Jacks, Terry – 1974E
Jackson Five – 1964C, 1970E
Jackson, Mississippi
  *Arts Center* – *1977L*
  *Harmoneers* – *1939C*
  *Music Association* – *1937L*
  *Symphony Orchestra* – *1944L*
Jackson Music Warehouse – 1821L
Jackson, Alan – 1958A
Jackson, Arthur
  *World of Big Bands, The* – 1977D
Jackson, Benjamin "Bullmoose" – 1989B
Jackson, Freddie – 1956A
Jackson, George K. – 1796K, 1797K, 1802I, 1812I,
  1822G
  *Choral Companion, The* – *1817M*
  *Collection of Choice Chants* – *1816M*
  *David's Psalms* – *1804N*
  *Freedom & Our President (Jefferson's March)* –
    *1801N*
  *Ode for General Hamilton's Funeral* – *1804N*
  *Ode for the Fourth of July* – *1808N*
  *Ode to Harmony* – *1805N*
  *Ode to Peace* – *1805N*
  *Overture with Double Fugue & March* – *1801N*

---

❖

---

**Vernacular/Commercial Music Scene**
A *Births*   B *Deaths*   C *Biographical*   D *Publications*
E *Representative Pieces*

*President Jefferson's March & Quick Step –*
   *1803N*
*Thirteen Easy Canons: Sacred to Masonry – 1807N*
Jackson, George Pullen – 1874A, 1953B
   *Another Sheaf of White Spirituals – 1952D*
   *Down East Spirituals & Others – 1943D*
   *Spiritual Folksongs of Early America – 1937D*
   *Story of the Sacred Harp, The – 1944M*
   *White & Negro Spirituals – 1943E*
   *White Spirituals in the Southern Uplands – 1933D*
Jackson, George
   *One Bad Apple – 1971E*
Jackson, Isaiah – 1945F, 1982I, 1987I
Jackson, Janet – 1966A, 1986E, 1989E, 1990E,
   1991E, 1993E
Jackson, Jermaine – 1954A
Jackson, John B.
   *Knoxville Harmony – 1838M*
Jackson, Judge – 1883F, 1958G
   *Colored Sacred Harp, The – 1934M*
Jackson, Laurence – 1991H
Jackson, Mahalia – 1911A, 1972B
Jackson, Michael – 1958A, 1972E, 1979E, 1980E,
   1983E, 1987E, 1988E, 1991E
Jackson, Millie – 1943A
Jackson, Milt – 1923A
Jackson, Milt, Quartet – 1951C
Jackson, Richard – 1936F
   *Democratic Souvenirs:...19th-Century American*
   *Music – 1988D*
   *Popular Songs in Nineteenth-Century America –*
   *1976D*
Jackson, Samuel P. – 1818F, 1830I, 1841I, 1861I,
   1885F
   *Sacred Harmony – 1848M*
Jackson, Stonewall – 1932A
Jackson, Tony – 1876A, 1921B
Jackson, Wanda – 1937A
Jacksonville, Florida
   *Civic Music Association – 1930L*
   College of Music – 1926L
Jazz Festival – 1983C
Jacob, Gordon
   *How to Read a Score – 1944M*
Jacob, J. H.
   *Grease – 1972E*
Jacobi, Frederick – 1891F, 1936I, 1952G
   *California Suite – 1917N*
   *Cello Concerto – 1932N*
   *Eve of St. Agnes, The – 1919N*
   *Fantasy Sonata for Piano – 1945N*
   *Introduction & Toccata, Piano – 1946N*
   *Piano Concerto – 1935N*
   *Pied Piper, The – 1915N*
   *Poet in the Desert, The – 1925N*
   *Prodigal Son, The – 1944N*
   *String Quartet No. 1 – 1924N*
   *String Quartet No. 2 – 1933N*
   *String Quartet No. 3 – 1945N*

   *Suite Fantasque – 1948N*
   *Symphony No. 1 – 1924N*
   *Symphony No. 2 – 1948N*
   *Violin Concerto – 1937N*
Jacobs, Paul – 1930F, 1951H, 1983G
Jacobson, Robert
   *Magnificence: Onstage at the Met – 1985M*
Jacoby, Josephine – 1875F
Jadlowker, Hermann – 1910H
Jaëll, Alfred – 1852H
Jaffe, David A.
   *Silicon Valley Breakdown – 1982N*
Jaffe, Stephen – 1954F
   *Double Sonata – 1989N*
   *Fort Juniper Songs – 1989N*
   *Four Images – 1983N*
   *Four Songs with Ensemble – 1988N*
   *Pedal Point – 1992N*
   *Rhythm of the Running Plough – 1985N*
   *String Quartet No. 1 – 1991N*
   *Triptych – 1993N*
Jaffee, Michael – 1938F
Jagel, Frederick – 1897F, 1924H, 1927H,
   1982G
Jaggerz, The – 1965C
Jag Panzer – 1981C
Jakobowski, Edward
   *What the Dickie-Birds Say – 1886E*
Jamal, Ahmad – 1930A
Jamal's, Ahmad, Three Strings – 1951C
James Gang – 1967C
James, Dorothy – 1901F
   *Paolo & Francesca – 1932N*
   *String Quartet in One Mvt. – 1932N*
James, Elmore – 1918A, 1963B
James, Etta – 1938A
James, Henry Fillmore
   *Songs of Gratitude – 1877M*
James, Harry – 1916A, 1983B
James, Harry, Big Band – 1938C
James, Joni – 1930A
James, Philip – 1898F, 1922I, 1930J, 1933J
   *Bret Harte Overture – 1925N*
   *By the Water of Babylon – 1921N*
   *Gen. Booth Enters..Heaven – 1932N*
   *Missa Imaginum – 1929N*
   *Nun, The – 1922N*
   *Organ Sonata – 1929N*
   *Sea Symphony, A – 1928N*
   *Song of the Night – 1930N*
   *Stabat Mater Speciosa – 1921N*
   *Station WGZBX – 1914N*
   *Symphony No. 1 – 1943N*
   *Symphony No. 2, "Seria" – 1947N*
   *Te Deum in C Major – 1913N*
James, Rick – 1948A
James, Sonny – 1929A
James, Tommy – 1947A
James, Tommy, and the Shondells – 1965C

---

## Cultivated/Art Music Scene

F *Births*   G *Deaths*   H *Debuts*   I *New Positions*   J *Honors and Awards*
K *Biographical*   L *Musical Beginnings*   M *Publications*   N *Compositions*

James, Uriah/Joseph
  *Aeolian Songster, The* – 1832M
Jan and Dean – 1963E
Jander, Owen – 1930F
Jane's Addiction – 1986C
Janis, Byron – 1928F, 1943H, 1967K
Janis, Elsie – 1956B
Janowitz, Gundula – 1967H
Janowski, Marek – 1984H, 1988H
Janssen, Herbert – 1939F, 1946K, 1965G
Janssen, Werner – 1899F, 1934H, 1937I, 1946I,
  1947I, 1990G
  *Louisiana Symphony* – 1932N
  *String Quartet No. 1* – 1934N
  *String Quartet No. 2* – 1935N
Jardine, George – 1837K, 1882G
Jardine, George, & Son – 1839L
Jarreau, Al – 1940A
Jarrell, Tommy – 1901A, 1985B
Jarrett, Keith – 1945A
Järvi, Neeme – 1980K, 1990I
Jarvis, Charles H. – 1837F
Jasen, D. A.
  *Rags & Ragtime: a Musical History* – 1978D
Jason and the Scorchers – 1981C
Jay and the Americans – 1961C
*Jazz and Pop: The Magazine about Music* – 1962C
Jazz Artists Guild – 1960C
Jazz at the Philharmonic – 1944C
Jazz Composer's Orchestral Association – 1966C
Jazz Composer's Guild – 1964C
Jazz in July – 1985C
*Jazz Line* – 1981C
*Jazz Magazine* – 1976C
Jazz Messengers – 1954C
Jazz Orchestra, New – 1963C
*Jazz Review, The* – 1958C
Jazz Workshop Ensemble (Brubeck) – 1946C
Jazz World Society – 1977C
*Jazzmen* – 1939C
Jazzmobile – 1965C
*Jazzologist, The* – 1963C
Jazztet (Art Farmer) – 1959C
Jazzy Jeff and the Fresh Prince – 1986C
Jean, Kenneth – 1984J
Jean, Norma – 1938A
Jeffers, Ronald – 1943F
Jefferson Airplane – 1965C
Jefferson, Blind Lemon – 1897A, 1930B
Jeffreys, Garland – 1944A
Jehin-Prume, Frantz – 1865H
Jeleznov, Irina/Maxim – 1990H
Jellinek, George – 1941K
  *History Through the Opera Glass* – 1994M
Jellyfish – 1990C
*Jelly's Last Jam* – 1992E
Jenkins, Gordon – 1910A, 1984B
  *Manhattan Towers* – 1945E
Jenkins, Graeme – 1993I

Jenkins, J. W., Co. (KC) – 1878L
Jenkins, Leroy – 1932A
Jenkins, Newell – 1915F
Jenkins, Speight –1983I
Jenkins, Timothy – 1951F, 1974H, 1979H, 1989K
Jenks, Stephen – 1772F, 1829K, 1856G
  *Delights of Harmony, The* – 1805M
  *Harmony of Zion, or Union Compiler* – 1818M
  *Hartford Collection of Sacred Harmony* –
  1807M
  *Laus Deo* – 1806M
  *New England Harmonist, The* – 1799M
Jennings, Waylon – 1937A
Jenson, Dylana – 1961F, 1973H, 1978JK
Jepson, Harry B. – 1878F, 1895I, 1952G
Jepson, Helen – 1905F, 1928H, 1935H
Jeritza, Maria – 1921H, 1943K, 1982G
Jerome, M. K., Publishers – 1931C
Jerome, William – 1865A, 1932B
Jerusalem, Siegfried – 1980H
Jessup, G. H.
  *Mavourneen* – 1891E
Jessye, Eva – 1895F
Jesus Jones – 1988C
Jesus Lizard – 1989C
Jet Set (The Byrds) – 1964C
Jeter-Phillars Orchestra – 1933C
Jethro Tull – 1969C
Jets, The – 1984C
Jett, Joan – 1960A, 1982E
Jewell, Kenneth, Chorale – 1962L
Jewell, Fred – 1875F, 1936G
Jewell, Fred, Music Publishing Co. – 1920L
Jewels (Impala) – 1961C
Jewish Liturgical Music Society – 1962L
Jewish Music Forum – 1939L
Jewish Music Research Center – 1964L
Jirák, K. B. – 1947K
Jive Bombers – 1948C
Jive Five, The – 1959C
Jo, Sumi – 1988H
Jochum, Veronica – 1981H
Jocelyn/Doolittle
  *Chorister's Companion, The* – 1788M
Jodeci – 1988C
Joel, Billy – 1949A, 1980E, 1983E, 1989E
Joffrey Ballet Co. – 1956L
Johannesen, Grant – 1921F, 1944H, 1949J, 1963K,
  1973I, 1977I
Jóhannson, Kristián – 1993H
Johanos, Donald – 1928F, 1962I, 1979I
Johansen, David (Buster Poindexter) – 1950A
Johansen, Gunnar – 1929HK, 1991G
Johansen, Mlle. – 1856H
John, Elton – 1970C, 1973E, 1974E, 1975E, 1976E,
  1992E
John, Little Willie – 1937A, 1968B
John, Robert – 1979E
Johnny and the Jammers – 1957C

---

---

❄

---

### Cultivated/Art Music Scene

F *Births*     G *Deaths*     H *Debuts*     I *New Positions*     J *Honors and Awards*
K *Biographical*     L *Musical Beginnings*     M *Publications*     N *Compositions*

Jones, Charles (continued)
   *String Quartet No. 3* – 1951N
   *String Quartet No. 4* – 1954N
   *String Quartet No. 5* – 1961N
   *String Quartet No. 6* – 1970N
   *String Quartet No. 7* – 1978N
   *String Quartet No. 8* – 1984N
   *Symphony No. 1* – 1939N
   *Symphony No. 2* – 1957N
   *Symphony No. 3* – 1962N
   *Symphony No. 4* – 1965N
   *Symphony No. 5* – 1969N
Jones, Darius
   *Plymouth Collection of Hymns & Tunes* – 1851M
Jones, David Lynn – 1950A
Jones, Della – 1986H
Jones, Edwin Arthur – 1853F, 1911G
   *Dedication March* – 1881N
   *Easter Concert, Opus 28* – 1890N
   *String Quartet No. 1* – 1880N
   *String Quartet No. 2* – 1887N
   *Suite Ancienne, Opus 17* – 1886N
Jones, Elvin – 1927A
Jones, F. O.
   *Handbook of American Music & Musicians...* –
   1886D
Jones, George – 1931A, 1980C, 1991C, 1992C
Jones, Grace – 1952A
Jones, Grandpa – 1913A, 1978C
Jones, Gwyneth – 1966H, 1972H
Jones, Hank – 1918A
Jones, Isham – 1894A, 1956B
   *I'll See You In My Dreams* – 1924E
   *Indiana Moon* – 1923E
   *It Had To Be You* – 1924E
Jones, Isola – 1949F, 1977H
Jones, Jack – 1938A
Jones, Jo – 1911A, 1985B
Jones, Lazarus J. – 1897G
   *Southern Minstrel, The* – 1849M
Jones, LeRoi
   *Black Music* – 1967D
   *Blues People: Negro Music in White America* –
   1963D
Jones, Mason – 1919F
Jones, Philly Joe – 1923A, 1985B
Jones, Quincy – 1933A
   *Color Purple, The* – 1985E
Jones, Quincy, Big Band – 1959C
Jones, Ricky Lee – 1954A
Jones, Shirley – 1934A
Jones, Sissieretta – 1869F, 1888H, 1933G
   *Gaiety Girl, A* – 1894E
Jones, Spike – 1911A, 1965B
Jones, Stan
   *Ghost Riders in the Sky* – 1949E
Jones, Thaddeus – 1923A, 1986B
Jones, Tommy – 1966E, 1969E
Joó, Arpád – 1968K, 1973I

Joplin, Janis – 1943A, 1970B, 1971E
Joplin, Scott – 1868A, 1896H, 1907K
   *Breeze from Alabama Rag, A* – 1902E
   *Cascades Rag, The* – 1904E
   *Chrysanthemum Rag* – 1904E
   *Country Club Rag* – 1909E
   *Easy Winner Rag* – 1901E
   *Elite Syncopations Rag* – 1902E
   *Entertainer, The, Rag* – 1902E
   *Eugenia Rag* – 1905E
   *Euphonic Sounds Rag* – 1909E
   *Favorite Rag, The* – 1904E
   *Fig Leaf Rag* – 1908E
   *Gladiolus Rag* – 1907E
   *Guest of Honor, The* – 1903E
   *Heliotrope Bouquet Rag* – 1907E
   *Joplin's New Rag* – 1912E
   *Leola Rag* – 1905E
   *Lily Queen Rag* – 1907E
   *Maple Leaf Rag* – 1899E
   *Original Rag* – 1899E
   *Palm Leaf Rag* – 1903E
   *Paragon Rag* – 1909E
   *Peacherine Rag* – 1901E
   *Pine Apple Rag* – 1908E
   *Rose Leaf Rag* – 1907E
   *School of Ragtime—Six Exercises for Piano* –
   1908D
   *Scott Rag* – 1912E
   *Slow Drag Rag* – 1901E
   *Something Doing Rag* – 1903E
   *Stoptime Rag* – 1910E
   *Sugar Cane Rag* – 1908E
   *Sunflower Rag* – 1901E
   *Sycamore Rag, The* – 1904E
   *Treemonisha* – 1911N
   *Wall Street Rag* – 1909E
   *Weeping Willow Rag* – 1903E
Joplin, Scott, Ragtime Festival – 1974C
Jordá, Enrique – 1954I
Jordan, Arthur, Conservatory of Music – 1928L
Jordan, Irene – 1919F, 1946H
Jordan, Joe – 1882A, 1971B
   *Brown Buddies* – 1930N
   *Deep Harlem* – 1929N
   *Double Fudge Rag* – 1902E
   *J. J. J. Rag* – 1905E
   *Lovey Joe* – 1910E
Jordan, Jules – 1850F, 1880I, 1927G
Jordan, Louis – 1908A, 1975B
Jordan, Philip D.
   *Singin' Yankees* – 1946D
Jordan, Sheila – 1928A
Jordan, Stanley – 1959A
Jordanaires, The – 1948C
Jörn, Carl – 1909H, 1947G
Joselson, Tedd – 1954F, 1974H
Josephson, Kim – 1992H
Joshua – 1981C

---

**Vernacular/Commercial Music Scene**
A  *Births*   B  *Deaths*   C  *Biographical*   D  *Publications*
E  *Representative Pieces*

---

## Cultivated/Art Music Scene

F *Births*    G *Deaths*    H *Debuts*    I *New Positions*    J *Honors and Awards*
K *Biographical*    L *Musical Beginnings*    M *Publications*    N *Compositions*

❀

Vernacular/Commercial Music Scene
A  *Births*    B  *Deaths*    C  *Biographical*    D  *Publications*
E  *Representative Pieces*

---

## Cultivated/Art Music Scene

F *Births*   G *Deaths*   H *Debuts*   I *New Positions*   J *Honors and Awards*
K *Biographical*   L *Musical Beginnings*   M *Publications*   N *Compositions*

Kern, Jerome (continued)
  *Centennial Summer* – 1946E
  *Girl from Utah, The* – 1914E
  *Good Morning, Dearie* – 1921E
  *Have a Heart* – 1917E
  *Ladies & Gentlemen, Jerome Kern* – 1986E
  *Last Time I Saw Paris, The* – 1940E
  *Leave It to Jane* – 1917E
  *Left-All-Alone-Again Blues* – 1920E
  *Mark Twain Suite* – 1942E
  *Miss Information* – 1915E
  *Music in the Air* – 1932E
  *Nobody Home* – 1915E
  *Oh, Boy* – 1917E
  *Oh, I Say!* – 1913E
  *Oh Lady! Lady!* – 1918E
  *Red Petticoat, The* – 1912E
  *Roberta* – 1933E
  *Rock-a-Bye Baby* – 1918E
  *Sally* – 1920E
  *Show Boat* – 1927E
  *Stepping Stones* – 1923E
  *Sunny* – 1925E
  *Sweet Adeline* – 1929E
  *Swing Time* – 1936E
  *Very Good, Eddie* – 1915E
  *Very Warm for May* – 1939E
  *Way You Look Tonight, The* – 1936E
Kern, Patricia – 1969H
Kern, Robert – 1933F
Kernfeld, B.
  *New Grove Dictionary of Jazz, The* – 1988D
Kernis, Aaron Jay
  *Before Sleep & Dreams* – 1990N
  *Brilliant Sky, Infinite Sky* – 1990N
  *Invisible Mosaic II* – 1988N
  *Love Scenes* – 1987N
  *Morningsongs* – 1983N
  *Poisoned Nocturnes* – 1987N
  *String Quartet, "Musical Celestis"* – 1990N
  *Symphony in Waves* – 1989N
Kerr, Anita – 1927A
Kerr, Harrison – 1897F, 1949I, 1978G
  *Dance Suite* – 1940N
  *Four Piano Preludes* – 1943N
  *Piano Sonata No. 1* – 1929N
  *Piano Sonata No. 2* – 1943N
  *String Quartet No. 1* – 1935N
  *String Quartet No. 2* – 1937N
  *Symphony No. 1* – 1929N
  *Symphony No. 2* – 1945N
  *Symphony No. 3* – 1954N
  *Tower of Kel, The* – 1960N
  *Violin Concerto* – 1951N
Kersands, Billy – 1842A, 1915B
Kershaw, Doug – 1936A
Kershaw, Sammy – 1958A
Kessel, Barney – 1923A
  *Guitar, The: a Tutor* – 1967D

Kertész, István – 1970K
Ketchum, Hal – 1953A
*Keynote, The* – 1883L
*Keyboard Classics* – 1981L
Keyes, John – 1964F, 1995H
Keynote Records – 1940C
Khachaturian, Aram – 1968H
Khan, Chaka – 1953A
Kharitonov, Dimitri – 1990H
Kid Creole and the Coconuts – 1974C
Kid Ory – 1973B
Kid Ory Band – 1911C
Kieffer, Aldine S. – 1840F, 1904G
Kiepura, Jan – 1930H, 1931H, 1966G
Kiesler, Kenneth – 1953F
Kihn, Greg, Band – 1975C
Kik Tracee – 1990C
Kilduff, Barbara Jane – 1959F
Kilenyi, Edward, Jr. – 1910F, 1940H
Kilenyi, Edward, Sr. – 1968G
Kilgen, George – 1902G
Kilgen, George, Organ Co. – 1851L
Killebrew, Gwendolyn – 1939F, 1967H
Kill for Thrills – 1990C
Kim, Andy – 1946A, 1974E
Kim, Earl – 1920F, 1952I, 1965J, 1967I, 1971J
  *12 Caprices* – 1980N
  *Violin Concerto* – 1979N
Kim, Lisa – 1995J
Kim, Young-Mi – 1980H
Kim, Young-Uck – 1947F, 1963H
Kimball, Jacob, Jr. – 1761F, 1780K, 1826G
  *Essex Harmony, The* – 1800M
  *Rural Harmony, The* – 1793M
  *Village Harmony, The* – 1798M
Kimball, W. W., Co., Publishers – 1857L
Kimball Music Store (Chicago) – 1858L
Kincaid, Bradley – 1895A, 1989B
Kincaid, William – 1895F, 1967G
Kincses, Veronica – 1981H
Kinder, Ralph – 1876A
Kindler, Hans – 1914K, 1927H, 1931I, 1949G
King Diamond – 1985C
King Musical Instrument Co. – 1893L
King, Albert – 1923A, 1992B
King, B. B. – 1925A, 1995C
King, Ben E. – 1938A
King, Carole – 1940A, 1971E
King, Elisha J. – 1820F, 1844G
King, Evelyn "Champagne" – 1960A
King, Freddie – 1934A, 1976B
King, James – 1925F, 1961H, 1966H
King, Karl – 1891F, 1920I, 1953J, 1971G
  *Barnum & Bailey's Favorite* – 1913N
  *Emblem of Freedom March* – 1910N
  *March, Invictus* – 1921N
  *Robinson's Grand Entry* – 1911N
King, Pearl
  *I Hear You Knockin'* – 1955E

---

**Vernacular/Commercial Music Scene**
A *Births*    B *Deaths*    C *Biographical*    D *Publications*
E *Representative Pieces*

King, Pee Wee – 1914A
King, Robert A. – 1862A, 1932B
　Anona – 1903E
　Beautiful Ohio – 1918E
　I Ain't Nobody's Darling – 1921E
　While Strolling Through the Park One Day –
　　1884E
King, Wayne – 1901A, 1985B
　Waltz You Saved For Me, The – 1930E
King Records – 1944C
Kings of Dixieland (Chicago) – 1949C
Kingsmen, The – 1958C
Kingston Trio – 1957C, 1958E
Kingston, Morgan – 1917H
King's X – 1980C
Kinkeldey, Otto – 1878F, 1914I, 1923I, 1927I,
　1930I, 1966G
Kinkle, Roger
　Complete Encyclopedia of Popular Music & Jazz
　　– 1974D
Kinscella, Hazel
　History Sings – 1940M
　Music in the Small School – 1939M
Kipnis, Alexander – 1923H, 1931K, 1940H, 1978G
Kipnis, Igor – 1930F, 1959H
Kirana Center for Indian Classical Music – 1971L
Kirby, John – 1908A, 1952B
Kirby, John, Sextet – 1937C
Kirchner, Leon – 1919F, 1951J, 1954I, 1961I, 1962J,
　1977J
　Cello Concerto – 1992N
　Concerto, Violin, Cello, Winds & Percussion –
　　1960N
　Five Pieces for Piano – 1984N
　Interlude for Piano – 1989N
　Lily – 1976N
　Little Suite – 1949N
　Music for Cello & Orchestra – 1994N
　Music for Flute & Orchestra – 1978N
　Music for Orchestra – 1969N
　Piano Concerto No. 1 – 1953N
　Piano Sonata – 1948N
　String Quartet No. 1 – 1949N
　String Quartet No. 2 – 1958N
　String Quartet No. 3 – 1966N
　Sinfonia – 1951N
　Twilight Stood, The – 1983N
　Variations on "L'homme armé" – 1947N
Kirchoff, Walter – 1927H
Kirchschlager, Angelika – 1995H
Kirk, Andy – 1898A, 1992B
Kirk, Roland – 1936A, 1977B
Kirkby-Lunn, Louise – 1902H
Kirkby, Emma – 1978H
Kirkpatrick, John – 1905F, 1931H, 1949I, 1968I,
　1991G
Kirkpatrick, Ralph – 1911F, 1930H, 1940I, 1984G
　Interpreting Bach's Well-tempered Clavier –
　　1984M

Kirkpatrick, William J. – 1838F, 1921G
　He Hideth My Soul – 1890N
　Jesus Saves – 1882N
　Lord, I'm Coming Home – 1892N
　Redeemed, How I Love to Proclaim It – 1882N
　'Tis So Sweet to Trust in Jesus – 1882N
Kirshbaum, Ralph – 1946F, 1959H, 1969J, 1970J
Kirsten, Dorothy – 1917F, 1940H, 1945H, 1992G
Kislan, Richard
　Musical: A Look at the American Musical Theater,
　　The – 1980D
Kiss – 1972C
Kiss, Janos – 1956K, 1973K
　Quo Vadis – 1982N
Kissin, Evgeny – 1990H
Kitchen Minstrels – 1844L
Kitt, Eartha – 1928A
Kittredge, W.
　Tenting on the Old Camp Grounds – 1863F
　Union Song Book, The – 1862M
Kitziger, Frederick E. – 1865K, 1881I, 1903G
Kivy, Peter
　Music Alone:...Reflections on the...Musical
　　Experience – 1990M
　Osmin's Rage:...Reflections on Opera, Drama &
　　Text – 1988M
　Sound & Semblance – 1984M
　Sound Sentiment: An Essay on the Musical
　　Emotions – 1989M
Kix – 1980C
Kjos, Neil A., Music Co. – 1936L
Klafsky, Katharina – 1895H
Klaus, Kenneth
　Romantic Period in Music, The – 1970M
Klauser, Karl
　Half Hours with the Best Composers – 1894M
Kleiber, Carlos – 1988H
Klein, Andreas – 1976H
Klein, Bruno Oscar – 1878K, 1911G
Klein, Kenneth – 1939F, 1981I, 1982I, 1983I
Klein, Peter – 1949H
Kleinknecht, Daniel – 1960F
Kleinsinger, George
　Shinbone Alley – 1957E
　Symphony No. 1 – 1946N
　Western Rhapsody, A – 1942N
Klemm, Johann Gottlob – 1733K, 1757K, 1819K
Klemm & Brothers, Publishers – 1819L
Klemperer, Otto – 1927H, 1933IK
Kletzki, Paul – 1958I
Klibonoff, Jon – 1984J
Kline, Jack T. – 1974I
Klohr, John N.
　Billboard March – 1901N
Kmen, Henry A.
　Music in New Orleans: The Formative Years,
　　1791-1841 – 1966D
Knabe & Gaehle, Piano Makers – 1835L
Knabe Brothers Co. – 1911L

---

## Cultivated/Art Music Scene

F *Births*　　G *Deaths*　　H *Debuts*　　I *New Positions*　　J *Honors and Awards*
K *Biographical*　　L *Musical Beginnings*　　M *Publications*　　N *Compositions*

Knabe, William – 1883K
Knack, The – 1978C, 1979E
Knapp, Phebe Palmer – 1909G
  *Bible School Songs* – 1873M
  *Notes of Joy* – 1869M
Knauff, George P.
  *Wait for the Wagon* – 1851E
Kneisel Quartet – 1905K
Kneisel String Quartet – 1886L
Kneisel, Franz – 1885K, 1911J, 1915J, 1926G
Knickerbockers – 1964C
Knie, Roberta – 1938F, 1963H, 1975H
Knight, Edward
  *Big Shoulders* – 1991N
Knight, Gladys – 1944A, 1973E
Knight, Gladys/Pips – 1952C
Knight, Joseph P.
  *Rocked in the Cradle of the Deep* – 1839N
Knopf, Alfred – 1984G
Knote, Heinrich – 1904H
Knox, Buddy – 1933A, 1957E
Knoxville, Tennessee
  *Bijou Theater* – *1888L*
  *Civic Auditorium* – *1961L*
  *Opera Co.* – *1978L*
  *Philharmonic Society* – *1867L*
  *Staub's Opera House* – *1872L*
  *Symphony Orchestra* – *1935L*
  *Tuesday Morning Musical Club* – *1898L*
Kobbé, Gustav – 1857F, 1918G
  *Famous American Songs* – 1906M
  *How to Appreciate Music* – 1906M
  *Kobbé's Complete Opera Book* (posthumous) –
    1919M
  *Opera Singers* – 1901M
Kobler, Linda – 1952F, 1984H
Kochański, Paul – 1921HK, 1924H, 1934G
Koch, Caspar – 1872F, 1904I, 1914I
  *Organ Student's Gradus ad Parnassum* – 1945M
Kocian, Jaroslav – 1902H
Kocsis, Zoltán – 1971H
Koechlin, Charles – 1918K
Koehler, Ted – 1894A, 1973B
Koemmenich, Louis – 1917I
Koenen, Tilly – 1909H
Kogan, Leonard – 1958H
Kogan, Pavel – 1975H
Köhler, Axel – 1990H
Kohn, Karl – 1939K, 1945K
  *Impromptus for Wind Octet* – 1968N
  *Innocent Psaltery* – 1973N
  *Interlude I & II* – 1969N
  *Partita for Piano* – 1963N
  *Prophet Bird* – 1973N
  *Recreations, Piano, 4 Hands* -1968N
  *Sinfonia Concertante* – 1951N
Kohs, Ellis – 1916F, 1946J, 1950I
  *Cello Concerto* – 1947N
  *Concerto for Orchestra* – 1941N

*Lord of the Ascendant* – 1955N
*Musical Composition: Projects in Ways & Means*
  – 1980M
*Musical Form: Studies in Analysis & Synthesis* –
  1976M
*Music Theory* – 1961M
*String Quartet No. 1* – 1940N
*String Quartet No. 2* – 1948N
*String Quartet No. 3* – 1984N
*Symphony No. 1* – 1950N
*Symphony No. 2* – 1957N
*Violin Concerto* – 1981N
Kojian, Varujan – 1957K, 1967K, 1980I
Kolar, Victor – 1904K
Kolb, Barbara – 1939F, 1969J, 1973J, 1987J
  *All In Good Time* – 1994N
  *Appello* – 1976N
  *Enchanted Loom, The* – 1989N
  *Extremes* – 1989N
  *Grisaille* – 1979N
  *Trobar Clus* – 1970N
  *Voyants* – 1989N
Kolisch, Rudolf – 1935K, 1944I, 1978G
Kollo, René – 1976H
Kolodin, Irving – 1908F, 1932I, 1947I, 1988G
  *Composer as Listener: a Guide to Music, The* –
    1958M
  *Continuity of Music, The* – 1969M
  *Critical Composer, The* – 1940M
  *In Quest of Music* – 1980M
  *Kingdom of Swing, The* – 1939D
  *Metropolitan Opera, 1883-1936, The* – 1936M
  *Musical Life, The* – 1958M
  *Opera Omnibus: 4 Centuries of Critical Give &*
    *Take* – 1976M
  *Orchestral Music* – 1955M
Kondrashin, Kyrill – 1958K
Konetzni, Anny – 1934H
Konetzni, Hilde – 1938H, 1980G
König, Klaus – 1988H
Konitz, Lee – 1927A
Kontski, Antoine de – 1883H
Konya, Sándor – 1961H
Kool and the Gang – 1964C, 1981E
Koptchak, Sergei – 1983H
Korbay, Francis – 1871H
Kord, Kazimierz – 1980K
Korean Classical Music & Dance Co. (LA) – 1973L
Korevaar, David – 1988J
Korn, Artur – 1984H
Korn, Clara Anna – 1866F, 1940G
Korn, Peter Jona – 1941K, 1944K
  *Horn Sonata* – 1952N
  *Saxophone Concerto* – 1956N
  *String Quartet No. 1* – 1950N
  *String Quartet No. 2* – 1963N
  *Symphony No. 1* – 1946N
  *Symphony No. 2* – 1951N
  *Symphony No. 3* – 1956N

---

❂

## Vernacular/Commercial Music Scene
A *Births*    B *Deaths*    C *Biographical*    D *Publications*
E *Representative Pieces*

Trumpet Concerto – 1979N
Variations, from Beggar's Opera – 1955N
Korngold, Erich W. – 1934K, 1943K, 1957G
  Adventures of Robin Hood – 1938E
  Cello Concerto – 1946N
  Kathrin, Die – 1939N
  String Quartet No. 2 – 1935N
  String Quartet No. 3 – 1945N
  Symphony in F-sharp – 1952N
  Tomorrow – 1942N
  Violin Concerto – 1945N
Korte, Karl – 1928F, 1969J, 1971I
  Hill Country Birds – 1982N
  Piano Concerto – 1977N
  Piano Trio – 1979N
  Symphony No. 2 – 1961N
  Symphony No. 3 – 1968N
Kortschak String Quartet – 1913L
Koshetz, Nina – 1920K, 1921H, 1965G
Koshgarian, Richard
  American Orchestral Music – 1992M
Kostelanetz, André – 1922K, 1928K, 1930I, 1938K
Kostelanetz, André, Presents – 1932V
Kostelanetz, Richard – 1940G, 1965J
  On Innovative Musicians – 1989M
Kottke, Leo – 1945A
Kotzschmar, Hermann – 1848K, 1849I, 1851I,
  1869I, 1909G
Kountz, Richard – 1896F, 1950G
Koussevitzky Music Foundation (N.Y.) – 1942L
Koussevitzky Foundation (Library of Congress) –
  1949L
Koussevitzky, Olga – 1963J
Koussevitzky, Serge – 1924IK, 1941K, 1947JK,
  1951G
Koutzen, Boris – 1923K, 1966G
  String Quartet No. 2 – 1936N
  String Quartet No. 3 – 1944N
  Valley Forge – 1931N
  Violin Sonata – 1928N
Kozar, John – 1946F, 1978H
Kozlowska, Joanna – 1990H
Kraft, Edwin Arthur – 1883F, 1901I, 1904I, 1907I,
  1962G
Kraft, Jean – 1960H, 1970H
Kraft, Leo – 1922F, 1947I
  Concerto, Flute, Clarinet, Trumpet – 1950N
  Concerto No. 2 for 13 Instruments – 1966N
  Concerto No. 3, Cello, Winds & Percussion –
    1969N
  Concerto No. 4, Piano & 14 Instruments – 1979N
  Concerto No. 5, Oboe & Strings – 1986N
  Concerto No. 6, Clarinet & Orchestra – 1986N
  Gradus:...Harmony, Counterpoint and Analysis –
    1976M
  New Approach to Ear Training, A – 1967M
  New Approach to Keyboard Harmony, A – 1978M
  Pacific Bridges – 1989N
  Piano Sonata – 1956N

Piano Variations – 1951N
Statements & Commentaries – 1965N
String Quartet No. 1 – 1950N
String Quartet No. 2 – 1959N
String Quartet No. 3 – 1966N
Sublime & the Beautiful, The – 1979N
Symphony in One Movement – 1985N
Ten Short Pieces for Piano – 1976N
Variations for Orchestra – 1958N
Washington Square – 1990N
Kraft, William – 1871F
Kraft, William – 1923F, 1981I, 1984J, 1991J
  American Carnival Overture – 1962N
  Contextures II: The Final Beast – 1985N
  Gallery 83 – 1983N
  Interplay for Cello & Orchestra – 1982N
  Melange – 1985N
  Of Ceremonies, Pageants & Celebrations –
    1986N
  Piano Concerto – 1973N
  Quartet for Percussion – 1988N
  Quartet for the Love of Time – 1987N
  Settler's Suite – 1981N
  Silent Boughs – 1963N
  Three Pieces for Orchestra – 1963N
  Timpani Concerto – 1984N
  Tuba Concerto – 1978N
  Veils & Variations – 1986N
  Vintage Renaissance – 1989N
  Vintage 1990-91 – 1990N
  Weavings – 1984N
Krainik, Ardis – 1981I, 1991I
Kramer, A. Walter – 1910I, 1929I, 1969G
  Symphonic Rhapsody – 1915N
  Two Symphonic Sketches – 1914N
Kramer, Alex C.
  Far Away Places – 1948E
Kramer, Jonathan D. – 1942F, 1978I, 1988I
  Listen to the Music – 1988M
  Notta Sonata – 1993N
  Time of Music, The – 1988M
Kramer, Toni – 1988H
Kramer, Walter – 1890F
Kramer-Whitney Co. – 1947C
Krane, Julia E.
  Music Teacher's Manual – 1887M
Kranich & Bach Piano Co. – 1864L
Krasker, Tommy
  Catalog of the American Musical – 1988D
Krasnapolsky, Yuri – 1934F, 1969I, 1974I
Krasner, Louis – 1903F, 1976I, 1995G
Krásová, Marta – 1937H
Kraus, Alfredo – 1962H, 1966H
Krause, Tom – 1967H
Kraus, Ernst – 1903H
Kraus, Lili – 1949H, 1968I, 1986G
Krauss, Allison – 1971A
Kravis Center for the Performing Arts – 1992L
Kravitz, Lenny – 1964A

---

❈

## Cultivated/Art Music Scene

F *Births*    G *Deaths*    H *Debuts*    I *New Positions*    J *Honors and Awards*
K *Biographical*    L *Musical Beginnings*    M *Publications*    N *Compositions*

---

Vernacular/Commercial Music Scene

A *Births*    B *Deaths*    C *Biographical*    D *Publications*

E *Representative Pieces*

---

## Cultivated/Art Music Scene

F *Births*    G *Deaths*    H *Debuts*    I *New Positions*    J *Honors and Awards*
K *Biographical*    L *Musical Beginnings*    M *Publications*    N *Compositions*

---

Vernacular/Commercial Music Scene
A *Births*    B *Deaths*    C *Biographical*    D *Publications*
E *Representative Pieces*

---

### Cultivated/Art Music Scene

F *Births*    G *Deaths*    H *Debuts*    I *New Positions*    J *Honors and Awards*
K *Biographical*    L *Musical Beginnings*    M *Publications*    N *Compositions*

---

**Vernacular/Commercial Music Scene**
A *Births*    B *Deaths*    C *Biographical*    D *Publications*
E *Representative Pieces*

LeBaron, Anne – 1953A
*E & O Line, The* – 1989N
*Metamorphosis* – 1977N
*Strange Attractors* – 1987N
Leblanc, G., Corporation – 1946L
Ledbetter, Huddie
*Goodnight, Irene* – 1936jE
Lederer, Charles
*Timbuktu (Kismet)* – 1978E
Lee & Walker, Publishers – 1848L
Lee, Alfred
*Man on the Flying Trapeze* – 1868E
Lee, Aung-Sook – 1973H
Lee, Brenda – 1944A, 1960E
Lee, Dai-Keong – 1915F
Lee, Dickey – 1941A
Lee, Edward
*Jazz: An Introduction* – 1972D
Lee, Noel – 1959J
Lee, Peggy – 1920A, 1970C
*Mañana* – 1948E
Leech, Richard – 1956F, 1988J, 1989H
Leedy, Douglas – 1938F
Leedy & Cooley Co. – 1900L
Lees, Benjamin – 1924F
*Concerto for Brass Choir* – 1983N
*Concerto for Orchestra* – 1959N
*Concerto, Piano & Chamber Group* – 1961N
*Concerto for String Quartet* – 1964N
*Concerto for Woodwind Quintet* – 1976N
*Double Concerto* – 1982N
*Fantasy Variations* – 1983N
*Kaleidoscope* – 1959N
*Mobiles for Orchestra* – 1979N
*Oboe Concerto* – 1963N
*Piano Concerto No. 1* – 1955N
*Piano Sonata No. 1* – 1949N
*Piano Sonata No. 2* – 1950N
*Piano Sonata No. 3* – 1956N
*Piano Sonata No. 4* – 1963N
*Six Ornamental Etudes* – 1957N
*Sonata for 2 Pianos* – 1951N
*String Quartet No. 1* – 1952N
*String Quartet No. 2* – 1955N
*String Quartet No. 3* – 1981N
*Symphony No. 1* – 1953N
*Symphony No. 2* – 1958N
*Symphony No. 3* – 1968N
*Symphony No. 4* – 1985N
*Symphony No. 5* – 1986N
*10 Pieces for Piano* – 1954N
*Three Piano Preludes* – 1962N
*Variations, Piano & Orchestra* – 1976N
*Violin Concerto* – 1958N
Lefèbvre, Pierre – 1994H
Leffler-Burckard, Martha – 1892H, 1908H
Lefkowitz, Mischa – 1984H
Left Banke, The – 1965C
Legendary Blues Band – 1980C

Legends of Jazz – 1973C
Legg Brothers Music Store – 1890L
Leginska, Ethel – 1907K, 1913H, 1970G
Legs Diamond – 1977C
Lehigh Valley Chamber Orchestra – 1979L
Lehman String Quartet – 1892L
Lehman, Mark Louis
*Pilgrim Songs* – 1989N
Lehmann, Lilli – 1885H
Lehmann, Liza – 1910H
Lehmann, Lotte – 1930H, 1934H, 1945K
Lehrer, Tom – 1928A
Leiber, Jerry – 1933A, 1994E
Leichtentritt, Hugo – 1890K, 1891K, 1894K,
    1933IK, 1951G
*Geschichte der Motette* – 1908M
*Music, History & Ideas* – 1938M
*Serge Koussevitzky...& the New American Music* –
    1946M
Leider, Frida – 1928H, 1933H
Leiferkus, Sergei – 1987H, 1992H
Leigh, Carolyn – 1926A, 1983B
Leigh, Mitch – 1928A
*Man of La Mancha* – 1965E
Leimer, Kurt – 1956II
Leinsdorf, Erich – 1930H, 1938I, 1942K, 1943I,
    1947I, 1956I, 1962I, 1963J
*Composer's Advocate, The* – 1982M
Leisner, David – 1953F, 1979H
Lemare, Edwin – 1900H, 1917I, 1924I, 1934G
Lemonheads, The – 1986C
Lemon Pipers, The – 1967E
Lennon, John – 1974F, 1980BCE
Lennon, John Anthony – 1950F, 1980J
*Ghostfires* – 1983N
*Zingari* – 1990N
Lenox String Quartet I – 1922L
Lenox String Quartet II – 1958L
Lenski, Kathleen – 1969J
Lenya, Lotte – 1935C
Leon, Harry
*Little Drummer Boy, The* – 1959E
León, Tania – 1967K
*Scourge of Hyacinths* -1994N
Leonard, Charles
*Foundations & Principles of Music Education* –
    1959M
Leonard, Eddie – 1875A, 1941B
*Ida, Sweet As Apple Cider* – 1903E
*Oh, Didn't It Rain* – 1923E
Leonard, Hal, Music Inc. – 1946L
Leonard, Neil
*Jazz: Myth & Religion* – 1987D
Leoncavallo, Ruggiero – 1906K
LePage, Jane
*Women Composers, Conductors...of the 20th
    Century I* – 1980M
*Women Composers, Conductors..of the 20th
    Century II* – 1980M

---

✿

---

## Cultivated/Art Music Scene
F *Births*    G *Deaths*    H *Debuts*    I *New Positions*    J *Honors and Awards*
K *Biographical*    L *Musical Beginnings*    M *Publications*    N *Compositions*

---

✿

## Vernacular/Commercial Music Scene
**A** *Births*   **B** *Deaths*   **C** *Biographical*   **D** *Publications*
**E** *Representative Pieces*

❀

## Cultivated/Art Music Scene
F *Births*  G *Deaths*  H *Debuts*  I *New Positions*  J *Honors and Awards*
K *Biographical*  L *Musical Beginnings*  M *Publications*  N *Compositions*

Little Rock, Arkansas (continued)
*Musical Coterie* – *1883L*
*Symphony Orchestra* – *1933L*
Little Walter – 1930A, 1958B
Little, Jack
*In a Shanty in Old Shanty Town* –
1933E
Little, William
*Easy Instructor, The* – 1801M
Litton, Andrew – 1959F, 1989H, 1994IK
Litvinne, Félia – 1885H, 1896H
Lively, David – 1953F, 1968H
Living Colour – 1983C
Livingston, Jay – 1915A
*Bonanza Theme* – 1959E
*Buttons & Bows* – 1948E
*Mona Lisa* – 1950E
*Que Sera, Sera* – 1956E
*Silver Bells* – 1950E
*To Each His Own* – 1946E
Livingston, Jerry – 1909A, 1987B
*It's the Talk of the Town* – 1933E
*Mairzy Doats* – 1943E
Lizzie Borden – 1983C
Ljunberg, Göta – 1932H
Lloyd, Bill – 1955A
Lloyd, David – 1920F, 1950H
Lloyd, Edward – 1888H
Lloyd, Norman – 1909F, 1980G
*Fireside Book of Favorite American Songs* –
1947D
*Fireside Book of Love Songs* – 1954D
*Piano Sonata* – 1958N
Lloyd, Robert – 1975H
Lloyd Webber, Andrew
*Aspects of Love* – 1990E
*Evita* – 1979E
*Jesus Christ, Superstar* – 1971E
*Joseph & the Amazing Technicolor Dream Coat* –
1976E
*Starlight Express* – 1984E
*Song & Dance* – 1985E
Lo Presti, Ronald – 1933F
Locke, Alain
*Negro & His Music, The* – 1936D
Lockhart, Eugene
*World is Waiting for the Sunrise, The* – 1919E
Lockhart, Keith – 1995I
Locklair, Dan S. – 1949F
*Breakers Pound, The* – 1985N
*Brief Mass* – 1994N
*Creation's Seeing Order* – 1987N
*Fantasy Brings the Day* – 1989N
*Hues for Orchestra* – 1994N
*Rubrica* – 1988N
*Voyage* – 1991N
Lockwood, Lewis – 1970J, 1985I
Lockwood, Normand – 1906F
*Piano Sonata* – 1944N

*Prairie, The* – 1953N
*Scarecrow, The* – 1945N
*Symphony* – 1941N
Loder, George – 1836KG
*New York Glee Book, The* – 1843M
Lodge, Henry
*Temptation Rag* – 1909E
Loeb, John Jacob – 1910A, 1970B
Loeffler, Charles M. – 1881K, 1887K, 1903K,
1908J, 1919J, 1926J, 1931J, 1935G
*Divertimento in a, Opus 1* – 1894N
*Divertissement Espagnol* – 1900N
*Evocation* – 1930N
*Fantastic Concerto* – 1894N
*Five Irish Fantasies* – 1920N
*Four Poems, Op. 15* – 1905N
*Hora Mystica* – 1915N
*Memories of My Childhood* – 1924N
*Morceau Fantastique* – 1893N
*Mort de Tintagiles, La, Opus 6* – 1897N
*Pagan Poem, A* – 1906N
*Passion of Hilarion, The* – 1913N
*String Quartet in A Minor* – 1889N
*String Sextet* – 1891N
*Veillées de L'Ukraine, Les* – 1890N
Loesser, Arthur – 1894F, 1913H, 1969G
*Humor in American Song* – 1943M
*Men, Women & Pianos: a Social History* – 1954M
Loesser, Frank – 1910A, 1969B
*Baby, It's Cold Outside* – 1948E
*Greenwillow* – 1960E
*Guys & Dolls* – 1950E
*Hans Christian Andersen (film)* – 1952E
*Hans Christian Andersen (stage)* – 1974E
*How to Succeed in Business...* – 1961E
*I'd Love to Get You on a Slow Boat to China* –
1948E
*Most Happy Fella* – 1956E
*Perfectly Frank* – 1980E
*Praise the Lord & Pass the Ammunition* – 1942E
*Spring Will Be a Little Late This Year* – 1943E
*Thank Your Lucky Stars* – 1943E
*They're Either Too Young or Too Old* – 1943E
*Where's Charley* – 1948E
Loewe, Frederick – 1924C, 1988B
*Great Lady* – 1938E
*Life of the Party, The* – 1942E
Lofgren, Nils – 1951A
Logan, Ella – 1932C, 1969B
Logan, Frederick K. – 1871A, 1928B
*Missouri Waltz* – 1914E
Logan, James, Library – 1751L
Logan, Joshua – 1908B
Loggins, Kenny – 1948A, 1984E
Lohse, Otto – 1876K
Lollapalooza Music Festival – 1991C
Lomax, Alan – 1915A, 1986C
*American Folk Song & Folk Lore* – 1942D
*Folk Songs of North America* – 1960D

---

❄

**Vernacular/Commercial Music Scene**
A  *Births*    B  *Deaths*    C  *Biographical*    D  *Publications*
E  *Representative Pieces*

Folk Song Style & Culture – 1968D
Folk Song, U.S.A. – 1947D
Leadbelly: A Collection of World Famous Songs – 1959D
Our Singing Country – 1941D
Lomax, John Avery – 1867A, 1948B
American Ballads & Folksongs – 1934D
Negro Folk Songs as Sung by Leadbelly – 1936D
Lombardo, Guy – 1902A, 1977B
Lombardo, Guy, Band – 1923C
London, George – 1919F, 1941H, 1951H, 1960K, 1975I, 1985G
London, Julie – 1926A
Lone Justice – 1983C
Lone Star – 1975C
Long Playing Record Catalog – 1949L
Long-Playing Record, Columbia – 1948L
Longfellow, Samuel
Book of Hymns & Tunes, A – 1860M
Longstreet, Stephen
Real Jazz, Old & New, The – 1956D
Longines Symphonette    1941L
Long Ryders – 1982C
Longy School of Music – 1916L
Looking Glass – 1972E
Loomis, Clarence    1965G
Captive Woman, The – 1953N
Fall of the House of Usher – 1941N
Piano Concerto – 1915N
String Quartet No. 1 – 1953N
String Quartet No. 2 – 1963N
String Quartet No. 3 – 1965N
Yolanda of Cyprus – 1929N
Loomis, Clarence – 1889F
Loomis, Harvey Worthington – 1865F, 1930G
Lopardo, Frank – 1958F, 1974H
Lopatnikoff, Nikolai – 1939K, 1944K, 1945I, 1953J, 1963J, 1976G
Cello Sonata – 1929N
Concerto for Orchestra – 1964N
Concerto for 2 Pianos – 1951N
Danton – 1932N
Festival Overture – 1960N
Melting Pot Ballet – 1976N
Music for Orchestra – 1958N
Piano Concerto No. 1 – 1921N
Piano Concerto No. 2 – 1930N
Piano Sonata – 1943N
String Quartet No. 1 – 1920N
String Quartet No. 2 – 1928N
String Quartet No. 3 – 1955N
Symphony No. 1 – 1928N
Symphony No. 2 – 1939N
Symphony No. 3 – 1954N
Symphony No. 4 – 1971N
Violin Concerto – 1941N
Lopez, Trini – 1937A
Lopez, Vincent – 1894A, 1975B
Lopez, Vincent, Big Band – 1918C

López-Cobos, Jesús – 1972H, 1978H, 1986I
Lorengar, Pilar – 1955H, 1966H
Lorenz Publishing Co. – 1890L
Lorenz, Max – 1931H
Loriod, Yvonne – 1949H
Lorraine, Lillian – 1955B
Los Angeles, California
Ambassador Auditorium – 1974L
American Youth Orchestra – 1944L
(Philharmonic) Auditorium – 1906L
Bohemian Composers Group – 1957L
Chamber Music in Historic Sites – 1981L
Chamber Orchestra – 1969L
Chandler, Dorothy, Pavilion – 1964L
Child's Grand Opera House – 1884L
Classic Jazz Festival – 1984C
Conservatory of Music – 1883L
Ellis Club – 1888L
Festival Negro Chorus – 1936L
Grand Opera Association – 1924L
Janssen Symphony Orchestra – 1940L
Japanese Philharmonic Orchestra – 1961L
Korean Classical Music & Dance Co. – 1973L
Master Chorale & Sinfonia – 1965L
Merced Theater – 1870L
Music Center Opera – 1986L
Music Festival – 1947L
Musical Association – 1871L
Negro Chorus of L.A. – 1936L
New Orchestra – 1948L
Opera Repertory – 1980L
Oratorio Society – 1912L
Piano Quartet – 1977L
Philharmonic Orchestra – 1919L
Philharmonic Society – 1878L
Shrine Auditorium – 1927L
Symphony Orchestra – 1898L
Treble Clef Club – 1889L
Turnverein Hall – 1872L
Zoellner Conservatory of Music – 1922L
Los Lobos – 1973C, 1987E
Losey's Military Band School – 1914L
Lost City Ramblers, New – 1958C
Lott, Felicity – 1986H, 1990H
Loudermilk, John – 1934A
Louisiana Five – 1915C
Louisiana Shakers – 1932C
Louisville, Kentucky
Academy of Music – 1954L
Bach Society – 1964L
Chamber Music Society – 1938L
Conservatory of Music – 1915L
Greater L. Foundation – 1949L
Kentucky Center for the Arts – 1983L
Kentucky Opera Association – 1952L
Macauley's Theater – 1873L
Orchestra – 1937L
Orchestra Commissioning Project – 1948L
Philharmonic Society – 1866L

---

❂

## Cultivated/Art Music Scene

F *Births*    G *Deaths*    H *Debuts*    I *New Positions*    J *Honors and Awards*
K *Biographical*    L *Musical Beginnings*    M *Publications*    N *Compositions*

Louisville, Kentucky (continued)
  *Records – 1953L*
Lounge Lizards – 1979C
Loup, François – 1991H
Love – 1965C
Love of Life Orchestra – 1977C
Love, Darlene – 1938A
Love, Shirley – 1940F, 1962H, 1963H
Loveberg, Aase – 1957H
Lovecraft, H. P. – 1967C
Loveless, Patty – 1957A
Lovely Music, Ltd. – 1978C
Lovett, Lyle – 1957A, 1989C
Love Unlimited – 1969C
Lovin' Spoonful – 1965C, 1966E
Lowe, Ruth
  *I'll Never Smile Again* – 1940E
Lowens, Irving – 1916F, 1972J, 1977J, 1983G
  *Bibliography of Songsters...in America before
    1821* – 1976M
  *Music & Musicians in Early America* – 1964M
  *Source Readings in American Music History* –
    1966M
Lowenthal, Jerome – 1932F, 1945H, 1957J, 1963H
Lowinsky, Edward – 1940K, 1947K, 1973J
Lowry, Robert – 1826F, 1899G
  *I Need Thee Every Hour* – 1872N
  *Low in the Grave He Lay* – 1875N
  *Shall We Gather at the River* – 1865N
  *Where is My Wandering Boy Tonight?* – 1877E
L 7 – 1985C
Lübeck, Ernst – 1849H
Lubin, Steven – 1942F, 1977H
Luboff, Norman – 1917F, 1987G
Luboff, Norman, Choir – 1963L
Luboshutz & Nemenoff – 1937H
Luboshutz, Léa – 1924K, 1927I, 1965G
Luboshutz, Pierre – 1926K, 1931K, 1971G
Luca, Sergiu – 1961K, 1965H, 1966K
Lucas, Sam – 1850F, 1916B
Lucca, Pauline – 1872H
Luchesi, Joseph – 1844I
Luchetti, Veriano – 1988H
Lucier, Alvin – 1931F
  *Amplifiers & Reflectors* – 1990N
  *Ghosts* – 1978N
  *Music for Piano &..Sonorous Vessels* – 1990N
  *Music for Pure Waves* – 1980N
  *Music on a Long Thin Wire* – 1977N
  *Seesaw* – 1983N
  *Serenade* – 1985N
  *Silver Streetcar* – 1988N
  *Spinner* – 1984N
  *Solar Sounder No. 1* – 1979N
  *Whistlers* – 1967N
Ludden & Bates Co. – 1884L
Luders, Gustav – 1899C, 1913B
  *Burgomaster, The* – 1900E
  *Fair Co-ed, The* – 1909E

  *Gypsy, The* – 1912E
  *King Dodo* – 1901E
  *Marcello* – 1908E
  *Prince of Plsen, The* – 1903E
  *Shogun, The* – 1904E
  *Somewhere Else* – 1913E
  *Woodland* – 1904E
Ludgin, Chester – 1925F, 1956H
Ludikar, Pavel – 1913H, 1926H
Ludwig, Christa – 1959H, 1993K, 1994J
Ludwig, Leopold – 1958I, 1970H
Ludwig, Thomas
  *Violin Concerto* – 1994N
Ludwig, W. F., Drum Co. – 1936L
Ludwig, William F. – 1973G
Luening, Otto – 1900F, 1934I, 1944I, 1946J, 1970K,
  1981J
  *Dynamophonic Suite* – 1958N
  *Electronic Tape Music* – 1952M
  *Evangeline* – 1932N
  *Fantasy in Space* – 1952N
  *Gargoyles* – 1960N
  *Louisville Concerto* – 1951N
  *Music for Orchestra* – 1923N
  *Poem in Cycles & Bells* – 1954N
  *Sister Beatrice* – 1926N
  *Sonority Forms I* – 1983N
  *String Quartet No. 1* – 1920N
  *String Quartet No. 2* – 1923N
  *String Quartet No. 3* – 1928N
  *Symphonic Fantasia I* – 1924N
  *Symphonic Fantasia II* – 1939N
  *Symphonic Fantasia III* – 1975N
  *Symphonic Fantasias V, VI* – 1985N
  *Symphonic Fantasias VII, VIII* – 1986N
  *Symphonic Fantasia IX* – 1989N
  *Symphonic Fantasia X* – 1990N
  *Symphonic Interlude No. 4* – 1985N
  *Symphonic Interlude No. 5* – 1986N
  *Theater Piece No. 2* – 1956N
  *Two Symphonic Interludes* – 1935N
  *Wisconsin Symphony* – 1975N
Luke, Ray – 1926F
  *Medea* – 1979N
  *Orchestra Suite No. 1* – 1958N
  *Orchestra Suite No. 2* – 1967N
  *Piano Concerto* – 1969N
  *Symphony No. 1* – 1959N
  *Symphony No. 2* – 1963N
  *Symphony No. 3* – 1964N
  *Symphony No. 4* – 1970N
Lulu – 1967E
Lummis, Charles F. – 1859F, 1928G
Lunceford, Jimmy – 1902A, 1947B
Lunceford, Jimmie, Band – 1929C
Lund, John R. – 1885H
Lunden, Jeffery
  *Another Midsummer Night* – 1995E
  *Wings* – 1992E

---

### Vernacular/Commercial Music Scene
A  *Births*    B  *Deaths*    C  *Biographical*    D  *Publications*
E  *Representative Pieces*

Luperi, Mario – 1988H
LuPone, Patti – 1949A
Lupu, Radu – 1972H
Lurie, Elliot – 1948A
Lussan, Zélie de – 1862F, 1878H, 1894H, 1895K
Lutkin, Peter C. – 1858F, 1883I, 1895I, 1900J,
  1931G
Lutoslawski, Witold
  *Chaim I* – 1983N
  *Chaim II* – 1985N
  *Chaim III* – 1986N
  *Piano Concerto* – 1987N, 1988N
  *Symphony No. 4* – 1992N
Lutoslawski Composition Competition – 1990L
Luxon, Benjamin – 1980H
Lybbert, Donald – 1923F
  *Monica* – 1952N
Lyford, Ralph – 1882F, 1927G
  *Castle Agrazant* – 1926N
  *Piano Concerto* – 1917N
Lyman, Abe – 1957B
Lyman, Abe, Band – 1921C
Lymon, Frankie – 1942A, 1968B
Lymon, Frankie, and the Teenagers – 1955C
Lympany, Moura – 1948H
Lynch, Vincent
  *Jukebox: The Golden Age* – 1981D
Lyne, Felice – 1887F, 1911H, 1935G
Lynn, Cheryl – 1957A
Lynn, Loretta – 1935A, 1972C, 1988C
Lynes, Frank – 1858F, 1913G
Lynne, Shelby – 1968A
Lynryd Skynryd – 1966C
Lyon & Healy Co. (Chicago) – 1864L
Lyon & Healy Harp Co. – 1899L
Lyon, James – 1735F, 1759K, 1762JK, 1764K,
  1794G
  *Urania* – 1761M
Lyons Musical Academy – 1854L
Lyons, James – 1925F, 1953I, 1957I, 1973G
  *Modern Music* – 1957M
Lyons, Julius J.
  *Lady or the Tiger?, The* – 1888D
Lyons, Leonard
  *Great Jazz Pianists, The* – 1989D
Lyras, Panayis – 1979J, 1981J
Lyric Art Quartet-Quintet – 1953L
Lyric Opera of Baton Rouge – 1985L

# M

M – 1979E
Ma, Yo-Yo – 1955F, 1978J
Maag, Peter – 1959H, 1972H
Maas, Joseph – 1873H
Maas, Louis – 1880K, 1889G
  *Symphony, "On the Prairie"* – 1882N
Maazel, Lorin – 1938F, 1942K, 1960K, 1970K,
  1972I, 1984I, 1987K
Mácal, Zdenek – 1986I, 1988I

MacArdle, Donald – 1897F, 1964G
MacArthur, Edwin – 1967I
Macbeth, Florence – 1891F, 1913H, 1914H, 1966G
Macbride, David – 1951F
  *Chartres* – 1989N
  *Three Dances* – 1987N
MacCarthy, Harry
  *Bonnie Blue Flag, The* – 1861E
MacCarthy, Maud – 1898H
MacColl, Hugh F. – 1885F, 1953G
  *Ballad* –1934N
  *Romantic Suite* – 1935N
  *Sahara Suite* – 1927N
  *String Quartet No. 1* – 1928N
  *String Quartet No. 2* – 1945N
  *Variations in F* – 1934N
MacCombie, Bruce – 1993I
MacDermot, Galt
  *Hair* – 1967E
  *Human Comedy, The* – 1984E
  *Two Gentlemen of Verona* – 1971E
  *Via Galactica* – 1972E
MacDonald, Ballard – 1882A, 1935B
  *Trail of the Lonesome Pine* – 1913E
MacDonald, Harl – 1955G
MacDonald, Jeanette – 1903F, 1965G
MacDonough, Glen – 1870A, 1924B
  *The Midnight Sons* – 1909E
MacDowell Chorus – 1909L
MacDowell Colony (NH) – 1907L
MacDowell Festivals – 1910L
MacDowell, Edward – 1861F, 1869K, 1876K,
  1879K, 1881K, 1882K, 1884K, 1888K, 1896IK,
  1904JK, 1908G, 1960J
  *Eight Chansons Fugitives, Opus 2* – 1876N
  *Eight Songs, Opus 47* – 1893N
  *Etude de Concert, Opus 36* – 1887N
  *Fireside Tales, Op. 61* – 1902N
  *Five Songs, Opus 11, 12* – 1881N
  *Four Pieces, Opus 24* – 1886N
  *Four Songs, Opus 56* – 1898N
  *Hamlet* – 1885N
  *Idyllen: Six Little Pieces, Opus 28* – 1887N
  *Lamia, Opus 29* – 1887N
  *Lancelot & Elaine, Opus 25* – 1886N
  *Marionetten, Opus 38* – 1888N
  *Modern Suite No. 1, Opus 10* – 1881N
  *Modern Suite No. 2, Opus 14* – 1882N
  *New England Idylls, Op. 62* – 1902N
  *Ophelia* – 1885N
  *Orchestra Suite No. 1, Opus 42* – 1891N
  *Orientales Les, Opus 37* – 1888N
  *Piano Concerto No. 1* – 1882N
  *Piano Sonata No. 1, "Eroica"* – 1892N
  *Piano Sonata No. 2, "Eroica"* – 1895N
  *Piano Sonata No. 3, "Norse"* – 1899N
  *Piano Sonata No. 4, "Keltic"* – 1900N
  *Piano Suite, Opus 5* – 1876N
  *Prelude & Fugue in D Minor, Opus 13* – 1881N

❖

## Cultivated/Art Music Scene

F *Births*    G *Deaths*    H *Debuts*    I *New Positions*    J *Honors and Awards*
K *Biographical*    L *Musical Beginnings*    M *Publications*    N *Compositions*

MacDowell, Edward (continued)
   *Romance for Cello & Orchestra* – 1887N
   *Sea Pieces, Opus 55* – 1898N
   *Serenade, Opus 16* – 1882N
   *Six Love Songs, Opus 40* – 1890N
   *Six Poems after Heine, Opus 31* – 1887N
   *Suite No. 2, "Indian," Opus 48* – 1895N
   *Three Petits Morceaux, Opus 4* – 1876N
   *Three Poesien, Opus 20* – 1885N
   *Three Songs, Opus 33* – 1888N
   *Three Songs, Opus 58* – 1899N
   *Three Songs, Op. 60* – 1901N
   *Twelve Etudes, Opus 39* – 1890N
   *Twelve Virtuoso Etudes, Opus 46* – 1894N
   *Two Northern Songs, Opus 43* – 1891N
   *Two Fantasie Pieces, Opus 17* – 1883N
   *Two Pieces for Piano, Opus 18* – 1884N
   *Wald Idyllen, Opus 19* – 1884N
   *Woodland Sketches, Opus 51* – 1896N
MacDowell, Edward, Medal – 1960L
MacGregor, Mary – 1977E
Machlis, Joseph – 1906F, 1938I, 1976I
   *American Composers of Our Time* – 1963M
   *Enjoyment of Music, The* – 1955M
   *Introduction to Contemporary Music* – 1961M
Machover, Tod – 1953F, 1984I, 1987I
   *Bounce* – 1992N
   *Desires* – 1989N
   *Electronic Etudes* – 1983N
   *Extended Orchestra, The* – 1985M
   *Forever & Ever* – 1993N
   *Nature's Breath* – 1985N
   *Some Thoughts on Computer Music* – 1984M
   *Spectres Parisiens* – 1984N
   *String Quartet No. 1* – 1981N
   *Valis* – 1987N
Macintyre, Marguerite – 1901H
Mack, Andrew
   *Heart of My Heart* – 1899R
Mack, Cecil – 1883A, 1944B
Mack, Edward
   *Centennial March Series* – 1875N
   *Dirge for President Lincoln* – 1865N
   *General Grant's Grand March* – 1868N
   *General McClellan's Grand March* – 1861N
   *President Lincoln's Funeral March* – 1865N
Mack, Lonnie – 1941A
Mackey, Stephen – 1946F
   *Among the Vanishing* – 1989N
   *Banana/Dump Truck* – 1995N
   *Deal* – 1995N
   *Eating Greens* – 1994N
   *No Two Breaths* – 1995N
   *On All Fours* – 1990N
   *Physical Property* – 1992N
   *TILT* – 1992N
MacKenzie, Giselle – 1927A
Mackie, Neil – 1988H
Mackinac Island Music Festival – 1986L

Maclaglen, T.
   *Captain Jinks of the Horse Marines* – 1901E
Maclennan, Francis – 1879F, 1902H, 1904HK,
   1935G
MacLellan, Gene
   *Put Your Hand in the Hand* – 1971E
Macmillan, Francis – 1885F, 1903H, 1906H, 1973G
MacMillan, James
   *Kiss on Wood* – 1994N
MacMurrough, Dermot
   *Macushla* – 1910E
MacNeil, Cornell – 1922F, 1950F, 1959F
Macon, Uncle Dave – 1870A, 1952B
MacRae, Gordon – 1921A, 1986B
Macurdy, John – 1929F, 1952H, 1962H
Madden, Edward – 1877A, 1952B
   *Moonlight Bay* – 1912E
Maddox Brothers and Rose – 1946C
Maddy, Joseph – 1891F, 1966G
Madeira, Francis – 1917F, 1945I
Madeira, Jean – 1918F, 1943H, 1948H, 1972G
Madeira, Paul
   *I'm Glad There Is You* – 1941E
Mader, Clarence – 1904F
Maderna, Bruno – 1965K
Madison Civic Center (WI) – 1980L
Madison Choral Union – 1893L
Madison, Dolley – 1809K
Madison, Dorothy – 1956F, 1986H
Madonna – 1958A, 1984E, 1985E, 1986E, 1987E,
   1989E, 1990E, 1991E
Mad River – 1965C
Maganini Chamber Symphony – 1932L
Maganini, Quinto – 1897F, 1939I, 1974G
   *Argonauts, The* – 1935N
   *Night in the Tropics, A* – 1933N
   *Symphony in G* – 1932N
Magee, Emily – 1994J
Magnussen, Lars – 1990H
Mahavishnu Orchestra – 1971C
Mahler, Fritz – 1936K, 1939K, 1947I, 1953I
Mahler, Gustav – 1908I, 1909I
Maier, Guy – 1891F, 1956G
Mailman, Martin – 1932F
   *Autumn Landscape* – 1954N
   *Hunted, The* – 1959N
   *Sinfonietta* – 1964N
   *String Quartet* – 1962N
   *Suite in 3 Movements* – 1961N
   *Symphony No. 1* – 1969N
   *Symphony No. 2* – 1979N
   *Symphony No. 3* – 1983N
   *Violin Concerto* – 1982N
Maine Music Festival – 1897L
Maison, René – 1927H, 1936H
Majors – 1959C
Malaco Records – 1975C
Malas, Spiro – 1933F, 1959H, 1983H
Malas-Godlewska, Ewa – 1991H

---

❁

Vernacular/Commercial Music Scene
A *Births*   B *Deaths*   C *Biographical*   D *Publications*
E *Representative Pieces*

Malcolm, Alexander – 1749K, 1754K, 1763G
Malcuzynski, Witold – 1942H
Malfitano, Catherine – 1948F, 1972H, 1979H
Malibran, Maria – 1825H
Maliponte, Adriana – 1963H, 1971H
Malkin Conservatory – 1933L
Malkin, Joseph – 1909H
Malko, Nikolai – 1946K
Mallet & Graupner Musical Academy – 1801L
Mallet, François – 1834G
Mallinger, Mathilde – 1873H
Malneck, Matty – 1903A
  *Goody, Goody* – 1936E
  *Park Avenue Fantasy* – 1935E
Malone, Bill C.
  *Country Music, U.S.A.* – 1968D
Malotte, Albert Hay – 1895F, 1964G
  *Ferdinand, the Bull* – 1939E
  *Lord's Prayer, The* – 1935N
Mamas and the Papas, The – 1965C, 1966E
Mamikonian, Vardan – 1993H
Mamlok, Ursula – 1941K, 1945K, 1981J, 1989J
Mana-Zucca – 1885F, 1981G
  *Hypatia* – 1920N
  *I Love Life* – 1923E
  *Piano Concerto* – 1919N
  *Violin Concerto* – 1955N
Manassas – 1971C
Manassas Jazz Festival – 1985C
Manchester, Melissa – 1951A
  *I Sent a Letter to My Love* – 1995E
Mancinelli, Aldo – 1954J
Mancinelli, Luigi – 1893H
Mancini, Henry – 1924A, 1969E, 1994B
  *Breakfast at Tiffany's* – 1961E
  *Charade* – 1963E
  *Days of Wine & Roses* (film) – 1962E
  *House Calls* – 1978E
  *Moon River* – 1961E
  *Nightwing* – 1979E
  *Peter Gunn Theme* – 1958E
  *Pink Panther Theme* – 1963E
  *Shot In the Dark, A* – 1964E
  *Silver Streak* – 1976E
  *Victor-Victoria* – 1982E
  *Victor-Victoria* (musical) – 1995E
  *10 (film music)* – 1979E
Mandac, Evelyn – 1968H, 1975H
Mandel, Mel
  *My Old Friends* – 1980E
Mandel, Alan – 1935F, 1948H
Mandel, Johnny A. – 1935A
  *Being There* – 1979E
  *M*A*S*H* – 1970E
  *Shadow of Your Smile, The* – 1965E
Mandelbaum, Joel – 1932F
Mandingo Griot Society – 1977C
Mandrake Memorial – 1967C
Mandrell, Barbara – 1948A

Mandrell, Louise – 1954A
Mandrill – 1968C
Mangione, Chuck – 1940A
Mangione, Chuck, Quartet – 1968C
Manhattan – 1962C
Manhattan Chamber Orchestra – 1984L
Manhattan String Quartet – 1970L
Manhattan Transfer – 1969C
Manhattans, The – 1961C, 1976E
Manilow, Barry – 1946A, 1975E, 1976E, 1977E
Manly, Basil, Jr.
  *Baptist Chorals: a Hymn & Tune Book* – 1859N
Mann, Barry – 1939A
Mann, Elias – 1750F, 1825G
  *Massachusetts Collection of Sacred Harmony* –
    1807M
Mann, Herbie – 1930A
Mann, Herbie, Music – 1981C
Mann, Manfred – 1964E
Mann, Robert – 1920F, 1941HJ
Manne, Shelly – 1920A, 1984B
Manne, Shelly, Quintet – 1956C
Mannes College of Music – 1916L
Mannes Trio – 1949L
Mannes, Clara Damrosch – 1869F, 1948G
Mannes, David – 1866F, 1959G
Mannes, Leopold D. – 1899F, 1922H, 1940I, 1964G
  *Orchestral Suite* – 1924N
  *String Quartet* – 1927N
Manning, Dick
  *It Takes Two to Tango* – 1952E
Manning, Kathleen Lockhart – 1890F, 1951G
Manowar – 1981C
Manship, Paul – 1909J
Manski, Dorothée – 1927H, 1967G
Manson, Anne – 1993K
Mansouri, Lotfi – 1988I
Mantelli, Eugenia – 1894H
Mapleson, Helen – 1902H
Marable, Fate – 1890A, 1947B
Marák, Otakar – 1914H
Marcel, Lucille – 1885F, 1903H, 1912H, 1921G
Marcels, The – 1961E
Marchesi, Blanche – 1899H
Marchesi, Salvatore – 1848H
Marcoux, Vanni – 1912H
Marcovici, Silvia – 1977H
Mardiello, Catherine – 1958F
Mardones, José – 1913H, 1917H
Mares, Paul – 1949B
Maretzek, Max – 1848I
  *Sleepy Hollow* – 1879E
Margison, Richard Charles – 1991H, 1995H
Margita, Stefan – 1992H
Margulies, Adele – 1881H
Margun Music – 1975L
Mariano, Charlie – 1923A
Marie, Tina – 1956A
Marimon, Marie – 1879H

---

Cultivated/Art Music Scene

F *Births*     G *Deaths*     H *Debuts*     I *New Positions*     J *Honors and Awards*
K *Biographical*     L *Musical Beginnings*     M *Publications*     N *Compositions*

Marin, Ion – 1992H
Marine Band, U.S. – 1799L
Marine Fife & Drum Corps, U.S. – 1798L
Marini, Ignacio – 1850H
Marino, Amerigo – 1925F, 1964I, 1988G
Mario, Giovanni – 1854H
Mario, Queena – 1896F, 1918H, 1922H, 1951G
Mark Educational Recordings – 1967L
Mark, Marky – 1991E
Mar-Keys, The – 1957C
Markoe, Peter
  *Reconciliation, The* – 1790N
Markov, Alexander – 1982J
Markowitz, Richard Allen – 1994B
Marks, Alan – 1949F, 1966H, 1973J
Marks, Edward B. – 1865F, 1945G
  *December & May* – 1893E
Marks, Gerald
  *All of Me* – 1931E
Marks, Godfrey
  *Sailing, Sailing, Over the Bounding Main* – 1880E
Marks, Johnny – 1909A, 1985B
  *I Heard the Bells on Christmas Day* – 1956E
  *Rudolph, the Red-Nosed Reindeer* – 1949E
Marks, Walter
  *Golden Rainbow* – 1968E
  *I've Got To Be Me* – 1969E
Marlboro Festival (VT) – 1950L
Marlowe, Sylvia – 1908F, 1981G
Marriner, Neville – 1979I
Marrocco, W. Thomas – 1909F
Marsalis, Branford – 1960A
Marsalis, Wynton – 1961A
  *In This House, On This Morning* – 1994E
  *Majesty of the Blues* – 1989E
Marsh, Calvin – 1954H
Marsh, J. B. T.
  *Story of the Jubilee Singers, The* – 1881D
Marsh, Jane – 1945F, 1965H, 1966J
Marshall, Lois – 1952H
Marshall, Margaret – 1980H
Marshall, Robert L. – 1939F
Marsick, Martin Pierre – 1895H
Marteau, Henri – 1893H
Martika – 1969A, 1989E
Martin & Morris Music Co. – 1940C
Martin, C. J., & Co., Guitars – 1833L
Martin, Dean – 1917A, 1956E, 1964E
Martin, Freddy – 1906A, 1983B
Martin, Henry
  *Enjoying Jazz* – 1986D
Martin, Hugh – 1914A
  *Best Foot Forward,* 1941E
  *High Spirits* – 1964E
Martin, Janis – 1939F, 1962H
Martin, Julian – 1975J
Martin, Marilyn – 1985E
Martin, Mary – 1913A, 1989C, 1990B

Martin, Riccardo – 1874F, 1904H, 1906H, 1907H, 1952G
Martin, Roberta – 1907A
Martin, Roberta, Singers – 1933C
Martin, Sallie – 1896A, 1988B
Martin, Tony – 1912A
Martin-Frye Quartet – 1933C
Martinelli, Giovanni – 1913H, 1969G
Martinez, R. J.
  *Portraits of New Orleans Jazz* – 1971D
Martini, Nino – 1931H, 1933H
Martino, Al – 1927A
Martino, Donald – 1931F, 1967J, 1981J, 1987J
  *Cello Concerto* – 1972N
  *Concerto for Wind Quintet* – 1964N
  *Contemplations* – 1956N
  *Fantasies & Impromtus* – 1981N
  *From the Other Side* – 1988N
  *Mosaic* – 1967N
  *Notturno* – 1973N
  *Pianissimo* – 1970N
  *Piano Concerto* – 1965N
  *Piano Fantasy* – 1958N
  *Saxophone Concerto* – 1987N
  *String Quartet* – 1983N
  *Triple Clarinet Concerto* – 1977N
  *Twelve Piano Preludes* – 1991N
  *White Island, The* – 1985N
Martinon, Jean – 1963I
Martinů, Bohuslav – 1941K, 1948I, 1955K, 1956K
  *Cello Concerto* – 1944N
  *Concerto da Camera* – 1947N
  *Double Violin Concerto No. 2* – 1950N
  *Memorial to Lidice* – 1943N
  *Piano Concerto No. 3* – 1948N
  *Symphony No. 1* – 1942N
  *Symphony No. 2* – 1943N
  *Symphony No. 3* – 1944N
  *Symphony No. 4* – 1945N
  *Symphony No. 5* – 1946N
  *Symphony No. 6* – 1953N
Martinucci, Nicola – 1988H
Martirano, Salvatore – 1927F, 1960J, 1963I
  *Cherry Orchard, The* – 1949N
  *Fast Forward* – 1977N
  *Fifty One* – 1978N
  *Lon/dons* – 1989N
  *Magic Stone, The* – 1951N
  *O, O, O, O, that Shakespeherian Rag* – 1958N
  *She Spoke* – 1979N
  *Shop Talk* – 1974N
  *Three Electronic Dances* – 1963N
  *Underworld* – 1965N
Marton, Eva – 1975H, 1976H
Martucci, Paolo – 1911K, 1980G
Martzy, Johanna – 1957H
Maruzin, Yuri – 1991H
Marvelettes, The – 1960C, 1961E
Marvelows – 1959C

---

**Vernacular/Commercial Music Scene**

A *Births*    B *Deaths*    C *Biographical*    D *Publications*
E *Representative Pieces*

Marvin, Frederick – 1923F, 1948H
Marvin, M. W.
  *History of the American Film, A* – 1978E
Marx, Richard – 1964A, 1988E, 19889E
Maryland Handel Festival – 1981L
Mascagni, Pietro – 1902K
Masekela, Hugh – 1968E
Masi, Francesco
  *Sonata, Battles of Lake Champlanin & Plattsburg*
    – 1815N
Mason & Colburn Co. – 1849L
Mason & Hamlin Organ Co. – 1854L
Mason & Hamlin Piano Co. – 1882L
Mason & Thomas Chamber Music Soirées –
  1855L
Mason Brothers, Publishers – 1855L
Mason Proffitt – 1969C
Mason, Daniel Gregory – 1873F, 1891K, 1905I,
  1953G
  *Art of Music, The* – 1915M
  *Artistic Ideals* – 1925M
  *Chanticleer Overture* – 1926N
  *Clarinet Sonata, Op. 14* – 1923N
  *Dilemma of American Music, The* – 1928M
  *Divertimento, Op. 26* – 1927N
  *Four Love Songs, Op. 4* – 1906N
  *From Grieg to Brahms* – 1902M
  *Great Modern Composers* – 1916M
  *Guide to Music, A* – 1909M
  *Music as a Humanity* – 1920M
  *Music in My Time* – 1938M
  *Orchestral Instruments, The* – 1908M
  *Passacaglia & Fugue, Op. 10* – 1912N
  *Piano Quartet, Op 7* – 1911N
  *Piano Sonata* – 1895N
  *Prelude & Fugue, Op. 12* – 1914N
  *Prelude & Fugue, Op. 20* – 1920N
  *Romantic Composers, The* – 1906M
  *Sentimental Sketches* – 1935N
  *Serenade for String Quartet* – 1931N
  *Six Love Songs, Op. 15* – 1915N
  *Soldiers, Op. 42* – 1949N
  *Songs of the Countryside* – 1923N
  *String Quartet on Negro Themes* – 1919N
  *Suite After English Folk Songs* – 1934N
  *Symphony No. 1* – 1914N
  *Symphony No. 2* – 1929N
  *Symphony No. 3, "Lincoln"* – 1936N
  *Tune In, America!...Our Coming Musical
    Independence* – 1931M
  *Variations on a Quiet Theme* – 1939N
  *Variations on a Theme of Powell* – 1925N
  *Violin Sonata* – 1908N
Mason, Edith – 1921H, 1973G
Mason, Lowell – 1792F, 1812K, 1818K, 1820I,
  1827IK, 1835J, 1837K, 1838I, 1855J, 1872G
  *Address on Church Music* – 1826M
  *Boston Academy's Collection of Choruses* –
    1836M

*Boston Academy Collection of Church Music* –
  1835M
*Boston Anthem Book, The* – 1839M
*Boston Glee Book, The* – 1838M
*Cantica Laudis* – 1850M
*Carmina Sacra* – 1841M
*Carmina Sacra Enlarged: American Tune Book* –
  1869M
*Choir, The: or, Union Collection* – 1832M
*Choral Harmony* – 1830M
*Choralist, The* – 1847M
*Glee Hive, The* – 1851M
*Hallelujah, The* – 1854M
*Handel & Haydn Society's Collection of Church
  Music* – 1822M
*Juvenile Lyre, The* – 1831M
*Juvenile Psalmist, The* – 1829M
*Lyra Sacra* – 1832M
*Manual of Christian Harmony* – 1832M
*Manual of Christian Psalmody* – 1831M
*Manual of the Boston Academy of Music* – 1834M
*Mason's Handbook of Psalmody* –
  1852M
*Missionary Hymn* – 1823N
*Modern Psalmist, The* – 1839M
*Musical Letters from Abroad* – 1853M
*Musical Notation in a Nutshell* – 1854M
*National Psalmist, The* – 1848M
*New Carmina Sacra, The* – 1852M
*Odeon, The: Collection of Secular Melodies* –
  1837M
*People's Tune Book, The* – 1860M
*Pestalozzian Music Teacher, The* –
  1871M
*Psaltery, The* – 1845M
*Sabbath School Songs* – 1833M
*Sabbath School Harp, The* – 1837M
*Sacred Harp, The* – 1835M
*Sacred Melodies* – 1833M
*Union Hymns* – 1834M
*Vocalist, The* – 1844M
Mason, Luther Whiting – 1818F, 1853I, 1856I,
  1864I, 1880K, 1896G
Mason, Marilyn – 1925F, 1946I
Mason, Thomas
  *Devotional Hymns & Religious Poems* – 1850M
Mason, Timothy B.
  *Ohio Sacred Harp, The* – 1834M
Mason, William G. – 1829F, 1846H, 1855K, 1869J,
  1908G
  *Method for Piano, A* – 1867M
  *Pianoforte Technics* – 1878M
Mason Dixon – 1988C
Masselos, William – 1920F, 1939H, 1976I, 1992G
Masser, Michael
  *Theme from Mahogany* – 1976E
Massey, Andrew John – 1986I, 1987I
Massey, Louise
  *My Adobe Hacienda* – 1947E

---

❁

## Cultivated/Art Music Scene
F *Births*    G *Deaths*    H *Debuts*    I *New Positions*    J *Honors and Awards*
K *Biographical*    L *Musical Beginnings*    M *Publications*    N *Compositions*

Master Jazz Recording Co. – 1967C
Masterson, Valerie – 1980H
Mastersounds Jazz Quartet – 1957C
Masterwork Chorus & Orchestra – 1955L
Mastilović, Danica – 1963H, 1975H
Masur, Kurt – 1974HK, 1993J
Masurok, Yuri – 1977H
Mata, Edouardo – 1974I, 1977I, 1988K, 1995G
Material – 1979C
Material Issue – 1986C
Materna, Amalie – 1882H, 1885H
Mates, Julian
   *American Musical State before 1800, The –*
    *1962M*
Mather, Cotton
   *Accomplished Singer..., The –* 1721M
Mathews, William S. B. – 1837F, 1878I,
   1912G
   *Great in Music, The –* 1902M
   *How to Understand Music –* 1888M
   *Hundred Years of Music in America, A –* 1889M
   *Music, Its Ideals & Methods –* 1897M
   *Outline of Music Form, An –* 1868M
   *Popular History of the Art of Music, A –*
    1891M
   *Primer of Musical Forms –* 1890M
   *Pronouncing & Defining Dictionary of Music –*
    1896M
Mathis, Edith – 1970H
Mathis, Johnny – 1935A, 1978E
Mathushek Piano Co. – 1863L
Matorin, Vladimir – 1994H
Mattea, Kathy – 1959A, 1990C
Mattfeld, Julius
   *Folk Music of the Western Hemisphere –* 1925D
Mattfeld, Marie – 1901H
Matthews, Andrea – 1956F, 1984H
Matthews, Artie – 1888A, 1958B
   *Weary Blues –* 1915E
Matthews, W. S. B.
   *Hundred Years of Music in America, A –* 1899M
Mattila, Karita – 1983H, 1990H
Mattox, Janis – 1949F
Matzenauer, Margarete – 1911H, 1918K, 1963G
Matzka, George – 1876I
Maubourg, Jeanne – 1909H
Mauceri, John – 1945F, 1984H
Maultsby, Nancy – 1993J
Maurel, Victor – 1873H, 1894H, 1909K
Maurer, Marie – 1902H
Mauriat, Paul – 1968E
Mauro, Ermanno – 1975H, 1978H
Mavericks, The – 1962C
Maw, Nicholas
   *Odyssey –* 1994N
   *Piano Trio –* 1991N
Maxfield, Richard
   *5 Movements for Orchestra –* 1959N
Maxi Priest – 1990E

Maxim, Abraham – 1773F, 1829G
   *Oriental Harmony –* 1802M
May, Billy – 1916A
May, Billy, Band – 1950C
Maybrick, Michael – 1884H
Mayer, Oscar, Auditorium (Madison) – 1980L
Mayer, Steven – 1992J
Mayer, William – 1925F
   *Death in the Family, A –* 1983N
   *Enter Ariel –* 1980N
   *Eve of St. Agnes –* 1967N
   *Inner & Outer Strings –* 1982N
   *Octagon –* 1971N
   *Of Rivers & Trains –* 1988N
   *One Christmas Long Ago –* 1983N
   *Overture for an American –* 1958N
   *Passage –* 1981N
   *Snow Queen –* 1963N
   *Spring Came On Forever –* 1975N
Mayfield, Curtis – 1942A
Mayfield, Percy – 1920A, 1984B
Maylath, Heinrich – 1867K, 1883G
Maynor, Dorothy – 1910F, 1939H
Mayr, Richard – 1927H
Mazura, Franz – 1980H
M'Boom – 1970C
MC5 – 1967C
McAfee, Rhonda Jackson – 1956F, 1984H
McAllester, David – 1916F
McArthur, Edwin – 1907F, 1941HK, 1950H
McAuliffe, Leon – 1912A, 1988B
McBeth, W. Francis – 1933F
   *Band Suite No. 2 –* 1962N
   *Chant & Jubilee –* 1963N
   *Five Projections for Piano –* 1962N
   *Symphony No. 1 –* 1955N
   *Symphony No. 2 –* 1957N
   *Symphony No. 3 –* 1963N
   *Symphony No. 4 –* 1970N
   *Three Pieces for Piano –* 1958N
McBride, Robert – 1911F, 1942J, 1957I
   *Country Music Fantasy –* 1965N
   *Mexican Rhapsody –* 1934N
   *Pumpkin Eater's Little Fugue –* 1952N
   *Symphonic Melody –* 1968N
McCabe, Robin – 1949F, 1975H
McCall, C. W. – 1976E
McCalla, James – 1946F, 1985J
   *Jazz: A Listener's Guide* -1982D
McCarthy, Albert
   *Big Band Jazz –* 1974D
McCarthy, Daniel
   *Hat Me Father Wore, The –* 1876E
McCarthy, Joseph – 1885A, 1943B
   *They Go Wild, Simply Wild Over Me –* 1917E
McCartney, Paul – 1971E, 1973E, 1974E, 1980E,
   1983E
McCauley, Barry – 1950F, 1977H, 1985H, 1980J
McCawley, Leon – 1993J

---

❁

Vernacular/Commercial Music Scene
A *Births*   B *Deaths*   C *Biographical*   D *Publications*
E *Representative Pieces*

❁

### Cultivated/Art Music Scene

McKay, George Frederick (continued)
*Evocation Symphony* – 1951N
*Organ Sonata No. 1* – 1930N
*Pioneers* – 1942N
*Suite on 16th C. Hymns* – 1960N
*Violin Concerto* – 1940N
McKee, M.
*Beale Street Black & Blue* – 1993D
McKinley, Carl – 1895F, 1966G
*Blue Flower, The* – 1920N
*Indian Summer Idyll* – 1917N
*Masquerade* – 1925N
*String Quartet in One Mvt.* – 1942N
McKinley, Ray – 1995B
McKinley, William – 1895A
McKinley, William Thomas
*Boston Overture* – 1986N
*Concert Variations, Violin & Viola* – 1993N
*6 Romances* – 1990N
*Viola Concerto* – 1993N
McKinney, William – 1969B
McKinney's Cotton Pickers – 1926C
McLaughlin, Marie – 1984H, 1986H
McLean, Barton – 1938F
*Electric Sinfonia* – 1982N
*Genesis* – 1973N
*Last Ten Minutes, The* – 1982N
*Sorcerer Revisited, The* – 1975N
McLean, Don – 1945A, 1972E
McLean, Priscilla – 1942F
*Dance of Dawn* – 1974N
*Invisible Chariots* – 1977N
*Night Images* – 1973N
*Spectra I* – 1971N
*Spectra II* – 1972N
McLennan, John – 1985J
McMurtry, James – 1962A
McNabb, Michael – 1952F
*Dreamsong* – 1978N
*Love in the Asylum* – 1981N
*Solstice* – 1975N
McNair, Barbara – 1939A
McNair, Sylvia – 1956F, 1980H, 1990J, 1992H
McNally, John J. – 1931B
McPartland, Jimmy – 1907A, 1991B
McPhatter, Clyde – 1933A, 1972B
McPhee, Colin – 1900F, 1926K, 1931K, 1934K,
1954J, 1964G
*Four Iroquois Dances* – 1944N
*Four Piano Sketches, Op. 1* – 1916N
*Kinesis* – 1930N
*Piano Concerto No. 1* – 1920N
*Piano Concerto No. 2* – 1923N
*Sea Shanty Suite* – 1929N
*Symphony No. 1* – 1930N
*Symphony No. 2* – 1957N
*Symphony No. 3* – 1962N
*Tabuh-Tabuhan* – 1936N
*Transitions* – 1954N

McRae, Barry
*Jazz Handbook, The* – 1990D
McRae, Carmen – 1922A, 1994B
McShann, Jay "Hootie" – 1909A
McVea, Jack
*Open the Door, Richard* – 1947E
Meacham, F. W.
*American Patrol* – 1891E
Meacham, Horace – 1789F, 1861G
Meacham, John, Jr. – 1785F, 1844G
Mead, Elizabeth – 1979H
Mead, Olive, String Quartet – 1902L
Mead, Smith
*Hymns & Spiritual Songs* – 1805M
Meader, George – 1888F, 1911H, 1919H, 1921H
Meadow Brook Festival (MI) – 1964L
Meadowmount School for String Players – 1944L
Meanstreak – 1985C
Meatloaf (Marvin Aday) – 1948A, 1993E
Meat Puppets, The – 1980C
Mechanical Orguinette Co. – 1878L
Mechem, Kirke – 1925F
*Symphony No. 1* – 1959N
*Symphony No. 2* – 1967N
*Tartuffe* – 1980N
Medeiros, Glenn – 1990E
Medley, Bill – 1987E
Meet the Composer Program – 1974L
Megadeth – 1983C
Mehlig, Anna – 1869H
Mehta, Mehli – 1959K
Mehta, Zubin – 1962I, 1965H, 1978I, 1980J
Meier, Johanna – 1938F, 1969H, 1976H, 1981K
*Meier, Waltraud* – 1985H, 1987H
Meignen, Léopold – 1828K, 1873G
*Deluge, The* – 1856N
*Intro. & Variations, "Tho' You Leave Me"* –
1842N
*Symphonie Militaire* – 1845N
Meineke, Christopher
*Funeral March for General Lafayette* – 1834N
*Grand National March for General Jackson* –
1829N
*Harlem Waltz, The* – 1843N
*President Taylor's Inauguration March* – 1849N
*Rail Road March, The* – 1828N
*Te Deum* – 1821N
*Variations on "Araby's Daughter"* – 1826N
*Variations on "Au Clair de la Lune"* – 1827N
*Variations on "Brignal Banks"* – 1827N
*Variations on "Le Petit Tambour"* – 1828N
*Variations on "Malbrouk"* – 1829N
*Variations on Mozart's "Non Più Andrai"* –
1828N
*Variations on "My Heart & Lute"* – 1827N
*Variations on Weber's "Hunter's Chorus"* –
1826N
Meinken, Fred
*Wabash Blues* – 1922E

---

❖

---

**Vernacular/Commercial Music Scene**
A *Births*    B *Deaths*    C *Biographical*    D *Publications*
E *Representative Pieces*

Melanie (Safka) – 1947A, 1971E
Melba, Nellie – 1893H
Melbye, Mikael – 1983H
Melchior, Lauritz – 1926H, 1947K, 1950K, 1973G
Melis, Carmen – 1909H
Mellencamp, John – 1951A
Mellers, Wilfrid
  *Angels of the Night* – 1986D
  *Music in a New Found Land* – 1965D
Mello-Kings – 1956C
Melodears (Ina Ray Hutton) – 1934C
Melton, James – 1904F, 1932H, 1942H, 1961G
Melville Clark Piano Co. – 1900L
Melvin, Harold, and the Blue Notes – 1955C
Memphis, Tennessee
  *Beethoven Club – 1888L*
  *Greenlaw Opera House – 1866L*
  *Opera Theater – 1956L*
  *Blues Festival – 1966C*
  *Symphony Orchestra I – 1909L*
  *Symphony Orchestra II – 1947L*
Memphis Five, Original – 1917C
Memphis Jug Band – 1927C
Memphis Slim – 1915A, 1988B
Memphis Students – 1905C
Men at Work – 1982E, 1983E
Mendel, Arthur – 1905F, 1979G
Mendelssohn Quintet – 1858L
Mendocino Music Festival – 1987L
Meneely & Co., Bell Foundry – 1826L
Meneses, António – 1985H
Menga, Robert – 1966J
Mengelberg, Willem – 1905H, 1921I
Menges, Isolde – 1916H
Menken, Alan
  *Beauty & the Beast* – 1994E
  *Little Mermaid, The* – 1990E
  *Little Shop of Horrors* – 1982E
Mennin, Peter – 1923F, 1946J, 1947I, 1958I, 1962I,
  1970J, 1983G
  *Cantata de Virtute – 1969N*
  *Concertato "Moby Dick" – 1952N*
  *Flute Concerto – 1983N*
  *Piano Concerto – 1958N*
  *Piano Sonata – 1963N*
  *String Quartet No. 1 – 1941N*
  *String Quartet No. 2 – 1951N*
  *Symphony No. 1 – 1941N*
  *Symphony No. 2 – 1944N*
  *Symphony No. 3 – 1946N*
  *Symphony No. 4 – 1948N*
  *Symphony No. 5 – 1950N*
  *Symphony No. 6 – 1953N*
  *Symphony No. 7 – 1963N*
  *Symphony No. 8 – 1973N*
  *Symphony No. 9 – 1981N*
  *Violin Concerto – 1956N*
Mennini, Louis – 1920F, 1949J
  *Mass – 1953N*

*Rope, The* – 1955N
*String Quartet* – 1961N
*Symphony No. 1* – 1960N
*Symphony No. 2* – 1963N
*Well, The* – 1951N
Menotti, Gian Carlo – 1927K, 1935K, 1945J, 1984J,
  1991J
  *Amahl & the Night Visitors* – 1951N
  *Apocalypse* – 1952N
  *Bride From Pluto, A* – 1982N
  *Canti della lontananza* – 1967N
  *Consul, The* – 1949N
  *Dernier Sauvage, Le* – 1963N
  *Doublebass Concerto* – 1983N
  *For the Death of Orpheus* – 1990N
  *Goya* – 1986N
  *Help, Help, the Globolinks* – 1968N
  *Hero, The* – 1976N
  *Island God, The* – 1942N
  *Labyrinth* – 1963N
  *Loca, La* – 1979N
  *Maria Golovin* – 1958N
  *Martin's Lie* – 1964N
  *Medium, The* – 1945N
  *Most Important Man, The* – 1971N
  *Old Maid & the Thief, The* – 1939N
  *Piano Concerto No. 1* – 1945N
  *Piano Concerto No. 2* – 1982N
  *Saint of Bleecker Street, The* – 1953N
  *Sebastian* – 1944N
  *Singing Child, The* – 1993N
  *Symphony No. 1* – 1976N
  *Tamu-Tamu* – 1973N
  *Telephone, The* – 1946N
  *Triplo Concerto a tre* – 1970N
  *Unicorn, the Gorgon & the Manticore* – 1956N
  *Variations on a Theme of Schumann* – 1931N
  *Violin Concerto in a* – 1952N
Mentzer, Susanne – 1957F, 1981H, 1989H
Menudo – 1977C
Menuhin, Hephzibah – 1920F, 1928H, 1981G
Menuhin, Jeremy – 1951F
Menuhin, Yehudi – 1916F, 1924H, 1966J, 1985J,
  1986J
Mercer, Jesse
  *Cluster, The* (Baptist) – 1810M
Mercer, Johnny – 1909A, 1976B
  *Ac-cent-tchu-ate the Positive* – 1944E
  *Dream* – 1944E
  *I'm an Old Cowhand* – 1936E
  *Li'l Abner* – 1956E
  *On the Atchison, Topeka & Santa Fe* – 1946E
  *Top Banana* – 1951E
Mercer, Mabel – 1900A, 1938C, 1983C,
  1984B
Mercurio, Steven – 1956F, 1991I
Mercury Records – 1945C
Merli, Francesco – 1932H
Merman, Ethel – 1909A, 1984B

---

## Cultivated/Art Music Scene

F *Births*   G *Deaths*   H *Debuts*   I *New Positions*   J *Honors and Awards*
K *Biographical*   L *Musical Beginnings*   M *Publications*   N *Compositions*

Merola, Gaetano – 1899K, 1923I, 1953G
Mérö, Yolanda – 1909H
Merriam, A. P.
  *Bibliography of Jazz, A* – 1954D
Merrill, A.
  *Wesleyan Harp, The* – 1834M
Merrill, Bob – 1921A
  *Carnival* – 1961E
  *Henry, Sweet Henry* – 1967E
  *How Much Is That Doggie in the Window* – 1953E
  *If I Knew You Were Comin', I'd've Baked a Cake*
    – 1950E
  *My Truly, Truly Fair* – 1951E
  *New Girl in Town* – 1957E
  *Take Me Along* – 1959E
Merrill, David
  *Psalmodist's Best Companion* – 1799M
Merrill, George
  *How Will I Know* – 1986E
Merrill, Helen – 1930A
Merrill, Richard
  *Musical Practitioner, The* – 1797M
Merrill, Robert – 1917F, 1944H, 1945H
Merrimack Lyric Opera (MA) – 1985L
Merriman, Nan – 1920F, 1942H
  *New Look at 16th Century Counterpoint, A* –
    1982M
Merritt, A. Tillman – 1902F, 1932I
Merritt, Chris – 1952F, 1981H
Merry-Go-Round – 1966C
Merryman, Marjorie – 1991J
Mertons, William – 1897H
Merwe, Peter van der
  *Origins of the Popular Style* – 1989D
Merz, Karl – 1861I
  *Elements of Harmony & Composition* – 1881M
  *Katie Dean* – 1882N
  *Last Will & Testament* – 1882N
  *Musical Hints for the Millions* – 1875M
  *Runaway Flirt, The* – 1868N
  *Mesplé, Mady* – 1973H
  *Messiah Festival (KS)* – 1882L
  *Messiter, Arthur*
  *Literature of Music* – 1900M
  *Marion, Hymn Tune* – 1883N
Mester, Jorge – 1967I, 1968JK, 1971I, 1984I
Metal Church – 1984C
Metallica – 1981C
Metcalf, Frank – 1865F, 1945G
  *American Psalmody* – 1917M
  *American Writers & Compilers of Sacred Music* –
    1925M
  *Stories of Hymn Tunes* – 1928M
Metcalf, Samuel L.
  *Kentucky Harmonist, The* – 1817M
Meters, The – 1967C
Metheny, Pat – 1955A
*Metronome, The* – 1885L
Metropolitan Opera Auditions – 1936L

Metropolitan Opera Broadcasts – 1931L
Metropolitan Opera Guild – 1935L
Metropolitan Opera House (Lincoln Center) – 1966L
Metropolitan Opera Studio – 1960L
Metternich, Josef – 1953H
Metz, Julius
  *Alliance Waltz* – 1835N
  *Clermont Waltz with Variations* – 1820N
  *Tyrolean Waltz with Variations* – 1835N
  *Variations on the Vesper Hymn* – 1822N
  *West Point March* – 1825N
Metz, Theodore
  *Hot Time In the Old Town Tonight, A* – 1896E
Meyer, Conrad, Piano Maker – 1829L
Meyer, George W. – 1884A, 1959B
  *For Me & My Gal* – 1917E
Meyer, Hazel
  *Gold in Tin Pan Alley, The* – 1958D
Meyer, Joseph – 1894A, 1987B
  *California, Here I Come* – 1924E
  *Crazy Rhythm* – 1928E
Meyer, Kerstin – 1960H
Meyer, Leonard B. – 1845H, 1918k
  *Emotion & Meaning in Music* – 1956M
  *Rhythmic Structure of Music, The* – 1960M
  *Style & Music: Theory, History & Ideology* –
    1989M
Meyerhoff, Joseph – 1985J
Meyerhoff, Joseph, Symphony Hall – 1982L
Meyers, Anne Akiko – 1970F
Meyerson, Janice – 1950F
Meyerson, Morton, Symphony Center – 1989L
Mezzrow, Mezz
  *Really the Blues* – 1946D
MFSB – 1974E
MGM Records – 1946C
M'Guckin, Barton – 1887H
  *Miami, Florida*
  *Center for the Fine Arts* – 1984L
  *City Ballet* – 1986L
  *Classic Opera of Miami* – 1975L
  *Greater M. Opera Association* – 1941L
  *Greater M. Symphony Orchestra* – 1965L
  *Gusman, Maurice, Philharmonic Hall* – 1972L
Miami Beach Symphony Orchestra – 1953L
Miami Latin Boys – 1973C
Miami Sound Machine – 1975E
Michael, David Moritz – 1795K, 1815K
  *Psalm 103* – 1808N
Michael, George – 1987E, 1988E, 1990E, 1992E
Michael, Hermann – 1984H
Michaels, Lee – 1945A
Michaels-Moore, Anthony – 1989H
Michalak, Thomas – 1977I, 1986G
Michalski, Raymond – 1978G
Michigan State U. Music Dept. – 1927L
Michigan Opera Theater – 1971L
Mid-America Jazz Festival – 1982C
Midler, Bette – 1945A, 1989E

Midori – 1982HK
Midori Foundation – 1992L
Midwest National Band & Orchestra Clinic –
1947L
Miedél, Rainer – 1976I
Mielke, Antonia – 1890H
Migenes, Julia – 1945F, 1965H, 1979H
Mighty Blue Kings – 1994C
Mighty Clouds of Joy – 1960C
Mike and the Mechanics – 1989E
Milanov, Michail – 1995H
Milanov, Zinka – 1937H, 1977I
Milburn, Ellsworth – 1938F
Mildenberg, Albert – 1878F, 1918G
   *Love's Locksmith* – 1912N
   *Vathek, Op. 56* – 1903N
   *Wood Witch, The* – 1903N
Miles, Alastair – 1993H
Miles, Alfred H.
   *Anchors Aweigh* – 1906E
Miles, Barry – 1947A
Miles, Buddy – 1946A
Miles, C. Austin
   *I Come to the Garden Alone* – 1912N
Miles, Lizzie – 1895A, 1963B
Milestone Records – 1966C
Miley, Bubber – 1903A, 1932B
Milhaud, Darius – 1922K, 1940K, 1971K
   *Aspen Serenade* – 1957N
   *Kentuckiana* – 1948N
   *Petite Suite* – 1955N
   *Piano Concerto No. 2* – 1941N
   *Piano Sonata No. 2* – 1949N
   *String Quartet No. 15* – 1949N
   *Symphony No. 2* – 1944N
   *Symphony No. 3* – 1946N
   *Symphonies 6 & 7* – 1955N
Milhaud, Darius, Archive (Mills) – 1985L
Millard, Harrison – 1829F, 1895G
Millenium – 1967C
Miller & Beecham, Publishers – 1853L
Miller, Henry, & Sons, Piano Co. – 1863L
Miller, Arthur – 1984C
Miller, Dayton
   *Anecdotal History of the Science of Sound* –
   1935M
   *Science of Musical Sounds, The* – 1916M
Miller, Glenn – 1904A, 1944B
   *Method for Orchestral Arranging* – 1943D
   *Moonlight Cocktail* – 1942E
   *Moonlight Serenade* – 1939E
Miller, Glenn, Band – 1937C
Miller, Marilyn – 1936B
Miller, Mildred – 1924F, 1949H, 1951H
Miller, Mitch – 1911A
Miller, Robert – 1957H
Miller, Roger – 1936A, 1964C, 1965C, 1992B
   *Big River: Adventures of Huckleberry Finn* –
   1985E

Miller, Steve – 1943A
   *Abracadabra* – 1982E
   *Joker, The* – 1973E
Miller, Steve, Band – 1966C, 1974E, 1976E, 1982E
Millett, William E., & Sons – 1834L
Milli Vanilli – 1989E
Millo, Aprile – 1958F, 1977J, 1978J, 1980H, 1984H,
1985J
Mills Blue Rhythm Band – 1930C
Mills Brothers – 1930C
Mills College Music Dept. – 1894L
Mills Music Publishers – 1919L
Mills, Charles – 1914F
   *Crazy Horse Symphony* – 1958N
   *Piano Sonata No. 1* – 1941N
   *Piano Sonata No. 2* – 1942N
   *String Quartet No. 1* – 1939N
   *String Quartet No. 2* – 1942N
   *String Quartet No. 3* – 1943N
   *Symphonic Ode* – 1976N
   *Symphony No. 1* – 1941N
   *Symphony No. 2* – 1942N
   *Symphony No. 5* – 1980N
   *Theme & Variations* – 1957N
   *30 Penitential Preludes* – 1945N
Mills, Eric – 1953F, 1978H, 1988H
Mills, Frederick A.
   *Red Wing* – 1907E
Mills, Irving – 1884A, 1985B
Mills, Frederick A. "Kerry" – 1869A, 1948B
   *Any Old Port in a Storm* – 1908E
   *At a Georgia Camp Meeting* – 1897E
   *Kerry Mills' Cake Walk* – 1915E
   *Let Bygones Be Bygones* – 1897E
   *Meet Me in St. Louis* – 1904E
   *Rufus On Parade* – 1895E
   *Whistling Rufus* – 1899E
Mills, Mary – 1988H, 1994H
Mills, Sebastian Bach – 1856K, 1859H
Mills, Stephanie – 1959A
Milnes, Sherrill – 1935F, 1965H
Milsap, Ronnie – 1944A, 1974C, 1976C, 1981C,
1985C
Milstein, Nathan – 1929H, 1942K, 1983J, 1987J,
1992G
Milwaukee, Wisconsin
   *Civic Orchestra* – 1921L
   *College of Music* – 1874L
   *Conservatory of Music* – 1878L
   *Grand Opera House* – 1871L
   *Liederkranz* – 1878L
   *Liedertafel* – 1858L
   *Music Hall* – 1864L
   *Musikverein* – 1851L
   *Opera Co.* – 1932L
   *Performing Arts Center* – 1969L
   *School of Music* – 1884L
   *Symphony Orchestra* – 1958L
   *Summerfest* – 1968C

---

### Cultivated/Art Music Scene

F *Births*   G *Deaths*   H *Debuts*   I *New Positions*   J *Honors and Awards*
K *Biographical*   L *Musical Beginnings*   M *Publications*   N *Compositions*

Mimaroglu, Ilhan – 1955K
  *Agony* – 1966N
  *Twelve Preludes for Piano* – 1967N
Mimms, Garnet, and the Enchanters –
  1963C
Mindfunk – 1990C
Mindwarp, Zodiac, & the Love Reaction – 1985C
Mineo, Sal – 1939A, 1976B
Mingus, Charlie – 1922A, 1979B
Minneapolis, Minnesota
  *Academy of Music* – *1871L*
  *Auditorium (Lyceum)* – *1905L*
  *Orchestral Hall* – *1974L*
  *Pence Opera House* – *1867L*
  *School of Fine Arts* – *1886L*
  *Symphony Orchestra* – *1903L*
Ministry – 1981C
Mink Deville – 1974C
Minnelli, Liza – 1946A
Minnesota Composers Forum – 1973L
Minnesota Opera Co. – 1962L
Minnigerode, M.
  *Whiffenpoof Song, The* – 1911E
Minot Opera Ass'n – 1975L
Minton, Yvonne – 1970H, 1973H
Mintz, David S.
  *Spiritual Song Book* – 1805M
Mintz, Shlomo – 1973H
Minutemen, The – 1979C
Mirabella, Giovanni – 1883H
Miracles, The – 1955C, 1970E, 1976E
Miranda, Carmen – 1939C, 1955B
Miron, Emmy – 1888H
Mirtova, Elena – 1991H
Mischakoff, Mischa – 1981G
Mischakoff, Mischa – 1921K, 1927K
Misfits – 1977C
Missing Persons – 1980C
Mission of Burma – 1979C
Mississippi Opera Ass'n – 1945L
*Mississippi Rag: The Voice of Traditional Jazz &*
  *Ragtime* – 1974C
Mississippi River Festival – 1969C
Mister Big – 1988C
Mitchell, Chad, Trio – 1958C
Mitchell, Guy – 1927A, 1956E, 1959E
Mitchell, Howard – 1911F, 1949I, 1988G
Mitchell, Joni – 1943A
Mitchell, Leona – 1949F, 1972H, 1975H
Mitchell, Nahum – 1769F, 1853G
  *Brattle Street Collection* – 1810M
  *Templi Carmina* – 1812M
Mitchell, Nellie Brown, Concert Co. – 1886L
Mitchell, Sidney B. – 1888A, 1942B
Mitchell, William J. – 1906F
  *Elementary Harmony* – 1939M
Mitropoulos, Dimitri – 1936HI, 1946K, 1949I
Mittelhauser, Albert – 1888H
Mobile Opera Guild (AL) – 1946L

Mobo Band – 1983C
Moby Grape – 1966C
Modarelli, Antonio – 1926I
Modern Jazz Quartet – 1951C
*Modern Liturgy* – 1973L
Modern Lovers – 1979C
Modern Music Co. – 1945C
Modern Music Masters Society – 1952L
Modern Music Society – 1912L
Mödl, Martha – 1957H
Mödlinger, Ludwig – 1888H
Modugno, Domenico – 1958E
Moe and the Mavericks – 1962C
Moennig, William & Son – 1909L
Moevs, Robert – 1920F, 1952J, 1956J, 1964I
  *Concerto Grosso* – 1968N
  *Main-travelled Roads* – 1973N
  *Pandora* – 1983N
  *Piano Sonata* – 1950N
  *Piano Sonatina* – 1947N
  *Prometheus* – 1980N
  *String Quartet* – 1957N
  *Symphonic Piece No. 5* – 1984N
  *Three Symphonic Pieces* – 1955N
  *14 Variations for Orchestra* – 1952N
Moffatt, Hugh – 1948A
Moffo, Anna – 1932F, 1955H, 1957H, 1959H, 1984I
Moiseiwitsch, Benno – 1919H
Moldenhauer, Hans – 1938K, 1987G
Mole, Irving "Miff" – 1898A
Molinari, Bernadino – 1928H
Moll, Kurt – 1974H, 1978H
Mollenhauer, Eduard – 1853K, 1914G
  *Corsican Bride, The* – 1861N
  *Manhattan Beach* – 1878N
Mollenhauer, Emil – 1855F, 1889I, 1892I, 1899I,
  1927G
Mollenhauer, Frederic – 1853K
Mollenhauer, Frederic, Studio of Music –
  1865L
Mollenhauer, Heinrich, Conservatory – 1867L
Moller, John Christopher – 1785K, 1786I, 1790HK,
  1796IG
  *Dank und Gebet* – 1794N
  *Quartet, Glass Harmonica & Strings* – 1795N
  *Sinfonia* – 1793N
Moller & Capron Music Store & School – 1793L
Möller, M. P., Organ Builder – 1875L
Molly Hatchet – 1975C
Monaco, Jimmy – 1885A, 1945B
  *You Made Me Love You* – 1913E
Money, Eddie – 1949A
Monk, Meredith – 1943F, 1995J
  *Atlas* – 1991N, 1992N
Monk, Meredith, Vocal Ensemble – 1978L
Monk, Thelonious – 1917A, 1982B
  *Bolivar Blues* – 1962N
  *Criss Cross* – 1951N
  *Five Spot Blues* – 1962N

---

✿

---

*Misterioso* – 1948N
*'Round Midnight* – 1957N
Monk, Thelonious, Big Band – 1959C
Monk, Thelonious, Jr. – 1950A
Monkees, The – 1965C, 1966E, 1967E
Monotones – 1955C
Monroe, Bill – 1911A, 1970C, 1988C, 1995C
Monroe, Vaughn – 1912A, 1973B
Monroe, Vaughn, Band – 1940C
Montague, Diana – 1984H, 1987H
Montana String Quartet – 1957L
Montana, Patsy – 1914A
Montarsolo, Paolo – 1974H
Monterey International Pop Festival – 1967C
Monterey Jazz Festival – 1958C
Monteux, Pierre – 1916K, 1917HI, 1919I, 1936I,
    1942K
Montgomery, Dave – 1870A
Montgomery, Elizabeth
    *Story Behind Popular Songs, The* – 1958D
Montgomery, Kathryn – 1952F, 1972H, 1985II
Montgomery, Little Brother – 1906A
Montgomery, Wes – 1923A, 1968B
Montgomery, Wes, Trio – 1959C
Montoya, Carlos – 1993G
Montreux-Detroit International Jazz Festival –
    1980C
Montrose – 1974C
Montrose, Percy
    *Oh, My Darling Clementine* – 1884E
Moody, James – 1925A
Moody, James, Sextet – 1951C
Moog, R. A., Co. – 1954L
Moog, Robert – 1934F
Moon, David
    *Three Etudes for Piano* – 1982N
Moonglows – 1952C
Moore, Carman
    *Franklin & Eleanore* – 1989E
Moore, Douglas – 1893F, 1926I, 1940I, 1967J,
    1969G
    *Ballad of Baby Doe, The* – 1956N
    *Carry Nation* – 1966N
    *Devil & Daniel Webster* – 1938N
    *Farm Journal* – 1947N
    *From Madrigal to Modern Music* – 1042M
    *Giants in the Earth* – 1949N
    *Headless Horseman, The* – 1936N
    *In Memoriam* – 1943N
    *Listening to Music* – 1932M
    *Moby Dick* – 1928N
    *Overture on an American Tune* – 1932N
    *Pageant of P. T. Barnum* – 1924N
    *Piano Suite* – 1948N
    *String Quartet* – 1933N
    *Symphony in Autumn, A* – 1930N
    *Symphony No. 2 in A* – 1945N
    *White Wings* – 1935N
    *Wings of the Dove, The* – 1961N

Moore, Grace – 1898F, 1928H, 1947G
Moore, Henry E. – 1803F, 1841G
    *New Hampshire Collection* – 1835M
Moore, John W. – 1807F, 1889G
    *Complete Encyclopedia of Music...* – 1852M
    *Dictionary of Musical Information* – 1876M
    *Sacred Minstrel* – 1842M
    *Sentimental Songbook, The* – 1878M
Moore, Mary Carr – 1873F
    *Beyond These Hills* – 1924N
    *David Rizzio* – 1928N
    *Flaming Arrow, The* – 1920N
    *Flutes of Jade Happiness* – 1933N
    *Harmony* – 1917N
    *Ka-mi-a-kin* – 1930N
    *Legende Provençule* – 1935N
    *Leper, The* – 1912N
    *Memories* – 1914N
    *Narcissa* – 1911N
    *Piano Concerto* – 1934N
    *Rubios, Los* – 1931N
    *String Quartet in G* – 1926N
    *String Quartet in F* – 1930N
Moore, Melba – 1945A
Moore, Samuel – 1935A
Moore, Undine Smith – 1905F
Moore, Victor – 1962B
Moore, William
    *Columbian Harmony* – 1825M
Moots, Hezekiah
    *Province Harmony, The* – 1809M
Mora, Helene
    *Kathleen* – 1894E
Moran, Karl – 1888H
Moran, John
    *Jack Benny* – 1979N
    *From the Towers of the Moon* – 1991N
    *Manson Family, The* – 1990N
Moran, Peter K. – 1817K, 1831G
    *Carrier Pigeon, The* – 1822N
    *National Guards March & Rondo* – 1830N
    *Variations on "Ach du lieber Augustin"* –
        1817N
    *Variations on "Ah Beauteous Maid"* –
        1826N
    *Variations on "Coal Black Rose"* – 1835N
    *Variations on "Kinlock of Kinlock"* –
        1825N
    *Variations on Stantz Waltz* – 1817N
    *Variations on a Swiss Waltz* – 1810N
Moran, Robert – 1937F
    *Desert of Roses* – 1992N
    *Dracula Diary, The* – 1994N
Morath, Max – 1926A
Moravec, Ivan – 1964H
Moravec, Paul – 1957F, 1984J
    *Missa Miserere* – 1981N
Moravian Music Foundation – 1956L
Morbid Angel – 1984C

---

❄

## Cultivated/Art Music Scene

F *Births*     G *Deaths*     H *Debuts*     I *New Positions*     J *Honors and Awards*
K *Biographical*     L *Musical Beginnings*     M *Publications*     N *Compositions*

Mordden, Ethan
   *Demented: The World of the Opera Diva* – 1985M
   *Hollywood Musical, The* – 1983D
   *Opera in the Twentieth Century* – 1978M
Mordred – 1985C
Morel, Jean – 1955H
Morell, Barry – 1927F, 1955H, 1958H
Morelli, Carlo – 1932H, 1935H
Moren-Olden, Fanny – 1888H
Morena, Berta – 1908H
Moret, Neil (Charles Daniels) – 1878A, 1943B
   *Chloe* – 1927E
   *Hiawatha* – 1901E
   *She's Funny That Way* – 1928E
Morey, Larry
   *Snow White & the 7 Dwarfs* – 1937E
Morgan, Beverly – 1952F
Morgan, Dennis – 1994B
Morgan, George – 1975B
Morgan, Helen – 1900A, 1941B
Morgan, Jaye P. – 1932A
Morgan, John Paul – 1841F, 1867I
Morgan, Justin – 1747F, 1798G
Morgan, Lorrie – 1959A
Morgan, M. H.
   *Bless This House* – 1927E
Morgan, Maud – 1875H
Morgan, Michael – 1957F, 1982H
Morgan, Russ – 1904A, 1969B
Morgan, Russ, Band – 1936C
Morgana, Nina – 1920H
Morgenstern, Dan
   *Jazz People* – 1976D
Morini, Erika – 1921H, 1943K
Morissey, Bill – 1962A
Moroccos – 1952C
Moross, Jerome
   *Concerto, Flute & Strings* – 1978N
   *Gentlemen, Be Seated* – 1957N
   *Golden Apple, The* – 1954E
   *Last Judgment, The* – 1953N
   *Piano Sonata, 4 Hands* – 1975N
   *Sorry, Wrong Number* – 1977N
   *Symphony* – 1942N
   *Variations on a Waltz* – 1966N
Morricone, Enio
   *Wolf* – 1994E
Morris, Gary – 1948A
Morris, Harold C. – 1890F, 1922I, 1964G
   *American Epic* – 1942N
   *Contemporary American Music* – 1934M
   *Piano Concerto* – 1927N
   *String Quartet* – 1928N
   *Symphony No. 1, "Prospic"* – 1925N
   *Symphony No. 2, "Victory"* – 1943N
   *Symphony No. 3, "Amaranth"* – 1946N
   *Symphony No. 4* – 1952N
   *Violin Concerto* -1938N
Morris, James – 1947F, 1967H, 1971H

Morris, Joan – 1943F, 1973H, 1981I
Morris, Kenneth – 1917A
   *Just a Closer Walk with Thee* – 1940N
Morris, Robert – 1980I
   *Composition with Pitch-Classes* – 1987M
Morrison, Jim – 1943A, 1971B
Morrow, Buddy – 1919A
Morrow, Buddy, Band – 1951C
Morrow, Charlie – 1942F
Morse & Haviland, Publishers – 1905L
Morse Music Co. (NY) – 1897C
Morse Music Co. – 1910C
Morse, Charles H. – 1853F
Morse, H. W.
   *Dr. Syntax* – 1894E
   *Madame Piper* – 1884E
   *Wang* – 1891E
Morse, Theodore – 1873A, 1924B
   *Blue Bell* – 1904E
   *Daddy's Little Girl* – 1905E
   *Dear Old Girl* – 1903E
   *Down in Jungle Town* – 1908E
   *Hail, Hail, the Gang's All Here* – 1917E
   *M-O-T-H-E-R* – 1915E
   *Way Down in My Heart* – 1904E
Morse, Theodore, Publisher – 1898L
Morse, Woolson
   *Ask the Man in the Moon* – 1891E
   *Cinderella at School* – 1881E
   *Lost, Strayed or Stolen* – 1896E
   *Merry Monarch, The* – 1890E
   *Pretty Girl, A* – 1891E
Morton, Benny – 1907A
Morton, Jelly Roll – 1890A, 1917C, 1922C, 1941B
   *Black Bottom Stomp* – 1925E
   *Cannonball Blues* – 1926E
   *Grandpa's Spells* – 1911E
   *Jelly Roll Blues* – 1915E
   *Kansas City Stomp* – 1919E
   *New Orleans Blues* – 1902E
   *Pearls, The* – 1919E
Mosaic Records – 1983C
Mosca, Silvia – 1988H
Moscona, Nicola – 1937H, 1975G
Moseley, Carlos, Music Pavilion – 1990L
Moser, Edda – 1968H
Moser, Thomas – 1993H
Mosque Theater (Symphony Hall, Newark) – 1925L
Moss, Lawrence – 1927F
   *Ariel* – 1969N
   *Brute, The* – 1960N
   *Exchanges* – 1968N
   *Omaggio I* – 1966N
   *Orchestral Suite* – 1950N
   *Windows* – 1966N
Motels, The – 1972C
Moten, Bennie – 1894A, 1935B
   *Moten's Blues* – 1929E
Moten, Bennie, Trio – 1918C

---

### Vernacular/Commercial Music Scene
A *Births*    B *Deaths*    C *Biographical*    D *Publications*
E *Representative Pieces*

Mother Earth – 1966C
Mother Mallard's Portable Masterpiece Co. – 1969L
Mother's Finest – 1974C
Mothers of Invention – 1964C
Mötley Crüe – 1981C
Motown Records and Publishing Co. – 1960C
Mound City Blue Blowers – 1924C
Mountain – 1969C
Mozart in Monterey – 1987L
Mr. Big – 1992E
Mr. Mister – 1982C, 1985E, 1986E
MTV – 1981C
Mu Alpha Sinfonia Fraternity – 1898L
Mu Beta Psi Music Fraternity – 1925L
Mu Phi Epsilon Sorority – 1903L
Muck, Karl – 1906I, 1912I, 1919K
Muczynski, Robert – 1929F, 1958H, 1965I
  *Divertimento, Op. 2* – 1952N
  *Dream Cycle* – 1983N
  *Five Sketches for Piano* – 1952N
  *Flute Sonata* – 1959N
  *Masks* – 1990N
  *Maverick Pieces* – 1976N
  *Piano Concerto* – 1954N
  *Piano Sonata No. 1* – 1957N
  *Piano Sonata No. 2* – 1966N
  *Piano Sonata No. 3* – 1974N
  *Saxophone Concerto* – 1981N
  *Six Piano Preludes* – 1954N
  *Summer Journal, A* – 1964N
  *Symphonic Dialogues* – 1965N
  *Symphony, Op. 5* – 1953N
  *Woodwind Quintet* – 1981N
Muddy Waters – 1915A, 1983B
Mudge, Enoch
  *American Camp Meeting Hymn Book, The* –
    1817M
Mudhoney – 1988C
Mueller, Johann C. – 1803K, 1845G
Muir, Lewis F. – 1884A
  *Waiting for the Robert E. Lee* – 1911E
Muldaur, Maria – 1943A
Müller, George Godfrey – 1784K, 1821G
Müller, Maria – 1925H
Mullican, Moon – 1909A
Mulligan, Gerry – 1927A
Mulligan, Gerry, Quartet – 1952C
Mumma, Gordon – 1935F
  *Aleutian Displacement* – 1987NN
  *Beam* – 1969N
  *Conspiracy 8* – 1970N
  *Corbusier, Le* – 1965N
  *Cybersonic Cantilevers* – 1973N
  *Epoxy* – 1962N
  *Gestures II* – 1962N
  *Hornpipe* – 1967N
  *Megaton for Wm. Burroughs* – 1963N
  *Mesa* – 1966N
  *Passenger Pigeon 1776-1976* – 1976N

*Piano Suite* – 1959N
*Sinfonia* – 1960N
Munch, Charles – 1946H, 1949I, 1952K, 1968G
Münchinger, Karl – 1953H
Municipal Auditorium (Springfield, MA) – 1913L
Munsel, Patrice – 1925F, 1943H
Munz, Mieczyslaw – 1922H, 1976G
Muratore, Lucien – 1913H
Murgu, Corneliu – 1983H
Murphey, Michael M. – 1945A
Murphy, Elliott – 1949A
Murphy, Heidi Grant – 1989H
Murphy, J. B.
  *Nicodemus Johnson* – 1865E
Murphy, Rose – 1913A, 1989B
Murphy, Suzanne – 1985H
Murphy, Turk – 1915A, 1987B
Murphy, Walter
  *Fifth of Beethoven, A* – 1976E
Murray, Anne – 1947A, 1974C, 1978C, 1978E,
    1979H, 1980C, 1983C, 1985H
Murray, David – 1955A
Murray, John Horton – 1990H
Murray, Michael – 1943F
Murray, Thomas – 1943F, 1965I, 1973I, 1981I
Murray, William – 1935F
Mursell, James L.
  *Music & the Classroom Teacher* – 1951M
  *Music Education: Principles & Programs* –
    1956M
  *Music in American Schools* – 1943M
  *Human Values in Music Education* – 1934M
  *Principles of Musical Education* – 1927M
  *Psychology of Music, The* – 1937M
  *Psychology of School Music Teaching, The* –
    1931M
Murska, Ilma di – 1873H, 1880I
Muscle Shoals Sound Rhythm Section – 1967C
Musgrave, Thea – 1959K, 1970K, 1971K
  *Christmas Carol, A* – 1979N
  *Harriet, The Woman Called Moses* – 1984N
  *Last Twilight, The* – 1980N
  *Mary, Queen of Scots* – 1977N
  *Occurrence at Owl Creek Bridge* – 1981N
  *Simón Bolívar* – 1994N
*Music* – 1891L
Music Academy of the West – 1947L
Music Aeterna Orchestra & Chorus – 1961L
*Music & Drama* – 1882L
*Music & Musicians* – 1915L
Music Appreciation Hour (W. Damrosch) – 1928L
Music Associates of America – 1980L
Music at the Gainey Center – 1990L
Music at the Vineyards – 1958L
*Music: Books on Music and Sound Recordings* –
    1953C
Music Box Theater – 1921C
*Music Cataloging Bulletin* – 1970L
*Music City News* – 1963C

---

### Cultivated/Art Music Scene
F *Births*   G *Deaths*   H *Debuts*   I *New Positions*   J *Honors and Awards*
K *Biographical*   L *Musical Beginnings*   M *Publications*   N *Compositions*

*Music Critic & Trade Review* -1878L
Music Critics Association – 1958L
Music Education School (OR) – 1913L
*Music Educator's Journal* – 1914L
Music Festival of Arkansas – 1982L
*Music Forum* – 1967L
Music in Our Time Series – 1954L
*Music Index, The* – 1949L
*Music Journal of the West, Northwest & Southwest* – 1913L
*Musica judaica* – 1975L
Music Library Association – 1931L
Music Library Association Publication Prizes – 1977L
Music Machine – 1965C
*Music of the West* – 1945L
Music Publishers Association of the U.S. – 1895L
Music Publishers Protective Association – 1910C
Music School, Colored Children – 1912L
Music Teachers' National Association (NTNA) – 1876L
*Music Trade Review, The* – 1875L
*Music Trades* – 1890L
Music Vale Academy – 1835L
*Music Yearbook* – 1972C
*Musical America* – 1898L
*Musical Herald, The* – 1897L
*Musical Independent, The* – 1868L
*Musical Journal for the Piano Forte* – 1800L
*Musical Leader & Concert-goer* – 1895L
*Musical Life* – 1901L
*Musical Magazine, The* – 1792L
*Musical Magazine...* – 1839L
*Musical Messenger* – 1891L
*Musical Messenger (Chicago)* – 1904L
*Musical Million & Fireside Friend* – 1870L
*Musical Observer, The* – 1907L
*Musical Quarterly, The* – 1915L
*Musical Review (Pacific Coast M.R.-1907)* – 1903L
*Musical Review for the Blind* – 1930L
*Musical World* – 1863L
*Musical World & New York Musical Times* – 1850L
*Musician, The* – 1896L
Musicians' Club, Richmond, VA – 1915L
Musicians' Guild of America – 1956L
Musicians' National Protective Association – 1871L
Musicraft Records – 1937C
Musicwriter – 1954L
Musin, Ovide – 1883H, 1929G
Mustonen, Olli – 1986H
Muti, Riccardo – 1972H, 1975K, 1980I
Mutter, Anne-Sophie – 1980H
Muzak Co. – 1934C
Muzio, Claudia – 1916H
Myddleton, W. H.
　*Down South* – 1900E
Myers, Levi C.
　*Manual of Sacred Music* – 1853M
Myers, Michael – 1955F, 1977H

Myers, Pamela – 1952F, 1977H
Myles, Alannah – 1990E
Myrow, Joseph – 1910A, 1987B
　*You Make Me Feel So Young* – 1946E
Mysterians, The – 1966E

# N

Nabokov, Nicolas – 1939K, 1970J, 1978G
　*Cello Concerto* – 1953N
　*Don Quixote* – 1965N
　*Flute Concerto* – 1948N
　*Holy Devil, The* – 1958N
　*Love's Labor Lost* – 1973N
　*Piano Sonata No. 2* – 1940N
　*Return of Pushkin, The* – 1947N
　*String Quartet* – 1937N
　*Symphonic Variations* – 1967N
　*Symphony No. 2* – 1940N
　*Symphony No. 3* – 1967N
　*Union Pacific* (ballet) – 1934N
　*Vita Nuova, La* – 1950N
　*4 Poems by Pasternak* – 1959N
　*5 Poems by Anna Akhmatova* – 1964N
Nagano, Kent – 1951F, 1978I, 1994H, 1995K
Nágy, János – 1985H
Nagy, Robert – 1957H
Nakamatsu, Jon – 1995J
Nakamichi Baroque Music Festival – 1986L
Naked Prey – 1981C
Nancarrow, Conlon – 1912F, 1981K
　*String Quartet No. 1* – 1945N
Nanry, Charles
　*American Music from Storyville to Woodstock* – 1972D
Nantier-Didiée, Constance – 1855H
Napier, Marita – 1986H
Napoleao, Arthur – 1858H
Napoleon, Phil – 1901A
Nardiello, Catherine – 1985H
Narmour, Eugene – 1939F
　*Analysis & Cognition of Basic Melodic Structures* – 1990M
　*Analysis & Cognition of Melodic Complexity* – 1991M
Nash, Gary Powell
　*In Memoriam: Sojourner Truth* – 1992N
Nash, Johnny – 1940A, 1972E
Nashville (TN)
　*Jackson, Andrew, Hall* – 1980L
　*Symphony Orchestra* – 1904L
　*Symphony Orchestra II* – 1920L
　*Symphony Orchestra III* – 1946L
Nassau, Paul
　*Education of H\*Y\*M\*A\*N K\*A\*P\*L\*A\*N, The* – 1968E
Nasty Savage – 1983C
Nathan, Hans – 1936K, 1944K, 1946I, 1989G
　*Dan Emmett & the Rise of Early Negro Minstrelsy* – 1962D

---

## Vernacular/Commercial Music Scene
A *Births*　　B *Deaths*　　C *Biographical*　　D *Publications*
E *Representative Pieces*

---

### Cultivated/Art Music Scene

F *Births*   G *Deaths*   H *Debuts*   I *New Positions*   J *Honors and Awards*
K *Biographical*   L *Musical Beginnings*   M *Publications*   N *Compositions*

Nelson, Ron (continued)
   *Five Pieces after Wyeth* – 1976N
   *Hamaguchi* – 1981N
   *Savannah River Holiday* – 1953N
Nelson, Tracy – 1944A
Nelson, Willie – 1933A, 1975C, 1978C, 1982C,
   1983C, 1992C, 1993C
Nelsova, Zara – 1942H, 1955K, 1963K
Nemenoff, Genia – 1931K, 1989G
Nentwig, Franz – 1984H
Neon Cross – 1984C
Nero, Peter – 1934A, 1990C
Neruda, Wilma – 1899H
Nerves, The – 1976C
Nesterenko, Yevgeni – 1975H
Nestico, Sammy – 1924A
Nettl, Bruno – 1930F, 1953I, 1964I
   *Folk & Traditional Music of the Western*
     *Continents* – 1965D
   *North American Indian Musical Styles* –
     1953M
   *Theory & Method in Ethnomusicology* – 1964M
   *Western Impact on World Music, The* – 1985M
Nettl, Paul – 1939K, 1945K, 1946I, 1972G
   *Dance in Classical Music, The* – 1963M
   *Forgotten Musicians* – 1951M
   *Story of Dance Music, The* – 1947M
Nettleton, Asahel – 1783F, 1844G
   *Village Hymns for Social Worship* – 1824M
Neuendorff, Adolph – 1843F, 1854K, 1897G
   *Don Quixote* – 1882N
   *Minstrel, The* – 1892N
   *Prince Waldmeister* – 1887N
   *Rattenfänger von Hameln, Der* – 1880N
   *Symphony No. 1* – 1878N
   *Symphony No. 2* – 1880N
Neuendorff, Georgine – 1886H
Neuhaus, Max – 1939F
Neuman, Klauss-Gunter
   *Wonderland by Night* – 1961E
Neumann, Václav – 1985H
Neumann, Wolfgang – 1985H, 1988H
Neupert, Edmund – 1888G
Nevada, Emma – 1859F, 1880H, 1884H, 1887K,
   1940G
Neveu, Ginette – 1937H
Nevil, Robbie – 1960A
Neville Brothers – 1977C
Nevin, Arthur – 1871F, 1943G
   *Arizona* – 1935N
   *Daughter of the Forest, A* – 1918N
   *Djinns, The* – 1913N
   *Lorna Doone Suite* – 1897N
   *Love Dreams Suite* – 1914N
   *Miniature Suite* – 1902N
   *Night in Yaddo Land, A* – 1900N
   *Poia* – 1910N
   *Springs of Saratoga* – 1911N
   *String Quartet in D Minor* – 1929N

   *Symphonic Poem* – 1930N
   *Twilight* – 1911N
Nevin, Ethelbert – 1862F, 1870K, 1878K, 1879K,
   1883K, 1884K, 1886H, 1888K, 1891K, 1893K,
   1895K, 1898J, 1901G
   *Book of Songs, A* – 1893N
   *Captive Memories, Opus 29* – 1899N
   *Day in Venice, A* – 1898N
   *En Passant, Opus 30* – 1899N
   *Five Songs, Opus 5* – 1889N
   *Five Songs, Opus 12* – 1891N
   *Four Pieces for Piano, Opus 7* – 1890N
   *Guitare, maggio in Toscana, La* – 1896N
   *In Arcady, Opus 16* – 1892N
   *Maggio in Toscana* – 1895N
   *Mazurka in E-Flat* – 1894N
   *Melody & Habanera, Opus 8* – 1891N
   *Mighty Lak' a Rose* – 1901E
   *Milkmaid's Song, The* – 1881N
   *O'er Hill & Dale* – 1902N
   *Quest, The* – 1902N
   *Rosary, The* – 1898N
   *Songs from Vineacre, Opus 28* – 1899N
   *Three Piano Duets, Opus 4* – 1890N
   *Three Songs, Opus 17* – 1892N
   *Two Etudes for Piano, Opus 18* – 1892N
   *Water Scenes, Opus 13* – 1891N
New Albion Records – 1983L
New American Co. – 1791L
Newark, New Jersey
   *Amateur Glee Co.* – 1837L
   *Arion Men's Chorus* – 1859L
   *Boys' Choir* – 1966L
   *Chamber Orchestra* – 1956L
   *College of Music* – 1885L
   *Concert Hall* – 1847L
   *Eintracht* – 1846L
   *Germania Men's Chorus* – 1865L
   *Handel & Haydn Society* – 1831L
   *Harmonic Society I* – 1830L
   *Harmonic Society II* – 1860L
   *Harmonie Society* – 1883L
   *Krueger Auditorium* – 1884L
   *Little Symphony* – 1966L
   *Mozart Sacred Society* – 1834L
   *Music Festival* – 1915L
   *New Jersey Symphony Orchestra* – 1928L
   *New Jersey Symphony Chorus* – 1967L
   *Oratorio Society* – 1878L
   *Orpheus Club* – 1889L
   *Symphony Orchestra* – 1893L
Neway, Patricia – 1919F, 1946H
Newberry Consort – 1982L
Newborn, Ira – 1949A
New College Music Festival – 1965L
Newcomb, Billy
   *Big Sunflower, The* – 1866E
Newcomb, Ethel – 1875F, 1903H, 1959G
New Company, The – 1790L

---

❖

## Vernacular/Commercial Music Scene
A *Births*    B *Deaths*    C *Biographical*    D *Publications*
E *Representative Pieces*

New Christy Minstrels – 1961C
New Edition – 1981C
Newel Chamber Music Festival (VA) – 1972L
Newell, Norman
  *More (Mondo Cane)* – 1963E
New England Bach Festival – 1969L
New England Conservatory of Music – 1867L
New England Conservatory Opera Workshop –
  1942L
New England Conservatory Ragtime Ensemble –
  1972C
New England Conservatory/Piatigorsky Artist Award
  – 1992L
New England Contemporary Music Ensemble –
  1970L
New England Fiddling Contest – 1974C
New England Folk Festival – 1944C
New England Opera Theater – 1946L
New Friends of Music – 1936L
New Frontier – 1988C
New Grass Revival – 1974C
New Hampshire Music Festival – 1953L
New Hampshire Music Festival II – 1986L
New Haven, Connecticut
  *Mendelssohn Society* – 1858L
  *Musical Society* – 1832L
  *Oratorio Society* – 1903L
  *Symphony Orchestra* – 1894L
New Ipswich Military Band – 1804L
New Kids on the Block – 1985C, 1989E, 1990E
Newlin, Dika – 1923G
Newman, Alfred – 1900A, 1970B
  *All About Eve* – 1950E
  *Bell for Adano, A* – 1945E
  *Black Swan, The* – 1942E
  *Call of the Wild, The* – 1935E
  *Captain From Castile, The* – 1947E
  *Count of Monte Cristo, The* – 1934E
  *David & Bathsheba* – 1951E
  *Grapes of Wrath, The* – 1940E
  *How Green Was My Valley* – 1941E
  *I Cover the Waterfront* – 1933E
  *Indiscreet* – 1931E
  *Keys of the Kingdom, The* – 1944E
  *Love Is a Many-Splendored Thing* – 1953E
  *Misérables, Les* – 1935E
  *Razor's Edge, The* – 1946E
  *The Robe* – 1953E
  *Song of Bernadette, The* – 1943E
  *Tree Grows in Brooklyn, A* – 1945E
  *Twelve O'Clock High* – 1949E
  *Yellow Sky* – 1948E
Newman, Anthony – 1941F, 1967H, 1968I
  *Adagio & Rondo* – 1989N
  *Viola Concerto* – 1985N
Newman, Edward – 1977J, 1978J
Newman, Jimmy C. – 1927A
Newman, Joel
  *Kisses Sweeter Than Wine* – 1951E

Newman, Randy – 1943A
  *Faust* – 1995E
  *Natural, The* – 1984E
Newman, William S. – 1912F
New Mexico Opera Association – 1956L
*New Music* – 1982C
New Music America Festival – 1979L
New Music for Young Ensembles – 1974L
New Music Quartet – 1947L
New Orleans, Louisiana
  *Camp Street Theater* – 1824L
  *Classical Music Society* – 1855L
  *Conservatory* – 1919L
  *French Opera Co. II* – 1859L
  *French Opera House* – 1859L
  *Harmonic Association* – 1866L
  *Jazz and Heritage Festival* – 1969C
  *Jazz Club* – 1948C
  *Louisiana Philharmonic Orchestra* – 1992L
  *Mardi Grass* – 1857C
  *Onward Brass Band I* – 1885L
  *Opera Association* – 1943L
  *Philharmonic Society I* – 1824L
  *Philharmonic Society II* – 1906L
  *Philharmonic Society of the Friends of Art* –
    1853L
  *Philharmonic Symphony Orchestra* – 1936L
  *Preservation Hall* – 1961C
  *St. Charles Theater* – 1835L
  *Serenaders* – 1846L
  *Spectacle de la Rue St. Pierre* – 1792L
  *Theater of the Performing Arts* – 1973L
  *Théâtre d'Orléans* – 1811L
  *Théâtre d'Orléans (new)* – 1818L
  *Théâtre St. Philippe* – 1807L
New Orleans Feetwarmers – 1932C
New Orleans Gang (Louis Prima) – 1934C
New Orleans Jazz Band, Original (N.Y.) – 1918C
New Orleans Jazz Club of California – 1963C
New Orleans Rhythm Kings (Chicago) – 1922C
New Orleans Wanderers – 1926AC
Newport Classic Recordings – 1985L
Newport Folk Festival – 1959C
Newport Jazz Festivals (Kool) – 1954C
Newport Jazz Saratoga – 1978C
Newport Music Festival (RI) – 1969L
New Power Generation – 1991E
New Riders of the Purple Sage – 1969C
New School of Music (MA) – 1976L
Newton, Eddie
  *Casey Jones* – 1909E
Newton, Francis
  *Jazz Scene, The* – 1959D
Newton, J.
  *Olney Hymns* (American Edition) – 1787M
Newton, James – 1953A
Newton, Juice – 1952A, 1982C
Newton, Wayne – 1942A
Newton-John, Olivia – 1974CE, 1978E, 1980E, 1981E

---

## Cultivated/Art Music Scene
F *Births*     G *Deaths*     H *Debuts*     I *New Positions*     J *Honors and Awards*
K *Biographical*     L *Musical Beginnings*     M *Publications*     N *Compositions*

---

### Vernacular/Commercial Music Scene

A *Births*   B *Deaths*   C *Biographical*   D *Publications*
E *Representative Pieces*

---

## Cultivated/Art Music Scene

F *Births*      G *Deaths*      H *Debuts*      I *New Positions*      J *Honors and Awards*
K *Biographical*      L *Musical Beginnings*      M *Publications*      N *Compositions*

---

Vernacular/Commercial Music Scene
A *Births*    B *Deaths*    C *Biographical*    D *Publications*
E *Representative Pieces*

North Tonawanda Barrel Organ Works – 1893L
North, Alex – 1910A, 1986J, 1991B
  *Death of a Salesman* – 1951E
  *Streetcar Named Desire, A* – 1951E
  *Symphony No. 2* – 1968N
  *Symphony No. 3* – 1971N
  *Unchained Melody* – 1955E
  *Who's Afraid of Virginia Woolf?* – 1966E
Northwest Chamber Orchestra – 1973L
Northwest Grand Opera Association – 1951L
Northwest Regional Folklife Festival – 1972C
Northwestern Conservatory of Music (Minn.) –
  1885L
Northwestern U. Conservatory – 1873L
Northwestern U. School of Music – 1895L
Norup, Bent – 1980II
Norvo, Red – 1908A
Norvo, Red, Band    1935C
Norworth, Jack    1959B
  *Shine On, Harvest Moon* – 1908E
Noté, Jean – 1908H
*Notes* – 1943L
Notes From the Underground – 1965C
Novácek, Ottokar
  *Perpetuum Mobile* – 1895N
  *String Quartet No. 1* – 1890N
  *String Quartet No. 2* – 1898N
Novachord – 1939C
Novaës, Guiomar – 1915H
Noval, Tara – 1969F
Novara, Franco – 1883H
Novatna, Jarmila – 1994G
Novello's Sacred Music Store (NY) – 1852L
Novello, Ivor
  *Keep the Home Fires Burning* – 1915E
Novotná, Jarmila – 1939H, 1940H
Nowak, Lionel – 1911F
  *Concertino, Piano & Orch.* – 1944N
  *Flickers* – 1942N
  *String Quartet* – 1938N
  *Violin Sonatina* – 1944N
Norwich Anacreontic Society – 1795L
Norworth, Jack – 1879A
NRBQ – 1967
Nucci, Leo – 1980H
Nuclear Assault – 1985C
Nugent, Maude
  *Sweet Rosie O'Grady* – 1896E
Nugent, Ted – 1948A
Nuibo, Francisco – 1905H
Number One Hits:
  *ABC* – 1970E
  *Abracadabra* – 1982E
  *Addicted to Love* – 1986E
  *Africa* – 1983E
  *Afternoon Delight* – 1976E
  *Again* – 1993E
  *Against All Odds* – 1984E
  *Ain't Going Down* – 1993E

*Ain't No Mountain High Enough* – 1970E
*Alibis* – 1993E
*All 4 Love* – 1992E
*All for Love* – 1994E
*All I Have To Do Is Dream* – 1958E
*All Night Long* – 1983E
*All Shook Up* – 1957E
*All the Man That I Need* – 1991E
*All You Need Is Love* – 1967E
*Alley-Oop* – 1960E
*Alone* – 1987E
*Alone Again* – 1972E
*Alone with You* – 1992E
*Always* – 1987E
*Amanda* – 1986E
*American Pie* – 1972E
*American Woman* – 1970E
*Angie* – 1973E
*Angie Baby* – 1974E
*Annie's Song* – 1974E
*Another Brick in the Wall* – 1980E
*Another Day in Paradise*    1989E
*Another One Bites the Dust* – 1980E
*Anything For You* – 1988E
*Any Time, Any Place* – 1994E
*April Love* – 1957E
*Aquarius* – 1969E
*Are You Lonesome Tonight?* – 1960E
*Arthur's Theme* – 1981E
*At the Hop* – 1958E
*Babe* – 1979E
*Baby Baby* – 1991E
*Baby-Baby-Baby* – 1992E
*Baby Come Back* – 1978E
*Baby, Come to Me* – 1983E
*Baby Don't Forget My Number* – 1989E
*Baby Don't Get Hooked On Me* – 1972E
*Baby Got Back* – 1992E
*Baby, I Love Your Way* – 1988E
*Baby Love* – 1964E
*Back In My Arms Again* – 1965E
*Bad* – 1987E
*Bad, Bad Leroy Brown* – 1973E
*Bad Blood* – 1975E
*Bad Girls* – 1979E
*Bad Medicine* – 1988E
*Ballad of the Green Berets* – 1966E
*Bamba, La* – 1987E
*Band on the Run* – 1974E
*Batdance* – 1989E
*Battle of New Orleans, The* – 1959E
*Beat It* – 1983E
*Because I Love You* – 1990E
*Before the Next Teardrop Falls* – 1975E
*Be My Baby Tonight* – 1994E
*Ben* – 1972E
*Bennie and the Jets* – 1974E
*Best of My Love* – 1975E, 1977E
*Best Things in Life Are Free, The* – 1992E

---

## Cultivated/Art Music Scene

F *Births*     G *Deaths*     H *Debuts*     I *New Positions*     J *Honors and Awards*
K *Biographical*     L *Musical Beginnings*     M *Publications*     N *Compositions*

Number One Hits (continued)
- Bette Davis Eyes – 1981E
- Big Bad John – 1961E
- Big Girls Don't Cry – 1962E
- Big Hunk O'Love, A – 1959E
- Billie Jean – 1983E
- Billy, Don't Be a Hero – 1974E
- Black and White – 1972E
- Black Cat – 1990E
- Black or White – 1991E, 1992E
- Black Velvet – 1990E
- Black Water – 1975E
- Blame It on the Rain – 1989E
- Blaze of Glory – 1990E
- Blinded By the Light – 1977E
- Blue Moon – 1961E
- Blue Velvet – 1963E
- Boogie Fever – 1976E
- Boogie Oogie Oogie – 1978E
- Boot Scootin'Boogie – 1992E
- Brand New Key – 1971E
- Brandy – 1972E
- Breaking Up Is Hard To Do – 1962E
- Bridge Over Troubled Waters – 1970E
- Broken Wings – 1985E
- Brother Louis – 1973E
- Brown Sugar – 1971E
- Bump n' Grind – 1994E
- Calcutta – 1961E
- Call Me – 1980E
- Candy Man – 1972E
- Can I Trust You with My Heart? – 1993E
- Can't Buy Me Love – 1964E
- Can't Fight This Feeling – 1985E
- Can't Get Enough of Your Love, Babe – 1974E
- Can't Help Falling in Love – 1993E
- Can We Talk? – 1994E
- Car Wash – 1977E
- Careless Whisper – 1985E
- Caribbean Queen – 1984E
- Cat's in the Cradle – 1974E
- Cathy's Clown – 1960E
- Celebration – 1981E
- Centerfold – 1982E
- Chapel of Love – 1964E
- Chariots of Fire – 1982E
- Chattahoochee – 1993E
- Cherish – 1966E
- Chipmunk Song, The – 1958E
- Close to You – 1970E
- Close to You – 1990E
- Cold Hearted – 1989E
- Come On Eileen – 1983E
- Come See About Me – 1964E
- Come Softly to Me – 1959E
- Come Together – 1969E
- Coming Out of the Dark – 1991E
- Coming Up – 1980E
- Convoy – 1976E

- Could've Been – 1988E
- Cracklin' Rosie – 1970E
- Crazy for You – 1985E
- Crazy Little Thing Called Love – 1980E
- Cream – 1991E
- Creep – 1994E
- Crimson and Clover – 1969E
- Crocodile Rock – 1973E
- Cry for You – 1994E
- Da Doo Ron Ron – 1977E
- Dancing Queen – 1977E
- Dark Lady – 1974E
- Daydream Believer – 1967E
- December, 1963 – 1976E
- Deep Purple – 1963E
- Delta Dawn – 1973E
- Diana – 1957E
- Didn't We Almost Have It All – 1987E
- Died In Your Arms – 1987E
- Dirty Diana – 1988E
- Disco Duck – 1976E
- Disco Lady – 1976E
- Dizzy – 1969E
- Do It to Me – 1992E
- Do That To Me One More Time – 1980E
- Do Wah Diddy Diddy – 1964E
- Do Ya Think I'm Sexy – 1979E
- Dock of the Bay, The – 1968E
- Dominique – 1963E
- Don't Be Cruel – 1956E
- Don't Break the Heart That Loves You – 1962E
- Don't Give Up On Us – 1977E
- Don't Go Breaking My Heart – 1976E
- Don't I Beg of You – 1958E
- Don't Leave Me This Way – 1977E
- Don't Let the Sun Go Down On Me – 1992E
- Don't Stop 'Til You Get Enough – 1979E
- Don't Wanna Lose You – 1989E
- Don't Worry, Be Happy – 1988E
- Don't You Forget About Me – 1985E
- Don't You Want Me – 1982E
- Down Under – 1983E
- Downtown – 1965E
- Dreamlover – 1993E
- Dreams – 1977E
- Duke of Earl – 1962E
- Easier Said than Done – 1963E
- Easy Come, Easy Go – 1993E
- Ebony and Ivory – 1982E
- Eight Days a Week – 1965E
- El Paso – 1960E
- Emotions – 1991E
- End of the Road – 1992E
- Endless Love – 1981E
- Escapade – 1990E
- Escape (Piña Colada Song) – 1979E
- Eternal Flame – 1989E
- Eve of Destruction – 1965E
- Evergreen – 1977E

---

❈

## Vernacular/Commercial Music Scene
A *Births*   B *Deaths*   C *Biographical*   D *Publications*
E *Representative Pieces*

Every Breath You Take – 1983E
Every Rose Has Its Thorn – 1988E
Everybody Loves Somebody – 1964E
Everybody Wants to Rule the World – 1985E
Everybody's Somebody's Fool – 1960E
Everyday People – 1969E
Everything Is Beautiful – 1970E
Everything She Wants – 1985E
Everytime You Go Away – 1985E
Exhale – 1995E
Eye of the Tiger – 1982E
Faith – 1987E
Fame – 1975E
Family Affair – 1971E
Fantasy – 1995E
Father Figure – 1988E
Feel Like Makin' Love – 1974E
Fifth of Beethoven, A – 1976E
Fifty Ways to Leave Your Lover – 1976E
Fingertips – 1963E
Fire – 1975E
First Time, The – 1991E
First Time Ever I Saw Your Face – 1972E
Flame, The – 1988E
Flashdance – 1983E
Foolish Beat – 1988E
Footloose – 1984E
Forever Your Girl – 1989E
Frankenstein – 1973E
Freak, Le – 1978E
Freak Me – 1993E
Funkytown – 1980E
Game of Love – 1965E
Gangsta Lean – 1993E
Gangsta's Paradise – 1995E
Georgia On My Mind – 1960E
Get Back – 1969E
Get Down Tonight – 1975E
Get Off My Cloud – 1965E
Get Out of My Dreams, Get Into My Car – 1988E
Girl I'm Gonna Miss You – 1989E
Give Me Love – 1973E
Glory of Love – 1986E
Go Away Little Girl – 1963E
Go Away Little Girl – 1971E
Gonna Fly Now – 1977E
Gonna Make You Sweat – 1991E
Good Lovin' – 1966E
Good Luck Charm – 1962E
Good Thing – 1989E
Good Times – 1979E
Good Vibrations – 1966E, 1991E
Got My Mind Set On You – 1988E
Got to Give It Up – 1977E
Grazing in the Grass – 1968E
Grease – 1978E
Greatest Love of All – 1986E
Green Tambourine – 1968E
Groovin' – 1967E

Groovy Kind of Love – 1988E
Gypsys, Tramps and Thieves – 1971E
Half-Breed – 1973E
Hang on Sloopy – 1965E
Hangin' Tough – 1989E
Hanky Panky – 1966E
Happening, The – 1967E
Happy Organ, The – 1959E
Happy Together – 1967E
Hard Day's Night, A – 1964E
Hard Headed Woman – 1958E
Hard to Say I'm Sorry – 1982E
Harper Valley P.T.A. – 1968E
Have You Ever Really Loved a Woman? – 1995E
Having My Baby – 1974E
He Don't Love You (Like I Love You) – 1975E
He's a Rebel – 1962E
He's So Fine – 1963E
Head to Toe – 1987E
Heart of Glass – 1979E
Heart of Gold – 1972E
Heartache Tonight – 1979E
Heartaches By the Number – 1959E
Heartbreak Hotel – 1956E
Heaven – 1985E
Heaven Is a Place on Earth  1987E
Hello – 1984E
Hello, Dolly! – 1964E
Hello Goodbye – 1967E
Hello I Love You – 1968E
Help! – 1965E
Help Me Rhonda – 1965E
Here Comes the Hotstepper – 1994E
Here I Go Again – 1987E
Hero – 1993E, 1994E
Hey! Baby – 1962E
Hey Jude – 1968E
Hey Paula – 1963E
Higher Love – 1986E
Hip Hop Hooray – 1993E
Hit the Road Jack – 1961E
Hold On – 1990E
Hold On to the Nights  1988E
Holding Back the Years – 1986E
Honey – 1968E
Honeycomb – 1957E
Honky Tonk Women – 1969E
Horse With No Name, A – 1972E
Hot Child in the City – 1978E
Hot Stuff – 1979E
Hotel California – 1977E
Hound Dog – 1956E
House of the Rising Sun, The – 1964E
How Am I Supposed to Live Without You – 1990E
How Deep Is Your Love – 1977E
How Do You Mend a Broken Heart? – 1971E
How Do You Talk to an Angel? – 1992E
How Will I Know – 1986E
Hustle, The – 1975E

❀

## Cultivated/Art Music Scene
F Births    G Deaths    H Debuts    I New Positions    J Honors and Awards
K Biographical    L Musical Beginnings    M Publications    N Compositions

Number One Hits (continued)
  *I Adore Mi Amor – 1991E*
  *I Am Woman – 1972E*
  *I Can Help – 1974E*
  *I Can See Clearly Now – 1972E*
  *I Can't Get Next To You – 1969E*
  *I Can't Get No Satisfaction – 1965E*
  *I Can't Go for That – 1982E*
  *I Can't Help Myself – 1965E*
  *I Can't Stop Loving You – 1962E*
  *I Do for You – 1991E*
  *I Don't Have the Heart – 1990E*
  *I Don't Wanna Cry – 1991E*
  *I Feel Fine – 1964E*
  *I Get Around – 1964E*
  *I Got You Babe – 1965E*
  *I Hear a Symphony – 1965E*
  *I Heard It Through the Grapevine –
    1968E*
  *I Honestly Love You – 1974E*
  *I Just Called to Say I Love You – 1984E*
  *I Just Can't Stop Loving You – 1987E*
  *I Just Want To Be Your Everything – 1977E*
  *I Knew You Were Waiting – 1987E*
  *I Like It, I Love It – 1995E*
  *I Like the Way – 1991E*
  *I Love a Rainy Night – 1981E*
  *I Love Rock and Roll – 1982E*
  *I Shot the Sheriff – 1974E*
  *I Still Believe in You – 1992E*
  *I Still Haven't Found What I'm Looking For –
    1987E*
  *I Swear – 1994E*
  *I Think I Love You – 1970E*
  *I Think We're Alone Now – 1987E*
  *I Wanna Be Down – 1994E*
  *I Wanna Dance with Somebody –
    1987E*
  *I Want to Be Wanted – 1960E*
  *I Want to Hold Your Hand – 1964E*
  *I Want to Know What Love Is – 1985E*
  *I Want You Back – 1970E*
  *I Want You, I Need You, I Love You – 1956E*
  *I Will Always Love You – 1992E, 1993E*
  *I Will Follow Him – 1963E*
  *I Will Survive – 1979E*
  *I Wish – 1977E*
  *I Write the Songs – 1976E*
  *Ice Ice Baby – 1990E*
  *I'd Do Anything for Love – 1993E*
  *If I Can't Have You – 1978E*
  *If I Didn't Have You – 1992E*
  *If the Good Die Young – 1994E*
  *If Wishes Came True – 1990E*
  *If You Don't Know Me By Now – 1989E*
  *If You Leave Me Now – 1976E*
  *If You Wanna Be Happy – 1963E*
  *I'll Be Loving You – 1989E*
  *I'll Be There For You – 1989E*

  *I'll Be Your Everything – 1990E*
  *I'll Be There – 1970E*
  *I'll Be There – 1992E*
  *I'll Make Love to You – 1994E*
  *I'll Take You There – 1972E*
  *I'm a Believer – 1966*
  *I'm Henry VIII, I Am – 1965E*
  *I'm Leaving It Up to You – 1963E*
  *I'm Sorry – 1960E*
  *I'm Sorry – 1975E*
  *I'm Telling You Now – 1965E*
  *I'm Too Sexy – 1992E*
  *I'm Your Baby Tonight – 1990E*
  *I'm Your Boogie Man – 1977E*
  *In the Year 2525 – 1969E*
  *Incense and Peppermints – 1967E*
  *Indian Reservation- 1971E*
  *Informer – 1993E*
  *Invisible Touch – 1986E*
  *Island Girl – 1975E*
  *Islands in the Stream – 1983E*
  *It Must Have Been Love – 1990E*
  *It's All In the Game- 1958E*
  *It's My Party – 1963E*
  *It's Now or Never – 1960E*
  *It's Only Make Believe – 1958E*
  *It's Still Rock and Roll To Me – 1980E*
  *It's Too Late – 1971E*
  *Itsy Bitsy Teeny Weeny Yellow Polka Dot Bikini –
    1960E*
  *Jack and Diane – 1982E*
  *Jacob's Ladder – 1987E*
  *Jailhouse Rock – 1957E*
  *Jessie's Girl – 1981E*
  *Jive Talkin' – 1975E*
  *Johnny Angel – 1962E*
  *Joker, The – 1974E*
  *Joy to the World – 1971E*
  *Joyride – 1991E*
  *Judy in Disguise – 1968E*
  *Jump – 1984E*
  *Just Kickin' It – 1993E*
  *Just My Imagination – 1971E*
  *Justify My Love – 1991E*
  *Kansas City – 1959E*
  *Karma Chameleon – 1984E*
  *Keep On Loving You – 1981E*
  *Keep On Truckin' – 1973E*
  *Killing Me Softly with His Song – 1973E*
  *King of a Drag – 1967E*
  *Kiss – 1986E*
  *Kiss and Say Goodbye – 1976E*
  *Kiss From a Rose – 1995E*
  *Kiss On My List – 1981E*
  *Kiss You All Over – 1978E*
  *Knockin' da Boots – 1993E*
  *Knock On Wood – 1979E*
  *Knock Three Times – 1971E*
  *Kokomo – 1988E*

✦

**Vernacular/Commercial Music Scene**
A  *Births*    B  *Deaths*    C  *Biographical*    D  *Publications*
E  *Representative Pieces*

---

## Cultivated/Art Music Scene

F *Births*    G *Deaths*    H *Debuts*    I *New Positions*    J *Honors and Awards*
K *Biographical*    L *Musical Beginnings*    M *Publications*    N *Compositions*

---

✶

---

**Vernacular/Commercial Music Scene**
A   *Births*    B   *Deaths*    C   *Biographical*    D   *Publications*
E   *Representative Pieces*

* * *

## Cultivated/Art Music Scene

F *Births*    G *Deaths*    H *Debuts*    I *New Positions*    J *Honors and Awards*
K *Biographical*    L *Musical Beginnings*    M *Publications*    N *Compositions*

---

Vernacular/Commercial Music Scene
A *Births*    B *Deaths*    C *Biographical*    D *Publications*
E *Representative Pieces*

O'Connor, Sinead – 1990E
O'Day, Alan – 1977E
O'Day, Anita – 1919A
O'Day, Anita, Records – 1972C
O'Day, Molly – 1923A
Odell Brothers Organ Co. – 1859L
Odetta – 1930A
Oelze, Christiane – 1994H
Offenbach, Jacques – 1876K
Ogawa, Noriko – 1982H
Ogdon, John – 1963H
Ogdon, Will – 1921F
Oh, David
   *Music of the Canvas* – 1990N
O'Hara, Geoffrey – 1881A, 1967G
   *K-K-K-Katy* – 1918E
Ohio Express – 1968C
Ohio Players – 1959C, 1975E, 1976E
Ohio State U. School of Music – 1945L
Ohlsson, Garrick – 1948F, 1966J, 1968J, 1970HJK,
   1994J
Ohms, Elisabeth – 1930H
Oingo Boingo – 1979C
Oistrakh, David – 1955H
Ojai Music Festival – 1947L
O'Jays, The – 1958C, 1973E
OK Mozart Festival – 1985L
Okada, Yoshiko – 1991H
OKeh Records – 1920C
O'Kanes, The – 1907C
Oke, Alan – 1986H
Okeh Records – 1918C
Olcott, Chauncey – 1858A, 1932B
   *Garrett O'Magh* – 1901E
   *My Wild Irish Rose* – 1899E
   *Old Limerick Town* – 1902E
   *Romance of Athlone, A* – 1899E
   *Sweet Inniscarra* – 1897E
Olczewska, Maria – 1933H
Old American Co. (revival) – 1785L
Old & New Dreams – 1976C
Old Folks Concert Troupe – 1855C
Old Ship of Zion Music Co. – 1936C
Old Time Fiddler's Convention – 1924C
Oldberg, Arne – 1874F, 1899I, 1962G
   *Academic Overture* – 1909N
   *Paolo & Francesca* – 1908N
   *Piano Concerto No. 2* – 1931N
   *Piano Sonata* – 1909N
   *Sea, The* – 1934N
   *String Quartet in C* – 1900N
   *Symphony in F, Opus 23* – 1910N
   *Symphony No. 4* – 1939N
   *Symphony No. 6* – 1956N
   *Violin Concerto* – 1933N
Oldham, Kevin – 1993G
Oldmixon, Georgina – 1793H, 1835G
Old Town Records – 1952C
Olevsky, Julian – 1949H, 1985G

Oliphant, Thomas
   *Santa Lucia* – 1850N
Olitzka, Rosa – 1895H, 1949G
Olitzki, Walter – 1939H, 1949G
Oliveira, Elmar – 1950F, 1964H, 1975J, 1978J,
   1983J, 1990I
Oliver, Henry K. – 1800F, 1818K, 1883J, 1885G
   *Oliver's Collection of Hymn & Psalm Tunes* –
   1860M
Oliver, John, Chorale (MA) – 1977L
Oliver, King – 1885A, 1938B
   *Canal Street Blues* – 1923E
   *Doctor Jazz* – 1927E
   *New Orleans Stomp* – 1924E
   *Snake Rag* – 1923E
   *Sugar Foot Stomp* – 1923E
Oliver's, King, Creole Jazz Band – 1920C
Oliver, Paul
   *Aspects of the Blues Tradition* – 1970D
   *Blues Off the Record* – 1988D
   *Meaning of the Blues, The* – 1961D
   *New Grove Gospel, Blues & Jazz* – 1987D
Oliver, Sy – 1910A, 1988B
Olivero, Magda – 1967H, 1975H
Oliveros, Pauline – 1932F, 1967I
   *Beautiful Soop* – 1967N
   *Big Mother is Watching You* – 1966N
   *In Memoriam Mr. Whitney* – 1991N
   *Software for People: Collected Writings 1963-80* –
   1984M
   *Sound Patterns* – 1961N
   *Variations for Piano Sextet* – 1960N
Olivet Conservatory of Music (MI) – 1874L
Ollmann, Kurt – 1957F
Olman, Abe – 1888A, 1984B
   *Down Among the Sheltering Palms* – 1914E
   *Oh, Johnny, Oh!* – 1917E
Olmstead, Timothy – 1759F, 1848G
   *Martial Music* – 1807M
   *Musical Olio, The* – 1805M
Olsen, Stanford – 1986HJ
Olson, Keith – 1957F, 1982H
Olympia Brass Band – 1958C
Olympics – 1954C
Omaha, Nebraska
   *Festival of Contemporary Music* – 1986L
   *Opera Co.* – 1957L
   *Regional Ballet Co.* – 1965L
Omen – 1984C
Ondriczek, Franz – 1895H
O'Neal, Alexander – 1954A
Onégin, Sigrid – 1922H
Onward Brass Band I – 1885C
Opalach, Jan – 1980J
Opera America – 1970L
Opera Colorado – 1981L
Opera de Lyons – 1995K
Opera Ebony – 1976L
Opera for Youth (FL) – 1977L

---

❀

Cultivated/Art Music Scene
F *Births*    G *Deaths*    H *Debuts*    I *New Positions*    J *Honors and Awards*
K *Biographical*    L *Musical Beginnings*    M *Publications*    N *Compositions*

Opera in the Ozarks – 1950L
*Opera Journal, The* – 1968L
Opera Midwest – 1979L
Opera/Music Theater Institute (NJ) – 1987L
*Opera News* – 1936L
*Opera Quarterly, The* – 1983L
Opera St. Paul – 1981L
Opera San Jose – 1980L
Opera/South (Jackson, MS) – 1971L
Oppens, Ursula – 1944G, 1969J, 1976J
*Opus* – 1984L
Orange Blossoms – 1927C
Orange County Performing Arts Center – 1986L
Oratorio Society of Utah – 1914L
Orbach, Jerry – 1935A
Orbison, Roy – 1936A, 1961E, 1964E, 1988B
   *Oh, Pretty Woman* – 1949E
Orchestra USA – 1962C
Ordway Music Theater – 1985L
Ordway's Aeolian Vocalists – 1850L
Oregon – 1970C
Oregon Conservatory of Music II – 1945L
Oren, Daniel – 1995H
*Organ* – 1890L
Organ Historical Society – 1956L
Orgonosova, Luba – 1995H
Originals – 1966C
O'Riley, Christopher – 1956F, 1981H
Orioles – 1946C
Orion String Quartet – 1987L
Orlandi-Malaspina, Rita – 1969H
Orlando, Tony – 1944A, 1975E
Orleans – 1972C
Orlons, The – 1959C
Ormandy, Eugene – 1921K, 1924H, 1927K, 1931I,
   1934K, 1936I, 1944K, 1970J, 1973K,1975J, 1979J,
   1980K, 1982J, 1984K, 1985G
Ornstein School of Music – 1940L
Ornstein, Leo – 1907K, 1911H, 1920I
   *A La Mexicana* – 1920N
   *Arabesques* – 1921N
   *Biography in Sonata Form* – 1974N
   *Dwarf Suite* – 1913N
   *Five Water Colors* – 1935N
   *Fog, The* – 1915N
   *Impressions of Chinatown* – 1917N
   *Impressions of Notre Dame* – 1910N
   *Lysistrata Suite* – 1930N
   *Moods* – 1914N
   *Morning in the Woods, A* – 1971N
   *Nocturne & Dance of the Fates* – 1936N
   *Piano Concerto* – 1923N
   *Piano Quintet* – 1927N
   *Piano Sonata* – 1913N
   *Piano Sonata No. 4* – 1924N
   *Piano Sonata No. 6* – 1981N
   *Some New York Scenes* – 1971N
   *String Quartet No. 1* – 1929N
   *String Quartet No. 2* -1940N

   *String Quartet No. 3* – 1976N
   *Symphony* – 1934N
   *Ten Poems of 1917* – 1918N
Orpheon Free School – 1865L
*Orpheonist & Philharmonic Journal* – 1864L
Orpheus – 1972L
Orquesta Broadway – 1962C
Orrego-Salas, Juan – 1960K
   *Piano Concerto No. 2* – 1985N
   *Piano Sonata* – 1967N
   *Symphony No. 3* – 1961N
   *Symphony No. 4* – 1966N
   *Violin Concerto* – 1984N
Orth, John – 1850F, 1932G
Orth, Peter – 1976J, 1979J
Ortiz, Christina – 1971H
Ory, "Kid" – 1886A
Osborn-Hannah, Jane – 1873F, 1904H, 1910H,
   1943G
Osborne Brothers – 1953C
Osborne, Adrienne – 1873F
Osborne, Bobby – 1931A
Osborne, Jeffrey – 1948A
Osborne, John – 1792F, 1835G
Osborne, John, Piano Co. – 1815L
Osborne, Mary – 1992B
Osborne, Sonny – 1937A
Osbourn & Strail Musical Supplies – 1836L
Osgood, Emma – 1849F, 1873H, 1911G
Osgood, George – 1844F
Osgood, H. D.
   *So This Is Jazz* – 1926D
Oslin, K. T. – 1943A, 1987C, 1988C
Osmond, Donny – 1957A, 1971E
Osmond, Marie – 1959A
Osmonds, The – 1957C, 1971E
Osmosis – 1967C
Ossman, Vess L. – 1868A, 1923B
Ostransky, Leroy
   *Anatomy of Jazz, The* – 1960D
O'Sullivan, Denis – 1897H
O'Sullivan, Gilbert – 1972E
Oswald, Mark – 1991H
Ostinelli, Eliza – 1847H
Ostinelli, Sophia H. H. – 1845G
Otis, Johnny – 1921A
Ott, David
   *Piano Concerto* – 1994N
   *Symphony No. 1* – 1990N
   *Symphony No. 2* – 1991N
   *Symphony No. 3* – 1992N
Otten, Joseph – 1880I
Otter, Anne Sofie von – 1988H
Ottman, Robert – 1914F
   *Advanced Harmony, Theory & Practice* – 1961M
   *Elementary Harmony, Theory & Practice* –
   1961M
Otto, Melitta – 1879H
Oudin, Eugène E. – 1858F, 1886H, 1894G

---

### Vernacular/Commercial Music Scene
A *Births*   B *Deaths*   C *Biographical*   D *Publications*
E *Representative Pieces*

Outlaws – 1974C
*Ovation* – 1980L
Overkill – 1984C
Overlook Lyric Theatre – 1992L
Overstreet, Paul – 1955A
Overton, Hall – 1920F, 1964J, 1972G
  *Piano Sonata* – 1963N
  *Polarities No. 1* – 1959N
  *Polarities No. 2* – 1971N
  *Sonorities* – 1964N
  *String Quartet No. 1* – 1950N
  *String Quartet No. 2* – 1954N
  *String Quartet No. 3* – 1967N
  *Symphony No. 1 for Strings* – 1955N
  *Symphony No. 2* – 1962N
Owen, Anita
  *Daisies Won't Tell* – 1908E
  *Sweet Bunch of Daisies* – 1894E
Owen, Harold
  *Modal & Tonal Counterpoint: From Josquin to*
  *Stravinsky* – 1992M
Owen, Jimmy, Quartet Plus One – 1969C
Owen, Richard – 1922F
  *Abigail Adams* – 1987N
  *Death of the Virgin, The* – 1983N
  *May Dyer* – 1979N
  *Tom Sawyer* – 1989N
Owens, Buck – 1929A
Owens, Harry
  *Sweet Leilani* – 1937E
Owings, John – 1964H, 1968J
Ozark Folk Festival – 1947C
Ozark Mountain Daredevils – 1971C
Ozawa, Seiji – 1960K, 1961HK, 1970I, 1973I,
  1979K
Ozawa, Seiji, Hall (Tanglewood) – 1994L
Ozone – 1977C

# P

Pablo Cruise – 1973C
Pablo Recording Co. – 1973C
Pace Gospel Choral Union – 1936C
Pace-Handy Co. – 1908C
Pace Jubilee Singers – 1925L
Pace Music House (Chicago) – 1910C
Pace, Charles Henry – 1886A, 1963B
Pace, Charles H., Music Publishers – 1952C
Pachelbel, Charles T. – 1732K, 1737I, 1750G
Pachmann, Vladimir de – 1891H
Pacific Chamber Orchestra – 1985L
*Pacific Coast Musician* – 1911L
Pacific Contemporary Music Center – 1987L
Pacific Gas & Electric – 1968C
Pacific Jazz Records – 1952C
Pacific World Artists – 1968L
Packard Piano & Organ Co. – 1871L
Paderewski Prize – 1896L
Paderewski, Ignace Jan – 1891H, 1941G, 1992K
Paff, John/Michael, Publishing Co. – 1797L

Page, "Hot Lips" – 1908A, 1954B
Page, Hot Lips, Band – 1936C
Page, Patti – 1927A
Page, Paula – 1968J
Page, Tim
  *Music from the Road: Views & Reviews 1978-*
  *1992* – 1992M
Page, Tommy – 1990E
Page, Walter – 1900A, 1957B
Pagliughi, Lina – 1907F, 1927H, 1980G
Paige, Janis – 1922A
Paik, Kun-Woo – 1971H
Paillard, M. J., & Co. (NY) – 1850L
Paine, David
  *Portland Sacred Music Society's Collection* –
  1839M
Paine, John Knowles – 1839F, 1858K, 1861IK,
  1862I, 1869J, 1873K, 1875K, 1890J, 1898J,
  1906G
  *Azara* – 1898N
  *Birds, The* – 1900N
  *Centennial Hymn, Opus 27* – 1876N
  *Concert Variations on Star-Spangled Banner* –
  1861N
  *Concert Variations on the Austrian Hymn* –
  1860N
  *Columbus March & Hymn* – 1892N
  *Duo Concertante, Opus 33* – 1877N
  *Fantasia & Fugue in E Minor* – 1860N
  *Four Character Pieces, Opus 11* – 1866N
  *Four Character Pieces, Opus 25* –
  1876N
  *Funeral March in Memory of President Lincoln* –
  1865N
  *Hymn for Harvard Commencement* – 1862N
  *Hymn of the West* – 1903N
  *Island Fantasy, An, Opus 44* – 1888N
  *Lecture Notes* – 1885M
  *Mass in D, Opus 10* – 1865N
  *Nativity, The, Opus 38* – 1883N
  *Oedipus Tyrannus* – 1881N
  *Overture, As You Like It* – 1876N
  *Pesceballo, Il* – 1862N
  *Phoebus, Arise!* – 1882N
  *Piano Sonata No. 1 in A Minor* – 1859N
  *Piano Trio in D Minor* – 1874N
  *Prelude & Fugue in G Minor* – 1859N
  *Realm of Fancy, The, Opus 36* – 1882N
  *St. Peter, Opus 20* – 1872N
  *Song of Promise, Opus 43* – 1888N
  *String Quartet in D, Opus 5* – 1859N
  *Symphony No. 1, Opus 23* – 1875N
  *Tempest, The* – 1876N
  *Ten Sketches: In the Country* – 1873N
  *Three Piano Pieces, Opus 41* – 1884N
  *Two Preludes, Opus 19* – 1864N
  *Violin Sonata, Opus 24* – 1875N
Paine, Thomas D. – 1813F, 1895G
Paley, Alexander – 1991H

---

## Cultivated/Art Music Scene

F *Births*    G *Deaths*    H *Debuts*    I *New Positions*    J *Honors and Awards*
K *Biographical*    L *Musical Beginnings*    M *Publications*    N *Compositions*

---

**Vernacular/Commercial Music Scene**

A  *Births*     B  *Deaths*     C  *Biographical*     D  *Publications*
E  *Representative Pieces*

---

### Cultivated/Art Music Scene

F *Births*     G *Deaths*     H *Debuts*     I *New Positions*     J *Honors and Awards*
K *Biographical*     L *Musical Beginnings*     M *Publications*     N *Compositions*

---

Vernacular/Commercial Music Scene
A *Births*    B *Deaths*    C *Biographical*    D *Publications*
E *Representative Pieces*

Payne, Maggi – 1945F
Payne, Patricia – 1977H, 1980H
Paynter, John
  *Sound & Structure* – 1992M
Pazmor, Radiana – 1892F
Peabody Conservatory – 1857L
Peabody, George – 1795F, 1869G
Peaches and Herb – 1965C, 1979E
Peacock, Lucy – 1947F, 1959H
Peanut Butter Conspiracy – 1966C
Pearce, S. Austen – 1872K, 1900G
  *Columbia College Chapel Music* – 1877M
  *Pocket Dictionary of Musical Terms* – 1889M
Pearl Harbor & the Explosions – 1979C
Pearl Jam – 1990C
Pearl, Minnie – 1975C, 1992C
Pearls Before Swine – 1965C
Pears, Peter – 1974H
Pearson Electronic Sound Studio – 1969L
Pease, Alfred H. – 1838F, 1864H, 1882G
  *Piano Concerto* – 1875N
Pease, James – 1916F, 1967G
Pecchioli, Benedetta – 1983H
Pechner, Gerhard – 1940H, 1941H
Pedreira Music Academy – 1931L
Pedroni, Simone – 1993H
Peer-Southern Music Co. – 1928L
Peerce, Jan – 1904F, 1932K, 1938H, 1941H, 1981I, 1984G
Peinemann, Edith – 1962H
Pelham, Peter, III – 1721F, 1755I, 1805G
Pelissier, Victor – 1792K
  *Ariadne Abandoned on the Isle of Naxos* – 1797N
  *Columbian Melodies* – 1811M
  *Danaides, or, Vice Punished* – 1795N
  *Death of Captain Cook, The* – 1793N
  *Edwin & Angelina* – 1796N
  *Fille Hussar, La* – 1803N
  *Forêt noire, La* – 1795N
  *Fourth of July, The* – 1799N
  *Gil Blas* – 1802N
  *Harlequin Pastry Cook* – 1794N
  *Mother Goose* – 1810N
  *Mysterious Monk, The* – 1796N
  *Obi, or, Three-Fingered Jack* – 1801N
  *Raymond & Agnes* – 1804N
  *Robinson Crusoe* – 1796N
  *Sophia of Brabant* – 1794N
  *Sterne's Maria, or, The Vintage* – 1799N
  *Tale of Mystery, A* – 1803N
  *Valentine & Orson* – 1805N
  *Virgin of the Sun* – 1800N
Pellegrini, Maria – 1975H
Pellegrino, Ron
  *Electronic Arts of Sound & Light, The* – 1983M
Pelletier, Wilfred – 1928H
Peloubet, Chabrier – 1885G
Peloubet, Chabrier, Woodwind Maker – 1829L
Pendergrass, Teddy – 1950A

Penfield, Smith Newhall – 1837F
Penguins – 1954C
Peninsula Music Festival (WI) – 1953L
Penn, Arthur A.
  *Carissima* – 1905E
Pennario, Leonard – 1924F, 1936H
Pennsylvania Opera Theatre – 1975L
Pensacola Chamber Music Festival – 1985L
People – 1968C
People-to-People Music Committee – 1968L
People's Songs, Inc. – 1946C
*Pepper's, J. W., Musical Times* – 1877L
Pepper, J. W., Publisher – 1876L
Pepper, Art – 1925A, 1982B
Pepper, James W. – 1853F, 1919G
Perabo, Ernst – 1845F, 1865HK, 1920G
Perahia, Murray – 1947F, 1968H, 1972J, 1973J, 1975J, 1978J
Peralta, Frances – 1920H
Percussion – 1970C
Pere Ubu – 1975C
Perelman, S. J.
  *One Touch of Venus* – 1943E
Perera, Ronald – 1941F
  *Earthsong* – 1983N
  *Five Summer Songs* – 1972N
  *White Whale, The* – 1981N
  *Yellow Wallpaper, The* – 1989N
Peress, Maurice – 1930F, 1962I, 1970I, 1974I
Peretti, Burton W.
  *Creation of Jazz, The* – 1992M
Peretti, Hugo
  *Maggie Flynn* – 1968E
Perick, Christof – 1985H
Périer, Jean – 1908H
Perkins, C. C.
  *Grand Symphony* – 1850N
  *Pilgrim's Cantata* – 1855N
Perkins, Carl – 1932A
  *Blue Suede Shoes* – 1956E
Perkins, Henry S. – 1833F, 1891I, 1914G
  *Advance* – 1872M
  *Choir, The* – 1883M
  *College Hymns & Tune Book* – 1868M
  *Convention Choruses* – 1874M
  *Good Templar* – 1881M
  *Nightingale* – 1860M
  *Perkins' Class & Choir* – 1879M
  *Perkins' Graded Anthems* – 1880M
  *Perkins' Vocal Method* – 1868M
  *Song Echo* – 1871M
Perkins, John MacIvor – 1935F, 1970I
Perkins, Jule Edson – 1845F, 1869H, 1875G
Perkins, Walton – 1847F, 1869H, 1907I, 1929G
Perkins, William O. – 1831F, 1902G
  *Atlantic Glee Book* – 1861M
  *Choral Choir* – 1882M
  *Choral Harmony* – 1859M
  *Church Welcome* – 1872M

---

✺

## Cultivated/Art Music Scene
F *Births*   G *Deaths*   H *Debuts*   I *New Positions*   J *Honors and Awards*
K *Biographical*   L *Musical Beginnings*   M *Publications*   N *Compositions*

Perkins, William O (continued)
   *Laurel Wreath* – 1870M
   *Orpheon* – 1871M
   *Shining River* – 1875M
   *Perkins' Singing School* – 1875M
   *Starry Crown* – 1869M
   *Temple, The* – 1879M
   *Union Star Glee Book* – 1861M
Perl, Alfredo – 1993H
Perlea, Jonel – 1949H, 1955I, 1970G
Perle, George – 1915F, 1949I, 1957I, 1961I, 1978J,
   1985J, 1986J, 1989I
   *Cello Concerto* – 1966N
   *Concertino, Piano, Winds, Timpani* – 1979N
   *Dance Overture* – 1987N
   *Listening Composer, The* – 1990M
   *Piano Concerto No. 1* – 1990N
   *Piano Concerto No. 2* – 1992N
   *Piano Sonata* – 1950N
   *Piano Sonatina* – 1986N
   *Rhapsody for Orchestra* – 1954N
   *Serenade No. 1* – 1962N
   *Serenade No. 2* – 1968N
   *Serenade No. 3* – 1983N
   *Serial Composition & Atonality* – 1962M
   *Short Sonata* – 1964N
   *Short Symphony, A* – 1980N
   *Sinfonietta I* – 1988N
   *Sinfonietta II* – 1991N
   *Six Etudes for Piano* – 1976N
   *Songs of Praise & Lamentation* – 1974N
   *String Quartet No. 5* – 1960N
   *String Quartet No. 6* – 1969N
   *String Quartet No. 7* – 1973N
   *String Quartet No. 8* – 1989N
   *String Quintet* – 1958N
   *Suite in C* – 1970N
   *Symphony for Band* – 1959N
   *Symphony No. 2* – 1950N
   *Three Movements for Orchestra* – 1960N
   *Thirteen Dickinson Songs* – 1979N
   *Twelve-tone Tonality* – 1977M
   *Wind Quintet No. 1* – 1959N
   *Wind Quintet No. 2* – 1960N
   *Wind Quintet No. 3* – 1967N
   *Wind Quintet No. 4* – 1984N
Perlman, Itzhak – 1958H, 1964J, 1975I, 1986J
Perlonga, David – 1970J
Perotti, Julius – 1888H
Perrini, Giuletta – 1849H
*Perry's Musical Magazine* – 1881L
Perry, Edward B. – 1855F, 1924G
   *Descriptive Analyses of Piano Works* – 1902M
Perry, Eugene – 1955F, 1986H
Perry, Herbert – 1991H
Perry, Janet – 1947F, 1969H, 1983H
Perry, Julia – 1924F, 1979G
   *Symphony No. 3* – 1962N
   *Symphony No. 4* – 1964N

   *Symphony No. 6* – 1966N
   *Symphony USA* – 1967N
   *Symphony No. 8* – 1969N
   *Symphony No. 9* – 1970N
Persichetti, Vincent – 1915F, 1941I, 1948J, 1963I,
   1965J, 1975J, 1987G
   *Concertino, Piano & Orchestra* – 1941N
   *Creation, The* – 1969N
   *English Horn Concerto* – 1977N
   *Fairy Tale* – 1950N
   *Harmonium, Op. 51* – 1951N
   *Net of Fireflies, A* – 1970N
   *Organ Sonata* – 1960N
   *Piano Concerto* – 1962N
   *Piano Quintet* – 1956N
   *Piano Sonatas 1 & 2* – 1939N
   *Piano Sonata No. 3* – 1943N
   *Piano Sonatas 4 & 5* – 1949N
   *Piano Sonatas 6 – 8* – 1950N
   *Piano Sonata No. 9* – 1952N
   *Piano Sonata No. 10* – 1955N
   *Piano Sonata No. 11* – 1965N
   *Piano Sonata No. 12* – 1980N
   *Piano Sonatinas 1-3* – 1950N
   *Piano Sonatinas 4-6* – 1954N
   *String Quartet No. 1* – 1939N
   *String Quartet No. 2* – 1944N
   *String Quartet No. 3* – 1959N
   *String Quartet No. 4* – 1972N
   *Symphony No. 1 & 2* – 1942N
   *Symphony No. 3* – 1946N
   *Symphony No. 4* – 1951N
   *Symphony No. 5* – 1953N
   *Symphony No. 6 (Band)* – 1956N
   *Symphony No. 7* – 1958N
   *Symphony No. 8* – 1967N
   *Symphony No. 9* – 1970N
   *Twentieth Century Harmony* – 1961M
Persinger, Louis – 1887F, 1912H, 1930I, 1966G
*Perspectives of New Music* – 1962L
Persuasions, The – 1962C
Pertile, Aureliano – 1921H
Pertusi, Michele – 1992H
Peschka-Leutner, Minna – 1872H
Peskanov, Mark – 1973K, 1985J, 1987J
Peter and Gordon – 1964E
Peter, Johann F. – 1770K, 1813G
   *I Will Make An Everlasting Covenant* – 1782N
   *It Is a Precious Thing* – 1772N
   *Lord Is In His Holy Temple, The* – 1786N
   *Psalm of Joy, A* – 1783N
   *Six String Quintets* – 1789N
Peter, Simon – 1770K, 1819G
Peters, Cragg & Co. – 1851L
Peter, Paul and Mary – 1961C
*Peter's Sax-Horn Journal* – 1850L
Peters & Co., Publisher – 1846L
Peters, C. F., Music Publishers – 1948L
Peters, John L., & Brother, Publishers – 1851L

---

❁

### Vernacular/Commercial Music Scene
A *Births*   B *Deaths*   C *Biographical*   D *Publications*
E *Representative Pieces*

Peters, Roberta – 1930F, 1950H, 1993J
Peters, W. C.
    *Peter's Catholic Harp* – 1863M
    *Symphony in D* – 1831N
Peters, W. C., Music Store – 1829L
Peters, W. C., Publishers – 1851L
Petersilea, Carlyle – 1844F, 1878G
Peterson, Clara Gottschalk
    *Staccato Polka* – 1909N
Peterson, Claudette – 1953F, 1975H
Peterson, John – 1921A
Peterson, Oscar – 1925A
Peterson, Ray – 1939A
Peterson, Wayne – 1927F
    *Face of the Night, The Heart of the Dark* – 1991N
    *String Quartet No. 1* – 1984N
    *String Quartet No. 2* – 1992N
    *Trilogy* – 1987N
    *Widening Gyre, The* – 1990N
Petra – 1972C
Petrides, Frédérique J. – 1923K, 1933I
Petri, Egon – 1932H, 1938K, 1940I, 1947I, 1952I, 1962G
Petri, Michaela – 1982H
Petrie, Henry W. – 1857A, 1925B
    *Asleep In the Deep* – 1897E
Pettiford, Oscar – 1922A, 1968B
Pettis, Jack
    *Bugle Call Rag* – 1923E
Petty, Tom – 1950A
Petty, Tom, and the Heartbreakers – 1975C
Peyser, Ethel
    *Book of Culture: Basis of a Liberal Education* – 1934M
    *How Opera Grew* – 1956M
    *How to Enjoy Music* – 1933M
Peyser, Joan – 1931F, 1977I
    *Music of My Time* – 1995M
    *New Music: The Sense behind the Sound* – 1971M
    *Orchestra: Origins & Transformations, The* – 1986M
Pez Band – 1976C
Phair, Liz – 1968A
Phelps, Ellsworth – 1827F
    *American Legend* – 1885N
    *Hiawatha Symphony* – 1880N
Phelps, William L. – 1865F
Phi Beta Fraternity – 1912L
Phi Beta Mu – 1937L
Phi Mu Gamma Sorority – 1898L
Phi Mu Alpha Sinfonia Fraternity – 1898L
Philadelphia, Pennsylvania
    *Academy of Music* – 1825L
    *Adgate Free School* – 1785L
    *American Academy of Music* – 1857L
    *American Conservatorio* – 1823L
    *American Musical Fund Society* – 1849L
    *Arion Society* – 1854L
    *Bach Choir* – 1934L

    *Cecilia Club* – 1875L
    *Chamber Music Association* – 1917L
    *Chamber Orchestra* – 1961L
    *Chamber String Sinfonietta* – 1925L
    *Chamber Subscription Series* – 1757L
    *Chamber Symphony* – 1966L
    *Chesnut Street Opera House* – 1885L
    *Chestnut Street Theater* – 1794L
    *Choral Art Society* – 1922L
    *Choral Arts Society* – 1982L
    *Choral Society* – 1897L
    *City Concerts* – 1786L
    *Civic Opera Co.* – 1924L
    *Combs School of Music* – 1885L
    *Composers Concerts* – 1769L
    *Concerto Soloists* – 1965L
    *Conservatory of Music* – 1877L
    *Eurydice Chorus* – 1886L
    *Folk Festival* – 1962C
    *Germania Orchestra* – 1856L
    *Grand Opera Co.* – 1927L
    *Grand Opera House* – 1880L
    *Harmonie* – 1855L
    *Haydn Society* – 1809L
    *Hinrichs Opera Co* – 1888L
    *Little Symphony* – 1909L
    *Männerchor* – 1835L
    *Manuscript Music Society* – 1892L
    *Mendelssohn Glee Club* – 1874L
    *Musical Academy* – 1869L
    *Musical Association* – 1863L
    *Musical Fund Hall* – 1824L
    *Musical Fund Society* – 1820L
    *New Theater Opera House* – 1793L
    *Opera Theater* – 1976L
    *Orchestra* – 1900I
    *Orpheus Club* – 1872L
    *Palestrina Choir* – 1915L
    *Philharmonic Society* – 1837L
    *Settlement Music School* – 1908L
    *Singers* – 1971L
    *Singing City* – 1947L
    *Southwark Theater* – 1766L
    *Sternberg School of Music* – 1890L
    *String Quartet* – 1959L
    *Treble Clef Club* – 1884L
    *Uranian Society* – 1787L
    *Woodwind Quintet* – 1950L
Phile, Philip – 1793G
Philharmonia Baroque (Berkeley) – 1981L
Philipp, Adolf – 1890K, 1893C
Philipp, Robert – 1882H
Philips, Nathaniel, Publisher – 1839L
Phillips, Burrill – 1907F, 1944J, 1949I, 1988G
    *Cello Sonata* – 1946N
    *Commentaries* – 1983N
    *Concerto Grosso* – 1949N
    *Dr. Faustus* – 1957N
    *Don't We All* – 1947N

---

## Cultivated/Art Music Scene

**F** *Births*    **G** *Deaths*    **H** *Debuts*    **I** *New Positions*    **J** *Honors and Awards*
**K** *Biographical*    **L** *Musical Beginnings*    **M** *Publications*    **N** *Compositions*

Phillips, Burrill (continued)
  *Organ Sonata* – 1964N
  *Piano Concerto* – 1942N
  *Piano Sonata No. 1* – 1942N
  *Piano Sonata No. 4* – 1960N
  *Play Ball* – 1937N
  *Return of Odysseus, The* – 1956N
  *Scherzo for Orchestra* – 1944N
  *Selections from McGuffey's Reader* – 1933N
  *Sinfonia Brevis* – 1959N
  *Soleriana Concertante* – 1965N
  *String Quartet No. 1* – 1940N
  *String Quartet No. 2* – 1958N
  *Tom Paine Overture* – 1946N
  *Triple Concerto* – 1952N
  *Unforgiven, The* – 1981N
Phillips, Charlie
  *Sugartime* – 1958E
Phillips, Little Esther – 1935A, 1984B
Phillips, Harvey – 1929F, 1971I
Phillips, Henry – 1844H
Phillips, John – 1935A
Phillips, Liz – 1951F
Phillips, Philip – 1834F, 1895G
  *Hallowed Songs* – 1865M
  *Singing Pilgrim, The* – 1866M
Phillips, Philip, & Co., Pianos – 1863L
Phillips, Wilson – 1990E, 1991E
Phillipps, Adelaide – 1833F, 1852K, 1855H, 1882G
Philo (Aladdin) Records – 1945C
Philo International Records – 1971C
Phoenix, Arizona
  *Arizona Opera Co.* – 1971L
  *Bach & Madrigal Society* – 1958L
  *Boys' Choir* – 1949L
  *Lyric Opera Theater* – 1968L
  *Opera Co.* – 1965L
  *Orpheus Male Chorus* – 1929L
  *Scottsdale Center for the Arts* – 1976L
  *Symphony Hall* – 1972L
  *Symphony Orchestra* – 1947L
*Phonograph Monthly Review* – 1926L
Piaf, Edith – 1947C
Pianists Foundation of America – 1977L
Piano Technicians Guild – 1958L
Piantadosi, Al – 1884A, 1955B
Piastro, Mishel – 1920H, 1941I, 1970G
Piatigorsky, Gregor – 1929HK, 1942IK, 1962I, 1976G
Piccadilly Boys – 1947C
Piccolomini, Maria – 1858H
Pickens, Jo Ann – 1955F
Picker, Tobias – 1954F, 1977J, 1985I
  *Pian-o-rama* – 1984N
  *Piano Concerto No. 1* – 1980N
  *Piano Concerto No. 2* – 1983N
  *Piano Quintet* – 1988N
  *Symphony No. 1* – 1982N
  *Symphony No. 2* – 1986N

  *Viola Concerto* – 1991N
  *Violin Concerto* – 1981N
Pickett, Bobby – 1962E
Pickett, Wilson – 1941A
*Pickin': The Magazine of Bluegrass and Old-time Country Music* – 1974C
Picon, Molly – 1898A
Picou, Alphonse – 1878A, 1961B
Pied Pipers, The – 1938C
Pierce, Webb – 1926A, 1991B
Pierian Sodality – 1808L
Pierpont, James – 1822F, 1893B
  *Jingle Bells* – 1857E
Pi Kappa Lambda – 1918L
Pilarczyk, Helga – 1965H
Pilcher, Henry, Organ Builder – 1833L
Pilgrim, Neva – 1938F, 1965H
Pilkington, H. W.
  *Musical Dictionary, A* – 1812M
Pillow & Drew Music Store (OR) – 1850L
Pilou, Jeannette – 1967H
Pimsleur, Solomon – 1900F, 1962G
  *Miracle of Life & Mystery of Death* – 1932N
  *Neo-Classic Overture* – 1927N
  *Symphonic Ballad* – 1924N
  *Symphony of Disillusionment* – 1928N
  *Symphony of Terror & Despair* – 1947N
Pini-Corsi, Antonio – 1899H
Pink Floyd – 1980E
Pinkham, Daniel – 1923F, 1959I
  *Advent Cantata* – 1991N
  *Ascension Cantata* – 1970N
  *Christmas Cantata* – 1957N
  *Christmas Symphony* – 1992N
  *Conversion of Saul, The* – 1981N
  *Daniel in the Lion's Den* – 1973N
  *Dreadful Dining Car, The* – 1982N
  *Easter Cantata* – 1957N
  *Hezekiah* – 1979N
  *Jonah* – 1966N
  *Organ Concerto* – 1970N
  *Overture Concertante* – 1992N
  *Passion of Judas, The* – 1976N
  *Requiem* – 1963N
  *St. Mark Passion* – 1965N
  *String Quartet* – 1990N
  *Symphony No. 1* – 1961N
  *Symphony No. 2* – 1963N
  *Symphony No. 3* – 1985N
  *Symphony No. 4* – 1990N
Pinza, Ezio – 1926H, 1949C, 1957G
*Pioneer, The* – 1854L
Pioneer Trio (Sons of the Pioneers) – 1933C
Pips, The – 1952C, 1973E
Pires, Maria-João – 1988H
Pisk, Paul – 1936IK, 1937I, 1941K, 1948I, 1951I, 1963I, 1990G
  *History of Music & Musical Style, A* – 1963M

---

※

Vernacular/Commercial Music Scene
A *Births*    B *Deaths*    C *Biographical*    D *Publications*
E *Representative Pieces*

❂

### Cultivated/Art Music Scene

F *Births*    G *Deaths*    H *Debuts*    I *New Positions*    J *Honors and Awards*
K *Biographical*    L *Musical Beginnings*    M *Publications*    N *Compositions*

❊

Vernacular/Commercial Music Scene
A *Births*    B *Deaths*    C *Biographical*    D *Publications*
E *Representative Pieces*

Merry Wives of Windsor, The – 1954N
Midsummer Night's Dream – 1926N
Moving Tide, The – 1944N
Music for Strings – 1941N
Orchestra Suite in C – 1926N
Piano Quintet – 1927N
Piano Sonata – 1930N
Poem & Dance – 1932N
Quintet, Flute & Strings – 1940N
Sonata for Horn – 1946N
String Quartet No. 1 – 1923N
String Quartet No. 2 – 1925N
String Quartet No. 3 – 1930N
String Quartet No. 4 – 1931N
String Quartet No. 5 – 1935N
String Quartet No. 6 – 1937N
String Quartet No. 7 – 1943N
String Quartet No. 8 – 1950N
String Quartet No. 9 – 1958N
String Sextet, on Slavic Folk Songs – 1947N
Sweeney Agonistes – 1933N
Symphony No. 1 – 1934N
Symphony No. 2 – 1962N
Symptoms of Love – 1961N
Ukrainian Suite – 1925N
Viola Concerto – 1948N
Violin Sonata No. 1 – 1926N
Violin Sonata No. 2 – 1929N
Porter, Susan
  With an Air Debonair: Musical Theater in
    America – 1992D
Porter, William
  Musical Cyclopedia, The – 1834M
Portland, Maine
  Beethoven Musical Society – 1819L
  Chamber Music Society – 1982L
  Chandler's Band – 1867L
  Choral Arts Society – 1972L
  Concert Association – 1931L
  Handel Society of Maine – 1814L
  Handel & Haydn Society – 1828L
  Kotzschmar Club – 1900L
  Lyric Theater – 1953L
  Marston Club – 1887L
  Portland Band – 1827L
  Rossini Club – 1869L
  Sacred Music Society – 1836L
  String Quartet – 1969L
  Symphony Orchestra – 1923L
Portland, Oregon
  Apollo Club – 1883L
  Civic Auditorium – 1917L
  Junior Symphony – 1924L
  Marquam Grand Theater – 1890L
  Mechanics Band – 1864L
  Opera Association – 1950L
  Opera Co. – 1917L
  Oregon Conservatory of Music – 1898L

Oregon Repertory Singers – 1974L
Philharmonic Music Society – 1866L
Schnitzer, Arlene, Concert Hall – 1984L
School of Music – 1918L
Symphonic Choir – 1946L
Symphony Orchestra – 1896L
Posselt, Ruth – 1914F, 1935K
Possessed – 1983C
Post, Merriweather, Pavilion (MD) – 1967L
Postlewaite, J. W.
  St. Louis Quick Step – 1849N
Poulet, Michel – 1992H
Poulton, George R.
  Aura Lee – 1861E
Powell, Bud – 1924A, 1966B
Powell, Claire – 1990H
Powell, Dick – 1904A
Powell, Eleanor – 1910A, 1982B
Powell, Jane – 1929A
Powell, John – 1882F, 1907H, 1912H, 1924J, 1963G
  At the Fair (Piano) – 1907N
  At the Fair (Orchestra) – 1925N
  Babe of Bethlehem, The – 1934N
  Electronic Setting – 1960N
  In Old Virginia – 1921N
  In the South – 1906N
  Natchez-on-the-Hill – 1932N
  Piano Sonata No. 1 – 1907N
  Piano Sonata No. 3 – 1913N
  Rapsodie Nègre – 1917N
  Set of Three, A – 1935N
  Sonata Virginianesque – 1919N
  Sonate Noble, Op. 21 – 1907N
  String Quartet No. 1 – 1907N
  String Quartet No. 2 – 1922N
  Symphony in A – 1945N
  Symphony on Virginia Folk Themes – 1951N
  Variations & Double Fugue – 1906N
  Violin Concerto – 1910N
  Violin Sonata – 1928N
Powell, Maud – 1867F, 1885H, 1904K,
  1920G
Powell, Maud, String Quartet – 1894L
Powell, Maud, Trio – 1908L
Powell, Mel – 1933F, 1957I, 1963J, 1969I
  Cantilena – 1970N
  Duplicates – 1990N
  Electronic Setting No. 1 – 1961N
  Electronic Setting No. 2 – 1962N
  Events – 1963N
  Filigree Setting – 1959N
  Modules – 1985N
  Piano Quintet – 1957N
  Piano Trio – 1957N
  Setting – 1961N
  Settings for Small Orchestra – 1992N
  Stanzas – 1957N
  String Quartet 1982 (No. 2) – 1982N
  Three Synthesizer Settings – 1981N

---

※

## Cultivated/Art Music Scene

F *Births*    G *Deaths*    H *Debuts*    I *New Positions*    J *Honors and Awards*
K *Biographical*    L *Musical Beginnings*    M *Publications*    N *Compositions*

Powell, W. C.
  *Sweet Violets* – 1908R
Powell, Verne Q. – 1879F, 1968G
Powell, Verne Q., Flutes, Inc. – 1926L
Power Center for the Performing Arts (U. Michigan)
  – 1971L
Powers, Harold S. – 1973I
Powers, Marie – 1974G
Powley, John – 1816I
Pownall, Mary Ann – 1792HK, 1796G
Poznanski, Barrett – 1840F
Prado, Perez, Mambo Band – 1948C
Prang Edcational Co. – 1882L
Prater, David – 1937A, 1988B
Praticò, Bruno – 1994H
Pratt, Awadagin – 1992J, 1993H, 1992K
Pratt, Carroll – 1894F
  *Meaning of Music, The* – 1931M
  *Music as the Language of Emotion* –
  1952M
Pratt, Charles E.
  *Walking Down Broadway* – 1868E
Pratt, Paul – 1890A, 1948B
  *Hot House Rag* – 1914E
  *Springtime Rag* – 1916E
  *Vanity Rag* – 1909E
  *Walhalla Rag* – 1910E
Pratt, Silas G. – 1846F, 1868K, 1871IK, 1872I,
  1875K, 1888IK, 1906I, 1916G
  *America* – 1894N
  *Anniversary Overture* – 1876N
  *Antonio (Lucille)* – 1871N
  *Canon for String Orchestra* – 1877N
  *Caprice Fantastique* – 1879N
  *Centennial Hymn* – 1876N
  *Grand March Heroique* – 1867N
  *Grand Polonaise I* – 1874N
  *Grand Polonaise II* – 1878N
  *Grand Valse Etude* – 1875N
  *Homage to Chicago March* – 1873N
  *Inca's Farewell, The* – 1891N
  *Lucille* – 1887N
  *Maddalena's Lament* – 1870N
  *Meditation Religeuse* – 1881N
  *Musical Metempsychosis, The* – 1888N
  *Pianist's Mental Velocity, The* – 1905M
  *Prodigal Son, The* – 1885N
  *Serenade for String Orchestra* – 1879N
  *Shadow Thoughts* – 1870N
  *Shakesperian Grand March* – 1866N
  *Symphony No. 1* – 1871N
  *Symphony No. 2, "Prodigal Son"* – 1875N
  *Tragedy of the Deep, A* – 1912N
  *Triumph of Columbus, The* – 1892N
  *Variations on "Sweet Bye & Bye"* – 1877N
  *Zenobia, Queen of Palmyra* – 1882N
Pratt, Waldo Selden – 1857F, 1878K, 1881K, 1882I,
  1939G
  *Class Notes in Music History* – 1908M

*History of English Hymnody, The* –
  1895M
*History of Music, The* – 1907M
*Music of the French Psalter of 1562* – 1939M
*Music of the Pilgrims, The* – 1921M
*Musical Ministries in the Church* – 1901M
*New Encyclopedia of Music & Musicians* –
  1924M
  *Problem of Music in the Church, The* – 1930M
Pratt Institute of Music & Art – 1906L
Prausnitz, Frederik – 1920F, 1961I, 1971I, 1974J,
  1976I
  *Score & Podium: A Complete Guide to*
  *Conducting* – 1983M
Prescott, Abraham – 1789F, 1858G
Presley, Elvis – 1935A, 1956E, 1957E, 1958F,
  1959E, 1960E, 1961E, 1962E, 1969E, 1970C,
  1977B
Presleys' Mountain Music Jubilee Theater – 1987C
Presser Foundation – 1916L
Presser Home for Retired Music Teachers – 1906L
Presser, Theodore – 1848F, 1925G
Presser, Theodore, Co. – 1883L
Pressler, Menahem – 1955I
Prestige Records – 1949C
Preston, Billy – 1946A, 1969E, 1973E
Preston, Johnny – 1930A, 1960E
Pretenders, The – 1978C
Prêtre, Georges – 1959H, 1964H
Previn, André – 1939K, 1943K, 1962H, 1967I,
  1970K, 1976I, 1985I
  *Coco* – 1969E
  *Guitar Concerto* – 1971N
  *Honey and Rue* – 1992N
  *Piano Concerto* – 1987N
Previtali, Fernando – 1955H
Prévost, Eugène-Prosper – 1838IK, 1872G
  *Adolphe et Clari* – 1846N
  *Blanche et Renée* – 1871N
  *Chaste Suzanne, La* – 1845N
  *Esmeralda* – 1842N
  *Requiem* – 1857N
Preyer, Carl Adolph – 1947G
Prey, Hermann – 1960H
Price, Florence – 1888F, 1927K
  *Mississippi River Symphony* – 1934N
  *Piano Concerto in F Minor* – 1934N
  *Piano Sonata in E Minor* – 1932N
  *Songs to the Dark Virgin* – 1941N
  *Symphony No. 1* – 1932N
  *Symphony No. 3* – 1940N
  *Violin Concerto No. 2* – 1952N
Price, Leontyne – 1927F, 1949K, 1952K, 1961HJ,
  1965J, 1980J, 1985JK
Price, Lloyd – 1933A, 1959E
  *Lawdy Miss Clawdy* – 1950E
Price, Margaret – 1969H, 1985H
Price, Ray – 1926A, 1970C, 1991C
Price, Sammy – 1908A, 1992B

---

❖

Vernacular/Commercial Music Scene
A *Births*    B *Deaths*    C *Biographical*    D *Publications*
E *Representative Pieces*

---

Cultivated/Art Music Scene

F *Births*     G *Deaths*     H *Debuts*     I *New Positions*     J *Honors and Awards*
K *Biographical*     L *Musical Beginnings*     M *Publications*     N *Compositions*

Radio Music Co. – 1929C
Raffanti, Dano – 1980H, 1981H
Raftery, J. Patrick – 1951F, 1980H, 1981J, 1982H
*Rag Times* – 1968C
*Rag Time Review* – 1914C
Ragin, Derek Lee – 1958F, 1983H, 1988H
Rahn, John – 1944F, 1983I
   *Basic Atonal Theory* – 1980M
   *Kali* – 1986N
   *Miranda* – 1990N
Raiders, The – 1971E
Raim, Cynthia – 1979J
Raimondi, Gianni – 1957H, 1965H
Raimondi, Ruggero – 1970H
Rainer Family – 1839HK
Rainey, Gertrude "Ma" – 1886A, 1939B
Rainger, Ralph – 1901A, 1942B
   *Blue Hawaii* – 1937E
   *Love in Bloom* – 1934E
   *Thanks for the Memories* – 1938E
Rains, Leon – 1878F, 1898H, 1909H, 1954G
Raisa-Rimini Singing School – 1937L
Raisa, Rosa – 1913H, 1963G
Raitt, Bonnie – 1949E
Raitt, John – 1917E
Raksin, David – 1912E
   *Ben Casey Theme* – 1961E
   *Laura* – 1945E
   *Shocking Miss Pilgrim, The* – 1946E
Ralf, Torsten – 1945H
Ram, Samuel (Buck)
   *Twilight Time* – 1944E
Ramey, Samuel – 1942F, 1968K, 1973H, 1984H
Ramírez, Louie – 1938A
Ramones, The – 1974C
Ramrods – 1956C
Ran, Shulamit – 1962K, 1973I, 1991I, 1992J, 1994I
   *Capriccio, Piano & Orchestra* – 1963N
   *Concertpiece for Piano & Orchestra* – 1971N
   *Hyperbolae* – 1977N
   *Legends* – 1993N
   *Piano Concerto* – 1977N
   *String Quartet* – 1984N
   *Symphonic Poem, Piano & Orchestra* – 1967N
   *Symphony* – 1990N
Randall, James K. – 1929F
Randall, James R.
   *Maryland, My Maryland* – 1861E
Randle, Thomas – 1958F
Randolph, Anson D. F., Publisher – 1851L
Randolph, Harold – 1898I
Randová, Eva – 1981H
Rands, Bernard – 1975IK, 1983JK, 1989I
   *Canti del Sole* – 1982N
   *Canti Lunatici* – 1980N
   *Canzoni per orchestra* – 1995N
   *Ceremonial 3* – 1991N
   *Hiraeth* – 1987N
   *Mésalliance* – 1972N

   *Songs of the Eclipse* – 1993N
   *Suites 1 & 2* – 1984N
   *Symphony* – 1993N
   *...where the Murmurs die...*- 1993N
   *Wildtrack I* – 1969N
   *Wildtrack II* – 1973N
   *Wildtrack III* – 1975N
Randy & the Rainbows – 1959C
Range, The – 1984C, 1986E
Rank & File – 1981C
Rankin, Nell – 1926F, 1949H, 1951H
Rapchak, Lawrence – 1951F
   *Lifework of Juan Diaz, The* – 1988N
   *Sinfonia Antiqua* – 1989N
Rapee, Erno – 1912IK, 1931I, 1945G
   *Iron Horse, The* – 1924E
   *Motion Picture Moods* – 1925D
   *Robin Hood* – 1923E
   *Seventh Heaven* – 1927E
   *What Price Glory* – 1925E
Rappold, Marie – 1905H
Rare Earth – 1969C
Rasbach, Oscar – 1888F, 1975G
   *Trees* – 1922E
Rascals, The – 1965E
Rascher Saxophone Quartet – 1969L
Rascher, Sigurd – 1939HK
Raskin, Judith – 1928F, 1956H, 1962H, 1984G
Rasmussen, Paula – 1965F
Raspberries, The – 1970C
Rathaus, Karol – 1938K, 1946K, 1954G
Ratner, Leonard – 1916F
   *Classic Music: Expression, Form & Style* –
   1979M
   *Harmony: Structure & Style* – 1962M
   *Music: The Listener's Art* – 1957M
Ratt – 1981C
Rattle, Simon – 1976H, 1981K, 1988K
Raudenbush, George K. – 1899F, 1927I
Rautio, Nina – 1995H
Ravelli, Luigi – 1880H
Rawlins, Emily – 1950F, 1973H, 1980H
Rawls, Lou – 1935A
Ravel, Maurice – 1928K
Ravens, The – 1945C
Rawlins, Emily – 1973H, 1980H
Ray, Johnny – 1927A, 1990B
Raye, Don
   *Beat Me, Daddy, 8 to the Bar* – 1940E
   *This Is My Country* – 1940E
Raye, Susan – 1944A
Rays – 1955C
Razaf, Andy – 1895A, 1973B
   *That's What I Like About the South* – 1944E
RCA Victor Co. – 1929L
Read, Daniel – 1757F, 1782K, 1836G
   *American Singing Book, The* – 1785M
   *American Singing Book Supplement* – 1787M
   *Columbian Harmonist I, The* – 1793M

---

❖

**Vernacular/Commercial Music Scene**
A *Births*    B *Deaths*    C *Biographical*    D *Publications*
E *Representative Pieces*

---

## Cultivated/Art Music Scene

F *Births*    G *Deaths*    H *Debuts*    I *New Positions*    J *Honors and Awards*
K *Biographical*    L *Musical Beginnings*    M *Publications*    N *Compositions*

Reich, Steve  (continued)
 *Pendulum Music* – 1968N
 *Six Pianos* – 1973N
 *Tehillim* – 1981N
 *Three Movements for Orchestra* – 1986N
 *Vermont Counterpoint* – 1982N
 *Writings about Music* – 1974M
Reichmann, Theodor – 1889H
Reid, Donald
 *Remember Pearl Harbor* – 1941E
Reid, Mike – 1947A
Reid, Michael
 *Different Fields* – 1995N
Reidel, Deborah – 1994H
Reinagle, Alexander – 1786HK, 1787K, 1793K,
 1803K, 1809G
 *American, Commerce & Freedom* – 1794N
 *Arabs of the Desert, The* – 1799N
 *Columbus* – 1797N
 *Constellation, The* – 1799N
 *Double Disguise, The* – 1800N
 *Edwy & Elgiva* – 1801N
 *Federal March* – 1788N
 *Four Piano Sonatas* – 1790N
 *Gentle Shepherd, The* – 1798N
 *Harlequin Freemason* – 1800N
 *Harlequin Shipwreck'd* – 1795N
 *I Have a Silent Sorrow Here* – 1799N
 *Italian Monk, The* – 1798N
 *Mary, Queen of Scots* – 1806N
 *Masonic Ode* – 1803N
 *Masonic Overture* – 1800N
 *Miscellaneous Quartets* – 1791N
 *Occasional Overture, An* – 1794N
 *Overture, Auld Robin Gray* – 1795N
 *Overture, Harlequin's Invasion* – 1795N
 *Overture, The Lucky Escape* – 1796N
 *Overture, The Wife of Two Husbands* – 1805N
 *Paradise Lost* – 1809N
 *Piano Concerto* – 1794N
 *Piano Preludes in Three Classes* – 1794N
 *Pierre de Province & La Belle Magulone* – 1796N
 *Pizarro* – 1800N
 *Purse, The* – 1795N
 *Robin Hood* – 1794N
 *Rosa* – 1800N
 *Sailor's Daughter, The* – 1804N
 *St. Patrick's Day* – 1794N
 *Savoyard, The* – 1797N
 *Selection of the Most Favorite Scots Tunes* –
 1787M
 *Slaves in Algiers* – 1794N
 *Spanish Barber, The* – 1794N
 *Travellers, The* – 1807N
 *Voice of Nature, The* – 1805N
 *Volunteers, The* – 1795N
 *Warrior's Welcome, The* – 1796N
 *Witches of the Rock, The* – 1796N
 *Wreath for American Tars, A* – 1800N

Reimer, Bennett
 *Philosophy of Music Education, A* – 1970M
Reimers, Paul – 1913H, 1924I, 1942G
Reiner, Fritz – 1922IK, 1928K, 1931I, 1938I, 1948I,
 1949H, 1953I, 1962K
Reiner, Fritz, Center for Contemporary Music –
 1984L
Reinhardt, Delia – 1923H
Reining, Maria – 1938H
Reisenaur, Alfred – 1895H
Reisenberg, Nadia – 1922HK
Reisner, R. G.
 *Jazz Titans, The* – 1960D
 *Literature of Jazz, The* – 1954D
Reiss, Albert – 1901H
Reiter, Max – 1939I
Relache – 1977L
R.E.M. – 1980C
Remler, Emily – 1957A, 1990B
Reliance Brass Band – 1892C
Remains, The – 1965C
Remedios, Alberto – 1973H, 1976H
Reményi, Eduard – 1848K, 1850H, 1878K, 1898G
Remick, Jerome H. – 1868A, 1898K, 1931B
Remick, Jerome H., Co. – 1894C
Remoortel, Edouard van – 1958I
Renaud, Maurice – 1893H, 1906H, 1910H
Rendall, David – 1980H
Rene, Leon T.
 *When It's Sleepy Time Down South* – 1931E
Rentfro Valley Barn Dance – 1937C
Renzetti, Donato – 1988H
REO Speedwagon – 1967C, 1981E, 1985E
Répertoire International d'Iconographie Musicale –
 1971L
Répertoire International de Littérature Musicale –
 1966L
Replacements – 1980C
Reprise Records – 1961C
Residents, The – 1970C
Res Musica (MD) – 1980L
Resnik, Regina – 1922F, 1942H, 1944H, 1993I
Respighi, Ottorino – 1925K
Restless Heart – 1985C
Rethberg, Elisabeth – 1922H, 1976G
Réti, Rudolf – 1938K, 1957G
 *Thematic Process in Music, The* – 1951M
 *Tonality—Atonality—Pantonality* – 1958M
 *Tonality in Modern Music* – 1962M
Return to Forever – 1971C
Reuss-Belce, Luise – 1902H
Reuter, Rudolph E. – 1888F
Reuter Organ Co. – 1917L
Revel, Harry – 1929C, 1958B
 *Did You Ever See a Dream Walking?* – 1933E
Revelation Records – 1965C
Revelli, William D. – 1902F, 1935I, 1941I, 1971K,
 1994G
Revere, Paul – 1942A

---

※

---

**Vernacular/Commercial Music Scene**
A  *Births*    B  *Deaths*    C  *Biographical*    D  *Publications*
E  *Representative Pieces*

---

❋

---

Cultivated/Art Music Scene

F *Births*    G *Deaths*    H *Debuts*    I *New Positions*    J *Honors and Awards*
K *Biographical*    L *Musical Beginnings*    M *Publications*    N *Compositions*

❀

Vernacular/Commercial Music Scene

  A  *Births*     B  *Deaths*     C  *Biographical*     D  *Publications*
              E  *Representative Pieces*

---

## Cultivated/Art Music Scene

F *Births*   G *Deaths*   H *Debuts*   I *New Positions*   J *Honors and Awards*
K *Biographical*   L *Musical Beginnings*   M *Publications*   N *Compositions*

---

✷

---

Vernacular/Commercial Music Scene
A  *Births*     B  *Deaths*     C  *Biographical*     D  *Publications*
E  *Representative Pieces*

Rogers, Francis – 1870F, 1898H, 1924I, 1951G
  *Some Famous Singers of the Nineteenth Century* –
  1914M
Rogers, James H.
  *In Memoriam* – 1919N
Rogers, Kenny – 1938A, 1977C, 1979C, 1980E,
  1983E
Rogers, Roy – 1911A, 1988C
Rolandi, Gianna – 1952F, 1975H, 1979H
Rolling Stones – 1964C, 1965E, 1966E, 1967E,
  1969E, 1970E, 1971E,
*Rolling Stone* – 1967C
Rollini, Adrian – 1904A, 1956B
Rollins, Sonny – 1929A
Rollinson, Thomas H. – 1844F, 1888I, 1928G
Rolnick, Neil
  *ElectriCity* – 1991N
Roloff, Roger – 1984J
Roma, Caro – 1869F, 1937G
  *Can't Yo' Heah Me Callin', Caroline* – 1914E
Roman, Stella – 1941H, 1992G
Romantic Music Festival (IN) – 1968L
Romantics – 1977C
Romberg, Sigmund – 1909K
  *Blossom Time* – 1921E
  *Blue Paradise, The* – 1915E
  *Blushing Bride, The* – 1922E
  *Desert Song, The* – 1926E
  *East Wind* – 1931E
  *Katinka* – 1915E
  *Love Birds* – 1921E
  *May Wine* – 1935E
  *Maytime* – 1917E
  *New Moon* – 1928E
  *Nina Rosa* – 1930E
  *Passing Show III* – 1914E
  *Robinson Crusoe, Jr.* – 1916E
  *Student Prince, The* – 1924E
  *Up in Central Park* – 1945E
  *When I Grow Too Old to Dream* – 1935E
Rome, Harold – 1908A, 1993B
  *Bless You All* – 1950E
  *Destry Rides Again* – 1959E
  *Fanny* – 1954E
  *I Can Get It For You Wholesale* – 1962E
  *Let Freedom Ring* – 1942E
  *Pins & Needles* – 1937E
  *Sing Out the News* – 1938E
  *Wish You Were Here* – 1952E
  *Zulu & the Zayda, The* – 1965E
Romeo Void – 1979C
Romero, Angel – 1958K
Romero, Celedonio – 1958K
Romero, Celin – 1958K
Romero, Pepe – 1958K
Ronettes, The – 1959C
Roney, Wallace – 1960A
Ronstadt, Linda – 1946A, 1975CE
Rooftop Singers, The – 1963E

Rooney, Pat
  *Is That You, Mr. Riley?* – 1883E
Roosevelt, Hilborne L. – 1849F, 1886G
Root & Cady, Publishers – 1858L
Root & Sons Music Co. – 1875L
Root, Frederick W. – 1846F, 1862I, 1916G
  *F. W. Root's School of Singing* – 1873M
Root, George Frederick – 1820F, 1839K, 1844IK,
  1850K, 1881J, 1895G
  *Battle Cry of Freedom* – 1862E
  *Belshazzar's Feast* – 1860N
  *Bethlehem* – 1889N
  *Building of the Temple, The* – 1889N
  *Choicest Gift, The* – 1883N
  *Christian Graces, The* – 1862N
  *Columbus, the Hero of Fate* – 1892N
  *Coming of the Flowers, The* – 1888N
  *Daniel* – 1853N
  *David, the Shepherd Boy* – 1882N
  *Faith Triumphant* – 1886N
  *Festival of the Flowers, The* – 1893N
  *Florens, the Pilgrim* – 1890N
  *Flower Queen, The* – 1852N
  *Haymakers, The* – 1857N
  *Hazel Dell, The* – 1853E
  *Jacob & Esau* – 1890N
  *Just Before the Battle, Mother* – 1862E
  *Musical Curriculum, The* – 1864N
  *Normal Musical Handbook, The* – 1872M
  *Our Flag with the Stars & Stripes* – 1896N
  *Phillis, the Farmer's Daughter* – 1892N
  *Pilgrim Fathers, The* – 1854E
  *Pillar of Fire, The* – 1887N
  *Plough & Sickle* – 1894N
  *Root's Harmony & Composition* – 1892M
  *Rosalie, the Prairie Flower* – 1855E
  *Santa Claus' Mistake* – 1885N
  *Snow White & the Seven Dwarfs* – 1888N
  *Song Tournament, The* – 1878N
  *Star of Light, The* – 1896N
  *Story of a Musical Life: An Autobiography* –
  1891D
  *There's Music in the Air* – 1854E
  *Tramp! Tramp! Tramp!* – 1864E
  *Under the Palms* – 1880N
  *Vacant Chair, The* – 1861E
  *Young Ladies' Choir, The* – 1846M
  *Young Men's Singing Book* – 1855M
Rootering, Jan-Hendrik – 1987H
Rorem, Ned – 1923F, 1949K, 1968J, 1979J, 1980I
  *After Long Silence* – 1982N
  *Air Music* – 1974N
  *American Oratorio, An* – 1983N
  *Ariel* – 1971N
  *Bertha* – 1968N
  *Childhood Miracle, A* – 1952N
  *Concerto, Cello, Piano & Orchestra* – 1979N
  *Cycle of Holy Songs* – 1951N
  *Eagles* – 1958N

---

Cultivated/Art Music Scene
  F *Births*    G *Deaths*    H *Debuts*    I *New Positions*    J *Honors and Awards*
    K *Biographical*    L *Musical Beginnings*    M *Publications*    N *Compositions*

---

❀

## Vernacular/Commercial Music Scene

A *Births*    B *Deaths*    C *Biographical*    D *Publications*
E *Representative Pieces*

Rostropovich, Mstislav – 1956H, 1974K, 1975H, 1977I, 1987J, 1990JK, 1992J
Rosvaenge, Helge – 1962H
Rota, Nino
   *Romeo & Juliet* – 1966E
Rotary Connection – 1967C
Roth String Quartet – 1928L
Rothenberger, Anneliese – 1960H
Rothenberg, Ned – 1956F
Rothier, Léon – 1910H, 1951G
Rothmüller, Marko – 1948H, 1959H, 1993G
Rothwell, Walter Henry – 1904HIK, 1908I, 1919I, 1927G
Rouleau, Joseph – 1955H
Rouse, Charlie – 1988B
Rouse, Christopher – 1949F, 1978I, 1981I, 1985I, 1986I, 1991I
   *Cello Concerto* – 1992N
   *Concerto for Strings* – 1990N
   *Doublebass Concerto* – 1985N
   *Flute Concerto* – 1993N
   *Infernal Machine, The* – 1981N
   *Gorgon* – 1984N
   *Karolju* – 1990N
   *String Quartet No. 1* – 1981N
   *String Quartet No. 2* – 1988N
   *Symphony No. 1* – 1986N
   *Symphony No. 2* – 1994N
   *Trombone Concerto* – 1992N
   *Violin Concerto* – 1991N
Roussakis, Nicolas – 1949K, 1956K, 1969J, 1977I, 1994G
   *Fire & Earth & Water & Air* – 1983N
   *Ode & Cataclysm* – 1975N
Roussehère, Charles – 1906H
Rova Saxophone Quartet – 1977C
Rowe, Monk
   *Cheeks* – 1993N
Rowen, Ruth H.
   *Early Chamber Music* – 1949M
   *Music through Sources & Documents* – 1979M
Roxette – 1989E, 1990E, 1991E
Roxon, Lillian
   *Rock Encyclopedia* – 1969D
Royal, Billy Joe – 1942A
Royal Guardsmen – 1966C
Royal Teens – 1956C
Royaltones – 1957C
Royce, Rose – 1977E
Rôze, Marie Hippolyte – 1877H
Rózsa, Miklós – 1940K, 1995G
   *Ben Hur* – 1959E
   *Cello Concerto* – 1971N
   *Cid, El* – 1960E
   *Double Life, A* – 1948E
   *Green Berets, The* – 1968E
   *Ivanhoe* – 1952E
   *Jungle Book, The* – 1942E
   *King of Kings* – 1961E

   *Knights of the Round Table* –1954E
   *Lust for Life* – 1956E
   *Piano Concerto* – 1966N
   *Quo Vadis?* – 1951E
   *Sinfonia Concertante* – 1966N
   *Spellbound* – 1945E
   *String Quartet* – 1950N
   *Thief of Bagdad, The* – 1940E
   *Variations, Vintner's Daughter* – 1952N
   *Viola Concerto* – 1979N
   *Violin Concerto* – 1954N
Rozsnyai, Zoltán – 1956K, 1967I, 1978I, 1990G
Rubenstein, Bernard – 1984I
Rubinstein, Anton – 1872HK
Rubinstein, Artur – 1906H, 1946K, 1976JK, 1978J, 1982G
Rubinstein, Beryl – 1898F, 1916H, 1921I, 1952G
   *Outline of Piano Pedagogy* – 1929M
Rublowsky, John
   *Black Music in America* – 1971D
Rubsamen, Walter – 1911F, 1965I, 1973G
   *Literary Sources of Secular Music in Italy (ca. 1500)* – 1943M
Ruby and the Romantics – 1962E
Ruby, Harry – 1895A, 1974B
   *Animal Crackers* – 1928E
   *Come On, Papa* – 1918E
   *Five O'Clock Girl* – 1927E
   *Ramblers, The* – 1926E
   *Real McCoys, The* – 1957E
   *Town Clowns, The* – 1923E
Rudakova, Larissa – 1995H
Rudel, Julius – 1938K, 1944K, 1957I, 1958J, 1979I, 1985J
Rudersdorff, Hermine – 1871H, 1882G
Rudge, Olga – 1895F
Rudhyar, Dane – 1916K, 1926K
   *Catharsis* – 1923N
   *Cosmic Cycle* – 1977N
   *Dithyrambs* – 1919N
   *Four Pentagrams* – 1926N
   *Granites* – 1929N
   *Mosaics* – 1918N
   *Piano Quintet* – 1950N
   *Poèmes Ironiques* – 1914N
   *Sinfonietta* – 1931N
   *Soul Fire* – 1920N
   *Symphony* – 1928N
   *Syntony No. 1 & 2* – 1921N
   *Syntony No. 5* – 1954N
   *Theurgy* – 1976N
   *Three Paeans* – 1925N
   *Transmutation* – 1976N
   *Tripthong* – 1949N
   *Trois chansons de Bilitis* – 1918N
   *Warrior, The* – 1921N
Rudolf, Max – 1940K, 1945I, 1946K, 1958I, 1970I, 1995G
   *Grammar of Conducting, The* – 1950M

---

### Cultivated/Art Music Scene

F *Births*   G *Deaths*   H *Debuts*   I *New Positions*   J *Honors and Awards*
K *Biographical*   L *Musical Beginnings*   M *Publications*   N *Compositions*

---

Vernacular/Commercial Music Scene
A *Births*    B *Deaths*    C *Biographical*    D *Publications*
E *Representative Pieces*

---

Cultivated/Art Music Scene

F *Births*    G *Deaths*    H *Debuts*    I *New Positions*    J *Honors and Awards*
K *Biographical*    L *Musical Beginnings*    M *Publications*    N *Compositions*

---

❀

### Vernacular/Commercial Music Scene
A  *Births*    B  *Deaths*    C  *Biographical*    D  *Publications*
E  *Representative Pieces*

---

## Cultivated/Art Music Scene

F *Births*   G *Deaths*   H *Debuts*   I *New Positions*   J *Honors and Awards*
K *Biographical*   L *Musical Beginnings*   M *Publications*   N *Compositions*

Schech, Marianne – 1957H
Scheel, Fritz – 1895I, 1893K, 1900I, 1907G
Scheff, Fritzi – 1900H, 1903K, 1954G
Schein, Ann – 1939F, 1958H, 1962H, 1980I
Scheja, Steffan – 1972H
Schelle, Michael – 1950F
Schelling, Ernest – 1876F, 1882K, 1905K, 1913J,
   1919K, 1936I, 1939G
   *Divertimento* – 1925N
   *Fantastic Suite* – 1905N
   *Impressions from an Artist's Life* – 1913N
   *Légende Symphonique* – 1904N
   *Morocco* – 1927N
   *Suite Fantastique* – 1906N
   *Victory Ball, A* – 1923N
   *Violin Concerto* – 1916N
Schemtchuk, Ludmila – 1990H
Schenig, Francis – 1836I
Schenk, Andrew – 1992G
Scherchen, Hermann – 1964H
Scherman, Thomas – 1917F, 1960J, 1979G
Schermerhorn, Kenneth – 1929F, 1957I, 1963I,
   1968I, 1983I
Scherr, Emilius N. – 1822K, 1874G
Schertzinger, Victor – 1890A, 1941B
   *Civilization* – 1916E
   *Tangerine* – 1942E
Schetky, J. George – 1776F, 1787K, 1810K, 1831G
Schetky, J. George, Music Publisher – 1802L
Schexnayder, Brian – 1953F, 1980H
Schick, George – 1939K, 1958I, 1969I
Schiff, András – 1978H
Schiff, David – 1945F
   *Gimple the Fool* – 1978N
Schiff, Heinrich – 1981H
Schiffman, Harold
   *Rhapsody for Guitar* – 1991N
Schifrin, Lalo – 1958C
   *Mission Impossible* – 1967E
Schickele, Peter – 1935F
Schilke Music Products – 1956L
Schilke, Renold – 1910F, 1982G
Schiller, Madeline – 1911G
Schilling, Nina – 1897H
Schillinger, Joseph – 1928K, 1943G
   *Kaleidophone: New Resources of Melody &
   Harmony* – 1940M
Schindler, Kurt – 1904K, 1905K, 1907I, 1935G
Schiotz, Aksel – 1948H
Schipa, Tito – 1919H, 1932H, 1965G
Schipper, Emil – 1928H
Schippers, Thomas – 1930F, 1951I, 1955H, 1959K,
   1970I, 1977IK
Schirmer's Library of Musical Classics –
   1892L
Schirmer, Ernest C. – 1865F, 1958G
Schirmer, E. C., Publisher – 1921L
Schirmer, Gustav – 1837K, 1854I, 1861K, 1866K,
   1893G

Schirmer, Gustave, II – 1864F, 1907G
Schirmer, Gustave, III – 1890F, 1965G
Schlesinger, Daniel – 1836HK, 1837I, 1838G
Schlicker, Herman – 1925K, 1974G
Schlicker Organ Co. – 1932L
Schlöffler, Paul – 1950H
Schlusnus, Heinrich – 1927H
Schmedes, Erik – 1908H
Schmidt, Annerose – 1980H
Schmidt, Arthur P. – 1866K, 1921G
Schmidt, Arthur P., Co. – 1876L
Schmidt, Harvey – 1929A
   *Celebration* – 1969E
   *Fantasticks, The* – 1960E
   *I Do! I Do!* – 1966E
   *110 In the Shade* – 1963E
Schmidt, John Henry – 1797I
Schmidt, Wolfgang – 1993H
Schmiege, Marilyn – 1955F, 1978H, 1986H
Schmitz, Elie Robert – 1919H, 1949G
Schnabel, Artur – 1921H, 1939K, 1940I, 1944K,
   1951G
   *Music & the Line of Most Resistance* – 1942M
Schnaut, Gabriele – 1983H
Schnéevoigt, Georg – 1927I
Schneider, Alexander – 1938K, 1945J, 1988J, 1993G
Schneider, Edward F. – 1872F, 1901I, 1950G
Schneider, John – 1766K, 1771G
Schneider, John – 1954A
Schneider, Louis – 1873I
Schoebel, Elmer
   *Bugle Call Rag* – 1923E
Schoen-René, Anna – 1942G
Schoenberg (Columbia) String Quartet – 1977L
Schoenberg, Arnold – 1933I, 1934K, 1936I, 1941K,
   1946K, 1947J, 1951G
   *De Profundis* – 1950N
   *Dreimal Tausand Jahre* – 1949N
   *Fundamentals of Musical Composition* – 1948M
   *Genesis Prelude* – 1945N
   *Kol Nidre* – 1938N
   *Models for Beginners in Composition* – 1942M
   *Modern Psalm* – 1950N
   *Ode to Napoleon* – 1942N
   *Phantasy for Violin & Piano* – 1949N
   *Piano Concerto* – 1942N
   *Preliminary Exercises in Counterpoint* – 1950M
   *String Quartet No. 4* – 1936N
   *String Trio, Op. 45* – 1946N
   *Structural Functions of Harmony* – 1948M
   *Style & Idea* – 1950M
   *Survivor from Warsaw, A* – 1947N
   *Theme & Variations, Op. 43a* – 1943N
   *Variations on a Recitative* – 1941N
   *Violin Concerto* -1935N
Schoenberg, Arnold, Institute (USC) – 1974L
Schoenefeld, Henry – 1857F, 1875K, 1879K, 1936G
   *Suite Caractéristique for Strings* – 1890N
   *Symphony No. 1, "Rural"* – 1893N

---

❀

---

**Vernacular/Commercial Music Scene**
A *Births*    B *Deaths*    C *Biographical*    D *Publications*
E *Representative Pieces*

---

Cultivated/Art Music Scene
F *Births*    G *Deaths*    H *Debuts*    I *New Positions*    J *Honors and Awards*
K *Biographical*    L *Musical Beginnings*    M *Publications*    N *Compositions*

Vernacular/Commercial Music Scene
A *Births*    B *Deaths*    C *Biographical*    D *Publications*
E *Representative Pieces*

---

## Cultivated/Art Music Scene

F *Births*   G *Deaths*   H *Debuts*   I *New Positions*   J *Honors and Awards*
K *Biographical*   L *Musical Beginnings*   M *Publications*   N *Compositions*

Sedlmayer, Wilhelm – 1888H
Sedona Chamber Music Festival – 1985L
Seeds, The – 1965C
Seefried, Irmgard – 1953H
Seeger, Charles – 1886F, 1912I, 1921I, 1931K,
   1935I, 1941I, 1960I
   *Derdra* – 1914N
   *Essays for a Humanist* – 1977M
   *Harmonic Structure & Elementary Composition -*
   1916M
   *Music and Society* – 1953M
   *Music as Recreation* – 1940M
   *Parthema* – 1915N
   *String Quartet* – 1913N
   *Studies in Musicology, 1935-75* – 1977M
   *Violin Sonata* – 1913N
Seeger, Mike – 1933A
Seeger, Peggy – 1935A
Seeger, Pete – 1919A, 1994C
Seeger, Ruth Crawford – 1953B
   *American Folk Songs for Children* – 1948D
   *American Folk Songs for Christmas* – 1955D
   *Animal Folk Songs for Children* – 1950D
Seeley, Blossom – 1974B
Seely, Jeannie – 1966C
Seesaw Music Corporation – 1963L
Seger, Bob – 1947A, 1987E
Segovia, Andrés – 1928H
Seguin, Anne – 1838K, 1888G
Seguin, Arthur – 1838K
Seguin, Edward – 1838H, 1852G
Segurola, Andrés de – 1901H
Seidel, Toscha – 1918H, 1924K, 1962G
Seidl, Anton – 1885HI, 1889K, 1891II
Seidl-Krauss, Frau – 1884H
Seiffert, Peter – 1988H, 1993H
Seinemeyer, Meta – 1923H
Seitz, Roland F. – 1867F, 1946G
Selby, Kathryn – 1981H
Selby, William – 1771HIK, 1776I, 1778I, 1798G
   *Ten Organ Voluntaries* – 1767N
Seldom Scene, The – 1971C
Selena – 1995C
Selika, Marie – 1849F, 1937G
Sellars, James – 1943F, 1983J
   *World Is Round, The* – 1993N
Sellars, Peter – 1957F
Seller, Emma
   *Voice In Singing* – 1869M
Seltmann, Ernst T. – 1883G
Sembello, David – 1983E
Sembrich, Marcella – 1883H, 1935G
Semkow, Jerzy – 1968H, 1977I, 1985I
Sendrey, Alfred
   *Bibliography of Jewish Music* – 1951M
Senn, Marta – 1958F, 1982H
Senofsky, Berl – 1925F, 1947J, 1955J
Sensational Nightingales – 1945C
Sensations – 1954C

Sentinals – 1962C
Sentinel Beast – 1984C
Sequoia String Quartet – 1972L
Serafin, Tullio – 1924HI
Serebrier, José – 1956K, 1968I, 1976J
Sereni, Mario – 1957H
Serge Modular Music Systems – 1974L
Serkin, Peter – 1947F, 1958H, 1973K, 1983J, 1992I
Serkin, Rudolf – 1933H, 1939IK, 1963J, 1968I,
   1981J, 1985K, 1988J, 1991G
Serly, Tibor – 1901F, 1911K, 1978G
   *Modus Lascivus: the Road to Enharmonicism –*
   1976M
   *Pagan City, The* – 1938N
   *Pleiades, The* – 1975N
   *Second Look at Harmony, A* – 1965M
   *Sonata in Modus Lascivus* – 1946M
   *String Quartet* – 1924M
   *Symphony No. 1* – 1931M
   *Symphony No. 2* – 1932M
   *Viola Concerto* – 1929M
Servile, Roberto – 1994H
Sessions, Roger – 1896F, 1917IK, 1921I, 1928J,
   1935I, 1937J, 1944I, 1953IJ, 1958J, 1961J,
   1968JK, 1974J, 1985G
   *Black Maskers, The* – 1923N
   *Concertino 3 Times 3* – 1965N
   *Concerto for Cello & Violin* – 1971N
   *Concerto for Orchestra* – 1981N
   *Concerto for Two Pianos* – 1958N
   *Five Pieces for Piano* – 1977N
   *Harmonic Practice* – 1951M
   *Idyll of Theocritus* – 1954N
   *Lancelot & Elaine* – 1910N
   *Montezuma* – 1963N
   *Musical Experience of Composer, Performer,*
   *Listener- 1950M
   *Pages from My Diary* – 1939N
   *Piano Sonata No. 1* – 1930N
   *Piano Sonata No. 2* – 1946N
   *Piano Sonata No. 3* – 1965N
   *Questions about Music* – 1970M
   *Reflections on the Music Life in the United States*
   – 1956N
   *Rhapsody for Orchestra* – 1970N
   *Roger Sessions on Music: The Collected Essays –*
   1979M
   *String Quartet No. 1* – 1936N
   *String Quartet No. 2* – 1951N
   *String Quintet* – 1958N
   *Symphony in D* – 1917N
   *Symphony No. 1* – 1927N
   *Symphony No. 2* – 1946N
   *Symphony No. 3* – 1957N
   *Symphony No. 4* – 1958N
   *Symphony No. 5* – 1964N
   *Symphony No. 6* – 1966N
   *Symphony No. 7* – 1967N
   *Symphony No. 8* – 1968N

---

✵

Vernacular/Commercial Music Scene
A *Births*     B *Deaths*     C  *Biographical*     D *Publications*
E *Representative Pieces*

---

### ❋ Cultivated/Art Music Scene

F *Births*    G *Deaths*    H *Debuts*    I *New Positions*    J *Honors and Awards*
K *Biographical*    L *Musical Beginnings*    M *Publications*    N *Compositions*

Shavers, Charlie – 1917A, 1971B
Shaw Attractions, Inc. – 1978L
Shaw Concerts, Inc. – 1969L
Shaw, Alice J. – 1856F, 1918G
Shaw, Arnold – 1909F
  *Dictionary of American Pop/Rock* – 1985D
  *Honkers & Shouters: Golden Years of Rhythm &*
  *Blues* – 1978D
  *Lingo of Tin-Pan Alley* – 1950D
  *Rock Revolution, The* – 1969D
  *Street That Never Slept, The* – 1971D
  *World of Soul, The* – 1970D
Shaw, Artie – 1910A, 1938C
  *Concerto for Clarinet* – 1941E
  *Interlude in B-Flat* – 1936E
Shaw, Artie, Band – 1936C
Shaw, Artie, Band II – 1937C
Shaw, Artie, Band III – 1941C
Shaw, Artie, Band IV – 1944C
Shaw, David – 1940A
Shaw, Harold – 1923F
Shaw, Joseph P. – 1899G
Shaw, Joseph P., Music House – 1854L
Shaw, Oliver – 1779F, 1805K, 1809I, 1848G
  *Columbian Sacred Harmonist, The* – 1808M
  *Favorite Selection of Music, A* – 1806M
  *For the Gentleman: A Favorite Selection...* –
  1807M
  *Instructions for the Pianoforte* – 1831M
  *Melodia Sacra* – 1819M
  *Plain Introduction to...Playing the Pianoforte* –
  1811M
  *Providence Selection of Psalm & Hymn Tunes* –
  1815M
  *Sacred Melodies...from Handel, Haydn...& Others*
  – 1818M
  *Social Sacred Melodies* – 1835M
  *Thanksgiving Anthem* – 1809N
  *Welcome the Nation's Guest* – 1824N
Shaw, Robert – 1916F, 1967I, 1979I, 1988JK, 1991J,
  1992J, 1993J
Shaw, Robert, Chorale – 1948L
Shaw, Woody – 1944A, 1989B
Shear, Jules – 1952A
Shearing, George – 1947C
  *Lullaby of Birdland* – 1952E
Shearing, George, Quintet – 1949C
Sheehan, Joseph – 1895H
Sheila E – 1959A
Sheinfeld, David – 1906F
Shelley, Harry Rowe – 1858F, 1878I, 1898J, 1899I,
  1947G
  *Carnaval Overture* – 1893N
  *Death & Life* – 1898N
  *Inheritance Divine, The* – 1895N
  *Lochinvar's Ride* – 1915N
  *Old Black Joe* – 1911N
  *Pilgrims, The* – 1903N
  *Romeo & Juliet* – 1901N

  *Santa Claus Overture* – 1900N
  *Soul Triumphant, The* – 1905N
  *String Quartet No. 1* – 1946N
  *Symphony* – 1897N
  *Vexilla regis* – 1893N
  *Violin Concerto* – 1891N
Shells – 1957C
Shelter Records – 1969C
Shelton, Lucy – 1944F, 1980J
Shelton, Ricky Van – 1952A
Shelton, Robert
  *Country Music Story, The* – 1966D
Shenandoah Valley Boys – 1951C
Sheng, Bright – 1982K
  *H'UN (Lacerations)* – 1987N
  *Song of Majnun* – 1992N
  *String Quartets 1 & 2* – 1984N
Shep and the Limelites – 1961C
Shepherd, Adaline
  *Pickles & Peppers Rag* – 1906E
Shepherd, Arthur – 1880F, 1892K, 1897IK, 1901K,
  1909K, 1910I, 1919K, 1920K, 1927I, 1928I, 1937J,
  1941J, 1950K, 1958G
  *Ballad of Trees & the Master, A* – 1934N
  *Capriccio No. 1 for Piano* – 1938N
  *Capriccio No. 2 for Piano* – 1941N
  *Capriccio No. 3 for Piano* – 1943N
  *Choreographic Suite* – 1930N
  *City in the Sea, The* – 1913N
  *Eclogue No. 1* – 1931N
  *Fantasia on "The Garden Hymn"* – 1943N
  *Fantasie Humoreske* – 1916N
  *Fantasy Overture on...Spirituals* – 1946N
  *Festival of Youth Overture* – 1915N
  *Five Songs on Lowell, Op. 7* – 1909N
  *Fugue in C#* – 1920N
  *Hilaritas* – 1942N
  *Invitation to the Dance* – 1936N
  *Marche Solenelle* – 1918N
  *Nocturne in B* – 1908N
  *Nocturne No. 2 for Piano* – 1941N
  *Ouverture Joyeuse, Op. 2* – 1901N
  *Overture to a Drama* – 1919N
  *Piano Sonata No. 1* – 1907N
  *Piano Sonata No. 2* – 1930N
  *Prelude in B* – 1904N
  *Quintet, Piano & Strings* – 1940N
  *Sinfonia Domestica de Famiglia Blossom* – 1932N
  *Song of the Pilgrims, The* – 1932N
  *String Quartet in G* – 1926N
  *String Quartet No. 1* – 1933N
  *String Quartet No. 2* – 1936N
  *String Quartet No. 3* – 1944N
  *String Quartet No. 4* – 1955N
  *Symphony No. 1* – 1927N
  *Symphony No. 2* – 1938N
  *Two Movements (SQ)* – 1905N
  *Variations, Original Theme* – 1952N
  *Violin Concerto* – 1946N

---

❖

**Vernacular/Commercial Music Scene**
A *Births*    B *Deaths*    C *Biographical*    D *Publications*
E *Representative Pieces*

Sheppards – 1959C
Sherman & Hyde Music Store – 1871L
Sherman, Bobby – 1943A
Sherman, Garry
  *Coming Uptown* – 1979E
Sherman, John K. – 1926I
Sherman, Leander S. – 1847F, 1926G
Sherman, Richard M.
  *Chitty, Chitty, Bang Bang* – 1968E
  *Over Here* – 1974E
Sherman, Russell – 1930F, 1945H, 1967I
Sherriff – 1989E
Sherwin, William F. – 1826F, 1884I, 1888G
  *Heart & Voice* – 1881M
Sherry, Fred – 1948F, 1969H
Sherwood, Billy – 1981B
Sherwood, William Hall – 1911G
  *Harp of Zion, The* – 1893M
Shicoff, Neil – 1949F, 1975H, 1976H
Shields, Ren – 1868A, 1913B
Shifrin, Lalo
  *Jazz Faust* – 1963E
  *Jazz Suite on the Mass Texts* – 1965E
Shifrin, Seymour – 1926F, 1951I, 1957J,
  1979G
  *Cantata to Sophoclean Choruses* – 1958N
  *Chamber Symphony* – 1953N
  *Chronicles* – 1970N
  *Concerto of the Americas* – 1992N
  *Four Cantos for Piano* – 1948N
  *Five Last Songs* – 1979N
  *Modern Temper* – 1959N
  *Music for Orchestra* – 1948N
  *Piano Trio* – 1974N
  *Satires of Circumstance* – 1964N
  *Songs of the Aztecs* – 1988N
  *String Quartet No. 1* – 1949N
  *String Quartet No. 2* – 1962N
  *String Quartet No. 3* – 1966N
  *String Quartet No. 4* – 1967N
  *String Quartet No. 5* – 1972N
  *Trauermusik* – 1956N
  *3 Pieces for Orchestra* – 1958N
Shilkret, Nat – 1895F, 1916I, 1982B
Shilohs, The – 1963C
Shire – 1983C
Shire, David
  *Baby* – 1983E
  *Starting Here, Starting Now* – 1977E
Shirelles, The – 1958C, 1961E
Shirley, George – 1934F, 1959H, 1961H
Shirley-Quirk, John – 1974H
Shirreff, Jane – 1838K
Shocked, Michelle – 1962A
Shocking Blue – 1970E
Shoemaker, Carolie J. – 1963F
Shondells, The – 1965C, 1966E, 1969E
Shore, Clare – 1956F
Shore, Dinah – 1917A, 1994B

Short, Bobby – 1926A
Shorter, Wayne – 1933A
Shostakovich, Maxim – 1981K, 1986I
Shout – 1988C
Showalter, A. J. – 1858F, 1924G
  *Best Gospel Songs & Their Composers, The* –
  1904M
  *Choir & Congregation* – 1888M
  *Harmony & Composition* – 1882M
  *Rudiments of Music* – 1887M
Showalter, A. J., Co. – 1884L
Shulman, Alan – 1915F
  *Cello Concerto* – 1948N
  *Laurentian Overture, A* – 1951N
  *Pastorale & Dance* – 1944N
  *Theme & Variations* – 1940N
Shuman, Mort – 1936A, 1991B
Shumsky, Oscar – 1917F, 1925H
Shumway, Jeffrey – 1977J
Shumway, Nehemiah
  *American Harmony, The* – 1793M
Shure, Leonard – 1910F, 1927H, 1933H, 1995G
Sidlin, Murry – 1940F, 1978I
Siegel, Janis – 1952A
Siegel, Jeffrey – 1942F, 1958H, 1968J, 1985J
Siegling, John, Music Store – 1819L
Siegmeister, Elie – 1909F, 1927K, 1949I, 1978J,
  1990J, 1991G
  *Abraham Lincoln Walks at Midnight* – 1937N
  *American Holiday* – 1933N
  *American Sonata (Piano-# 1)* – 1944N
  *Figures in the Wind* – 1990N
  *Flute Concerto* – 1960N
  *Four Robert Frost Songs* – 1930N
  *Harmony & Melody* – 1965M
  *Invitation to Music* – 1961M
  *Lady of the Lake* – 1985N
  *Music Lover's Handbook, The* – 1943M
  *Negro Songs of Protest* – 1935D
  *Ozark Set* – 1943N
  *Piano Concerto* – 1974N
  *Piano Sonata No. 2* – 1964N
  *Piano Sonata No. 3* – 1979N
  *Prelude, Blues & Toccata* – 1980N
  *Strange Funeral in Braddock* – 1932N
  *String Quartet No. 1* – 1935N
  *String Quartet No. 2* – 1960N
  *String Quartet No. 3* – 1973N
  *Symphony No. 1* – 1947N
  *Symphony No. 2* – 1950N
  *Symphony No. 3* – 1957N
  *Symphony No. 4* – 1970N
  *Symphony No. 5* – 1975N
  *Symphony No. 6* – 1983N
  *Symphony No. 7* – 1986N
  *Symphony No. 8* – 1989N
  *Theme & Variations No. 1* – 1932N
  *Theme & Variations No. 2* – 1967N
  *Treasury of American Song, A* – 1940M

---

## Cultivated/Art Music Scene
**F** *Births*    **G** *Deaths*    **H** *Debuts*    **I** *New Positions*    **J** *Honors and Awards*
**K** *Biographical*    **L** *Musical Beginnings*    **M** *Publications*    **N** *Compositions*

---

❀

---

Vernacular/Commercial Music Scene
A *Births*     B *Deaths*     C *Biographical*     D *Publications*
E *Representative Pieces*

---

❖

---

## Cultivated/Art Music Scene

F *Births*    G *Deaths*    H *Debuts*    I *New Positions*    J *Honors and Awards*

K *Biographical*    L *Musical Beginnings*    M *Publications*    N *Compositions*

Smith, David Stanley (continued)
   *Prince Hal Overture* – 1912N
   *Rhapsody of St. Bernard* – 1915N
   *Songs of Three Ages* – 1936N
   *String Quartet No. 1* – 1906N
   *String Quartet No. 3* – 1920N
   *String Quartet No. 8* – 1936N
   *String Quartet No. 10* – 1944N
   *String Sextet* – 1931N
   *Symphony No. 1* – 1910N
   *Symphony No. 2* – 1917N
   *Symphony No. 3* – 1928N
   *Symphony No. 4* – 1937N
   *Symphony No. 5* – 1949N
   *Triumph & Peace* – 1943N
   *Violin Concerto* – 1933N
   *Violin Sonata* – 1921N
   *Vision of Isaiah* – 1926N
   *Witch's Daughter, The* – 1918N
   *1929—A Satire* – 1932N
   *4 & 20 Little Songs* – 1919N
Smith, Edgar – 1857A, 1938B
Smith, Ethel – 1910A
Smith, Gregg – 1931F
Smith, Gregg, Singers – 1955L
Smith, Geoff
   *New Voices: American Composers Talk...* –
   1995M
Smith, H. Augustine
   *Hymns of the Living Age* – 1923M
Smith, Hale – 1925F
   *Toussaint L'Ouverture 1803* – 1977N
Smith, Harry B. – 1860A, 1890E, 1936B
Smith, Hubbard T.
   *If You Love Me, Darling, Tell Me with Your Eyes* –
   1887E
   *Listen to My Tale of Woe* – 1884E
Smith, Huey "Piano" – 1934A
Smith, Jabbo – 1908A, 1991B
Smith, Jimmy – 1925A
Smith, Joe – 1902A
Smith, Joshua
   *Divine Hymns or Spiritual Songs...* – 1784M
Smith, Josiah – 1781G
Smith, Julia – 1911F
   *Characteristic Suite, Piano* – 1949N
   *Cockcrow* – 1953N
   *Cynthia Parker* – 1938N
   *Directory of American Women Composers* –
   1970M
   *Folkways Symphony* – 1948N
   *Piano Concerto* – 1939N
Smith, Kate – 1909A, 1982C, 1986B
Smith, Keely – 1932A
Smith, Lawrence Leighton – 1936F, 1964J, 1973I,
   1980I, 1983I
Smith, Leland – 1925F
   *Handbook of Harmonic Analysis* – 1963M
Smith, Mamie – 1883A, 1946B

Smith, Moses – 1901F, 1924I, 1934I, 1964G
Smith, N. Clark
   *Negro Choral Symphony* – 1933N
Smith, Nicholas
   *Stories of the Great National Songs* – 1889D
Smith, Patrick J. – 1932F, 1970I, 1977I
   *Tenth Muse, The* – 1970M
Smith, Patti – 1946A
Smith, Rex – 1956A
Smith, Robert B. – 1875A, 1951B
Smith, Russell – 1927F, 1970I
   *Piano Concerto No. 2* – 1957N
   *Songs of Innocence* – 1949N
Smith, Sammi – 1971C
Smith, Stuff – 1909A, 1967B
Smith, Terry – 1960A
Smith, "Whispering" Jack – 1951B
Smith, William – 1784K, 1821G
   *Assistant to the Evangelical Psalmodist* – 1816M
   *Churchmans' Choral Companion* – 1809M
   *Reasonableness of Setting Forth the...Praise of*
   *God* – 1814M
Smith, William O. – 1926F, 1954I, 1957J, 1966I
Smith, Willie Mae Ford – 1906A, 1994B
Smith, Willie "the Lion" – 1897A
Smith's Mandolin & Stringed Instrument Club –
   1904L
Smither, Howard – 1925F
Smithereens, The – 1980C
Smithers, Don – 1933F
SMU Summer Music Festival – 1976L
Snap! – 1989C
Snider, Dee – 1955A
Snow – 1993E
Snow, Hank – 1914A, 1979C
Snow, Phoebe – 1952A
Snyder, Barry – 1966J
Snyder, Ted – 1881A, 1965B
   *One Girl in a Million* – 1914E
   *Sheik of Araby, The* – 1921E
   *That Mysterious Rag* – 1911E
   *Who's Sorry Now* – 1923E
Snyder, Ted, Music Co. – 1908C
Sobolewski, Eduard – 1859K, 1860I, 1872G
Social Distortion – 1979C
Society for Asian Music – 1960L
Society for Contemporary Music – 1927L
Society for Electro-Acoustic Music – 1984L
Society for Ethnomusicology – 1955L
Society for Forgotten Music – 1948L
Society for the Preservation...of Barber Shop Quartet
   Singing – 1938C
Society for the Preservation of the American Musical
   Heritage – 1958L
Society for the Publication of American Music –
   1919L
Society of American Musicians & Composers –
   1889L
Society of Black Composers – 1968L

---

Vernacular/Commercial Music Scene
A *Births*   B *Deaths*   C *Biographical*   D *Publications*
E *Representative Pieces*

Society of Composers, Inc. – 1966L
Society of European State Authors & Composers –
1931L
Society of St. Gregory of America – 1914L
Society of the Classic Guitar – 1936L
Society of the Friends of Music – 1913L
Soderlund, Gustave F. – 1916K, 1928I
Söderström, Elisabeth – 1959H
Sohmer, Hugo – 1863K, 1913G
Sohmer & Co., Pianos – 1872L
Sojourn – 1983C
Sokoloff, Nicolai – 1886F, 1898K, 1914I, 1918I,
1938I, 1965G
Solar Records – 1978C
Soldier, Dave
*Ultraviolet Railroad* – 1992N
*War Prayer* – 1993N
Sollberger, Harvey – 1938F, 1965IJ, 1983H
*Flute & Drums* – 1977N
*Humble Heart, The* – 1983N
*Two & the One, The* – 1972N
Solly, Bill
*Great American Backstage Musical* – 1976E
Solomon – 1926H
Solomon, Izler – 1910F, 1932H, 1936I, 1941I,
1956I, 1987G
Solovox – 1940C
Solti, Georg – 1953H, 1960H, 1969I, 1993J
Somer, Hilda – 1938K
Something Else Press – 1964L
Somogi, Judith – 1937F, 1977I, 1984K, 1988G
Somogyi, László – 1964I
Sondheim, Stephen – 1930A, 1983C, 1992C, 1993C
*Anyone Can Whistle* – 1964E
*Assassins* – 1990E
*Company* – 1970E
*Follies* – 1971E
*Funny Thing Happened on the Way to the Forum*
 – 1962E
*Into the Woods* – 1987E
*Little Night Music, A* – 1973E
*Merrily We Roll Along* – 1981E
*Pacific Overtures* – 1976E
*Passion* – 1994E
*Putting It Together* – 1992E
*Seven Percent Solution, The* – 1977E
*Side by Side with Sondheim* – 1977E
*Sunday in the Park with George* – 1984E
*Sweeney Todd* – 1979E
*Song Hits* – 1942C
*Song Messenger of the Northwest* – 1863L
*Songsmith's Journal* – 1976C
Songwriters' Hall of Fame – 1977C
*Songwriters Magazine* – 1975C
*Songwriter's Market* – 1979C
*Songwriter's Museum* – 1803L
Songwriters' Protective Association – 1931C
*Songwriter's Review, The* – 1946C
Sonic Arts Union – 1966L

Sonic Youth – 1981C
Sonneck, Oscar G. – 1873F, 1899K, 1902I, 1915I,
1917I, 1928G
*Bibliography of Early Secular American Music* –
1905M
*Dramatic Music:...Scores in the...Library of*
*Congress* – 1908M
*Early Concert Life in America (1731–1800)* –
1907M
*Early Opera in America* – 1915M
*Miscellaneous Studies in the History of Music* –
1921M
*Suum cuique: Essays on Music* – 1916M
Sonneck Society – 1975I
Sonnier, Jo-el – 1946A
Sonny and Cher – 1963C, 1965E
Sons of the Pioneers – 1933C, 1980C
Sontag, Henriette – 1852H
Souter, Edward – 1966H, 1980H
Sophie von Otter, Anne – 1985H
Sopkin, Henry – 1903F, 1944I, 1988G
Sopwith Camel – 1965C
Sordello, Enzo – 1955H
S.O.S. Band – 1977C
SOS Productions – 1987C
Sotin, Hans – 1972H
Soul Asylum – 1981C
Soul City Symphony – 1975E
Soul Survivors – 1966C
Soul, David – 1943A, 1983E
Soul, Jimmy – 1983E
Souled America – 1987C
SoundCelebration – 1987L
Soundgarden – 1984C
*Soundings* – 1972L
Sousa, Antonio – 1854K
Sousa, John Philip – 1854F, 1861K, 1868K, 1875K,
1878K, 1879K, 1880I, 1892K, 1900K, 1910K,
1920J, 1923J, 1924K, 1929J, 1932G, 1973J
*Across the Danube March* – 1877N
*America First March* – 1916N
*American Maid, The* – 1913E
*At the King's Court* – 1904N
*Beau Ideal March, The* – 1893N
*Belle of Chicago, The* – 1892N
*Ben Bolt March* – 1888N
*Black Horse Troop* – 1924N
*Blending of the Blue & Gray, The* – 1877N
*Bonnie Annie Laurie March* – 1883N
*Boy Scouts of America* – 1916N
*Bride Elect, The* – 1898E
*Bullets & Bayonets* – 1919N
*Capitan, El* – 1896E
*Capitan March, El* – 1896N
*Century of Progress, A* – 1931N
*Charlatan, The* – 1898E
*Chris & the Wonderful Lamp* – 1899E
*Colonial Dames Waltzes* – 1896N
*Columbia's Pride* – 1914N

---

## Cultivated/Art Music Scene

F *Births*    G *Deaths*    H *Debuts*    I *New Positions*    J *Honors and Awards*
K *Biographical*    L *Musical Beginnings*    M *Publications*    N *Compositions*

Sousa, John Philip (continued)
  *Congress Hall March* – 1882N
  *Corcoran Cadets March* – 1890N
  *Crusader March, The* – 1888N
  *Dauntless Battalion March, The*
  *Désirée* – 1883N
  *Diplomat, The* – 1904N
  *Directorate March* – 1894N
  *Esprit de Corps March* – 1878N
  *Federal March* – 1910N
  *Flags of Freedom* – 1918N
  *Florine* – 1881N
  *Free Lance March* – 1906N
  *From Maine to Oregon* – 1913N
  *Gallant Seventh March* – 1922N
  *Gladiator March* – 1886N
  *Globe & Eagle March* – 1879N
  *Guide Right March* – 1881N
  *Hail to the Spirit of Liberty* – 1900N
  *Hands Across the Sea March* – 1899N
  *High School Cadets March* – 1898N
  *Homeward Bound March* – 1892N
  *Honored Dead March* – 1876N
  *Imperial Edward* – 1902N
  *In Memoriam March* – 1881N
  *In Parlor & Street* – 1880N
  *Invincible Eagle* – 1901N
  *Jack Tar March* – 1903N
  *Kansas Wildcats* – 1931N
  *Katherine* – 1879N
  *King Cotton March* – 1895N
  *Lady of the White House Waltzes* – 1897N
  *Lamb's Gambol Overture* – 1914N
  *Last Days of Pompeii, The* – 1893N
  *Liberty Bell March* – 1893N
  *Loyal Legion March* – 1890N
  *Magna Carta* – 1928N
  *Man Behind the Gun March* – 1899N
  *Manhattan Beach March* – 1893N
  *March of the Royal Trumpets* – 1892N
  *March, On the Tramp* – 1879N
  *March, Review* – 1873N
  *Marching Along* – 1928M
  *Mikado March* – 1885N
  *Moonlight on the Potomac Waltzes* – 1872N
  *Mother Goose March* – 1883N
  *Mother Hubbard March* – 1885N
  *National Fencibles March* – 1888N
  *National, Patriotic & Typical Airs of All Countries*
   – 1890M
  *New York Hippodrome* – 1915N
  *Nobles of the Mystic Shrine* – 1923N
  *Occidental March* – 1887N
  *On Parade (Lion Tamer March)* – 1892N
  *Our Flirtation* – 1880N
  *Overture, Tally-Ho* – 1886N
  *Overture, Vautour* – 1886N
  *Paroles d'amour Waltzes* – 1880N
  *Pet of the Petticoats March* – 1883N

  *Phoenix, The* – 1875N
  *Picador March, The* – 1889N
  *Powhattan's Daughter* – 1907N
  *Presidential Poloniase* – 1886N
  *Pride of Pittsburgh* – 1901N
  *Queen of Hearts, The* – 1885N
  *Quilting Party, The* – 1889N
  *Reine d'Amour Waltzes, La* – 1874N
  *Reine de la Mer Waltzes, La* – 1866N
  *Resumption March* – 1879N
  *Revival March* – 1876N
  *Rifle Regiment March* – 1886N
  *Right Forward March* – 1881N
  *Right-Left March* – 1883N
  *Rivals Overture, The* – 1877N
  *Sabre & Spurs March* – 1918N
  *Salutation March* – 1873N
  *Salute of the Nations, The* – 1893N
  *Sandalphon Waltzes* – 1886N
  *Sardanapolis Waltzes* – 1877N
  *Semper Fidelis* – 1888N
  *Smugglers, The* – 1882E
  *Songs of Grace & Songs of Glory* – 1892N
  *Sound Off March* – 1885N
  *Sounds from the Revivals* – 1876N
  *Stars & Stripes Forever* – 1896N
  *Suite, Looking Up* – 1902N
  *Thunderer March, The* – 1889N
  *Transit of Venus March* – 1883N
  *Triumph of Time March* – 1885N
  *University of Nebraska* – 1928N
  *U.S. Field Artillery* – 1917N
  *Washington Post March* – 1889N
  *Wildcats March* – 1930N
  *Wolf, The* – 1888N
  *Wolverine March* – 1881N
  *Yorktown Centennial March* – 1881N
Sousa Band – 1892L
South Memphis Jug Band – 1925C
South Mountain Concerts (MA) – 1919L
Southard, Lucien H. – 1827F, 1868I, 1881G
  *Course in Harmony, A* – 1855M
  *Union Glee Book* – 1852M
Southeastern Music Center Summer Festival – 1983L
Southeastern Composers' League – 1952L
Southernaires – 1929C
*Southern Folklore Quarterly* – 1937C
Southern Music Co. (San Antonio) – 1935L
Southern Music Publishing Co. (San Antonio) –
  1957L
*Southern Musical Advocate & Singer's Friend* –
  1859L
Southern Musical Convention – 1845L
Southern Pacific – 1985C
Southern Symphony Orchestra (Columbia, SC) –
  1938L
Southern, Eileen – 1920F, 1973I, 1976I
  *Biographical Dictionary of Afro-American*
  *Musicians* – 1982M

❁

## Vernacular/Commercial Music Scene
A *Births*    B *Deaths*    C *Biographical*    D *Publications*
E *Representative Pieces*

---

### Cultivated/Art Music Scene

F *Births*    G *Deaths*    H *Debuts*    I *New Positions*    J *Honors and Awards*
K *Biographical*    L *Musical Beginnings*    M *Publications*    N *Compositions*

Spielman, Fritz
   *Stingiest Man in Town, The* – 1956E
Spier & Coslow Publishing Co. – 1928C
Spies, Claudio – 1942K, 1958I, 1966K, 1969J,
   1970I
Spikes, John
   *Wolverine Blues* – 1923E
Spilman, James E.
   *Flow Gently, Sweet Afton* – 1838N
Spina, Harold
   *Annie Doesn't Live Here Anymore* – 1933E
Spin Doctors, The – 1988C
Spinners, The (Detroit) – 1957C
Spirit – 1967C
Spirits of Rhythm – 1932C
Spitalny, Phil – 1970G
Spitalny's All-Girl Orchestra – 1934L
Spivacke, Harold – 1904F, 1937I, 1977G
   *Archive of American Folk Song in the Library of
   Congress* – 1941D
Spivak, Charlie – 1905A, 1982B
Spivakov, Vladimir – 1975H
Spivakovsky, Tossy – 1940HK, 1974I
Spivey, Victoria – 1906A, 1976B
Spohr, Ludwig – 1936K
Spokane Conservatory of Music – 1942L
Spoorenberg, Erna – 1967H
Springfield, Massachusetts
   *Handel Chorus of Springfield* – 1874L
   *Orchestral Club (MA)* – 1875L
   *Orpheus Society* – 1873L
   *Symphony Chorus* – 1944L
   *Symphony Orchestra* – 1944L
   *Tonic Sol-Fa Association* – 1883L
   *Young People's Symphony Orchestra* – 1947L
Springfield, Rick – 1949A, 1981E
Springsteen, Bruce – 1949A
Spurgeon, Phillip – 1969I
Spy – 1979C
Spyro Gyra – 1975C
Squier, Billy – 1950A
Squire, Albert
   *Squire's Cornet Band Olio* – 1871M
Stabile, Mariano – 1928H
Stafford, Jo – 1920A
Stagno, Roberto – 1883H
Stahl, Richard
   *Contented Woman, A* – 1897E
Stair, Patty – 1869F, 1926G
Stambler, Irwin
   *Encyclopedia of Folk, Country & Western Music* –
   1969D
   *Encyclopedia of Popular Music* – 1965D
   *Encyclopedia of Pop, Rock & Soul* – 1974D
Stamenova, Galina – 1984H
Stamm, Haralm – 1979H
Stamper, Dave – 1883A, 1963B
Stamps Quartet Music Co. – 1945C
Stamps-Baxter Music Co. – 1924C

Stamps, Frank – 1896A, 1965B
Stamps, V. O. – 1892A, 1940B
Stamps, V.O., Music Co. – 1924C
Standells – 1962C
Stanford Center for Computer Research – 1975L
Stanley Brothers – 1946C
Stanley String Quartet – 1949L
Stanley, Albert A. – 1851F, 1888I, 1932G
Staples, The – 1953C, 1972E, 1975E
Staples, Samuel E.
   *Ancient Psalmody & Hymnology of New England*
   – 1880M
Stapp, Gregory Lee – 1954F, 1978H
Stapp, Olivia – 1940F, 1960H, 1982H
Starcastle – 1972C
Starer, Robert – 1947K, 1949I, 1979J, 1994J
   *Apollonia* – 1978N
   *Ariel: Visions of Isaiah* – 1959N
   *Cello Concerto* – 1988N
   *Clarinet Concerto* – 1988N
   *Concerto, Viola, Strings & Percussion* –
   1958N
   *Concerto, Violin & Cello* – 1967N
   *Dybbuk, The* – 1960N
   *Four Seasonal Pieces* – 1985N
   *Holy Jungle* – 1974N
   *Hudson Valley Suite* – 1974N
   *Images of Man* – 1973N
   *Intruder, The* – 1956N
   *Joseph & His Brothers* – 1966N
   *Kaaterskill Quartet* – 1987N
   *Kohelet (Ecclesiastes)* – 1952N
   *Lady of the House of Sleep, The* – 1968N
   *Last Lover, The* – 1974N
   *Mutabili: Variants for Orchestra* – 1965N
   *Pantagleize* – 1967N
   *People, Yes, The* – 1976N
   *Phaedra* – 1962N
   *Piano Concerto No. 1* – 1947N
   *Piano Concerto No. 2* – 1953N
   *Piano Concerto No. 3* – 1972N
   *Piano Quartet* – 1977N
   *Piano Sonata No. 1* – 1949N
   *Piano Sonata No. 2* – 1965N
   *Prelude & Dance* – 1949N
   *Rhythmic Training* – 1969M
   *Samson Agonistes* – 1961N
   *Sketches in Color I* – 1963N
   *Story of Esther* – 1960N
   *String Quartet* – 1947N
   *Symphonic Prelude* – 1984N
   *Symphony No. 1* – 1950N
   *Symphony No. 2* – 1951N
   *Symphony No. 3* – 1969N
   *Transformation* – 1978N
   *Violin Concerto* – 1980N
Stark, John – 1841F
Stark, John, & Son – 1882L
Starker, Janos – 1948K, 1954K, 1958I, 1959K

---

### Vernacular/Commercial Music Scene
A *Births*   B *Deaths*   C *Biographical*   D *Publications*
E *Representative Pieces*

---

### Cultivated/Art Music Scene

F *Births*   G *Deaths*   H *Debuts*   I *New Positions*   J *Honors and Awards*
K *Biographical*   L *Musical Beginnings*   M *Publications*   N *Compositions*

---

❁

Vernacular/Commercial Music Scene

A *Births*   B *Deaths*   C *Biographical*   D *Publications*
E *Representative Pieces*

---

## Cultivated/Art Music Scene

**F** *Births*    **G** *Deaths*    **H** *Debuts*    **I** *New Positions*    **J** *Honors and Awards*
**K** *Biographical*    **L** *Musical Beginnings*    **M** *Publications*    **N** *Compositions*

❀

Vernacular/Commercial Music Scene
A *Births*    B *Deaths*    C *Biographical*    D *Publications*
E *Representative Pieces*

I & Albert – 1973E
Nick & Nora – 1991E
Rags – 1986E
Superman – 1966E
Truth about Cinderella – 1974E
Strow-Picco!ɔ, Lynne – 1975H
Strube, Gustav – 1890K, 1900I, 1913I,
1916I
   Americana – 1930N
   Captive, The – 1914N
   Cello Sonata – 1925N
   Echo – 1913N
   Four Preludes for Orchestra – 1920N
   Harz Mountains – 1940N
   "Lanier" Symphony – 1925N
   Lazarus – 1926N
   Longing – 1905N
   Loreley – 1913N
   Narcissus – 1913N
   Overture Puck – 1910N
   Peace Overture – 1945N
   Piano Trio – 1925N
   Ramona (The Captive) – 1916N
   Rhapsody for Orchestra – 1901N
   Sinfonietta – 1922N
   String Quartet No. 1 – 1923N
   String Quartet No. 2 – 1936N
   Sylvan Scenes – 1930N
   Symphonic Prologue – 1927N
   Symphony in B – 1909N
   Theory & Use of Chords, The – 1928M
   Viola Sonata – 1924N
   Violin Concerto No. 1 – 1924N
   Violin Concerto No. 2 – 1930N
   Violin Sonatas 1 & 2 – 1923N
   Wind Quintet – 1930N
Struckmann, Falk – 1995H
Strummer, Peter – 1972H, 1985H
Strunk, Oliver – 1901F, 1927K, 1934I, 1937I,
1966K, 1980G
   Essays on Music in the Western World – 1974M
   Source Readings in Music History – 1950M
   State & Resources of Musicology in the United
     States – 1932M
Stryper – 1983C
Stuart, Leslie
   Tell Me, Pretty Maiden – 1900E
Stuart, Marty – 1958A
Stückgold, Grete – 1927H, 1977G
Stucky, Steven
   Double Flute Concerto – 1994N
Studer, Cheryl – 1955F, 1984H, 1988H
Stuff – 1976C
Stulberg, Neal – 1954F, 1985I
Stults, R. M.
   Sweetest Story Ever Told, The – 1892E
Stylistics, The – 1968C
Styne, Jule – 1905A, 1990C, 1994B
   Bells Are Ringing – 1956E

Do Re Mi – 1960E
Fade Out—Fade In – 1964E
Five Minutes More – 1946E
Funny Girl – 1964E
Gentlemen Prefer Blondes – 1949E
Gypsy – 1959E
Hallelujah, Baby – 1967E
High Button Shoes – 1947E
I Don't Want to Walk Without You – 1941E
It's Been a Long, Long Time – 1945E
I've Heard That Song Before – 1942E
Let It Snow – 1945E
Lorelei – 1974E
Peter Pan – 1954E
Saturday Night Is the Loneliest Night – 1944E
Say, Darling – 1958E
Standing on the Corner – 1956E
Subways Are for Sleeping – 1961E
Sugar – 1972E
There Goes That Song Again – 1944E
Three Coins in the Fountain – 1954E
Time After Time – 1947E
Two on the Aisle – 1951E
Styx – 1963C, 1979E
Subotnick, Morton – 1933F, 1959I, 1966I, 1969I,
1979J
   All My Hummingbirds... – 1991N
   And the Butterflies Began to Sing – 1989N
   Balcony, The – 1960N
   Danton's Death – 1966N
   Galileo – 1964N
   Jacob's Room – 1993N
   Key to Songs, The – 1985N
   Lamination – 1968N
   Liquid Strata – 1982N
   Percussion Symphony – 1978N
   Serenade No. 3 – 1965N
   Sidewinder – 1971N
   Silver Apples of the Moon – 1967N
   Two Butterflies – 1975N
Sucher, Rosa – 1895H
Suchoff, Benjamin – 1918F
Sudds, William F. – 1843F, 1850K, 1920G
Suderburg, Robert – 1936F, 1957K, 1974I,
1985I
   Chamber Music II – 1967N
   Concert Mass – 1960N
   Harp Concerto – 1981N
   Percussion Concerto – 1977N
   Piano Concerto, "mirror of time" – 1974N
   Orchestral Music I – 1969N
Suessdorf, Karl
   Moonlight in Vermont – 1944E
Sugarcreek – 1981C
Sugar Hill Gang, The – 1977C
Suicide – 1972C
Suk, Josef – 1964H
Sullivan, George M., Arena (Alaska) – 1982L
Sullivan, Joe – 1906A, 1971B

---

## Cultivated/Art Music Scene

F  *Births*     G  *Deaths*     H  *Debuts*     I  *New Positions*     J  *Honors and Awards*
K  *Biographical*     L  *Musical Beginnings*     M  *Publications*     N  *Compositions*

Sullivan, Joseph J.
  *Where Did You Get That Hat?* – 1888E
Sullivan, Maxine – 1911A, 1987B
Sumac, Yma – 1946K, 1955K
Summa Cum Laude Orchestra – 1939C
Summer Terrace Garden Concerts – 1866L
Summer, Donna – 1948A, 1978E, 1979E
  *Bad Girls* – 1949E
Summy, Clayton F., Publisher – 1888L
Summy-Birchard Co. – 1957L
Sun Records – 1951C
Sun Valley Music Festival – 1982L
Sunday School Union
  *Union Prayer Meeting Hymns* – 1858M
Sundelius, Marie – 1884F, 1910H, 1916H, 1958G
Sundine, Stephanie – 1954F, 1981H, 1990H
Sunny & the Sunglows – 1959C
Sunnyside Records – 1982C
Supersax – 1972C
Supervia, Conchita – 1915H
Supremes, The – 1959C, 1964E, 1965E, 1966E,
  1967E, 1968E, 1969E
Surette, Thomas Whitney – 1861F, 1941G
  *Course of Study...Development of Symphonic
    Music* – 1915M
  *Eve of Saint Agnes, The* – 1897N
  *Music & Life* – 1917M
  *Priscilla* – 1889N
Surface – 1983C, 1991E
Surfaris – 1962C
Surinach, Carlos – 1951K, 1959K, 1966J
  *Acrobats of God* – 1960N
  *Agathe's Tale* – 1967N
  *Chronique* – 1974N
  *David & Bathsheba* – 1960N
  *Feast of Ashes* – 1962N
  *Harp Concerto* – 1978N
  *Owl & the Pussycat, The* – 1978N
  *Piano Concerto* 1974N
  *Sinfonietta Flamenca* – 1954N
  *String Quartet* – 1974N
  *Symphonic Melismas* – 1993N
  *Symphonic Variations* – 1963N
  *Violin Concerto* – 1980N
Survival Records – 1973C
Survivor – 1978C, 1982E
Susa, Conrad
  *Dangerous Liasons, The* – 1994N
Susskind, Walter – 1968I, 1977I, 1980G
Sustaining Pedal for Piano – 1874L
Suthaus, Ludwig – 1953H
Sutherland, David, Harpsichord Shop – 1974L
Sutherland, Joan – 1960H, 1961H, 1990K
Sutro, Ottilie – 1872F, 1894H, 1970G
Sutro, Rose Laura – 1870F, 1894H, 1957G
Sutton, Harry O.
  *I Don't Care* – 1905E
Sutton, Ralph Earl – 1922A
Svanholm, Set – 1946H

Svéd, Sándor (Alexander) – 1940H
Svendsén, Birgitta – 1988H
Svoboda, Tomás – 1964K
SWA – 1985C
Swafford, Jan
  *Midsummer Variations* – 1985N
  *They Who Hunger* – 1985N
Swan, Billy – 1943A, 1974E
Swan, Marcus Lafayette – 1827F, 1869G
  *Harp of Columbia, The* – 1848M
  *New Harp of Columbia, The* – 1867M
Swan, Timothy – 1758F, 1842G
  *Federal Harmony* – 1788M
  *New England Harmony* – 1801M
  *Singster's Museum, The* – 1803M
  *Songster's Assistant* – 1800M
Swander, Don
  *Deep in the Heart of Texas* – 1941E
Swann, Frederick – 1966I
Swann, Jeffrey – 1972J, 1977J
Swanson, Howard – 1907F, 1978G
  *Concerto for Orchestra* – 1954N
  *Music for Strings* – 1952N
  *Piano Concerto* – 1956N
  *Piano Sonata No. 1* – 1948N
  *Piano Sonata No. 2* – 1970N
  *Piano Sonata No. 3* – 1978N
  *Short Symphony* – 1948N
  *Symphony No. 1* – 1945N
  *Symphony No. 3* – 1970N
Swanson, Robert
  *Piano Sonata No. 1* – 1948N
Swarthout, Gladys – 1900F, 1924H, 1929H, 1954K,
  1969G
Sweat, Keith – 1961A
Sweatman, Wilbur
  *Down Home Rag* – 1913E
Swedish Folkopera – 1993K
Sweeney, Joel Walker – 1810F, 1830K, 1860B
Sweet Honey in the Rock – 1973C
Sweet Sensation – 1986C, 1990E
Sweet, Rachel – 1963A
Sweet, Sharon – 1951F, 1985H, 1989H, 1990H
Sweethearts of the Rodeo – 1985C
Sweney, John R. – 1837F, 1899G
  *Tell Me the Story of Jesus* – 1880N
  *There is Sunshine in the Soul Today* –
    1887N
Swensen, Ruth Ann – 1991H, 1992J, 1993J
Swift, Kay – 1897A
Swoboda, Henry – 1939K, 1944K
SWV – 1993E
Sydeman, William – 1928F, 1959I, 1962J
  *Aria da Capo* – 1982N
  *Concerto da Camera I* – 1958N
  *Maledictions* – 1970N
  *Orchestral Abstractions* – 1958N
  *Piano Sonata* – 1961N
  *Piano Variations* – 1958N

---

❖

## Vernacular/Commercial Music Scene
A *Births*    B *Deaths*    C *Biographical*    D *Publications*
E *Representative Pieces*

---

### Cultivated/Art Music Scene

F *Births*      G *Deaths*      H *Debuts*      I *New Positions*      J *Honors and Awards*
K *Biographical*      L *Musical Beginnings*      M *Publications*      N *Compositions*

Tatum, Nancy – 1962H
Tau Beta Sigma Sorority – 1939L
Taub, Robert – 1955F, 1981H
Tauber, Richard – 1931H
Taubman, Howard – 1907F, 1929I, 1935I, 1955I
  *Music as a Profession* – 1939M
  *New York Times Guide to Listening Pleasure* –
    1968M
  *Opera: Front & Back* – 1938M
Taucher, Curt – 1922H
Tavares – 1959C
Tavárez, M. Gregorio – 1843F, 1883G
Tawa, Nicholas E.
  *Coming of Age of American Art Music, The* –
    1991M
  *Mainstream Music of Early 20th Century America*
    – 1992M
  *Music for Millions, A* – 1984D
  *Sweet Songs for Gentle Americans: The Parlor
    Song* – 1980D
  *Way to Tin Pan Alley, The* – 1990D
Taws, Charles – 1786K, 1833G
Taws, Joseph C. – 1803F, 1818H
  *Air with Variations* – 1820N
  *My Home* – 1825N
  *Pennsylvania LaFayette March* – 1824N
  *Triumphal March of General LaFayette* – 1824N
  *Variations on "The Knight Errant"* – 1821N
Taylor, Art – 1995B
Taylor, Billy – 1973C, 1975C, 1992C
  *Jazz Piano: History & Development* – 1982D
  *Suite for Jazz Piano & Orchestra* – 1973E
Taylor, Billy, Trio – 1952C
Taylor, Cecil – 1933A
  *Tetra Stomp: Eatin' Rain in Space* – 1979E
Taylor, Christopher – 1990J, 1993J
Taylor, Clifford – 1923F
  *Nine Studies for Piano* – 1962N
  *Piano Concerto* – 1974N
  *String Quartet No. 1* – 1960N
  *String Quartet No. 2* – 1978N
  *Symphony No. 1* – 1958N
  *Symphony No. 2* – 1965N
  *Symphony No. 3* – 1978N
  *Theme & Variations* – 1952N
  *Thirty Six More Ideas for Piano* – 1976N
  *Violin Sonata* – 1952N
Taylor, Deems – 1885F, 1921I, 1924J, 1927IJ,
  1931I, 1933I, 1935J, 1936I, 1942I, 1966G
  *Cap'n Kidd & Co.* 1908N
  *Chambered Nautilus, The* – 1914N
  *City of Joy, The* – 1916N
  *Five Inventions for Piano* – 1926N
  *Highwayman, The* – 1914N
  *Jurgen, Op. 17* – 1925N
  *King's Henchman, The* – 1926N
  *Music to My Ears* – 1949M
  *Of Men & Music* – 1937M
  *Peter Ibbetson* – 1930N

*Ramuntcho* – 1942N
*Siren Song, The* – 1912N
*Through the Looking Glass* – 1919N
*Well Tempered Listener, The* – 1940M
Taylor, Deems, Award – 1967L
Taylor, Guy – 1959I
Taylor, James – 1948A, 1971E
Taylor, Johnnie – 1938A, 1976E
Taylor, Marshall
  *Collection of Revival Hymns & Plantation
    Melodies* – 1883M
Taylor, Raynor – 1792K, 1795I, 1810K, 1825G
  *Aethiop, The* – 1814N
  *Capocchio & Dorinna* – 1793N
  *Iron Chest, The* – 1797N
  *Monody on the Death of George Washington* –
    1799N
  *New Overture* – 1796N
  *Ode to the New Year, An* – 1794N
  *Petite Piedmontese, La* – 1795N
  *Shipwrecked, The* – 1797N
  *Sonata for Piano with Violin* – 1797N
  *Symphony* – 1797N
  *Violin Concerto* – 1796N
Taylor, Samuel Coleridge – 1904K
Taylor, Samuel P. – 1806K, 1875G
  *Practical School for the Organ* –
    1830M
  *Uranian Harmony, The* – 1823M
Taylor, Tell
  *Down By the Old Mill Stream* – 1910R
  *Everybody Loves Somebody* – 1949E
T-Bones – 1964C
Tchaikovsky, Peter – 1891K
Tcherepnin, Alexander – 1926HK, 1948K, 1958K,
  1967K, 1974GJ
  *Eight Piano Pieces* – 1955N
  *Farmer & the Fairy, The* – 1952N
  *Lost Flute, The* – 1955N
  *Piano Concerto No. 5* – 1963N
  *Piano Concerto No. 6* – 1965N
  *Piano Sonata No. 2* – 1961N
  *Russian Sketches* – 1971N
  *Symphonic Prayer* – 1959N
  *Symphony No. 2* – 1951N
  *Symphony No. 3* – 1952N
  *Symphony No. 4* – 1957N
Tcherepnin, Alexander, Society – 1983L
Tcherepnin, Ivan – 1960K
Te Kanawa, Kiri – 1971H, 1974H
Teagarden, Jack – 1905A, 1964B
Teagarden, Jack, Band – 1938C
Teagarden, Jack, All Stars – 1951C
Tears for Fears – 1985E
Tebaldi, Renata – 1950H, 1955H
Teddy Bears, The – 1958CE
Teenagers, The – 1955C
Television – 1973C
Telmanyi, Emil – 1921H

---

❄

Vernacular/Commercial Music Scene
A *Births*    B *Deaths*    C *Biographical*    D *Publications*
E *Representative Pieces*

Cultivated/Art Music Scene

  F *Births*   G *Deaths*   H *Debuts*   I *New Positions*   J *Honors and Awards*
  K *Biographical*   L *Musical Beginnings*   M *Publications*   N *Compositions*

❖

Vernacular/Commercial Music Scene
A *Births*    B *Deaths*    C *Biographical*    D *Publications*
E *Representative Pieces*

---

Cultivated/Art Music Scene
F *Births*    G *Deaths*    H *Debuts*    I *New Positions*    J *Honors and Awards*
K *Biographical*    L *Musical Beginnings*    M *Publications*    N *Compositions*

Toch, Ernst, Archive (UCLA) – 1974L
Toczyska, Stefania – 1979H, 1988H
Todd, H. H.
   *Cokesbury Hymnal (Methodist)* –
   1923M
Todisco, Nunzio – 1978H, 1989H
Tokatyan, Armand – 1922H, 1960G
Tokens, The – 1958C, 1961E
Tokody, Ilona – 1986H
Tokyo String Quartet – 1969L
Toll, Robert C.
   *Blacking Up: The Minstrel Show...* – 1974D
Tollefsen, Carl H. – 1882F, 1963G
Tollefsen Trio – 1909L
Tomlinson, John – 1983H
Tomowa-Sintow, Anna – 1974H, 1978H
Tone, Yasunao – 1972K
*Tonic Sol-Fa Advocate* – 1881L
Topilow, Carl – 1947F, 1981I
Töpper, Hertha – 1960H, 1962H
Toradze, Alexander – 1977H, 1983K
Torkanowsky, Werner – 1948K, 1952K, 1961J,
   1963I, 1982I, 1992G
Torke, Michael – 1961F
   *Ash* – 1989N
   *Black & White* – 1988N
   *Copper* – 1988N
   *December* – 1995N
   *Guitar Concerto* – 1994N
   *Javelin* – 1994N
   *Piano Concerto* – 1991N
   *Rust* – 1989N
   *Slate* – 1989N
   *Telephone Book, The* – 1995N
Tormé, Mel – 1925A
   *Christmas Song, The* – 1946E
Tornadoes, The – 1962E
Tortelier, Yan Pascal – 1985H
Toscanini, Arturo – 1908I, 1915K, 1928I, 1937I,
   1940K, 1954K
Totenberg, Roman – 1935H, 1936K, 1943K, 1951I,
   1961I, 1978I
Toto – 1978C, 1983E
Totten, John C.
   *Collection of the Most Admired Hymns...* – 1809M
Tough, Dave – 1908A
Tourangeau, Huguette – 1973H
Tourel, Jennie – 1937H, 1946K, 1973G, 1992K
Tourjée, Eben – 1834F, 1861I, 1867I, 1869J, 1873I,
   1876I, 1891G
   *New England Conservatory's Pianoforte Method* –
   1870M
Tours, Frank E.
   *Mother o' Mine* – 1903E
Toussaint, Alain – 1938A
Tovey, Donald – 1925H
Tower of Power – 1967C
Tower, Joan – 1938F, 1955K, 1983J, 1985I, 1990J
   *Amazon I* – 1977N

   *Amazon II* – 1979N
   *Amazon III* – 1982N
   *Cello Concerto* – 1984N
   *Concerto for Orchestra* – 1991N
   *Duets* – 1994N
   *Island Rhythms Overture* – 1985N
   *Night Fields* – 1994N
   *Petroushskates* – 1980N
   *Piano Concerto* – 1986N
   *Sequoia* – 1981N
   *Silver Ladders* – 1986N
   *Stepping Stones* – 1993N
   *Violin Concerto* – 1992N
Towner, Daniel Brink – 1850F, 1885K, 1893I,
   1919G
   *Trust & Obey* – 1887N
Towner, Ralph – 1940A
Townsend, E. W.
   *Marquis of Michigan, The* – 1898E
Tozzi, Giorgio – 1923F, 1948H, 1955H
Tracey, Minnie – 1895H
Traetta, Filippo – 1799K, 1822K
   *Commodore Decatur's Turkish March* – 1817N
   *Daughters of Zion, The* – 1829N
   *Introduction to the Art & Science of Music* –
   1829M
   *Jerusalem in Affliction* – 1828N
   *Peace* – 1815N
   *Rudiments of the Art of Singing I* – 1829M
   *Rudiments of the Art of Singing II* – 1843M
   *Sinfonia Concertata* – 1803N
Trakas, Christopher – 1985J
Trammps – 1965C
Trashmen – 1962C
Traubel, Helen – 1899F, 1923H, 1926K, 1937H,
   1953K, 1972G
Traubman, Sophie – 1885H, 1888H
Traveling Wilburys, The – 1988C
Travers, Mary – 1937A
Travis, Merle – 1917A, 1970C, 1977C, 1983B
   *Sixteen Tons* – 1947E
   *Smoke! Smoke! Smoke! That Cigarette* – 1947E
Travers, Patricia – 1927F
Travis, Randy – 1959A, 1987C, 1988C
Travis, Roy – 1922F
Travolta, John – 1978E
Trebelli, Zélia – 1878H, 1883H
Treger, Charles – 1935F, 1962J, 1984I
Treigle, Norman – 1927F, 1947H, 1975G
Treitler, Leo – 1962I, 1975I
   *Music & the Historical Imagination* – 1990M
Tremaine, Henry B. – 1866F, 1932G
Tremaine, William B. – 1907G
Tremaine Brothers, Pianos – 1876L
Tremblay, George – 1911F, 1982G
   *Chaparral Symphony* – 1938N
   *Definitive Cycle of the 12-tone Row...* – 1974M
   *Modes of Transportation* – 1940N
   *Phoenix, The* – 1982N

---

❀

**Vernacular/Commercial Music Scene**
A *Births*   B *Deaths*   C *Biographical*   D *Publications*
E *Representative Pieces*

---

## Cultivated/Art Music Scene

F *Births*    G *Deaths*    H *Debuts*    I *New Positions*    J *Honors and Awards*
K *Biographical*    L *Musical Beginnings*    M *Publications*    N *Compositions*

Tufts, John Wheeler (continued)
*Normal Music Course, The* – 1885M
Tully, Alice – 1902F, 1927H, 1936H, 1969I, 1975J, 1985J, 1993G
Tulsa, Oklahoma
*Commercial Club Band* – 1902L
*Little Symphony* – 1979L
*Opera* – 1948L
*Performing Arts Center* – 1977L
*Philharmonic Orchestra* – 1947L
*Youth Symphony* – 1963L
Tumagian, Eduard – 1986H
Tumanyan, Barseg – 1989H
Turner, Tina – 1984E
Tureck Bach Institute – 1981L
Tureck, Rosalyn – 1914F, 1935H
*Introduction to the Performance of Bach, An* – 1960M
Turetzky, Bertram – 1933F
*Contemporary Contrabass, The* – 1974M
Turk, Roy – 1892A, 1934B
*Are You Lonesome Tonight?* – 1926E
Turner & Steere Organ Co. – 1867L
Turner, Eva – 1929H
Turner, Ike – 1931A
Turner, J. V. "Big Joe" – 1911A, 1985B
Turner, Joe – 1907A, 1990B
Turner, Tina – 1938A
Turok, Paul – 1929F, 1964I, 1980I
*Richard III* – 1975N
*Secular Masque, A* – 1979N
*String Quartet No. 1* – 1955N
*String Quartet No. 2* – 1969N
*String Quartet No. 3* – 1980N
*Symphony* – 1955N
*Three Transcendental Etudes* – 1970N
*Ultima Thule* – 1981N
*Violin Concerto* – 1953N
Turek, Ralph
*Elements of Music: Vol 1, Concepts & Applications* – 1988M
Turpin, Tom – 1873A, 1922B
*Bowery Buck Rag* – 1899E
*Buffalo Rag* – 1904E
*Harlem Rag* – 1897E
*Ragtime Nightmare, A* – 1900E
*St. Louis Rag* – 1903E
Turtles, The – 1965C, 1967E
Tuthill, Burnet C. – 1888F, 1922I, 1935I, 1937I, 1938I, 1943J, 1982G
*Big River* – 1942N
*Clarinet Concerto* – 1949N
*Clarinet Quintet* – 1936N
*Laurentia* – 1936N
*Nocturne* – 1933N
*Piano Trio* – 1933N
*Requiem* – 1960N
*String Quartet No. 1* – 1953N

*String Quartet No. 2* – 1955N
*Symphony in C* – 1940N
*Trombone Concerto* – 1967N
*Tuba Concerto* – 1975N
Tuxedo Brass Band – 1917C
Tweedy, Donald
*Manual of Harmonic Technique Based on...J.S. Bach* – 1928M
29th Street Saxophone Quartet – 1983C
Twisted Sister – 1973C
Twitty, Conway – 1933A, 1958E, 1993B
Two Nice Girls – 1989C
Tyers, William H. – 1876A, 1924B
Tyl, Noel – 1936F
Tyler, Bonnie – 1983E
Tyler, James
*Early Guitar, The* – 1980M
Tyler, T. Texas – 1916A, 1972B
Tymes, The – 1956C, 1963E
Tyner, McCoy – 1938A
Tyrannosaurus Rex – 1967C

# U

UB40 – 1988E, 1993E
Uchida, Mitsuko – 1987H
Ughi, Uto – 1967H
Ugly Kid Joe – 1990C
Uhde, Hermann – 1955H
Ulanov, Barry
*History of Jazz in America, A* – 1952D
Ulanowsky, Paul – 1935K, 1943K
Ulfung, Ragnar – 1967H, 1972H
Ullman & Strakosch Opera Co. – 1857L
Ulmer, James Blood – 1942A
Ulrich, Homer – 1906F, 1953I
*Education of a Concertgoer, The* – 1949M
*Music: A Design for Listening* – 1957M
*Survey of Choral Music* – 1973M
*Symphonic Music* – 1952M
Uncle Sam – 1987C
Uncle Tupelo – 1987C
Undisputed Truth – 1970C
Ung, Chinary – 1964K, 1989J
*Triple Concerto* – 1992N
United Artists Records – 1958C
United Jazz and Rock Ensemble – 1975C
United Nations Jazz Society – 1958C
United Records – 1951C
United States
*Amusement Co.* – 1906C
*Army Music School* – 1911L
Universities
*Arizona School of Music* – 1934L
*California, Berkeley, Music Dept.* – 1901L
*California, Davis, Music Dept.* – 1958L
*Chicago Press* – 1964L
*Hawaii Summer Music Festival* – 1979L
*Illinois School of Music* – 1895L
*Indiana Music Dept.* – 1910L

---

❖

**Vernacular/Commercial Music Scene**
A *Births*    B *Deaths*    C *Biographical*    D *Publications*
E *Representative Pieces*

Cultivated/Art Music Scene
F *Births*   G *Deaths*   H *Debuts*   I *New Positions*   J *Honors and Awards*
K *Biographical*   L *Musical Beginnings*   M *Publications*   N *Compositions*

*Distant Worlds* – 1985N
*Twelve Pieces for Piano* – 1986N
Van der Walt, Deon – 1990H
Van Dresser, Marcia – 1877F, 1903H, 1937G
Vandross, Luther – 1951A
Van Dyck, Ernest Marie – 1898H
Van Dykes – 1964C
Vaness, Carol – 1952F, 1977H, 1984H
Vangelis – 1982E
Vanguard Recording Society – 1949L
Van Hagen, Peter
 *Adopted Child, The* – 1797N
 *Columbus* – 1800N
 *Federal Overture* – 1797N
Van Halen – 1974C, 1984E
Van Heusen, Jimmy – 1913A, 1990B
 *All the Way* – 1957E
 *Call Me Irresponsible* – 1963E
 *High Hopes* – 1959E
 *Imagination* – 1940E
 *It Could Happen to You* – 1944E
 *Love & Marriage* – 1955E
 *Nellie Bly* – 1946E
 *Pennies From Heaven* – 1936E
 *Skyscraper* – 1965E
 *Sunday, Monday or Always* – 1943E
 *Tender Trap, The* – 1955E
 *Walking Happy* – 1966E
Van Hoose, Ellison – 1868F, 1897H, 1936G
Vanilla Fudge – 1967C
Vanilla Ice – 1990E
Van Peebles, Melvin – 1932A
Van Rooy, Anton – 1898H
Van Shelton, Ricky – see Shelton, Ricky Van
Van Slyck, Nicholas – 1962I
Van Vactor, David – 1906F, 1947I, 1994G
 *Flute Concerto* – 1932N
 *Masque of the Red Death* – 1952N
 *Overture to a Comedy I* – 1934N
 *Overture to a Comedy II* – 1941N
 *Quintet, Flute & Strings* – 1932N
 *Sinfonia Breve* – 1964N
 *String Quartet No. 1* – 1940N
 *String Quartet No. 2* – 1950N
 *Symphony No. 1* – 1937N
 *Symphony No. 2* – 1943N
 *Symphony No. 3* – 1959N
 *Symphony No. 4* – 1971N
 *Symphony No. 5* – 1975N
 *Symphony No. 6* – 1980N
 *Symphony No. 7* – 1983N
 *Symphony No. 8* – 1984N
 *Twenty-Four Etudes for Flute* – 1933N
 *Viola Concerto* – 1940N
 *Violin Concerto* – 1951N
Van Vechten, Carl – 1888F
 *Interpreters & Interpretations* – 1917M
 *Music after the Great War* – 1915M
 *Music & Bad Manners* – 1916M

*Music of Spain, The* – 1918M
 *Red: Papers on Musical Subjects* – 1925M
Van Vleck, Jacob – 1751F, 1831G
Van Zandt, Jennie – 1864H
Van Zandt, Marie – 1858F, 1879H, 1880K, 1891H, 1919G
Van Zandt, Townes – 1944A
Van Zanten, Cornelie – 1886H
Varady, Julia – 1978H
Varèse, Edgard – 1915K, 1955J, 1962J, 1965GJ
 *Amériques* – 1921N
 *Arcana* – 1927N
 *Density 21.5* – 1936N
 *Déserts* – 1954N
 *Ecuatorial* – 1934N
 *Etude pour Espace* – 1947N
 *Hyperprism* – 1923N
 *Intégrales* – 1925N
 *Ionisation* – 1931N
 *Nocturnal* – 1961N
 *Octandre* – 1923N
 *Offrandes* – 1921N
 *Poème électronique* – 1958N
Vargas, Ramon – 1994H
*Variety* – 1905C
Various composers
 *Amen Corner* – 1983E
 *Around the World in Eighty Days* – 1875E
 *Bubbling Brown Sugar* – 1976E
 *Enchantment* – 1879E
 *Five-Six-Seven-Eight...Dance* – 1983E
 *Gospel at Colonus, The* – 1988E
 *In Gay New York* – 1896E
 *Miss Manhattan* – 1897E
 *Oh, Calcutta* – 1970E
 *Passing Show, The* – 1894E
 *Pullman Palace Car, A* – 1879E
 *Show Is On, The* – 1936E
 *Star & Garter* – 1942E
 *Sugar Babies* – 1979E
 *Your Arms Too Short to Box with God* – 1976E
Varnay, Astrid – 1920K, 1941H
Varney, Pierre Joseph – 1840I
Varviso, Silvio – 1959H, 1961H
Vásáry, Tamás – 1962H
Vaudeville Managers Association – 1900C
Vaughan, James D. – 1864F, 1941B
 *Gospel Chimes* – 1890M
Vaughan, James D., Publisher – 1890L
Vaughan, Jimmie – 1951A
Vaughan Co. – 1912L
Vaughan, Sarah – 1924A, 1993B
Vaughan, Stevie Ray – 1954A, 1990B
Vaughan-Williams, Ralph – 1932K, 1954K
Vaughn, Billy – 1931A
Veasey, Josephine – 1968H
Vee, Bobby – 1943A, 1961E
Vee Jay Records – 1953C
Vega Co., Stringed Instruments – 1889L

---

❖

## Vernacular/Commercial Music Scene
A *Births*   B *Deaths*   C *Biographical*   D *Publications*
E *Representative Pieces*

---

### Cultivated/Art Music Scene

F *Births*    G *Deaths*    H *Debuts*    I *New Positions*    J *Honors and Awards*
K *Biographical*    L *Musical Beginnings*    M *Publications*    N *Compositions*

---

Vernacular/Commercial Music Scene

A *Births*      B *Deaths*      C *Biographical*      D *Publications*

E *Representative Pieces*

Walker, George – 1873A, 1911B
Walker, George – 1922F, 1945H, 1982J
   *Cello Concerto* – 1982N
   *Mass* – 1978N
   *Piano Concerto* – 1975N
   *Piano Sonata No. 1* – 1953N
   *Piano Sonata No. 2* – 1957N
   *Piano Sonata No. 3* – 1975N
   *Piano Sonata No. 4* – 1985N
   *Sinfonia No. 1* – 1984N
   *Sinfonia No. 2* – 1990N
   *String Quartet* – 1946N
   *Symphony* – 1961N
   *Violin Concerto* – 1984N
Walker, George Lee – 1856K
Walker, Jerry Jeff – 1942A
Walker, Joe Louis – 1949A
Walker, Jr. – 1995B
Walker, Jr., and the All Stars – 1961C
Walker, Sandra – 1948F, 1972H
Walker, Sarah – 1977H, 1986H
Walker, T-Bone – 1910A, 1975B
Walker, Thomas – 1811K
Walker, William – 1809F, 1856K
   *Christian Harmony, The* – 1867M
   *Fruits & Flowers* – 1873M
   *Southern Harmony & Musical Companion* –
   1835M
   *Southern & Western Pocket Harmonist* – 1846M
Wallace, Oliver
   *Der Führer's Face* – 1943E
Wallace, Stewart
   *Harvey Milk* – 1994N
Wallace, William V – 1841K
Wallenstein Sinfonietta – 1933L
Wallenstein, Alfred – 1898F, 1912H, 1935I, 1943I,
   1983G
Waller, Don
   *Motown Story, The* – 1985D
Waller, "Fats" – 1904A, 1943B
   *Ain't Misbehavin'* – 1928E
   *Ain't Misbehavin' (revue)* – 1978E
   *Connie's Hot Chocolates* – 1929E
   *Honeysuckle Rose* – 1929E
   *Keep Shufflin'* – 1928E
   *London Suite* – 1939E
Waller, Fats, and His Rhythm – 1934C
Wallers – 1958C
Wallfisch, Raphael – 1988H
Wallnöfer, Adolf – 1896H
Walsh, Diane – 1971J
Walsh, Joe – 1947A
Walter, Bruno – 1923H, 1939K, 1941H, 1947I,
   1962G
   *Of Music & Music-Making* – 1961M
Walter, Thomas – 1725G
   *Grounds & Rules of Music Explained* – 1721M
Walter, William E. – 1924I
Walton, Blanche W. – 1871F

Wand Records – 1961C
Wand, Günther – 1989H
Wann, James C.
   *Pump Boys & Dinettes* – 1981E
War – 1969C
Ward, Anita – 1979E
Ward, Billy, and His Dominoes – 1950C
Ward, Charles B.
   *Band Played On, The* – 1895E
Ward, Clara – 1924A, 1973B
Ward, David – 1964H
Ward, Frank E. – 1872F
Ward, Genevieve – 1862H
Ward, Helen – 1916A
Ward, John M. – 1917F, 1955I
Ward, Robert – 1917F, 1946J, 1956I, 1967IJ, 1972J,
   1979I
   *Abelard & Heloise* – 1981N
   *Appalachian Ditties & Dances* – 1989N
   *Byways of Memories* – 1991N
   *Claudia Legare* – 1973N
   *Concert Piece for Orchestra* – 1948N
   *Crucible, The* – 1961N
   *Dialogues* – 1983N
   *Fatal Interview* – 1937N
   *He Who Gets Slapped* – 1955N
   *Invocation & Toccata* – 1963N
   *Jubilation: An Overture* – 1948N
   *Lady from Colorado, The* – 1964N
   *Minutes till Midnight* – 1982N
   *Ode for Orchestra* – 1939N
   *Piano Concerto* – 1968N
   *Roman Fever* – 1993N
   *Sacred Songs for Pantheists* – 1951N
   *Saxophone Concerto* – 1984N
   *Scarlet Letter, The* – 1990N
   *Songs for Ravenscroft* – 1993N
   *Sonic Structure* – 1981N
   *String Quartet* – 1966N
   *Sweet Freedom Songs* – 1965N
   *Symphony No. 1* – 1941N
   *Symphony No. 2* – 1947N
   *Symphony No. 3* – 1950N
   *Symphony No. 4* – 1958N
   *Symphony No. 5* – 1976N
   *Symphony No. 6* – 1989N
   *Violin Sonata No. 2* – 1990N
   *3 Celebrations of God in Nature* – 1980N
Ward, Samuel A.
   *Maderna* – 1882N
Ward, Thomas – 1884K
Ward-Steinman, David – 1936F, 1961I
   *Arcturus* – 1972N
   *Cello Concerto* – 1966N
   *Intersections* – 1982N
   *Kaleidoscope* – 1971N
   *Now Music* – 1967N
   *Olympics Overture* – 1984N
   *Piano Sonata* – 1957N

---

❁

## Cultivated/Art Music Scene
F *Births*   G *Deaths*   H *Debuts*   I *New Positions*   J *Honors and Awards*
K *Biographical*   L *Musical Beginnings*   M *Publications*   N *Compositions*

Ward-Steinman, David (continued)
  *Sonata for Fortified Piano* – 1972N
  *Song of Moses* – 1964N
  *Symphony No. 1* – 1959N
  *Toward a Comparative Theory of the Arts* –
    1989M
  *Western Orpheus* – 1964N
Ware, Harriet – 1877F, 1962G
  *Artisan, The* – 1929N
Warfield, Sandra – 1929F, 1953H
Warfield, William – 1920F, 1950H, 1952K, 1974I
Wariner, Steve – 1954A
Waring Music Workshop – 1947L
Waring, Fred – 1900F, 1984G
Waring, Fred, Glee Club – 1938L
Waring, Fred, Pennsylvanians – 1916L
Warner Brothers Music – 1929C
Warner Brothers Records – 1958C
Warner, J.
  *Down in Alabam'* – 1858E
Warner, Wendy – 1991J
Warnes, Jennifer – 1947C, 1982E, 1987E
Warnick, Henry Clay, Jr.
  *Heidi* – 1955E
Warrant – 1984C
Warren School of Violinmaking (Chicago) –
  1975L
Warren, Diane – 1956A, 1995C
Warren, Earle – 1994B
Warren, Elinor Remick – 1900F, 1991G
  *Along the Western Shore* – 1963N
  *Crystal Lake, The* – 1958N
  *Fountain, The* – 1942N
  *Symphony in One Movement* – 1971N
Warren, George William – 1828F, 1860K, 1870K,
  1902G
  *National Hymn (God of Our Fathers)* – 1892N
Warren, Harry – 1893A, 1981B
  *Chattanooga Choo Choo* – 1941E
  *Don't Give Up the Ship* – 1935E
  *42nd Street* – 1933E
  *I Found a Million Dollar Baby* – 1931E
  *I Had the Craziest Dream* – 1942E
  *I'll String Along with You* – 1934E
  *I Only Have Eyes for You* – 1934E
  *Jeepers Creepers* – 1938E
  *Laugh Parade, The* – 1931E
  *Lullaby of Broadway* – 1935E
  *Shuffle Off to Buffalo* – 1933E
  *That's Amore* – 1953E
  *There Will Never Be Another You* – 1942E
  *We're In the Money* – 1933E
  *You Must Have Been a Beautiful Baby* – 1938E
  *You'll Never Know* – 1943E
Warren, Kenneth, Violin Dealer – 1926L
Warren, Leonard – 1911F, 1938H, 1960G
Warren, Nina – 1993H
Warren, Richard Henry – 1859F, 1886I, 1933G
Warren, Samuel Prowse – 1841F, 1867I, 1915G

Warriner, Solomon – 1801I
  *Springfield Collection of Sacred Music* – 1813M
Warrington, James – 1915G
  *Hymns & Tunes for the Children of the Church* –
    1886M
  *Short Titles of Books Relating to...Psamody...* –
    1898M
Warwick, Dionne – 1940A, 1974E
Washburn, Robert – 1928F, 1982I
  *North Country Sketch* – 1969N
  *St. Lawrence Overture* – 1962N
  *String Quartet* – 1963N
  *Symphony No. 1* – 1959N
  *Three Pieces for Orchestra* – 1959N
Washington, D.C.
  *Albaugh's Opera House* – 1884L
  *Amphion Glee Club* – 1891L
  *Cathedral Choir of Men & Boys* – 1912L
  *Cathedral Choral Society* – 1942L
  *Choral Arts Society* – 1965L
  *Choral Society* – 1869L
  *Community Opera* – 1918L
  *Contemporary Music Forum* – 1974L
  *Coolidge Aud., Library of Congress* – 1925L
  *Folger Music Consort* – 1976L
  *Friday Morning Music Club* – 1886L
  *Guitar Quintet* – 1986L
  *Inter-American Music Festival* – 1958L
  *Kennedy Center* – 1971L
  *Kennedy Center Awards* – 1978L
  *National Symphony* – 1931L
  *Opera* – 1980L
  *Opera Society* – 1956L
  *Performing Arts Society* – 1966L
  *Permanent Chorus* – 1899L
  *Sängerbund* – 1851L
  *Symphony Orchestra* – 1902L
  *Terrace Theater* – 1979L
  *20th Century Consort* – 1975L
  *Whittall Pavilion (Lib. of Congress)* – 1938L
Washington, Dinah – 1924A, 1963B
Washington, Grover, Jr. – 1943A
Washington, Ned – 1901A, 1976B
Washingtonians – 1923C
Wasserman, Ellen – 1972J
Was (Was Not) – 1981C
W.A.S.P. – 1984C
Watanabe, Ruth
  *Introduction to Music Research* – 1967M
Watanabe, Yoko – 1985H, 1986H
Water, Edward – 1972I
Waterloo Music Festival (NJ) – 1968L
Waters, Ethel – 1896A, 1977B
Waters, Horace – 1812F, 1893G
  *Athenaeum Collection* – 1863M
  *Waters' Golden Harp* – 1863M
Waters, Horace, Music Store – 1845L
Waters, Safford
  *Belle of Avenoo A, The* – 1895E

---

Vernacular/Commercial Music Scene
A *Births*    B *Deaths*    C *Biographical*    D *Publications*
E *Representative Pieces*

---

### Cultivated/Art Music Scene

F *Births*	G *Deaths*	H *Debuts*	I *New Positions*	J *Honors and Awards*
K *Biographical*	L *Musical Beginnings*	M *Publications*	N *Compositions*

Weidemaar, Reynold – 1945F
Weidig, Adolf – 1931G
　　*Concert Overture, Op. 65* – 1919N
　　*Harmonic Material & Its Uses* – 1923M
Weidinger, Christine – 1972H
Weidt, Lucie – 1910H
Weigel Hall (Ohio State U.) – 1980L
Weigl, Karl – 1938K, 1943K
　　*Festival Overture* – 1938N
　　*Old Vienna* – 1939N
　　*Piano Trio* – 1939N
　　*Rhapsody for Piano & Orchestra* – 1940N
　　*String Quartet No. 6* – 1939N
　　*String Quartet No. 7* – 1942N
　　*String Quartet No. 8* – 1949N
　　*Symphony No. 5* – 1945N
　　*Symphony No. 6* – 1947N
Weikert, Ralf – 1987H
Weikl, Bernard – 1977H
Weil, Hermann – 1911H
Weill, Kurt – 1950G
　　*Ballad of Magna Charta, The* – 1939N
　　*Down In the Valley* – 1948E
　　*Johnny Johnson* – 1936E
　　*Knickerbocker Holiday* – 1938E
　　*Lady in the Dark* – 1941E
　　*Lost in the Stars* – 1949E
　　*One Touch of Venus* – 1943E
　　*Three Walt Whitman Songs* – 1942N
　　*Weg der Verheissung, Der* – 1935N
Weill, Kurt, Foundation – 1962L
Weill, Kurt, Prize – 1995L
Weinberger, Jaromir – 1922IK, 1939K,
　　1967G
　　*Bible Poems* – 1939N
　　*Czech Rhapsody* – 1941N
　　*Dedications (organ)* – 1954N
　　*Lincoln Symphony* – 1941N
　　*Mississippi Rhapsody* – 1940N
　　*Organ Sonata* – 1941N
　　*Prelude & Fugue, Southern Folktune* – 1940N
　　*Six Religious Preludes* – 1946N
　　*Variations, "Spreading Chestnut Tree"* –
　　1939N
Weinberg, Henry – 1931F, 1966I, 1968J
Weinberg, Jacob – 1926K, 1956G
Weiner, Lazar – 1914K, 1929I, 1982G
　　*Golem, The* – 1956N
Weiner, Otto – 1962H
Weingartner, Felix – 1905H
Weinrich, Carl – 1904F, 1934I, 1942I
Weinstock, Herbert – 1905F, 1971G
　　*Men of Music* – 1939M
　　*Music as an Art* – 1953M
　　*Opera, The:...its Creation and Performance* –
　　1941M
Weintraub Music Co. – 1950L
Weirdos – 1976C
Weisberg, Arthur – 1931F

Weisgall, Hugo – 1920K, 1926K, 1931I, 1940K,
　　1949I, 1954J, 1957I, 1963I, 1975J, 1990I, 1994J,
　　1995J
　　*Appearances & Entrances* – 1960N
　　*Athaliah* – 1963N
　　*Esther* – 1990N
　　*Fancies & Inventions* – 1970N
　　*Four Impressions* – 1931N
　　*Gardens of Adonis, The* – 1959N
　　*Jennie* – 1976N
　　*Lillith* – 1934N
　　*Night* – 1932N
　　*Nine Rivers from Jordan* – 1968N
　　*Outpost* – 1947N
　　*Overture in F* – 1943N
　　*Piano Sonata in F#* – 1931N
　　*Piano Sonata No. 2* – 1982N
　　*Piano Variations* – 1939N
　　*Prospect* – 1983N
　　*Purgatory* – 1958N
　　*Quest* – 1938N
　　*6 Characters in Search of an Author* – 1956N
　　*Soldier Songs* – 1946N
　　*Song of Celebration* – 1975N
　　*Stronger, The* – 1952N
　　*Tekiator* – 1985N
　　*Tenor, The* – 1950N
　　*Translations* – 1972N
Weiss, Adolph – 1891F, 1926K, 1955J, 1971G
　　*Fantasie for Piano* – 1918N
　　*I Segreti* – 1923N
　　*Libation Bearers, The* – 1930N
　　*Piano Sonata* – 1932N
　　*Scherzo, American Life* – 1928N
　　*Seven Songs by Dickinson* – 1928N
　　*Sextet, Piano & Winds* – 1947N
　　*String Quartet No. 1* – 1925N
　　*String Quartet No. 2* – 1926N
　　*String Quartet No. 3* – 1932N
　　*Suite for Orchestra* – 1938N
　　*Theme & Variations* – 1933N
　　*Trumpet Concerto* – 1952N
　　*Twelve Preludes for Piano* – 1927N
　　*Violin Sonata* – 1941N
Weissenberg, Alexis – 1947HJ
Weisser, Albert – 1918F, 1982G
Weisshaar, Hans – 1937K
Weisshaar, Hans, Violin Maker – 1947L
Welcher, Dan
　　*Piano Concerto, "Shiva's Drums"* – 1994N
　　*Symphony No. 1* – 1992N
Weldon, Peter
　　*New York Serenading Waltz, The* – 1802N
　　*President Madison's March* – 1809N
Welk, Lawrence – 1903A, 1961E, 1992B
Wellitsch, Ljuba – 1949H
Wellman, W. F., Jr.
　　*Branigan's Band* – 1877E
Wells, Dickey – 1985B

---

❀

## Vernacular/Commercial Music Scene
A *Births*　　B *Deaths*　　C *Biographical*　　D *Publications*
E *Representative Pieces*

Wells, Jeffrey – 1988H
Wells, Junior – 1934A
Wells, Kitty – 1919A, 1976C
Wells, Mary – 1943A, 1964E, 1992B
Welser, Robert
   *Running with the Devil* – 1993D
Welser-Moest, Franz – 1989H
Welte Musical Instrument Co., New York – 1865L
Welte, Emil – 1923G
Welting, Ruth – 1949F, 1970H, 1976H
Wendling, Pete – 1974B
   *Chromatic Rag* – 1916E
Wendt, Larry – 1946F
Wendy and Lisa – 1986C
Wenkel, Ortrun – 1983H
Wenkoff, Spas – 1981H
Wenrich, Percy – 1887A, 1952B
   *Alamo Rag* – 1910E
   *Cotton Babes Rag* – 1909E
   *Egyptian Rag* – 1910E
   *Put On Your Old Grey Bonnet* – 1909E
   *Skeleton Rag* – 1911E
   *Sunflower Rag* – 1911E
   *When You Were a Tulip* – 1914E
   *Whipped Cream* – 1913E
Werlein Music Store (Vicksburg) – 1842L
Werlein, Philip – 1831K, 1850K, 1853K, 1885G
Werlein, P. F., Publisher – 1853L
Werner, Eric – 1939IK, 1988G
   *From Generation to Generation* – 1962M
   *Sacred Bridge, The* – 1959M
   *Sacred Bridge II* – 1984M
Wernick, Richard – 1934F, 1968I, 1976J
   *Cello Concerto* – 1980N
   *Emperor's Nightingale, The* – 1958N
   *4 Pieces for String Quartet* – 1955N
   *Maggie* – 1959N
   *Moonsongs from the Japanese* – 1969N
   *Piano Concerto* – 1989N
   *Poison Tree, A* – 1980N
   *Prayer for Jerusalem* – 1971N
   *Saxophone Quartet* – 1992N
   *Songs of Remembrance* – 1974N
   *String Quartet No. 1* – 1963N
   *String Quartet No. 2* – 1973N
   *String Quartet No. 3* – 1988N
   *Symphony No. 1* – 1987N
   *Symphony No. 2* – 1994N
   *Trojan Women, The* – 1953N
   *Viola Concerto* – 1986N
   *Violin Concerto* – 1984N
   *Visions of Wonder & Terror* – 1976N
Werrenrath, George – 1876K
Werrenrath, Reinald – 1883F, 1919H, 1953G
Wesley, John/Charles – 1735K
   *Collection of Psalms & Hymns, A* – 1737M
Wessel, Mark – 1894F
   *Piano Concerto* – 1942N
   *Prelude & Fugue for SQ* – 1931F

   *String Quartet* – 1931F
   *Symphony* – 1932F
West – 1967C
West Bay Opera of Palo Alto – 1955L
West Coast Festival of Sound Poetry – 1977L
West Coast Pop Art Experimental Band –
   1966C
West Virginia Opera Theater – 1972L
West, Arthur
   *See, Saw, Margery Daw* – 1893E
West, Dottie – 1932A, 1964C, 1991B
West, Shelly – 1958A
West, Stephen – 1995H
Westcott, Mark – 1971J
Westenburg, Richard – 1932F, 1964I, 1974I, 1977I,
   1990I
Westendorf, Thomas P. – 1848F, 1923G
   *I'll Take You Home Again, Kathleen* – 1875E
Westergaard, Peter – 1931F, 1958I, 1968I
   *Charivari* – 1953N
   *Introduction to Tonal Theory, An* – 1974M
   *Leda & the Swan* – 1961N
   *Mr. & Mrs. Discobbolos* – 1966N
   *Plot Against the Giant* – 1956N
   *String Quartet* – 1957N
   *Tempest, The* – 1990N
   *Tuckets & Sennets* – 1969N
   *Variations for 6 Players* – 1963N
Western Arts Music Festival – 1972L
*Western (Brainard's) Musical World* – 1864L
Western Wind – 1969L
Westminster Choir – 1921L
Westminster Choir College – 1926L
Westminster Presbyterian Church Choir – 1920L
Westminster Recordings – 1949L
Weston, Horace – 1825A, 1890B
Weston, Maury
   *Grand Hotel* – 1989E
Weston, Paul – 1912A
Wetmore, Truman S. – 1774F, 1861G
Wettergren, Gertrud – 1935H
Wetzler, Hermann – 1870F, 1897I, 1943G
   *Assisi* – 1924N
   *As You Like It* – 1917N
   *Baskische Venus, The* – 1928N
   *Symphonic Dance in Basque Style* – 1927N
   *Symphonic Fantasy* – 1922N
   *Symphonie Concertante* – 1932N
   *Visionen* – 1923N
Wham – 1984E, 1985E
Wharton Center for the Performing Arts – 1982L
Whear, Paul William – 1925F
Wheatstraw, Peetie – 1902A, 1941B
Whelpley, Benjamin L. – 1864F, 1886H
Whispers, The – 1962C
Whitaker, Howard
   *Prayers of Habakkuk* – 1993N
Whitcomb, Ian
   *After the Ball: Pop Music from Rag to Rock* – 1972D

---

## Cultivated/Art Music Scene

F *Births*   G *Deaths*   H *Debuts*   I *New Positions*   J *Honors and Awards*
K *Biographical*   L *Musical Beginnings*   M *Publications*   N *Compositions*

White Lion – 1983C
White Trash – 1969C
White Zombie – 1985C
White, Barry – 1944A, 1974E
White, Benjamin Franklin – 1800F, 1879G
  *Sacred Harp, The* – 1844M
White, Charles A. – 1829F, 1892G
  *Ise Gwine Back to Dixie* – 1874E
  *Marguerite* – 1883E
  *When the Leaves Begin to Turn* – 1878E
White, Charley – 1821F, 1891B
White, Clarence C. – 1880F, 1960G
  *Dance Rhapsody* – 1955N
  *Elegy* – 1954N
  *Kutamba Rhapsody* – 1942N
  *Ouanga* – 1932N
  *String Quartets 1 & 2* – 1931N
White, Cool – 1821F, 1891B
  *Lubly Fan (Buffalo Gals)* – 1844N
White, David – 1936F
White, Donald H. – 1981I
White, Edward L. – 1809F, 1851G
  *Bridge of Sighs, The* – 1846N
White, Ernest – 1925K, 1937I
White, George
  *Scandals* – 1919C
White, John – 1924F
White, John – 1855F, 1887I, 1902G
  *Missa Solemnis* – 1889N
White, Josh – 1908A, 1969B
White, Karyn – 1965A, 1991E
White, Michael
  *Songs From Another Time* – 1985N
White, Paul – 1895F, 1973G
  *Andante & Rondo* – 1945N
  *Feuilles Symphoniques* – 1920N
  *Five Miniatures for Orchestra* – 1933N
  *Pagan Festival Overture* – 1927N
  *String Quartet* – 1925N
  *Symphony in E* – 1932N
White, Richard Grant – 1851I
White, Ronnie – 1995B
White, Ruth – 1925F
White, Tony Joe – 1943A
White, Wendy – 1989H
White, William C. – 1881F, 1964G
White's Serenaders – 1846L
Whitefield, George
  *Collection of Hymns for Social Worship* – 1765M
Whitehill, Clarence – 1871F, 1898H, 1900H, 1909H,
  1932G
Whiteley, William – 1789F, 1871G
  *Instrumental Preceptor, The* – 1816M
Whiteley, William, Instrument Shop – 1810L
Whiteman, Paul – 1890A, 1967B
  *Jazz* – 1926D
Whiteman, Paul, Dance Band – 1918C
Whitesnake – 1987E
Whitewater Opera Co. – 1972L

Whithorne, Emerson – 1884F, 1907K, 1958G
  *Adventures of a Samurai* – 1919N
  *Aeroplane, The* – 1920N
  *Camino Real, El* – 1937N
  *Dream Peddler, The* – 1930N
  *Fata Morgana* – 1927N
  *Gate of Memory, The* – 1908N
  *Greek Impressions* – 1914N
  *Grim Troubadour, The* – 1927N
  *Moon Trail* – 1930N
  *New York Days & Nights* – 1922N
  *Piano Quintet* – 1928N
  *Poem, Op. 43* – 1927N
  *Rain, The* – 1912N
  *Ranga* – 1920N
  *Saturday's Child* – 1926N
  *Sierra Morena* – 1938N
  *Sooner or Later* – 1925N
  *String Quartet No. 1* – 1917N
  *String Quartet No. 2* – 1930N
  *Symphony No. 1* – 1929N
  *Symphony No. 2* – 1935N
  *Symphony No. 3* – 1937N
  *Violin Concerto* – 1931N
  *Violin Sonata* – 1932N
Whiting, Arthur B. – 1861F, 1883K, 1905J, 1936G
  *Concert Overture* – 1866N
  *Fantasia for Piano & Orchestra, Opus 11* –
  1897N
  *Golden Cage, The* – 1926N
  *Piano Concerto in D* – 1888N
  *Rubáiyát of Omar Khayyám* – 1901N
  *Suite for 4 Horns & Strings* – 1888N
  *Violin Sonata* – 1891N
Whiting, George E. – 1840F, 1876I, 1869I, 1923G
  *Dream Picture* – 1877N
  *Lenora* – 1893N
  *Mass In C Minor* – 1872N
  *Mass in F Minor* – 1874N
  *Organist, The* – 1879M
  *Prologue to "The Golden Legend"* – 1873N
Whiting, Margaret – 1924A
Whiting, Richard A. – 1891A, 1938B
  *Ain't We Got Fun* – 1921E
  *It's Tulip Time in Holland* – 1915E
  *Japanese Sandman* – 1920E
  *Louise* – 1929E
  *My Ideal* – 1930E
  *Sleepy Time Gal* – 1925E
  *Till We Meet Again* – 1918E
  *Too Marvelous for Words* – 1937E
Whiting, Samuel B. – 1842F
Whitley, Keith – 1955A, 1989B
Whitley, Ray – 1901A
Whitlock, Billy – 1813F, 1878B
Whitmer, T. Carl – 1873F, 1909I, 1916I
  *Art of Improvisation:...Principles and Methods* –
  1934M
  *Oh, Isabel* – 1951N

---

❖

**Vernacular/Commercial Music Scene**
A *Births*    B *Deaths*    C *Biographical*    D *Publications*
E *Representative Pieces*

---

### Cultivated/Art Music Scene

F *Births*    G *Deaths*    H *Debuts*    I *New Positions*    J *Honors and Awards*
K *Biographical*    L *Musical Beginnings*    M *Publications*    N *Compositions*

Williams, Roger – 1925A
Williams, Spencer – 1889A, 1965B
 Basin Street Blues – 1929E
 Boy Friend, The – 1954E
 I Ain't Got Nobody – 1916E
 Mahogany Hall Stomp – 1924E
 State Street Blues – 1922E
 Tishomingo Blues – 1918E
Williams, Tony – 1945A
Williams, Tony, Lifetime – 1969C
Williams, Vanessa – 1963A, 1992E
Williams, W. R.
 I'd Love to Live in Loveland – 1910E
Williamson, John Finley – 1887F, 1929K, 1932K,
 1964G
Williamson, John L. "Sonny Boy" – 1916A, 1948B
Williamson, R. Miller "Sonny Boy" – 1897A, 1965B
Willig, George – 1793K, 1851G
Willig, George, Music Pub. – 1794L
Willig, George, Jr., Publishing Co. – 1829L
Willimantic Brass Band (MA) – 1872L
Willis Music Co. – 1899L
Willis, Richard – 1816K, 1817I, 1830G
 Lone Fish (Meat) Ball, The – 1855E
Willis, Richard Storr – 1819F, 1852I, 1900G
 Carol (Upon the Midnight Clear) – 1850N
 Church Chorals & Choir Studies – 1850M
 Our Church Music – 1856M
 Waif of Song – 1876M
Willis, Thomas
 Chicago Symphony Orchestra, The – 1974M
Willows – 1953C
Wills, Bob – 1905A, 1968C, 1975B
 San Antonio Rose – 1938E
Wills' Fiddle Band – 1928C
Willson, John – 1811K
Willson, Meredith – 1902A, 1984B
 Here's Love – 1963E
 Music Man, The – 1957E
 Symphony No. 1 – 1936N
 Symphony No. 2 – 1940N
 Unsinkable Molly Brown, The – 1960E
Wilmer, Valerie
 Face of Black Music, The – 1976D
Wilson Phillips – 1989C
Wilson, Al – 1939A, 1974E
Wilson, Cassandra – 1955A
Wilson, Dana
 Piece of Mind – 1988N
Wilson, Donald M. – 1937F
Wilson, Grenville Dean – 1833F, 1897GI
Wilson, Harry Robert – 1901F
Wilson, Jackie – 1934A, 1984B
Wilson, John – 1838HK
Wilson, Nancy – 1937A
Wilson, Neal – 1956F, 1980H
Wilson, Olly – 1937F, 1970I, 1974J, 1995J
 City Called Heaven, A – 1989N
 Lumina – 1981N

Sinfonia – 1984N
Sometimes – 1976N
SpiritSong – 1974N
Wilson, Ransom – 1951F
Wilson, Richard – 1941F, 1966I, 1979I, 1986J
 Articulations – 1989N
 Bassoon Concerto – 1983N
 Eclogue – 1974N
 Fixations – 1985N
 Intercalation – 1985N
 Piano Concerto – 1991N
 Silhouette – 1988N
 String Quartet No. 1 – 1968N
 String Quartet No. 2 – 1977N
 String Quartet No. 3 – 1982N
 Suite for Small Orchestra – 1988N
 Symphony No. 1 – 1984N
 Symphony No. 2 – 1986N
Wilson, Teddy – 1912A, 1986B
Wilson, W.
 Ain't Dat a Shame? – 1901E
Winant, William – 1953F
Winbergh, Gösta – 1983H
Wincenc, Carol – 1949F, 1972H, 1978J, 1980I
Winchell, James
 Psalms, Hymns & Spiritual Songs of Watts –
 1818M
 Sacred Harmony – 1818M
Windgassen, Wolfgang – 1957H
Windingstad, Ole – 1913IK, 1940I, 1959G
Wingate, Philip
 I Don't Want to Play in Your Yard –
 1894E
 You Can't Play in Our Yard Any More – 1894E
Winger – 1986C
Wings – 1973E, 1974E, 1976E, 1978E
Wings Over Jordan – 1937C
Winkelmann, Hermann – 1884H
Winner Brothers Music Store – 1845L
Winner, Joseph E. – 1837F
 Little Brown Jug – 1869E
Winner, Septimus – 1827A, 1902B
 Deitcher's Dog, Der – 1864E
 Ellie Rhee – 1865E
 Gettysburg March, The – 1886N
 Give Us Back Our Old Commander – 1862E
 Listen to the Mocking Bird – 1855E
 Ten Little Indians – 1868E
 Whispering Hope – 1868E
Winograd, Arthur – 1920F, 1960I, 1964I
Winsor, Phil – 1938F
 Computer-Assisted Music Composition – 1987M
Winston, Jeannie – 1876H
Winter Park Bach Festival – 1935L
Winter, Banks
 White Wings – 1884E
Winter, Edgar, Group – 1973E
Winter, Johnny – 1944A
Winter, Paul – 1939A

---

Vernacular/Commercial Music Scene
A *Births*   B *Deaths*   C *Biographical*   D *Publications*
E *Representative Pieces*

---

## Cultivated/Art Music Scene

   F *Births*    G *Deaths*    H *Debuts*    I *New Positions*    J *Honors and Awards*
   K *Biographical*    L *Musical Beginnings*    M *Publications*    N *Compositions*

Woodbury, Isaac Baker (continued)
  *Thanksgiving, The* – 1857M
  *Timbrel, The* – 1848M
  *Uncle Tom's Lament for Eva* – 1852N
  *Variations on "The Watcher"* – 1847N
  *Willow Wood Quick Step, The* – 1850N
Woodman, Huntington – 1861F, 1894I, 1943G
Woods, Harry M. – 1896A, 1970B
  *I'm Looking Over a Four-Leaf Clover* – 1927E
  *Paddlin' Madelin' Home* – 1925E
  *Side by Side* – 1927E
  *When the Red, Red Robin...* – 1926E
Woods, Phil – 1931A
Woodstock Rock Festival – 1969C
Wooley, Sheb – 1958E
Woolf, Benjamin E. – 1836F, 1901G
Woolls, Stephen – 1799G
Worcester, Massachusetts
  *Festival Association* – 1850L
  *Glee Club* – 1810L
  *Music Festival* – 1858L
  *Philharmonic Society* – 1850L
Worcester, Samuel – 1770F, 1859G
  *Christian Psalmody* – 1815M
  *Psalms, Hymns & Spiritual Songs of..Watts* –
    1819M
Words & Music (Shawnee Press) – 1939L
Wordworth, G. Wallace – 1902F
Work, Frederick J. – 1880F, 1942G
Work, Henry Clay – 1832F, 1855K, 1863I, 1884G
  *Agnes by the River* – 1868E
  *Babylon is Fallen!* – 1863E
  *Beautiful Rose* – 1861E
  *Brave Boys Are They* – 1861E
  *Buckskin Bag of Gold, The* – 1869E
  *Columbia's Guardian Angels* – 1864E
  *Come Back to the Farm* – 1867E
  *Come to Me, Sunbeam!* – 1879E
  *Come, Pretty Schoolgirl* – 1883E
  *Corporal Schnapps* – 1864E
  *Crossing the Grand Sierras* – 1869E
  *Crying for Bread* – 1877E
  *Dad's a Millionaire* – 1867E
  *Days When We Were Young* – 1863E
  *Don't be Cruel to the Motherless Darlings* –
    1882E
  *Drop the Pink Curtains* – 1884E
  *Farewell, My Loved One!* – 1877E
  *Father, Dear Father, Come Home With Me Now* –
    1864E
  *Fire Bells Are Ringing, The* – 1877E
  *First Love Dream, The* – 1862E
  *Georgie Sails Tomorrow!* – 1870E
  *Girls at Home, The* – 1862E
  *God Save the Nation* – 1862E
  *Grafted into the Army* – 1862E
  *Grandfather's Clock* – 1875E
  *Grandmother Told Me So* – 1863E
  *I'm Dying* – 1879E

*Joy in Heaven!* – 1871E
*King Bibler's Army* – 1877E
*Kingdom Coming* – 1862E
*Lillie of the Snowstorm* – 1866E
*Lilly-willy-woken* – 1855E
*Little Hallie* – 1861E
*Little Major* – 1863E
*Lost Letter, The* – 1883E
*Lost on the Lady Elgin* – 1861E
*Mac O'Macorkity* – 1877E
*Marching Through Georgia* – 1865E
*Monkey & the Mule, The* – 1882E
*Mystic Veil, The* – 1876E
*Nellie Lost & Found* – 1861E
*No Letters from Home* – 1869E
*Now, Moses!* – 1865E
*Old Village Doctor, The* – 1879E
*Our Last Grand Camping Ground* – 1868E
*Our Captain's Last Words* – 1861E
*Parrot & the Billy Goat, The* – 1882E
*Phantom Footsteps* – 1877E
*Picture on the Wall, The* – 1864E
*Pity Me, Loo!* – 1878E
*Ring the Bell* – 1865E
*Sequel to Grandfather's Clock* – 1878E
*Shadows on the Floor* – 1877E
*Ship That Never Returned* – 1865E
*Silver Horn, The* – 1883E
*Sleeping for the Flag* – 1863E
*Song of the Red Men* – 1868E
*Song of a Thousand Years* – 1863E
*Sweet Echo Dell* – 1876E
*Take Them Away! They'll Drive Me Crazy* –
  1871E
*Tie the Knot Tightly* – 1877E
*'Tis Finished! or Sing Hallelujah* – 1865E
*Touch the Sleeping Strings* – 1876E
*Traveling Homeward* – 1872E
*Uncle Joe's "Hail Columbia!"* – 1862E
*Used-Up Joe* – 1876E
*Wake, Nicodemus!* – 1864E
*Washington & Lincoln* – 1864E
*Watching for Pa* – 1863E
*Watchman!* – 1865E
*We Are Coming, Sister Mary* – 1854E
*We'll Go Down Ourselves* – 1862E
*When You Get Home, Remember Me* – 1882E
*When the "Evening Star" Went Down* – 1866E
*Where's My Billy Goat Gone To?* – 1882E
*Who Shall Rule This American Nation?* – 1866E
Work, John W. – 1873F, 1898I, 1925G
  *Folk Song of the American Negro* – 1915D
Work, John W., Jr. – 1901F, 1933I, 1967G
  *American Negro Songs & Spirituals* – 1940D
  *Jubilee* – 1962D
  *Singers, The* – 1941N
Workman, William – 1940F, 1965H
World Cello Congress – 1988L
*World of Music* – 1843L

---

❖

**Vernacular/Commercial Music Scene**
A *Births*    B *Deaths*    C *Biographical*    D *Publications*
E *Representative Pieces*

---

### Cultivated/Art Music Scene

**F** *Births*    **G** *Deaths*    **H** *Debuts*    **I** *New Positions*    **J** *Honors and Awards*
**K** *Biographical*    **L** *Musical Beginnings*    **M** *Publications*    **N** *Compositions*

---

❖

**Vernacular/Commercial Music Scene**
A *Births*    B *Deaths*    C *Biographical*    D *Publications*
E *Representative Pieces*

---

### Cultivated/Art Music Scene

**F** *Births*   **G** *Deaths*   **H** *Debuts*   **I** *New Positions*   **J** *Honors and Awards*
**K** *Biographical*   **L** *Musical Beginnings*   **M** *Publications*   **N** *Compositions*